# Table of Contents

locates rapidly specific topics within each subject area.

# Study Guide 2-96

# Comprehensive Index

gives ready references to the information in Volumes 1 through 4.

# For Further Reference

identifies useful books for those who wish to read more about a subject.

## For Further Reference

Asimov, Isaac
    *The Universe*
    Walker and Co.
Jastrow, Robert
    *Red Giants and White Dwarfs*
    Harper & Row
Pasachoff, Jay
    *Astronomy Now*
    Saunders
Ploman, Edward W.
    *Space, Earth & Communication*
    Greenwood

Sagan, Carl
    *Cosmos*
    Random House
Shipman, Harry L.
    *Black Holes, Quasars, and the Universe*
    Houghton-Mifflin
Smith, Arthur
    *Planetary Exploration*
    Patrick Stevens
Spangenburg, Ray and Moser, Diane
    *Opening the Space Frontier*
    Facts on File

# FLAGS OF STATES AND POSSESSIONS: UNITED STATES

## UNITED STATES

| | |
|---|---|
| **AREA** | 3,623,420 sq. mi. (9,384,658 sq. km.) |
| **POPULATION** | 249,632,692 |
| **CAPITAL** | Washington |
| **LARGEST CITY** | New York |
| **HIGHEST POINT** | Mt. McKinley 20,320 ft. (6194 m.) |
| **MONETARY UNIT** | U.S. dollar |
| **MAJOR LANGUAGE** | English |
| **MAJOR RELIGIONS** | Protestantism, Roman Catholicism, Judaism |

## ALABAMA

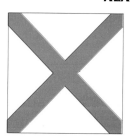

| | |
|---|---|
| **AREA** | 51,705 sq. mi. (133,916 sq. km.) |
| **POPULATION** | 4,062,608 |
| **CAPITAL** | Montgomery |
| **LARGEST CITY** | Birmingham |
| **HIGHEST POINT** | Cheaha Mtn. 2,407 ft. (734 m.) |
| **SETTLED IN** | 1702 |
| **ADMITTED TO UNION** | December 14, 1819 |
| **POPULAR NAME** | Heart of Dixie; Cotton State; Yellowhammer State |
| **STATE FLOWER** | Camellia |
| **STATE BIRD** | Yellowhammer |

## ALASKA

| | |
|---|---|
| **AREA** | 591,004 sq. mi. (1,530,700 sq. km.) |
| **POPULATION** | 551,947 |
| **CAPITAL** | Juneau |
| **LARGEST CITY** | Anchorage |
| **HIGHEST POINT** | Mt. McKinley 20,320 ft. (6194 m.) |
| **SETTLED IN** | 1801 |
| **ADMITTED TO UNION** | January 3, 1959 |
| **POPULAR NAME** | Great Land; Last Frontier |
| **STATE FLOWER** | Forget-Me-Not |
| **STATE BIRD** | Willow Ptarmigan |

## ARIZONA

| | |
|---|---|
| **AREA** | 114,000 sq. mi. (295,260 sq. km.) |
| **POPULATION** | 3,677,985 |
| **CAPITAL** | Phoenix |
| **LARGEST CITY** | Phoenix |
| **HIGHEST POINT** | Humphreys Pk. 12,633 ft. (3851 m.) |
| **SETTLED IN** | 1752 |
| **ADMITTED TO UNION** | February 14, 1912 |
| **POPULAR NAME** | Grand Canyon State |
| **STATE FLOWER** | Saguaro Cactus Blossom |
| **STATE BIRD** | Cactus Wren |

## ARKANSAS

| | |
|---|---|
| AREA | 53,187 sq. mi. (137,754 sq. km.) |
| POPULATION | 2,362,239 |
| CAPITAL | Little Rock |
| LARGEST CITY | Little Rock |
| HIGHEST POINT | Magazine Mtn. 2,753 ft. (839 m.) |
| SETTLED IN | 1685 |
| ADMITTED TO UNION | June 15, 1836 |
| POPULAR NAME | Land of Opportunity |
| STATE FLOWER | Apple Blossom |
| STATE BIRD | Mockingbird |

## CALIFORNIA

| | |
|---|---|
| AREA | 158,706 sq. mi. (411,049 sq. km.) |
| POPULATION | 29,839,250 |
| CAPITAL | Sacramento |
| LARGEST CITY | Los Angeles |
| HIGHEST POINT | Mt. Whitney 14,494 ft. (4418 m.) |
| SETTLED IN | 1769 |
| ADMITTED TO UNION | September 9, 1850 |
| POPULAR NAME | Golden State |
| STATE FLOWER | Golden Poppy |
| STATE BIRD | California Valley Quail |

## COLORADO

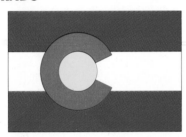

| | |
|---|---|
| AREA | 104,091 sq. mi. (269,596 sq. km.) |
| POPULATION | 3,307,912 |
| CAPITAL | Denver |
| LARGEST CITY | Denver |
| HIGHEST POINT | Mt. Elbert 14,433 ft. (4399 m.) |
| SETTLED IN | 1858 |
| ADMITTED TO UNION | August 1, 1876 |
| POPULAR NAME | Centennial State |
| STATE FLOWER | Rocky Mountain Columbine |
| STATE BIRD | Lark Bunting |

## CONNECTICUT

| | |
|---|---|
| AREA | 5,018 sq. mi. (12,997 sq. km.) |
| POPULATION | 3,295,669 |
| CAPITAL | Hartford |
| LARGEST CITY | Bridgeport |
| HIGHEST POINT | Mt. Frissell (S. Slope) 2,380 ft. (725 m.) |
| SETTLED IN | 1635 |
| ADMITTED TO UNION | January 9, 1788 |
| POPULAR NAME | Constitution State; Nutmeg State |
| STATE FLOWER | Mountain Laurel |
| STATE BIRD | Robin |

## DELAWARE

| | |
|---|---|
| AREA | 2,044 sq. mi. (5,294 sq. km.) |
| POPULATION | 668,696 |
| CAPITAL | Dover |
| LARGEST CITY | Wilmington |
| HIGHEST POINT | Ebright Road 442 ft. (135 m.) |
| SETTLED IN | 1627 |
| ADMITTED TO UNION | December 7, 1787 |
| POPULAR NAME | First State; Diamond State |
| STATE FLOWER | Peach Blossom |
| STATE BIRD | Blue Hen Chicken |

## FLORIDA

| | |
|---|---|
| **AREA** | 58,664 sq. mi. (151,940 sq. km.) |
| **POPULATION** | 13,003,362 |
| **CAPITAL** | Tallahassee |
| **LARGEST CITY** | Jacksonville |
| **HIGHEST POINT** | (Walton County) 345 ft. (105 m.) |
| **SETTLED IN** | 1565 |
| **ADMITTED TO UNION** | March 3, 1845 |
| **POPULAR NAME** | Sunshine State; Peninsula State |
| **STATE FLOWER** | Orange Blossom |
| **STATE BIRD** | Mockingbird |

## GEORGIA

| | |
|---|---|
| **AREA** | 58,910 sq. mi. (152,577 sq. km.) |
| **POPULATION** | 6,508,419 |
| **CAPITAL** | Atlanta |
| **LARGEST CITY** | Atlanta |
| **HIGHEST POINT** | Brasstown Bald 4,784 ft. (1458 m.) |
| **SETTLED IN** | 1733 |
| **ADMITTED TO UNION** | January 2, 1788 |
| **POPULAR NAME** | Empire State of the South; Peach State |
| **STATE FLOWER** | Cherokee Rose |
| **STATE BIRD** | Brown Thrasher |

## HAWAII

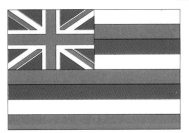

| | |
|---|---|
| **AREA** | 6,471 sq. mi. (16,760 sq. km.) |
| **POPULATION** | 1,115,274 |
| **CAPITAL** | Honolulu |
| **LARGEST CITY** | Honolulu |
| **HIGHEST POINT** | Mauna Kea 13,796 ft. (4205 m.) |
| **SETTLED IN** | —— |
| **ADMITTED TO UNION** | August 21, 1959 |
| **POPULAR NAME** | Aloha State |
| **STATE FLOWER** | Hibiscus |
| **STATE BIRD** | Nene (Hawaiian Goose) |

## IDAHO

| | |
|---|---|
| **AREA** | 83,564 sq. mi. (216,431 sq. km.) |
| **POPULATION** | 1,011,986 |
| **CAPITAL** | Boise |
| **LARGEST CITY** | Boise |
| **HIGHEST POINT** | Borah Pk. 12,662 ft. (3859 m.) |
| **SETTLED IN** | 1842 |
| **ADMITTED TO UNION** | July 3, 1890 |
| **POPULAR NAME** | Gem State |
| **STATE FLOWER** | Syringa |
| **STATE BIRD** | Mountain Bluebird |

## ILLINOIS

| | |
|---|---|
| **AREA** | 56,345 sq. mi. (145,934 sq. km.) |
| **POPULATION** | 11,466,682 |
| **CAPITAL** | Springfield |
| **LARGEST CITY** | Chicago |
| **HIGHEST POINT** | Charles Mound 1,235 ft. (376 m.) |
| **SETTLED IN** | 1720 |
| **ADMITTED TO UNION** | December 3, 1818 |
| **POPULAR NAME** | Prairie State; Land of Lincoln |
| **STATE FLOWER** | Native Violet |
| **STATE BIRD** | Cardinal |

## INDIANA

| | |
|---|---|
| AREA | 36,185 sq. mi. (93,719 sq. km.) |
| POPULATION | 5,564,228 |
| CAPITAL | Indianapolis |
| LARGEST CITY | Indianapolis |
| HIGHEST POINT | (Wayne County) 1,257 ft. (383 m.) |
| SETTLED IN | 1730 |
| ADMITTED TO UNION | December 11, 1816 |
| POPULAR NAME | Hoosier State |
| STATE FLOWER | Peony |
| STATE BIRD | Cardinal |

## IOWA

| | |
|---|---|
| AREA | 56,275 sq. mi. (145,752 sq. km.) |
| POPULATION | 2,787,424 |
| CAPITAL | Des Moines |
| LARGEST CITY | Des Moines |
| HIGHEST POINT | (Osceola Co.) 1670 ft. (509 m.) |
| SETTLED IN | 1788 |
| ADMITTED TO UNION | December 28, 1846 |
| POPULAR NAME | Hawkeye State |
| STATE FLOWER | Wild Rose |
| STATE BIRD | Eastern Goldfinch |

## KANSAS

| | |
|---|---|
| AREA | 82,277 sq. mi. (213,097 sq. km.) |
| POPULATION | 2,485,600 |
| CAPITAL | Topeka |
| LARGEST CITY | Wichita |
| HIGHEST POINT | Mt. Sunflower 4,039 ft. (1231 m.) |
| SETTLED IN | 1831 |
| ADMITTED TO UNION | January 29, 1861 |
| POPULAR NAME | Sunflower State |
| STATE FLOWER | Sunflower |
| STATE BIRD | Western Meadowlark |

## KENTUCKY

| | |
|---|---|
| AREA | 40,409 sq. mi. (104,659 sq. km.) |
| POPULATION | 3,698,969 |
| CAPITAL | Frankfort |
| LARGEST CITY | Louisville |
| HIGHEST POINT | Black Mtn. 4,145 ft. (1263 m.) |
| SETTLED IN | 1774 |
| ADMITTED TO UNION | June 1, 1792 |
| POPULAR NAME | Bluegrass State |
| STATE FLOWER | Goldenrod |
| STATE BIRD | Cardinal |

## LOUISIANA

| | |
|---|---|
| AREA | 47,752 sq. mi. (123,678 sq. km.) |
| POPULATION | 4,238,216 |
| CAPITAL | Baton Rouge |
| LARGEST CITY | New Orleans |
| HIGHEST POINT | Driskill Mtn. 535 ft. (163 m.) |
| SETTLED IN | 1699 |
| ADMITTED TO UNION | April 30, 1812 |
| POPULAR NAME | Pelican State |
| STATE FLOWER | Magnolia |
| STATE BIRD | Eastern Brown Pelican |

## MAINE

| | |
|---|---|
| AREA | 33,265 sq. mi. (86,156 sq. km.) |
| POPULATION | 1,233,223 |
| CAPITAL | Augusta |
| LARGEST CITY | Portland |
| HIGHEST POINT | Katahdin 5,268 ft. (1606 m.) |
| SETTLED IN | 1624 |
| ADMITTED TO UNION | March 15, 1820 |
| POPULAR NAME | Pine Tree State |
| STATE FLOWER | White Pine Cone & Tassel |
| STATE BIRD | Chickadee |

## MARYLAND

| | |
|---|---|
| AREA | 10,460 sq. mi. (27,091 sq. km.) |
| POPULATION | 4,798,622 |
| CAPITAL | Annapolis |
| LARGEST CITY | Baltimore |
| HIGHEST POINT | Backbone Mtn. 3,360 ft. (1024 m.) |
| SETTLED IN | 1634 |
| ADMITTED TO UNION | April 28, 1788 |
| POPULAR NAME | Old Line State; Free State |
| STATE FLOWER | Black-Eyed Susan |
| STATE BIRD | Baltimore Oriole |

## MASSACHUSETTS

| | |
|---|---|
| AREA | 8,284 sq. mi. (21,456 sq. km.) |
| POPULATION | 6,029,051 |
| CAPITAL | Boston |
| LARGEST CITY | Boston |
| HIGHEST POINT | Mt. Greylock 3,491 ft. (1064 m.) |
| SETTLED IN | 1620 |
| ADMITTED TO UNION | February 6, 1788 |
| POPULAR NAME | Bay State; Old Colony |
| STATE FLOWER | Mayflower |
| STATE BIRD | Chickadee |

## MICHIGAN

| | |
|---|---|
| AREA | 58,527 sq. mi. (151,585 sq. km.) |
| POPULATION | 9,328,784 |
| CAPITAL | Lansing |
| LARGEST CITY | Detroit |
| HIGHEST POINT | Mt. Curwood 1,980 ft. (604 m.) |
| SETTLED IN | 1650 |
| ADMITTED TO UNION | January 26, 1837 |
| POPULAR NAME | Wolverine State |
| STATE FLOWER | Apple Blossom |
| STATE BIRD | Robin |

## MINNESOTA

| | |
|---|---|
| AREA | 84,402 sq. mi. (218,601 sq. km.) |
| POPULATION | 4,387,029 |
| CAPITAL | St. Paul |
| LARGEST CITY | Minneapolis |
| HIGHEST POINT | Eagle Mtn. 2,301 ft. (701 m.) |
| SETTLED IN | 1805 |
| ADMITTED TO UNION | May 11, 1858 |
| POPULAR NAME | North Star State; Gopher State |
| STATE FLOWER | Pink & White Lady's-Slipper |
| STATE BIRD | Common Loon |

## MISSISSIPPI

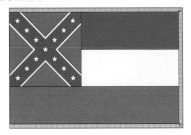

| | |
|---|---|
| AREA | 47,689 sq. mi. (123,515 sq. km.) |
| POPULATION | 2,586,443 |
| CAPITAL | Jackson |
| LARGEST CITY | Jackson |
| HIGHEST POINT | Woodall Mtn. 806 ft. (246 m.) |
| SETTLED IN | 1716 |
| ADMITTED TO UNION | December 10, 1817 |
| POPULAR NAME | Magnolia State |
| STATE FLOWER | Magnolia |
| STATE BIRD | Mockingbird |

## MISSOURI

| | |
|---|---|
| AREA | 69,697 sq. mi. (180,515 sq. km.) |
| POPULATION | 5,137,804 |
| CAPITAL | Jefferson City |
| LARGEST CITY | St. Louis |
| HIGHEST POINT | Taum Sauk Mtn. 1,772 ft. (540 m.) |
| SETTLED IN | 1764 |
| ADMITTED TO UNION | August 10, 1821 |
| POPULAR NAME | Show Me State |
| STATE FLOWER | Hawthorn |
| STATE BIRD | Bluebird |

## MONTANA

| | |
|---|---|
| AREA | 147,046 sq. mi. (380,849 sq. km.) |
| POPULATION | 803,655 |
| CAPITAL | Helena |
| LARGEST CITY | Billings |
| HIGHEST POINT | Granite Pk. 12,799 ft. (3901 m.) |
| SETTLED IN | 1809 |
| ADMITTED TO UNION | November 8, 1889 |
| POPULAR NAME | Treasure State; Big Sky Country |
| STATE FLOWER | Bitterroot |
| STATE BIRD | Western Meadowlark |

## NEBRASKA

| | |
|---|---|
| AREA | 77,355 sq. mi. (200,349 sq. km.) |
| POPULATION | 1,584,617 |
| CAPITAL | Lincoln |
| LARGEST CITY | Omaha |
| HIGHEST POINT | (Kimball Co.) 5,246 ft. (1654 m.) |
| SETTLED IN | 1847 |
| ADMITTED TO UNION | March 1, 1867 |
| POPULAR NAME | Cornhusker State |
| STATE FLOWER | Goldenrod |
| STATE BIRD | Western Meadowlark |

## NEVADA

| | |
|---|---|
| AREA | 110,561 sq. mi. (286,353 sq. km.) |
| POPULATION | 1,206,152 |
| CAPITAL | Carson City |
| LARGEST CITY | Las Vegas |
| HIGHEST POINT | Boundary Pk. 13,143 ft. (4006 m.) |
| SETTLED IN | 1850 |
| ADMITTED TO UNION | October 31, 1864 |
| POPULAR NAME | Silver State; Sagebrush State |
| STATE FLOWER | Sagebrush |
| STATE BIRD | Mountain Bluebird |

## NEW HAMPSHIRE

| | |
|---|---|
| **AREA** | 9,279 sq. mi. (24,033 sq. km.) |
| **POPULATION** | 1,113,915 |
| **CAPITAL** | Concord |
| **LARGEST CITY** | Manchester |
| **HIGHEST POINT** | Mt. Washington 6,288 ft. (1917 m.) |
| **SETTLED IN** | 1623 |
| **ADMITTED TO UNION** | June 21, 1788 |
| **POPULAR NAME** | Granite State |
| **STATE FLOWER** | Purple Lilac |
| **STATE BIRD** | Purple Finch |

## NEW JERSEY

| | |
|---|---|
| **AREA** | 7,787 sq. mi. (20,168 sq. km.) |
| **POPULATION** | 7,748,634 |
| **CAPITAL** | Trenton |
| **LARGEST CITY** | Newark |
| **HIGHEST POINT** | High Point 1,803 ft. (550 m.) |
| **SETTLED IN** | 1617 |
| **ADMITTED TO UNION** | December 18, 1787 |
| **POPULAR NAME** | Garden State |
| **STATE FLOWER** | Purple Violet |
| **STATE BIRD** | Eastern Goldfinch |

## NEW MEXICO

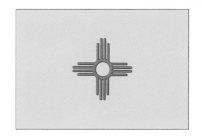

| | |
|---|---|
| **AREA** | 121,593 sq. mi. (314,926 sq. km.) |
| **POPULATION** | 1,521,779 |
| **CAPITAL** | Santa Fe |
| **LARGEST CITY** | Albuquerque |
| **HIGHEST POINT** | Wheeler Pk. 13,161 ft. (4011 m.) |
| **SETTLED IN** | 1605 |
| **ADMITTED TO UNION** | January 6, 1912 |
| **POPULAR NAME** | Land of Enchantment |
| **STATE FLOWER** | Yucca |
| **STATE BIRD** | Road Runner |

## NEW YORK

| | |
|---|---|
| **AREA** | 49,108 sq. mi. (127,190 sq. km.) |
| **POPULATION** | 18,044,505 |
| **CAPITAL** | Albany |
| **LARGEST CITY** | New York |
| **HIGHEST POINT** | Mt. Marcy 5,344 ft. (1629 m.) |
| **SETTLED IN** | 1614 |
| **ADMITTED TO UNION** | July 26, 1788 |
| **POPULAR NAME** | Empire State |
| **STATE FLOWER** | Rose |
| **STATE BIRD** | Bluebird |

## NORTH CAROLINA

| | |
|---|---|
| **AREA** | 52,669 sq. mi. (136,413 sq. km.) |
| **POPULATION** | 6,657,630 |
| **CAPITAL** | Raleigh |
| **LARGEST CITY** | Charlotte |
| **HIGHEST POINT** | Mt. Mitchell 6,684 ft. (2037 m.) |
| **SETTLED IN** | 1650 |
| **ADMITTED TO UNION** | November 21, 1789 |
| **POPULAR NAME** | Tarheel State |
| **STATE FLOWER** | Flowering Dogwood |
| **STATE BIRD** | Cardinal |

## NORTH DAKOTA

| | |
|---|---|
| AREA | 70,702 sq. mi. (183,118 sq. km.) |
| POPULATION | 641,364 |
| CAPITAL | Bismarck |
| LARGEST CITY | Fargo |
| HIGHEST POINT | White Butte 3,506 ft. (1069 m.) |
| SETTLED IN | 1780 |
| ADMITTED TO UNION | November 2, 1889 |
| POPULAR NAME | Flickertail State; Sioux State |
| STATE FLOWER | Wild Prairie Rose |
| STATE BIRD | Western Meadowlark |

## OHIO

| | |
|---|---|
| AREA | 41,330 sq. mi. (107,045 sq. km.) |
| POPULATION | 10,887,325 |
| CAPITAL | Columbus |
| LARGEST CITY | Cleveland |
| HIGHEST POINT | Campbell Hill 1,550 ft. (472 m.) |
| SETTLED IN | 1788 |
| ADMITTED TO UNION | March 1, 1803 |
| POPULAR NAME | Buckeye State |
| STATE FLOWER | Scarlet Carnation |
| STATE BIRD | Cardinal |

## OKLAHOMA

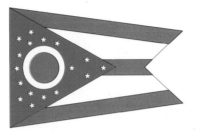

| | |
|---|---|
| AREA | 69,956 sq. mi. (181,186 sq. km.) |
| POPULATION | 3,157,604 |
| CAPITAL | Oklahoma City |
| LARGEST CITY | Oklahoma City |
| HIGHEST POINT | Black Mesa 4,973 ft. (1516 m.) |
| SETTLED IN | 1889 |
| ADMITTED TO UNION | November 16, 1907 |
| POPULAR NAME | Sooner State |
| STATE FLOWER | Mistletoe |
| STATE BIRD | Scissor-Tailed Flycatcher |

## OREGON

| | |
|---|---|
| AREA | 97,073 sq. mi. (251,419 sq. km.) |
| POPULATION | 2,853,733 |
| CAPITAL | Salem |
| LARGEST CITY | Portland |
| HIGHEST POINT | Mt. Hood 11,239 ft. (3426 m.) |
| SETTLED IN | 1810 |
| ADMITTED TO UNION | February 14, 1859 |
| POPULAR NAME | Beaver State |
| STATE FLOWER | Oregon Grape |
| STATE BIRD | Western Meadowlark |

## PENNSYLVANIA

| | |
|---|---|
| AREA | 45,308 sq. mi. (117,348 sq. km.) |
| POPULATION | 11,924,710 |
| CAPITAL | Harrisburg |
| LARGEST CITY | Philadelphia |
| HIGHEST POINT | Mt. Davis 3,213 ft. (979 m.) |
| SETTLED IN | 1682 |
| ADMITTED TO UNION | December 12, 1787 |
| POPULAR NAME | Keystone State |
| STATE FLOWER | Mountain Laurel |
| STATE BIRD | Ruffed Grouse |

| | |
|---|---|
| **AREA** . . . . . . . . . | 1,212 sq. mi. (3,139 sq. km.) |
| **POPULATION** . . . . . . | 1,005,984 |
| **CAPITAL** . . . . . . . | Providence |
| **LARGEST CITY** . . . . . | Providence |
| **HIGHEST POINT** . . . . . | Jerimoth Hill 812 ft. (247 m.) |
| **SETTLED IN** . . . . . . . | 1636 |
| **ADMITTED TO UNION** . . | May 29, 1790 |
| **POPULAR NAME** . . . . | Little Rhody; Ocean State |
| **STATE FLOWER** . . . . . | Violet |
| **STATE BIRD** . . . . . . . | Rhode Island Red |

| | |
|---|---|
| **AREA** . . . . . . . . . | 31,113 sq. mi. (80,583 sq. km.) |
| **POPULATION** . . . . . . | 3,505,707 |
| **CAPITAL** . . . . . . . | Columbia |
| **LARGEST CITY** . . . . . | Columbia |
| **HIGHEST POINT** . . . . . | Sassafras Mtn. 3,560 ft. (1085 m.) |
| **SETTLED IN** . . . . . . . | 1670 |
| **ADMITTED TO UNION** . . . | May 23, 1788 |
| **POPULAR NAME** . . . . | Palmetto State |
| **STATE FLOWER** . . . . . | Carolina (Yellow) Jessamine |
| **STATE BIRD** . . . . . . . | Carolina Wren |

| | |
|---|---|
| **AREA** . . . . . . . . . | 77,116 sq. mi. (199,730 sq. km.) |
| **POPULATION** . . . . . . | 699,999 |
| **CAPITAL** . . . . . . . | Pierre |
| **LARGEST CITY** . . . . . | Sioux Falls |
| **HIGHEST POINT** . . . . . | Harney Pk. 7,242 ft. (2207 m.) |
| **SETTLED IN** . . . . . . . | 1856 |
| **ADMITTED TO UNION** . . | November 2, 1889 |
| **POPULAR NAME** . . . . | Coyote State; Sunshine State |
| **STATE FLOWER** . . . . . | Pasqueflower |
| **STATE BIRD** . . . . . . . | Ring-Necked Pheasant |

| | |
|---|---|
| **AREA** . . . . . . . . . | 42,144 sq. mi. (109,153 sq. km.) |
| **POPULATION** . . . . . . | 4,896,641 |
| **CAPITAL** . . . . . . . | Nashville |
| **LARGEST CITY** . . . . . | Memphis |
| **HIGHEST POINT** . . . . . | Clingmans Dome 6,643 ft. (2025 m.) |
| **SETTLED IN** . . . . . . . | 1757 |
| **ADMITTED TO UNION** . . | June 1, 1796 |
| **POPULAR NAME** . . . . | Volunteer State |
| **STATE FLOWER** . . . . . | Iris |
| **STATE BIRD** . . . . . . . | Mockingbird |

## TEXAS

| | |
|---|---|
| AREA | 266,807 sq. mi. (691,030 sq. km.) |
| POPULATION | 17,059,805 |
| CAPITAL | Austin |
| LARGEST CITY | Houston |
| HIGHEST POINT | Guadalupe Pk. 8,749 ft. (2667 m.) |
| SETTLED IN | 1686 |
| ADMITTED TO UNION | December 29, 1845 |
| POPULAR NAME | Lone Star State |
| STATE FLOWER | Bluebonnet |
| STATE BIRD | Mockingbird |

## UTAH

| | |
|---|---|
| AREA | 84,899 sq. mi. (219,888 sq. km.) |
| POPULATION | 1,727,784 |
| CAPITAL | Salt Lake City |
| LARGEST CITY | Salt Lake City |
| HIGHEST POINT | Kings Pk. 13,528 ft. (4123 m.) |
| SETTLED IN | 1847 |
| ADMITTED TO UNION | January 4, 1896 |
| POPULAR NAME | Beehive State |
| STATE FLOWER | Sego Lily |
| STATE BIRD | Sea Gull |

## VERMONT

| | |
|---|---|
| AREA | 9,614 sq. mi. (24,900 sq. km.) |
| POPULATION | 564,964 |
| CAPITAL | Montpelier |
| LARGEST CITY | Burlington |
| HIGHEST POINT | Mt. Mansfield 4,393 ft. (1339 m.) |
| SETTLED IN | 1764 |
| ADMITTED TO UNION | March 4, 1791 |
| POPULAR NAME | Green Mountain State |
| STATE FLOWER | Red Clover |
| STATE BIRD | Hermit Thrush |

## VIRGINIA

| | |
|---|---|
| AREA | 40,767 sq. mi. (105,587 sq. km.) |
| POPULATION | 6,216,568 |
| CAPITAL | Richmond |
| LARGEST CITY | Norfolk |
| HIGHEST POINT | Mt. Rogers 5,729 ft. (1746 m.) |
| SETTLED IN | 1607 |
| ADMITTED TO UNION | June 26, 1788 |
| POPULAR NAME | Old Dominion |
| STATE FLOWER | Dogwood |
| STATE BIRD | Cardinal |

# WASHINGTON

AREA . . . . . . . . . . . 68,139 sq. mi. (176,480 sq. km.)
POPULATION . . . . . . 4,887,941
CAPITAL . . . . . . . . Olympia
LARGEST CITY . . . . . Seattle
HIGHEST POINT . . . . . Mt. Ranier 14,410 ft. (4392 m.)
SETTLED IN . . . . . . . 1811
ADMITTED TO UNION . . November 11, 1889
POPULAR NAME . . . . . Evergreen State
STATE FLOWER . . . . . Western Rhododendron
STATE BIRD . . . . . . . Willow Goldfinch

# WEST VIRGINIA

AREA . . . . . . . . . . 24,231 sq. mi. (62,758 sq. km.)
POPULATION . . . . . . 1,801,625
CAPITAL . . . . . . . . Charleston
LARGEST CITY . . . . . Charleston
HIGHEST POINT . . . . . Spruce Knob 4,863 ft. (1482 m.)
SETTLED IN . . . . . . . 1774
ADMITTED TO UNION . . June 20, 1863
POPULAR NAME . . . . . Mountain State
STATE FLOWER . . . . . Big Rhododendron
STATE BIRD . . . . . . . Cardinal

# WISCONSIN

AREA . . . . . . . . . . 56,153 sq. mi. (145,436 sq. km.)
POPULATION . . . . . . 4,906,745
CAPITAL . . . . . . . . Madison
LARGEST CITY . . . . . Milwaukee
HIGHEST POINT . . . . . Timms Hill 1,951 ft. (595 m.)
SETTLED IN . . . . . . . 1670
ADMITTED TO UNION . . May 29, 1848
POPULAR NAME . . . . . Badger State
STATE FLOWER . . . . . Wood Violet
STATE BIRD . . . . . . . Robin

# WYOMING

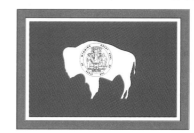

AREA . . . . . . . . . . 97,809 sq. mi. (253,325 sq. km.)
POPULATION . . . . . . 455,975
CAPITAL . . . . . . . . Cheyenne
LARGEST CITY . . . . . Casper
HIGHEST POINT . . . . . Gannett Pk. 13,804 ft. (4207 m.)
SETTLED IN . . . . . . . 1834
ADMITTED TO UNION . . July 10, 1890
POPULAR NAME . . . . . Equality State
STATE FLOWER . . . . . Indian Paintbrush
STATE BIRD . . . . . . . Meadowlark

## AMERICAN SAMOA

| | |
|---|---|
| **AREA** . . . . . . . . . . | 77 sq. mi. (199 sq. km.) |
| **POPULATION** . . . . . . . | 43, 052 |
| **CAPITAL** . . . . . . . . | Pago Pago |
| **LARGEST CITY** . . . . . | Pago Pago |
| **LOCATION** . . . . . . . | South Pacific Ocean |
| **CLIMATE** . . . . . . . . . | Tropical Marine |
| **MONETARY UNIT** . . . . . | U. S. Dollar |
| **LANGUAGE** . . . . . . . | Samoan; English |

## GUAM

| | |
|---|---|
| **AREA** . . . . . . . . . . | 209 sq. mi. (541 sq. km.) |
| **POPULATION** . . . . . . . | 144,978 |
| **CAPITAL** . . . . . . . . | Agana |
| **LARGEST CITY** . . . . . | Agana |
| **LOCATION** . . . . . . . | North Pacific Ocean |
| **CLIMATE** . . . . . . . . . | Tropical Marine |
| **MONETARY UNIT** . . . . . | U. S. Dollar |
| **LANGUAGE** . . . . . . . | English; Chamorro; Japanese |

## PUERTO RICO

| | |
|---|---|
| **AREA** . . . . . . . . . . | 3,535 sq. mi. (9104 sq. km.) |
| **POPULATION** . . . . . . . | 3,294,997 |
| **CAPITAL** . . . . . . . . | San Juan |
| **LARGEST CITY** . . . . . | San Juan |
| **LOCATION** . . . . . . . | Caribbean Sea |
| **CLIMATE** . . . . . . . . . | Tropical Marine |
| **MONETARY UNIT** . . . . . | U. S. Dollar |
| **LANGUAGE** . . . . . . . | Spanish; English |

## VIRGIN ISLANDS

| | |
|---|---|
| **AREA** . . . . . . . . . . | 133 sq. mi (344 sq. km.) |
| **POPULATION** . . . . . . . | 99,404 |
| **CAPITAL** . . . . . . . . | Charlotte Amalie |
| **LARGEST CITY** . . . . . | Charlotte Amalie |
| **LOCATION** . . . . . . . | Caribbean Sea |
| **CLIMATE** . . . . . . . . . | Subtropical |
| **MONETARY UNIT** . . . . . | U. S. Dollar |
| **LANGUAGE** . . . . . . . | English; Spanish; Creole |

# Student Handbook

Including
## Science for Fun Experiments
and
## The Knowledge Factory

Volume **1**

# Student Handbook

Including
## Science for Fun Experiments
and
## The Knowledge Factory

Volume **1**

**THE SOUTHWESTERN COMPANY**
Nashville, Tennessee

**Science for Fun Experiments** and **The Knowledge Factory**
© Aladdin Books Ltd 1996

Designed and produced by
Aladdin Books Ltd
28 Percy Street
London W1P 0LD

First published in the United States by
Copper Beech Books, an imprint of
The Milbrook Press
2 Old New Milford Road
Brookfield, Connecticut 06804

Printed in the United States of America

# Preface

This new edition of the *Student Handbook* is among the most practical and appealing student aids ever published. Consisting of 850 pages (402 in Volume One and 448 in Volume Two), it brings together information on the major subjects taught in every elementary, junior high, and high school.

For this new edition, the most important information on each subject has been distilled and presented in a visually interesting and easy-to-use way. Both volumes are filled with tables, informative line drawings, brief "dictionaries" of terms used in special fields, chronologies showing major national or world events year by year, time lines showing the life spans of important men and women in history, and many other features. All information is up to date.

The *Student Handbook* has been organized to present material usually taught in the fourth to eighth grades in Volume One and material taught in ninth grade or above in Volume Two. Useful information for all ages will be found in both volumes, however. Each *Student Handbook* is organized in two major parts. PART ONE includes material designed to help students do better in school. PART TWO features a complete reference work that readers of all ages will find useful and enjoyable.

The major headings in PART ONE of Volume One are:

       Study Guide (with special emphasis on grammar and writing)

       Social Studies (U.S. history and U.S. geography)

       Mathematics and Science (basic arithmetic and science)

       Sports and Entertainment (sports, music, film, and television)

PART TWO of Volume One contains two great references useful for students: *Science for Fun Experiments* and *The Knowledge Factory*. Factual and current, these references help children see that learning really is fun.

The major headings in PART ONE of Volume Two are:

       Social Studies (world history and geography, U.S. government, including the Constitution and the Presidents, and a color atlas of the world)

       Science and Mathematics (laboratory sciences and algebra, geometry, etc.)

       English and Literature (writing research papers and book reports and understanding poetry, drama, and fiction)

PART TWO of Volume Two is *The Young Reader's Companion*, an illustrated A-to-Z guide to books, authors, and subjects of special interest to young people. Its more than 2000 concise, lively entries are as entertaining as they are informative. The entries are carefully crafted to help young people find the books they will enjoy reading, provide them with useful information that will increase their enjoyment of the books they choose, and encourage them to broaden and deepen their reading experiences.

The two volumes are designed to complement each other. For example, a reader using the algebra section in Volume Two may find it helpful to review parts of arithmetic in Volume One. Similarly, a reader who has found basic material in "Physical Sciences" in Volume One will find additional, more advanced material in "Physics" in Volume Two. The Index at the end of each volume helps locate all major information on a given topic.

In summary, the *Student Handbook* offers students and those out of school essential information on basic skills (reading, writing, mathematics) *and* a vast collection of easy-to-use data on all major school subjects. We are certain that this set of books will contribute to increased success in school and to the enjoyment of learning.

*The Editors*

# Table of Contents

# Study Guide 2-96

# Social Studies 104-155

## United States History 106

## United States Today 134

# Mathematics and Science 156-319

# Sports and Entertainment 320-370

ILLUSTRATION CREDITS *Pages 2-3* Richard Hutchings/PhotoEdit; *4-5* Tony Freeman/PhotoEdit; *7* Leslie Dunlap/Publishers' Graphics, Inc.; *8* Rafael Macia/Photo Researchers; *9* Leslie Dunlap/Publishers' Graphics, Inc.; *11* Richard Hutchings/Photo Researchers; *12* Robert E. Daemmrich/Tony Stone Worldwide; *16* Lloyd Birmingham; *18-19* Doug Pensinger/Allsport USA; *20* Richard Hutchings/Photo Researchers; *25* Lloyd Birmingham; *28* Michael Newman/PhotoEdit; *32* Lloyd Birmingham; *35* Michael Tamborino/Leo de Wys; *37* Mark Burnett/PhotoEdit; *40* Vanessa Vick/Photo Researchers; *43* Michael Newman/PhotoEdit; *56-57* Lenore Serra; *74* Michael Newman/PhotoEdit; *76* Joel Snyder/Publishers' Graphics, Inc.; *78* Myrleen Ferguson Cate/PhotoEdit; *79 (left)* Frank Siteman/PhotoEdit, *(right)* Richard Hutchings/Photo Researchers; *80* Kip Forde; *81 (left)* Monkmeyer/Grantpix, *(right)* Laurence Monneret/Tony Stone Images; *82* John Killgrew/Mulvey Associates; *83* Lauren Serra; *84 (both)* Joel Snyder/Publishers' Graphics, Inc.; *90* Lauren Serra; *94* Joel Snyder/Publishers' Graphics, Inc.; *97 (left)* The Granger Collection, *(right) Charlie and the Chocolate Factory*—illustration by Joseph Schindelman, copyright © 1964 by Roald Dahl, by permission of Random House, Inc.; *99 (left)* The Granger Collection, *(right) Charlotte's Web*—illustration by Garth Williams, copyright © 1952 by E. B. White, by permission of Harper & Row Publishers, Inc.; *100 The Arabian Nights*—illustration by Eric Pape, copyright © 1923 by Padraic Colum, by permission of The Macmillan Company; *101 (left) The Complete Nonsense Book*, copyright © 1964 by Edward Lear, by permission of Dodd, Mead and Company, *(right) The Little Prince*, copyright © 1943 by Antoine de Saint-Exupéry, by permission of Harcourt Brace Jovanovich; *103 (left)* Bantam Books, *(right)* reprinted by permission of Four Winds Press, a division of Scholastic, Inc., from *The Hodge-Podge Book* by Emrich Ohlsson, copyright © 1972 by Duncan Emrich; *104-105* Mark Burnett/PhotoEdit; *106 (top)* Paul Conklin/PhotoEdit; *108 (left)* The Granger Collection, *(right)* Library of Congress; *110 (left)* New York Public Library, *(right)* The Granger Collection; *111* New York Public Library; *112* Valley Forge Historical Society/Heritage-Horizon; *113* New York Public Library; *115* Betty Whelan; *116* New York Historical Society/Heritage-Horizon; *118* Wide World Photos; *119* Culver Pictures; *120* National Archives; *123* UPI; *125 (left)* Keystone View Company, *(right)* Culver Pictures; *127* UPI; *129* Wide World Photos; *130 (left)* Wide World Photos, *(right)* Larry Mulvehill/Photo Researchers; *131* Jason Laure/Woodfin Camp & Associates; *132* UPI/Bettmann; *133* James Shaffer/PhotoEdit; *134* Jan Halaska/Photo Researchers; *135* David Lindroth; *136* Betty Whelan; *139* David Lindroth; *140 (left)* Kent and Donna Danny/Photo Researchers, *(right)* Sylvain Grandadam/Photo Researchers, Inc ; *141 (left)* Dirck Halstead/Gamma Liaison, *(right)* A&L Sinibaldi/Tony Stone Images; *143* David Lindroth; *144 (left)* Willard Clay/FPG International, *(right)* John Gaps III/AP/Wide World Photos; *145 (left)* Andy Sacks/Tony Stone Images, *(right)* Charles Thatcher/Tony Stone Worldwide; *147* David Lindroth; *148 (left)* Cosmo Condina/Tony Stone Images, *(right)* Roberto Borea/AP/Wide World Photos; *149 (left)* Jim Zipp/Photo Researchers, Inc., *(right)* Patsy Lynch/Corbis; *151* David Lindroth; *152 (left)* E. Johnson/Leo de Wys, *(right)* Jeff Greenberg/PhotoEdit; *153 (left)* Joseph Nettis/Photo Researchers, Inc., *(right)* Bachmann/Photo Researchers; *154-155* NASA; *156* Ann Purcell/Photo Researchers; *159* Focus On Sports; *165* Leslie Dunlap/Publishers' Graphics, Inc.; *167* William Munoz/Photo Researchers, Inc.; *170* Robert Brenner/PhotoEdit; *180* Michael Newman/PhotoEdit; *185-187* Leslie Dunlap/Publishers' Graphics, Inc.; *189* David Young-Wolff/PhotoEdit; *195, 197 (both)* Leslie Dunlap/Publishers' Graphics, Inc.; *216 (left)* Jeffrey Sylvester/FPG, *(right)* David Young-Wolff/PhotoEdit; *220 (top)* Peter Loewer, *(bottom)* Russ Lappa/The Picture Cube, Inc.; *222* NASA; *223* Leslie Dunlap/Publishers' Graphics, Inc.; *227* Jean Loewer; *228-243* Leslie Dunlap/Publishers' Graphics, Inc.; *244 (right)* Richard Cash/PhotoEdit, *(top center)* SIU School of Medicine/Photo Researchers, Inc., *(bottom center)* Kathie Kelleher/Publishers' Graphics, Inc., *(bottom)* John Kaprielian/Photo Researchers, Inc.; *246* Leslye Borden/PhotoEdit; *248* Phillip Jones/Mulvey Associates, *(bottom)* Peter Loewer; *250 (left)* Rue/Monkmeyer, *(center, map)* David Lindroth, *(right)* Rue/Monkmeyer; *252-253* Phillip Jones/Mulvey Associates; *254 (top)* Pfletschinger/Peter Arnold, *(center, top)* Scott Camazine/Photo Researchers, *(center, bottom)* Gerard/Monkmeyer, *(bottom)* Everett Collection; *256* NASA; *257* Grant Le Duc/Monkmeyer; *261 (top)* John Killgrew/Mulvey Associates, *(bottom far left)* Bonnie Kamin/PhotoEdit, *(bottom center left)* Mark Richards/PhotoEdit, *(bottom center right)* Jennifer Lyden, *(bottom far right)* John Kelly/Tony Stone Images; *262* Peter Loewer; *263* Tim Davis/Photo Researchers, Inc.; *266-267* Kathie Kelleher/Publishers' Graphics, Inc., *(bottom)* David Young-Wolff/PhotoEdit, *(center, top)* Barbara Burnes/Photo Researchers, *(center left, bottom)* Tony Freeman/PhotoEdit, *(center right, bottom)* Myrleen Ferguson/PhotoEdit, *(bottom, left)* David Young-Wolff/PhotoEdit, *(bottom, center left, art)* Peter Loewer, *(bottom, center right, right)*, David Young-Wolff/PhotoEdit; *270* Kathie Kelleher/Publishers' Graphics, Inc. *271-272* Peter Loewer; *273* Leslie Dunlap/Publishers' Graphics, Inc.; *274 (top, center top)*, Kathie Kelleher/Publishers' Graphics, Inc., *(center bottom)* Leslie Dunlap/Publishers' Graphics, Inc., *(bottom)* Peter Loewer; *276* Jack Zehrt/FPG; *277* David Lindroth; *278* Lloyd Birmingham; *279 (top)* Lloyd Birmingham, *(bottom)* Peter Loewer; *280* Lloyd Birmingham; *281* Joel Snyder/Publishers' Graphics, Inc.; *282* Lloyd Birmingham; *283* David Lindroth; *284-285* Lloyd Birmingham; *286* David Lindroth; *287* Lloyd Birmingham; *289* Phillip Jones/Mulvey Associates; *290-291* Peter Loewer; *293* Wide World Photos; *294 (top)* Kathie Kelleher/Publishers' Graphics, Inc., *(center, bottom)* Photo Researchers; *296* NASA/PhotoEdit; *297* Lloyd Birmingham; *298 (left)* U.S. Geological Survey/Science Photo Library/Photo Researchers, *(center, right)* Mark Marten/NASA/Photo Researchers; *299 (left)* Mark Marten/NASA/Photo Researchers, *(right)* NASA/Science Source/Photo Researchers; *300 (top)* Sanford/Monkmeyer, *(bottom, left)* Photo Researchers, *(bottom, right)* University of Arizona; *301 (top, left)* John Sanford/Photo Researchers, *(right)* Rue/Monkmeyer; *302 (both)* Lloyd Birmingham; *303 (top)* NASA, *(bottom, left)* NASA/Photo Release, *(bottom, right)* Photo Researchers; *304* Phillip Jones/Mulvey Associates; *306* The Folio Press, London; *307* Leslie Dunlap/Publishers' Graphics, Inc.; *308* Peter Loewer; *309 (top)* NASA, *(bottom)* Francois Gohier/Photo Researchers; *311 (both)* Jet Propulsion Laboratory; *312* UPI/Bettmann; *313* NASA TV/AP/Wide World Photos; *314* Dennis O'Brien/Joseph, Mindin & Mulvey, Inc.; *315* NASA; *316 (art)* Peter Loewer, *(center, bottom)* NASA; *320-321* Rhoda Sidney/Leo de Wys; *323* Patrick Vielcanet/Photo Researchers; *323 (left)* Peter Loewer, *(right)* Jeff Greenberg/Photo Researchers; *325 (top)* New York Yankees, *(top center)* Focus on Sports, *(bottom center)* Manuello Paganelli/Corbis, *(bottom)* Michael Caulfield/AP/Wide World Photos; *326* Peter Loewer; *327 (left)* Clifford Hausner/Leo de Wys; *328* AP/Wide World Photos; *329 (top)* Culver Pictures, *(center, top)* Scott Halleran/Allsport USA, *(center, bottom)* Vernon Biever/Green Bay Packers, *(bottom)* Reuters/Bettmann; *330* Peter Loewer; *331* Focus On Sports; *332 (left)* Focus On Sports, *(right)* Peter Loewer; *333 (top)* Bruce Bennett, *(bottom)* Focus On Sports; *334 (top)* Peter Loewer, *(bottom)* Tony Freeman/Photo Edit; *335* New York Cosmos; *336 (top)* Peter Loewer, *(bottom)* Gary M. Prior/Allsport; *337* Clive Brunskill/Allsport; *338* Peter Loewer; *339 (top)* Everett Collection, *(bottom)* J. D. Cuban/Allsport USA; *340* Yann Guichaoua/Photo Researchers; *341* Kathy Willens/AP Photos; *342 (top)* Frank A. Cezus/FPG; *343 (bottom)* David Young-Wolff/PhotoEdit; *344 (top)* Photo Researchers, *(bottom)* Kathie Kelleher/Publishers' Graphics, Inc.; *345 (top)* Peter Loewer, *(center)* Vandvstadt/Photo Researchers, *(bottom)* Tony Freeman/PhotoEdit; *346* Robert Brenner/PhotoEdit; *347* Michael Austin Photo Researchers; *348* Dennis Hallinan/FPG; *349 (top left, top right, bottom left)* Peter Loewer, *(bottom right)* Kathie Kelleher/Publishers' Graphics, Inc.; *350 (strings, all)* C.G. Conn, *(woodwinds, left to right)* C.G. Conn, C.G. Conn, King Musical Instruments, C.G. Conn, King Musical Instruments; *351 (brass, top, middle, bottom left)* C.G. Conn, *(bottom right)* King Musical Instruments, *(percussion, top left)* David Strickler/Monkmeyer, *(top right, bottom left, bottom right)* Selmer; *352* Bob Krist/Leo de Wys; *353-355* Peter Loewer; *356* Austria National Library, Vienna; *357* Everett Collection; *358 (top)* Paula Lerner/The Picture Cube, Inc., *(top center, center, bottom center)* Peter Loewer, *(bottom)* Bill Stanton/International Stock Photography; *360* Tony Freeman/PhotoEdit; *361* New York Public Library; *363* Culver Pictures; *364* Paramount Pictures/Photofest; *365* Culver Pictures; *366* Photofest; *367* David Young-Wolff/PhotoEdit; *368 (top)* Hi Tech Toons/Photofest, *(center)* Bob Krist/Tony Stone Worldwide, *(bottom)* Tri-Star Pictures/Photofest.

Editorial development of the Student Handbook was directed by
The Hudson Group, Inc., Pleasantville, New York 10570

| | |
|---|---|
| *Administrative editors*: | Gorton Carruth and Eugene Ehrlich |
| *Editors-in-chief*: | Lawrence T. Lorimer and Bryan Bunch |
| *Managing editor*: | Hayden Carruth |
| *Administrative assistant*: | Nicole Grandjean |
| *Copy-editing and indexing*: | Felice Levy and Chris Carruth/AEIOU, Inc. |
| *Contributors*: | Frances Barth, Nance J. Davidson, Marcia Golub, Raymond V. Hand, John Harrington, Mary Hicks, Seymour Levine, Howard Liss, Don Lorimer, Janet McHugh, Sam Plummer, Bertram Siegel, Bruce Wetterau, Richard Worth |
| *Design and art direction*: | Pam Forde Graphics |
| *Production*: | Rachelle Engelman |
| *Illustrations and maps*: | David Lindroth, H. Peter Loewer, Jean Loewer/Graphos Studio, Ric Del Rossi/Mulvey Associates, Phillip Jones/Mulvey Associates, Leslie Dunlap/Publishers' Graphics, Inc., Lloyd Birmingham, Betty Whelan, Joel Snyder/Publishers' Graphics, Inc., Kathie Kelleher/Publishers' Graphics, Inc. |
| *Photo researchers*: | Pat Vestal, Carousel Research |

# Student Handbook

Including
## Science for Fun Experiments
and
## The Knowledge Factory

Volume 1

# Study Guide

# Grammar and Writing

Even though the purpose of your writing may change in each assignment you get, the main goal always stays the same: to express ideas clearly and effectively. Unless readers can understand what you write, they will not appreciate your special ideas on a subject. This is where knowing good grammar becomes important. Knowledge of the rules of language helps you to write clearly, express ideas effectively, and avoid being misunderstood.

This section tells about the basics of writing. It begins with an easy-to-use introduction to grammar. Printed in large type and containing many examples, it tells you how words are used to make sentences. The following part on combining sentences will help you write about more complicated ideas. A section on diagramming will help you understand the structure of sentences. In addition, the section on spelling and punctuation will aid you in spelling and punctuating correctly. Finally, a dictionary of synonyms and antonyms will let you choose just the right words for what you want to say.

# Parts of speech

Words are like certain types of lizards that change color to fit their surroundings. Words can change their meaning and the job they do, depending on when, where, and how they are used. Because words can be used in so many ways, people have created labels that show how words work in different surroundings. These labels are called *parts of speech*. There are eight parts of speech: nouns, pronouns, verbs, adjectives, adverbs, prepositions, conjunctions, and interjections. Knowing how to identify each part of speech will help you understand the parts of a sentence and write clearly and effectively.

## Parts of speech

This box reviews the parts of speech. More detailed coverage appears in the following pages.

A **noun** is a word that names *people, places, things,* or *ideas.*

| | | | |
|---|---|---|---|
| **people** | mother, carpenter, Amy | **places** | city, beach, France |
| **things** | tree, book, building | **ideas** | honesty, freedom, hope |

A **pronoun** is a word that takes the place of a noun, a group of words acting like a noun, or another pronoun.

you, me, their, himself, this, who, any, something

A **verb** is a word that expresses *action* or a *state of being.* It tells what a noun does or helps to tell what or how it is. Some verbs link the subject of a sentence with other verbs; these are called *linking* verbs.

| | |
|---|---|
| **action** | run, fly, rest, think, give |
| **being, linking** | be, have, appear, smell |

An **adjective** is a word that modifies the meaning of a noun or pronoun.

quiet, large, nasty, purple, glorious

An **adverb** is a word that modifies a verb, an adjective, or another adverb by making its meaning more specific. It can answer the questions *when, where, how, how much,* or *to what extent or degree.*

| | | | |
|---|---|---|---|
| **when** | now, soon, early, never | **to what extent or degree** | very, somewhat, not |
| **where** | here, inside, everywhere | | |
| **how** | carefully, happily | | |

A **preposition** is a word that shows the relationship of a noun or a pronoun to some other word in a sentence.

under, before, to, of, with, by, at

A **conjunction** is a word or a group of words that joins single words or sentence parts together.

and, but, or, when, as, wherever, although, however

An **interjection** is a word or a group of words that expresses emotion or exclamation. It has no grammatical connection to other words.

well, ouch, ah, wow

# NOUNS

A *noun* is one of the most important words used in speaking and writing. It is the word that tells what is being talked about. Nouns name people, places, things, or ideas.

## Characteristics of nouns.

Nouns change their form to show the number of people, places, things, or ideas being talked about. They also change form to show ownership.

**Number.** Nouns can be either singular or plural. A *singular noun* refers to only one person, place, thing, or idea. A *plural noun* refers to more than one. Most plural nouns are formed by adding -s or -es to the singular noun.

SINGULAR

hat     orange     torpedo     gas

PLURAL

hats     oranges     torpedoes     gases

Other nouns become irregular in the plural and do not follow the rules.

SINGULAR

woman     loaf     spacecraft     sheep

PLURAL

women     loaves     spacecraft     sheep

When you are in doubt about the spelling of a plural form of a noun, look it up in the dictionary.

**Possessive form.** Nouns change form to show possession, or ownership. To form the possessive of a singular noun or a plural noun that does not end in *s,* add -'s.

the astronaut<u>'s</u> helmet
the church<u>'s</u> steeple

To form the possessive of a plural noun that ends in *s,* add the apostrophe only.

two girl<u>s'</u> books
several countrie<u>s'</u> flags

However, when a person's or place's name (a proper noun) ends in *s,* add -'s.

Mr. Jones<u>'s</u> car
Kansas<u>'s</u> tornadoes
Davis<u>'s</u> raincoat

Possessive nouns are frequently used as modifiers that give additional information about other nouns. Although they often come before the nouns they

## What is a noun?

| people | places | things | ideas |
|---|---|---|---|
| Ramón | horizon | computer | leadership |
| mother-in-law | universe | piano | curiosity |
| Harriet Tubman | village | snow | knowledge |
| pilot | Sunshine State | dog | hope |

modify, they can also appear in other places in the sentence.

Larry's book is on the table.
This book is Larry's.
This book of Larry's is interesting.

# Kinds of nouns.
Understanding the differences between proper and common nouns, abstract and concrete nouns, general and specific nouns, and compound and collective nouns will help you to write more clearly.

**Common and proper nouns.** All nouns are either common or proper. A *common noun* refers to a general person, place, thing, or idea. Usually, a common noun is not capitalized unless it begins a sentence. A *proper noun* is the name or title of a specific person, place, thing, or idea. Proper nouns include the names of religions, languages, historical events, documents, days of the week, and months of the year. The first letter of a proper noun is capitalized.

COMMON NOUNS

scientist        city
cat              actor

PROPER NOUNS

Marie Curie      Denver
Thailand         Robin Williams

Proper nouns help to focus your writing. In the following example, notice how much more information the revised sentence gives you.

ORIGINAL

One day last week the doctor visited a large city.

REVISED

Last Tuesday Dr. Michaels visited Chicago.

*It is much clearer to say, "A chickadee sat on my hand," than it is to say, "A bird sat on my hand."*

**General and specific nouns.** All nouns are either general or specific. A *general noun* names any person, place, thing, or idea. A *specific noun* names particular people, places, things, or ideas

GENERAL NOUNS

park             animal
building         flower

SPECIFIC NOUNS

Mellon Park      zebra
Eiffel Tower     rose

Specific nouns create clearer images than general nouns do. Notice how much more you can see in the revised sentence in the following example.

ORIGINAL

The two dogs traveled down the street.

REVISED

The poodle and the cocker spaniel traveled down Oak Street.

**Concrete and abstract nouns.** All nouns are either concrete or abstract. A *concrete noun* names something that can be experienced through the senses of sight, sound, taste, smell, or touch. *Abstract nouns* name qualities, feelings, conditions, and attitudes. Sometimes abstract nouns seem difficult to identify since they do not refer to things that you can see or touch. Remembering the tip about putting *a, an,* or *the* before a noun will help you be more sure of abstract nouns.

*"Statue" is a concrete noun, but this particular statue symbolizes "liberty," an abstract noun.*

CONCRETE NOUNS

| | | |
|---|---|---|
| steak | jeans | waves |
| noise | garbage | |

ABSTRACT NOUNS

| | | |
|---|---|---|
| truth | freedom | democracy |
| joy | anger | |

Even though abstract nouns may mean different things to different people—for example, most everyone will have a different definition of joy—they are necessary in most forms of writing. If you use abstract nouns along with details and examples that show what they mean to you, your writing will be clearer and more interesting.

**Collective nouns.** A *collective noun* is a singular noun that names a group of people or things (a collection). These nouns may take a singular or a plural verb, depending on meaning.

| | | |
|---|---|---|
| bunch | cast | club |
| committee | herd | family |

**Compound nouns.** A *compound noun* is made up of two or more words used together to form a single noun. One kind of compound noun consists of two or more words joined together.

| | |
|---|---|
| sunglasses | backpack |
| spacecraft | sunscreen |

Another kind of compound noun has words joined by one or more hyphens.

| | |
|---|---|
| passers-by | life-style |
| light-year | sister-in-law |

A third kind of compound noun consists of two or more words that create a single noun even though they are not joined together in any way.

| | |
|---|---|
| jet engine | stars and stripes |
| air force | blue jeans |

Check a dictionary to make sure you are using the correct form of compound noun.

8

**Grammar and Writing**

# PRONOUNS

*Pronouns* are words that replace nouns, groups of words acting as nouns, or other pronouns. The word or words that a pronoun replaces is called the *antecedent* of that pronoun. Pronouns identify people, places, things, and ideas without renaming or repeating them. As the following two sentences show, pronouns make it possible to eliminate awkward repetition in writing.

First person refers to the person speaking, second person refers to the one spoken to, and third person is the one spoken about.

AWKWARD

The paper is finished, but the paper must still be typed.

REVISED

The paper is finished, but <u>it</u> must still be typed.

In the above example, *paper* is the antecedent of *it*.

## Kinds of pronouns.
There are seven kinds of pronouns: personal, demonstrative, reflexive, intensive, interrogative, relative, and indefinite.

**Personal pronouns.** A *personal pronoun* refers to a specific person or thing by indicating the person speaking (the first person), the person being addressed (the second person), or any other person or thing being discussed (the third person). In addition, personal pronouns have forms that indicate possession or ownership. These *possessive pronouns* take the place of possessive nouns (see Pronoun Usage on page 11 for more information on possessive pronouns).

Bill called to <u>me</u> just as <u>I</u> opened the door so <u>I</u> waved to <u>him</u>.

Visitors to the museum were disappointed because <u>they</u> could not see the exhibit <u>they</u> had heard so much about.

## Personal pronouns

|  | SINGULAR | PLURAL | POSSESSIVE |  |
|---|---|---|---|---|
|  |  |  | SINGULAR | PLURAL |
| FIRST PERSON | I, me | we, us | mine | ours |
| SECOND PERSON | you | you | yours | yours |
| THIRD PERSON | he, him | they, them | his | theirs |
|  | she, her | they, them | hers | theirs |
|  | it | they, them | its | theirs |

**Demonstrative pronouns.** A *demonstrative pronoun* is used to point out a specific person, place, or thing. It identifies which one or which group is being referred to.

We bought several of <u>those.</u>

<u>This</u> is my favorite pair of boots.

**Reflexive pronouns.** A *reflexive pronoun* indicates that a person or thing performs actions to, for, or on behalf of herself, himself, or itself. Reflexive pronouns are formed by adding -self or -selves to certain personal pronouns.

She sometimes talks to <u>herself</u> as she works.

They let <u>themselves</u> into the house.

## Demonstrative pronouns

| | |
|---|---|
| this | that |
| these | those |

## Reflexive pronouns

| | |
|---|---|
| FIRST PERSON | myself, ourselves |
| SECOND PERSON | yourself, yourselves |
| THIRD PERSON | himself, herself, itself, oneself, themselves |

## Interrogative pronouns

| | |
|---|---|
| who | whom |
| which | what |
| whose | |

## Relative pronouns

| | |
|---|---|
| who | whom |
| whose | which |
| that | |

**Intensive pronouns.** An *intensive pronoun* draws special attention to a noun or pronoun in a sentence. Intensive pronouns are the same words as reflexive pronouns, but they are used for different purposes. You will notice in the following examples that the intensive pronouns could be left out without changing the meaning of the sentences. They simply emphasize their noun antecedents.

The cast <u>itself</u> wrote the play and designed the scenery.

In this example, the intensive pronoun *itself* draws attention to the word *cast*.

We were greeted by the owner of the shop <u>himself</u>.

The intensive pronoun *himself* draws special attention to the word *owner*.

**Interrogative pronouns.** An interrogative pronoun introduces a question.

<u>What</u> does this word mean?

<u>Who</u> is going with you?

**Relative pronouns.** A *relative pronoun* introduces an adjective clause, which modifies a noun or pronoun by telling which, what kind, or how many.

The flat tire, <u>which</u> was caused by a nail, took an hour to repair.

Notice that the adjective clause *which was caused by broken glass* begins with the relative pronoun *which* and tells which tire took an hour to repair.

Someday we may have personal robots <u>that</u> do our chores.

The adjective clause *that do our chores* begins with the relative pronoun *that*

      **Grammar and Writing**

and tells what kind of robots we may have.

**Indefinite pronouns.** An *indefinite pronoun* refers to a person, place, or thing in a more general (or indefinite) way than a noun does. Unlike other pronouns, indefinite pronouns have no antecedents. They are used when the appropriate noun is unknown or unspecified.

> The Lions Club sent invitations to <u>everyone</u> in the community.

> The Denburgs returned from their vacation with <u>plenty</u> of gifts and souvenirs.

# Pronoun usage.
Many people make mistakes in using pronouns because some pronouns have a number of different forms. This section will help you learn how and when to use these different forms of pronouns.

**Pronoun and antecedent agreement.** All pronouns, whether they are personal, demonstrative, reflexive, intensive, interrogative, relative, or indefinite, must agree with their antecedents in number, gender, and person.

*"This is one of my favorite books. I'd recommend it to anyone. Most of the books I like best are about horses." In this quotation, the words "one," "anyone," and "Most" are indefinite pronouns.*

**Agreement in number.** Use a singular pronoun to refer to or replace a singular antecedent. Use a plural pronoun to refer to or replace a plural antecedent.

> <u>Kameko</u> decided that <u>she</u> would pack a picnic lunch.

> Kameko's <u>sisters</u> decided that <u>they</u> would pack a picnic lunch.

## Indefinite pronouns

| SINGULAR | | PLURAL | SINGULAR OR PLURAL |
|---|---|---|---|
| another | much | both | all |
| anybody | neither | few | any |
| anyone | nobody | many | more |
| anything | no one | others | most |
| each | nothing | plenty | none |
| either | one | several | some |
| enough | other | | |
| everybody | somebody | | |
| everyone | someone | | |
| everything | something | | |

Use a plural pronoun to refer to or replace two or more singular antecedents joined by *and*. Use a singular pronoun to refer to or to replace two or more singular antecedents joined by *or* or *nor*.

Shannon and Travis have seen their favorite movie six times.

Either Shannon or Travis will bring his photographs to school.

Some indefinite pronouns, such as *all, any, more, most, none,* and *some,* can be either singular or plural. Use either singular or plural pronouns to refer to or replace them, depending on the meaning of the sentence.

All of the color in the painting had lost its glow.

In the example shown above, *All* refers to *color,* which is singular; *its* refers to *all.*

All of the students are required to bring their permission slips.

*All* refers to *students,* which is plural; *their* refers to *all.*

When an antecedent is a collective noun, you need to determine whether the collective noun is singular or plural in meaning. If it is singular, use a singular pronoun to refer to it or replace it. If it is plural, use a plural pronoun.

The club voted to change its meeting time and location.

The singular is used above because the meeting time and location are for the entire club as one unit.

The city council argued among themselves.

The plural is correct in this example because the individual council members were arguing.

*Susan, David, and Mark agreed that they would bring only recyclable packaging with their lunches each day. Susan said that at home she and her family recycle everything. (In these sentences, the pronouns "they" and "she" agree in number and gender with their antecedents, "Susan, David, and Mark" and "Susan."*

**Grammar and Writing**

**Agreement in gender.** The gender of a pronoun is either masculine, feminine, or neuter (neither masculine nor feminine).

| | | | |
|---|---|---|---|
| MASCULINE | he | him | his |
| FEMININE | she | her | hers |
| NEUTER | it | its | |

Use a pronoun that agrees in gender with its antecedent.

<u>Dave</u> leaned <u>his</u> bike against the fence.

Occasionally, it is unclear whether the gender of a singular antecedent is masculine or feminine. If a neuter pronoun will not work, use the phrase *his or her* to show that the antecedent could be either masculine or feminine. When this kind of sentence becomes awkward, rewrite it so that the antecedent and all words that refer to it are plural.

AWKWARD

A pet owner should care about his or her animal.

REVISED

Pet owners should care about their animals.

**Agreement in person.** Pronouns are in either the first, second, or third person. Use a pronoun that agrees in person with its antecedent.

FIRST PERSON

I get home before <u>my</u> parents do.

SECOND PERSON

Will you get home before <u>your</u> parents do?

THIRD PERSON

Noel will get home before <u>his</u> parents do.

**Agreement of reflexive and intensive pronouns.** Reflexive and intensive pronouns must also agree with their antecedents in number, gender, and person. Reflexive and intensive pronouns are always used with antecedents. Do not use them alone to replace a noun or a personal pronoun.

INCORRECT

Dina and I will travel to New Jersey by themselves.

INCORRECT

Dina and myself will travel to New Jersey.

CORRECT

Dina and I will travel to New Jersey by <u>ourselves</u>.

**Pronoun case.** To show the grammatical use of a pronoun in a sentence, you must use the proper form, or *case*.

Use the *nominative case* when a pronoun acts as a subject or as a complement.

SUBJECT

<u>I</u> am the only one who knows how to get there.

COMPLEMENT

That was <u>she</u> on the telephone.

You will often find that pronouns in the nominative case are not used as complements in casual conversation.

For example, many people say, "It's me" instead of "It is I." You will also hear "That's him" instead of "That is he." Be sure to use pronouns in the nominative case in your own writing for school.

Use the *objective case* when a pronoun acts as a direct object, as an indirect object, or as an object of a preposition.

If a pronoun answers the question *Whom?* after an action verb, it is a direct object.

Whom did I see at the dance?
I saw him at the dance.

A pronoun used as an indirect object comes before the direct object and answers the question *To whom?* or *For whom?*

To whom did Suzette give the credit?

Suzette gave us all the credit.

For more information about direct and indirect objects, see page 38.

Use a pronoun in the objective case when the pronoun is the object of a preposition (*to, in, with*, etc.).

The police officer motioned to them to cross the street.

She has confidence in me.

George went to the store with me.

For more information about prepositions, see page 31.

Use the *possessive case* pronouns *mine, yours, his, hers, its, ours,* and *theirs* to refer to or replace nouns. These pronouns function in the same way as nouns do: as subjects, complements, direct or indirect objects, or objects of prepositions.

## Pronoun case

| | SINGULAR | PLURAL |
|---|---|---|
| NOMINATIVE CASE | I | we |
| | you | you |
| | he, she, it | they |
| OBJECTIVE CASE | me | us |
| | you | you |
| | him, her, it | them |
| POSSESSIVE CASE | mine | ours |
| | yours | yours |
| | his, hers, its | theirs |

**TIP**

To check the correct case of pronouns in compound direct objects, indirect objects, and objects of the preposition, break the sentence down into parts.

The Norris's collie always barks at Gwen and (I, me).

The Norris's collie always barks at Gwen.

The Norris's collie always barks at me.

The Norris's collie always barks at Gwen and me.

SUBJECT

<u>Theirs</u> is the party that everyone wants to attend.

COMPLEMENTS

The best short story is <u>his</u>.

DIRECT OBJECT

Although Kate lost her ring almost immediately, Sara wore <u>hers</u> for years.

INDIRECT OBJECT

Despite the rest of the boring speeches, Dwight gave <u>yours</u> his full attention.

OBJECT OF THE PREPOSITION

The twins will be upset that he did not pay attention to <u>theirs</u>.

**Determining the case of *who* and *whom*.** You can use forms of the pronoun *who* either as an interrogative pronoun or as a relative pronoun. The way that you use the pronoun determines the case, or form, that should be chosen.

NOMINATIVE CASE who, whoever
OBJECTIVE CASE whom, whomever
POSSESSIVE CASE whose

Use *who* when an interrogative pronoun acts as a subject or as a predicate nominative. Use *whom* when an interrogative pronoun acts as an object of a verb or as an object of a preposition.

NOMINATIVE

<u>Who</u> is playing the lead in the school play?

*Who* is the subject of the verb *playing*.

OBJECTIVE

To <u>whom</u> did you speak when you called the doctor's office?

*Whom* is the object of the preposition *to*.

If the interrogative pronoun *who* or *whom* is followed by a phrase that is not essential to the meaning of the sentence, remove the phrase for a moment to determine the use of the pronoun in the sentence and the form of the pronoun to use.

(Who, Whom) do you think will win the election.

Think: Who will win the election? *Who* is the subject.

Use *who* or *whoever* when a relative pronoun is the subject of a subordinate clause (a dependent clause that functions as a single part of speech). Use *whom* or *whomever* when a relative pronoun is an object within the subordinate clause.

The new student, <u>who</u> has already made a number of friends at our school, has been here little more than a week.

*Who* is the subject of the clause *who has already made a number of friends our school*.

The writer, <u>whom</u> many people respect, was honored at the conference.

*Whom* is the direct object of *respect*.

**Pronouns in comparisons.** In some comparisons using *than* or *as*, part of the phrase or clause is implied rather than stated. To choose the correct pronoun, think of the missing words to determine how the pronoun is used. In the following examples, you will see how the case of the pronoun used in an incomplete comparison can change the intended meaning.

Gary spends more time with Jeff than I.

Think: *than I spend with Jeff. I* is the subject of the implied clause; therefore, use the nominative form of the pronoun.

OBJECTIVE

Gary spends more time with Jeff than me.

Think: *than he spends with me. Me* is the object of the implied preposition *with*; therefore, use the objective form of the pronoun.

**Clear pronoun reference.** When you go over something you have written, check to see whether the pronouns are in the correct case and whether there is agreement between pronouns and their antecedents. Also check for pronoun shifts and unclear or missing antecedents. Incorrect pronoun usage will confuse your readers. Do not use a pronoun that can refer to more than one antecedent even if it means repeating the antecedent.

UNCLEAR

Susan chose Lily to be on her team because she knows the game well.

CLEAR

Susan chose Lily to be on her team because Lily knows the game well.

In the first example, we are unsure of which of the two girls knows the game well.

Avoid using the pronouns *it, they, you,* or *your* without a clear antecedent.

UNCLEAR

Before you give the lamb its bottle, be sure to shake it.

*"Before you give the lamb its bottle, be sure to shake it." The unclear pronoun reference in this sentence make for a very silly sentence.*

CLEAR

Before you give the lamb its bottle, be sure to shake the bottle.

In the first example, we do not know whether to shake the lamb or the bottle.

Avoid unnecessary pronoun shifts that may change the meaning you intended.

INCORRECT

I like summer best because you can swim in the ocean.

CORRECT

I like summer best because I can swim in the ocean.

Do not use the pronoun *your* in place of an article (*a, an,* or *the*) if possession is not involved.

INCORRECT

Many of your athletes have been training for years.

CORRECT

Many of the athletes have been training for years.

**Grammar and Writing**

# VERBS

The *verb* is sometimes considered the part of speech that is at the heart of a sentence, mostly because it affects meaning more than any other element. It determines the number of nouns needed, and it guides the action that takes place. Verbs can indicate a state of being as well as a physical action. They can even focus a reader's attention on a particular part of a sentence.

**Kinds of verbs.** There are five kinds of verbs that allow you to make a complete statement about something or someone.

**Action verbs.** An *action verb* describes the behavior, or action, of someone or something. It may express physical action or mental activity.

PHYSICAL

The band <u>marched</u> down Northfield Avenue.

The batter <u>hit</u> the ball to left field.

Louise <u>skates</u> very fast on the smooth ice.

MENTAL

Malcolm <u>thought</u> about his wood-working project.

He <u>believes</u> in working hard.

**Linking verbs.** A *linking verb* connects a noun or a pronoun with a word or words that identify or describe the noun or pronoun. Forms of the verbs *be* and *have* are the most common linking verbs.

Marnie <u>was</u> the winner of the race.

*Was* links *winner* with *Marnie; winner* identifies who Marnie is.

My parents <u>were</u> anxious about rush hour traffic.

*Were* links *anxious* with *parents; anxious* describes the word *parents*.

Mary <u>has</u> chicken pox.

*Has* links *Mary* with *chicken pox* and *chicken pox* describes Mary's condition.

Babette and Nicole <u>are</u> the twins in school.

*Are* links *twins* with *Babette* and *Nicole; twins* tell who *Babette* and *Nicole* are.

The verbs in the following list may also be used as linking verbs.

| | | |
|---|---|---|
| appear | feel | look |
| seem | sound | taste |
| become | grow | remain |
| smell | stay | turn |

The first speaker <u>appeared</u> nervous.

All of a sudden Alice <u>became</u> sad.

The long-distance runner <u>looks</u> tired.

The cookies <u>tasted</u> like root beer.

Some verbs can be either action verbs or linking verbs, depending on their use in a sentence.

ACTION

The whistle <u>sounded</u> a warning.

Deborah <u>stayed</u> home from school.

LINKING

His comments <u>sounded</u> really sarcastic.

Robert <u>stayed</u> very still.

**Auxiliary verbs.** Sometimes a verb needs the help of another verb, called an *auxiliary* or *helping verb*. The verb that it helps is called the *main verb*. The main verb and the helping verb form a *verb phrase*. A verb phrase may have more than one auxiliary verb.

<u>Will</u> you <u>be waiting</u> for me after school?

*Waiting* is the main verb, *will* and *be* are the helping verbs, and *will be waiting* is the verb phrase.

My sister <u>should have taken</u> that job.

*Taken* is the main verb, *should* and *have* are the helping verbs, and *should have taken* is the verb phrase.

The teacher <u>is obeyed</u> by her students.

*Obeyed* is the main verb, *is* is the helping verb, and *is obeyed* is the verb phrase.

Susan <u>ought</u> to study her grammar more.

*To study* is the main verb, *ought* is the helping verb, and *ought to study* is the verb phrase.

## Common auxiliary verbs

| | | |
|---|---|---|
| am | do | must |
| are | does | ought |
| be | had | shall |
| being | has | should |
| been | have | was |
| can | is | were |
| could | may | will |
| did | might | would |

**Transitive and intransitive verbs.** All action verbs are either transitive or intransitive. A *transitive verb* needs an object, called the *object of the verb*, to complete its meaning. An *intransitive verb* has no object. Linking verbs, such as *be* and *have*, are always intransitive. Some action verbs can be either transitive or intransitive, depending on their meaning and whether an object is necessary.

TRANSITIVE

Mr. Abeed <u>photographed</u> the Great Wall of China.

*Great Wall of China* is the object of the verb *photographed*.

*Li Xiaoshuang gave a fine performance at the 1996 Olympics (*a fine performance *is the object of* gave, *so* gave *is a transitive verb).*

Wally <u>painted</u> his house during the summer.

*House* is the object of the verb *painted.*

The old house <u>seems</u> haunted.

*Seems* is a linking verb and therefore has no object.

The blackbird <u>hid</u> in the bushes.

*Hid* is intransitive because it has no object.

We <u>stopped</u> a stranger on the street to ask for directions.

The object of *stopped* is *stranger*.

*Li Xiaoshuang felt proud to have won a gold medal at the 1996 Olympics (felt is a linking verb and has no object and therefore is intransitive).*

Jane <u>smiled</u> a wide, happy grin.

The object of *smiled* is *grin*.

The subway <u>stopped</u> abruptly.

*Stopped* has no object.

Jane <u>smiled</u> with pleasure.

*Smiled* has no object.

# How to use verbs.

Verbs have several characteristics, such as tense, that other parts of speech do not. If you understand the forms and tenses of verbs, you will be able to choose the ones that best explain what is going on in your sentences and use them correctly.

**Principal parts of verbs.** The four basic forms of a verb are called its *principal parts*. Knowing the principal parts of a verb is important because all the tenses of a verb are formed from them. The principal parts of a verb are the *infinitive*, the *present participle*, the *past*, and the *past participle*. By using these forms alone or with helping (auxiliary) verbs, you can express the various tenses of a verb.

The infinitive and the present participle are formed in the same way for all verbs. The *infinitive* is the basic verb form. The word *to* usually precedes the infinitive in a sentence. The *present participle* is always a combination of the infinitive and -ing. It is used in a sentence with a form of *be* as an auxiliary verb.

Five miles is a long way <u>to walk</u> in the snow.

Jared is walking home from school.

**Regular and irregular verbs.** Most verbs are *regular verbs*. They form their past and their past participle the same way, by adding -ed or -d to the infinitive. In a sentence, the past participle takes a form of the verb *have* as an auxiliary verb. When certain endings are added to the infinitive, a spelling change may be necessary. Check a dictionary if you are unsure of a particular spelling.

*The students rode their bicycles to and from school every day. (Ride is irregular. Its past tense is "rode," not "rided.")*

## Common irregular verbs

| INFINITIVE | PAST | PAST PARTICIPLE |
|---|---|---|
| awake | awoke | (have) awakened |
| beat | beat | (have) beat or beaten |
| become | became | (have) become |
| begin | began | (have) begun |
| bite | bit | (have) bitten |
| bleed | bled | (have) bled |
| blow | blew | (have) blown |
| break | broke | (have) broken |
| bring | brought | (have) brought |
| build | built | (have) built |
| buy | bought | (have) bought |
| catch | caught | (have) caught |
| choose | chose | (have) chosen |
| come | came | (have) come |
| dig | dug | (have) dug |
| dive | dived or dove | (have) dived |
| do | did | (have) done |
| drink | drank | (have) drunk |
| drive | drove | (have) driven |
| eat | ate | (have) eaten |
| fall | fell | (have) fallen |
| fly | flew | (have) flown |
| forget | forgot | (have) forgotten |
| freeze | froze | (have) frozen |
| get | got | (have) gotten |
| give | gave | (have) given |
| go | went | (have) gone |

*Irregular verbs* do not follow the standard rules for forming the past and the past participle. The only way to master the past and past participial forms of irregular verbs is to memorize the main parts of the verbs that you use frequently and check your dictionary for those that you do not use as often. You will find the list of common irregular verbs below useful as an everyday reference.

**Verb tense.** Various forms of verbs show whether an action or condition takes place in the present, took place in the past, or will take place in the future. The forms of a verb that express time are called *tenses.* There are six different verb tenses: *present; past; future; present perfect; past perfect;* and *future perfect.* To form all but the present and past tenses, combine the principal parts of verbs with auxiliary verbs.

| INFINITIVE | PAST | PAST PARTICIPLE |
|---|---|---|
| hang | hung | (have) hung |
| | hanged | (have) hanged |
| have | had | (have) had |
| hear | heard | (have) heard |
| hide | hid | (have) hidden |
| hurt | hurt | (have) hurt |
| know | knew | (have) known |
| lay | laid | (have) laid |
| lie | lay | (have) lain |
| lose | lost | (have) lost |
| make | made | (have) made |
| pay | paid | (have) paid |
| prove | proved | (have) proven, (have) proved |
| ride | rode | (have) ridden |
| ring | rang | (have) rung |
| rise | rose | (have) risen |
| say | said | (have) said |
| sell | sold | (have) sold |
| show | showed | (have) shown, (have) showed |
| sink | sank | (have) sunk |
| speak | spoke | (have) spoken |
| take | took | (have) taken |
| teach | taught | (have) taught |
| tear | tore | (have) torn |
| throw | threw | (have) thrown |
| wear | wore | (have) worn |
| write | wrote | (have) written |

In the following examples, the six tenses of the verb *see* are used to express action at different times.

PRESENT

I <u>see</u> at least one movie a week.

PAST

I <u>saw</u> a good movie two days ago.

FUTURE

I <u>will see</u> the new Disney movie this weekend.

PRESENT PERFECT

I <u>have seen</u> two movies so far this month.

PAST PERFECT

I <u>had</u> not <u>seen</u> many movies before last year.

FUTURE PERFECT

By the end of this year, I <u>will have seen</u> over 50 movies.

To *conjugate* a verb means to list all of

## Conjugation of *to fall*

### PRINCIPAL PARTS

| PRESENT | PRESENT PARTICIPLE | PAST | PAST PARTICIPLE |
|---------|--------------------|------|-----------------|
| fall | (is) falling | fell | (have) fallen |

| | SINGULAR | PLURAL |
|---|----------|--------|
| PRESENT TENSE | I fall<br>you fall<br>he, she, it falls | we fall<br>you fall<br>they fall |
| PAST TENSE | I fell<br>you fell<br>he, she, it fell | we fell<br>you fell<br>they fell |
| FUTURE TENSE | I will/shall fall<br>you will fall<br>he, she, it will fall | we will/shall fall<br>you will fall<br>they will fall |
| PRESENT PERFECT | I have fallen<br>you have fallen<br>he, she, it has fallen | we have fallen<br>you have fallen<br>they have fallen |
| PAST PERFECT | I had fallen<br>you had fallen<br>he, she, it had fallen | we had fallen<br>you had fallen<br>they had fallen |
| FUTURE PERFECT | I will/shall have fallen<br>you will have fallen<br>he, she, it will have fallen | we will/shall have fallen<br>you will have fallen<br>they will have fallen |

the forms for its six tenses. The conjugation of a verb also shows how the verb forms change for the first person, the second person, and the third person and for the singular and the plural.

To form the *present tense* of a verb, use its infinitive. To form the third person singular, add -s or -es to the infinitive in most cases. Use the present tense to show an action that takes place now, to show an action that is repeated regularly, or to show a condition that is true at any time.

We <u>walk</u> the Livingston High School track.

We <u>walk</u> every day for exercise.

Walking <u>is</u> always good exercise.

Also use the present tense in statements about literary works or other works of art.

This book <u>is</u> about a young girl's adventures growing up in England.

To form the *past tense* of a regular verb, add -d or -ed to the infinitive. Use the past tense to express action that occurred in the past and was entirely completed.

Yesterday we <u>walked</u> the track in the rain.

To form the *future tense*, combine *will* or *shall* with the infinitive form of the main verb. Use the future tense to describe action that will occur in the future.

They <u>will walk</u> with us tomorrow.

The *present perfect tense* is formed by using *has* or *have* with the past parti-ciple of the main verb. Use the present perfect tense to describe action that was completed recently or at an indefinite time in the past.

I <u>have walked</u> farther today than I have ever walked before.

To form the *past perfect tense*, use *had* with the past participle of the main verb. The past perfect tense describes an action that was completed by a certain time in the past or before another action was completed.

We <u>had walked</u> the required distance before we realized that we should have stopped to rest.

Form the *future perfect tense* by using *will have* or *shall have* with the past participle of the main verb. Use the future perfect tense to describe an action that will be completed before another action will be.

They <u>will have walked</u> three miles before the rest of the group joins them.

**The progressive forms of verbs.** Each of the six tenses has an additional form that is used to express continuing action. To form the progressive, use the appropriate tense of the verb *be* with the present participle of the main verb.

PRESENT PROGRESSIVE

We <u>are walking</u> to raise money for charity.

PAST PROGRESSIVE

He <u>was walking</u> faster than we were.

FUTURE PROGRESSIVE

I <u>will be walking</u> for the next 20 minutes.

#### PRESENT PERFECT PROGRESSIVE
They <u>have been walking</u> all morning.

#### PAST PERFECT PROGRESSIVE
We <u>had been walking</u> for only a short time when he joined us.

#### FUTURE PERFECT PROGRESSIVE
By the time they arrive, she <u>will have been walking</u> for an hour.

***The emphatic form of verbs.*** The emphatic form is used to make the present and past tenses of a verb stronger. To use the emphatic form, combine the present or the past tense of the verb *do* with the infinitive form of the main verb.

We <u>do walk</u> every day when the weather is nice.

We <u>did walk</u> during the winter.

***Modals.*** The auxiliary verbs *can, could, may, might, must, will,* and *should* are known as *modals*. These verbs are used with main verbs to add emphasis to a sentence or to provide shades of meaning. Use *can* (present tense) and *could* (past tense) to express the ability to perform the action of the main verb.

We <u>can walk</u> faster if you like.

She <u>could have walked</u> with us yesterday if we had called her.

Use *may* to mean "have permission to" or to express a possibility.

The doctor said my mother <u>may walk</u> now that her ankle has healed.

I <u>may walk</u> this weekend if I have time.

Use *might* (the past tense of *may*) to express a possibility that is less likely than one expressed by *may*.

There is always a chance that the test <u>might be canceled</u>.

Use *must* to show that the action of the main verb is required or to suggest a possible explanation.

Sheila <u>must call</u> her parents immediately.

Gunnar <u>must have been</u> wrong about the date of the meeting.

Use *should* (the past tense of *shall*) to suggest that something ought to happen.

Sheila <u>should call</u> home immediately.

***Consistency of tenses.*** Using verb tenses consistently makes writing clear. A shift in tense often causes confusion and misunderstanding.

When two or more actions take place at the same time, use verbs that are in the same tense.

#### INCORRECT
Connie <u>collected</u> firewood, and Hugh <u>builds</u> the fire.

#### CORRECT
Connie <u>collected</u> firewood, and Hugh <u>built</u> the fire.

#### INCORRECT
Martha's interest in art <u>grows</u> steadily as time <u>went</u> by.

#### CORRECT
Martha's interest in art <u>grew</u> steadily as time <u>went</u> by.

**Grammar and Writing**

INCORRECT

The train <u>passed</u> Pleasantville when it <u>is</u> exactly noon.

CORRECT

The train <u>passes</u> Pleasantville when it <u>is</u> exactly noon.

***Active and passive voice.*** In addition to tense, transitive verbs have voice. A verb is in the *active voice* when it has a direct object. A verb is in the *passive voice* when the direct object is converted into the subject.

ACTIVE

The audience <u>applauded</u> the violinist's solo.

The batter <u>hits</u> the ball.

PASSIVE

The violinist's solo <u>was applauded</u> by the audience.

The ball <u>is hit</u> by the batter.

Intransitive verbs are always in the active voice because they do not take objects. As you can see from the examples above, when a verb in the active voice is changed to the passive voice, its direct object becomes the subject of the sentence. The subject of the sentence becomes the object of a preposition.

The active voice is generally the more direct and effective way of expressing action. You should use the passive voice only to emphasize the receiver of the action, or when the person or thing performing the action is unknown. Overusing the passive voice makes writing dull.

**Choosing effective verbs.** In your writing, select the most specific verbs that you can. Strong verbs give your readers precise images.

DULL VERB CHOICE

The puppy <u>walked</u> into the kitchen and <u>lay</u> down.

VIVID VERB CHOICE

The puppy <u>waddled</u> into the kitchen and <u>sprawled</u> on the floor.

*Choosing a vivid verb over a dull one will help make your writing more exciting. "The puppy waddled into the kitchen and sprawled on the floor" is a more interesting sentence than "The puppy walked into the kitchen and lay down."*

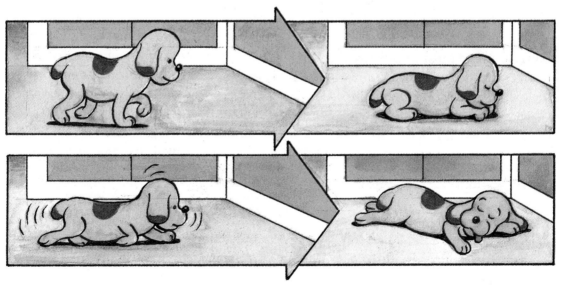

# WHAT ARE MODIFIERS?

Modifiers can change the meaning of nouns, pronouns, and verbs by adding information or limiting a meaning. Adjectives and adverbs, the two most common kinds of modifiers, give color and life to language, helping you to create clearer images in your writing.

**Adjectives.** An *adjective* is a word that modifies a noun or a pronoun. To modify means to change. An adjective changes the meaning of a noun or a pronoun by describing it or making it more specific. An adjective answers one of three questions: *which? what kind?* or *how many?*

WHICH?

Jodi found a <u>red</u> shoe in front of her <u>gym</u> locker.

WHAT KIND?

We bought <u>fresh</u> vegetables at the <u>farmers'</u> market.

HOW MANY?

<u>Two thousand</u> people attended the concert.

**Articles.** The most frequently used adjectives are the *definite article* (*the*), and the *indefinite articles* (*a* and *an*). Use *a* when the noun it modifies begins with a consonant sound. Use *an* when the noun begins with a vowel sound.

The woman carried <u>a</u> purse and <u>an</u> overnight bag.

It is <u>an</u> honor to serve my country.

Did you find <u>the</u> stamps I bought yesterday?

**Proper adjectives.** A *proper adjective* is formed from a proper noun. It is always capitalized and can be used to modify a noun or pronoun. The names of products are proper adjectives because the specific name limits the type of general product.

Two sailboats glided into <u>Boston</u> harbor.

Glenda washes her face with <u>Luxury</u> soap.

**Nouns used as adjectives.** Some nouns function as adjectives without changing form.

The whistle of the <u>freight</u> train interrupted my sleep.

*Possessive nouns* show ownership, answering the question *which?* When you use them to show possession, change their form by adding 's or just an apostrophe.

<u>Keith's</u> house is at the bottom of the hill.

The <u>cars'</u> headlights bother my eyes.

**Possessive adjectives.** Use the possessive adjectives *my, your, his, its, our,* and *their* to modify nouns and to show possession.

<u>Their</u> shouts warned us of the fire.

The cat rolled <u>its</u> ball across the floor.

**Placement of adjectives.** Adjectives usually come before the nouns or pronouns that they modify. Sometimes they are separated from the words that they modify by a comma.

Dull and repetitious, the speech put the audience to sleep.

*Dull* and *repititious* modify the noun *speech.*

Adjectives may follow linking verbs, modifying the subject of the sentence.

The cat is frisky and playful.

Sometimes adjectives follow the words that they modify and are separated from them by commas.

The cat, frisky and playful, tore through the house.

## Adverbs.

Like adjectives, adverbs are modifiers. An *adverb* is a word that modifies a verb, an adjective, or another adverb. An adverb answers one of five questions about the word or phrase that it modifies: *how? when? where? how often?* or *to what extent?*

Claus and Yoshio shook hands firmly.

*Firmly* modifies the verb *shook.*

We will see the Borgese family soon.

*Soon* modifies the verb *will see.*

Noreen looked everywhere for her lost bracelet.

*Everywhere* modifies the verb *looked.*

Their family rarely eats dinner together.

*Rarely* modifies the verb *eats.*

Barry was rather doubtful about getting a part in the play.

*Rather* modifies the adjective *doubtful.*

**Placement of adverbs.** An adverb does not have to appear next to the verb that it modifies. Notice the different positions of the adverbs *silently* and *slowly* in these sentences.

Silently and slowly, the snow covered the yard.

The snow silently and slowly covered the yard.

The snow covered the yard silently and slowly.

An adverb usually comes directly before the adjective that it modifies.

Josh discovered that the map was fairly easy to read.

Adverbs usually come right before the other adverbs that they modify.

Raisa crossed the balance beam quite slowly.

## Common adverbs

| | | |
|---|---|---|
| again | just | seldom |
| almost | later | so |
| alone | never | soon |
| already | not | then |
| also | now | there |
| always | nowhere | today |
| away | often | too |
| even | perhaps | very |
| ever | quite | yet |
| here | rather | |
| indeed | really | |

**Distinguishing between adjectives and adverbs.** Sometimes it is difficult to tell the difference between an adjective and an adverb. Many adverbs end in -ly, but so do some adjectives.

ADJECTIVE

The <u>daily</u> newspaper has excellent local sports coverage.

ADVERB

Arden delivers the newspaper <u>daily</u>.

# How to use modifiers. Lively
modifiers can vastly improve your writing. However, the adjectives and adverbs that you choose must be used correctly to avoid confusing your readers.

**Comparison of modifiers.** By using different forms of adjectives and adverbs, you can compare two or more persons or things. The three degrees of

comparison are positive, comparative, and superlative.

Use a modifier in the *positive degree* to add some information about a person, a thing, an action, or an idea. Use a modifier in the *comparative degree* to compare a person, a thing, an action, or an idea with another one. Do not use the comparative when more than two things are being compared. Use a

*"I've looked everywhere for my other running shoe." In this sentence "everywhere" is an adverb, modifying the verb "looked," and "other" and "running" are adjectives modifying "shoe."*

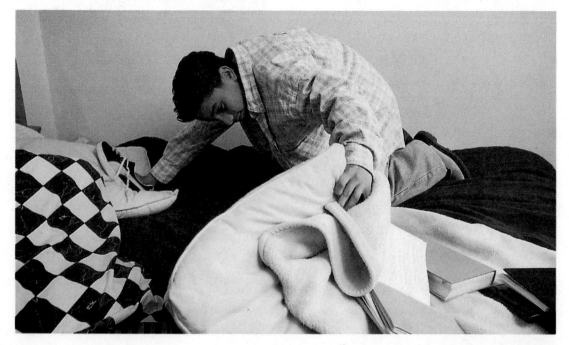

28          **Grammar and Writing**

modifier in the *superlative degree* to compare a person, a thing, an action, or an idea with at least two others.

## ADJECTIVES

### POSITIVE

That program was <u>long</u>.

### COMPARATIVE

That program was <u>longer</u> than last week's.

### SUPERLATIVE

That program was the <u>longest</u> I've seen.

## ADVERBS

### POSITIVE

Teddy works <u>fast</u>.

### COMPARATIVE

Teddy works <u>faster</u> than Eric does.

### SUPERLATIVE

Teddy works the <u>fastest</u> of any boy in our grade.

Add -er to form the comparative and -est to form the superlative of modifiers with one or two syllables. In some cases, to form the comparative correctly, you must drop the final *e*, double the final consonant, or change a final *y* to *i* before adding an ending to a word.

clean, cleaner, cleanest
funny, funnier, funniest
old, older, oldest

Use *more* to show the comparative degree and *most* to show the superlative degree in three cases: with all three-syllable words, with two-syllable words that would otherwise be difficult to pronounce, and with adverbs that end in -ly.

dreadful, more dreadful, most dreadful
fragrant, more fragrant, most fragrant
serious, more serious, most serious

Use *less* and *least* to form the comparative and superlative degrees of comparisons showing less.

funny, less funny, least funny
healthy, less healthy, least healthy
hopeful, less hopeful, least hopeful

The comparative and superlative degrees of some modifiers are formed irregularly. Since there are only a few, memorizing them will ensure that you use them correctly.

Certain adjectives, such as *perfect, unique, dead, round, full,* and *empty,* do not have a comparative or superlative degree. These adjectives refer to conditions about which no more can be said. Logically, nothing can be described as

## Irregular comparisons

| POSITIVE | COMPARATIVE | SUPERLATIVE |
|---|---|---|
| bad/badly | worse | worst |
| far | farther/further | farthest/furthest |
| good/well | better | best |
| little | less | least |
| many/much | more | most |

"more perfect" or "more empty." You should also avoid double comparisons. Use either the word *more* or *most* or else the correct ending; do not combine the two.

INCORRECT

Which is the <u>most highest</u> mountain?

CORRECT

Which is the <u>highest</u> mountain?

Avoid incomplete comparisons by clearly indicating the things being compared. When you compare one member of a group with the rest of the group, you can avoid being unclear or misleading by using the comparative degree and the word *other* or *else*.

UNCLEAR

Anita plays softball better than anyone in the class.

The sentence above says either that Anita plays softball better than anyone in the class, including herself, or that Anita plays softball better than anyone in a class of which she is not a part.

CLEAR

Anita can play softball better than anyone <u>else</u> in the class.

Now we know that Anita is the best softball player in her class.

Be sure to avoid using double negatives. A *double negative* is the use of two negative words to express only one negative idea. Negative words include *no, none, nothing, not,* and *never*. A contraction ending in *n't* is also a negative word.

INCORRECT

We did <u>not</u> find <u>nothing</u> on the radio worth listening to.

CORRECT

We did <u>not</u> find <u>anything</u> on the radio worth listening to.

CORRECT

We found <u>nothing</u> on the radio worth listening to.

The words *scarcely, hardly,* and *barely* all mean almost not at all. They carry the force of negatives. Therefore, avoid using these words with another negative to express a single idea.

INCORRECT

Connie did <u>not hardly</u> know how to do her math homework.

CORRECT

Connie did <u>not</u> know how to do her math homework.

CORRECT

Connie <u>hardly</u> knew how to do her math homework.

**Placement of modifiers.** Putting modifiers in the wrong place can create unclear sentences. To avoid misplacing modifiers, put the adjective or adverb as close as possible to the word you wish to modify, while keeping your intended meaning.

Strolling by the lake, a family of geese walked in front of Jaime.

In the above example, we do not know who was strolling by the lake.

CLEAR
Strolling by the lake, Jaime noticed a family of geese in front of him.

In this version, Jaime is doing the strolling by the lake.

CLEAR
In front of him, Jaime noticed a family of geese strolling by the lake.

In this version, the family of geese is doing the strolling.

A *dangling modifier* is a phrase or clause that does not clearly or sensibly modify any word in the sentence. To avoid dangling modifiers, provide an antecedent for every modifying phrase or clause.

UNCLEAR
Grilled over charcoal, we particularly enjoy vegetables like zucchini.

Here, the modifying phrase *grilled over charcoal* appears to modify the pronoun *we*.

UNCLEAR
We particularly enjoy vegetables grilled over charcoal like zucchini.

The modifying phrase *like zucchini* seems to modify *charcoal*.

CLEAR
We particularly enjoy vegetables like zucchini grilled over charcoal.

**Using effective modifiers.** You should practice using precise adjectives and adverbs to create colorful details in your writing. Strong verbs are essential, but even strong verbs often need adverbs to tell more. Your readers will more easily understand what you have to say if your adverbs are specific. When you write, try to avoid using vague adverbs such as *very, really, only, well, hard,* and *often.*

ORIGINAL
She wore a very nice dress.

REVISED
She wore a stylish lace mini dress.

# WHAT ARE CONNECTING WORDS?

In many sentences, special words join or show the connections between other words. Prepositions and conjunctions are these special words.

**Prepositions.** A *preposition* is a word that shows the relationship between a noun or a pronoun and another word in the sentence. The preposition is usually followed by a noun or a pronoun that is called the *object of the preposition.* Together, the preposition, the object, and the modifiers of that object form a *prepositional phrase.*

Cardinals and robins nest <u>in</u> thickets.

The preposition *in* relates *cardinals* and *robins* to *thickets,* which is the object of the preposition; *in thickets* is the prepositional phrase.

Prepositions usually state direction, time, or position.

The deer are running <u>toward</u> the woods.

The audience became restless <u>during</u> his speech.

Please place the book <u>on</u> that table.

The most common prepositions are at, by, for, from, in, of, on, to, and with.

A *compound preposition* consists of more than one word.

The Chulaks bought two turkeys <u>instead of</u> just one.

The child is hiding <u>back of</u> the bookcase.

<u>Because of</u> the cold weather, Susie stayed indoors.

*Maria hid her frog in her T-shirt drawer. (In this sentence* in her T-shirt drawer *is a prepositional phrase.)*

A prepositional phrase functions as an adjective if it modifies a noun or a pronoun. A prepositional phrase functions as an adverb if it modifies a verb, an adjective, or another adverb.

ADJECTIVE

Their housing development has a picnic area <u>for the residents.</u>

In this case, the prepositional phrase *for the residents* modifies the noun *area.*

ADVERB

The exhausted tennis player sat <u>on the grass.</u>

## Common prepositions

| | | | | | |
|---|---|---|---|---|---|
| aboard | at | but (except) | inside | out | underneath |
| about | before | by | into | over | until |
| above | behind | concerning | like | past | up |
| across | below | down | near | since | upon |
| after | beneath | during | of | through | via |
| against | beside | except | off | throughout | with |
| along | besides | for | on | to | within |
| among | between | from | onto | toward | without |
| around | beyond | in | opposite | under | |

## Common compound prepositions

| | | | |
|---|---|---|---|
| according to | as of | in addition to | instead of |
| ahead of | back of | in back of | in view of |
| apart from | because of | in front of | next to |
| as far as | by means of | in place of | out of |
| aside from | contrary to | in spite of | prior to |

**Grammar and Writing**

The prepositional phrase *on the grass* modifies the verb *sat*.

Some words can function as prepositions or as adverbs, depending on their use in a sentence. Remember that every preposition must have an object.

PREPOSITION

Hank saw Marilyn <u>outside</u> the theater.

The children are running <u>around</u> the house.

ADVERB

Please don't go <u>outside</u> without your jacket.

The children are somewhere <u>around</u>.

# Conjunctions.

A *conjunction* is a word that connects words or groups of words. There are three kinds of conjunctions: coordinating, correlative, and subordinating.

**Coordinating conjunctions.** When you want to connect individual words or groups of words (phrases and clauses) that perform the same function in a sentence, you use a *coordinating conjunction*.

The boys raced across the street <u>and</u> into the house.

The conjunction connects two prepositional phrases.

I remembered his face, <u>but</u> I forgot his name.

The conjunction connects two independent clauses.

You may use a pen <u>or</u> a pencil.

The conjunction connects two words.

**Correlative conjunctions.** Like coordinating conjunctions, *correlative conjunctions* connect words that perform equal functions in a sentence. Correlative conjunctions consist of two or more words that work together.

## Coordinating conjunctions

| | | | | | |
|---|---|---|---|---|---|
| and | but | for | nor | or | yet |

## Correlative conjunctions

| | | | | | |
|---|---|---|---|---|---|
| both/and | either/or | neither/nor | not only/but also | so/as | whether/or |

## Subordinating conjunctions

| | |
|---|---|
| TIME | after, as, as long as, as soon as, before, since, until, when, whenever, while |
| MANNER | as, as if, as though |
| CAUSE | because |
| CONDITION | although, as along as, even if, even though, if, provided that, though, unless, while |
| COMPARISON | as, than |
| PURPOSE | in order that |

We had <u>both</u> snow <u>and</u> sleet during the skiing trip.

The conjunction connects two words.

<u>Not only</u> were we cold, <u>but</u> we were <u>also</u> lost.

The conjunction connects two clauses. Here are some more examples:

Do not become <u>so</u> hungry <u>as</u> to faint.

<u>Either</u> you stay home <u>or</u> you go to school.

You may <u>neither</u> stay home <u>nor</u> go to the movies.

We do not know <u>whether</u> you are going to school or are staying at home.

**Subordinating conjunctions.** A *subordinating conjunction* introduces a subordinate clause, which is a clause that cannot stand by itself as a complete sentence. A subordinating conjunction connects the subordinate clause to an independent clause, which <u>can</u> stand by itself as a complete sentence. Subordinating conjunctions usually show relationships of time, manner, cause, condition, comparison, or purpose.

<u>Because</u> the sneakers are expensive, we cannot afford to buy them.

The subordinating conjunction *because* introduces the subordinate clause and connects it to the independent clause that follows it.

The stores are extremely crowded with holiday shoppers <u>unless</u> you go first thing in the morning.

The subordinating conjunction *unless* introduces the subordinate clause and connects it to the independent clause that precedes it.

<u>As</u> tall as Adam is, Betty is taller.

The subordinating conjunction *as* introduces the subordinating clause and connects it to the independent clause that follows it.

**Conjunctive adverbs.** A *conjunctive adverb* functions like a coordinating conjunction because it usually connects independent clauses. A semicolon precedes the conjunctive adverb and a comma usually follows it.

CONJUNCTIVE ADVERB
The races were exciting; <u>therefore</u>, we stayed until the end.

COORDINATING CONJUNCTION
The races were exciting, <u>and</u> we stayed until the end.

More examples of the use of conjunctive adverbs follow:

## Frequently used conjunctive adverbs

| | | | |
|---|---|---|---|
| also | furthermore | later | still |
| besides | however | moreover | then |
| consequently | indeed | nevertheless | therefore |
| finally | instead | otherwise | thus |

**Grammar and Writing**

Charles dislikes vegetables; <u>furthermore</u>, he especially dislikes spinach.

They went swimming in the morning; <u>later</u>, they had lunch on the terrace.

In the afternoon, they walked and read magazines; <u>otherwise</u>, there was nothing else to do.

# INTERJECTIONS

There are a number of words or phrases that are used to express strong feeling or sudden emotion. Words that serve this purpose are called *interjections*. Many interjections stand alone and are followed by exclamation points. Others appear within a sentence and are set off with a comma or commas.

<u>Wow!</u> That taco was really spicy.

<u>Oh</u>, I beg your pardon.

<u>Ouch!</u> You stepped on my toe.

<u>No! No!</u> I won't do it.

**Using interjections.** Although interjections add variety to writing, you should use them sparingly. The strong feeling in your writing should come from the words you choose, the sentences you construct, and the ideas you express, not just from interjections.

Weak interjections should be avoided.

WEAK

Well, well, what's the use. It won't work.

BETTER

What's the use! It won't work.

*Wow! Look at him move! I've never seen someone do that on a skateboard before. (In these sentences, Wow, is an interjection.)*

# What are sentences?

When a number of words are put together to express a complete thought, they produce a sentence. By learning the jobs of different kinds of sentences and by understanding their individual parts, you will be able to choose the best ways to express your ideas.

## What can a sentence do?

A *sentence* is a group of words that has a subject and a verb and that expresses a complete thought. It describes an action or states something about a person, place, or thing. Even so, some sentences are difficult to define, especially those that consist of only one word: Welcome. Yes. Why? Notice that even these one-word sentences express a complete thought. Two-word sentences are common: Dogs bark. She cried. They sat. You will see, however, that most sentences consist of many words.

There are four types of sentences and each has a different purpose. A *declarative sentence* makes a statement and ends with a period. An *interrogative sentence* asks a question and ends with a question mark. An *exclamatory sentence* shows strong feeling and ends with an exclamation point. An *imperative sentence* gives an order or makes a request. A mild command or request ends with a period, but a strong command or request ends with an exclamation point.

| | |
|---|---|
| DECLARATIVE | *Xavier's best friend is a talented artist.* |
| INTERROGATIVE | *Have you decided to enter the essay contest?* |
| EXCLAMATORY | *What a tragedy that was!* |
| IMPERATIVE | *Clear the halls at once!* (strong command) |
| IMPERATIVE | *Please shut the door.* (mild request) |

## Parts of a sentence.
To express a complete thought, a sentence must have a subject and a verb. However, there are other parts as well that help to provide further information. A sentence may or may not include all the parts of speech described above. These parts of speech can be used in a sentence in many expanded ways. For example, the function of a noun may be modified by several words and the function of a verb may likewise be modified by other words. In order for you to understand how a sentence is put together, you must learn how these larger functions work.

**Simple subjects.** The *simple subject* of a sentence is the noun or pronoun that names the person, place, thing, or idea that the sentence is about. The simple subject does not include modifiers.

> *Mr. Wong's fried <u>dumplings</u> are the best I've ever tasted.*
> *The <u>stack</u> of dirty dishes in the sink must be washed.*
> *Yesterday <u>they</u> took a boat across Lake Champlain.*
> *Tomorrow <u>he</u> will go alone.*

The simple subject of an imperative sentence is always *you*. Often, *you* is understood rather than stated.

> *Bring your camera to school tomorrow.*

As you can see in the example above, *you* is the understood simple subject of the sentence, as in *you bring your camera.*

> *Wake up!*

Again, *you* is the understood simple subject of the sentence: *You wake up!*

A *compound subject* is a simple subject that has two or more nouns or pronouns of equal rank.

> *<u>Lemonade</u> and <u>iced tea</u> were the only drinks.*
> *The twins <u>John</u> and <u>Mary</u> go to different schools.*
> *The <u>knives</u> and <u>forks</u> are made of silver.*
> *<u>We</u> and <u>you</u> are going to the police station.*

**Simple predicates.** A *simple predicate* is the verb or verb phrase that describes the action or states something about the subject. The simple predicate does not include modifiers and words that complete the meaning of the verb. It also does not include the adverbs *not* or *never*.

> *Each student <u>collected</u> several kinds of wildflowers.*
> *Lisa and Alan <u>will try</u> to be here on time.*
> *Mary <u>will have received</u> the letter by the time you get there.*

A *compound predicate* is a simple predicate that is made up of two or more verbs or verb phrases of equal importance.

*DeVona <u>measured</u> the fabric and then <u>cut</u> out the pieces of the vest.*
*Mike <u>carried</u> the ball down the football field and <u>crossed</u> the goal line jubilantly.*
*Dan <u>had worked</u> hard and <u>had saved</u> his money.*

**Complete subjects and complete predicates.** The *complete subject* consists of the simple subject and all the words that modify or identify it.

<u>*Union Street, which is in San Francisco,*</u> *is known for its restaurants and art galleries.*
<u>*Popular with all their classmates, Len and Lyle, who are identical twins,*</u> *are the newest students in the school.*
<u>*High on a mountain, often hidden by clouds, the monastery*</u> *is rarely visited.*

The *complete predicate* consists of the simple predicate and all the words that modify it or complete its meaning.

*Union Street, which is in San Francisco, <u>is known for its restaurants and art galleries.</u>*
*Popular with all their classmates, Len and Lyle, who are identical twins, <u>are the newest students in the school.</u>*
*High on a mountain, often hidden by clouds, the monastery <u>is rarely visited.</u>*

**Placement of subjects and predicates.** Subjects and predicates may be arranged in a variety of ways in sentences. Where you place the subject and the predicate often depends on the purpose of the sentence. In the examples that follow, the complete subjects are underlined and the complete predicates not underlined.

DECLARATIVE    <u>*The giant tortoise, the animal with the longest life span,*</u> *lives in a pond·in the zoo.*
Here, the subject precedes the predicate.

DECLARATIVE    *Here are <u>the athletic socks that you ordered from the catalogue</u>.*
The sentence above is written in inverted order; that is, the subject follows the predicate.

DECLARATIVE    *Into the street rolled <u>the car</u>.*
This sentence has inverted word order.

DECLARATIVE    *Because they had studied Native American jewelry techniques, <u>Paula and Diane, who both love silver and turquoise,</u> were particularly interested in the exhibit.*
In this example, the subject is between the two parts of the predicate.

*The simple subject of the sentence "The woman is walking toward the bus" is "woman." The verb "walk" supplies the action in the form of the simple predicate, "is walking."*

INTERROGATIVE *How were you able to fix the plugged drain in the kitchen?* The subject is between two parts of the predicate.

IMPERATIVE *Try to finish painting the window frames by noon.* Here, the entire imperative sentence is the complete predicate because the subject, *you*, is understood.

EXCLAMATORY *The pictures that you took are fantastic!* The subject precedes the predicate.

EXCLAMATORY *What a fascinating book that was!* The subject is between two parts of the predicate.

**Complements.** A *complement* is a word or group of words that completes the meaning of a verb. Complements are always part of the complete predicate. Without complements, the meaning of the following sentences would be incomplete and unclear.

*The oranges that the DiNardos brought back from Florida were sweet and juicy.*
*Soon we must begin chopping wood for the winter.*
*This winter seems especially cold.*

There are three types of complements: direct and indirect objects, objective complements, and subject complements. Sometimes you will have to analyze a sentence carefully to determine which word or words are complements.

A *direct object* is a noun or a pronoun that follows an action verb in the active voice and receives the action of the verb. It answers the question *what?* or *whom?* Verbs that take direct objects are called transitive verbs. (You can learn more about transitive and intransitive verbs under the section Verbs above.) Modifiers are not part of the object.

*Mrs. Duryea will visit her great aunt.*
This answers the question, will visit *whom?*

*Our neighbors have a blower for clearing leaves and snow from their property.*
In the example above, the direct object answers the question, have *what?*

*The birthday boy ate his cake greedily.*
In this example, the question is, the boy ate *what?*

An *indirect object* is a noun or a pronoun that names the person or thing *to* whom or *for* whom something is done. An indirect object follows an action verb in the active voice. In most cases, an indirect object is used with a direct object. The indirect object comes immediately after the verb and before the direct object.

*We will show Jared as many historical sites as we have time for.*
Think: We will show historical sites *to* Jared.

*Her grandmother knitted Sonya a red sweater.*
Think: Grandmother knitted a sweater *for* Sonya.

Like subjects and predicates, objects may be compound. A *compound object* consists of two or more objects that complete the same predicate.

COMPOUND DIRECT OBJECT *Jake read several books and articles about icebergs.*

COMPOUND INDIRECT OBJECT *Marlene offered Carol and her brother tickets to the game.*

An *objective complement* is a noun or an adjective that follows a direct object and explains, identifies, or describes that object. Only certain verbs take an objective complement: *appoint, call, choose, consider, elect, find, make, name, think,* and other verbs that have the same meaning.

*The board of trustees has appointed Mr. Gearhart the director of the research department.*
*Director* is the objective complement of the verb *appointed*; it further identifies Mr. Gearhart.

*We considered the dancer's performance inspiring.*
*Inspiring* is the objective complement of the verb *considered*; it describes the direct object, *performance*.

A *subject complement* is a word that comes after a linking verb and identifies or describes the subject of a sentence or a clause. Subject complements often follow forms of the verb *be* as well as *appear, become, feel, grow, look, remain, seem, smell, sound, stay,* and *taste.*

There are two types of subject complements. A *predicate nominative* is a noun or a pronoun that follows a linking verb and identifies the subject of the sentence. The predicate nominative renames the subject.

*Owen is a volunteer at the local hospital.*

In the example above, *volunteer* identifies the subject, *Owen*.

> *After working with a trainer, Phineas became an obedient <u>dog.</u>*

*Dog* renames the subject of the sentence, *Phineas*.

A *predicate adjective* follows a linking verb and modifies the subject of the sentence.

> *The book that I read was <u>hard</u> to follow.*

Here, the predicate adjective *hard* modifies the subject, *book*.

> *Micki felt <u>relaxed</u> and <u>sleepy</u> after reading for only ten minutes.*

The predicate adjectives *relaxed* and *sleepy* modify the subject, *Micki*.

# What are phrases? A *phrase* is a group of related words that functions as a single part of speech. But a phrase is different from a sentence because it lacks a subject, or a predicate, or both. Phrases can add variety to your writing and enable you to use fewer words.

**Prepositional phrases.** A *prepositional phrase* is made up of a preposition and its object and any modifiers of that object. A prepositional phrase that modifies a noun or a pronoun is called an *adjective phrase*. A prepositional phrase functions as an adverb if it modifies a verb, an adjective, or another adverb. This kind of phrase is sometimes called an *adverb phrase*.

ADJECTIVE PHRASE

> *The newspaper will list the location <u>of the next meeting</u>.*

The prepositional phrase *of the next meeting* modifies the noun *location*.

ADVERB PHRASE

> *Mr. Whiteside will not leave <u>before dinner</u>.*

The prepositional phrase *before dinner* modifies the verb *will not leave*, making it an adverb phrase.

ADVERB PHRASE AND ADJECTIVE PHRASE

> *The entire class was curious <u>about methods of conserving energy.</u>*

Here, the prepositional phrase *about methods* modifies the adjective *curious*; it is an adverb phrase. The prepositional phrase *of conserving energy* modifies the noun *methods*; it is an adjective phrase.

ADVERB PHRASE AND ADJECTIVE PHRASE

> *A boy or girl <u>with dirty hands</u> is not welcomed <u>at the table</u>.*

The prepositional phrase *with dirty hands* modifies the nouns *boy* and *girl*; thus, it is an adjective phrase. The prepositional phrase *at the table* modifies the verb *is not welcomed*; it is an adverb phrase.

**Appositive phrases.** An *appositive* is a noun or a pronoun placed near another noun or pronoun to explain it or identify it. Like an appositive, an *appositive phrase* explains or identifies a noun or a pronoun. It includes all the words or phrases that modify an appositive.

APPOSITIVE

> *The class secretary, <u>Anton Berrioz</u>, read the meeting notes aloud.*

The appositive *Anton Berrioz* identifies the class secretary.

APPOSITIVE PHRASE

> *The movie, <u>a science fiction thriller with special effects</u>, was exciting.*

The appositive phrase *a science fiction thriller with special effects* further describes the movie.

An *essential appositive phrase* is an appositive that is necessary to the meaning of the sentence. This kind of appositive should not be separated from the rest of the sentence with a comma. A *nonessential appositive phrase* is an appositive that is not necessary to the meaning of the sentence. This appositive phrase should be separated from the rest of the sentence with a comma or commas.

ESSENTIAL APPOSITIVE PHRASE

> *Edgar Allen Poe's short story "The Telltale Heart" has been recorded many times.*

Poe wrote more than one short story. Therefore, the appositive "The Telltale Heart" is necessary to identify which story has been recorded many times.

NONESSENTIAL APPOSITIVE PHRASE

> *Poe also wrote "The Pit and the Pendulum," <u>a story that gives me nightmares every time I read it</u>.*

In this case, the appositive is not necessary to identify the story.

*The students, searching diligently on the banks of the pond, found many interesting things. (In this sentence* searching diligently on the banks of the pond *is a participial phrase.)*

**Verbal phrases.** *Verbals* are verb forms that function as nouns, adjectives, or adverbs but keep some of the properties of verbs. They express action or a state of being, and may take complements. There are three kinds of verbals: participles, gerunds, and infinitives.

**Participial phrases.** A *participial phrase* consists of a participle and its modifiers and complements. The participial phrase functions as an adjective to modify a noun or a pronoun. Both present and past participles may be used to form participial phrases.

> *Cooing softly to herself, the baby played with her toes.*

The participial phrase shown above modifies *baby.*

> *The instructions, written in poorly translated Japanese, were impossible to understand.*

The participial phrase modifies *instructions.*

Always place a comma after an introductory participial phrase. If the information in a phrase within a sentence is essential, you do not need to use commas. Essential information identifies a person, place, or thing. If the information in a

phrase is nonessential, however, commas are used to separate it from the rest of the sentence. A nonessential phrase contains information that could be removed without changing the basic meaning of the sentence.

ESSENTIAL PARTICIPIAL PHRASE

> *The person talking to the coach is Peter Boland.*

No commas are used because the phrase is needed to identify the person.

NONESSENTIAL PARTICIPIAL PHRASE

> *Peter Boland, talking to the coach, is a friend.*

Commas are needed because the phrase could be removed from the sentence.

**Gerunds and gerund phrases.** A *gerund* is a verbal that ends in -ing and functions as a noun. It has some of the properties of a verb in that it expresses action or being, and it may take a complement such as a direct object or an indirect object.

**Grammar and Writing**

| | |
|---|---|
| SUBJECT | *Pointing is impolite.* |
| DIRECT OBJECT | *Nell enjoys <u>skating</u> and <u>biking</u>.* |
| INDIRECT OBJECT | *She gives her <u>practicing</u> one hour a day.* |
| OBJECT OF THE PREPOSITION | *Gil went the whole day without <u>eating</u>.* |
| PREDICATE NOMINATIVE | *Last year my favorite winter sport was <u>skiing</u>.* |
| APPOSITIVE | *Tina has a new interest, <u>sewing</u>.* |

A *gerund phrase* is a gerund with its modifiers and complements all working together as a noun.

<u>*Singing together*</u> *is a treat for them.*
*The Carrs surprised us by <u>visiting for a week</u>.*
<u>*Painting scenery*</u> *is Rick's specialty.*

The possessive form of a noun or a pronoun is used before a gerund and is considered part of the phrase.

<u>*Talia's winning the debate tournament*</u> *was a shock.*

*His parents encouraged <u>his studying chemistry</u>.*

**Infinitives and infinitive phrases.** An *infinitive* is a verbal form that consists of the first principal part of the verb. The word *to* usually, though not always, precedes the infinitive. An infinitive may function as a noun, an adjective, or an adverb. Like a participle and a gerund, an infinitive has some of the characteristics of a verb. It expresses action or being, and it may take a complement.

| | |
|---|---|
| NOUN | <u>*To make*</u> *a mistake is human.* Here the infinitive is the subject. *Everyone should learn <u>to change</u> a tire.* The infinitive is a direct object in this instance. |
| ADJECTIVE | *North Caldwell is the team <u>to beat</u>.* *To beat* modifies the noun *team.* |

---

TIP

Because an infinitive begins with the word *to*, it is sometimes confused with a prepositional phrase. An infinitive ends with a verb form, but a prepositional phrase ends with a noun or a pronoun.

---

| | |
|---|---|
| ADVERB | *Young children are quick <u>to learn</u>.* *To learn* modifies the adjective *quick.* |

An *infinitive phrase* consists of an infinitive and its modifiers and complements. It can function as a noun, an adjective, or an adverb.

| | |
|---|---|
| NOUN | <u>*To win at chess*</u> *requires concentration.* |
| ADJECTIVE | *The best time <u>to cut flowers</u> is early in the morning.* |
| ADVERB | *It's fun <u>to try different foods</u> in new restaurants.* |

*To* is sometimes omitted when an infinitive follows such verbs as *dare, feel, hear, help, let, make, need, see,* or *watch.*

*Mr. Hussein helped me <u>put up the badminton net</u>.*

Think: helped me *to* put up the badminton net.

# What are clauses?
A *clause* is a group of related words that contains both a subject and a verb. There are two kinds of clauses: independent and subordinate. Understanding clauses and being able to include them in your writing is valuable because clauses show important relationships between ideas. Clauses also let you combine ideas to create clearer sentences.

**Independent clauses.** An *independent* or *main clause* can stand alone as a sentence because it expresses a complete thought. When an independent clause stands by itself, it is called a *sentence.* When it appears in a sentence with another clause, it is called a clause. In the following example, you will notice how each clause has a subject and a predicate. Each could be a separate sentence.

*Janice raked the leaves, and Dwight bagged them.*

You can use a comma and a coordinating conjunction like *and* or *but* to join the clauses. *And* is not part of either clause. It coordinates, or connects, the independent clauses. You can also join independent clauses with either a semicolon or a semicolon and a conjunctive adverb.

*This sounds like a tall tale, <u>but</u>, believe it or not, it's true.*
*This sounds like a tall tale<u>;</u> believe it or not, it's true.*
*This sounds like a tall tale<u>; however</u>, believe it or not, it's true.*

**Dependent clauses.** A *dependent* or *subordinate clause* cannot stand alone as a sentence because it does not express a complete thought. Even though it has a subject and a predicate, it depends on the rest of the sentence for meaning.

*Because we were late, we missed the kickoff.*

*Carly goes to the beach whenever she has the chance.*

A dependent clause functions as an *adjective clause* if it modifies a noun or a pronoun. Most adjective clauses begin with a relative pronoun: *that, which, who, whom,* or *whose.*

*Teddy wants a pet that he can play with.*

*Ramona looked for Mrs. Weinstein, who was holding tryouts in the auditorium.*

Adjective clauses can be either *essential* or *nonessential.* Separate a nonessential clause from the rest of the sentence with a comma or commas, but do not separate an essential adjective clause from its independent clause.

A dependent clause functions as an *adverb clause* when it modifies a verb, adjective, or another adverb. An adverb clause always begins with a subordinating conjunction, a word that shows the relationship between the dependent clause and the independent clause. Adverb clauses tell *how, when, where, to what extent,* and *why.*

*We will go whenever you're ready.*

*Alan is taller than I am.*

*As long as its chin is being tickled, the cat will sit quietly.*

Place a comma after an introductory adverbial clause. If an adverbial clause interrupts an independent clause, place a comma before and after it.

*If you win, will you give your prize money to charity?*

*The Senate, after the President vetoed the bill, overrode the veto.*

A dependent clause functions as a *noun clause* when it is used like a noun: as a subject, a direct object, an indirect object, an object of the preposition, or a predicate nominative. Noun clauses are introduced with interrogative pronouns, subordinating conjunctions, or the relative pronoun *whose.*

SUBJECT  *Whatever you choose is fine with me.*

DIRECT OBJECT  *Did you realize that Lamar won?*

INDIRECT OBJECT  *Give whoever comes to the door the samples.*

OBJECT OF THE PREPOSITION  *Bridget was overwhelmed by what she had heard.*

PREDICATE NOMINATIVE  *Helen's reason for leaving early was that she was sick.*

# Subject/verb agreement. For
a sentence to be clear, the subject and its verb must agree. The forms of nouns, pronouns, and verbs can be changed to show whether they are singular or plural. If the subject is singular, the form of the verb should be singular. If the subject is plural, the form of the verb should be plural. This is called making the subject and verb agree in number.

SINGULAR  *Peter lives in a small town near the border of Tennessee.*

PLURAL  *Three of my relatives live in the same town.*

For a verb phrase to agree with its subject, the helping verb must agree in number with the subject.

SINGULAR  *Peter has lived there only since March.*

PLURAL  *My relatives have lived there all their lives.*

Sometimes words and phrases come between a subject and its verb. These words or phrases do not change the number of the subject. Be sure to make the verb agree in number with the subject of the sentence, not with some word in another phrase.

SINGULAR  *Lisa, new to the life of babysitters, was unprepared for her lack of free time on weekends.*

PLURAL  *The contestants waiting backstage for a cue were becoming restless.*

**Determining the number of the subject.** In some sentences, you may find it difficult to determine the number of the subject. These guidelines will help you.

**Compound subjects.** A *compound subject* is made up of two or more subjects that are connected by a coordinating conjunction. A compound subject may take a singular or a plural verb, depending on which conjunction is used and whether the words in the compound subject are singular or plural. Use a plural

**Grammar and Writing**

verb with most compound subjects connected by *and*.

PLURAL    *The <u>coach and the principal were expected</u> to attend the meeting.*

Use a singular verb with a compound subject that refers to one person or one thing, or to something that is generally considered as a unit—plural in form but singular in meaning.

SINGULAR    *This year's most popular <u>player and speaker is planning</u> to sign autographs.*

The singular is used in the above example because the player and speaker are the same person.

Use a singular verb with a compound subject that has a singular noun or pronoun connected by *or* or *nor*.

SINGULAR    *Either her <u>aunt or</u> her <u>cousin plans</u> to attend the concert.*

Use a plural verb with a compound subject that is composed of plural nouns or pronouns connected by *or* or *nor*.

PLURAL    *Neither the old <u>televisions nor</u> the broken <u>radios have been fixed</u>.*

When a compound subject is composed of a singular subject and a plural subject connected by *or* or *nor*, use the verb that agrees in number with the subject that is closer to the verb in the sentence.

SINGULAR    *Neither the cellists nor the <u>violinist has</u> sheet music.*

PLURAL    *Neither the violinist nor the <u>cellists have</u> sheet music.*

**Nouns with plural forms.** Nouns such as *economics, mathematics, measles,* and *news* are plural in form but singular in meaning. Although they end in <u>s</u>, they refer to a single thing or to a unit and therefore take a singular verb.

SINGULAR    *<u>Physics is</u> a challenging branch of science.*

Other nouns, such as *clothes, congratulations, pliers, shears,* and *scissors,* end in <u>s</u> but take a plural verb, even though they refer to one thing.

PLURAL    *His garden <u>shears are</u> on the porch.*

Some nouns, such as *athletics, dramatics,* and *politics* end in <u>s</u> but may be singular or plural depending on their meaning in the sentence. It is important to use your dictionary to find out whether a noun that ends in <u>s</u> takes a singular or a plural verb.

**Inverted word order.** In some sentences, especially questions or sentences beginning with *Here* or *There*, you may have difficulty locating the subject because the verb comes before it. Rearrange the sentence in its normal subject-verb order to find the subject and make the verb agree with it in number.

SINGULAR    *Beside the building was a tiny park.*
            Think: park *was*.

PLURAL    *There are many caves in those mountains.*
          Think: caves *are*.

**Sentences with predicate nominatives.** Using a predicate nominative can confuse subject-verb agreement when the subject and the predicate nominative differ in number. You should always use a verb that agrees in number with the subject, not the predicate nominative.

INCORRECT    *Roses is one of her favorite flowers.*

CORRECT    *Roses are one of her favorite flowers.*

**Every and many a(n).** As adjectives, *every* and *many a(n)* emphasize separateness when they modify subjects. *Every* means every single one and *many a(n)* means each item separate from all other items. Therefore, use a singular verb with a single subject or a compound subject modified by *every* or *many a(n)*.

*Every shirt and vest <u>is</u> on sale this weekend.*
*Many a cat <u>dislikes</u> milk and fish.*

*Clothes are fun to shop for.* (Clothes *is a plural noun and takes a plural verb,* are.)

# Combining sentences

So far, we have been looking only at simple sentences; yet we all know that not all sentences are simple; they can be highly complex. Writing, indeed, would be very dull if it were nothing but one simple sentence after another after another.

## Sentence combining.
Simple sentences, of the kinds we have been looking at, can be combined with other simple sentences. The results of these combinations are more complex sentences. In fact, every sentence, no matter how complex, can be thought of as the combining of two or more simple sentences.

There are many ways in which sentences can be combined. In the following pages, we shall look at a number of them. Learning to combine sentences can be of great help in two important ways:

1. Practicing ways of combining sentences will help you learn how the language works; its grammar, its general rules, and its oddities. Start with two simple sentences you have made up. Combine them in as many ways as you can. Although not every pair of sentences can be combined in every way, you will be surprised at how many ways there are to modify the sentences' meanings by combining them. Then try more complex combinations, of three, four, five, and even more sentences. This practice will be a great help in teaching you to write more clearly.
2. Combining sentences can help you clarify your own thinking. When you know what you want to say, but can't get it down on paper, turn to sentence combining. Take the idea that you are having trouble with, and write out its parts in simple sentences. Then try various ways of putting the simple sentences together, being sure that you keep the sentences' main ideas unchanged. Sooner or later (probably sooner than you expect), you will find the right way to say what you want to.

## Compounding.
The simplest way of combining sentences is called compounding. Compounding combines sentences by joining them together with coordinating conjunctions.

Consider these two simple sentences:
*My mother is a dentist.*
*My father is a writer.*
These two sentences can be put together by simply joining them with *and*:
*My mother is a dentist, and my father is a writer.*
Notice that neither of the original sentences has been changed; they have just been joined together. Notice, too, the comma before *and*, which is important. When two simple sentences are joined in this way, forming what is called a compound sentence, a comma always comes before the word that joins them.

Other conjunctions besides *and* can join sentences in this way:
*or, nor, but, for, either/or, neither/nor, both/and, not only/but also*
Suppose, for example, that you have these two simple sentences. One of them is true, but you do not know which one it is.
*His father is a bus driver.*
*His uncle is a bus driver.*
These sentences can be combined using *either/or*:
*Either his father is a bus driver, or his uncle is a bus driver.*
Again, notice that the original sentences have not changed; they have just been joined by the conjunctions and the comma.

Now cover the page with a sheet of paper. Write out the combinations of each of these pairs of sentences, using the conjunction given after the second sentence. Do not look at the combined versions until you have written your own.

SENTENCES: *Yesterday was beautiful.*
*Today is cold and rainy. (but)*
COMBINED: *Yesterday was beautiful, but today is cold and rainy.*

SENTENCES: *We took a long walk.*
*It was a lovely day. (because)*
COMBINED: *We took a long walk, because it was a lovely day.*

SENTENCES: *We shall leave today.*
*We shall leave tomorrow.*
*(either/or)*
COMBINED: *Either we shall leave today, or we shall leave tomorrow.*

**Grammar and Writing**

**Compounding sentence parts.** Look again at that last pair of sentences. Notice that they are the same except for the adverbs at the end. When two sentences have some words that are identical, as here, the identical words can be crossed out of the second sentence and the remainder of the sentence can be combined with the first.

SENTENCES: *We shall leave today.*
*We shall leave tomorrow.*
*(either/or)*

COMBINED: *We shall leave either today or tomorrow.*

This kind of combining can be done with all kinds of sentence parts. Whatever parts are combined in the two sentences are said to be compound. These two sentences, for example,

*Jerry is ready.*
*I am ready. (and)*

combine to produce a sentence with a compound subject:

*Jerry and I are ready.*

(Notice that *Jerry and I*, being two people, require the plural verb *are*.)

Other sentence parts can be compounded:

VERBS: *The departing guests smiled.*
*The departing guests waved.*
*(and)*

COMBINED: *The departing guests smiled and waved.*

DIRECT OBJECTS: *They will choose Jennifer.*
*They will choose me. (or)*

COMBINED: *They will choose Jennifer or me.*

ADJECTIVES: *The day was bright.*
*The day was sunny.*

COMBINED: *The day was bright and sunny.*

PREPOSITIONAL PHRASES:
*She walked across the street.*
*She walked into the house.*

COMBINED: *She walked across the street and into the house.*

OBJECTS OF PREPOSITIONS:
*This gift is for Carol.*
*This gift is for her husband.*

COMBINED: *This gift is for Carol and her husband.*

**Parallelism.** In forming compounds of this kind, it is important that the sentence elements that are compounded be of the same kind. In the following pair of sentences, for example, a compound cannot be correctly formed.

*He likes tennis.*
*He likes to swim.*

*Tennis* and *to swim* are not the same kind of sentence element; they are said to be not parallel. Thus the sentence *He likes tennis and to swim* is incorrect. To combine the sentences, the form of one of them must first be changed.

SENTENCES: *He likes tennis.*
*He likes swimming.*

COMBINED: *He likes tennis and swimming.*

**Compounding with semicolons.** The two sentences below could be combined using *and*:

SENTENCES: *Finish your breakfast.*
*Then we can go.*

COMBINED: *Finish your breakfast, and then we can go.*

There is, however, another way they can be joined. Simply put them next to each other and join them with a semicolon:

COMBINED: *Finish your breakfast; then we can go.*

It is important that the punctuation mark be a semicolon. Connecting the sentences with only a comma (or with no punctuation at all) produces a "run-on" sentence and is incorrect.

**Series.** Supposing that, instead of two sentences with some identical words, you have three:

*The day was bright.*
*The day was cold.*
*The day was windy.*

These three sentences can be combined in exactly the same way as can two sentences:

*The day was bright and cold and windy.*

Usually, combinations of this kind are taken a step further. First, every conjunction except the last one is taken out; second, commas are inserted after all but the last of the combined elements. This is called a series:

*The day was bright, cold, and windy.*

Series can be made from any kind of sentence elements so long as the elements are parallel. Just be sure to include the commas.

# Complex transformations.

Compounding is the simplest kind of sentence combining. Other ways produce sentences that are more complex.

## Relative clauses.

One of the most important ways of combining two sentences is the way that produces a relative clause. A relative clause helps identify or modify a noun. There are two kinds of relative clauses, nonrestrictive and restrictive.

**Nonrestrictive clauses.** Nonrestrictive clauses modify a noun or a noun phrase without being necessary to identify it. Consider these:

*Mr. Johnson is my teacher.*

*Mr. Johnson is standing on the corner.*

The sentences could be combined into a compound sentence:

*Mr. Johnson is my teacher, and Mr. Johnson is standing on the corner.*

Or, more likely,

*Mr. Johnson is my teacher, and he is standing on the corner.*

An even more likely way to combine these two sentences is to transform one of them into a relative clause. It's done this way. First, change the part of one sentence that is the same as part of the other sentence—in this case *Mr. Johnson*—to a relative pronoun. The relative pronouns are *who, whom, whose, which,* and *that.* In this case, use *who.* The second sentence of the pair,

*Mr. Johnson is standing on the corner.*

thus becomes

*who is standing on the corner*

This group of words can then be inserted into the middle of the first sentence to produce:

*Mr. Johnson, who is standing on the corner, is my teacher.*

The words *who is standing on the corner* constitute a relative clause. In this case, the relative clause is nonrestrictive; it simply adds the information that he is standing on the corner. Nonrestrictive relative clauses are set off from the rest of the sentence by commas.

**Restrictive clauses.** A restrictive clause is necessary to identify the particular noun or noun clause it modifies. Start this time with two somewhat different sentences:

*The man is my teacher.*

*The man is standing on the corner.*

Here the second sentence can again be transformed into the relative clause,

*who is standing on the corner*

The relative clause can then be inserted into the first sentence to produce the combined sentence

*The man who is standing on the corner is my teacher.*

In this case, a restrictive relative clause tells us *which man* we are talking about. It suggests that *the man standing on the corner,* rather than the man walking down the street, is the speaker's teacher. A restrictive relative clause is *not* set off from the rest of the sentence by commas.

**Other relative clauses.** The relative pronoun *who* is used when it replaces the subject of a sentence, as in the above examples.

When the noun phrase that the relative pronoun replaces is a direct object, use either *whom* or *that.* For example, in the sentences

*The woman is my mother.*

*You saw the woman.*

the second of the sentences can be changed to *whom you saw* or *that you saw,* producing either of these combined sentences:

*The woman whom you saw is my mother.*

*The woman that you saw is my mother.*

When the relative pronoun replaces the object of a preposition, use *whom* or *which.*

SENTENCES: *The person was grateful.*
*You wrote to the person.*

COMBINED: *The person to whom you wrote was grateful.*

SENTENCES: *The company is out of business.*
*George worked for the company.*

COMBINED: *The company for which George worked is out of business.*

In speech it is acceptable to leave the preposition at the end of the relative clause, as in *the company that George worked for,* but such usage is best avoided in writing.

The relative pronoun *that* can be used only in restrictive clauses. Generally, it is best to use *which* only in nonrestrictive clauses. The other relative pronouns—*who, whom,* and *whose*—are correct when used in both restrictive and nonrestrictive clauses.

RESTRICTIVE: *The article that I read was very interesting.*

NONRESTRICTIVE: *The article, which I read, was very interesting.*

## Deletion transformations.

To delete something is to take it out. At certain times it is possible to delete the beginning of a relative clause, producing a number of different kinds of sentence structures. Deletion transformations are only possible when:

1. The relative pronoun is the subject of the relative clause.
2. The word immediately following the relative pronoun is a form of *be*; that is, *am, is, are, was,* or *were.*

**Appositives.** Look again at these two sentences from the previous page:

*Mr. Johnson is standing on the corner.*

*Mr. Johnson is my teacher.*

By changing the second sentence to a relative clause, *who is my teacher,* and inserting it into the first sentence, we produce the combined sentence

*Mr. Johnson, who is my teacher, is standing on the corner.*

A further change, a deletion transformation, is possible. By deleting *who* and *is,* we can produce:

*Mr. Johnson, my teacher, is standing on the corner.*

In this last sentence, the noun phrase *my teacher* is what is called an appositive. An appositive is a noun phrase that identifies or renames another noun phrase, which it immediately follows. Notice that the appositive, like the nonrestrictive clause from which it was made, is set off from the rest of the sentence by commas.

**Participles.** Remember that every verb has two forms called participles. They are the present participle, or *-ing* form (*seeing, showing, looking*), and the past participle (*seen, shown, looked*). As verbs, these forms are used only with auxiliaries. Often the auxiliary is a form of *be.*

Sentences containing participles can be made into relative clauses and combined with other sentences.

SENTENCES: *The boy spoke to me.*
*The boy was standing.*

The combining of these sentences differs, depending on whether the clause with the participle is restrictive or nonrestrictive.

| | RESTRICTIVE | NONRESTRICTIVE |
|---|---|---|
| COMBINED: | *The boy who was standing spoke to me.* | *The boy, who was standing, spoke to me.* |

Because the relative clause begins with *who was,* those two words can be deleted.

| | RESTRICTIVE | NONRESTRICTIVE |
|---|---|---|
| DELETION: | *The boy standing spoke to me.* | *The boy, standing, spoke to me.* |

Without its auxiliary, the participle in the sentence on the left is now a word by itself, modifying the noun *boy.* It has, in fact, become an adjective. Since it is an adjective, it can be moved (and usually is) to a position before the noun. In the sentence on the right, the participle must continue to be set off by commas, but it can move to the beginning of the sentence.

| | RESTRICTIVE | NONRESTRICTIVE |
|---|---|---|
| MOVE PARTICIPLE: | *The standing boy spoke to me.* | *Standing, the boy spoke to me.* |

The same series of combinations and deletions can be made with a past participle:

| | RESTRICTIVE | NONRESTRICTIVE |
|---|---|---|
| SENTENCES: | *Our car looked like new.* *That car was washed.* | *Our car looked like new.* *Our car was washed.* |
| COMBINED: | *Our car that was washed looked like new.* | *Our car, which was washed, looked like new.* |
| DELETION: | *Our car washed looked like new.* | *Our car, washed, looked like new.* |

## Participial phrases.

The examples above show how a participle can, by itself, become a noun modifier—an adjective. But participles often are not words by themselves. When they are functioning as verbs in simple sentences, they often have complements.

*The girl is washing the car.*
*The man is standing near the door.*

In these sentences, *the car* is the direct object of *washing*, and *near the door* is an adverbial complement of *standing*.

Participles with complements can also be made into noun modifiers. As usual, begin with two sentences, and transform one of them into a relative clause.

SENTENCES: *The girl is my neighbor.*
*The girl is washing the car.*
COMBINED: *The girl who is washing the car is my neighbor.*
DELETION: *The girl washing the car is my neighbor.*

In this sentence, the words *washing the car*, a participle and its complement, are what is called a participial phrase. The phrase follows the noun that it modifies, *girl*. Because the relative clause was restrictive, the participial phrase is also restrictive; there are no commas.

Participial phrases can also be made from nonrestrictive relative clauses:

SENTENCES: *The small child smiled shyly.*
*The small child was waving at me.*
COMBINED: *The small child, who was waving at me, smiled shyly.*
DELETION: *The small child, waving at me, smiled shyly.*

In the last sentence above, *waving at me* is a participial phrase modifying *child*. Because it was made from a nonrestrictive relative clause, it, too, is nonrestrictive, and so is set off by commas.

A nonrestrictive participial phrase (unlike a restrictive one) can be moved to a position in front of the noun phrase it modifies:

*Waving at me, the young child smiled shyly.*
As usual, it is set off by commas.

## Gerunds and gerund phrases.

Gerunds are a form of verb used as a noun. Because a gerund, like a participle, uses the *-ing* form of a verb, the two are often confused. But they are not the same thing at all. A gerund is, by itself, the *-ing* form of a verb used as a noun. It can fill any of the noun phrase positions in simple sentences:

SUBJECT: *Cooking is his hobby.*
PREDICATE NOMINATIVE: *His hobby is cooking.*
DIRECT OBJECT: *He enjoys cooking.*
INDIRECT OBJECT: *He gives cooking all his time.*
OBJECT OF PREPOSITION: *He takes pride in his cooking.*

Sentences with gerunds are, like other complex sentences, formed by first changing the form of one sentence, and then inserting the transformed sentence into a second sentence. To form the first of the gerund sentences above, for example, begin with these two sentences:

*Something is his hobby.*
*He cooks.*

The problem is to transform *he cooks* so that it can take the place of *something* in the first sentence. This is done by changing the verb to its gerund form, *cooking*. The subject of the sentence, *he*, can be transformed to its possessive form, *his*. Thus the sentence *he cooks* has been transformed into the gerund phrase *cooking* or *his cooking*, which can now replace the word *something* in the first sentence:

*His cooking is his hobby.*
*Cooking is his hobby.*

When a verb has a complement, the transforming and combining process remains the same:

SENTENCES: *Something was a pleasant surprise.*
*Jason won the race.*
TRANSFORM THE SECOND SENTENCE:
*Jason's winning the race . . .*
AND INSERT IT INTO THE FIRST SENTENCE:
*Jason's winning the race was a pleasant surprise.*

## Infinitive phrases.

Remember that an infinitive is a verb form that begins with the preposition *to*: *to see, to have seen, to be seen,* and so on. An infinitive, like a gerund, can fill certain noun phrase positions in a sentence:

SUBJECT: *To sing is a pleasure.*
PREDICATE NOMINATIVE: *His greatest pleasure is to sing.*

As with other complex sentences, a sentence with an infinitive is built from two simple sentences.

SENTENCES: *His greatest pleasure is something.*
*He sings.*

To make an infinitive phrase of the second sentence, two changes must take place:

1. Change the verb *sings* to the infinitive form *to sing*.
2. Change the subject *he* to the prepositional phrase *for him*. That produces the infinitive phrase *for him to sing*, which can now be inserted into the other sentence:

*His greatest pleasure is for him to sing.*

Again, if there is no question as to who is doing the singing, the phrase *for him* can be deleted:

*His greatest pleasure is to sing.*

## Noun clauses.

A noun clause is yet another way to transform a sentence so that it can act as a noun phrase in another sentence. Consider these sentences:

*Something is a surprise.*
*Jan is here.*

The second sentence can be transformed into a noun clause simply by adding the word *that* to the beginning of it:

*That Jan is here. . .*

The resulting noun clause can then be inserted into the first sentence:

*That Jan is here is a surprise.*

Sometimes a noun clause is introduced by a word like *whoever* or *whomever*:

SENTENCES:  *Someone must light the fire.*
            *Someone arrives first.*

Transform the second sentence by changing *someone* to *whoever*:

*Whoever arrives first. . .*

Insert the noun clause into the first sentence:

*Whoever arrives first must light the fire.*

*Whomever* is used when it replaces the direct object in one of the original sentences:

SENTENCES:  *Give these books to someone.*
            *You can find someone.*
TRANSFORM:  First: *You can find whomever. . .*
            Second: *Whomever you can find. . .*
INSERT:     *Give these books to whomever you can find.*

Sometimes a noun clause begins with an adverb like *when* or *where*.

SENTENCES:  *I do not know something.*
            *You got that idea somewhere.*
TRANSFORM:  *Where you got that idea. . .*
INSERT:     *I do not know where you got that idea.*

## Adverbial clauses.

When two sentences are joined by a subordinating conjunction (pages 33-34), one of the sentences becomes an adverbial (or subordinate) clause. Look at the following sentences:

*We arrived.*
*The movie had begun.*

You can guess that there is some time relationship between the two events that the sentences tell about. A subordinating conjunction such as *after* will make that relationship clear. Adding the subordinating conjunction transforms one sentence into an adverbial clause:

*After the movie had begun. . .*

This clause can be attached to the first sentence:

*We arrived after the movie had begun.*

Adverbial clauses usually occupy the adverb slot at the end of a sentence. Like adverbs and adverbial phrases, they can also move to the beginning of a sentence, separated from the rest of the sentence by a comma:

*After the movie had begun, we arrived.*

## Subjunctive mood.

The subjunctive mood is a special verb form that is required in certain adverbial or noun clauses.

The present subjunctive is used in noun clauses that are the direct objects of verbs like *demand, ask,* or *move*. It uses the unmarked form of the verb:

*I request that I be allowed to leave.*
*They demanded that George resign.*

The past subjunctive is used in adverbial clauses that begin with such conjunctions as *if* or *as if*. It is used when the statement made in the adverbial clause is clearly contrary to fact:

*I would not do that if I were you.*

Since I am *not* you, the past subjunctive is used.

For most nouns and pronouns, the past subjunctive is the same as the past tense. Its only difference is that it uses *were* instead of *was* for singular nouns and pronouns as well as for plural.

Note that clauses beginning with *if* do not always have subjunctive verbs:

*If he was there, I did not see him.*

(Maybe he was there, maybe he wasn't; the subjunctive is not used.)

*If he were there, I would have told you.*

(He was not there; the subjunctive is used.) Notice, too, that when the past subjunctive is used, the main verb always has the auxiliary *would*.

# Sentence diagrams

A sentence diagram has been compared to a map of a sentence. It arranges the words of a sentence on a page in a way that makes it easy to see their relationships. (Caution: a diagram does not necessarily show the word order of the sentence.)

Always begin a diagram with a horizontal line bisected by a vertical line:

**Simple sentence:** On the left side of the horizontal line, write the simple subject of the sentence. The simple subject is either the main noun in a noun phrase or a pronoun. On the right side of the line, write the verb, including any auxiliaries.

*Snow is falling.*

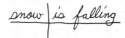

**Direct object:** When the verb is transitive, draw a vertical line to the right of the verb. The vertical line should meet but not cross the base line. To the right of this line, write the main noun or pronoun of the direct object.

*Liz likes me.*

**Linking verbs:** If the sentence has a linking verb, draw a diagonal line to the right of the verb. The line should meet but not cross the base line. To the right of this line, write the adjective complement or the predicate nominative.

*People can be nice.*
*We are students.*

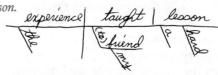

**Modifiers:** If there are adjectives (including determiners) modifying a noun, put them on a diagonal line beneath the noun. Do the same with adverbs modifying the verb.

*A light snow fell softly.*

**Prepositions:** When diagramming a prepositional phrase, write the preposition on a diagonal line beneath the word that the phrase modifies. Then write the noun or pronoun on a horizontal line, and put any adjective modifiers on diagonal lines below.

*The woman in the red dress hurried from the room.*

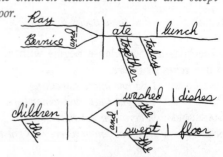

**Indirect object:** Diagram an indirect object as if it were a prepositional phrase with the preposition *to* understood. Put *to* in parentheses.

*The experience taught my friend a hard lesson.*

**Compound subjects or predicates:** To diagram compound sentence elements, place them on parallel lines. Connect the two lines with a dotted vertical line, and write the coordinating conjunction on it.

*Ray and Bernice ate lunch together today.*
*The children washed the dishes and swept the floor.*

**Compound sentences:** To diagram a compound sentence—that is, two simple sentences joined by a coordinating conjunction—diagram each of the simple sentences, one above the other. Then connect them with a vertical dotted line, and write the conjunction on that line.

*The mail has come, but that letter was not in it.*

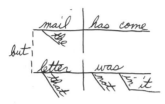

**Appositives:** To diagram an appositive, put the appositive noun or pronoun in parentheses after the noun that it renames or identifies.

*Sam, an old friend of mine, sent this book.*

**Relative clauses:** To diagram a relative clause, diagram the clause on its own line below the main line. With a dotted line, connect the noun that is being modified to the relative pronoun or relative adverb.

*Those apples that you sent me were delicious.*
*This is the place where we saw him last.*

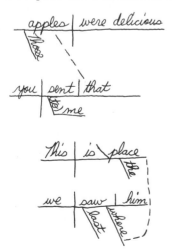

**Participles and participial phrases:** A participle is diagrammed in a curve along a diagonal and a horizontal line. The complement of the participle, if any, is to the right on the horizontal line.

*Laughing, Judy handed me the squirming puppy.*
*The man scratching his head is your new teacher.*

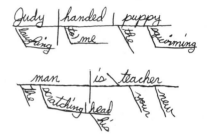

**Gerunds:** A gerund is diagrammed the same way as a participle, except that it is placed on a pedestal. The bottom of the pedestal rests on the base line in a noun's position.

*His being the culprit surprised everyone.*

**Infinitive phrases:** An infinitive phrase occupying a noun position is diagrammed the same way as a gerund.

*Nobody wants to leave the game yet.*

**Adverbial clauses:** An adverbial clause is diagrammed on a line below the base line. The subordinating conjunction is written along a diagonal dotted line that connects the word modified to the clause's verb.

*If I were you, I would be careful.*

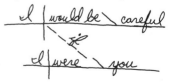

# Spelling rules

<table>
<tr><td></td><td>Examples</td><td>Exceptions</td></tr>
</table>

**Rule 1.** Remember this verse:
Use *i* before *e*,
Except after *c*,
Or when sounded like *a*,
As in *neighbor* or *weigh*.

*Examples*
*friend, fiend*
*piece, tie;*
*receipt, deceive*

*Exceptions*
*ei* exceptions:
*either, foreign,*
*forfeit, height,*
*leisure, neither*
*ie* exceptions:
*ancient, efficient*

**Rule 2.** Form the plurals of nouns and the *-s* forms of verbs ending in *y* in these ways:

**a.** When a noun or verb ends in *y* preceded by a consonant, change the *y* to *i* and add *-es*:
*mystery, mysteries;*
*berry, berries;*
*carry, carries*

**b.** When a word ends in *y* preceded by a vowel, add *-s*:
*boy, boys; key, keys;*
*pay, pays*

**c.** When a proper noun ends in *y*, add *-s*:
*Kennedy, Kennedys*

**Rule 3.** Do the following when adding a suffix to a word that ends in a silent *e*:

**a.** When the suffix begins with a vowel, drop the silent *e*:
*live, living, livable;*
*bake, baker, baking*

**b.** When a word ends in *ce* or *ge*, keep the silent *e* when it is needed to maintain the soft sound of *c* or *g*:
*manage, manageable*

**c.** When the suffix begins with a consonant, keep the final *e*:
*care, careful;*
*aware, awareness*

*judge, judgment;*
*acknowledge,*
*acknowledgment*

**Rule 4.** When adding a suffix that begins with a vowel, it sometimes is necessary to double the consonant.

**a.** When a one-syllable word ends with a consonant preceded by a single vowel, double the consonant:
(Applies only when the suffix begins with a vowel.)
*hop, hopping;*
*win, winner;*
*star, starred*

**b.** When a word of two or more syllables ends in a single consonant preceded by a single vowel, and when the final syllable is accented, double the consonant when adding a suffix:
*rebel, rebellious;*
*control, controlled*

**c.** When a word of two or more syllables does not have the accent on the final syllable, the consonant should not be doubled:
*travel, traveler*

**Rule 5.** To form noun plurals and the third-person singular form of present tense verbs

**a.** In most cases, add *-s*:
*pencil, pencils;*
*jump, jumps*

**b.** When the word ends in *s, sh, ch, x,* or *z*, add *-es*:
*brush, brushes;*
*box, boxes;*
*watch, watches*

**Grammar and Writing**

## Spelling tables

### Homophones.
Homophones are words that are pronounced the same but spelled differently. Many spelling errors result from an incorrect choice of homophones. If you are unsure which word is which in a pair, look the word up in a dictionary.

| | | | | | | | | | | | | |
|---|---|---|---|---|---|---|---|---|---|---|---|---|
| aisle | isle | fair | fare | lead | led | real | reel | stake | steak | | |
| ant | aunt | flea | flee | loan | lone | right | write | rite | stationary | stationery | |
| ate | eight | flour | flower | made | maid | road | rode | rowed | steal | steel | |
| bare | bear | foul | fowl | mail | male | role | roll | tail | tale | | |
| be | bee | guest | guessed | meat | meet | sail | sale | their | there | they're | |
| blew | blue | heal | heel | night | knight | scene | seen | threw | through | | |
| brake | break | hear | here | one | won | sea | see | to | too | two | |
| buy | by | heir | air | pail | pale | sew | sow | so | vain | vane | vein |
| capital | capitol | hole | whole | pair | pare | pear | shone | shown | waist | waste | |
| cell | sell | hour | our | peace | piece | sight | site | cite | wait | weight | |
| cellar | seller | in | inn | plain | plane | soar | sore | way | weigh | | |
| cent | sent | scent | its | it's | pray | prey | sole | soul | week | weak | |
| chord | cord | knew | new | principal | principle | some | sum | whose | who's | | |
| dear | deer | knot | not | rain | rein | reign | son | sun | wood | would | |
| die | dye | know | no | read | red | stair | stare | your | you're | | |

### Commonly misspelled words.
The words on the following list are often misspelled. In some cases this list indicates suffixes that can be added without other spelling changes. Thus, for example, the list's *anxious, -ly* indicates the correct spellings of two words, *anxious* and *anxiously*.

| | | | | | | | |
|---|---|---|---|---|---|---|---|
| absence | awkward | confident | enemy | holiday | marriage | receipt | suit |
| absolute, -ly | balance | conscience | enough | honor | mileage | receive | surprise |
| accept, -ance | balloon | control, -led | envelope | huge | mirror | recognize, -d | syllable |
| accident, -ally | bandage | cooperate | especially | humor | mischief | recommend | symbol, -ize |
| accurate, -ly | bargain | cough | evidence | hundredth | miserable | refrigerator | synonym |
| ache | bass | could | exceed, -ed | imagine | missile | relieve | system |
| achieve | beauty | courage, -ous | excellent, -ly | imitation | muscle | religious | technical |
| acknowledge | beginning | courtesy | exception | immediate, -ly | necessary | responsibility | temperature |
| across | behavior | cousin | exercise, -d | importance | necessity | restaurant | temporary |
| actual | belief | daily | experience | interest | nickel | rhythm | theater |
| advantage | believe | deceive | explanation | interrupt | niece | ridiculous | therefore |
| advice | bicycle | decision | familiar | investigate | nuclear | roommate | thief |
| advise | breath | defense | favorite | invitation | nuisance | sandwich | though |
| afraid | breathe | definite, -ly | February | island | occur, -red | sanitary | thought |
| against | brief | definition | federal | jealous | opposite | satellite | tobacco |
| alcohol | broad | delicious, -ly | foreign, -er | jewelry | parallel | scene | tomorrow |
| all right | bruise | desert, -ed | forty | journal, -ism | particular | schedule | tongue |
| already | burglar | design, -ing | forward | journey | peculiar | science | transistor |
| altogether | bury | dessert | fourth | judgment | peninsula, -r | scissors | truly |
| among | business | develop, -ed | freight | juicy | perspiration | secretary | tying |
| ancient | busy | -ment | friend | knowledge | physical | seize | typical |
| anniversary | captain | diamond | garage | laugh | physician | sense | usual, -ly |
| answer | celebrate | difference | gasoline | league | picnic, -king | separate | valuable |
| antenna | cemetery | difficult, -y | generous | length | possession | shoulder, -s | variety |
| anxiety | certain, -ly | disappear | genuine | liable | possibility | siege | vegetable |
| anxious | character | disappoint, -ed | government | library | practice | similar | vicinity |
| appear, -ance | chief | disease | governor | license | precede | sincere, -ly | view |
| appetite | chocolate | divide, -d | grammar | lightning | prefer, -red | solemn | villain |
| appreciate | climate | doctor | grateful | liquid | prejudice, -d | sophomore | visible |
| approval | climb | doubt | grocery | liquor | probably | specific | Wednesday |
| arctic | clothe, -s | duplicate | guarantee | literature | procedure | sphere | weight |
| area | clothing | easily | guess | loneliness | proceed | statue | weird |
| article | college | effect, -ive | guilt, -y | lonely | psychology | straight | whether |
| artificial | comfortable | eighth | gymnasium | loose | pursue, -r | strenuous | whose |
| athlete | competition | either | handkerchief | lose, -r | pursuit | suburb | width |
| athletic | complexion | electricity | happiness | lovable | qualified | success | witch |
| attorney | compliment | embarrass, -ing | height | machine | quite | sugar | withhold |
| audience | confidence | -ment | heroes | magazine | realize | suggestion | yield |

# Punctuation review

**End punctuation.** There are three kinds of end punctuation: the period, the question mark, and the exclamation point. Every sentence must end with one of these marks.

The exclamation point ends an exclamatory sentence (page 36), and the question mark is at the end of a question. All other sentences end with a period.

*What a good boy Paul is!*
Is Paul a good boy?
*Paul is a good boy.*

The most common mistake in end punctuation usage is to punctuate as a sentence a group of words that is not a sentence. A sentence must, as a minimum, have a subject and a verb. In addition, it must not have been transformed into an adjective clause by the addition of a subordinate conjunction, nor into a relative clause by the use of a relative pronoun. Such clauses should not be punctuated as separate sentences, but only as parts of some other, longer sentence.

SENTENCE FRAGMENT
*Although I like the design.*

CORRECTION
(1) *I like the design.*
(2) *Although I like the design, I don't care to use it in a living room.*

**Periods.** Besides its use at the end of a sentence, the period is used after initials (*T.S. Eliot*) and after many other abbreviations, including those of months (*Feb.*), countries (*U.S.A.*), states (*Tenn.*), and other commonly abbreviated forms (*St., Ave., Dr., Mr.,* and so on).

**Commas.** The most common mistake in comma usage is to use too many. Limit comma usage to the following situations.

**Compound sentences.** When two simple sentences are joined together by a coordinating conjunction, put a comma before the conjunction (page 33). (This comma is often omitted when the clauses being joined are especially short.) Do not use commas when only a part of the sentence has been compounded.

*She got up to close the window, but he asked her to sit down again.*

**Series**. Use commas after all but the last item in a series (page 45).

**Nonrestrictive relative clauses**. A nonrestrictive relative clause is set off from the rest of the sentence (page 46). So, too, are expressions that derive from nonrestrictive clauses, such as the appositive (pages 39 and 47) and nonrestrictive participles and participial phrases (pages 47-48).

*Mr. Jackson, standing on the makeshift platform, gave a rousing campaign speech.*

**Adverbial clauses.** An adverbial clause at the beginning of a sentence is set off from the rest of the sentence by a comma (page 49). Such a clause at the end of a sentence is not set off.

*When we got back from the beach, we were too tired to eat dinner.*
*We were too tired to eat dinner when we got back from the beach.*

**Parenthetical expressions.** Parenthetical expressions are set off by commas. These include *yes, no,* and mild interjections (those not followed by an exclamation point), such as *well* and *oh.*

*Well, it's time to leave.*

nouns of address,

*How is your garden growing, Mary?*

and such expressions as *of course* and *however.*

*We will, of course, be ready; others, however, may not be.*

**Clarity.** Sometimes—but very rarely—a comma is needed to avoid confusion and to make a sentence clearer:

*To John, Matilda would always be a mystery.*

**Semicolons.** Use a semicolon to join two sentences without using a conjunction (page 45), or when two sentences are joined by such an expression as *therefore* or *however.*

*He was ill; however, he worked anyway.*

The semicolon is also used to separate the items in a series (page 45) when there are already commas within the series:

*He has lived in Moline, Illinois; Boulder, Colorado; and Seattle, Washington.*

**Colons.** The main use of a colon is to introduce a list, an example, a question, or a long quotation:

*The question is this: What should we do next?*

A colon used in this way should always follow a noun or a pronoun, never a verb or a preposition. It may also come after the expressions *as follows* and *the following.*

**Dashes.** The dash indicates a sudden break or change of emphasis in a sentence:

*I have here a—now, where did I put that thing?*

Dashes can also be used to set off an appositive when the appositive is to be emphasized or when it contains commas within it.

**Parentheses.** Parentheses set off material in a sentence that is separate or apart from the main thought.

*She traveled through Davenport (a city she once lived in) and on toward Chicago.*

**Quotations.** A direct quotation—the exact words that someone has said or written—is enclosed in quotation marks. If the quotation is included within another sentence, it is set off from the rest of the sentence by commas:

*"I think," he said, "that you are right."*

When more than one person is being quoted, as in a conversation, begin a new paragraph for each change of speaker.

Question marks and exclamation points are placed inside the quotation marks as long as they are a part of the quote:

*"Who are you?" she asked*

and outside if they apply to the sentence as a whole:

*Who was it that said, "I shall return"?*

Periods and commas are always placed inside quotation marks, while the semicolon and colon are always placed outside, unless they are a part of the quote.

Do not use quotation marks for an indirect quotation, that is, one that does not report someone's exact words:

*He said that it was raining.*

**Italics.** Words to be set in italics are indicated in typed or handwritten material by an underline. Italics are used to single out words, phrases, or even sentences for special emphasis. Titles of books, plays, magazines, and newspapers, and the names of ships, trains, and airplanes are italicized. (Shorter works like poems and stories are put in quotation marks.)

*The Adventures of Tom Sawyer*
*Hamlet*
*National Geographic*
the *Titanic*
"Annabel Lee"
"The Masque of the Red Death"

**Capitalization.** All proper nouns (names of persons, places, or things) are capitalized. In addition, capitalize the first word of every sentence; the first word of a direct quotation embedded in another sentence; the names of groups, associations, and businesses; the letters of some abbreviations; and all historic events, buildings, monuments, and documents. Titles used with proper nouns are capitalized, as are the first, last, and important words in titles of printed texts.

Prepositions, articles, and conjunctions are not capitalized unless they are the first or last word of the title.

*General Motors*
*NASA*
*World War II*
*Grant's Tomb*
*Declaration of Independence*
*Dr. Brown*
*Senator Douglas*

# Writing a paper

Writing a paper is seldom easy. Even the most experienced writers find it hard work. There are, however, some things that can be done to make the work less difficult and to write a better paper at the same time. If you are writing an advanced research paper, see also Volume 2, page 318.

**Planning.** The first, and perhaps most important, step in writing is to do some good, hard thinking. As you think, keep a sheet of paper in front of you and a pencil in your hand, and make some notes. These notes are just that: notes you are writing to yourself. No one else will ever see them.

Think about the subject of your paper. Think of the various things you could tell about that subject, and make a list of them. Do not worry about the order of things on the list; you can sort that out later. The main point now is not to forget anything that might belong in the paper.

Second, with your list in front of you, think about *why* you are writing the paper. Are you describing someone or something? Are you telling about something amusing that happened, or something that taught you a lesson? Are you arguing for or against something? Are you reporting on something that you have read? As you think about the purpose of your paper, go over your checklist. Look for items on the list that have little or nothing to do with your purpose, and cross them out. Add anything that seems likely to help you carry out the purpose of your paper.

Third, think about the reader of your paper. You are going to write something to be read by *someone*. Think of that person. If, as is likely, there will be more than one reader, think of one individual in that group, and imagine that you are writing the paper for that one reader.

Now go back over your checklist with that reader in mind. Put a ($+$) by items that you consider it important for that person know about, and a ($-$) beside things that you can pass over lightly, probably because your reader knows about them already. Make any other additions to your list, or changes, that come to mind as you think about your reader.

Now you are ready to plan your paper. Rewrite

*An outline is one way to organize material for a written report. It can help you decide which of your topics are most important (deserving a II or III), and which should be placed under a more important topic (receiving an A or B).*

your list in the order that seems best—in terms of carrying out your purpose and of making things clear to your reader. One of the best ways to organize your list of thoughts is through an outline. An outline encourages you to put related ideas together and to assign levels of importance to each (see box).

**Drafting.** Write a first draft of your paper. Your purpose in writing this draft is to get what you have to say down on a piece of paper. You should not try to make it perfect or expect it to be perfect. When you cannot think of the best way to say something, write it down anyway as best you can and keep on going.

Keep two things in mind as you write the first draft:

- *Use your own language.* Do not try to be "cute." Do not try to sound like a learned college professor, either. Write as yourself, a person who is telling something interesting to another person, in as clear and uncomplicated way as you can.

- *Think of your reader.* Remember that the reader is the person for whom you are writing in the first place.

**Grammar and Writing**

**Report: Draft #1** Februa[ry]

Title
~~Name~~ of report
The report should be ~~written~~
~~My teacher has told me~~
paper 8 by 11. The
~~of paper to use and~~
~~the~~ final draft ~~draft~~
written in ink with
~~gins and no eras[ures]~~

---

Lenore Serra
March 1
Page #1

Report Requirements

Reports for Mrs. Harpers' English class should be written on lined paper, 8½ by 11 inches. The final draft should be written in ink with no erasures.

Together with the final draft, Mrs. Harper required a copy of the outline for the report on a separate piece of paper and a list of books that you consulted.

*A final draft offers a chance to get your information down on paper. You may rewrite parts of it, making it more specific and easier to understand. If there are many corrections, you may need a second draft before preparing the final draft, which is to be turned in. In addition to following the teacher's requirements, take enough time to make the report neat and readable.*

**Revising.** When you have finished your draft, put it away for a day or two, if possible. Then read the paper aloud to a friendly listener. Usually it is best to read it once straight through. Then read it a second time, asking your listener to point out to you

- parts that are hard to follow and understand;
- parts that leave your listener curious to know more than you have told about; and
- parts that are particularly good: interesting, clear, and complete.

Now go back over the paper yourself. Besides remembering your listener's comments, imagine yourself as your reader and be critical.

Look also at the flow of ideas in your paper. Is it clear how each thing that you are saying relates to what has gone before? Look for places where such expressions as *therefore, however, on the other hand, next,* or *meanwhile* might help your reader follow your train of thought. When you start a new paragraph, use language in the first sentence that ties the new paragraph to what has gone before.

Look, too, for opportunities to say things more clearly and more precisely than in the first draft. Look for words that may be unnecessary, and take them out. Look for ways to replace several words with one precise, exact one. Look for sentences that can be rewritten so that their relationship to what has gone before and to what follows will be as clear as possible.

Finally, go over your paper for

- *spelling*: check in a dictionary any words about which you are not sure;
- *usage*: be sure there are no mistakes in pronoun case forms, irregular verb forms, and the like; and
- *punctuation*: check commas in particular, being sure that you have them where they belong; be sure that what begins with a capital letter and ends with a period is in fact a sentence, not two sentences or a piece of a sentence punctuated as one.

Last of all, copy your paper in its final form. Use only one side of the paper, and be sure that your margins are adequate: at least an inch at the sides and bottom, more at the top. Number your pages. If you are writing by hand, write in ink. If you type, be sure to double space. Remember that the neat appearance of your paper may encourage your reader to take you and your ideas seriously.

# Synonyms and antonyms

Synonyms are words having the same or nearly the same meaning in one or more senses. Thus, after the entry word **beautiful** in the following list, these words are shown as synonyms: fine, handsome, pretty, bewitching, attractive, comely.

The synonyms share one characteristic: they all, in one or more senses, have the meaning or nearly the meaning of **beautiful**. Antonyms—words with meanings opposite or nearly opposite the entry—follow in parentheses.

## A

**abandon,** leave, forsake, desert, renounce, surrender, relinquish, quit, forgo, waive (keep, hold, maintain, cherish)

**abate,** decrease, ebb, dwindle, subside, moderate, reduce, lessen (increase, revive, enlarge, aggravate, enhance)

**abbreviate,** shorten, abridge, curtail, contract, condense, reduce (extend)

**abdicate,** give up, resign, renounce, abandon, forsake, relinquish, quit, forgo

**abide,** endure, tolerate, bear, continue, wait (avoid, resist, abandon, shun)

**ability,** capability, talent, faculty, capacity, qualification, aptitude, aptness, expertness, skill, efficiency, accomplishment, attainment (incompetency)

**able,** strong, powerful, muscular, stalwart, vigorous, athletic, robust, brawny, skillful, adroit, competent, efficient, capable, clever, qualified, fitted (weak)

**abolish,** destroy, revoke, cancel, annihilate, nullify, end, remove, repeal (establish, continue, support, sustain, enforce)

**abominable,** hateful, detestable, odious, vile, execrable (lovable)

**about,** concerning, regarding, relative to, with regard to, as to, respecting, referring to, around, nearly, approximately

**absent,** inattentive, abstracted, not present, away, dreamy (present)

**absolute,** entire, complete, unconditional, unqualified, unrestricted, despotic, arbitrary, tyrannous, imperative, authoritative, imperious, autocratic, positive, unequivocal (limited, conditional, accountable)

**absorb,** engross, swallow up, engulf, imbibe, consume, merge (eject, exude, emit, disgorge)

**absurd,** silly, foolish, preposterous, ridiculous, irrational, unreasonable, nonsensical, inconsistent, ludicrous (logical, sensible)

**abuse,** *n.,* scurrility, ribaldry, contumely, obloquy, opprobrium, foul invective, vituperation, ill-usage (praise, protection)

**accelerate,** hasten, hurry, expedite, forward, quicken, dispatch (retard)

**accept,** receive, take, admit (refuse)

**acceptable,** agreeable, pleasing, gratifying, pleasurable, welcome (displeasing)

**accident,** casualty, incident, contingency, mishap, adventure, chance

**accommodate,** serve, oblige, adapt, adjust, fit, suit (disoblige, impede)

**accomplice,** confederate, accessory, abettor, coadjutor, assistant, ally, associate, helper (adversary)

**accomplish,** do, effect, finish, execute, achieve, complete, perfect, consummate (fail)

**account,** narrative, description, relation, detail, recital, reckoning, bill, charge

**accountable,** punishable, answerable, amenable, responsible, liable

**accumulate,** bring together, amass, collect, gather (scatter, dissipate)

**accurate,** correct, exact, precise, nice, truthful (erroneous, careless)

**achieve,** do, accomplish, effect, fulfill, execute, gain, win

**achievement,** feat, exploit, accomplishment, attainment, performance, acquirement, gain (failure)

**acknowledge,** admit, confess, own, avow, grant, recognize, allow, concede (deny)

**acquaint,** inform, enlighten, apprise, make aware, make known, notify, communicate (deceive)

**acquaintance,** familiarity, intimacy, cognizance, fellowship, companionship, friendship, knowledge (unfamilarity)

**acquit,** pardon, forgive, discharge, set free, clear, absolve (condemn, convict)

**act,** do, operate, make, perform, play, enact

**action,** deed, achievement, feat, exploit, accomplishment, battle, engagement, agency, instrumentality

**active,** lively, sprightly, alert, agile, nimble, brisk, quick, supple, prompt, vigilant, bustling, energetic, busy, laborious, industrious (lazy, idle, inactive, slow, sluggish, indolent, passive)

**actual,** real, positive, genuine, certain (fictitious)

**adapt,** accommodate, suit, fit, conform

**addition,** increase, accession, augmentation, reinforcement (subtraction, separation)

**adequate,** fit, equal, capable, able, suited, qualified, competent (inferior, unfit, unequal, inadequate, incompetent)

**adjourn,** defer, postpone

**adjust,** set right, fit, accommodate, adapt, arrange, settle, regulate, organize (confuse)

**admirable,** striking, surprising, wonderful, astonishing (detestable)

**admire,** esteem, love, extol, respect, venerate, honor, adore, approve, enjoy, applaud (abhor, detest, scorn, execrate, dislike, despise, abominate)

**admit,** allow, permit, suffer, tolerate (deny)

**advantageous,** beneficial, useful, helpful, valuable (hurtful)

**adverse,** opposed, unfavorable, inimical, antagonistic, contrary, hostile (helpful, favorable, aiding, assisting, cooperative)

**afraid,** apprehensive, scared, fearful, timid, alarmed, cautious, anxious (audacious, brave, confident, bold, gallant, heroic, intrepid, valiant, daring, courageous)

**agree,** accord, acquiesce, concur, harmonize, assent, coincide (contradict, differ, oppose, disagree, dissent)

**alarm,** fright, panic, terror, fear, dread, dismay, affront (confidence, assurance, calmness, security)

**alert,** nimble, active, prompt, brisk, lively (dull, inactive, slow, sluggish)

**amazement,** surprise, awe, wonder, bewilderment, confusion, astonishment (indifference, steadiness, coolness, stoicism, calmness, composure)

**amend,** improve, correct, better, mend, rectify, repair (impair, harm, spoil, injure)

**anger,** ire, wrath, indignation, resentment, animosity, displeasure, rage (good nature, amiability)

**argue,** debate, dispute, reason upon (agree)

**artful,** disingenuous, sly, tricky, insincere (candid)

**association,** combination, company, partnership, society (isolation, solitude, separation)

**attack,** assail, assault, encounter (defend)

**austere,** rigid, rigorous, severe, stern (dissolute)

**aversion,** antipathy, dislike, hatred, repugnance (affection)

**awe,** wonder, amazement, dread, fear, reverence (familiarity)

**awkward,** clumsy, uncouth, ungainly (graceful, adroit)

# B

**babble,** chatter, prattle, prate, murmur, cackle

**bad,** wicked, evil (good)

**baffle,** confound, defeat, disconcert

**beautiful,** fine, handsome, pretty, bewitching, attractive, comely (homely, ugly, hideous, horrid, unattractive)

**becoming,** decent, fit, seemly, suitable, befitting, graceful (unbecoming, unsuitable, unfitting, misplaced)

**beg,** beseech, crave, entreat, implore, solicit, supplicate (give)

**behavior,** carriage, conduct, deportment, bearing, manner, demeanor

**belief,** credit, faith, trust (doubt)

**benefit,** favor, advantage, kindness, civility (injury)

**blame,** censure, condemn, reprove, reproach, upbraid (praise)

**bleak,** cheerless, bare, dismal, blank, desolate, waste, unsheltered, dreary (cheery, balmy, sunny, warm, mild)

**blemish,** defect, disfigurement, imperfection, flaw, speck, spot, stain (ornament)

**bold,** brave, daring, fearless, intrepid, undaunted (timid)

**brave,** daring, bold, courageous, adventurous, heroic, intrepid, fearless, valiant, dauntless (afraid, timid, cowardly, fearful)

**break,** crack, split, smash, bruise, crush, pound

**breeze,** blast, gale, gust, hurricane, storm, tempest

**bright,** brilliant, luminous, resplendent, clear, radiant, shining (dull)

# C

**calm,** cool, mild, quiet, peaceful, still, tranquil, composed, placid, serene (stormy, disturbed, agitated, excited, violent, unsettled)

**cancel,** nullify, abolish, annul, rescind, quash, revoke, repeal (maintain, establish, sustain, uphold, approve)

**candid,** sincere, honest, truthful, frank, fair, impartial, unbiased (cunning, adroit, crafty, sly, shrewd, tricky, wily, subtle, deceitful, artful)

**catch,** grasp, grip, capture, clutch, clasp, seize, snatch, secure, take (miss, lose, restore, release)

**cause,** motive, reason (effect, consequence)

**cease,** finish, quit, stop, terminate, discontinue, end (continue, begin, inaugurate, start)

**certain,** secure, sure (doubtful)

**chance,** fate, fortune (design)

**changeable,** fickle, inconstant, mutable, variable (unchangeable)

**character,** reputation, repute, standing

**charm,** captivate, enchant, enrapture, fascinate (repel, offend)

**cheap,** inexpensive, inferior, common (dear)

**cheerful,** gay, merry, sprightly (mournful)

**chief,** head, leader (subordinate, attendant, follower)

**class,** degree, order, rank

**clear,** bright, lucid, vivid (opaque, ambiguous, dim, obscure, vague)

**clever,** adroit, dexterous, expert, skillful (stupid, awkward, bungling)

**command,** injunction, order, precept

**compassion,** sympathy, pity, clemency (cruelty, severity)

**compel,** force, oblige, necessitate, make, coerce (coax, lead)

**complain,** lament, murmur, regret, repine (rejoice)

**comprehend,** comprise, include, embrace, grasp, understand, perceive (exclude, mistake)

**conceal,** hide, secrete (uncover)

**conceive,** start, begin, imagine

**conclusion,** inference, deduction, end (beginning, start)

**condemn,** censure, blame, disapprove, reprove (justify, exonerate, acquit, approve)

**confirm,** corroborate, approve, attest (contradict)

**conflict,** combat, contest, contention, struggle (peace, quiet)

**conquer,** master, beat, overcome, subdue, surmount, vanquish (defeat, lose, capitulate)

**consequence,** effect, event, issue, result (cause)

**consider,** reflect, ponder, weigh (forget, leave out)

**consistent,** constant, compatible (inconsistent)

**console,** comfort, solace (harrow, worry)

**contaminate,** corrupt, defile, pollute, taint

**continual,** constant, perpetual, incessant (intermittent)

**continue,** persist persevere, pursue, prosecute (cease)

**contradict,** deny, gainsay, oppose (confirm)

**contrast,** discriminate, differentiate

**cowardice,** fear, timidity, pusillanimity (courage)

**crime,** sin, vice, misdemeanor (virtue)

**criminal,** convict, culprit, felon, malefactor

**crooked,** bent, curved, oblique (straight)

**cruel,** barbarous, brutal, inhuman, savage (kind)

**custom,** fashion, manner, practice

# D

**danger,** hazard, peril (safety)

**dark,** somber, gloomy, dismal, opaque, obscure, dim (light, bright, clear, radiant)

**deadly,** fatal, destructive, mortal

**deceive,** delude, gull, dupe, cheat

**decide,** determine, settle, adjudicate, resolve

**decision,** determination, conclusion, resolution, firmness (vacillation)

**decrease,** diminish, lessen, wane, decline, retrench, curtail, reduce (grow)

**dedicate,** devote, consecrate, offer, set, apportion

**deed,** act, commission, achievement, instrument, document

**deep,** profound, subterranean, submerged (shallow)

**deface,** mar, spoil, injure, disfigure (beautify)

**defect,** imperfection, flaw, fault, blemish (beauty, improvement)

**defend,** guard, protect, justify (attack)

**defense,** excuse, plea, vindication, bulwark, rampart

**defer,** delay, postpone, put off, adjourn (force, expedite)

**define,** fix, settle, determine, limit

**delicate,** tender, fragile, dainty, refined (coarse)

**delicious,** sweet, palatable, luscious, savory (bitter, unpalatable)

**delight,** enjoyment, pleasure, happiness, gladness, rapture, bliss (annoyance)

**deliver,** liberate, free, rescue, pronounce, give, hand over (retain)

**demonstrate,** prove, show, exhibit, illustrate

**depart,** leave, quit, decamp, retire, withdraw, vanish (remain)

**describe,** delineate, portray, explain, illustrate, define, picture

**deserve,** merit, earn, justify, win

**design,** *n.,* delineation, sketch, drawing, cunning, artfulness, contrivance

**desirable,** expedient advisable, valuable, acceptable, proper, judicious, beneficial, profitable, good

**desire,** *n.,* longing, affection, craving, coveting, wish

**desolate,** bereaved, forlorn, forsaken, deserted, wild, waste, bare, bleak, lonely (pleasant, happy)

**desperate,** wild, daring, audacious, determined, reckless

**destiny,** fate, decree, doom, end

**destructive,** detrimental, hurtful, noxious, injurious, deleterious, baleful, baneful, subversive (creative)

**develop,** unfold, amplify, expand, enlarge

**devoted,** attached, fond, absorbed, dedicated

**dictate,** prompt, suggest, enjoin, order, command

**dictatorial,** imperative, imperious, domineering, arbitrary, tyrannical, overbearing (submissive)

**die,** perish, decease, expire, depart, decline, languish, wane, sink, fade, decay (live)

**difference,** variation, contrast, disparity, separation, disagreement, discord, dissent, estrangement, variety

**different,** various, manifold, diverse, unlike, separate, distinct (similar)

**difficult,** severe, arduous, laborious, trying, hard, intricate, involved, perplexing, obscure, unmanageable (easy)

**diligence,** care, assiduity, attention, heed, industry (negligence)

**diminish,** lessen, reduce, contract, curtail, retrench (increase)

**discipline,** order, strictness, training, coercion, punishment, organization (confusion, demoralization)

**discover,** disclose, detect, make known, find, invent, contrive, expose, reveal

**discreet,** cautious, prudent, wary, judicious (indiscreet)

**disease,** illness, unhealthiness, complaint, malady, disorder, ailment, sickness

**disgrace,** *n.,* disrepute, reproach, dishonor, shame, odium (honor)

**disgust,** dislike, distaste, loathing, abomination, abhorrence (admiration)

**display,** show, spread out, exhibit, expose (hide)

**dispute,** *n.,* argument, debate, controversy, quarrel, disagreement (harmony)

**dispute,** *v.,* argue, contest, contend, question, impugn (assent)

**dissent,** disagree, differ, vary (assent)

**distinct,** clear, plain, obvious, different, separate (obscure, indistinct)

**distinguish,** perceive, discern, mark out, divide, discriminate

**distinguished,** famous, glorious, noted, illustrious, eminent, celebrated (obscure, unknown, ordinary)

**distribute,** allot, share, dispense, apportion, deal (collect)

**disturb,** agitate, rouse, interrupt, confuse, trouble, annoy, vex, worry (pacify, quiet)

**doctrine,** tenet, belief, creed, dogma, teaching, conviction

**doubt,** *n.,* uncertainty, suspense, hesitation, scruple, ambiguity (certainty)

**dread,** *n.,* fear, horror, terror, alarm, dismay, awe (assurance, calm)

**dress,** *n.,* clothing, attire, apparel, garments, costume, garb, livery, raiment

**drown,** inundate, swamp, submerge, overwhelm, engulf

**dry,** arid, parched, lifeless, dull, tedious (moist, interesting, succulent)

**dull,** stupid, gloomy, sad, dismal, commonplace (bright)

**durable,** lasting, permanent, abiding, continuing (ephemeral, perishable)

**dwindle,** pine, waste, diminish, decrease, fall off (grow)

# E

**eager,** fervent, desirous, hot, ardent, impassioned, forward, impatient (diffident, apathetic, indifferent, unconcerned)

**earn,** acquire, obtain, win, gain, achieve

**easy,** light, comfortable, unconstrained (difficult, hard)

**economical,** sparing, saving, provident, thrifty, frugal, careful, niggardly (wasteful)

**effect,** consequence, result, issue, event, execution, operation

**effective,** efficient, operative, serviceable (vain, ineffectual)

**efficient,** effectual, effective, competent, capable, able, fitted

**eliminate,** drive out, expel, thrust out, eject, cast out, oust, dislodge, banish, proscribe

**embarrass,** shame, distress, trouble (assist)

**eminent,** distinguished, conspicuous, noted, prominent, elevated, renowned, famous, glorious, illustrious (obscure, unknown)

**emit,** give out, throw out, exhale, discharge

**emotion,** feeling, sentiment, passion, warmth, excitement

**employment,** business, vocation, office, trade, profession, occupation, calling

**enclose,** surround, shut in, fence in, cover, wrap (free)

**encourage,** countenance, sanction, support, foster, cherish, inspirit, embolden, animate, cheer, incite, urge, impel, stimulate (deter)

**endure,** last, continue, support, bear, sustain, suffer, brook, submit to, undergo, tolerate (perish, succumb, yield)

**enemy,** foe, antagonist, adversary, opponent (friend)

**energetic,** industrious, effectual, efficacious, powerful, binding, forcible, nervous (lazy)

**engage,** employ, busy, occupy, attract, invite, allure, entertain, engross, take up, enlist

**enjoyment,** pleasure, gratification (grief, sorrow, sadness)

**enlarge,** increase, extend, augment, broaden, swell (diminish)

**enlighten,** illuminate, instruct, inform (befog, becloud)

**enormous,** gigantic, colossal, huge, vast, immense, prodigious (insignificant)

**enroll,** enlist, list, register, record

**enterprise,** undertaking, endeavor, venture, energy

**entertain,** beguile, amuse, cheer, divert, interest, please (annoy, disturb, tire, bore, weary, distract)

**enthusiasm,** fervor, warmth, intensity, earnestness, devotion, zeal, ardor (ennui, timidity, wariness, lukewarmness)

**entrance,** ingress, access, door, approach, inlet, entry, gate, opening, portal (ejection, refusal, expulsion, exit, egress, withdrawal)

**equal,** even, like, uniform (unequal)

**error,** blunder, mistake (truth)

**especially,** chiefly, particularly, principally (generally)

**establish,** build up, confirm (overthrow)

**eternal,** perpetual, undying, timeless, unceasing, endless, everlasting (finite)

**even,** level, plain, smooth (uneven)

**event,** accident, adventure, incident, occurrence

**evil,** ill, harm, mischief, misfortune (good)

**examination,** investigation, inquiry, research, search, scrutiny

**exceed,** excel, outdo, surpass, transcend (fall short)

**exceptional,** uncommon, rare, extraordinary (common)

**excite,** awaken, provoke, rouse, stir up (lull)

**execute,** fulfill, perform

**exhaustive,** thorough, complete (cursory)

**explain,** expound, interpret, illustrate, elucidate

**express,** declare, signify, utter, tell

**extravagant,** lavish, profuse, prodigal (parsimonious)

# F

**face,** visage, countenance

**fail,** fall short, be deficient (accomplish)

**faint,** weak, irresolute, faltering, feeble, languid (forcible, fresh, hearty, resolute)

**fair,** equitable, honest, reasonable (unfair)

**faith,** belief (disbelief)

**faithful,** staunch, devoted, trusty, true, loyal, constant (faithless, false, untrue)

**fall,** drop, droop, sink, tumble (rise)

**fame,** renown, reputation, distinction, eminence

**famous,** celebrated, renowned, illustrious (obscure)

**fast,** rapid, quick, fleet, expeditious (slow, sluggish)

**fatigue,** weariness, lassitude (vigor)

**fear,** timidity, fright, apprehension, trepidation (bravery)

**Grammar and Writing**

**feeling,** sensation, sense

**ferocious,** fierce, savage, wild, barbarous (mild)

**fertile,** fruitful, prolific, plenteous, productive (sterile)

**feud,** bitterness, contest, affray, animosity, brawl, dispute, fray, enmity, riot, quarrel, strife, row, controversy, dissension

**firm,** constant, solid, steadfast, fixed, stable (weak, flabby)

**first,** foremost, chief, earliest (last)

**fit,** accommodate, adapt, adjust, suit

**flame,** blaze, flare, flash, glare

**flat,** level, even

**flexible,** pliable, ductile, supple (inflexible)

**flourish,** prosper, thrive (decay)

**follow,** succeed, ensue, imitate, copy, pursue

**follower,** partisan, disciple, adherent, retainer, pursuer, successor (critic, dissenter)

**folly,** silliness, foolishness, imbecility, weakness (wisdom)

**fond,** enamored, attached, affectionate (distant)

**foolhardy,** venturesome, incautious, hasty, adventurous, rash (cautious)

**foolish,** simple, silly, irrational, brainless, imbecilic, crazy, absurd, preposterous, ridiculous, nonsensical (discreet, wise)

**forecast,** forethought, foresight, premeditation, prognostication

**foregoing,** antecedent, anterior, preceding, previous, prior, former

**forerunner,** herald, harbinger, precursor, omen

**foresight,** forethought, forecast, premeditation

**forgive,** pardon, remit, absolve, acquit, excuse, except (blame)

**forlorn,** forsaken, abandoned, deserted, desolate, lone, lonesome

**form,** *n.*, ceremony, solemnity, observance, rite, figure, shape, conformation, fashion, appearance, representation, resemblance

**form,** *v.*, make, create, produce, constitute, arrange, fashion, mold

**formal,** ceremonious, precise, exact, stiff, methodical, affected (informal, natural)

**former,** antecedent, anterior, previous, prior, preceding, foregoing

**forsaken,** abandoned, forlorn, deserted, desolate, lone, lonesome

**fortunate,** lucky, happy, auspicious, prosperous, successful (unfortunate)

**fortune,** chance, fate, luck, doom, destiny, property, possession, riches

**fragile,** brittle, frail, delicate, feeble (strong)

**fragments,** pieces, scraps, leavings, chips, remains, remnants

**frailty,** weakness, failing, foible, imperfection, fault, blemish (strength)

**frank,** artless, candid, sincere, free, easy, familiar, open, ingenuous, plain (tricky, insincere)

**frantic,** distracted, mad, furious, raving, frenzied (quiet, subdued)

**fraud,** deceit, deception, duplicity, guile, cheat (honesty)

**free,** *a.*, liberal, generous, bountiful, bounteous, munificent, frank, artless, candid, familiar, open, independent, unconfined, unreserved, unrestricted, exempt, clear, loose, easy, careless (slavish, stingy, artful, costly)

**free,** *v.*, release, deliver, rescue, liberate, emancipate, exempt (enslave, bind)

**freedom,** liberty, independence, unrestraint, familiarity, license, franchise, exemption, privilege (slavery)

**frequent,** often, common, usual, general (rare)

**friendly,** cordial, fond, companionable, affable, amicable, genial, kind, hearty, neighborly, sociable, social (antagonistic, belligerent, cold, alienated, frigid, hostile, distant, unfriendly, unkind, indifferent)

**frugal,** provident, economical, saving (wasteful, extravagant)

**fruitful,** fertile, prolific, productive, abundant, plentiful, plenteous (barren, sterile)

**fruitless,** vain, useless, idle, abortive, unavailing (productive)

**furious,** violent, boisterous, vehement, dashing, sweeping, rolling, impetuous, frantic, distracted, stormy, angry, raging, fierce (calm)

# G

**gain,** *n.*, profit, emolument, advantage, benefit, winnings, earnings (loss)

**gain,** *v.*, get, acquire, obtain, attain, procure, earn, win, achieve, reap, realize, reach (lose)

**gallant,** brave, bold, courageous, fine, showy, intrepid, heroic, fearless (cowardly)

**game,** play, diversion, sport, amusement

**gang,** band, horde, company, troop, crew

**gap,** breach, chasm, hollow, cavity, cleft, crevice, rift, chink

**gather,** pick, cull, assemble, muster, infer, collect (scatter)

**gaudy,** showy, flashy, tawdry, gay, glittering, bespangled (somber)

**gaunt,** emaciated, scraggy, skinny, meager, lank, attenuated, spare, lean, thin (well-fed)

**gay,** cheerful, merry, lively, jolly, sprightly, blithe (solemn)

**generous,** beneficent, noble, honorable, bountiful, liberal, free, magnanimous (niggardly, greedy, miserly, stingy, parsimonious)

**gentle,** placid, bland, mild, meek, tame, docile (rough, uncouth)

**get,** obtain, earn, gain, attain, procure, achieve, acquire

**gift,** donation, benefaction, grant, alms, bequest, present, gratuity, boon, faculty, talent

**gigantic,** colossal, huge, enormous, vast, prodigious, immense (diminutive)

**give,** cede, deliver, grant, bestow, confer, yield, impart

**glad,** pleased, cheerful, joyful, gratified, cheering (sad)

**glee,** gaiety, merriment, mirth, joviality, joy, hilarity (sorrow)

**gloom,** cloud, darkness, dimness, blackness, dullness, sadness (light, brightness, joy)

**gloomy,** lowering, lurid, dim, dusky, sad, glum (bright, clear)

**glorify,** magnify, celebrate, adore, exalt

**glory,** honor, fame, renown, splendor, grandeur (infamy)

**go,** depart, proceed, move, budge, stir

**good,** *a.,* virtuous, righteous, upright, just, true (wicked, bad)

**good,** *n.,* benefit, weal, advantage, profit, boon (evil)

**gorgeous,** superb, grand, magnificent, splendid (plain, simple)

**govern,** control, rule, direct, manage, command

**government,** rule, state, control, sway

**graceful,** becoming, comely, elegant, beautiful (awkward)

**grand,** majestic, stately, dignified, lofty, elevated, exalted, splendid, gorgeous, superb, magnificent, sublime, pompous (shabby)

**grant,** bestow, impart, give, yield, cede, allow, confer, invest

**grasp,** catch, seize, grip, clasp, grapple

**grateful,** agreeable, welcome, thankful

**grave,** *a.,* serious, sedate, solemn, sober, pressing, heavy (giddy)

**grave,** *n.,* tomb, sepulcher, vault

**great,** big, huge, large, majestic, vast, grand, noble, august (small)

**grief,** affliction, sorrow, trial, woe, tribulation, sadness, melancholy (joy)

**grieve,** mourn, lament, sorrow, pain, hurt, wound, bewail (rejoice)

**grievous,** painful, afflicting, heavy, baleful, unhappy

**gross,** coarse, outrageous, unseemly, shameful, indelicate (delicate)

**group,** assembly, cluster, collection, clump, order, class

**grow,** increase, vegetate, expand, advance (decay, diminish)

**growl,** grumble, snarl, murmur, complain

**gruff,** rough, rugged, blunt, rude, harsh, surly, bearish (pleasant)

**guilty,** culpable, sinful, criminal (innocent)

# H

**habit,** custom, practice, fashion, routine, system

**happiness,** beatitude, blessedness, bliss, felicity, contentment, joy, merriment, rapture, pleasure, enjoyment (unhappiness)

**hard,** firm, solid, arduous, difficult (soft, easy)

**harm,** injury, hurt, wrong, affliction (benefit)

**harmless,** safe, innocuous, innocent (hurtful)

**harsh,** rough, rigorous, severe (gentle)

**harvest,** crop, fruit, growth, result, return, yield, proceeds, product, increase

**hasten,** accelerate, dispatch, expedite, speed (delay)

**hasty,** hurried, ill-advised (deliberate)

**hatred,** enmity, ill will, rancor, animosity, hostility, revenge, spite, hate (friendship)

**hazard,** peril, chance, risk, venture

**healthy,** hale, vigorous, well, salubrious, salutary, wholesome (unhealthy, diseased, fragile, ill, sick)

**hearty,** vigorous, cordial, sincere, warm (insincere)

**heavy,** burdensome, ponderous, weighty (light)

**heighten,** enhance, exalt, elevate, raise

**help,** abet, encourage, aid, assist, relieve, succor (hinder, oppose, thwart, discourage)

**hesitate,** falter, stammer, stutter

**hide,** cover, disguise, cloak, conceal, bury, veil, suppress, screen, entomb, secrete (confess, admit, divulge, expose, show, reveal, publish, advertise, tell, uncover)

**hint,** allude, refer, suggest, intimate, insinuate

**hold,** detain, keep, retain

**home,** habitation, dwelling, fireside, hearth, house, residence, domicile, abode

**homely,** plain, ugly, coarse (beautiful)

**honesty,** integrity, probity, uprightness (dishonesty)

**honor,** respect, reverence, esteem (dishonor)

**hope,** confidence, expectation, trust

**hot,** ardent, burning, fiery (cold)

**however,** nevertheless, notwithstanding, yet

**humble,** *a.*, modest, submissive, plain, unostentatious, simple (haughty)

**humble,** *v.*, degrade, humiliate, mortify, abase (exalt)

**hunt,** pursue, search, seek, chase

**hypocrite,** cheat, deceiver, dissembler, impostor

# I

**idea,** thought, imagination

**ideal,** imaginary, fancied, perfect (actual, imperfect)

**idle,** indolent, lazy (industrious)

**ignorant,** illiterate, uninformed, uneducated (knowing)

**illegal,** unlawful, illicit, contraband, illegitimate (legal)

**illiterate,** unlettered, unlearned, untaught, uninstructed (learned, educated)

**illusion,** fallacy, deception, phantasm

**image,** likeness, picture, representation, effigy

**imaginary,** ideal, fanciful, illusory (real)

**imagine,** conceive, fancy, think, picture, presume

**imitate,** copy, ape, mimic, mock, counterfeit

**immediate,** pressing, instant, next, proximate

**immediately,** instantly, forthwith, directly, presently (later)

**immense,** vast, enormous, huge, prodigious, monstrous (small)

**impartial,** just, equitable, unbiased (partial)

**imperfection,** fault, blemish, defect, vice

**importance,** significance, avail, consequence, weight, gravity, moment

**impressive,** stirring, forcible, exciting, affecting, moving

**imprison,** incarcerate, shut up, immure, confine (liberate)

**improve,** amend, better, mend, reform, rectify, ameliorate, apply, strengthen (damage, weaken, deteriorate)

**impulsive,** rash, hasty, forcible, violent (deliberate)

**incentive,** motive, inducement, impulse

**incline,** slope, lean, slant, tend, bend, turn, bias, dispose

**include,** comprise, contain, embrace, take in

**incompetent,** incapable, unable, inadequate, insufficient (competent)

**increase,** extend, enlarge, augment, dilate, expand, amplify, raise, enhance, aggravate, magnify, grow (diminish)

**indefinite,** vague, uncertain, unsettled, loose, lax (definite)

**indicate,** point out, show, mark

**indignation,** anger, wrath, ire, resentment

**inequality,** disparity, disproportion, dissimilarity, unevenness (equality)

**infamous,** scandalous, shameful, ignominious, opprobrious, disgraceful (honorable)

**infinite,** eternal, absolute, boundless, countless, limitless, unbounded, numberless, unlimited, unfathomable (brief, bounded, restricted, small, moderate, limited, little, measurable)

**inhuman,** cruel, brutal, savage, barbarous, ruthless, merciless, ferocious (humane)

**injure,** damage, hurt, deteriorate, wrong, aggrieve, harm, spoil, mar, sully (benefit)

**injustice,** wrong, iniquity, grievance, unfairness (right)

**innocent,** guiltless, inoffensive, innocuous, exemplary, stainless, virtuous (guilty)

**inquiry,** investigation, examination, research, scrutiny, disquisition, question, query, interrogation

**insane,** mad, deranged, delirious, demented (sane)

**inspire,** animate, exhilarate, enliven, cheer, breathe, inhale

**instruct,** inform, teach, educate, enlighten, initiate

**insult,** affront, outrage, indignity, blasphemy (honor)

**integrity,** uprightness, honesty, probity, entirety, completeness, rectitude, purity (dishonesty)

**intellect,** understanding, sense, mind, intelligence, ability, talent, genius

**intense,** ardent, earnest, glowing, fervid, burning, vehement

**intent,** design, purpose, intention, drift, view, aim, purport, meaning

**interfere,** meddle, interpose

**interpret,** explain, expound, elucidate, unfold, decipher

**intimidate,** dishearten, alarm, frighten, scare, appall, daunt, cow, browbeat (encourage)

**invasion,** incursion, inroad, aggression, raid, fray

**invent,** devise, contrive, frame, find out, discover, design

**investigation,** examination, search, inquiry, research, scrutiny

**invincible,** unconquerable, impregnable, insurmountable

**invisible,** unseen, imperceptible, impalpable, unperceivable (visible)

**invite,** ask, call, bid, request, allure, attract, solicit

**invoke,** call upon, implore, beseech

**involve,** implicate, entangle, compromise, envelop

**irritate,** aggravate, worry, embitter, madden, exasperate

**issue,** emerge, rise, proceed, flow, spring, emanate

# J

**jarring,** conflicting, discordant, inconsonant, inconsistent

**jaunt,** ramble, excursion, trip

**jealousy,** suspicion, envy

**jeopardy,** hazard, peril, danger

**jest,** joke, sport, divert, make game of

**journey,** travel, tour, passage, excursion, voyage, trip

**joy,** happiness, gladness, mirth, delight (grief)

**judge,** justice, referee, arbitrator, arbiter

**judgment,** discernment, discrimination, understanding

**justice,** equity, right; justice is right as established by law; equity according to the circumstances of each particular case (injustice)

# K

**keep,** preserve, save (abandon)

**kill,** execute, massacre, assassinate, murder, slay, cancel, cross out

**knowledge,** intelligence, wisdom, comprehension, erudition, learning, science (ignorance, illiteracy, unfamiliarity)

# L

**labor,** toil, work, effort, drudgery (idleness)

**lack,** need, deficiency, scarcity, insufficiency (plenty)

**lament,** mourn, grieve, weep (rejoice)

**language,** dialect, idiom, speech, tongue

**large,** ample, big, capacious, abundant, coarse, colossal, commodious, enormous, vast, huge, gigantic, great, massive, spacious (little, petty, paltry, scanty, small, tiny, trivial, brief, diminutive, insignificant)

**last,** final, latest, ultimate (first)

**laughable,** comical, droll, ludicrous (serious)

**leave,** quit, relinquish

**life,** existence, animation, spirit, vivacity (death)

**lift,** erect, elevate, exalt, raise (lower)

**light,** clear, bright (dark)

**likeness,** resemblance, similarity (unlikeness)

**linger,** lag, loiter, tarry, saunter (hasten)

**little,** diminutive, small (great)

**livelihood,** living, maintenance, subsistence, support

**lively,** jocund, sprightly, vivacious, merry, sportive (slow, languid, sluggish)

**long,** extended, extensive (short)

**look,** gaze, discern, behold, glance, see, stare, view, watch, scan, inspect

**lose,** miss, forfeit (gain)

**loss,** detriment, damage, deprivation (gain)

**loud,** clamorous, high-sounding, noisy (low, quiet)

**love,** fondness, attachment, devotion, affection (hate)

# M

**mad,** crazy, insane, delirious, rabid, violent, frantic (sane, rational, quiet)

**make,** form, create, produce, build, construct (destroy)

**manage,** contrive, direct

**management,** direction, superintendence, care, economy

**mania,** obsession, madness, insanity, lunacy

**manly,** masculine, vigorous, courageous, brave, heroic (effeminate)

**manner,** habit, custom, way, air, look, appearance

**mar,** spoil, ruin, disfigure (improve)

**march,** tramp, tread, walk, step

**margin,** edge, rim, border, brink, verge

**marvelous,** wondrous, wonderful, amazing, miraculous

**masculine,** manly, mannish, virile, male, manful, manlike

**massive,** bulky, heavy, weighty, ponderous, solid, substantial (flimsy)

**mastery,** dominion, rule, sway, ascendancy, supremacy

**matchless,** unrivaled, unequaled, unparalleled, peerless, incomparable, inimitable, surpassing (common, ordinary)

**meaning,** signification, import, acceptation, sense, purport

**meek,** unassuming, mild, gentle, soft, demure, humble (proud, arrogant, bold, haughty, impudent, presumptuous)

**melancholy,** low-spirited, dispirited, dreamy, sad (jolly, buoyant)

**melodious,** tuneful, musical, silver, dulcet, sweet (discordant)

**memory,** reminiscence, remembrance, recollection

**mend,** repair, amend, correct, better, ameliorate, improve, rectify (break)

**mention,** tell, name, communicate, impart, divulge, reveal, disclose, inform, acquaint

**merciful,** compassionate, lenient, clement, tender, gracious, kind (cruel)

**merciless,** hard-hearted, cruel, unmerciful, pitiless, remorseless, unrelenting (kind)

**mercy,** favor, grace, kindness, leniency, pardon, tenderness, pity, compassion, benevolence, clemency, benignity, blessing (revenge, cruelty, harshness, severity, sternness, punishment, implacability, hardness)

**merry,** cheerful, mirthful, joyous, gay, lively, sprightly, hilarious, jovial, blithe, sportive, jolly (sad)

**mimic,** imitate, ape, mock

**mind,** intellect, brain, instinct, reason, sense, soul, thought, understanding, intelligence

**mischief,** injury, harm, damage, evil, hurt, ill (benefit)

**miserable,** unhappy, wretched, distressed, afflicted (happy)

**misery,** wretchedness, woe, destitution, penury, privation, beggary (happiness)

**mix,** blend, combine, amalgamate, associate, fuse, join, unite, mingle, compound (divide, sift, part, segregate, sort, unravel, disjoin, classify, assort, analyze)

**moderate,** temperate, abstemious, sober, abstinent (immoderate)

**modest,** chaste, virtuous, bashful, reserved (immodest)

**moist,** wet, damp, dank, humid (dry)

**monotonous,** unvaried, dull, undiversified, tiresome (varied)

**monstrous,** shocking, dreadful, horrible, huge, immense

**monument,** memorial, record, remembrance

**mood,** humor, disposition, vein, temper

**mournful,** sad, sorrowful, lugubrious, grievous, doleful, heavy (happy)

**move,** actuate, impel, induce, prompt, instigate, persuade, stir, agitate, propel, push

**music,** harmony, melody, symphony

**musical,** tuneful, melodious, harmonious, dulcet, sweet

**mute,** dumb, silent, speechless

**mutual,** reciprocal, interchanged, correlative (sole, solitary)

**mysterious,** dark, obscure, hidden, secret, dim, mystic, enigmatic, unaccountable, inexplicable, abstruse (open, clear)

**mystify,** confuse, perplex, puzzle (explain)

# N

**naked,** nude, bare, uncovered, rude, unclothed, rough, simple (covered, clad)

**narrate,** tell, relate, detail, recount, describe, enumerate, rehearse, recite

**nation,** country, tribe, people, community, realm, state

**native,** indigenous, inborn, vernacular

**neat,** natty, nice, orderly, clean, dapper, tidy, trim, prim, spruce (dirty, rough, disorderly, unkempt, soiled, untidy, negligent)

**necessary,** needful, expedient, essential, requisite, indispensable (useless)

**necessity,** need, exigency, emergency, urgency, requisite

**need,** *n.,* necessity, distress, poverty, indigence, want, penury

**need,** *v.,* require, want, lack

**neglect,** *n.,* omission, failure, default, negligence, remissness, carelessness, slight

**neglect,** *v.,* disregard, slight, omit, overlook

**neighborhood,** environs, vicinity, adjacency, nearness, proximity

**nimble,** spry, active, brisk, lively, alert, quick, agile, prompt (awkward, slow, clumsy)

**notable,** plain, evident, remarkable, signal, striking, rare (obscure)

**note,** token, symbol, mark, sign, indication, remark, comment

**notice,** *n.*, advice, notification, intelligence, information

**notice,** *v.*, mark, note, observe, attend to, regard, heed

**notify,** publish, acquaint, apprise, inform, declare

**notorious,** conspicuous, open, obvious, ill-famed (unknown)

**nourish,** nurture, cherish, foster, supply (starve, famish)

**nourishment,** food, diet, sustenance, nutrition

**novel,** modern, new, fresh, recent, unused, strange, rare (old)

**nutrition,** food, diet, nutriment, nourishment

# O

**obedient,** compliant, submissive, dutiful, respectful (obstinate)

**obey,** conform, comply, submit (rebel, disobey)

**object,** oppose, except to, contravene, impeach, deprecate (assent)

**obnoxious,** offensive (agreeable)

**obscure,** dense, deep, undistinguished, unknown (distinguished)

**obsolete,** old, rare, ancient, disused, antiquated, archaic

**obstruct,** block, hinder, clog, bar, arrest, retard, stay, barricade, impede, oppose, interrupt (aid, clear, promote, facilitate, free, advance, accelerate)

**offense,** affront, misdeed, misdemeanor, transgression, trespass

**offensive,** insolent, abusive, obnoxious (inoffensive)

**old,** aged, ancient, antiquated, obsolete, old-fashioned, senile, elderly, venerable (young, new)

**open,** candid, unreserved, clear, fair (hidden, dark)

**opinion,** notion, view, judgment, belief, sentiment

**oppose,** resist, withstand, thwart (give way)

**option,** choice

**origin,** cause, occasion, source, beginning, birth (end, conclusion)

**overbearing,** haughty, pround, arrogant (gentle)

**overflow,** inundation, deluge

**overrule,** supersede, suppress

**overturn,** invert, overthrow, reverse, subvert (establish, fortify)

**overwhelm,** crush, defeat, vanquish

# P

**pain,** suffering, qualm, pang, agony, anguish, torment, ache, torture (pleasure, delight, rapture)

**part,** division, portion, share, fraction (whole)

**perceive,** note, observe, discern, distinguish, comprehend, understand

**perfect,** ideal, sinless, spotless, stainless, holy, complete, immaculate, unblemished, consummate, correct, faultless (bad, defaced, corrupt, blemished, spoiled, worthless, perverted, inferior, marred, defective, faulty, deficient, imperfect)

**peril,** danger, pitfall, snare (safety)

**permanent,** fixed, constant, lasting, perpetual, stable, steadfast, unchanging, imperishable, durable, enduring, changeless

**permission,** liberty, leave, permit, license, allowance, authority (denial, objection, refusal, prevention)

**permit,** allow, tolerate (forbid)

**perplexity,** confusion, doubt, distraction, amazement, astonishment, bewilderment

**persuade,** coax, convince, urge, allure, entice, prevail upon

**physical,** corporeal, bodily, material (mental)

**picture,** engraving, print, representation, illustration, image

**pitiful,** mournful, pathetic, pitiable, woeful, sorrowful, abject, lamentable, mean, miserable, wretched (glorious, great, grand, mighty, lofty, noble, superb, exalted, commanding, august, superior)

**pity,** mercy, condolence, compassion, sympathy (cruelty, brutality, harshness, severity, sternness, barbarity)

**plain,** open, manifest, evident (secret)

**play,** game, sport, amusement (work)

**plead,** beseech, ask, beg, entreat, implore, urge, solicit, argue, advocate

**plentiful,** abundant, ample, copious, plenteous, rich, teeming, luxuriant, full, bountiful, affluent (scarce, deficient, impoverished, scant)

**polite,** cultured, courtly, elegant, genteel, civil, urbane, gracious, obliging, courteous, accomplished (awkward, coarse, boorish, raw, rude, uncivil, insulting, uncouth, impolite, impudent)

**positive,** absolute, peremptory, decided, certain (negative)

**possessor,** owner, proprietor

**possible,** practical, practicable, likely (impossible)

**poverty,** penury, indigence, need, want (wealth)

**power,** authority, force, strength, dominion

**praise,** acclaim, approbation, commendation, eulogy, plaudit, extol, laud (blame)

**prayer,** entreaty, petition, request, suit

**prevent,** obviate, preclude

**previous,** antecedent, introductory, preparatory, preliminary (subsequent)

**pride,** haughtiness, arrogance, vanity, conceit (humility)

**principal,** chief, main, essential

**principle,** ground, reason, motive, impulse, maxim, rule, rectitude, integrity

**privilege,** immunity, advantage, favor, prerogative, exemption, right, claim

**profession,** business, trade, occupation, vocation, office, employment, engagement, avowal

**profound,** deep, fathomless, penetrating, solemn, abstruse, recondite (shallow)

**prohibit,** forbid, hinder, prevent, debar, disallow, interdict (permit, license, sanction, allow, tolerate, authorize)

**prominent,** eminent, marked, important, conspicuous, leading (obscure)

**proper,** legitimate, right, just, fair, equitable, suitable, decent, becoming, befitting, adapted, pertinent, appropriate (wrong)

**prosper,** flourish, succeed, grow rich, thrive, advance (fail)

**prosperity,** well-being, weal, welfare, happiness, good luck (poverty)

**prudence,** carefulness, judgment, discretion, wisdom (indiscretion)

**punctual,** exact, precise, nice, particular, prompt, timely (dilatory)

**puzzle,** perplex, confound, embarrass, bewilder, confuse, pose, mystify (enlighten)

## Q

**quack,** imposter, pretender, charlatan (savant)

**quaint,** artful, curious, farfetched, fanciful, odd, singular

**qualified,** competent, fitted, adapted (incompetent)

**quality,** attribute, rank, distinction

**queer,** odd, peculiar, singular, quaint, unique, strange, unusual, ridiculous, preposterous, bizarre, curious, eccentric, ludicrous, fantastic, funny (common, natural, usual, normal, ordinary, regular)

**question,** query, inquiry, interrogatory

**quick,** lively, brisk, expeditious, impetuous, adroit, fleet, rapid, swift, sweeping, dashing, clever, sharp, ready, prompt, alert, nimble, agile, active (slow)

**quote,** note, repeat, cite, adduce

## R

**radiance,** splendor, brightness, brilliance, luster, glare (dullness)

**rank,** order, degree, dignity, nobility, consideration

**ransack,** rummage, pillage, overhaul, explore, plunder

**rare,** curious, unique, unusual, strange, peculiar, odd, extraordinary, scarce, singular, uncommon (ordinary)

**rascal,** scoundrel, rogue, knave, vagabond, scamp

**rash,** hasty, precipitate, foolhardy, adventurous, heedless, reckless, careless (deliberate)

**rate,** value, compute, appraise, estimate, chide, abuse

**ratify,** confirm, establish, substantiate, sanction (protest, oppose)

**rational,** reasonable, sagacious, judicious, wise, sensible, sound (unreasonable)

**ravage,** overrun, desolate, despoil, destroy

**reach,** touch, stretch, attain, gain, arrive at

**ready,** prepared, ripe, apt, prompt, adroit, handy (slow, dilatory)

**real,** authentic, actual, literal, practical, positive, certain, genuine, true (unreal)

**realize,** accomplish, achieve, effect, gain, get, acquire, comprehend

**reap,** gain, get, acquire, obtain

**reason,** *n.,* motive, design, end, proof, cause, ground, purpose

**reason,** *v.,* deduce, draw from, trace, infer, conclude, think

**reasonable,** rational, wise, honest, fair, right, just (unreasonable)

**rebellion,** insurrection, revolt

**rebellious,** mutinous, seditious, refractory, disobedient, ungovernable, insubordinate, contumacious (docile, obedient, yielding, tractable, subservient, compliant, gentle)

**recreation,** sport, pastime, amusement, play, game, fun

**redeem,** ransom, recover, rescue, deliver save, free

**reduce,** abate, lessen, decrease, lower, shorten, conquer (increase)

**refined,** polite, courtly, polished, cultured, genteel, purified (boorish)

**reflect,** consider, meditate, cogitate, think, ponder, muse

**reform,** amend, correct, better, restore, improve (corrupt)

**refute,** disprove, falsify (affirm)

**regard,** mind, heed, notice, behold, view, consider, respect

**regret,** grief, sorrow, lamentation, repentance, remorse

**regular,** orderly, uniform, customary, ordinary, stated (irregular)

**regulate,** methodize, arrange, adjust, organize, govern, rule (disorder)

**reliance,** trust, hope, dependence, confidence (suspicion)

**relief,** succor, aid, help, redress, alleviation

**relinquish,** give up, forsake, resign, surrender, quit, leave, forego (retain)

**remedy,** help, relief, redress, cure, reparation

**remote,** distant, far, secluded, indirect (near)

**renounce,** disown, recant, refute, reject, retract, revoke, repudiate, recall, discard, deny, abandon, disclaim, disavow (assert, avow, advocate, acknowledge, cherish, claim, uphold, defend, vindicate, proclaim, retain)

**report,** record, rumor, story, tale, statement, narrative, account, description, recital

**reproduce,** propagate, imitate, represent, copy

**repulsive,** forbidding, odious, ugly, disagreeable, revolting (attractive)

**reverence,** honor, respect, awe, veneration, deference, homage, worship (execration)

**revise,** review, reconsider

**revive,** refresh, renew, renovate, animate, resuscitate, vivify, cheer, comfort

**rich,** wealthy, affluent, opulent, copious, ample, abundant, exuberant, plentiful, fertile, fruitful, superb, gorgeous (poor)

**rival,** antagonist, opponent, competitor

**road,** way, highway, route, course, path, pathway

**roam,** ramble, rove, stray, wander, stroll

**robber,** bandit, brigand, burglar, pirate, thief, raider, plunderer, pillager, marauder, forager, buccaneer

**robust,** strong, lusty, vigorous, sinewy, stout, sturdy, stalwart, able-bodied (puny)

**rout,** beat, defeat, overthrow, scatter

**route,** road, course, way, path, journey, direction

**rude,** rugged, rough, uncouth, unpolished, harsh, gruff, impertinent, impudent, saucy, flippant, insolent, churlish (polished, polite)

**ruthless,** cruel, savage, barbarous, inhuman, merciless, remorseless, relentless (considerate)

# S

**sacred,** holy, hallowed, divine, consecrated, dedicated, devoted (profane)

**safe,** secure, harmless, trustworthy, reliable (perilous, dangerous)

**sane,** sober, lucid, sound, rational (crazy)

**scandalize,** shock, disgust, offend, vilify, revile, malign, traduce, defame, slander

**scanty,** bare, pinched, insufficient, slender, meager (ample)

**scatter,** strew, spread, disseminate, disperse, dissipate, dispel (collect)

**secret,** clandestine, concealed, hidden, sly, underhand, latent, private (open)

**send,** fling, hurl, emit, drive, dispatch, cast, delegate, throw, launch, project (get, bring, carry, convey, hand, keep, receive, retain, hold)

**sense,** discernment, appreciation, perception, view, opinion, feeling, sensibility, susceptibility, thought, judgment, import, significance, meaning, purport, wisdom

**sensible,** wise, intelligent, reasonable, sober, sound, conscious, aware (foolish)

**settle,** arrange, adjust, regulate, conclude, determine

**several,** sundry, many, various

**severe,** austere, inexorable, strict, harsh, stern, stringent, unmitigated, rough, unyielding (lenient, affable, easy, indulgent)

**shake,** tremble, shudder, shiver, quiver, quake

**shallow,** superficial, flimsy, slight (deep, thorough)

**shame,** disgrace, dishonor (honor)

**shameless,** immodest, impudent, indecent, indelicate, brazen

**shape,** form, fashion, mold, model

**share,** portion, lot, division, quantity, quota, contingent

**sharp,** acute, keen (dull)

**shine,** glare, glitter, radiate, sparkle

**short,** brief, concise, succinct, summary (long)

**sick,** diseased, ill, unhealthy, morbid (healthy)

**sickness,** illness, indisposition, disease, disorder (health)

**significant,** expressive, material, important (insignificant)

**silent,** dumb, mute, speechless (talkative)

**simple,** single, plain, artless (complex, compound)

**sincere,** candid, frank, honest, pure, genuine, real (insincere)

**situation,** condition, plight, predicament, state, position

**size,** bulk, greatness, magnitude, dimension

**slander,** defame, detract, revile, vilify, traduce, libel, malign, disparage, decry, calumniate (defend, extol, laud, praise, eulogize)

**slavery,** servitude, bondage, thralldom (freedom)

**sleep,** doze, drowse, nap, slumber (wake)

**slow,** dilatory, tardy, lingering, sluggish (fast)

**smell,** fragrance, odor, scent, perfume

**smooth,** even, level, mild (rough)

**soak,** drench, imbue, steep

**social,** friendly, communicative (unsocial)

**solicit,** importune, urge

**solitary,** sole, only, single

**sound,** *a.,* healthy, sane (unsound)

**sound,** *n.,* tone, noise

**sparse,** scanty, thin (luxuriant)

**speak,** converse, talk, say, tell, confer, articulate, express, utter

**spend,** expend, exhaust, consume, dissipate, waste, squander (save)

**spread,** disperse, diffuse, expand, disseminate, scatter

**stain,** soil, discolor, spot, tarnish, color, blot

**state,** commonwealth, realm

**sterile,** barren, unfruitful (fertile)

**stormy,** rough, boisterous, tempestuous (calm)

**straight,** direct, right (crooked)

**stranger,** alien, foreigner (friend)

**strengthen,** fortify, invigorate, encourage (weaken)

**strong,** robust, sturdy, powerful (weak)

**stupid,** dull, foolish, obtuse, witless (clever)

**subsequent,** succeeding, following (previous)

**substantial,** solid, durable (insubstantial)

**suit,** accord, agree (disagree)

**surrender,** cede, give, yield, sacrifice, relinquish, abandon, capitulate, alienate

**surround,** encircle, encompass, environ

**sustain,** maintain, support

**sympathy,** commiseration, compassion, condolence

**system,** rule, manner, method, plan, order

# T

**take,** accept, receive (give)

**talkative,** garrulous, communicative, loquacious (silent)

**taste,** flavor, relish, savor (tastelessness)

**tax,** custom, duty, impost, excise, toll

**tease,** taunt, tantalize, torment, vex

**temporary,** fleeting, transient, transitory (permanent)

**term,** boundary, limit, period, time

**territory,** dominion

**thankful,** grateful, obliged (thankless)

**thaw,** melt, dissolve, liquefy (freeze)

**theatrical,** dramatic, showy, ceremonious, meretricious

**theft,** robbery, depredation, spoliation

**theme,** subject, topic, text, essay

**theory,** speculation, scheme, hypothesis, conjecture

**therefore,** accordingly, consequently, hence

**thick,** dense, close, compact, solid, coagulated, muddy, turbid, misty, foggy, vaporous (thin)

**thin,** slim, slender, slight, flimsy, attenuated, lean, scraggy (fat, heavy)

**think,** cogitate, consider, reflect, ponder, contemplate, meditate, conceive, imagine, apprehend, hold, consider, regard, believe

**thorough,** accurate, correct, trustworthy, reliable, complete (superficial)

**thought,** idea, conception, imagination, fancy, conceit, notion, supposition, care, provision, consideration, opinion, view, sentiment, reflection, deliberation

**thoughtful,** considerate, careful, reflective, cautious, heedful, contemplative, provident, pensive, dreamy (thoughtless)

**thoughtless,** inconsiderate, rash, improvident, precipitate, heedless

**tie,** bind, restrain, restrict, oblige, secure, unite, join (loosen)

**time,** duration, season, period, era, age, date, span, spell

**tolerate,** allow, admit receive, suffer, permit, let, endure, abide (oppose)

**top,** summit, apex, head, crown, surface (bottom, base)

**torture,** torment, anguish, agony

**touching,** tender, affecting, moving, pathetic

**trade,** traffic, commerce, dealing, occupation, employment, office

**tranquil,** still, unruffled, peaceful, quiet, hushed (noisy, boisterous)

**transaction,** negotiation, occurrence, proceeding, affair

**trash,** nonsense, twaddle, trifle

**travel,** trip, ramble, peregrination, excursion, journey, tour, voyage

**treacherous,** traitorous, treasonable, disloyal, faithless, false, perfidious, sly (trustworthy, faithful)

**trite,** stale, old, ordinary, commonplace, hackneyed (novel)

**triumph,** achievement, ovation, victory, conquest, jubilation (failure, defeat)

**trivial,** trifling, petty, small, frivolous, unimportant, insignificant (important)

**true,** genuine, actual, sincere, unaffected, honest, upright, veritable, real, veracious, authentic, exact, accurate, correct (false)

**tune,** tone, air, melody, strain

**type,** emblem, symbol, figure, sign, letter, sort, kind

# U

**ugly,** unsightly, plain, homely, ill-favored, hideous (beautiful)

**umpire,** referee, arbitrator, judge, arbiter

**uncertain,** doubtful, dubious, questionable, equivocal, ambiguous, indistinct, variable, fluctuating

**uncommon,** rare, strange, scarce, singular, choice (common, ordinary)

**uncouth,** strange, odd, clumsy, ungainly (graceful)

**under,** below, beneath, subordinate, lower, inferior (above)

**understanding,** knowledge, intellect, intelligence, faculty, comprehension, mind, reason, brains

**undertake,** engage in, embark on, agree, promise

**undo,** annul, frustrate, unfasten, destroy

**uneasy,** restless, disturbed, stiff, awkward (quiet)

**unequaled,** matchless, unique, novel, new, unheard of

**unfortunate,** calamitous, ill-fated, unlucky, wretched, unhappy, miserable (fortunate)

**uniform,** regular, symmetrical, even, equal, alike, unvaried (irregular)

**union,** junction, combination, alliance, confederacy, league, coalition, agreement, concern (disunion, separation)

**unique,** unequal, uncommon, rare, choice, matchless (common, ordinary)

**unite,** join, combine, add, attach, incorporate, embody, clench, merge (separate, disrupt, sunder)

**universal,** general, all, entire, total, catholic (sectional)

**unlimited,** absolute, boundless, undefined, infinite (limited)

**unreasonable,** foolish, silly, absurd (reasonable)

**unusual,** rare, unwonted, singular, uncommon, remarkable, strange, extraordinary (common)

**uphold,** maintain, defend, sustain, support, vindicate (desert, abandon)

**upright,** vertical, perpendicular, just, erect, equitable, fair, pure, honorable (prone, horizontal)

**urge,** incite, impel, push, drive, instigate, stimulate, press, solicit, induce

**urgent,** pressing, important, imperative, immediate, serious, wanted (unimportant)

**use,** *n.,* usage, practice, habit, custom, avail, advantage, utility, benefit, application (disuse, desuetude)

**use,** *v.,* employ, exercise, occupy, accustom, practice, inure (abuse)

**useful,** advantageous, serviceable, available, helpful, beneficial, good (useless)

**usual,** ordinary, common, accustomed, habitual, customary, prevalent, regular (unusual, exceptional, rare, singular, strange)

# V

**vacant,** empty, unfilled, unoccupied, thoughtless, unthinking, void, vacuous (occupied, crowded, full, jammed, packed)

**vague,** unsettled, undetermined, uncertain, pointless, indefinite (definite)

**vain,** useless, fruitless, empty, worthless, inflated, proud, conceited, unreal, unavailing, frivolous (effectual, humble, real)

**valiant,** brave, bold, valorous, courageous, gallant (cowardly)

**valid,** weighty, strong, powerful, efficient, sound, binding (invalid)

**valor,** courage, gallantry, boldness, bravery, heroism (cowardice)

**value,** appraise, assess, reckon, appreciate, estimate, prize, treasure, esteem (despise, condemn)

**vanish,** disappear, fade, melt, dissolve

**vanity,** conceit, egotism, affectedness (humility)

**variable,** changeable, unsteady, shifting, inconstant, wavering, fickle, fitful, restless (constant)

**variety,** difference, diversity, change, diversification, mixture, medley, miscellany (sameness, monotony)

**vast,** spacious, boundless, mighty, immense, enormous, colossal, gigantic, huge, prodigious (confined)

**verbal,** oral, spoken, literal, unwritten (written)

**verdict,** judgment, finding, decision, answer

**vicious,** corrupt, depraved, bad, profligate, faulty (virtuous, gentle)

**victim,** sacrifice, food, prey, sufferer, dupe, gull

**view,** prospect, survey

**violent,** destructive, furious (gentle)

**virtue,** honesty, morality, honor, truth, worth, uprightness, probity, purity, integrity, chastity, goodness, duty, rectitude, faithfulness (vice, viciousness, evil, wrong, wickedness)

# W

**wander,** range, ramble, roam, rove, stroll, stray, deviate

**wary,** circumspect, cautious (foolhardy)

**wash,** clean, rinse, wet, moisten, tint, stain

**waste,** squander, dissipate, lavish, destroy, decay, dwindle, wither

**way,** method, plan, system, means, manner, mode, form, fashion, course, process, road, route, track, path, habit, practice

**wealth,** money, pelf, plenty, opulence, means, riches, prosperity, lucre, luxury, assets, abundance, affluence, property (need, destitution, lack, beggary, misery, poverty, privation, want, scarcity)

**win,** get, obtain, gain, procure, effect, realize, accomplish, achieve (lose)

**wisdom,** prudence, foresight, sagacity, far-sightedness, judiciousness, sense (foolishness, absurdity, idiocy, silliness, stupidity, nonsense)

**wit,** humor, satire, fun, raillery

**wonder,** marvel, miracle, prodigy

**work,** labor, task, toil, occupation, business, employment, exertion (play)

**worthless,** valueless (valuable)

**wrong,** injustice, injury (right)

# Y

**yearn,** long for, desire, crave

**yell,** bellow, cry out, scream

**yield,** bear, give, afford, impart, communicate, confer, bestow, abdicate, resign, cede, surrender, relinquish, relax, quit (withdraw, withhold, retain, deny, refuse, vindicate)

**youthful,** young, juvenile, boyish, girlish, puerile, immature, adolescent (aged, mature, decrepit, venerable, antiquated)

# Z

**zeal,** energy, fervor, ardor, earnestness, enthusiasm, eagerness (indifference, apathy, torpor, coldness, carelessness, sluggishness)

**zero,** nothing, naught, cipher

**zest,** flavor, appetizer, gusto, pleasure, enjoyment, relish, sharpener, enhancement (distaste, disgust, disrelish)

## For Further Reference

Brandt, Sue R.
*How to Improve Your Written English*
Franklin Watts
Newman, Gerald
*How to Write a Report*
Franklin Watts
Strunk, William, Jr., and White, E.B.
*The Elements of Style*
Macmillan
Tchudi, Susan and Tchudi, Stephen
*The Young Writer's Handbook*
Macmillan
Yates, Elizabeth
*Someday You'll Write*
E.P. Dutton

# Speaking

The section on studying, pages 78–103, focuses on the ways that we absorb information in school. The most important ways are through listening and through reading. This section and the prior section concentrate on the way we express ourselves—how we communicate what we have learned to others. The two main ways are by speaking and by writing. This section is on speaking, expecially in school situations.

Almost everyone knows how to speak. We say our first words when we are less than a year old, and by the time we reach four, we can form sentences and let people know about our needs and feelings without much trouble. At the same time, however, we do not always know how to speak well. When students give class reports, some mumble and stumble over their words. Others speak too loudly or have irritating mannerisms. This section takes a look at speaking and offers some pointers on how you can become a more effective speaker. It also shows how you can make sure that your listeners hear what you have to say.

# How speaking works

The first thing we need to know is how we make the noises that result in speech. Even though we all speak all the time, we are not always aware of how we do so. There are four main components in producing spoken sounds:

**Breathing.** As we are drawing breath into our lungs, we cannot speak—although it is possible for us to make odd ghostly sounds. Speaking is possible when we are pushing air out of our lungs. We force the air to pass through the noise-making part of our throats called the *larynx* or *voice box.*

Once in awhile we become aware of how important breath is to speaking. If you have just run half a mile and are out of breath, you will find it difficult to speak because you are breathing too rapidly. If you are bending down to tie your shoe, your lungs and breathing muscles are cramped, and you cannot speak very loudly or clearly.

Many speakers could improve their speech just by remembering the importance of breathing. If you stand in front of the class slouched down or hunched over a lectern or desk, your breathing muscles are cramped, and you cannot use them properly to push air through your larynx. If you stand up straight, and breathe deeply before you start speaking, your words will be much more clear and forceful.

**Vibration.** The second element in speaking is the actual creation of sound in the larynx, or voice box. When you start to speak, you unconsciously pull your two vocal cords tight, and push air from your lungs between them. The air causes them to vibrate in much the same way that a bow causes the string on a violin to vibrate. You control the loudness of your voice by controlling the amount of air you push between the cords. You control the pitch of your voice (shrill, deep, or in between) by controlling how tightly the cords are stretched.

You can actually feel your vocal cords in action by feeling your throat as you make a continuous sound of "ah." If you make a deep sound, then a shrill sound, you will feel the muscles that pull the cords tight and that allow you to change pitch.

**Resonance.** The third component in speaking may suprise you: it is your head. Just as a violin has a wooden case that gives resonance to the sound of vibrating string, so the nasal passages, mouth, and throat, and the upper chest are resonators for the vibrating vocal cords. The resonators help make the sound of your voice both louder and more pleasing than it would otherwise be. You can feel how they vibrate if you make a loud "mmm" sound and feel your chest, throat, and head. When a person has a bad cold, all the nasal passages are shut, so the voice sounds hollow and weak.

**Articulation.** The last element in speaking is articulation—the many different ways in which you can vary the sound of your vocal cords to form words. Some sounds (*t* and *p*, for example) do not even require vocal sound. When vocal sound is used, *t* becomes *d*, and *p* becomes *b*. Most of our vocal sounds are used on vowels (a, e, i, o, u), although some consonants (m, n, r) are also sounded.

One of the most common speech problems is lazy articulation. Words get slurred together, and sometimes meanings can be lost altogether. Lazy speech is not usually a problem in informal conversation, but it can be a serious problem when a person is speaking to more than one or two others. When lazy speech is printed out, it looks odd on the page, but we are all used to hearing it. For example: I dough wancha t'go.

I don't want you to go.

# Improving your speech

When students in a class give an oral book report, teachers and students alike notice that some have read their books more carefully than others and some have more interesting things to say about their books. But there are always a few who speak so badly that it is difficult to know how carefully they have read or how much they have to say. Even the best student will not be recognized unless he can communicate his knowledge and opinions effectively.

Like listening skills, speaking skills are often ignored because it seems that everyone knows how to listen and speak. But a wise student will put some time and energy into considering basic speaking skills, which can be as important to success in school as the writing skills described in the next section. The following paragraphs will list some of the important things to consider when preparing and giving an oral report in front of the class.

**Nonverbal speech.** Much of the success of a good speaker may not even be in his words. Listeners are alert not only for what is said but for how the speaker stands and how he delivers his words.

Many students are nervous about giving a report, and they let the audience know this before they speak a word. They may slouch, sway back and forth, crack their knuckles, or keep their eyes down on their notes to avoid looking at anyone. Mannerisms of this kind detract greatly from a speech. They say to the audience, "I don't even know that you're here, and I do not really have anything I want to tell you." If you are in the audience when someone does this, you probably have the same negative reaction.

Even good speakers are normally a little nervous when they get up in front of a group. But they learn to use their nervousness to advantage. They come to the front of the class, put their notes on the lectern, and look perhaps toward a particular friend in the class, waiting until the class is paying attention before beginning.

Even if you are reading from notes, look up at the audience once in a while. Your glance tells the audience that you are thinking about them. You may also notice some reaction that will tell you how you are doing. If half the class is yawning, perhaps you have gone on too long. If people look puzzled, perhaps there is some important fact you have left out or not explained clearly. With your eyes, you can stay in contact with your listeners and can encourage them to stay in contact with you.

*There is a wrong way* (left) *and a right way* (right) *to give an oral report. Which speaker would you rather listen to?*

Gestures are another important tool. For a class report, throwing your arms around and jumping up and down may not be appropriate, but if there is something visual in your report that you want to explain—a spiral staircase, the size of the fish you caught—use your hands to help. In some cases, you may be able to demonstrate by walking from one side of the room to another or by showing something you have brought. An audience often listens better when it also has something to watch.

Your face is the most expressive part of your body, and listeners will be watching for expressions that will help them understand what you are explaining. For example, if you are reporting on a funny book you have read, a solemn, slow recital of the plot with no hint of a smile and no twinkle in the eye will probably not be very effective. If you are telling a suspenseful story, your expressions help reflect the growing excitement.

Finally, your voice itself is a very expressive tool. Listeners will try to understand what you are saying partly by the pitch, the tone, and the cadence of your voice. If you always speak at the same pitch and never vary the tone or the cadence (speed), your listeners will soon be lulled to sleep.

In telling about a book or a personal experience, think about what parts should be told slowly and what parts more rapidly. If there is suspense, you might speak more and more softly. If there is a surprise, a sudden change of tone can make it more surprising.

There are many good examples of the way good speakers use their bodies, faces, and tones of voice to help get their messages across. Television announcers, advertisers, politicians, and ministers are often expert in the use of nonverbal communication. Watch them and listen carefully to them, and you may find new things that will work for you.

**Speaking**

# Preparing a report

In many ways, speaking is easier than writing because you needn't worry about all the mechanics of writing: spelling, punctuation, etc. But a good oral report does require planning.

The first planning step is to consider any requirements—in a book report, you may be asked to begin with the title and author, then tell about the book, then evaluate it. A second step is to decide how to balance the report—about how much time do you want to spend on each of the major topics? Speakers who get up without a plan often waste all their time on one topic and do not have time to finish.

A third step is to consider your audience. For example, if you are reporting on a new home computer, you should consider what others in the class are likely to know about computers in general. If you start at a level that is too advanced, they will not be able to understand you; if you start at a level that is too elementary, they will be bored or even resentful.

**Organization.** Once you have your general presentation in mind, sit down and write out its main points. Many speakers prefer to use outline form. Like a written report, an oral report often has three main parts: I. Introduction
II. Body
III. Conclusion

For a book report, the introduction might consist of the name and author of the book and a brief description of its type—mystery, science fiction, historical fiction, biography, etc. An introduction also may include a general statement of your point of view. For example: "I thought this was the best mystery I had ever read until I came to the last ten pages. Then I changed my mind because the ending was not believable." This helps your listeners know where your report is going and makes it easier to follow.

The body of the report may deal with some aspect of the topic. Unless you have a great deal of time, you probably will not be able to consider all aspects. With a book report, for example, you may have time to consider the plot (it may be the most important item in a mystery), or the characters (they may be most important in an historical novel or a biography), or the mood and style. Pick an aspect and concentrate on it.

Some experience at giving reports will help you judge how much material you can cover in the time you are allowed. Try to isolate the important points so that you do not get bogged down in trying to tell too much. In order to report clearly, you will have to simplify, leaving out the less important topics. Otherwise your listeners may be hopelessly confused.

The conclusion of the report may be the place where you give your personal reactions. Or you may come back to the statement you made in the introduction—illustrating, for example, why the end of the mystery was not believable. Another kind of conclusion summarizes the body of the report in a sentence or two. Always have the introductory material and the conclusion well in mind (or even written down). Do not be like the legendary minister who had at least three conclusions in every sermon.

**Practice.** Perhaps the most important part of preparing for an oral report is to practice it out loud. Go into a room and start to give the report, listening to the way it sounds. The first time, you are likely to stumble from one point to the next. The second time through, time yourself—if the report is too long, go back and find places where it can be shortened. One of the most useful tools for practicing is a cassette recorder. If you have (or can borrow) one, record your second or third practice run, then listen as if you were sitting in the audience. Where does the report work, and where does it fall down? Experiment with varying your tone of voice and the speed of your delivery. Also listen for signs of lazy speech, such as words or phrases that get lost.

## For Further Reference

Detz, Joan
  *You Mean I Have to Stand Up and Say Something?*
  Atheneum
Monroe, Alan and Ehninger, Douglas
  *Principles of Speech Communication*
  Scott, Foresman & Co.
Otfinoski, Steven
  *Speaking Up, Speaking Out*
  Millbrook Press
Silverstein, Alvin and Silverstein, Virginia
  *Wonders of Speech*
  William Morrow

# How to Study

Schools are set up to teach many subjects and many skills. But one skill is important as a beginning—knowing *how to learn.* A serious student soon discovers that he needs to master a few basic skills in order to take advantage of time spent in school. Most important are the skills of planning, listening, reading, and test taking. With these skills a student can absorb most of what school has to offer. In fact, these basic study skills will be useful all through life, because learning does not end when school ends. The ability to take in new information, digest it, and then use it is the most important skill in a wide variety of occupations and jobs. In school, these same skills can make the difference between being happy and successful and being fearful and unsuccessful. If you know how to study, you are much more likely to succeed and to enjoy your school years. The *Student Handbooks* are filled with information on a wide variety of subjects, but pointers on how to study are equally important because they lay the groundwork for effective learning.

# Make a plan

All students want to do their best in school, but many do not succeed. Is it just that others are smarter? Is it that others spend every hour of every day on homework and never have any fun? Some students do pick up and store information more easily than others, and some students do spend huge amounts of time studying; but the real difference between a good student and a bad one comes down to one thing: planning.

Men and women in many professions have learned that they must know how to plan in order to succeed. Many regret that they did not learn this lesson sooner so that they could have profited more from their years in school. Regardless of career, the difference between success and failure is often planning.

Making a good plan is hard work, but it needn't take very long. The most important advantage of a plan is that it helps you to make the best use of your time. Often it may save you hours or days of needless study and worry. When you do study, you learn to do so efficiently and rapidly; then, when the studying is done, you are free to enjoy yourself.

There are six important steps to good planning. They are:
1. Know what you want to accomplish.
2. Decide what steps are necessary to accomplish it.
3. Gather necessary material.
4. Organize your time.
5. Coordinate your plan with other activities.
6. Stick to your plan.

To illustrate how planning works, consider a family planning a trip to a distant town by car. First, they decide where they want to go. This may involve deciding whether there is time for a side trip to visit a friend or to accomplish some other business. Second, they decide on their route. No sensible traveler sets out to stop at each crossroad to decide which way to turn; instead, he finds out ahead of time how far his destination is and what roads he must take to get there. Third, the family gathers the necessary materials for the trip. This may involve being sure that the car is in good working order, filling it with gas, and packing a lunch to eat on the way. Fourth, the travelers plan their time. They estimate how long the trip will take, how far along they should be by midday, and how many stops they can afford to make along the way. Fifth, they coordinate their trip with other plans. Perhaps there is a store along the way where they want to buy clothes or a business associate to meet with. Finally, the family sets out. They are more relaxed because they know where they are going and how they will get there. They stick to their plan unless something occurs outside of their control. If the car breaks down, for example, they will revise their schedule—make a new plan that will work in the changed situation.

A plan for a trip that will take place over a few days is simpler than a plan for a whole school year, but it is really not so very different. How does this planning method work for a student? **What do you want to accomplish?** Answering this question is the most important step. Like the travelers, you must know the direction in which

you want to go, or there will be no reason for a plan. Perhaps your objective is to improve your grades in each subject or to get your highest grade in social studies. Thinking about what you most want to do must come first. A good plan should be ambitious—every student can find lots of room to improve. At the same time, however, you should aim at a realistic goal. If you failed in math last year, planning to become the top student this year may be unrealistic. Set your sights on a goal that is challenging but reachable.

**How will you get there?** Perhaps you think that if your aim is a higher grade in a class, the best plan is to study harder. But a real plan requires more detailed thinking. What steps will you take? Perhaps you should start with your knowledge about the class. When will the tests be given? What will you be expected to know at the end of the first month? How will you be sure that you are ready by then? Must you do a special report? When is it due, and what steps will you take to do it well and complete it on time?

**What materials do you need?** Now that you have a basic idea of your plan, you may have some preparations to make. The materials you need may be simple supplies like paper and pencils. For an art project, you will need paints or special paper. For a research report, you may need particular books. Make a list of needed materials and begin to gather them.

*A balanced study plan should set aside plenty of time for both study and play. Studying in a group turns learning into a team effort that sharpens your learning skills and increases your knowledge, just as playing a team sport improves your athletic skills and strengthens your body. Physical exercise and other enjoyable activities also help refresh your mind and sharpen your ability to learn.*

## MY SCHEDULE

| Date | School | outside | home |
|------|--------|---------|------|
| Monday | study period 2:00 Math | Library on way home from school | Make bed [every day] |
| Tuesday | MATH TEST | Scouts 4:00 | Late Supper |
| Wednesday | Clubs [study period] | | Judy's club [close door] |
| Thursday | French quiz [study period] 2:00 Book Report | Davis after school Piano Session 7:00 | Finish Book Report |
| Friday | BOOK REPORT DUE | | |
| Saturday | | [Don here] 2:00 football | CHORES |
| Sunday | | | [Church] check scout project |

**How will you budget your time?** This question is often the hardest one for students to answer. Not all study assignments are pleasant, and it is human to want to postpone dull or difficult assignments. When such things are postponed, time always seems to run out before they are done.

If you really want to accomplish a goal and are willing to make some sacrifices to do so, you must budget time for it. The best way is to do it *first* and to devote the time left over to other enjoyable but less important activities. Although it will be difficult to start with study, you will have more fun after your work is done because you know that you have already made the necessary progress toward your goal. Many students seem worried even when supposedly enjoying themselves because they have left important projects undone.

**How does your plan fit with other activities?** In planning your time, you might sit down and list all the activities in which you are engaged. Your goal may be a better grade in social studies, but social studies is only a part of your schoolwork; perhaps you also practice a musical instrument, and want to try out for the basketball team.

Once you have listed all your activities, put a number beside each one: "1" for the most important, "2" for the next most important, and so on. This is called setting priorities, and it is a very important part of planning. Both students and adults often find that they must choose between two or more activities because there just is not time or energy for all. If you know ahead of time what is most important, and you pay attention to that activity first, chances are you will succeed in accomplishing your aims.

If you choose an ambitious study goal, you will soon discover that it will have to be high on your list of priorities if it is to be reached. If study is always left until last, and if it gets left out altogether when time is short, then no amount of planning is likely to help you reach your goal.

**Can you stick to your plan?** There are two kinds of planners: the first likes to make a plan on paper but never follows through; the second makes plans so that he can accomplish them. The first kind of planner usually ends up disappointed in himself or looking for someone to blame. The second kind knows that a plan is no better than its execution. The successful planner is the one who actually sticks to the plan and reaches his goal.

## Talent and success.

Thomas Edison, inventor of the electric light, the phonograph, and many other modern devices, was often called a genius. But Edison himself always insisted that "genius is one percent inspiration and ninety-nine percent perspiration." "Perspiration," or hard work, is often a matter of planning—approaching a task in an orderly way—and concentration—sticking to the plan. Anyone who can master the arts of planning and concentration can realize his or her full potential, both in school and in other pursuits.

**How to Study**

# Learn to listen

Of all the skills important to students, listening may be the most valuable. It is surprising that schools themselves spend much time and money on teaching reading but scarcely anything on teaching listening.

Of course, everyone has ears, and listening isn't exactly like reading. There is no alphabet to learn, no special process of sounding out words, recognizing punctuation, and so on. But just because we all have ears does not mean that we are all good listeners. In school and in everyday situations, all of us miss words spoken to us because we are not paying attention; or we hear the words but immediately forget them. Even when we hear and remember, we can often get the information confused. Fortunately, however, with a little work, anyone can improve his listening. For a student, this can mean improving performance in school not by spending hours doing extra work but simply by making better use of class time.

## Basic listening.

The first important fact about listening is that it is *not* all done with the ears. Understanding spoken language can be greatly improved by watching as well. A teacher may tell a great deal about his subject by posture, facial expression, gestures, and eye contact. Sensitive students get to know their teachers and to understand this language of *visual cues.* It helps students to understand precisely what the teacher is saying and to remember not only the words but the mood or the tone surrounding a particular piece of information. When studying for a test, a student may remember an important phrase by first recalling the teacher's excitement when mentioning it.

A second fact about listening is that it is *not* all a matter of understanding words. Teachers and others communicate a great deal by the loudness, pace, and tone of their voices. For example, one teacher may stress an important point by speaking more loudly and more slowly than normal. Another may stress a point by speaking very quietly, requiring the class to listen intently.

If you listen only to the words, you may mistake the meaning altogether. Many speakers use *irony* or *sarcasm,* employing a tone of voice that tells listeners that they mean exactly the opposite of what they are saying. For example, a student spills milk on the teacher's desk and says, "I hope you are not angry." The teacher replies, "Of course I'm not angry." If she says this in a calm, quiet tone, she means what she says; but if she says it loudly, with her fists clenched and her eyes flashing, she is probably sarcastic and means, "I am not angry—I am furious!"

A third fact about listening is that a good listener must be almost as alert and active as the person being listened to. The listener must note words, tone of voice, and visual cues, and make sense of them as a whole. Many teachers encourage their students to be alert by frequently asking questions. This requires the listener to keep track of more than one speaker and sometimes to speak himself, to give an answer or an opinion. Most students could save themselves time spent studying outside of class by listening more closely in class. Good listening takes energy and attention.

## Gestures and facial expressions

*Gestures, such as this teacher's motion for quiet in her classroom* (left), *and signs of emotion, such as this girl's expression of surprise and joy* (right), *are good ways to communicate without using words.*

Get the assignment in writing so you won't have to wonder what you are supposed to do.

## Different kinds of teachers.

Every student has two different jobs in a classroom. One is to understand and master the material being taught—history, spelling, math, and so on. The other is to understand the teacher—how he teaches and what he requires of a student. One teacher may place great emphasis on learning basic principles of a subject. Another may require the mastery of a large body of small facts. Still another may be most interested in encouraging students to think for themselves or to solve problems themselves.

All of these approaches are valid, and it is the responsibility of the student to adapt to each of them. By listening carefully, you can usually understand which approach a teacher is following so that on tests, papers, and other assignments you can meet his or her expectations. This does not mean that you must always say or do exactly what pleases a teacher, but that there is usually room for individual differences within a teacher's general approach.

Listening skills also help a student to find out how he is doing in the teacher's estimation. Whether in a classroom or in a teacher conference, an attentive student uses all his listening skills. These include "listening" for what is *not* said as well as for what is said. For example, a teacher might say, "You have a great aptitude for math," in a way that also suggests a criticism: "but you are too careless in your computations."

## Getting the facts. Important as all
the general listening skills are, many students fall down on the most basic skill of all—getting the facts. In most classrooms, assignments are given out every day, and every day one or more of the students manages not to hear or to hear wrong.

For specific assignments, use a pencil and paper to assist your memory. In early grades, teachers often require students to write down assignments. But even if the teacher does not require this, do it anyway. You cannot do a good job on an assignment you have forgotten or misunderstood. If you do not understand the assignment, ask questions. Chances are that someone else in the class also does not understand.

## Taking notes. Probably the best way
to improve your listening is to get into the habit of taking notes. Note-taking will become more and more important as you progress in school, and learning how to do it early on can be very helpful.

If your teacher is presenting new material, you will be taking "lecture notes." The secret of lecture notes is that you must first work hard to *understand* what the teacher is saying. Unless you can take shorthand, you cannot copy down even half of what is said. Even if you could, the results would probably not be worthwhile. Instead, you must get a sense of how the teacher's material is organized.

**Getting the organization.** A presentation on history might be organized *chronologically*, moving from one event to a later event, and so on. If so, your notes should be organized accordingly, with dates or the names of major events down the left side of the page.

Another presentation might be organized around people—for example, the leaders of World War II. If so, the main headings in your notes would be the names of these people.

*Notes from a teacher's presentation may look like an informal outline—with each thought or topic on a new line.*

Scientific presentations may follow a step-by-step process. An English lesson may be planned to illustrate all the uses of a comma or all the forms of a verb. These would then become main headings.

Listening at the beginning of a teacher's presentation is especially important, because often he will introduce the subject by describing the organization that is to be used. Even without such an introduction, however, a note-taker can almost always find the organizational pattern in the first few minutes.

Nearly all school presentations have some sort of basic structure, and it is the job of the note-taker to get that structure down on paper. At first, you may have trouble deciding what is important and what is not. Teachers often enliven their presentations with little stories or anecdotes to illustrate or demonstrate a point. If the basic point is a difficult one, they may use several illustrations. You may have time to get some of the illustrations down, but it is most important that you get down the *main points,* even if you miss some of the detail.

**How should the notes look?** The teacher is the one who sets the organization of your notes, but you are the one who must learn how best to get the information down on paper. Usually, the only person you have to please in note-taking is yourself. If the finished notes recall the teacher's presentation, their purpose has been served. Only you will ever read and evaluate them.

You may want to adopt some personal code to help distinguish between important and less important points. For example, the most important might be written all in capitals. Many note-takers prefer to work in outline form—they may even pretend that they are trying to reproduce the teacher's outline for the presentation. Space is not a serious concern, so you may want to skip lines between the end of one topic and the beginning of another so that when you read through the notes later the breaks will be easily spotted.

In a complicated presentation, you may even want to distinguish between several kinds of notes. For a very important phrase, you might take down the teacher's exact words and put them in quotation marks to remind yourself. Sometimes you might try to rephrase an idea in your own words and underline it as a reminder. There may also be times when you put down your reactions to the teacher's point (disagreement, questions, approval); these might best be put in parentheses so that you do not later confuse your ideas with your teacher's. Even drawings or diagrams can help and save writing time. Many note-takers use arrows, boxes, and other such devices to set off certain material.

As in all listening skills, the important part of note-taking is to remain active—alert for the important points, framing questions about the material, and trying to make connections. If you merely write down an odd part of what you hear now and then, your notes will almost certainly be useless.

At their best, notes can be one of the most worthwhile study aids. You may be reading similar material in your textbook, but your notes are your own—you took them down and they bring back to you information that you have absorbed, whether you are studying for an examination, writing a paper, or preparing for an oral report. Notes can preserve the things you have learned because of your listening skills.

# Improve your reading

*Your reading will improve if you find a place to read with no distractions.*

Listening is one way to gain information in school. As we have seen, a student can improve his listening skills with a little practice and attention. The other major way to gain information is through reading. Unlike listening, reading is not a natural skill. Beginning in the early grades, a student must learn to read.

Nearly all students learn the basics of reading in the early grades. Slowly they recognize words that occur often, such as "dog," "cat," and "house." At the same time, students are learning the sound of each letter in the alphabet so that they can sound out unfamiliar words. By third or fourth grade, most students can read simple passages and understand them.

But learning the basic skills is not the end. Many students never go further, however, and for them reading is always a slow, difficult procedure. As they progress in school, they may fall further and further behind because they cannot read well enough. Reading becomes a more and more important learning tool. To be a good student, you must be a good reader.

## Using your equipment.
If you are having trouble with reading, your first step should be to check out the equipment you use. The most obvious equipment for reading is your eyes. If you have trouble focusing as you read, or if a few minutes of reading gives you a headache or makes your eyes water or burn, you should have your eyes checked by an ophthalmologist without delay. Nearly all common sight problems can be corrected, and it may surprise you how much easier reading can be with correctly prescribed glasses.

Another important tool for good reading is good hearing. This may seem surprising, but students of reading have discovered that a surprising number of students with reading problems have hearing problems. Learning to read is a process of translating symbols on a page (visual information) into sounds (aural information). This translation is difficult for those who do not hear well.

A third piece of equipment necessary for good reading is a sound processing center in the brain. Modern reading researchers have found that

**How to Study**

some students see and hear well enough but have some problem in *processing* the information they see on the printed page. For example, they may see letters in reverse order or be tempted to read some lines from right to left. Such processing problems are known as *dyslexia*, a term that simply means "problems learning to read." Reading specialists have developed special programs of instruction to help those who are *dyslexic*.

There is also the possibility that trouble with reading may have emotional causes. A good reader knows how to concentrate. But someone who is extremely sad or angry cannot concentrate very well on such a demanding task as reading. His mind may constantly wander to personal problems or feelings; as a result, the reader may lose track of a sentence in the middle or forget an important fact within moments of having read it. Even good readers have trouble concentrating sometimes. But if you have had trouble concentrating or have had trouble remembering what you read for weeks or months, you should consider asking for help in solving the problem.

Finally, reading difficulties can be caused by a person's surroundings. One student may grow up in a home where everyone reads—for information, for pleasure, and for learning. Such a student will develop the habit of reading at an early age, and it will seem a natural activity. Another student may grow up in a home where reading is less common. As a result, this student does not develop a reading habit and may come to see reading as unpleasant and seek to do as little of it as possible. In order to become a better reader, such a student must exercise some self-discipline and set aside some time each day—at home, at school, or at a library—to read.

Physical surroundings can also play a part in discouraging reading. Noise and activity in the same room distract many readers. Poor lighting can make reading an unpleasant chore. Other conditions including extreme heat and cold and poor ventilation can also slow down even a good reader. For many students a proper reading environment would increase reading skills without any further effort.

**Reviewing basic skills.** One common cause for reading difficulties is a gap in some important part of the process of learning to read. The student may have been sick and missed the important lessons, or may have been too young to fully understand them. If this is the case, it is always possible to go back and relearn or review these lessons—and the result may be a dramatic improvement in reading.

**Sounds.** The first step in reading is to translate a group of written symbols into a word. Simple words may be easy to recognize, but longer words probably need to be sounded out, especially if they are unfamiliar. If a student has never thoroughly learned the sounds of all the letters, he may not be able to sound out such words. This job would be simpler if all letters always had the same sound. But in English, many letters have quite different sounds in different situations. Some letter combinations have a sound quite different from the sound of either of the letters standing alone. For example, the letters *c* and *h* each have their own sounds when used alone. Yet when they are together, they have still another sound, as in *children* or *chief*. The vowel sounds—a, e, i, o, and u—have a still wider variety of sounds, depending on their position in a word and on various combinations. One example is the combination *ai* in *pair* and *wait*.

If the sounds of letters are sometimes confusing to you, you may feel embarrassed about this problem, since letter sounds are taught mainly in the early grades. But you can review the letter sounds all by yourself. The table on this page shows some of the most common sound changes. The dictionary in this volume has much more information. If you have trouble telling what a word is from its letters, this kind of review may be a first step toward better reading.

**Sentence meaning.** A second problem for many who find reading difficult is making sense of a group of words strung together. As long as a reader only moves along one word at a time, the meaning of a sentence can get lost. For example, a beginning reader might group words together like this: Jack . . . and . . .

Jill . . . went . . .
up . . . the . . . hill . . . to . . .
fetch . . . a . . .
pail . . . of . . .
water . . . .

In order to keep track of the meaning, every word must be remembered because the words are not grouped in a reasonable way.

## Vowel sounds

| Sound | Letters that can make this sound (example) |
|---|---|
| **a** as in cat | **a**, ai (plaid) |
| **a** as in cake | **a**, ai (paid), ea (break), ey (obey), ay (say) |
| **a** as in care | **a** + **r**, ai + r (fair), ea + r (wear), e + r (there) |
| **a** as in father | **a**, o (stop) |
| **a** as in saw | **a**, au (caught), oa (broad), ou (fought) |
| **e** as in bed | **e**, ea (heavy), ie (friend), ai (said) |
| **e** as in we | **e**, ei (receive), ey (key), ie (field) |
| **i** as in it | **i**, ee (been), u (busy), ui (build), y (hymn) |
| **i** as in kite | **i**, ie (tie), ei (height), ey (eye), uy (buy), y (fly) |
| **o** as in go | **o**, oa (goat), oe (toe), ou (soul), ew (sew), ow (grow) |
| **oo** as in tool | **oo**, ue (blue), ui (fruit), ew (threw), ough (through) |
| **oo** as in book | **oo**, o (wolf), ou (would), u (pull) |
| **ow** as in now | **ow**, ou (out), ough (bough) |
| **oy** as in boy | **oy**, oi (toil) |
| **u** as in cuff | **u**, o (son), oo (flood), oe (does), ou (double) |
| **u** as in hurt | **u** + **r**, ea + r (heard), i + r (bird), o + r (worry), ou + r (courage) |
| **u** as in fuse | **u**, ue (cue), eau (beauty), ew (few), iew (view), yu (yule), you (youth) |
| **ə** (an unaccented *uh* sound) | a (asleep), e (voted), o (confession), u (focus), etc. |

**How to Study**

A more skilled reader would naturally group the words in his mind:

Jack and Jill            (who?)
went up the hill         (did what?)
to fetch a pail of water (why?)

Good readers learn to see words in clusters. If you read word for word, and sometimes lose track of a sentence's meaning, try some exercises in seeing clusters of words together. At the beginning, read a simple paragraph word for word. Then go back and read it again, putting the words in groups that help them make sense. When you have done this several times, try reading a new paragraph by clusters the first time—without going through it word for word. Reading words in clusters becomes more important as you begin to read passages with longer, more complicated sentences.

**Word meaning.** Many readers begin to have trouble when they start to read passages about unfamiliar subjects. These readers may be able to recognize or pronounce all the words and they may be able to see how the words cluster in a sentence, but they cannot tell what a sentence means because they do not know the meaning of an essential word.

For such readers, an important step toward improving their reading is to increase their vocabulary. The box on the following pages provides a basic understanding of the way in which many long words are put together; this can help in learning new words. There are also other ways to increase your knowledge of the meanings of words. The most important are the following:

*Learn from context.* Readers can often learn a great deal about the meaning of a word simply by paying attention to what the rest of the passage says. Consider the word *perambulator* in the following paragraph, for example.

---

In the mornings, our nurse would take us to the playground in Central Park. I tagged along, holding onto her skirts, and she pushed my brother along in a great old-fashioned perambulator. It was much bigger and more luxurious than the baby carriages other nannies pushed, and nurse seemed proud of it. She only complained when we went up the big hill, when she used to mutter over and over, "Too heavy! Too heavy!"

---

A reader who does not know the meaning of *perambulator* can learn a great deal about it from this paragraph. It is compared with other baby carriages, so it must be a thing of that kind. This perambulator is larger and heavy, so it may be that in general perambulators are heavier than baby carriages. There is also the suggestion that a perambulator is an old-fashioned kind of baby carriage.

There are many other cases where the context will help define an unfamiliar word. Schoolbooks are often particularly careful to help a reader with unfamiliar terms.

*Use a dictionary.* Many students do not understand why teachers stress using a dictionary. It is the one quickest way for anyone to increase his vocabulary. Even if you can gain the basic meaning of a word from context, it is often wise to look the word up to be sure that you have the correct meaning.

If you look up *obstruction* in the dictionary in this volume, you may see that the word just before *obstruction* is o*bstruct*, which means "to fill and block," or "to stand or be in the way of." You can guess from this that an *obstruction* is something that blocks or stands in the way of something else. Note that the entries for both words present sample sentences to help you understand what the words mean.

Most people use dictionaries to look up long, difficult words. It is worth remembering that a dictionary may also be useful for looking up everyday words that are used in unfamiliar ways. For example, a reader may be confused by this sentence:

She greeted us warmly at the door, but we had the feeling she felt *put upon.*

Under *put* in the dictionary, you can learn that *put upon* means to "take advantage of," so you can conclude that the woman in the sentence felt that her guests had taken advantage of her.

*Write down new words.* A fast way to increase your word power is to keep a set of index cards or slips of paper. Each time you hear or read a word that you do not know, write the word down on a card. On the back of the card, write down its definition. Often, just writing the word and definition are enough to make it stick in your memory. If you keep the cards, you can go back through them later and review the new words and meanings.

# Increasing your vocabulary

Few people have trouble learning everyday words such as *house, man, dog, run.* The ones that give trouble are less common words that are long and that often refer to *abstract* ideas and pursuits.

These long words are often made up of smaller pieces whose meanings are easy to learn. These parts are *roots, prefixes,* and *suffixes.*

For example, consider the word *transportation.* Its root is *port,* a word that comes to English from Latin and that means "to carry." Its prefix is *trans-,* which also comes from Latin and which means "across." Its suffix, *-ation,* tells us that the word is a noun. If we had to "translate" *transportation* into other English words, we might suggest "across-carrying," which is close to the usual meaning of the word, "a carrying of things or people from one place to another."

Once you learn some of the common roots, prefixes, and suffixes, you can reason about the meanings of many other unfamiliar words.

**Using the root.** Knowing the one root *port,* you can probably think of other words of which port is a part: *import, export, deport, report.* This shows that there are several other common prefixes that can be used with this root. There are also suffixes such as the *-er* in *porter, importer, exporter, reporter.*

**Using the prefix.** A prefix like *trans-* can be used with many roots: *transatlantic, transcribe, translate, transmit,* and so on. The prefix table gives many of the more common prefixes, their basic meanings and examples.

**Using the suffix.** A suffix like *-ation* or *-tion* also has many uses with other roots. It always tells us that the word it is part of is a noun. If *translate* means to change from one language to another, *translation* is the result or the process of translating. The suffix table shows how other suffixes change words from one part of speech to another.

## Common English roots

| Root | Meaning | Examples |
|---|---|---|
| **act** | do, drive | act, action, actor, react, reaction, reactor |
| **aud** | hear | audio, audience, auditorium, audition |
| **cap (cip, cept, ceiv, ceit)** | seize, hold | capture, anticipate, accept, receive, reception, deceit, deception |
| **ced (ceed, cess)** | yield, go | secede, recede, proceed, process, procession, recess, recession |
| **clude (clus)** | close, shut | conclude, conclusion, seclude, include, recluse |
| **dict** | say, speak | dictate, dictation, predict, diction, dictionary |
| **fac (fic, fact, fect)** | make, do | manufacture, factory, efficient, perfect, affect |
| **grad (gress)** | step | grade, graduate, progress, progression, progressive |
| **jac (ject)** | throw | adjacent, inject, reject, subject |
| **mit (miss)** | send | transmit, emit, mission, missionary |
| **pel, puls** | push | propel, repel, compel, propellant, repulsion, compulsion |
| **pend** | hang | pendant, depend, dependent, append, appendix |
| **port** | carry | transportation, porter, portable |
| **posit (pos)** | put, place | deposit, repose, depose, exposure |
| **scrib (script)** | write | describe, subscribe, scripture, manuscript |
| **spec, spic** | look | inspect, suspect, spectacle, conspicuous |
| **ven (vent)** | come | convene, convent, convention, invent, intervene |
| **vid (vis)** | see | video, vision, provide |
| **voc (vok)** | call | vocal, vocation, advocate, invoke |

**How to Study**

# Common English prefixes

| Prefix | Meaning | Examples |
|---|---|---|
| **ab-** | away (from) | abnormal, abstract |
| **ad-*** | to, toward | admonish, accept, affect, appear, assign |
| **com-, con-,*** | with, together | companion, communication, conclude, collect, correct |
| **de-** | down, away from | decay, defect, default |
| **ex-, e-*** | out, (from) | exhale, exhaust, eject, effervescent |
| **in-, im-, en-, em-** | in, into | include, inspect, immigrate, enact, emboss |
| **in-, im-*** | not | inoffensive, imbalance, irreligious |
| **inter-** | between | intercept, intercede, intervene |
| **non-** | not | nonsense, nonentity |
| **per-** | through | perceive, permit, perseverance |
| **post-** | after | postscript, postpone |
| **pre-** | before | prescribe, precede, predict |
| **pro-** | forward | proceed, progress, project, propose, provide, provoke |
| **sub-*** | under | submarine, substitute, succeed, suffer, suppose |
| **trans-** | across, over | transact, transgress, transmit, transcribe |

* Sometimes made by first letter (or consonant and vowel) *plus* a double letter, as shown in illustration.

# Common English suffixes

| Purpose | Suffix | Examples |
|---|---|---|
| to make a noun from a verb | **-ation, -ion,** | transportation, suspension |
| | **-ment** | judgment, agreement |
| to make a noun from a verb, showing who or what is the *doer* | **-or, -er** | actor, porter, transmitter |
| | **-ent, -ant** | superintendent, commandant |
| to make a noun from an adjective | **-ness** | goodness, blackness |
| | **-ence, -ance** | independence, radiance |
| to make a verb from a noun | **-ize** | criticize |
| to make a verb from an adjective | **-en** | lighten, redden |
| to make an adjective from a verb | **-y** | scary, runny |
| to make an adjective from a verb, showing possibility | **-ical** | practical |
| | **-able, -ible** | breakable, edible |
| to make an adjective from a noun | **-ary** | revolutionary, fragmentary |
| | **-en** | wooden, golden |
| | **-ious, -ous** | mysterious, gracious, grievous |
| | **-ic** | harmonic, graphic |
| to make an adverb from an adjective | **-ly, -ally** | slowly, comically |

*Basic Reading Skills*
*1. Review — did I miss something when I learned to read?*
*2. Sounds — Sounding out words helps to recognize them.*
*(Table: shows many different combinations of letters that can make the same sound. I knew most of them but there were a few surprises.)*
*3. Sentences — Group of words together.*

These are a student's notes about pages 86 and following in this book. The note taker has recorded his reactions as well as the content.

# Reading strategies.

If you have reviewed the basics of reading and do not seem to have any trouble with them, but are still only a fair reader, your next step should be to consider the way you go about reading. Perhaps you are using a wrong approach—reading schoolbooks too fast, for example, or reading simpler material too slowly.

There are several kinds of reading, and each has its place. The important thing is to use the right method at the right time.

**Reading for fun.** If you are reading for fun, of course you can read at any speed that suits you. This kind of reading offers you a good chance to experiment at reading faster, trying to see words in larger clusters, seeing if you can guess the meaning of an unfamiliar word by its context. Usually reading for pleasure is comfortable and easy, and goes faster than reading a history book or a math textbook.

Recreational reading is most important for the practice it gives. Like swimming or playing a musical instrument, reading is a skill that improves with use—the more you do it, the better you are likely to be. Like other skills, reading gradually comes to seem natural and easy.

**School texts.** Much of the reading you do for school is for the purpose of extracting information. Some schoolbooks—those on mathematics or on English grammar, for example—are very *dense.* They are not meant to be read through quickly. Often you read only a page or two at a time. For this kind of reading, speed is not important. You may read some sentences several times to be sure you understand them. You may want to do written exercises or answer review questions as you go, making sure you understand one step before going on to the next.

**Book reports.** Another kind of informational reading is the kind you do for a book report. With this kind of assignment, you can save time by taking a few minutes before starting the first chapter to examine the book and see what it covers. The box on the next page suggests seven steps to follow in previewing a book.

**Reference reading.** Still other informational reading may have a particular aim. For example, you may be preparing a report on the architecture of the Aztecs. Many of the books you find will tell also about Aztec history, society, customs, and other topics. In this case, it is even more important to preview the book. If you just start reading, you may have to go through dozens of pages before you reach any information about architecture. If you check the table of contents, however, you may find that there is one chapter about your subject. The index may show you where there are references to particular buildings. Leafing through the book may reveal a collection of architectural illustrations.

When you are gathering information for a report, you will want to make notes. It is always best to read a whole passage or chapter first before writing anything down, so that you understand what the writer is saying. After reading the whole passage, go back and summarize it in your mind. Put down this summary in your notes. Then, if there is particular information—a date, a name, or a specific idea—write it down afterward. Be sure that each note has the name of the book and the pages you read so that you can find the passage again.

**How to Study**

# How to preview a book

You will be able to understand the material in a book much more quickly if you examine it before you actually start to read. Here are some suggested steps and questions to answer.

1. **Look at the jacket.** If the book has a jacket, its illustration may help you to understand the mood or content of the book. On the *flaps*—the parts that fold inside the front and back covers—there is often a brief description of the book, and a brief sketch of the author.

2. **Look at the title page.** The title page has the full, official name of the book. Often there is a subtitle that is not on the jacket or on the cover of the book. The title page will also tell the publisher of the book and the date of publication.

3. **Look at the copyright page.** The copyright notice almost always appears on the back of the title page. It will tell you when the book was originally published. This might be very important if you are looking up the latest information on astronomy, for example. If the book was first published in 1945, it will not have up-to-date information. The copyright page may also have information on where the book's illustrations came from and where it was prepared and published. This might be important, too. A British dictionary would not be a good source for everyday language usage in the United States because British English differs from American English in many small ways.

4. **Study the table of contents.** The table of contents is the framework of most books. A few minutes spent studying it will show you how the book is put together. It will often show you where the material you are looking for can be found. If you are doing research for a report and only need a few facts, the contents can help lead you straight to your material.

5. **Look for a foreword or introduction.** Writers of books often put important information in an introduction. They may tell you how to use the book, or that they have left out certain topics—perhaps even the one you are most interested in. Especially if the introduction is short, it is a good idea to read it.

6. **Page through the book quickly.** Starting at the front, turn the pages, getting yourself familiar with the look and "feel" of the volume. Pay special attention to chapter headings and to other headings in the text—they will help you see how the material is organized. Look for illustrations. Sometimes they fall on the same page as the text on your subject, but sometimes they are all in one place, bound into the middle of the book, for example. If you see illustrations that are particularly interesting, note their page numbers so that you can find them again easily. Also note the pages of any chapters or headings that you want to go back to read.

7. **Check the back of the book.** Several kinds of information are often found in the back of a book. Sometimes there are notes that include valuable information. Often there is a *bibliography*, a list of other books on related topics. In most nonfiction books there is an index. The index can be especially helpful if you are looking for specific information. It can direct you to the page where the information is discussed and even to specific illustrations.

After you have followed these steps, you will be able to decide how to use the book. If you plan to read it through, you already have a kind of road map—you know where the book starts and where it is going. If you are using the book for reference, you may not start at the beginning. Instead, you may go directly to the chapter or page that interests you.

This job of previewing a book, which should only take between ten minutes and half an hour, can save you hours of unnecessary time and add to your enjoyment of each book.

**Reading tests.** Most students are tested at least once a year for reading comprehension. These tests usually consist of short passages on various subjects and a set of multiple-choice questions on each passage. Many students find it helpful to read such a passage twice—once very quickly to get the general idea, then a second time more slowly to get more detailed information. When answering the questions, read them carefully and be sure you understand them. Even if you understood the reading passage, you will do poorly if you misunderstand the questions.

**Reading fiction.** Most fiction has been written to entertain the reader as well as to provide information. The great pleasure of many stories is to find out what happens next. Many young readers prefer action stories, where the plot moves along quickly and keeps the reader in suspense.

Fiction from other eras can be more difficult than modern fiction to understand. Stories from long ago can show how people in other times and places felt and thought. Many famous short stories and novels were written many years ago, and they may contain unfamiliar words or ideas, and word-pictures.

The most important skill a reader needs for enjoying fiction is the skill of imagining—of picturing along with the author the time, the place, the emotions of the characters. The reader must provide the picture, the voices, and even the sound effects for himself and be ready to travel anywhere—even into the mind of a character.

Reading fiction is a good way to improve general reading skills. The passage in the box on the next page is the opening of a story by Edgar Allan Poe. At first it may seem difficult, but the reader who masters it will find that it raises many questions and makes him want to read on.

## Sample reading comprehension test

It might be best to let sleeping sea lions lie. At least this is what Mr. Snow, an explorer, thinks.

One July during the breeding season, he rowed up to an Arctic island through schools of sea lions. They showed no fright and no desire to fight. When he landed he came near the animals and called, "Come on there, you! Come on!"

A sudden roar and a great sea lion was hurtling toward him, his white tusks gleaming. Mr. Snow ran. This big fellow followed. It seemed easy to keep out of reach of the awkward animal. But straight ahead lay a cow with a young one! Mr. Snow knew that he was trapped. He struck frantically at the cow's head with a boat hook. She caught it out of the air and wrenched it from his hand. There was a great crunching and grinding. She was chewing the boat hook to splinters!

Now was Mr. Snow's chance to run. The bull was after him again, but he kept dodging round and round until the sea lion was tired out by the chase. The explorer finally returned to the boat, a wiser man.

1. **The selection is chiefly about**   Ⓐ a boat hook   Ⓑ a young sea lion   Ⓒ a mother   Ⓓ an explorer
2. **At first the sea lions were**   Ⓐ afraid   Ⓑ angry   Ⓒ peaceful   Ⓓ playful
3. **Which is most probable? The sea lion**   Ⓐ did not like the sound of the man's voice   Ⓑ was afraid of the man   Ⓒ knew he could trap the man   Ⓓ liked to fight
4. **Most probably the mother was angry because**   Ⓐ she wanted to protect her baby   Ⓑ she was a sea lion   Ⓒ she lay in the path   Ⓓ she did not like the explorer
5. **Sea lions have very strong**   Ⓐ tusks   Ⓑ tails   Ⓒ flippers   Ⓓ babies
6. **Sea lions move**   Ⓐ gracefully   Ⓑ clumsily   Ⓒ swiftly   Ⓓ crunching and grinding
7. **We may infer from the selection that the mother sea lion**   Ⓐ liked to eat wood   Ⓑ was playing with the explorer   Ⓒ wanted to keep Mr. Snow away   Ⓓ was showing one of her tricks
8. **As a result of Mr. Snow's narrow escape he was a**   Ⓐ jollier man   Ⓑ wiser man   Ⓒ more energetic man   Ⓓ kinder man

D C A A A B C B

**How to Study**

**Reading poetry.** Poetry is language that has been condensed and that often uses special effects of sound and appearance to make an emotional impression on the reader. Much early poetry was set to music, and even modern poetry sometimes is particularly musical. Most poetry is meant to be *heard*, even when it is read silently, so it should be read slowly. Since its meanings may be very condensed, poetry usually must be read over several times before its full impact is felt.

Often the meanings of poetry are difficult to put into other words because the poetry appeals to the reader's emotions as well as to his mind. Emotions and feelings are personal matters for every reader of poetry. This is why readers will often disagree about the meaning of a poem.

The box on this page lists some of the special uses of language favored by poets. These uses may also be found in some kinds of prose.

## Special language in poetry

**alliteration.** Deliberate repetition of sounds.
> *The fair breeze blew, the white foam flew,*
> *The furrow followed free. . . .*

**hyperbole.** Obvious and deliberate exaggeration, used to emphasize but not deceive.
> *It rained all night the day I left,*
> *The weather it was dry,*
> *It was so cold I froze to death,*
> *Susanna don't you cry.*

**metaphor.** A figure of speech in which a word or phrase is applied to an object, idea, or person to which it is not literally related.
> *Tiger! Tiger! burning bright*
> *In the forests of the night . . .*

**onomatopoeia.** Use of words that suggest by their sounds the object or idea being named; for example, *sizzle, twitter, buzz, hiss, coo, roar.*

**personification.** A figure of speech giving human qualities to animals, objects, or ideas.
> *His life was so gentle, and the elements*
> *So mix'd in him, that Nature might stand up*
> *And say to all the world, This was a man!*

**simile.** A metaphor employing *like* or *as.*
> *My love is like a red, red rose . . .*
> *I wandered lonely as a cloud . . .*

---

### Edgar Allan Poe
### "Ligeia"

I cannot, for my soul, remember how, when, or even precisely where, I first became acquainted with the lady Ligeia. Long years have since elapsed, and my memory is feeble through much suffering. Or, perhaps, I cannot *now* bring these points to mind, because, in truth, the character of my beloved, her rare learning, her singular yet placid cast of beauty, and the thrilling and enthralling eloquence of her low musical language, made their way into my heart by paces so steadily and stealthily progressive that they have been unnoticed and unknown. Yet I believe that I met her first and most frequently in some large, old, decaying city near the Rhine. Of her family—I have surely heard her speak. That it is of a remotely ancient date cannot be doubted. Ligeia! Ligeia! Buried in studies of a nature more than all else adapted to deaden impressions of the outward world, it is by that sweet word alone—by Ligeia—that I bring before mine eyes in fancy the image of her who is no more.

---

### Emily Dickinson (A train)

I like to see it lap the miles,
And lick the valleys up,
And stop to feed itself at tanks;
And then, prodigious, step

Around a pile of mountains,
And, supercilious, peer
In shanties by the sides of roads;
And then a quarry pare

To fit its sides
And crawl between
Complaining all the while
In horrid, hooting stanza;
Then chase itself down hill

And neigh like Boanerges;
Then punctual as a star,
Stop—docile and omnipotent—
At its own stable door.

# Improve your test-taking

Some students learn more than they are ever able to show on school tests because they are "test-shy." They may actually perform more poorly than students who know less than they do. Everyone wants to do as well as possible on tests, and good test-takers often have an advantage over classmates who do not test well. For these reasons, it is worthwhile to learn about tests and to become "test-wise."

## Attitude.
The first big step in improving your test-taking is to adopt the right attitude. Tests are designed to *measure* your mastery of a skill or your knowledge of a subject. They are not designed to embarrass you, fool you, or terrify you. In a sense, taking a test should be no harder than taking your temperature or measuring your feet for a new pair of shoes.

Forget about the students around you—what they do is of no concern. Forget about the teacher, about the plans you have for after school, and about anything else that may be on your mind. Until the test is over, the only two things that are important are you and the subject of the test. With this single-minded attitude, you are ready to concentrate and to do your very best. You may feel keyed up, like an athlete before a game. This can make you more alert and ready, but you should not feel anxious or worried.

## Preparation.
There are two kinds of preparation for any test. The first is study of the subject matter. If you do not know the subject matter, nothing else will help. Some students do study, but do not seem to master the material. They may read a chapter over and over, desperately trying to memorize hundreds of facts, or they may run in circles, trying over and over again to master a new kind of problem without having understood it first.

If the test is on subject matter from a book, try a different approach. Instead of reading the material over and over, read it once, then spend some time organizing it on a piece of paper. What are the two or three major facts or themes of the material? What are the important names or dates or other facts—those necessary to understanding the whole? Many of the other

*A good breakfast on the day of a test will help give you the energy you need to do well.*

names and dates may be less important—in fact, some of them probably needn't be committed to memory at all.

If you are learning a skill, go back to an example—either in the book or in your notes—and follow it step by step, making sure that you see how the right answer was arrived at. Then take a new problem and follow exactly the same steps. If you still do not understand, ask for help from a classmate or teacher.

If you are having trouble, it is important that you start preparing for your test early. Otherwise, there will not be time to ask for help. Starting early is a good idea in any case. Especially when learning vocabulary in a foreign language or basic facts such as the multiplication table, your mind needs time and many repetitions to fix the information firmly. No amount of cramming the night before the test is likely to make up for work not done ahead of time. Even if you do manage to remember part of the material for the test, you will forget it soon afterward.

The second kind of preparation for any test has nothing at all to do with subject matter. It consists of making sure that you are ready physically and mentally to do well. One important factor is a good night's sleep. The day before a test, remember to take a few minutes now and then to relax. Finish your studying early so that you can get to bed and be ready to sleep on time. In the morning, eat a good breakfast. At the same time, train yourself to put aside any other worries or excitements for the few hours until the test is over. You need all your concentration skills for it.

## How to take a test

There are many kinds of tests, and each requires a slightly different technique. There are a few tips, though, that apply to nearly all tests:

**1. Take a moment or two to look through the whole test.** Read all instructions carefully. Notice how many questions there are altogether, and try to get a sense of how much time you will have for each question. If one part is multiple choice, and a second part is an essay question, decide how much time you will spend on each part.

**2. Read each question carefully.** If you misunderstand the question, you will answer it wrong, no matter how much you know about the subject. Some tests have questions with tricky wording just to test your understanding. Especially if the question is complicated, read it a second time just to be sure.

**3. Skip questions you are not sure about.** It is best to answer all the questions that seem easy first; then you can use the remaining time to consider the more difficult questions. This will keep you from getting a mental block and will assure that you answer everything you know best before time runs out.

**4. Take the last two or three minutes to read through your answers.** This is especially important on essay tests. When you write quickly, you may leave out an important word, leaving a sentence or paragraph that makes no sense. In multiple-choice tests, be sure that you have put your answers in the right space or column and (if there is time) that each answer seems reasonable.

# Kinds of tests.

The two main kinds of tests are multiple choice and essay tests.

**Multiple choice tests.** Multiple choice tests are most often used to test your mastery of facts. Be sure to read the question and each possible answer carefully. Sometimes, more than one answer may seem to be correct; in that case, choose the one that seems most accurate.

On short multiple-choice tests, you usually are graded on the number of right answers. This means that if you do not know the answer to a question, you can guess at the answer without being penalized.

On long multiple-choice tests—especially standardized reading, math, and other such tests—you are penalized for guessing. In this kind of test, you *should not* guess at an answer if you have no idea what the answer is. You *should* guess if you can eliminate one or more of the possible answers as being wrong.

**Essay tests.** Essay tests require you to put your ideas down on paper clearly. If there are several essay questions, it is important that you budget your time so that you will finish them all. Do not try to be the one who writes the most: quality is usually better than quantity. Take a few moments to organize your answers before you start to write. Then write slowly enough so that your handwriting is legible.

# Learning from results.

In one sense, the test is over the moment you turn it in. But if you want to improve your test-taking, it's not really over until you get the test back. Then is the time to go over the results carefully to see just what errors or mistakes you may have made. Did you misunderstand one of the questions? Did you make any careless error? If there are more wrong answers toward the end, did you run out of time or energy?

If you can determine what you did wrong, you will be able to work on that particular aspect of test-taking and improve accordingly. As you do better, you will also begin to relax and to concentrate until you learn to do your very best in all testing situations.

# Guide to good reading

One of the best ways to improve your reading is to take up reading as a hobby. Books are not just for study: millions find them a source of great entertainment as well. In fact, a well-written book can entertain and inform at the same time. It can be the most painless way to learn.

The following lists suggest over 100 books on a wide variety of subjects. No reader will find all of them interesting, but almost every reader will find some to his or her liking. The first (and longest) list is of fiction. Then come two shorter lists—one of poetry and folk tales and the second of books of nonfiction.

The reading level of the books varies—from intermediate (suitable for fourth or fifth grade) to difficult (suitable for ninth grade and above). No reading level markings have been given, however, because interest often dictates reading level. You may read at a fourth grade level if a subject is boring to you, then read on an eighth grade level when the book's subject is one you really care about. If you find that a book on this list is too difficult, ask a teacher or librarian to recommend a less difficult book.

Many of the books listed here are easily available for purchase. Children's classics are often published in many editions. Some books, however—especially those on the nonfiction list—may be available only in libraries. If you are eager to find a particular book, try the library first. If you want to know whether a book can be purchased, ask a librarian to help you look it up in *Books in Print*, a huge catalog published each year that lists all books currently available.

For more ideas on good reading, see the section on Literature in Volume 2.

---

**Fiction.** Most good fiction is entertaining while at the same time offering food for thought. Some stories help a reader understand the way people think and feel today. Others give a glimpse into the thoughts and feelings of people who lived in other times and places. Many of the books on this list are classics—stories that have been read and loved by generations of young readers. A few represent newer books about contemporary life. If they are good enough, these new books may also become classics someday. Good books seem to grow better with age. Mediocre books, on the other hand, soon seem dated and are forgotten by later generations.

---

*Alcott, Louisa May*
**Little Women**
A classic American novel about four sisters growing up during the 1860's in New England. Other books by Alcott include *Eight Cousins* and *Little Men*.

*Alexander, Lloyd*
**The High King**
Newbery Award winner, the last of five fantasy novels about an imaginary kingdom that resembles ancient Wales.

*Armstrong, William*
**Sounder**
A black sharecropper must steal to support his family and his dog Sounder. His son is trying to understand his father's choices.

*Asimov, Isaac*
**The Best New Thing**
Science fiction about two children who live on a different planet.

*Barrie, Sir James*
**Peter Pan and Wendy**
Classic story about a flight to Never-Never land with Peter Pan, the boy who refuses ever to grow up.

*Baum, Lyman Frank*
**The Wizard of Oz**
Fantasy about Dorothy, who is carried off by a tornado from Kansas to the Land of Oz; subject of a famous movie version. Baum wrote many sequels.

*Blume, Judy*
**Are You There, God? It's Me, Margaret**
A contemporary story about the hopes and fears of an eleven-year-old girl. First of many books by a popular author for young readers.

*Blume, Judy*
**It's Not the End of the World**
How three children react when they learn that their parents are about to be divorced.

*From Carroll,* Alice's Adventures in Wonderland

*From Dahl,* Charlie and the Chocolate Factory

**Boston, Lucy M.**
### The Children of Green Knowe
First of a series about an old house where present-day children can meet children of the past.

**Burnford, Sheila**
### The Incredible Journey
The epic travels of two dogs and a cat in search of their masters.

**Byars, Betsy**
### The Summer of the Swans
A girl searches for her lost brother, who is mentally retarded. A Newbery Award book.

**Carroll, Lewis**
### Alice's Adventures in Wonderland
Classic fantasy about a girl's adventures in a strange and illogical land.

**Chew, Ruth**
### The Wednesday Witch
A witch rides a flying vacuum cleaner instead of a broom and meets mystery and adventure.

**Cleary, Beverly**
### Ramona the Brave
A popular writer tells about the terrors of being in first grade.

**Dahl, Roald**
### Charlie and the Chocolate Factory
Charlie discovers the amazing factory of Willie Wonka in a modern fantasy classic.

**Defoe, Daniel**
### Robinson Crusoe
The adventures of a man cast ashore on a desert island. Among the most popular books in English for more than 250 years.

**Dixon, Franklin W.**
### The Hardy Boys
This huge series of detective stories has appealed to readers for decades. Frank and Joe Hardy catch the imagination at first, but their adventures become repetitive.

**Dodge, Mary Mapes**
### Hans Brinker, or The Silver Skates
Classic story about a Dutch family and Hans's wonderful ice skates.

**Edmonds, Walter D.**
### The Matchlock Gun
A suspense-packed story about how a boy and his mother fight off Indians on the American frontier.

**Farley, Walter**
### The Black Stallion
First of a series of appealing horse stories; subject of a prize-winning movie.

**Fitzhugh, Louise**
### Harriet the Spy
The diary of a sharp-tongued eleven-year-old falls into the wrong hands.

**Forbes, Esther**
**Johnny Tremain**
An apprentice to a silversmith becomes a courier in the American Revolution.

**Gipson, Fred**
**Old Yeller**
A stray dog adopts a Texas family in the 1860's and defends them against all dangers.

**Grahame, Kenneth**
**The Wind in the Willows**
Classic fantasy about animals who live like human beings and have human problems.

**Heinlien, Robert**
**Podkayne of Mars**
Adventures of a 16-year-old girl on Mars by a master of science fiction.

**Hitchcock, Alfred, editor**
**Alfred Hitchcock's Daring Detectives**
An anthology of great detective stories by well-known mystery writers. One of several Hitchcock anthologies.

**Juster, Norton**
**The Phantom Tollbooth**
Milo discovers a fantasy land filled with odd creatures and questions about language.

**Keene, Carolyn**
**Nancy Drew**
A huge series about a girl detective. Interesting at first, but her adventures become repetitious.

**Knight, Eric**
**Lassie Come Home**
A classic dog story about Lassie's long journey in search of her master.

**Konigsburg, E.L.**
**From the Mixed-Up Files of Mrs. Basil T. Frankweiler**
Claudia and her younger brother run away and hide in the Metropolitan Museum of Art in New York. A Newbery Award winner.

**Lagerlöf, Selma**
**The Wonderful Adventures of Nils**
A fanciful tour of Sweden taken by Nils with the help of friendly animals.

**Lawson, Robert**
**Ben and Me**
A humorous look at the life of Ben Franklin, told by his resident mouse.

**LeGuin, Ursula**
**A Wizard of Earthsea**
First of a trilogy about the land of Earthsea by an important science fiction writer.

**L'Engle, Madeleine**
**A Wrinkle in Time**
A sister and brother travel to the far reaches of the universe. First book of a trilogy.

**Lewis, C.S.**
**The Chronicles of Narnia**
A seven-book series about the mystical land of Narnia, popular both for its adventure and for its serious moral quest. The first book is *The Lion, The Witch, and the Wardrobe.*

**Lindgren, Astrid**
**Pippi Longstocking**
Pippi is a girl who lives with a monkey and a horse. Together they create fun and excitement wherever they go.

**Lofting, Hugh**
**The Adventures of Dr. Doolittle**
Delightful fantasy about an amazing—and magical—doctor. First of a series.

**London, Jack**
**Call of the Wild**
Classic story of a dog named Buck who returns to the wild to join a pack of wolves in Alaska.

**McCloskey, Robert**
**Homer Price**
The humorous adventures of a boy in a turn-of-the-century Ohio town.

**Milne, A.A.**
**Winnie the Pooh**
Whimsical stories about the stuffed bear Pooh and his friends, including the boy Christopher Robin.

**North, Sterling**
**Rascal**
The story of a boy and his pet raccoon.

**Norton, Mary**
**The Borrowers**
First of four volumes on a family of tiny people who live in the nooks and crannies of big people's houses.

**O'Dell, Scott**
**Island of the Blue Dolphin**
An Indian girl is cast away on an island off California, where she lives for 18 years.

**Rawlings, Marjorie Kinnan**
**The Yearling**
A classic story about a boy and his pet fawn.

**Rogers, Mary**
**Freaky Friday**
A 13-year-old girl suddenly becomes her own mother and must deal with adult problems.

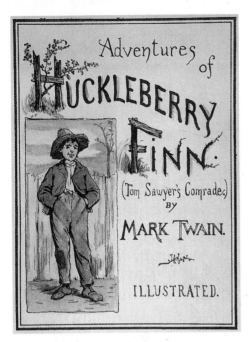

*From Twain*, The Adventurers Of Huckleberry Finn

*From White*, Charlotte's Web

**Sobol, Donald**
**Encyclopedia Brown Saves the Day**
First of a series about a boy detective.

*Spyri, Johanna*
**Heidi**
A young Swiss girl is uprooted from her mountain home, but succeeds in making friends wherever she goes.

*Steinbeck, John*
**The Red Pony**
The story of a boy and a horse by one of America's great writers.

*Stevenson, Robert Louis*
**Treasure Island**
A boy's adventures among pirates, the most popular of Stevenson's many adventure stories.

*Swift, Jonathan*
**Gulliver's Travels**
Famous satire about Gulliver's visits to strange lands; it is available in many editions for all ages.

*Thurber, James*
**The Thirteen Clocks**
A tale by America's great humorist about a wicked duke, a beautiful princess, and a handsome prince.

*Tolkien, J.R.R.*
**The Hobbit**
A fanciful creature must find a treasure guarded by a dragon. Tolkien's three-volume fantasy *Lord of the Rings* is also popular.

*Travers, P.L.*
**Mary Poppins**
Adventures of an English nursemaid who can fly. The first of a series.

*Twain, Mark*
**The Adventures of Huckleberry Finn**
Classic American novel about a footloose boy, son of the town drunk, who runs away on a raft down the Mississippi River with Jim, a runaway slave.

*Twain, Mark*
**The Adventures of Tom Sawyer**
Mischievous Tom is growing up in a small Missouri town in the mid-1800's. Filled with humor and adventure.

*Verne, Jules*
**20,000 Leagues Under the Sea**
This adventure story imagined submarines before one had ever been built.

*White, E.B.*
**Charlotte's Web**
A story of the friendship between a girl, her prize pig, and a spider named Charlotte. Also by White: *Stuart Little* and *Trumpet of the Swan*.

*Wilder, Laura Ingalls*
**Little House in the Big Woods**
First of a classic series of "Little House" books following the travels of a pioneer family in the 1870's and 1880's. The books were the basis of a popular television series.

## Poetry and folk tales.

The earliest literature that came down to us was in poetic form. Before the invention of writing, the rhythm of poetic lines helped singers and storytellers remember the words. Often, this early literature told of great heroes of the past, preserving the memories for a tribe or a people. Many modern writers and poets have imitated the approach of folk literature, so the style is familiar even today. Folklore continues to survive and to be read and enjoyed all over the world. In fact, familiar stories and themes continue to reappear in new versions. Many of the world's cultures have a story like Cinderella, for example.

The books listed here are the works of both ancient and modern writers. Some are collections of poetry. Others are retellings in prose of the stories of old poems and legends. Still others are modern imitations of folklore.

*From Colum,* Arabian Nights

*Aesop*

**Aesop's Fables**

Famous animal fables from ancient Greece with morals that still make sense today.

*Andersen, Hans Christian*

**Fairy Tales and Stories**

Written by Andersen in the 1800's in the style of traditional fairy tales, these stories are filled with humor and pathos. Among the most popular are "The Ugly Duckling" and "The Emperor's New Clothes."

*Arbuthnot, May Hill, and Sheldon L. Root, Jr., editors*

**Time for Poetry**

Poems and verse from the time of Mother Goose to the present.

*Bernos de Gasztold, Carmen*

**Prayers from the Ark**

Amusing, often moving prayers of 26 animals on Noah's ark, translated by Rumer Godden.

*Cole, William, editor*

**The Birds and the Beasts Were There: A Book of Nature Poems**

One of several appealing anthologies compiled by this editor.

*Colum, Padraic*

**The Children's Homer**

A prose version of the great stories told by the Greek poet Homer in the *Iliad* and the *Odyssey,* telling of the war at Troy and of the legendary heroes and gods who fought there.

*Colum, Padraic, editor*

**The Arabian Nights**

Colum's retelling of tales from the Middle East. Includes stories of Aladdin, Sinbad the Sailor, and others. Many other editions.

*Felton, Harold W.*

**Pecos Bill and the Mustang**

American tall tales about a Southwestern cowboy legend. Felton's other books tell about Mike Fink, John Henry, and other legendary heroes.

*Frost, Robert*

**You Come Too**

A selection by the great American poet of his own poetry for young readers.

*Grimm, Jakob and Wilhelm*

**Grimm's Fairy Tales**

These very old stories and fables were collected in Germany by the Grimm brothers around 1800. They include "Hansel and Gretel," "Snow White," and many other dramatic and amusing tales.

*Harris, Joel Chandler*

**Nights with Uncle Remus**

Classic stories from black American folklore about Br'er Rabbit, Br'er Fox, and other animal heroes.

*Kipling, Rudyard*

**Just So Stories**

Humorous explanations of natural facts: how the camel got its hump and others.

There was a Young Lady whose chin
Resembled the point of a pin;
So she had it made sharp, and purchased a harp,
And played several tunes with her chin.

*From Lear,* Complete Nonsense Book

*From St. Exupery,* The Little Prince

*La Fontaine, Jean de*
**Fables**
The great verse fables by this French writer are available in verse translation by American poet Marianne Moore.

*Lang, Andrew, editor*
**The Blue Fairy Book**
One of a series of tales collected by Lang from many parts of the world. Other collections have other colors: red, yellow, etc.

*Larrick, Nancy, editor*
**I Heard a Scream in the Street**
Poems by—and for—city kids.

*Larrick, Nancy, editor*
**Piper, Pipe That Song Again**
A much admired anthology of poetry for all ages.

*Lear, Edward*
**The Complete Nonsense Book**
Story poems, limericks, and nonsense from a great humorist of the 1800's.

*Malory, Sir Thomas (Sidney Lanier, editor)*
**The Boy's King Arthur**
A modern adaptation of Malory's telling of the legend of King Arthur and his Knights of the Round Table. Many other adaptations are available.

*McCord, David*
**All Day Long: Fifty Rhymes of the Never Was and Always Is**
Modern verses, both amusing and serious.

*Merriam, Eve*
**There Is No Rhyme for Silver**
One of several volumes of lively free verse by this writer.

*Milne, A.A.*
**Now We Are Six**
Whimsical verse about Pooh Bear and Christopher Robin. Appeals to readers older than six.

*Perrault, Charles*
**Perrault's Complete Fairy Tales**
The standard versions of many classic tales, collected 200 years ago by Perrault.

*Pyle, Howard*
**The Merry Adventures of Robin Hood**
One retelling of the great legends of Robin Hood's adventures in Sherwood Forest as an outlaw hero.

*St. Exupery, Antoine*
**The Little Prince**
A whimsical fable that appeals to all ages, by a famous French writer and aviator.

*Stevenson, Robert Louis*
**A Child's Garden of Verses**
The classic collection of poems by the gifted turn-of-the-century writer. Available in many editions.

*White, Ann Terry*
**The Golden Treasury of Myths and Legends**
Legends from Greece, Scandinavia, and other parts of the world.

**Nonfiction.** The range of books on real people, places, and things is huge. Readers who are interested in a particular subject should learn to use a library, where books are carefully arranged by subject category for easy reference.

This list can give only a sampling of the richness of nonfiction books, ranging from science to art and music, from biography to ancient history.

---

*Asimov, Isaac*
**Asimov's Guide to Science**
A survey by a well-known science writer.

*Asimov, Isaac*
**The Egyptians**
The lives, beliefs, and activities of the residents of ancient Egypt.

*Betterbury, Ariane and Michael*
**The Pantheon Story of American Art for Young People**
A historical survey of the visual arts in the United States; heavily illustrated.

*Bliven, Bruce, Jr.*
**The American Revolution**
An exciting account of America's war for independence.

*Bliven, Bruce, Jr.*
**The Story of D-Day: June 6, 1944**
The story of the Allied landing in France during World War II.

*Boorstin, Daniel*
**The Landmark History of the United States**
A lively, heavily illustrated two-volume history by a distinguished historian.

*Britten, Benjamin, and Imogen Holst*
**The Wonderful World of Music**
Musical history and language, explained by a great modern composer.

*Carson, Rachel*
**Silent Spring**
Classic explanation of the effects of pollution and pesticides on plant and animal life.

*Carson, Rachel*
**The Sea Around Us**
A moving yet scientific look at the importance of the sea to world ecology.

*Clayton, Ed*
**Martin Luther King: The Peaceful Warrior**
Biography of the Nobel Prize winner and his struggle for civil rights.

*Cohen, Robert*
**The Color of Man**
What determines the skin and hair color and how racial prejudices have evolved.

*Coit, Margaret*
**Andrew Jackson**
Biography of a colorful and courageous President and military hero.

*Coolidge, Olivia*
**Women's Rights: The Suffrage Movement in America 1840–1920**
An account of women's long struggle to receive the right to vote.

*Elting, Mary*
**All Aboard: The Trains That Built America**
A lively account of the construction of the railroads and their colorful history.

*Emrich, Duncan*
**The Hodge-Podge Book**
An entertaining collection of folk wisdom, riddles, puzzles, verses, and nonsense.

*Foster, Genevieve*
**George Washington's World**
How people lived and what they believed in during Washington's lifetime. Foster also wrote about the times of Julius Caesar and other heroes.

*Frank, Anne*
**The Diary of a Young Girl**
The moving account of a Jewish family hiding from the Nazis during World War II.

*Fritz, Jean*
**And Then What Happened, Paul Revere?**
An amusing but accurate biography of the American patriot.

*Gidal, Sonia*
**My Village in Hungary**
One of a series of books on villages in many parts of the world. All are attractively illustrated with photographs.

*Graham, Frank, Jr.*
**Since Silent Spring**
A sequel to Rachel Carson's book *Silent Spring*, reporting on man's efforts to end water and air pollution.

*Gutman, Bill*
**Duke Ellington**
Biography of the great jazz performer and composer.

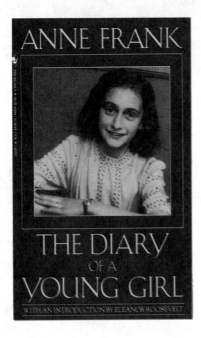

*From Frank,* The Diary of A Young Girl

**Eat cooked chicken feet behind a door and throw or poke the bones through the crack of the door. This will make you pretty.**

*From Emrich,* The Hodge-Podge Book

*Kelly, Regina Z.*
**John F. Kennedy**
Biography of a President who especially appealed to young people.

*Krementz, Jill*
**A Very Young Dancer**
A photographic account of the rigorous life of a young ballet student.

*Lorimer, Lawrence, editor*
**Breaking In**
First-person accounts by nine well-known athletes, telling of their early struggles to succeed.

*Macauley, David*
**Cathedral**
An illustrated description of the way a medieval cathedral was built. Also by this author, similar books on an Egyptian pyramid and a skyscraper.

*McHargue, Georgess*
**Meet the Werewolf**
A look at the lore and superstition about werewolves.

*McNeer, Mary*
**The California Gold Rush**
An exciting account of a colorful period in American history.

*McWhirter, Norris and Ross*
**The Guinness Book of World Records**
A vast compendium of useful and not-so-useful facts. There are many shorter Guinness collections for young readers.

*Renault, Mary*
**The Lion in the Gateway**
The story of the great ancient war between the Greeks and the Persians by a famous novelist.

*Sarnoff, Jane, and Reynolds Ruffins*
**The Code and Cipher Book**
Explanations and examples of secret writing.

*Savage, Katharine*
**The Story of World Religion**
How the major religions began and grew, and what they believe and practice today.

*Shaw, Arnold*
**The Rock Revolution**
The story of the growth of rock music in the 1950's and 1960's.

## For Further Reference

Fry, Ronald W.
*How to Study*
Career Press
Gilbert, Sara
*How to Take Tests*
William Morrow
James, Elizabeth and Doty, Roy
*How to Be School Smart*
Lothrop, Lee & Shepard
Kornhauser, Arthur William
*How to Study*
University of Chicago Press
Wikler, Janet
*How to Study and Learn*
Franklin Watts

# Social Studies

# United States History

The United States of America has a shorter history than that of the countries of Europe or Asia. The land was discovered less than 1000 years ago. Settlement began less than 500 years ago, and the country itself has been independent barely 200 years. But in that time, it has grown rapidly in population, power, and influence.

The following pages provide a brief outline of U.S. history, beginning with the earliest explorers and ending at the present day. Following the outline, there is a special time line of important Americans, showing their birth and death dates. For more information about the government and people of the United States, see Volume 2.

# Explorers and colonies

The early history of the North American continent is lost in time. Descendants of the American Indians arrived in North America perhaps 10,000 years ago from Asia. By 1500, there were some 1.5 million of them in North America. They were divided into hundreds of tribes, spoke many different languages, and kept no written records.

In the late 1400's, the kingdoms of Europe were seeking to expand. They explored both land and sea in search of treasure, trade, and new possessions. In seeking a better route to the Orient, they discovered the Americas. But for 100 years, they sent only explorers to North America.

Then, beginning in 1587, the English began serious attempts to send colonists to the new lands. Within 200 years, there were nearly 4 million Europeans along the Atlantic coast, forming the nucleus of what was soon to become the United States.

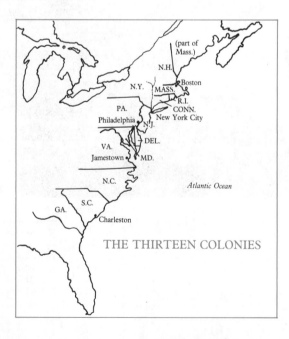

THE THIRTEEN COLONIES

**c 1000**     **The Vikings,** sailing under the leadership of Leif Ericsson, reach the continent of North America. They make landfalls in Labrador and Newfoundland.

**1492–1502**     **Christopher Columbus,** searching for a water route to Asia to the west, makes four voyages to the western hemisphere. He reaches the islands of the Caribbean and the Central and South American coasts. He claims the newly found lands for Spain, under whose flag he sails.

**1497–1498**     **John Cabot,** sailing for England, explores the coast of North America in search of a water route across North America to Asia. He claims the land for England.

**1513**     **Ponce de Leon,** having already found gold in Puerto Rico, explores Florida in search of the legendary "fountain of youth."

**1524**     **Giovanni da Verrazano,** sailing for France, explores the North American coast while searching for a waterway west. Because of his explorations, France claims North America.

**1534–1536**     **Jacques Cartier** penetrates the North American continent by traveling southward and westward along the St. Lawrence River.

**1539–1542**     **Hernando De Soto,** searching for gold, explores from Florida westward to Oklahoma.

**1540–1542**     **Francisco Coronado** leads an expedition in search of the legendary "Seven Cities of Gold" through the Southwest. In his travels, he comes upon the Grand Canyon.

**1565**     **The Spanish establish the first permanent settlement** in what will become the United States, at St. Augustine in Florida.

**1587**     **The English establish a settlement on Roanoke Island** off the coast of North Carolina. It fails and its inhabitants disappear, including the first child born of English parents in North America, Virginia Dare.

**1607**     **The English establish their first permanent settlement in America,** at Jamestown in Virginia. Captain John Smith is its leader.

**1608**     **Samuel de Champlain** establishes a French settlement at Quebec on the St. Lawrence River.

**1609**     **Henry Hudson,** sailing for the Dutch East India Company, explores the Chesapeake, Delaware, and New York bays and sails up the Hudson River, claiming the region for the Dutch.

        **The Spanish establish a settlement at Santa Fe** in New Mexico to serve as the center of Spanish government in northern Mexico.

**1619**     **The House of Burgesses** is established in Virginia. It is North America's first colonial legislature.

        **The first blacks arrive in America,** as indentured servants. Within a few years, blacks are brought to North America as slaves.

**1620**     **The Pilgrims,** seeking religious freedom they do not have in England, land on the coast of Massachusetts. Led by William Bradford, they draw up a plan of government, the Mayflower Compact, and found the settlement of Plymouth.

| Date | Event |
|---|---|

Left, *a replica of the Mayflower.* Right, *Peter Minuit buys Manhattan Island from the Indians.*

**1626**     **Peter Minuit,** acting for the Dutch, buys the island of Manhattan from the Indians for $24 worth of goods. The Dutch establish the settlement of New Amsterdam there and found other settlements in New Netherland, an area extending from Delaware Bay in the south northward up the Hudson River.

**1628–1630**     **The Puritans,** also seeking the religious freedom denied them in England, establish the Massachusetts Bay Colony under the leadership of John Winthrop.

**1634**     **George Calvert, Lord Baltimore,** an English Catholic, founds the colony of Maryland, where Catholics find religious freedom.

**1636**     **Roger Williams,** who disagrees with the religious practices of the Puritans in the Massachusetts Bay Colony, is driven out of the colony and founds the colony of Rhode Island.

    **Thomas Hooker,** also in disagreement with Massachusetts Puritans, leaves and founds the colony of Connecticut.

    **Harvard College** is founded, the first college in the English colonies in North America.

**1639**     **The Fundamental Orders of Connecticut,** considered the first written constitution in America, are drawn up to govern the colony.

**1647**     In Massachusetts, the first laws providing for the establishment of **public schools** are passed.

**1649**     **The Maryland Toleration Act** grants religious freedom to all Christians who settle in the colony.

**1660, 1663**     **England passes the Navigation Acts,** which place restrictions on colonial trade. The acts make it necessary to transport goods only in English-owned ships, to pay taxes to England on colonial goods, and to ship certain goods only to Britain.

**1664**     **The English gain control of New Netherland** by ousting the Dutch governor, Peter Stuyvesant. New Amsterdam is renamed New York.

**1673**     **Father Jacques Marquette and Louis Jolliet,** sailing for France, travel up the St. Lawrence River, through the Great Lakes, and down the Mississippi to the Gulf of Mexico.

**1676**     **Bacon's Rebellion** begins as Nathaniel Bacon leads a small group of farmers to rise up against the English governor of Virginia. The farmers claim that they are not adequately represented in the colony's government, that their taxes are too high, and that they are not protected by the government from Indian attacks.

**1682**   **Robert de La Salle** follows a route similar to Marquette's and Jolliet's and claims the Mississippi River valley for France. He names it Louisiana after the French King Louis XIV.

**William Penn,** a wealthy English Quaker, establishes the colony of Pennsylvania, where Quakers, as well as other Protestants, Catholics, and Jews can enjoy religious freedom.

**1699**   **The French begin to establish trading posts** along the Mississippi River and the Gulf coast. They also begin moving into the valley of the Ohio River.

**1712**   Twelve wealthy British proprietors establish **North and South Carolina.**

**1732**   **James Oglethorpe** establishes the colony of Georgia as a place where people imprisoned for debt in Great Britain can settle and start life anew.

**1733**   **The British pass the Molasses Act** in an attempt to force the colonists to buy molasses only from the British West Indies.

**1735**   **John Peter Zenger,** a newspaper publisher, is placed on trial for printing articles criticizing the British governor of New York. He is acquitted and the principle of freedom of the press is established in the colonies.

**1754**   **Several colonies send representatives to Albany** in New York to try to adopt a plan to unite the 13 colonies under one central government. The colonial governments reject the Albany Plan of Union, first proposed by Benjamin Franklin.

**1754–1763**   **The French and Indian War.** Britain and France, long-time enemies, wage war in both Europe and North America; each claims ownership of the same territory. From 1754 to 1763, the British and the colonists fight the French and their Indian allies in North America in battles that come to be called the French and Indian War.

1754   A force of Virginia militia, under the command of 22-year-old George Washington, builds Fort Necessity, near the French Fort Duquesne (the site of present-day Pittsburgh) to establish a British presence in the Ohio River valley. The French attack and defeat Washington near Fort Necessity.

1755   General Edward Braddock, in command of 2500 British redcoats, marches on Fort Duquesne to attack the French. French and Indian troops defeat them soundly, killing Braddock and nearly half his force.

1758   Generals Jeffrey Amherst and James Wolfe capture Louisbourg, a French fortress in Canada. General James Forbes captures Fort Duquesne and drives the French out.

1759   General James Wolfe attacks the French city of Quebec, defended by Louis Joseph de Montcalm. Both commanders are killed but the British are victorious and capture Quebec.

1763   The Treaty of Paris ends the war and grants Britain control of Canada and lands east of the Mississippi River.

# A nation is born

Disagreements between the British government and its colonies in America grew serious in the 1760's. The British saw the colonies as possessions. The colonists, however, sought to govern themselves. The arguments led to war in 1775, and on July 4, 1776, the colonies declared their independence. Five years later, the British were defeated and soon recognized the United States.

The new nation then turned its attention to its two major jobs. The first was to form a lasting government. In 1787, a new Constitution was drawn up, providing a stronger central government. The second job was to develop the vast American lands. By 1814, the United States controlled more than half the continent and had gained new respect among world nations.

| Date | Event |
|------|-------|
| **1763** | **Britain's Proclamation of 1763** prohibits American settlers from moving west of the Appalachian Mountains because British soldiers cannot protect them from unfriendly Indians there. This is the first of several British acts that will anger the American colonists and turn them against Britain. |
| **1764–1765** | **Parliament passes the Grenville Acts**—the Sugar, Currency, Quartering, and Stamp acts. The acts call for new duties and taxes from the colonists, forbid colonists from issuing paper money, and force them to house British soldiers. |
| **1766** | **Parliament repeals the Stamp Act** after colonists resist paying the taxes it calls for and threaten tax collectors with violence. |
| **1767** | **Parliament passes the Townshend Acts,** imposing new duties on colonists for tea and other goods and giving British troops the right to search any colonist's property. |
| **1769–1782** | **Father Junípero Serra** and other Franciscan friars establish 21 missions in California. |
| **1770** | **The Boston Massacre** erupts as Bostonians, angry at British acts, taunt British soldiers and are fired upon. Five colonists are killed. |
| | **All the Townshend Acts are repealed except for the tax on tea.** The British leave that tax to show that they still claim the right to tax the colonists. |

Above, *the stamp Britain required colonists to buy to put on all newspapers and documents (1765). Right, the Boston Tea Party (1773).*

| Date | Event |
|------|-------|
| **1773** | **The Boston Tea Party** takes place as 50 American patriots dressed as Indians board three ships in Boston harbor. Angry over a new Tea Act that forces them to buy British tea, they throw all the tea the ships carry overboard into the harbor. |
| **1774** | **Parliament passes the Coercive, or Intolerable, Acts,** closing Boston Harbor to shipping, placing Massachusetts under military rule, and forcing Massachusetts colonists to house British soldiers sent to carry out the acts. |
| | **The First Continental Congress** meets in Philadelphia as twelve colonies send representatives to protest British actions and to urge the formation of a Massachusetts militia. |
| **1775** | **The first military conflicts** between the British and Americans occur at Lexington and Concord in Massachusetts as British soldiers attempt to capture a storehouse of American weapons. |
| | **The Second Continental Congress** meets in Philadelphia and names George Washington to command American troops fighting around Boston, which the British have under siege. Before he arrives, British and American troops clash at Breed's Hill and Bunker Hill. |
| **1776** | **Thomas Paine,** a writer recently arrived from Britain, publishes *Common Sense*, a pamphlet that urges the American colonies to throw off British rule. |
| | **The Declaration of Independence** is signed in Philadelphia after the Second Continental Congress decides that the colonies must break away from British rule. |

### DECLARATION OF INDEPENDENCE

Wʜᴇɴ in the Course of human Events, it becomes necessary for one People to dissolve the Political Bands which have connected them with another, and to assume among the Powers of the Earth, the separate and equal Station to which the Laws of Nature and of Nature's God entitle them, a decent Respect to the Opinions of Mankind requires that they should declare the causes which impel them to the Separation.

We hold these Truths to be self-evident, that all Men are created equal, that they are endowed by their Creator with certain unalienable Rights, that among these are Life, Liberty, and the Pursuit of Happiness—That to secure these Rights, Governments are instituted among Men, deriving their just Powers from the Consent of the Governed, that whenever any Form of Government becomes destructive of these Ends, it is the Right of the People to alter or to abolish it, and to institute new Government, laying its Foundation on such Principles, and organizing its Powers in such Form, as to them shall seem most likely to effect their Safety and Happiness. Prudence, indeed, will dictate that Governments long established should not be changed for light and transient Causes; and accordingly all Experience hath shewn, that Mankind are more disposed to suffer, while Evils are sufferable, than to right themselves by abolishing the Forms to which they are accustomed. But when a long Train of Abuses and Usurpations, pursuing invariably the same Object, evinces a Design to reduce them under absolute Despotism, it is their Right, it is their Duty, to throw off such Government, and to provide new Guards for their future Security. Such has been the patient Sufferance of these Colonies; and such is now the Necessity which constrains them to alter their former Systems of Government.

(Here follows a list of specific complaints against the King and the British government.)

We, therefore, the Representatives of the UNITED STATES ᴏꜰ AMERICA, in Gᴇɴᴇʀᴀʟ Cᴏɴɢʀᴇꜱꜱ, Assembled, appealing to the Supreme Judge of the World for the Rectitude of our Intentions, do, in the Name, and by Authority of the good People of these Colonies, solemnly Publish and Declare, That these United Colonies are, and of Right ought to be, Fʀᴇᴇ ᴀɴᴅ Iɴᴅᴇᴘᴇɴᴅᴇɴᴛ Sᴛᴀᴛᴇꜱ; that they are absolved from all Allegiance to the British Crown, and that all political Connection between them and the State of Great-Britain, is and ought to be totally dissolved; and that as Fʀᴇᴇ ᴀɴᴅ Iɴᴅᴇᴘᴇɴᴅᴇɴᴛ Sᴛᴀᴛᴇꜱ, they have full Power to levy War, conclude Peace, contract Alliances, establish Commerce, and to do all other Acts and Things which Iɴᴅᴇᴘᴇɴᴅᴇɴᴛ Sᴛᴀᴛᴇꜱ may of right do. And for the support of this Declaration, with a firm Reliance on the Protection of divine Providence, we mutually pledge to each other our Lives, our Fortunes, and our sacred Honor.

**1775–1783**  **The American Revolution.** Even before the Declaration of Independence was signed, British troops began arriving to put down the rebellion. They would not leave for another five years.

1776  The British finally leave Boston, but they capture New York City after fighting General Washington and his troops. The Americans retreat to Pennsylvania.

1776–1777  In a surprise move on the British and their Hessian mercenaries, Washington captures British garrisons at Trenton and Princeton, New Jersey, taking weapons and ammunition.

American troops defeat combined forces of the British at Saratoga, New York. A turning point in the war, this victory strengthens American morale and convinces the French to send military aid and supplies to the Americans.

1777–1778  During the bitter winter, American soldiers face starvation and disease at Valley Forge, Pennsylvania. However, they also receive solid military training and come out a stronger army.

1778  The war moves south as the British capture the port city of Savannah, Georgia.

1779  The most famous naval battle of the war is fought as the American ship *Bonhomme Richard*, under Captain John Paul Jones, defeats and captures the British ship *Serapis*.

1780  The British capture a second major port city in the South, Charleston, South Carolina.

1780–1781  In a series of running battles in the Carolinas at Camden, King's Mountain, Cowpens, and Guilford Court House, the British withdraw to the Atlantic coast.

1781  British troops are trapped at Yorktown, Virginia, as the French fleet cuts off any resupply or escape and as American armies surround them. The British surrender, convincing the British government to end the long and costly war.

1783  The Treaty of Paris, drawn up by the British and American representatives Benjamin Franklin, John Adams, and John Jay, is signed. Through it, the British recognize American independence and cede rights to the rich Ohio valley to the new nation.

*Washington visits his troops during the winter at Valley Forge.*

**1781**  The Articles of Confederation are adopted by the Continental Congress. They unite the new states and organize a central government.

**1785**  The Land Ordinance is passed by Congress. It tells how the lands to the west of the 13 states will be settled and governed.

**1786**  Shays's Rebellion erupts as Daniel Shays, a Massachusetts farmer, leads other farmers in an armed revolt against the Massachusetts legislature, protesting heavy taxes. The state militia puts down the rebellion.

**1787**  The Northwest Ordinance is passed. It creates the Northwest Territory, made up of part of the Ohio and Mississippi valleys, and provides that it will be divided into several states (eventually Ohio, Indiana, Illinois, Michigan, and Wisconsin).

A Constitutional Convention is called in Philadelphia when it becomes clear that the government set up by the Articles of Confederation cannot deal adequately with the nation's problems. Fifty-five delegates from twelve states attend, and George Washington serves as president of the convention. In September, the delegates adopt the Constitution, but the states must ratify it.

*The Federalist* begins publication. It is a series of essays written by Alexander Hamilton, James Madison, and John Jay in support of the Constitution.

**1788**  The Constitution is ratified by three-fourths of the states and becomes the law of the land.

**1789**  George Washington is elected the first President of the United States and takes the oath of office in the temporary national capital at New York City.

**1791**  The Bill of Rights is ratified and becomes the first ten amendments to the Constitution.

The Bank of the United States receives its first government charter, to run until 1811.

Two political parties emerge—Federalists and Democratic-Republicans.

**1793**  Eli Whitney invents the cotton gin. It makes raising cotton highly profitable and causes a demand for more and more slaves, as new southern lands are planted with cotton.

War between Britain and France leads to their harassment of American shipping and to British impressment of sailors from American ships. A period of crisis among the countries arises.

**1794**  The Whiskey Rebellion erupts in western Pennsylvania as whiskey-producing frontier people protest a new whiskey tax. A federal militia puts down the rebellion with no loss of life.

The Jay Treaty, negotiated by John Jay with the British, fails to end British impressment of American sailors but does extract a promise to clear British troops out of the Northwest Territory, where many of them are still stationed.

**1795**  The Pinckney Treaty, negotiated by Charles C. Pinckney with Spain, gives Americans free use of the Mississippi River and allows them to set up warehouses for American goods in New Orleans.

| Date | Event |
|------|-------|
| **1797** | **The XYZ Affair** occurs when three agents of the French government (referred to as X, Y, and Z) demand huge bribes from the United States in return for peaceful relations between the French and American nations. |
| **1798** | **The Alien and Sedition Acts** are passed as President John Adams and other Federalists attempt to quiet criticism of their administration with new laws. Kentucky and Virginia pass resolutions saying that such laws are null and void. |
| **1800** | **Thomas Jefferson,** a Democratic-Republican, defeats John Adams for the Presidency in a very close vote. Aaron Burr is Jefferson's Vice President. |
| **1801** | **John Marshall** becomes chief justice of the Supreme Court, a post he will hold for the next 34 years, during which many important and lasting decisions will be made. In 1803, Marshall's decision in ***Marbury v. Madison*** establishes the principle that the Supreme Court has the right to decide whether laws passed by Congress are constitutional. |
| **1803** | **The Louisiana Purchase** is made when President Jefferson buys the Louisiana Territory from France for $15 million. The purchase doubles the nation's size. |
| **1804–1806** | On instructions from President Jefferson, **Meriwether Lewis and William Clark** lead a party of 30 to explore the Louisiana Territory. They travel beyond it, to the Pacific. |
| **1807** | **Congress passes the Embargo Act,** forbidding American ships to call on any foreign port after France and Britain both interfere with American shipping. |
|  | **Robert Fulton** develops the first successful steamboat, inaugurating an era of steamboat shipping and travel on the nation's rivers, lakes, and coastal waterways. |
| **1812–1814** | **The War of 1812.** Continued British interference with American shipping, as well as British encouragement of Indians to attack American frontier settlements, finally causes President Madison and Congress to declare war. Britain, involved in war with France, can spare few troops to fight the war. |
| 1812 | A three-pronged American attack on British-held Canada fails. |
|  | The *U.S.S. Constitution* ("Old Ironsides") defeats the British *Guerriere* in sea battle. |
| 1813 | Captain Oliver Hazard Perry scores a naval victory on Lake Erie and forces the British to leave Detroit. |
|  | General William Henry Harrison attacks British troops retreating from Detroit and the Indian allies. The Indian leader Tecumseh is killed, and the Indians desert the British cause. |
| 1814 | The British attack Washington, D.C., and burn the White House. |
|  | The British bombard Fort McHenry near Baltimore, and Francis Scott Key writes "The Star-Spangled Banner" after witnessing the bombardment. |
|  | The Treaty of Ghent is signed in Belgium, ending the War of 1812. |
|  | General Andrew Jackson defeats a British attack on New Orleans. Neither side knows that the war has already been ended by the Treaty of Ghent. |

**United States History**

# Expansion and Civil War

The period from 1815 to 1880 was one of amazing growth for the United States. Huge parts of the continent were settled; millions of new immigrants arrived from Ireland, Germany, and many other countries. The nation became increasingly connected by new roads, canals, railroads, and telegraph wires. By 1880, the United States had acquired all its present territory except Hawaii.

At the same time, the country suffered its most disastrous war. The great Civil War was fought over the issue of black slavery and over many political and economic disagreements between North and South. For four years, the nation was divided, and brother fought against brother. Finally the North won, and the country was reunited, but scars of the war took decades to heal.

| Date | Event |
|------|-------|
| **1816** | **The Tariff of 1816** is passed by Congress to encourage the manufacture of American goods. |
| | **The Second Bank** of the United States is chartered. |
| | **The Era of Good Feelings** begins as James Monroe is elected to the Presidency. |
| **1816–1817** | **The American Colonization Society** is founded to transport free slaves back to a newly founded country in Africa called Liberia. It is an early attempt to abolish slavery. |
| **1818** | The United States and Great Britain agree to joint occupation of the **Oregon Territory.** |
| **1819** | In *McCulloch v. Madison,* the Supreme Court determines that the Second Bank of the United States is constitutional. |
| | **Through the Adams-Onis Treaty,** the United States gains Florida from Spain for $5 million. |

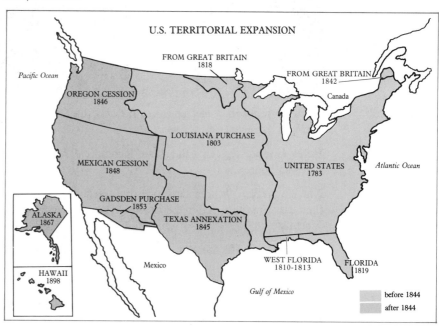

U.S. TERRITORIAL EXPANSION

| Date | Event |
|------|-------|

**1820**      **The Missouri Compromise,** proposed in Congress by Henry Clay of Kentucky, is reached, maintaining the balance between northern and southern states in Congress by admitting Maine as a free state and Missouri as a slave state. The compromise also states that slavery will not be allowed in any other territory that is part of the Louisiana Purchase.

**1821**      **Stephen Austin** establishes an American colony in Texas, a part of Mexico.

         **Emma Willard** opens the Troy Female Seminary, offering collegiate education to American women for the first time.

**1823**      **The Monroe Doctrine** is proclaimed. President Monroe declares that there shall be no more conquest or colonization in the western hemisphere by European nations.

**1825**      **John Quincy Adams** is elected President by the House of Representatives after the electoral college is unable to provide a clear winner.

         **The Erie Canal,** linking the Hudson River to the Great Lakes, is completed.

*The Erie Canal as it passes through Rochester, New York.*

**1828**      **Andrew Jackson** is elected President and the Democratic Party emerges in the two-party system.

**1830**      **Peter Cooper** develops the steam locomotive *Tom Thumb,* capable of going 10 miles an hour.

         **Nat Turner,** a Virginia slave preacher, leads his followers in a rebellion against their slave masters. After the deaths of over 50 whites, Turner is captured and executed.

         **The Webster-Hayne debates** take place on the floor of Congress as Daniel Webster of Massachusetts and Robert Y. Hayne of South Carolina debate states' rights and whether any state has the right to nullify a federal law.

         ***The Liberator,*** a newspaper that demands the abolition of slavery, is founded by William Lloyd Garrison. It strengthens the abolition movement.

| Date | Event |
|---|---|
| **1832** | **The forceable removal of Indians from their homes** in Georgia to lands in the West is ordered by President Jackson, defying a Supreme Court decision. |
| **1833** | President **Jackson smashes the Second Bank** of the United States, which leads to the strengthening of Democratic-owned state banks, soon called "pet banks." |
| **1834** | **Cyrus McCormick** patents the mechanical reaper, which will soon increase farm production. |
| **1836** | **The Whig Party** emerges in the two-party system. |
|  | **Texas declares itself independent of Mexico,** fights the Battle of the Alamo against Mexican troops, and forms the Texas, or Lone Star, Republic. |
| **1837** | **John Deere** introduces the steel plow, which at last makes it possible to farm the Great Plains. |
|  | **The Panic of 1837** begins when a boom in land speculation and easy credit ends in depression. |
| **1839** | **The Liberty Party** is founded to foster antislavery movements. |
|  | **Charles Goodyear** develops the vulcanization process that will start a thriving rubber industry. |
| **1842** | **The Webster-Ashburton Treaty** settles a dispute with Britain over Maine's boundaries. |
| **1844** | **Samuel F. B. Morse** puts the telegraph into operation between Washington, D.C., and Baltimore, Maryland. |
| **1845** | **Texas** is added to the Union. |
| **1846** | **The Oregon Treaty** divides Oregon between Britain and the United States along the 49th parallel. |

| | |
|---|---|
| **1846–1848** | The Mexican War. Eager to see the nation stretch across the continent, several American Presidents offer to buy the Mexican lands of the West and Southwest, but Mexico does not want to sell. To many, war seems the way to get the lands once and for all. |
| 1846 | American troops are sent to Texas when a border dispute erupts with Mexico over Texas's rightful boundaries. Mexican troops cross the Rio Grande and attack the American troops. Congress declares war on Mexico and Mexico replies in kind. |
|  | The Bear Flag Revolt erupts in California, a part of Mexico, as American settlers there proclaim their independence from Mexican rule. |
| 1847 | General Zachary Taylor and his American troops capture the Mexican cities of Matamoras and Monterey. General Winfield Scott and his troops take the city of Veracruz and begin a march toward the capital, Mexico City. After defeating Mexican troops under General Antonio Santa Anna, they capture the capital. |
| 1848 | The Treaty of Guadalupe Hidalgo ends the war. Mexico cedes the entire Southwest to the United States, for $15 million. |

| Date | Event |
|---|---|

**1846**  The **Wilmot Proviso** is declared on the floor on Congress, stating that "neither slavery nor involuntary servitude shall ever exist" in lands acquired from Mexico.

**1847**  The **Mormons** end their long trek westward when they reach the Great Salt Lake in Utah.

**Elias Howe** patents the sewing machine.

**1848**  The **Seneca Falls Convention** meets in New York to demand equal rights for women, including the right to vote.

**Gold** is discovered at Sutter's mill near Sacramento, California, touching off a gold rush.

*Gold miners in California.*

**1850**  The **Compromise of 1850,** proposed by Henry Clay, is reached when California tries to enter the Union as a free state. To maintain the North-South balance in the Senate, California is allowed in, but New Mexico and Utah are allowed to choose for themselves whether they want slavery. A tough new Fugitive Slave Law is passed to help slave owners recapture their slaves who have escaped to the North.

**1851**  **Congress adopts the first reservation policy for Indians,** setting off certain lands for them.

**1851–1856**  **Henry Bessemer and William Kelly** each discover the same process for producing large quantities of steel. The development of a giant steel industry begins.

**1852**  *Uncle Tom's Cabin,* a novel by Harriet Beecher Stowe about the cruelties of slavery, is published. It triggers a great new surge of antislavery feeling in the North.

**Elisha Otis** develops the electric elevator, which will make skyscrapers possible.

**1853**  The **Gadsden Purchase** is approved by Congress. Fifteen million dollars is paid to Mexico for a piece of land that will become part of Arizona and New Mexico.

| Date | Event |
|---|---|

**1854**     **The Kansas-Nebraska Act** is passed, a compromise between slavery and antislavery forces. It creates two new territories—Kansas and Nebraska—and says that the territories can decide for themselves whether to have slavery.

**The Republican Party** is formed as antislavery forces from both the Whigs and Democrats unite.

**1856**     **"Bleeding Kansas"** begins as proslavery and antislavery forces battle each other in bloody ambushes and attacks in the Kansas Territory.

**1857**     **In the Dred Scott decision,** the Supreme Court rules that slaves are not citizens of the United States, that living in free states does not free slaves, and that the Missouri Compromise was unconstitutional because Congress did not have the right to exclude slavery.

**1858**     **Abraham Lincoln and Stephen A. Douglas,** running for Congress from Illinois, hold a series of debates in which matters related to slavery figure importantly. The debates give Lincoln a national reputation.

**1859**     **John Brown,** an antislavery fighter from "Bleeding Kansas," leads a raid on a federal arsenal at Harpers Ferry, Virginia, to seize guns and ammunition for a slave revolt. U.S. Army troops under Colonel Robert E. Lee capture Brown and his followers. Brown is executed for his actions.

**Edwin Drake** builds the nation's first oil derrick in Titusville, Pennsylvania, signaling the beginning of the American oil industry.

**1860**     **Abraham Lincoln,** running as the candidate of the Republican Party, is elected President.

**1860–1861**     **South Carolina secedes** from the Union and all the other states of the lower South—Mississippi, Florida, Alabama, Georgia, Louisiana, and Texas—follow suit.

**1861**     Representatives of the seven states that seceded meet in Montgomery, Alabama, to form a new nation, **the Confederate States of America,** with Jefferson Davis of Mississippi as President.

**The Confederates attack federally held Fort Sumter** in the harbor of Charleston, South Carolina, triggering the Civil War. Virginia, Tennessee, Arkansas, and North Carolina join the Confederacy. The Confederate capital moves from Montgomery, Alabama, to Richmond, Virginia (see next page).

**1862**     **The Homestead Act** is passed; the government will grant 160 acres of public land to anyone who pays a small registration fee and lives on the homestead for five years. This measure helped settle the plains states.

**The Morrill Act** is passed. The government grants the states large tracts of land for them to sell and utilize the proceeds for agricultural and industrial education.

**1863**     **The Emancipation Proclamation** is signed by President Lincoln, granting freedom to all slaves living in states still involved in rebellion.

**1864**     **George M. Pullman** develops a sleeping car for the railroads.

**1861–1865**   **The Civil War.** Slavery is one point of disagreement between the North and the South, but there are others. There are quarrels over tariffs and over the rights that states have as part of the Union, as well as differences between the highly industrial North and the highly agricultural South. With secession and the attack on Fort Sumter, the disagreements finally bring on war.

1861   The first battle of Bull Run begins as Union forces marching from Washington, D.C., clash with Confederate troops at Manassas Junction in Virginia. The Union army is forced to retreat.

1862   At Shiloh, Tennessee, a Confederate attack on General Ulysses S. Grant and his Union army fails, and the Confederate troops withdraw after two days of bloody fighting.

The second battle of Bull Run takes place as Union troops, trying to capture the Confederate capital at Richmond, Virginia, are defeated by Confederate troops under General Robert E. Lee.

A Union fleet defeats a Confederate fleet on the Mississippi River near Memphis, takes Memphis, and gains control of the entire upper Mississippi.

At Antietam Creek in Maryland, Confederate troops marching to attack Pennsylvania are stopped by Union troops under General George B. McClellan. They retreat to Virginia.

At Fredericksburg, Virginia, Union forces are defeated again as they try for Richmond.

1863   At Chancellorsville, Virginia, another Union attempt on Richmond is defeated by Lee's troops.

At Gettysburg, Lee is again defeated in his march on Pennsylvania and he retreats to Virginia.

Vicksburg, Mississippi, falls to Union forces. This puts the entire Mississippi River under Union control.

1863–1864   "Sherman's March to the Sea" begins as Union troops under the command of General William T. Sherman march from Chickamauga, Georgia, to Atlanta to Savannah, cutting a path of destruction as they march.

1864–1865   Union troops under Grant repeatedly engage Confederate troops under Lee in Virginia at the Wilderness, Spotsylvania, Cold Harbor, and Petersburg.

1865   Lee surrenders to Grant at Appomattox Courthouse in Virginia and the Civil War ends.

*A Civil War cemetery at Andersonville, Georgia.*

**1865** The **Freedmen's Bureau** is established by Congress to help recently freed slaves to start life anew.

**President Lincoln is assassinated** at Ford's Theater in Washington, D.C., by an actor and Confederate sympathizer, John Wilkes Booth. Andrew Johnson succeeds him.

The **13th Amendment** is ratified, abolishing slavery in the United States.

**1865–1877** The defeated South goes through a period of **Reconstruction** as Congress decides when the states will be readmitted to national government. Federal troops occupy the South.

**1866** **Cyrus Field** lays a cable under the Atlantic extending to Europe, making it possible to send messages between the continents in minutes rather than days or weeks.

**1867** **The United States buys Alaska** from Russia for over $7 million.

**Christopher Sholes** develops the typewriter, which will revolutionize office work before the turn of the century.

**The Grange Movement** is founded by farmers who want to better their lives and gain more sympathetic treatment from the government.

**1868** The **14th Amendment** is ratified, granting citizenship to former slaves and to anyone else born in the United States.

**President Johnson is impeached** and stands trial in the U.S. Senate. He is acquitted of the "high crimes and misdemeanors" of which some members of Congress accuse him.

**1869** The **first transcontinental railroad** is completed at Promontory Point, Utah. It links railroads in the East with the Central and Pacific railroads, stretching from Omaha, Nebraska, to Sacramento, California.

**George Westinghouse** patents the air brake, replacing the harder to use railroad hand brake.

**The Knights of Labor** is formed in an attempt to bring workers together in a union.

**1870** The **15th Amendment** is ratified, granting black adult males the right to vote.

**1871** **The Chicago fire** destroys one-third of the city and kills at least 300 people.

**1876** **The United States celebrates the Centennial** of its independence with a lavish exhibition in Philadelphia.

**Alexander Graham Bell** applies for a patent for the telephone.

**The Battle of Little Big Horn**—Custer's last stand—is fought. The Sioux and Cheyenne, angered over railroad building through their land, wipe out General George Custer and his men.

**1878** **Thomas Alva Edison** develops the first practical incandescent light bulb. He had patented the phonograph the year before and would patent many other inventions in the years following.

# Growing and changing

Between 1890 and 1920, the United States changed from a pioneer nation to a world power. Huge industrial empires produced coal, steel, and oil. Inventors perfected the use of electricity, and such conveniences as the telephone, the phonograph, the automobile, and the airplane. The government began assembling an empire of possessions in Asia and the Caribbean.

At the same time, these changes caused serious growing pains. Labor unions were organized to demand fair pay and better working conditions. Farmers protested low prices. And the United States was reluctantly drawn into world politics. In 1917, millions of American troops fought in Europe for the first time, helping to bring victory to the Allied powers.

| Date | Event |
|------|-------|
| **1880–1881** | **James A. Garfield** is elected President. Four months after taking office, he is assassinated by Charles J. Guiteau, a mentally unbalanced and disappointed seeker of a government job. Chester A. Arthur succeeds Garfield. |
| **1881** | **Tuskeegee Institute** in Alabama is founded by Booker T. Washington. Its aim is to provide education for young black men and women for immediate and practical application. |
| | **Clara Barton,** a Civil War nurse called "the Angel of the Battlefield," founds the American Red Cross and remains its president until 1904. |
| **1883** | **The Civil Service Reform Act,** or Pendelton Act, is passed to assure that many government jobs are given out on the basis of competitive examination rather than political appointment. |
| **1886** | **The American Federation of Labor** is founded in Columbus, Ohio. It quickly replaces the Knights of Labor as the leading American labor organization. |
| | **The Haymarket Riot** erupts in Chicago as 1500 workers demonstrate for an eight-hour workday. A bomb explodes and seven police officers and four others are killed; 100 are wounded. |
| **1887** | **The Interstate Commerce Act** is passed to stop railroads from engaging in monopolistic practices that give large corporations advantages over smaller ones. |
| | **The Dawes Act** is passed in an attempt to "Americanize" the Indians by granting them small tracts of land and eventually ending the reservation system. |
| **1888** | **George Eastman** invents a small, inexpensive camera for popular use. |
| **1889** | **Jane Addams** opens Hull House in Chicago in an early attempt to provide recreational and educational opportunities for slum dwellers in the nation's growing cities. |
| **1890** | **The Sherman Antitrust Act** is passed to protect the public against monopolies and other business abuses. |
| | **Jacob Riis,** a New York City reporter, publishes *How the Other Half Lives*, a description of the wretched conditions in which slum dwellers live. It brings cries for reform. |
| **1892** | **The Populist Party** is formed by farm and labor groups who demand reforms to give citizens a larger and more direct voice in government. |

| Date | Event |
|---|---|

**The Homestead strike** occurs near Pittsburgh as 3800 workers walk out. Fighting with company police results in the deaths of twelve men. The state militia defeats the strike.

**1893**    **The Panic of 1893** begins causing business failures and unemployment.

**1894**    **"Coxey's Army,"** led by General Jacob S. Coxey of Ohio, marches on Washington, D.C., to demand a huge federal railroad building program to provide jobs for the unemployed. Coxey is arrested.

**1896**    **William Jennings Bryan** of Nebraska, a Populist hero, is nominated for President but loses to Republican William A. McKinley.

**1898**    **Hawaii** is annexed by the United States at the request of Americans living there.

**1898**    **The Spanish-American War.** Like other Western countries, America seeks an empire, eyeing especially the Spanish possessions in the Caribbean and the Pacific. The battleship *U.S.S. Maine*, sent to Havana, Cuba, to protect American citizens there, is blown up in the harbor. Two months later, Congress declares war on Spain, after Spain refuses to relinquish Cuba. American forces attack the Spanish fleet in the Philippines and land in Cuba. U.S. Navy ships destroy the Spanish fleet and bombard Santiago. The Spanish surrender. Americans occupy Puerto Rico, another Spanish possession. Spain gives up Cuba and Puerto Rico and sells the Philippine Islands to the United States for $20 million.

**1901**    **President McKinley is assassinated** by Leon Czolgosz, a crazed anarchist. Theodore Roosevelt succeeds McKinley.

**The United States Steel Corporation** is formed by financier J. Pierpont Morgan. It is the world's first billion-dollar corporation.

**1902**    **President Roosevelt** intervenes in a coal strike in Pennsylvania in support of the labor unions.

**1903**    **Orville and Wilbur Wright,** from Ohio, accomplish the first heavier-than-air flight in a motor-powered plane, at Kitty Hawk, North Carolina.

*The first airplane at Kitty Hawk.*

**1904–1914**    **The Panama Canal** is constructed to link the Atlantic and Pacific oceans between North and South America.

**1906**    ***The Jungle,*** a novel by Upton Sinclair that depicts unsanitary conditions in Chicago meat-packing houses, brings reforms in food-processing plants.

| Date | Event |
|---|---|

**1909**      **The National Association for the Advancement of Colored People** (NAACP) is organized to eliminate segregation and secure civil rights for blacks through legislation and court action.

**1912**      **Democrat Woodrow Wilson** is elected President when Republican votes are split between Taft and Roosevelt.

**1913**      **The 16th Amendment** is ratified, giving Congress the power to tax individual incomes.

**1914**      **The Clayton Antitrust Act** protects the right of labor unions to organize and negotiate.

     **World War I breaks out in Europe** as Archduke Francis Ferdinand of Austria-Hungary is assassinated. This spark sets off a war between rival alliances: the Allies led by Britain, France, and Russia; and the Central Powers, led by Germany and Austria-Hungary.

**1915**      **The *Lusitania*,** a British passenger liner, is sunk off the Irish coast by a German submarine. Among passengers lost are 128 Americans, but Germany pledges to restrict its submarine warfare and stop sinking passenger ships.

     **The Ku Klux Klan** is organized in Georgia and begins to terrorize immigrants, Catholics, Jews, and especially blacks.

**1917**      **Germany** resumes unrestricted submarine warfare.

     **Communists overthrow the Russian government,** and Russia withdraws from the war against Germany.

     **The Zimmermann note,** suggesting that Germany is encouraging Mexico to go to war against the United States, is revealed.

**1917–1918**      **The United States in World War I.** In April 1917, President Wilson asks Congress for a declaration of war against Germany and Congress responds.

1917      The Selective Service Act is passed, providing for the eventual draft of 3 million men. General John J. Pershing is named to command the American Expeditionary Forces (A.E.F.). President Wilson presents his Fourteen Point plan for world peace. The points advocate open diplomacy, freedom of the seas, removal of tariffs, arms reduction, and a league of nations.

1918      At Cantigny, France, American troops achieve the first clear-cut American victory. At Chateau-Thierry, Americans help block a German advance. At Belleau Wood, they drive the Germans out of an important position. In the Battle of the Marne, American and French troops drive the Germans far back, marking the turning point of the war. At St. Mihiel, American troops mount the first distinctly American offensive and capture the town.

In the Meuse-Argonne offensive, more than a million American troops join British and French troops. They defeat the enemy and the Germans surrender. An armistice is signed, ending the war on November 11, 1918. In 1919, the Treaty of Versailles is signed, providing for the creation of the League of Nations, but Congress opposes American membership. The League of Nations is formed, but the United States never joins it.

# Boom, bust, war

Between 1920 and 1954, the United States grew into the most prosperous land on Earth. During the 1920's, the country turned away from world affairs and found excitement at home—the popular entertainment of radio and the movies, jazz, and the promise of ever greater prosperity.

The excitement ended suddenly in the early 1930's, however. A Great Depression wrecked the economy and millions lost their jobs. Even before recovery was complete, the country faced another world war, successfully defending against the aggression of Germany and Japan.

Peace was short-lived, however. The United States was soon competing with the Soviet Union for world dominance, and still another war broke out in Korea within five years.

| Date | Event |
|---|---|
| **1919** | **The 18th Amendment** is ratified, prohibiting the manufacture and sale of alcoholic beverages. It will be repealed by the 21st Amendment in 1933. |
| | **The "Red scare"** erupts as antigovernment bombings occur in the United States. The bombings are blamed on Communist influences. The "Palmer raids," ordered by the attorney general, bring about the arrest and deportation of suspected radicals. The scare dies down. |
| **1920** | **The 19th Amendment** is ratified, giving adult women the right to vote. In the first Presidential election in which they vote, Warren G. Harding is elected. |
| | **The nation's first radio station,** KDKA in Pittsburgh, goes into operation. |
| **1921–1922** | **The Washington Naval Conference** is held. The United States, Britain, and Japan seek to limit naval armaments. |
| **1921–1929** | **Congress begins passing laws to restrict immigration,** including the Emergency Quota Act of 1921 and the Immigration Act of 1924. Immigration shrinks to 150,000 a year by 1929. |
| **1923** | **President Harding dies** and Calvin Coolidge succeeds him. |
| **1924** | **The Teapot Dome** scandal comes to light as the American people learn that several members of the Harding administration are guilty of corruption. Among their crimes is taking bribes to rent government oil-producing land at Teapot Dome, Wyoming, and Elk Hills, California, to private oil interests. |

Left, *police watch as illegal liquor is dumped.* Right, *a cartoonist's view of the 1920's dance craze, the Charleston.*

**1924**    **Indians are granted American citizenship,** partly in recognition of Indian wartime service.

**1927**    **The first talking picture** is released, *The Jazz Singer*, starring Al Jolson.

**Charles A. Lindbergh** becomes the first person to fly across the Atlantic alone. His plane, *The Spirit of St. Louis*, makes the trip from New York to Paris in 33 hours.

**1929**    **The stock market crashes** as sellers find no buyers for their highly overpriced stocks. Falling farm prices, an oversupply of manufactured goods, and a loss of foreign trade also help to bring on the Great Depression, the worst in U.S. history.

**1929–1932**    **Farm income shrinks** by 50 percent; industry drops to one-half production; 85,000 businesses fail; thousands of banks close after losing their depositors' money; unemployment reaches $12\frac{1}{2}$ million, one-quarter of the nation's work force.

**1932**    **The "Bonus Army"** marches on Washington. Ten thousand World War I veterans demand the $1000 bonuses the government has promised them although the bonuses are not yet due. U.S. Army troops drive them away under orders of President Herbert Hoover.

**Democrat Franklin Delano Roosevelt** runs against Hoover for the Presidency, promising the American people a "New Deal" that will bring relief and recovery form the Great Depression. Roosevelt wins by a landslide.

**1933**    **Roosevelt is inaugurated** and immediately declares a "bank holiday," closing banks temporarily to determine which are sound enough to handle depositors' money.

**1933–1938**    **The New Deal** begins as Congress passes an amazing number of programs during Roosevelt's first hundred days in office, including the Emergency Banking Relief Act, the Agricultural Adjustment Act, the Tennessee Valley Act, and the National Industrial Recovery Act. Later legislation includes the Social Security Act and the Fair Labor Standards Act.

**1939**    **World War II begins in Europe** as Adolf Hitler, fascist dictator of Germany, sends troops into Poland, part of an Allied alliance led by Britain and France. Hitler's partners in the Axis alliance, Italy and Japan, also commit aggressive acts—Italy in Africa and Japan in China.

**1940**    **The Selective Service Act** is passed, the first peacetime draft in American history.

**1941**    **The Lend-Lease Act** is passed to supply Britain with guns, tanks, ships, and planes.

**The nation's first commercial television** broadcasting begins, in New York City.

**The Japanese attack** the U.S. Navy Pacific fleet at Pearl Harbor in Hawaii, sinking or badly damaging 19 ships and killing 2300 Americans. Congress declares war on Japan, and Germany and Italy declare war on the United States.

**1941–1945**    **The United States in World War II.** When the United States enters the war, Allied powers Britain and Russia are fighting Axis powers Germany and Italy in Europe and Africa. (France had fallen to Germany in 1940.) In Asia, Axis power Japan is fighting in China and is conquering Southeast Asia and the Pacific. The United States faces war in both Europe and the Pacific.

1942    Wartime agencies are established to mobilize for war. They include the War Production Board and the Office of War Mobilization.

The draft is extended, eventually helping to raise a military force of 16 million.

All people in the United States of Japanese ancestry are sent to relocation camps.

*War in Europe and North Africa*

1942–1943    The Allies battle the Germans and Italians in North Africa and drive them out.

1943    The Allies invade Italy. After several bloody campaigns, Italy surrenders.

1943–1944    The Russians drive the Germans out of the Soviet Union and back into Poland.

1944    The Allies begin the D-Day invasion of Europe and drive nearly to the German border.

1945    The Allies invade Germany and Germany surrenders on V-E (Victory-Europe) Day.

*War in the Pacific*

1942    Manila, Bataan, and Corregidor all fall to the Japanese and the Philippines are lost. But the U.S. Navy wins the battle of the Coral Sea and of Midway and prevents the capture of Guadalcanal.

1943–1945    American forces drive the Japanese from the Aleutian Islands and begin recapturing other Pacific islands—the Solomons, the Gilberts, the Marshalls, New Guinea, Saipan, Guam, and the Philippines.

1945    American forces begin the invasion of Japan, capturing Iwo Jima and Okinawa. Atomic bombs are dropped on Hiroshima and Nagasaki and Japan surrenders on V-J Day.

*American troops come ashore on Normandy beach, 1944.*

**1944**
**The GI Bill of Rights** is passed, offering government aid and loans to veterans for education, housing, and business ventures.

**1945**
**President Roosevelt dies** and is succeeded by Harry S. Truman.

**The United Nations** is founded in San Francisco. It begins with 50 member nations.

**1947**
A **"Cold War"** develops between the Soviet Union, which is seeking to spread communism, and anti-communist nations led by the United States. The Truman Doctrine is announced, offering American economic and military aid to any nation threatened by communist takeover. The Marshall Plan follows, offering economic aid to help war-torn countries of Europe.

**The Taft-Hartley Act** is passed. It seeks more control over labor unions in a response to the great number of labor strikes since the end of the war.

**1948–1949**
**The Berlin blockade** begins as the Soviet Union tries to drive Britain, France, and the United States out of Berlin, which the four powers jointly occupy. The Western powers fly in enough supplies to maintain their parts of the city. The Russians finally end the blockade.

**1949**
**NATO,** the North Atlantic Treaty Organization, is founded to thwart Communist moves against the Western nations. The United States, Canada, Britain, and France are some of the members.

**1950–1953**
War in Korea. In 1949, after a long civil war, Communist forces finally succeed in winning China. Americans grow fearful that other areas of Asia will also fall to communism. In 1950, China's neighbor Communist North Korea invades non-Communist South Korea. President Truman asks the United Nations to send a force to repel the North Koreans. American troops make up most of the force.

1950
U.S. forces attack at Inchon, throwing the North Korean troops back over the South Korean border and almost as far back as North Korea's border with China.

1950–1951
Chinese troops cross their border and drive UN forces south of the South Korean border. UN forces fight their way to back near the border.

1951–1953
Truce talks begin, but the fighting drags on with great loss of life.

1953
An armistice is reached, leaving the border through Korea as it was before the war.

**1950–1954**
**McCarthyism** is rampant as American fears of communism create fears of possible Communist traitors within the country. Senator Joseph McCarthy of Wisconsin accuses many people of "un-Americanism." He is finally censured by the Congress and McCarthyism fades away.

**1952**
**Dwight D. Eisenhower is elected President** on the Republican ticket. He serves two terms, presiding over a period of general prosperity. During his first years in office, the Korean War is ended by negotiation and McCarthyism weakens and dies. At the same time, new problems arise.

# Modern America

From 1954 to the present, the United States has remained a world power. At the same time, it has struggled to solve many serious problems of its own. The civil rights campaigns of the 1950's and 1960's sought to follow through on promises made to black Americans after the Civil War. In the 1960's and 1970's, citizens debated how best to help the poor; how far the country should in-volve itself in the long war in Vietnam; and just what a country could expect of its leaders.

The Cold War with the Soviet Union contin-ued with confrontations in Berlin and in Cuba. But gradually attention shifted to crises brought on by smaller countries, such as the oil crisis brought on by Arab nations in the Middle East and the painful hostage crisis in Iran.

| Date | Event |
|---|---|
| **1954–1955** | **The black civil rights struggle** begins as the Supreme Court decides in *Brown v. Board of Education of Topeka* that school segregation must end. The next year, a bus boycott in Montgomery, Alabama, led by Rev. Martin Luther King, leads to bus desegregation there. Sit-ins lead to desegregation of public places. "Free-dom riders" bring on desegregation of interstate buses. |
| **1958** | **The National Defense Education Act** is passed, giving federal aid to schools to strengthen their science and math programs in an effort to maintain U.S. techno-logical supremacy. |
| **1961** | **The Peace Corps,** to send Americans to help in developing countries, and the Alliance for Progress, offering $10 billion in aid for developing Latin American countries, are inaugurated by President John F. Kennedy. |
| | **The Bay of Pigs invasion** takes place as exiled Cubans, driven from their country by the Communist government of Fidel Castro, land in Cuba to over-throw Castro. The American-trained and supplied army of exiles is quickly de-feated, and Cuban-American relations grow worse. |
| **1962** | **The Cuban missile crisis** occurs as Soviet-built missiles are discovered in Cuba. President Kennedy demands that the Soviet Union remove the missiles and threatens to turn back any other weapons-carrying Soviet ship headed for Cuba. After a few tense days, the Soviet Union agrees to remove the missiles. |
| **1963** | **A march on Washington** is staged by more than 200,000 civil rights supporters who demand that Congress pass civil rights legislation. |
| | **President Kennedy is assassinated** in Dallas, Texas, by Lee Harvey Oswald, an alleged Cuban sympathizer. Lyndon B. Johnson succeeds to the Presidency. |
| **1964–1965** | **"Great Society"** legislation is passed as President Johnson declares a "War on Poverty." The Economic Opportunity Act creates the Office of Economic Oppor-tunity, which provides job training; VISTA, a domestic Peace Corps; and Head Start programs for children. The Elementary and Secondary Education Act pro-vides federal grants for schools in low-income districts. The Medicare Act pro-vides federal health benefits for those over 65. |
| **1964–1968** | **The Civil Rights Act of 1964** is passed to outlaw racial discrimination in em-ployment and public accommodations. The Voting Rights Act of 1965 follows, to protect black people's right to vote. The Civil Rights Act of 1968 aims to guaran-tee blacks open housing. |

*President Kennedy.*

| Date | Event |
|------|-------|

**1964–1975**     **War in Vietnam.** Communist North Vietnam fights to take over non-Communist South Vietnam. Presidents Eisenhower and Kennedy send military advisers and supplies to help South Vietnam, but the South keeps losing. President Johnson decides to increase American involvement.

1964    The Gulf of Tonkin Resolution is passed by Congress, giving the President expanded powers to commit American troops and supplies to South Vietnam.

1965–1968    American planes begin flying regular bombing missions over North Vietnam. By the end of 1968, 536,000 American troops have been sent to Vietnam and 25,000 have been killed. The Communist Tet offensive in February, 1968, shows how unsuccessful American involvement has been.

1968–1969    Anti-Vietnam War protest gathers strength. A national moratorium is held in October, 1968, demanding an end to American involvement.

1969–1972    President Richard M. Nixon takes office and promises to have the Vietnamese take over more of the fighting and thus reduce American involvement. By 1972 American troops in Vietnam are down to 60,000.

1973    "An Agreement on Ending the War and Restoring Peace in Vietnam" is signed, providing for a cease-fire and the withdrawal of all American troops.

1975    The last American troops withdraw from South Vietnam; it is soon overrun by the North.

Left, *a medical evacuation during the Vietnam War.* Right, *an antiwar protest in the United States.*

**1966**    **The National Organization for Women (NOW)** is founded, signaling the start of a new women's movement to gain equal social, political and economic rights.

**1968**    **Martin Luther King** is assassinated in Memphis, Tennessee, by James Earl Ray.

       **Robert Kennedy,** brother of John F. Kennedy and Presidential candidate, is assassinated in Los Angeles by Sirhan Sirhan, an Arab nationalist.

**1969**    U.S. astronauts Neil Armstrong, Edwin Aldrin, and Michael Collins succeed in making **the first manned landing on the moon,** the aim of a space program begun in 1961 by President Kennedy.

**1970**    **An Ohio National Guard unit** kills four students and wounds nine others during antiwar demonstrations at Kent State University.

**1972**    **President Nixon visits China,** ending a 20-year period of separation between China and the United States. He and Chinese leaders agree to allow scientific and cultural ties and to foster trade between their countries. Three months later, Nixon visits the Soviet Union to ease tensions. He and Soviet leaders sign an arms control agreement and agree to more international cooperation.

**1972–1974**    **The Watergate crisis** is brought on when Democratic National Headquarters in the Watergate complex in Washington, D.C., are broken into. The intruders are later connected with the White House and the Committee to Re-elect the President. President Nixon denies any involvement, but congressional and judicial investigations find proof of Nixon's participation.

**1973**    **Vice President Spiro Agnew** is forced to resign after pleading no-contest to a charge of tax evasion. Gerald R. Ford, member of Congress from Michigan, is selected as Vice President.

**An oil crisis** erupts as several Arab oil-producing nations refuse to ship oil to the United States. Oil shortages continue even after Arabs start shipping oil again. Oil prices rise, fueling worldwide inflation and threatening the health of the American and world economies.

*A common sight during the 1973 oil crisis.*

*Roe* v. *Wade*, a Supreme Court ruling, bans state restrictions on abortions.

**1974**    **Nixon resigns** from the Presidency after the House Judiciary Committee approves articles of impeachment. Gerald Ford succeeds him as President. One of Ford's first acts is to pardon Nixon.

**1976**    **The United States celebrates its Bicentennial** with events across the country, including a parade of tall ships from all over the world up the Hudson River.

**1978**    **The Panama Canal Treaty** is ratified by Congress, providing for the turnover of control of the canal to Panama by the year 2000.

**1979**    **The Camp David accords** are reached after President Jimmy Carter calls the leaders of Israel and Egypt together and they agree to a framework for arriving at peace between their nations.

| Date | Event |
|------|-------|
| **1979-1981** | **Iranians take 53 American Embassy personnel hostage** in Teheran and hold them for 444 days in retaliation for American protection of the overthrown Iranian leader Shah Pahlevi. |
| **1980** | **Mount Saint Helens,** a volcano in Washington State, erupts, killing 26 people and spreading volcanic ash over 120 square miles. |
| **1981** | **President Reagan is shot** by John W. Hinckley, Jr., who is found innocent by reason of insanity. Reagan recovers and returns to work. |
| | **Sandra Day O'Connor** becomes the first woman named to the Supreme Court. |
| **1981-1998** | **Acquired immune deficiency syndrome (AIDS)** is first reported in the United States in 1981. The virus that causes AIDS is finally discovered in 1986. In the 17 years following the discovery of the syndrome, more than 660,000 people are diagnosed in the United States. Of these cases, about 400,000 deaths are reported. |
| **1982** | **Strategic Arms Reduction Talks (START)** begin in Geneva, Switzerland, and attempt to limit the number of nuclear warheads in the world. |
| **1983** | **Sally K. Ride** becomes the first American woman in space as a member of the crew of the space shuttle *Challenger*. |
| | **A terrorist bomb** at the headquarters of the U.S. peacekeeping force in Beirut, Lebanon, kills 241 American servicemen. |
| **1986** | **The space shuttle *Challenger* explodes** on takeoff, killing all aboard, including schoolteacher Christa McAuliffe. |
| **1987** | **The Iran-Contra congressional hearings** expose a plot by U.S. government officials to sell arms to Iran in an effort to obtain the release of hostages and to use the money received to support the Contra rebels in Nicaragua. |
| **1988** | **A terrorist bomb** explodes aboard a Pan American Boeing 747 jumbo jet flying over Lockerbie, Scotland, killing all 259 passengers and crew and 11 people on the ground below. |
| **1989** | **An earthquake** measuring 6.9 on the Richter scale hits the San Francisco area, causing 67 deaths and considerable damage. |
| | **U.S. troops invade Panama** in order to install a democratically elected government and to apprehend dictator Manuel Noriega, indicted in the United States on drug-related charges. |
| | **The Exxon Valdez** supertanker spills over 11 million gallons of crude oil into Prince William Sound, Alaska. |
| **1990-1991** | **The United States responds to the Iraqi invasion of Kuwait** by leading a military coalition of some 527,000 soldiers from 30 nations against Iraq. On January 16, 1991, coalition forces launch a six-week military campaign that decimates Iraq and forces its troops out of Kuwait. |

**1992**      **A relief mission to Somalia,** under UN auspices, is led by U.S. forces to help deliver relief supplies and restore order to the war-torn country.

**1993**      **The worst floods in a century** strike the Mississippi and Missouri river basins, causing some $12 billion in damage and leaving tens of thousands homeless.

*Flooding along the Mississippi River in 1993.*

**1994**      **A major earthquake,** measuring 6.6 on the Richter scale, devastates the Los Angeles, California, area, destroying or damaging thousands of buildings, buckling freeways, and leaving some 51 dead and tens of thousands homeless.

**1996**      **Bill Clinton** becomes the first Democratic President to gain reelection to a second term since Franklin D. Roosevelt in 1936. The Republicans, who gained control of Congress in 1994 for the first time in 40 years, retain majorities in both houses.

**1997**      **The U.S. economy booms.** In May, unemployment drops below 5 percent for the first time in 24 years, and in July the Dow Jones industrial average rises above 8000 for the first time.

**1998-1999**      **Impeachment.** In December, 1998, the House of Representatives votes two articles of impeachment against Bill Clinton, charging him with perjury and obstructing justice in relation to a White House sex scandal. In February, 1999, the Senate acquits Clinton on both counts.

**2000**      **George W. Bush** is elected president in one of the closest U.S. elections ever. For only the second time in history, a son follows his father to the White House.

## For Further Reference

Durant, Will and Ariel
    *Story of Civilization.* 11 volumes.
    Simon & Schuster
Grun, Bernard
    *The Timetables of History: A Historical Linkage of Peoples and Events*
    Simon & Schuster
Kirkler, Bernard
    *A Reader's Guide to Contemporary History*
    Quadrangle

McNeill, William H.
    *A World History*
    Oxford University Press
Palmer, R. R. and Colton, Joel
    *A History of the Modern World*
    Simon & Schuster
Wetterau, Bruce
    *The Macmillan Concise Dictionary of World History*
    Macmillan

# United States Today

The United States today is made up of 50 states. Of these, 48 make up a central band across the continent of North America between Mexico and Canada. The other two states are Alaska, in the northwest corner of the continent, and Hawaii, a chain of islands in the Pacific Ocean some 2200 miles west and south of the American mainland. This section briefly describes the land and people of the United States. It then presents information on each of the states in the Union by region, beginning with the West and ending with the Northeast.

# The land

The land of the continental United States is divided into major land regions by its mountain chains. The largest and most important of these are the Rocky Mountains, which run from north to south through the Western states from Montana to Alaska. A second major chain is the Appalachian Mountains, which run through the Northeastern states and into the South, from Maine to Alabama. Smaller mountain ranges include the Coastal Mountains, which run parallel to the Pacific coast in Washington, Oregon, and California; and an isolated highland region called the Ozark-Ouachitas, mainly in Arkansas and Missouri.

Between the Coastal Ranges and the Rockies lies the great Basin and Range region of the Far West. It is a generally dry and barren area of high plateaus. Between the Rockies and the Appalachians lies the Great Plains region, covering almost all of the Midwest from the Dakotas to Ohio. The Plains region is drained by the largest U.S. river system, which includes the great Mississippi and its tributaries, especially the Missouri and the Ohio. The region is one of the richest farming areas in the world, producing huge crops of corn, wheat, and other grains and millions of beef cattle and hogs each year. East of the Appalachians and following the seacoast from Maine to Texas are the Coastal Plains. These lowlands were the site of many early American settlements, and today they have many large cities and much fertile farmland.

Along the eastern half of the country, the northern border with Canada is formed by the Great Lakes, five of the largest freshwater lakes in the world. Four of them—Superior, Huron, Erie, and Ontario—are shared with Canada. The fifth lake, Michigan, is the largest body of fresh water wholly in the United States.

Alaska is a vast wilderness bordering Canada

# U.S. landforms

mountains and highlands

basin and range, plateau

central plains

coastal plains

on the east and facing the Pacific and Arctic oceans and the Bering Sea on its other sides. It includes Mt. McKinley, the highest point in North America. Hawaii is a chain of small volcanic islands, featuring both warm, sandy beaches and snowcapped volcanic peaks.

The climate of the United States is generally *temperate*—neither extremely hot nor extremely cold. The warmest places are in the south—in Florida, Texas, Arizona, California, and Hawaii. The coldest places are in the north—in Minnesota, the Dakotas, and, of course, Alaska. The highest rainfall occurs along the Pacific coast of Washington and in the southeast. The driest regions are the deserts of the southwest.

## Area.

In area, the United States is the fourth largest country in the world, behind Russia, Canada, and China. The continental United States averages 2500 miles from east to west and some 1200 miles from north to south.

The Western region is the largest by far, containing more than 2 million square miles and all of the ten largest states. It is larger than all the rest of the country combined. The largest state,

Alaska, has 615,230 square miles and is more than twice as large as the second largest state, Texas. The smallest state is Rhode Island, with just over 1500 square miles. Alaska is 500 times as large as Rhode Island.

## U.S. area *(land and water, in square miles)*

| U.S. total | | 3,717,796 |
|---|---|---|
| **Regions** | West | 2,149,119 |
| | Midwest | 821,762 |
| | South | 569,998 |
| | Northeast | 176,917 |
| **Largest states** | 1. Alaska | 615,230 |
| | 2. Texas | 267,277 |
| | 3. California | 158,869 |
| | 4. Montana | 147,046 |
| | 5. New Mexico | 121,598 |
| **Smallest states** | 50. Rhode Island | 1,231 |
| | 49. Delaware | 2,396 |
| | 48. Connecticut | 5,544 |
| | 47. Hawaii | 6,459 |
| | 46. New Jersey | 8,215 |

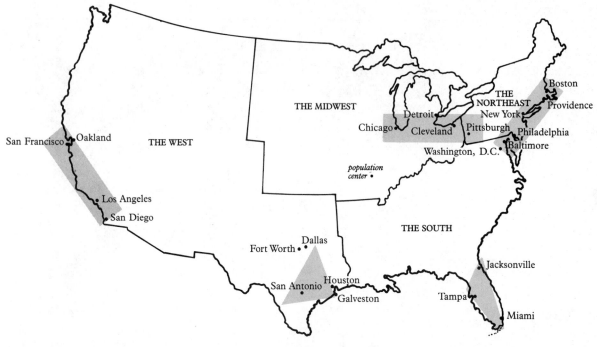

MAJOR U.S. POPULATION CENTERS

# The people

The United States is the third largest country in the world in population, behind China and India. According to 1996 estimates, there are 265 million Americans, distributed fairly evenly among the four great regions. The West led with 81 million, followed closely by the South and Midwest and trailed by the Northeast.

Because of differences in area, however, far more people live on less land in the Northeast. This can be measured by calculating how many people there are per square mile in each region:

| Region | Persons per square mile |
|---|---|
| Northeast | 292 |
| South | 124 |
| Midwest | 76 |
| West | 38 |

The table shows that there are about eight times as many people per square mile in the Northeast as there are in the West. The most densely populated state, New Jersey, has 1077 people per square mile. Alaska actually has more square miles than it has people!

The most populous state in the United States is California, with almost 32 million people. One person out of eight in the country is a Californian. Other large states are New York, which actually lost population between 1970 and 1990; Texas, whose population was estimated to have passed that of New York in 1994; Florida; and Pennsylvania. The two least populous states, Wyoming and Vermont, each have fewer than 600,000 people. For every Alaskan, there are 53 Californians. The average population of a state is about 5 million. Eleven states have between 3 and 5 million residents, and eight more have between 5 and 7 million.

The people of the United States are a rich, diverse group made up of many races and nationalities. Individuals whose roots lie on every continent are included in the group we call Americans. While English is the language used most commonly, a large percentage of the population speaks Spanish. In any American city, one is likely to hear many languages (Russian, French, and German among them) spoken by American citizens.

## U.S. population *(1990 census)*

| | | |
|---|---|---|
| **U.S. total** | | 248,709,873 |
| **Regions** | West | 72,919,000 |
| | Midwest | 59,669,000 |
| | South | 65,313,000 |
| | Northeast | 50,809,000 |
| **Largest states** | 1. California | 29,760,021 |
| | 2. New York | 17,990,455 |
| | 3. Texas | 16,986,510 |
| | 4. Florida | 12,937,926 |
| | 5. Pennsylvania | 11,881,643 |
| **Smallest states** | 50. Wyoming | 453,588 |
| | 49. Alaska | 550,043 |
| | 48. Vermont | 562,758 |
| | 47. North Dakota | 638,800 |
| | 46. Delaware | 666,168 |

# Cities.

For nearly 200 years, more and more people have been living in cities. Today, nearly 80 percent of the U.S. population lives in a metropolitan area—a city or a suburb near a large city. Many of the large urban areas are close together in one of three corridors of population.

• BOS-WASH stretches from Boston, Massachusetts, to Washington, D.C., along the Atlantic coast. It includes such major cities as Providence, New York, Philadelphia, and Baltimore.

• CHI-PITTS stretches from Chicago, Illinois, to Pittsburgh, Pennsylvania, along the southern shores of the Great Lakes. It includes Detroit and Cleveland.

• SAN-SAN runs along California's Pacific coast from San Francisco to San Diego. It includes the sprawling Los Angeles region, which is made up of several metropolitan areas.

Another cluster of large cities is growing up in Texas in a triangle whose corners are Houston-Galveston, Dallas-Fort Worth, and San Antonio. There are also three metropolitan areas in Florida with a million or more people. Other large cities such as St. Louis, Minneapolis-St. Paul, and Atlanta serve as important regional capitals.

There are 43 metropolitan areas in the United States with populations of more than 1 million. The three largest are Los Angeles, New York, and Chicago.

## Largest cities *(metro. pop., 1990)*

| | |
|---|---|
| 1. Los Angeles-Long Beach CA | 8,863,000 |
| 2. New York NY-NJ | 8,547,000 |
| 3. Chicago IL | 6,070,000 |
| 4. Philadelphia PA-NJ | 4,857,000 |
| 5. Detroit MI | 4,382,000 |
| 6. Washington DC-MD-VA | 3,924,000 |
| 7. Dallas-Fort Worth TX | 3,885,000 |
| 8. San Francisco-Oakland CA | 3,667,000 |
| 9. Houston TX | 3,302,000 |
| 10. Boston MA | 2,871,000 |
| 11. Atlanta GA | 2,834,000 |
| 12. Nassau-Suffolk Counties NY | 2,609,000 |
| 13. Riverside-San Bernadino-Ontario CA | 2,589,000 |
| 14. San Diego CA | 2,498,000 |
| 15. Anaheim-Santa Ana-Garden Grove CA | 2,471,000 |
| 16. Minneapolis-St. Paul MN-WI | 2,464,000 |
| 17. St. Louis MO-IL | 2,444,000 |
| 18. Baltimore MD | 2,382,000 |
| 19. Phoenix AZ | 2,122,000 |
| 20. Tampa-St. Petersburg-Clearwater FL | 2,068,000 |

## Index to the states

# The West

The Western United States consists of 13 states in the main continental region, stretching from Texas in the southeast to Washington in the northwest. In addition, the region includes the two states that are separated from the other 48—Alaska and Hawaii.

The Western region was scarcely known in 1776 when the United States was formed. The only European settlements were Spanish missions in present-day California and New Mexico. As late as 1900, this huge region had only about 8.3 million people. By 1980, it was the most populous of the four regions, with more than 60 million people. California and Texas are by far the most populous Western states. Nearly two-thirds of all Westerners—about 51 million in 1996—live in these two states.

The Western states include vast areas of mountain and desert wasteland. But they also include most of the oil and natural gas deposits in the United States and immense treasures in timber. California is the most important and most diversified agricultural state in the country. Light manufacturing is of growing importance.

The Western region is growing at a faster rate than any other region, especially along its southern half. Between 1970 and 1990, California gained more new residents than any other state, and Nevada and Arizona had the highest percentage increases.

| State name<br>Date entered union | Area<br>Population<br>Est. 1990 | Capital<br>Principal cities | Bird<br>Flower<br>Tree |
|---|---|---|---|
| **Alaska**<br>Jan. 3, 1959 (49th) | 591,004 sq. mi.<br>551,947 | ★Juneau,<br>Anchorage | Willow ptarmigan<br>Forget-me-not<br>Sitka spruce |
| **Arizona**<br>Feb. 14, 1912 (48th) | 114,000 sq. mi.<br>3,677,985 | ★Phoenix,<br>Tucson, Mesa,<br>Tempe | Cactus wren<br>Saguaro blossom<br>Paloverde |
| **California**<br>Sept. 9, 1850 (31st) | 158,706 sq. mi.<br>29,839,250 | ★Sacramento,<br>Los Angeles,<br>San Francisco,<br>San Diego, San Jose | California valley quail<br>Golden poppy<br>California redwood |
| **Colorado**<br>Aug. 1, 1876 (38th) | 104,091 sq. mi.<br>3,307,912 | ★Denver,<br>Colorado Springs,<br>Aurora | Lark bunting<br>Rocky Mountain columbine<br>Blue spruce |
| **Hawaii**<br>Aug. 21, 1959 (50th) | 6471 sq. mi.<br>1,115,274 | ★Honolulu,<br>Hilo | Hawaiian goose<br>Hibiscus<br>Kukui (candlenut) |
| **Idaho**<br>July 3, 1890 (43rd) | 83,564 sq. mi.<br>1,011,986 | ★Boise,<br>Pocatello,<br>Idaho Falls | Mountain bluebird<br>Syringa<br>White pine |
| **Montana**<br>Nov. 8, 1889 (41st) | 147,046 sq. mi.<br>803,655 | ★Helena,<br>Billings,<br>Great Falls | Western meadowlark<br>Bitterroot<br>Ponderosa pine |

| Land/Climate | Economy |
|---|---|
| Southern coastal ranges, extensive interior plateau, and northern mountains to Arctic slope; arctic north and mild summers in south | Drilling of oil and natural gas; limited agriculture, commercial fishing, and tourism |
| Central mountain highlands with northeast plateau and southwest desert basin; hot and dry at low elevations and milder in highlands | Manufacturing of electrical, metal, and aircraft products; tourism; mining of copper, gold, and silver; cattle and sheep ranching |
| Coastal ranges, central valley, inland Sierra Nevada Mountains, southern desert; rainfall and temperature variation increasing toward north | Leader in manufacturing, with machinery, electric, and food goods; also leading farm state, with both livestock and varied crop yields; tourism |
| Eastern plains, central spine of Rocky Mountains, western plateau; mild and dry except in mountains; peaks are snow-covered all year | Manufacturing of food goods and electronic equipment; oil, natural gas, molybdenum; tourism; cattle ranching and wheat |
| Chain of volcanic islands with sandy beaches broken by coastal cliffs; coastal areas warm year-round, inland areas wetter and cooler | Tourism; crops of pineapple and sugar cane; cattle ranches; manufactures based on food processing |
| Rocky Mountains in northern half, plains in southern half; dry continental climate of cold winters and warm summers | Agriculture based on potato crop and cattle; manufacturing of processed foods and lumber products; tourism |
| Rocky Mountains in west and Great Plains over eastern two-thirds; dry, with severe winters and hot summers | Agriculture based on wheat, cattle, and feed crops; mining of copper and coal; timber; tourism |

Colorado mountains

Hollywood Boulevard, Los Angeles

| State name<br>Date entered union | Area<br>Population<br>Est. 1990 | Capital<br>Principal cities | Bird<br>Flower<br>Tree |
|---|---|---|---|
| **Nevada**<br>Oct. 31, 1864 (36th) | 110,561 sq. mi.<br>1,206,152 | ★Carson City,<br>Las Vegas,<br>Reno | Mountain bluebird<br>Sagebrush<br>Single-leaf piñon |
| **New Mexico**<br>Jan. 6, 1912 (47th) | 121,593 sq. mi.<br>1,521,779 | ★Santa Fe,<br>Albuquerque,<br>Las Cruces | Roadrunner<br>Yucca<br>Piñon |
| **Oklahoma**<br>Nov. 16, 1907 (46th) | 69,956 sq. mi.<br>3,157,604 | ★Oklahoma City,<br>Tulsa | Scissor-tailed flycatcher<br>Mistletoe<br>Redbud |
| **Oregon**<br>Feb. 14, 1859 (33rd) | 97,073 sq. mi.<br>2,853,733 | ★Salem,<br>Portland,<br>Eugene | Western meadowlark<br>Oregon grape<br>Douglas fir |
| **Texas**<br>Dec. 29, 1845 (28th) | 266,807 sq. mi.<br>17,059,805 | ★Austin,<br>Houston, Dallas,<br>San Antonio, El Paso | Mockingbird<br>Bluebonnet<br>Pecan |
| **Utah**<br>Jan. 4, 1896 (45th) | 84,899 sq. mi.<br>1,727,784 | ★Salt Lake City,<br>Ogden,<br>Provo | Seagull<br>Sego lily<br>Blue spruce |
| **Washington**<br>Nov. 11, 1889 (42nd) | 68,139 sq. mi.<br>4,887,941 | ★Olympia,<br>Seattle, Spokane,<br>Tacoma | Willow goldfinch<br>Rhododendron<br>Western hemlock |
| **Wyoming**<br>July 10, 1890 (44th) | 97,809 sq. mi.<br>455,975 | ★Cheyenne,<br>Casper,<br>Laramie | Meadowlark<br>Indian paintbrush<br>Cottonwood |

**United States Today**

*Microsoft office, Redmond, Washington*

*Sandstone buttes, Monument Valley, Utah*

| *Land/Climate* | *Economy* |
| --- | --- |
| Predominantly desert basin with low ranges of hills running north-south; arid climate of hot days and cool nights | Tourism; mining of ores including copper and gold; cattle ranches; electronic and chemical manufactures |
| Mountains in north, Great Plains in east, arid plateau in west; dry and sunny, with warm days and cool nights throughout the year | Oil, natural gas, and mining of specialized ores including uranium; cattle ranching; tourism; manufacture of food goods and electrical parts |
| Central lowland, with high plains to west and hilly plateau to east; moderate climate, with rainfall greater in east than west | Drilling of oil and natural gas, with related refining industries; extensive farmland devoted to livestock and feed grains |
| Coastal ranges and Cascade Mountains in west, with elevated plateau in east; mild and rainy near coast, with drier continental climate inland | Wheat, potatoes, cattle, and sheep; lumber; tourism; mining of nickel ore |
| Complex topography surrounding southern Gulf Plain and central high plains; warm and rainy near coast, cooler and drier inland | Oil and natural gas; mineral refining and diversified manufacturing; U.S. leader in beef cattle, sheep, and cotton |
| Mountains in northeast, plateau in southeast, arid basin in west; extremely dry, with mild winters and hot summers | Manufacture of transportation and aerospace equipment, and food goods; copper, oil, and coal mining; dairy livestock and sheep; tourism |
| Coastal ranges and central Cascade Mountains with eastern plateau; mild and rainy in west, with drier continental climate in east | Manufacture of aircraft and transportation equipment, and lumber products; wheat crops and livestock; tourism; timber |
| Central mountains, southwest arid basin, eastern plains; generally cool and dry, with variations with elevation | Drilling of oil and natural gas and mining of ores; cattle ranching; tourism; wheat |

# The Midwest

The Midwestern region takes in twelve states that stretch from the edge of the Rocky Mountains in the west to the Appalachians in the east. The half of the region west of the Mississippi River is mainly devoted to agriculture, while the half to the east is a major industrial region. These states, clustering around the Great Lakes, were all part of the Northwest Territories, which became part of the United States in the settlement ending the Revolutionary War. The lands west of the Mississippi were part of the Louisiana Purchase and were bought from France in 1803.

The three most populous Midwestern states are Illinois, Ohio, and Michigan. These three are the industrial giants of the region. They are the homes of several major steel companies and of the major U.S. automobile manufacturers. The less densely populated western states constitute the greatest food-producing region in the country and one of the most productive in the world. The major crops include wheat, corn, hogs, and cattle. The northern parts of Minnesota, Wisconsin, and Michigan are heavily wooded and filled with small lakes. The only mountains in the region are the Ozarks, which cover the southern half of Missouri and extend south into Arkansas.

In area, the Midwest is about a third the size of the Western region. In population, with about 62 million, it is four-fifths as large. The people in the Midwest are concentrated especially around such large cities as Chicago, Detroit, Cleveland, St. Louis, and Minneapolis-St. Paul. Between 1970 and 1990, however, the region's industries lost out to foreign competition and laid off thousands of workers. As a result, the region has lost millions of its residents to migration. These migrants have moved to the South and Southwest, leaving the Midwest with only a very small population increase from the excess of births over deaths and migration.

The northern reaches of the Midwest have the most severe cold in the country outside of the interior of Alaska. The Dakotas and northern Minnesota often register the coldest temperatures in the nation. The states west of the Mississippi are accustomed to occasional violent weather: tornadoes and thunderstorms in the warm months and blizzards in the winter.

| State name<br>Date entered union | Area (rank)<br>Population (rank)<br>Est. 1990 | Capital<br>Principal cities | Bird<br>Flower<br>Tree |
|---|---|---|---|
| **Illinois**<br>Dec. 3, 1818 (21st) | 56,345 sq. mi.<br>11,466,682 | ★Springfield,<br>Chicago, Peoria,<br>Rockford | Cardinal<br>Violet<br>White oak |
| **Indiana**<br>Dec. 11, 1816 (19th) | 36,185 sq. mi.<br>5,564,228 | ★Indianapolis,<br>Gary, Evansville,<br>South Bend | Cardinal<br>Peony<br>Tulip poplar |
| **Iowa**<br>Dec. 28, 1846 (29th) | 56,275 sq. mi.<br>2,787,424 | ★Des Moines,<br>Cedar Rapids,<br>Davenport | Eastern goldfinch<br>Wild rose<br>Oak |
| **Kansas**<br>Jan. 29, 1861 (34th) | 82,277 sq. mi.<br>2,485,600 | ★Topeka,<br>Kansas City,<br>Wichita | Western meadowlark<br>Sunflower<br>Cottonwood |
| **Michigan**<br>Jan. 26, 1837 (26th) | 58,527 sq. mi.<br>9,328,784 | ★Lansing,<br>Detroit, Flint,<br>Grand Rapids | Robin<br>Apple blossom<br>White pine |

| Land/Climate | Economy |
|---|---|
| Predominantly rolling plains with elevations rising toward south; temperate climate of hot summers and cold, snowy winters | Major manufacturer of food and machine products; large corn harvest and extensive dairy farming; mining of coal, oil, natural gas |
| Central lowland plateau with Great Lakes Plain in north; long, hot summers and cold snowy winters | Manufacturing of primary metal, electrical, and food products; corn crops and hog farms; tourism; mineral fuels and stone quarrying |
| Uniform plain breaking into rolling lands in east; humid continental climate with long warm summers | Leading agricultural state with largest U.S. yield of corn and hogs; manufacturing sector based on farm machinery and meat packing |
| Plains throughout, with higher elevations at east and west extremes; variable continental climate notable for sudden changes | Major agricultural state, with largest U.S. wheat crop; manufacturing of food goods and aircraft; mining of natural gas |
| Upper peninsula of mountains and uplands and lower peninsula of lowland plains; warm summers and cold winters, most severe in north | Manufacturing of automobiles, machinery, chemicals; orchard crops and dairy farming; tourism; mining of iron ore, stone, natural gas |

Midwestern cornfields

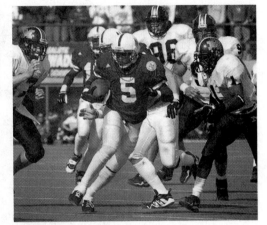
Football, Nebraska

| State name<br>Date entered union | Area<br>Population<br>Est. 1990 | Capital<br>Principal cities | Bird<br>Flower<br>Tree |
|---|---|---|---|
| **Minnesota**<br>May 11, 1858 (32nd) | 84,402 sq. mi.<br>4,387,029 | ★St. Paul,<br>Minneapolis,<br>Duluth | Common loon<br>Showy lady's slipper<br>Red pine |
| **Missouri**<br>Aug. 10, 1821 (24th) | 69,697 sq. mi.<br>5,137,804 | ★Jefferson City,<br>St. Louis,<br>Kansas City | Bluebird<br>Hawthorn<br>Dogwood |
| **Nebraska**<br>March 1, 1867 (37th) | 77,355 sq. mi.<br>1,584,617 | ★Lincoln,<br>Omaha | Western meadowlark<br>Goldenrod<br>Cottonwood |
| **North Dakota**<br>Nov. 2, 1889 (39th) | 70,702 sq. mi.<br>641,364 | ★Bismarck,<br>Fargo | Western meadowlark<br>Wild prairie rose<br>American elm |
| **Ohio**<br>March 1, 1803 (17th) | 41,330 sq. mi.<br>10,887,325 | ★Columbus,<br>Cleveland, Cincinnati,<br>Toledo, Dayton | Cardinal<br>Scarlet carnation<br>Buckeye |
| **South Dakota**<br>Nov. 2, 1889 (40th) | 77,116 sq. mi.<br>699,999 | ★Pierre,<br>Sioux Falls,<br>Rapid City | Ring-necked pheasant<br>Pasqueflower<br>Black Hills spruce |
| **Wisconsin**<br>May 29, 1848 (30th) | 56,153 sq. mi.<br>4,906,745 | ★Madison,<br>Milwaukee,<br>Racine | Robin<br>Wood violet<br>Sugar maple |

Automobile assembly line, Michigan

Mt. Rushmore, South Dakota

| *Land / Climate* | *Economy* |
|---|---|
| Hill and lake region with plain to northwest and mountainous uplands to northeast; cold and dry climate, most severe in north | Extensive dairy farming and largest U.S. oat crop; iron ore mining in northeast Mesabi range; food processing; tourism |
| Plains and rolling hills in north, rugged Ozark Plateau in south; cold winters and long, hot summers with rain heaviest in north | Agricultural state with northern corn crop, southern cotton crop, cattle and dairy livestock throughout; manufacturing; zinc mining |
| Great Plains over 80 percent of state area, with central lowlands to the east; dry climate with long, warm summers and severe winters | Major agricultural state, second only to Texas in beef cattle; grower of large corn and wheat harvests; manufacturing of food goods |
| Eastern river lowland rising to central prairie and western plateau; dry continental climate with cool summer nights and severe winters | 95 percent of state farmland devoted to livestock and feed crops; coal and oil fuels; mineral refining |
| Rolling plains of central lowland with Great Lakes Plain in north; temperate climate with hot, humid summers and cold winters | Manufacturing of steel, machinery, transportation equipment; dairy farming; tourism; mining of fuels and stone |
| Predominantly Great Plains, with Black Hills in west and Prairie-plains in east; dry climate of dramatic seasonal temperature extremes | Farms principally devoted to livestock, wheat, and corn for feed; manufacturing based on food processing; first in United States in gold mining |
| Northern rolling uplands and southern lowland plains; long, cold winters with heavy snows and short, warm summers | Manufacturing of machinery, foods, and paper goods; dairy farms and corn and oat crops; tourism; lumber |

# The South

The South consists of 14 states and the District of Columbia, and occupies the southeastern part of the United States. It is bordered on two sides by water: the Atlantic Ocean is to the east and the Gulf of Mexico is to the south. Most of its northern border is defined by the Ohio River. The region is divided into eastern and western sections by the crest of the Appalachian Mountains.

Six Southern states were among the original 13 states—Delaware, Maryland, Virginia, North Carolina, South Carolina, and Georgia. Important battles of the Revolutionary War were fought in North and South Carolina, and the final surrender of British troops took place at Yorktown, Virginia.

Less than 100 years later, most of the South-ern states seceded from the Union to form the Confederate States of America, setting in motion the Civil War. After the defeat of the Confederacy, in 1865, the Southern states joined the Union once again.

The most populous state in the South today is Florida, followed by Georgia, North Carolina, and Virginia. These states grew rapidly between 1970 and 1990, attracting many new residents from the Northeast and Midwest. The region's total population in 1996 was almost 71 million, about 9 million more than that of the Midwest. The region's largest cities include Baltimore, Md.; Memphis, Tenn.; Washington, D.C.; New Orleans, La.; and Atlanta, Ga., which was the host city for the 1996 Summer Olympics.

| State name<br>Date entered union | Area<br>Population<br>Est. 1990 | Capital<br>Principal cities | Bird<br>Flower<br>Tree |
|---|---|---|---|
| **Alabama**<br>Dec. 14, 1819 (22nd) | 51,705 sq. mi.<br>4,062,608 | ★Montgomery,<br>Birmingham, Mobile,<br>Huntsville | Yellowhammer<br>Camellia<br>Southern pine |
| **Arkansas**<br>June 15, 1836 (25th) | 53,187 sq. mi.<br>2,362,239 | ★Little Rock,<br>Pine Bluff,<br>Hot Springs | Mockingbird<br>Apple blossom<br>Pine |
| **Delaware**<br>Dec. 7, 1787 (1st) | 2044 sq. mi.<br>668,696 | ★Dover,<br>Wilmington,<br>Newark | Blue hen chicken<br>Peach blossom<br>American holly |
| **Florida**<br>March 3, 1845 (27th) | 58,664 sq. mi.<br>13,003,362 | ★Tallahassee,<br>Miami, Tampa,<br>Jacksonville | Mockingbird<br>Orange blossom<br>Sabal palm |
| **Georgia**<br>Jan. 2, 1788 (4th) | 58,910 sq. mi.<br>6,508,419 | ★Atlanta,<br>Columbus, Savannah,<br>Macon | Brown thrasher<br>Cherokee rose<br>Live oak |
| **Kentucky**<br>June 1, 1792 (15th) | 40,409 sq. mi.<br>3,698,969 | ★Frankfort,<br>Louisville,<br>Lexington | Cardinal<br>Goldenrod<br>Coffeetree |
| **Louisiana**<br>April 30, 1812 (18th) | 47,752 sq. mi.<br>4,238,216 | ★Baton Rouge,<br>New Orleans,<br>Shreveport | Eastern brown pelican<br>Magnolia blossom<br>Bald cypress |

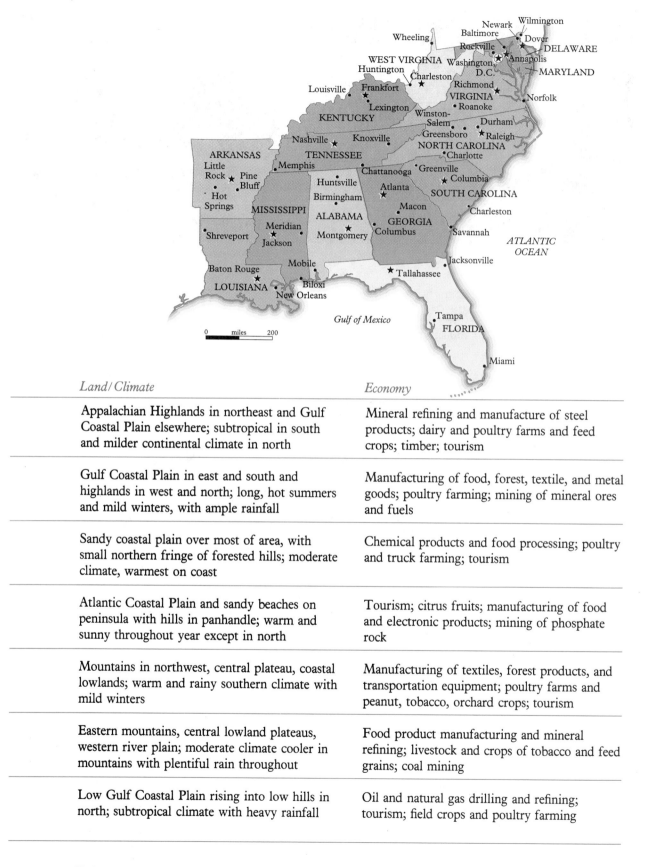

| Land/Climate | Economy |
|---|---|
| Appalachian Highlands in northeast and Gulf Coastal Plain elsewhere; subtropical in south and milder continental climate in north | Mineral refining and manufacture of steel products; dairy and poultry farms and feed crops; timber; tourism |
| Gulf Coastal Plain in east and south and highlands in west and north; long, hot summers and mild winters, with ample rainfall | Manufacturing of food, forest, textile, and metal goods; poultry farming; mining of mineral ores and fuels |
| Sandy coastal plain over most of area, with small northern fringe of forested hills; moderate climate, warmest on coast | Chemical products and food processing; poultry and truck farming; tourism |
| Atlantic Coastal Plain and sandy beaches on peninsula with hills in panhandle; warm and sunny throughout year except in north | Tourism; citrus fruits; manufacturing of food and electronic products; mining of phosphate rock |
| Mountains in northwest, central plateau, coastal lowlands; warm and rainy southern climate with mild winters | Manufacturing of textiles, forest products, and transportation equipment; poultry farms and peanut, tobacco, orchard crops; tourism |
| Eastern mountains, central lowland plateaus, western river plain; moderate climate cooler in mountains with plentiful rain throughout | Food product manufacturing and mineral refining; livestock and crops of tobacco and feed grains; coal mining |
| Low Gulf Coastal Plain rising into low hills in north; subtropical climate with heavy rainfall | Oil and natural gas drilling and refining; tourism; field crops and poultry farming |

*Jazz band, New Orleans*

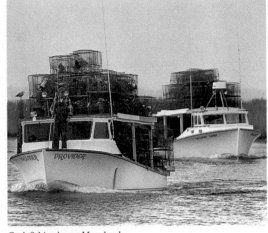

*Crab fishing boats, Maryland*

| State name<br>Date entered union | Area<br>Population<br>Est. 1990 | Capital<br>Principal cities | Bird<br>Flower<br>Tree |
|---|---|---|---|
| **Maryland**<br>April 28, 1788 (7th) | 10,460 sq. mi.<br>4,798,622 | ★Annapolis,<br>Baltimore,<br>Rockville | Baltimore oriole<br>Black-eyed Susan<br>White oak |
| **Mississippi**<br>Dec. 10, 1817 (20th) | 47,689 sq. mi.<br>2,586,443 | ★Jackson,<br>Biloxi,<br>Meridian | Mockingbird<br>Magnolia blossom<br>Magnolia |
| **North Carolina**<br>Nov. 21, 1789 (12th) | 52,669 sq. mi.<br>6,657,630 | ★Raleigh,<br>Charlotte, Greensboro,<br>Winston-Salem,<br>Durham | Cardinal<br>Dogwood blossom<br>Pine |
| **South Carolina**<br>May 23, 1788 (8th) | 31,113 sq. mi.<br>3,505,707 | ★Columbia,<br>Charleston,<br>Greenville | Carolina wren<br>Yellow jasmine<br>Palmetto |
| **Tennessee**<br>June 1, 1796 (16th) | 42,144 sq. mi.<br>4,896,641 | ★Nashville,<br>Memphis, Knoxville,<br>Chattanooga | Mockingbird<br>Iris<br>Tulip poplar |
| **Virginia**<br>June 25, 1788 (10th) | 40,767 sq. mi.<br>6,216,568 | ★Richmond,<br>Norfolk,<br>Roanoke | Cardinal<br>Dogwood blossom<br>Flowering dogwood |
| **West Virginia**<br>June 20, 1863 (35th) | 24,231 sq. mi.<br>1,801,625 | ★Charleston,<br>Huntington,<br>Wheeling | Cardinal<br>Big rhododendron<br>Sugar maple |
| **Washington, D.C.** | 68 sq. mi.<br>607,000 | | Wood thrush<br>American beauty rose<br>Scarlet oak |

*Blue Ridge Mountains, Virginia*

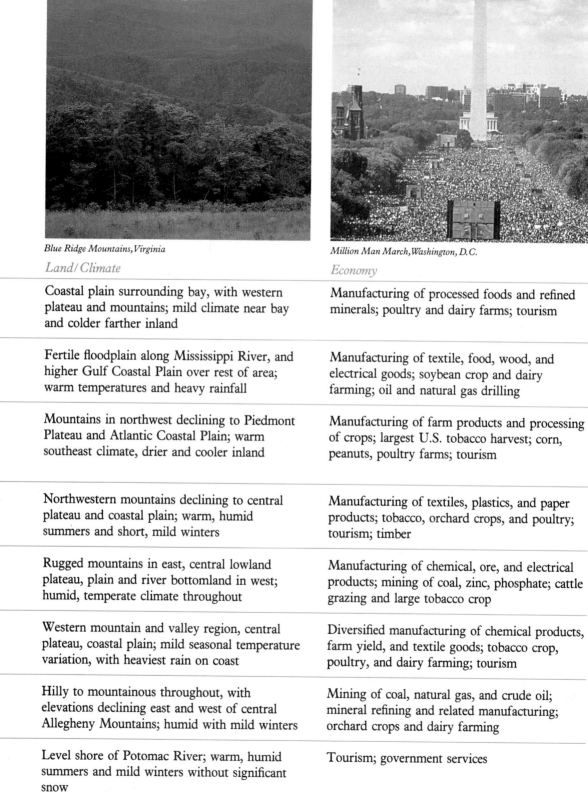
*Million Man March, Washington, D.C.*

| *Land/Climate* | *Economy* |
| --- | --- |
| Coastal plain surrounding bay, with western plateau and mountains; mild climate near bay and colder farther inland | Manufacturing of processed foods and refined minerals; poultry and dairy farms; tourism |
| Fertile floodplain along Mississippi River, and higher Gulf Coastal Plain over rest of area; warm temperatures and heavy rainfall | Manufacturing of textile, food, wood, and electrical goods; soybean crop and dairy farming; oil and natural gas drilling |
| Mountains in northwest declining to Piedmont Plateau and Atlantic Coastal Plain; warm southeast climate, drier and cooler inland | Manufacturing of farm products and processing of crops; largest U.S. tobacco harvest; corn, peanuts, poultry farms; tourism |
| Northwestern mountains declining to central plateau and coastal plain; warm, humid summers and short, mild winters | Manufacturing of textiles, plastics, and paper products; tobacco, orchard crops, and poultry; tourism; timber |
| Rugged mountains in east, central lowland plateau, plain and river bottomland in west; humid, temperate climate throughout | Manufacturing of chemical, ore, and electrical products; mining of coal, zinc, phosphate; cattle grazing and large tobacco crop |
| Western mountain and valley region, central plateau, coastal plain; mild seasonal temperature variation, with heaviest rain on coast | Diversified manufacturing of chemical products, farm yield, and textile goods; tobacco crop, poultry, and dairy farming; tourism |
| Hilly to mountainous throughout, with elevations declining east and west of central Allegheny Mountains; humid with mild winters | Mining of coal, natural gas, and crude oil; mineral refining and related manufacturing; orchard crops and dairy farming |
| Level shore of Potomac River; warm, humid summers and mild winters without significant snow | Tourism; government services |

# The Northeast

The Northeast is the smallest of the four U.S. regions, both in area and population. Its nine states take up an area just slightly larger than that of California. Although it is smaller in population than the other regions, its 52 million people are more densely settled than those in other regions. The Northeast has nearly 20 percent of the country's people on less than 5 percent of its land.

The Atlantic shores of the Northeast were settled in the 1600's, mostly by English colonists. Seven of its states were among the original 13. The Declaration of Independence was proclaimed in Philadelphia, and the Revolutionary War began near Boston. During the Civil War, all the Northeastern states were part of the Union. The only major battle of that war fought in the Northeast was the battle of Gettysburg in Pennsylvania.

Before and after the Civil War, the Northeast became the settling place for millions of immigrants from Europe. Even today, the region claims a large proportion of descendants from Ireland, Italy, Germany, and Eastern Europe.

The most populous state in the region is New York. Other populous states are Pennsylvania, New Jersey, and Massachusetts. New Jersey is the most densely populated state in the Union, with almost 1100 residents per square mile. New York and Rhode Island both lost population between 1970 and 1980. All of the states gained population between 1980 and 1990. New Hampshire and Vermont had the highest percentage of gains.

The region's most important city is New York, which is the largest in the United States. Most of its other large cities lie in a corridor that stretches from New York north to Boston and south to Philadelphia and Washington, D.C. Important cities to the west include Pittsburgh and Buffalo.

| State name<br>Date entered union | Area<br>Population<br>Est. 1990 | Capital<br>Principal cities | Bird<br>Flower<br>Tree |
|---|---|---|---|
| **Connecticut**<br>Jan. 9, 1788 (5th) | 5018 sq. mi.<br>3,295,669 | ★Hartford,<br>Bridgeport,<br>New Haven | American robin<br>Mountain laurel<br>White oak |
| **Maine**<br>March 15, 1820 (23rd) | 33,265 sq. mi.<br>1,233,223 | ★Augusta,<br>Portland, Lewiston,<br>Bangor | Chickadee<br>White pine cone and tassel<br>White pine |
| **Massachusetts**<br>Feb. 6, 1788 (6th) | 8284 sq. mi.<br>6,029,051 | ★Boston,<br>Springfield, Worcester,<br>Lowell | Chickadee<br>Mayflower<br>American elm |
| **New Hampshire**<br>June 21, 1788 (9th) | 9279 sq. mi.<br>1,113,915 | ★Concord,<br>Manchester, Nashua,<br>Portsmouth | Purple finch<br>Purple lilac<br>White birch |
| **New Jersey**<br>Dec. 18, 1787 (3rd) | 7787 sq. mi.<br>7,748,634 | ★Trenton,<br>Newark, Camden,<br>Paterson | Eastern goldfinch<br>Purple violet<br>Red oak |
| **New York**<br>July 26, 1788 (11th) | 49,108 sq. mi.<br>18,044,505 | ★Albany,<br>New York, Buffalo,<br>Rochester, Syracuse | Bluebird<br>Rose<br>Sugar maple |

| Land/Climate | Economy |
|---|---|
| New England Uplands to east and west of central river valley; moderate climate, coldest in northwest areas | Diversified manufactures, including aircraft engines; national insurance companies; dairy farming; tourism |
| Northeast uplands, central White Mountains, southeast coastal lowlands; cold winters with heavy snows inland and cool summers | Manufacturing of wood pulp, leather, and textile goods; tourism; dairy farming and potato crop |
| New England Uplands in interior and sandy seaboard lowlands along eastern coast; temperate in east and colder and drier inland | Manufacturer of electrical, textile, machine, and printing goods; tourism; dairy farms and greenhouse vegetables |
| All hilly uplands surrounding White Mountains except for coastal lowland; severe winters in uplands, with moderate temperatures on coast | Manufacturing of leather, wood pulp, and electronic equipment; tourism; dairy farming |
| Hilly, forested northern half and flat, sandy south; moderate northeastern climate | Diversified manufacturing notable for chemical products; tourism at coastal beaches; truck farming in south |
| Appalachian Plateau and mountains over most of area, with Great Lakes Plain to north; moderate climate southeast, colder inland | Second only to California in diversified manufactures; tourism; dairy livestock with orchard, vineyard, and greenhouse crops |

Theater, New York City

Yale University, New Haven

| State name Date entered union | Area Population Est. 1990 | Capital Principal cities | Bird Flower Tree |
|---|---|---|---|
| **Pennsylvania** Dec. 12, 1787 (2nd) | 45,308 sq. mi. 11,924,710 | ★Harrisburg, Philadelphia, Pittsburgh, Scranton, Erie | Ruffed grouse Mountain laurel Hemlock |
| **Rhode Island** May 29, 1790 (13th) | 1212 sq. mi. 1,005,984 | ★Providence, Warwick, Pawtucket | Rhode Island red hen Violet Red maple |
| **Vermont** March 4, 1791 (14th) | 9614 sq. mi. 564,964 | ★Montpelier, Burlington, Rutland | Hermit thrush Red clover Sugar maple |

# U.S. territories

The United States held numerous overseas possessions early in the 1900's. Today, however, it retains possession of only a few. The largest by far is the Caribbean island of Puerto Rico.

Near Puerto Rico are the U.S. Virgin Islands.

The remainder of U.S. territories are in the Pacific Ocean. The largest of these is the western Pacific island of Guam.

| Official name | Location | Area/Population Est. 1990 |
|---|---|---|
| **American Samoa** | In south Pacific 2500 miles east of Australia | 77 sq. mi.; 43,052 |
| **Guam** | In west Pacific 1200 miles east of the Philippines | 209 sq. mi.; 144,978 |

152

*Liberty Bell, Philadelphia*

*Vermont village*

| Land/Climate | Economy |
|---|---|
| Central Allegheny Mountains with rugged plateau north and west and plain to southeast; moderate climate in east and colder in western interior | Manufacturing ranging from heavy coal industries in west to food and electronic products in east; dairy livestock; tourism |
| Sandy seaboard lowlands rising to hill and lake region in northwest; moderate climate influenced by inland bay | Manufactures include machinery, textiles, and electronics; tourism; truck and dairy farming |
| Hilly throughout with central spine of Green Mountains; short, warm summers and long winters with heavy snowfall | Manufacturing of machine tools and electronic equipment; tourism; dairy farms and maple syrup |

| Official name | Location | Area/Population |
|---|---|---|
| **Midway Islands** | In Pacific Ocean 1000 miles northwest of Hawaii | 2 sq.mi.; 453 |
| **Puerto Rico** | Caribbean island east of Dominican Republic | 3535 sq.mi.; 3,294,997 |
| **Virgin Islands** | Caribbean islands 40 miles east of Puerto Rico | 133 sq.mi.; 99,404 |
| **Wake Island** | In Pacific Ocean 2000 miles west of Hawaii | 3 sq.mi.; 302 |

# Mathematics

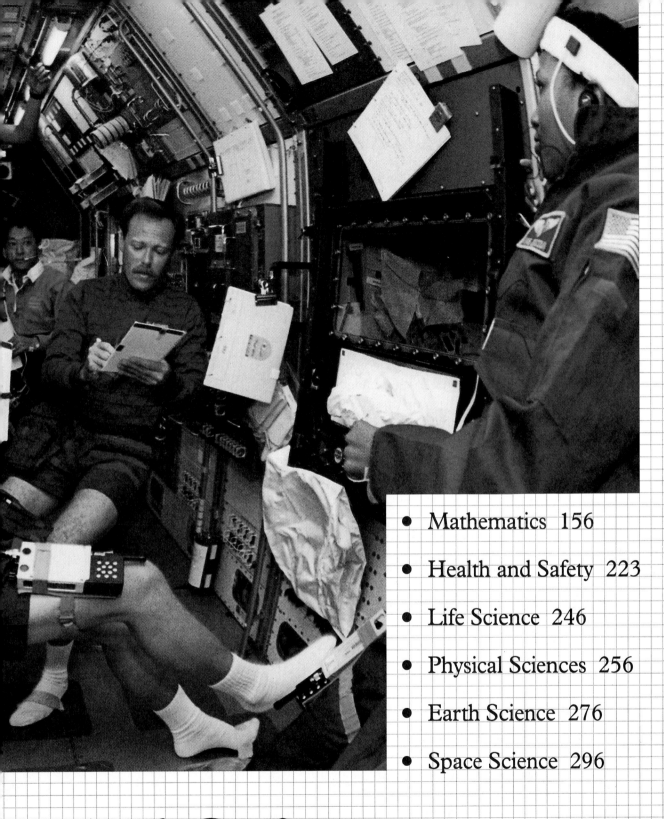

# and Science

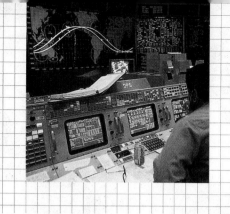

# Mathematics

As you learn mathematics in school, you may find that it takes longer and longer to understand some problems. Or you may forget how to do a certain problem. Or you may need another way to work a problem. You will find the help you need in these pages. There are examples and problems like the ones you have in school, all worked out. When you need help in memorizing the basic facts of addition, subtraction, multiplication, and division, you will find that help in these pages as well.

# Whole numbers

When you do arithmetic, you use ten digits, or numerals: 0, 1, 2, 3, 4, 5, 6, 7, 8, and 9. So we say that our system of numbering is a decimal system — a base-ten system.

**Place value.** A number like 5 is read 5. But what happens to that number when you write a 1 before it, or a 0 after it? Its value changes. The value of a digit or numeral, or its place value, depends on its place in a number. So the 1 before 5 becomes 15, with 5 in the ones place. Writing 0 after 5 makes it 50, with the 5 in the tens place. As you can see, a number's position makes quite a differ-

ence. In order to add, subtract, multiply, and divide numbers correctly, you must pay careful attention to place value.

To see how place value works, look at the number 37.

$$37 = 3 \text{ tens} + 7 \text{ ones}$$
$$= 30 + 7$$

The place, or position, of the 7 tells you that its value is seven ones—or 7. The position of the 3 tells you that its value is three tens—or 30. The 7 is in

**Mathematics**

the ones place or ones column and the 3 is in the tens place or tens column.

In a three-digit number like 204, the position of the 2 tells you that its value is two hundreds. The position of the 0 is that of a place holder, meaning that there are no tens in this number. The value of 4 is four ones.

In a four-digit number like 4932, the position of the 4 tells you that its value is four thousands, the position of the 9 tells you that its value is nine hundreds, the position of the 3 tells you that its value is three tens, and 2 is in ones place.

**Using place value in renaming numbers.** Renaming numbers is just another way of breaking them down into smaller parts, or expanding them. Knowing how to write a number in expanded form or expanded notation will help you to add, subtract, multiply, and divide. For example, 37 in expanded notation would look like this:

30 + 7.

The three-digit number 204 is 200 + 0 + 4 in expanded notation. And 4932 would look like this:

4000 + 900 + 30 + 2.

**Using place value in rounding numbers.** You round numbers to remember them more easily. For example, 400 is easier to remember than 378.

Numbers can be rounded to the nearest tens place, hundreds place, thousands place, ten thousands place, and so on. You use place value by finding the number's position on the chart.

*Example 1*:   Round 23 to the nearest ten.

The number to the right of 2 is 3, and 3 is less than 5. Replace 3 with 0. 23 rounded to the nearest ten becomes 20.

*Example 2*:   Round 27 to the nearest ten.

The number to the right of 2 is 7, and 7 is more than 4. The rounded number is 30.

In each of these examples, find the place in the number to which you are rounding. In 23 and 27, 2 is in the tens place. Look one place to the right, or to the ones place in the examples above. If the digit or number in that place is less than 5, *round down*. To round down, replace the digit to the right of the place you found in the first step with 0. The 0 mean that there are no ones. So 23 is rounded down to 20.

In 27, the 2 is in the tens place, and the 7 at the right is greater than 5. In that case, *round up*. To round up, increase the digit in the tens place, or 2 in this example, to 3 and replace the digit to the right with 0. So 27 rounded up becomes 30.

These rules for rounding apply to all numbers and whatever places they are rounded to. More examples are shown below:

*Example 3:* Round 7245 to the nearest ten.

Four is in the tens place, and the number to the right of 4 is 5. You must round up, so 7245 becomes 7250.

*Example 4:* Round 843 to the nearest hundred.

Four is in the tens place, and the number to the right of 4 is 3. Since both 3 and 4 are less than 5, you must round down. So 843 is rounded to 800.

Visualize it this way: 843 is between 800 and 900.

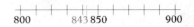

850 is halfway between 800 and 900. 843 is closer to 800.

## Rounding numbers with your calculator

Most calculators do not round numbers. If you divide 10 by 6, the answer will be given as 1.666666. In some cases, you can correct the calculator's rounding to improve accuracy. Most of the time, however, you can use one less place and round the answer that is shown on the calculator. For example, change 1.666666 to 1.66667.

# Addition

**Everyday addition.** You use addition when you find out how much several gifts cost altogether. You also add to find the number of hours you studied in one week. If you are a member of a team, you must add to find the total number of points of your team's score. If you wish to place a border around your garden, you must add the length of each side of the plot of land to find the perimeter. As you can see, addition is used in many ways.

**Adding whole numbers.** Addition is a binary operation, which means that you can add only two numbers at a time. These numbers tell the size of a group and are called addends. Your answer is called a sum or total. This number tells you how many or how much you have altogether.

Addition is based on a set of basic facts that you should memorize. If you forget a fact, you can still find the answer. Here are some hints:

1. **Use doubles or near doubles.** You may find facts such as 2 + 2 = 4 or 8 + 8 = 16 easy to remember. These facts are known as doubles. Facts such as 6 + 7 and 7 + 9 are near doubles. To find sums such as 6 + 7, think of 6 + 6 = 12, so 6 + 7 = 13. Even 7 + 9 is easy to remember when you start with 7 + 7 = 14. Then add 2 and you will have the answer, 16. So 7 + 9 = 16. To understand how this works, try other doubles, such as 4 + 4 = 8. In an example like 4 + 5 = 9, you count one more. In 4 + 6 = 10, you count two more.

2. **Use tens.** To add 8 + 5, think 8 + 2 = 10 and 5 = 2 + 3, so 8 + 5 = 10 + 3, or 13.

3. **Count if you have to.** Addition is based on counting. For example, add 7 + 4 by counting to the answer: 8, 9, 10, 11.

4. **Switch addends.** If you have forgotten the answer to 6 + 4, all you have to do is turn this problem around to 4 + 6. You can change the order of the addends and still get the same sum.

## Basic addition facts

| + | 0 | 1 | 2 | 3 | 4 | 5 | 6 | 7 | 8 | 9 |
|---|---|---|---|---|---|---|---|---|---|---|
| 0 | 0 | 1 | 2 | 3 | 4 | 5 | 6 | 7 | 8 | 9 |
| 1 | 1 | 2 | 3 | 4 | 5 | 6 | 7 | 8 | 9 | 10 |
| 2 | 2 | 3 | 4 | 5 | 6 | 7 | 8 | 9 | 10 | 11 |
| 3 | 3 | 4 | 5 | 6 | 7 | 8 | 9 | 10 | 11 | 12 |
| 4 | 4 | 5 | 6 | 7 | 8 | 9 | 10 | 11 | 12 | 13 |
| 5 | 5 | 6 | 7 | 8 | 9 | 10 | 11 | 12 | 13 | 14 |
| 6 | 6 | 7 | 8 | 9 | 10 | 11 | 12 | 13 | 14 | 15 |
| 7 | 7 | 8 | 9 | 10 | 11 | 12 | 13 | 14 | 15 | 16 |
| 8 | 8 | 9 | 10 | 11 | 12 | 13 | 14 | 15 | 16 | 17 |
| 9 | 9 | 10 | 11 | 12 | 13 | 14 | 15 | 16 | 17 | 18 |

5. **Use the table.** *Example:*

$$\begin{array}{r} 5 \\ +3 \\ \hline \end{array}$$

You can solve this problem by using the table of basic addition facts. Read down to row 5 (see the arrow on the side of the table) and across to column 3 (see the arrow at the top of the table.) Row 5 and column 3 meet at the number 8, which is the answer.

$$\begin{array}{r} 5 \\ +3 \\ \hline 8 \end{array}$$

*A baseball scoreboard is an example of simple addition. Add the number of runs for each inning to get the final score.*

**Memorizing the basic addition facts**. In order to do addition problems quickly, you should memorize the basic addition facts. These facts are 1 + 1 = 2, 1 + 2 = 3, 1 + 3 = 4, and so on. All of them appear in the table of basic addition facts on page 159.

The best way to memorize the addition facts is by using them as much as possible.

*Example:*
```
   4
   3
 +6
```

You can use the table of basic addition facts to solve this problem if you break it up into two steps.

Add one pair of numbers.

```
  4 }
  3 } 7
+6
```

Add this sum to the third number.

```
   7
 +6
 ──
  13
```

**Adding two-digit numbers.** To add two-digit numbers, such as 27, to other numbers, you can use counters. They often help you understand how whole numbers are used:

▪ stands for, or represents, one unit.

▮ stands for, or represents, ten units.

A number, such as 23, can be shown as

You can use counters to add 23 to other numbers.

*Example:*
```
   23
 + 5
```

First show 23 as two ten units and three one units and place five units on the other side:

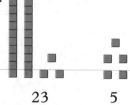

23          5

Count the smaller units, or ones, first, and get 8 as the answer. The number of ten units is still 2. The answer to this problem is 28.

Often, you will be adding two larger numbers, such as the numbers below:

```
   23
 +12
```

Show 23 as two ten units and three one units. Then show 12 as one ten unit and two one units.

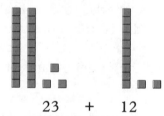

23     +     12

Add the single units first.

```
 ▪                    23
▪▪ ▪▪                +12
                      ──
3  +  2                5
```

Next, combine and add the tens units. There are three ten units. The answer to this problem is 35.

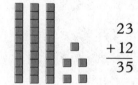

```
   23
 +12
 ──
  35
```

# Ten hints on memorizing addition facts

1. Do not try to memorize all of the facts at one time. Doing this makes it too hard to remember them later.

2. Do memorize a few at a time, say, five or ten facts in a week.

3. Do remember that changing the order of the numbers you add will not change the answer. For example, 2 + 4 is the same problem as 4 + 2. If you know that 2 + 4 equals 6, you also know that 4 + 2 equals 6. Now you only have half as many facts to remember.

4. Learn with a friend. Let your friend answer your questions on the facts. Then switch turns. How many facts does your friend know? How many do you know?

5. Make an addition table and fill it in. But do not stop there. Look at it more closely and you will see patterns.

6. Play games of addition by yourself. For example, toss two dice and add the dots that come up. Make or buy addition facts bingo to play with a friend. Let each game won be worth seven or twelve points. At the end of three or four games, you and the other player can add up your scores.

7. Make an addition diary. How did you use addition today? How did you see addition used by your family, friends, and teachers? Were large numbers used? In what other ways could the same answer have been obtained?

8. Use things to help you practice. On separate 3 x 5 cards, copy one fact without the answer. On the other side of each card, write the answer. Now mix up the cards and place them on a table facedown. Look at each card and write the answer to the fact. After you have used all of the cards, compare your answers. Then practice only those facts you answered incorrectly.

9. Use your clock. Work with one number at a time. For example, start with 2, add 3 and get 5. Start with 3, add 4 and get 7.

10. Begin practicing using difficult facts. Instead of studying what you probably know, such as 1 + 2 = 3, begin with facts such as 7 + 6 = 13.

$$\begin{array}{r} 23 \\ +\ 4 \\ \hline \end{array}$$

**A.** Add the numbers in the ones column. Then write the 7 at the bottom of the ones column.

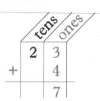

**B.** Add the numbers in the tens column.

$$\begin{array}{r} 2 \text{ tens} \\ +0 \text{ tens} \\ \hline 2 \text{ tens} \end{array}$$

**C.** Write the 2 at the bottom of the tens column. Your answer is 27.

$$\begin{array}{r} 27 \\ +\ 9 \\ \hline \end{array}$$

**A.** Add the ones.

$$\begin{array}{r} 7 \\ +9 \\ \hline 16 \end{array}$$

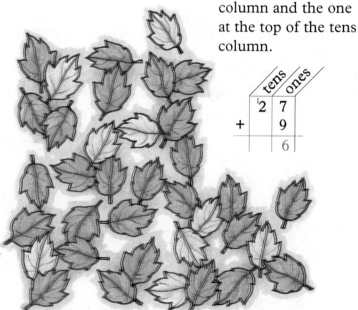

**B.** Rename 16 as one ten and six ones. Write the 6 at the bottom of the ones column and the one at the top of the tens column.

**C.** Add the tens.

$$\begin{array}{r} 2 \text{ tens} \\ +1 \text{ ten} \\ \hline 3 \text{ tens} \end{array}$$

**D.** Write the 3 at the bottom of the tens column. Your answer is 36.

Another way of adding this problem is counting nine numbers up from 27: 28, 29, 30, 31, 32, 33, 34, 35, 36.

$$\begin{array}{r} 13 \\ +44 \\ \hline \end{array}$$

**A.** Add the numbers in the ones column.

$$\begin{array}{r} 3 \\ +4 \\ \hline 7 \end{array}$$

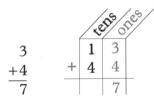

**B.** Add the numbers in the tens column.

$$\begin{array}{r} 1 \text{ ten} \\ +4 \text{ tens} \\ \hline 5 \text{ tens} \end{array}$$

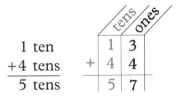

Write the 5 at the bottom of the tens column. Your answer is 57.

---

## Special help with carrying in addition

In many addition problems, you will have to bring a digit into the next value place. For example, if you are adding a column of numbers in the ones place and get 29 as the answer, write this answer with 9 in the ones place and bring, or "carry," 2 to the tens place. Once you have done this, you can add the column of numbers in the tens place.

Suppose you have to add
$$\begin{array}{r} 11 \\ +19 \end{array}$$

Begin adding in the ones place. Your answer will be 10. If you write the whole number 10 as shown, it will be wrong.

$$\begin{array}{r} 11 \\ +19 \\ \hline 10 \end{array}$$

This is incorrect because 10 means one ten and zero ones. The 1 belongs in the tens place column:

This is the one you carried ⟶

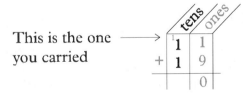

Now add the numbers in the tens column. Do not forget to add the one you carried to the tens place! The problem is done.

163

$$\begin{array}{r} 37 \\ +26 \\ \hline \end{array}$$

**A.** Add the numbers in the ones column.

$$\begin{array}{r} 7 \\ +6 \\ \hline 13 \end{array}$$

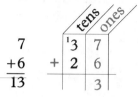

Rename 13 as one ten and three ones. With the 3 at the bottom of the ones column, write the 1 at the top of the tens column.

**B.** Add the numbers in the tens column.

1 ten
3 tens
+2 tens
___
6 tens

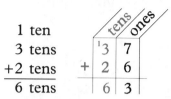

Write the 6 at the bottom of the tens column.

---

$$\begin{array}{r} 57 \\ +88 \\ \hline \end{array}$$

**A.** Add the numbers in the ones column.

$$\begin{array}{r} 7 \\ +8 \\ \hline 15 \end{array}$$

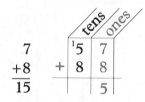

Rename 15 as one ten and five ones. Write the 5 at the bottom of the ones column and the 1 at the top of the tens column.

**B.** Add the numbers in the tens column.

1 ten
5 tens
+8 tens
___
14 tens

Rename 14 tens (or 140) as one hundred and four tens. Write the 4 at the bottom of the tens column and write the 1 at the top of the hundreds column.

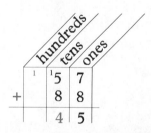

**C.** Add the numbers in the hundreds column.

1 hundred
+0 hundreds
___
1 hundred

Write the 1 at the bottom of the hundreds column.

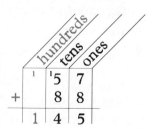

$$731$$
$$+569$$

**A.** Add the numbers in the ones column.

$$\begin{array}{r} 1 \\ +9 \\ \hline 10 \end{array}$$

Write the 0 at the bottom of the ones column and the 1 at the top of the tens column.

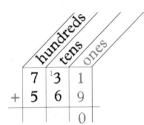

**B.** Add the numbers in the tens column.

$$\begin{array}{r} 1 \text{ ten} \\ 3 \text{ tens} \\ +6 \text{ tens} \\ \hline 10 \text{ tens} \end{array}$$

Write the 0 at the bottom of the tens column and the 1 at the top of the hundreds column.

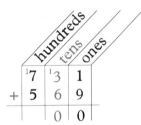

**C.** Add the numbers in the hundreds column.

$$\begin{array}{r} 1 \text{ hundred} \\ 7 \text{ hundreds} \\ + 5 \text{ hundreds} \\ \hline 13 \text{ hundreds} \end{array}$$

Write the 3 at the bottom of the hundreds column and the 1 at the top of the thousands column.

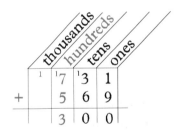

**D.** Add the numbers in the thousands column.

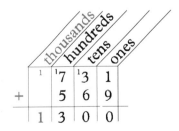

**Column addition:** Remember, you are still adding two numbers at a time. This means that you will always get the same answer no matter the order in which you add a group of addends.

Add    3
          4
     +6

To add this column, group any two numbers at a time.

1.    3 ⎫
       4 ⎭7
    +6
     ——
     13

2.    3
       4 ⎫
    +6 ⎭10
     ——
     13

---

768
395
+288

**A.** Add the numbers in the one column.

   8 ones
   5 ones
   8 ones
  ———
  21 ones

Rename 21 as two tens and one 1. Write the one in the ones column.

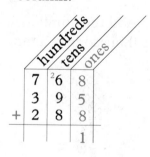

**B.** Add the numbers in the tens column.

   2 tens
   6 tens
   9 tens
   8 tens
  ———
  25 tens

Rename 25 as two tens and five ones. Write the 5 in the tens column.

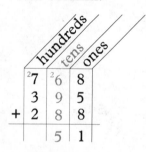

**C.** Add the numbers in the hundreds column.

   2 hundreds
   7 hundreds
   3 hundreds
   2 hundreds
  ———
  14 hundreds

Write down the 4 in the hundreds place and the 1 in the thousands place.

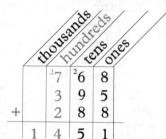

# Other ways to add

1. If you do not have time to find the exact sum, yet need an idea of the answer, round off and add the addends to get an estimate.

   *Example:* Round each number to the hundreds place. Find the hundreds place in each number and look at the digit to the right.

   $$2893$$
   $$532$$
   $$+1539$$

   Rounds to hundreds. Becomes

   $$2900$$
   $$500$$
   $$+1500$$
   $$\overline{4900}$$

2. Adding long columns of large numbers is not so hard when you add one column at a time and do not carry digits to the next place.

*Estimating is a way to count when an approximate sum is close enough, as for instance when counting the number of apples on the branches of a tree.*

*Example:*

$$3462$$
$$1048$$
$$9367$$
$$5290$$
$$+4738$$

| 25 | the sum of the ones |
| 28 | the sum of the tens |
| 16 | the sum of the hundreds |
| 22 | the sum of the thousands |
| 23905 | sum |

## Checking answers

If you are adding a column of numbers, start at the top of the first column and add down. To check your work, start at the bottom of the first column and add up. Or, if you began adding at the bottom originally, check your work by starting to add at the top of the first column and adding down.

Use estimation by rounding off numbers. Use a calculator.

## Using your calculator to check your work

Begin by pressing the first number, or addend, then the + button, then the next addend, and so on, until you have added the column. To get the answer, press the = symbol. The answer will appear in the display. Compare it with your written answer.

**Solving addition word problems**. In word problems, you are asked to use your knowledge of addition in various situations. To solve these problems, read each problem carefully. Then look at the problem's question. What is it asking you to find? If it asks you to tell how many there are in all, or the sum or total, you must add to find the answer.

---

José borrowed three books from the library on Wednesday, and two books on Friday. How many books did he borrow in all?

In this problem, you are asked to find the total of all the books José borrowed from the library in two days.

To find this number, add up the number of books.

3 books + 2 books = 5 books

---

One addend is 18. The sum is 46. Find the missing addend.

A. In this problem, you are given only one addend, 18, and the answer, or sum of 46. Show this information in the following way:

18 + □ = 46

B. To find the missing addend, you could count to 46 from 18 to find out how much more would be needed to get the sum. The answer is 28.

---

In some problems, you are told that someone has 18 cents and wants to buy an item that costs 46 cents. How much more money does he need? Or someone has traveled 18 miles on a trip that is 46 miles long. How many more miles does this person have to travel? To find the answer, write the problem in the same way as the one shown above and solve. Then check your answer by adding the addends and comparing your findings to the total given.

---

Kerry sold 140 tickets to the local trading card show on Monday, 215 tickets on Tuesday, 134 tickets on Wednesday, 322 tickets on Thursday, and 277 tickets on Friday. How many tickets did he sell in all?

A. In this problem, you are given all of the addends. You must simply add them to find the total number of tickets.

B. 140 + 215 + 134 + 322 + 277 = ?
The answer is 1088.

---

**Mathematics**

Donna and Kim made up and played a dice game.
On Donna's first turn, she scored 18 points, on her second turn,
10 points, and on her last turn, 24 points. When Kim played, she scored
15 points on her first turn, 30 points on her second turn, and 12 points
on her third turn. How many points did Donna score in all? What was
Kim's total score? Who would you say is winning the dice game?

**A.** This problem has more than one part. It first asks you to find Donna's total score. Remember that the word "total" means addition. So for the first part of this problem, add Donna's scores:

18 + 10 + 24 = 52

**B.** In the second part of this problem, you are asked to find Kim's total score. Again, this means add:

15 + 30 + 12 = 57

**C.** Finally, you are asked to compare the two total scores and decide who is winning so far. Kim has more points than Donna.

---

A sponsor of rock concerts estimated that at least 50,000 tickets would
be sold in 1994. During that year, the rock star performed in six
concerts. The number of tickets sold were 14,320, 26,089, 18,159,
17,763, 10,842, and 20,611. Was the sponsor's estimate correct?

**A.** One way of solving this problem is by rounding each number of tickets and adding these amounts. You will not get an exact number, but an estimate. The rounded amounts are:
14,000 + 26,000 + 18,000 + 18,000 + 11,000 + 21,000 = 108,000 estimated number of tickets sold.

**B.** If you compare the sponsor's estimate to the rounded total, you will see that the sponsor's estimate was well under the actual total. To find out the *exact* number of tickets sold, add the amounts.
14,320 + 26,089 + 18,159 + 17,763 + 10,842 + 20,611 = 107,784 actual number of tickets sold.

**C.** The problem only asked you if the sponsor was correct, not how many tickets were actually sold. All you needed to do was round off the number of tickets and add. The sponsor's estimate was actually very much under the estimated number of tickets sold.

In a spelling bee, Mark spelled 56 words, JoAnn spelled 58 words, Carrie spelled 42 words, Eddie spelled 63 words, Bob spelled 39 words, and Sue spelled 25 words. How many words were spelled altogether?

**A.** In this problem, the word "altogether" is an addition word. To do this problem, add up all of the words spelled by all of the children named to get the total number of words spelled by all of the children.

**B.** Mark's words + JoAnn's words + Carrie's words + Eddie's words + Bob's words + Sue's words = total number of words spelled. 56 + 58 + 42 + 63 + 39 + 25 = 283 words spelled altogether.

---

For a homework assignment, Rodney kept a record of the length of a number of commercials. His record is 20 seconds, 35 seconds, 19 seconds, 42 seconds, and 31 seconds. What was the total number of seconds of these commercials?

The word "total" is also an addition word. You must add to find the total amount: 20 + 35 + 19 + 42 + 31 = 147 seconds.

---

# Subtraction

**Everyday subtraction.** When you take away an item from a larger group, a smaller number of items is left. If you take a book from a shelf, there is one less book on the shelf. If you pay for a 29-cent item with a dollar bill, you will receive change of 71 cents. When your teacher subtracts 3 points for an incorrect answer from a total score of 100, you are left with 97. You use subtraction every day.

**Subtracting whole numbers.** The number you subtract from, such as the shelf of books, is called the *minuend*. The number of books you remove is the *subtrahend*. The answer is called the *difference* or the *remainder*.

*In order not to get a ticket a driver must subtract the time away from the car from the total time paid for on the parking meter.*

Subtraction, like addition, is based on a set of basic facts that should be memorized. If you have forgotten one of the basic subtraction facts, there are a number of different ways to remember or relearn the fact.

1. **Count back.** Like all arithmetic, subtraction is based on counting. If you cannot remember what a fact such as 9 – 2 is, start with the larger number, 9, and count back as many steps as the smaller number: 9, 8, (1 step), 7 (2 steps); the fact is 9 – 2 = 7.

2. **Compare subtraction with addition.** If you cannot remember what 17 – 9 is, try to remember the related addition fact: 9 + □ = 17. What number added to 9 is 17? If you remember the addition fact, you can find that 9 + 8 = 17, so the subtraction fact is 17 – 9 = 8.

3. **Use tens.** There are a number of ways to use tens in subtraction. In 17 – 9, for example, you can think 17 – 7 = 10; 9 = 7 + 2, so 17 – 9 is the same as 10 – 2, or 8. In a problem like 11 – 6, 11 is 1 more than ten, so 11 – 6 is 1 more than 10 – 6. Since 10 – 6 = 4, 11 – 6 is 5.

4. **Use doubles**. Another way to solve 11 – 6 is to think, two 6's are 12, one 6 and 6 less 1 are 11. The fact is 11 – 6 = 5.

5. **Use a number line.** You can find the answer to 8 – 5 by drawing a number line diagram similar to the one below:

8 – 5 = 3

6. **Use the table of basic subtraction facts.** To find the answer to a problem such as 8 – 5, read down the left side of the table to row 8 and across to column 5. Row 8 and column 5 meet at the number 3, so 8 – 5 = 3.

You will see that some boxes in the chart are blank. These blank boxes show that some subtraction problems, such as 5 – 8, do not have an answer in whole numbers. The table also shows that such problems as 18 – 5 = 13 are not basic facts.

## Basic subtraction facts

| – | 0 | 1 | 2 | 3 | 4 | 5 | 6 | 7 | 8 | 9 |
|---|---|---|---|---|---|---|---|---|---|---|
| **0** | 0 | | | | | | | | | |
| **1** | 1 | 0 | | | | | | | | |
| **2** | 2 | 1 | 0 | | | | | | | |
| **3** | 3 | 2 | 1 | 0 | | | | | | |
| **4** | 4 | 3 | 2 | 1 | 0 | | | | | |
| **5** | 5 | 4 | 3 | 2 | 1 | 0 | | | | |
| **6** | 6 | 5 | 4 | 3 | 2 | 1 | 0 | | | |
| **7** | 7 | 6 | 5 | 4 | 3 | 2 | 1 | 0 | | |
| **8** | 8 | 7 | 6 | 5 | 4 | 3 | 2 | 1 | 0 | |
| **9** | 9 | 8 | 7 | 6 | 5 | 4 | 3 | 2 | 1 | 0 |
| **10** | 10 | 9 | 8 | 7 | 6 | 5 | 4 | 3 | 2 | 1 |
| **11** | 11 | 10 | 9 | 8 | 7 | 6 | 5 | 4 | 3 | 2 |
| **12** | 12 | 11 | 10 | 9 | 8 | 7 | 6 | 5 | 4 | 3 |
| **13** | 13 | 12 | 11 | 10 | 9 | 8 | 7 | 6 | 5 | 4 |
| **14** | 14 | 13 | 12 | 11 | 10 | 9 | 8 | 7 | 6 | 5 |
| **15** | 15 | 14 | 13 | 12 | 11 | 10 | 9 | 8 | 7 | 6 |
| **16** | 16 | 15 | 14 | 13 | 12 | 11 | 10 | 9 | 8 | 7 |
| **17** | 17 | 16 | 15 | 14 | 13 | 12 | 11 | 10 | 9 | 8 |
| **18** | 18 | 17 | 16 | 15 | 14 | 13 | 12 | 11 | 10 | 9 |

**Memorizing the basic subtraction facts.** You will learn the basic subtraction facts by figuring answers to them first. Later on, you will save time by memorizing these facts. The best way to remember subtraction facts is by using them as much as possible.

# Ten hints on memorizing subtraction facts

1. Do not try to memorize all of the facts at one time.

2. Choose a few subtraction facts to memorize, such as five or ten in a week.

3. Remember that you cannot change the order of numbers to be subtracted and still get the same answer. For example, 12 − 5 will not give you the same answer as 5 − 12.

4. Write the subtraction facts on a sheet of paper and cover the answers. Then write the answers without looking. Time yourself. Try this activity again. Were you able to get the right answer in less time?

5. Try to see the fact. What does 6 subtracted from 10 look like? Use pennies or buttons to find out. Or draw 10 things and cross out 6.

6. Play with patterns. Do the following examples in the order shown. What did you notice about the answers?

$$
\begin{array}{cccccccccc}
10 & 10 & 10 & 10 & 10 & 10 & 10 & 10 & 10 & 10 \\
-\,9 & -\,8 & -\,7 & -\,6 & -\,5 & -\,4 & -\,3 & -\,2 & -\,1 & -\,0 \\
\hline
\end{array}
$$

What other patterns can you find or make?

7. Play subtraction pick-up sticks. Use pick-up sticks for this activity. How many sticks do you have now? Play the game. How many sticks were left when you were finished playing? Play the game again. Are more or less sticks left this time?

8. Try calendar subtraction. Use any month and circle a special day, such as a friend's birthday or a holiday. If that day is the 17th, for example, cover two days. How many days are left? Cover three days. Remember to write the combination, such as 17 − 2, and the answer.

9. Count down. Begin with a number, such as 22. Starting with this number, count down to zero. For a challenge, skip count by twos to zero.

10. Play subtraction rummy. Write a number on separate 3 x 5 cards. Shuffle and place all of the cards facedown. Pick up the first card and the card underneath. Does the second card have a lower number than the first? Subtract to find the answer. Use this answer as your score.

# Help with borrowing in subtraction

In many examples, you will not be able to subtract the numbers in the problem as they are written. You will have to rename those numbers. For example, 330 becomes three hundreds, three tens and zero ones.

Borrowing is not hard if you understand how place value works. Remember that each number, no matter how large or small, has its own place. When you borrow, you are putting numbers in their right places before subtracting.

Suppose you have this problem:

$$\begin{array}{r} 2\,1 \\ -\ \ 8 \end{array}$$

Before you subtract, write each number in the problem in its right place as shown:

Now look at the ones place. You cannot subtract 8 from 1 in whole numbers. Think about it. If you have one pencil in your hand, there is no way you can take away, or subtract, eight pencils from it. To subtract, you must do something about the 1 in the ones place. This means you will have to go to the tens place for one 10. One 10 can be changed to 10 ones.

Adding these 10 ones to the 1 gives you 11. You can write a small 1 to show 11.

So far, you have renamed the 10 to ones. You can subtract 8 from 11. The answer is 3.

Now look at the tens column. After taking a 10 from it in this problem, you will have only one 10 left. You can write this in the shorthand shown below and finish subtracting.

You have transferred a 10 from the tens place and added it to the 1 in the ones place. You have 11.

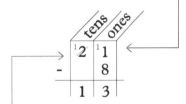

You have one 10 left. Cross out the 2 and write a 1.

$$\begin{array}{r} 17 \\ -\ 8 \\ \hline \end{array}$$

*Using the table of basic subtraction facts:*

**A.** Although you cannot subtract 8 from 7, 17 – 8 is in the table.

**B.** Read down the left side of the table to row 17.

**C.** Read across the row to column 8. The answer is 9.

   Another way to find the answer is by counting down from 17 to 8 on the number line.

---

$$\begin{array}{r} 47 \\ -\ 5 \\ \hline \end{array}$$

*Using a place value chart:*

**A.** Subtract in the ones column.

Write the 2 at the bottom of the ones column.

**B.** Subtract in the tens column.

Write the 4 at the bottom of the tens column.

*Using counters:*

Show the larger number first. Then cross out the counters for the smaller number.

$$\begin{array}{r} 47 \\ -\ 5 \\ \hline \end{array}$$

---

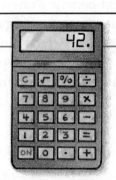

## Using your calculator to subtract

Press the number to the minuend first, then the – button, and the number of the subtrahend. Then press the = button. The number appearing on the display will be your answer, or the difference.

$$\begin{array}{r} 37 \\ -\ 9 \\ \hline \end{array}$$

*Using a place value chart:*

**A.** Before subtracting in the ones column, you must do some borrowing, since 9 cannot be subtracted from 7. Rename the three as two tens and ten ones. This gives you 17 ones in the ones column.

37 = 3 tens + 7 ones
37 = 2 tens + 17 ones

**B.** Now you can subtract in the ones column.

$$\begin{array}{r} 17 \\ -\ 9 \\ \hline 8 \end{array}$$

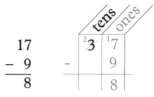

**C.** Subtract in the tens column.

$$\begin{array}{r} 2\ \text{tens} \\ -0\ \text{tens} \\ \hline 2\ \text{tens} \end{array}$$

| | tens | ones |
|---|---|---|
| | ²3 | ¹7 |
| − | | 9 |
| | 2 | 8 |

*Using counters:*

If you have to rename with counters, rename a ten counter as ten ones.

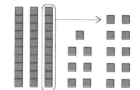

---

$$\begin{array}{r} 68 \\ -52 \\ \hline \end{array}$$

*Using a place value chart:*

**A.** Subtract in the ones column.

$$\begin{array}{r} 8 \\ -2 \\ \hline 6 \end{array}$$

| | tens | ones |
|---|---|---|
| | 6 | 8 |
| − | 5 | 2 |
| | | 6 |

**B.** Subtract in the tens column.

$$\begin{array}{r} 6\ \text{tens} \\ -5\ \text{tens} \\ \hline 1\ \text{tens} \end{array}$$

| | tens | ones |
|---|---|---|
| | 6 | 8 |
| − | 5 | 2 |
| | 1 | 6 |

68 snacks... 52 kids want an ⬤... how many want an 🍎?

$$\begin{array}{r} 70 \\ -45 \\ \hline \end{array}$$

*Using a place value chart:*

**A.** Before subtracting in the ones column, you must rename because 5 cannot be subtracted from 0. Rename seven tens as six tens and ten ones. This gives you ten ones in the ones column.
70 = 7 tens + 0 ones
70 = 6 tens + 10 ones

**B.** Now you can subtract in the ones column.

$$\begin{array}{r} 10 \\ -\ 5 \\ \hline \end{array}$$

| | tens | ones |
|---|---|---|
| | $^{6}\cancel{7}$ | $^{1}0$ |
| - | 4 | 5 |
| | | 5 |

**C.** Subtract in the tens column.

$$\begin{array}{r} \text{6 tens} \\ \text{-4 tens} \\ \hline \text{2 tens} \end{array}$$

| | tens | ones |
|---|---|---|
| | $^{6}\cancel{7}$ | $^{1}0$ |
| - | 4 | 5 |
| | 2 | 5 |

$$\begin{array}{r} 682 \\ -\ \ 47 \\ \hline \end{array}$$

*Using a place value chart:*

**A.** Before subtracting in the ones column, rename eight tens as seven tens and ten ones. This gives you twelve ones in the ones column. Now you can subtract.

$$\begin{array}{r} 12 \\ -\ 7 \\ \hline 5 \end{array}$$

| | hundreds | tens | ones |
|---|---|---|---|
| | 6 | $^{7}\cancel{8}$ | $^{1}2$ |
| - | | 4 | 7 |
| | | | 5 |

**B.** Subtract in the tens column.

$$\begin{array}{r} \text{7 tens} \\ \text{-4 tens} \\ \hline \text{3 tens} \end{array}$$

| | hundreds | tens | ones |
|---|---|---|---|
| | 6 | $^{7}\cancel{8}$ | $^{1}2$ |
| - | | 4 | 7 |
| | | 3 | 5 |

**C.** Subtract in the hundreds column.

$$\begin{array}{r} \text{6 hundreds} \\ \text{-0 hundreds} \\ \hline \text{6 hundreds} \end{array}$$

| | hundreds | tens | ones |
|---|---|---|---|
| | 6 | $^{7}\cancel{8}$ | $^{1}2$ |
| - | | 4 | 7 |
| | 6 | 3 | 5 |

$$503$$
$$-\ 46$$

*Using a place value chart:*

**A.** Before subtracting in the ones column, rename by going to the hundreds column. Rename the five hundreds as four hundreds and ten tens.

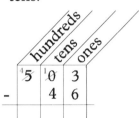

**B.** Now you have ten tens, which can be renamed as nine tens and ten ones. Subtract.

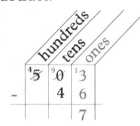

**C.** Subtract in the tens column.

    9 tens
  −4 tens
    5 tens

Write the 5 at the bottom of the tens column.

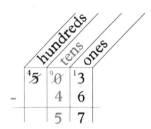

**D.** Subtract in the hundreds column.

  4 hundreds
 −0 hundreds
  4 hundreds

Write the 4 at the bottom of the hundreds column.

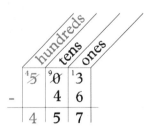

---

## Checking answers

To see if your answers are correct, add the difference, or answer, to the subtrahend (number being subtracted). If this number is the same as the minuend, your answer is correct.

      791 minuend
    −398 subtrahend
      393 difference, or remainder

Check:    393 difference
       + 398 subtrahend
       791

**How to solve subtraction word problems.** You must first read the problem carefully, then find out what is being asked for. If you see terms such as *difference*, *remainder*, *less*, or a question asking how many are left, you will need to subtract. But be careful here! Sometimes the problem will ask you to find the difference between the two numbers and sometimes you may be given the difference and asked to find the subtrahend.

### Tom is 14 years old and Laura is 8. How many years older is Tom than Laura?

In this problem, you are given the ages of two youngsters. You have to find the difference in their ages. This problem asks you to compare by finding the number of years that separate Tom's age from Laura's.

Tom's age – Laura's age = difference in ages

14 – 8 = 6 years

Tom is 6 years older than Laura.

### At a local animal shelter 144 animals were adopted in July. 24 were cats. The remaining animals were dogs. How many dogs were adopted?

This problem asks you to find out how many dogs were adopted. To do this, subtract the number of cats from the total number of animals.

Total number of animals – number of cats = number of remaining animals, or dogs.

144 – 24 = 120 dogs were adopted.

### Tanya's coat has ten buttons altogether. If she loses three buttons the first time she wears the coat, and two more buttons the next time, how many buttons will be left on her coat?

This problem involves more than one step. You can do this problem in two ways:

**1.** Write 10 – 3 = number of buttons left after the first time Tanya wears the coat, or 7 buttons. Use the new answer, 7, to figure that 7 – 2 = 5 buttons are left after the next time.

**2.** First add to get the total number of lost buttons, or 3 + 2 = 5. Then subtract this number from the ten buttons that used to be on Tanya's coat: 10 – 5 = 5.

A delivery man carried a crate of 24 bottles of seltzer water to a deli. He lost his balance at the door. The crate tipped and 6 bottles fell out and broke on the sidewalk. How many bottles were actually delivered?

In this problem, 24 bottles of seltzer were supposed to reach the deli. Despite the accident, most of the bottles were safely delivered. The question is, how many bottles were left?

To do this problem, you must subtract. The number of bottles before the accident – number of bottles broken = number of bottles left.
24 bottles – 6 bottles = 18 bottles left.

About 6540 people paid to enter a popular amusement park. At closing time, only 4692 people had left the park. How many people were still in the amusement park at closing time?

In this problem, you are given the approximate number of people who entered the park. At closing time, not all of the people who came had left the park. You are asked to find the number of people who did not leave.

The total number of people entering the park – number of people who left at closing time = number of people left. 6540 people – 4692 people who left at closing time = 1848 people still in the park.

## Relating addition and subtraction

When you add two groups together, you will get a sum, or total as your answer. If you subtract either number, minuend or subtrahend, from this total, you will get one of the numbers in the problem, never a different number. The following shows how this works:

$$
\begin{array}{r}
12 \\
+38 \\
\hline
50
\end{array}
$$

Subtract 12 from the answer

$$
\begin{array}{r}
50 \\
-12 \\
\hline
38
\end{array}
$$

Subtract 38 from the total

$$
\begin{array}{r}
50 \\
-38 \\
\hline
12
\end{array}
$$

As you can see, there are no other numbers than 12, 38, or 50. Since no other numbers are possible, you can say that this so-called "family" has closure in the set of whole numbers. Addition increases, or builds up, numbers, and subtraction decreases, or breaks down, numbers. Addition and subtraction may seem like two different operations, but they are not.

# Multiplication

## Everyday multiplication.

People use multiplication as a shortcut. If a person travels 18 miles for 4 days, he can find the total number of miles traveled by multiplying 18 × 4. The number of miles traveled is 72. Since multiplication is repeated addition, the traveler could have added 18 + 18 + 18 + 18 to get 72. But this is a longer calculation. Multiplication is also useful for finding out the number of all possible combinations of items. For example, if you have three kinds of bread and four sandwich fillings, how many different sandwiches could you make for a family outing? Instead of adding four three times, multiply 3 × 4 and you will find that there are twelve possible sandwich combinations.

**Multiplying whole numbers.** In multiplication, you are finding the total amount of groups of items. For example, a classroom has six large tables and six chairs at each table. How many students can sit at these tables? The long way to find the answer to this problem is by adding 6 + 6 + 6 + 6 + 6 + 6. To save time, write 6 tables × 6 chairs = total number of students, or 36.

In multiplication, the two numbers that are combined are called *factors.* The two sixes that were multiplied in the problem above are factors. The answer to a multiplication problem, or in this case, 36, is called the *product.*

Sometimes, you will see the terms "multiplicand" and "multiplier." When you multiply 361 × 22, the 361 is the *multiplicand,* or number to be multiplied by another, and the 22 is the

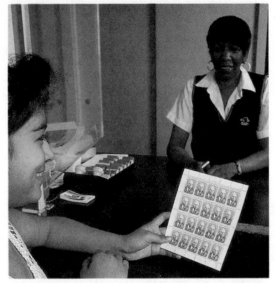

*Multiplication is used in every day activities like purchasing stamps. This sheet contains four rows of five, or 20, stamps.*

*multiplier,* or number by which another is multiplied. The answer is called the *product.*

Just as you memorized the addition and subtraction facts, you also should memorize the multiplication facts. Memorizing these facts may seem like a lot of work now, but you will save time later. You will be able to recall these facts and do problems faster. If you do have trouble trying to remember, here are some hints that do not involve using a table or repeated addition.

1. **Add to a fact that you know.** To find 6 × 7, you can think 6 × 6 is 36, so 6 × 7 is 36 + 6, or 42.
2. **Subtract from a fact that you know.** To find 8 × 9, you can think ten 8's are 80, so nine 8's are 80 - 8 = 72.
3. **Change the order of factors.** As in addition, in multiplication it does not matter whether you multiply 2 × 8 or 8 × 2. Both of these problems have the same answer, or product, 16.

**Mathematics**

**4. Use the patterns in products.** This means that the answer, or product, will be even when multiplied by 2, 4, 6, and 8. It also means that a factor, such as 3 or 5, multiplied by another number can be divided evenly by 3 or 5. A factor can also divide a number evenly.

**Factor of 2:** Product is even; for example, $2 \times 1 = 2$, $2 \times 2 = 4$, $2 \times 3 = 6$, $2 \times 4 = 8$; 2, 4, 6, and 8 are even.

**Factor of 3:** Digits can be added by 3; $3 \times 1 = 3$, $3 \times 2 = 6$, $3 \times 3 = 9$, $3 \times 4 = 12$.

**Factor of 4:** Product is even; for example, $4 \times 1 = 4$, $4 \times 2 = 8$, $4 \times 3 = 12$.

**Factor of 5:** Last digit is either 0 or 5; for example, $5 \times 1 = 5$, $5 \times 2 = 10$, $5 \times 3 = 15$, $5 \times 4 = 20$.

**Factor of 6:** Product is even and digits sum to 3; $6 \times 1 = 6$, $6 \times 2 = 12$, $6 \times 3 = 18$, $6 \times 4 = 24$.

**Factor of 8:** Product is even; $8 \times 1 = 8$, $8 \times 2 = 16$, $8 \times 3 = 24$, $8 \times 4 = 32$.

**Factor of 9:** Digits can be added by 9; $9 \times 1 = 9$, $9 \times 2 = 18$, $9 \times 3 = 27$, $9 \times 4 = 36$.

There is no easy way to recognize products that have a factor of 7.

**Memorizing the basic multiplication facts.** As you learn multiplication, you will probably use repeated addition and other ways to figure out answers. Multiplication facts such as $2 \times 2$ are easy. Perhaps you have some of them memorized already. Write out all the facts and try to memorize them. Remember that the best way to memorize them is by using them.

*Example:*
$$\begin{array}{r} 4 \\ \times 3 \\ \hline \end{array}$$

**A.** You can solve this by using the table of basic multiplication facts. Read down to row 4 and across to column 3. Row 4 and column 3 meet at the number 12, which is the answer.

### Basic multiplication facts

| × | 0 | 1 | 2 | 3 | 4 | 5 | 6 | 7 | 8 | 9 |
|---|---|---|---|---|---|---|---|---|---|---|
| **0** | 0 | 0 | 0 | 0 | 0 | 0 | 0 | 0 | 0 | 0 |
| **1** | 0 | 1 | 2 | 3 | 4 | 5 | 6 | 7 | 8 | 9 |
| **2** | 0 | 2 | 4 | 6 | 8 | 10 | 12 | 14 | 16 | 18 |
| **3** | 0 | 3 | 6 | 9 | 12 | 15 | 18 | 21 | 24 | 27 |
| **4** | 0 | 4 | 8 | 12 | 16 | 20 | 24 | 28 | 32 | 36 |
| **5** | 0 | 5 | 10 | 15 | 20 | 25 | 30 | 35 | 40 | 45 |
| **6** | 0 | 6 | 12 | 18 | 24 | 30 | 36 | 42 | 48 | 54 |
| **7** | 0 | 7 | 14 | 21 | 28 | 35 | 42 | 49 | 56 | 63 |
| **8** | 0 | 8 | 16 | 24 | 32 | 40 | 48 | 56 | 64 | 72 |
| **9** | 0 | 9 | 18 | 27 | 36 | 45 | 54 | 63 | 72 | 81 |

**B.** You can also find the answer by adding three fours or by counting the elements of three sets of four.

$$\begin{array}{r} 4 \\ 4 \\ + 4 \\ \hline 12 \end{array}$$

12 elements

**C.** Or you can use a number line.

0 1 2 3 4 5 6 7 8 9 10 11 12 13 14

# Ten hints on memorizing multiplication facts

1. Do not try to memorize all of the facts at one time.

2. Do memorize one set of tables at a time before moving on to others. For example, begin with the six or seven times tables.

3. Do practice multiplication every day. For example, use multiplication to find the total number of an array of stamps.

4. Do let a change in the order of factors help you. For example, $6 \times 8$ and $8 \times 6$ both have the same answer, 48. If you know the answer to $6 \times 8$, you know the answer to $8 \times 6$. So now you only have half as many—or 50—facts to memorize.

5. Double the fun by counting by two, threes, fives. For example, 2 groups of 2 can be written as $2 \times 2$. Three groups of two look like $3 \times 2$. Write down the combinations you use, such as $3 \times 7 = 21$.

6. Copy the playing board at the right. Taking turns with a partner, toss a paper clip on the board and write the number it lands on. Toss the clip again and multiply the two numbers. This number is your score.

| 14 | 2 | 10 | 8 |
|----|---|----|---|
| 3 | 0 | 4 | 6 |
| 7 | 1 | 9 | 11 |
| 28 | 5 | 0 | 4 |
| 12 | 8 | 9 | 7 |

7. Write the multiplication facts on a piece of paper with the right answers. Cover the answers and try to fill in the correct ones. How many do you have correct? Time yourself. Can you beat your own record?

8. Fold or rule off a piece of paper to look like the one at right. How many boxes do you have at the top and on one side? Multiply these two numbers. Now try folding this paper so that you have more boxes. Again, count one row and one column of boxes. Multiply these two numbers. Can you fold this paper again so that you have more boxes?

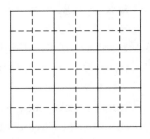

9. Select a partner for a game. Pick any number and tell your partner to multiply it by another number, say, 6. For example, you can pick 3, and tell your partner to multiply it by 6. In the example, 18 ($6 \times 3 = 18$) is one score. You can make this game as easy or as hard as you wish.

10. Glue two toothpicks at a time on heavy paper or cardboard to design a building or invention. Count how many pairs of toothpicks you used after you have completed the project. Then count how many single toothpicks you used altogether.

**Mathematics**

$$26$$
$$\times\ 3$$

The number 26 does not appear in the table of basic multiplication facts. But 2 and 6 do. You can solve this problem by multiplying ones and tens separately.

**A.** Multiply ones by three ones.

$$6$$
$$\times\ 3$$
$$\overline{18}$$

Write the partial product.

**B.** Multiply tens by three ones.

2 tens
×3 ones
$\overline{\text{6 tens}} = 60$

Write the partial product.

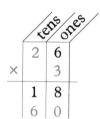

Note that two tens × three ones is six tens — not six ones.

**C.** Add the partial products.

$$18$$
$$+60$$
$$\overline{78}$$

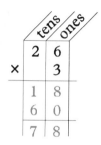

You will find the following method faster.

---

**A.** Multiply ones by ones.

$$6$$
$$\times\ 3$$
$$\overline{18} = \text{one ten and}$$
eight ones

Write the 8 at the bottom of the ones column and write the 1 in the tens column.

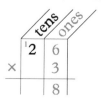

**B.** Multiply tens by ones.

$$20$$
$$\times\ 3$$
$$\overline{60}$$

**C.** Now add the 10 shown by the small 1 in the tens column.

$$60$$
$$+10$$
$$\overline{70} = \text{7 tens}$$

Write the 7 in the tens column.

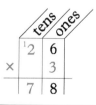

**Commutative law**

Multiplication and addition are *commutative*. The order in which one multiplies or adds does not make any difference in the answer. Therefore, since 3 × 26 = 78, it is also true that 26 × 3 = 78.

183

## 45
## ×23

**A.** Multiply ones by ones.

5
× 3
15 = 1 ten and 5 ones

Write the 5 at the bottom of the ones column, and the 1 in the tens column.

**B.** Multiply tens by ones.

4 tens
× 3 tens
12 tens

Now add to this the 10 shown by the small 1 in the tens column:

120
+ 10
130 = 1 hundred and 3 tens

Write the 1 in the hundreds column and the 3 in the tens column.

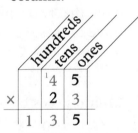

**C.** Multiply ones by tens.

5 ones
× 2 tens
10 tens

Write a 0 in the tens column and a 1 at the top of the hundreds column.

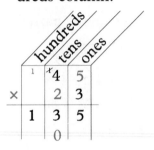

**D.** Multiply tens by tens.

4 tens
×2 tens
8 hundreds

Add to this the hundred shown by the small 1.

8 hundreds
+1 hundred
9 hundreds

Write the 9 in the hundreds column.

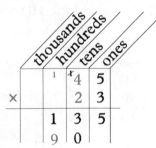

**E.** Add the columns together.

| | thousands | hundreds | tens | ones |
|---|---|---|---|---|
| | | ˣ4 | 5 | |
| × | | | 2 | 3 |
| | | 1 | 3 | 5 |
| | | 9 | 0 | |
| | 1 | 0 | 3 | 5 |

**Mathematics**

**Using counters in multiplication.**
Counters may be used to show how renaming in multiplication works.

26
× 3

This example shows three groups of 26. To add them together, take 10 of the ones counters (■) and combine them in a tens counter. You end up with 7 tens counters and 8 ones counters. Add the tens counters together (10+10+10+10+10+10+10) to get 70. Then add the remaining 8 ones counters to 70 to get 78.

319
×524

**A.** Multiply ones, tens, and hundreds by ones.

319
×524
1276

**B.** Then multiply by tens:

319
×524
1276
638

**C.** Finally, multiply ones, tens, and hundreds by hundreds.

319
×524
1276
638
1595

**D.** Add partial products.

319
×524
1276
638
1595
167156

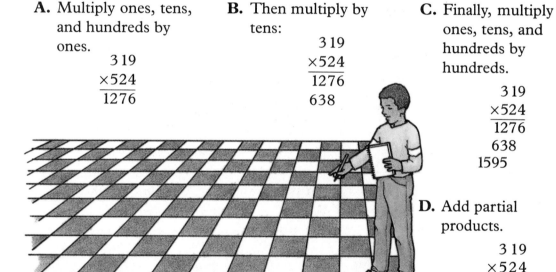

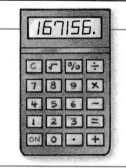

167156.

**Using your calculator to multiply**

Press the number of the multiplicand, the × sign, the number of the multiplier, and the = sign. Your answer should match the answer shown in the display.

**How to solve multiplication word problems.** You will use the basic multiplication facts as well as the information given to you in the problem. Read the problem and question carefully. In some problems, you may find words that mean multiply, such as *times, how many, how much,* and *product.*

---

**Maria's new garden will have 12 columns of plants on one side and 36 rows of plants on the other. How many plants will be in Maria's garden altogether?**

**A.** Sometimes drawing a picture will help you to solve the problem. In this problem, you are given the number of plants for two sides of the garden. You are asked to find how many plants there are in all.

**B.** To find the number of plants, multiply 12 × 36. Your product will be 432.

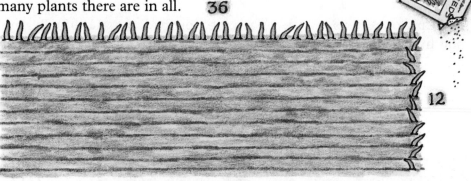

36

12

---

**George wanted to multiply 7 × 3 on his calculator, but lost track of the number of three's he pressed. When he pressed the = sign, he was surprised to see 567 on the display. What answer should George have seen on the calculator's display? What problem did George actually solve when he lost count?**

**A.** In the first part of this problem, all you have to do is multiply 7 × 3. If you forgot what 7 × 3 is, switch the factors and write 3 × 7. You will still get 21, which is the answer, or product to the first part of this problem.

**B.** The second part of this problem asks you to write the problem George solved instead. The question here is how many extra threes did George press to get 567?

7×3×3×3×3
21 ×3×3×3

**C.** Press 21 on your calculator, the × sign, and 3. You will get 63. Press the × sign and 3 again and you will get 189. Press the × sign and 3 once more and you will get 567.

---

Dana is helping to unpack six cartons of new books. Each carton has twelve books inside. How many new books will Dana have to unpack and place on the shelves?

In this problem, you are asked to find the total number of books in all of the cartons. To solve this problem, write:

6 cartons × 12 books = 72 books

A go-cart for a popular ride can hold an average weight of 510 pounds. Three men weighing 160 pounds each get into the cart. In the meantime, a friend decides to ride, too. This man weighs 130 pounds. Will all of these men be able to ride in the cart together?

**A.** This is a two-step problem. You are given the number of pounds that the cart can hold and have to find out whether the total weight of the men is under or over this limit. If the men's weight is over this limit, one of the men will have to leave or ride in another cart. So the first step in this problem is to find out how much the first three men weigh together.

Since they each weigh 160 pounds, you need only to multiply to find the answer.

160 pounds, or the weight of one of the men × 3 men = total weight of the three men.

160 × 3 = 480 pounds.

This is the total weight of the first three men. So far, they can all ride in the cart.

**B.** Now you have to add the last man's weight to the 480 pounds to get the weight of the four men.

480 + 130 = 610 pounds.

This is the total weight of the four men. Not all of these men will be able to ride in the cart together. 610 pounds is over the cart's weight limit of 510 pounds.

## Checking answers

There are several ways to check multiplication. In the first, *reverse the order of the factors*. If you do not remember the product of 9 × 6, try 6 × 9. Either way, you will get 54.

Another way is to *estimate the product* before or after doing the problem. You will not get an exact answer, but a reasonable guess.

**Estimating.** To estimate in multiplication, round each factor to the place of its first, or leading, digit.

$$\begin{array}{r} 5983 \\ \times\ 236 \end{array} \text{ rounds to } \begin{array}{r} 6000 \\ \times\ 200 \end{array}$$

Multiply using the rounded factors.

$$\begin{array}{r} 6000 \\ \times\ 200 \\ \hline 1200000 \end{array}$$

The estimated product of 1,200,000 is fairly close to the actual product, which is 1,411,988. This is enough information to be able to tell whether a product obtained on a calculator is likely to be free of mistakes.

One way to get a closer estimate is to include a second estimate as a "correction factor." Estimate the effect of the part of the problem that was lost in rounding.

$$\begin{array}{r} 236 \\ -200 \\ \hline 36 \end{array}$$

Round 36 to 40.

$$\begin{array}{r} 6000 \\ \times\ 40 \\ \hline 240000 \end{array}$$

Add or subtract the correction factor to or from your previous estimate to obtain a closer estimate.

$$\begin{array}{r} 1,200,000 \\ +\ 240,000 \\ \hline 1,440,000 \end{array}$$

The estimate of 1,440,000 is close enough to the true answer of 1,411,988 for most purposes that do not require a computed answer.

For a quick estimate, just multiply the leading digits and write the correct number of zeros. Since 5 × 2 = 10, the quick estimate tells you that the answer will be greater than 1,000,000. You can improve that estimate by rounding both numbers up. If you round 5983 up to 6000 and 236 up to 300, then multiplying the leading digits will give you an estimate of 1,800,000. Now you know that the actual answer will be between 1,000,000 and 1,800,000.

**Factors.** Factors can also be used to check your work. Factor the multiplier, then multiply using the factors.

*Example:*

$$\begin{array}{r} 24 \\ \times\ 12 \\ \hline 48 \\ +24 \\ \hline 288 \end{array}$$

12 can be factored into 4 × 3, therefore:

$$\begin{array}{r} 24 \\ \times\ 4 \\ \hline 96 \\ \times\ 3 \\ \hline 288 \end{array}$$

# Division

**Everyday division.** Whenever you cut a slice of pizza or a piece of cake, or any whole item into one or more parts, you are dividing. You are also using division when you place separate items in two or more containers in equal amounts.

**Dividing numbers.** In division, the number you are dividing by is called the *divisor*, the number you are dividing into is called the *dividend*, and the answer is called the *quotient*.

There are only 90 division facts because division by zero is not possible in whole numbers (see the basic division table on page 190). Because there are less facts, you might suppose that division facts would be easier to learn than those of addition, subtraction, or multiplication (there are 100 facts for each of those operations). But many people have difficulty estimating in division, or guessing how many times a number "goes into" another number. Division also involves addition, subtraction, and multiplication.

To be able to divide easily, you will need to memorize the facts. But if you are unable to remember a fact, there are various tips you can use.

1. **Relate division to multiplication.** For example, if you cannot recall the answer to $3\overline{)9}$ , you can ask, 3 times what number equals 9? Or how many sets of 3 are in 9?

   Since $3 \times 3 = 9$, then

   $$\begin{array}{r} 3 \\ 3\overline{)9} \end{array}$$

   is the correct fact.

*Even simple everyday things like pouring equal shares of milk from a jug into glasses is a kind of division.*

2. **Use the number line.** To find the answer to $4\overline{)12}$ , you can draw a picture that is just like a multiplication line except that the jumps go in the other direction.

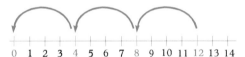

   In this case, the answer is the number of jumps it takes to get to 0. Therefore,

   $$\begin{array}{r} 3 \\ 4\overline{)12} \end{array}$$

3. **Use an array.** If you want to find the answer to $7\overline{)28}$ , you can draw rows of 7 dots until you have 28 dots in all. This may be more work than memorizing the fact.

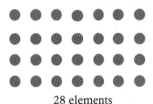

28 elements

The array shows that 28 divided by 7 is 4.

**Use the basic division table.** The easiest kind of division table to use is just a multiplication table with one column deleted. The 0 column is deleted to show that you cannot divide by 0.

## Basic division table

| × | 1 | 2 | 3 | 4 | 5 | 6 | 7 | 8 | 9 |
|---|---|---|---|---|---|---|---|---|---|
| 0 | 0 | 0 | 0 | 0 | 0 | 0 | 0 | 0 | 0 |
| 1 | 1 | 2 | 3 | 4 | 5 | 6 | 7 | 8 | 9 |
| 2 | 2 | 4 | 6 | 8 | 10 | 12 | 14 | 16 | 18 |
| 3 | 3 | 6 | 9 | 12 | 15 | 18 | 21 | 24 | 27 |
| 4 | 4 | 8 | 12 | 16 | 20 | 24 | 28 | 32 | 36 |
| 5 | 5 | 10 | 15 | 20 | 25 | 30 | 35 | 40 | 45 |
| 6 | 6 | 12 | 18 | 24 | 30 | 36 | 42 | 48 | 54 |
| 7 | 7 | 14 | 21 | 28 | 35 | 42 | 49 | 56 | 63 |
| 8 | 8 | 16 | 24 | 32 | 40 | 48 | 56 | 64 | 72 |
| 9 | 9 | 18 | 27 | 36 | 45 | 54 | 63 | 72 | 81 |

To find the answer to a problem such as $8\overline{)56}$ using this table, first locate the divisor, 8, at the top of the table. Go down the column headed 8 until you find the dividend, 56, in the body of the table. It is in row number 7. Therefore,

$$7$$
$$8\overline{)56}$$

**Memorizing the basic division facts.** Like addition, subtraction, and multiplication basic facts, division facts are learned — and memorized — better by using them often. You will save much time if you can just look at a fact and know the answer to it. There are many ways to memorize facts. Using division facts in different ways will help you to memorize them faster.

$$6\overline{)39}$$

**A.** Use the division table if you do not remember the division facts when the divisor is 6. There is <u>no</u> division fact for $6\overline{)39}$ , but it is between two division facts.

$$6$$
$$6\overline{)36}$$ and $$7$$
$$6\overline{)42}$$

**B.** Subtract the lesser dividend from the dividend in the original problem.

$$6$$
$$6\overline{)39}$$
$$\underline{36}$$
$$3$$

**C.** Write the result as a quotient with a *remainder*, shown by writing R.
A remainder is the number left over after the last subtraction.

$$6\text{ R }3$$
$$6\overline{)39}$$
$$\underline{36}$$
$$3$$

This means that $(6 \times 6) + 3 = 39$.

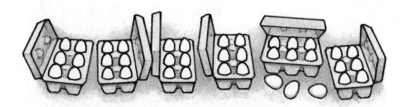

# Ten hints on memorizing basic division facts

1. Do not try to memorize all of the division facts at the same time.

2. Do memorize a few facts at a time. then move on to others. Look for ways that one set of facts is related to another in division.

3. Do remember that $16 \div 4$ and $4 \div 16$ give two different quotients!

4. Practice using division. Pick a number, any number. Can you divide it evenly by 2, 3, 4, 5, 6, 7, 8, or 9? Try dividing other numbers. Does the same thing happen?

5. Another way to practice is to spill a pile of beans or buttons on the table. Count how many there are. Take turns making groups of 2, 3, 4, etc. Did you have any beans or buttons left over each time? Why or why not?

6. Find a book you will enjoy reading, such as a mystery. Write down the number of pages in the whole book. Read the book. How many days did it take you to finish it? Divide this number into the total number of pages. You will get the number of pages you read each day.

7. Write down the division facts on a piece of paper with the answers. Cover the answers and try to write the correct answers in the shortest amount of time, say five minutes. Try this again tomorrow and see if you can beat your own record.

8. Try to share something when you have four items, such as four pieces of fruit, and two friends. Or four containers for 20 eggs. Think of other situations and practice them on your friends. Then try to help with your friends' division dilemmas.

9. Find examples of the ways people use division every day. Begin by asking your friends and family how they use division. Ask them to show you an example, if possible. If you have a favorite sport, find out if division can be used to figure records of scores and other information.

10. Try using averages. You get an average by first adding, say, six things and dividing this total number by six. To start, keep a record of the time you watch television for five days. Try to use even numbers, such as 30, 60, or 90 minutes. At the end of five days, add up these times. Then divide your answer by five. You will get the *average* time spent watching television. What other ways are averages used?

$$2\overline{)80}$$

**A.** One approach is to think of the dividend as 8 tens.

$$
\begin{array}{r}
4 \text{ tens} = 40 \\
2\overline{)8 \text{ tens}} \\
\underline{8 \text{ tens}} \\
0 \text{ tens}
\end{array}
$$

**B.** Place value can be used to write the same procedure in a more familiar way.

$$
\begin{array}{r}
40 \\
2\overline{)80} \\
\underline{8} \\
0
\end{array}
$$

In effect, if you can solve the problem $2\overline{)8}$, you can solve any of the following problems:

$$
2\overline{)800} = 2\overline{)8 \text{ hundreds}} \quad \begin{array}{l} 4 \text{ hundreds} = 400 \\ \\ \underline{8 \text{ hundreds}} \\ 0 \end{array}
$$

$$
2\overline{)8000} = 2\overline{)8 \text{ thousands}} \quad \begin{array}{l} 4 \text{ thousands} = 4000 \\ \\ \underline{8 \text{ thousands}} \\ 0 \end{array}
$$

and so on. This fact makes it possible to attack division problems digit by digit.

---

$$2\overline{)88}$$

**A.** The problem can be rewritten as follows:

$$2\overline{)8 \text{ tens} + 8 \text{ ones}}$$

**B.** Divide the tens.

$$
\begin{array}{r}
4 \text{ tens} \\
2\overline{)8 \text{ tens} + 8 \text{ ones}} \\
\underline{8 \text{ tens}} \\
0
\end{array}
$$

**C.** Divide the ones.

$$
\begin{array}{r}
4 \text{ tens} + 4 \text{ ones} = 44 \\
2\overline{)8 \text{ tens} + 8 \text{ ones}} \\
\underline{8 \text{ tens}} \quad \underline{8 \text{ ones}} \\
0 \qquad 0
\end{array}
$$

---

**D.** You can write the problem using place value instead of the words "tens" and "ones."

$$
\begin{array}{r}
4 \\
2\overline{)88} \\
\underline{8} \\
8
\end{array}
$$

**E.** Note that there is really nothing new in this. The first 8 merely shows that you are subtracting 8 tens from the 88.

The second 8 is a remainder — you have not yet taken away as many twos as you can.

$$
\begin{array}{r}
44 \\
2\overline{)88} \\
\underline{8} \\
8 \\
\underline{8} \\
0
\end{array}
$$

**Using counters in division.** When using counters in division, ring each group that is being removed and then count the rings. For example, to divide 88 by 2, remove groups of 2.

The first step is shown in removing groups of two tens. There are four such groups. The second step is shown as removing groups of two ones. There are also four groups of two ones. Therefore, the quotient, when you divide 88 by 2, is four tens and four ones, or 44.

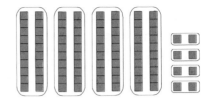

$$3\overline{)78}$$

**A.** This sort of problem can be attacked by dividing each digit separately.

Divide the tens.

$$\begin{array}{r} 2 \\ 3\overline{)78} \\ 60 \\ \hline 18 \end{array}$$

**B.** Divide the remainder.

$$\begin{array}{r} 26 \\ 3\overline{)78} \\ 60 \\ \hline 18 \\ 18 \\ \hline 0 \end{array}$$

$$3\overline{)528}$$

**A.** Divide the first digit.

$$\begin{array}{r} 1 \\ 3\overline{)528} \\ 3 \\ \hline 2 \end{array}$$

Here, we write only a 3 to note that we have subtracted three hundreds. We write the remainder as 2, although the remainder at this point is actually 228.

**B.** Bring down the second digit.

$$\begin{array}{r} 1 \\ 3\overline{)528} \\ 3 \\ \hline 22 \end{array}$$

**C.** Divide the 22 by 3.

$$\begin{array}{r} 17 \\ 3\overline{)528} \\ 3 \\ \hline 22 \\ 21 \\ \hline 1 \end{array}$$

**D.** Bring down the third digit.

$$\begin{array}{r} 17 \\ 3\overline{)528} \\ 3 \\ \hline 22 \\ 21 \\ \hline 18 \end{array}$$

**E.** Divide the 18 by 3.

$$\begin{array}{r} 176 \\ 3\overline{)528} \\ 3 \\ \hline 22 \\ 21 \\ \hline 18 \\ 18 \\ \hline 0 \end{array}$$

$$24\overline{)294}$$

**A.** In this case, there is a two-digit divisor, making it a much more complicated division problem than one with a one-digit divisor. The first step is to estimate what the first partial quotient will be. It is easiest to round the divisor to 20 to make such an estimate. Think:

$$20\overline{)294}^{?}$$

Since 20 will divide into 29 once, the first partial quotient is 1.

**B.** The next part of the problem is to determine where the partial quotient of 1 should be written. Think: Will the answer be more than 1? More than 10? More than 100? You can look at the related multiplication facts.

$$1 \times 24 = 24$$
$$10 \times 24 = 240$$
$$100 \times 24 = 2400$$

The first digit will be in the tens place.

$$24\overline{)294}^{1}$$

**C.** Now multiply the divisor by the first partial quotient.

$$\begin{array}{r} 24 \\ \times\ 1 \\ \hline 24 \end{array}$$

Write the product under the first two digits of 294.

$$24\overline{)294}^{1}$$
$$24$$

**D.** Subtract the product from the dividend. Remember that the 1 showing as a partial quotient is really one ten — which is shown by its place value in the quotient.

$$24\overline{)294}^{1}$$
$$\underline{24}$$
$$5$$

**E.** Bring down the next digit of the dividend, in this case the 4 in 294.

$$24\overline{)294}^{1}$$
$$\underline{24}$$
$$54$$

**F.** Use the rounded version of 24 to estimate how many 24s there are in 54. Since there are two 20s in 50, make 2 the next estimate of a digit in the quotient.

$$24\overline{)294}^{12}$$
$$\underline{24}$$
$$54$$

*continued on next page*

194

**G.** Again multiply the partial quotient by the divisor.

$$
\begin{array}{r}
24 \\
\times\ 2 \\
\hline
48
\end{array}
$$

Write the product under the earlier difference, 54.

$$
\begin{array}{r}
12\phantom{9} \\
24\overline{)294} \\
24\phantom{9} \\
\hline
54 \\
48
\end{array}
$$

**H.** Subtract the product from the remainder.

$$
\begin{array}{r}
12\phantom{9} \\
24\overline{)294} \\
24\phantom{9} \\
\hline
54 \\
48 \\
\hline
6
\end{array}
$$

**I.** Since 6 is less than 24, the division cannot continue, so write the quotient with a remainder of 6.

$$
\begin{array}{r}
12\ \text{R}6 \\
24\overline{)294} \\
24\phantom{9} \\
\hline
54 \\
48 \\
\hline
6
\end{array}
$$

The answer to the problem is 12 remainder 6.

---

**How to solve division word problems.** When you are trying to solve word problems it helps to follow certain steps:
- Read the problem carefully.
- Read the question and write a math sentence for it.
- Look out for words that will give you a hint meaning divide. Some of these words are *per, average,* and *part of.*

---

During January, Vanessa tried to lose weight. In the first week, she weighed 130 pounds; in the second, 128 pounds; in the third, 131; and in the fourth, 131. What was Vanessa's average weight in January?

**A.** This is a two-step problem. Begin solving this problem by adding all of Vanessa's weights. You can write a math sentence as follows:
130 + 128 + 131 + 131 = 520 pounds, total weight.

**B.** To find the average weight, count the weeks Vanessa weighed herself, which is four, and divide:

$$
\begin{array}{r}
130 \\
4\overline{)520} \\
4\phantom{9} \\
\hline
12 \\
12 \\
\hline
0
\end{array}
$$

Vanessa's average weight in January was 130 pounds.

Darryl bought three pizzas for a class party. Each pizza had eight slices. There are 15 students in Darryl's class. According to Darryl, each student will be able to have two slices of pizza. Is he right?

**A.** This is a multistep problem. First you have to find how many pizza slices there are altogether:
  3 pizzas × 8 slices = 24 slices.
There are 24 slices of pizza to be shared among the students.

**B.** Darryl thinks each student will be able to get exactly two slices of pizza and that there are 15 students, including Darryl. Write this information this way:

$$24 \div 5 \text{ or } 15\overline{)24}$$
$$\underline{15}$$
$$9$$

(with quotient 1 above)

**C.** The quotient shows that each student will certainly get one slice of pizza. Since there is a remainder, it is possible that some students will get two slices of pizza, but not all, as Darryl supposed.

---

Sally traveled 237 miles in three days to a business convention in another state. How many miles did she travel per day?

This problem gives you the total number of miles Sally traveled and asks you to find the number of miles she traveled each day.

To solve this problem, you must divide. You can write the following math sentence:
  237 ÷ 3 = number of miles traveled per day.

$$3\overline{)237}$$
quotient 79
$$\underline{21}$$
$$27$$
$$\underline{27}$$

---

A salesman spoke to 1350 customers in ten business days, or two weeks. How many customers did he speak to per day?

In this problem you have to use the total number of customers, or 1350. If you do not read this problem carefully, you might use the two weeks as the divisor. You have to find how many customers were spoken to in a single day.

So if you divided 1350 by the two weeks, your answer would be 675 customers, which is much too large. Besides, such a large number would not make a lot of sense.

Instead, you have to divide 1350 by 10.
  1350 customers ÷ 10 days = number of customers salesman spoke to in one day.
  1350 ÷ 10 = 135

**Mathematics**

**Estimating.** Estimating in division has more roles than it does in any other part of arithmetic. First, you must estimate to determine where the first digit of the product should be shown. Next, you must estimate trial quotients when the divisor has more than one digit. Finally, you may need to estimate the answer to check a calculation on a calculator, or simply because you do not have the time or the need to find the actual answer. Often, the best way to begin estimating in division is to find how many digits will be in the quotient. You can do this by multiplying the divisor by 10, 100, 1000, and so forth. The product can then be compared with the dividend.

For example, to find how many digits are in the quotient of 528 divided by 3, think 3 × 10 is 30;

528 is greater than 30;
3 × 100 is 300;
528 is greater than 300;
3 × 1000 is 3000;
528 is less than 3000,

so the quotient is between 100 and 1000. It will have three digits. The quotient is 176.

## Relating multiplication and division

When you multiply two numbers, or factors, you will get a product as your answer.

If you divide the product by either factor, you will get one of the numbers in the problem, never a different number. The following shows how this works.

*Example:* 8 x 2 = 16.
Now divide 16 by 2.

$$\begin{array}{r} 8 \\ 2\overline{)16} \end{array}$$

Now divide 16 by 8.

$$\begin{array}{r} 2 \\ 8\overline{)16} \end{array}$$

There are no other numbers than 8, 2, and 16. Also, you have probably noticed that multiplication increases, or builds up, numbers, and division decreases, or breaks down, numbers. Multiplication and division may seem like two different operations, but they are not.

## Using your calculator to divide

To divide, press the number of the dividend, the ÷ sign, and the number of the divisor on your calculator. The calculator will display the quotient, or answer.

## Checking answers

Even after you have completed a division problem, you should be able to check its accuracy. The following ways show you how to do this.

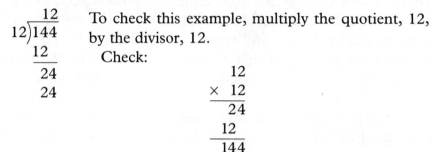

*Example 1:*

$$12\overline{)144}$$
12 (quotient above)
  12
  ——
  24
  24

To check this example, multiply the quotient, 12, by the divisor, 12.

Check:

```
    12
×   12
  ———
    24
    12
  ———
   144
```

*Example 2:*

```
     12R 2
 12)146
    12
   ——
    26
    24
   ——
     2
```

To check a division problem with a remainder, multiply the quotient by the divisor, then add the remainder to your answer.

Check:

```
    12
×   12
  ———
    24
    12
  ———
   144
+    2  remainder
  ———
   146
```

You can also check answers by finding factors of the divisor and dividing each factor separately.

*Example:*

```
     12
 12)144
    12
   ——
    24
    24
```

The divisor, 12, can be factored as 3 × 4.

First use 4 as a divisor:     4⌐144

Then use 3 as a divisor:     3⌐36 the quotient to 144 ÷ 4

12 the quotient to 36 ÷ 3, which matches the quotient in the original problem!

The last answer you got dividing by 3 was 12, which is the answer shown in the original example. Since these answers match, they are correct.

**Mathematics**

# Fractions

*Fractions* are the quotients of whole numbers (division by zero is, of course, excluded). Instead of writing $4\,\overline{)\,3}$, however, a fraction is written as $\frac{3}{4}$. The bottom number in a fraction, the *denominator*, tells how many parts are being considered in all. The top number, the *numerator*, specifies some of those parts. For example, $\frac{3}{4}$ could refer to 3 pieces of a pie that had been divided into 4 parts. Operations with fractions are made easier by factoring the numerators and denominators.

**Factoring.** To *factor* a number, you find its factors: the whole numbers that can be multiplied together to give the number. For many purposes, it is most useful to find the factors that are *prime*—those numbers such as 2, 3, 5, 7, 11, 13, 17, and so forth that have only themselves and 1 as factors. For example, 12 has factors of 1, 2, 3, 4, 6, and 12, but only 2 and 3 are prime factors. When you factor 12, the factor 2 must be included twice: $12 = 2 \times 2 \times 3$.

## Factor 30.

**A.** Successive division by prime numbers, starting with the smallest and working up, is a sure method of finding all the prime factors. Divide 30 by the smallest prime, 2.

$$2\,\overline{)\,30}\phantom{0}$$
$$\phantom{0}15\phantom{00}$$

In factoring, it is easier to turn the division upside down.

$$2\,\overline{)\,30}$$
$$15$$

**B.** Continue with either 2 again or the next higher prime. Since 15 is not divisible by 2, use 3.

$$2\,\overline{)\,30}$$
$$3\,\overline{)\,15}$$
$$5$$

**C.** Since 5 is a prime number, you can stop. You read the factors from the left-hand side of the division (and include the last quotient) to get the factored form.

$$30 = 2 \times 3 \times 5.$$

## Factor 735.

**A.**
$$2\,\overline{)\,735}$$
$$?$$

2 is not a factor of 735, since 735 is an odd number. Try the next higher prime, 3.

**B.**
$$3\,\overline{)\,735}$$
$$245$$

**C.** Since 2 was not a factor of 735, it cannot be a factor of 245, so try 3 again.

$$3\,\overline{)\,735}$$
$$3\,\overline{)\,245}$$
$$?$$

3 is not a factor of 245.

**D.**
$$3\,\overline{)\,735}$$
$$5\,\overline{)\,245}$$
$$49$$

**E.** You should recognize that 5 is not a factor of 49. Try 7.

$$3\,\overline{)\,735}$$
$$5\,\overline{)\,245}$$
$$7\,\overline{)\,49}$$
$$7$$

**F.** You can stop because the quotient is a prime number. Reading the divisors and the last quotient gives the factored form.

$$735 = 3 \times 5 \times 7 \times 7.$$

# Simplifying

## Reduce $\dfrac{12}{16}$.

**A.** Factor the numerator and the denominator.

$$\frac{12}{16} = \frac{2 \times 2 \times 3}{2 \times 2 \times 2 \times 2}$$

**B.** Cross out common factors.

$$\frac{12}{16} = \frac{\cancel{2} \times \cancel{2} \times 3}{\cancel{2} \times \cancel{2} \times 2 \times 2}$$

**C.** Rewrite.

$$\frac{12}{16} = \frac{3}{2 \times 2} = \frac{3}{4}$$

## Reduce $\dfrac{105}{110}$.

**A.** Factor the numerator and the denominator.

$$\frac{105}{110} = \frac{3 \times 7 \times 5}{2 \times 5 \times 11}$$

**B.** Cross out common factors.

$$\frac{105}{110} = \frac{3 \times 7 \times \cancel{5}}{2 \times \cancel{5} \times 11}$$

**C.** Rewrite.

$$\frac{105}{110} = \frac{3 \times 7}{2 \times 11} = \frac{21}{22}$$

## Reduce $\dfrac{4}{4}$.

It might seem from the earlier problems on this page that the answer would be

$$\frac{4}{4} = \frac{2 \times 2}{2 \times 2} =$$

since the common factors all cancel out.

If all the factors are canceled, a factor of 1 (not written) always remains, so

$$\frac{4}{4} = \frac{1}{1}$$

The form $\frac{1}{1}$ is not considered the simplest form, however. Notice that if you divide any number by itself, the result is 1. Since fractions are another way of writing division, the simplest form is

$$\frac{4}{4} = 1.$$

## Reduce $\dfrac{127}{8}$.

Whenever the numerator is larger than the denominator, you can use the definition of a fraction as division to simplify. The simplified form will be either a whole number or a *mixed number,* such as $1\frac{1}{2}$, which is a way of writing $1 + \frac{1}{2}$ without using a $+$ sign.

**A.** Divide the numerator by the denominator.

$$8 \overline{)127}$$
$$\phantom{8)}\underline{\phantom{1}8}$$
$$\phantom{8)1}47$$
$$\phantom{8)1}\underline{40}$$
$$\phantom{8)11}7$$

This takes care of 120 of the 127 eighths, since $8 \times 15$ is 120. The remainder is 7 eighths.

**B.** Write the whole number and the fractional remainder.

$$\frac{127}{8} = 15\frac{7}{8}$$

# Finding the least common multiple (LCM)

You need to be able to find the *least common multiple* of two numbers. The multiples of a number are the products of that number and each of the whole numbers. For example, multiples of 2 are 0, 2, 4, 6, 8, 10, 12, and so forth, and multiples of 3 are 0, 3, 6, 9, 12, and so forth.

*Common* multiples of 2 and 3 are those that are in both lists: 0, 6, 12, and so forth. By definition, the least common multiple does not include 0 (since 0 is a common multiple of every pair of numbers), so the least common multiple (LCM) of 2 and 3 is 6.

---

## Find the LCM of 4 and 6.

**A.** List the nonzero multiples of both numbers.
Multiples of 4: 4, 8, 12, 16, 20
Multiples of 6: 6, 12, 18, 24, 30

**B.** Find the LCM.
Multiples of 4: 4, 8, 12, 16, 20
Multiples of 6: 6, 12, 18, 24, 30

The LCM of 4 and 6 is 12. This method can be used to find the LCM of any two numbers.

---

# Finding the least common denominator (LCD)

The least common multiple of the denominators of two or more fractions is known as the *least common denominator* (LCD) of the fractions. The LCD is used in addition.

---

## Find the LCD for $\frac{1}{6}$ and $\frac{3}{4}$.

**METHOD 1**
Find the least common multiple of the denominators.

Multiples of 6: 6, 12, 18
Multiples of 4: 4, 8, 12

The least common multiple of 6 and 4 is 12. Therefore, the LCD is 12.

---

**METHOD 2**

**A.** Factor each of the denominators.
$$6 = 2 \times 3$$
$$4 = 2 \times 2$$

**B.** The LCD must contain all of the factors of the two denominators as many times as they occur in the denominator in which each factor occurs the most.

**C.** The factor 3 occurs the most (1 time) in 6; the factor 2 occurs the most (2 times) in 4. Therefore, the LCD is
$$2 \times 2 \times 3 = 12.$$

---

## Multiplying fractions by 1

When you multiply any number by 1, the product is the same as the original number. This is as true of fractions as it is of whole numbers. With fractions, however, you can change the meaning of the fraction by multiplying by 1 without changing the value of the fraction.

The fraction $\frac{2}{3}$ is shown on the left. On the right, the same diagram is shown with each of the thirds separated into two pieces. Now there are 4 parts shaded, and 6 parts in all, but the same

amount of the square is shaded. In other words, if you multiply the numerator of the fraction by the same nonzero number as you multiply the denominator by—in this case,
$$\frac{2 \times 2}{3 \times 2}$$
the result has the same value as the original fraction.

# Renaming

$$\frac{2}{3} = \frac{?}{6}$$

To add or subtract fractions, you often have to rename one or both as a fraction with a different denominator. You do this by multiplying the fraction by some fraction equal to 1.

Because 1 is the identity element for multiplication, multiplying a number by 1 does not change its value.

$$\frac{2}{2} \times \frac{2}{3} = \frac{2 \times 2}{2 \times 3} = \frac{4}{6}$$

Multiplying $\frac{2}{3}$ by $\frac{2}{2}$ changes its denominator to 6; but it does not change its value, because $\frac{2}{2}$ is simply a name for 1.

---

$$\frac{3}{5} = \frac{?}{20}$$

The following fractions are equal to 1.

$$\frac{2}{2}, \frac{3}{3}, \frac{4}{4}, \frac{5}{5}, \frac{6}{6}, \frac{7}{7}, \cdots$$

One of them can be used to change $\frac{3}{5}$ to a fraction with a denominator of 20.

$$\frac{\square}{\square} \times \frac{3}{5} = \frac{?}{20}$$

Therefore $\frac{4}{4}$ is the fraction we must use to change $\frac{3}{5}$ to a fraction with a denominator of 20.

$$\frac{4}{4} \times \frac{3}{5} = \frac{4 \times 3}{4 \times 5} = \frac{12}{20}$$

We see it must be $\frac{4}{4}$, since $4 \times 5 = 20$. We could also reach this by division:

$$20 \div 5 = 4$$

---

$$\frac{4}{9} = \frac{?}{45}$$

**A.** Divide 45 by 9.

$$45 \div 9 = 5$$

**B.** Write a fraction equal to 1 that has the denominator 5.

$$1 = \frac{5}{5}$$

**C.** Multiply $\frac{4}{9}$ by $\frac{5}{5}$.

$$\frac{5}{5} \times \frac{4}{9} = \frac{5 \times 4}{5 \times 9} = \frac{20}{45}$$

---

$$4 = \frac{?}{3}$$

**A.** Rename 4 as a fraction with the denominator 1.

$$4 = \frac{4}{1}$$

**B.** Rename $\frac{4}{1}$ as thirds.

$$\frac{3}{3} \times \frac{4}{1} = \frac{12}{3}$$

### Improper fractions

If the numerator is greater than the denominator in a fraction, it is an *improper fraction.* You can think of the improper fraction $\frac{12}{3}$ as 4 objects, each of which has been divided into 3 parts. Clearly, the number of parts will be $3 \times 4$, or 12.

**Mathematics**

$$257 = \frac{?}{4}$$

**A.** Rename 257 as a fraction with the denominator 1.
$$257 = \frac{257}{1}$$

**B.** Rename $\frac{257}{1}$ as fourths.
$$\frac{4}{4} \times \frac{257}{1} = \frac{1028}{4}$$

$$2\frac{1}{3} = \frac{?}{3}$$

**A.** Rename 2 as a fraction with the denominator 3.
$$\frac{3}{3} \times \frac{2}{1} = \frac{6}{3}$$

**B.** Add $\frac{6}{3}$ to $\frac{1}{3}$.
$$\frac{6}{3} + \frac{1}{3} = \frac{6+1}{3} = \frac{7}{3}$$

$$4\frac{2}{7} = \frac{?}{7}$$

**A.** Rename 4 as a fraction with the denominator 7.
$$\frac{7}{7} \times \frac{4}{1} = \frac{28}{7}$$

**B.** Add $\frac{28}{7}$ to $\frac{2}{7}$.
$$\frac{28}{7} + \frac{2}{7} = \frac{28+2}{7} = \frac{30}{7}$$

### A shortcut

Here is an easy way to rename a mixed number as an improper fraction. Multiply the whole-number part of the mixed number by the denominator of the fraction. Add the product to the numerator of the fraction part of the mixed number. The sum is the numerator of the improper fraction. For example, to rewrite $2\frac{1}{3}$ as a fraction, think $(2 \times 3) + 1 = 7$, so $2\frac{1}{3} = \frac{7}{3}$. Similarly, to rewrite $4\frac{2}{7}$ as a number of sevenths, think $(4 \times 7) + 2 = 30$, so $4\frac{2}{7} = \frac{30}{7}$. The same shortcut will work for changing a whole number to an improper fraction. In that case, the number to be added to the product is 0.

## Sets of numbers

There are several sets of numbers that are used in arithmetic. Here is a summary of the types used in this section:

**Counting numbers or natural numbers**
The numbers you use to count with: 1, 2, 3, 4, 5, and so forth.

**Whole numbers**
The counting numbers and 0: 0, 1, 2, 3, 4, and so forth. The whole numbers are the numbers that tell how many members are in a set.

**Fractions or nonnegative rational numbers**
Numbers formed when any whole number is divided by any counting number. These numbers can be used to describe the relation of part of a set to a whole set. They also can be used to measure quantities that cannot be measured with whole numbers.

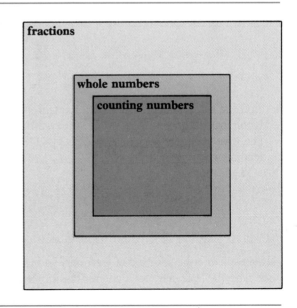

# Addition of fractions

$$\frac{1}{5} + \frac{3}{5}$$

Adding fractions that have a common denominator is very simple.

**A.** Rewrite the numerator addends over the common denominator.

$$\frac{1}{5} + \frac{3}{5} = \frac{1+3}{5}$$

**B.** Add the numerators.

$$\frac{1+3}{5} = \frac{4}{5}$$

---

$$\frac{3}{8} + \frac{2}{8}$$

**A.** Rewrite the numerator addends over the common denominator.

$$\frac{3}{8} + \frac{2}{8} = \frac{3+2}{8}$$

**B.** Add the numerators.

$$\frac{3+2}{8} = \frac{5}{8}$$

---

$$\frac{1}{3} + \frac{1}{2}$$

Before adding two fractions with different denominators, you must rewrite them as fractions with a common denominator.

**A.** Find the least common denominator for $\frac{1}{3}$ and $\frac{1}{2}$. The least common denominator for $\frac{1}{3}$ and $\frac{1}{2}$ is 6.

**B.** Rename $\frac{1}{3}$ and $\frac{1}{2}$ as sixths.

$$\frac{2}{2} \times \frac{1}{3} = \frac{2}{6} \text{ and } \frac{3}{3} \times \frac{1}{2} = \frac{3}{6}$$

**C.** Add $\frac{2}{6}$ and $\frac{3}{6}$.

$$\frac{2}{6} + \frac{3}{6} = \frac{2+3}{6} = \frac{5}{6}$$

---

$$\frac{2}{5} + \frac{3}{7}$$

**A.** Find the least common denominator for $\frac{2}{5}$ and $\frac{3}{7}$. The least common denominator for $\frac{2}{5}$ and $\frac{3}{7}$ is 35.

**B.** Rename $\frac{2}{5}$ and $\frac{3}{7}$ as thirty-fifths.

$$\frac{7}{7} \times \frac{2}{5} = \frac{14}{35} \text{ and } \frac{5}{5} \times \frac{3}{7} = \frac{15}{35}$$

**C.** Add $\frac{14}{35}$ and $\frac{15}{35}$.

$$\frac{14}{35} + \frac{15}{35} = \frac{14+15}{35} = \frac{29}{35}$$

Any two fractions with unlike denominators can be added in this way.

## Picturing addition of fractions

If you picture the addition of fractions, you can see why the least common denominator is needed.

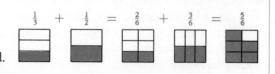

$$\frac{1}{3} + \frac{1}{2} = \frac{2}{6} + \frac{3}{6} = \frac{5}{6}$$

**Mathematics**

$$2\frac{1}{9} + \frac{4}{9}$$

Adding a mixed number and a fraction is easy once you have renamed the mixed number as a fraction.

**A.** Rename $2\frac{1}{9}$ as a fraction.
$$2\frac{1}{9} + \frac{4}{9} = \frac{19}{9} + \frac{4}{9}$$

**B.** Add.
$$\frac{19}{9} + \frac{4}{9} = \frac{23}{9}$$

**C.** Simplify.
$$\frac{23}{9} = 2\frac{5}{9}$$

---

$$2\frac{1}{9} + 16\frac{4}{9}$$

**A.** Rename both addends as fractions.
$$2\frac{1}{9} + 16\frac{4}{9} = \frac{19}{9} + \frac{148}{9}$$

**B.** Add.
$$\frac{19}{9} + \frac{148}{9} = \frac{19 + 148}{9} = \frac{167}{9}$$

**C.** Simplify.
$$\frac{167}{9} = 18\frac{5}{9}$$

---

$$3\frac{1}{8} + 6\frac{2}{5}$$

**METHOD 1**

**A.** Rename both addends as fractions.
$$3\frac{1}{8} + 6\frac{2}{5} = \frac{25}{8} + \frac{32}{5}$$

**B.** Rewrite as fractions with a common denominator.
$$\frac{25}{8} + \frac{32}{5} = \frac{125}{40} + \frac{256}{40}$$

**C.** Add.
$$\frac{125}{40} + \frac{256}{40} = \frac{125 + 256}{40} = \frac{381}{40}$$

**D.** Simplify.
$$\frac{381}{40} = 9\frac{21}{40}$$

---

**METHOD 2**

**A.** Write in vertical form as you do for the addition of whole numbers.
$$3\frac{1}{8}$$
$$+6\frac{2}{5}$$

**B.** Add the fractions.

$$3\frac{1}{8} \qquad 3\frac{5}{40}$$
$$+6\frac{2}{5} \qquad +6\frac{16}{40}$$
$$\overline{\phantom{+6}\frac{21}{40}}$$

**C.** Add the whole numbers.
$$3\frac{1}{8}$$
$$+6\frac{2}{5}$$
$$\overline{9\frac{21}{40}}$$

---

$$2\frac{3}{5} + 5\frac{7}{8}$$

**A.** Add in vertical form
$$2\frac{3}{5}$$
$$+5\frac{7}{8}$$

**B.** First rewrite the fractions with the lowest common denominator and add.
$$2\frac{24}{40}$$
$$+5\frac{35}{40}$$
$$\overline{7\frac{59}{40}}$$

**C.** The fraction part is improper. Change it to a mixed number and add the whole number part to 7.
$$7\frac{59}{40} = 7 + 1\frac{19}{40}$$
$$= 8\frac{19}{40}$$

# Subtraction of fractions $\dfrac{1}{2} - \dfrac{1}{3}$

**A.** Find the least common denominator for $\frac{1}{2}$ and $\frac{1}{3}$. The least common denominator for $\frac{1}{2}$ and $\frac{1}{3}$ is 6.

**B.** Rename $\frac{1}{2}$ and $\frac{1}{3}$ as sixths.
$$\frac{3}{3} \times \frac{1}{2} = \frac{3}{6}$$
$$\frac{2}{2} \times \frac{1}{3} = \frac{2}{6}$$

**C.** Subtract the numerators and write them over the common denominator.
$$\frac{3}{6} - \frac{2}{6} = \frac{3-2}{6} = \frac{1}{6}$$

---

$$\dfrac{30}{7} - 3\dfrac{3}{7}$$

**A.** Rewrite $3\frac{3}{7}$ as a fraction.
$$\tfrac{30}{7} - 3\tfrac{3}{7} = \tfrac{30}{7} - \tfrac{24}{7}$$

**B.** Subtract.
$$\tfrac{30}{7} - \tfrac{24}{7} = \tfrac{30-24}{7} = \tfrac{6}{7}$$

---

$$2\dfrac{5}{8} - 1\dfrac{1}{3}$$

**METHOD 1**

**A.** Rename both mixed numbers as fractions.
$$2\tfrac{5}{8} - 1\tfrac{1}{3} = \tfrac{21}{8} - \tfrac{4}{3}$$

**B.** Rewrite as fractions with a common denominator.
$$\tfrac{21}{8} - \tfrac{4}{3} = \tfrac{63}{24} - \tfrac{32}{24}$$

**C.** Subtract.
$$\tfrac{63}{24} - \tfrac{32}{24} = \tfrac{63-32}{24} = \tfrac{31}{24} \text{ or } 1\tfrac{7}{24}$$

**METHOD 2**

**A.** Write in vertical form as you do for whole numbers.
$$2\tfrac{5}{8}$$
$$-1\tfrac{1}{3}$$

**B.** Rename the fraction parts and subtract the fractions.
$$2\tfrac{15}{24}$$
$$-1\tfrac{8}{24}$$
$$\overline{\quad\tfrac{7}{24}}$$

**C.** Subtract the whole numbers.
$$2\tfrac{15}{24}$$
$$-1\tfrac{8}{24}$$
$$\overline{1\tfrac{7}{24}}$$

---

$$2\dfrac{5}{8} - 1\dfrac{2}{3}$$

**A.** Write in vertical form and rename.
$$2\tfrac{5}{8} \qquad 2\tfrac{15}{24}$$
$$-1\tfrac{2}{3} \qquad -1\tfrac{16}{24}$$
However, you cannot subtract $\frac{16}{24}$ from $\frac{15}{24}$ because 16 is greater than 15.

**B.** Rename $2\frac{15}{24}$ as follows:
$$1 + (1 + \tfrac{15}{24}) = 1\tfrac{24+15}{24}$$
$$= 1\tfrac{39}{24}$$

**C.** Now subtract the fractions first and then the whole numbers.
$$1\tfrac{39}{24}$$
$$-1\tfrac{16}{24}$$
$$\overline{\quad\tfrac{23}{24}}$$

---

**Mathematics**

# Multiplication of fractions

Multiplication of fractions is a very simple process:
you simply multiply numerators and denominators.

$$\frac{2}{9} \times \frac{6}{7}$$

**A.** Multiply numerators and denominators.
$$\frac{2}{9} \times \frac{6}{7} = \frac{2 \times 6}{9 \times 7} = \frac{12}{63}$$

**B.** Simplify.
$$\frac{12}{63} = \frac{4}{21}$$

$$6 \times \frac{3}{8}$$

**A.** To multiply a whole number by a fraction, you can rewrite the whole number as a fraction.
$$6 = \frac{6}{1}$$

**B.** Then go on to multiply and simplify.
$$\frac{6}{1} \times \frac{3}{8} = \frac{18}{8} = 2\frac{2}{8} = 2\frac{1}{4}$$

$$2\frac{3}{7} \times 9$$

**A.** Rename both factors as fractions.
$$2\frac{3}{7} \times 9 = \frac{17}{7} \times \frac{9}{1}$$

**B.** Multiply.
$$\frac{17}{7} \times \frac{9}{1} = \frac{17 \times 9}{7} = \frac{153}{7}$$

**C.** Simplify.
$$\frac{153}{7} = 21\frac{6}{7}$$

$$5\frac{2}{13} \times 2\frac{3}{9}$$

**A.** Rename both factors as fractions.
$$5\frac{2}{13} \times 2\frac{3}{9} = \frac{67}{13} \times \frac{21}{9}$$

**B.** Multiply.
$$\frac{67}{13} \times \frac{21}{9} = \frac{67 \times 21}{13 \times 9} = \frac{1407}{117}$$

**C.** Simplify.
$$\frac{1407}{117} = 12\frac{3}{117}$$

## Fractions and whole numbers

You may have learned to find $\frac{1}{3}$ of 6 this way:
Divide 6 by 3.
The quotient is 2, so $\frac{1}{3}$ of 6 is 2. That method is correct, but $\frac{1}{3}$ of 6 also means $\frac{1}{3} \times 6$. Therefore, you can also find $\frac{1}{3}$ of 6 by rewriting 6 as the fraction $\frac{6}{1}$ and multiplying:
$$\frac{1}{3} \times \frac{6}{1} = \frac{6}{3} = 2 .$$
The multiplication method is more general because you can also use it to find $\frac{1}{3}$ of $\frac{1}{2}$ more easily than by the division method. Furthermore, the division method is not effective for finding $\frac{2}{3}$ of 6.

## The size of the answer

Pam found $\frac{1}{2}$ of a pizza in the refrigerator. She ate $\frac{1}{3}$ of it for lunch. How much of a whole pizza did she eat?

Experience with whole numbers suggests that the answer to multiplication should be *greater* than any of the numbers in the problem. When both of the factors are less than 1, as in this problem, however, the answer will be *less* than either number in the problem. The answer is $\frac{1}{6}$.

# Division of fractions $\quad\dfrac{1}{2} \div \dfrac{2}{3}$

It is useful to know that dividing by a fraction gives the same result as multiplying by its *reciprocal*.

The reciprocal of $\frac{2}{3}$ is $\frac{3}{2}$. Therefore,

$$\frac{1}{2} \div \frac{2}{3} = \frac{1}{2} \times \frac{3}{2}$$

Dividing fractional numbers than becomes a simple problem of multiplication.

$$\frac{1}{2} \times \frac{3}{2} = \frac{1 \times 3}{2 \times 2} = \frac{3}{4}$$

---

$$\dfrac{2}{3} \div \dfrac{4}{7}$$

**A.** Rewrite as a multiplication problem.

$$\tfrac{2}{3} \div \tfrac{4}{7} = \tfrac{2}{3} \times \tfrac{7}{4}$$

**B.** Multiply.

$$\tfrac{2}{3} \times \tfrac{7}{4} = \tfrac{14}{12}$$

**C.** Simplify.

$$\tfrac{14}{12} = 1\tfrac{2}{12} = 1\tfrac{1}{6}$$

---

$$2\dfrac{5}{8} \div 3$$

**A.** Rename $2\frac{5}{8}$ and 3 as fractions.

$$2\tfrac{5}{8} \div 3 = \tfrac{21}{8} \div \tfrac{3}{1}$$

**B.** Rewrite as a multiplication problem.

$$\tfrac{21}{8} \div \tfrac{3}{1} = \tfrac{21}{8} \times \tfrac{1}{3}$$

**C.** Multiply.

$$\tfrac{21}{8} \times \tfrac{1}{3} = \tfrac{21 \times 1}{8 \times 3} = \tfrac{21}{24}$$

**D.** Simplify.

$$\tfrac{21}{24} = \tfrac{7}{8}$$

---

$$1\dfrac{5}{6} \div 4\dfrac{2}{7}$$

**A.** Rename $1\frac{5}{6}$ and $4\frac{2}{7}$ as fractions.

$$1\tfrac{5}{6} \div 4\tfrac{2}{7} = \tfrac{11}{6} \div \tfrac{30}{7}$$

**B.** Rewrite as a multiplication problem.

$$\tfrac{11}{6} \div \tfrac{30}{7} = \tfrac{11}{6} \times \tfrac{7}{30}$$

**C.** Multiply.

$$\tfrac{11}{6} \times \tfrac{7}{30} = \tfrac{11 \times 7}{6 \times 30} = \tfrac{77}{180}$$

---

## Estimation: Fractions and mixed numbers

Close estimates for operations with fractions are generally not needed. Often, it is just as easy to compute the answer to multiplication or division of fractions as it is to estimate. For checking purposes, the most important rules are:

- When adding or dividing two fractions, the answer will be *greater* than either of the fractions.
- When subtracting fractions, the answer will be *less* than the greatest number in the problem.
- When multiplying two fractions, the answer will be *less* than either number in the problem.

For mixed numbers, the best strategy is to estimate by rounding each number in the problem to the nearest whole number. Thus, $5\frac{1}{3} + 2\frac{1}{2}$ is about 8 (rounding $2\frac{1}{2}$ up to 3), $8\frac{1}{4} - 3\frac{7}{8}$ is about 4, $2\frac{1}{6} \times 3\frac{1}{8}$ is about 6, and $5\frac{3}{4} \div 2\frac{5}{6}$ is about $\frac{6}{3}$, or 2.

**Mathematics**

# Exponents

## Find the value of $4^3$.

**A.** Rewrite $4^3$ as a multiplication problem.
$4^3 = 4 \times 4 \times 4$

**B.** Multiply.
$4 \times 4 \times 4 = 64$

## Simplify $2^4 \times 2^5$.

**A.** Rewrite $2^4$ and $2^5$ as multiplication problems.
$2^4 = 2 \times 2 \times 2 \times 2$
$2^5 = 2 \times 2 \times 2 \times 2 \times 2$

**B.** Multiply.
$2^4 \times 2^5 = (2 \times 2 \times 2 \times 2) \times (2 \times 2 \times 2 \times 2 \times 2)$

**C.** Count how many twos are being multiplied together. There are 4 twos, then 5 twos being multiplied together.
$2^{4+5} = 2^9$
This could be written as
$2^4 \times 2^5 = 2^{4+5} = 2^9$.

## Simplify $3^7 \div 3^4$.

**A.** Rewrite $3^7$ and $3^4$ as multiplication problems.
$3^7 = 3 \times 3 \times 3 \times 3 \times 3 \times 3 \times 3$
$3^4 = 3 \times 3 \times 3 \times 3$

**B.** Divide.
$$\frac{3^7}{3^4} = \frac{\cancel{3} \times \cancel{3} \times \cancel{3} \times \cancel{3} \times 3 \times 3 \times 3}{\cancel{3} \times \cancel{3} \times \cancel{3} \times \cancel{3}}$$

**C.** Count how many threes are left. There are 3 threes.
$3 \times 3 \times 3 = 3^{7-4} = 3^3$
This could be written as
$3^7 \div 3^4 = 3^{7-4} = 3^3$.

## Simplify $(5^3)^2$.

**A.** Rewrite $5^3$ as a multiplication problem.
$5^3 = 5 \times 5 \times 5$

**B.** Rewrite as $(5 \times 5 \times 5)^2$.
$(5 \times 5 \times 5) \times (5 \times 5 \times 5)$

**C.** Count how many fives are being multiplied together. There are six fives.
$(5 \times 5 \times 5) \times (5 \times 5 \times 5) = 5^{3 \times 2} = 5^6$
This could be written as
$(5^3)^2 = 5^{3 \times 2} = 5^6$.

---

## Rules for exponents

The examples on this page suggest general rules for operating with exponents. If $a$ represents a number, and $m$ and $n$ are whole numbers greater than 1, then

$$a^m \times a^n = a^{m+n}$$
$$a^m \div a^n = a^{m-n}$$
$$(a^m)^n = a^{m \times n}$$

# Decimals

**11.6**
**+ 3.34**

Using a place value chart is a good way of solving problems like this.

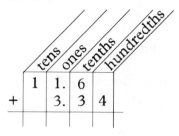

**A.** Add the numbers in the four columns, as before. Write the answer at the bottom.

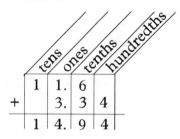

## Reading decimals

When reading a decimal, use either one of two different methods.

METHOD 1
The places after the decimal point are differentiated from those before the decimal point by adding -th to the end of the place name. The decimal point is read as *and*. Therefore, to read 3.34, say, "three and thirty-four hundredths."

METHOD 2
Many people prefer to read decimals by saying the name of each digit and saying *point* to indicate the placement of the decimal point. Using this system, 3.34 would be read as "three point three four."

**6.14**
**−2.05**

**A.** Subtract the numbers in the three columns, as before.

Write the answer at the bottom.

```
  6.14
 −2.05
  4.09
```

**20.**
**− 0.37**

**A.** Enter two zeros to the right of the decimal in the first number. This does not change the value of the number since
20. = 20.00

**B.** Subtract the numbers in the four columns, as before. Write the answer at the bottom.

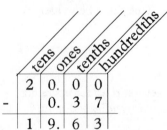

You may have noticed that we entered a zero in the ones column in the number 0.37. This was done to emphasize the location of the decimal.

**Mathematics**

$$\begin{array}{r} 12.96 \\ \times \quad 1.8 \end{array}$$

The number 12.96 is close to 13 and the number 1.8 is close to 2 so the product of these two numbers should be close to $13 \times 2 = 26$. This method of estimating can be used to check on the final location of the decimal point.

**A.** Multiply the numbers, temporarily forgetting the decimal points.

$$\begin{array}{r} 1296 \\ \times \quad 18 \\ \hline 10368 \\ 1296 \\ \hline 23328 \end{array}$$

**B.** Count the number of places that are used on the right of the decimal.

12.96 (two places)
1.8 (one place)

**C.** Add the number of places.

12.96 (two places)
1.8 +(one place)
(three places)

**D.** Enter a decimal point in the product so that number of places on the right of the decimal is the same as that found in step C.

23.328

23.328 has three places to the right of the decimal. Notice that 23.328 is near the approximate product of 26, which we found earlier.

$$6.1 \overline{)43.31}$$

The number 6.1 is close to 6 and the number 43.31 is close to 42. The quotient of these two numbers should be close to $42 \div 6 = 7$.

**A.** Divide the numbers as you would have done earlier, by temporarily forgetting the decimal points.

$$\begin{array}{r} 71 \\ 61 \overline{)4331} \\ 427 \\ \hline 61 \\ 61 \\ \hline 0 \end{array}$$

**B.** Count the number of places that are used on the right of the decimal in each number.

43.31 (two places)
6.1 (one place)

**C.** Subtract the number of places in the divisor from the number of places in the dividend.

43.31 (two places) (dividend)
6.1 −(one place) (divisor)
(one place)

**D.** Enter a decimal point in the quotient so that it has the same number of places to the right of the decimal point as found in step C. This gives us the quotient 7.1.

7.1 has one place to the right of the decimal. Notice that 7.1 is near the approximate quotient of 7, which we found earlier.

## Decimals and place value

Exponents can be used to make the meaning of decimals clearer. For whole numbers, the powers of 10 descend from left to right when you look at expanded form.

$$60,419 = 6 \times 10^4 + 0 \times 10^3 + 4 \times 10^2 + 1 \times 10 + 9$$

For decimals, the part to the left of the decimal point is just like a whole number, but the part to the right uses powers of $1/10$; also, the exponents *increase* as you read from left to right.

$$5.287 = 5 + 2 \times (1/10) + 8 \times (1/10)^2 + 7 \times (1/10)^3$$

# Decimals and fractions.

All fractions can be rewritten as decimals. There are, however, two kinds of decimals that result.

If the denominator of the fraction, when written in reduced form, can divide exactly into 10 or a power of 10 (i.e., 100, 1000, 10,000, . . .), then the decimal will end. If the denominator of the fraction, when written in reduced form, cannot divide exactly into 10 or a power of 10, then the decimal will continue without end and the numbers to the right of the decimal will repeat. The next two problems show an example of each kind.

## Write $\dfrac{21}{56}$ as a decimal.

**A.** Reduce the fraction.
$\frac{21}{56} = \frac{3}{8}$

**B.** Divide the denominator, 8, into 10 or one of its powers.
Since 8 divides exactly into 1000, the decimal will end.

**C.** Divide the denominator into the numerator. Add zeros to the right of the decimal point in the dividend, as needed.

$$
\begin{array}{r}
375 \\
8\overline{)3.000} \\
2\,4\phantom{00} \\
\hline
60\phantom{0} \\
56\phantom{0} \\
\hline
40 \\
40 \\
\hline
\end{array}
$$

**D.** Position the decimal point. There are three places in the dividend and no places in the divisor. Therefore, there will be three places in the quotient.

$$\frac{21}{56} = 0.375$$

## Write $\dfrac{10}{12}$ as a decimal.

**A.** Reduce the fraction.
$\frac{10}{12} = \frac{5}{6}$

**B.** Divide the denominator into 10 or one of its powers. Since 6 will not divide exactly into 10, 100, 1000, . . ., the decimal will not end.

**C.** Divide the denominator into the numerator. Add zeros to the right of the decimal point in the dividend, until the decimal begins to repeat.

$$
\begin{array}{r}
83\ldots \\
6\overline{)5.00} \\
4\,8\phantom{0} \\
\hline
20 \\
18 \\
\hline
20 \\
18 \\
\hline
2 \\
\end{array}
$$

**D.** Position the decimal point. We can use approximation to check on the final location of the decimal point. $6 \div 5$ is close to $6 \div 6$, which is 1. Our answer should be close to 1, which it is.
$$\frac{10}{12} = 0.833 \ldots$$

## Fraction-decimal equivalents

| | | | | |
|---|---|---|---|---|
| $\frac{1}{16} = 0.0625$ | $\frac{3}{8} = 0.375$ | $\frac{11}{16} = 0.6875$ | $\frac{1}{10} = 0.1$ | $\frac{3}{5} = 0.6$ |
| $\frac{1}{8} = 0.125$ | $\frac{7}{16} = 0.4375$ | $\frac{3}{4} = 0.75$ | $\frac{1}{5} = 0.2$ | $\frac{7}{10} = 0.7$ |
| $\frac{3}{16} = 0.1875$ | $\frac{1}{2} = 0.5$ | $\frac{13}{16} = 0.8125$ | $\frac{3}{10} = 0.3$ | $\frac{4}{5} = 0.8$ |
| $\frac{1}{4} = 0.25$ | $\frac{9}{16} = 0.5625$ | $\frac{7}{8} = 0.875$ | $\frac{2}{5} = 0.4$ | $\frac{9}{10} = 0.9$ |
| $\frac{5}{16} = 0.3125$ | $\frac{5}{8} = 0.625$ | $\frac{15}{16} = 0.9375$ | $\frac{1}{2} = 0.5$ | $\frac{10}{10} = 1.0$ |

**Mathematics**

## Write $2.56$ as a fraction.

**A.** Expand the decimal.
2.56 = 2 ones + 5 tenths + 6 hundredths
$2.56 = 2 + \frac{5}{10} + \frac{6}{100}$

**B.** Add the numbers.
$$2 + \frac{5}{10} + \frac{6}{100} = \frac{200}{100} + \frac{50}{100} + \frac{6}{100} = \frac{256}{100}$$

**C.** Reduce the fraction.
$$\frac{256}{100} = \frac{64}{25}$$

## Write $1.376376\ldots$ as a fraction.

**A.** Count the number of places in the part of the decimal that repeats. Since 376 repeats, there are 3 places.

**B.** Multiply the decimal by 10 raised to that power. 3 places means $10^3$ or $10 \times 10 \times 10$.
$1.376376\ldots \times 10 \times 10 \times 10 = 1376.376\ldots$

**C.** Subtract the smaller decimal from the larger.
$$\begin{array}{r} 1376.376\ldots \\ -\phantom{00}1.376376\ldots \\ \hline 1375. \end{array}$$

**D.** Divide the result by the power of 10 used in step B ($10^3$) minus one.
$$(10 \times 10 \times 10) - 1 = 999$$
$$1375 \div 999 = \frac{1375}{999}$$

# Ratio and percent

**Ratio.** A *ratio* is a comparison of two quantities by division; frequently, a ratio is also a rate, such as miles per gallon. If you get 37 miles per gallon, then for each gallon of gasoline you use, you can expect to drive 37 miles. Such a ratio is often written as a fraction.

$$\frac{\text{number of mi.}}{\text{number of gal.}} = \frac{37}{1} \text{ or } \frac{\text{number of gal.}}{\text{number of mi.}} = \frac{1}{37}$$

When two ratios are equal, the statement of that equality is a *proportion*. For example, if you can buy 4 apples for a dollar and 1 apple for a quarter, this can be shown by a proportion.

$$\frac{\text{apples}}{\text{cost}} = \frac{4}{1.00} = \frac{1}{0.25} \text{ or } \frac{\text{cost}}{\text{apples}} = \frac{1.00}{4} = \frac{0.25}{1}$$

Proportions are often useful in problem solving situations.

$$\frac{3}{4} = \frac{6}{?}$$

**METHOD 1**

**A.** Rename $\frac{3}{4}$ by multiplying by a fraction form for 1.

**B.** Since the numerator of the renamed fraction must be 6, the fraction form needed for 1 is $\frac{2}{2}$.

**C.** $\frac{3}{4} \times \frac{2}{2} = \frac{6}{8}$ so $\frac{3}{4} = \frac{6}{8}$.

**METHOD 2**

**A.** In a proportion, the product of the numerator of one ratio and the denominator of the other is equal to the product of the denominator of the first with the numerator of the second.

**B.** Therefore, $3 \times ? = 4 \times 6$
$= 24$

**C.** If 3 times some number is 24, determine the unknown number by dividing 24 by 3. The answer is $\frac{3}{4} = \frac{6}{8}$.

**Percent.** A *percent* is a ratio of some quantity to 100. Percents are usually written with a percent sign, %, instead of as fractions. A percent is also equivalent to hundredths, since hundredths are a way of writing fractions with denominators of 100.

---

## Write $37\%$ as a fraction and as a decimal.

**A.** The numerator of the fraction is 37 and the denominator is 100.
$$37\% = \tfrac{37}{100}$$

**B.** 37% is the same as 37 hundredths.
$$37\% = 0.37$$

---

## Find $40\%$ of $150$.

**METHOD 1**

**A.** Rewrite 40% as a fraction.
$$40\% = \tfrac{40}{100}$$

**B.** Simplify.
$$\tfrac{40}{100} = \tfrac{2}{5}$$

**C.** Multiply.
$$\tfrac{2}{5} \times 150 = \tfrac{300}{5} = 60$$

**METHOD 2**

**A.** Rewrite 40% as hundredths.
$$40\% = 0.40$$

**B.** Multiply.
$$
\begin{array}{r}
150 \\
\times\, 0.40 \\
\hline
60.00
\end{array}
$$

**METHOD 3**

**A.** A percent problem can always be rewritten as a proportion.
$$\tfrac{40}{100} = \tfrac{?}{150}$$

**B.** Rewrite the proportion as a multiplication problem.
$$40 \times 150 = 100 \times ?$$
$$\text{or} \quad 100 \times ? = 6000$$

**C.** Solve by dividing 6000 by 100. The quotient is 60.

---

## What percent is $40$ of $64$?

**METHOD 1**

**A.** Use the proportion idea.
$$\tfrac{40}{64} = \tfrac{?}{100}$$

**B.** Rewrite as
$$40 \times 100 = 64 \times ?$$
$$\text{or} \quad 64 \times ? = 4000.$$

**C.** Divide by 64.
$$4000 \div 64 = 62.5$$
40 is 62.5% of 64.

**METHOD 2**

**A.** Think of the unknown percent as a decimal.
$$? \times 64 = 40$$

**B.** Divide 40 by 64.
$$
\begin{array}{r}
0.625 \\
64\,\overline{)\,40.000}
\end{array}
$$

**C.** Rewrite the quotient as a percent. The answer is 62.5%.

---

## $18$ is $24\%$ of what number?

**A.** Write a proportion.
$$\tfrac{18}{?} = \tfrac{24}{100}$$

**B.** Rewrite as a multiplication problem.
$$18 \times 100 = ? \times 24$$
$$\text{or} \quad ? \times 24 = 1800$$

**C.** Divide by 24. The quotient is 75. Therefore, 18 is 24% of 75.

---

**Mathematics**

# Problem solving with percents

## A shirt that normally sells for $18 is offered at a 15% discount. How much will you have to pay?

**METHOD 1**

**A.** Find 15% of 18 by one of the methods shown earlier. Here conversion to a decimal and multiplication will be used.

$$\begin{array}{r} 18 \\ \times\,0.15 \\ \hline 2.7 \end{array}$$

**B.** The answer is the amount of the discount: $2.70. A discount is a *percent of decrease*, which means that the *percentage* (the amount that is a percent of a number) must be

subtracted from the original amount.

$$\begin{array}{r} 18.00 \\ -\,\,2.70 \\ \hline 15.30 \end{array}$$

The amount that you will pay is $15.30.

**METHOD 2**

**A.** A percent of decrease may be subtracted from 100% before calculating the amount after the decrease. This is often easier to do than subtracting the percentage of decrease from the original amount, since, for example, most people can subtract 15 from 100 in their heads to get 85.

**B.** Find 85% of 18 by any of the methods used earlier. Here, for comparison, the proportion method will be used instead of the multiplication method that was used in Method 1.

$$\frac{85}{100} = \frac{?}{18}$$

**C.** Complete the solution.

$$85 \times 18 = 100 \times ?$$

or $100 \times ? = 1530$

Dividing by 100 can be accomplished by "moving the decimal point" to the left 2 places, so the answer is $15.30.

## In a state where sales tax is 5¼%, what amount must you pay on a purchase of $16.50?

**METHOD 1**

**A.** Find the percentage. Here the proportion method is used.

$$\frac{5.25}{100} = \frac{?}{16.5}$$

$$100 \times ? = 86.625$$

$$? = 0.86625$$

**B.** Since this is a money problem, the percentage must be rounded *up* to the next higher cent. The percentage is $0.87.

**C.** A sales tax is a *percent of increase*, so the percentage must be *added* to the original amount to get the answer.

$$\begin{array}{r} 16.50 \\ +\,\,0.87 \\ \hline 17.37 \end{array}$$

**METHOD 2**

**A.** For a percent of increase, you can add the percent to 100% before you begin to compute. This is easy to do in your head. Therefore, you can compute the final amount by using $105\frac{1}{4}$%.

**B.** A percent greater than 100 percent may be written as a decimal that is greater than 1. For example, $105\frac{1}{4}$% is equivalent to 1.0525.

**C.** Complete the solution by finding $105\frac{1}{4}$% of $16.50.

$$\begin{array}{r} 16.5 \\ \times\,1.0525 \\ \hline 17.36625 \end{array}$$

The answer is $17.37.

# Hand-held calculators

*Calculators are useful in many different situations. Most people use one at least sometimes in the home, and many schools now permit students to use calculators to help them with their homework and during exams.*

Hand-held calculators are so inexpensive that most families and many schools now have them. These calculators make problems with addition, subtraction, multiplication, and division of whole numbers very easy. Calculators can also be used to solve problems involving decimals and percents, but special techniques must be employed to solve problems involving fractions.

Although no two calculators are exactly alike, all have some characteristics in common. For example, on all calculators, problems involving decimals are solved in the same way as problems involving whole numbers. The only difference is that the decimal point key must be depressed when needed.

Simple addition, subtraction, multiplication, and division problems are solved by depressing the correct keys for the numbers, operations, or symbols. Often a more complicated problem must be broken down into a series of simpler problems, but in many cases problems can be solved more easily by attacking the complicated problem in the proper manner. Some methods are detailed on the two pages that follow.

Here are some specific things to look for on the calculator you are using.

**Does it have a percent key?** Most calculators have a percent key that permits percents to be entered as whole numbers in multiplication. If your calculator has a percent key, you can find the percent of a number by entering the number, entering $\times$, entering the amount of the percent, and then using the percent key instead of $=$. To find 25% of 60, you would enter

$$\boxed{6}\,\boxed{0}\,\boxed{\times}\,\boxed{2}\,\boxed{5}\,\boxed{\%}.$$

If your calculator does not have a percent key, you must convert the percent to a decimal, enter the number, the $\times$, the decimal, and the $=$.

$$\boxed{6}\,\boxed{0}\,\boxed{\times}\,\boxed{.}\,\boxed{2}\,\boxed{5}\,\boxed{=}$$

**Which key causes the calculator to keep repeating an operation?** All calculators have a key that will cause the same number to be added, subtracted, multiplied, or divided over and over, but the key that does this varies from calculator to calculator. The most common key for this is $=$. You can check to see if this works on your calculator by pressing

$$\boxed{2}\,\boxed{\times}\,\boxed{3}\,\boxed{=}\,\boxed{=}\,\boxed{=}$$

If $=$ is the *accumulator key*, the display panel should show

2   3   6   12   24.

Notice that on most calculators, the number that is held constant is the *first* number entered, not the second. If the second number entered had been held constant, the display would have been

2   3   6   18   54.

**Does your calculator use a floating decimal point display for large numbers?** On more expensive calculators, an answer may surprise you by being written in a different notation from the familiar one. In that case, the calculator has

**Mathematics**

gone into a "floating-point" notation because it does not have enough room on the display to give the answer. If a calculator has the ability to display up to eight digits, which is common, it will give a floating-point answer for any product greater than 9999 × 10,000. For example, try

$$\boxed{1}\,\boxed{0}\,\boxed{0}\,\boxed{0}\,\boxed{0}\,\boxed{\times}\,\boxed{1}\,\boxed{0}\,\boxed{0}\,\boxed{0}\,\boxed{0}\,\boxed{=}.$$

In the floating-point system, the display will read something like
$$1. \times 10\ 08 \text{ or } 1.\ E\ 8.$$

If the calculator is not a floating-point calculator and has room to display only eight digits, an error message will appear, for example E, along with a decimal such as 1.000000; or the calculator may be unable to provide an answer.

# Using your calculator.

**Reading floating-point notation.** The first number in a floating-point system is a factor. The number after the × 10 or the E is an exponent. The base of the exponent is always 10. Thus the number 1. E 8 means 1 times $10^8$. The number $10^8$ is written as 1 followed by 8 zeros, so
$$1.\ E\ 8 = 100,000,000.$$
A number such as 2.8374 E 10 means
$$2.8374 \times 10,000,000,000 = 28,374,000,000.$$

**Understanding about rounding.** The calculator has only a limited space to display answers, so infinite decimals and all of the digits of a floating-point factor cannot be displayed. Most calculators do not round, however. If you divide 10 by 6, the answer will be given as 1.6666666, although the answer to the nearest ten millionth is actually 1.6666667. Similarly, if you multiply 13,131,131 by 20 in a floating-point system, the answer will be shown as 2.6262 E 8, although the correct answer to the nearest ten thousand is 262,630,000. In some cases, you will want to correct the calculator's rounding to improve accuracy. Most of the time, however, it is satisfactory to use one less place and round the answer that is shown on the calculator; in other words, change 1.6666666 to 1.666667 or 2.6262 E 8 to 262,600,000. Notice that in a series of calculations, the errors produced by dropping digits will all tend to be in the same direction, while rounded subcalculations will sometimes be too great and sometimes be too small, tending to average out the error.

The most common errors are the result of one of two mistakes.

1. You may punch the wrong key accidentally. These errors can be minimized by using as few keys as possible and by always checking your result by estimating the answer in your head as you do the problem.

2. You may set up the problem the wrong way. Make sure that the answer you get is reasonable for the problem situation. For example, determine in advance whether the answer will be larger or smaller than the largest number in the problem.

**Adding columns.** Adding on a calculator is more accurate and faster if you can punch in fewer numbers. You can perform easy operations mentally as you go along. For example, here is a way to group an addition problem.

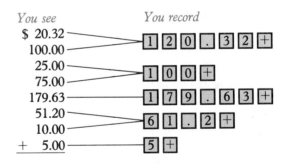

The display should show 466.15, the correct answer. Note that you do not need to enter decimal points and zeros if there are only zeros after the decimal point.

**Using the distributive property.** The product of a sum is equal to the sum of the products. For example,
$$(3 \times 2) + (3 \times 5) = 3 \times (2 + 5)$$
$$6 \quad + \quad 15 \quad = 3 \times \quad 7$$
$$21 = 21$$

Technically, this is known as *the distributive property of multiplication over addition*. It also applies for multiplication over subtraction.
$$(4 \times 6) - (4 \times 1) = 4 \times (6 - 1)$$
$$24 \quad - \quad 4 \quad = 4 \times \quad 5$$
$$20 = 20$$

Here is an example of how this property can save time and work. Suppose you know the daily amount 5 persons earned in a small business:

| Harold | $ 9 |
| Marianne | $31 |
| Dale | $21 |
| Al | $27 |
| Kathy | $25 |

You need to calculate the total amount paid by the company for a 5-day work week. The most obvious way is to multiply each daily salary by 5 and then add the totals:

$$5 \times \$ 9 = \$ 45$$
$$5 \times \$31 = \$155$$
$$5 \times \$21 = \$105$$
$$5 \times \$27 = \$135$$
$$5 \times \$25 = \underline{\$125}$$
$$\$565$$

Since all the daily income figures are to be multiplied by the same factor, however, you can add the daily salary figures and then multiply the total by 5. Enter:

$$\boxed{9}\,\boxed{+}\,\boxed{3}\,\boxed{1}\,\boxed{+}\,\boxed{2}\,\boxed{1}\,\boxed{+}\,\boxed{2}\,\boxed{7}$$
$$\boxed{+}\,\boxed{2}\,\boxed{5}\,\boxed{\times}\,\boxed{5}\,\boxed{=}$$

The display should show 565, which means $565. Both ways give the same result, but the second is much shorter and less likely to produce errors, especially on a calculator.

**Converting fractions to decimals.** Since calculators do not work with fractions, you must convert any fraction problems to decimals. This is easily accomplished by dividing the numerator of each fraction in the problem by the denominator. In most cases (unless the denominator contains factors of 2 and 5 only), the fraction will have a nonterminating decimal expansion and the computer will drop all digits after the seventh or eighth. Therefore, your answer will be approximate instead of exact.

$$\frac{3}{4} \times \frac{2}{3} = .75 \times 0.6666666 = 0.4999999$$

If you need a more accurate answer, however, you can save the conversion to decimals to the end of the problem. For example, the more accurate way to multiply $\frac{2}{3}$ by $\frac{3}{4}$ is to punch in

$$\boxed{3}\,\boxed{\times}\,\boxed{2}\,\boxed{=}$$

record the answer and punch in

$$\boxed{4}\,\boxed{\times}\,\boxed{3}\,\boxed{=}$$

and record the answer, then divide the first an-

swer by the second. In this case, however, you can probably perform the first operations in your head and proceed to directly punch in

$$\boxed{6}\,\boxed{\div}\,\boxed{1}\,\boxed{2}\,\boxed{=},$$

which will give a display of 0.5. This answer is the exact one.

**Using percents of increase and decrease.** When a percentage is to be added to an amount (as in a sales-tax situation), it is a *percent of increase*. When a percentage is to be subtracted from an amount (as in a discount situation), it is a *percent of decrease*. In both cases, it is generally better to solve problems by first adding the given percent to 100% or subtracting it from 100% before performing the calculation. For example, if you want to find the amount of a purchase when the sales tax is $5\frac{1}{4}\%$, multiply the amount before the tax by 105.25 and then press the $\boxed{\%}$ key (if you do not have a $\boxed{\%}$ key, multiply by 1.0525 and press the $\boxed{=}$ key). The result is the same as multiplying by $5\frac{1}{4}\%$ and then adding the result to the original amount, but the calculation is much easier. Similarly, to find the amount of a purchase after a discount of 20%, it is easier to first subtract 20% from 100% to get 80% (which you can do in your head). Then multiply the amount of the purchase by 80 and press the $\boxed{\%}$ key (or multiply the amount of the purchase by .8 and press the $\boxed{=}$ key).

**Learning to use the calculator's memory.** Almost all hand-held calculators have a memory feature, but surveys have shown that most people do not use it. The memory features of calculators usually differ. Use the instructions that come with the calculator. Here is an example of how one calculator works. To calculate $(47 \times 12) + (58 \div 4) - (69 \times 8)$, first clear the memory and then press the following keys:

$$\boxed{4}\,\boxed{7}\,\boxed{\times}\,\boxed{1}\,\boxed{2}\,\boxed{M+}\,\boxed{5}\,\boxed{8}$$
$$\boxed{\div}\,\boxed{4}\,\boxed{M+}\,\boxed{6}\,\boxed{9}\,\boxed{\times}\,\boxed{8}\,\boxed{M-}\,\boxed{RM}.$$

The advantage of using the memory over working without it is in what you see displayed on the screen. After you press $\boxed{M+}$ for the first time, you will see 564, which is the product of 47 and 12; the second time you press $\boxed{M+}$ you will see the quotient of 58 divided by 4, 14.5; when you press $\boxed{M-}$ you will see the product of 69 and 8, 552. Only when you press $\boxed{RM}$ will the final answer, 26.5, appear.

**Mathematics**

# List of symbols

## Arithmetic

| | |
|---|---|
| . | decimal point |
| $\div$ | divided by |
| $\overline{\phantom{)}}$ | divided into |
| $=$ | equals |
| $(\ )$ | grouping |
| $-$ | minus |
| $\times$ | multiplied by or times |
| $\%$ | percent |
| $+$ | plus |

## Geometry

| | |
|---|---|
| $\angle$ | angle |
| $\odot$ | circle |
| $\cong$ | congruent |
| $\overleftrightarrow{AB}$ | line $AB$ |
| $\overline{AB}$ | line segment $AB$ |
| $m\,(\angle A)$ | measure of angle $A$ |
| $\|\|$ | parallel to |
| $\perp$ | perpendicular to |
| $\pi$ | pi (about 3.14159) |
| $\overrightarrow{AB}$ | ray $AB$ |
| $\sim$ | similar to |
| $\therefore$ | therefore |
| $\triangle$ | triangle |

## Algebra

| | |
|---|---|
| $\|a\|$ | absolute value of $a$ |
| $\approx$ | approximately equal to |
| $^3$ | cubed |
| $>$ | greater than |
| $\geq$ | greater than or equal to |
| $<$ | less than |
| $\leq$ | less than or equal to |
| $\neq$ | not equal to |
| $-3$ | negative 3 |
| $\ldots$ | not all members shown |
| $\pm$ | plus or minus |
| $+3$ | positive 3 |
| $'$ | prime (changes the meaning of a variable) |
| $\sqrt{\phantom{x}}$ | square root |
| $^2$ | squared |

## Sets

| | |
|---|---|
| $\varnothing$ | empty (or null) set |
| $\cap$ | intersection |
| $\subset$ | (proper) subset of |
| $\in$ | member of |
| $\{\ \}$ | set |
| $\cup$ | union |

$$\frac{3}{5} = \frac{6}{10}$$

fraction

# Dictionary of mathematics

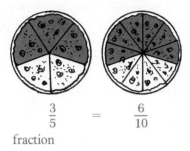

## Roman numerals

The ancient Romans used seven letters in their number system. The letters and their values are:

| I | V | X | L | C | D | M |
|---|---|---|---|---|---|---|
| 1 | 5 | 10 | 50 | 100 | 500 | 1000 |

In Roman numerals a number is written from left to right, with the symbols added together to determine the value of the number. For example, the value 56 in Roman numerals is LVI (50 + 5 + 1). When a smaller numeral is to the left of a larger one, the smaller is subtracted from the larger. For example, the number 90 is written as XC (10 *subtracted* from 100).

**addend.** Any one of a set of numbers that are being added.

**addition.** Process of finding the number of members in two or more sets that have been combined.

**alogorithm.** Any formal method for performing a computation.

**area.** Two-dimensional measure of the surface inside a plane (flat) geometric figure.

**base.** When an exponent is used, the number to which the exponent is applied.

**basic fact.** For addition, subtraction, multiplication, and division of whole numbers, the sums, differences, products, and quotients formed when two numbers less than 10 are added or multiplied, or when a subtrahend and difference are both less than 10, or when a divisor and quotient are less than 10.

**circle.** Plane figure that is the set of points equidistant from a given point.

**common denominator.** For two or more fractions, a denominator with which each fraction may be shown.

**counting number.** One of the numbers 1, 2, 3, . . . that are used to count with; also called a *natural number*.

**cubed.** Taken as a factor three times.

**decimal.** Number shown using a decimal point to indicate fractions whose denominators are powers of 10.

**denominator.** In a fraction, the number that tells the number of parts into which something has been divided.

**difference.** In subtraction, the answer; sometimes called the

*remainder.* A distinction is maintained between subtraction used to show comparison (when *difference* is used) and subtraction to show part of a set taken away (when *remainder* is used).

**digit.** Whole number less than 10.

**dividend.** In division, the quantity that is to be divided.

**division.** Operation that can be either treated as repeated subtraction or as the inverse (opposite operation) of multiplication.

**divisor.** Quantity by which the dividend is divided.

**element.** Another name for a member of a set.

**expanded form.** Method of writing a number as the sum of powers of 10, either with or without using exponents.

**exponent.** Small numeral (superscript) written above and to the right of a number. Exponents that represent counting numbers tell how many times the number is used as a factor.

**factor.** In multiplication, any one of the numbers to be multiplied to form a product.

**factoring.** Process of finding the counting numbers that when multiplied will form a given number.

**fraction.** Number formed by dividing a whole number by a counting number.

**greatest common factor.** Number that is the largest factor shared by two or more numbers.

**least common denominator.** Least common multiple of the denominators of a set of fractions.

**least common multiple.** Smallest nonzero number that is a multiple of all numbers in a set of numbers.

**minuend.** In subtraction, the number from which you subtract or the larger of two amounts being compared by subtraction.

**mixed number.** Sum of a whole number and a fraction that is written by adjoining the numeral for the fraction to the numeral for the whole number.

**multiple.** Product of a given number and a whole number.

**multiplicand.** Number that you are multiplying; when multiplication is viewed as repeated addition, the addend that is repeated.

**multiplication.** Operation that for counting numbers may be viewed as repeated addition.

**multiplier.** Number by which you are multiplying; when multiplication is viewed as repeated addition, the number that indicates how many times the repeated addend will be used.

**number line.** Line on which a scale of numbers is indicated.

**numeral.** Written symbol for a number.

**numerator.** In a fraction, the number of parts represented by the fraction.

**parallel.** For lines, two or more lines in a plane that do not meet.

**percent.** Ratio of a number to 100 that is shown as a whole number or mixed number with a percent sign.

**percent of decrease.** Percent used to indicate that the per-

centage must be subtracted from the original amount.

**percent of increase.** Percent used to indicate that the percentage must be added to the original amount.

**percentage.** Quantity found by taking a percent of a number.

**perimeter.** Distance around a plane figure (usually called the *circumference* if the figure is a circle).

**perpendicular.** For lines or line segments, two lines (segments) that meet at right angles.

**place value.** System of representing numbers in which the place a digit has in a numeral indicates the value of the digit.

**power.** Number formed by using the same number as a factor more than once; more generally, any number indicated by an exponent.

**product.** The answer in multiplication.

**proportion.** Statement that two ratios are equal.

**quotient.** Answer in division.

**ratio.** Comparison of two quantities by division, often expressed as a rate.

**real number.** Any positive or negative number that can be shown on a number line.

**remainder.** In division, the whole number left over in addition to the quotient.

Sometimes used to name the answer in subtraction.

**right angle.** When two lines intersect to form four equal angles, one of the four angles.

**set.** Any collection of objects or ideas such that you can tell whether a given object or idea is a member of the collection.

**square.** Plane figure formed of four equal line segments that share endpoints and also make four right angles.

**squared.** Taken as a factor two times.

**subtraction.** Operation that can be viewed as finding the number when objects are taken away from a set or as a comparison to determine how much greater one amount is than another; the inverse (opposite) of addition.

**subtrahend.** Either the number that is taken away in subtraction or the smaller of two amounts being compared.

**sum.** Answer in addition.

**triangle.** Plane figure formed from three different line segments that share endpoints.

**whole number.** Either a counting number or zero.

**zero.** A number that tells the number of members in a set that is empty (a set that has no members).

---

## For Further Reference

Hogben, Lancelot
*Mathematics for the Million*
W.W. Norton
Prindle, Anthony and Prindle, Katie
*Math the Easy Way*
Barron's

Sperling, Abraham P. and Levison, Samuel D.
*Arithmetic Made Simple*
Doubleday
Trivieri, Lawrence A.
*Basic Mathematics*
HarperCollins

---

# Health and Safety

A healthier and happier lifestyle is within reach of everyone who understands and follows sensible health practices. To enjoy a high level of "wellness," it is essential to eat sufficient nutritional foods; obtain enough rest and relaxation; exercise sensibly; attend to personal grooming; and cultivate a positive outlook on life. You should also learn to avoid dangerous situations and know the proper procedures to follow in an emergency.

It is equally important to be aware of potential threats to good health (such as persistent pain or bleeding), and to report promptly such distress signals to your physician. Regular medical checkups, as recommended by your family physician, provide the best possible method of detecting medical problems as they arise. For more information about good health, see the sections on Health and Fitness and You and Modern Medicine in Volume 3.

## Common distress signals

*If any of the following conditions arise and are persistent, severe, or unexplained, check with your physician without delay.*

**Pain** (the foremost danger signal especially when the cause is not known)
**Fatigue** (without obvious cause)
**Weight change** (gain or loss)
**Headache** (especially if it recurs)
**Fever** (almost always a sign of infection)
**Hemorrhage** (bleeding)
**Indigestion** (especially if it recurs often)
**Insomnia** (sleeplessness)
**Skin changes** (rashes or ulcers)
**Personality changes** (abnormal restlessness or aggression)
**Vision changes** (seeing double or poorly)

**Edema** (swelling)
**Lumps or growths** (especially if they get larger)
**Breathlessness** (especially after slight exertion)
**Coughing and hoarseness** (if continued for a period of time)
**Sore throat** (if not relieved within a few days)
**Loss of appetite** (or difficulty in swallowing)
**Excessive thirst** (especially if there is excessive or painful urination)
**Dizziness, giddiness, or vertigo**
**Bowel-habit changes** (especially unaccustomed constipation or diarrhea)

# Nutrition

The human body requires adequate amounts of basic foods together with their nutrients to keep it functioning properly and to stay healthy and strong. Some foods are needed to supply energy or growth, while others are necessary to regulate body processes. There are also some foods whose use should be restricted.

Because no one food contains all the nutrients (proteins, carbohydrates, fats, vitamins, and minerals) needed for good health, it is important you select the right amounts and combinations of foods. Proper nutrition consists of eating well-balanced meals that include daily servings from each of five major food groups.

The United States Department of Agriculture (USDA) has developed the Food Guide Pyramid, which illustrates the five major food groups and identifies the number of servings from each that you need for a healthful, well-balanced diet.

No single food group is more important than another—all are needed to achieve a balanced diet.

The Food Guide Pyramid is also a good guide to limiting the amount of fat in your diet. The top of the pyramid represents fats, oils, and sweets, items that add calories and little else to the diet. These have so little nutritional value that you should eat them sparingly.

The base of the pyramid represents low-fat, high-energy foods that come from grains. Above this are the food groups for fruits and vegetables, also low-fat foods that are important for vitamins and minerals and for dietary fiber. Above these are the food groups for milk, yogurt, and cheese and for meat, poultry, fish, beans, and nuts. Both are higher in fat but are good sources of protein and such minerals as calcium, zinc, and iron.

## The USDA Food Guide Pyramid

The pyramid shape reflects the relative number of servings you need from each food group daily. Eat more cereals, grains, vegetables, and fruits, less dairy foods and meat. Limit fat and sweets.

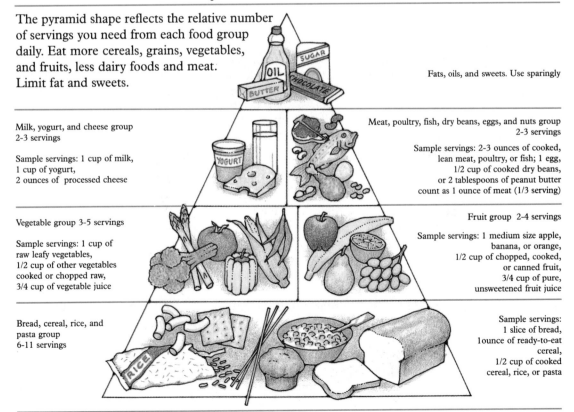

Fats, oils, and sweets. Use sparingly

Milk, yogurt, and cheese group
2-3 servings

Sample servings: 1 cup of milk,
1 cup of yogurt,
2 ounces of processed cheese

Meat, poultry, fish, dry beans, eggs, and nuts group
2-3 servings

Sample servings: 2-3 ounces of cooked,
lean meat, poultry, or fish; 1 egg,
1/2 cup of cooked dry beans,
or 2 tablespoons of peanut butter
count as 1 ounce of meat (1/3 serving)

Vegetable group 3-5 servings

Sample servings: 1 cup of
raw leafy vegetables,
1/2 cup of other vegetables
cooked or chopped raw,
3/4 cup of vegetable juice

Fruit group 2-4 servings

Sample servings: 1 medium size apple,
banana, or orange,
1/2 cup of chopped, cooked,
or canned fruit,
3/4 cup of pure,
unsweetened fruit juice

Bread, cereal, rice, and
pasta group
6-11 servings

Sample servings:
1 slice of bread,
1 ounce of ready-to-eat
cereal,
1/2 cup of cooked
cereal, rice, or pasta

# Vitamins and nutrition.

In themselves, vitamins are not sources of energy but they help to process carbohydrates, fats, and proteins so that they can be turned into energy or be used in the body to build cells and restore tissues. Vitamins are divided into two groups, depending on whether they can dissolve in fat (fat-soluble) or in water (water-soluble). The water-

## Vitamins

### Fat-soluble vitamins

| Vitamin | Good sources | Recommended daily allowances* | Average serving in some foods |
|---|---|---|---|
| Vitamin A | butter, cheese, whole milk liver green leafy and yellow vegetables apricots, peaches, persimmons | infants and children: 375 to 700 mcg RE** males and females: 800 to 1000 mcg RE pregnant and lactating women: 800 to 1300 mcg RE | 1/2 cup raw, or 1 cup cooked carrots 1 apricot or peach 1 large egg 1 cup whole milk 3 oz. Cheddar cheese 1 cup dandelion or turnip greens |
| Vitamin D | cod-liver or other fish-liver oils dairy products | infants and children: 300 to 400 I.U. males and females: 200 to 400 I.U. pregnant and lactating women: 400 I.U. | 4 8-oz. glasses whole milk 14 tbsp. butter 12 large egg yolks |
| Vitamin E alpha-tocopherol | green leafy vegetables fish and other oils butter rice | infants and children: 3 to 7 mg alpha-TE** males and females: 8 to 10 mg alpha-TE pregnant and lactating women: 10 to 12 mg alpha-TE | 9 to 15 tbsp. olive oil 2 tbsp. safflower oil 3/4 lb. beet top greens 5 to 6 large stalks broccoli 18 Brussels sprouts 2/3 lb. spinach |

### Water-soluble vitamins

| Vitamin | Good sources | Recommended daily allowances* | Average serving in some foods |
|---|---|---|---|
| Thiamine vitamin B$_1$ | whole grain cereals peas, beans many fruits and vegetables brewer's yeast liver, kidney | infants and children: 0.3 to 1.0 mg males and females: 1.0 to 1.5 mg pregnant and lactating women: 1.5 to 1.6 mg | 2 1/2 cups cooked peas 1 tbsp. brewer's yeast 10 stalks broccoli 5 large oranges 3 oz. liver, calf |
| Riboflavin vitamin B$_2$ | enriched foods green leafy vegetables liver, kidney lean meat eggs, milk wheat germ, yeast | infants and children: 0.4 to 1.2 mg males and females: 1.2 to 1.8 mg pregnant and lactating women: 1.6 to 1.8 mg | 2 2/3 cups whole milk 3 cups low-fat yogurt 2 cups cottage cheese 3/4 cup broccoli 4 oz. liver, calf 1/4 cup peanut butter |

**Health and Safety**

soluble vitamins, unlike the fat-soluble vitamins, are not stored effectively in the body and must be obtained from the daily diet. The fat-soluble vitamins can cause disease if taken in excessive amounts. When taking vitamin supplements, it is wise to check with your physician regarding your special needs. Each average serving meets the daily allowance

## Water-soluble vitamins (cont.)

| Vitamin | Good sources | Recommended daily allowances* | Average serving in some foods |
|---|---|---|---|
| **Niacin** nicotinic acid | beefsteak, liver fish legumes whole grain cereals peanuts, soybeans | infants and children: 5 to 13 mg males and females: 13 to 20 mg pregnant and lactating women: 17 to 20 mg | 3 cups fresh peas 3 cups cooked lentils 2 cups cottage cheese 3 cups soybeans, uncooked 1/2 cup bran or oatmeal 1/4 cup peanuts |
| **Vitamin B$_{12}$**\*** cyanocobalamin | liver, kidney dairy products brewer's yeast fish eggs | infants and children: 0.3 to 1.4 mcg males and females: 2.0 mcg pregnant and lactating women: 2.2 to 2.6 mcg | 3 cups whole or skim milk 1 1/2 cups cottage cheese 3 eggs 12 oz. Cheddar cheese 6 oz. Swiss or cream cheese |
| **Vitamin C** ascorbic acid | most fruits and vegetables, especially citrus fruits and juices | infants and children: 30 to 45 mg males and females: 50 to 60 mg pregnant and lactating women: 70 to 95 mg | 1 apple or orange 1/2 cantaloupe or grapefruit 1/2 cup collards, raw or cooked 2 tomatoes 2 boiled potatoes with jackets 2 cups raw spinach |
| **Vitamin B$_6$** pyridoxine | blackstrap molasses liver, kidney, heart whole grains wheat germ | infants and children: 0.3 to 1.4 mg males and females: 1.4 to 2.0 mg pregnant and lactating women: 2.1 to 2.2 mg | 2 1/2 lbs. raw spinach 1 cup peas 2 cups dry lentils 1 medium baked potato 1 tbsp. molasses 4 oz. liver, beef |
| **Folic acid** folate | liver, kidney brewer's yeast green leafy vegetables legumes | infants and children: 25 to 100 mcg males and females: 150 to 200 mcg pregnant and lactating women: 260 to 400 mcg | 6 stalks broccoli 15 large Brussels sprouts 9 beets 1/2 lb. spinach 1 3/4 cups dry chick peas or kidney beans |

*The average requirements shown are taken from *Recommended Daily Dietary Allowances* (revised 1989), Food and Nutrition Board, National Academy of Sciences. These allowance levels are estimated to be adequate for practically all healthy people in the United States.
**Synthetic vitamins are measured by weight, with the main weight measurement called a gram (about 1/28 of an ounce). The vitamins shown here are recommended in a certain number of units (I.U.), or by weight in grams or parts of grams (milligrams or micrograms).

    I.U.—International Unit (amount of vitamin necessary to produce the identifying action of the vitamin).
    mg—milligram (one-thousandth of a gram).            RE—retinol equivalent (1 mcg retinol or 6 mcg beta-carotene).
    mcg—microgram (one-thousandth of a milligram).      alpha-TE—alpha-tocopherol equivalent.
***Note that there are no vegetable sources for Vitamin B$_{12}$. Strict vegetarians should take B$_{12}$ supplements.

**Faulty food habits.** It is well recognized that many Americans eat far too many "empty calories" (refined flour, highly milled rice, refined sugar, and alcohol) in their daily diets. Nutritionists recommend that such foods be avoided, or greatly limited, especially in growing children and in adults with severe nutritional problems (for example, alcoholics and the aging). In the United States today, the emphasis on good nutrition has shifted from the problem of getting enough of the right nutrients to getting too much of some ingredients.

```
NUTRITION INFORMATION PER SERVING
SERVING SIZE .........(8 OZ. AS PREPARED - 226 G)
CALORIES ............................................. 75
PROTEIN (GRAMS) ................................. 3
TOTAL CARBOHYDRATES (GRAMS).................... 8
FAT (GRAMS)........................................ 4
SODIUM............................ 960 MG/SERVING
INGREDIENTS: CHICKEN STOCK, CHICKEN,
POTATOES, WATER, SALT, PEPPER, CARROTS,
CELERY, PEAS, CORN STARCH, MONOSODIUM
GLUTAMATE, CHICKEN FAT, DEHYDRATED
ONIONS, YEAST EXTRACT AND PLANT PROTEIN.
```

*By law, ingredients are listed in order of the amount used, so there is more salt than carrots in this soup. Monosodium glutamate also adds to the sodium count.*

## Hard facts about sugar and salt (sodium)

### Sugar

- Foods containing white sugar, white flour, or refined cereals account for more than 50 percent of the calories in the average American diet.
- Refined sugar is 100 percent carbohydrate. It supplies nothing more than "empty calories." It has no proteins, vitamins, or minerals.
- Refined sugar is truly a starvation food. At first, it satisfies the call for food and the blood sugar level rises very rapidly. Then, however, this level drops far below normal limits, resulting in hypoglycemia (abnormally low blood sugar), which is often accompanied by extreme fatigue.
- Refined sugar is hidden in many popular and processed foods such as bakery products, cereals, soups, salad dressings, jams and jellies, and soft drinks.
- Bacteria that thrive on refined white sugar create acids that are chiefly responsible for tooth decay. Dentists recommend not eating sweets between meals and rinsing the mouth after eating or drinking to remove anything sweet from the teeth.
- The names given sugars end in "-ose." Fructose (fruit sugar), glucose (found in honey and corn syrup), dextrose (bread sugar), and lactose (milk sugar) are sugars found in food. Sucrose (a molecular combination of fructose and glucose) is table sugar. Check product labels to see the amount of sugar content in processed foods.

### Salt (sodium)

- Sodium salts are necessary to perform various functions in the body. It takes about 230 milligrams of sodium every day to maintain a healthy balance of water and minerals. The U.S. Surgeon General has established 2000 milligrams as the daily allowance; this is slightly more than nine times actual body needs.
- Most Americans consume at least 5000 milligrams of sodium every day. This amounts to 20 times actual body needs and is at least $2\frac{1}{2}$ times the recommended daily sodium intake.
- Since World War II, Americans have relied more and more on processed and fast foods. Such foods are often greatly overloaded with sodium. For example, one tablespoon of canned peas contains as much salt as $5\frac{1}{2}$ pounds of fresh peas. A McDonald's Big Mac contains 962 milligrams of sodium, just about half the recommended daily allowance.
- The greatest source of sodium in the American diet today can be found in cereals and breads, cakes, pies, and cookies, baking powder, and baking soda. This is reason enough to not use salt in cooking or at the table. Yet many people habitually reach for the salt shaker before even tasting the food they are about to eat.
- In checking product labels, it is important to recognize sodium in its various forms: sodium chloride (table salt); monosodium glutamate (a flavor enhancer); and sodium benzoate and sodium nitrate (preservatives).

**Health and Safety**

*A chicken leg has about 260 Calories fried, but only 230 stewed. Most of the fat is in the skin; without the skin the same chicken leg has only about 190 Calories.*

*There is about the same amount of alcohol in a can of beer, a glass of wine, and a highball. Two of any of them can become the cause of impaired driving.*

## Hard facts about fats and alcohol

### Fats

- Like carbohydrates and proteins, fats are energy-producing foods. In addition, fats have various other important functions, such as heat insulation under the skin and protective support to various parts of the body. Fats also serve as a vehicle for fat-soluble vitamins.

- There are three principal dietary sources of fat supply: animal fats, dairy products, and plant oils. Fat contains over twice as many calories as an equal amount of protein or carbohydrate. In a good diet, fats should constitute only about 25 percent of the body's total caloric needs.

- Excessive amounts of fat stored in the body cause people to be overweight. This overworks the heart and circulatory system. The strain is tremendous; it takes 4000 feet of blood vessels to nourish every pound of extra fat.

- Animal fats (beef, pork, lamb, dairy products) are high in saturated fatty acids. Vegetable fats (vegetable oils, fish, poultry) contain large amounts of polyunsaturated acids.

- While the matter of polyunsaturated (soft) fats versus unsaturated (hard) fats in preventing heart disease has not yet been completely resolved, there is general agreement that total fat intake should be limited. The American Heart Association suggests that animal fats be limited to 10 percent of daily caloric intake, and that vegetable fats constitute 10 to 15 percent of daily caloric intake.

### Alcohol

- There are an estimated 10 million alcoholics in the United States; these people affect the lives of more than 40 million nonalcoholics. Almost half of all alcoholics are women; men in their early 20's make up the largest number of problem drinkers.

- Alcohol is absorbed directly into the bloodstream without digestion. The body oxidizes alcohol slowly, only $\frac{1}{2}$ ounce an hour. If too much alcohol is taken too quickly, intoxication results. A blood alcohol level of 80 mg per 100 ml (0.08 percent) can be expected when a man of average weight drinks two double whiskeys or two pints of beer. At this level, driving may be seriously impaired.

- Alcohol is alcohol, no matter what the form. There are equal amounts of alcohol in 12 ounces of beer, 4 ounces of wine, and $1\frac{1}{2}$ ounces of whiskey.

- Alcoholism is a sickness and a social problem. It is well to learn in young adulthood that alcohol is not a necessity of life, nor does it add to one's total social acceptability. For some people drinking is no problem, but for others it can result in serious harm.

- The longer alcoholism continues untreated, the greater the risk of damage to the liver, heart, and brain. A number of special problems of chronic alcoholism are related to nutritional deficiencies caused by the ability of alcohol to supply calories and depress the appetite without supplying needed vitamins or amino acids.

# Good nutrition and healthy teeth

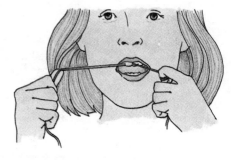

*Both brushing up-and-down thoroughly and flossing are needed after each meal.*

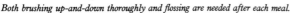

It is not known exactly how dental caries (tooth decay) are caused, but dental authorities agree that the best way to prevent dental problems is with twice daily cleaning of the teeth (using a brush and floss), attention to diet, and twice-a-year visits to the dentist. Decayed teeth interfere with proper chewing of food and may contribute to digestive disorders.

The purpose of brushing the teeth is to remove fermentable debris (especially carbohydrates such as sugar) on which acid-forming bacteria flourish. Toothpastes or powders (used only to aid the brush) are a matter of choice, but the toothbrush must be of a suitable design and construction to permit proper cleaning of the teeth.

A sufficient intake of calcium and vitamins, especially in infancy and childhood, will help the normal development of teeth and jaws. Regular visits to the dentist should start early in life, especially to correct the overcrowding of teeth or improper growth.

# Exercise

Every healthy person needs regular exercise to keep physically fit and enjoy robust health. The benefits of even a fair amount of exercise are many: improved digestion and blood circulation; more efficient functioning of the lungs and heart; increased muscle tone; and an easing of tension.

Keeping physically fit does not mean having to join an expensive health spa or buy special equipment. The benefits of exercise can be obtained just by pursuing your favorite sport, by taking an exercise break instead of a coffee break, or by doing ordinary chores in and about the home. When sweeping, dusting, making beds, or gardening, make a conscious effort to bend and stretch. Break up your day with a brisk walk. Walking uses most of the vital muscles, and it can be done anytime, anywhere, in almost any kind of weather.

Whatever the sport or exercise program chosen, your age, weight, and physical condition are important factors to consider. Start slowly and build up your exercises as your endurance increases. Ease into an exercise period with some simple warm-up exercises (stretching and bending) and cool down the same way at the end of an exercise period. In general, aerobic exercises provide the most benefits.

**Weight control.** Regular exercise can help the body to burn up unnecessary fat and should be a part of any weight-control process. It is the combination of improved eating habits (notably, cutting out empty calories) and regular exercise that will make for the success and permanent value of a weight-reduction program.

Eating less of high-fat meats, sauces, and pastries, and substituting more cereal products, vegetables, and fruits, will not only reduce the number of calories, but will afford the body needed vitamins and minerals. To be safe, an exercise and diet program should be approved by your physician.

Exercise does more than merely burn off calories. Studies have shown that regular exercise helps moderate the appetite by changing the levels of hormones in the body. As a result, lost weight is not regained the way it often is when a weight-loss diet ends.

## Varieties of  exercise

| Type | Example | Effects |
|------|---------|---------|
| **Aerobic** | walking<br>jogging<br>cycling<br>swimming<br>aerobic dancing | This type of activity helps the lungs process more air, which in turn strengthens the heart and builds up endurance. |
| **Anerobic** | tennis<br>handball<br>sprinting | Activity of short, intense duration, followed by a period of rest, places a sudden high demand on the heart and lungs. These sports also have an aerobic effect. |
| **Isometric** | hand, arm or leg pulls and presses principle involves pitting one muscle group against another, or against an object that does not move, for about 10 to 15 seconds | These exercises, having very little or no movement connected with them, are intended to increase the strength of the muscles exercised. |
| **Isotonic** | calisthenics, such as toe touches, jumping jacks, sit ups, leg lifts, push ups | This form of exercise permits considerable free body movement. |

## Energy costs for different kinds of activities

| Home activities | Calories spent per minute | Sports and hobbies | Calories spent per minute |
|-----------------|---------------------------|--------------------|---------------------------|
| bringing in laundry | 3.2 | basketball | 8.6 |
| hanging laundry | 4.7 | bowling | 8.1 |
| ironing clothes | 4.2 | cycling | 8.0 |
| machine sewing | 1.5 | fencing | 4.0 |
| making beds | 5.3 | golfing | 5.5 |
| mopping floors | 5.3 | horseback riding | 3.0 |
| peeling vegetables | 2.0 | jogging | up to 17.0 |
| scrubbing floors | 6.0 | Ping-Pong | 4.8 |
| sweeping floors | 1.7 | swimming | 12.1 |
| stirring, mixing foods | 3.0 | tennis | 7.0 |
| washing clothes | 2.9 | walking outdoors | 6.1 |

# Drugs and disease

## Drug Abuse

| Drug group | Drugs | Effects of occasional use | Effects of chronic use |
|---|---|---|---|
| CNS (central nervous system) general depressant | Alcohol | Slurred speech; hangover; impaired coordination and judgment; increased tolerance | Addiction; loss of responsibility; tremors; shakes; depression; seizures; delirium; possible liver damage. |
| | Barbiturates Called downers, yellow jackets, red or blue devils; swallowed or injected. | Sluggishness; impaired thinking and speech; poor memory and judgment; personality changes. | Anxiety; nausea; weakness and insomnia; possible convulsions; delirium; hallucinations; death from overdose. |
| | Inhalants (aerosols/volatile hydrocarbons) | Lowered pulse and respiration; exhilaration; confusion; delirium; coma; heart failure. | Weight loss; fatigue; brain, kidney, and liver damage. |
| CNS (central nervous system) general stimulant | Amphetamines Called speed or uppers; swallowed or injected. | Elevated mood; sense of ability and energy; nervousness; less need for food and sleep. | Fatigue; depression; loss of appetite; paranoia; convulsions; death from overdose. |
| | Cocaine Inhaled, smoked, or injected; crack, a crystalline form is smoked. | Short-term high followed by depression; restlessness; irritability; loss of appetite; less need for sleep; anxiety. | Psychological dependence; sleeplessness; loss of appetite; nasal passage damage. |
| | Nicotine Smoked, snuffed, or chewed. | Tobacco smell; increased heart rate; stained teeth and hands. | Addiction; respiratory problems; lung and heart disease; cancer. |
| Hallucinogen | LSD (lysergic acid diethylamide) Called acid; swallowed or injected. | Hallucinations; mood swings; enhanced senses; time distortion; bad trips can be terrifying. | Psychological dependence; time distortion; flashbacks; lapses in sense of reality; panic reactions. |
| | Marijuana Called pot, grass, or joints; smoked or eaten. | Relaxed feeling; enhanced senses; anxiety; paranoia; time distortion. | Psychological dependence; memory impairment; lack of motivation; respiratory problems; chromosome damage. |
| | Ecstasy (MDMA) Swallowed. | Hallucinations; sense of well-being; euphoria; nervousness; increased blood pressure and heartbeat; sweating; insomnia. | Possible brain damage; other long-term effects not determined. |
| Narcotic analgesic (pain-relieving medicine) | Heroin Morphine Methadone Swallowed, smoked, or injected. | Drowsiness; changes in mood; mental clouding; unrealistic sense of well-being, or the opposite. | Addiction; suppression of pain, hunger, aggression, and sexual drive; coma or death from overdose. |
| Dissociative anesthetic (block all bodily sensations) | PCP Special K (phencyclidine hydrochloride) Swallowed, smoked, injected, or snuffed. | Blockage of bodily sensations, particularly sense of pain; clouded thinking; delusions; aggression; mood swings; nausea; coma. | Interference with normal growth; inhibition of cognitive abilities and learning; psychological dependence. |

**Health and Safety**

# Communicable diseases.
Infection can only be conveyed by contact with the infecting organism.

*Direct contact* means actually touching, or being touched by, the person having the infection or the natural source of the infection. Such contact also includes breathing in air exhaled by the person within a range of 3 feet or less.

*Indirect contact* occurs mainly by means of contaminated vehicles of infection (food, clothing, etc.), air convection, and insects or animals.

## Suggested vaccination schedule

| Age | Vaccine |
|---|---|
| Birth–2 months | Hepatitis B shot |
| 2 months | DTP (diphtheria, tetanus, pertussis) shot<br>Hib (H. influenzae type b) shot<br>IPV (inactivated polio virus) shot |
| 2–4 months | Hepatitis B shot |
| 4 months | DTP shot<br>Hib shot<br>IPV shot |
| 6 months | DTP shot<br>Hib shot*<br>OPV (oral polio vaccine) dose |
| 6–18 months | Hepatitis B shot |
| 12–15 months | Hib shot<br>MMR (measles, mumps, rubella) shot |
| 12–18 months | DTP; or DTaP (diphtheria and tetanus toxoids and acellular pertussis vaccine) at 15 months<br>VZV (varicella zoster virus) shot |
| 18 months | OPV dose |
| 4–6 years | DTP or DTaP shot |
| 4–6 years or 11–12 years | MMR shot (consistent with state immunization requirements) |
| 11–12 years | Hepatitis B series (for those who have not already received three doses) |
| 11–16 years | Tetanus-diphtheria booster |
| 13 years | VZV (for those who have not already received the vaccine) |

* May not be required, depending on the type of vaccine administered

Source: Public Health Service,
Centers for Disease Control and Prevention, Atlanta, Georgia 30333

## Some communicable diseases

| Method of transfer | Disease |
|---|---|
| By respiratory discharges (droplet infection) and/or contact | chicken pox<br>common cold<br>diphtheria<br>German measles (rubella)<br>mumps<br>pneumonia/influenza<br>streptococcal sore throat<br>tuberculosis<br>whooping cough |
| By discharges from intestinal tract (therefore, often by contaminated soil or water) | cholera<br>dysentery (amoebic and bacillary)<br>hookworm<br>paratyphoid fever<br>typhoid fever |
| By contaminated food or milk | botulism<br>cholera<br>food infections (salmonellosis)<br>intestinal worms<br>streptococcal infections<br>tuberculosis<br>typhoid fever<br>undulant fever |
| By association with animals | anthrax<br>plague (e.g., from rats)<br>tularemia (e.g., from rabbits)<br>undulant fever (e.g., from cows) |
| By insects (usually the bite of an insect) | sleeping sickness (tsetse fly)<br>dengue fever (mosquito)<br>malaria (mosquito)<br>plague (rat-flea)<br>typhus (louse)<br>yellow fever (mosquito) |
| By intimate contact or, usually, by sexual intercourse | gonorrhea<br>syphilis<br>herpes (genital)<br>AIDS |

# Human anatomy

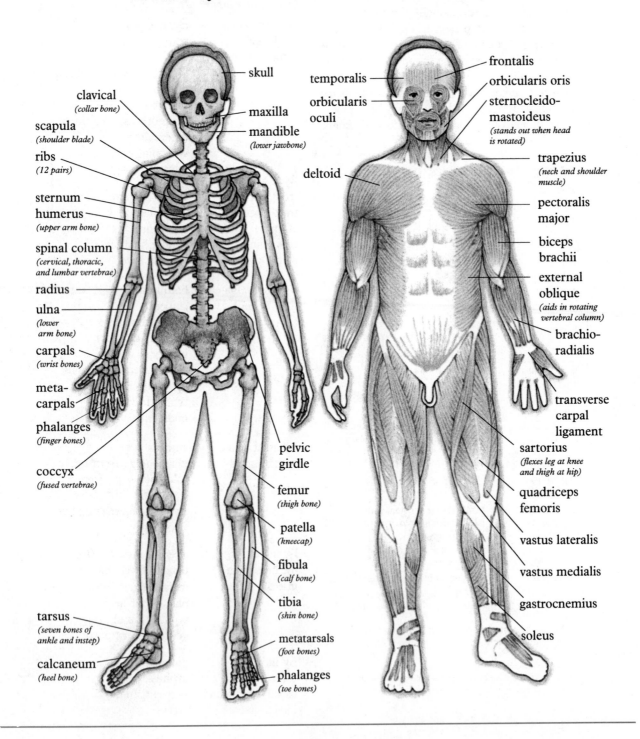

## Skeletal system

skull

clavical
*(collar bone)*

scapula
*(shoulder blade)*

maxilla

mandible
*(lower jawbone)*

ribs
*(12 pairs)*

sternum

humerus
*(upper arm bone)*

spinal column
*(cervical, thoracic, and lumbar vertebrae)*

radius

ulna
*(lower arm bone)*

carpals
*(wrist bones)*

meta-carpals

phalanges
*(finger bones)*

coccyx
*(fused vertebrae)*

pelvic girdle

femur
*(thigh bone)*

patella
*(kneecap)*

fibula
*(calf bone)*

tibia
*(shin bone)*

tarsus
*(seven bones of ankle and instep)*

calcaneum
*(heel bone)*

metatarsals
*(foot bones)*

phalanges
*(toe bones)*

## Muscular system

frontalis

temporalis

orbicularis oris

orbicularis oculi

sternocleido-mastoideus
*(stands out when head is rotated)*

deltoid

trapezius
*(neck and shoulder muscle)*

pectoralis major

biceps brachii

external oblique
*(aids in rotating vertebral column)*

brachio-radialis

transverse carpal ligament

sartorius
*(flexes leg at knee and thigh at hip)*

quadriceps femoris

vastus lateralis

vastus medialis

gastrocnemius

soleus

**Health and Safety**

# Respiratory system

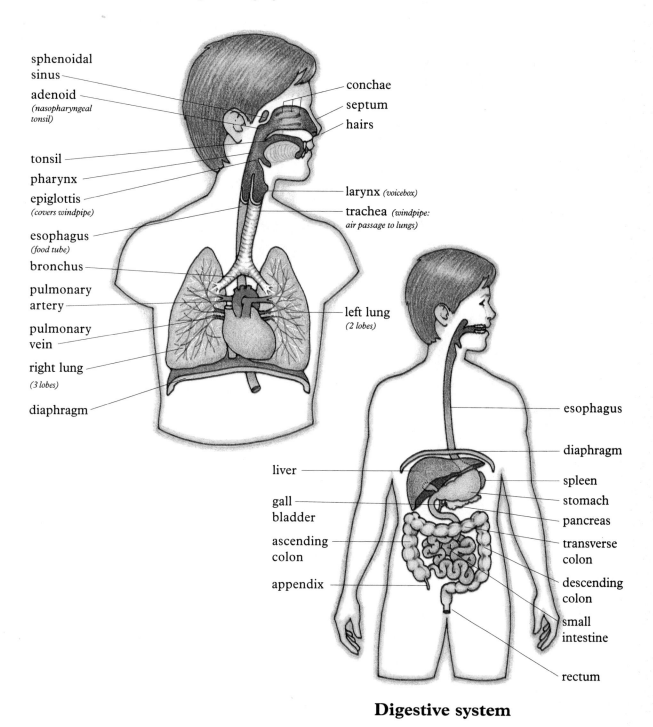

sphenoidal sinus

adenoid
*(nasopharyngeal tonsil)*

tonsil

pharynx

epiglottis
*(covers windpipe)*

esophagus
*(food tube)*

bronchus

pulmonary artery

pulmonary vein

right lung
*(3 lobes)*

diaphragm

conchae

septum

hairs

larynx *(voicebox)*

trachea *(windpipe: air passage to lungs)*

left lung
*(2 lobes)*

liver

gall bladder

ascending colon

appendix

esophagus

diaphragm

spleen

stomach

pancreas

transverse colon

descending colon

small intestine

rectum

# Digestive system

# Nervous System

# Human brain

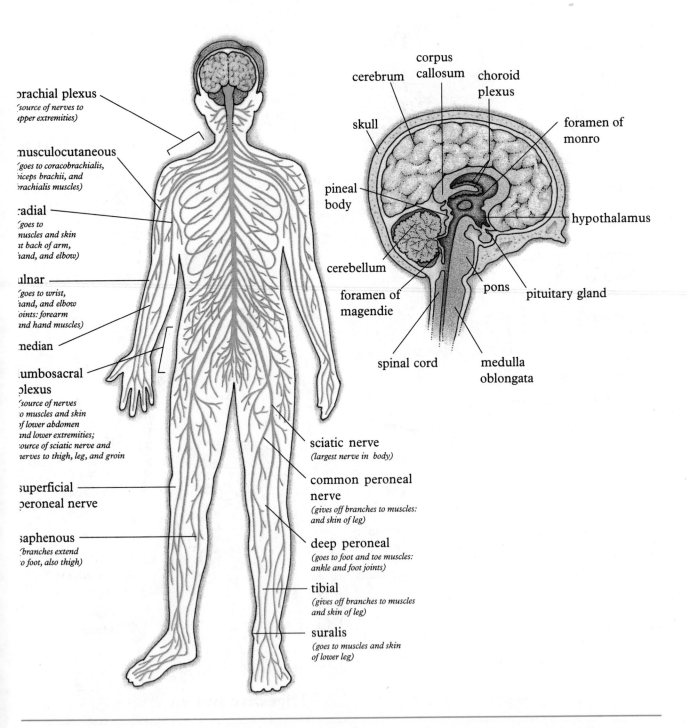

**brachial plexus**
*(source of nerves to upper extremities)*

**musculocutaneous**
*(goes to coracobrachialis, biceps brachii, and brachialis muscles)*

**radial**
*(goes to muscles and skin at back of arm, hand, and elbow)*

**ulnar**
*(goes to wrist, hand, and elbow joints: forearm and hand muscles)*

**median**

**lumbosacral plexus**
*(source of nerves to muscles and skin of lower abdomen and lower extremities; source of sciatic nerve and nerves to thigh, leg, and groin*

**superficial peroneal nerve**

**saphenous**
*(branches extend to foot, also thigh)*

**sciatic nerve**
*(largest nerve in body)*

**common peroneal nerve**
*(gives off branches to muscles: and skin of leg)*

**deep peroneal**
*(goes to foot and toe muscles: ankle and foot joints)*

**tibial**
*(gives off branches to muscles and skin of leg)*

**suralis**
*(goes to muscles and skin of lower leg)*

cerebrum

corpus callosum

choroid plexus

skull

foramen of monro

pineal body

cerebellum

hypothalamus

foramen of magendie

pons

pituitary gland

spinal cord

medulla oblongata

**Health and Safety**

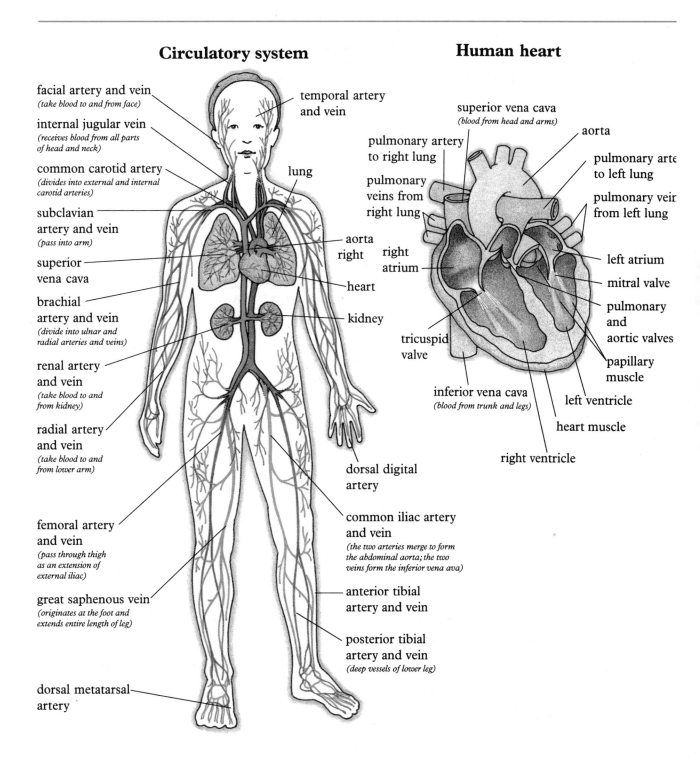

# Circulatory system

facial artery and vein
*(take blood to and from face)*

internal jugular vein
*(receives blood from all parts of head and neck)*

common carotid artery
*(divides into external and internal carotid arteries)*

subclavian artery and vein
*(pass into arm)*

superior vena cava

brachial artery and vein
*(divide into ulnar and radial arteries and veins)*

renal artery and vein
*(take blood to and from kidney)*

radial artery and vein
*(take blood to and from lower arm)*

femoral artery and vein
*(pass through thigh as an extension of external iliac)*

great saphenous vein
*(originates at the foot and extends entire length of leg)*

dorsal metatarsal artery

temporal artery and vein

lung

aorta

right

heart

kidney

dorsal digital artery

common iliac artery and vein
*(the two arteries merge to form the abdominal aorta; the two veins form the inferior vena ava)*

anterior tibial artery and vein

posterior tibial artery and vein
*(deep vessels of lower leg)*

# Human heart

superior vena cava
*(blood from head and arms)*

aorta

pulmonary artery to right lung

pulmonary arte to left lung

pulmonary veins from right lung

pulmonary veir from left lung

right atrium

left atrium

mitral valve

tricuspid valve

pulmonary and aortic valves

papillary muscle

inferior vena cava
*(blood from trunk and legs)*

left ventricle

heart muscle

right ventricle

# Safety

Everyone is aware of the great numbers of serious and fatal accidents on the highway, but not everyone realizes that many more accidents happen at home. Most often, children under five years of age and adults over 65 are involved. Much can be done to prevent accidents in the home: it is usually just a matter of combining common sense and good housekeeping.

## Safety at home

| *Area* | *Safety precautions* |
|---|---|
| **Kitchen and laundry** (The kitchen may well be the most dangerous room in the house. All types of accidents occur there: e.g., falls, burns, explosions, and poisonings.)  | • Keep lye, bleach, and all cleaning supplies in locked, or tightly secured, cabinets out of the reach of children and away from food.<br>• Use well-balanced pots and pans, and keep handles turned away from stove edges.<br>• Wipe up spilled grease, water, and bits of food at once.<br>• Never mix cleaning aids. Dangerous fumes can be released.<br>• Use well-made pot-holders, not dish towels, to handle hot pots and pans.<br>• Use sturdy stepladders or stools to reach high places. |
| **Bathroom**  | • Use nonskid mat or strips in tub or shower.<br>• Install handrails on bathtub.<br>• Never leave a tub of hot water unattended.<br>• Never leave a young child unattended in the tub.<br>• Never use electrical appliances while taking a bath. |
| **Stairways and halls**  | • Keep well-lit and litter-free (no toys or other objects strewn about) so that passageways are clear at all times.<br>• Be sure handrails or banisters on all stairways are adequate and in good repair.<br>• Be sure stair pads or carpeting are securely fastened.<br>• Be sure throw rugs are nonskid or secured to the floor. |
| **Basement, attic, garage, and other storage areas** 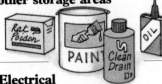 | • Store flammable liquids, charcoals, paints, and poisons in tightly covered, labeled, original containers out of the reach of children.<br>• Keep area free of oily rags and combustible litter.<br>• Be sure furnace, flue, and chimneys are checked and cleaned once a year. |
| **Electrical**  | • Be sure there are enough outlets and circuits for all lighting and appliances without dangerous overload.<br>• Keep unused outlets covered by dummy plugs, or block access with furniture.<br>• Be sure major electrical appliances are grounded.<br>• Follow manufacturer's recommendations on all lighting equipment and appliances. Use only where specifically stated. |

# Fire emergencies

## Solid fuel fires

Solid fuel fires can usually be put out with water or a multi-purpose extinguisher.

## Liquid fires

Liquid fires are either flammable or combustible (gasoline, solvents, paints, cooking oil, grease). If such fires spread, you must leave the premises at once and call the fire department.

## Electrical fires

Electrical fires are doubly difficult to control because it is imperative to avoid electric shock while putting out the fire. Do *not* throw water on an electrical appliance until it is unplugged.

**Clothing on fire.** DO NOT RUN. Drop to the floor. Roll over and over. If a heavy blanket or rug is at hand, wrap yourself in it to smother the flames.

**Mattress on fire.** Saturate with water. Call the fire department and have them remove it. If the mattress is in flames, leave the premises and call the fire department.

**Oven or broiler fire.** Turn off the heat. Close the oven door and keep it closed.

**Pan-on-the-stove fire.** Turn off the heat. Cover the pan with a lid, or throw salt or baking soda at the *base* of the flames in the pan. Do *not* pick up or move the pan, or throw water on it.

**Fireplace or wood-burning stove fire.** Do not close the damper (located in the flue). Leave the premises at once and call the fire department.

**Grease fire (deep fat fryer or pan).** Do *not* move the appliance or pan. Turn off the heat. Cover with a metal lid; if flames are too high, throw baking soda or salt into the pan. Cover with a lid after flames have died down.

**Gasoline, acetone, benzene fire.** Do *not* try to put out such fires. Leave the premises at once and call the fire department. Take off any clothing that has come into contact with gasoline.

**Charcoal lighter fluid (used in barbecues) fire.** If fire is confined to barbecue, try to cover with a large metal lid, or throw sand or dirt on the barbecue.

**Lacquer thinner, alcohol, turpentine fire.** If fire has not spread, smother it with baking soda, sand, or a multipurpose extinguisher.

**Kerosene heater or lamp fire.** Use sand, baking soda, or a multi-purpose extinguisher to smother.

**Television smoking.** Keep away from the TV set as the picture tube may burst. Shut off power to the circuit from a switch or the fuse box and call the fire department.

**Faulty wiring.** If switch outlets and plugs feel warm to the touch, disconnect all electricity. Call the fire department.

**Shock from an electrical appliance.** This could be from a defective plug or loose wiring in the outlet or the appliance. Unplug at once, or shut off power to the circuit from a switch or from the fuse box, as continued use of the appliance may result in fire.

**Shock.** Shock is brought on by a sudden and dangerous drop in blood pressure. It may be caused by a variety of conditions: bleeding, infection, injuries, drug reaction, poisoning, and heart damage. No matter what the cause, shock demands prompt treatment. If shock is not treated, it may prove fatal. *When present, stoppage of breathing, severe bleeding, or poisoning must be treated first.*

**Signs**

- The skin is pale and cold and clammy.
- Lips and fingernails may have a bluish-gray tinge.
- Breathing is rapid and weak; the pulse is fast and faint.
- The victim may be restless or drowsy, partly or totally unconscious, and there may be internal bleeding.

**Treatment**

- *A physician should be called at once.*
- Do not let victim sit, walk, or stand.
- Keep victim lying down and prop up legs about 12 inches (except in case of broken leg or possible head injury).
- Do not move victim unless necessary.
- Keep him warm but apply no heat of any kind.
- Give nothing by mouth.
- Stay calm and attentive.

**Electric shock.** This happens when a person has been in contact with electricity (including lightning).

- Do *not* touch the person, but turn off power at source if possible. It may be necessary to call the power company.
- Call an ambulance or doctor.
- After person is clear of contact, assistance may be given, if needed, for unconsciousness and lack of breathing or heartbeat.
- If possible, free person from electrical contact with dry nonconducting material such as wood or cloth. Be certain not to use metal.

## How to treat for shock

1. Call a physician before beginning treatment if possible.
2. Free shock victim from electric contact if necessary.

 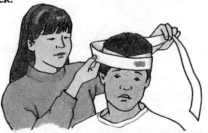

3. Treat stoppage of breathing or bleeding before treating shock.

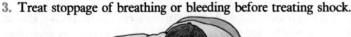

4. Keep victim lying down, with feet elevated, and warm.

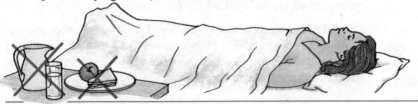 

# Choking.

When a person is choking on food, his face turns blue, and he cannot speak or make any noise (that is, groan, wheeze, or move air). The person may then collapse.

## First aid for choking

### When standing

1. Give victim four sharp blows on the back. (Omit this step for children.)
2. Stand behind the choking victim and wrap your arms around his waist.
3. Place a fist against the victim's abdomen between the navel and the breastbone. Grasp the fist with other hand.
4. *Press your fist in and upward* sharply into the victim's abdomen.

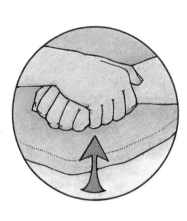

### When sitting

Stand behind the chair, and follow the same procedure outlined above.

### When lying down

1. Place the victim on his back with head turned. Straddle victim's legs and face him.
2. Put one hand on top of the other with the heel of your bottom hand placed slightly above the victim's navel and just below the rib cage.
3. Press your hand into the victim's abdomen with a *quick upward push*. Repeat the procedure several times, if necessary.

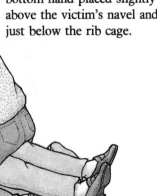
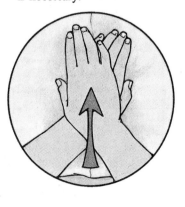

**Restoring breathing.** When a person has stopped breathing (from drowning, electric shock, carbon monoxide or other gaseous poisoning, or disease), start artificial respiration to restore breathing as quickly as possible. Check for someone with CPR training first.

## Mouth-to-mouth (or nose) method

1. Lay the victim on his back. Wipe or remove foreign matter from his mouth.

2. Tilt head backward; chin up. To keep tongue out of air passage, lift the chin with one hand and use other hand to push back on forehead.

3. Take hand placed on forehead and pinch the nose shut. Or press your cheek against the nose to close it.

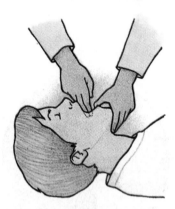
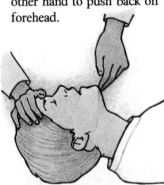
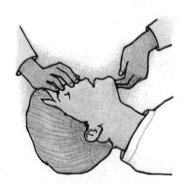

4. Open your mouth wide and take a deep breath. Cover victim's mouth with yours and give four deep quick breaths. Take your mouth away after each breath.

5. When victim's chest has expanded, stop blowing and listen for exhalation. Watch to see that chest falls. Repeat the blowing cycle.

6. For mouth-to-nose method, tilt head back as before but close mouth with other hand. Open your mouth wide, seal it around victim's nose, and blow.

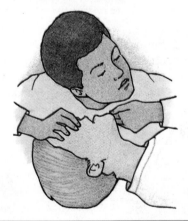

**Learning about CPR.** Cardio-Pulmonary Resuscitation (CPR) must be given to someone who is unconscious and in whom the heart and/or breathing may have stopped. However, CPR can only be done properly by a trained person, or damage may be caused by the technique.

CPR courses are widely available and, depending upon the community, may be given at hospitals, fire departments, or colleges. Generally, the local office of the American Heart Association or the American Red Cross can tell you where to enroll in a well-taught CPR course.

**Health and Safety**

# Poisoning.

The symptoms of poisoning vary with the type of poison. Most suspected poisonings do not require hospitalization.

1. Look for poison, medication, or liquid swallowed or its container.
2. Note if there are any marks or odors on the person. Corrosives may leave marks on face or clothes. Gasoline and other petroleum products have a characteristic odor.
3. Call Poison Control Center or hospital emergency room.
4. Give all available information; the name and the ingredients of the poison, the amount swallowed, how long ago, the condition of the victim.
5. Follow instructions given. You may be guided to treat the poisoning at home, but if you go to the hospital, be sure to take the poison container with you.
6. Do *not* give antidotes or induce vomiting unless so instructed by a medical professional. Causing vomiting after ingesting acid, lye or other corrosives, or petroleum products such as lighter fluid, would only do more harm.
7. Do *not* give salt solution. It can prove dangerous to the victim.
8. Do *not* dilute the poison by giving lots of milk or water. It may make things worse by speeding up the rate at which the poison is absorbed by the body.

**Poison control centers.** There are many Poison Control Centers throughout the country. Check your local telephone book for a listing of these centers under Poison Control Center (in the white pages), Emergency Numbers, or Community Service Numbers, or dial "O" and have the operator assist you. Check your local hospital listings for Emergency Room numbers. Note these numbers with other emergency numbers and keep readily available.

## Poisoning by plants and animals

| | |
|---|---|
| **Poison ivy, poison oak, poison sumac dermatitis** | If there has been known exposure to any of these plants, a thorough washing of the skin with soap and water, and a complete change of clothing is advisable. If the skin inflammation is mild, applying a soothing lotion is usually sufficient. In more severe cases, cool wet dressings or baths may help give relief. Check with a physician to see if medication is needed. |
| **Snakebite, scorpion, and spider stings** | Have person lie down. Wipe away from the bite area any venom on the skin. Wash area with soap and water. Pat dry. Do not rub. Apply clean dressing. Watch breathing. Get person to hospital immediately. Do *not* suck wound area, cut into area, or apply tourniquet or chemicals. |

**First aid.** A first-aid kit will help you be ready to deal with emergency situations when they happen. First-aid kits may be purchased at your local pharmacy, or put together on your own. A good-sized metal box, brightly colored to make it quickly visible on a shelf, is suitable. Keep the kit in one place at all times. Here are suggested supplies for your kit:

**Bandages and dressings.** Include assorted sizes of adhesive and sterile vaseline gauze band-

## First aid remedies

**Animal bites**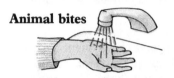

Wash the wound freely with water (under a running tap for a few minutes, if possible). Cover with sterile gauze dressing or compress. Get to a physician or to a hospital emergency room without delay. The offending animal should be caught and tested for rabies.

**Blisters**

Do not puncture blister. Apply a sterile dressing and bandage. If the blister is broken, clean the wound with soap and water. Blot dry with clean towel. Cover with sterile dressing and bandage.

**Bruises**

Apply cold cloths or icebag for about 25 minutes. If the injury is severe, have it examined by a physician.

**Burns**

DO NOT APPLY BUTTER, GREASE, OR OINTMENTS.
*First-degree burns* (like sunburn, red and painful): submerge burned part in cold water or apply cold-water bottle.
*Second-degree burns* (red and painful with blisters): submerge burned part in cold water. Put cold, wet dressings on burn, using clean, freshly pressed cloths if possible. Get medical help.
*Third-degree burns* (skin destroyed, white or charred): do not remove clothing on burn area or apply wet packs. Elevate burned limbs to keep burn higher than heart. Get medical help quickly.

**Cuts or scrapes**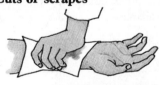

For minor injuries with no bleeding, sponge off area gently. Blot dry and cover with a simple bandage. In deeper cuts, apply direct constant pressure on the wound to stop the bleeding. Use a sterile pad and press down with your hand. If blood seeps through, place more padding over the first pad and continue pressure. If the bleeding persists or the wound is severe, call a doctor.

**Fainting**

If a person feels faint, have him sit down and lower his head between his knees or, preferably, have him lie down with head lower than his body. If the person has already fainted, lay him flat on his back, tilt head back, and elevate feet. Loosen tight clothing around neck and waist. Person should be seen by a doctor to determine the cause of fainting.

**Foreign bodies**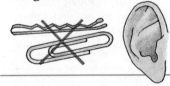

*Ear.* If there is an insect in the ear, lay person on side and pour a little warm water or oil into the ear. This will allow the insect to float out. However, if there is any chance that eardrum is perforated, do not put fluid into ear. Do not attempt to remove any other object. Call a doctor.

**Health and Safety**

ages; 1″ adhesive tape; cotton-tipped swabs; gauze bandage rolls (1″ × 4″ wide), and triangular bandages (37″ × 37″) cut or folded diagonally.
**Medicine.** Include hydrogen peroxide, aspirin or acetaminophen tablets, and children's aspirin; anesthetic ointment and antibiotic ointment; ipecac syrup and/or activated charcoal.
**Other aids.** The kit should also contain a thermometer, a tourniquet, safety pins, tweezers, and scissors.

---

**Foreign bodies**

*Eye.* Do not let person rub eye. Seat person in good light and, if object can be seen, try to remove it by touching it *gently* with a dry corner of a handkerchief. If it does not come out with the first try, or cannot be seen, cover eye with a clean pad or compress and take person to a physician or hospital emergency room.
*Nose.* Have person blow nose carefully, but not hard. If this does not remove the object, call doctor. Do not try to poke the object loose.

**Frostbite**

Frostbite usually begins as patches of white or grayish-yellow skin after exposure to extreme cold. Rewarm person slowly in air at room temperature. Gently cover frozen part with hand, or place in warm (not hot) water. Do not apply heat or expose person to heat from stove. Do not rub (especially not with snow or ice). Warm drinks may be given (tea, coffee, or beef tea), but no alcohol.

**Heat exhaustion**

Help person lie down in cool place, loosen clothes, and apply cool, wet cloths. Keep in lying position with head low. Give salt water to drink (1 teaspoon of salt to a pint of water) in small amounts at frequent intervals, and large amounts of fruit juices.

**Heatstroke or sunstroke**

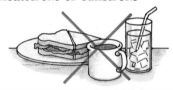

Heatstroke is characterized by an extremely high body temperature (106° F) and a lack of sweating to relieve temperature. Remove person to cool place and remove most clothing. Reduce temperature by covering skin with cold cloths or towels, changing frequently. Place person in tub of cold water, keeping head above water. Give nothing by mouth.

**Insect bites and stings**

If swelling is severe, or person has allergic reaction (pallor, collapse), get medical help at once. Allergic reactions to insect bites can be fatal. Generally, the sting is not serious. If stinger is embedded in skin, remove with tweezers and then apply a soothing cream or paste of baking soda.
*Embedded ticks.* Kill the tick with a few drops of turpentine, or touch it with a hot needle to make it release its hold. Then carefully remove tick with tweezers, being careful not to crush the insect or only half pull it out.

**Sprains**

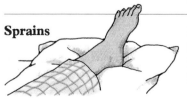

If the victim's leg or foot is sprained, do not allow walking. Elevate the joint (ankle, wrist, finger, knee) and apply cold compresses. Give firm support by using thick pads and then firm bandaging (elastic bandage).

---

She has her father's eyes and her mother's smile. She also has AIDS.

Reduce your risk of getting or giving the AIDS virus.

AIDS

# Dictionary of health and safety

DIRECTIONS: as a dietary supplement take 6 tablets daily, preferably with meals.
Six (6) tablets per day supply:

| Nutrient | Source | Potency | %USRDA* |
|---|---|---|---|
| Calcium | calcium carbonate, calcium phosphate | 900 mg. | 90 |
| Phosphorus | brewer's yeast, oat meal, calcium phosphate | 75 mg. | 7.5 |
| Vitamin D | cholecalciferol | 400 I.U. | 100 |
| Magnesium | brewer's yeast, oxide | 4.3 mg. | |

Sulfur (oat meal, brewer's yeast) 6.9mg.; Potassium (citrate, brewer's yeast) 29mg.; Silicon (brewer's

minerals

PLAGUE WARNING
PRAIRIE DOGS and other rodents are infected with PLAGUE.
Do not feed or approach ANY wildlife.
Stay out of meadows.

plague

poison ivy

**acquired immune deficiency syndrome (AIDS).** Caused by a retrovirus that attacks the immune system and so enables life-threatening diseases to flourish. AIDS is transmitted primarily through sexual activity and sharing of needles by drug users.

**anthrax.** Acute infectious disease that usually attacks cattle and sheep. Man contracts it by handling contaminated animal hair or hides, most often through wounds or skin abrasions.

**bacteria.** One-celled microorganisms without nuclei that may cause such diseases as cholera, syphilis, and typhoid fever.

**botulism** (food poisoning). The growth of pathogenic organisms in food itself causes the poisoning, while the toxins produced by the organisms result in the illness. It may be hours after contaminated food is eaten before abdominal pain, vomiting, and diarrhea appear.

**chancroid.** Infectious venereal disease that begins as a pustule or ulcer and spreads.

**chicken pox** (varicella). Highly contagious but mild infectious disease occurring mostly in children. There is slight fever, and a sparse red rash develops that becomes blistery and finally crusts. Itching may be intense.

**cholera.** Acute epidemic infectious disease that is marked by profuse watery diarrhea.

**cholesterol.** Sterol (fatlike substance) widely found in animal tissues and occurring in egg yolk, various oils, fats, and nerve tissue.

**germ.** Common name for agents of disease, including bacteria, viruses, and protozoans.

**herpes simplex** (Type I and Type II). Virus that causes cold sores or fever blisters, but which may also cause many other complications. Type I is usually found on the upper half of the body where it is most common around the mouth. Type II (genital herpes) is more common on the lower part of the body. Both types can be sexually transmitted.

**lymphogranuloma venereum.** Venereal disease that is caused by a virus and is readily transmitted by sexual contact.

**measles** (rubeola). Highly contagious disease in which there is fever, catarrhal symptoms, and a typical skin eruption. It usually occurs before adolescence. German measles (rubella) resembles measles but its course is short, fever is slight, and there are no aftereffects.

**minerals.** Inorganic elements (calcium, phosphorus, iron, sodium, etc.) that in general are the regulators of the metabolic processes.

**mumps.** Acute, contagious, and feverish disease in which there is inflammation of the parotid (below the ear) glands and other salivary glands.

**nutrients.** Food components that supply the body with necessary elements. Some nutrients (carbohydrates, fats, proteins) provide energy; others (water, minerals, vitamins) are needed for regulatory processes.

**plague** (Black Death). Bubonic plague is primarily transmitted to man by the bite of fleas having fed on infected animals.

**pneumonia.** Characterized by cough, chest pain, and fever, pneumonia is an acute illness resulting from inflammation or infection of the lungs either bacterial or viral.

**poison ivy.** A climbing vine, *Rhus toxidendrom,* causes a severe form of skin inflammation on contact.

**proteins.** Essential for growth and repair of body tissues; of the utmost importance in body functioning.

**protozoans.** One-celled animals. Some cause such diseases as malaria, sleeping sickness, and dysentery.

**sleeping sickness** (African trypanosomiasis). Endemic disease caused by the bite of a tsetse fly. The main symptoms are an increasing tendency to drowse or sleep, tremors, fever, wasting, and weakness.

**smallpox.** Contagious disease caused by a virus found in the oral and nasal secretions and skin lesions of infected persons. Smallpox, however, has been completely eliminated all over the world. The only known viruses are kept in medical laboratories for research purposes.

**stroke** (apoplexy). There is a sudden loss of consciousness (coma) followed by paralysis, usually of the side of the body opposite the side of the brain affected.

**syphilis.** Infectious venereal disease that can result in destructive lesions almost anywhere in the body. When fully developed, soft tissue tumors appear and there is damage to the heart, brain, and blood vessels.

**tetanus.** Disease marked by painful muscular contractions. At first, there is an inability to move the jaw (lockjaw); this is followed by tetanic spasm, another characteristic of the disease.

**tuberculosis.** Infectious disease caused by the tubercle bacillus. It may affect almost any body tissue or organ, but it occurs most commonly in the lungs.

**tularemia** (rabbit fever, deer fly fever). Man acquires the disease from rodents through the bite of an infected tick or other blood-sucking insect, by handling of infected animal tissues, or by eating undercooked meat or contaminated water.

**typhoid fever.** This illness, caused by the bacillus *Salmonella typhosa,* is marked by continued fever, the eruption of rose-colored spots on the chest and abdomen, and an enlarged spleen.

**typhus** (epidemic and endemic). One of a group of rickettsial infectious diseases marked by high fever, severe prostration and headache, and a generalized rash.

**undulant fever.** An infectious disease in which fever rises to 104° or 105° F (40° to 40.6° C) in the evening, gradually returning to normal by morning. Other symptoms include weakness, sweating, chills, anorexia, malaise, and nervousness.

**viruses.** Microorganisms smaller than cells that cause such diseases as herpes, measles, and colds.

**vitamins.** These organic substances perform a specific metabolic function, depending upon the vitamin, and are essential to the diet.

**whooping cough.** Acute infectious disease marked by a peculiar recurrent spasm of coughing that ends in whooping.

**yellow fever.** Acute infectious disease that is marked by jaundice, tenderness in the pit of the stomach, vomiting, hemorrhage, and recurrent fever. It is transmitted by the bite of a female mosquito.

## For Further Reference

American Red Cross
 *The American Red Cross First Aid
  and Safety Handbook*
 Little, Brown
Bosco, Dominick
 *The People's Guide to Vitamins and
  Minerals, From A to Zinc*
 Contemporary Books
Consumer Guide Editors
 *Emergency First Aid for Your Child*
 Publications International
Dunne, Lavon J.
 *Nutrition Almanac*
 McGraw-Hill

Madison, Arnold
 *Drugs and You*
 Julian Messner
Nardo, Don
 *Vitamins and Minerals*
 Chelsea House
Null, Gary
 *The Complete Guide to Health and
  Nutrition*
 Delacorte
Peavy, Linda S. and Smith, Ursula
 *Food, Nutrition and You*
 Scribner's

# Life Science

Life sciences have become both better understood and more relevant in the past few years, after decades dominated by the physical sciences. Since the 1960's it has become increasingly clear that the environment is in danger and that we must maintain the other living creatures in our environment to maintain both our health and a sound economy. In this brief article, the focus is on the environment; other important topics in life science are treated in that context.

One major focus is the different natural environmental regions that comprise North America. Another is natural recycling. Understanding the environment requires knowledge of how such natural resources as air and water are recycled by nature. This process involves several steps. So does the process by which part of an environment that has been destroyed restores itself.

The relationship of living things to their environment is one of the basic ways that life science can be approached. In Volume 2, the biology article takes another one of the basic approaches, starting with the cell and working up to the organism in its environment.

# Natural resources

**Wildlife.** Among our planet's most valuable natural resources is its great variety of wildlife—plants and animals. Unfortunately, some types of wildlife are threatened with extinction, and they have been declared *endangered species*. An endangered species is any type of plant or animal that is protected by law from being killed. It is protected so that it will not become *extinct* (cease to exist as a living species). Endangered species in North America include the California condor, the whooping crane, the star cactus, the manatee, and the Steller sea-lion.

It is important to preserve as many species of wildlife as possible because of the species' potential use to the human race. Wild varieties of plants or animals often have useful properties that can be bred into domestic plants or animals.

**Land and forests.** Productive farmland contains a substantial layer of fertile topsoil that is rich in the vital nutrients needed by plants to grow. Many years are necessary to build up this topsoil. According to the U.S. Department of Agriculture, about 5 tons of topsoil per acre per year are being lost in the United States from erosion caused by poor farming practices.

To reduce erosion, farmers often resort to *strip cropping*, in which different types of crops are planted in alternate strips. Typically, corn alternates with grass, which cuts down on water run-off. Some farmers also build *terraces*—platforms with plants growing on them. These terraces catch the water and prevent erosion.

Planting wheat or corn in the same field each year removes vital nutrients from the topsoil and makes the land less productive. In *crop rotation*, the crop is changed from year to year.

National and state forests are another vital land resource. These precious lands are carefully administered so they can fulfill a variety of important functions:

- Provide a habitat for wildlife.
- Protect important watershed areas.
- Prevent soil erosion.
- Serve as recreation areas.
- Provide timber for building and other purposes.

Timber can be removed from forests in different ways, depending on the species of trees involved. *Clear-cutting* removes large blocks of trees, but this method disrupts the natural beauty of the forest and can lead to soil erosion. *Selection cutting* is used for species that can thrive in shade. In selection cutting, older trees are cut down while younger ones are left to grow taller.

## Air.

The quality of our air is affected by pollution, which creates a variety of problems. *Hydrocarbons*, which are released when coal or oil is burned as fuel, have been linked to cancer. Pollutants have also been cited as a cause of such lung diseases as emphysema.

Another type of pollution, which often blankets cities like Los Angeles, is called *smog*. Smog is a yellowish haze produced by the reaction of oxygen, hydrocarbons, and other pollutants in sunlight. One of the elements in smog is *ozone*, a type of oxygen with a pungent odor. Ozone causes coughing and eye irritation in humans and damages plants.

A serious problem created by air pollution is *acid rain*. Pollutants, especially those released by coal-burning power plants in the Midwest, mix with moisture in the air to produce nitric and sulfuric acids. These fall as acid rain or snow, destroying vegetation, polluting waterways, and killing fish. At present, many lakes in New York, New England, and Canada have been polluted by acid rain.

Over the past few years, progress has been made in reducing air pollution through legislation such as the Clean Air Act and the efforts of the Environmental Protection Agency. Pollution control devices on automobiles are one example of this progress.

## Water.

Fresh, clean water is essential for residential use, agriculture, and industry, but the water quality in many lakes and rivers has been destroyed by pollution. The Great Lakes, for example, were polluted by industries dumping chemicals and heavy metals into them. A massive cleanup program was initiated to save the lakes and to restore the quality of their water. Similar programs have been started in other parts of the country, as on Ohio's Cuyahoga River and along the Maine coast.

In some of the Western states the problem is not so much pollution as it is the threat of water shortages. Limited amounts of rainfall in that part of the U.S. are insufficient to fill all the needs of an expanding population.

Vast quantities of water are necessary to irrigate dry areas in the West for agriculture. Although irrigation ditches are commonly used to transport water, some of the water is lost through seepage and evaporation. An alternate method of irrigation, called the *drip system*, brings water to plants through pipes and reduces waste.

| Sources of air and water pollution | | Average water consumption |
|---|---|---|
| **Air** | **Water** | |
| Transportation (cars, etc.) | Industrial wastes | residential 60 |
| Fuel combustion for heating | Fertilizers and pesticides | industrial 50 |
| Industrial pollutants | Oil spills | 150 gallons per person per day |
| Dust from land | Sewage | commercial 20 |
| Volcanic eruptions | Nuclear wastes | public 10 |
| Burning solid wastes | Heat from power stations | leakage 10 |
| Forest fires | Strip mining | |

# The ecosystem

sun energy

secondary (and tertiary) consumer

producer organism

primary consumer

secondary consumer

Survival of all living things depends on a carefully balanced system called an *ecosystem*. All life needs energy, and the original source of energy in an ecosystem is the sun. Green plants, called *producer organisms*, use the sun's energy to make their food. Animals, which get their energy by eating plants or other animals, are called *consumers*. There are different kinds of consumers. A rabbit, which eats plant material, is called a *primary* consumer. An eagle is called a *secondary* consumer when it gets its energy from eating animals that eat plants. A snake is also called a secondary consumer because it eats animals that eat plants. When an eagle eats a snake, the eagle is

called a *tertiary* consumer. There are other organisms in an ecosystem, such as bacteria that decompose dead animals and plant material. Such organisms, called *decomposers*, return minerals and organic material to the air and soil. They are not shown here.

Green plants are the producers because only they can manufacture their own food by a process called *photosynthesis*. The raw materials of photosynthesis are carbon dioxide, water, and sunlight, all of which are absorbed by the plants. Inside plant cells is a pigment called *chlorophyll* that gives green plants their color. Chlorophyll also captures the sun's energy and plays an essential

**Life Science**

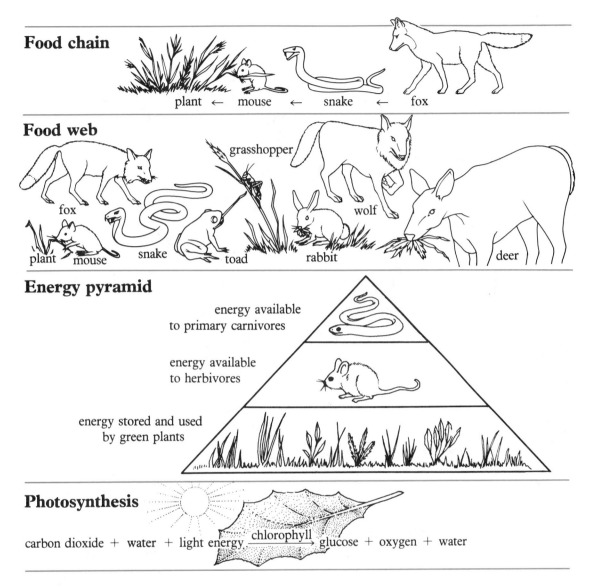

**Food chain**

plant ← mouse ← snake ← fox

**Food web**

grasshopper

fox

wolf

plant mouse snake toad rabbit deer

**Energy pyramid**

energy available
to primary carnivores

energy available
to herbivores

energy stored and used
by green plants

**Photosynthesis**

carbon dioxide + water + light energy $\xrightarrow{\text{chlorophyll}}$ glucose + oxygen + water

role in the chemical reactions that occur during photosynthesis. These reactions produce a sugar called *glucose* and release oxygen and water.

Glucose is a food that provides energy necessary to sustain life. Plants use some of the glucose for their own life functions and store the rest. When plants are eaten by primary consumers, the consumers obtain the stored glucose and their cells convert it into energy.

In the ecosystem, the relationship between producers and consumers is often illustrated by a *food chain* such as the one shown at the top of this page. But the relationship between living organisms is often far more intricate than a chain sug-

gests. For example, plants are eaten by other animals besides mice. Snakes prey not only on mice, but on toads and prairie dogs as well. A fox's diet consists of more than just snakes. The complex feeding pattern linking organisms together is called a *food web*.

In food webs and food chains, energy is transferred from one living thing to the next. However, only about 10 percent of the energy contained in a plant ever reaches a primary consumer. An even smaller amount is eventually passed on to secondary and tertiary consumers. This transfer of energy is called the *energy pyramid*.

# Biomes

Prairie dogs live in towns in the grasslands.

Snow geese fly south after summering in the tundra.

## Biomes of North America

| | Plant life | Animal life |
|---|---|---|
| **Tundra** cold and dry | lichens; mosses; grasses | caribou; wolves; foxes; lemmings; ptarmigan; ducks and geese (summer only) |
| **Taiga** cool and less dry than tundra | pines; spruces; firs; cedars; redwoods; wood sorrel; sphagnum moss | moose; mule deer; bobcats; lynx; snowshoe hare; red crossbill |
| **Temperate-deciduous forest** moderate temperatures and wet | oak; elm; maple; birch; mountain laurel; ferns; aspen | chipmunks; rabbits; bears; squirrels; deer; raccoons; |
| **Grasslands** moderate temperatures and less wet than forests | big bluestem grasses; cordgrass; little bluestem; psoralea; clover | bison; pronghorn antelope; prairie dogs; prairie chickens; mice |
| **Desert** moderate to hot and very dry | cactus; yucca; sagebrush; desert palms; mesquite; desert dandelions | jackrabbits; owls; snakes; kangaroo rats; lizards; roadrunners |

**Life Science**

A *biome* is an ecological unit that has a certain general type of vegetation. Many of the natural biomes of North America have been changed by the process of civilization. Without the interference of human beings, biomes are determined by temperature, moisture, and soil. There are five large natural biomes in America north of Mexico. In the southern part of North America is a sixth biome, the rain forest (not discussed here).

## Tundra.

The North American series of six biomes begins in the Arctic region with the *tundra*. The tundra is a cold plain where average temperatures remain below freezing. During the short summer, however, the tundra becomes warmer, allowing ponds and marshes to thaw. Here water fowl such as ducks and geese reside before migrating south for the long winter.

Rainfall is sparse in the tundra, and only hardy plants such as mosses and lichens, which require little water, can survive.

An unusual type of bird found in the tundra is the ptarmigan. The ptarmigan is brown in summer but white in winter to blend with its snowy environment.

## Taiga.

South of the tundra is the coniferous forest, or *taiga*. The beginning of this biome is marked by the timber line, the point at which trees begin to grow. Average temperatures are higher than in the tundra and there is more rainfall, so certain species of trees can thrive. The coniferous forest takes its name from the word *conifer*, meaning "cone-bearing," which describes the trees of this biome.

The conifers have needlelike leaves, and most are evergreen. This means that only part of the leaves fall at any one time, so the trees always remain green. Conifers include pines, spruces, firs, and cedars. Along the west coast is another species of conifer—the giant redwood. Some redwood trees are thousands of years old.

Among the animals that inhabit the taiga are herbivores (plant eaters) such as deer and beaver. Carnivores (meat eaters) include wolves and bobcats. There are also varieties of birds and insects.

## Forest.

In the eastern United States is the *temperate-deciduous forest*. This biome receives large amounts of precipitation, and temperatures are generally moderate. These conditions allow many species of wildlife to flourish.

Throughout the year the deciduous forest changes dramatically. In autumn the leaves turn color; in winter the leaves drop to expose bare limbs; in spring new leaves return.

Many types of flowering plants can be found in the deciduous forest. The rich flora provide food for vast numbers of herbivores. These, in turn, support a large population of higher level consumers such as foxes and owls.

## Grasslands.

In the central part of the United States, rainfall begins to decrease, and we enter the biome known as *grasslands*. In the eastern part of the grasslands, where there is the most moisture, tall bluestem grasses grow. These are sometimes 8 feet high with very deep roots. Farther west, where there is less precipitation, the grasses are shorter. These grasses include little bluestem, western wheatgrass, and short blue gramma. The grasses provide food for grazing animals such as white-tailed deer.

A variety of animals in the grasslands make their homes underground. These include gophers, moles, and prairie dogs. The prairie dogs live in large communities, or "towns," with huge populations. Many prairie animals are endangered by the replacement of grasses by crops.

## Desert.

A biome that receives very little precipitation is called a *desert*. Perhaps the most familiar type of desert plant is the cactus, which adapted itself to survive in dry conditions. The Giant Desert Cactus, for example, has no leaves; this reduces the amount of water lost through evaporation. It has a wide root system that can absorb the small amounts of rain that fall. The cactus also has the ability to store water for long periods of time.

Desert temperatures are very hot during the day because there is little moisture to reflect the sunlight. At night temperatures drop rapidly because there are few clouds to prevent the heat from leaving the earth. As a result of the extreme daytime heat, many desert animals are *nocturnal*—active mainly at night.

One of the most common desert species is the jackrabbit, which plays an important role in the food web.

# Cycles

## Water cycle

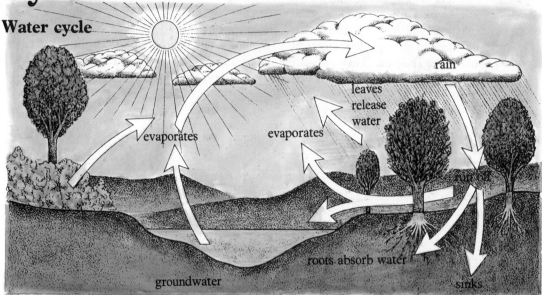

In the water cycle, water is evaporated into the atmosphere by the sun's energy. The water vapor is then carried by the wind, condenses, and forms clouds. Eventually, the water falls as precipitation—rain or snow. Some of the water is absorbed by plants; some sinks into the ground or flows as runoff into lakes and streams. Evaporation occurs again, and the cycle continues.

## Oxygen–carbon dioxide cycle

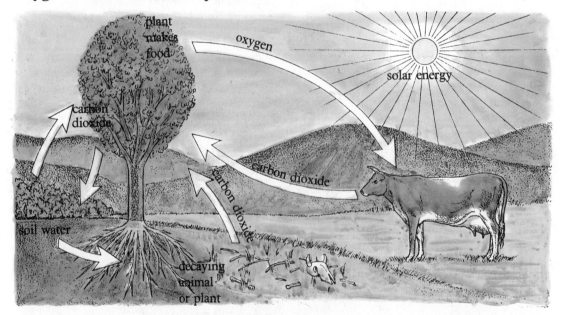

Green plants absorb carbon dioxide ($CO_2$) and release oxygen in the process of photosynthesis. Oxygen is used by both plant and animal cells during respiration, and carbon dioxide is released in the process. Carbon dioxide also enters the atmosphere from decaying organic material.

**Life Science**

# Succession

When an ecosystem has been destroyed by fire, glacier, wind, volcano, or human intervention, the pattern of life that existed before the destruction is not immediately restored. Instead, a step-by-step process gradually follows. This process is called *succession*. Here are a few examples of succession in different settings. Each example leads to a *climax* forest, one that is stable.

## A glacial lake

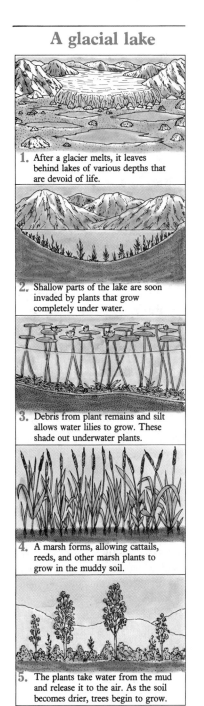

1. After a glacier melts, it leaves behind lakes of various depths that are devoid of life.

2. Shallow parts of the lake are soon invaded by plants that grow completely under water.

3. Debris from plant remains and silt allows water lilies to grow. These shade out underwater plants.

4. A marsh forms, allowing cattails, reeds, and other marsh plants to grow in the muddy soil.

5. The plants take water from the mud and release it to the air. As the soil becomes drier, trees begin to grow.

## A cleared field

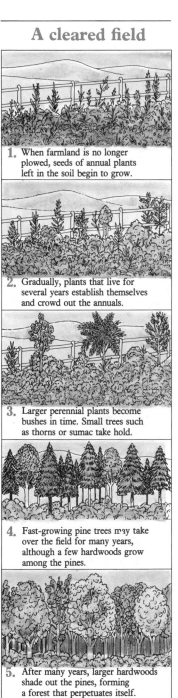

1. When farmland is no longer plowed, seeds of annual plants left in the soil begin to grow.

2. Gradually, plants that live for several years establish themselves and crowd out the annuals.

3. Larger perennial plants become bushes in time. Small trees such as thorns or sumac take hold.

4. Fast-growing pine trees may take over the field for many years, although a few hardwoods grow among the pines.

5. After many years, larger hardwoods shade out the pines, forming a forest that perpetuates itself.

## A lava flow

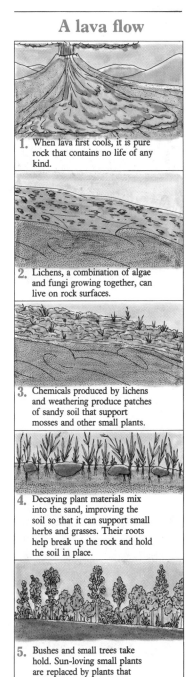

1. When lava first cools, it is pure rock that contains no life of any kind.

2. Lichens, a combination of algae and fungi growing together, can live on rock surfaces.

3. Chemicals produced by lichens and weathering produce patches of sandy soil that support mosses and other small plants.

4. Decaying plant materials mix into the sand, improving the soil so that it can support small herbs and grasses. Their roots help break up the rock and hold the soil in place.

5. Bushes and small trees take hold. Sun-loving small plants are replaced by plants that thrive in partial shade.

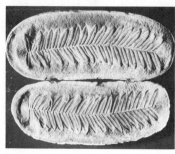

fossil
*reveals fern from the past*

# Dictionary of life science

instinct
*shapes the wasps' nest*

metamorphosis
*of tadpole into frog*

symbiosis
*red-billed oxpeckers and warthog*

**abiotic.** Parts of the environment that are not living.

**acquired characteristic.** Physical trait of an organism that is brought about by its environment.

**adaptations.** Features of structure and function that make an organism better suited for living and reproducing in a particular environment.

**algae.** Simple plants that carry on photosynthesis. Most are single-celled.

**anatomy.** Study of the structure of organisms.

**angiosperms.** Plants that form true flowers as their structures of reproduction. The seeds of angiosperms are enclosed in structures of the parent plant. These structures are usually called fruits.

**antibiotic.** Substance produced by one organism that is used to kill another organism. Penicillin was the first antibiotic to be discovered.

**asexual reproduction.** Reproduction from one parent organism without the union of germ cells.

**bacteria.** Microscopic organisms found throughout the environment. They are neither plants nor animals.

**balance of nature.** Natural condition in which plant and animal communities continue unchanged in either numbers or composition.

**biogeography.** Study of the plants and animals found in various climatic and geographic zones.

**biome.** Largest ecological unit. A biome includes all of the plants and animals of a particular region of Earth.

**carnivore.** Organism that eats meat.

**cell.** Smallest unit of living matter, usually composed of a nucleus, cytoplasm, and a membrane or wall.

**cell membrane.** Thin outer layer of animal cells.

**cell wall.** Outer layer of plant cells.

**chlorophyll.** Green pigment in plants that transforms sunlight into usable energy for the process of photosynthesis.

**chloroplast.** Cellular structure in plants that contains chlorophyll.

**conifer.** Cone-bearing shrub or tree.

**conjugation.** Form of sexual reproduction in which two cells join and transfer genetic material. Conjugation is usually associated with single-celled organisms.

**consumer.** Organism that survives by eating other organisms.

**cytoplasm.** Semifluid material surrounding the nucleus of a cell and enclosed by the cell membrane.

**deciduous.** Type of plant that sheds all its leaves after a growing season.

**ecology.** Study of organisms in relation to each other and to their environment.

**ecosystem.** Living community that contains an energy source, abiotic chemicals, and organisms that function as producers, consumers, and decomposers.

**environment.** Total surroundings of a living thing.

**evolution.** Genetic change in a species that, over a period of time, better adapts it to its environment.

**food web.** Feeding pattern of organisms in the ecosystem.

**fossil.** Organism's remains or traces that have been preserved.

**genus.** Group of related species.

**gymnosperm.** Seed plant that has exposed ovules. Gymnosperms are often referred to as conifers or evergreens.

**habitat.** Natural home of an animal or plant.

**herbivore.** Plant-eating organism.

**heredity.** Traits that are genetically passed from parent to offspring; biological inheritance.

**hermaphrodite.** Animal or plant possessing both male and female reproductive organs.

**hybrid.** Cross between different species.

**instinct.** Type of behavior that is inborn.

**invertebrate.** Organism that lacks a backbone.

**lichen.** Alga and a fungus living together and depending on each other for survival.

**mammal.** Vertebrate with milk-producing (mammary) glands, such as a dog or cat.

**meiosis.** Special kind of cell division in organisms that have sexual reproduction. Meiosis reduces the chromosome number in the mature germ cells by half.

**metabolism.** Set of interrelated chemical processes characteristic of life.

**metamorphosis.** Radical changes in the development of some animals as they mature. Metamorphosis is usually associated with insects and amphibians.

**mitosis.** Cell division in which two daughter cells have the same genetic material as the parent cell.

**morphology.** Study of the form and structure of living things.

**mutation.** Inheritable change in a chromosome or gene.

**niche.** Organism's role in the ecosystem.

**nucleus.** Inner body in a cell that contains the cell's hereditary material (chromosomes, genes, and DNA) and controls the activity of the cytoplasm.

**omnivore.** Organism that consumes both plants and animals. Humans are omnivores.

**parasite.** Organism that takes its food from another living organism.

**photosynthesis.** Process by which green plants manufacture food (glucose) from carbon dioxide, water, and light.

**predator.** Animal that feeds on other animals.

**protoplasm.** All the material in a living cell.

**respiration.** Chemical reactions in a cell that release energy.

**sexual reproduction.** Reproduction that requires the combination of genetic material from the germ cells of two individuals.

**species.** Particular group of plants or animals that maintains its distinctness over many generations.

**spontaneous generation.** Living things emerging from nonliving material.

**spore.** Single-celled reproductive body.

**succession.** Gradual replacement of plant and animal species at a given site in a regular pattern after removal of an existing ecosystem at the site by a disaster such as fire, flood, or removal of the ecosystem by human beings. Succession also occurs at new sites, such as lakes, which gradually change to bogs and then to land.

**symbiosis.** Relationship in which two dissimilar organisms live together and benefit each other.

**taxonomy.** Classification of plants and animals according to evolutionary relationships.

**transpiration.** Process by which plants lose water through evaporation.

**vertebrate.** Animal having a segmented spinal column, a skull surrounding the brain, and an internal skeleton.

**zygote.** Egg cell at the moment of fertilization.

---

## For Further Reference

Allen, Durward
*The Life of Prairies and Plains*
McGraw-Hill
Attenborough, David
*Life on Earth*
Little, Brown
Clement, Roland C.
*Nature Atlas of America*
Hammond

Peck, Robert McCracken
*Land of the Eagle: A Natural History of North America*
Summit Books
Teal, John and Teal, Mildred
*Life and Death of the Salt Marsh*
Ballantine Books
Wagner, Frederic H.
*Wildlife of the Deserts*
Harry N. Abrams

---

**Life Science**

# Physical Sciences

Although knowledge about nature can be divided into the life sciences and the physical sciences, it is common to define the expression *physical science* as the combined study of topics in physics and chemistry. This convention is adopted here. You will learn how scientists work, the principal units of measurement, the basic meaning of matter and energy, the way that energy can be changed by machines or transmitted by waves, and how waves can be modified. And you will find the answers to many often-asked questions, such as: What is the difference between heat and temperature? What causes rainbows? And why is the sky blue? See also the sections on Chemistry and Physics in Volume 2.

# The scientific method

## What is science?
Science is one of the branches of knowledge that requires systematic study and method. In an attempt to answer questions about the nature of things, scientists ask "what" and "how" questions. *What* questions are usually answered by a description. "What kind of animals live in that pond?" Answer: "Frogs, fish, and reptiles." *How* questions often require the study of a particular natural phenomenon. "How is energy conducted?" The answer, "Energy is transferred from atom to atom in a conductor," requires the study of a number of different substances. Many substances have to be compared and measurements taken.

Measurement is extremely important in science. Questions of how much and how fast can only be answered by measurement. Measurement allows scientists to compare the results of their experiments. Measurement has been called the "language of science."

Science and scientists, in an attempt to explain nature, use facts to formulate laws and theories. *Facts* are particular pieces of information. *Laws* describe regular natural occurrences; they are records of what happens. *Theories* use facts in an organized way to explain both laws and facts, and to predict what will occur in similar situations. In order for a theory to be acceptable, it must predict correctly how something will react before it happens. If a theory does not predict properly, it must be changed or a new theory must take its place. Science is cumulative and self-correcting.

## How scientists work.
Scientists test theories by performing experiments and making their results known so that other scien-

tists can view the results and repeat the experiments. This system is called *the scientific method*.

The scientific method has been divided into a series of steps, a blueprint for action; but not all scientists follow this blueprint all of the time. There is no single method or way that scientists work, but the scientific method has helped many people.

# What is an experiment? An
experiment is a controlled procedure carried out to test or discover something. It is the process of making something happen under conditions controlled by the observer. The key word for a scientific experiment is *controlled*.

Let us assume we wish to answer the question, "Do seeds need water to germinate?" We buy a package of seeds and place one in a bottle that has some dry soil in it. We allow it to stand for several days without watering. We observe that the seed did not germinate (sprout). However, we cannot tell why the seed did not sprout. Perhaps it needed water; perhaps the seed was dead; perhaps the soil was poor; perhaps the bottle was inadequate; perhaps it was too hot or cold or too light or dark. All of these are possible answers to why the seed did not germinate. There were too many *variables* in this experiment.

Now let us design another experiment to answer the same question, only this time we will attempt to eliminate as many variables as possi-

ble. This time we take two identical, clean bottles and put the same amount of soil from the same location in each one. Next we plant a seed from the same package in each bottle. For convenience, we label one bottle A and the other B. We place both bottles in the same place and water the soil in bottle A, but not in bottle B. Bottle A is our control. After several days, the seed in bottle A germinates, but not the one in bottle B. By using a control, we have eliminated the variables of the bottle, soil, temperature, and light. The possibility that the particular seed in bottle B was dead still exists, however. This last variable can be eliminated by using many seeds and bottles in both the control and experimental setups. After several days we can compare the number of seeds that germinated in each group. All experiments must be planned and controlled to eliminate variables so that the results provide only one answer to the question being asked.

A scientific experiment is not performed in a vacuum, however. First the scientist must learn enough about a subject to identify a problem and to find out what others have done to solve the problem. If the problem has not been solved, or if the scientist thinks there is a better solution for the problem, then the scientist can work on a possible solution for the problem in a form that can be tested by experiment. A solution is not considered "scientific" unless an experiment can be devised to test it.

## The scientific method

*Gathering information and recording your observations are important steps in the scientific method that are often overlooked.*

1. **Identify** or state the problem.

2. **Analyze** the problem: gather information, find out what is known about the problem. It may have been solved.

3. **Form a hypothesis:** make an "educated guess" as to what the answer may be. This can be based on a hunch or past experience.

4. **Test the hypothesis:** design and carry out an experiment or experiments.

5. **Record** observations and measurements, interpret them, and form conclusions.

6. **Revise** the hypothesis based on data.

# Measurement.

Scientists constantly compare things. It may be easy to say that one object is bigger or heavier than another; or that a place is farther away than another without measuring them. But to answer questions like "How big?"; "How much bigger?"; "How heavy?" requires measuring—a more exact way of comparing. The measurements scientists gather must be available to other scientists so that they can repeat the experiment or use the information in their own work. The units of measurement must be standard, that is, they must mean the same everywhere. There are two standard systems in use today. We commonly use the customary system (also known as the English system). In the customary system, the *yard* is the basic unit of length. You know this system and probably use it quite easily. However, it was difficult to learn because the units within the system are not related.

**Metric system.** The *metric system* is in common use in most countries and by scientists all over the world. This system of measurement is a decimal system. Each unit is related by a factor of 10. The basic unit of length is the *meter*. All other units are 10, 100, or 1000 times larger than the meter or $\frac{1}{10}$, $\frac{1}{100}$, or $\frac{1}{1000}$ of a meter.

The units of 10 meters (dekameter), 100 meters (hectometer), and $\frac{1}{10}$ meter (decimeter) are not commonly used. The key to using the metric system is understanding the prefixes used to designate the decimal fractions. "Kilo-" means 1000 times the basic unit; "cent-" means 0.01 or $\frac{1}{100}$ of the basic unit; and "milli-" means 0.001 or $\frac{1}{1000}$ of the basic unit. The basic unit of liquid volume in the metric system is the *liter* and the basic unit of mass is the *gram*.

**Temperature.** Temperature is measured on the Fahrenheit or Celsius scales. On the Fahrenheit scale, water freezes at 32 degrees and boils at 212 degrees. The Celsius (formerly the centigrade scale) is used in scientific work. On this scale, water freezes at 0 degrees and boils at 100 degrees. There are 180 degrees between boiling and freezing on a Fahrenheit thermometer, and 100 degrees between the same points on a Celsius thermometer. To convert a Fahrenheit value to the Celsius, subtract 32 from the Fahrenheit value and multiply by $\frac{5}{9}$. $C = \frac{5}{9}(F - 32)$. To convert a Celsius temperature to Fahrenheit, multiply the Celsius value by $\frac{9}{5}$ and add 32 to it. $F = \frac{9}{5}C + 32$.

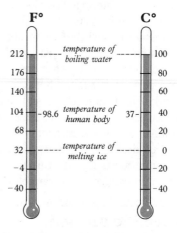

## Principal units of measurement

### The customary system of length

1 mile = 1760 yards = 5280 feet
1 yard =       3 feet =      36 inches
                1 foot =      12 inches

### The metric system of length

| | | | |
|---|---|---|---|
| kilometer | km | 1000 meters | 1000 × meter |
| meter | m | 1 meter | — |
| centimeter | cm | 0.01 meters | $\frac{1}{100}$ meter |
| millimeter | mm | 0.001 meters | $\frac{1}{1000}$ meter |

### Metric units of liquid volume

| | | | | |
|---|---|---|---|---|
| kiloliter | kl | 1000 liters | 1000 × liter |
| liter | l | 1.0 liter | — |
| centiliter | cl | 0.01 liters | $\frac{1}{100}$ liter |
| milliliter | ml | 0.001 liters | $\frac{1}{1000}$ liter |

### Metric units of mass

| | | | | |
|---|---|---|---|---|
| kilogram | kg | 1000 grams | 1000 × gram |
| gram | g | 1.0 gram | — |
| centigram | cg | 0.01 grams | $\frac{1}{100}$ gram |
| milligram | mg | 0.001 grams | $\frac{1}{1000}$ gram |

**Physical Sciences**

# Equivalents

**1 acre** = 43,560 square feet = 4840 square yards
**1 bushel (U.S.)** = 2150.42 cubic inches
         = 32 quarts
**1 cord** = 128 cubic feet
**1 cubic centimeter** = 0.061 cubic inch
**1 cubic foot** = 7.481 gallons = 1728 cubic inches
**1 cubic inch** = 0.554 fluid ounce
         = 16.387 cubic centimeters
**1 cubic meter** = 1.308 cubic yards
**1 cubic yard** = 0.765 cubic meter = 27 cubic feet
**1 cup** = 8 fluid ounces = 0.5 liquid pint
**1 gallon (U.S.)** = 231 cubic inches
         = 128 U.S. fluid ounces
         = 4 liquid quarts
**1 liter** = 1.057 liquid quarts
**1 meter** = 39.37 inches = 1.094 yards
**1 micron** = 0.001 millimeter = 0.00003937 inch
**1 mile, nautical** = 1.852 kilometers
         = 1.151 statute miles
         = 6076.1155 feet
**1 milliliter** = 0.061 cubic inch
**1 pint, dry** = 33.600 cubic inches = 0.551 liter
**1 pint, liquid** = 28.875 inches = 0.473 liter
         = 2 cups = 16 ounces
**1 pound, avoirdupois** = 7000 grains = 16 ounces
         = 453.59237 grams
**1 quart, dry (U.S.)** = 67.201 cubic inches
         = 1.101 liters
**1 quart, liquid (U.S.)** = 57.75 cubic inches
         = 0.946 liter
         = 2 pints = 32 ounces
**1 square foot** = 929 square centimeters
         = 144 square inches
**1 square inch** = 6.45 square centimeters
**1 square kilometer** = 0.386 square miles
         = 247.105 acres
**1 square meter** = 1.196 square yards
         = 10.764 square feet
**1 square mile** = 640 acres
**1 square yard** = 0.836 square meter
         = 9 square feet
         = 1296 square inches
**1 tablespoon** = 3 teaspoons = 0.5 fluid ounce
**1 ton, metric** = 2204.623 pounds
         = 1.102 net tons
**1 ton, net or short** = 2000 pounds
         = 0.907 metric ton
**1 yard** = 0.9144 meter = 3 feet = 36 inches

# Conversions

| To convert | into | multiply by |
|---|---|---|
| angstroms | microns | 0.0001 |
| centimeters | feet | 0.03281 |
| centimeters | inches | 0.3937 |
| cubic cm | cubic inches | 0.06102 |
| cubic feet | cubic meters | 0.02832 |
| days | seconds | 86,400.0 |
| degrees (angle) | radians | 0.01745 |
| fathoms | feet | 6.0 |
| feet | centimeters | 30.48 |
| feet | meters | 0.3048 |
| feet/min. | cm/sec. | 0.5080 |
| feet/sec. | knots | 0.5921 |
| feet/sec. | statute mi./hr. | 0.6818 |
| furlongs/hr. | statute mi./hr. | 0.125 |
| furlongs | feet | 660.0 |
| gallons (liq.) | liters | 3.785 |
| gal of water | pounds of water | 8.3453 |
| grams | oz. (avoirdupois) | 0.03527 |
| grams | pounds | 0.002205 |
| hours | days | 0.04167 |
| hours | weeks | 0.005952 |
| inches | centimeters | 2.540 |
| kilograms | pounds | 2.205 |
| kilometers | feet | 3280.8 |
| kilometers | mi. (statute) | 0.6214 |
| knots | feet/hr. | 6080.0 |
| knots | nautical mi./hr. | 1.0 |
| knots | statute mi./hr. | 1.151 |
| liters | gallons (liq.) | 0.2642 |
| liters | pints (liq.) | 2.113 |
| meters | feet | 3.281 |
| meters | mi. (nautical) | 0.0005396 |
| meters | mi. (statute) | 0.0006214 |
| microns | meters | 0.000001 |
| mi. (nautical) | feet | 6076.115 |
| mi. (statute) | feet | 5280.0 |
| mi. (nautical) | kilometers | 1.852 |
| mi. (statute) | kilometers | 1.609 |
| mi. (nautical) | mi. (statute) | 1.1508 |
| mi. (statute) | mi. (nautical) | 0.8684 |
| mi. (statute)/hr. | feet/min. | 88.0 |
| millimeters | inches | 0.03937 |
| oz. (avoirdupois) | grams | 28.3495 |
| oz. (avoirdupois) | lb. (avoirdupois) | 0.0625 |
| pints (liq.) | gallons (liq.) | 0.125 |
| pints (liq.) | quarts (liq.) | 0.5 |
| lb. (avoirdupois) | kilograms | 0.4536 |

# The physical sciences

The word "science" comes from the Latin word *scire*, which means "to know." The attempt "to know" the universe involves the study of many different subjects. For this reason, science is divided into different branches. The *physical sciences* form one of these major branches. The word "physical" comes from the Greek word *physika*, meaning "natural things." Today the physical sciences involve the study of matter and energy. There are two main branches of the physical sciences. *Chemistry* is the study of the substances found in nature and the ways new substances can be formed. *Physics* deals with energy and the way it changes from one form to another. Physics also studies the basic nature of the physical world.

Both chemistry and physics study *matter* from different points of view. Matter is anything that takes up space, that has volume and weight. Both volume and weight are measurements. Weight is the measure of the force of gravity on an object. The gravitational force on an object depends on the quantity of matter that makes up the object. The quantity of matter is called *mass*. All matter has mass.

Different kinds of matter are often described in terms of their properties. Properties are characteristics or qualities that allow us to put substances into groups, to identify them, and to predict how the substances will act under certain conditions. There are two kinds of properties. A *physical* property of a substance can be determined without changing that substance into an-

## Melting and boiling points of some substances

| Substance | Melting point (°C) | Boiling point (°C) |
|---|---|---|
| Neon | −248.0 | −246 |
| Ethyl alcohol | −117.3 | + 78.5 |
| Chlorine | −101 | − 34.6 |
| Water | 0 | 100 |
| Sodium | 98 | 882.9 |
| Sodium chloride | 801 | 1413 |
| Silver | 961.9 | 2212 |
| Copper | 1083 | 2567 |
| Iron | 1535 | 2750 |

other. The temperatures at which substances freeze and boil are physical properties. The *phase* of a substance is another common property. Phase is the form that a substance normally exists in at room temperature. There are three common phases of matter—solid, liquid, and gas. A solid has a definite shape and a definite volume; a liquid has a definite volume but no definite shape; a gas has neither a definite shape nor a definite volume. Liquids and gases are fluids—they take the shape of their container.

Another physical property is the *solubility* of a substance; that is, the ability of that substance to dissolve in water or other liquids.

The *density* of a substance is an important physical property because it allows us to compare

## Densities of some common substances *(in grams per cubic centimeter)*

| | | | | | |
|---|---|---|---|---|---|
| balsa wood | 0.11 to 0.14 | alcohol | 0.791 | marble | 2.6 to 2.84 |
| cork | 0.22 to 0.26 | kerosene | 0.82 | granite | 2.64 to 2.76 |
| oak | 0.60 to 0.80 | paraffin | 0.87 to 0.91 | aluminum | 2.70 |
| walnut | 0.64 to 0.70 | ice | 0.917 | diamond | 3.01 to 3.52 |
| ash | 0.65 to 0.85 | water | 1.00 | steel | 7.6 to 7.8 |
| gasoline | 0.66 to 0.69 | sea water | 1.025 | iron | 7.85 |
| cardboard | 0.69 | milk | 1.028 to 1.035 | brass | 8.2 to 8.7 |
| beech | 0.70 to 0.90 | rubber | 1.19 | copper | 8.89 |
| paper | 0.7 to 1.15 | sugar | 1.59 | lead | 11.3 |
| ether | 0.736 | clay | 1.8 to 2.6 | mercury | 13.6 |
| dogwood | 0.76 | glass | 2.4 to 2.8 | gold | 19.3 |

equal volumes of different substances. Density is the mass of a definite volume of a substance. It is usually measured in grams (units of mass) per cubic centimeter or per milliliter (both units of volume). The density of water under normal pressure at room temperature is 1.0g/cc.

*Chemical properties* describe how a substance reacts with other substances. Iron will rust when it combines with oxygen. The metal iron has changed into a new substance, iron oxide.

# Types of matter.
Scientists have learned that matter can be divided into three different groups. *Elements* are substances that cannot be divided into any other substance. Ninety occur naturally, and scientists have created 25 others in the laboratory for a total of 115 elements (including 6 yet-unnamed elements). Most elements are solids at room temperature. Hydrogen, helium, oxygen, and a few others are gases. Mercury and bromine are the only elements that are liquids at normal room temperature. Each named element has been given a symbol or abbreviation that is related to its English, Greek, or Latin name. (For more information about chemical elements, see the Chemistry section in Volume 2.)

Many kinds of matter are made up of two or more elements that are chemically combined. Water is one example. It is made up of hydrogen and oxygen. Sugar is made up of carbon, hydrogen, and oxygen. Salt is composed of sodium and chlorine. A substance that is made up of two or

*A miner uses the different densities of substances in the mixture that is sand and gravel to separate the very heavy element gold from the lighter compounds of silicon that form most of the mixture.*

more elements that have been chemically combined is a *compound*. A chemical change occurs when elements combine to form a compound. The elements lose their identity and a new substance is formed. Each compound has its own chemical formula that uses the symbols of the elements forming it.

*Mixtures* are a third kind of matter. A mixture is made up of two or more elements or compounds that are mixed together. No chemical change takes place, so the individual components do not lose their identity and can be separated from each other physically. Soil and air are mixtures. Soil is mostly a mixture of compounds, while air is mostly a mixture of elements.

## Some common compounds

*The number of elements is small compared to the vast number of compounds that can be made from them. Here are four very different compounds formed out of only five elements: sodium (Na), hydrogen (H), carbon (C), oxygen (O), and nitrogen (N).*

$NaHCO_3$ baking soda    $C_{12}H_{22}O_{11}$ sugar    $NH_4OH$ ammonia    $H_2O$ water

# The particle theory.

In order to explain the different kinds of matter and how matter changes, scientists assume that all matter is made up of tiny particles. Elements are made up of *atoms*. An atom is the smallest particle of an element that still has the properties of that element. When elements combine chemically to form a compound, their atoms usually become bonded together. Atoms of elements bonded together may form *molecules* of compounds. A molecule is made up of two or more atoms bonded together. A molecule is the smallest particle of a compound that has all the properties of that compound. When two atoms of hydrogen, H, combine with one atom of oxygen, O, one molecule of water, $H_2O$, is formed. Some compounds are formed without molecules, strictly speaking. In ionic compounds such as table salt, NaCl, the particles of sodium, Na, and chlorine, Cl, are loosely bonded when dissolved in water.

In addition to assuming that all matter is made up of particles, scientists also state that these particles are constantly moving and that there are spaces between the particles. These three statements allow us to offer an explanation for the differences between the phases of matter, how substances boil and melt, how substances change phase, and other basic questions about matter.

*Although scientists cannot see individual atoms, they use mental models of what atoms are like to predict their behavior. A picture of such a mental model of the helium atom shows four heavy particles at the atom's center—two protons and two neutrons. Two much lighter particles—electrons—are thought of as moving in regions outside the heavy center.*

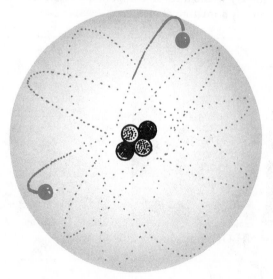

## How to read a chemical equation

Chemical equations provide a compact way to represent the reactions that occur when two compounds are combined. A typical chemical equation is

$$SO_2 + H_2O \rightarrow H_2SO_3$$

The + sign means that the two compounds are combined. The $\rightarrow$ means "yields." This equation, then, means sulfur dioxide ($SO_2$) combined with water ($H_2O$) yields sulfurous acid ($H_2SO_3$).

Frequently, the amount of one compound that enters into the combination is different from the amount of the other compound. In that case, the chemical equation is "balanced" by writing numbers indicating the amounts involved before the symbol for the compound.

$$P_4 + 5\ O_2 \rightarrow 2\ P_2O_5$$

In this equation, one part of phosphorus, which occurs as a molecule of four phosphorus atoms, is combined with five parts of oxygen, which occurs as a molecule of two oxygen atoms, to yield two parts of a compound named phosphorus pentoxide. Often you see arrows pointing up or down in chemical equations. Arrows pointing up indicate that the substance is formed as a gas, while arrows pointing down mean that the substance is formed as a solid when two liquids are combined. For example,

$$AgNO_3 + NaCl \rightarrow AgCl \downarrow + NaNO_3$$

means that when silver nitrate ($AgNO_3$) in solution is added to salt (NaCl) in solution the silver chloride (AgCl) is formed as a solid that collects at the bottom of the mixture. The sodium nitrate ($NaNO_3$) that also forms stays in solution. Similarly,

$$3NO_2 + H_2O \rightarrow 2HNO_3 + NO \uparrow$$

means that three parts of nitrogen dioxide ($NO_2$) dissolved in one part of water yields two parts of nitric acid ($HNO_3$) and one part of the gas nitric oxide (NO).

A small triangle written over the "yields" arrow means that the chemicals must be heated for the reaction to occur. Similarly, a small "D.C." over the arrow means that direct current (electricity) must be applied.

**Physical Sciences**

# Matter

The smaller particles that make up atoms are called electrons, protons, and neutrons. The simplest kind of atom is the hydrogen atom, which is built from just one proton and one electron. One might expect that the next simplest atom would consist of a pair of protons and a pair of electrons, but the forces in the central part of the atom, called the nucleus, do not permit this atom to exist. In fact, the next-most-complicated atom is another form of hydrogen, called heavy hydrogen or deuterium. Its atoms each contain one proton, one neutron, and one electron. A third form of hydrogen, called tritium, can also exist; it has two neutrons, a proton, and an electron.

The type of element is normally given by the number of electrons. Only electrons enter into chemical reactions. However, the number of electrons in an atom may be easily changed, while the number of protons is more constant. Therefore, physical scientists say that the element is determined by the number of protons.

When the elements are arranged in order by the number of protons, called the *atomic number*, there is an element for each whole number of protons. Hydrogen has the atomic number 1, helium has the atomic number 2, carbon has the atomic number 6, oxygen has the atomic number 8, and so forth, up to uranium, the last naturally occurring element, which has the atomic number 92. But 25 elements, with atomic numbers between 93 and 118, have been created.

Neutrons occur in all atomic nuclei heavier than hydrogen. The number of protons and neutrons, which are both much heavier than electrons, gives the *mass number* of each element. Deuterium has a mass number of 2, tritium of 3, and helium of 4. From this information (helium's atomic number of 2 and mass number of 4), one can determine that helium must consist of two protons, two neutrons, and two electrons.

Most elements found in nature are a mixture of atoms that all have the same number of protons, but have different numbers of neutrons. Such different versions of the same element are called *isotopes*. For example, the most common isotope of carbon is the one with a mass number of 12, which is called carbon 12. Since the atomic number of carbon is 6, carbon 12 has six protons, six

*Elements with smaller atomic masses tend to be very light. Helium, the element with the second lowest atomic mass, is used in modern blimps to make them lighter than the air they displace.*

neutrons, and six electrons. There exist in nature, however, small amounts of both carbon 13 and carbon 14. Carbon 13 has seven neutrons and carbon 14 has eight.

When the mass of an atom is adjusted for small differences in the mass of the proton and neutron, for the mass of the electrons in the atom, and for the relative abundance of isotopes, a number close to—but not equal to—the mass number results. Since this number, called the *atomic mass*, can be measured directly, the atomic mass is often used by chemists or physicists instead of the mass number. (The mass number cannot be directly measured.) For example, the atomic mass of carbon, which reflects the amount of carbon 13 and carbon 14, is 12.01115.

Although the only forms of matter that we normally experience are elements, compounds, and mixtures, the individual particles that make up atoms are considered matter as well. In addition to electrons, protons, and neutrons, matter also includes such particles as muons, pions, kaons, and many other *subatomic* particles. Most subatomic particles are very short-lived, however. After tiny fractions of a second, they change into other particles or into energy.

# Some important elements

A *mass number* is the mass of the atom compared with carbon 12, an isotope of carbon whose mass has been assigned the value 12. The *atomic mass* is the average mass number of the different forms of the element.

The *atomic number* is the number of protons in the nucleus of the atom. Atomic number is the most important factor in determining the chemical properties of the element.

| Element | Symbol | Atomic mass | Atomic number | Properties, uses |
|---|---|---|---|---|
| **aluminum** | Al | 26.9815 | 13 | White metal, used in construction where light weight is important. As oxide, used as abrasive. |
| **bismuth** | Bi | 208.98 | 83 | Brittle metal used in electric fuses, fire sprinkler systems, safety valves. |
| **bromine** | Br | 79.909 | 35 | Red corrosive liquid used to make organic compounds, medicines, photographic film. |
| **cadmium** | Cd | 112.40 | 48 | Blue-white metal used in electroplating, bearings, batteries, atomic reactors. |
| **calcium** | Ca | 40.08 | 20 | Silvery, active metal. Compounds used in mortar, plaster, cement, agriculture. |
| **carbon** | C | 12.011 | 6 | Black or transparent nonmetal. As diamond, used in jewelry, abrasives; as graphite, in lubricants. Forms innumerable compounds. Basis of all life. |
| **chlorine** | Cl | 35.453 | 17 | Green corrosive gas. Used in bleach, germicides, drugs, manufacture of organic chemicals. |
| **copper** | Cu | 63.54 | 29 | Reddish metal used as electrical conductor, to make brass, bronze, other alloys. Compounds used in water purification. |
| **fluorine** | F | 18.9984 | 9 | Yellow gas, very corrosive. Used to make refrigerants, plastics. As hydrofluoric acid, etches glass. |
| **gold** | Au | 196.97 | 79 | Yellow metal, used in coins, jewelry, dentistry. |
| **helium** | He | 4.003 | 2 | Inert gas, used in balloons. |
| **hydrogen** | H | 1.008 | 1 | Gas used for heat, to make ammonia, many chemical processes. |
| **iodine** | I | 126.90 | 53 | Black solid, used as germicide, for organic chemicals, photography. |
| **iron** | Fe | 55.85 | 26 | White, hard metal. Chief component of steel. Compounds used in medicine, blueprints. |
| **lead** | Pb | 207.21 | 82 | White metal used in plumbing, solder, type metal, batteries. Compounds used as pigments. |
| **lithium** | Li | 6.940 | 3 | Light, very active metal. Salts used in medicine, fireworks. |

| Element | Symbol | Atomic mass | Atomic number | Properties, uses |
|---|---|---|---|---|
| **magnesium** | Mg | 24.32 | 12 | Light, white metal, used to make light alloys for airplanes. Salts used in medicine. |
| **manganese** | Mn | 54.938 | 25 | Gray-white, brittle metal. Used in stainless steel, other alloys. |
| **mercury** | Hg | 200.59 | 80 | Liquid, silvery metal, used in thermometers, barometers, other instruments. |
| **neon** | Ne | 20.183 | 10 | Inert gas used in electric signs. |
| **nitrogen** | N | 14.007 | 7 | Colorless gas, used to make ammonia, nitric acid, many organic compounds. |
| **oxygen** | O | 15.999 | 8 | Colorless gas, essential for life, used in oxyacetylene flames, aid to respiration. |
| **phosphorus** | P | 30.98 | 15 | Yellow, waxy form; red, crystalline form. Compounds used in fertilizer, detergents. |
| **platinum** | Pt | 195.09 | 78 | Silvery metal used in jewelry, instruments, laboratory ware, catalysts. |
| **potassium** | K | 39.096 | 19 | Soft, silvery, very active metal. Salts used in fertilizers, medicine. |
| **radium** | Ra | 226.05 | 88 | Radioactive metal, used in medicine, to make luminous watch dials. |
| **silicon** | Si | 28.086 | 14 | Brown nonmetal. Compounds used in glass, cement, ceramics, photoelectric cells. |
| **silver** | Ag | 107.870 | 47 | White metal used in jewelry, coins, tableware, photography, medicine, electroplating. |
| **sodium** | Na | 22.9898 | 11 | Silvery, very active metal. Salts used in seasoning, fertilizers, detergents. |
| **sulfur** | S | 32.064 | 16 | Yellow solid, used to vulcanize rubber, make sulfuric acid; sulfur dioxide used as fumigant, bleach. |
| **tin** | Sn | 118.70 | 50 | White metal, used to plate steel, make pewter, solder, bronze, type metal. Salts used in textiles. |
| **titanium** | Ti | 47.90 | 22 | Lustrous white metal used in alloys. Oxide used as paint pigment. |
| **uranium** | U | 238.029 | 92 | White, dense metal, radioactive, used in glass and china, source of atomic energy. |
| **zinc** | Zn | 65.37 | 30 | Blue-white metal used in brass, many other alloys, metal plating. Compounds used in paints, antiseptics. |

# Energy

Physics is the branch of physical science that deals with energy, its forms, and the way it changes. In science, energy is the ability to do work. There are several types of energy and each type can be transformed into another. A common example can be found in the automobile. The source of energy is the gasoline used as fuel. The gasoline is burned in the engine. The chemical energy of the fuel is transformed into heat. The heat energy causes other parts to move, causing the car to move. The heat energy is converted or tranformed into mechanical energy.

Many different experiments performed over many years have shown scientists that energy can neither be created nor destroyed by chemical or mechanical methods, but can be transformed from one type to another.

Energy is the ability to do work. For work to be done, an object must move or be moved over a distance. A *force* is required to move or lift an object. A force is a push or pull. There are several kinds of forces. You can exert force on a wall by pushing on it, but no work will be done if the wall does not move. More work is done when you lift a pencil than when you push on a wall! The amount of work that is done by a force depends on two factors: the weight of the object to be lifted or moved and the distance it is lifted or moved. The amount of work done (W) is equal to the force (F) required to lift or move an object multiplied by the distance (d) through which the force is exerted. The relationship between work done, force, and distance is expressed by the formula $W = F \times d$.

## Forms of energy.
Each type of energy can exist in two different *forms*. Electrical energy can be stored in a cell. A bicycle at the top of a hill has stored energy to coast down. Food has energy stored within the molecules that make it up. The cell, bicycle, and food have energy that is stored up owing to the composition of the material or the position of the object. This energy is called *potential energy*. Potential energy is commonly called energy of position. A hammer that has been raised to hit a nail has potential energy. When you drop the hammer, it has the energy of motion. The potential energy has become *kinetic* energy. Kinetic energy is the energy of motion. Since both potential and kinetic energy are associated with motion, they are often considered as kinds of mechanical energy.

## Energy conversions

*Energy can be changed from one form to another. The energy of the sun, stored by green plants millions of years ago in what has become coal or oil, is recaptured in part by burning. The heat energy released is used to produce steam, which turns the blades of a turbine, converting the heat energy into mechanical energy. The turbine drives a generator, which converts the mechanical energy into electrical energy. The electrical energy can then be converted by machines, tools, or appliances into heat, light, or mechanical energy.*

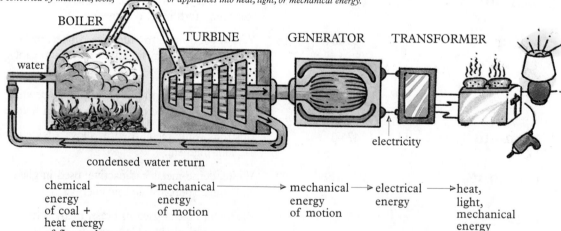

**Heat energy.** According to the particle theory, all matter is made up of particles that are always moving. All matter has this internal kinetic energy called *heat energy*. The amount of heat an object contains is measured in either of two units, the *calorie* or the *British thermal unit* (Btu). The calorie is the amount of heat required to raise the temperature of 1 gram of water 1 degree Celsius. The Btu is used in heating and air-conditioning systems. One Btu is the amount of heat required to raise the temperature of 1 pound of water 1 Fahrenheit degree.

Temperature is a measurement of how hot something is, not how much heat something contains. The amount of heat something contains will vary with the mass of the object. A bathtub full of water will melt more ice than a cup full of water at the same temperature. Temperature is a measurement of the average kinetic energy of the particles in an object. When the average kinetic energy increases, the temperature will increase. A thermometer usually is made up of a glass tube from which the air has been removed and partially replaced with a small amount of alcohol or mercury. When a thermometer is placed in hot water, it absorbs energy from the water. The particles of the alcohol or mercury begin to move faster and move away from each other. The mercury or alcohol expands up the tube.

In addition to the Celsius and Fahrenheit temperature scales, the Kelvin scale is used to measure very high or low temperatures. The Kelvin, or absolute, scale is based on the assumption that there is a temperature at which all particle motion stops. At this temperature there is no heat. This temperature has been calculated to be about 273 degrees below zero on the Celsius scale and is called *absolute zero*. Absolute zero equals -273.16° C. Water freezes at 273.16° Kelvin (K) and boils at 373.16° K.

Heat energy always moves from a substance with a higher temperature to a substance with a lower one. Heat can be transferred in three different ways: *conduction, convection,* and *radiation*.

In *conduction,* an object must be in direct contact with another. Heat energy will be transferred, or conducted, from the hotter object to the cooler.

Heat is transferred through liquids or gases by *convection*. When water is heated in a pan, the water at the bottom is heated first. It expands and becomes less dense. Cooler, denser water sinks and replaces the warmer water. Convection currents of rising warm water and settling cooler water are set up. This movement of the fluid will continue until the entire container of water is equally heated.

Both conduction and convection involve particles of matter. *Radiation* does not. Heat can be transferred through space in the form of waves that move at the speed of light. When these waves are absorbed by an object, they are converted to heat energy.

## Heat transfer

*The hot water or steam produced in a boiler transfers heat to a radiator through* conduction, *then flows back to the boiler for reheating. The radiator warms the air around it through* convection. *The warm air rises and cooler air sinks, producing* convection *currents. The radiator also heats the air and objects in a room through* radiation, *by which energy waves emitted by the radiator directly heat the molecules they strike.*

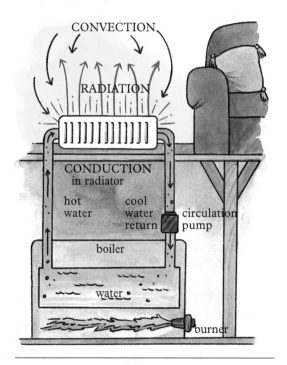

# Machines.

Mechanical energy is the energy an object has from its position or motion. The moving parts of an automobile engine are an example of mechanical energy. A hammer hitting a nail also has mechanical energy.

When you think of mechanical energy and machines, you may think of motors and engines, such as the engine in an automobile. The actions of such motors, however, are based in part on fundamental arrangements that transfer mechanical energy. These arrangements are known as *simple machines.*

People have always sought ways to make the work they do easier or faster. Simple machines can make work easier or faster, but cannot increase the amount of work done. The operator of a simple machine must do work in order to operate it. This work is called the *input* or *work input.* The work the machine does is the *output* or *work output.* The output is never greater than the input. In fact, the input work is usually greater than the output work. Some of the input is used to overcome *friction.* Friction is a force that resists movement between two surfaces. Friction converts mechanical energy into heat energy as parts of machines rub against each other, in the same way that heat is generated when hands are rubbed together.

There are six simple machines: levers, pulleys, wheels and axles, inclined planes, wedges, and screws. These machines help us do work by multiplying the force we put into them or by changing the direction of that force. With any machine, the user must apply a force to overcome the resistance of the object being moved. The force the user applies is called the *effort.* The distance the effort moves through is the *effort distance.* Work is force times distance, so the work input is equal to the effort times the effort distance.

The object being moved exerts a force, the *resistance*, that must be overcome by the effort. The distance that the machine moves the resistance is the *resistance distance.* The work output is the product of the force of the resistance times the resistance distance. If friction and other resistances are ignored, the work input should equal the work output. This is the *law of machines.* Machines can increase or multiply the effort that is applied to them, making work easier. This is usually done by increasing the effort distance. The work done by a small effort over a large distance will equal the work done when a large resistance is moved over a small distance.

**Levers.** A lever is a simple machine consisting of a bar that is supported at one position while a force is applied at another position. The place where the lever is supported is the *fulcrum.* There are three classes of levers, depending on the positions of the effort, fulcrum, and resistance.

*1st class levers*: the fulcrum is between the effort and resistance. These levers multiply effort.

*2nd class levers*: the resistance is between the fulcrum and the effort. These levers also multiply the effort applied to them.

*3rd class levers*: the effort is between the fulcrum and the resistance. This arrangement multiplies the effort distance.

**Pulleys.** A pulley is a grooved wheel supported in a frame with a rope placed in the groove of the wheel. The simplest pulley is one that is fixed. This machine does not increase the force applied but does allow a change in the direction of the force. If the pulley is fixed to a ceiling or bar, one can pull down on the rope to lift a resistance. Movable pulleys, where a pulley or combination of pulleys is attached to the resistance, allow us to decrease the force applied to produce the same force on the resistance.

**Wheels and axles.** These simple machines are made up of a large wheel attached to a smaller wheel, the *axle*, so that both wheels turn together. A small effort applied to the large wheel can overcome a large resistance on the axle. However, the effort must move through a greater distance. The steering wheel of a car is a wheel and axle, as is a screwdriver attached to the head of a screw.

**Inclined planes.** It is easier to push an object up a gradual slope than to lift it directly. It might take three men to lift a 400-pound object to the back of a truck that is 3 feet high. One man can raise the object to that height by rolling it along a 10-foot ramp.

**Wedges.** A wedge is an inclined plane that moves into or under a resistance. A small ax or wedge can be used to split a large log.

**Screws.** A screw is often described as an inclined plane wrapped around a post. The ridges of a screw are called the *threads* and the distance between threads is the *pitch.* The smaller the pitch of a screw, the more times it must be turned to fasten it in place. The number of turns equals the effort distance.

**Physical Sciences**

# Simple machines

## levers

The fulcrum of a bottle opener rests atop the cap. The fulcrum of a scissors is where the two halves are connected.

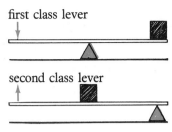

first class lever

second class lever

third class lever

↓ effort

▲ fulcrum

▨ resistance

## pulleys

A system of pulleys enables the winch on this tow truck to lift the weight of an automobile.

fixed pulley

movable pulley

pulley system

## wheels and axles

Doorknobs and screwdrivers are both combinations of axles (the shafts) and wheels (the handles).

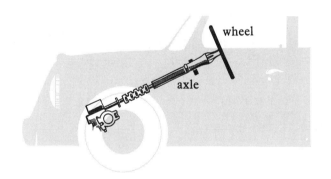

wheel

axle

## inclined planes

It is much easier to roll an automobile up a ramp — an inclined plane — than to lift it up and carry it forward.

## screws

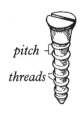

pitch

threads

A screw is an inclined plane around a cylinder.

## wedges

A drillbit tip is a wedge, and its threaded shaft is an inclined plane. A wedge separates objects or splits material apart.

# Electromagnetism

## Static electricity.
Another form of energy is electromagnetism. One kind of electromagnetism is *static electricity*. Atoms have no electric charge since the number of negatively charged electrons equals the number of positively charged protons. Electrons can be transferred to or from certain substances when they are rubbed, producing static electricity. A substance that gains electrons becomes negatively charged. It has more electrons than protons. A substance that loses electrons becomes positively charged since it now has more protons than electrons. Experiments have shown that substances that have like charges will repel each other.

Some substances can become electrically charged when they touch a charged object. Those substances that allow electrons to move freely, such as metals, are *conductors*. Materials that do not allow electric charges to move easily, such as glass, are *insulators*.

## Electric circuits.
When a stream of electrons can be made to move through a device that uses their energy, useful work can be done by the moving charges. Electric charges in motion produce *current*. The force or push required to move electrons through a conductor is called *voltage*. The higher the voltage (the greater the number of volts), the more work the electrons can do.

Electrons require a closed pathway in order for them to flow. This closed pathway is called a *circuit*. A circuit requires three components: a source of electrons, a conducting pathway, and a device that will use the energy of the moving electrons. The device that uses the energy is called the *load* or *resistance*.

Two or more resistances can be connected so that there is only one path for the electric energy. This is a *series circuit*. Since there is only one pathway, a break anywhere in the circuit will open the entire circuit. If light bulbs in a house were connected in series, the loosening or burning out of one bulb would cause all the bulbs in the house to go out. In a *parallel circuit* there is more than one path for electrical energy to follow. Each pathway can operate a different appliance or room in a house.

## Electromagnetism.
A *magnet* is a substance that attracts iron. Some materials are natural magnets. Others can become magnetized when they are stroked several times in the same direction with a magnet. Magnets can attract objects without touching them. A magnetic field extends around each magnet. When a bar magnet is suspended freely and allowed to come to rest, it will point in a north-south direction. This happens because Earth itself has a magnetic field. The end pointing north is the north-seeking or

---

## Electrical circuits

**Series**

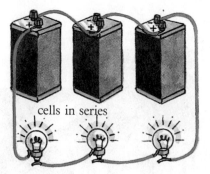

cells in series

resistances in series

**Parallel**

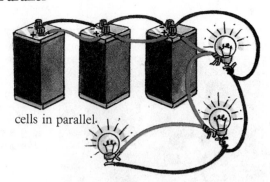

cells in parallel.

resistances in parallel

---

**Physical Sciences**

north pole. The opposite end is the south-seeking or south pole. When two bar magnets are brought near each other, unlike poles will attract each other while like poles will repel each other.

When a compass is placed parallel to a wire conducting an electric current, the compass needle, a small bar magnet, will move sideways. This indicates that there is a magnetic field around a wire conducting electricity. The direction of the magnetic field depends on the direction in which the current is flowing in the conductor.

When a conducting wire is formed into a coil, the strength of the magnetic field is increased. This electromagnetic effect can be made even stronger if a piece of iron is placed inside the coil of wire. Electromagnets are used to lift heavy metal objects, in telephones, electric motors, and electric generators.

*Electric motors* convert electrical energy into mechanical energy. A motor is made up of a moving electromagnet and a fixed magnet. The electromagnet spins on an axle. This magnet and axle are called the *armature*. When current flows through the electromagnet, the armature is attracted to and turns toward the opposite pole of the fixed magnet. As the armature moves toward the opposite pole, the direction of current flowing in it is reversed. This causes the magnetic field to be reversed. Instead of being attracted to the pole of the fixed magnet, the armature is now repelled

*A magnet such as the bar magnet shown at the left produces a magnetic field around it, a field that can be shown as lines of force. When the north pole of one magnet is placed near the north pole of another, the lines of force interfere with each other, causing the magnets to repel one another. When the north pole of one magnet is placed near the south pole of another, however, the lines of force work together to make the two magnets attract each other.*

by it. The armature is kept spinning by alternating the direction of the current flowing through the electromagnet.

Just as an electric current produces a magnetic field, a magnetic field can produce an electric current. An electric current can be *induced* in a conductor when the conducting wire is moved within a magnetic field. A *generator* uses this principle to convert mechanical energy into electrical energy. In a generator, a coil of wire is made to turn within the magnetic field of a U-shaped magnet. When the coils cut across the lines of force in the field, a current is induced to flow in the coil. As the coil continues to turn, it again cuts across the lines of force, but the induced current flows in the opposite direction. Such generators produce the *alternating current* we use in our homes, industries, and schools.

## Electrical generators

*When the field of a magnet moves with respect to a loop of conducting wire (1), an electric current is produced in the wire. This effect can be enhanced by using a coil of wire, since the more times the wire cuts the magnetic lines of force, the greater will be the electric current (2). The direction of motion controls the direction of the current in the wire.*

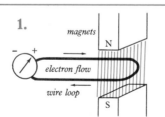

**1.**

magnets

electron flow

wire loop

*By mounting a coil of wires on an axle inside a magnet (3), a generator can be produced. As the axle is turned by an engine or by waterpower, the wire continually cuts across the lines of magnetic force, first in one direction, then in the other. The same principle, but reversed, is used in electric motors.*

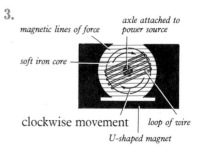

**3.**

magnetic lines of force

axle attached to power source

soft iron core

clockwise movement | loop of wire

U-shaped magnet

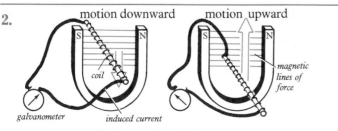

**2.**

motion downward    motion upward

coil

magnetic lines of force

galvanometer    induced current

# Wave motion

Energy is often transmitted or transferred in the form of waves. A *wave* is a series of back and forth or up and down vibrations. The energy in a wave travels but the material that the wave travels through only vibrates. A boat bobs up and down as waves pass. The boat moves at right angles to the direction of the waves. This is an example of *transverse waves*. Light, television, radio, and x-rays are transverse waves. Sound is an example of a *longitudinal wave*. In longitudinal waves, the material that the wave is traveling through vibrates parallel to the direction of the wave.

## Sound energy. Sound is produced when an object is made to vibrate (move rapidly back and forth). We perceive these vibrations as sounds when they are transmitted by our ears to our brains.

Sound requires a *medium*; that is, a substance to carry the energy. A medium can be a solid, liquid, or gas. Sound is transmitted when the vibrating object disturbs the particles that make up the medium. When an object is made to vibrate, it collides with the particles of the medium. These particles receive energy from the vibrating object and pass the energy to the particles with

which they collide. The energy of the vibrating object is transferred to particles around it with each back and forth movement. In this way, sound is transmitted in all directions.

The speed of sound depends on the density of the medium through which it is traveling. In general, sound has a greater velocity in solids than in liquids or gases.

The rate at which vibrations of an object are produced is called the *frequency* of that sound. Frequency is the number of *cycles* per second. A cycle is one sound wave. One *hertz* is equal to one cycle per second.

The human ear can detect sounds from about 20 hertz to 20,000 hertz. Sounds with a greater frequency than 20,000 hertz are called *ultrasonic*. *Pitch* is the highness or lowness of a sound. Pitch is related to frequency in that the greater the frequency, the higher the pitch produced.

*Wavelength* is also related to the pitch. The wavelength is the length of one cycle. Greater frequency means a shorter wavelength and a higher pitch of the sound produced. The *amplitude* of a sound wave is the distance that the particles of the medium were displaced. Greater amplitude means a greater intensity, or loudness, of the sound produced.

## Types of wave motion

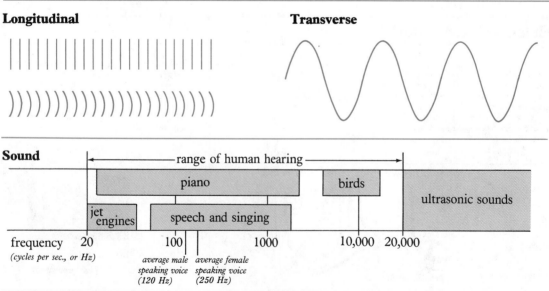

**Longitudinal**

**Transverse**

Sound

range of human hearing

piano

birds

ultrasonic sounds

jet engines

speech and singing

frequency   20          100                    1000          10,000   20,000
(cycles per sec., or Hz)

*average male speaking voice (120 Hz)*    *average female speaking voice (250 Hz)*

# Light energy.

The speed of light is accepted today as approximately 300,000 kilometers per second in a vacuum. This is equal to about 186,000 miles per second. In a more dense medium, such as glass, light will slow down, causing a change in the direction of the wave. This change of direction of waves as they pass in a slanted path from one medium to another is called *refraction*.

Refraction enables us to bend and focus light, making telescopes, cameras, and microscopes possible. Prisms allow us to separate visible light in the various wavelengths we see as colors.

**Color.** White light is actually a group of wavelengths and frequencies. Each frequency is refracted differently as it passes from air into glass and from glass into air again. The higher frequencies are refracted more than the lower ones. Violet is refracted most, followed by blue, green, yellow, orange, and red.

*Rainbows* are caused by the refraction of sunlight by raindrops. Rainbows are usually visible when the sun and rain are opposite each other and the sun is low in the sky. Usually, we must be facing the falling rain with the sun behind us to see a rainbow. In addition, the raindrops must be of a certain size to act as tiny prisms.

The color that an object appears to be depends on the frequency of the light that reaches the eye from that object. A red apple appears red because to our eyes it reflects only red light. It absorbs all other colors of light. If the same apple were placed in green light, it would appear black to us. The apple would absorb the green light; since there would be no red light to reflect, it would appear black. This is true for all *opaque* objects. Opaque objects do not allow light to pass through.

*Transparent* objects, such as glass, do allow light to pass through. They appear to be the color of the wavelength of light that passes through them. Green glass transmits or sends through light in the green frequency range and absorbs or filters out other colors.

The sky appears blue to our eyes when the particles of dust and gas in the atmosphere scatter the wavelengths of blue light. During midday, when the sun is most directly overhead, its light passes through a minimum of atmosphere. The light we receive appears white. The sun is close to the horizon in the evening and morning. Its light passes through more atmosphere. Dust particles in the air block off or scatter the shorter (blue) wavelengths of light and the sky around the sun appears to be orange or red.

## Light

**Lenses**

nearsightedness
*image formed
in front of retina*

*correction
concave lens*

farsightedness
*image blurred
on retina*

*correction
convex lens*

**Rainbows**

sunlight

**Why sky is blue**

sunlight

*scattering by
air molecules*

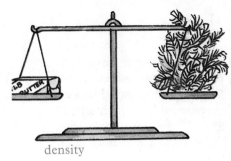
density

## Dictionary of physical sciences

physical change

pitch

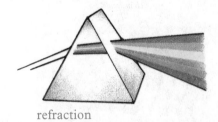
refraction

**ampere.** Unit of measurement used to describe the rate of flow of current in an electric circuit.

**amplitude.** Height of a crest of a wave; the maximum displacement of the medium through which a wave is traveling.

**atom.** Smallest particle of an element that retains the properties of that element.

**atomic mass.** Average of the mass numbers of an element for forms found in nature.

**atomic number.** Number of protons in the nucleus of an atom.

**chemical change.** Change in which the substances involved lose their identities to form different substances with different properties.

**compound.** Substance consisting of two or more elements that are chemically combined by weight in definite proportions.

**concave.** Surface (lens or mirror) that is hollowed inward like a bowl, thicker at the edges than in the center.

**conservation of mass-energy, law of.** In any change, the sum of the amount of matter and the amount of energy remains constant.

**control.** Part of an experiment for which all conditions except the one being tested are kept the same as in the experimental setup; that condition, which is the one being changed in the experiment, is left unchanged in the control.

**convex.** Surface (lens or mirror) that is thicker in the center than at its edges.

**density.** Mass of a definite volume of a substance, usually expressed in grams per cubic centimeter.

**effort.** Force put into a machine in order for it to do useful work.

**effort arm.** In a lever, the distance the effort must act over to provide the input work.

**electromagnetic waves.** Transverse waves produced by vibrations of electric charges. Electromagnetic waves travel at the speed of light and do not need a medium to travel through.

**element.** One of 112 substances that are composed of only one kind of atom.

**energy.** Ability to perform work.

**force.** Push or pull that will cause an object to change its motion or direction.

**frequency.** Number of cycles of a wave per unit time.

**friction.** Force that resists motion between two surfaces.

**heat.** Energy transferred from one place to another owing to differences in temperature; the kinetic energy of the particles of a substance owing to their random motion.

**hypothesis.** Possible solution to a scientific problem that can be tested by an experiment.

**image, real.** Image formed when light passes from an object through a convex lens. The image is on the opposite side of the lens from the object, is always inverted, and can be projected on a screen.

**incident ray.** Incoming light ray that strikes a surface.

**Physical Sciences**

**isotope.** Form of an element with the same atomic number but a different mass number.

**law.** In science, laws describe naturally occurring events. They are records of what happens.

**lens.** Transparent material designed to cause light to converge or diverge when passing through it.

**longitudinal waves.** Waves in which the vibration of the moving particles is parallel to the wave direction; that is, sound.

**magnetic field.** Area around a magnet in which the effects of its magnetism can be detected.

**mass.** Amount of matter in a body. It is a measure of the inertia of an object.

**mass number.** Weight of an atom compared with the weight of an atom of carbon that has been assigned the value of 12.

**matter.** Anything that has mass and occupies space.

**mixture.** Two or more elements or compounds that have been mixed together. The components of a mixture retain their properties and no chemical change takes place.

**nucleus.** Central, positively charged portion of an atom, made up of protons and neutrons.

**Ohm's law.** Electric current is equal to the ratio of voltage and resistance.

**phase.** Form that a substance normally exists in at room temperature; that is, solid, liquid, gas.

**physical change.** Change in a substance that does not change its chemical characteristics or composition.

**pitch.** Frequency of a sound wave.

**power.** Rate at which work is done.

**prism.** Device used to separate visible light into different wavelengths.

**radioactivity.** Spontaneous breakdown of atomic nuclei.

**reflection, law of.** Angle between an incident ray of light and the normal is always equal to the angle between the reflected ray and the normal.

**refraction, law of.** When light passes at an oblique angle from one medium into another of greater density, the velocity of light decreases and is bent toward the normal.

**resistance.** Opposition offered to the flow of electric current by a substance through which it is passing; an opposing force.

**simple machine.** Any one of the six basic devices used to change the direction, intensity, or distance traveled of a force.

**sound waves.** Compressional waves of audible frequencies move through an elastic medium by compressions and rarefactions of the particles.

**spectrum.** Continuous series of wavelengths.

**subatomic particle.** Any of the particles of matter that are smaller than an atom such as electrons, protons, neutrons, photons, or mesons.

**telescope.** Arrangement of lenses or mirrors used to see distant objects.

**temperature.** Condition of a substance that determines the direction of heat flow from one object to another; a measurement of the kinetic energy of the particles of a substance.

**theory.** General explanation that describes the results of many confirmed hypotheses.

**transverse waves.** Waves in which the particles move perpendicular to the direction of the wave; that is, light.

**ultrasonic.** Sound waves having a frequency of more than 20,000 hertz.

**wave.** Cyclic disturbance traveling through a medium.

**wavelength.** Distance between adjacent peaks of a wave.

**weight.** Measure of the pull of the force of gravity on a body.

**work.** Product of a force and the displacement of an object in the direction of the force.

## For Further Reference

Adler, Irving
  *The Story of Light*
  Harvey House
Clark, John
  *Matter and Energy: Physics in Action*
  Oxford University Press
Newton, David E.
  *The Chemical Elements*
  Franklin Watts

Sobel, Michael I.
  *Light*
  University of Chicago Press
Stevens, S.S. and Warshofsky, Fred
  *Sound and Hearing*
  Time-Life Books
Trefil, James
  *From Atoms to Quarks: An Introduction to the Strange World of Particle Physics*
  Doubleday

# Earth Science

Over the past few decades, science has changed our perceptions and expanded our horizons. Astronauts have walked on the surface of the moon. Satellites hover above Earth sending back photographs that aid in weather forecasting. Other satellites travel through the solar system, transmitting photographs of Venus, Jupiter, and Saturn. Oceanographers have mapped the sea floor and discovered huge deposits of valuable minerals. Scientists have theorized about the forces that set Earth's surface in motion, unleashing the awesome power of earthquakes and volcanoes. What scientific discoveries will revolutionize our world in the future?

# Plate tectonics

### Continental drift.
By looking at a map of the world, you will notice that Africa and South America seem to fit together. Fossil remains of the same animals have been found on both continents, and both share the same rock formations. Is this just coincidence?

A German scientist named Alfred Wegener did not think so. In 1912 he proposed his theory of continental drift. According to Wegener, about 200 million years ago all the land on Earth was one large continent that he called Pangaea. Approximately 180 million years ago, Pangaea began to break apart to form three separate continents. The large block to the north (which later became Europe, Asia, North America, and Greenland) is called Laurasia. It broke away from the other two land masses, which together are called Gondwanaland.

The northern block of Gondwanaland was to become South America and Africa; the southern block would become Antarctica, Australia, and New Zealand. A small piece broke away between the northern and southern parts of Gondwanaland and began moving northward. This would be India.

These land masses continued to drift. About 65 million years ago, the continents began to look as they do today. South America and Africa had drifted apart, and soon North America and Greenland would break away from Laurasia. India was about to collide with Asia. The southern block of Gondwanaland would soon break apart into separate pieces, forming Antarctica, Australia, and New Zealand.

Although Wegener's theory of continental drift was disbelieved at first, eventually it came to be accepted in a modified form. Increasingly, geologists found geological, fossil, and magnetic evidence that the continents were no longer in the same relationship to each other as before. More recently, evidence has turned up to show that the continents themselves have been built in part from large islands that have drifted and stuck to the continents' shorelines.

# Continental drift

### 200 million years ago

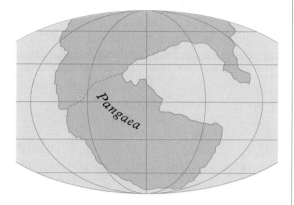

### 135 million years ago

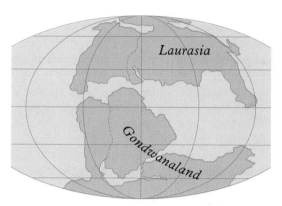

### 65 million years ago

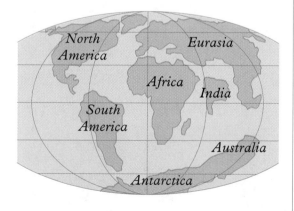

### today

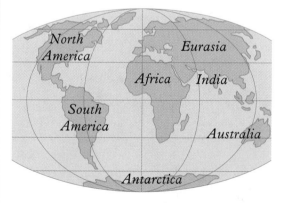

# The moving crust.

Today Earth's surface continues to be in motion. According to the *plate tectonics theory*, Earth's surface—or *crust*—is broken into pieces called plates. A crustal plate may carry only ocean floor, only continent, or some combination of both. Some plates are huge, such as the Pacific Plate, which carries most of the Pacific Ocean. Others are much smaller, like the Nazca Plate, which lies off the west coast of South America. These plates move around on a layer of molten rock beneath Earth's surface much as a boat floats on water.

Plates are involved in three different types of movement. On the floor of the Atlantic Ocean, the plates are moving apart in a process called *sea-floor spreading*. The amount of movement is about 2 inches a year, which means that the Atlantic is constantly growing wider, and Europe is moving farther away from the United States. As the plates move apart, molten rock wells up from beneath the surface to form new ocean floor.

Sea-floor spreading in the Atlantic occurs along a huge underwater mountain range called the *mid-ocean ridge*. Within the ridge is an opening called a *rift valley*, through which the molten rock pours out. Rift valleys can be found in other parts of the world too. In East Africa a large rift valley has formed; it may indicate that the African continent is beginning to break apart. The Red Sea may have appeared as a result of the Arabian Peninsula separating from Africa.

In some parts of the world, crustal plates are converging. Here crust is being destroyed, offsetting the new crust being formed in other regions, thereby keeping the size of Earth's surface constant. When a plate carrying oceanic crust collides with a plate carrying continental crust, the sea floor sinks beneath the continent, forming a deep ocean trench. Such trenches are found along Japan and the Aleutian Islands. In these areas volcanoes are common. For example, the volcanic Andes Mountains in South America and the deep trench in the nearby Pacific may have been produced when two plates converged.

The collision of two plates carrying continental crust may also lead to the formation of huge mountain ranges. An example is the Himalayas, which were created when India collided with Asia millions of years ago.

When two plates carrying oceanic crust converge, one is forced beneath the other. This results in the formation of an ocean trench accompanied by undersea volcanic activity and earthquakes.

Instead of separating or coming together, two plates may simply move past each other. This type of movement is occurring along the San Andreas fault in California.

## Theory of plate tectonics

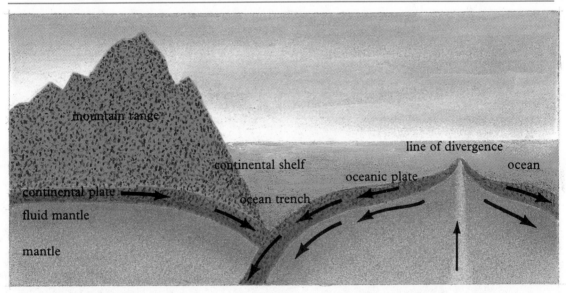

mountain range

continental shelf

line of divergence

oceanic plate

ocean

continental plate

ocean trench

fluid mantle

mantle

# Earthquakes.

An earthquake is a sudden trembling of Earth's crust. Earthquakes generally occur as a result of the movement of crustal plates. The crust cracks along a line called a *fault*, such as the San Andreas fault, which is at the boundary between two plates. As the crust moves apart, rocks on either side bend until they finally break, creating the vibrations that are called an earthquake.

A particularly powerful earthquake struck Alaska on March 27, 1964, causing the death of 114 people. Many died as a result of the *tsunami*, or giant wave, created when the sea floor moved during the earthquake. Tsunamis can travel across the ocean at speeds of 600 mph and reach heights of 100 feet as they crash into coastal towns and cities. Earthquakes also produce landslides and fires that cause enormous damage.

The spot under Earth's surface where an earthquake originates is called the *focus*. The *epicenter* is the point on the surface directly above the focus. When a quake occurs, waves radiate out from the focus. There are several types of waves. **P** (primary) waves are longitudinal, or push-pull, waves that travel through the earth. They can penetrate solid and liquid material. **S** (secondary) waves are transverse, or shake, waves. They also travel through the earth, but cannot penetrate liquids very well. **L** waves travel along the surface and do the most damage.

Earthquake waves are recorded on an instrument called a *seismograph*. Since **S** waves travel more slowly than **P** waves, we can tell how far away an earthquake occurred by computing the difference in time it takes for the two waves to arrive at the seismograph. Using seismographs at three or more locations enables scientists to calculate where an earthquake has occurred.

The strength of an earthquake is indicated on a scale called the *Richter scale*, which is based on the magnitude of the waves recorded by the seismograph. A magnitude of 2.5 is enough to be recorded but not felt; 6.0 may cause great damage; a very large earthquake registers over 8.0. The Alaska earthquake registered 8.4 to 8.6 on the Richter scale.

# Earth's interior.

By studying **S** and **P** waves, scientists have learned about the structure of Earth's interior. For example, they have concluded that Earth's *outer core* is liquid mate-

## The inner Earth

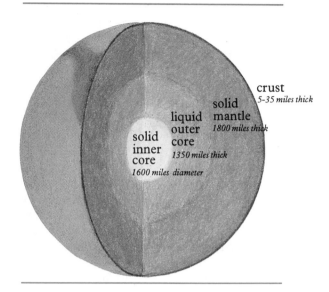

crust
*5-35 miles thick*

solid mantle
*1800 miles thick*

liquid outer core
*1350 miles thick*

solid inner core
*1600 miles diameter*

## Earthquake belts

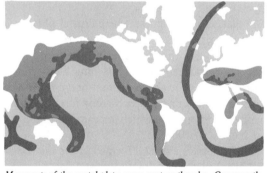

*Movements of the crustal plates cause most earthquakes. Consequently, belts of earthquake activity can be found near the edges of the plates.*

rial, because **S** waves cannot travel through it very well. The outer core is thought to be iron and nickel, which is kept in a liquid state because of the enormous heat inside Earth. The *inner core*, also made up of nickel and iron, is solid as a result of the enormous pressure on Earth's interior.

Above the core is a mostly solid layer called the *mantle*. It consists of rocks containing iron, magnesium, and silicon. The upper layer of mantle is partially molten, and it is in this material that the crustal plates "float." Convection currents set up within the liquid part of the mantle are thought to be the force that moves the plates. Above the mantle is Earth's *crust*. The crust is the part of Earth that can be directly observed as rock and soil.

# Volcanoes.

Volcanic activity occurs along the boundaries between plates, just as earthquakes do. In fact, surrounding the Pacific Ocean, in the same area as the earthquake belt is a circle of volcanoes that is called the "Ring of Fire."

When crustal plates come together, one plate often sinks, forming a deep ocean trench. The material in this plate is heated by the high temperatures found within Earth's interior and transformed into a molten substance. This molten substance is called *magma*. Pressure exerted on the magma from above may force it up through a chamber. Eventually the magma may pour out through an opening, or *vent*, in the earth and flow onto the surface. As the magma pours out, it changes and becomes a substance called *lava*.

The flow of lava creates a cone that grows larger and that may rise above the surface of the water. In this way island chains, such as Japan and the Aleutians, were created adjacent to the deep ocean trenches.

Volcanoes also appear where crustal plates are separating, such as at the mid-ocean ridge. As the lava pours out through openings, it forms new sea floor and may build up into huge cones. Sometimes a cone above the mid-ocean ridge also breaks the water's surface, thereby forming an island such as Surtsey, which appeared off the coast of Iceland in 1963.

Volcanoes can also be formed in the middle of a crustal plate. Perhaps the most famous examples are the volcanoes in the Pacific Plate that form the Hawaiian Islands.

There are different types of volcanic eruptions, resulting in various kinds of volcanic cones. Sometimes the lava flows quietly along the surface, creating a *shield cone*. An example of a shield cone is Mauna Loa on the island of Hawaii. This huge volcano is over 27,000 feet in height. The island of Hawaii is composed of five shield volcanoes.

Magma does not always flow easily, and it can plug up an opening to the surface. If gases from the magma build up, they may eventually force it through the opening with a violent explosion. Volcanic materials can then be seen shooting into the sky creating a spectacular display. These materials include cinders, ash, and larger fragments called bombs. They build up around the volcanic opening forming a *cinder cone*. An example of a cinder cone is Parícutin, which erupted outside of Mexico City in 1943.

A third type of volcanic cone is a combination of lava and cinders. It is called a *composite cone*. Two composite cones found in North America are Mt. Rainier and Mt. Hood.

At the top of a volcano is a depression called a *crater*. When a volcano becomes inactive, the crater may fill with water forming a lake. Crater Lake in Oregon was created in this way. Wizard Island, which is found in the lake, is part of a volcanic cone.

In the United States, active volcanoes are found in Hawaii, Alaska, and along the Pacific coast. Mount St. Helens in the state of Washington began erupting on May 18, 1980, and continues to erupt frequently.

## Volcanoes

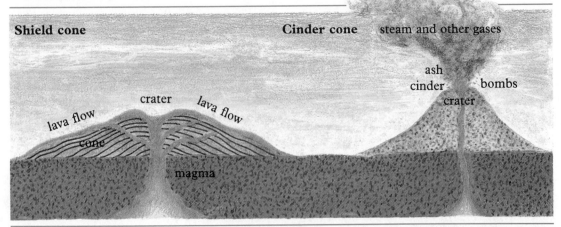

Shield cone      Cinder cone    steam and other gases

ash cinder bombs crater crater lava flow lava flow cone magma

# Rocks and minerals

**The rock cycle.** The rock cycle shows the relationship between the three types of rocks. *Igneous* rocks are formed when magma or lava cools and solidifies. Common igneous rocks are granite, pumice, and obsidian. When igneous rocks are broken down, they form sediments. After these sediments are compacted under pressure or cemented together by dissolved minerals, they form *sedimentary* rocks. These include sandstone, shale, and limestone. Some sedimentary rocks are also formed almost entirely from the remains of living organisms. Coal is a well-known example. The action of pressure, heat, and chemicals in the environment can transform igneous and sedimentary rocks into *metamorphic* rocks. Common metamorphic rocks are marble and slate.

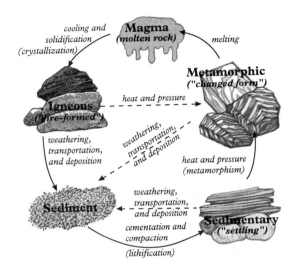

## Common minerals

| Group | Member | Formula | Description/use |
|---|---|---|---|
| **Silicates** | Feldspar (orthoclase) | $KAlS_{13}O_8$ | most common mineral |
| | Quartz | $S_1O_2$ | used in radios, clocks, etc. |
| | Garnet | $Mg_3Al_2S_{13}O_{12}$ | jewelry |
| **Carbonates** | Calcite | $CaCo_3$ | chief minerals in limestone |
| | Dolomite | $CaMg(CO_3)_2$ | found in limestone and marble |
| **Oxides** | Hematite | $Fe_2O_3$ | ore of iron |
| | Magnetite | $Fe_3O_4$ | ore of iron |
| | Corundum | $Al_2O_3$ | used as an abrasive |
| | Ice | $H_2O$ | solid form of water |
| **Sulfides** | Galena | $PbS$ | ore of lead |
| | Sphalerite | $ZnS$ | ore of zinc |
| | Pyrite | $FeS_2$ | fool's gold |
| | Chalcopyrite | $CuFeS_2$ | ore of copper |
| **Sulfates** | Gypsum | $CaSO_4 \cdot 2\,H_2O$ | used for plaster |
| | Anhydrite | $CaSO_4$ | used for plaster |
| **Native elements** | Gold | $Au$ | |
| | Copper | $Cu$ | |
| | Diamond | $C$ | |
| | Sulfur | $S$ | |
| | Graphite | $C$ | |
| **Halides** | Halite | $NaCl$ | common salt |
| | Fluorite | $CaF_2$ | used in steel making, chemicals, ceramics |

# Glaciers

Approximately 2 million years ago, during the Pleistocene epoch, vast sheets of ice called *glaciers* advanced southward covering large parts of North America and Northern Europe. The glaciers alternately advanced and retreated, creating a series of ice ages. These ice ages apparently ended between 10,000 and 15,000 years ago, when the glaciers began to recede. Many scientists believe, however, that the ice may yet return.

Glaciers occur where temperatures are low enough to permit a large and lasting snow accumulation. As pressure builds up on the lower layers of snow, the layers turn to ice and eventually begin to move.

There are two types of glaciers. Huge *continental glaciers*, like those of the ice ages, still cover Antarctica and most of Greenland. The Antarctic glacier stretches for about 8 million miles and contains 80 percent of the world's ice. Continental glaciers can move as fast as 100 feet a day.

Much more common are *Alpine glaciers*, which are found in mountainous regions. These glaciers are smaller and move more slowly, generally only a few inches a day. Glaciers begin to retreat when more ice starts to melt than is accumulated.

All glaciers cause erosion. At its head, a glacier may carve out a basin called a *cirque*. Sometimes a few cirques may cut into the side of a mountain, creating a sharp peak. This is known as a *horn*, or matterhorn, like the spectacular mountain in Switzerland called the Matterhorn.

When a glacier moves along, it picks up pieces of rock and other material and carries these pieces forward. Thus, a glacier can have the effect of broadening and deepening a narrow valley. When the glacier recedes, a wide glacial trough, or U-shaped valley, remains. Waterfalls often can be seen tumbling into a glacial trough from shallower valleys above.

A particular type of glacial trough found near the sea is a *fjord*. The fjords were created during the ice ages. As the ice retreated and sea level rose, the fjords filled with water to form deep ocean inlets.

Glaciers deposit the rocks and other material they accumulate as *till*. When a glacier retreats, it leaves behind layers of till called *moraine*. On the side of the moraine away from the ice is a rela-

## Glacial formations

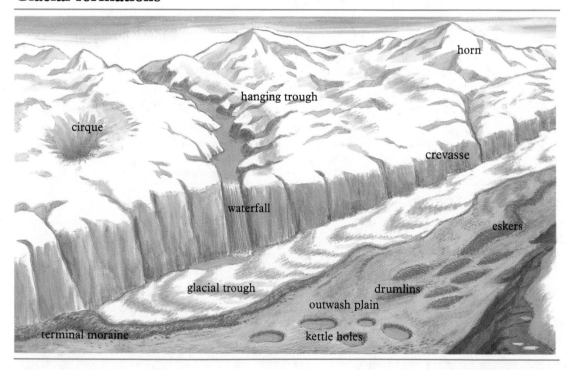

cirque

hanging trough

horn

crevasse

waterfall

eskers

glacial trough

drumlins

outwash plain

terminal moraine

kettle holes

tively level area called an *outwash plain*. This is composed of fine material washed away from the moraine by glacial meltwater. Found in the moraine and outwash plain are pits called *kettle holes*. These are formed by the melting of buried blocks of ice. Lakes, created when the kettle holes fill with water, can be seen in New York and New England.

Continental glaciers also form groups of hills called *drumlins*, which are composed of till. Drumlins may be as high as 200 feet. They occur in New York, Wisconsin, and other areas. Ridges of till, called *eskers*, are found along the Mississippi River valley.

# Pleistocene ice ages.

There have been many ice ages in the remote past, such as 200 million and 600 million years ago. About 1 million years ago, another series of advances and retreats of the continental ice sheets began. Geologists equate the first advance of the ice with the beginning of the Pleistocene epoch, the epoch that saw the development of modern human beings. In between the first four advances, there were long warm periods, which led to retreat of the ice. These times are known as interglacial periods. It is not known whether the present is the early part of an interglacial period or a temporary retreat during a glacial period.

## Area covered by ice during last ice age

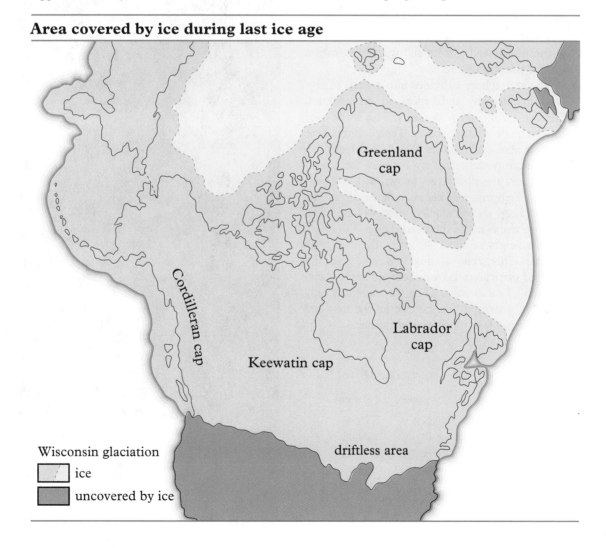

Greenland cap

Cordilleran cap

Keewatin cap

Labrador cap

driftless area

Wisconsin glaciation
ice
uncovered by ice

# Climate

The planet Earth is surrounded by a layer of air that is called the *atmosphere*. This is largely composed of two gases—*nitrogen* and *oxygen*. But other vital substances are found in the atmosphere too. *Carbon dioxide*, for example, absorbs heat that leaves Earth's surface. This helps keep the atmosphere warm. *Ozone*, which is found mainly in the higher reaches of the atmosphere, absorbs the sun's ultraviolet rays and prevents most of them from reaching Earth. The small amounts of *water vapor* found in the atmosphere are extremely important because they are the source of precipitation. And *dust particles* serve as the nuclei around which raindrops form. In fact, the atmosphere is where Earth's climate and weather happen. Therefore, the place to begin to understand climate and weather is with a tour of the atmosphere.

The atmosphere is divided into a series of layers separated by differences in temperature. Nearest Earth is the *troposphere*. This is the zone in which our weather occurs. Temperatures here drop at about 3.5 degrees F per 1000 feet. The tropopause is the boundary between the troposphere and the next layer, known as the *stratosphere*. Temperatures begin to level off in the stratosphere and gradually start to rise. The stratosphere contains the ozone layer.

At a height of about 40 miles, the *ionosphere* begins. This zone is filled with electrically charged particles called *ions*. Ions aid in the transmission of radio waves. The waves, which only travel in a straight line, bounce off the ions and are deflected over much greater distances.

## Elements in the atmosphere

| Component | Symbol | Percent |
|---|---|---|
| Nitrogen | $N_2$ | 78.08 |
| Oxygen | $O_2$ | 20.95 |
| Argon | A | 0.93 |
| Carbon dioxide | $CO_2$ | 0.03 |
| All others | | variable |

neon Ne, water vapor $H_2O$, helium He, dust, ozone $O_3$

## Earth's atmosphere

400 miles
exosphere

Satellite

Space shuttle: 200 mi.

Landsat: 200 mi.

thermosphere

Highest manned aircraft: 60 mi.

Highest manned balloon: 21.5 mi.

50 mesosphere
ionosphere

30 stratosphere

Ozone layer: 12 mi.

Highest mountain: 5.5 mi.

10 troposphere

## Seasons

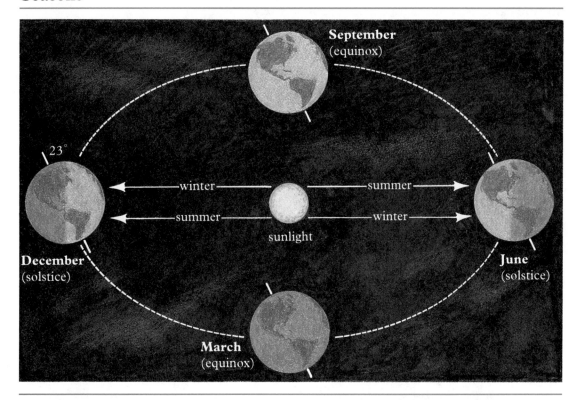

September
(equinox)

23°

winter — summer —

summer — winter —

sunlight

December
(solstice)

June
(solstice)

March
(equinox)

**The seasons.** The climate over much of Earth is characterized by seasons. In some parts of the world these are summer, fall, winter, and spring; in other parts, these are simply a wet, or rainy, season and a dry season. Each year at a particular place on the surface of Earth the seasons change much as they did the year before. But these changes are different in different parts of the world. When it is summer in New York City, it is winter in Buenos Aires, Argentina. In fact, the pattern of the seasons is reversed completely on the different sides of the equator. At the equator itself, and in the region on both sides of the equator that is called the *tropics*, there is almost no seasonal change. Seasonal changes in weather occur outside the tropics for two reasons. First, the Earth tilts on its axis at $23\frac{1}{2}$ degrees. Second, Earth revolves around the sun. As a result, most areas of Earth receive different amounts of sunlight throughout the year. During summer, the northern hemisphere is tilted toward

the sun and receives longer periods of light. The sun's rays also strike more directly, producing more heat. During winter, opposite conditions prevail.

The reverse conditions occur in the southern hemisphere, of course. When the northern hemisphere is tilted toward the sun, the southern hemisphere is tilted away from it. The positions are shown in the diagram above.

Many people assume that winter is colder because Earth is farther from the sun during the winter. A little thought would show that that cannot be the case because if it were, winter would occur all over Earth at the same time. In fact, Earth is closest to the sun around January 1, a time when most of the northern hemisphere experiences some of its coldest weather.

Other seasonal changes are caused in part by the tilt of Earth with respect to the sun. If Earth did not tilt, each place would have the same season all year long.

# U.S. climate zones.

Climate refers to the average weather conditions of a region over a long period of time. These conditions include temperature, precipitation, and humidity. A variety of factors affect the climatic conditions of a particular region. One of these is latitude, or distance from the equator. Regions lying closer to the equator receive more of the sun's direct rays for longer periods of time, and their average temperatures are generally higher than regions farther away. Another factor is altitude. A city perched high in the mountains usually has lower average temperatures than another one lying in a valley, even if both are located at the same latitude. Other factors affecting climate are prevailing winds, mountain ranges, and oceans.

The United States experiences different types of climate in various parts of the country. Since the southern part of the United States lies closest to the equator, average temperatures tend to be warmer here than in other areas. The climate in the southern region is called *humid subtropical*. The climate is a variation of the hot, rainy conditions found in the tropics. Air masses traveling in from the Gulf of Mexico and the Atlantic Ocean bring humid weather and high precipitation. Summers are hot, and winters tend to be relatively mild.

Around the city of San Francisco, California, and northward into Oregon and Washington, is a climate zone known as *marine west-coast*. This zone is characterized by mild summers and winters because of the prevailing westerlies—winds that blow inland from the Pacific Ocean. The westerlies bring large amounts of precipitation to the Pacific Northwest, allowing huge coniferous forests to flourish there.

In southern California, winters are mild, but summers are hotter and drier. The climate here, called *Mediterranean*, after similar climatic areas in Europe, results from seasonal shifts in the winds.

East of the Sierra Nevada mountain range lie the deserts of southern California, Nevada, and Arizona. As the westerlies rise over the mountains, they lose their moisture. Regions on the

## Climate zones of the continental United States

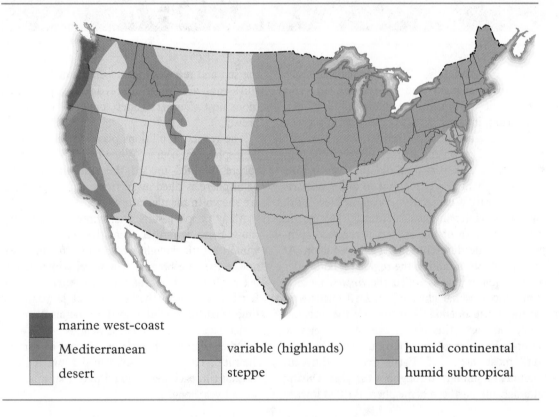

marine west-coast

Mediterranean

desert

variable (highlands)

steppe

humid continental

humid subtropical

other side of the mountains are said to be in the "rain shadow," receiving little or no precipitation. Winds blowing off the mountains are hot and dry, absorbing any moisture that may be found in the atmosphere.

Northward is a climate zone called the *steppe*, after the vast plains of central Europe. It includes parts of Utah, Colorado, Kansas, and all the states north to the Canadian border. Although this region receives more rain than desert regions, it is still quite dry because the huge Rocky Mountains act as a barrier to rainfall. This is an area of vast grasslands for grazing cattle and other animals.

The rest of the country experiences a *continental climate*. Frigid air masses from the north bring cold winters and high accumulations of snow. Warm air masses from the south bring hot, muggy weather during summer.

# Winds.
Winds result from differences in pressure owing to the unequal heating of Earth's atmosphere by the sun. The direction of wind flow is always from an area of high pressure to an area of low pressure. Giant wind systems, powered by the sun, travel across the globe and influence our weather.

Along the equator, the sun's rays shine directly from above for longer periods of time than they do farther north or south. Here the air is heated and begins to rise, creating an area of low pressure. The warm air travels north and south to a latitude of about 30 degrees, where, after being cooled, it begins to descend. These areas of high pressure, called *horse latitudes*, often have very little wind.

Air flows along the surface from the areas of high pressure at the horse latitudes to the areas of low pressure along the equator. This air flow is called the *trade winds*. Instead of flowing directly to the equator in a straight line, the winds are deflected to the right in the northern hemisphere and to the left in the southern hemisphere. This phenomenon, which is caused by Earth's rotation, is called the *Coriolis force*.

Some of the air descending in the horse latitudes flows away from the equator. This flow of air is known as the *prevailing westerlies*, because the winds come from a general westerly direction. Winds are always named for the direction from which they flow.

## Wind belts of Earth

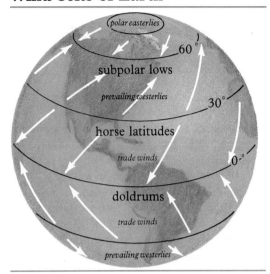

The third great wind system, called the *polar easterlies*, consists of cool air blowing from the polar regions. The easterlies meet the westerlies at about 60 degrees N and S latitude.

High above Earth's surface flow the *jet streams*. These are high-velocity winds that circle the globe in both hemispheres. Jet streams over North America often change position, dipping into the southern part of the United States, and then receding northward. Such changes may lead to storms in various parts of the country.

Local winds operate according to the same principles as the world's great wind systems. One example is a land-sea breeze. During the day the sun's rays heat the land more rapidly than a nearby body of water. Warm air rises over the land creating a low pressure area, and cool air flows inland from the sea. At night the flow of air is reversed as the land cools more rapidly than the water.

The *monsoon* is a giant land-sea breeze that occurs in the Indian subcontinent as well as other areas of the world. During summer the land heats up faster than the ocean. Monsoon winds blow inland bringing torrential rains.

Local winds are also created in mountainous regions. During the day the exposed slopes of a mountain are heated faster than the surrounding valley. Warm air along the slopes rises, and cool air pushes up from the valley below. At night the flow of air is down the mountain.

# Weather

## Rain, snow, and dew.
Water is constantly circulating throughout the atmosphere in a cycle that involves evaporation, condensation, and precipitation. This is called the *water cycle*. The energy that runs the water cycle comes from the sun.

When heat from the sun is applied to the molecules of water found in a lake or stream, the molecules begin to move more rapidly. Eventually some of these molecules evaporate; that is, they enter the air as a gas called *water vapor*. Evaporation is a cooling process. Heat is absorbed by the water molecules that evaporate, and the water remaining is cooled. This same principle applies when perspiration is evaporated from the skin, a process that makes one's body cooler.

The amount of water vapor in the air is known as its *humidity*. During a weather report, one generally hears the forecaster refer to *relative humidity*. This is a percentage that compares the amount of water vapor actually in the air at a particular temperature with the amount of water the air could hold if it were filled to capacity. When the temperature is high and the relative humidity is over 90 percent, most people feel very uncomfortable. This is because the air is almost filled to capacity and cannot absorb much perspiration. When the air reaches capacity, it is said to be *saturated*.

Relative humidity is measured by a device called a *psychrometer*. It consists of two thermometers called a wet-bulb and a dry-bulb. The wet-bulb thermometer is covered with a water-soaked cloth. As air passes over, it absorbs some of the water. Cooling occurs, lowering the temperature on the wet-bulb thermometer. When the air is dry, it can absorb more water, creating a greater temperature difference between the wet-bulb and dry-bulb thermometers. (The dry-bulb simply records air temperature.) This difference in temperature is correlated with relative humidity by using a chart.

How much water vapor can be contained in a volume of air? This depends on the air temperature. The warmer the air, the more water vapor it can hold. The temperature at which the air becomes saturated is called the *dew point*. If any more water vapor enters the air, the vapor will begin to condense, forming a liquid. If the temperature of the air lowers, so that its holding capacity is reduced, condensation will occur.

**Dew and frost.** During the night, as the land cools, the temperature of the air near the surface may fall below the dew point. In the morning, moisture appears on the grass in the form of *dew*. If the temperature of the grass drops below freezing, *frost* occurs.

**Fogs.** When warm, saturated air passes over a cool surface, the air temperature may fall beneath the dew point. Then the water vapor condenses to form *fog*. This type of fog is *advection fog*. During the winter months, as warm, moist air from the Gulf of Mexico is blown over the cold ground of the Midwest, advection fogs occur frequently. Another type of fog is common in river valleys. This type of fog is produced by the cooling of a moist layer of air just above Earth's surface.

**Clouds.** As a parcel of warm, moist air rises into the atmosphere, the air expands and cools. Eventually the temperature of the air may drop below the dew point. Then the water vapor condenses as cloud droplets. These water droplets are so small and light that they can float through the air.

**Rain and snow.** Precipitation occurs when cloud droplets become large and heavy enough to fall. To explain this process, scientists have proposed two different theories. In some high clouds, the droplets are *supercooled*. This means that their temperature falls below freezing without the droplets turning to ice. Sometimes an ice crystal is present in the cloud, and the supercooled droplets may attach themselves to it. When the droplets strike this colder surface, they freeze. Gradually, the ice crystal grows larger and begins to fall. Sometimes the crystal breaks apart, creating surfaces to which other droplets can attach themselves. If temperatures near Earth's surface are cold enough, ice crystals will land as snow. Otherwise, the crystals will melt and fall as rain.

In lower-level clouds, precipitation is formed differently. Droplets often coalesce around particles of dust or grains of salt called *condensation nuclei*. As the droplets coalesce and grow larger,

**Earth Science**

**Clouds**

30,000 ft.

cirrus ("mares' tails")

anvil cirrus

cirrus

25,000

cirrostratus ("sun halo")

20,000

cirrocumulus

cirrostratus

15,000

cumulus

cumulonimbus

10,000

stratocumulus

nimbostratus

alto cumulus

5,000

stratus

ground

they begin to fall, picking up more droplets along the way. These reach the ground as rain.

**Hail and sleet.** Two other common types of precipitation are *hail* and *sleet*. Hailstones are ice pellets. They are created from supercooled water that freezes inside huge cumulonimbus clouds.

The frozen drops are carried repeatedly throughout the cloud, picking up more ice and growing larger.

Sleet occurs when rain passes through a layer of air that is below freezing. The rain is turned to ice before reaching the ground.

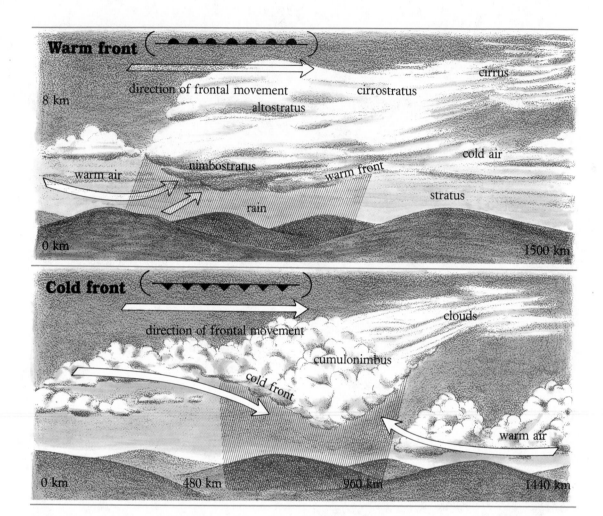

Warm front

8 km

direction of frontal movement

warm air

nimbostratus

rain

0 km

cirrus

cirrostratus

altostratus

cold air

warm front

stratus

1500 km

Cold front

direction of frontal movement

cold front

cumulonimbus

clouds

warm air

0 km        480 km        960 km        1440 km

## Air masses and fronts.

Large bodies of air with uniform temperature and humidity are called *air masses*. Air masses form over a particular surface area—either land or ocean—and assume the characteristics of that area. Thus, an air mass that forms over the Arctic tundra will be cooler and drier than one that originates in the Gulf of Mexico.

Weather conditions in North America are influenced by several types of air masses. *Continental polar* air forms over the frigid landscape of Canada and Alaska. This cool, dry air mass is carried southward by the polar easterlies. It brings clear, crisp weather to the eastern United States during the winter, and relief from the hot spells of summer.

*Continental tropical* air masses originate in Mexico. They are blown by the westerlies into the southwestern United States, creating hot, dry weather conditions.

*Maritime tropical* air masses form over the Caribbean Sea and the Atlantic Ocean. They absorb moisture from the sea and carry it to the southeastern United States. Maritime tropical air brings humid weather and precipitation to the South, the Atlantic coastal states, and farther inland.

*Maritime polar* air masses can be found over the northern Pacific Ocean and the icy north Atlantic. A polar air mass may be blown inland by the easterlies, creating a heavy storm called a *northeaster*.

As air masses move across North America, they frequently bump into each other. The boundary line between two different air masses is called a *front*.

**Warm fronts.** When a cold air mass is being replaced by a warm air mass, its leading edge is called a *warm front*. As the warm air gradually rises over the cold air, clouds begin to appear.

*Cirrus* clouds foretell the approach of the front. These are followed by *cirrostratus* and *altostratus* clouds. Eventually, the low *nimbostratus* clouds appear, followed by periods of rain or snow. As the warm air mass settles in a region, the weather clears; temperatures rise; and the winds shift to the southwest.

**Cold fronts.** When warm air is replaced by a cold air mass, its leading edge is called a *cold front*. A cold front travels rapidly. Owing to friction, the air travels more slowly along Earth's surface than in the atmosphere. As a result, the cold front takes on a very steep slope. Moist air is pushed high into the atmosphere, forming huge *cumulonimbus* clouds. These bring a short period of heavy thunderstorms accompanied by brisk winds. As cold air settles in a region, temperatures drop and wind direction changes to the north or northwest.

**Stationary fronts.** Sometimes two air masses remain in a region for some time without either one replacing the other. The boundary line between them is called a *stationary front*.

**Lows.** In the United States, air masses often meet along a boundary known as the *polar front*. This front extends worldwide in the middle latitudes. Typically, tropical air from the south meets polar air from the north, with the wind in each air mass blowing in a different direction.

Eventually, a wave may develop along the front. Cold air begins pushing into warm air, creating a cold front. The warm air mass tries to displace the cold air mass, producing a warm front. As the warm air rises, it creates an area of low pressure. This gives the entire weather system its name—a *low*.

When a low enters a region, weather conditions change rapidly. A storm will begin with the rainy weather generally associated with a warm front. This will be followed by clearing and higher temperatures. Soon a cold front will arrive, bringing more rain. Then skies will clear.

As moist air ascends along the fronts and water condenses to form precipitation, large amounts of heat are released. This deepens the low-pressure area. The winds flowing into this area increase, and the storm grows in intensity. A satellite photo of the storm system would show that the winds are spiraling in a counter-clockwise rotation. For this reason, the low is called a *cyclone*.

The faster moving cold front often overtakes the warm front, lifting it off the ground. This creates an *occluded front*. As the warm air rises, more heat is released. Winds are especially strong in this area, and the storm is intense. Eventually, the low will run its course, and the polar front will return to its original condition.

Storm systems generally originate in the south or west and move toward the northeast. Their speeds vary, making the task of predicting the arrival time of a storm especially difficult.

## Developing low

The four diagrams here show a "weather-map" picture of a low developing and beginning to disperse; that is, you are looking at the map as the low moves eastward (toward the right of the page). In the first diagram, there is no low. In the second and third diagrams, the low develops rapidly and begins to move east. The cold front moves faster than the warm front. In the last diagram, the air from the cold front has begun to mix with the air from the warm front, dissipating the low.

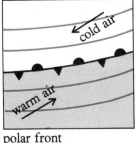

polar front

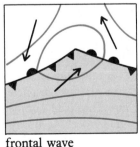

frontal wave

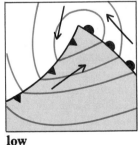

**low**

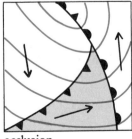

occlusion

**Storms.** The large cumulonimbus clouds that accompany cold fronts often produce *thunderstorms*. These storms are short-lived, generally lasting for no more than an hour. Perhaps the most spectacular aspect of a thunderstorm is *lightning*. This is a discharge of electricity within a cloud, between clouds, or between a cloud and Earth.

Although scientists cannot fully explain how lightning occurs, they believe that two areas of oppositely charged particles are created within a cumulonimbus cloud. Positively charged ions are gathered at the top of the cloud; at its bottom are mostly negatively charged ions. When these charges build up to a certain point, a stroke of lightning will pass between them. A similar process occurs when lightning strikes Earth.

A discharge of lightning creates enough heat to expand the air in an explosive way. This sends out sound waves that are heard as *thunder*. Since light travels much faster than sound, lightning is seen before thunder is heard. To determine the distance of a storm from a given location, count the number of seconds between the lightning and the thunder. For every 5 seconds, the storm is about 1 mile away.

**Tornadoes.** The *tornado* is a funnel-shaped storm characterized by rapidly twisting winds. For this reason it is often called a "twister." Wind speeds in a tornado may exceed 400 mph. The winds swirl around an area of extremely low pressure created at the center of the storm. The storm's dark cloud is due to the condensation of moisture inside it.

When tornadoes strike, they can cause enormous damage. This results in part from the high velocity of the winds. The destruction is also due to the low pressure area inside the funnel. As the funnel passes over a building, the difference in pressure inside and outside causes the walls to explode.

Tornadoes can move very rapidly, sometimes at speeds of 70 mph, although they generally travel more slowly. The diameter of the funnel averages anywhere from 500 to 2000 feet. Tornadoes occur most often during the spring. While they may strike any part of the United States, they are most common in the South and the Midwest. The leading tornado states are Texas, Oklahoma, and Nebraska.

Probably the most destructive tornado on re-

cord occurred in March, 1925. It traveled along the ground for over 200 miles through the states of Missouri, Illinois, and Indiana. In the tornado's wake, the storm left 695 people dead, and over 2000 injured.

**Hurricanes.** A *hurricane* is a large tropical storm that originates in the ocean. Hurricanes that strike the United States start in the Atlantic Ocean near the Caribbean Sea. These storms are most common in the summer during the months of August and September.

Hurricanes form around a low-pressure area. Within a hurricane, large amounts of water vapor are condensing and releasing heat. This causes air to rise, reducing the already low pressure even further. More moist air rushes into the storm, giving it a constant supply of heat. At the hurricane's center is an area of calm called the "eye." From a satellite photo, winds can be seen whirling about the eye in a counter-clockwise direction typical of a cyclone. Wind speeds in a hurricane are 75 mph or more.

Hurricanes move at speeds of 10 to 20 mph. They are carried from their point of origin by the trade winds. Eventually a hurricane in the Atlantic Ocean may strike the islands of the Caribbean or the mainland of the United States. Some hurricanes follow a path that takes them from Florida northward along the Atlantic coast into New England. The strong winds, high sea waves, and flooding that accompany the storm wreak tremendous damage.

# Weather prediction. A meteorologist relies on a variety of instruments to predict the weather. A *barometer* is used to measure air pressure. Perhaps you have heard a forecaster say that the barometric pressure is 30.62 inches and steady. This pressure reading refers to the height of a column of mercury. In a mercury barometer, air pushes down on liquid mercury in a dish, forcing it up a glass tube. The height of the column in the tube corresponds to the amount of pressure exerted by the air. At sea level, the standard air pressure is 29.92 inches of mercury. If a low approaches the area, the pressure will drop and the barometer will record a lower reading. Thus, the barometer can be used to forecast an approaching storm.

A barometer that does not use liquid is called an *aneroid barometer*. It relies on a metal con-

*Meteorologists today have at their disposal a great deal of information collected from ground stations and satellites alike. All of this information is combined to produce computerized weather maps such as this one, which shows the devastating hurricane Andrew approaching Florida in August, 1992*

tainer with most of the air removed. This container is very sensitive to changes in air pressure. A *barograph* consists of an aneroid barometer attached to a recording device. It provides a continuous written record of barometric changes.

The *rain gauge* measures levels of precipitation. A *wind vane* indicates wind direction. The most common wind vane is an arrow with a large tail. This arrow rotates freely on a fixed base and points into the wind in the direction from which the wind is blowing.

An instrument used to measure wind speed is called an *anemometer*. The cup anemometer is made up of three or four hollow cups attached to horizontal arms extending from a vertical axis. The force of the wind on the cups causes the apparatus to turn on the axis; the higher the wind speed, the faster the cups turn. The spinning apparatus is linked to a pointer that moves over a scale and indicates wind speed in knots or in miles per hour.

Another device is the *thermograph*, a metal thermometer that keeps a written record of temperature changes. During a weather forecast, you may hear temperature given according to two scales, Fahrenheit and Celsius. Freezing is 32 degrees on the Fahrenheit scale and 0 degrees on the Celsius scale.

Located throughout the country are weather stations that record local conditions on their instruments. To determine conditions in the atmosphere, the stations launch weather balloons that contain thermometers and barometers.

Each station records such things as wind conditions, temperature, the amount of cloud cover, dew point, and precipitation. This information is then transmitted to the National Meteorological Center in Maryland, run by the National Weather Service. The Weather Service also relies on satellite pictures and radar. Satellite pictures show the movement of entire weather systems. All the information is analyzed with the aid of computers. The data are then used to design a weather map for the entire country.

Lines called *isobars* are drawn to connect areas with the same barometric pressure. *Isotherms* are drawn to connect points with the same temperature. The map shows the location of any fronts, storm systems, and high pressure zones (areas of clear, dry weather).

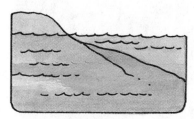

continental shelf

# Dictionary of earth science

fjord

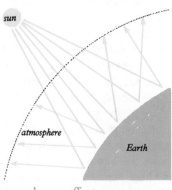

greenhouse effect

**absolute humidity.** Weight of water vapor in a specific amount of air.

**adiabatic change.** Temperature change of air when it expands or is compressed without any heat being added from outside sources.

**advection fog.** Fog created when warm, moist air moves over a cool surface.

**air mass.** Large body of air with uniform temperature and humidity.

**alluvial plain.** Fan-shaped plain formed by materials deposited from a river.

**altimeter.** Instrument that measures altitude.

**anemometer.** Device that measures the velocity of wind.

**aneroid barometer.** Barometer that does not contain a liquid.

**anticline.** Upfolded region of layers of rock.

**aquifer.** Rock structure that contains groundwater.

**arête.** Sharp divide between glacial cirques.

**barometer.** Device used to measure air pressure.

**caldera.** Large crater in a volcano.

**chinook.** Warm wind that blows down the eastern slope of the Rocky Mountains.

**cinder cone.** Steep cone formed by the cinders from an explosive volcanic eruption.

**cirque.** Basin found at the head of a glacier.

**cirrus clouds.** High, feathery clouds.

**climate.** Average weather conditions in a region over a long period of time.

**cold front.** Leading edge of a

cold air mass that is displacing a warm air mass.

**composite cone.** Cone produced by a combination of lava and cinders.

**condensation.** Change from a gas to a liquid.

**continental drift.** Movement of the continents on pieces of Earth's crust called plates.

**continental shelf.** Gently sloping part of a continent that extends under the sea to the continental slope.

**continental slope.** Steep slope that extends from the continental shelf to the ocean bottom.

**core (inner).** Solid layer inside the earth composed of iron and nickel.

**core (outer).** Liquid layer outside the inner core.

**Coriolis force.** Force caused by Earth's rotation.

**crater.** Depression found at the top of a volcano.

**crevasse.** Large and deep crack in a glacier.

**cyclone.** Area of low pressure in which winds rotate in a counter-clockwise direction.

**delta.** Sediment deposited where a river enters a lake or ocean.

**density.** Weight per unit volume.

**dew point.** Temperature at which the air can hold no more water.

**dike.** Region in which magma has forced itself into vertical cracks in the crustal rock.

**epicenter.** Spot on Earth's surface directly above the focus of an earthquake.

**esker.** Long ridge composed of till.

**evaporation.** Conversion of liquid to gas.

**eye of the hurricane.** Area of

calm in the center of a hurricane.

**fault.** Crack in rock along which movement has occurred.

**firn.** Grainy snow or ice in a glacier.

**fjord.** Valley that has been created by a glacier and later filled by the sea.

**focus.** Point under Earth's surface where an earthquake originates.

**front.** Boundary line between two different air masses.

**glacier.** Large sheet of ice.

**greenhouse effect.** Process of trapping heat waves radiated from Earth.

**hail.** Lumps of ice.

**high.** Area of high air pressure.

**horn.** Sharp peak created by a series of cirques.

**horse latitudes.** Areas of high pressure located at 30 degrees N and S latitude.

**hurricane.** Tropical storm with very high winds that begins in the Atlantic Ocean near the Caribbean Sea.

**hygrometer.** Device used to measure relative humidity.

**igneous rock.** Rock formed when magma or lava cools.

**ionosphere.** That part of the atmosphere that contains many ions.

**isobar.** Line on a map that connects points with the same atmospheric pressure.

**jet streams.** Upper atmosphere winds that move at very high velocity.

**joint.** Large crack in crustal rock.

**kettle holes.** Pits created by the melting of buried blocks of ice deposited by glaciers.

**lava.** Magma that has flowed onto Earth's surface.

**low.** Storm center that is characterized by an area of low pressure.

**magma.** Molten rock found beneath Earth's surface.

**mantle.** Layer of earth found just beneath the crust in Earth's interior.

**metamorphic rock.** Rock that has been changed by pressure, heat, or chemicals.

**mineral.** Crystalline substance occurring naturally in the environment.

**monsoon.** Huge land-sea breeze found in India and other areas of the world.

**moraine.** Layers of till.

**occluded front.** Front created when a warm front is lifted by a cold front.

**plate tectonics.** Theory that continents and oceans are contained in crustal plates that move continually.

**polar easterlies.** Cold winds that blow from the poles.

**polar front.** Boundary line between warm air masses and cold air masses.

**prevailing westerlies.** Winds that blow out of the west in the mid latitudes.

**psychrometer.** Device that measures relative humidity.

**relative humidity.** Percent that expresses the relationship between the amount of water vapor contained in a volume of air and the amount the air can hold when saturated.

**Richter scale.** Measure of earthquake intensity.

**seismograph.** Device that records earthquake waves.

**shield cone.** Volcanic cone created by lava flow.

**stationary front.** Boundary between two air masses that are not moving.

**subpolar lows.** Low pressure areas located at about 60 degrees N and S latitude.

**syncline.** Layers of rock folded into a U-shape.

**till.** Rocks and other material carried or deposited by glaciers.

**tornado.** Violent, twisting wind that forms a funnel cloud.

**trade winds.** Winds that blow from a general easterly direction from the horse latitudes to the equator.

**troposphere.** Lower part of Earth's atmosphere.

**tsunami.** Giant wave produced by an earthquake or other force that affects the sea floor.

**warm front.** Leading edge of a warm air mass that is displacing a cold air mass.

**water table.** Part of the upper level of earth that is saturated with groundwater.

**weathering.** Process by which rocks are broken down by natural forces in the environment.

**wind vane.** Device that indicates wind direction.

## For Further Reference

Burroughs, William James
*Weather*
Time-Life Books
National Geographic Society
*Powers of Nature*

Sullivan, Walter
*Continents in Motion*
McGraw-Hill
Williams, Jack
*The Weather Book*
Vintage Books

# Space Science

It is astonishing that people have learned so much about stars and galaxies that are so far away that we see them as tiny points of light. Today scientists can often tell how far away a star or galaxy is, the elements from which it is made, its true brightness, its mass, and even its history over several million years merely by examining the light. In fact, all that we know about distant stars and galaxies has been learned from the record of electromagnetic waves. These waves are often millions of years old when they reach Earth.

Closer to home, the sun and six of the nine planets (counting Earth) can be seen with the naked eye, although the planets, too, are millions of miles from us. What is more, we have been able to reach out to the planets with space probes that have landed on Mars and Venus and also provided close-up views of all the planets visible without a telescope. These close-up pictures have dramatically changed our knowledge of the solar system.

# The solar system

Earth is one of nine planets that revolve around a star we call the sun. There are also 45 known moons that revolve around the various planets. In addition, there are asteroids, meteors, comets, dust, and gas. Taken together, these make up the *solar system*.

**The sun.** The sun is the power center of the solar system. Its gravitational pull keeps the planets in their orbits. Its energy provides heat and light to the planets. According to one estimate, the sun produces more energy in a single second than the human race has used in its entire existence.

How is this energy created? The sun is made up largely of hydrogen atoms. Under the high temperatures that exist on the sun, these atoms move very rapidly. The nuclei of four hydrogen atoms come together, or fuse, to form one atom of an element called helium. This process is known as *nuclear fusion*. The helium atom contains less mass than did the original four hydrogen atoms. According to Einstein's well-known equation $E = mc^2$, the mass that is lost during fusion is converted into energy.

The sun is a fiery ball of hot gases. On the yellow surface, or *photosphere*, temperatures average about 10,000 degrees F. Although the photosphere may appear uniform, closer observation reveals many bright spots. These spots are caused by hotter gases emerging from inside the sun. Temperatures in the solar interior are thought to reach as high as 27,000 degrees F.

Dark spots are also found on the sun's surface. Such dark spots, which are more easily seen than bright spots, are called *sunspots*. The sunspots are areas of cooler temperatures. The number of sunspots varies according to an eleven-year cycle.

Explosions on the sun's surface, called *solar flares*, occur in conjunction with the sunspots. During these explosions, a glow may appear in the sky at Earth's poles. This glow is called an *aurora*. The colorful night sky of the aurora borealis, or northern lights, can be seen from Canada and the United States. The northern aurora is called the *aurora borealis*.

The sun's surface is enveloped by the solar atmosphere. The lower part of the atmosphere—called the *chromosphere*—appears red because of the hydrogen set aglow there by the high temperatures. The upper atmosphere, or *corona*, is the white halo seen during a solar eclipse. Electrically charged particles are emitted by the corona and travel rapidly into the solar system. These particles, known as *solar winds*, blow across our moon, scarring its landscape.

The sun is by far the largest part of our solar system. The mass of the sun is about 700 times as large as the rest of the solar system. Its diameter is so large that 110 Earths could be strung along the disk we see at its widest point. Its volume is more than 1 million times that of Earth.

**The planets.** Mercury, Venus, Earth, and Mars are called the *inner planets*. Mercury, the smallest planet, is the one closest to the sun. This nearness to the sun, combined with Mercury's long days, produces very high temperatures on the planet's surface. Mercury has an extremely thin atmosphere that may have been created by the solar winds. Thus, meteors encounter little resistance and bombard the surface, producing huge craters.

In contrast to Mercury, the planet Venus has a thick atmosphere comprised mainly of carbon dioxide ($CO_2$). This creates a "greenhouse effect," so-called because of the similarity to what happens inside a greenhouse. The sun radiates short-wave energy that passes through the $CO_2$ and heats the surface of the planet. But the heat is radiated back from the surface in longer waves, which are trapped by the $CO_2$ layer, creating tremendously high temperatures.

During the 1970's and 1980's, the Soviet Venera satellites landed on Venus. They photographed a parched, rocky surface filled with many rounded and sharp boulders.

## The solar system

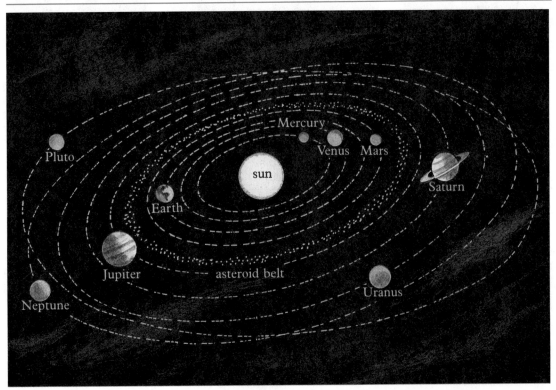

In some ways the planet Mars resembles Earth. Its day lasts just over 24 hours. The planet inclines on its axis at 24 degrees creating a change in seasons, although the seasons are about double Earth's in length. At each of the poles is a huge ice cap that grows during the winter and recedes in the summer. These ice caps are comprised largely of frozen carbon dioxide.

Photographs taken during the Viking and Mariner space missions launched by the United States in the 1970's revealed many features of the Martian surface. Some areas have large craters, much like the planet Mercury. In other areas are huge volcanoes similar to the shield cones found on Earth. One cone, called Olympus Mons, is over 360 miles wide.

In addition to volcanic activity, Mars shows signs of erosion from wind and water, although no water presently flows on the surface. Erosion has produced gigantic canyons and gullies, as well as other land formations.

The *outer planets* include Jupiter, Saturn, Uranus, Neptune, and Pluto. Jupiter is the largest of the planets of the solar system, with a greater mass than the combined total of all the others. Encircling Jupiter are bands of clouds that con-

## Facts about the solar system

Mars, the red planet

Venus, taken by the Magellan probe

Earth, seen from space

|  | **Mercury** | **Venus** | **Earth** | **Mars** |
|---|---|---|---|---|
| *Distance from sun* | 36,000,000 mi. | 67,000,000 mi. | 93,000,000 mi. | 142,000,000 mi. |
| *Length of year* | 87.96 days | 224.70 days | 365.26 days | 687 days |
| *Diameter* | 3000 mi. | 7500 mi. | 7900 mi. | 4200 mi. |
| *Length of day* | 58.65 Earth days | about 243 Earth days | 23 hr., 56 min. | 24 hr., 37 min. |
| *Mass relative to Earth* | 0.056 | 0.815 | 1.00 | 0.108 |
| *Surface temperature (average)* | 332° F | 854° F | 59° F | -67° F |
| *Atmosphere* | solar wind | carbon dioxide, nitrogen | nitrogen, oxygen, carbon dioxide, argon | carbon dioxide, argon, nitrogen, water |
| *Weight of 150 lbs* | 58 lbs. | 130 lbs. | 150 lbs | 58 lbs. |
| *Number of moons* | none | none | 1 | 2 |

**Space Science**

tain the planet's most prominent feature—the Great Red Spot. Scientists are still uncertain about its cause but the Spot seems to be a storm that has persisted for hundreds of years.

Jupiter has 16 known satellites. On Ganymede, enormous craters pit the surface. Volcanoes have been observed on Io, while extensive fractures break up the landscape of Europa.

Beyond Jupiter is the planet Saturn, which is distinguished by its extensive ring system. Photographs relayed by the Voyager space probes show that the system is composed of almost 1000 small rings. Vast numbers of tiny particles comprise the rings, which are about 10 miles thick. Information gathered during the Voyager mission indicates that the moon Titan's atmosphere is similar to that of Earth's during its very early stages.

The planet Uranus appears as a greenish-blue disk. In 1977 scientists discovered that Uranus is encircled by rings.

In 1989 Neptune was visited by Voyager 2. It was learned that Neptune also has rings, that it is swept by violent storms, and that it apparently generates part of its own internal heat. To date, little is known about Pluto.

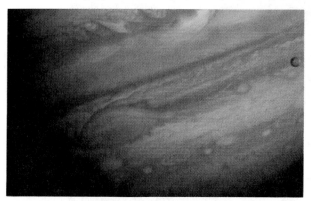

*Jupiter and the Great Red Spot*

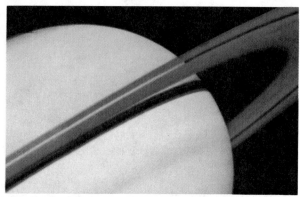

*Saturn and its rings*

| Jupiter | Saturn | Uranus | Neptune | Pluto | Sun |
|---|---|---|---|---|---|
| 484,000,000 mi. | 887,000,000 mi. | 1,800,000,000 mi. | 2,800,000,000 mi. | 3,700,000,000 mi. | |
| 11.86 yr. | 29.46 yr. | 84.01 yr. | 164.79 yr. | 247.7 yr. | 200 million yr. |
| 89,000 mi. | 75,000 mi. | 32,000 mi. | 31,000 mi. | 1400 mi. | 860,000 mi. |
| 9 hr., 50 min | 10 hr., 14 min. | 17 hr., 12 min. | 16 hr., 3 min. | 6.39 Earth days | 25 days |
| 317.9 | 95.2 | 14.6 | 17.2 | 0.2 | 333,000 |
| -128° F* | -148° F* | -344° F | -365° F | -355° F | 10,000° F |
| hydrogen, helium, methane, ammonia, water | hydrogen, helium, methane, ammonia | hydrogen, helium | hydrogen, helium, methane | methane (trace) | hydrogen, helium |
| 380 lbs. | 160 lbs. | 155 lbs. | 210 lbs. | 24 lbs. | |
| 16 known | 18 known | 15 known | 8 known | 1 | |

* Effective temperature, a measure of the amount of energy given off by the planet

*A comet, such as the one shown in the top photograph, is one of the most spectacular sights in the heavens. Visitors from space, in the form of meteorites, sometimes bombard Earth, as Meteor Crater in Arizona demonstrates. Most meteors, such as those shown in the shower (lower right), burn up in the atmosphere and do not reach Earth.*

# The minor planets. *Asteroids* are
the minor planets of our solar system. Most of them can be found orbiting the sun in a zone between Mars and Jupiter. The vast majority of asteroids are small, measuring less than a mile in diameter. But the largest, Ceres, is approximately 500 miles across. Asteroids may have resulted from the destruction of larger bodies.

In 1986 a bright light was seen shooting across the sky. This was Halley's Comet, which has appeared at regular intervals for centuries. A *comet* consists of tiny particles of frozen gases. As a comet approaches the sun, these particles melt and begin to glow, creating the bright head known as a *coma*. Some of the particles escape the coma and flow outward, producing the comet's *tail*. Each time a comet approaches the sun and returns to space, it loses some of its mass; eventually it will totally disintegrate.

*Meteoroids* are tiny particles traveling through space. Sometimes they enter our atmosphere, where they are set aglow by friction. These glowing particles are called *meteors* or, more popularly, "shooting stars." A vast number of meteors, called a meteor shower, may be created from the remains of a passing comet. Generally, meteoroids are quite small and disintegrate in the atmosphere, but a few may be large enough to reach the surface of Earth. These are called *meteorites*. When they strike the surface, meteorites can produce enormous craters such as the one found in Arizona that is approximately 4000 feet wide.

**Space Science**

**The moon.** Earth's only natural satellite is called the *moon*. The moon is an average distance of 238,857 miles from Earth. The moon orbits Earth once every 27⅓ days; during that time it makes a single rotation on its axis. This means that the same side of the moon is always facing Earth.

From our position on Earth, the moon appears as a patchwork of light and dark areas. The light areas are created by sunlight reflecting off the craggy lunar mountains. Some of the mountains are over 5 miles high. The lunar surface is also deeply pitted with craters that result from the impact of numerous meteors. Since there is no atmosphere on the moon, meteors have been able to reach the surface easily. One crater, called Clavius, is about 148 miles in diameter.

The dark areas are the lunar seas, or *maria*. These are not actual bodies of water, for no water exists on the moon's surface. The maria were created by volcanic activity that occurred millions of years ago. As lava flowed onto the surface, it solidified into dark rock. The maria have been given names such as the Sea of Rains, the Sea of Tears, and the Sea of Serenity.

Various types of rocks were found on the moon during the lunar landings. The maria are comprised of dark basalts. The highlands contain other types of igneous rock such as breccia.

Because of its orbit, the moon is constantly changing position with respect to Earth and the sun. Consequently, the amount of sunlight reflected by the moon to Earth changes. This creates the *phases of the moon*. For example, at new moon, half of the lunar surface is lighted by the sun, but the moon appears dark to us because of its position between Earth and the sun. The moon *waxes* as it reflects more light to Earth, and *wanes* as the amount of light diminishes. An entire cycle (new moon to new moon) takes 29½ days, which is two days longer than the period of the moon's revolution. The reason for this time difference is that Earth has been moving in its orbit.

## The moon

The moon and its changes have always fascinated people on Earth. Although there are many myths to explain the phases of the moon, the ancient Greeks had long ago found the true explanation: the changes are caused by the motions of the sun, Earth, and moon. Today men have walked on the moon's surface.

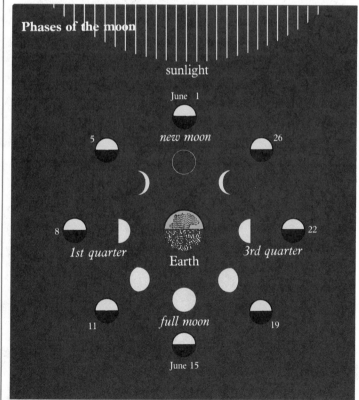

Phases of the moon

sunlight

June 1

new moon

5     26

8     22

1st quarter     Earth     3rd quarter

11     19

full moon

June 15

## Eclipses.

A celestial body casts a shadow into space when it is lighted from one side. The light usually comes from a sun. If another celestial body passes into this shadow, it is eclipsed. For example, when Earth passes between the sun and the moon, a lunar *eclipse* occurs. When the moon passes between the sun and Earth, a solar eclipse occurs.

The shadow that is cast by Earth or the moon is really of two different darknesses. The inner shadow, which is very dark, is called the *umbra*. Outside the umbra is a shadow of semidarkness called the *penumbra*.

A lunar eclipse can only occur during a full moon, when sun, Earth, and moon are in a straight line. Most of the time, the moon's orbit takes it out of Earth's shadow. When Earth's umbra covers the moon's surface, a total eclipse of the moon can be seen from an entire hemisphere on Earth.

A solar eclipse occurs when sun, moon, and Earth are in a straight line. Because of the sun's size compared with the moon's, the umbra cast by the moon is small, covering an area about 167 miles wide. The penumbra covers an area about 2000 miles wide. People in the area where the umbra falls see a total solar eclipse. Those in the area of the penumbra see a partial solar eclipse. Solar eclipses happen less often than lunar eclipses and are over more quickly.

## Eclipses

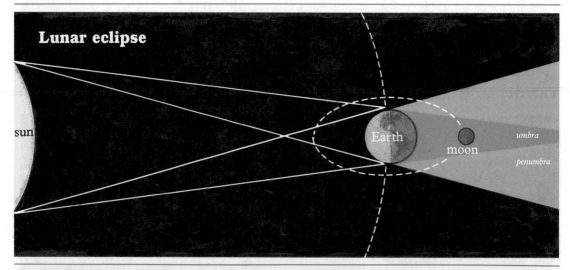

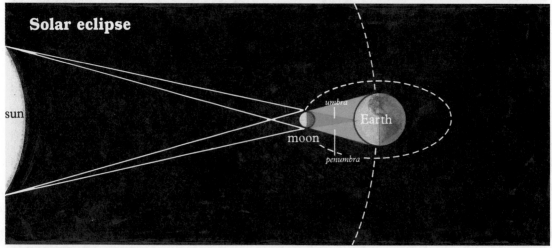

# Galaxies

Our solar system is a small part of a *galaxy*. A galaxy is a very large collection of stars, gas, dust, and other objects traveling through space as a unit. Our galaxy is called the *Milky Way* because we see millions of stars whose light gives a milky haze when we look at the night sky. The Milky Way is relatively thin and flat, something like a wristwatch, but it also has spiral arms, something like a pinwheel. Our sun is located in one of these arms, far from the center of the galaxy.

The universe consists of many galaxies. Some, like Andromeda, are spiral-shaped. Andromeda is visible to the naked eye, but it is very faint because of its great distance. Many galaxies have an elliptical shape, while others appear formless and are called irregular galaxies. These include the Large and Small Magellanic Clouds, which are the galaxies located closest to the Milky Way.

Distances in astronomy are so great that the unit of measurement most often used is the *light-year*. A light-year is the distance that light travels in a year, or about 6 trillion miles. Another unit is the *parsec*, which is 3.26 light-years. The Milky Way has a diameter of about 100,000 light-years and is believed to be about 10,000 light-years thick. It contains about 100 billion stars, as well as huge amounts of dust and gas. The entire galaxy rotates very slowly, taking about 200 million years to complete one revolution.

The distance to a nearby star can be deter-

*The Milky Way galaxy is a disk with spiral arms, representing one of the more common types of galaxies.*

mined by using a method known as *parallax*. This refers to the apparent shift in a star's position when viewed from two different locations. Astronomers observe a star at an interval of six months, when Earth is at two different locations in its orbit. Using trigonometry, a star's distance is then calculated. The nearest star is Alpha Centauri, about 4.3 light-years away.

*In the galaxy M100, in this photograph made by the Hubble Space Telescope, spiral arms are prominent. The Horsehead Nebula is a cloud of dust and gas.*

# Stars

Stars are born in a rotating cloud of gas and dust called a *nebula*. The laws of physics predict that such a cloud will break up into many smaller clouds under the influence of gravity, and that gravity will also cause the smaller clouds to contract. As the hydrogen atoms in such a cloud fall faster and faster toward the center, the cloud becomes hot and starts to glow. Finally it becomes so hot at the core that a nuclear reaction begins: hydrogen atoms are fused to form helium. This is the same reaction that occurs in the sun, producing huge amounts of energy. The energy exerts an outward pressure that balances the force of gravity; at this point the gas cloud stops contracting. This is how stars are created. New stars are still being born from the nebulas in our galaxy.

## Luminosity.

One of the most important facts about a star is its brightness, or *luminosity*. Luminosity is the rate at which a star radiates energy. Astronomers generally use the term *magnitude* to express the brightness of a star. There are two kinds of magnitude. *Apparent magnitude* is the brightness as it appears to us, without corrections for the distance of the star from Earth. *Absolute magnitude* is brightness after allowing for the fact that stars are at different distances from us. The bright stars are given a magnitude of one and are first-magnitude stars. A first-magnitude star is about 2.5 times as bright as a second-magnitude star and $2.5 \times 2.5 = 6.25$ times as bright as a third-magnitude star, and so on. The human eye can see stars down to the sixth apparent magnitude, which is about 100 times fainter than the first magnitude. Some stars are brighter than first magnitude; these stars are given a negative magnitude. Apparent magnitudes range from $-26.5$ for the sun to about $+20$, which can be detected only by the largest telescopes.

To calculate absolute magnitude, one must correct for the different distances of the stars. One star may look much fainter than another although it is actually putting out far more energy. It appears fainter because it is farther away. The apparent brightness of a star is inversely proportional to the square of its distance. That is, the farther away a star is, the less its apparent brightness. The absolute magnitude is the value one would measure if the star or other celestial object were at a distance of 10 parsecs (32.6 light-years). On this scale, the stars show a magnitude range of $-10$ to $+20$. Our sun is somewhere in the middle with $+5$. It is an average star.

## Constellations

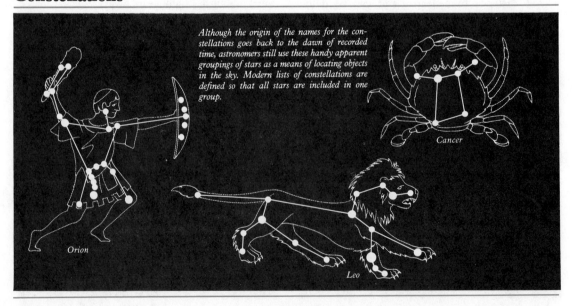

Although the origin of the names for the constellations goes back to the dawn of recorded time, astronomers still use these handy apparent groupings of stars as a means of locating objects in the sky. Modern lists of constellations are defined so that all stars are included in one group.

Orion

Cancer

Leo

# Stars: H–R diagram

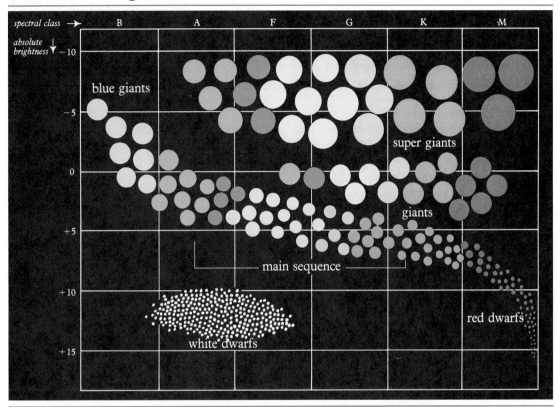

spectral class →
absolute brightness ↓

## Classification of stars.

Stars appear to us as luminous dots that "twinkle." This is due to their distance from Earth and to the effect of our atmosphere on the light that they emit. Stars glow in various colors of the spectrum depending on their surface temperatures. The hottest stars glow a brilliant blue-white; others glow yellow; while the coolest stars glow red. A spectroscope is a device that breaks down the light coming from a star and helps scientists obtain a fairly accurate measure of a star's surface temperature. Scientists have used letters to classify stars into the following spectral groups based on temperature:

| | | | |
|---|---|---|---|
| O | 50,000 C | G | 5,500 C |
| B | 20,000 C | K | 4,500 C |
| A | 10,000 C | M | 3,000 C |
| F | 7,500 C | | |

Each major group is further subdivided. Our sun is class $G_2$, temperature 6000 degrees C.

The astronomers Ejnar Hertzsprung and Henry Russell plotted the absolute magnitude (brightness) of many stars and compared it to the stars' spectral classes (surface temperatures). This resulted in the *H-R diagram*. Most stars fall into a regular order known as the *main sequence*. It was found that a star's position along the main sequence depends on its mass. The very massive stars have a high temperature and appear blue, whereas the smaller stars have lower temperatures and appear yellow or red.

## Life cycle of a star.

The H-R diagram provides an effective way to chart the life cycle of a star. After a star is born and becomes stable, it eventually enters the main sequence. Massive stars, such as Vega and Sirius, show up on the left. An average-size star, such as our sun, can be found near the center of the main sequence. Smaller stars join at the right.

The length of time that a star remains stable is a function of its mass. The more massive stars consume their hydrogen faster. Those similar to our sun burn much more slowly.

As a star begins to run out of hydrogen, it becomes unstable. Its surface cools, and its size may grow enormously. A massive star may expand to become one of the supergiants shown in the upper part of the H-R diagram. These stars glow very brightly because of their enormous surface area. An example of a supergiant is the star Betelgeuse, which is found in the constellation Orion.

An average-size star, such as our sun, will not expand so much as the supergiants; it will become a giant. In time the giant sun will use up all its energy and begin to contract. Finally, the sun will enter its last stage and become a cold star that emits only a faint glow. Such a star is called a *white dwarf*.

The end of a supergiant can occur in different ways. The supergiant may explode and become very bright, forming a spectacular *supernova*. In 1054 Chinese astronomers observed such a supernova in our galaxy; today we can still see the cloud of expanding gas that remains from the explosion. It forms the Crab nebula in the constellation Taurus. A more recent supernova occurred in our galaxy in 1604.

Following the explosion of a supernova, the remains of the star that exploded may collapse. Its protons and electrons may be pushed so closely together that they fuse to produce neutrons. Such a star is called a *neutron star*, and it is very small in size. For example, if the planet Earth were to become a neutron star, it would be only 100 yards in diameter.

Some neutron stars emit bursts, or pulses, of radio waves. These stars are called *pulsars*. In the Crab nebula, astronomers have found a pulsar that gives off radio waves and flashes of light. Other pulsars emit x-rays.

After its explosion as a supernova, a large part of a star—perhaps three times or more as massive as our sun—may still remain and begin to collapse. Eventually it may become even smaller than a neutron star and have a gravitational force so strong that light cannot escape from its surface. As a result, the star will simply disappear. The result is a *black hole*. Of course, black holes cannot be observed directly, but their existence can be inferred from the way they affect visible stars nearby. The gravitational attraction of a black hole makes its visible neighbor move abnormally. Astronomers believe a black hole may be present in the constellation Cygnus, although it is difficult to prove that black holes exist.

# Other phenomena

The heavens include many different types of phenomena. Astronomers have observed that two stars often revolve around each other because of their gravitational attraction. These stars are called *binary* stars. If more than two are involved, they are called *multiple* stars.

Stars known as *cepheid variables* glow lighter and darker according to a definite pattern. The cepheids have been helpful in calculating the distances to stars that are too far away to allow for the use of the parallax method. Astronomers have discovered that the absolute magnitude of a cepheid is directly related to the time interval between its bright and dark periods. By comparing absolute magnitude to apparent magnitude, they can calculate the distance to a cepheid, or to a galaxy with a cepheid. The distance to the Andromeda galaxy was determined in this way.

During the 1960's, astronomers observed faint stars that emitted radio waves. They called these starlike objects *quasars*, short for quasi-stellar radio sources. Astronomers estimate that quasars are billions of light-years away. Since they still appear to us as faint stars even at this distance, it must mean that they are many times brighter than our sun. As yet there is no accepted theory to explain quasars. A quasar may be the center of a dense galaxy, or it may have giant stars.

*Astronomers are still puzzled by quasars, but they think that pulsars are neutron stars. The pulses of the first one discovered were so regular that some astronomers thought at first that they were signals sent by intelligent life forms millions of years away.*

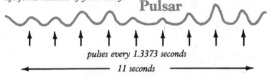

**Pulsar**

*pulses every 1.3373 seconds*

*← 11 seconds →*

**Space Science**

# Cosmology

*Cosmology* is the study of the way the universe as a whole is organized, how it began, and what will eventually happen to it. One of the most important events in the history of cosmology occurred during the 1920's. The American astronomer Edwin Hubble discovered that the universe is expanding. Evidence for this was provided by the so-called *red shift*. Stars moving away from us appear to emit longer waves of light. In other words, the light is shifted toward the red end of the spectrum. Stars approaching us seem to give off shorter waves of light.

Hubble observed that light from distant galaxies is shifted in its wavelength toward the red; the farther away the galaxy, the greater the shift. Apparently, the galaxies—including our own—are receding from one another, and those most distant from us are traveling the fastest. The situation can be likened to the effect of inflating a ball. As the ball expands, all the points on it move farther apart.

How did the expansion of the universe begin? Some astronomers theorize that all matter was concentrated in a huge ball that exploded. This idea is called the *big-bang theory*. It postulates that the explosion is still occurring, which accounts for the continuous expansion of the universe that Hubble observed.

As a result of evidence discovered over the past two decades, the big-bang theory is now widely accepted. Calculations show that the universe is 15 to 20 billion years old. In 1965, scientists working at Bell Laboratories discovered a type of radiation coming from the universe. This is exactly the form of radiation that would remain following a giant explosion to form the universe.

## Origins of solar system.
For centuries scientists have speculated about the origins of our solar system. One theory, formulated during the 18th century, was called the *nebular hypothesis*. This stated that the sun was originally a nebula of gases whirling in space. As the nebula condensed, it spun more and more rapidly, becoming a flat disk. Eventually the disk began to discharge rings of material that condensed to become the planets. If this theory were accurate, we

*As the universe expands, the galaxies become farther apart, like points on a vast inflating balloon.*

might expect the sun to be still revolving at very high velocities. But it is not. In addition, the rings of gaseous material would expand, not contract. Consequently, this theory was rejected.

Other scientists proposed the *close-encounter* theory. They speculated that at some point in the past, the sun had encountered another huge body and created enormous turbulence within the gaseous material that constitutes the sun. They further speculated that some of the material was ejected and later condensed to become the planets. A major flaw in the theory is that the material could not have been pulled out with enough force to produce planets at such great distances from the sun as Pluto.

The currently accepted theory about the origins of the solar system is a variation of the nebular hypothesis. Scientists now believe that a huge nebula contracted and slowly started to rotate. A large whirlpool inside the nebula eventually condensed and became the sun. Smaller whirlpools, known as protoplanets, formed and broke away. These contracted to produce the planets. A planet's gravitational force might be strong enough to hold tiny eddies around it in place. These eddies condensed to form the satellites.

# Space exploration

Many people think that the age of space exploration began with the launch of the first space vehicles in the 1950's and 1960's. In fact, astronomers, using only the naked eye or a telescope, had been exploring the universe long before the beginning of space flight. To this day, telescopes are still the primary means of learning more about the universe, its galaxies, and our solar system.

## Telescopes.
Galileo constructed the first optical telescope used for astronomy in 1609. Since then, astronomical telescopes have grown much larger and more complex. Still, there are only two basic types of optical telescopes: refracting and reflecting.

**Refracting telescopes.** This type of telescope is generally a long tube with an objective lens at one end and an eyepiece at the other. The objective lens gathers light and focuses an image in front of the eyepiece at a point called the focus. The eyepiece acts like a magnifying glass, enlarging the image at the focus for the eye to see.

**Reflecting telescopes.** A reflecting telescope uses mirrors to capture and magnify an image. Light passes down a tube to the mirror, which gathers the light and focuses it to form an image. The image is often reflected on another mirror to an eyepiece on the side of the tube.

Until the end of the 19th century, the largest telescopes were the refracting type. However, there is a practical limit to the size of an objective lens. Above a diameter of about 40 inches, the glass becomes very thick, and the thickness begins to limit the amount of light that passes through the lens.

Therefore, the largest optical telescopes today are reflecting. Not only can mirrors be made larger without loss of image, but several mirrors can be combined to create an even more powerful telescope.

Astronomers can learn much from direct observation of stars and planets. Details of the surfaces of the closest celestial objects, the planets, can be discerned using powerful optical telescopes. Astronomers can also track the movement of stars and planets, plotting their positions and determining their effects on one another.

A great deal can also be learned about the sun and the stars by analyzing the light a star emits. The light that reaches Earth from a star is made up of a spectrum of light of different colors. (See page 273 for a more complete discussion of the light spectrum.) Different patterns in the

## Telescopes

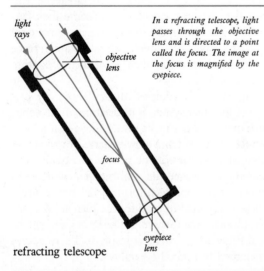

*In a refracting telescope, light passes through the objective lens and is directed to a point called the focus. The image at the focus is magnified by the eyepiece.*

light rays
objective lens
focus
eyepiece lens
refracting telescope

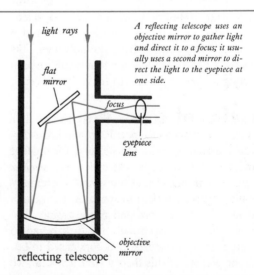

*A reflecting telescope uses an objective mirror to gather light and direct it to a focus; it usually uses a second mirror to direct the light to the eyepiece at one side.*

light rays
flat mirror
focus
eyepiece lens
objective mirror
reflecting telescope

spectrum of a star can provide information about its chemical composition, and shifts in the colors in the spectrum can indicate the velocity and direction of the movement of a star.

**Radio telescopes.** These telescopes are used to detect radio waves. Radio waves are given off naturally by many different bodies in the universe. By studying the waves, astronomers have made important discoveries about stars, distant galaxies, quasars, pulsars, and other mysteries of the universe.

There are many different kinds of radio telescopes. One of the most common is similar to, though much larger than, the satellite dishes that people use to receive television signals. Often, astronomers will connect many such dishes together in a long line, or even in different parts of the world, in order to achieve images of greater detail and precision.

**Telescopes in space.** Earth's atmosphere causes distortion in the images received by telescopes on the ground. Placing telescopes in orbit aboard satellites eliminates the interference that the atmosphere causes. The most famous orbiting telescope is the Hubble Space Telescope, which was placed into orbit in 1990. After a 1993 space shuttle mission repaired flaws in the telescope's main mirror that greatly reduced its

*In 1993 the Hubble Space Telescope was repaired by the crew of the space shuttle Endeavour, greatly improving the quality of its images.*

effectiveness, the Hubble telescope began providing the best images ever made of deep-space objects.

Scientists have also learned a great deal about the universe by using orbiting telescopes that detect infrared waves, x-rays, and gamma rays.

*The two most common types of telescopes used by astronomers are optical and radio. These dish antennae are part of the Very Large Array radio telescope in New Mexico.*

# Planetary space probes.

Much has also been learned about the solar system and its planets from the information returned to Earth by interplanetary probes. Probes are unmanned space capsules that carry photographic and sensing equipment as well as equipment that transmits information back to Earth.

From the beginning of the space age, both the United States and the Soviet Union were active in the exploration of the solar system using probes. Indeed, the competition between the two countries was a spur to both their space programs, since neither wanted the other to be first in the accomplishment of space feats.

**The moon.** The United States sent four different series of probes to the moon. The first, four Pioneer probes launched in 1958 and 1959, was not notably successful in returning information about the moon. The remaining three programs were designed to return information that would be useful to the manned Apollo lunar missions.

Nine Ranger probes were launched from 1961 to 1965. They were designed to return photographs of the surface of the moon during the few minutes before the probe would crash into the surface. The first six Ranger missions were unsuccessful; however, *Ranger 7, 8,* and *9* returned thousands of photos of the moon's surface.

The five Lunar Orbiter probes were designed to remain in orbit around the moon and photograph its surface, focusing particularly on areas of interest to the Apollo program. In all, the Orbiter craft were able to map about 95 percent of the surface of the moon.

Surveyor, a series of seven missions launched from 1966 to 1968, was the first U.S. probe designed to soft-land on the moon. Although two of the missions were unsuccessful, the others sent back thousands of photos and performed tests of the soil, temperature, and the effects of the sun's radiation on the moon's surface.

During this time the Soviet Union was also sending probes to the moon. The Luna series of 24 missions lasted from 1959 until 1976. Many of the early milestones in lunar exploration were first achieved by Luna craft. They were the first to pass near the moon, impact on it, return photographs of it, soft-land on it, and take soil samples and return them to Earth.

**Venus.** Both the Soviet Union and the United States have sent many probes to Venus. The first Venus probe was the Soviet *Venera 1;* however, the probe missed the planet, and radio contact was lost. The first probe to reach the planet was *Mariner 2,* launched by the United States in 1962. It confirmed the planet's high surface temperature and established that Venus has no magnetic field or radiation belt.

In all, the Soviet Union sent 13 Venera probes to Venus, beginning in 1961 and ending in 1983. Some of these craft were orbiters and some landed on the surface. In 1985 the Halley's comet probes *Vega 1* and *Vega 2* dropped a total of four probes, two landers and two atmospheric balloons, during a flyby of Venus.

Two more Mariner missions visited Venus, *Mariner 5* in 1967 and *Mariner 10* in 1974. They provided information about the planet's atmosphere. Two Pioneer Venus craft reached Venus in 1978, orbiting the planet and sending probes to the surface. The *Magellan* probe, which reached the planet in 1990, used radar to map the entire planet.

**Mars.** The Mariner program also sent four missions to Mars. *Mariner 4, 6,* and *7* were flyby visits designed to take and transmit photographs back to Earth. *Mariner 9* became the first probe to orbit another planet when it reached Mars in 1971. The probe took thousands of pictures and mapped the entire surface of the planet. From 1971 to 1973 the Soviet Union sent a series of Mars probes to the planet, but they were not particularly successful in sending back information to Earth.

The most successful missions to Mars were the *Viking 1* and *2* orbiter-lander combinations. The landers set down on the surface in 1976 and continued to transmit data for six and four years, respectively. They analyzed soil and atmosphere, monitored the weather, tested for the presence of life, and returned images of the surface. The orbiters returned over 50,000 photographs of the planet.

**The outer planets.** Two pairs of very important probes have taught us a great deal about the planets beyond the asteroid belt. *Pioneer 10,* launched in 1972, and *Pioneer 11,* launched in 1973, became the first interplanetary craft to visit one of the outer planets. *Pioneer 10* returned hundreds of images of Jupiter and its moons and carried instruments to study cosmic radiation and other phenomena. *Pioneer 10* passed beyond Jupiter and in 1984 became the first man-made object to leave the solar system. *Pioneer 11*, after transmitting images of Jupiter, traveled on to become the first probe to visit Saturn.

But even these two hugely successful missions were dwarfed by the success of the next two Voyager missions. Both probes encountered Jupiter in 1979; *Voyager 1* went on to fly by Saturn in 1980. *Voyager 2* passed Saturn in 1981 and went on to encounter Uranus in 1986 and Neptune in 1989. The astonishingly clear images of these planets and their satellites captured the imaginations of scientists and amateur astronomers the world over.

In 1989 the United States launched Galileo, which took up orbit around Jupiter in 1995 and sent a probe to study the planet's atmosphere.

## Highlights of unmanned space probes

*The Voyager space probe* (above right) *visited Jupiter, Saturn, Uranus, and Neptune and sent back valuable information. The Viking lander missions sent back images of the surface of Mars* (above).

1964 **Ranger 7** (US). Photographs the moon.
 **Mariner 4** (US). Photographs Mars from 6000 miles away.
1965 **A-1 Diamant** (France). First French satellite is in orbit.
1967 **Mariner 5** (US). Passes within 2500 miles of Venus.
1969 **Mariner 6** (US). Passes within 2000 miles of Mars.
1970 **Ohsumi** (Japan). Satellite is placed in orbit.
1971 **Mariner 9** (US). Orbits Mars.
1972 **Pioneer 10** (US). Passes Jupiter; becomes the first man-made object to leave the solar system.
1973 **Mariner 10** (US). Reaches Mercury.
1976 **Viking 1** (US). Lands on the surface of Mars.
1977 **Voyager 1** (US). Passes Jupiter and then Saturn.
 **Voyager 2** (US). Passes Jupiter, Saturn, and Uranus.
1978 **Pioneer Venus 1** (US). Enters orbit of Venus.
 **Pioneer Venus 2** (US). Probes reach the surface of Venus.
1984 **Ariane 3** (European Space Agency). Launch vehicle developed by French scientist deploys two satellites.
1985 **Giotto** (European Space Agency). Passes within 335 miles of Halley's comet's nucleus.
1990 **Hubble Space Telescope** (US, European Space Agency). Greatly enhances the resolution for viewing stars.
 **Magellan** (US). Orbits Venus, provides detailed radar mapping of the planet's surface.
 **Ulysses** (US, European Space Agency). Launched to study the sun's poles in 1994 and 1995.
1995 **Galileo** (US). Enters orbit of Jupiter to study the planet's atmosphere and moons.
1997 **Mars Pathfinder** (US). Sends back soil analyses and 16,000 photos of Martian surface.
 **Cassini** (US). Launched to provide detailed study of Saturn and its moons.
2000 **Image** (US). Launched to study Earth's magnetosphere's response to changes in solar wind.

# Manned space flights.

The first manned flight took place on April 12, 1961, when Yuri Gagarin went into orbit in the Soviet *Vostok 1* spacecraft. Gagarin made one revolution of Earth; his total flight time was 1 hour, 48 minutes.

On May 5, 1961, the United States sent up its first astronaut, Alan B. Shepard, Jr. In a Mercury capsule boosted by a Redstone launch vehicle, Shepard made a suborbital, 15-minute flight that took him to an altitude of 117 miles.

**Vostok (U.S.S.R.).** Vostok was a cylindrical spacecraft weighing slightly more than 5 tons. It was an elementary one-man vehicle designed to prove man's survivability in space. The spacecraft was lowered to Earth by parachute after reentry. The cosmonaut ejected at a low altitude and parachuted separately. The Vostok program consisted of six flights between 1961 and 1963, including the first manned flight, the first missions of more than 24 hours in space *(Vostok 2)*, and the first piloted by a woman *(Vostok 6)*.

**Mercury (U.S.).** Like Vostok, Mercury was an elementary spacecraft designed only for the initial steps of manned spaceflight. Mercury was a bell-shaped capsule. Its weight was about 3000 pounds, varying slightly with each mission. The small capsules used parachutes during their descent inside the atmosphere before splashing down in the ocean, where astronaut and capsule were recovered by U.S. ships and helicopters. The program consisted of six flights between 1961 and 1963, two of them suborbital and the rest orbital. The program included the first U.S. orbital flight *(Mercury-Atlas 6)* and the first flight of more than 24 hours by a U.S. spacecraft *(Mercury-Atlas 9)*.

**Voskhod (U.S.S.R.).** The second-generation Soviet manned spacecraft Voskhod made only two flights (1964–1965), but it represented a considerable advance over its predecessor. Voskhod's first flight, on October 12, 1964, marked the first multiman space mission. A crew of three made the 24-hour flight. The second flight, on March 18 and 19, 1965, was notable because the copilot, Alexei Leonov, became the first space walker. He spent 10 minutes outside the spacecraft in a special multilayered extravehicular suit.

*The Gemini spacecraft were a great improvement over the earlier Mercury craft.*

**Gemini (U.S.).** The United States's second-generation manned spacecraft Gemini offered a great many improvements over Mercury. Among the most important, it was a two-man craft and was maneuverable. All previous manned spacecraft had been unable to change course.

The first Gemini was launched March 23, 1965, and the program continued through ten manned flights; the last was launched November 11, 1966. The program included a number of highlights: the first orbital maneuvering by a manned spacecraft *(Gemini 3)*; the first U.S. multiman flight *(Gemini 3)*; the first U.S. space walk *(Gemini 4)*; a flight of exceptionally long duration—330 hours and 30 minutes—for that time *(Gemini 7)*; the first rendezvous between two spacecraft *(Gemini 6 and 7)*; the first docking in space *(Gemini 8)*.

**Soyuz (U.S.S.R.).** In 1967 the Soviet Union introduced its third-generation manned spacecraft, Soyuz. The first flight, on April 23 of that year, ended tragically when the parachute de-

**Space Science**

# International space station

*During a space walk in December, 1998, astronauts Jerry Ross and Jim Newman worked on the Russian-made module* Zarya. *The linking of the Russian module with the U.S.* Unity *module (lower left) marked the beginning of the station's construction, which was scheduled to continue for five years. Twelve other countries, including Japan, Canada, and the member nations of the European Space Agency, are working with the United States and Russia to build the station.*

scent system failed, killing Vladimir Komarov, the first man to die during a space mission. Soyuz was the first Soviet manned spacecraft capable of maneuvering, rendezvousing, and docking. It is also capable of almost unlimited time in space. Among the highlights of the Soyuz program are the first Soviet rendezvous and docking (the manned *Soyuz 3* docked with an unmanned *Soyuz 2*); the first transfer of men from one spacecraft in orbit to another (*Soyuz 4* and *5*); and the first triple launch and rendezvous of manned spacecraft (*Soyuz 6, 7,* and *8*).

*Soyuz 11* was part of a three-spacecraft experiment in space station development. The first segment, a prototype space laboratory called *Salyut 1*, was sent into orbit unmanned on April 19, 1971. *Soyuz 10*, launched April 22 and carrying a three-man crew, docked with *Salyut* and the cosmonauts transferred to the laboratory, where they conducted experiments for almost two days. They returned to Earth in *Soyuz 10*. On June 7, *Soyuz 11* docked with *Salyut*. Its three astronauts worked in the laboratory for 23 days, but they died during their return flight to Earth.

In later Soyuz flights, the Soviets continued docking maneuvers with Salyut space stations and conducting experiments. During 1984, Russian astronauts sent aloft in a Soyuz mission set a record of 237 days for space endurance.

In the 1980's the Soviet space program was centered on the development of a permanently manned space station. The *Mir* space station was launched in 1986 and continued to function into 2000, well past its planned life span. With six docking ports, *Mir* had a much greater capacity for expansion than the Salyut stations.

In 1988 the Soviet Union completed *Buran*, a craft similar to the U.S. space shuttle. *Buran* made one unmanned orbital flight but it is unlikely that it will ever fly again.

**Apollo (U.S.).** Apollo, the third generation of U.S. manned spacecraft, represented a great advance, as demonstrated in repeated lunar landings. Apollo included a command module; the reentry capsule, which also served as crew quarters and command post; the lunar module, in which two of the three astronauts descended to the lunar surface; and the service module, a jettisonable segment that contained much of the fuel, expendables, and other equipment. The lunar module had separate descent and ascent engines for its trip to the lunar surface.

The first manned Apollo mission (*Apollo 7*), an eleven-day Earth-orbital flight, was flown October 11-21, 1968. The highlight of the program was the first manned lunar landing, on July 20, 1969. *Apollo 11* astronauts Neil A. Armstrong and Edwin A. (Buzz) Aldrin were the first men to set foot on the moon. There were six Apollo landings on the moon before the program was concluded.

**Skylab (U.S.).** Skylab used modified Apollo hardware to create a prototype manned space station. Skylab was a large orbital laboratory weighing close to 85 tons. Its major elements were a large workshop with laboratory and living quarters; an astronomical observatory; and a docking port for manned spacecraft.

Skylab was launched on May 14, 1973, as a single unmanned unit. On May 25, 1973, the *Skylab 1* astronauts—Charles Conrad, Jr., Joseph P. Kerwin, and Paul J. Wertz—were launched to the space station for a 28-day stay in space.

On July 28, 1973, the *Skylab 2* astronauts—Alan L. Bean, Jack R. Lousma, and Owen K. Garriott—set out to link up with the station. After being in space for 59 days, they returned on September 25, 1973. The astronauts brought back 77,600 pictures of the sun's corona, 14,000 pictures of Earth, and 18 miles of magnetic tape data.

**Space shuttle (U.S.).** On April 12, 1981, the space shuttle *Columbia* was launched from Cape Canaveral, Florida, on its first journey into space. Two astronauts, John Young and Robert Crippin, piloted the vehicle through 36 orbits of Earth at 200 miles above the surface. After 54 hours, *Columbia* touched down safely on a runway at Edwards Air Force base in California.

The space shuttle is about the size of a DC-9 airplane, 122 feet long with a wingspan of 78 feet. The plane is linked to an external fuel tank and two solid-fuel booster rockets. On launch, the boosters provide 2,650,000 pounds of thrust

for 2 minutes. Afterward, the booster rockets fall away into the ocean, from which they are recovered and reused. The shuttle receives liquid fuel from the external tank until the tank is ejected about 8 minutes into the flight. After the shuttle finishes orbiting Earth and reenters the atmosphere, it glides downward toward the surface. When its journey is complete, the vehicle can be refueled and prepared for another trip.

The space shuttle has been designed for a variety of uses. With its large cargo hold, it can carry a satellite and place it in space. In fact, over the past few years, a primary purpose of the shuttle has been to place communications satellites in orbit around Earth.

Following the explosion of the space shuttle *Challenger* in 1986, the program's schedule was delayed pending a thorough investigation. The program was resumed with a successful launching in September, 1988. Seventy successful shuttle missions were completed between 1988 and the end of 1999. Space shuttle crews began assembling the new International Space Station at the end of 1998.

## Space shuttle

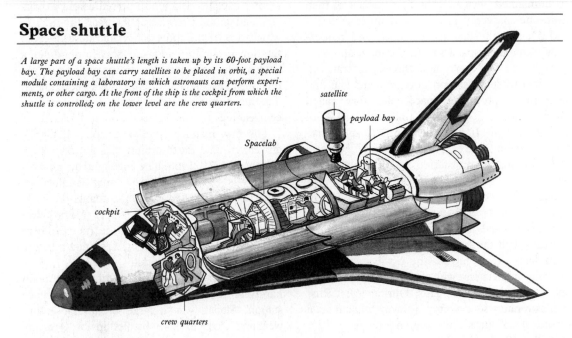

*A large part of a space shuttle's length is taken up by its 60-foot payload bay. The payload bay can carry satellites to be placed in orbit, a special module containing a laboratory in which astronauts can perform experiments, or other cargo. At the front of the ship is the cockpit from which the shuttle is controlled; on the lower level are the crew quarters.*

satellite

payload bay

Spacelab

cockpit

crew quarters

**Space Science**

# Highlights of manned space missions

*The Apollo moon landings, during which astronauts walked on the surface of the moon, are considered by many to be the most important achievement in the history of space exploration.*

1961 **Vostok 1** (USSR). Yuri Gagarin is the first to orbit the Earth.
     **Mercury 3** (US). Alan Shepard becomes the first American in space.
1962 **Mercury 6** (US). John Glenn is the first American to orbit Earth.
1963 **Vostok 6** (USSR). Valentina Tereshkova becomes the first woman in space.
1965 **Voskhod 2** (USSR). A cosmonaut is the first to leave a spacecraft for a space walk.
     **Gemini 3** (US). Becomes first manned spacecraft to maneuver out of its regular orbital path.
1967 **Apollo 1** (US). Launchpad fire kills Virgil Grissom, Edward White, and Roger Chafee.
     **Soyuz 1** (USSR). Cosmonaut is killed when parachute fails during reentry.
1968 **Apollo 8** (US). First manned flight orbits moon.
1969 **Soyuz 5** (USSR). Crew members transfer to *Soyuz 4* after space docking.
     **Apollo 11** (US). First manned moon landing; Neil Armstrong and Edwin Aldrin walk on moon.
1971 **Apollo 14** (US). Astronauts explore the surface of the moon for 9 hours.
     **Soyuz 11** (USSR). Docks with Salyut space station; craft orbit Earth together for 23 days; crew of three is killed during reentry.
1973 **Skylab 2** (US). Mission established Skylab in Earth's orbit; crew conducts experiments aboard Skylab.
1975 **Apollo 18** (US) **and Soyuz 19** (USSR). After docking, U.S. and Soviet crews cooperate in experiments.
1979 **Soyuz 34** (USSR). Launched unmanned and returns with the crew from the *Salyut 6* space station
1981 **Space shuttle Columbia** (US). Reusable spacecraft enters space for first time and returns safely.
1982 **Space shuttle Columbia** (US). Deploys satellites from its payload.
1983 **Space shuttle Challenger** (US). Sally Ride becomes the first American woman in space.
     Remote Manipulator Structure (mechanical arm) retrieves a satellite.
1984 **Space shuttle Challenger** (US). Jet-propelled backpacks allow astronauts to fly free of their spacecraft.
1986 **Space shuttle Challenger** (US). Explodes shortly after launch, killing crew of seven.
     **Soyuz T15** (USSR). Launches a new space station, *Mir*, into Earth's orbit.
1988 **Space shuttle Discovery** (US). Shuttle program resumes with a successful mission.
1989 **Space Shuttle Atlantis** (US). Launches Magellan radar-mapping spacecraft to Venus.
     **Space Shuttle Atlantis** (US). Launches Galileo probe to Jupiter.
1990 **Space shuttle Discovery** (US). Shuttle places the Hubble Space Telescope in orbit.
1991 **Space shuttle Discovery** (US). Launches the Gamma Ray Observatory.
1993 **Space shuttle Endeavour** (US). Repairs Hubble telescope in space.
1995 **Space shuttle Atlantis** (US). Successfully docks with Russian space station *Mir*; is 100th US manned mission.
2000 **Space shuttle Atlantis** (US). Successfully launches International Space Station living quarters.

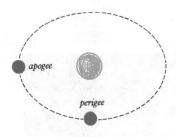

apogee/perigee

# Dictionary of space science

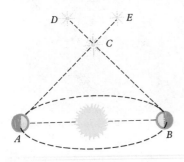

parallax

satellite

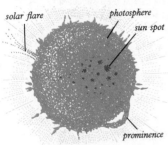

sun

**absolute magnitude.** Apparent brightness of a star viewed from a distance of 32.6 light-years.

**active satellite.** Communications satellite that includes equipment to re-broadcast radio or television signals.

**albedo.** Amount of light reflected by a heavenly body that does not produce its own light.

**altitude of a star.** Angle of a star above the horizon.

**angular resolution.** A measure of the sharpness of an image obtained by a telescope.

**aperture.** Diameter of the objective lens or the primary mirror of a telescope. The larger the aperture, the better its light-gathering power and angular resolution.

**aphelion.** Point in a planet's orbit when it is at the greatest distance from the sun.

**apogee.** Point in the orbit of a satellite when it is farthest from Earth.

**apparent magnitude.** Brightness of a star as it appears to us on Earth.

**artificial satellite.** Object that is placed into orbit around Earth or some other body in space.

**asteroids.** Small planetlike bodies that orbit the sun.

**astronaut.** Name given by the United States to a traveler in a spacecraft.

**astronautics.** Scientific study of the principles and technology of space travel.

**astronomical unit.** Unit of measurement equal to the mean distance from the sun to Earth, about 93,000,000 miles.

**astrophysics.** Study of the physics and evolution of the universe.

**aurora.** Colorful display of light caused by solar radiation that occurs at the poles.

**big bang theory.** Theory stating that the universe was created when a large mass of matter exploded.

**binary stars.** Two stars that orbit around each other because of their gravitational attraction.

**black hole.** Very dense object that may form from an exploded star. A black hole does not emit light.

**Bode's law.** Series of numbers equivalent to the approximate distances of the planets from the sun.

**booster.** Rocket used to propel a vehicle other than the rocket itself.

**capsule.** Type of spacecraft that has just enough room for one or two persons.

**cepheid variable.** Type of pulsating star that glows with varying amounts of intensity.

**chromosphere.** Lowest level of the sun's atmosphere.

**close-encounter theory.** Theory that states that the solar system was formed when the sun encountered another huge body. This event caused the sun to eject gaseous material that formed the planets.

**cluster.** Close grouping of stars of the same age. *Globular clusters* are spherical groupings of stars found in galaxies that contain up to several hundred thousand stars. Large groupings of galaxies are also called clusters.

**color index.** Number that indicates the color of a star. It is equal to the difference between the magnitude of a star measured in blue light and one measured in yellow light.

**coma.** Bright head of a comet.

**comet.** Mass of frozen gases orbiting the sun. On approaching the sun, the comet's material begins to melt and glow.

**command module.** Part of the Apollo system that remained in orbit around the moon while the lunar module landed.

**communications satellite.** Satellite used to relay signals from one point on Earth to another.

**conjunction.** One of two planetary configurations. The *superior conjunction* is the one in which the sun is between Earth and a planet. The *inferior conjunction* occurs when a planet is between Earth and the sun.

**constellation.** Apparent grouping of stars named after a mythical character.

**corona.** Outer layer of the sun's atmosphere.

**cosmic background radiation.** Microwave radiation coming from all directions in the universe. It is believed to be a remnant of the big bang.

**cosmic radiation.** Vast stream of atomic nuclei and electrons moving at very high speeds that reach Earth from all directions.

**cosmology.** Study of the general structure, origin, and development of the universe.

**cosmonaut.** Name given by the Soviet Union to a traveler in a space vehicle.

**docking.** Linking two spacecraft.

**Doppler effect.** Apparent change in the wavelength of radiation owing to the motion of the source and the observer.

**Doppler tracking.** Technique used to chart the progress of space probes. The changing frequency of the radio waves received from a spacecraft is measured to determine the craft's position and velocity in the solar system.

**Earthshine.** Light seen from Earth that is caused by the reflection of sunlight to the moon from the surface of Earth. It is a faint illumination of the moon's surface most easily seen when the moon is a crescent.

**eclipse.** Darkening of one celestial body when its light is cut off by another.

**ecliptic.** Apparent path of the sun among the stars.

**ephemeris.** Published table of the daily positions of the sun, moon, planets, artificial satellites, and selected stars. It also provides other data necessary for astronomical and navigational observations.

**equinox.** Two times of the year (March 21 and September 23) when day and night are of equal length.

**escape velocity.** Velocity required for a spacecraft to overcome the gravity of

Earth or any other body in the solar system.

**event horizon.** Boundary of the region around a black hole from which no light or matter can escape.

**extravehicular activity.** Activity outside a spacecraft that has left the atmosphere of Earth.

**field stars.** Stars in our galaxy that are found outside stellar clusters.

**free fall.** Any condition in which the force of gravity is not opposed by another force. In space, free fall occurs when the propulsion system of a space vehicle is turned off.

**galactic halo.** Region surrounding a galaxy filled with gas and globular clusters that appears to glow.

**galaxy.** Giant system of stars, dust, and gas.

**geosynchronous orbit.** Orbit used for communications satellites in which the satellite stays at the same place over Earth's surface.

**Hertzsprung-Russell diagram.** Chart that compares a star's absolute magnitude and its spectral class.

**interstellar matter.** Dust and gas found between the stars.

**jet aircraft.** Aircraft propelled by heating air to produce a stream of particles that gives the aircraft thrust.

**jettison.** Release part of a space vehicle so that it does not continue on a mission.

**Jovian planets.** Planets with orbits beyond that of Mars: Jupiter, Saturn, Uranus, Neptune, and Pluto.

**Kepler's law of equal areas.** One of the laws of planetary motion that the astronomer Kepler deduced from studying the planets. Kepler found that the path of a planet is such that a line from the sun to the planet sweeps out equal areas in equal times.

**Lagrange point.** The point between two celestial bodies at which the gravitational pulls of the two bodies on a third body cancel each other out.

**launch vehicle.** Rocket used to lift a satellite or probe into space.

**libration.** The oscillation in the motion of a celestial body traveling about another body.

**light-year.** Distance light travels in a year—about 6 trillion miles.

**lunar module.** In the Apollo program, the vehicle that landed on the moon.

**magnitude.** The brightness of a star or other celestial object. *Apparent magnitude* is the brightness of a star as it appears to an observer on Earth. *Absolute magnitude* is the apparent magnitude that a star would have if it were observed from a distance of 10 parsecs.

**mare.** Latin word for sea that refers to a dark area on the moon. Plural is maria.

**meteor.** Light produced by a meteoroid after entering Earth's atmosphere.

**meteorite.** Meteor that strikes Earth's surface.

**meteoroid.** Solid particle traveling through space.

**meteor shower.** Large group of falling meteors.

**Milky Way.** Galaxy in which our solar system is located.

**nebula.** Originally thought to be great clouds of dust and gas, but better telescopes revealed that many nebulae were actually vast collections of stars. Today the word "nebula" is generally replaced by "galaxy" for patches in the sky that resolve into stars. Consequently, the old meaning of "nebula" has returned, but sometimes well-known galaxies, such as Andromeda, are still called "nebula."

**nebular hypothesis.** Theory that states that the solar system was formed from a nebula of gases whirling in space.

**neutron star.** Very dense star composed of neutrons.

**nova.** Star that flares from obscurity to great brilliance and then sinks back to obscurity. *See also* **supernova.**

**objective lens.** Lens mounted at the front end of a telescope. It gathers light from a celestial object and focuses it in front of the eyepiece.

**occultation.** The hiding of one celestial body by another. Eclipses of a star or planet by the moon are occultations.

**orbit.** Travel in a closed path around some body in space; the path of a revolving body. A *heliocentric orbit* is an orbit with the sun as its center.

**parallax.** Distance an object appears to move when viewed from two different locations.

**parsec.** Distance equivalent to 3.26 light-years.

**passive satellite.** Communications satellite from which radio or television signals can be reflected.

**penumbra.** Part of a shadow that is partly lighted, as during an eclipse.

**perigee.** Point in the orbit of a satellite when it is nearest Earth.

**perihelion.** Point in a planet's orbit when it is closest to the sun.

**period (of an orbiting body).** Amount of time for one orbit.

**perturbation.** Disturbance in the orbit of a celestial body caused by the gravitational force of another body. Perturbations in the orbit of Uranus led to the discovery of Neptune and Pluto.

**photosphere.** Surface of the sun.

**plasma.** Gas that is almost completely ionized, that is, one or more electrons are split off each atom. Most of the matter in the universe, such as that inside stars, is plasma.

**primary.** Larger object around which a smaller object revolves. In a binary star, the primary is the larger of the two stars.

**probe.** Unmanned spacecraft that is not put into orbit around Earth.

**prominence.** Cloudlike structure that appears as a bright flame above the sun.

**pulsar.** Celestial body that emits pulses of light and radio waves.

**quasar.** Quasi-stellar radio source; a celestial body similar to a star that is intensely bright.

**radiation belt.** Zone around a planet that contains high-speed charged particles. The radiation belts around Earth are called *Van Allen belts.*

**radio telescope.** Device for collecting radio waves emitted from space.

**red shift.** Shift toward the red end of the spectrum caused by a body moving away from an observer.

**reentry.** Return to the atmosphere of Earth from space.

**remote manipulator system.** U.S. space shuttle's mechanical arm. It is used mainly for deploying and retrieving satellites.

**retrograde motion.** Motion in the opposite direction of Earth's rotation.

**revolution.** Orbital motion of a planet or satellite about its primary.

**Roche's limit.** Closest point to which a satellite can approach its primary without being pulled apart by the tidal effects of the gravitational fields of the primary.

**rocket.** Device that internally generates a stream of gases or particles to propel itself.

**rotation.** Turning of an object on its axis.

**satellite.** Small body orbiting a larger one.

**scintillation.** Irregular variation in the brightness of a star caused by variations in the density of the clouds of gases in Earth's atmosphere. This makes stars appear to twinkle.

**solar flare.** Explosion on the sun's surface.

**solar wind.** Electrically charged particles emitted by the corona.

**solstices.** Two points at which the sun is at its maximum distance from the equator. These two points correspond to the longest and shortest days of the year.

**space station.** Satellite designed for long-term use by several different teams.

**space transportation system.** Official name of the space shuttle.

**spectroscope.** Instrument that breaks down light into its colors.

**spectrum.** Band of different wavelengths that has been produced by separating the light or other electromagnetic radiation.

**suborbital.** Space mission that leaves the atmosphere but returns to Earth without going into orbit.

**sunspot.** Dark area of relatively cool temperatures on the sun's surface.

**supercluster.** Cluster of clusters of galaxies.

**supernova.** Exceptionally bright nova caused by the explosion of a star during the final stage of its development.

**terrestrial planets.** Planets with orbits within the orbit of Jupiter: Mercury, Venus, Earth, and Mars.

**trajectory.** Path that a rocket or spacecraft takes, especially the path after the propulsion engine has been jettisoned and the spacecraft is in free fall.

**transit.** Passing of a planet between Earth and the sun so that the planet can be seen crossing the face of the sun.

**umbra.** Darkest part of a shadow, as in an eclipse.

**Van Allen belt.** *See* **radiation belt.**

**Vernier engine.** Small motor used to steer booster rockets during flight or a spacecraft attempting to land on a planet.

**wane.** Decrease in brightness.

**wax.** Increase in brightness.

**white dwarf.** Small, extremely dense star that emits only a faint glow.

## For Further Reference

Asimov, Isaac
*The Universe*
Walker and Co.
Chetty, P.R.K.
*Satellite Technology and its Applications*
TAB Books
Jastrow, Robert
*Red Giants and White Dwarfs*
Harper & Row
Pasachoff, Jay M. and
Menzel, Donald H.
*A Field Guide to the Stars and Planets*
Houghton Mifflin

Sagan, Carl
*Cosmos*
Random House
Shipman, Harry L.
*Humans in Space:*
*Twenty-First Century Frontiers*
Plenum Press
Smith, Arthur
*Planetary Exploration*
Patrick Stevens
Spangenburg, Ray and Moser, Diane
*Opening the Space Frontier*
Facts on File

# Sports and

# Entertainment

# Sports

Sports has become an important part of modern life. Millions compete in amateur events, and tens of millions keep track of major professional sports. Sports stars are often major public figures, and some have later served with distinction in government and business. This section provides brief introductions to the most popular American games, beginning with the most widely followed team sports and concluding with major individual events. The major sports have sections on the history, the principal rules, and the current major competitions. Where possible, important records have been included. In each case, brief dictionaries of terms used in the sport have been included.

# Baseball

Baseball evolved from *rounders*, an old British game in which a ball was hit with a stick. The American Alexander Cartwright wrote the first rules of baseball, sketched the first diamond, and organized the first team, the New York Knickerbockers. The first baseball game was played in 1846 on a picnic field in Hoboken, New Jersey, between the Knickerbockers and a team called the New York Nine. The Knickerbockers lost, 23-1.

In 1869 the Cincinnati Red Stockings became baseball's first professional team. Soon other pro teams were formed. The National League was organized in 1876, and in 1901 the year-old American League began challenging the National League for fans. The first World Series was played in 1903, with Boston of the American League defeating Pittsburgh of the National League, five games to three.

The modern major league baseball season lasts from early April to the beginning of October. There are now 30 teams, 16 in the National

League, 14 in the American League. Each league is divided into Eastern, Central, and Western divisions. At the end of the season the leaders of each division and a single "wild card" team hold two playoff rounds to determine the league champion. Then the two league champions play a best-four-out-of-seven World Series to determine the year's national champion.

In July, an All-Star game is played between the two leagues. The starting lineups are determined by the votes of fans. The teams are managed by the managers of the previous season's pennant winners. These managers choose reserve players and the pitching staff for the game.

In addition to the major leagues, there are a number of minor leagues, ranging from Class-A through Class-AAA, the latter for players almost ready for major league competition. High schools and colleges also field varsity teams. Younger players participate in such organized leagues as Little League, Babe Ruth League, American Legion baseball, and others.

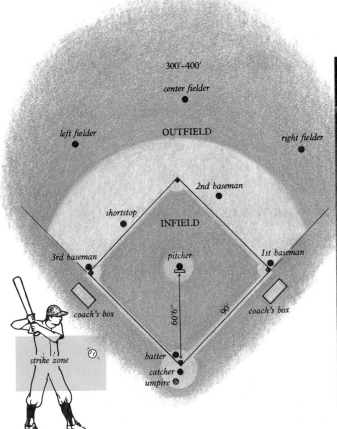

Baseball is one of America's favorite sports, both to watch and to play.

**Rules.** Baseball teams consist of nine players per side. In the American League, the pitcher does not bat for himself. His turn at the plate is taken by a tenth man, the *designated hitter,* who does not play in the field. The fielders are the pitcher, catcher, first baseman, second baseman, shortstop, third baseman, left fielder, center fielder, and right fielder. They are positioned as shown in the diagram. The bases are fixed 90 feet apart, while the pitching rubber is located 60 feet 6 inches from the plate. The outfield area varies from stadium to stadium.

At the beginning of the game, the home team takes the field while the visiting team is at bat. The batter stands in the *batter's box* (left or right side) located alongside home plate. A batter may be *put out* in several ways: if the pitcher delivers three *strikes* (pitched balls that cross some portion of the plate between the knees and armpits) that the batter does not hit or hits foul (out of the playing area); if the batter hits a ball, fair or foul, that is caught before it touches the ground; if the batter hits the ball on the ground and a fielder throws it to first base before the batter reaches the base. Base runners may be put out if they are tagged with the ball when not touching a base; or

in certain circumstances, if the ball is thrown to a fielder touching the base that the runner must reach. If a base runner and a batter are put out on the same play, it is called a *double play.*

A batter may reach first base safely if the pitcher delivers four *balls* (pitches not within the strike zone); if the batter is struck by a pitched ball; if he hits the ball into fair territory (within the foul lines) and it is not caught on the fly or thrown to first base before he arrives there. If the ball is hit far enough, the batter can try for more than one base. A ball hit over the fence in fair territory is a *home run.*

When runners are on first and second base, or when the bases are "loaded" (runners on first, second, and third), they must try to advance to the next base when a fair ground ball is hit. However, when a base immediately *behind* a runner is not occupied, he is not forced to run to the next base. On fly balls (fair or foul), a base runner returns to his original base but he can try to advance after the ball is caught.

Baseball umpires determine whether a pitched ball is a strike or a ball, whether batted balls are fair or foul, and whether a base runner is safe or out.

# Reading a box score

A surprising amount of information is detailed in a baseball box score. Only a knowledge of baseball abbreviations is necessary in order to read one:

| | | | |
|---|---|---|---|
| ab | at bat | r | runs scored |
| h | hit | rbi | runs batted in |
| avg. | batting average | E | error |
| DP | double plays | LOB | left on base |
| 2B | two base hits | 3B | three base hits |
| HR | home runs | SB | stolen bases |
| S | sacrifice | IP | innings pitched |
| ER | earned runs | BB | bases on balls |
| SO | strikeouts | ERA | earned run average |
| L | losing pitcher | W | winning pitcher |
| dh | designated hitter (American League only) | S | save |

The symbols after players' names show their position in the field.

The team lineups at the top of the box score show the performance of each player at bat. The paragraph after the lineups gives information about other aspects of the game—fielding, extra base hits, base running.

**VISITORS**

| | ab | r | h | rbi | avg. |
|---|---|---|---|---|---|
| Able—1b | 4 | 0 | 1 | 0 | .256 |
| Baker—2b | 3 | 1 | 1 | 0 | .277 |
| Charlie—3b | 3 | 0 | 0 | 0 | .301 |
| David—ss | 4 | 1 | 1 | 2 | .321 |
| Easy—lf | 4 | 0 | 1 | 0 | .250 |
| Fox—cf | 4 | 0 | 0 | 0 | .226 |
| George—rf | 4 | 1 | 0 | 0 | .304 |
| Henry—c | 4 | 0 | 2 | 1 | .282 |
| Inger—dh | 4 | 0 | 0 | 0 | .223 |

**HOME TEAM**

| | ab | r | h | rbi | avg. |
|---|---|---|---|---|---|
| John—1b | 4 | 1 | 1 | 0 | .213 |
| King—2b | 4 | 0 | 0 | 0 | .244 |
| Long—3b | 4 | 1 | 1 | 1 | .276 |
| Mike—ss | 3 | 0 | 1 | 0 | .282 |
| Norman-lf | 4 | 0 | 2 | 1 | .248 |
| Oscar—cf | 4 | 1 | 1 | 1 | .199 |
| Peter—rf | 4 | 0 | 0 | 0 | .302 |
| Quick—c | 3 | 1 | 2 | 0 | .254 |
| Roger—dh | 3 | 0 | 1 | 1 | .238 |

E—King. DP—Home Team, 2. LOB—Visitors 5, Home Team, 7. 2B—Henry. 3B—Roger. HR—David. SB—George.

| | | R | H | E |
|---|---|---|---|---|
| VISITORS: | 200 100 000 = | 3 | 6 | 0 |
| HOME TEAM: | 000 110 02x = | 4 | 9 | 1 |

**VISITORS:**

| | ip | H | R | ER | BB | SO | ERA |
|---|---|---|---|---|---|---|---|
| Sugar—L | 7 1/3 | 8 | 4 | 4 | 2 | 2 | 4.18 |
| Tommy | 2/3 | 1 | 0 | 0 | 0 | 0 | 3.56 |

**HOME TEAM:**

| | ip | H | R | ER | BB | SO | ERA |
|---|---|---|---|---|---|---|---|
| Uncle—W | 8 | 6 | 3 | 2 | 1 | 4 | 3.26 |
| Victor—S | 1 | 0 | 0 | 0 | 1 | 0 | 2.82 |

Next comes the line score—the score by inning in condensed form. The last lines give detailed information about the pitchers. This game was played by American League rules, so the pitchers do not appear in the batting lineup.

# The Major Leagues

## National League

| East | Central | West |
|---|---|---|
| Atlanta Braves | Chicago Cubs | Arizona Diamondbacks |
| Florida Marlins | Cincinnati Reds | Colorado Rockies |
| Montreal Expos | Houston Astros | Los Angeles Dodgers |
| New York Mets | Milwaukee Brewers | San Diego Padres |
| Philadelphia Phillies | Pittsburgh Pirates | San Francisco Giants |
| | St. Louis Cardinals | |

## American League

| East | Central | West |
|---|---|---|
| Baltimore Orioles | Chicago White Sox | Anaheim Angels |
| Boston Red Sox | Cleveland Indians | Oakland Athletics |
| New York Yankees | Detroit Tigers | Seattle Mariners |
| Tampa Bay Devil Rays | Kansas City Royals | Texas Rangers |
| Toronto Blue Jays | Minnesota Twins | |

## Lifetime records

*Highest batting average:*
| | |
|---|---|
| Ty Cobb (1905-1928) | .367 |
| Rogers Hornsby (1915-1937) | .358 |

*Most home runs:*
| | |
|---|---|
| Henry Aaron (1954-1976) | 755 |
| Babe Ruth (1914-1935) | 714 |

*Lowest earned run average:*
| | |
|---|---|
| Ed Walsh (1904-1917) | 1.82 |
| Addie Joss (1902-1910) | 1.88 |

*Most victories (pitcher):*
| | |
|---|---|
| Cy Young (1890-1911) | 511 |
| Walter Johnson (1907-1927) | 416 |

*Most consecutive games played:*
| | |
|---|---|
| Cal Ripken, Jr. (1982-1998) | 2632 |
| Lou Gehrig (1925-1939) | 2130 |

## Season records *(since 1900)*

*Highest batting average:*
| | |
|---|---|
| Rogers Hornsby (1924) | .424 |
| Nap Lajoie (1901) | .422 |

*Most home runs:*
| | |
|---|---|
| Mark McGwire (1998) | 70 |
| Sammy Sosa (1998) | 66 |
| Mark McGwire (1999) | 65 |
| Sammy Sosa (1999) | 63 |
| Roger Maris (1961) | 61 |
| Babe Ruth (1927) | 60 |

*Lowest earned run average:*
| | |
|---|---|
| Dutch Leonard (1914) | 1.01 |
| Three-Finger Brown (1906) | 1.04 |

*Most victories (pitcher):*
| | |
|---|---|
| Jack Chesbro (1904) | 41 |
| Ed Walsh (1908) | 40 |

## Team records *(since 1900)*

*Most pennants won:*
| | |
|---|---|
| New York Yankees | 37 |
| Brooklyn/Los Angeles Dodgers | 18 |

*Most World Series won (began 1903)*
| | |
|---|---|
| New York Yankees | 26 |
| St. Louis Cardinals | 9 |
| Philadelphia/Kansas City/ Oakland A's | 9 |

## Manager records

*Most pennants won:*
| | |
|---|---|
| Casey Stengel (1934-1965) | 10 |
| John McGraw (1899-1932) | 10 |

Joe DiMaggio

# Dictionary of baseball

Ken Griffey, Jr.

Cal Ripken, Jr.

Sammy Sosa

**assist.** Fielding help in putting out an opponent. A player who fields a ground ball and throws to first base to put out a batter is credited with an assist.

**balk.** An illegal move by a pitcher when there are runners on base. All base runners advance one base.

**batting average.** A decimal obtained by dividing a batter's number of hits by his number of official at bats. A batter getting 3 hits in 10 at-bats is batting .300.

**bull pen.** Where pitchers warm up before coming in to pitch.

**bunt.** A ball hit gently into the infield. It is most often used to advance a base runner. *See also* sacrifice.

**change-up.** A pitch delivered with less speed than a fast ball or slider.

**fielder's choice.** A situation where a fielder may put out either a base runner or the batter.

**force play.** A play in which the ball is thrown to a base ahead of a base runner to force him out.

**infield fly.** If a batter hits a fly to the infield when there are base runners on first and second, or first, second, and third, and not more than one out, the batter is out automatically. Otherwise, an infielder could drop the ball intentionally, then make a double or triple play.

**leadoff man.** The first batter in the batting order, or in an inning.

**passed ball.** A pitched ball that gets past the catcher that he could have stopped.

**pinch hitter.** A batter substituted for the player scheduled to bat. The batter who is being replaced may not reenter the game.

**pitchout.** A pitch deliberately delivered wide of the plate in order to give the catcher freedom to throw to a base to put out a runner.

**pull hitter.** A batter who "pulls the ball." A left-handed batter pulls the ball to right field, a right-handed hitter pulls to left field.

**run-down.** A situation in which a base runner is trapped off base, and two (or more) infielders try to tag him out.

**sacrifice.** A bunt with a runner on base and less than two out in which the runner advances a base but the batter is put out at first.

**sacrifice fly.** A fly ball with less than two out that allows a runner on third base to tag up after the out and score.

**signals.** The third base coach uses hand signals to relay the manager's orders. A catcher uses finger signals for various types of pitches to be delivered by the pitcher.

**squeeze play.** Trying to score a runner from third base by means of a batter's bunt.

**switch hitter.** A batter who can bat left-handed and right-handed.

**utility man.** A substitute who can play several positions.

**wild pitch.** A pitch delivered by a pitcher that is so wide of the plate (high, low, outside, inside) that the catcher has no chance to block it.

**windup.** The pitcher's motion before he throws the ball.

# Football

American football, first played in the 1800's, is a relative of soccer and rugby. Early football was a violent game, with few rules and much pushing, punching, and piling on. Serious injuries were common. Early in the 1900's, President Theodore Roosevelt threatened to ban the game unless the violence was lessened. The forward pass, legalized in 1906, was a step in that direction. Additional rules have since been added to minimize injuries, but they still occur.

**College football.** The first intercollegiate football game (really more like a violent soccer game) was played between Rutgers and Princeton universities on November 6, 1869. Other schools became interested in the game and it spread throughout the United States. College football today is governed by the National Collegiate Athletic Association (NCAA). Most universities are members of various *conferences,* such as the Ivy League, the Big Ten, the Pacific Ten, the Southwest Conference, and numerous others. Some schools, such as Notre Dame, elect to remain independent and belong to no conference. The college football season runs from early September to mid-December, with the best teams participating in post-season games.

**Professional football.** Professional football was born on August 31, 1895, in Latrobe, Pennsylvania, when Latrobe played against the neighboring town of Jeanette. Other pro teams were formed, and in 1920 the National Football League (NFL) was organized. Several rival leagues have merged with the NFL or gone out of business.

The professional football season begins with an exhibition schedule in August. The regular season starts early in September and lasts until mid-December, after which a series of playoffs determine the pro football championship.

**Post season play.** At the conclusion of the regular college season, various teams are invited to play in "bowl" games. The oldest of these is the *Rose Bowl,* in Pasadena, California. Others of major importance are the *Sugar Bowl* in New Orleans, Louisiana, the *Orange Bowl* in Miami, Florida, and the *Cotton Bowl* in Dallas, Texas.

At the conclusion of the regular professional season, ten teams participate in a series of play-

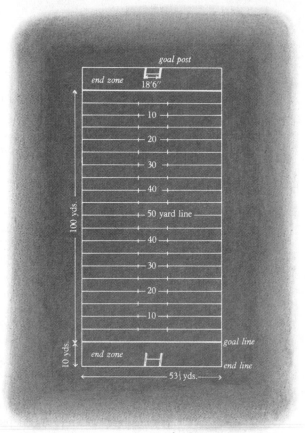

*A football field is 120 yards long and 53⅓ yards wide.*

off games. They include six division champions plus two "wild card" teams from each conference—the teams with the next best record. These playoffs determine the champion of each conference, and the two champions clash in the annual *Super Bowl* to determine the championship of professional football.

## Rules.

Football teams are composed of eleven players per side, with frequent substitutions permitted. The modern football is made of grainy plastic material, about 11 inches long from point to point and just over 21 inches in circumference in the middle.

The field measures 120 yards long by 53⅓ yards wide. The actual playing area is 100 yards long, with 10-yard *end zones* at each end. White stripes run across the width of the field at 5-yard intervals. The mid-field line is the 50-yard line, with other lines numbering down toward the *goal lines.* At the back of each end zone is the goal post, the target for kickers on certain scoring plays.

The game begins with one team kicking the ball to the other, then trying to tackle the ball carrier, who is protected by blockers. The spot where the runner is tackled or steps out of bounds becomes the *scrimmage line*. The team with the ball has four tries (downs) to advance the ball 10 yards or more. Its aim is to move the ball into the opposing team's end zone for a *touchdown*, worth 6 points. Failure to gain at least 10 yards in four tries results in loss of the ball. Usually, when a team has used three downs and has little chance to gain the remaining yards, it will *punt* (kick) the ball away, thus giving up possession to the other team.

A team may advance the ball by running or passing. A team may score via a *place kick* (field goal, worth 3 points); a similar kick after a touchdown has been scored (*conversion*, worth 1 point); running or passing the ball over the goal line following a touchdown (worth 2 points in college football only); or grounding an opponent with the ball behind his own goal line (*safety*, worth 2 points). Teams can be penalized yardage for various infractions of rules, including unnecessary roughness and pass interference. Penalties vary from 5 to 15 yards.

College and professional football games are divided into four 15-minute quarters. The clock is stopped when a runner steps out of bounds, a forward pass is incomplete, or a team calls a time out.

**Football positions.** The offensive team *must* have a seven-man line at the line of scrimmage: two ends, each eligible to receive a forward pass, two tackles stationed inside the ends, two guards stationed inside the tackles, and a center who snaps the ball to his quarterback. The offensive backfield may use several different formations (straight-T, slot-T, split-T, etc.). Usually, the quarterback is positioned directly behind the center. Behind him are the halfback and the fullback. The flanker back is usually split to one side of the offensive line. All backfielders are eligible to receive a pass.

The defensive team can use various formations, but most often (especially in professional football) there are four linemen, three linebackers, two cornerbacks, and two safety men. The linemen generally rush the ball carrier; backfield men stay back watching for passes.

*Football is a popular high school sport.*

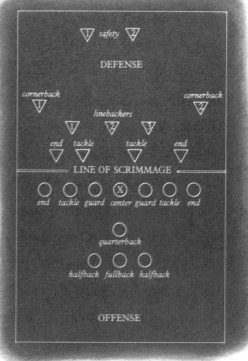

*The lineup for a play from scrimmage.*

# National Football League roster of teams

## American Conference

*Eastern Division*
Buffalo Bills
Indianapolis Colts
Miami Dolphins
New England Patriots
New York Jets

*Central Division*
Baltimore Ravens
Cincinnati Bengals
Cleveland Browns
Jacksonville Jaguars
Pittsburgh Steelers
Tennessee Titans

*Western Division*
Denver Broncos
Kansas City Chiefs
Oakland Raiders
San Diego Chargers
Seattle Seahawks

## National Conference

*Eastern Division*
Arizona Cardinals
Dallas Cowboys
New York Giants
Philadelphia Eagles
Washington Redskins

*Central Division*
Chicago Bears
Detroit Lions
Green Bay Packers
Minnesota Vikings
Tampa Bay Buccaneers

*Western Division*
Atlanta Falcons
Carolina Panthers
New Orleans Saints
St. Louis Rams
San Francisco 49ers

*The Green Bay Packers' Brett Favre*

# Professional football records

*Super Bowl victories:*
5—Dallas Cowboys, 1972, '78, '93, '94, '96
5—San Francisco 49ers, 1982, '85, '89, '90, '95
4—Pittsburgh Steelers, 1975, '76, '79, '80
3—Oakland Raiders, 1977, '81, '84
3—Washington Redskins, 1983, '88, '92
3—Green Bay Packers, 1967, '68, '97
2—Miami Dolphins, 1973, '74
2—New York Giants, 1987, '91
2—Denver Broncos, 1998, '99
1—New York Jets, 1969
1—Kansas City Chiefs, 1970
1—Baltimore Colts, 1971
1—Chicago Bears, 1986
1—St. Louis Rams, 2000
1—Baltimore Ravens, 2001

*Yards gained rushing:*

| | | |
|---|---|---|
| 1. Walter Payton | 16,726 |
| 2. Barry Sanders | 15,269 |
| 3. Emmitt Smith | 15,166 |

*Most yards gained rushing, one season:*
Eric Dickerson (1984)  2,105

*Yards gained passing:*

| | |
|---|---|
| 1. Dan Marino | 61,361 |
| 2. John Elway | 51,475 |
| 3. Warren Moon | 49,325 |

*Most yards gained passing, one season:*
Dan Marino (1984)  5,084

*Yards gained receiving:*

| | |
|---|---|
| 1. Jerry Rice | 19,247 |
| 2. James Lofton | 14,004 |
| 3. Henry Ellard | 13,777 |

*Most yards gained receiving, one season:*
Jerry Rice (1995)  1,848

**Sports**

Red Grange

# Dictionary of football

Coach Vince Lombardi

Dan Marino

Joe Montana

**audible.** A shouted signal changing an offensive play at the line of scrimmage before the ball is snapped.

**blitz.** A charge at the ball carrier by members of the defensive backfield.

**bootleg.** A fake handoff by the quarterback to another running back, in which the quarterback keeps the ball; also called "keeper."

**clip.** An illegal block in which an offensive player blocks a defensive player from behind.

**draw play.** A play in which the quarterback drops back as if to pass, then suddenly hands off to a running back who has been pretending to block for him.

**endlines.** White lines at the rear of both end zones.

**end zone.** Touchdown area. It runs the width of the field and is 10 yards deep.

**extra point.** The point after touchdown by place kick.

**fair catch.** When a team punts or kicks off the ball, the receiver may elect not to attempt to run with the ball but merely to catch it. He raises his arm overhead to signal "fair catch." No tackler may touch him, but if the receiver fumbles the ball, an opponent is permitted to recover it if possible.

**fumble.** Drop the ball.

**hand-off.** The handing of the ball from the quarterback to a running back.

**huddle.** Circle of players ready to receive instructions or signals between plays.

**in motion.** A running back on the offensive team may run laterally, parallel to the line of scrimmage before the ball is snapped. He is "in motion."

**line of scrimmage.** An imaginary line, the "no man's land" about a foot wide, between the offensive and defensive lines before the ball is snapped.

**offside.** When an offensive or defensive lineman crosses the line of scrimmage before the ball is snapped. The offender's team is penalized 5 yards.

**play action pass.** A fake handoff to a running back by the quarterback, who then passes the ball.

**punt.** A kick by the offensive team when it has not gained 10 yards in three of its four tries.

**roughing.** When a kicker has kicked the ball away, or a passer has passed the ball, he cannot be hit. If he is, a penalty for roughing is assessed.

**safety.** When an offensive player in possession of the ball is tackled behind his own goal line, the defense has scored a safety, worth 2 points.

**shotgun.** A formation in which the quarterback stands about 5 yards behind his center. It is almost always a passing formation.

**touchback.** When the ball is grounded by a team in its own end zone on a punt or kickoff reception or on the interception of a pass, a touchback is called: the team takes possession of the ball at its 20-yard line.

**zone defense.** A strategy in which each defensive backfield player is responsible for a definite area or "zone."

# Basketball

Basketball, the most widely played team sport in the world, was invented by Dr. James Naismith, an instructor at the International Young Men's Christian Association Training School (now Springfield College) in Massachusetts, in 1891. Naismith fixed peach baskets 10 feet off the ground at both ends of the gym, devised a set of rules, and used a group of students as players.

Today, nearly all American colleges field varsity teams. Men's professional basketball is played under the auspices of the National Basketball Association (NBA) and women's professional basketball is played under the auspices of the relatively new Women's National Basketball Association (WNBA). The college sport is governed by the National Collegiate Athletic Association (NCAA).

**Postseason play.** The most important postseason tournament in college basketball is the NCAA tournament, which includes the best independent and conference teams. Regional eliminations among 64 teams are held in March, and the final 4 teams play an elimination tournament early in April. The NCAA champion is usually considered the nation's best team.

In NBA basketball, the best teams in each of the divisions compete in a post-season tournament culminating in a championship playoff between the two remaining clubs.

## Rules.

The size of a basketball court varies. It can be no larger than 94 by 50 feet and no smaller than 74 by 42 feet. The inflated basketball is made of leather or rubberized plastic material, measures between $29\frac{1}{2}$ and 30 inches in circumference, and weighs between 20 and 22 ounces. Baskets, affixed to a backboard, are 10 feet above the floor.

A basketball team consists of five players: two guards, two forwards, and one center. The object of the game is to score points by throwing the ball through the hoop of the opponent's basket, which counts 2 points. A ball thrown through the hoop from behind the *3-point line* scores 3 points. Foul shots, taken from the *free throw line,* count 1 point each.

The game begins with a center jump as the referee tosses the ball up between the opposing

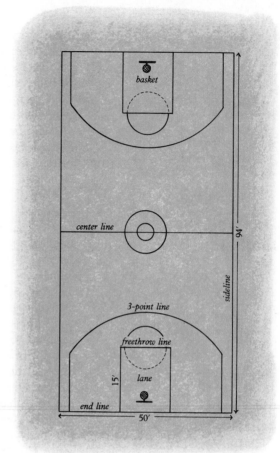

*A regulation basketball court.*

centers at mid-court. They leap, trying to tap the ball to a teammate. The ball is advanced by passing from one player to another or by bouncing the ball on the run (dribbling). Following a score of any kind, the opposing team puts the ball in play from behind its own end line.

Free throws are awarded for personal or technical fouls. Personal fouls include pushing, hacking (interfering with an opponent's arm in the act of shooting), and tripping. The fouled player is awarded one or two foul shots depending on the situation. Technical fouls are awarded for unsportsmanlike conduct, delay of a game, or abuse of an official. Technical violations by the offensive team cause the ball to be awarded to the other team. These violations include double dribbling (dribbling, holding the ball, then dribbling again), traveling (running without dribbling), or remaining in an opponent's foul lane too long.

Time of play varies. High-school games consist of four 8-minute periods. College games consist of two 20-minute periods. Professional games consist of four 12-minute periods.

# National Basketball Association

## Eastern Conference

| Atlantic Division | Central Division |
|---|---|
| Boston Celtics | Atlanta Hawks |
| Miami Heat | Charlotte Hornets |
| New Jersey Nets | Chicago Bulls |
| New York Knicks | Cleveland Cavaliers |
| Orlando Magic | Detroit Pistons |
| Philadelphia 76ers | Indiana Pacers |
| Washington Wizards | Milwaukee Bucks |
| | Toronto Raptors |

## Western Conference

| Midwest Division | Pacific Division |
|---|---|
| Dallas Mavericks | Golden State Warriors |
| Denver Nuggets | Los Angeles Clippers |
| Houston Rockets | Los Angeles Lakers |
| Minnesota Timberwolves | Phoenix Suns |
| San Antonio Spurs | Portland Trail Blazers |
| Utah Jazz | Sacramento Kings |
| Vancouver Grizzlies | Seattle SuperSonics |

# Women's National Basketball Association

## Eastern Conference

| | |
|---|---|
| Charlotte Sting | Miami Sol |
| Cleveland Rockers | New York Liberty |
| Detroit Shock | Orlando Miracle |
| Indiana Fever | Washington Mystics |

## Western Conference

| | |
|---|---|
| Houston Comets | Portland Fire |
| Los Angeles Sparks | Sacramento Monarchs |
| Minnesota Lynx | Seattle Storm |
| Phoenix Mercury | Utah Starzz |

# Dictionary of basketball

Shaquille O'Neal

**assist.** When a player passes to a teammate who scores, the passer is credited with an assist.

**back court.** The defensive part of the court for each team.

**bonus shot.** An extra free throw awarded to a team when its opponents have committed a certain number of fouls in a period of play.

**charging.** Personal contact by one player who moves against an opponent who is not moving. Usually, it is an offensive foul.

**fast break.** A quick attack after a score or a rebound.

**foul out.** After a college player has committed five personal fouls, he fouls out and must leave the game (six fouls in pro basketball).

**goal tending.** A defensive violation in which the defender taps a shot from the basket or backboard while the ball is descending toward the basket.

**loose foul ball.** A foul committed by a player when neither team is in possession of the ball.

**press.** Playing defense closely against the opposing team.

**screen.** An offensive play in which one player takes position between the player in possession of the ball and the guarding player.

**technical foul.** An infraction of the rules that is not a personal foul. Failure to report to the officials when entering the game and abusive language are examples.

**tip-in.** A leaping tap of an unsuccessful shot, resulting in a score.

**twenty-four-second rule.** A rule in pro basketball requiring the team in possession to take a shot within 24 seconds or lose possession to the other team.

# Hockey

There are hockey leagues for even the youngest players.

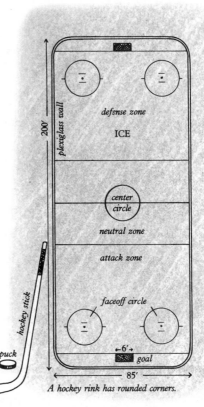

A hockey rink has rounded corners.

Ice hockey in crude form was first played by soldiers of the Royal Canadian Rifles stationed near Kingston, Ontario, Canada, during the 1850's. In 1879, W.F. Robertson and R.F. Smith devised some rules based on field hockey and other goal games. By the 1890's hockey had spread to the northern United States.

In 1917 the National Hockey League (NHL) was formed. The championship trophy of the NHL is the Stanley Cup, first offered in 1893 by Canada's governor-general, Lord Stanley of Preston. Ice hockey is one of the major sports of the winter Olympics.

## Rules. Hockey rinks vary in size, but the average is 200 feet long by 85 feet wide. The rink is surrounded by a 4-foot wall topped by plexiglass, which allows spectators to see the game while being protected from errant pucks. Ten feet from each end of the rink are goals with nets affixed to them. The goal measures 4 feet high by 6 feet wide. The rink is divided into three zones, the one nearest a team's goal being their defense zone, the middle the neutral zone, and the far-

thest the attack zone. The puck is made of hard rubber and is an inch thick by 3 inches in diameter. Sticks are not more than 53 inches long, with a "blade" not more than $14\frac{3}{4}$ inches wide.

Teams consist of six players: three forwards, two defensemen, and a goalkeeper. Games are divided into three 20-minute periods, with a change of goals after each period. Games can (and often do) end in ties, but in playoff and championship games, the winner is decided in overtime play, with the first team to score winning.

Play begins with a *face-off*. The referee drops the puck at center ice between the two centers. The puck is batted along the ice with the sticks. No player except the goalkeeper may touch the puck with his gloved hand. If a player crosses the blue line ahead of the puck, an offside is called, and a new face-off occurs.

Penalties are assessed for various infractions, such as tripping, high sticking, spearing, slashing, or other unnecessarily rough play. The player committing the violation must leave the ice for a specified time (2 minutes or more) and his team must play "short-handed."

# National Hockey League

## Eastern Conference

| Atlantic Division | Northeast Division | Southeast Division |
|---|---|---|
| New Jersey Devils | Boston Bruins | Atlanta Thrashers |
| New York Islanders | Buffalo Sabres | Carolina Hurricanes |
| New York Rangers | Montreal Canadiens | Florida Panthers |
| Philadelphia Flyers | Ottawa Senators | Tampa Bay Lightning |
| Pittsburgh Penguins | Toronto Maple Leafs | Washington Capitals |

## Western Conference

| Central Division | Northwest Division | Pacific Division |
|---|---|---|
| Chicago Blackhawks | Calgary Flames | Anaheim Mighty Ducks |
| Columbus Blue Jackets | Colorado Avalanche | Dallas Stars |
| Detroit Red Wings | Edmonton Oilers | Los Angeles Kings |
| Nashville Predators | Minnesota Wild | Phoenix Coyotes |
| St. Louis Blues | Vancouver Canucks | San Jose Sharks |

## Dictionary of hockey

Wayne Gretsky

**assist.** A player gets an assist when he passes the puck to a teammate who scores. Two or more players can be credited with an assist on the same scoring play.

**bench minor penalty.** A penalty in which a player must sit in the penalty box even though he did not commit a foul. If a club official (coach, etc.) uses profanity or otherwise interferes with play, the referee can impose a penalty. The coach can designate a player to serve the penalty.

**blue line(s).** The line(s) dividing each attack zone from the neutral zone.

**change on the fly.** While play is going on, a whole new forward line enters the game while the other line returns to the bench.

**face-off circle.** One of four circles in the corners of the rink where face-offs occur after icing, offside, and other minor violations.

**forecheck.** To check an opponent in his own defensive zone.

**hat trick.** A player's scoring of three goals in one game.

**icing.** Intentionally shooting the puck across the center line and over the opponent's goal line. A face-off results, in a circle near the offending team's goal.

**offside.** A violation in which a player crosses into his team's attack zone ahead of the puck. Play is suspended and a face-off occurs.

**penalty shot.** A free shot on goal. Only the goalkeeper is permitted to block the shot.

**power play.** When one team is short-handed, the opposing team sets up special plays to take advantage of its greater numbers.

**red line.** The line across the rink dividing the playing area in half.

**washout.** The disallowance of a goal because of a foul or other infraction.

# Soccer

Soccer is the most popular spectator sport in the world. Except in America, it is usually known as "football." The Chinese played a crude form of the game about 2500 years ago, calling it "tsu chu," meaning "kicking a ball with the foot." The Romans called their version of the game "harpastum," and it was played with an inflated pig's bladder. According to legend, in medieval times Danish raiders invaded an English town and the people fought off the Danes until help arrived from London. The Danish leader's head was cut off and kicked through the town. Since the incident occurred on Shrove Tuesday, that event has been celebrated annually with a kicking game.

Soccer was a rough game at first with few rules. In 1846 Cambridge University formulated a set of rules that eliminated some of the rugged aspects, and in 1863, representatives of eleven clubs met to form the Football Association in England. Not until 1890 did officials take complete control of the game.

Several other kicking games are relatives of soccer, including American football, Gaelic football, Irish hurling, and rugby. International soccer is governed by the *Federation Interna-*

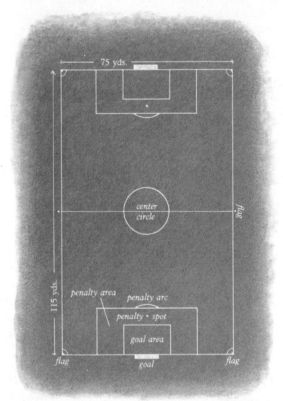

*A soccer field is about as long as a football field, but more than 20 yards wider.*

*tionale de Football Association.* Soccer's version of the World Series is the World Cup match, held every four years, which pits teams from many nations against each other. The final

*One of the most popular games around the world, soccer is only recently beginning to attract large numbers of players and fans in the United States.*

games of the World Cup Series are watched by more than a billion people on television. In 1994 the United States was the site of the Men's World Cup Series, and in 1999 it hosted the Women's World Cup Series.

# Rules.

A soccer field is 115 yards long by 75 yards wide. The ball is kicked into play from a line at midfield. At each end of the field is a goal backed by a net, 24 feet wide, 8 feet high, and 3 feet deep. The object of the game is to put the ball into the opponent's goal. The soccer ball is 27 to 28 inches in circumference and weighs 14 to 16 ounces. A game lasts 90 minutes, divided into two 45-minute periods.

A soccer team consists of eleven players: five forwards, three halfbacks, two fullbacks, and a goalkeeper. Only the goalkeeper may use his or her hands; the others may control the ball using their feet, knees, torso, or head. Substitutions are usually made only in case of injury.

There are relatively few rules in soccer. An attacking player cannot get between the ball and the opponents' goal unless there are at least two defenders between him or her and the goal. If not, an offside is called and the defensive team gets the ball. The rule does not apply if the ball was last touched by an opponent.

There are three basic types of "free kicks" in soccer. One is the *indirect* free kick, awarded in cases of offside, intentionally blocking or charging an opponent not in possession of the ball. The indirect free kick is taken at the point at which the infraction occurred, but the ball must be played by a teammate before it is kicked at the goal. A *direct* free kick is awarded for more serious infractions, such as charging from behind, tripping, hitting, holding, etc. The ball may be kicked directly at the goal, defenders must be at the goal, and all defensive players must be at least 10 yards from where the ball is kicked. If a foul is committed inside the penalty area (see diagram), a *penalty* kick is awarded. The ball is placed on the penalty spot and the kicker shoots for the goal with only the goalkeeper defending.

If a game ends in a tie, an overtime period is played in which the first team to score wins. If two overtime periods are played with no scoring, the tie stands. In the North American Soccer League, a "shootout" is held. Each team takes five penalty kicks, and the team with the most goals wins.

## Dictionary of soccer

Pelé

**corner area.** The small arc at the corners of the field from which corner kicks are taken. A corner kick is used to put the ball in play after the ball has gone over the goal line and out of play if it was last touched by a player defending that goal.

**dribbling.** Advancing the ball with a series of short kicks.

**goal kick.** When the attacking team kicks the ball over its opponent's goal line, the goalkeeper gets the ball and may kick it far downfield.

**half volley.** A ball kicked just as it is bouncing up from the ground.

**screening.** Keeping a player's body between an opponent and the ball.

**tackle.** Using the feet to try to take the ball away from an opponent.

**throw-in.** When the ball goes across the touch line, possession is awarded to the opponent of the last player to touch the ball. The throw-in is made with an overhand motion using both hands.

**touch line.** The sidelines running the length of the field.

**trapping.** Gaining control of the ball using some part of the body other than the hands or arms.

**volley.** A ball kicked while it is still in the air.

# Tennis

Some crude forms of paddle-and-ball games were played before the Christian era in ancient civilizations such as those in Egypt, Greece, Rome, and Mexico. The French of six centuries ago enjoyed a court game called "Jeu de Paume," and other European countries tried similar games (*see also* Wall and net games on page 346).

During the 1860's and 1870's there was a renewed interest in sports, but most were only for men. People wanted a game both sexes could enjoy. In 1873 Walter C. Wingfield of England devised some rules for a "net game" that was the basis for *lawn tennis.* It spread to France, the United States, and other countries. Many changes were made in Wingfield's rules, including the shape of the court (an hourglass in his rules).

The game dropped "lawn" from its name and gained popularity through the early 1900's. Then during the late 1960's and 1970's the game's popularity increased when television began featuring world-class matches. It was during that time that amateurs and professionals were allowed to compete in the same "open" tournaments. The four great tournaments, constituting a "grand slam of tennis," are Wimbledon (the British Open), the U.S. Open, and the Australian and French championships. Today's professionals play in tournaments that offer huge sums of money to the winner.

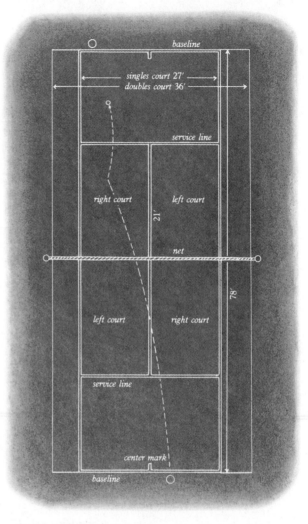

The diagram shows the path of a first serve.

## Major tennis victories (since 1945)

*British Open, men's and women's singles:*

| | |
|---|---|
| Won 9 times: | Martina Navratilova, 1978, '79, '82, '83, '84, '85, '86, '87, '90 |
| Won 7 times: | Steffi Graf, 1988, '89, '91, '92, '93, '95, '96 |
| | Pete Sampras, 1993, '94, '95, '97, '98, '99, 2000 |
| Won 6 times: | Billie Jean King, 1966, '67, '68, '72, '73, '75 |
| Won 5 times: | Bjorn Borg, 1976, '77, '78, '79, '80 |
| Won 4 times: | Louise Brough, 1948, '49, '50, '55 |
| | Rod Laver, 1961, '62, '68, '69 |
| Won 3 times: | Maureen Connolly, 1952, '53, '54 |
| | Maria Bueno, 1959, '60, '64 |
| | Margaret Smith Court, 1963, '65, '70 |
| | John Newcombe, 1967, '70, '71 |
| | Chris Evert Lloyd, 1974, '76, '81 |
| | John McEnroe, 1981, '83, '84 |
| | Boris Becker, 1985, '86, '89 |

*United States Open, men's and women's singles:*

| | |
|---|---|
| Won 6 times: | Chris Evert Lloyd, 1975, '76, '77, '78, '80, '82 |
| Won 5 times: | Margaret Smith Court, 1962, '65, '69, '70, '73 |
| | Jimmy Connors, 1974, '76, '78, '82, '83 |
| | Steffi Graf, 1988, '89, '93, '95, '96 |
| Won 4 times: | Maria Bueno, 1959, '63, '64, '66 |
| | Billie Jean King, 1967, '71, '72, '74 |
| | John McEnroe, 1979, '80, '81, '84 |
| | Pete Sampras, 1990, '93, '95, '96 |
| Won 3 times: | Margaret Osborne DuPont, 1948, '49, '50 |
| | Maureen Connolly, 1951, '52, '53 |
| | Ivan Lendl, 1985, '86, '87 |

Steffi Graf

336

**Rules.** A tennis ball is an inflated, hollow rubber ball with a tight flannel covering, weighing 2 to $2\frac{1}{16}$ ounces and measuring $2\frac{1}{2}$ to $2\frac{5}{8}$ inches in diameter. Rackets are oval shaped and strung with nylon or gut. Tennis courts may have surfaces of grass, clay, asphalt, or concrete. Each surface subtly affects the strategy of the game.

The court is rectangular, 78 feet long and 27 feet wide for singles, extending to 36 feet wide for doubles. A net strung across the center of the court is 3 feet 6 inches high (see diagram). A 2-inch white line running parallel to the net 21 feet from it on each side marks off the *service area*.

A match is divided into points, games, and sets. At least 4 points must be won in order to win a game, but it is necessary to win each game by at least 2 points. Three of the points have a determinate number: the first is called "15," the second "30," the third "40." The fourth point is called "game." No points (zero) has a special name—*love*. If a game comes to be tied at 40, the score is "deuce." The next player to win a point has the "advantage." If he wins the next point, he has won the game.

A set is won by the first player to win six games and lead his opponent by at least two games. Until recently, if a set were tied at six games all, a player had to win two games in a row to win the set. One tournament match in the 1940's went to 59–57. Today, most tournaments have a tie-breaker, a special game for use when the set is tied at six all.

In a tie-breaker, players alternate serve. There are two types of tie-breakers. In the 9-point or "sudden death" version, the first player to score 5 points wins the game and the set. The 12-point tie-breaker, used in major tournaments, requires that a player score at least six points and be ahead of his opponent by two points to win. If the game is tied at six, it is at deuce, and continues until one player gains a 2-point advantage.

A match consists of a maximum of three sets in women's and doubles matches (first player to win two wins the match); in major men's tournaments, there are a maximum of five sets (first player to win three).

The game begins when one player, with both feet behind the baseline, serves the ball diagonally into the service area of his opponent. A ball not landing in the proper service court, or one that hits into the net, is called a *fault*. Two consecutive faults loses the point. A ball hitting the net but bouncing into the service court is called a *let* and is served over. After serving from the right, the server serves from the left, and continues alternating until the game is over. The player who hits the ball into the net or outside the confines of the court loses the point.

## Dictionary of tennis

Pete Sampras

**ace.** A serve that an opponent finds impossible to return.

**advantage.** The point scored after deuce.

**backhand.** A stroke in which the player who is right-handed hits the ball from the left side (and vice versa for a left-handed player).

**break service.** When a player wins a game against his opponent's serve.

**forehand.** A stroke in which a right-handed player hits the ball from the right side (and vice versa for a left-handed player).

**ground stroke.** A ball hit after it has bounced.

**half volley.** A ball hit immediately after it has bounced and is on the rise (also called pick-up).

**lob.** A ball arched high into the air over the opponent's head.

**rally.** Hitting the ball back and forth across the net until one player loses the point.

**smash.** A hard overhand stroke.

**volley.** A stroke, usually made near the net, in which the ball has not bounced.

# Golf

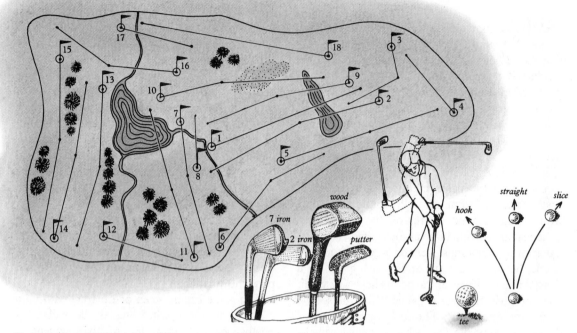

*The layout of a typical 18-hole course* (left), *representative clubs* (center), *and a diagram showing a hook and a slice, common golfing faults* (right).

Golf probably began as a team field game, called *paganica*, played by the Romans. There is no record as to when the first hole was introduced, but an illustrated book published in the year 1500 shows golfers standing around a hole.

The Scots were the first to formalize the game. In 1754 the St. Andrews Society of Golfers established a set of rules. The United States Golf Association (USGA) was organized in 1894; it offered a national championship tournament, the National Open. The U.S. Amateur tournament and a women's amateur tournament followed shortly.

For many years golf was considered "a rich man's game," but after World War II the game began to boom. Many public courses and less expensive private courses made the game affordable for millions of new players.

Tournament golf is governed in the United States by the USGA, and in England by the Royal Academy of Golf Clubs (St. Andrews, Scotland). The Professional Golfers Association (PGA) was formed in 1916. Although there are many tournaments during a year, the four that make up the "grand slam" of golf are the U.S. Masters Tournament, the PGA, the U.S. Open, and the British Open. In addition, there are im-portant tournaments for women, such as the Ladies PGA, and team matches, such as the Walker Cup (the United States vs. Great Britain and Ireland) and the Ryder Cup (for professionals of the United States and Great Britain).

## Rules.
Golf rules are quite uniform, except for the ball. By U.S. rules, the ball is 1.68 inches in diameter; the British ball is slightly smaller.

A golf course can be any size, varying from about 7000 to 7800 yards from the first tee to the 18th hole. Interspersed over all courses are many *hazards,* such as sand traps, bodies of water, high grass, or clumps of trees. A "round" of golf consists of 18 holes. *Par* for each hole may be three, four, or five strokes, depending on the distance from tee to hole.

A player is permitted a maximum of 14 clubs in his bag. Usually they consist of four *woods* (which years ago had wooden heads but now usually have steel heads), nine *irons*, and a *putter*, the last club used, to stroke the ball into the hole.

Different types of penalties add strokes to a golfer's score. Penalties are accrued for replacing a lost ball (often when it drops into a water hazard), moving a ball (even unintentionally), hitting a ball with an object other than a club, etc.

# Major golf victories (since 1945)

*United States Open:*
    Won 4 times: Ben Hogan, 1948, '50, '51, '53
                    Jack Nicklaus, 1962, '67, '72, '80

*PGA Tournament:*
    Won 5 times: Jack Nicklaus, 1963, '71, '73, '75, '80

*U.S. Masters Tournament:*
    Won 6 times: Jack Nicklaus, 1963, '65, '66, '72, '75, '86
    Won 4 times: Arnold Palmer, 1958, '60, '62, '64
    Won 3 times: Sam Snead, 1949, '52, '54
                    Gary Player, 1961, '74, '78
                    Nick Faldo, 1989, '90, '96

*U.S. Women's Open:*
    Won 4 times: Betsy Rawls, 1951, '53, '57, '60
                    Mickey Wright, 1958, '59, '61, '64
    Won 3 times: Babe Zaharias, 1948, '50, '54
                    Susie Maxwell Berning, 1968, '72, '73
                    Hollis Stacy, 1977, '78, '84
    Won 2 times: Louise Suggs, 1949, '52
                    Donna Caponi, 1969, '70
                    JoAnne Carner, 1971, '76
                    Betsy King, 1989, '90
                    Patty Sheehan, 1992, '94
                    Annika Sorenstam, 1995, '96

Betsy King

# Dictionary of golf

Tiger Woods

**ace.** A hole-in-one.

**address.** A player's position as he prepares to hit the ball.

**approach.** A stroke following the drive from the tee, intended to get the ball close to or onto the green putting surface.

**birdie.** Scoring one stroke under par for a hole.

**bogey.** Scoring one stroke over par for a hole. Two strokes over par is a double bogey, three is a triple bogey, etc.

**bunker.** A sand trap.

**caddie.** The person carrying the golfer's bag of clubs.

**chip shot.** A short approach shot, toward the green.

**divot.** A piece of turf torn from the ground by a stroke.

**dog leg.** A hole with a fairway that turns to the left or right.

**duffer.** An inept golfer.

**eagle.** Scoring two strokes under par.

**fairway.** A corridor between tee and green where the grass is closely cropped. Higher grass on either side is called the rough.

**fore.** The warning cry called out by a golfer so that others on that fairway know a ball is being hit in their direction.

**green.** The area of close-cut grass surrounding the hole.

**handicap.** A system of rating golfers. It is a method of "spotting" less skilled golfers a number of strokes against more skilled golfers.

**hook.** For a right-handed golfer, a drive that curves from right to left.

**lie.** The position of the ball after it has been hit and stops rolling.

**pitch.** A short approach shot.

**putt.** A stroke made on the putting green with the putter, intended to drop the ball into the hole.

**scratch golfer.** A skilled golfer who has no handicap.

**slice.** For a right-handed golfer, a ball that curves from left to right.

**tee.** A small wooden or plastic peg, inserted into the ground, on which the ball is placed before driving off. Also, the area from which the golfer tees off.

**whiff.** To swing and miss the ball completely.

# Olympics

The first Olympics were held in the Olympic Valley of Greece in 776 B.C. They only lasted a day and consisted of a 200-yard (one *stade*) race. The first champion was Coroebus of Elis, a young cook. The games grew and prospered in the years after 776, but by Roman times they had become a travesty. The emperor Nero was declared the winner of the chariot race, for example, even though he fell out of the cart. "Professional" athletes were entered. At last, in 394 A.D., the games were outlawed by Theodosius I, the Christian emperor of Rome.

**Modern games.** During the 1800's A.D., German archaeologists uncovered the area in Greece that had been the site of the temples and stadium of the ancient Olympics. A French scholar, Baron Pierre de Coubertin, visited the excavation and was so impressed that he began a campaign to have the Olympics restored. He was successful, and in 1894 the "new" or "modern" Olympiad was held in Athens, Greece. Athletes from 13 nations competed. The United States' "unofficial" team won nine out of the twelve track and field events held that year. The new Olympics were a success. It was decided that future Olympics should be held in different cities of the world rather than in Greece.

The Olympics have been held every four years since 1896 with only a few exceptions. A special Olympics was staged in Athens in 1906; all events were canceled in 1916 owing to World War I, and in 1940 and 1944, owing to World War II. The 1980 Olympics were boycotted by the United States and many other nations to protest the invasion of Afghanistan by the Soviet Union.

Over the years the Olympics have changed greatly. Women first competed in 1910, but they were only allowed to compete in golf, an event no longer part of the Olympics. In 1928 they were permitted to take part in track and field. There were no winter Olympics until 1924, when they were first held in Chamonix, France. Many additional events have been added.

## Sites of modern Oympic Games

| Year | Summer games | Winter games |
| --- | --- | --- |
| 1896 | Athens, Greece | |
| 1900 | Paris, France | |
| 1904 | St. Louis, USA | |
| 1906 | Athens, Greece | |
| 1908 | London, England | |
| 1912 | Stockholm, Sweden | |
| 1920 | Antwerp, Belgium | |
| 1924 | Paris, France | Chamonix, France |
| 1928 | Amsterdam, Holland | St. Moritz, Switzerland |
| 1932 | Los Angeles, USA | Lake Placid, USA |
| 1936 | Berlin, Germany | Garmische-Partenkirchen, Germany |
| 1948 | London, England | St. Moritz, Switzerland |
| 1952 | Helsinki, Finland | Oslo, Norway |
| 1956 | Melbourne, Australia | Cortina d'Ampezzo, Italy |
| 1960 | Rome, Italy | Squaw Valley, USA |
| 1964 | Tokyo, Japan | Innsbruck, Austria |
| 1968 | Mexico City, Mexico | Grenoble, France |
| 1972 | Munich, Germany | Sapporo, Japan |
| 1976 | Montreal, Canada | Innsbruck, Austria |
| 1980 | Moscow, USSR | Lake Placid, USA |
| 1984 | Los Angeles, USA | Sarajevo, Yugoslavia |
| 1988 | Seoul, S. Korea | Calgary, Canada |
| 1992 | Barcelona, Spain | Albertville, France |
| 1994* | | Lillehammer, Norway |
| 1996 | Atlanta, USA | |
| 1998 | | Nagano, Japan |
| 2000 | Sydney, Australia | |
| 2002 | | Salt Lake City, USA |
| 2004 | Athens, Greece | |
| 2006 | | Turin, Italy |

*Starting in 1994, Olympic summer and winter games were staggered at two-year intervals.

*Olympic women's hockey, U.S. vs. Canada*

**Olympic sports.** Olympic events fall into two categories, team sports and individual sports. Among the team sports are basketball, field hockey, rowing, soccer, volleyball, and water polo during the summer games; bobsled and ice hockey during the winter games. Figure skating can be an individual sport, or the competitors can be a man and woman paired for the event. Bobsleds can have two or four sledders. Women and men do not compete in all the same sports. For example, women do not box, wrestle, or compete in the decathlon.

It is not required that the host nation have all the possible sports; some, in the past, have been dropped and then reinstated. The decathlon, an individual competition in ten track and field events, is an outstanding event in any Olympiad. The most grueling race, the marathon, is the traditional conclusion of the summer games. The race is named for the legendary feat of Phidippides, a Greek warrior who ran from Marathon to Athens with news of victory.

Today the Olympics are a major international event attracting competitors from more than 100 nations. Cities from around the world seek the honor of playing host.

## Olympic events

### Summer Games

*Men*

| | |
|---|---|
| Archery | Rowing |
| Badminton | Shooting |
| Baseball | Swimming |
| Basketball | Table Tennis |
| Boxing | Taekwondo |
| Canoeing/Kayaking | Tennis |
| Cycling | Track and Field |
| Diving | Triathlon |
| Equestrian | Volleyball |
| Fencing | Water Polo |
| Field Hockey | Weight Lifting |
| Football (Soccer) | Wheelchair Events |
| Gymnastics | Wrestling |
| Handball | Yachting |
| Judo | |

*Women*

| | |
|---|---|
| Archery | Shooting |
| Badminton | Softball |
| Basketball | Swimming |
| Canoeing/Kayaking | Synchronized Swimming |
| Cycling | Table Tennis |
| Diving | Taekwondo |
| Equestrian | Tennis |
| Fencing | Track and Field |
| Field Hockey | Triathlon |
| Football (Soccer) | Volleyball |
| Gymnastics | Water Polo |
| Handball | Weight Lifting |
| Judo | Wheelchair Events |
| Pentathlon | Yachting |
| Rowing | |

### Winter Games

*Men*

| | |
|---|---|
| Biathlon | Luge |
| Bobsled | Skiing |
| Curling | Ski Jumping |
| Figure Skating | Snowboarding |
| Ice Hockey | Speed Skating |

*Women*

| | |
|---|---|
| Biathlon | Luge |
| Bobsled | Skiing |
| Curling | Snowboarding |
| Figure Skating | Speed Skating |
| Ice Hockey | |

# Other sports

## Auto racing.
Auto racing began in Europe in 1894 with a series of town-to-town races. In 1895 a group of cars raced between Chicago and Evanston, Illinois. All these were relatively minor events. The first important American race was run in 1903 on a 3-mile track at Grosse Pointe, Michigan. The driver was Barney Oldfield; the builder of the car was Henry Ford. Since then auto racing has become a popular sport throughout the world, with different types of cars competing in various races.

*Grand Prix* events are staged over courses in Holland, France, England, Italy, Mexico, and other countries. Drivers compete through a special point system for the title of Drivers' World Championship. Only Formula I cars—"pure" racing cars—may compete in these events. The Grand Prix courses are usually several miles long and are irregular in shape, requiring drivers to negotiate a variety of curves and hills. Grand Prix races are governed by the *Federation Internationale de l'Automobile*. The American arm of the body is the Automobile Competition Committee of the United States.

*Action in the Indianapolis 500*

Many races in the United States are held on paved or dirt tracks. The most famous track is the Indianapolis International Speedway, home of the Indianapolis 500. Stock car racing features modified production cars. Stock car events are sponsored by the National Association for Stock Car Auto Races. Other types of racing, as with sports cars, are governed by the Sports Car Club of America and the United States Auto Club.

## Bowling.
Bowling was known to exist around 5000 B.C. in Egypt. Modern-type bowling was developed by the Germans about the fourth century A.D. as part of their religious services. The Dutch brought the game to America. A part of Manhattan Island is still called Bowling Green.

Bowlers try to knock down ten pins that are arranged within a 36-inch triangle. The ball travels along a lane of polished wood, 60 feet from foul line to the headpin. The lane is 42 inches wide with gutters on either side. A bowling ball can be no more than 8.59 inches in diameter or 27 inches in circumference and can weigh not more than 16 pounds. Each ball has two or three finger holes. A game consists of ten frames. A perfect score is 300, meaning that the bowler has knocked down all ten pins in each frame with his first ball. The game is under the sanction of the American Bowling Congress.

### Bowling scores

*A strike is noted by an × in the left small box; no score for that frame is entered until the bowler bowls his next two balls. The bowler receives a score of 10 for the strike plus the total pins knocked down on his next two rolls.*

| FRAME | 1 | | 2 | | | |
|---|---|---|---|---|---|---|
| you | × | 19 | 6\|9 | 28 | | |
| me | 7/ | 16 | 6\|3 | 25 | | |

*A spare is noted by a slash (∕) in the right small box. A spare earns 10 points plus the pins knocked down on the next roll.*

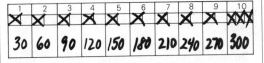

| 1 | 2 | 3 | 4 | 5 | 6 | 7 | 8 | 9 | 10 |
|---|---|---|---|---|---|---|---|---|---|
| 30 | 60 | 90 | 120 | 150 | 180 | 210 | 240 | 270 | 300 |

*A perfect game consists of 12 strikes in a row; the bowler receives a score of 30 for each frame, for a total of 300.*

# Boxing and martial arts.

Modern boxing originated in England with the adoption of the Marquess of Queensbury rules in 1867; the rules were intended to eliminate the more brutal aspects of the sport. Essentially the same rules are in effect today. Boxers compete in matches that are divided into 3-minute rounds (2 minutes in some amateur bouts), with a minute of rest between rounds. Bouts last from 3 rounds in the Olympics to 15 rounds in professional championship matches. Certain blows are outlawed, such as rabbit or kidney punches, or those struck below the waist. A bout may terminate through a decision of the judges or by a knockout. Boxers compete according to various weight limitations.

The martial arts are a series of unarmed combat styles originating in Far Eastern cultures.

| Weight classifications | |
|---|---|
| *Flyweight:* | not over 112 lbs. |
| *Bantamweight:* | not over 118 lbs. |
| *Junior featherweight:* | not over 122 lbs. |
| *Featherweight:* | not over 126 lbs. |
| *Junior lightweight:* | not over 130 lbs. |
| *Lightweight:* | not over 135 lbs. |
| *Junior welterweight:* | not over 140 lbs. |
| *Welterweight:* | not over 147 lbs. |
| *Junior middleweight:* | not over 154 lbs. |
| *Middleweight:* | not over 160 lbs. |
| *Light heavyweight:* | not over 175 lbs. |
| *Cruiserweight:* | not over 195 lbs. |
| *Heavyweight:* | over 195 lbs. |

The most popular are karate, judo, jujitsu, and kung fu. Judo is an Olympic event.

# Figure skating.

Figure skating was invented by a ballet teacher named Jackson Haines, an American who went to Vienna in 1863 to escape the Civil War and further his profession. As he watched skaters move about aimlessly, he conceived the idea of setting skating to waltz music and "dancing on ice." The first noted figure skater in America was one of his pupils, Louis Rubinstein of Canada. His exhibitions led to the formation of the Amateur Skating Association of Canada and the Skating Club of the United States.

*Speed skates* (left) *have long straight blades; figure skates are turned up at the toe for sudden starts and stops.*

In Olympic figure skating, skaters perform two programs: a short program incorporating eight different moves and a long program, in which each skater selects his or her own routine of jumps, spins, or other moves.

# Gymnastics.

Gymnastics stems from *gymna-zein*, a word of Greek origin that means to "exercise naked." Although the sport was popular during Greek and Roman days, gymnastics disappeared and did not surface again until late in the 1700's, when Frederick Jahn of Germany introduced some of the equipment now used in the sport. A few years later gymnastics was introduced in the United States. Today, the U.S. Gymnastics Federation is the governing body, in charge of events featuring side horse, calisthenics, horizontal bars, rings, parallel bars, and long horse. Gymnastics is an Olympic sport.

*Competitive gymnastics requires intense physical preparation.*

# Equestrian sports.

Horse racing can be divided into three types of events: *flat racing* around an oval track (or part of it); *harness racing* for "gaited" horses pulling light two-wheeled carts called "sulkies"; and *steeplechase racing*, in which horses must hurdle hedges and water hazards. Flat racing features *thoroughbred horses*, which are bred and trained only for racing. *Quarter horses*, an American offshoot of this breed, are trained only for short sprints. Harness racing horses are called *standardbreds* and are trained not to gallop. A *trotter* moves its left front leg and and right back leg simultaneously, while a *pacer* uses both legs on the same side of its body in unison. Steeplechase horses are bred and raced in Europe.

In equestrian events, speed is of no importance. Horses are judged on conformation, which includes height, weight, and form, soundness of bone and limb, training and fitness. Horses compete in jumping events, leaping hurdles of various heights. *Dressage* is an obedience event. Responding to barely perceptible movements by the rider, the horses execute various maneuvers and gaits.

*Jumping fences is part of many equestrian events.*

# Skiing.

Skiing is by far the most popular of all winter sports. Recreational skiing began in Austria toward the end of the 1700's, but competitive skiing started in Norway during the middle of the 1800's. Modern competitive skiing, as sanctioned in the Olympics, consists of Alpine and Nordic events.

Alpine events include the *downhill*, a run down a course in the fastest possible time. Some courses are 2 miles long. The *slalom* is shorter than the downhill. "Gates"—a set of two flags of the same color—are set in a zigzag pattern down a slope. The skier must pass through the gates in the fastest possible time. The *giant slalom* and the *super-g* are shorter than the downhill but longer than the slalom. A giant slalom race consists of two runs, a super-g one run.

Nordic events include *jumping*, in which the skier zooms down an inclined ramp and off its lip into the air. Jumps are judged for form and distance. *Cross-country* races are run over courses that include level, uphill, and downhill stretches. *Nordic combined* competitions include ski jumping and cross-country racing.

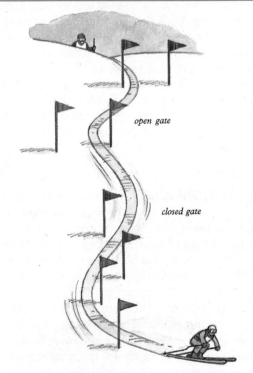

*open gate*

*closed gate*

*A slalom course: a winning skier must follow the irregular course through the "gates" and finish in the best time.*

**Sports**

# Swimming and diving.

Although humans have probably always known how to swim, the first nation to take swimming seriously was Japan, where the emperor ordered schools to compete against each other in that sport. However, the English developed swimming on a worldwide basis, beginning in the 1800's. Modern swimming uses four basic strokes in competition: freestyle (usually the Australian crawl), backstroke, breaststroke, and butterfly. In Olympic competition, races vary from 50 to 1500 meters.

"Fancy" diving began in England in 1905. Modern divers use both a stationary platform and a springboard. There are three classifications of dives: the layout (a swan dive); the pike (a jackknife); and the tuck (contained in somersaulting). Divers are judged on the difficulty and form of their dives.

*pike*

*layout*

*tuck*

*Three basic diving positions*

# Track and field.

Track events consist of running various distances, from short sprints (100 meters) to middle distances (400 to 1500 meters) to the marathon (26 miles, 385 yards). Also included in track events are *hurdles*—races in which runners leap obstacles placed in each running lane at regular intervals. Hurdles vary in height from 2 feet 6 inches to 3 feet 6 inches, according to the length of the race and the sex of the competitors.

Field events include the throwing of the *discus*, a flattened disk made of wood with a metal center and rim. It is thrown with one hand The *shot put* is a brass or iron ball, which is also thrown with one hand, with a pushing-out motion. The *javelin* is a spear thrown overhand for the greatest distance. Jumping events include the *high jump*, in which the jumper takes a short run at a bar that he or she must clear, and the *long jump*, in which the jumper takes a running start to a set mark and then leaps forward, landing in a sand pit. In the *pole vault*, the jumper takes a running start and uses a flexible pole to vault high up and over a bar. In the *triple jump* (also called hop-skip-and-jump), the athlete gets a running start to a mark, then leaps forward and lands on his takeoff foot, leaps forward again landing on the opposite foot, and leaps ahead a third time landing on both feet.

*Track events include the hurdles (above); field events include the high jump (below).*

Handball is a game popular in many cities. It is played against a wall by two or four players, who hit the ball with the flat of their hands.

# Wall and net games. 
Wall and net games have a number of similarities. All involve the use of a ball of varying size that is thrown or batted either against a wall or over a net using a racket, a paddle, a kind of basket, or a gloved hand (*see also* Tennis).

**Badminton** was invented during the 1870's by British army officers. It is a simple game involving light rackets, a shuttlecock (which is mostly cork with feathers stuck into the "head"), and a net. The shuttlecock is batted back and forth over the net until a player fails to return it, allowing the opponent to score a point. Usually, 15 points wins the game.

**Handball** was invented by the Irish in the 900's. In its modern form, it is played against walls on three sides of the player. The ball is hard rubber, $1\frac{7}{8}$ inches in diameter, and weighing 2.3 ounces. Gloves are worn to protect the hands. Only the server can score points. The server puts the ball in play by serving from behind a line; his opponent attempts to return the ball against the wall. Failure to return the serve scores a point for the server. A variation of the game is played in a four-wall court.

**Jai alai** was invented in the 1600's by the Basques of the Pyrenees Mountains. It has become popular in the Philippines, Mexico, and the United States. The game resembles handball to a great extent. Instead of a glove, players use a curved basket called a cesta. The pelota (ball) is made of rubber with a layer of nylon thread; it rebounds from the wall at extremely high speeds.

**Paddle tennis** is a smaller form of lawn tennis. The court is smaller and paddles are used instead of rackets. The ball is a deadened tennis ball. Overhand smashes are outlawed. Scoring is the same as in tennis, except that there is no tie-breaker.

**Ping-Pong** (table tennis) was invented by an American named James Gibb in 1899. As now played, the game involves a table 9 feet 5 inches long, 6 feet wide, and 30 inches high. The ball is made of celluloid, the paddles are wood covered with some kind of stippled or foam rubber. The server hits the ball so that it bounces first on his side of the net, then onto the opponent's side. Failure to return gives the opponent a point. Both server and opponent can score points in Ping-Pong. Service is alternated after each 5

*Volleyball is played at all levels of skill, from pickup games on the beach and local leagues to the Olympics.*

points; 21 points wins the game. If the score is tied at 20 all, the winner must score 2 additional points.

**Racquetball** is a combination of tennis and handball. A standard four-wall handball court is used. The racket resembles the one used in tennis except that the handle is shorter. The ball is very lively.

**Squash** was invented by students at Harrow School, England, during the 1800's. A modern squash court (singles) has walls 32 feet long on the sides and $18\frac{1}{2}$ feet wide to the front. The front wall is 16 feet high. A floor service line is marked 22 feet from the front wall, and a line bisects the back court in half, similar to a tennis court. A front wall service line is marked $6\frac{1}{2}$ feet above the floor, and all serves must hit above it. Returns must hit above a metal strip called the *telltale*, 17 inches above the floor. A score of 15 points usually wins.

**Volleyball** was invented in 1895 by Dr. William G. Morgan, a YMCA instructor. A volleyball court measures 30 by 60 feet; it is divided by a net 8 feet off the floor. A team consists of six players. It is similar to tennis in that the aim is to hit the ball over the net and to try to force the opposing team to hit the ball into the net or out of bounds. Only the hands or arms may be used to bat the ball, and it may be hit only three times on the same side of the net, never twice by the same player. Only the serving team may score. Game is usually 15 points. World-class volleyball is an extremely demanding sport which is a regular Olympic event, but the game is also enjoyed as a recreation by millions.

## For Further Reference

Baker, William
    *Sports in the Western World*
    Rowman and Littlefield
Diagram Group
    *Rules of the Game: Complete Illustrated Encyclopedia of
        All the Sports in the World*
    Paddington
Ritter, Lawrence S.
    *The Story of Baseball*
    William Morrow
Sullivan, George
    *All About Football*
    Dodd, Mead

# Music

Music—along with drama and dance—is one of the performing arts. Its history runs further into the past than written language, but because it was not written down or recorded, nearly all early music is lost to us. We know, for example, that early Greek drama included music and dance as well as spoken words, but only the words have been preserved. Biblical psalms and songs may have been written to be sung with musical accompaniment, but if so, the music has been lost. In the 1500's, musicians began to perfect a means of writing down their compositions, but even these early musical manuscripts are difficult to understand, and we cannot always be certain how they sounded when performed.

Today, music is everywhere. Performers record their music, making sure that they will be remembered as long as there is recording equipment to play back their performances. Great works from the past have been recorded hundreds of times.

No special knowledge is required to listen to music, but much study is required to become a performer. The following section briefly describes the mechanics of music, the elements of musical language and notation, and the major types of music important today. A dictionary of common musical terms is also provided.

## Time line of music

| Classical music | | American music |
|---|---|---|
| **Baroque** (1700–1760) | 1700 | |
| | 1750 | |
| **Classical** (1760–1790) | | |
| **Romantic** (1790–1890) | 1800 | |
| | | **Minstrel shows** (c 1830–1890) |
| | 1850 | |
| **Modern** (1890–    ) | | **Vaudeville** (1890–1925) |
| **Sound recording** | 1900 | **Jazz** (1900–    ) |
| **Radio** (1922) | | **Musical comedy** (1925–    ) |
| **Long-play records, high fidelity** (1950) | 1950 | **Rock** (1955–    ) |
| **Stereophonic sound** (1960) | | |
| **Digital recordings** (1980) | 2000 | |

# Mechanics of music

Music consists of sound; to understand it, one must understand how sound is made.

## Vibrations.
All sound is made by vibration. If you strike a drum, the drum head vibrates, sending sound waves out through the air. If you pluck a guitar string, it vibrates, sending out similar waves. These waves, which we perceive with our ears, we call sound. When the guitar string is at rest, it looks like this:

When it is plucked, it vibrates in a wave motion, first one way, then the others:

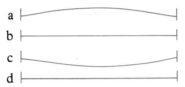

One complete movement through these stages is called a *cycle*.

## Frequency.
How high or low the guitar's sound is—its *pitch*—depends on its *frequency,* or the number of cycles it goes through in a second. A frequency of 440 cycles per second has the pitch of the A above middle C on the piano; a frequency of 220 cycles per second (half of 440) has the pitch of the A below middle C; and one of 880 cycles per second (twice 440) has the pitch of the second A above middle C.

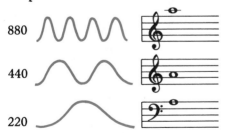

## Amplitude.
Amplitude is a measure of how far the guitar string (or other vibrating material) moves in a single cycle. If the amplitude is large, the sound is loud. If the amplitude is small, the sound is soft.

= loud
= soft

Some musical sounds, such as that of a trumpet, are steady in loudness. As long as the trumpeter's breath holds out, he can keep the sound at the same level. Other musical sounds, such as those of a guitar or piano, start out loud as the string is plucked or struck, but begin immediatey to die out or *decay*:

## Complex sounds.
Each sound maker or musical instrument has its own particular sound. The actual vibrations that cause the sounds are much more complex than the simple wave forms illustrated above. These complex vibrations give each sound maker its particular sound quality or *timbre*. Actual wave representations of familiar musical instruments are shown below.

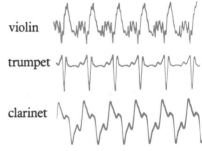

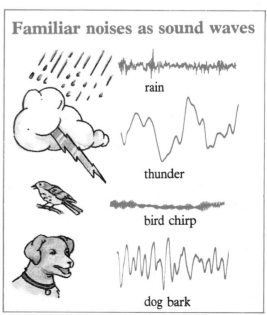

**Familiar noises as sound waves**

rain

thunder

bird chirp

dog bark

# Musical instruments

People have used hundreds of different objects to make musical sounds. The following list considers those most common today: the human voice, the four "families" of orchestral instruments, keyboard instruments, other nonorchestral instruments, and the growing number of electronic and electronically enhanced instruments.

## Human voice.

Perhaps the original musical instrument was the human voice. Vocal sound is created by forcing air between the vocal cords. A singer can vary the pitch of the voice by tightening or loosening the cords and can also vary its quality and loudness. The singer's chest and head act as a *resonator,* increasing the volume and affecting the timbre of the sound.

In general, men's voices are of lower pitch than women's. Choral groups are divided into sections by the pitch levels of the singers' voices. Men with the lowest voices are basses; men with higher voices are tenors; women with the highest voices are sopranos; women with lower voices are altos.

## Strings.

The strings are the first of the four families of orchestral instruments. They include the violin, viola, cello, and string bass. Each is normally played by drawing a bow over strings of different thickness and tautness, giving a sound of even loudness. The strings can also be plucked like those of a guitar; in that case, the sound decays rapidly. Different pitches on string instruments are produced by shortening the vibrating length of a string with a finger on the fingerboard. The wood sounding case under the strings acts as a resonator, increasing the volume of the sound and helping to give it its distinctive quality. The most valued string instruments were made in Italy in the 1700's—their rich sound has never been equaled by modern instruments. As with voices, string instruments are arranged according to their pitch from the string bass (the lowest) to the violin (the highest).

## Woodwinds.

The woodwinds include the bassoon, oboe, clarinet, flute, and piccolo. The flute and piccolo are tubes of metal or wood

## Orchestral instrument families

### Strings

### Woodwinds

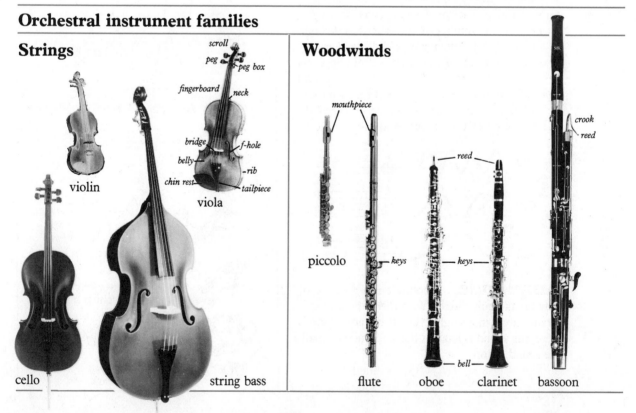

scroll
peg
peg box
fingerboard
neck
mouthpiece
bridge
f-hole
belly
rib
chin rest
tailpiece
reed
crook
reed
keys
keys
violin
viola
piccolo
bell
cello
string bass
flute
oboe
clarinet
bassoon

with small mouthpieces. The performer blows air over the hole in the mouthpiece, causing the air in the tube to vibrate, just as one blows air over the mouth of a bottle to produce a sound. The other woodwinds have mouthpieces with a reed. Performers put the reed between their lips and blow in a way that causes the reed to vibrate. Woodwind players change the pitch of their instruments by working levers that open and close holes along the length of the instruments, changing the length of the column of air inside them. The bassoon is the bass member of the woodwind family. The oboe, clarinet, and flute play in the alto and soprano range, and the piccolo has the highest range of any orchestral instrument.

## Brass.

The brass instruments include the trumpet, French horn, trombone, and tuba. Each of these instruments is a long tube of metal with a circular metal mouthpiece. Performers purse their lips and blow into the mouthpiece so that their lips vibrate. These vibrations are amplified by the long tube of air in the instrument.

Brass players change the pitch of their instruments partly by changing the tightness of their lips and partly by pressing valves that change the length of the column of air in the instrument. The trombone has a slide instead of valves to change the length of the column of air—the farther it is extended, the lower the note of the instrument. The brass instruments with the pitch range from the lowest to the highest are the tuba, trombone, French horn, and trumpet.

## Percussion.

The percussion section in an orchestra contains a wide variety of instruments that are most often used for rhythmic effect rather than for producing particular pitches or melodies. The section includes various drums, xylophone, cymbals, triangle, and special noise-making devices such as maracas and castanets. Nearly all percussion instruments are *struck* to make sound. Some percussion instruments have variable pitch (timpani, xylophone), and others do not (cymbals, snare drum). The piano is sometimes considered a percussion instrument.

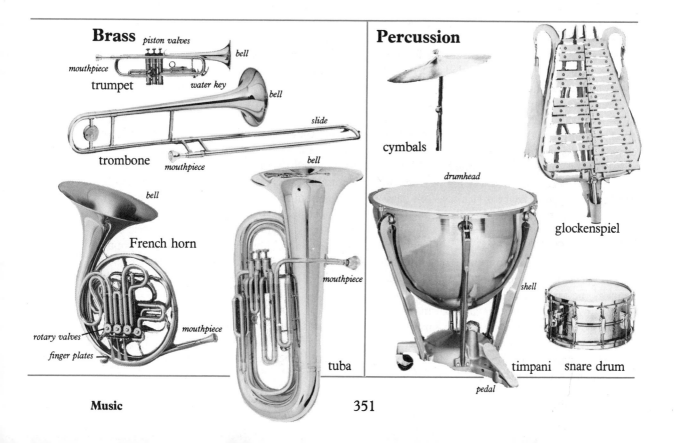

**Brass**
piston valves
mouthpiece
trumpet
bell
water key
bell
trombone
mouthpiece
slide
bell
bell
French horn
rotary valves
finger plates
mouthpiece
mouthpiece
tuba

**Percussion**
cymbals
drumhead
glockenspiel
shell
timpani   snare drum
pedal

*A classic configuration for a jazz combo includes piano, bass, saxophone, trumpet, and drums.*

# Keyboard instruments. Perhaps

the most popular solo instruments are those with a keyboard. The keyboard instruments have a much wider range of pitches than the orchestral instruments, and more than one note can be struck at a time, producing rich harmonies as well as melody.

Keyboard instruments use different methods to produce sound. The organ is a wind instrument related to the woodwinds. Pressing a note on its keyboard releases air into a pipe of a certain length and thickness, creating a woodwindlike sound. Large pipe organs may have hundreds of separate pipes, including many that have the same pitch but different sound qualities. The piano is both a percussion and a string instrument. Pressing a note on its keyboard causes a felt hammer to strike a string inside the piano.

# Other instruments. There are

many nonorchestral instruments important in music. They include such popular string instruments as the guitar and banjo, which are played by plucking the strings rather than bowing them; such woodwind instruments as the saxophone, which is widely used in jazz and in bands; and such brass instruments for band as the cornet, baritone, and sousaphone.

# Electronic instruments. The

development of electricity has produced a growing number of new musical instruments. Perhaps the most familiar is the electronic organ, which was designed to resemble the pipe organ in sound. When a key is depressed on an electronic organ, a pitch is produced by an oscillator and amplified by a speaker—there are no pipes or wind-producing mechanisms.

Other electronic keyboard instruments have been developed with a wide range of special abilities. These new instruments are called *synthesizers* and they can mimic the sounds of nearly any instrument. In addition, synthesizers can create sound qualities and effects never produced by any natural instrument or group of instruments.

Electronics has also been used to amplify many conventional instruments, creating sounds that are partly old and partly new. The electric guitar has become an important instrument in popular music, and the microphone has allowed singers to achieve new effects that would be impossible without amplification.

Finally, the tape recorder has helped modern musicians create many new musical sounds. A recording may be slowed down, speeded up, played backward, or superimposed to produce many exotic and revolutionary sound effects.

**Music**

# Materials of music

Most music has certain characteristics in common. These characteristics include melody, rhythm, and harmony. The following section explains each of them and illustrates how they are shown in traditional musical notation.

## Melody.
Melody consists of a number of pitches in a row. A melody may be long and complex or short and simple, consisting of only two or three notes.

Each pitch is represented in musical notation by a *note* placed on a staff:

The notes of the staff have letter names as shown below. They represent the pitches that can be played by all conventional instruments and are arranged on two *clefs:* the bass clef for lower pitches and the treble clef for higher pitches.

treble clef     bass clef

Any combination of pitches on the staff can create a melody. Those below are the opening pitches of "Three Blind Mice" and "Taps."

A melody may be performed by itself, or it may have accompaniment, which provides harmonies matching the melody.

## Rhythm.
Rhythm consists of several musical notes held for varying amounts of time or separated by silences called *rests.*

The major rhythmic pattern of a piece of music is shown at the beginning of the piece. The top number of the *time signature* shows how many beats there will be in a *measure*, a unit set off in written music by bar lines. The first beat of a measure is often stressed.

Two beats to the measure
Count 1-2 1-2 1-2
May be a march: left-right left-right

Three beats to the measure
Count 1-2-3 1-2-3
May be a waltz:
oom-pah-pah oom-pah-pah

The rhythmic pattern of the notes themselves is shown by the shadings of the notes and by a system of flags (see "Note values" below).
The two melodies shown earlier are both in $\frac{4}{4}$ time. The bottom number in the time signature tells what kind of note is to receive one beat. The bottom "4" in this signature says that the *quarter* note gets one count. With time signature and note values, the two melodies look like this:

---

## Pitch names

## Note values

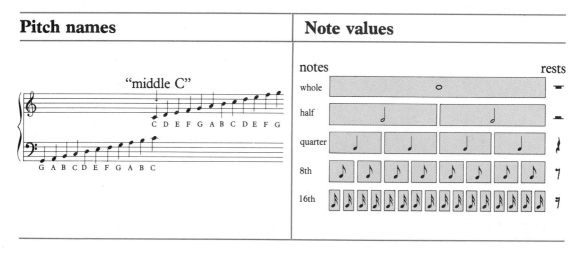

Rhythm is also affected by the speed at which the music is played—its *tempo*. Some indication of the proper speed is often given in the *tempo marking* at the beginning of the piece. Traditional Italian terms are recognized internationally by musicians. Among the most common are:

allegro: fast, lively

andante: moderately, at a walking speed

adagio: slowly

Some compositions also provide a metronome marking:

♩ = 120

This marking says that the composition should be played so that there are 120 quarter-note counts per minute.

# Harmony.
A third element of music is harmony, which consists of the sound of two or more notes played at the same time. For example, one might add a bass line to "Three Blind Mice" to create simple harmony:

Traditional harmony is based on chords—harmonious combinations of notes. Accompaniments to many simple songs may consist of only three chords:

I IV V

These may be broken up in any way. For example, the following measures are a series of I chords that could accompany the opening measures of a waltz:

Guitar accompaniments consist only of chords that are appropriate to a particular melody. Many pianists learn to accompany popular songs by following the chord patterns rather than by playing the melody.

# Other elements of music.
Among other elements of music are key, dynamics, and articulation.

**Key.** The examples given above have all been given in the key of C major. The C major scale consists of the white notes on a piano, running upward or downward from one C to the next. However, any melody may be written and performed in any of twelve major keys. For example, the opening of "Three Blind Mice" may appear as follows:

key of C        key of G        key of F

In the key of G, the F is always sharped—raised one half a step (to the next highest black note on a piano). In the key of F, the B is always flatted—lowered one half a step (to the next lowest black note on a piano).

Each major key has a *relative minor* key. A minor scale has a different, "sadder" sound. "Three Blind Mice" in the key of C minor would look like this:

The following box shows the key signatures (number of sharps or flats), key names, and relative minors for each major key.

Sharps and flats may also be used to raise and lower particular notes in a composition. When used this way, they are called *accidentals*. Other accidentals are the natural sign ( ♮ ), which tells the performer to use the natural pitch for a note that has been sharped or flatted; the double sharp ( 𝄪 ), which calls for a note already sharped to be

# Key signatures

sharp signatures

C maj.  G maj.  D maj.  A maj.  E maj.  B maj.  F♯ maj.  C♯ maj.

A min.  E min.  B min. F♯ min.  C♯ min. G♯ min. D♯ min. A♯ min.

flat signatures

F maj.  B♭ maj.  E♭ maj.  A♭ maj.  D♭ maj. G♭ maj.  C♭ maj.

D min.  G min.  C min.  F min.  B♭ min.  E♭ min.  A♭ min.

sharped still another half step; and the double flat (bb), which calls for a note already flatted to be lowered still another half-step. The relation of these accidentals is shown below:

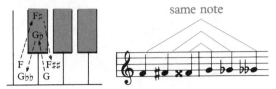

**Dynamics.** Musical notation has a system of alerting the performer to the loudness or softness desired by the composer or editor of the music. Like tempo markings, dynamic markings are in Italian. They are shown in the following table.

| | | | |
|---|---|---|---|
| *ppp* | (pianississimo) | = | as soft as possible |
| *pp* | (pianissimo) | = | very soft |
| *p* | (piano) | = | soft |
| *mp* | (mezzo piano) | = | moderately soft |
| *mf* | (mezzo forte) | = | moderately loud |
| *f* | (forte) | = | loud |
| *ff* | (fortissimo) | = | very loud |
| *fff* | (fortississimo) | = | as loud as possible |
| ———————— | (crescendo) | = | get louder |
| ———————— | (diminuendo) | = | get softer |

**Articulation.** Traditional notation may also have marks suggesting the way in which a note or series of notes should be performed. Among the articulation marks are the following:

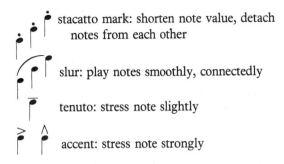

staccato mark: shorten note value, detach notes from each other

slur: play notes smoothly, connectedly

tenuto: stress note slightly

accent: stress note strongly

Traditional notation has been the way of preserving music from the distant past. Since the 1890's, however, music has been even more carefully preserved by recordings. A recording can save not only the notes and the general playing instructions, but an exact performance of a particular piece. By comparison, even the best edition of written music is only a blueprint for a performance. Modern composing synthesizers produce both a printed score and a recording.

# Kinds of music

More kinds of music are available to interested listeners today than ever before—on records, on tape, and in live performances. There are two major traditions of music, generally known as *classical* and *popular,* although the line between them is not always clear.

## Classical music. This term is often used to describe the long tradition of "serious" music from the European Middle Ages to the present. The classics are often associated with orchestral music, but they also include solo music for instruments, opera, and choral music.

**Early music.** European music grew from the music of the Christian church in the Middle Ages. The church used *chants* in its services— simple music for one voice, intoning words from the psalms or from ancient services of worship. In time, some churches added a second voice, producing a kind of harmony. By 1400, composers were writing music for four or more voices.

By the year 1600, music both for the church and for the courts of kings and nobles was highly developed. During the 1600's the pipe organ was perfected for church use. Court entertainments included the use of other instruments and the production of elaborate musical plays that gradually developed into opera and ballet. Composers wrote many pieces for two or more parts (either voices or instruments) and developed a style of music called *polyphonic,* or many-voiced.

The composer and performer who acted as a bridge between this early style and later, more "modern" styles was Johann Sebastian Bach (1685-1750). He was a great organist and composed many pieces for the organ. As a director of church music, he wrote hundreds of *cantatas* for small orchestra, solo voices, and chorus. For his wealthy patrons he wrote much instrumental music for groups of instruments that were coming to resemble the modern orchestra. The most famous of these are the six *Brandenburg Concertos.*

The other great composer of the age was George Frederick Handel (1685-1759). Although born in Germany, Handel spent most of his life in England. His greatest works were *oratorios*, dramatic works that often told a biblical story for orchestra, solo voices, and chorus. His *Messiah* is the most popular of all oratorios.

**Classic and Romantic.** By 1750, composers were tired of the complicated many-voiced music of Bach and Handel. They were looking for a simpler musical language. The result was the music of the classical period (about 1760 to 1790): symphonies, concertos for solo instruments with orchestra, and an increasing amount of music for the newly developed *pianoforte*. This instrument is an early version of the modern piano.

The classical period produced two great composers: Franz Joseph Haydn (1732-1809) and Wolfgang Amadeus Mozart (1756-1791). Haydn wrote over a hundred symphonies and scores of works for chamber groups—quartets, trios, and other small groups. The *chamber music* was played in the halls of noblemen for the enjoyment of the players and for a small audience of friends.

Mozart was a great musical prodigy who began performing in public at age five and who had written whole symphonies before he was ten. In his short life (he died at 35), he wrote symphonies, many great piano concertos, and several operas, including *The Marriage of Figaro*, perhaps the first great modern opera.

By 1790, still another style was beginning to take over from the classical style. Composers were seeking a musical language that would more nearly express their innermost thoughts and feelings. The new style came to be called Romantic, and it influenced serious musicians for more than 100 years.

The first great Romantic composer was Ludwig van Beethoven (1770–1827). His early works owed much to Haydn and Mozart, but he gradually learned to express his own tempestuous and dramatic feelings in his music. His nine symphonies are among the most important orchestral works ever written, and his 32 piano sonatas are the first great works for the modern solo instrument. Early in his career, Beethoven became almost completely deaf; he never really heard many of his great compositions performed except in his own mind.

Among later Romantic composers in Germany

*Johannes Brahms, a great orchestral composer, was also a pianist.*

were Franz Schubert, whose songs for voice and piano are still widely loved and played; Robert Schumann, a great composer for the piano; and Johannes Brahms, whose orchestral works seek to outshine even Beethoven's. The Polish-French pianist Frédéric Chopin and the Hungarian Franz Liszt wrote challenging new pieces for piano, while the Russian Peter Ilyich Tchaikovsky became a master of the symphony and other orchestral forms.

Meanwhile, opera became the great national music of Italy. Gioacchino Rossini and Giuseppe Verdi made opera perhaps the most satisfying of all musical experiences, combining great music with the color and spectacle of the stage. Late in the 1800's, Richard Wagner developed a form of grand opera in Germany, and his daring compositions greatly influenced modern composers.

**Modern period.** Since 1900, serious music has undergone rapid changes. Claude Debussy and Maurice Ravel sought to make music more like painting, seeking new "colors" and sounds in the orchestra. Igor Stravinsky's early compositions were so filled with unfamiliar timbres, rhythms, and harmonies that they caused riots in their first performances. Arnold Schoenberg and Alban Berg gave up traditional scales and harmonies and composed in a new musical language. The Hungarian Béla Bartók and others searched for folk themes and used them in new and surprising ways. Among the modern experimenters were Americans Charles Ives and Aaron Copland.

*The Beatles began with American rhythm and blues music, then added new influences to rock 'n' roll.*

## Popular music.

From earliest times, there has been a lively popular music tradition. Early church composers often used popular songs of their day as the basis for their serious compositions. During the late 1700's, musicians in many parts of Europe began to take their national folk music and ballads seriously.

The popular tradition has been especially strong in the United States since the late 1800's. It includes folk music, jazz, and rock.

**Folk music.** Immigrants to the United States brought folk music from their native countries. For example, English and Scottish folk ballads were kept and developed by isolated communities in the Appalachian Mountains until recent times. Sometimes words were changed to suit new situations, and many new tunes were developed and handed down from one generation to the next. In the 1900's, various folk music traditions contributed to revivals of "bluegrass" and country and Western music.

The blacks of the South also developed their own special folk materials. Combining African and Western forms, they created *blues, spirituals,* and a wide variety of music for dancing, from the *ragtime* of the 1890's to the later jazz and rock forms. Perhaps their greatest contribution was the development of jazz.

**Jazz.** Just how jazz came to be is not clear. By 1900, black musicians playing in clubs and on riverboats around New Orleans had created this new kind of music. It differed from both serious and popular music of the day in its intense rhythm and in its encouragement of *improvisation.* Jazz compositions were not written down; great jazz performers played by ear and improvised, never performing the same tune the same way twice. Fortunately, early efforts at sound recording have preserved some of these early jazz performances.

By the 1920's the popularity of jazz had spread far beyond the black community. European composers were studying and imitating it. George Gershwin, a composer of Broadway musicals, adapted jazz elements for "Rhapsody in Blue." His popular *Porgy and Bess* is a folk opera about black people.

The mainstream of jazz was made up of black performers. Louis Armstrong, who started with an early New Orleans band, became an international celebrity. Duke Ellington, leader of a jazz "big band," gradually became a serious and widely respected composer. Charlie "Bird" Parker developed a new kind of jazz called *bop* in the 1940's. More recent jazz giants include Miles Davis, Thelonius Monk, and Charlie Mingus.

Many jazz students believe that jazz has become a new "classical" music for the United States. At the same time, however, the language of jazz has so influenced popular American music that it is often difficult to tell where jazz ends and other popular forms begin.

**Rock 'n' roll.** Rock music came to public attention in the 1950's. Its insistent, rhythmic style probably originated in the traditions of black Americans, but a young white singer named Elvis Presley helped make rock a household word. Rock appealed to teenagers and sometimes angered their parents, but it gradually attracted a wide and knowledgeable audience. A British group, the Beatles, adopted rock, then mixed it with musical ideas from other parts of the world. Later "fusion" groups experimented with combinations of rock, jazz, and other popular styles.

**Recording.** This rapid musical development was all made possible by the art of recording. Until 1900, a musician knew about other musicians in distant places only by reputation or by written copies of their music. Today, widely available recordings allow new musical ideas and styles to spread worldwide within weeks or months. American popular music is becoming a musical tradition with an international following.

chamber music

# Dictionary of music

chords

monophonic music

polyphonic music

an octave

synthesizer

**accelerando.** Tempo marking: speed up.

**accidental.** Musical sign that instructs the player to alter the pitch of a note. The signs include sharps, flats, and naturals.

**adagio.** Tempo marking: slowly.

**allegro.** Tempo marking: quickly, in a lively mood.

**alto.** Pitch range below soprano and above tenor and bass.

**andante.** Tempo marking: moderately, at a walking pace.

**arpeggio.** Method of playing a chord, note after note from the bottom up.

**articulation.** Class of music instructions telling how notes or phrases should be played.

**Baroque.** Name for the musical period from 1600-1750 that culminated in the music of Bach and Handel.

**bass.** Lowest pitch range; a singer or instrument in this range.

**brass.** Family of instruments, including the trumpet, French horn, trombone, and tuba.

**cadenza.** Difficult, showy passage at the end of a solo or concerto for the soloist.

**cantata.** Setting of a religious text for soloists, chorus, and instruments.

**chamber music.** Instrumental music for a small group to be performed in an intimate setting.

**chord.** Three or more notes sounded at the same time; the basic unit of harmony.

**clef.** Sign at the beginning of a musical staff showing the pitch levels on that staff.

**coda.** Final section ending a work or movement.

**concerto.** Composition in three of four movements for solo instrument and orchestra.

**counterpoint.** Music in which two or more voices have melodic lines at the same time; polyphonic music.

**diatonic scale.** Traditional scale (major or minor) consisting of a combination of whole and half steps. There are seven notes between octaves (or eight including the octave); for example, C, D, E, F, G, A, B, (C). *See also* twelve-tone music; whole-tone scale.

**dissonance.** Chords or melodic intervals that are disagreeable to the ear and that tend to produce tension.

**dynamics.** Volume level of music, expressed in musical notation by terms such as *forte, piano,* etc.

**forte.** Dynamic marking: loud.

**harmony.** Sounding of two or more different tones at the same time; chords that are agreeable to the ear and tend to resolve tension.

**interval.** Distance between two tones.

**key signature.** Sharps or flats written at the beginning of a musical staff to show what key the music is in.

**largo.** Tempo marking: very slowly.

**mass.** Musical setting of the traditional Christian service of communion.

**measure.** Rhythmic unit in musical notation. Measures are separated by bar lines.

**meter.** Organization of beats into measure as dictated by a composition's time signature.

**moderato.** Tempo marking: in moderate time.

**modulation.** Changing from one key to another in a piece.

**monophonic.** Music consisting of one melodic line without accompaniment.

**octave.** Interval that contains eight steps of the conventional (diatonic) scale.

**oratorio.** Dramatic composition for soloists, chorus, and orchestra, usually on a religious theme and designed for concert performance.

**percussion.** Family of instruments that produces sounds by being struck: drums, etc.

**pitch.** Highness or lowness of a tone that can be measured in cycles per second. Pitch is shown in musical notation by the position of a note on a staff.

**presto.** Tempo marking: very fast.

**quartet.** Group of four musicians or music written for such a group. A string quartet consists of two violins, a viola, and a cello.

**rest.** Sign that corresponds to the value of a musical note and that indicates a similar period of silence.

**rondo.** Musical form in which a theme section is repeated several times, separated by contrasting sections; often used in the last movement of a sonata, concerto, or symphony.

**round.** Polyphonic song in which a second voice begins the first line as the first voice begins the second line; for example, "Three Blind Mice."

**scale.** Arrangement of tones between one note and its octave in ascending or descending order. A diatonic scale (major or minor) includes eight tones from base note to octave; a chromatic scale contains 13 notes from base note to octave.

**scherzo.** Musical form in lively $\frac{3}{4}$ or $\frac{3}{8}$ tempo, often used as the third of four movements in a symphony, sonata, or string quartet.

**sonata.** Composition in three or four movements for piano, or for solo instrument and piano; a common form in the classic and Romantic periods.

**sonata form.** Musical form in which two or more themes are stated, then developed, then repeated in their original form; often used in the first movement of a sonata, concerto, or symphony.

**soprano.** Highest of the four traditional pitch ranges; a voice or instrument that plays in this range.

**strings.** Family of instruments including the violin, viola, cello, and string bass.

**symphony.** Extended composition of three or four movements for full orchestra; a common form in the classic and Romantic periods.

**syncopation.** Strong rhythmic accents on normally weak beats; important in jazz and other popular forms.

**synthesizer.** Electronic instrument with an almost unlimited range of sound qualities or timbres.

**tempo.** Rate of speed of a composition. A general tempo is indicated by tempo markings above the staff (*allegro, andante,* etc.).

**tenor.** Pitch range above bass and below alto and soprano; a voice or instrument in this range.

**timbre.** Sound quality of a particular instrument or voice.

**time signature.** Two numbers placed after the key signature at the beginning of a piece of music showing the rhythmic organization of the piece.

**triad.** Chord with three notes: key note, third, and fifth.

**trill.** Rapid alternation between the note printed and the note above it.

**twelve-tone music.** Music using a chromatic scale with twelve notes between octaves rather than the traditional diatonic scale (which has only seven notes).

**whole-tone scale.** Scale with only whole-tone intervals consisting of only six notes from octave to octave; for example, C, D, E, F♯, G♯, A♯, (C).

**woodwinds.** Family of instruments including the piccolo, flute, clarinet, oboe, and bassoon.

## For Further Reference

Britten, Benjamin and Holst, Imogene
*The Wonderful World of Music*
Doubleday

Hurd, Michael and Scholes, Percy
*The Oxford Junior Companion to Music*
Oxford University Press

Machlis, Joseph
*The Enjoyment of Music*
W.W. Norton

Miller, Jim
*The Rolling Stone Illustrated History of Rock and Roll*
Rolling Stone Press

# Entertainment

Nearly everyone enjoys entertainment, and some people enjoy even more being entertainers—actors, comedians, dancers, singers. This section takes a brief look at the world of entertainment, from its earliest days to the present. Only in the last hundred years have we been able to record sound and pictures and to broadcast them through wire or air. These improvements have brought entertainment to every corner of the world and into most of our homes. They have also made it possible for us to store our memories. Actors and singers long dead seem to come to life again every time their films or records are played. The world of entertainment has grown tremendously, and it can teach us as well as entertain us. The first part of the section provides a thumbnail history of live entertainment—the only kind that existed until 100 years ago. The second part looks at movies, a new dramatic entertainment that has also become an art form. The third part describes radio and television, the most recent and widespread form of all.

# Live entertainment

The beginnings of popular entertainment go back to primitive societies, when dance and music, magic, and storytelling were created to celebrate the societies' rituals and gods. At first, men tried to gain control of their world through the magic of imitation. They believed that if they could create the sound of rain falling, real rain would fall. This belief in the magic of imitation gradually led to the arts of acting, theater, and popular entertainment.

**Greece and Rome.** The traditions of Western entertainment began in Greece over 2500 years ago with the development of Greek drama. Festivals were held to worship Dionysus (Bacchus), the Greek god of wine and new life, with song and dance. By the seventh century B.C., poets began to write stories for a large group of performers, known as a chorus, and a lead actor

to recite. By 500 B.C., Aeschylus added a second actor, making possible dialogue between characters. Within 50 years yet another character was added.

Even now, the plays that were written for ancient Greek theater are among the most powerful known. There were two main forms of classical Greek drama—tragedy and comedy. Tragedy tells the story of a great man who by the end of the story is destroyed by a flaw in his own character. Comedies made fun of the shortcomings of individuals and society.

There were other kinds of entertainment too. "Mimus" presented scenes from common life using stock comic characters who would act out familiar situations by improvising. The humor was often rough and crude. This form of popular entertainment appears again and again throughout history.

The Romans continued the traditions of Greece and developed other forms of entertainment as well. The beginnings of the circus appeared when conquering generals brought to Rome rare animals and strangely dressed captives from the farthest reaches of the Roman Empire. Chariot races were held and gladiators fought to the death in public arenas.

## Middle Ages.

After the fall of the Roman Empire, entertainment and drama was considered pagan and sinful by the Christian church. For hundreds of years, there is little evidence of public entertainment of any kind, but by the 1200's drama reappeared. On special occasions the church added dialogues to its service. Gradually these dialogues became more complex and theatrical. They became so popular that they began to interrupt the rest of the service, so these performances were moved out onto the steps of the church.

Trade unions or guilds took on the responsibility of producing these dramas. The themes were always religious. The stories based on the life of Christ were known as mysteries. Miracle plays told of the lives of saints. Morality plays emphasized the error of wicked ways and the triumph of virtue.

## Renaissance.

In theater, the Renaissance began in the 1500's. The theater became less religious. Interest in long lost comedies and tragedies of classical Greek and Roman theater were rediscovered and the nobles used them as models for courtly entertainments. But for popular entertainment, nothing could equal the commedia dell'arte, a refinement of the early Greek Mimus. The commedia dell'arte was performed by a traveling group of actors, each of whom played the same standard character throughout his career. The costume of each character was traditional so that the audiences could easily pick out the familiar types. There were about twelve stock characters in all, including a clown, a beggar, a vain young man, a merchant deceived by his wife, and various servants, one cunning, one witty, and one cruel and mean-spirited. There was no script for the actors, only a rough outline of what was to happen—and how the story was to end. The dialogue was made up as the actors performed, filling the story with traditional jokes, speeches, and stories. As long as each actor stayed within the limits of his character, anything was allowed. The commedia was improvised, fast-paced, and unpredictable. The actors usually performed from wooden platforms raised above the street for the general public, but the nobility also built special theaters for private performances.

## Golden age of theater.

Before the late 1500's in England, there were small bands of actors who traveled from town to town performing in the courtyards of inns and taverns. These actors offered entertainments, which included plays, songs, and dances, that became so popular that by the 1580's, special theaters resembling inn courtyards were built in London. The building of these theaters were the beginning of the golden age of Elizabethan theater. Among the writers for this theater was William Shakespeare, probably the greatest dramatist in any language. His plays were written for the general public, most of whom were neither cultivated nor learned but wildly enthusiastic nevertheless. Shakespeare created a great dramatic literature, but at the same time he provided his audience with popular entertainment of wide and lasting appeal.

In Spain and France, the 1600's also became a golden age of theater. Thousands of plays were written and performed for both the nobility and the general public. There were fewer tragedies and more comedies, satires, melodramas, and farces. Theater became a main source of diversion for the middle class and a truly popular entertainment while at the same time entering the great tradition of Western literature. For more information on the history of dramatic literature see *Literature* in Volume 2.

*A stock character from commedia dell'arte.*

# American entertainment.

Theater and entertainment were not well regarded in the early years of colonial America. Professional actors were looked upon with suspicion and mistrust and play acting was considered immoral. In New England theater was banned, but the Southern colonies were more tolerant. By 1716 the first theater in America was built in Williamsburg, Virginia. There are few records of theatrical productions before the Revolutionary War. What theater there was, was dominated by English producers and actors. At the outbreak of the war, Congress ordered that the theaters be closed because they were controlled by the English. Some states kept these anti-theatrical laws for many years after the war was over.

During the 1800's, new forms of popular entertainment grew rapidly. Every decade, thousands of immigrants arrived from different countries, each bringing his own ideas about entertainment. Scenes from Shakespearean plays were popular as well as melodramas and sentimental plays such as *Uncle Tom's Cabin*. Plays about firemen and Indians were in vogue during the 1840's and 1850's. Operas were brought from Italy and circuses began to tour from town to town. Variety shows featured comedy skits, singing, and dancing. Stars brought from Europe were in great demand. They included actors and actresses, opera singers, and variety performers.

**Medicine shows.** The advent of railroads allowed troupes of actors and musicians to easily travel from place to place, bringing entertainment to more and more people. Productions became larger and more elaborate. At the same time, many prosperous towns built theaters where these entertainments could be performed. In towns that were too small to build a theater, the entertainers would set up a tent outside of town. The traveling entertainers offered music, skits, and comedy routines and often full plays. In the middle of a performance or at the end, a "doctor" or an "Indian" would come on stage and sell patent medicine that was promised to cure almost anything. The shows that came to be called *medicine shows* were a major source of entertainment in small-town America.

**Circuses.** The circus also started to move across the country by train. There were lion tamers and elephants, high-wire artists and clowns, acrobats and magicians, music, parades, cotton candy, and sideshows. By the end of the 1800's, the circus had become big business and a circus train often had 20 cars or more. The Wild West Show was an American variation of the circus; it featured trick riding, shooting exhibitions, and Indians. The most famous of these shows was the *Buffalo Bill Cody Wild West Show*. Annie Oakley and Sitting Bull often traveled with the show.

**Minstrel shows.** The minstrel show was a new kind of variety show that made use of music and dance that had been brought to America by black slaves. The performers were all white at first, and much of the humor was at the expense of blacks. The singers and dancers appeared on stage in black-face, dressed in tuxedos and top hats. The central character and comic was called "Mr. Interlocutor." On either side of the stage were the "endmen," who were given standard names like Mr. Bones or Sambo. The comedy routines centered on the dialogue among these three characters. Behind them was the chorus. Minstrel shows reached their height of popularity in the 1880's, when some of the larger shows employed over 100 performers to tap dance and sing, joke, and fiddle. Some later minstrel shows were made up of all-black performers.

**Vaudeville.** Before the Civil War, a new kind of variety show was developed for all-male audiences. After 1865, these shows opened their doors to women and children and began to emphasize wholesome family entertainment. Dishes and sewing patterns were offered as door prizes to encourage ladies to attend. This new form came to be known as vaudeville. It consisted of many short acts introduced by a master of ceremonies, and usually included comedy skits, dancing bears, acrobats, black-face entertainers, and music. Almost anything that would keep the audience's attention was allowed on stage, no matter how silly.

Burlesque developed in the late 1860's, when vaudeville became family entertainment. Many familiar forms of American performance prospered in vaudeville, including tap dancing, the soft shoe, and the two-man comedy team. Vaudeville disappeared in the 1930's owing to the popularity of motion pictures. But some great vaudeville performers are still remembered for their later performances in radio, television, or the movies. They include George Burns and Gracie Allen, W.C. Fields, Mae West, and Jack Benny.

# Movies

The next big revolution in entertainment came about because of a new invention—the motion picture. Motion pictures made it possible for the first time to *record* a performance for viewing by hundreds or thousands of people.

In the mid-1800's, the still camera was being developed. Almost immediately there were experiments to try and make photographs appear to move. The first man to fully succeed was Thomas Edison, who invented the Kinetoscope, a small coin-operated machine that was cranked by hand and that showed the viewer a few seconds of motion, usually someone falling down or undressing.

In 1896, Edison held the first public showing of motion pictures projected onto a screen in this country. The exhibition caused a sensation. Movie houses called nickelodeons opened across the country, offering short features for a nickel. These shorts were no more than silent scenes from stage plays or vaudeville with subtitles; music was provided by a piano player in the theater. By 1910 the shorts were making more money than vaudeville and live theater together.

*Al Jolson is* The Jazz Singer *in the first full-length movie with sound. The enormous success of this pioneering movie signaled the beginning of the end of the era of the silent movie.*

## Camera language.
The American film director D.W. Griffith was the first to learn how to use the full potential of movies. His *Birth of a Nation* was the first great American screen epic. Griffith developed a technique that allowed him to place the audience into the middle of a story, thereby involving them emotionally. By using three different kinds of camera shots—the long shot, the medium shot, and the close-up—he gave the viewer a feeling of participation. The long shot was used to show the viewer location and situation at the beginning of a scene. The medium shot was then used to follow the action. The close-up could show the subtle emotion on a character's face or an important detail of the action, especially at the climax of a scene. By linking these shots together in a meaningful and rhythmic fashion, Griffith and others learned to increase the emotional pace of the story and show the action from many points of view. The film makers learned that, like a novelist, they could choose whether their audience would see all of the action in a scene or see the action only from one character's point of view.

## Sound.
The next major advance in movies came in 1927 with the addition of sound. The craft of recording sound had a history of its own, and by 1927, many American households had simple mechanical phonographs and recordings of popular or classical music. Matching sound to action on film was a difficult problem. Finally, a process was developed of placing recorded sound on movie film itself; when it was run through the projector, the sound could be amplified to match the motion on the screen.

The first major movie to use the sound-on-film process was *The Jazz Singer,* starring Al Jolson. When Jolson sat at a piano and began to sing, the theater was filled with the sound of his music. The new sound films, called "talkies," made movies more popular than ever. Movies began to replace live theater and vaudeville. Movie makers also began to explore the world of special sound effects. They found they could express the mood of a scene through the sound of birds singing or of hurricane winds. Suspense could be heightened by the intelligent use of sound as well as image.

**Color.** The new talkies were more realistic, but they were still only in black and white. Then, in 1939, *Gone With the Wind*, one of the first major movies filmed in color, was released. The beauty and realism of this film amazed audiences. *Gone With the Wind* became the most popular movie of all time. From 1939 on, movie makers learned that color, too, could be used to set a mood or create a special atmosphere.

## The golden age.

From the late 1920's until about 1950, movies were the most popular of all American entertainments. The new film industry, centered around Hollywood, California, employed thousands of people. More than half of all Americans went to the movies every week. In towns and cities across the country movie palaces were built—elaborately decorated theaters focused on a white screen. Other forms of popular entertainment disappeared. Vaudeville and traveling shows could not compete with the emotionally charged stories and musicals that were brought to town every week. Vaudeville comedians, actors, and actresses, stunt men and daredevils went to Hollywood, and many became movie stars.

## Since 1950.

The movies continue to be a major form of entertainment, but their popularity began to fall in the 1950's. When television became widespread, people began to stay home. There seemed to be less reason to go out when they could be entertained in their own living rooms. By 1980 only one American out of ten went to the movies in a given week.

At the same time, however, millions of viewers see movies every week on television. Even movies that are 40 years old continue to play on television to enthusiastic audiences. They include such classics as *The Wizard of Oz, Snow White, Gone With the Wind,* and *Casablanca*.

Movies have grown into a serious art form. New films and old by great directors are studied and admired—and often imitated by new film makers. The movies have shown that they can move an audience in many of the same ways as a great live drama or a great painting or sculpture. Even as they entertain millions around the world, they have entered the arena of serious artistic concern.

## Recent Academy awards

| 1999 | American Beauty *(comedy)* |
|------|---|
| 1998 | Shakespeare in Love *(comedy/drama)* |
| 1997 | Titanic *(drama)* |
| 1996 | The English Patient *(drama)* |
| 1995 | Braveheart *(drama)* |
| 1994 | Forrest Gump *(comedy/drama)* |
| 1993 | Schindler's List *(drama)* |
| 1992 | Unforgiven *(drama)* |
| 1991 | The Silence of the Lambs *(drama)* |
| 1990 | Dances with Wolves *(drama)* |
| 1989 | Driving Miss Daisy *(comedy/drama)* |
| 1988 | Rain Man *(drama)* |
| 1987 | The Last Emperor *(drama)* |
| 1986 | Platoon *(drama)* |
| 1985 | Out of Africa *(drama)* |
| 1984 | Amadeus *(drama)* |
| 1983 | Terms of Endearment *(drama)* |
| 1982 | Gandhi *(drama)* |
| 1981 | Chariots of Fire *(drama)* |
| 1980 | Ordinary People *(drama)* |
| 1979 | Kramer vs. Kramer *(drama)* |
| 1978 | The Deer Hunter *(drama)* |
| 1977 | Annie Hall *(comedy)* |
| 1976 | Rocky *(drama)* |
| 1975 | One Flew Over the Cuckoo's Nest *(comedy)* |
| 1974 | The Godfather Part II *(drama)* |
| 1973 | The Sting *(drama)* |
| 1972 | The Godfather *(drama)* |
| 1971 | The French Connection *(drama)* |
| 1970 | Patton *(drama)* |
| 1969 | Midnight Cowboy *(drama)* |
| 1968 | Oliver *(musical)* |
| 1967 | In the Heat of the Night *(drama)* |
| 1966 | A Man for All Seasons *(drama)* |
| 1965 | The Sound of Music *(musical)* |
| 1964 | My Fair Lady *(musical)* |
| 1963 | Tom Jones *(comedy)* |
| 1962 | Lawrence of Arabia *(drama)* |
| 1961 | West Side Story *(musical)* |
| 1960 | The Apartment *(drama)* |
| 1959 | Ben Hur *(drama)* |
| 1958 | Gigi *(musical)* |
| 1957 | Bridge Over the River Kwai *(drama)* |

*Titanic won the Academy Award for best picture in 1997.*

# Broadcasting

## Early history.

The movie and sound-recording revolution changed popular entertainment in important ways, allowing performances to be preserved and reproduced over and over again. But there was still another revolution to come. Today we call it broadcasting, and it has brought entertainment from public places into the home.

The telegraph was the first invention that allowed the instant transmission of information over long distances. Telegraph communications were in wide use by 1860. In the 1870's, the telephone allowed transmission of voices by wire, making it possible for a household to communicate with any of hundreds of other households. Perhaps some inventor would have found a way to send music and other entertainment into homes by telephone wire; but before that could happen, an even better system was developed.

## Radio.

Early radio was called "wireless." Sending messages through the air by the broadcast of electromagnetic (or radio) waves was seen as a wonderful tool for communication between ships at sea. At first, only code signals could be sent and received, but soon voice communication was also possible. Radio equipment was greatly improved during World War I (1914–1918). In 1919, a few enterprising Americans got the idea of sending music and other entertainment out over the air waves. At first, the only listeners were a few other radio technicians who had transmitting and receiving equipment. But the general public soon wanted this home entertainment, too, and inexpensive radio receivers were soon on sale.

Between 1920 and 1927, several million radio receivers were sold, and radio stations sprang up across the country. Radio executives set up the first *network*, which sent programs to scores of local stations.

**The golden age.** Radio's golden age ran from 1927 to about 1950, the same years as the golden age of movies. Radio programs were paid for by sponsors, who advertised their goods and hoped that listeners would respond by buying their products.

*Actors in an early radio drama surround the magic microphone. Their vast audiences used their imaginations to supply the details of scenery and costume that made radio drama so convincing.*

Early radio developed important new forms of entertainment: the musical variety show (using many vaudeville stars); the soap opera, a serial about the problems of everyday life that got its name because it was sponsored by soap companies; and the situation comedy, a series in which the same characters appeared each week. In addition, radio brought news and play-by-play accounts of big sports events.

In the 1930's, President Franklin Roosevelt was the first President to use radio regularly as a means of addressing all (or nearly all) Americans at the same time. His broadcasts were not called speeches; instead, he called them "fireside chats," and spoke in a quiet conversational tone. During World War II (1939-1945), radio became a major source of war news.

In the 1930's, still another improvement was being made in radio. A new way of transmitting, called *frequency modulation*, or FM for short, was invented. Beginning in the 1950's, FM transmission brought hundreds of new stations to radio. It was also chosen as the system for transmitting television sound.

*The so-called golden age of television in the 1950's produced such great television shows as "The Honeymooners."*

# Television.

The developers of radio were soon supporting research into television—transmitting pictures and sound together. A working electronic television system had been developed in 1926 by a 20-year-old inventor named Philo T. Farnsworth, but the introduction of television to home audiences was slowed first by patent lawsuits, then by World War II. After the war ended a great television boom began. Between 1946 and 1952, some 7 million sets were sold in the United States alone.

Television borrowed most of its programming from radio or from the movies. Like radio, television broadcasting was paid for by the sale of advertising. Also like radio, television offered musical variety shows, soap operas, and, especially, situation comedies. It also took many radio stars and made them television stars.

From the movies, television borrowed old movies. Old movies were the least expensive way to fill time, and they ran late at night, early in the morning, and at other off hours. Television also borrowed the most popular movie types. Westerns and action dramas were soon being made for television, bringing excitement and adventure to the home screen.

Most important, television "borrowed" radio listeners and moviegoers. At first, it seemed that radio and the movies might disappear. Many movie theaters closed, and radio stations were near bankruptcy. Soon, however, both "old" mediums learned to survive by attracting special audiences. Radio turned to music—helped by the new and improved method of transmission called FM. And film makers were free to appeal to adult audiences.

Meanwhile, television developed some new strengths of its own. It learned to broadcast sports events with great skill, even showing important plays over and over again through video recording. Television news became the most important news medium. It covered many historic events, such as a President's funeral or a moon landing, live, as it happened.

In early television, almost all shows were broadcast live. Recording techniques were crude, and filming was too expensive. New video recording made possible not only instant replay for sports, but also a new, inexpensive way to record drama and variety shows.

Television drama also grew into an important entertainment form. Camera language was

**Entertainment**

*The rise in popularity of cable television over the last decade has revolutionized television watching, providing, among other options, 24-hour news channels.*

borrowed from the movies, but it was revised to suit a smaller screen. Television was less impressive than movies in long shots showing a huge battlefield or natural panorama, but it was more effective in close-ups. Television stars became almost like friends to many viewers, appearing each week or each evening in the viewers' own homes.

**The future.** Today, broadcasting is the most important form of popular entertainment. But now it is being challenged by still newer inventions. Video playback and recording equipment make it possible for home viewers to buy or record their favorite shows. Many classic movies are already available for home viewing. This new equipment may encourage many viewers to spend fewer hours watching network offerings of situation comedies and action dramas.

At the same time, cable television may revolutionize viewing habits in another way. Cable companies offer hundreds of channels rather than three or four. They bring their programs directly into the home by cable, offering high-quality sound and picture. Cable television may offer every viewer programs on his or her special interest—sports events played on any given day,

news at any time, music or drama of any style, or special information such as stock market reports, weather, or congressional hearings. Improvements such as high definition television (HDTV) and interactive television will revolutionize broadcasting as well as viewers' habits.

Modern popular entertainment is a combination of ancient performing arts and new technology. Each time the technology changes, performers change with it, providing both pleasure and information in a form that suits the new medium. Many productions appear in many different media at once. For example, a Broadway musical may first appear as a live show in New York, then as a touring show in various cities; its music may be available on disc or tape recording. Then it may appear as a movie or as a made-for-television production. Viewers may see this new form in a movie theater or at home, by way of conventional television, cable TV, or their own videotape players.

Never in recorded history have the entertainment arts been so important in the lives of so many. Modern inventions have put nearly every person within reach of music and drama all day, every day, at home, and away from home.

animation

## Dictionary of entertainment

makeup

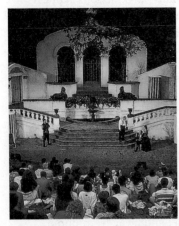
set design

**act.** (1) A main division of a play, usually broken down into one or more scenes. Modern plays often have three acts. (2) An individual performance in a variety show.

**animation.** Drawing objects on each frame of motion picture film so that when the film is run through a projector the objects will seem to move. Walt Disney has made the best known animated movies, including *Snow White* and *Cinderella*.

**audio.** (1) The sound portion of television broadcasts. (2) The equipment that plays back sound recordings.

**backdrop.** The rear curtain of a stage set; it is often painted and lighted so that it appears to be a view of the real world.

**backstage.** Behind or to the side of the stage. This is where the actors wait to go on stage. It is also where the dressing rooms are and where the stagehands, makeup artists, and lighting technicians work.

**ballet.** A dance performance that usually tells a story through dance and music alone. The ballet style was developed in the 1800's; it requires a large corps (company) of dancers and features two to eight solo dancers. One famous ballet is the *Nutcracker Suite*.

**cable television.** Television that is brought into the home by wire (cable). Cable television offers better reception, many channels and programs, and noncommercial broadcasting paid for by the user.

**cast.** All the actors and actresses in a play, movie, or television show. *To cast* a show is to find and hire the actors and actresses.

**character actor.** An actor (male or female) who plays supporting roles, portraying people of widely differing ages, backgrounds, and mannerisms.

**choreographer.** The dance director who invents the dances and teaches them to the dancers by showing them when, where, and how to move.

**chorus.** The singers and dancers in a show who do not have leading parts. In the theater they are sometimes called gypsies. After the choreographer has taught them the dances, the dance master is in charge of their performance.

**cinematographer.** The director of photography for a film. With the director, he plans how the action in a movie will be photographed, determining the placement of cameras, the length of each shot, and the lighting. During filming, he controls the operation and movement of the camera.

**comedy.** A play, movie, or TV show that is written and acted in a light or humorous way and that ends cheerfully.

**comic relief.** A comic character or situation in a play, movie, or TV show that prevents the audience from being too depressed by the more serious parts of the story.

**costume.** Special clothing required for a dramatic

production. The costume designer selects and designs the clothes. The wardrobe master/mistress makes sure that the costumes are repaired, cleaned, and available on cue. The dresser helps actors change costumes between scenes.

**cue.** A signal to an actor to begin his next line or action. If an actor misses his cue, the other actors may have to ad-lib or make up lines until he begins.

**curtain.** Most theaters have curtains between the stage and the audience. The play starts when the curtain is raised. At the end of the play, the curtain falls, marking the end. When the curtain is raised to allow the cast to accept the audience's applause, this is called the curtain call.

**director.** The person responsible for deciding how the story is to be presented, when and how the characters will move on the stage or screen, and how they will read their lines. It is the director's overall idea of the story that guides the cast and stage and film technicians in creating the performance. In the movies, the director also supervises the cinematographer and helps decide how the story will be photographed.

**dub.** In movies originally made in a foreign language, the actors' lines are recorded again in English. Special attention is given to matching the movement of the actors' lips on screen to the sound of the new language. This is called dubbing or *lip*

*synching.* Dubbing is also used when a singer's voice replaces that of an actor who cannot sing very well.

**extra.** A person in a play or movie who has no speaking part. Often he is a part of a crowd scene.

**film editor.** Movies are shot on hundreds of separate pieces of film. The job of a film editor is to assemble the movie by attaching the best pieces of film in a pattern that tells the story in the most dramatic and interesting way. If film editing is done poorly, the movie may appear jumpy or confusing.

**gaffer.** In movies, the chief electrician who designs and sets up the lighting. He works closely with the cinematographer.

**grip.** In movies and television, the person in charge of the props.

**green room.** A room backstage in a theater or television studio where actors and guests wait before going on stage. It is also used as a reception room after performances.

**laughtrack.** Prerecorded laughter added to the soundtrack of some television shows. The volume of the laughter is electronically controlled.

**lighting designer.** In the theater the lighting designer works closely with the set designer and in the movies he works closely with the cinematographer. Lighting can focus the audience's attention on specific areas of action, provide realistic atmosphere, and create moods.

**location.** Movies that are made "on location" are filmed in real places with natural surroundings, not on sets or sound stages.

**makeup.** In the theater, makeup is often exaggerated so that the expressions on the actors' faces will not wash out in the bright stage lights. In movies and television, makeup is usually less exaggerated. Makeup is an art of illusion. Men can be made into very real looking monsters, and young actresses can age 30 years between the acts of a play.

**melodrama.** An exaggerated, sentimental, and often emotional story that is neither a comedy nor a tragedy. Many television shows are melodramas.

**musical comedy.** Movies and plays in which the characters sing and dance and in which musical production numbers are the main attraction.

**network.** The original national television broadcasting companies, NBC, CBS, and ABC, and, since 1986, Fox Broadcasting. Two additional networks, UPN and WB, began operations in the 1990's.

**prime time.** The evening hours, when the greatest number of people are watching television. The most popular shows are usually broadcast during this time by the national networks.

**producer.** The person who chooses a play or screenplay, raises the money, and hires the main people involved, including the director, set designer, cinematographer, and often the stars. Since he has raised the money and is responsible for the show's success, he has the last word on all things.

**prompter.** The person who stands backstage in the theater where the actors can see him so that he can help them with their lines if they forget them.

**props.** All of the objects on the stage except the scenery. Stage props include furniture and hand props include swords or guns. The property manager makes sure that all the props are in place for the performance.

**rehearsal.** A run-through of a show without an audience. In the theater, the *dress rehearsal* is the last rehearsal; it is performed as if it were a public performance.

**repertory theater.** A theatrical company that performs several different plays during the same season, alternating them each week or each night. The same actors usually play parts in all or most of the plays.

**road show.** An entertainment that travels from town to town.

**scene.** In the theater, a subdivision of an act. Usually each scene takes place at a different time or in a different location from the scene before it. In the movies, a scene usually takes place in one location and shows one complete situation or action. However, movies can switch between two scenes that are taking place at the same time in different places.

**screenplay.** The script of a movie. The *shooting script* includes the stage directions and camera directions.

**set design.** A set is the surrounding in which a play or film takes place. The set designer makes drawings of a new set, allowing for the script's requirement for proper entrances, exits, and props. He then builds a scale model that must be approved by the director and producer. The sets are built by the master carpenter, then furnished and lighted to create the right atmosphere.

**shot.** In movies, a single piece of film photographed at one time. The shot is the basic building block of a movie. By connecting shots together, the film editor is able to tell a story in a pleasing way. He varies the length and rhythm of individual shots and connects them in different ways.

**situation comedy.** A common type of television show where the character and situation remain the same from week to week. Usually 30 minutes long, it deals with the comic side of family or work life.

**soundtrack.** The sound portion in movies and television. It is often made of several tracks mixed together: the dialogue, sound effects, and background music.

**special effects.** Any number of tricks used in movie making to produce visual illusion. Some common effects mix animation with real life action, create elaborate robots, and photograph scale models as if they were actual size (a trick especially useful in disaster pictures).

**stagehands.** The workers backstage who change the scenery, operate the curtain, and, in smaller theaters, control the stage lights during a performance.

**stage manager.** In the theater, the person who is in charge of everything once the play has opened.

**technical director.** In television, the person who works the control board and decides which picture out of several will be broadcast.

**tragedy.** A play or movie that deals with the serious side of life and in which the main character comes to an unhappy end.

**understudy.** The actor who is prepared to take over a role if the actor who plays the part cannot go on stage.

**video.** The picture part of a television production.

**voice over.** In television, the voice of an announcer who is not seen on the screen. Most often, the voice over is used in commercials.

## For Further Reference

Barnouw, Eric
*Tube of Plenty: The Evolution of American Television*
Oxford University Press
Brooks, Tim and Marsh, Earle
*The Complete Directory to Prime Time Network and Cable TV Shows, 1946 to the Present*
Ballantine Books

Halliwell, Leslie
*Halliwell's Filmgoer's Companion*
Hill and Wang
Lewis, Tom
*Empire of the Air*
HarperCollins
Monaco, James
*How to Read a Film*
Oxford University Press

# Index

Electroencephalograms
(EEGs). **4:** 445
**Electromagnetic
induction. 4:** 438
**Electromagnetic spectrum.
4:** 433, 438
**Electromagnetic waves.
1:** 365; **2:** 239-241, 244-
246; **4:** 392, 433-434, 438
**Electromagnetism. 1:** 270-
271, 274; **4:** 432-433
**Electromotive force. 4:** 438
**Electron. 1:** 263, 270;
**2:** 216-217, 219-224, 230-
231, 242, 244
**Electronic card catalogs.
2:** 400
**Electron configurations.
4:** 393, 406
**Electronegativity. 4:** 395
**Electronic instruments
(musical). 1:** 352. *See also*
specific instruments
**Electronic skills. 4:** 531-534
**Electronics. 3:** 23, 56. *See
also* Data processing
**Electron microscope.** *See*
Microscope
**Electrons. 4:** 368, 391, 406
**Electron shell. 4:** 392
**Electron transport chain.
4:** 373
**Electroweak force
(physics). 2:** 244
**Elementary and Secondary
Education Act. 1:** 129
**Elements. 4:** 390, 406
**Element (math). 2:** 313
**Elements (chemical).
1:** 261-265, 274; **2:** 214-
215, 218-219, 221-224,
228, 230
**Elephant. 2:** 148
**Elevator. 1:** 118
**Elicit. 4:** 456
**Eliot, George. 4:** 48
**Eliot, George (Mary Ann
Evans). 2:** 375, 379
**Eliot, Thomas Stearns
(T.S.). 2:** 351, 353, 356
**Elizabethan period. 1:** 361
**Elizabeth I (England).
4:** 294, 298
**Elizabeth I (Queen of
England and Ireland).
2:** 92
**Elk Hills (Calif.). 1:** 125
**Ellington, Duke. 1:** 357
**Ellipse (math). 2:** 282
**Ellipsis points. 4:** 91
**Ellis, Albert. 4:** 452
**El Salvador. 2:** 165
**E-mail. 3:** 17
**Emancipation**

Proclamation. **1:** 119;
**2:** 37, 59-60
**Embargo Act. 1:** 114; **2:** 31
**Embargos. 4:** 359
**Embedded. 4:** 491
**Embezzlement. 3:** 174
**Embolism. 3:** 99, 105
**Embryonic stage. 4:** 446
**Emergency Banking Relief
Act. 1:** 126
**Emergency Quota Act.
1:** 125
**Emic analysis. 4:** 504
**Eminent domain. 3:** 152,
174
**Emotion. 4:** 452, 456
**Emphysema. 1:** 247; **3:** 99
**Empirical formulas.
4:** 397, 406
**Empiricism. 4:** 442
**Employment. 1:** 123, 126,
129, 133; **2:** 41; **3:** 46, 164-
165
**Empty set. 2:** 313
**Encoding. 4:** 456
**Enculturation. 4:** 504
**Encyclopedia. 2:** 318, 322,
325, 399; **3:** 317
*Encyclopedia Britannica.*
**4:** 104
*Encyclopédie.* **4:** 298
**Endangered species. 1:** 246
**End notes. 4:** 108
**Endocrine system. 2:** 196-
197, 212; **4:** 384, 386, 445
**Endogamy. 4:** 494
**Endoplasmic reticulum
(ER). 2:** 182-183, 212;
**4:** 371-372, 388
**Endosperm. 4:** 388
**Endosperm mother cell.
4:** 381
**Endothermic changes.
4:** 391
**Endothermic processes.
4:** 400
**Endothermic reactions.
4:** 399
**End punctuation. 4:** 91
**Energy, Department of
(U.S.). 2:** 11
**Energy. 4:** 391, 438;
and chemical reactions,
**4:** 369-370;
electric potential, **4:** 431;
internal, **4:** 428;
kinetic, **4:** 391, 427;
law of conservation of,
**4:** 427;
mechanical, **4:** 427;
potential, **4:** 391, 427;
and reactions, **4:** 399;
and work, **4:** 427
**Energy (physics). 1:** 266-

269, 272-274; **2:** 232, 234-
235, 238, 244-246
**Energy (power). 3:** 121, 133
**Engels, Friedrich. 2:** 99;
**4:** 300-301
**Engel V. Vitale. 2:** 12
**Engineering. 3:** 22, 23, 29,
52, 54
basic considerations, **4:** 30-
34;
college classes in, **4:** 539;
**4:** 538;
genetic, **4:** 376
getting ready to write, **4:** 35-
45;
grammar review, **4:** 81-92;
improving your style, **4:** 97-
99;
other assignments, **4:** 79-80;
preparing final copy, **4:** 62-
66;
reasons for studying, **4:** 46-
64, 107;
research paper, **4:** 100-111;
rules and superstitions,
**4:** 93-96;
tests, homework, and
projects, **4:** 111-112;
usage guide, **4:** 113-115;
writing about literature,
**4:** 67-78;
writing paper, **4:** 46-61
**English composition.**
**England.** *See* United
Kingdom
**English-French dictionary.
3:** 367-373
**English-German
dictionary. 3:** 398-403
**English language. 3:** 44,
196, 234-235. *See*
Grammar; Reading; Speech
and speaking; Synonyms
and antonyms; Usage
dictionary; Vocabulary;
Writing; specific parts of
speech
**English Revolution of 1641.
4:** 298
**English-Spanish
dictionary. 3:** 432-437
**ENIAC (computer). 3:** 4, 5
**Enlightenment. 4:** 298, 312
**Enlightenment, The. 2:** 89-
96
**Ensure, assure, insure.
4:** 113
**Entertainment. 1:** 360-370;
**3:** 44, 54. *See also* specific
mediums, e.g., Television
**Enthalpy. 4:** 399, 406;
of reaction, **4:** 399
**Entrepreneurs. 4:** 316-317,
320;

18

Index

Hershey, Milton. **2:** 56
Hertzsprung, Ejnar. **1:** 305
Hertzsprung-Russell
  diagram. **1:** 305-306, 317
Herzegovina. *See* Bosnia and
  Herzegovina
Hesse, Hermann. **2:** 375,
  380
Heterogeneous. **4:** 390
Heterotrophs. **2:** 186, 212;
  **4:** 370, 389
Heterozgous. **4:** 375
Heuristic method. **4:** 451,
  457
Heuristics. **4:** 451
Hexagon. **2:** 296, 313
Hierarchy-of-needs model.
  **4:** 452
Hieroglyphics. **2:** 71
Hi-fi. *See* Sound recording
Higher-degree polynomial
  functions. **4:** 119
Higher-order derivatives.
  **4:** 143-144
High school, transition
  from. **4:** 508
Himalayas (mountains).
  **1:** 278; **2:** 127, 132
Hinckley, John W., Jr.
  **1:** 132
Hindbrain. **4:** 444
Hippocrates. **2:** 77
Hiring strategy. **4:** 327
Hiroshima (Japan). **1:** 127;
  **2:** 43, 106, 108
Hispanic-Americans.
  **1:** 136; **2:** 65-68; **3:** 297
Historicism. **4:** 489
History. **2:** 3-125, 417; **3:** 13.
  *See also* Ancient
  civilizations; History
  (U.S.); names of people,
  places, battles, wars, and
  events
History of Western
  civilization.
  ancient world, **4:** 266-276;
  early modern Europe,
    **4:** 287-296;
  glossary, **4:** 312-313;
  Medieval Europe, **4:** 277-
    286;
  modern Europe, **4:** 297-309;
  reasons for studying, **4:** 270,
    296, 307;
  tests, homework, and
    projects, **4:** 310-311
History (U.S.). **1:** 106-132
Hitchcock, Alfred. **1:** 98
Hitler, Adolf. **1:** 126; **2:** 61,
  105, 108; **4:** 305-306
Hittites. **2:** 72; **4:** 268
HMO (Health
  Maintenance

Organization). **3:** 124
Hobbes, Thomas. **4:** 476
Ho Chi Minh. **2:** 112
Hockey (field). **1:** 332, 341
Hockey (ice). **1:** 332-333,
  341
Hodgkin's disease. **3:** 101
Hogan, Ben. **1:** 339
Hogs. *See* Pigs
Hohenstaufen dynasty.
  **2:** 86
Holding companies. **4:** 318-
  319
Holidays. **4:** 329
Holland. *See* Netherlands
Hollerith, Herman. **3:** 3
Hollywood (Calif.). **1:** 364
Holmes, Oliver Wendell.
  **4:** 61
Holocaust. **4:** 306
Holophrases. **4:** 451
Holotrophs. **4:** 382
Holy Roman Empire.
  **2:** 84-86, 91-93, 95; **4:** 279
Home computers. **3:** 5
Homeless people. **4:** 466
Homeostasis. **2:** 213; **4:** 382,
  389
Home-owner's insurance.
  **3:** 124, 125
Homer. **2:** 73-74, 351-352,
  357, 389, 392
Homes. *See* Home-owner's
  insurance; Housing;
  Mortgages
Homestead Act. **1:** 119
Homestead strike. **1:** 123
Homework. **4:** 528;
  in biology, **4:** 387;
  in business administration,
    **4:** 360;
  in calculus, **4:** 212;
  in chemistry, **4:** 405;
  in cultural anthropology,
    **4:** 503;
  in economics, **4:** 258;
  in English composition,
    **4:** 111-112;
  in geology, **4:** 421;
  in physics, **4:** 437;
  in political science, **4:** 485;
  in psychology, **4:** 455;
  in sociology, **4:** 471;
  in Western civilization,
    **4:** 310
Homogeneous. **4:** 390
Homonyms. **3:** 222-223
Homophone. **1:** 53
Homo sapiens. **2:** 199
Homozygous. **4:** 375
Honduras. **2:** 166
Hong Kong. **2:** 98, 117
Hood, Mount (Ore.). **1:** 280
Hooker, Thomas. **1:** 108

Hoover, Herbert. **1:** 126;
  **2:** 40-41
Hopkins, Gerard Manley.
  **2:** 353, 357-358
Hormones. **2:** 196; **4:** 386,
  389, 445, 457
Hornsby, Rogers. **1:** 324
Hornworts. **2:** 205
Horse racing. **1:** 344
Horses. **1:** 341, 344
Horticulture. **4:** 492, 504
Hospitals. **3:** 82-86. *See also*
  Medicine and health
Hostile takeovers. **4:** 319
Hotels. *See* Motels and hotels
Household. **4:** 505
House of Burgesses (U.S.).
  **1:** 107
House of Representatives
  (U.S.). **4:** 479. *See also*
  Congress (U.S.)
Housing. **1:** 129; **3:** 121,
  147-153, 216, 292. *See also*
  Condominium; Home-
  owner's insurance;
  Mortgages; Real estate
Housing and Urban
  Development,
  Department of (U.S.).
  **2:** 11
Housman, A.E. **2:** 353, 358
Houston (Tex.). **1:** 137
Howard University. **2:** 60
Howe, Elias. **1:** 118
Hsüan T'ung (Emp. of
  China). **2:** 101
Hubble, Edwin. **1:** 307
Hubble Space Telescope.
  **1:** 309, 311, 315
*Hubris.* **4:** 69
Hudson, Henry. **1:** 107
Hudson River (N.Y.).
  **1:** 107-108, 116
Hughes, Langston. **2:** 61,
  353, 358
Hugo, Victor. **2:** 374
Huguenots. **2:** 53, 92;
  **4:** 293-294
Hull House (Chicago).
  **1:** 122
Human anatomy. **1:** 232-
  235. *See also* Skeleton
  (human)
Human development.
  **4:** 446-448
Human Engineering
  Laboratory. **3:** 206
Humanism. **4:** 288, 297,
  443, 452, 457;
  and art, **4:** 289-290;
  civic, **4:** 288-289;
  courtly, **4:** 289;
  spread of, in Italy, **4:** 288-
    289;

Rock 'n' roll. **1:** 357
**Rocky Mountains. 1:** 134,
287; **2:** 162
**Rocky Mountain spotted
fever. 3:** 106
**Rocks. 4:** 409
**Roebling, John A. 2:** 56
**Roe v. Wade. 1:** 131; **2:** 12
**Rogers, Carl. 4:** 443, 452
**Roles. 4:** 454, 463, 473
**Rolling admissions. 4:** 581
**Roman Catholic Church.
1:** 108, 124; **2:** 77, 82,
85-86, 88, 90-94, 97, 168;
**3:** 301
abuses in. **4:** 291-292;
beliefs of, **4:** 291;
and counter-reformation,
**4:** 291-293;
and the inquisition, **4:** 293
**Roman Empire. 1:** 361;
**2:** 77, 79-83
**Roman Empire and
Christianity. 4:** 272-275
**Romania. 2:** 109, 116, 146
**Roman numerals. 1:** 220
**Roman Republic. 4:** 272
**Romanov dynasty. 2:** 93
**Romanov, Michael.** *See*
Michael (Czar of Russia)
**Romanticism. 1:** 356;
**4:** 301
**Rome (Italy). 1:** 340; **2:** 74-
75, 77-80, 82, 87, 99, 108,
364-365. *See also* Roman
Empire
**Rommel, Erwin. 2:** 107
**Romulus and Remus. 2:** 74
**Romulus Augustulus
(Emp. of Rome). 2:** 81;
**4:** 274-275
**Roosevelt, Franklin
Delano. 1:** 126, 128, 133,
365; **2:** 29, 31, 41-43, 61,
105, 108; **4:** 307-308, 330
**Roosevelt, Theodore. 1:**
120-121, 123-124, 326;
**2:** 29
**Root. 4:** 213
**Root hairs. 4:** 379
**Root system. 4:** 379
**Root test. 4:** 207
**Root (word). 1:** 88, 90
**Rosaldo, Michelle. 4:** 494
**Rose. 2:** 204
**Ross, Jerry. 1:** 313
**Rossetti, Dante Gabriel.
2:** 353, 360
**Rossini, Gioacchino.
1:** 356; **2:** 364
**Rotational motion. 4:** 426-
427
**Roth IRA. 3:** 118
**Rounded characters. 4:** 70

**Round lot. 4:** 354
**Roundworms. 2:** 208
**Rousseau, Jean-Jacques.
2:** 374; **4:** 298, 304, 476
**Routing. 4:** 334
**Rowing and sculling. 1:** 341
**Rows in periodic table.
4:** 393
**Rubber. 1:** 117
**Rubella.** *See* German
measles
**Rubidium. 4:** 87, 418
**Rubinstein, Louis. 1:** 343
**Rumania.** *See* Romania
**Rumors. 4:** 470
**Runners. 4:** 380
**Russell, Henry. 1:** 305
**Russia. 2:** 13, 117, 127, 140,
146; **4:** 276. *See also* Soviet
Union
**Russo-Finnish War. 2:** 107
**Russo-Japanese War. 2:** 101
**Russworm, John. 2:** 59
**Rusts (fungi). 2:** 204
**Rutgers University. 1:** 326
**Ruth, Babe. 1:** 324
**Rutherford, Ernest. 2:** 216,
228-229
**Rwanda. 2:** 158

# S

**Saccharides. 3:** 77
**Sacramento (Calif.). 1:** 118
**Sacred. 4:** 505
**Sadat, Anwar el-. 2:** 114
**Safety. 1:** 236-245; **2:** 5-6;
**3:** 41, 160-163, 164
**Sahara Desert. 2:** 127, 148
**Salary.** *See* Wages
**Sales.** *See* Selling
**St. Andrews Society of
Golfers. 1:** 338
**St. Augustine. 4:** 288
**St. Augustine (Fla.).
1:** 107; **2:** 52, 65
**St. Bartholomew's Eve.
4:** 294
**St. Benedict. 4:** 281
**St. Exupery, Antoine.
1:** 101
**St. Helena. 2:** 175
**St. Helens, Mount (Wash.).
1:** 132, 280
**St. Ignatius of Loyola.
4:** 293
**St. Jerome. 4:** 291
**St. Kitts and Nevis. 2:** 167
**St. Lawrence River. 1:** 107-
108
**St. Lô (France). 2:** 108
**St. Louis (Mo.). 1:** 137
**St. Lucia. 2:** 167
**St. Mihiel (Fr.). 1:** 124

**St. Moritz (Switz.). 1:** 340
**St. Paul. 4:** 274
**St. Paul (Minn.). 1:** 137
**St. Peter's basilica. 4:** 291
**St. Pierre and Miquelon.
2:** 175
**St. Vincent and the
Grenadines. 2:** 167
**St. Vitus' dance. 2:** 194
**Saipan (Northern
Marianas). 1:** 127
**Salamander. 2:** 211
**Salary. 4:** 329
**Sales offices. 4:** 341
**Sales promotion. 4:** 342-
343
**Salinger, J.D. 2:** 386
**Salmonellosis. 3:** 106
**Salt. 1:** 226, 261-262; **2:** 186,
214-215, 220-221, 224,
231; **3:** 70, 71
**Salyut (space station).
1:** 313, 315
**Samarkand (Uzbekistan).
2:** 88
**Samoa. 2:** 137
**Sampras, Pete. 1:** 336
**San Andreas fault (Calif.).
1:** 278-279; **4:** 413
**Sanctions. 4:** 464
**Sand dollar. 2:** 209
**Sanders, Colonel. 3:** 47
**San Diego (Calif.). 1:** 137
**San Francisco (Calif.).
1:** 133, 137, 286; **2:** 63;
**3:** 309
**San Marino. 2:** 140, 146
**San of Southern Africa.
4:** 491
**Santa Anna, Antonio.
1:** 117
**Santa Fe (N.M.). 1:** 107
**Santiago (Cuba). 1:** 123
**São Paulo (Brazil). 2:** 168
**São Tomé and Principe.
2:** 158
**Sapporo (Japan). 1:** 340
**Sarajevo (Yugo.). 1:** 340
**Saratoga (N.Y.). 1:** 112
**Sardinia (Italy). 2:** 99
**Sargon I. 2:** 71
**Sargon II. 2:** 74
**Sarnoff, David. 2:** 104
**Satellite (artificial). 1:** 309,
314, 316, 318-319; **2:** 110
**SAT's.** *See* Scholastic
Assessment Tests
**Satire. 4:** 69
**Saturn (planet). 1:** 297-299,
311
**Saudi Arabia. 2:** 115, 148,
158
**Savannah (Ga.). 1:** 112
**Savings accounts. 3:** 115,

48

Index

# SCIENCE
## *for* FUN
# EXPERIMENTS

© Aladdin Books Ltd 1998
Designed and produced by
Aladdin Books Ltd
28 Percy Street
London W1P OLD

First published in the United States by
Copper Beech Books,
an imprint of
The Millbrook Press
2 Old New Milford Road
Brookfield, Connecticut 06804

*Design:* David West Children's Book Design
*Illustrator:* Tony Kenyon
*Photography:* Roger Vlitos
*Models:* David Millea

**Library of Congress
Cataloging-in-Publication Data**
Gibson, Gary, 1957–
Science for fun experiments / by Gary Gibson; illustrated by Tony Kenyon.
p. cm. Includes index.
Summary: Provides instructions for a selection of hands-on experiments
introducing basic scientific principles,
in such areas as magnetism, electricity, and water.
ISBN 0-7613-0517-3 (pbk.)
1. Science---Experiments---Juvenile
literature. [1. Science--Experiments.
2. Experiments.] I. Kenyon, Tony. Ill. II. Title.
Q164.G524 1996 96-13908
507' .8--dc20 CIP AC

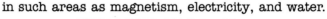

# SCIENCE
## *for* FUN

# EXPERIMENTS

GARY GIBSON

# COPPER BEECH BOOKS
## Brookfield, Connecticut

# CONTENTS

# INTRODUCTION

Have you ever wondered what would happen to the Earth if there were no sunlight? Have you thought about where magnetism comes from, or what life would be like without electricity?

You will probably have tried to walk as a weightless astronaut, and come down to Earth with a bump and wondered why that happens. But have you wondered why a submarine can both sink and float? Do you understand how musical instruments make sounds?

For centuries scientists have worked to find out more about these things. They have investigated light and color, shapes, pushing and pulling, and why and how things change. They have also experimented with floating and sinking,

electricity, magnetism, and sound.

*Science for Fun Experiments* introduces you to some of the fascinating discoveries that have been made about these scientific phenomena. It takes you step-by-step through fun, "hands-on" experiments, giving you a brief explanation of why they work, so you can impress your friends with your scientific knowledge! You will learn how to make useful gadgets – a stethoscope, a banger, a compass, a jet boat, a motor, even 3-D glasses – to name just a few of the exciting projects.

Whenever this symbol appears, adult supervision is required.

# CONTENTS

# CHAPTER *One*

# LIGHT AND COLOR

# LIGHT FOR LIFE

Green plants need sunlight to live and grow. They use the light's energy to grow. All animals get their food from plants, either directly or indirectly. Since plants need sunlight to grow, all living things depend on the sun.

GROWING WATERCRESS

**1** Put a layer of cotton in the bottom of two clean dishes. Add a little water. Sprinkle watercress seeds evenly over the cotton.

**2** Put the dishes on a sunny windowsill and cover each dish with a cardboard box. Make a hole in the side of one box and leave for several days. Check daily that the cotton is damp.

**3** The seeds under the box with no hole have grown straight up looking for light. The watercress under the box with the hole has grown toward the light.

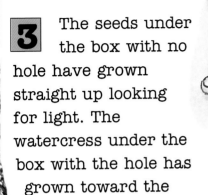

# WHY IT WORKS

Green plants contain a chemical called chlorophyll. Chlorophyll traps light, which combines with water and air to help make plants grow. This process is called "photosynthesis." Plants cannot see light but can bend and grow toward where it comes from.

FURTHER IDEAS
Follow step 1 again. Cover one dish with a large, clean glass jar to make a "greenhouse." Compare the growing roots and shoots with the uncovered dish. Which seedlings grow the best?

# DAY AND NIGHT

Half the world is in daylight and the other half in darkness. As the Earth spins around, each part takes its turn to face the sun. Parts of the Earth facing away from the sun can be lit only by the moon. Sometimes the moon passes between the sun and the Earth, so the sun's rays are blocked and the sky grows dark. This is called an eclipse.

## MAKE A SUNDIAL

**1** You need a piece of wood, or thick cardboard, and a length of dowel. Make a hole near one edge of the wood for the dowel.

**2** Stand the dowel in the hole (fix with glue if necessary). Decorate using waterproof paints.

**3** On a sunny morning put the sundial outside. The dowel casts a shadow; paint along the shadow.

4

3

12

**4** Repeat step 3 every hour. Paint the time next to each shadow. The sundial will only work on sunny days. Remember to keep it in the same place, facing the same way.

# WHY IT WORKS

The stick blocks the sun and casts a shadow. The shadow's position changes as the sun moves across the sky.

As the Earth spins around, the sun appears to move across the sky.

FURTHER IDEAS
Make a shadow animal with your hands. In a darkened room, get a friend to shine a flashlight onto the wall. Put your hands in front of the flashlight and see if you can make an animal-shaped shadow on the wall.

# SEEING IMAGES

An image is a likeness of something or someone. What we see in photographs or a movie are images. A camera is a box that can make an image on photographic film. The film contains chemicals that will keep the image for years.

## MAKE A PINHOLE CAMERA

**1** Find a small cardboard box that does not let light through. Use a pair of scissors to cut out one side of the box.

**2** Tape a piece of tracing paper over the cutout side of the box. Make sure that the tracing paper is kept as smooth as possible.

**3** Make a pinhole in the side of the box opposite the tracing paper. Point the pinhole at a window. Move toward the window until you see its image on the tracing paper.

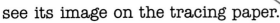

# WHY IT WORKS

Light rays in air do not bend or curve; they always travel in straight lines. Rays of light from the window enter the pinhole in straight lines and hit the tracing paper. The light rays from the bottom and the top of the window cross over as they pass through the hole, so the image appears upside down.

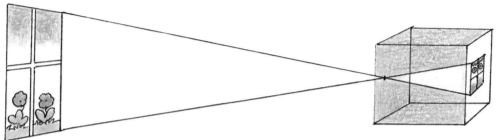

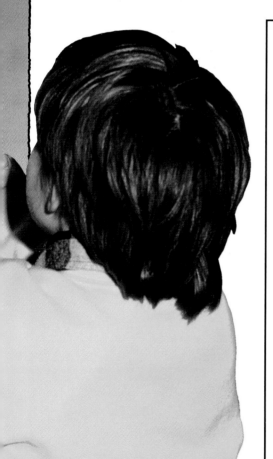

FURTHER IDEAS

Make the pinhole a little bigger so more light enters the camera. The image becomes brighter but less clear. A magnifying glass in front of the pinhole can sharpen the image. The image will be faint, so point the pinhole at a bright object such as a lightbulb.

# BOUNCING LIGHT

Rays of light can be bounced off an object like a rubber ball bouncing off a wall. We call this "reflection." Light rays are reflected best by flat, shiny surfaces such as shiny spoons, cans, bottles, or mirrors.

MAKE A KALEIDOSCOPE

**1** Carefully tape together three identical-sized small mirrors. Make a triangle-shaped tube with the shiny sides facing inside.

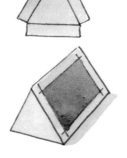

**2** Cut out a triangle-shaped piece of paper, allowing for flaps. Tape it over one end of the triangle of mirrors to form a box.

GET AN ADULT TO HELP YOU

**3** Cut out small pieces of brightly colored paper from a magazine and drop them into the bottom of the box.

**4** Tape another triangle of paper over the other end of the tube. Using a pencil, make a hole to look through. The kaleidoscope is finished.

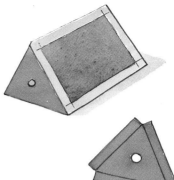

**5** Hold the kaleidoscope level, and point it at a bright light. Look at the pattern through the eye piece. Shake and look again.

# WHY IT WORKS

Light rays from the colored paper are reflected back and forth between the mirrors. Each image is doubled by the mirrors before the light rays reach your eye.

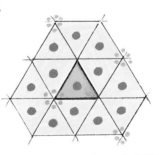

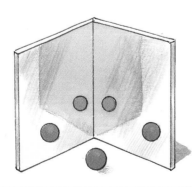

## FURTHER IDEAS
Stand two mirrors up at right angles, using modeling clay. Place a marble between the mirrors. How many images can you see?

# UP PERISCOPE!

Submarine crews want to know what is going on above the waves without being seen. Instead of rising to the ocean's surface, the submarine raises its periscope. On land you can use periscopes to see over walls and around corners!

## MAKE A PERISCOPE

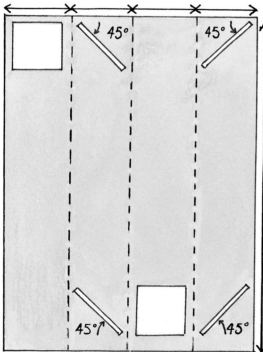

45° 45° 45° 45°

**1** Copy the pattern onto cardboard. Cut around the outline. Cut out the slots and squares. Fold on the dotted lines.

18

**2** Tape the edges of the cardboard together to form a box. Make sure that the slots line up. Paint to decorate.

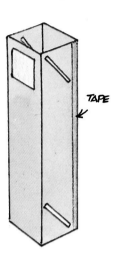

TAPE

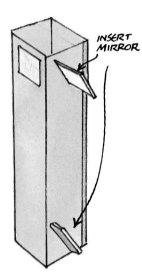

INSERT MIRROR

**3** Insert two mirrors into the slots, top mirror facing down, bottom mirror facing up. Look into the lower mirror.

# WHY IT WORKS

Light rays above and ahead of you hit the upper mirror. It reflects the rays down to the lower mirror, which in turn reflects the light rays into your eyes.

## FURTHER IDEAS

Make a periscope to see around corners. Copy the design shown below. Follow instructions 1 and 2 as before. But this time the angles of the mirror slots are different. Make sure the top mirror faces down and the bottom mirror faces up.

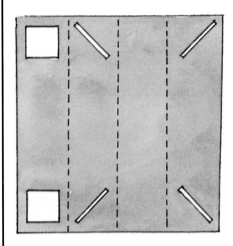

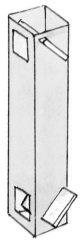

# MOVING PICTURES

Cartoon films are made out of many drawings. These are photographed one after another by a movie camera. When the film is projected onto a screen, the images seem to move. If you move your eyes quickly over the pictures on the right, the ball seems to bounce.

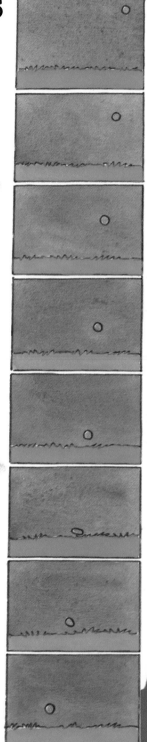

MAKE A FLICK BOOK

**1** Draw a background picture. Trace it onto at least 12 pages of the same size. Leave a margin down one side of each drawing.

**2** Draw the sun high in the sky on the first page. Draw it slightly lower on the second page. Repeat until the sun has set on the last page.

**3** Stack the pages neatly and staple them together with two staples along the edge of the margin.

# WHY IT WORKS

Your eyes see each image for a fraction of a second. If the images are shown fast enough, the eye runs the images together. Differences in the separate images appear as movement.

## FURTHER IDEAS

Copy the two faces (below) onto two sheets of tracing paper. Staple the two sheets together. Roll the upper sheet tightly around a pencil. Move the pencil up and down to roll and unroll the upper sheet.

**4** Hold the flick book by the margin and watch the sun go down as you flick the pages.

# SPLITTING LIGHT

More than 300 years ago, Sir Isaac Newton proved that white light is made from the colors of the rainbow. Newton split white light into a rainbow using a wedge of glass called a prism. We see rainbows in the sky because water droplets in the air split the sunlight before it reaches us.

**2** Angle a mirror in a bowl of water. Bend a large piece of white posterboard away from the bowl.

## MAKE A RAINBOW

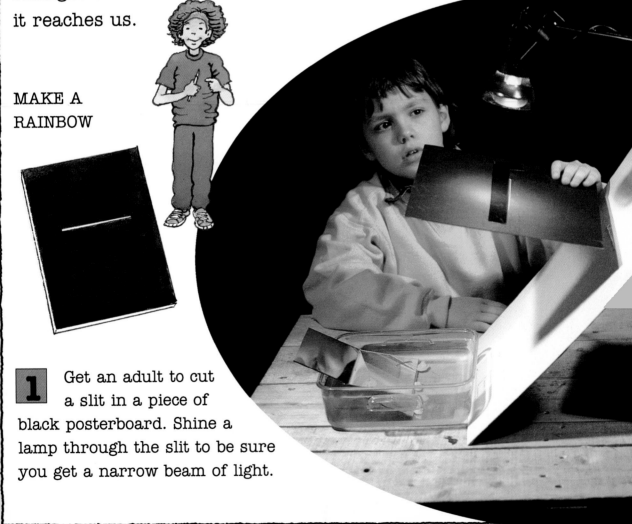

**1** Get an adult to cut a slit in a piece of black posterboard. Shine a lamp through the slit to be sure you get a narrow beam of light.

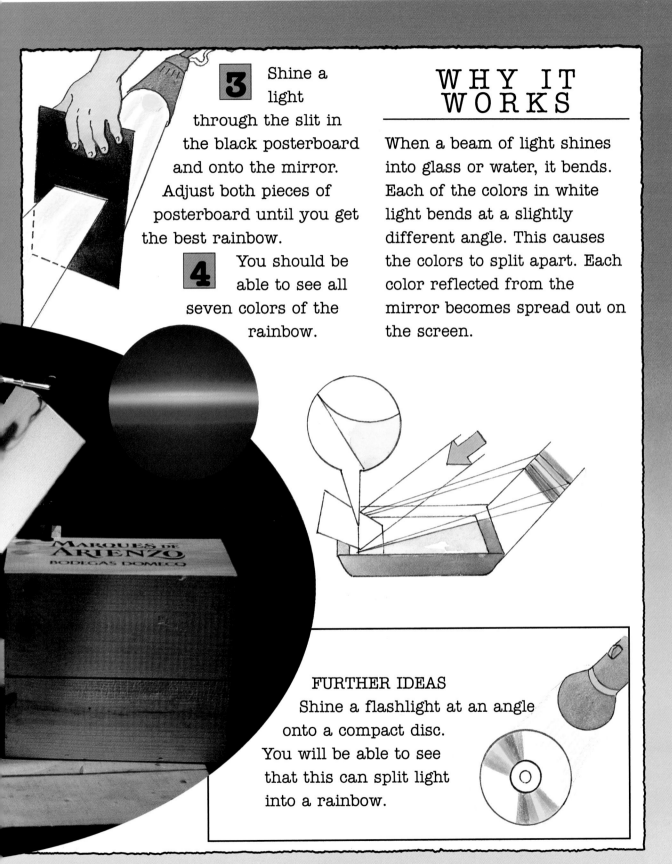

**3** Shine a light through the slit in the black posterboard and onto the mirror. Adjust both pieces of posterboard until you get the best rainbow.

**4** You should be able to see all seven colors of the rainbow.

# WHY IT WORKS

When a beam of light shines into glass or water, it bends. Each of the colors in white light bends at a slightly different angle. This causes the colors to split apart. Each color reflected from the mirror becomes spread out on the screen.

## FURTHER IDEAS

Shine a flashlight at an angle onto a compact disc. You will be able to see that this can split light into a rainbow.

# MIXING COLORS

Look closely at a color TV or the photographs in this book. The pictures are made up of lots of tiny, colored dots. Because we see books or TV from a distance, the dots seem to mix to make colors.

MAKE A COLOR SPINNER

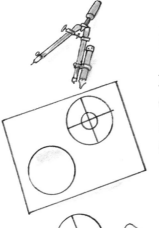

**1** Use a pencil and a pair of compasses to draw circles of different sizes onto white posterboard. Cut them out with scissors.

**2** Divide the circles into equal sections and decorate each section with different colors. Push a sharp pencil or stick through a hole in the center of each circle.

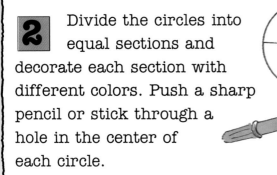

**3** Spin the spinner as fast as you can on a tabletop and watch the different colors merge. If you color a spinner with the colors of the rainbow, it may appear white when you spin it.

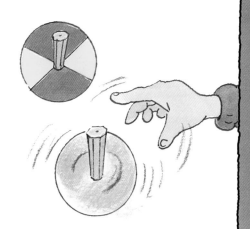

# WHY IT WORKS

The spinner is turning so fast that instead of seeing separate colors, our eyes see a mixture. White light is made up of the colors of the rainbow, so a spinner decorated with these colors appears white.

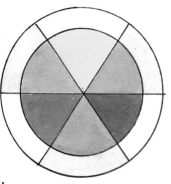

## FURTHER IDEAS

Cover three flashlights with red, blue, and green cellophane. Shine them onto white paper (or a white floor). Allow the light beams to overlap. See how many new colors you can make.

# SEEING IN THREE-DIMENSION

Animals usually have two eyes. Close one eye and look at an object. Guess how far away it is. Try again with both eyes open. It is much harder to judge distances using only one eye. Having two eyes gives us a sense of depth.

## MAKE 3-D GLASSES

**1** Measure the distances A and B around your head with a tape measure.

**2** Use the distances to draw out your glasses onto cardboard. Cut out the glasses and fold along the dotted lines.

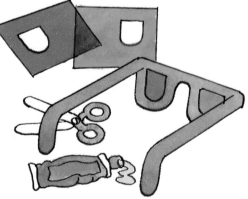

**3** Cut out red and green cellophane for the eyeholes. Glue the green over the right eyehole and red over the left. Try on the glasses. Look at the insect picture opposite.

## WHY IT WORKS

The left eye covered with red cellophane only sees the green image; the right eye only sees the red. Each eye sees a different view. The brain combines both images to give the illusion of depth.

### FURTHER IDEAS

Close one eye. Hold your hands out in front of you at arm's length. Bring your index fingers together so they touch. Can you thread a needle with one eye closed?

# SEPARATING COLORS

In printing and painting there are three primary colors – red, blue, and yellow. The enormous variety of colored dyes, paints, and inks are made by mixing different amounts of two or more of the primary colors.

FIND THE HIDDEN COLORS

**1** With a pair of compasses draw some circles onto paper towels. Cut them out with scissors.

**2** Using marker pens, draw a dot of color in the middle of each circle. Black, purple, green, brown, and orange are good colors to use.

**3** Place each circle of paper towel over the top of a clean, dry jar.

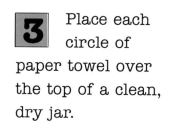

**4** Add drops of water to the dot of color. Dip a straw into water. Block the top with your finger. Touch the ink dot with the straw.

# WHY IT WORKS

Some inks are made up of several colors. These can separate as the water spreads, carrying the colors at different speeds.

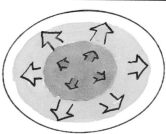

FURTHER IDEAS
Take a long strip of paper towel. Draw a large dot near the bottom. Hang the strip up so the end just dips into a bowl of water. Watch the colors separate as the water rises up the paper.

# COLORED DYES

Today we can buy clothes in an enormous variety of colors. These colors come from modern artificial dyes made from oil. Before the nineteenth century, people had always used natural dyes made from plants, animals, or materials in the ground.

## TIE-DYE A HANDKERCHIEF

GET AN ADULT TO DO THIS FOR YOU

**2** Tie some string around a white cotton handkerchief as tightly as you can.

**1** Collect lots of brown onion skins. Ask an adult to boil them in water for 20 minutes.

**3** Soak the tied handkerchief in the onion skin water for five minutes. Use an oven glove to protect yourself.

**4** Cut the string from the dyed handkerchief when cool. Fasten the handkerchief to a clothesline until it is dry.

FURTHER IDEAS
Many vegetables contain different colored pigments. See what color beet juice or spinach water dye fabric.

# WHY IT WORKS

Onion skins contain a chemical called a pigment. Boiling brings out the pigment, which in onion skin is yellow. Compare how well the pigment dyes fabrics other than cotton.

# COLOR CHANGES

Lemons taste sour because they contain acid ("acid" means sour). Hundreds of chemicals are acidic. It would be very dangerous if scientists had to taste chemicals to identify them. Instead they use a chemical that changes color when acid is added.

GET AN ADULT TO DO THIS FOR YOU

TESTING FOR ACIDS

**1** Ask an adult to chop up half a red cabbage. Boil the chopped cabbage in a pan of water for about five minutes.

**2** Remove the cabbage from the water. Cut paper towels or filter paper into strips.

**3** Dip each strip into the cabbage water. Allow the strips to soak the water up.

**4** Let the strips dry. When dry, try adding drops of vinegar, lemon, soap, and other harmless substances to each strip.

# WHY IT WORKS

Red cabbage contains a chemical called an indicator. Indicators change color when an acid or alkali is added. Red cabbage juice turns red in acids and green in alkalis. Litmus is an important indicator commonly used by scientists.

**5** Note the different colors you see on each strip.

FURTHER IDEAS
You can use geranium petals instead of red cabbage. Geranium petals also contain an indicator that changes color when an acid or alkali is added.

# CONTENTS

# CHAPTER *Two*

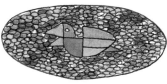

# MAKING SHAPES

# MYSTERIOUS SHAPES

We can learn a lot about materials and their shapes from nature. All of these shapes are solids, and have at least two sides. What about a one-sided shape? What special properties does it have?

## MAKE A MÖBIUS STRIP

**1** Color both sides of three paper strips. Tape together the first strip to make a band.

**2** Repeat with the second strip, but twist the strip once before sticking the ends together.

# WHY IT WORKS

The first strip will make two new bands, the second a single long band and the third, two linked bands. This is a trick of mathematics. The second and third strips are called *Möbius strips*, after their inventor.

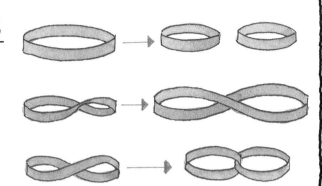

**3** Twist the third strip twice before taping the ends together.

**4** Finally, cut each band in half lengthwise.

## FURTHER IDEAS
Draw a pencil line along each of the bands. You will find that the line continues along both "sides" of the second band!

# SHAPES IN NATURE

You can find crystals everywhere around you. Gemstones, like emeralds, have always fascinated people. Salt, sand, and sugar are also made from crystals. Then there are the quartz crystals in your watch and the silicon in your computer.

### GROW SOME CRYSTALS

**1** Pour some hot tap water into a clean glass jar. Stir in one spoonful of potash of alum at a time.

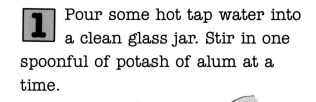

**2** Keep adding alum until no more will dissolve. You now have a *saturated solution*. Leave it for two days.

**3** Drain the saturated solution through a strainer. Save the water for later and keep the crystals.

# WHY IT WORKS

When the alum dissolved, the particles it was made up of spread out in the water. As the water evaporated, there was not enough water to dissolve the rest of the alum. The particles of alum were forced back together again to make crystals.

**4** Look at the crystals with a magnifying glass. They are different sizes. Are they the same shape?

FURTHER IDEAS
Pour the spare saturated solution into a jar. Hang a crystal from a pencil and lower it into the jar. Watch it grow over a few days.

# HANGING ROCKS

Rainwater can dissolve some types of solid rock. Sometimes the water drips into an underground cave, leaving a solid behind.

Over time this solid slowly builds up to form columns, which hang down from the roof of the cave, called *stalactites*.

GROW A STALACTITE

**1** Make a saturated solution with Epsom salts in a jar of hot water.

**2** Fill two glasses with the saturated solution.

**3** Attach paper clips to the ends of some wool. Hang the ends in the two glasses.

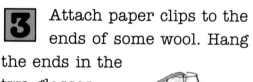

**4** Place a saucer under the wool. Leave in a warm, safe place for one week.

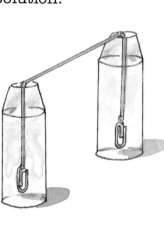

**5** Watch as the stalactite grows down from the wool to the saucer, over a number of days.

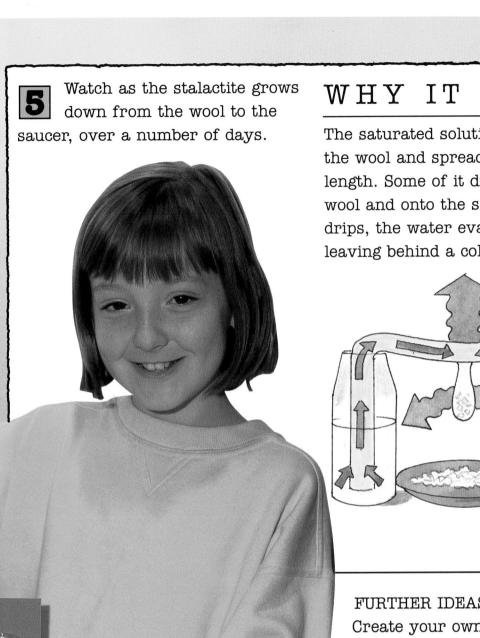

# WHY IT WORKS

The saturated solution soaks into the wool and spreads along its length. Some of it drips off the wool and onto the saucer. As it drips, the water evaporates, leaving behind a column of salts.

### FURTHER IDEAS

Create your own crystalline sculpture. Make a letter by bending a clean pipe cleaner. Dip it into a jar of saturated solution for a few minutes. Leave it to dry slowly.

# SHAPE AND STRENGTH

Everybody knows how easy it is to break an egg, because of its very thin shell. However, the egg can also be very strong. It must withstand the impact of falling to the ground when the egg is laid. The egg shape has been produced by nature to be both light and strong.

TEST THE STRENGTH OF AN EGG

**1** Find a large tray. Stand up the egg at one side of the tray using clay to hold it in place.

**2** At the other side of the tray place two piles of coins exactly the same height as the egg. The egg and two piles should make a triangle.

**3** Wrap some books in plastic wrap for protection. Support one book on the coins and egg.

**4** Add another book. Watch the egg carefully as you add each book. How many books can the egg help support before it breaks?

# WHY IT WORKS

The shape of the egg makes it both hollow and light. It has an arch at each end, a good structure for supporting weight. The egg has a lot of strength lengthwise because the tall arches spread more weight. It is much easier to break when on its side because these arches are weaker.

## FURTHER IDEAS

Repeat the test. This time compare the egg's strength to that of some paper shapes, such as a box and a cone.

# HANGING AROUND

One of the most important properties of any material is its strength. A material that snaps under the slightest weight is not much use. Nature has made some of the strongest materials around. For example, the silken strands in a spider's web are stronger than steel of the same thickness.

## FIND THE STRONGEST STRIP

**1** Cut three strips of paper, tissue paper, and plastic from a plastic bag, making them the same length and width.

**2** Using tape, fasten a wooden dowel to each end of the strips.

GET AN ADULT TO DO THIS FOR YOU

**3** Ask an adult to cut two small holes on each side of the top of three plastic bowls, to make three baskets.

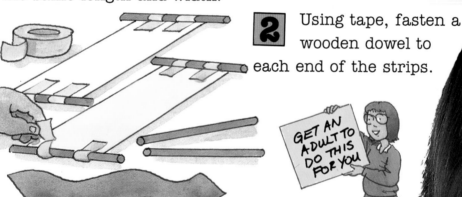

**4** Attach a basket to one of the wooden dowels. Tie string around the other wooden dowel.

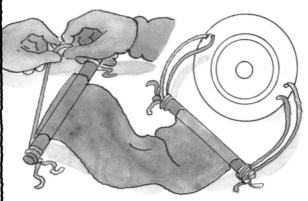

**5** Hang each strip from a wall. Slowly add weights to the baskets until each strip breaks.

# WHY IT WORKS

Plastic is the strongest because its particles are held together by very strong bonds. Paper is made from densely packed fibers that can be split apart quite easily. Tissue paper fibers are not as densely packed, making it the weakest of the three.

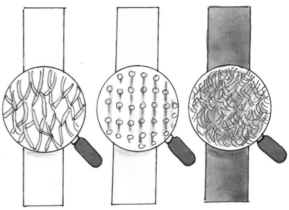

### FURTHER IDEAS
Repeat the test with plastic strips of different widths. How does this affect the strength?

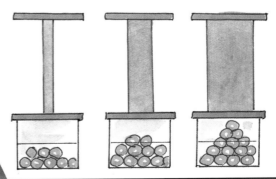

# MAKING MATERIALS

The materials we find in nature are called *raw materials*. We use many of these and change them to make other products. Glass is made from sand, and paper from wood. We can usually improve a material by changing its properties.

MAKE A PAPIER-MÂCHÉ BOWL

**1** Mix some flour and water in a large plastic bowl, keeping the mixture runny.

**2** Tear up strips of newspaper, and soak them in the mixture.

**3** Inflate a balloon. Starting near the balloon's middle, apply the soaked paper in layers.

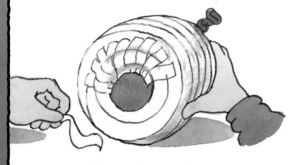

**4** To make the bowl's base, sit the balloon on a plastic lid. Cover the lid with more papier-mâché.

**5** Leave overnight, then remove the balloon. Paint the finished bowl for decoration. Varnish it for extra protection.

# WHY IT WORKS

Paper is made up of thousands of tiny strands of wood fibers. The mixture of flour and water fills the gaps between these fibers. As the mixture dries it becomes hard and makes the paper strong and more rigid. It keeps its new shape until soaked again in water.

## FURTHER IDEAS
You can use a real bowl as a mold. Cover the bowl with plastic wrap first to make the papier-mâché easy to remove.

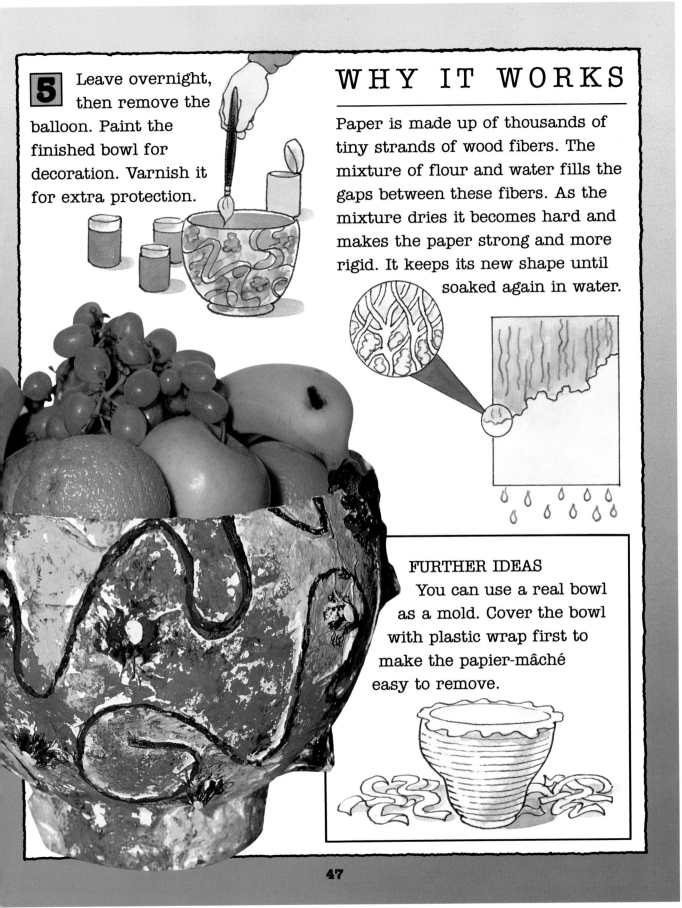

# FILLING SHAPES

Like papier-mâché, materials such as cement, plaster, and gypsum alter their form when mixed with water and allowed to dry. Unlike papier-mâché, these substances can be poured into molds and used to form shapes, from small statues to enormous buildings.

PLASTER OF PARIS

**1** Lubricate the inside of a clean, rubber glove with a few drops of liquid soap.

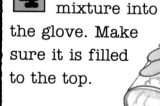

**2** Hang the glove upside down with a couple of clips to hold it open.

**3** Use a wooden stick to mix some plaster of Paris with cold water in a glass jar. Mix thoroughly until creamy.

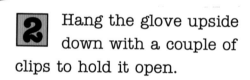

**4** Pour the mixture into the glove. Make sure it is filled to the top.

**5** Leave overnight to dry out. Gently peel off the glove from the plaster underneath. Be careful! The plaster is quite fragile.

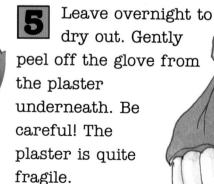

**6** Paint the plaster to brighten it up. Use your hand sculpture for holding jewelry.

# WHY IT WORKS

Plaster of Paris is made by heating crushed gypsum. The water evaporates away leaving behind a dry powder. When you add water to this powder you cause a chemical reaction. The powder is changed back to gypsum, which will set hard when the water has evaporated.

### FURTHER IDEAS
Hollow out the shape of a face in some clay. Pour plaster of Paris into the mold and leave it to dry overnight, making a plaster cast of the face.

# ELASTIC MATERIALS

One of the reasons metals are so useful is because of their springiness, or *elasticity*. This means that as you pull the material out of shape it tries to return to that shape. Most things have some springiness, especially elastic bands, which are very strong. Glass is also strong, but instead of being elastic it is brittle and shatters.

## MAKE A JACK-IN-THE-BOX

**1** Ask an adult to coil a piece of stiff wire around a broom handle to make a spring.

**2** Cut the neck from a plastic bottle. Attach the spring to the bottom with tape.

**3** Ask an adult to secure a lid with paper fasteners.

GET AN ADULT TO DO THIS FOR YOU

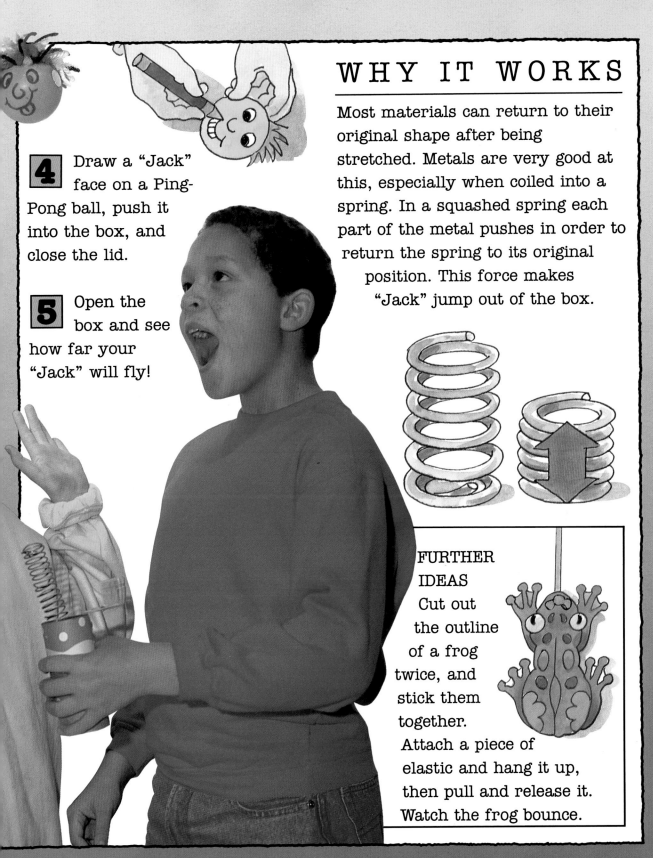

# WHY IT WORKS

Most materials can return to their original shape after being stretched. Metals are very good at this, especially when coiled into a spring. In a squashed spring each part of the metal pushes in order to return the spring to its original position. This force makes "Jack" jump out of the box.

**4** Draw a "Jack" face on a Ping-Pong ball, push it into the box, and close the lid.

**5** Open the box and see how far your "Jack" will fly!

FURTHER IDEAS
Cut out the outline of a frog twice, and stick them together. Attach a piece of elastic and hang it up, then pull and release it. Watch the frog bounce.

# SHAPELESS PLASTICS

Some materials can be pulled into new shapes which they then keep. They do not return to their previous shape as an elastic material would. Such materials are called "plastic." For example, wet clay is plastic because you can mold it into any shape you want and it stays that way.

MAKE SOME PLASTIC MILK

**1** Ask an adult to warm some milk in a pan.

**2** When the milk starts to boil, slowly stir in a little vinegar.

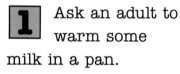

GET AN ADULT TO HELP YOU WITH THESE

**3** Keep stirring. Within seconds the mixture should become rubbery.

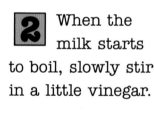

**4** Let this rubbery mixture cool. Wash it under the cold water tap, and examine the "plastic."

# WHY IT WORKS

Vinegar is a member of the chemical family called *acids*. When it is added to the warm milk, it sets up a chemical reaction which rearranges the particles in the milk. Instead of being "runny" and free to move, they clump together. It is this clump that becomes the lump of "plastic."

FURTHER IDEAS
Put a plastic container in a saucepan. Ask an adult to boil water. Pour the boiling water to cover the container, and watch it lose its shape.

# FIBERS AND THREADS

Fibers are long, thin, flexible strands of material like threads. Each of your hairs is a fiber. Natural fibers also include animal fur, cotton, and wool. Fibers can be twisted together to make yarn, which can be woven in turn to make fabrics or cloth.

## MAKE A LOOM

**1** Cut an odd number of notches along the top and bottom of some cardboard.

GET AN ADULT TO DO THIS FOR YOU

**2** Wind a piece of string around each pair of notches. Knot it together at the back of the loom.

**3** Weave some thick wool across the loom, in and out of the string. To change color, tie another strip to the old one.

**4** When you have filled the loom, tie off the last strip of fabric. Lift the weaving off the cardboard.

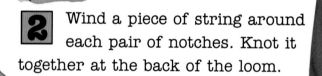

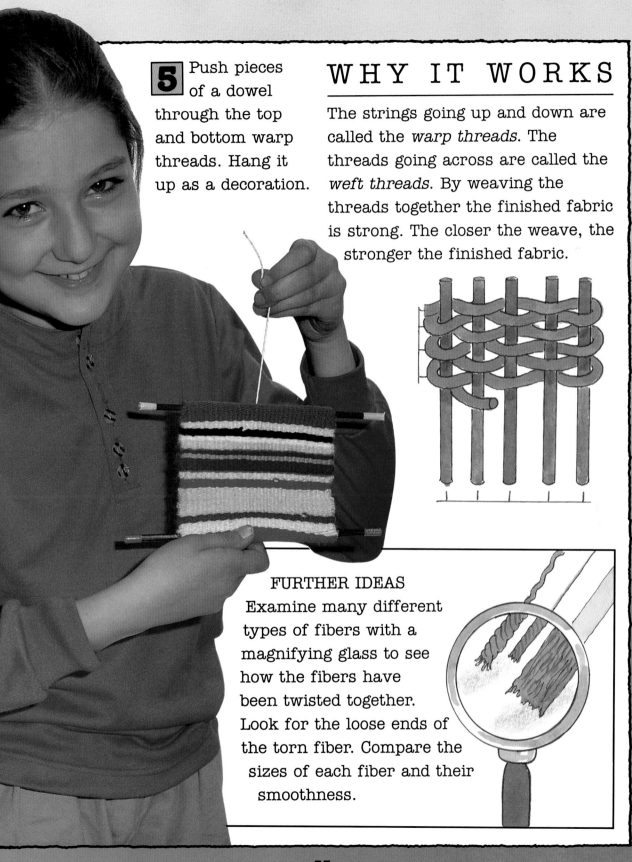

**5** Push pieces of a dowel through the top and bottom warp threads. Hang it up as a decoration.

# WHY IT WORKS

The strings going up and down are called the *warp threads*. The threads going across are called the *weft threads*. By weaving the threads together the finished fabric is strong. The closer the weave, the stronger the finished fabric.

### FURTHER IDEAS
Examine many different types of fibers with a magnifying glass to see how the fibers have been twisted together. Look for the loose ends of the torn fiber. Compare the sizes of each fiber and their smoothness.

# FITTING IT TOGETHER

Some shapes fit neatly together to cover an area without overlapping or leaving spaces. This is called *tessellation*. Examples are the bricks in a wall and the squares on a chessboard. An example in nature is the honeycomb in a beehive, where hexagonal cells fit snugly together.

## MAKE A TRIANGLE PUZZLE

**1** On a large sheet of white cardboard, draw a triangle with sides 12 inches long.

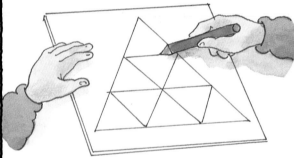

**2** Divide the large triangle into nine smaller ones. Each side should be 4 inches long.

**3** On each of the triangles draw a circle, a square, and a triangle as shown.

GET AN ADULT TO HELP YOU WITH THIS

**4** Use sharp scissors to carefully cut out each of the nine small triangles.

# WHY IT WORKS

A tessellated structure, like a beehive, must have no gaps or overlapping shapes. Only certain shapes, such as triangles and hexagons, will tessellate. To cover a surface with circles, which do not tessellate, you would have to overlap the shapes, or leave gaps.

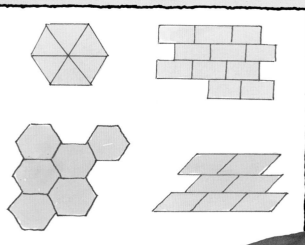

**5** Challenge a friend with your triangle puzzle. They should be able to match up the pattern to correctly put the big triangle back together again.

## FURTHER IDEAS

A mosaic is like a tessellation, but the shapes that fit together are not the same. Cut out a lot of small cardboard shapes. Glue them down to fit the outline of a drawing on cardboard. Make the gaps as small as possible.

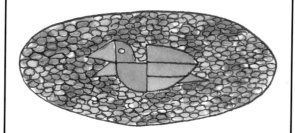

# BRIDGES

Since earliest times people have built bridges to cross rivers and other obstacles. The first bridges were probably tree trunks laid across a stream. Later, bridges were built from arches to carry heavier loads. Modern bridges use either steel girders or suspension cables, for support.

## BUILD MODEL BRIDGES

**1** Find six blocks of wood to make three bridges. Tape pencils to two of the corners on each block.

**2** Ask an adult to cut some strips of thick cardboard the same width as the blocks.

GET AN ADULT TO HELP YOU WITH THIS

**3** Place a strip of cardboard between two blocks to make a beam bridge. With the second, use an arch as a support.

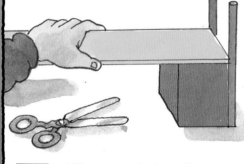

**4** On the third, tie string to the pencils, and tape the string to the strip to make a suspension bridge.

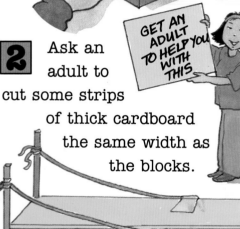

**5** Draw a river on a sheet of cardboard. Place it under your bridges.

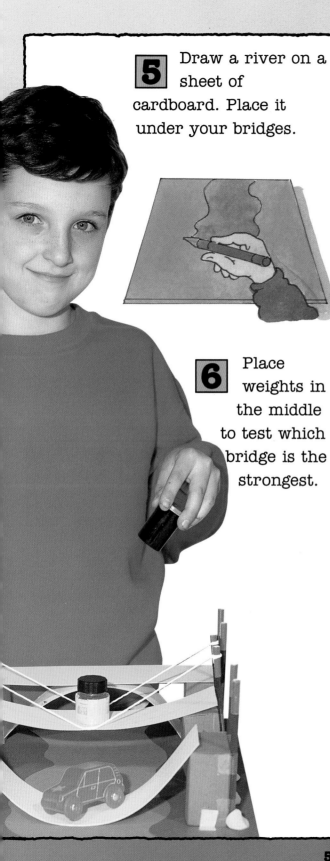

**6** Place weights in the middle to test which bridge is the strongest.

# WHY IT WORKS

The beam bridge is the weakest because the weight is not spread. The string in the suspension bridge takes some of the weight. The arch is strongest because the weight is spread out over its whole length.

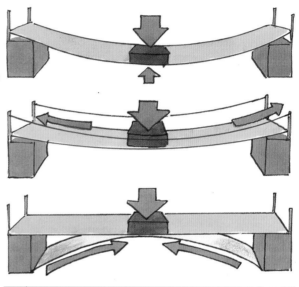

## FURTHER IDEAS

Try making a bridge frame out of plastic straws. Join the straws together by pushing the end of one into another.

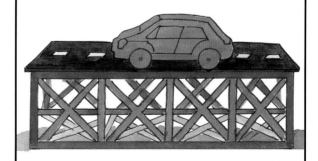

# CONTENTS

# CHAPTER *Three*

# PUSHING AND PULLING

# WHAT IS A FORCE?

If you want to make anything move you have to give it a push or a pull. Scientists call this push or pull a force. Sir Isaac Newton was inspired to write about the force of gravity after an apple landed on his head. The unit of force is called a newton – roughly the force or weight of one apple!

MAKE A FORCE METER

**1** Cut out three rectangles from a thick sheet of cardboard. Tape two together to make a "T." Tape the third to support the base.

**2** Make a small hole near the top of the cardboard. Push through a wooden dowel about six inches long. Secure firmly.

**3** Find a circular-shaped box or can. Attach two strong threads to the box. Hang the threads from a paper clip.

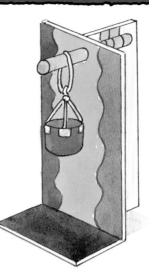

**4** Loop a rubber band through the paper clip. Hang the box from the wooden dowel using the rubber band.

**5** Place one object at a time in the box. Note how far the rubber band stretches.

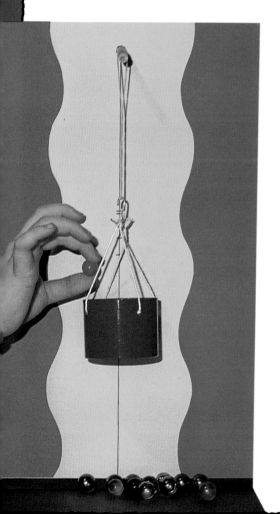

## WHY IT WORKS

We can measure how big forces are by seeing how far the rubber band stretches each time. The band must return to its original length after each stretch.

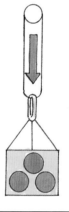

### FURTHER IDEAS
Measure the forces made by your own muscles with a set of bathroom scales. Squeeze as hard as you can and check how far the scale goes around. Can you push as hard as your own weight?

# THE PULL OF GRAVITY

Gravity is the mysterious force: Everybody knows it is there but it is very difficult to understand. Planet Earth keeps everything attracted to it quite firmly, because of the pull of gravity. When you see pictures of astronauts floating around in space apparently weightless, they are not being subjected to the Earth's pull of gravity.

## RACE WITH GRAVITY

**1** Lay a 12-inch ruler flat on a sheet of white cardboard. Use a pencil to draw a line all around the ruler.

**2** Use a pair of scissors to carefully cut out the shape from the cardboard.

**3** Divide the cardboard into six equal parts. Color each part brightly with markers.

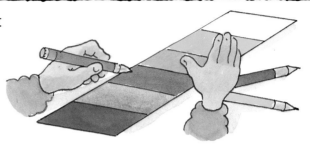

**4** Ask a friend to hold the cardboard hanging down just above your outstretched hand. When your friend releases it, try to catch the cardboard as quickly as you can.

# WHY IT WORKS

This is a race between gravity and your body. By the time the message has traveled

from your brain to your hand, gravity has pulled the cardboard down by many inches.

FURTHER IDEAS
Ask a friend to drop a small (Ping-Pong) ball down a cardboard tube. Hold a ruler ready near the bottom of the tube. You have to swat the ball before it hits the ground.

# BALANCING WEIGHT

We take the art of balance for granted once we have learned to walk as babies. Tightrope walkers have only the thin rope keeping them in the air. Everyone marvels as they balance carefully and defy gravity. This takes great skill as well as courage.

MAKE A BALANCING MAN

**1** Draw a "man" shape onto some thick white cardboard. Carefully cut out the shape with scissors.

**2** Color in the man to make him look more human. Carefully glue a thumbtack to the bottom of the cardboard.

**3** Ask an adult to cut off a piece of coat hanger wire. Glue it into place.

**4** Make two small clay balls of the same size. Wrap one ball around each end of the wire.

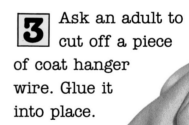

**5** Carefully stand the balancing man on top of a bottle. He may wobble slightly but should keep his balance.

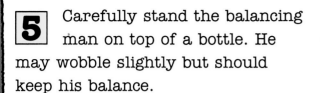

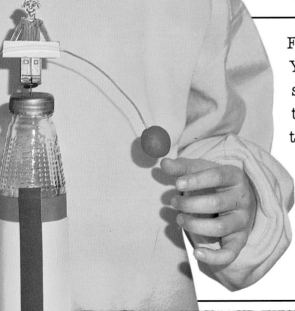

# WHY IT WORKS

Gravity keeps everything resting on the ground. In this experiment most of the pulling force of gravity is due to the two heavy balls. It is because these balls are low that the man has a low center of gravity. Any object will balance when its center of gravity is low.

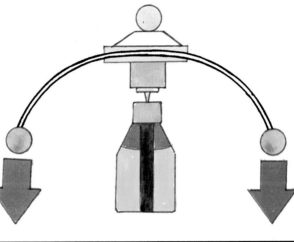

## FURTHER IDEAS

You can make a simpler balancing sculpture. Ask an adult to stick a long pin through a cork.

Push a fork into each side of the cork. Stand your sculpture on top of a bottle to balance.

# SMALL WEIGHTS

You probably see people weighing goods every time you go shopping. They expect to pay only for what they get. "How much" you have of something is normally measured by its weight. Everything has weight, no matter how small, because of the pull of gravity.

MAKE A MICROBALANCE

**1** Cut some thick cardboard into this diamond shape. Fold along the dotted lines.

**2** Cut out this shape (slightly over three times the width of a drinking straw) twice from cardboard. Fold into triangular shapes and slide one over each end of a straw.

**3** Fold the thick cardboard diamond into a support. Push a steel pin through the cardboard and straw. Strengthen the base with tape.

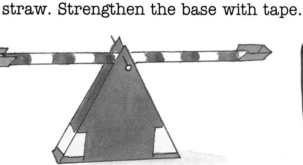

**4** Glue the triangular shapes to the ends of the straw. Make sure they balance each other.

**5** Remove the front of a cardboard box to screen your microbalance from drafts. Compare the weights of small objects like a pea or bean.

# WHY IT WORKS

The heavier an object is, the bigger the force of gravity tugging on it. The side of the straw that is pulled harder will tilt down. When the weights on both sides are equal, then the two forces balance out.

## FURTHER IDEAS

Balance a ruler on a pencil. Place an object on each end of the ruler. You can balance two objects of unequal weight by sliding the pencil closer to the lighter object.

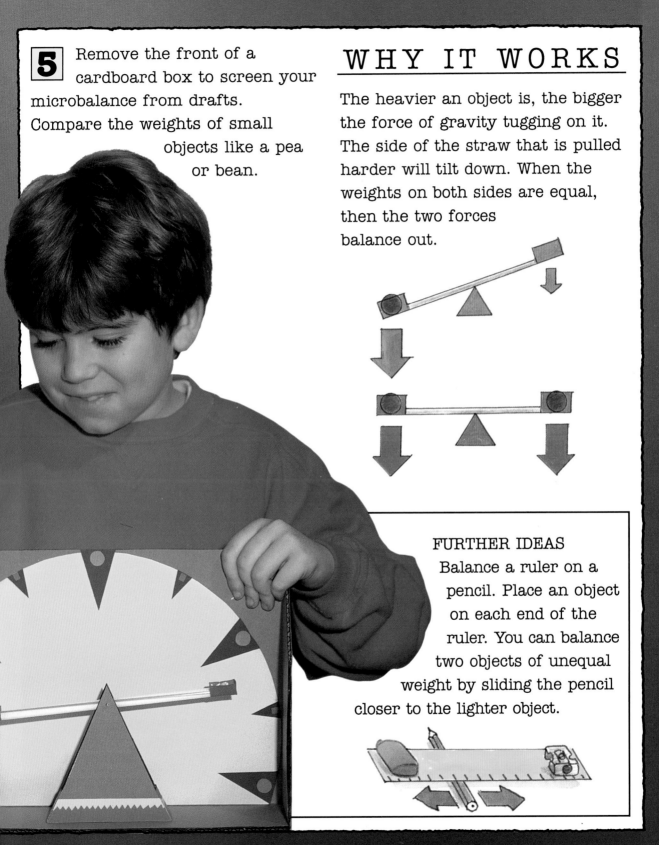

# FRICTION

Whenever any two things rub against each other, the force of friction tries to stop them. Rubbing your hands together warms them because of friction. Friction is useful because without it there would be no grip! Things would just slip and slide away from each other. Friction can also be a problem because it causes things to overheat.

## MEASURING FRICTION

**1** Draw the seven shapes A to G on thick cardboard. Carefully cut them out. They will be the parts of your ramp.

**2** Fold shape A along the dotted lines into a prism and stand it on shape C. Tape shape E to shape C. Position shape D between shapes A and E.

**3** Fold shape B along the dotted lines into a box. Position it at the end of the ramp. Glue shapes F and G into place. Flip up shape D to make your runway (shape E) steeper.

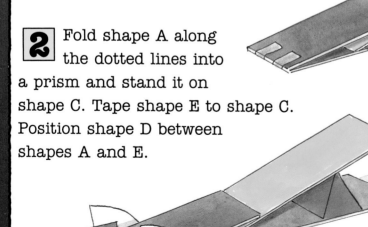

**4** Place a coin at the top of the runway. Slowly make the runway steeper until the coin slides down. Compare with a wooden block, an eraser, and a cork.

There is more friction, or grip, between rough surfaces than between smooth ones. Even though the eraser and the cardboard feel smooth, they have tiny rough edges. Only when the runway is steep enough can this grip between eraser and cardboard be overcome.

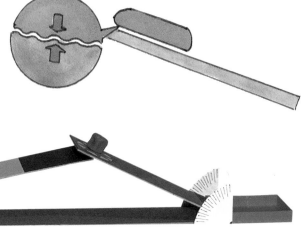

## FURTHER IDEAS

Cut out a piece of aluminum foil to fit your runway. Carefully lay it flat and into place. Repeat your tests. Is there more friction from the aluminum compared to the cardboard? Compare other surfaces, such as felt, plastic, or paper. Can you tell which surface has the most friction?

# GETTING A GRIP

Grip is very important to drivers. The wheels of a vehicle can slide, especially on slippery surfaces like mud, and may cause an accident. Tractors' wheels are very big and knobbly to increase their grip on muddy fields.

## MAKE A SPOOL TRACTOR

**1** Ask an adult to remove the wick from a candle and cut off a disc from the end of the candle.

**2** Cut out two circles of cardboard to fit the ends of a spool of thread. Make a small hole in the center and tape each into place.

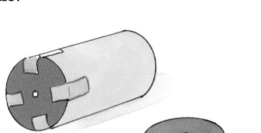

**3** Thread a small rubber band through the wax disc. Stop it from going all the way through by looping the end around a pencil.

**4** Thread the other end of the rubber band through the spool. A straightened paper clip will help with threading. Attach the end of the rubber band to half of a matchstick.

**5** Wind up the pencil tightly without breaking the rubber band. Place the tractor on the floor, and let the matchstick push it along.

# WHY IT WORKS

The wound up rubber band stores energy. As the rubber band starts to unwind, it makes the pencil rotate. The matchstick presses against the ground. Since one end of the matchstick cannot move against the ground, the energy is used up by making the spool of thread rotate instead. This is what pushes the tractor forward.

FURTHER IDEAS
Wrap rubber bands around the spool to act as rubber tires and improve the grip. See what is the steepest slope it can climb up. (Use the friction tester on pp 70 and 71).

# HYDRAULIC FORCES

Powerful machines like cranes, forklifts, and fire engines use hydraulic forces to lift heavy things quite easily. "Hydro" means water, although in practice these machines use other liquids in their hydraulics.

MAKE A HYDRAULIC FORCE

**1** Ask an adult to cut the necks off two large plastic bottles, then to cut a hole near the bottom of each.

**2** Thread a plastic tube through the bottles. Tie the neck of a balloon over one end of the tube. Fill the other end of the tube with water.

**3** Fill another balloon with water. Tie this balloon to the free end of the tube. Both balloons and the tube must be filled with water.

**4** Find two empty cans that just fit into the bottles. Place them above the balloons. Gently push down on one can with the palm of your hand.

**5** The second can rises by the same distance that you pressed down the first. You can reverse this by pressing down on the second can.

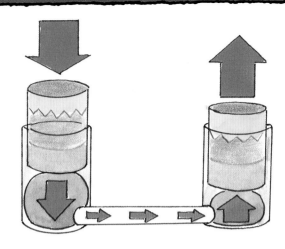

# WHY IT WORKS

It is very difficult to squash water. If you squeeze it hard in one place, it will push out just as hard in another place. The water transmits the force from one can to the other. This is the principle used by all hydraulic machines.

## FURTHER IDEAS

Glue a small plastic toy to a balloon. Connect the balloon to a plastic syringe with a tube. Lay the balloon flat in a glass tumbler and inflate with the syringe. This pump uses air, which is springy compared to water, to make the balloon inflate.

# WHAT A DRAG!

It is quite hard to move quickly under the water. The water gets in your way and before you can move forward you must push it out of the way. The water exerts a special force of friction called "drag." Birds and airplanes have wings designed to reduce "drag" in the air.

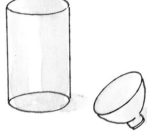

TESTING MOVING SHAPES

**1** Find a large plastic bottle and ask an adult to cut off the neck. Otherwise use a long plastic tube.

**2** Find a small but sturdy box. Cut a piece of thick cardboard and tape it to the back of the box.

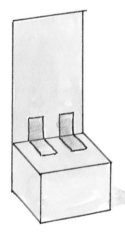

**3** Use a funnel to carefully fill the bottle with cooking oil. Stand the bottle on the box.

**4** Mold the same amount of clay into different shapes. Attach a piece of cotton to each shape.

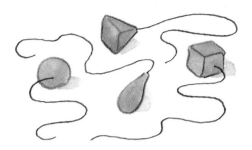

**5** Hold the shapes just above the bottle, release, and start timing. Make sure you hold on to the cotton. Stop timing when the shapes reach the bottom.

# WHY IT WORKS

Cooking oil has more drag than water so it is easier to see how much the shapes are slowed down. A shape has to push the oil out of its path to move forward. Shapes with a rounded front allow liquids to pass around them with little drag.

## FURTHER IDEAS

Try some of these shapes. Predict which will move the fastest before you test them. Add a small weight to the front of each shape to stop it from turning around as it falls.

# PULLEYS

A pulley is a machine to help you lift very heavy loads. Cranes are useful machines with a system of pulleys that make lifting heavy objects easier. You can see cranes almost everywhere – on building sites, at docks and railroad stations.

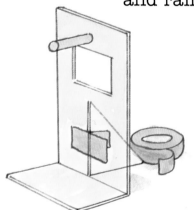

## MAKE A SIMPLE PULLEY

**1** Cut out a window from cardboard. Fold it and tape a triangle to the back to help it stand up. Push a short wooden dowel through the top.

**3** Bend three pieces of thin wire into shape. Attach the circles to the wire to make one double pulley and one single pulley.

**2** Cut four circles of cardboard, each with a hole in the middle. Push a piece of straw through each pair of circles.

**4** Hang the pulleys as shown. Make sure you loop the thread around the lower pulley, back over the top pulley, and out through the window.

**5** Hang a small weight from the hook on the lower pulley. Pull the thread from behind the window to lift the weight.

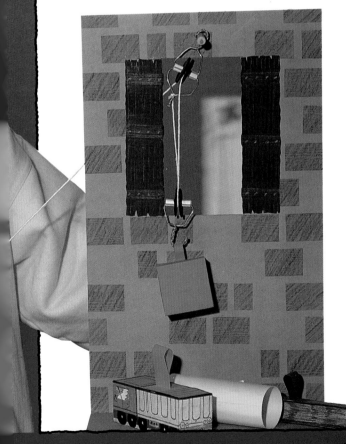

# WHY IT WORKS

A pulley system allows a force to be transferred from one place to another. As you pull on the thread, the force is transferred along the thread all the way to the weight. You can lift the weight with half the effort but it only moves half the distance.

FURTHER IDEAS
Make a winch from a cardboard base and clay-filled straw. Hold the straw in place with wire. Wrap thread around the straw, and tie a hook to the other end. Attach weights to the hook and pull them in by winding the winch.

# AROUND AND AROUND

Electric mixers, washing machines, and dryers all operate by spinning forces. A gyroscope is a terrific toy that seems to defy gravity while it spins. The spinning force balances out the force of gravity and makes the spinning object hard to push over.

MAKE SPINNING TOPS

**1** Find a large sheet of thin white cardboard. Use a pair of compasses to draw some circles of different sizes.

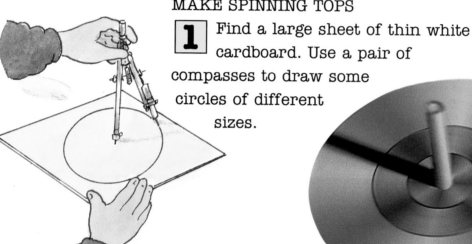

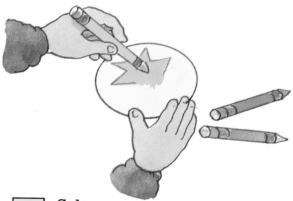

**2** Use a pair of scissors to cut out each circle carefully.

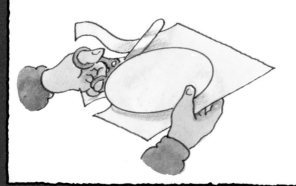

**3** Color each circle with bright markers. Create a different design for each one.

**4** Make a small hole through the center of each circle. Then push a sharp pencil through each hole.

# WHY IT WORKS

When you start the top spinning, you give it a lot of spinning energy. The top spins for minutes before this energy is all used up. The top actually stores some of the energy during this time so that it can go on spinning. The energy you gave it is only gradually released.

**5** Hold the top of the pencil between two fingers and spin it as fast as you can. Release it and let it spin on a smooth tabletop.

FURTHER IDEAS

Place an egg on a plate and start it spinning fast. Suddenly grab the egg to stop its spinning. Quickly release it and it will start spinning again all by itself!

# TRANSFERRING FORCES

All of the power in a modern car comes from the engine. The forces made by the engine are then transferred to where they are needed – mainly to make the wheels turn. One of the most common ways of transferring forces is through gearwheels.

## MAKE MODEL GEARS

**1** Draw and cut out four equal circles with teeth all the way around them using thick cardboard. These are your gearwheels.

**2** Make a small hole in the middle of each wheel. Add another close to the middle of one wheel. Draw and cut out the other shapes shown here.

**3** Use a thumbtack to attach one wheel to a piece of cardboard. Insert an extra piece of cardboard between the cardboard and paper clip for a tight fit.

**4** Attach the other wheel to the bar and hammer with a thumbtack. Attach these to the first wheel so that the teeth match.

**5** Rotate the upper wheel slowly. Watch how the hammer moves from side to side.

# WHY IT WORKS

As you turn the first gearwheel, this turning movement is passed on to the second gearwheel. The bar moves from side to side as the wheel turns and this sets up the sideways movement of the hammer.

FURTHER IDEAS
Try using different-sized wheels in your gear system. Notice how they move at different speeds: The larger gears move more slowly than the smaller gears.

# EQUAL AND OPPOSITE

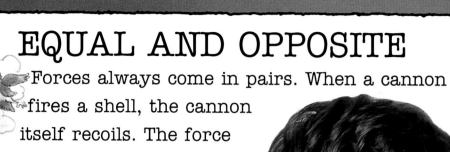

Forces always come in pairs. When a cannon fires a shell, the cannon itself recoils. The force pushing the shell FORWARD has an equal but opposite force.

## MAKE A JET ENGINE

**1** Cut out these shapes from thin cardboard. Tape the strip into a circle. Attach a drinking straw.

**2** Tape together all of the shapes to make up the outline of a rocket like the one illustrated below.

**3** Place a balloon in the cardboard. Slowly inflate it until it is a tight fit inside the rocket outline. Keep holding the neck of the balloon.

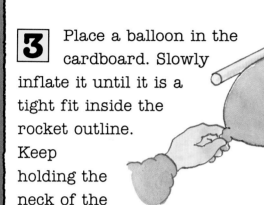

**4** Thread string through the straw. Fasten the ends of the string across the room. Release the balloon to be jet-propelled along the string.

# WHY IT WORKS

Over 300 years ago, Sir Isaac Newton found that every force has an equal but opposite reaction. As the air rushes out of the back of your balloon in one direction, the balloon itself is pushed forward in the opposite direction. This is the principle on which all jet engines work.

FURTHER IDEAS
Sit in a chair with wheels, and hold a soccerball. Try to throw it without moving. The harder you throw it, the stronger is the opposite force that pushes you backward.

# CONTENTS

# CHAPTER *Four*

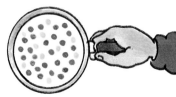

# MAKING THINGS CHANGE

# FREEZING AND MELTING

When the weather becomes cold, it can change many of the things around us. It can cause water to freeze, or solidify, into ice or snow. This change is easy to reverse; warmed ice will thaw, or melt, back into water.

EXPANDING ICE

**1** Find two large empty plastic bottles. Tape a paper marker around each about half way up.

**2** Using a large pitcher of water, carefully fill each of the bottles exactly to the mark on the paper.

**3** Place one bottle in a warm room and the other in your freezer. Leave them overnight.

**4** Take out the frozen bottle and compare the water level in each of them.

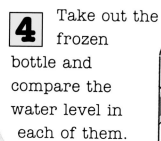

# WHY IT WORKS

There seems to be more ice. This is because water expands, gets larger, when it freezes. Pipes sometimes burst in winter because the water inside freezes and expands.

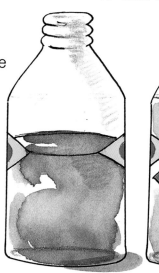

FURTHER IDEAS
Find lumps of chocolate, butter and wax from a candle, about the same size as an ice cube. Place them on a tray. Leave the tray in a warm place to compare how they melt. Place the tray in the freezer to reverse the changes.

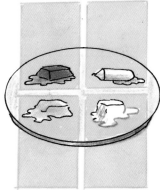

# THE ACID TEST

Chemicals are split into families of *acids*, *alkalis* or *neutrals*. These chemicals are everywhere – even in soil. The color of the Hydrangea flower depends on the levels of acid or alkali in the soil. Blue flowers mean there is more acid in the soil; pink, more alkali.

MAKE A CHEMICAL INDICATOR

**1** Take a red cabbage, tear it into shreds, and place these shreds into a bowl.

GET AN ADULT TO HELP YOU WITH THIS

**2** Pour hot water into the bowl. The cabbage color dissolves to make an indicator.

**3** Strain the juice, and pour the liquid into three small jars.

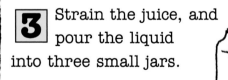

**4** Add a different liquid to each jar, such as vinegar or liquid soap. Compare the colors.

# WHY IT WORKS

A chemical that changes color in acids and alkalis is called an indicator. Red cabbage juice turns red when in acids, like vinegar, and green when in alkalis, like soap.

FURTHER IDEAS
Make indicator paper by soaking blotting paper in the indicator. Then test household items.

# BUBBLES AND FIZZ

Carbon dioxide is the gas in carbonated drinks which keeps them full of bubbles. When you shake a carbonated drink, then suddenly release the cap, the gas inside bubbles up and escapes. Carbon dioxide gas is important in other ways. It can be used to put out fires and it also makes cakes rise. Here you can make your own bubbles of gas.

MAKE AN ERUPTING VOLCANO

**1** Find a small glass jar. Stand it on a saucer. This will be your volcano.

**2** Cover the sides of the jar with clay to make the volcano.

**3** Carefully fill half the jar with baking soda. Add a few drops of red food coloring. Then add vinegar, a spoonful at a time.

**4** Stand back and watch as the mixture bubbles up and over the sides of the volcano.

## WHY IT WORKS

A mixture of the acid in vinegar and alkali in baking soda makes bubbles of gas. The thousands of bubbles are very light and this causes the mixture to fizz. The eruption of bubbles is similar to lava erupting from a volcano.

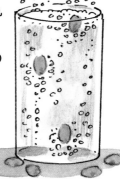

### FURTHER IDEAS
Fill a glass with vinegar and add a tablespoonful of baking soda. Drop in mothballs. Bubbles of gas make them rise back to the surface.

# PRETTY FLOWERS

Plants, like animals, need water to stay alive. The roots of plants are especially good at taking water from the ground. Water moves through the plant in tiny tubes, which are similar to the blood vessels in an animal.

CHANGE FLOWER COLORS

**1** Fill three glass bottles with water. Add a few drops of different food coloring to each.

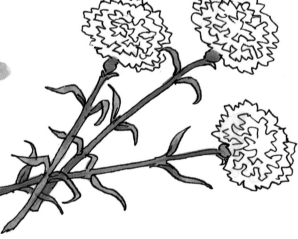

**2** Find three freshly cut flowers, preferably white or light-colored.

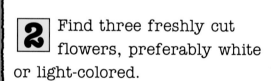

**3** Trim the stem of each flower before placing them into the three bottles.

**4** Leave the flowers overnight. Each becomes the color of the water in which it was placed.

# WHY IT WORKS

Water travels up the stem of each flower and spreads to all parts of the plant, including the petals. The water then escapes from the plant into the air by evaporation. Fresh water is continually drawn up to replace the lost water.

### FURTHER IDEAS

Repeat with a fresh stalk of celery. When the water has risen through it, ask an adult to slice the stalk. With a magnifying glass you should see the thin tubes that carry the water.

# FLOWING CURRENTS

Currents of hot air rise from warm valleys to the cooler hilltops. These are called *thermals*. They are very useful to hot air balloons, gliders, and even birds. The rising warm air helps to keep them aloft.

SEE HOT WATER CURRENTS

**1** Find a small jar with a metal screw-on lid. Ask an adult to make some small holes in the lid.

GET AN ADULT TO DO THIS FOR YOU

**2** Tie a piece of string tightly around the neck of the jar. Make sure the string can support the jar.

**3** Place a few drops of food coloring in the jar and fill it with hot water. Screw the lid on tightly.

**4** Fill a glass jug with cold water. Holding the string, gently lower the jar into the glass jug.

**5** Watch as the colored water swirls around in the cold water.

# WHY IT WORKS

Hot liquids expand and become less dense than the cold liquid around them. This causes the hot liquid to rise into the jug. Eventually the heat is spread out, and the cooled, denser liquid sinks to the bottom of the pitcher. This movement of the liquid is known as a *convection current.*

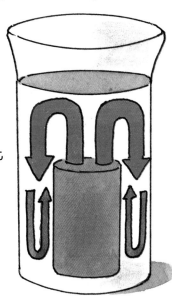

FURTHER IDEAS
Cut out some strips from circles of paper. Hold them above a heater. Rising warm air causes the strips to rotate.

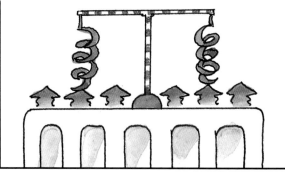

# RISING TEMPERATURES

On a hot day, you can see the temperature rise if you watch a thermometer carefully. As the air gets hotter, the liquid inside the thermometer expands up the glass tube. All liquids expand when heated, but usually only by a tiny amount.

## MAKE A BOTTLE FOUNTAIN

**1** Find a small glass jar with a screw-on lid. Fill the jar half full with cold water. Add a few drops of food coloring.

GET AN ADULT TO HELP YOU WITH THIS

**2** Ask an adult to make a hole in the lid just big enough for a thin straw. Seal the straw in place with some clay.

**3** Plug the end of the straw with clay. Use a pin to make a tiny hole in the plug.

**4** Fill a large bowl with hot tap water. Stand the small jar upside-down in the bowl on some clay, with the straw sticking above the water level.

**5** Wait for the small jar to heat up, and stand back to admire the fountain of colored water spraying out of the top.

# WHY IT WORKS

The heat from the hot water bowl warms up the air inside the jar, and this air expands. As it does so, it pushes on the water below. The water can only escape one way – by spraying out of the top of the straw.

FURTHER IDEAS
Fill a jar with water. Put a straw through a hole in the lid and seal with clay. Turn the jar upside-down. See how the level in the straw changes when the jar is put in hot water and in a refrigerator.

# SEPARATING MIXTURES

Tap water has been filtered many times to remove all impurities before you drink it. Filtering is like straining; it is a way of purifying a liquid by removing any solids that do not dissolve naturally.

MAKE MUDDY WATER CLEAR

**1** Mix some mud, clay, or soil with water in a jar. Make a cone shape out of a coffee filter.

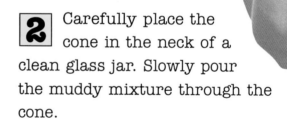

**2** Carefully place the cone in the neck of a clean glass jar. Slowly pour the muddy mixture through the cone.

**3** See how much clearer the filtered water appears. Warning: Do not drink the filtered water – it still contains germs.

# WHY IT WORKS

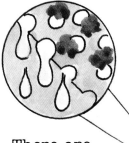

There are
tiny holes in
the paper that
only allow
water droplets
to squeeze
through. The
pieces of solid
are larger and
get trapped.

## FURTHER IDEAS

Dissolve some salt in a tall,
clean glass of water. Leave it in
a warm place for a few days.
See how salt is left behind when
all the water has evaporated.

# RUST OR BUST

Though many metals are strong, tough materials, they do not last forever. When iron is constantly damp it will rust; pieces of iron turn brown and crumble away. Rust can be a terrible problem. It can attack your car, bicycle, or anything else made from iron. The iron is changed into a new chemical that we call *rust*, or "iron oxide."

A RUST RACE

**1** Set up five glass jars with some steel wool in each. Add nothing to the first jar. Fill half the second jar with tap water. Fill the third to the brim with boiled water and tighten the lid. In the fourth, put the steel wool on a piece of damp cloth. Put tap water in the last jar, and add a pinch of salt.

**2** Leave the jars for at least a week. Regularly examine the steel wool for signs of rust.

# WHY IT WORKS

So-called "steel wool" is really made of iron. The steel wool rusts in jars 2 and 4, but especially in jar 5. Iron needs water and air to rust. The air and water particles attach to the iron particles to form iron oxide. Boiled water has no air in it. Salt makes iron rust faster.

FURTHER IDEAS
Scratch away some of the surface of some empty cans. See if the cans rust when damp.

# INVISIBLE INK

Have you ever wanted to write a secret message that only you can read? This project lets you write your message on a sheet of paper. When you have finished, the message is invisible – the paper just looks blank. Nobody can read it unless they know the method for making the message visible.

SEND A SECRET MESSAGE

**1** Squeeze some lemon juice into a glass.

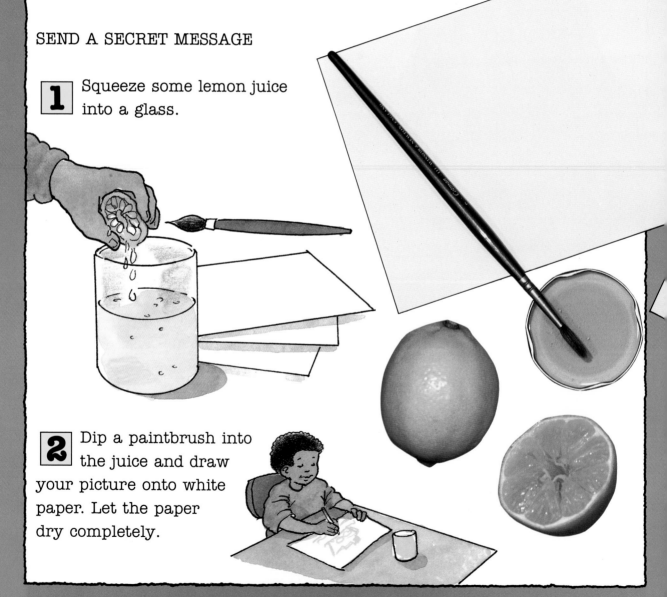

**2** Dip a paintbrush into the juice and draw your picture onto white paper. Let the paper dry completely.

104

**3** Ask an adult to place the paper in the oven for a few minutes, and the picture will reappear.

GET AN ADULT TO DO THIS

# WHY IT WORKS

When the lemon juice is heated, water evaporates away. The compounds that remain combine with oxygen in the air. This turns the juice brown and makes the picture visible.

## FURTHER IDEAS

Draw on white paper using a wax candle. Warm the paper on a radiator until the wax melts and the picture is revealed.

# SPLITTING COLORS

If you look very carefully with a magnifying glass at the colored dots that make up the colors in this book, you may notice that there are only four colors. All of the other colors are made by mixing these colors together.

SEPARATE COLORED INKS

**1** Cut some blotting paper into strips, 1 inch wide and 6 inches long.

**2** Make a large dot just above the bottom of each strip with several different-colored felt-tip pens.

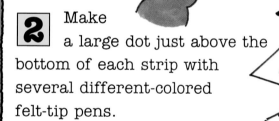

**3** Tape the other end of the strips to a string. Hang the string over a bowl with two pencils set in clay. Fill the bowl with water until it touches the strips.

**4** Watch the water rise half way up the strips. Remove them, and see how the colors have separated.

# WHY IT WORKS

The inks are made from different colors. These are separated by the rising water because some travel through the paper faster than others. For example, green is made from blue and yellow.

FURTHER IDEAS
Mix some food coloring together. Repeat the experiment with one drop of this mixture and watch the coloring separate.

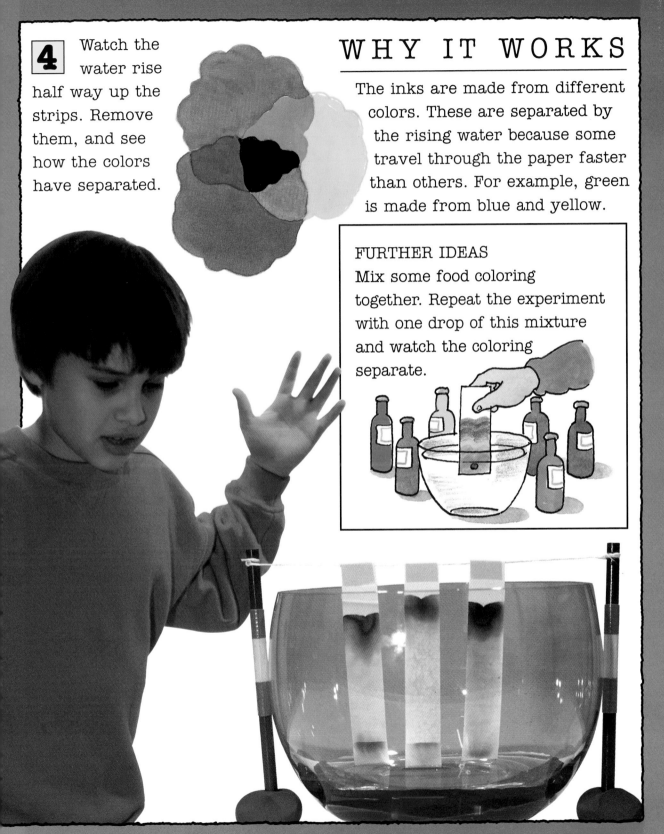

# BURNING AND BREATHING

Air is really a mixture of many gases. Most of the air is made up of nitrogen. One fifth is made up of oxygen. Oxygen is needed for fires and for people to breathe. Without oxygen, fires wouldn't burn and people would suffocate and die.

INVESTIGATE A BURNING CANDLE

**1** Use clay to stand a candle upright in the middle of a small, shallow saucer.

**2** Place four piles of coins around the clay so that a jar can sit over the candle.

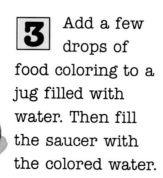

**3** Add a few drops of food coloring to a jug filled with water. Then fill the saucer with the colored water.

**4** Ask an adult to light the candle and lower the jar over it. Watch the water level in the jar rise as the candle goes out.

# WHY IT WORKS

The burning candle flame uses up the particles of oxygen. Water is sucked up into the jar to replace the used oxygen. Water rises about one fifth up the jar. The burning stops when all of the oxygen in the jar has been used up.

FURTHER IDEAS
Compare how long similar candles burn when different jars are placed over them. The longer they burn, the more oxygen is present.

# LIVING YEAST

Most germs, or "microbes," are bad for us, because they cause illness and disease. However, some microbes can be useful to us. We use microbes to make yogurt, cheese, bread, and beer. Yeast is a microbe that looks like a yellow powder, but under a microscope you can see that it is made of living cells.

SEE YEAST BREATHING

**2** Pour in some warm water. Swirl the bottle to mix the water, sugar, and yeast.

**1** Find a glass bottle and pour in a teaspoonful of sugar and some dried yeast.

**3** Fit a balloon over the neck of the bottle and make sure it is sealed tightly.

**4** Stand the bottle in a large bowl of hot water to keep it warm. Watch the mixture for bubbles of gas. Eventually, the balloon will fill with gas and inflate.

# WHY IT WORKS

When you add the warm water, the yeast "wakes up" and feeds on the sugar. As it feeds, it breathes out carbon dioxide and fills the balloon.

### FURTHER IDEAS

Stir a spoonful of sugar and dried yeast in warm water. Mix half a pound of flour with half an ounce of butter and a little salt. Add the yeast and water and knead into a dough. Bake the bread for fifteen minutes at 425°F (220°C).

# CONTENTS

# CHAPTER *Five*

# UNDERSTANDING ELECTRICITY

# WHAT IS ELECTRICITY?

All things are made up of tiny particles called atoms. Atoms are made from even smaller particles, some of which are electrically charged. This charge may be negative or positive. Electricity is a flow of the negatively charged particles. You can see a flow of charge in the form of a spark.

## LISTENING TO ELECTRICITY

**1** Find a metal tray or a cookie tin lid. Place a lump of clay, large enough to use as a handle, in the middle of the tray.

**2** Place the tray on a large plastic bag. Grip the clay firmly with one hand, press down, and rotate the tray vigorously for two minutes on the plastic.

**3** Be very careful not to touch the tray with your hands. Lift the tray off the plastic with the clay grip.

**4** Pick up a metal fork with your free hand. Touch the edge of the tray with it. Hear the sparks crackle!

# WHY IT WORKS

As the tray is rubbed on the plastic, it becomes negatively charged. The fork is positively charged and when it is brought close to the tray it attracts the negative charges. They jump through the air to the fork as a spark.

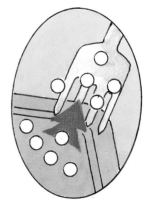

FURTHER IDEAS
Charge up a plastic comb by rubbing it vigorously on a clean, dry cloth. Adjust a faucet to give a thin stream of running water. Bring the comb close to the stream. The comb pulls at the water! Make the water dance by jiggling the comb.

# STATIC ELECTRICITY

The ancient Greeks noticed that when amber (fossilized tree resin) is rubbed, it attracts light objects, such as feathers. This is because the amber has become electrically charged. The word *electricity* comes from the Greek word *elektron*, meaning amber. Scientists use an electroscope to check if an object is electrically charged.

## MAKE AN ELECTROSCOPE

**1** Find a clean jar. Cut a circle of cardboard big enough to fit over the top of a glass jar. Cut two $\frac{1}{2}$ inch-long parallel slots in the middle of the cardboard.

**2** Cut out two strips of aluminum foil. They should each be about $\frac{1}{2}$ inch wide and 2 inches long.

**3** Insert one strip through each slot so the strips overlap at the top. Tape the cardboard to the top of the jar so the strips hang downward.

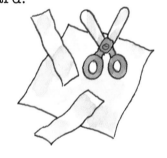

**4** Charge up a plastic comb by rubbing it vigorously for a couple of minutes with a clean, dry cloth.

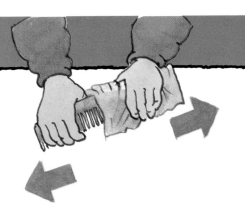

**5** Test the comb for charge with your electroscope. Touch the top of the aluminum strips with the comb. Watch what happens to the two strips.

# WHY IT WORKS

Electricity cannot move through plastic or amber. But they can hold a *static* (not moving) electric charge. When the comb touches the strips, the electric charge is released because electricity can move through metal. Both strips receive the same kind of charge, and because like charges repel (push away) each other, the strips move apart.

### FURTHER IDEAS

Inflate two balloons. Tie a piece of nylon thread to the end of each balloon. Rub each balloon on a wool sweater. Hang both balloons together from their threads. Watch how they repel each other.

# BATTERY POWER

Static electricity is not very useful for powering machines, so we use *current* electricity. An electric current is a controlled flow of electric charge. Batteries produce electric currents from chemicals. Alessandro Volta made the first battery in 1800. The volt, a unit of electric measurement, is named after him.

MAKE A BATTERY

**1** Find 12 copper coins and zinc washers of similar size. They will need to be stacked. Cut out 12 same-sized circles of blotting paper.

**2** Pour vinegar into a glass with a tablespoonful of salt. Soak each piece of blotting paper in the mixture. Stack a coin, then a washer, on a piece of blotting paper. Finish with a washer.

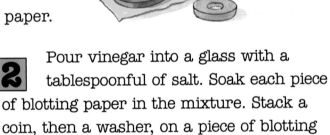

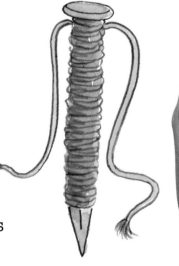

**3** Take 6 ½ feet of thin plastic-coated copper wire. Coil it tightly around an iron nail as many times as you can.

**4** Attach one end of the copper wire to the bottom coin and the other to the top washer.

# WHY IT WORKS

The salt and vinegar start a chemical reaction. Negatively charged particles flow through the coins to the washers, around the wire coil, and back to the battery. The electric current creates a magnetic field that affects a compass needle (see pages 134-135).

**5** Test your battery by bringing the nail close to a small compass. The nail should make the compass needle spin.

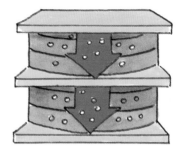

FURTHER IDEAS
Find a juicy lemon. Push one copper and one zinc nail into it. Touch both nails with your tongue. You will feel a tingle from the flow of current in the lemon "battery."

# SIMPLE CIRCUITS

The path an electric current takes is called a circuit. Electric current flows from the power supply, to the lightbulb, and back to the power supply. As long as there are no gaps in the circuit, the electric current will flow.

MAKE A CIRCUIT

**1** Ask an adult to open up a coat hanger. Bend it into a wavy shape. Push the ends of the wire into a cardboard base. Hold each end in place with clay.

**2** Make a loop out of thin wire. Connect it to a long piece of insulated wire. Thread this through a plastic straw to form a handle. Slip the loop onto the wavy wire.

**3** Attach a 6-volt lightbulb and 6-volt battery to the base. Wire the battery and bulb to the wavy wire as shown (right).

**4** Connect the other end of the bulb to the loop. The wire needs to be long enough to reach both ends of the wavy wire.

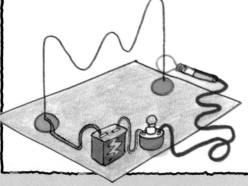

**5** Check that the bulb lights when you touch the loop to the wavy wire. Now try and move the loop along the path of the wavy wire without letting the two touch!

# WHY IT WORKS

Current electricity only flows if there is a complete circuit back to the battery. The gap in this circuit is between the loop and the wavy wire. The wires will touch if your hand is not steady. The gap is closed, the circuit is completed, and the bulb lights up.

FURTHER IDEAS
Try replacing the bulb in this circuit with a small electric buzzer. When you touch the wavy wire, the buzzer will buzz. You could make the game harder by making the wavy wire longer or even more wavy.

# CONDUCTORS AND INSULATORS

Some materials allow electricity to flow through them easily. These materials are called electrical conductors. Most metals are good conductors. Other materials, like plastic, do not easily let electricity flow through them. These materials, called insulators, are used to prevent electricity from reaching places where it would be dangerous.

## TEST FOR ELECTRICAL CONDUCTORS

**1** Find a thick cardboard base. Cut out two squares of aluminum foil. Glue them onto the base. Leave a small gap between them (see right).

**2** Attach a piece of thin plastic-coated copper wire to one square. Glue it to the board as shown. Repeat for the other square.

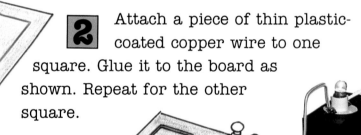

**3** Connect one of the wires to a 6-volt lightbulb (right). Glue the bulb to the base.

**4** Connect the other wire to a 6-volt battery. Now connect the battery and bulb to a small plastic-coated copper wire.

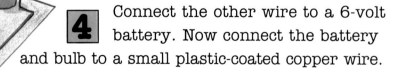

**5** Test a range of objects, such as keys, pencils, or erasers by placing them across the two squares.

# WHY IT WORKS

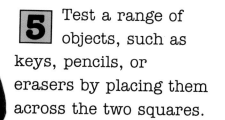

If an object is a conductor, it completes the circuit. The bulb lights up because conductors allow electricity to flow through them. All metals are conductors. Carbon is an unusual non-metal because it also conducts electricity. Pencil "lead" contains carbon in the form of graphite.

### FURTHER IDEAS
Make up another circuit without a base. Test water to see if it can conduct electricity. Keep the squares close together in the container. Stir in lots of salt to help the water to conduct. Watch the bulb get brighter as you add more salt.

# RESISTANCE

Good conductors of electricity allow electricity to flow easily. A thick wire can conduct more electricity than a thin wire, just like a wide road can carry more cars than a narrow road. The thin wire resists the flow of electricity or has a higher resistance.

MAKE A DIMMER SWITCH

**1** Attach a 6-volt battery and 6-volt bulb to a thick cardboard base. Use two long wires and one short one to make a circuit as shown (right).

**2** Remove the graphite from a mechanical pencil. Tape or glue together half a dozen graphite rods. Attach the wire from the battery to the bundle.

**3** Attach a square of aluminum foil to the wire from the bulb. Check that the circuit is complete and the bulb lights when you touch the square to the graphite.

# WHY IT WORKS

Graphite is made of carbon, which is a conductor. As you slide the square along the graphite toward the battery, the electricity travels less distance. This means less resistance, so the bulb gets brighter.

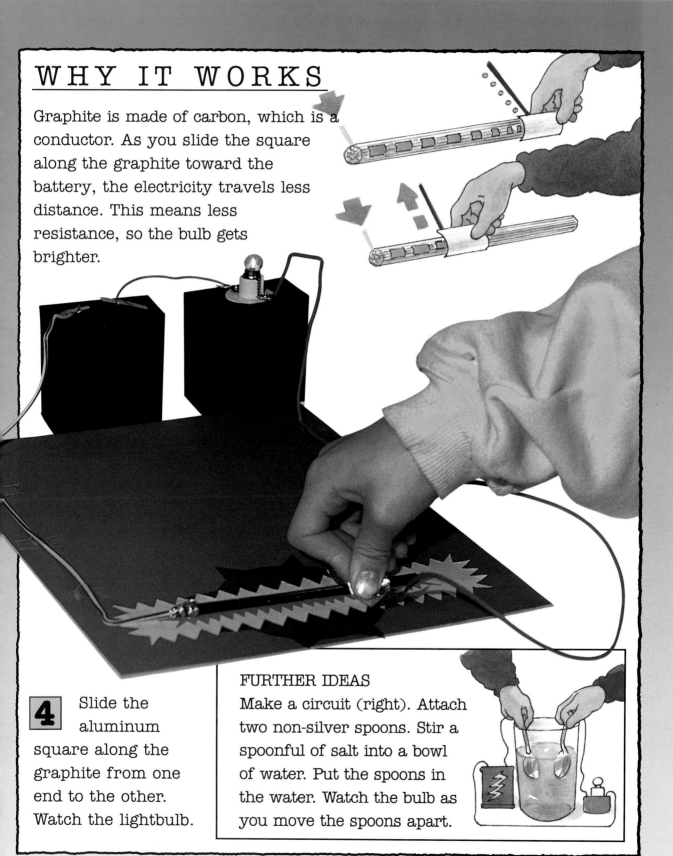

**4** Slide the aluminum square along the graphite from one end to the other. Watch the lightbulb.

## FURTHER IDEAS
Make a circuit (right). Attach two non-silver spoons. Stir a spoonful of salt into a bowl of water. Put the spoons in the water. Watch the bulb as you move the spoons apart.

# OPEN CIRCUITS

Every time you turn on a light you are completing a circuit. As soon as a switch is closed (turned on), the circuit is completed and the electricity operates the bulb or electrical appliance. In 1837, Samuel Morse had the idea of completing and breaking an electrical circuit to send messages.

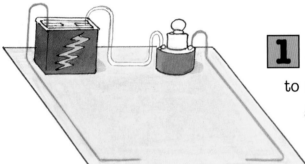

### SEND A MESSAGE

**1** Make a circuit using a 6-volt battery and 6-volt bulb attached to a thick cardboard base. Leave a gap between the two wires (see left).

**2** Make a switch out of a steel paper clip. Attach it to the end of the wire running from the battery. Tape a square of aluminum foil over the top (see right). Tape another aluminum square over the end of the other wire. Make sure the paper clip reaches this square.

**3** Press the paper clip down to touch the square and switch on the bulb. Practice long and short flashes to send a Morse code message.

# WHY IT WORKS

Electricity cannot flow when a circuit is open. Closing the switch completes the circuit. The bulb lights immediately because electricity can travel so quickly.

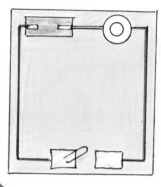

FURTHER IDEAS
Make a burglar alarm using your circuit board as a base. Tape some pencils or straws along the side edges. Place a second board on top of the pencils leaving the bulb and battery clear. Cover the boards with a mat. When the "intruder" steps on the mat, the switch will be pressed and the burglar alarm will light up.

# TURNED ON

Being able to turn a light on or off from two different places can be very useful. If a light can be turned on or off from both the top and the bottom of a staircase then not only is it safer at night but energy is also saved. This kind of switch is called a two-way switch.

MAKE A TWO-WAY SWITCH

**1** Fold a piece of cardboard into a wedge shape (shown right). Draw a line down the center. Stick down two pieces of cardboard on each side of the line and draw a staircase.

**2** Make a circuit using a 6-volt battery and light-bulb. Push a tack through each piece of cardboard. Attach the wires to them.

**3** Push four more tacks into the cardboard (shown below). Connect the upper two with a short piece of wire and repeat for the lower two.

**4** Attach a paper clip under each of the first two tacks so that they can turn to touch either the upper or lower tack.

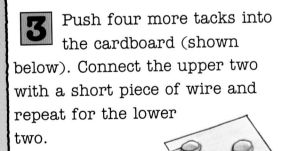

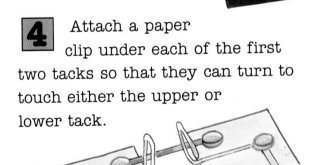

# WHY IT WORKS

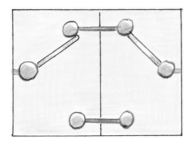 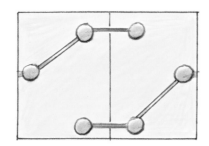 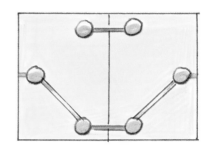

The two-way switch allows two alternative paths for an electric current. Electricity can flow only when both paper clips are touching the same wire. Removing one of the paper clips from the wire breaks the circuit.

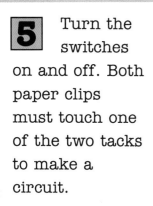

**5** Turn the switches on and off. Both paper clips must touch one of the two tacks to make a circuit.

FURTHER IDEAS

Make a three-way switch quiz game (see right). When the paper clips point to the same letter, the bulb lights up. When your friend chooses the correct answer (A, B, or C), the bulb lights up.

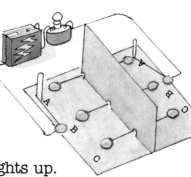

# BIGGER CIRCUITS

All the circuits you have built so far have been small and simple, requiring only one piece of wire. Electric circuits in your home consist of many more wires. Finding which wire is connected to which source can be like finding your way through a maze.

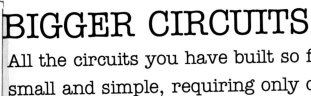

MAKE A MAZE

**1** Find a large piece of thick cardboard. Cut out ½ inch-wide strips of aluminum foil about the same length as the cardboard.

**2** Flatten the aluminum strips, glue them to the cardboard, then make a criss-cross pattern with the strips.

**3** Attach a 6 inch-long wire to one side of a 6-volt lightbulb. Then attach a 3.5 ft-long wire to a dowel "pointer," leaving the copper exposed at the end.

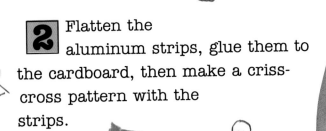

**4** Make a circuit (left). Wire the battery to the aluminum at one corner of the board. Test the circuit by touching the pointer to the foil.

**5** Cover parts of the aluminum with insulating tape. Copy the pattern shown at the bottom of the page. The gray shaded areas show where the tape should go.

**6** Challenge a friend to find a way through the maze keeping the bulb lit. The pointer must touch only the aluminum to complete the circuit.

## WHY IT WORKS

When the pointer touches any part of the aluminum connected to the battery, a circuit is created. Electricity can flow and light the bulb. If the pointer touches other parts of the maze, the bulb goes out.

# HOUSE LIGHTS

A simple way to arrange more than one lightbulb is in a series, so the electricity flows through one bulb to the next. But if a bulb fails, the circuit is broken, and all the lights go out. In a parallel circuit, each bulb has its own connection to the battery, so if one bulb fails the others are unaffected. House lights work this way.

MAKE A RING CIRCUIT

**1** Ask an adult to bend two pieces of wire into two rings, one larger than the other. Use some cardboard as a base for your circuit.

**2** Make a circuit out of the two rings and a 6-volt battery (left). Connect the outer ring to one battery terminal, and the inner ring to the other terminal.

**3** Connect two pieces of thin plastic-coated copper wire to the ends of a 6-volt bulb. Check that there is plenty of bare wire showing at the free ends.

# WHY IT WORKS

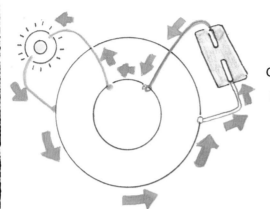

Wherever the battery and bulb are placed on the rings, there is always a complete circuit. This type of parallel circuit is called a ring circuit.

**4** Attach one of the wires running from the lightbulb to the outer ring, and one to the inner ring. It forms a circuit and the bulb lights up.

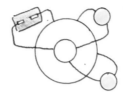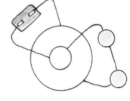

FURTHER IDEAS
Try adding another bulb to your ring circuit. Does one affect the other? Can you find a place on the rings where the circuit does not work?

# MOVEMENT FROM ELECTRICITY

Electric motors do all sorts of useful work in the home: They are found in household items such as washing machines, electric heaters, and food processors. The movement produced is usually a spinning motion. The electric motor uses electricity and magnetism to produce movement.

MAKE A SIMPLE MOTOR

**1** Wrap four 3.5-foot pieces of wire together to form a loop (see right). Secure the wires with insulation tape.

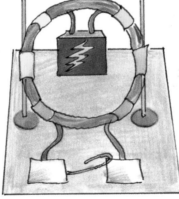

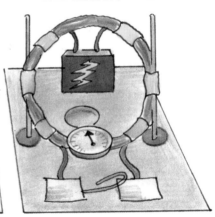

**2** On a cardboard base, attach two dowels in an upright position with clay. Tape the wire to the dowels (shown above).

**3** Attach the two top wires to a 6-volt battery. Attach the bottom wires to two aluminum squares at the base. Make a switch out of a paper clip.

**4** Leave the switch open. Hold a small pocket compass level in the middle of the wire loop. Note the direction the compass points to.

**5** Now turn off the switch and watch the effect on the compass. It should spin around until you turn the switch on again.

## WHY IT WORKS

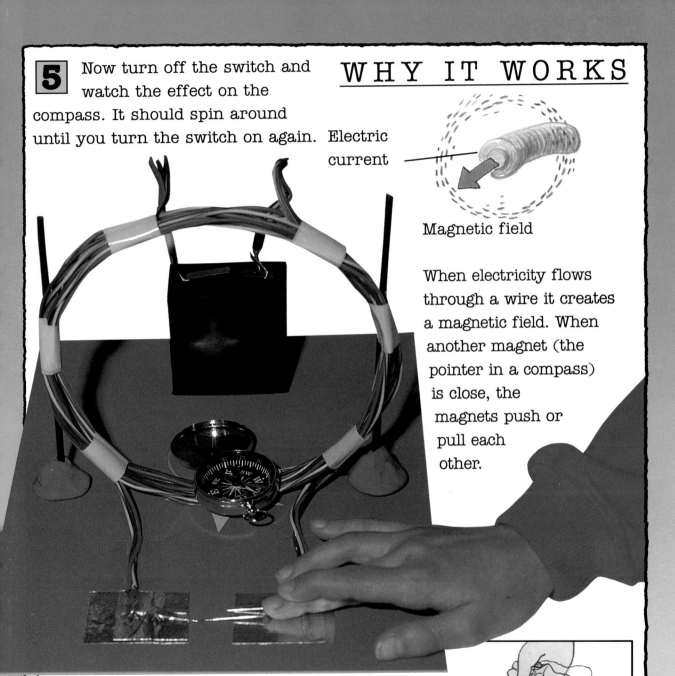

Electric current

Magnetic field

When electricity flows through a wire it creates a magnetic field. When another magnet (the pointer in a compass) is close, the magnets push or pull each other.

FURTHER IDEAS
Coil about three and a half feet of copper wire around an iron nail. Attach the ends of the wire to the terminals of a 6-volt battery. The nail will become an electromagnet which is strong enough to attract steel paper clips.

# ELECTROPLATING

An electric current can be used to split chemicals into the elements that they are made of. If an electric current is passed through a liquid called an electrolyte, charged particles will move through it. This is called electrolysis. Cutlery and jewelry are silverplated using electrolysis.

## COPPERPLATE A SILVER COIN

**1** Fill a clean glass jar with water. This will act as your electrolyte.

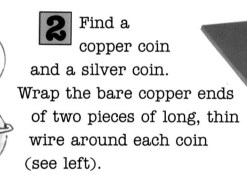

**3** Put the coins into the water. Wrap the two wires around a pencil balanced over the top of the jar.

**2** Find a copper coin and a silver coin. Wrap the bare copper ends of two pieces of long, thin wire around each coin (see left).

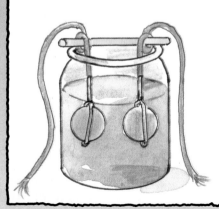

**4** Connect the copper coin to the positive (+) terminal of a 6-volt battery, and the silver coin to the negative (-) terminal.

**5** Make sure the coins are close but not touching. Leave the circuit set up for five minutes. Take out the two coins and observe.

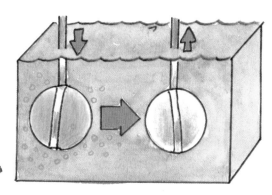

# WHY IT WORKS

Electric current enters the water through the positive terminal, attached to the copper coin. It carries some of the copper with it. The current carries the copper through the water to the silver coin. The copper is left as a thin layer over the silver coin. The copper can easily be scraped off afterwards. Dispose of the water carefully afterwards as it is poisonous.

## FURTHER IDEAS
Try using vinegar with lots of salt stirred into it as the electrolyte instead of water. Using a more powerful battery produces faster and thicker plating.

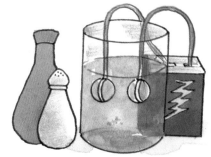

# CONTENTS

# CHAPTER *Six*

# MAKING THINGS FLOAT AND SINK

# WHY DO THINGS FLOAT?

Wood, cork and ice all float no matter what size or shape they are. However, materials such as modeling clay or steel, sometimes float and sometimes sink. With these materials, it is their shape that decides whether they float or sink.

MAKE A CLAY BOAT

**1** Fill a large plastic bowl with water from the tap.

**2** Try to float a lump of modeling clay on the surface of the water. Try floating marbles too. Watch them sink.

**3** Using your thumbs, press the clay into a boat shape. Hollow out the inside.

**4** Draw a sailor on a sheet of cardboard. Color him in and cut out. Fold along the dotted lines as shown so he can sit up.

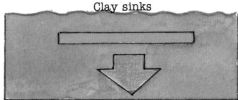
Clay sinks

**5** Sit the sailor in the boat. Now float the boat on the water. Put a marble in your boat. It will sink slightly but remains upright.

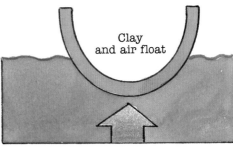
Clay and air float

## FURTHER IDEAS
Have a boat-building competition with some friends. Each make a boat using the same amount of clay. Whose boat can hold the most marbles?

# WHY IT WORKS

One ounce of water takes up more space than one ounce of clay. Because clay is denser than water it sinks. Shaped into a boat, clay fills with air. Air and clays together are less dense than water, so the boat floats.

# ICEBERG AHOY!

When most liquids freeze to solids they become more dense. Water is different. When water freezes it expands (causing burst pipes in winter) and becomes less dense. Ice floats because it is less dense than water. Giant blocks of ice floating in the sea are called icebergs. Ships must take care to avoid icebergs.

## WATCH AN ICE-CUBE MELT

**1** Add some food coloring to a jar of water. Add enough coloring to turn the water a bright color.

**2** Pour the colored water into an ice-cube tray. Put it in a freezer overnight.

**3** Fill up a large container with hot tap water. Ask an adult to help you.

**5** As the ice becomes water, the color moves around in the warmer water. It sinks to the bottom of the container.

**4** Take one of the colored ice-cubes and carefully float it on the surface of the hot water.

# WHY IT WORKS

As the ice melts to water its density increases. This makes it sink to the bottom of the container. There it mixes with the water in the jar and warms up. It becomes less dense and moves back toward the surface.

Melted ice

FURTHER IDEAS Make a volcano. Fill a jar with hot water. Add coloring. Cover the top of the jar with paper held in place with a rubber band. Put the jar in a bowl of cold water. Pierce the paper. Watch the volcano erupt.

# COLORFUL PAPER

It is not only boats and icebergs that float on water. Oil-based liquids that are less dense than water also float on top of water. We sometimes see escaped crude oil floating on the sea in a thin layer that stretches for miles. Such oil slicks can harm the seabed, fish, and birds.

## MAKE COLORED PAPER

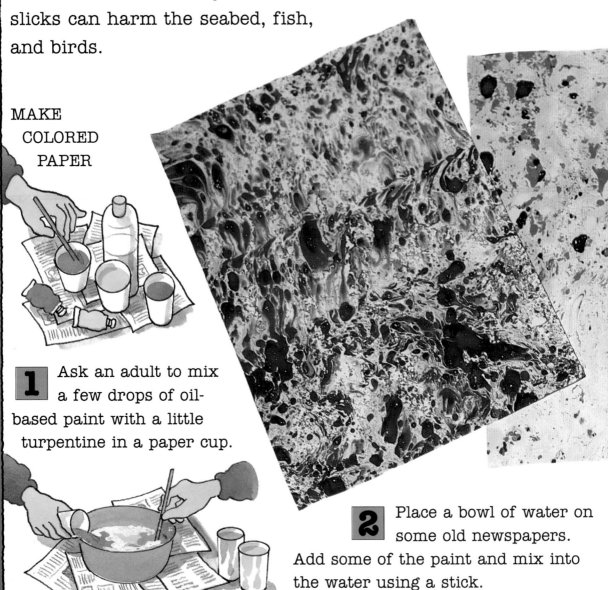

**1** Ask an adult to mix a few drops of oil-based paint with a little turpentine in a paper cup.

**2** Place a bowl of water on some old newspapers. Add some of the paint and mix into the water using a stick.

**3** Carefully lower a sheet of plain paper onto the surface of the water. Let the paper soak up the paint.

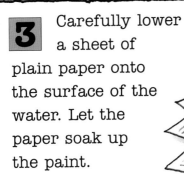

# WHY IT WORKS

Oil paints are less dense than water so they float on the surface. For this reason salad oil floats on top of vinegar. You can make the separate layers mix together by shaking them hard.

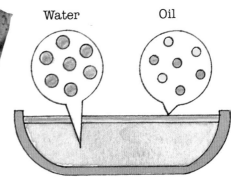

Water    Oil

**4** Remove the paper and leave it to dry. Repeat using fresh paper. Stir the water to get different patterns.

## FURTHER IDEAS
Try making different patterns by changing the colors of paint. Let the papers dry. Use your favorite patterns for writing paper.

# FLOATING LIQUIDS

Many liquids are like water and mix easily with it. But some liquids do not mix with water unless they are forced to. Oils and syrups do not mix well with water. Some liquids are less dense and float on top of water (see pages 144-145). Others are denser so water floats on top of them.

## MAKE LAYERS OF FLOATING LIQUIDS

**1** Find a clean, empty plastic soda bottle. Ask an adult to cut the top off with a sharp knife.

GET AN ADULT TO DO THIS FOR YOU

**2** Slowly pour in some syrup so there is a ¾ inch layer in the bottom. Let the syrup settle.

**3** Next, slowly pour ¾ inch of cooking oil over the layer of syrup.

**4** Finally, carefully pour in about ¾ inch of water.

**5** Examine the three layers. They float on top of each other without mixing. See what happens if you stir gently with a spoon.

# WHY IT WORKS

The layers of liquid refuse to mix with each other. The syrup is at the bottom because it is the densest. The oil is the least dense of the three and so floats on the very top.

FURTHER IDEAS
Try floating different objects on your layers of liquid. Experiment with things that you would expect to sink in water.

# FLOATING EGGS

How can you tell whether an egg is good or bad without breaking it? Fresh eggs sink if placed in a bowl of fresh water because they are denser than water. But if an egg turns bad, it floats in water. This is because the yolk and white have dried up, which makes it less dense than a good egg.

## MAKE AN EGG FLOAT

GET AN ADULT TO DO THIS FOR YOU

**1** Find two large containers. Fill one with hot tap water and the other with cold tap water. Get an adult to help.

**2** Add a spoonful of table salt to the hot water. Stir in the salt until it has all dissolved.

**3** Put a fresh egg into the salty water to see if it floats. If it doesn't, add more salt until it does.

# WHY IT WORKS

Salt dissolved in water increases the density of water. Denser liquids are better at keeping objects afloat. This is why many things that sink in fresh water will float in salted water.

**4** You cannot float the egg in fresh water but in salty water the same egg floats. Challenge your friends to explain it!

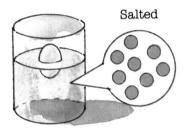

Salted

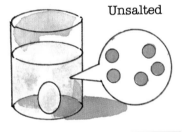

Unsalted

### FURTHER IDEAS
See how long it takes for a fresh egg to go bad when not refrigerated. Test it in a vase of fresh water each day. Dispose of the bad egg *carefully* when you've finished.

# DIFFERENT DEPTHS

We have seen that each liquid has its own particular density. The denser or "heavier" the liquid, the better it is at making things float in it. Brewers of beer need to know the exact density of beer to ensure the beer tastes just right. A hydrometer is used to test its density.

MAKE A HYDROMETER

**1** Pour equal amounts of syrup, cooking oil and hot water into three containers of the same size.

**2** Cut a plastic drinking straw into three equal lengths. Each will make a hydrometer.

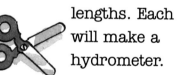

**3** Make three small balls out of clay. Attach one to the end of each straw.

Float your hydrometer in a bowl of water. Add salt or sugar to the water. What effect does this have on the hydrometer?

**4** Carefully place each hydrometer into the liquids. Compare the different levels at which the hydrometers float.

# WHY IT WORKS

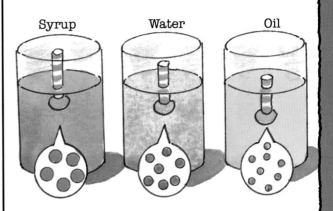

Syrup      Water      Oil

The particles of dense liquids are bigger or closer together. Dense liquids push harder on the hydrometer. The harder the push, the higher up in the liquid the hydrometer floats.

# UNSINKABLE

Boats and ships are always built to be as stable as possible. This means that they do not get pushed over easily by waves in rough seas. Most boats and ships capsize and sink if they are pushed too far. A buoy is a channel marker. Because it is there to warn of danger, it is vital that it never gets pushed over.

MAKE A BUOY

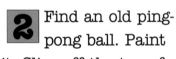

**1** Half fill a large container with water.

**2** Find an old ping-pong ball. Paint it. Slice off the top of it. Make a hole in its center.

GET AN ADULT TO DO THIS FOR YOU

**3** Fill the inside of the buoy with clay and tape the top back on.

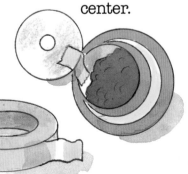

**4** Make a flag out of a triangle of paper and a drinking straw.

**5** Stick the flag into the hole in the top of the buoy.

**6** Put the buoy in the water. Make some waves. See how difficult it is to push the buoy over.

# WHY IT WORKS

The clay acts as "ballast." Ballast is spare weight. The ballast pulls downward into the water and keeps the buoy upright. Boats carry ballast to keep them stable at sea.

FURTHER IDEAS Compare the stability of your buoy with the boat you made on page 141. Waves lapping over the side of the boat can easily cause it to capsize.

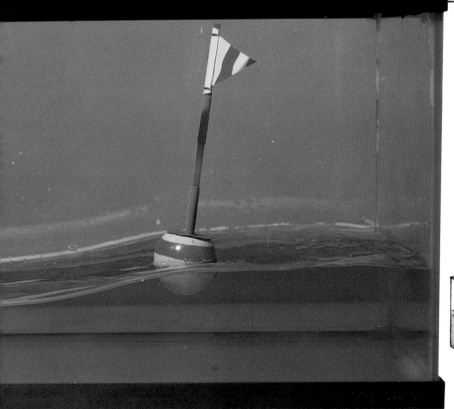

# PORT AND STARBOARD

You may have noticed that ships and large boats have steering wheels. Smaller boats have a tiller instead. Both wheel and tiller are used to control a "rudder." The rudder is used to steer the boat.

At sea, sailors say "port" for left and "starboard" for right.

MAKE A BOAT WITH A RUDDER

GET AN ADULT TO HELP YOU WITH THIS

**1** Ask an adult to cut a boat shape from a piece of styrofoam. Make two holes as shown.

**2** Make a brightly colored sail out of thin paper. Push a wooden stick through the sail.

**3** Push the stick into the hole at the pointed end of the boat. Hold in place with clay.

**4** Cut a rudder out of a waterproof milk carton. Tape it to a drinking straw.

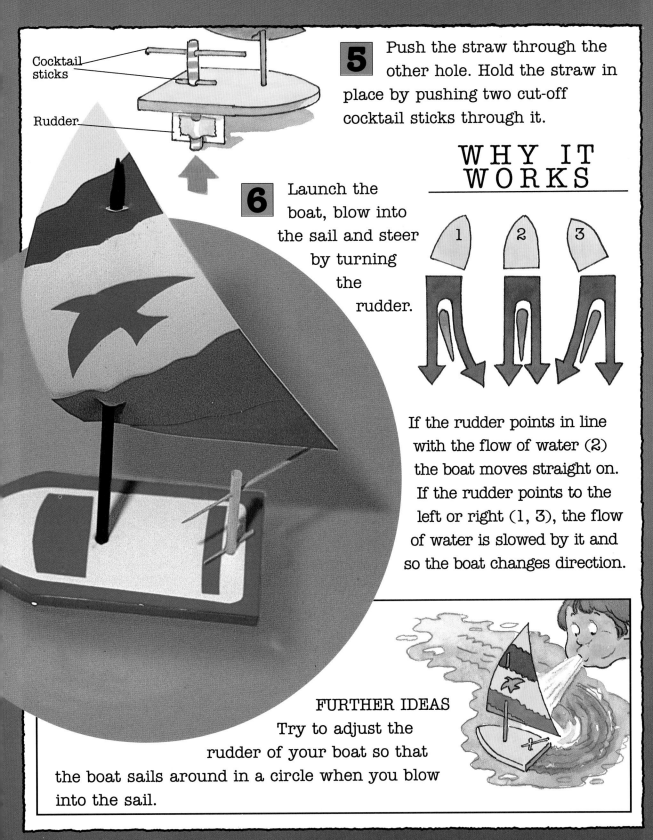

Cocktail sticks

Rudder

**5** Push the straw through the other hole. Hold the straw in place by pushing two cut-off cocktail sticks through it.

# WHY IT WORKS

**6** Launch the boat, blow into the sail and steer by turning the rudder.

1

2

3

If the rudder points in line with the flow of water (2) the boat moves straight on. If the rudder points to the left or right (1, 3), the flow of water is slowed by it and so the boat changes direction.

## FURTHER IDEAS

Try to adjust the rudder of your boat so that the boat sails around in a circle when you blow into the sail.

# JET POWER

Most boats and ships have propellers which push them along. The propeller cuts through the water, pushing it back behind the vessel. This push against the water "propels", or makes the vessel move forward. A jet-propelled boat can travel at high speeds without a propeller. The "jet", or fast-moving flow of water, pushes the boat along.

## MAKE A JET BOAT

**1** Decorate an old plastic soda bottle. Weight the bottom of the bottle with clay.

**2** Ask an adult to make a hole near the bottom of the bottle (right).

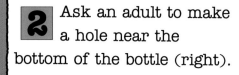

**3** Place a balloon inside the bottle. Make sure you do not drop the balloon.

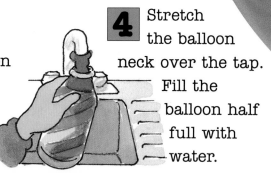

**4** Stretch the balloon neck over the tap. Fill the balloon half full with water.

**5** Pinch the balloon neck closed. Put clay around the bottle neck to weight the bottle.

**6** Still holding the end of the balloon, put the bottle in the bath.

**7** Let go of the balloon. Watch the jet of water shoot out and push the boat along.

## WHY IT WORKS

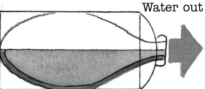

Boat moves forward

Water out

When the water shoots out of the balloon, it pushes against the water in the bath. This pushing force propels the jet boat forward. The quicker the water escapes from the balloon, the faster the boat travels.

### FURTHER IDEAS

Cut a boat shape out of cardboard. Make a hole near the stern of the boat. Cut from the stern of the boat to the hole. Float the boat. Drop liquid soap in the hole. The boat will shoot forward.

# DIVE DEEP!

Deep under the oceans are some of the last unexplored places on Earth. Deep-sea divers use vessels which can sink to the bottom and then float back to the surface again. Some marine animals such as jellyfish are also able to dive to great depths, then surface again.

MAKE A DIVING JELLYFISH

**1** Find a large, clean plastic soda bottle. Fill it up to the top with tap water.

**2** Cut both ends off a flexible plastic drinking straw to make a "U" shape.

**3** Unbend a paper clip. Bend it into shape (shown at right). Push it into the ends of the straw.

# WHY IT WORKS

When you squeeze the bottle, water is pushed into the straw, compressing the air. Water weighs more than air so the jellyfish gets heavier and sinks.

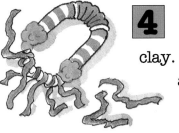

**4** Roll out three thin strips of clay. Loop them around the paper clip.

**5** This is your jellyfish. Drop it into the bottle and screw the top back on. To make the jellyfish dive, squeeze the bottle.

FURTHER IDEAS
Try making a diver from a small eye-dropper. Fill the dropper almost to the top with water then put it into the bottle of water.

# FLOATING UNDERWATER

Submarines are special floating vessels because they can sink and then return to the surface. Ballast tanks control how deep they dive. To make the submarine sink, the tanks are filled with water. To make the submarine rise, the water is pumped out and replaced with air.

FLOATING UNDERWATER

**1** Fill an aquarium or large tank with tap water.

GET AN ADULT TO DO THIS FOR YOU

**2** Cut four square holes in a plastic soda bottle (left).

**3** Put clay around the neck and base of the bottle to weight it.

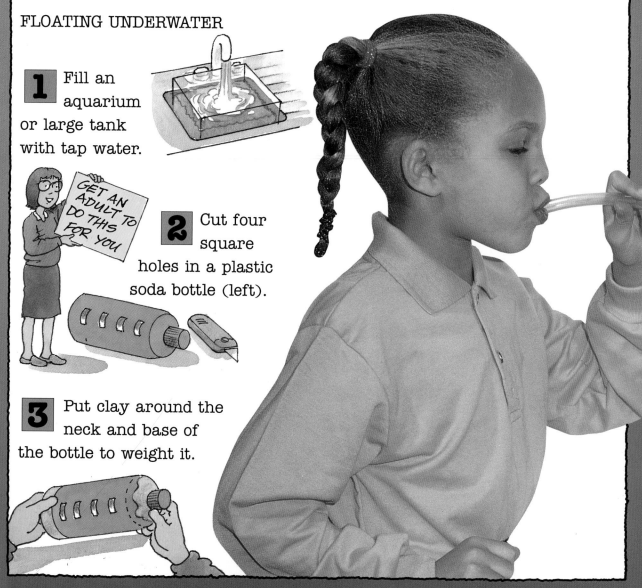

**4** On the other side of the bottle make three holes. Make one large enough to fit a plastic tube.

**5** Decorate your submarine. Push the end of the tube into the larger of the three holes.

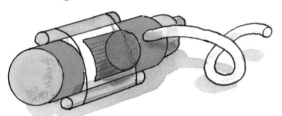

**6** Try out your submarine. It will fill with water and sink. Blow into the tube to make it rise.

# WHY IT WORKS

The submarine sinks when it fills with water (ballast). When you blow into the tube, the water is forced out and replaced by the air. Air is less dense than water so the submarine surfaces.

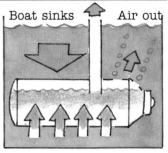

Boat sinks    Air out

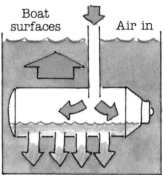

Boat surfaces    Air in

FURTHER IDEAS
Put an empty bottle in the bottom of your aquarium. Let it fill with water. Now blow air into it with a straw to make the bottle rise.

# FLOATING ON AIR

The hovercraft is one of the great inventions of the twentieth century. It can travel on water or on land. The engines suck in air and then pump it downward. This creates a cushion of air that keeps the hovercraft from touching the surface over which it is traveling. The passengers enjoy a smooth and bump-free journey.

GET AN ADULT TO DO THIS FOR YOU

## MAKE A HOVERCRAFT

**1** Ask an adult to cut the top off a plastic soda bottle for you.

**2** Wrap some clay around the base of the cut-off bottle top.

**3** Make a skirt of paper to go around the clay. Make sure it hangs over it.

**4** Blow up a balloon. Pinch the end. Carefully wrap the balloon around the bottle neck without letting it deflate.

**5** Find a smooth surface. Place the hovercraft on it and let go of the balloon. Watch your hovercraft glide along.

# WHY IT WORKS

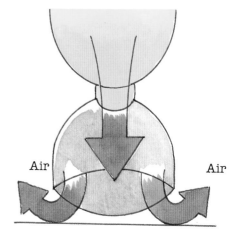

Air                    Air

Air from the balloon escapes into the bottle top. The air pressure builds up until it creates a cushion that lifts the bottle slightly. It is the downward force of air that makes the hovercraft hover.

### FURTHER IDEAS

Cut a hole in the bottom of a plastic margarine tub. Turn it upside down and fill it with air from a hairdrier. Watch it hover. Fill a paper bag with hot air from a hairdrier. What happens?

# CONTENTS

# CHAPTER
## *Seven*

# PLAYING WITH MAGNETS

# WHAT IS A MAGNET?

People have known about magnets for thousands of years. The first magnets were made out of black rocks called lodestones which are found naturally in the ground. Some metal objects are attracted to this rock. Modern magnets are made from steel. They can be made into almost any shape – horseshoe, bar or ring.

## MAKE A FISHING GAME

**1** Draw some fish shapes on thin cardboard. Color them in and cut them out. Attach a steel paper clip to each fish.

**2** Find a large, clean cardboard box. Decorate the outside so that it looks like the water in a pond.

**3** Make two fishing rods. Tie a 30 inch-long piece of string to each stick. Tape a magnet to the end of the string.

**4** Using the fishing rods, compete with a friend to see who can "catch" the most fish.

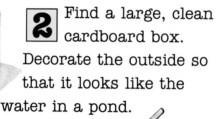

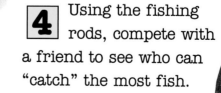

# WHY IT WORKS

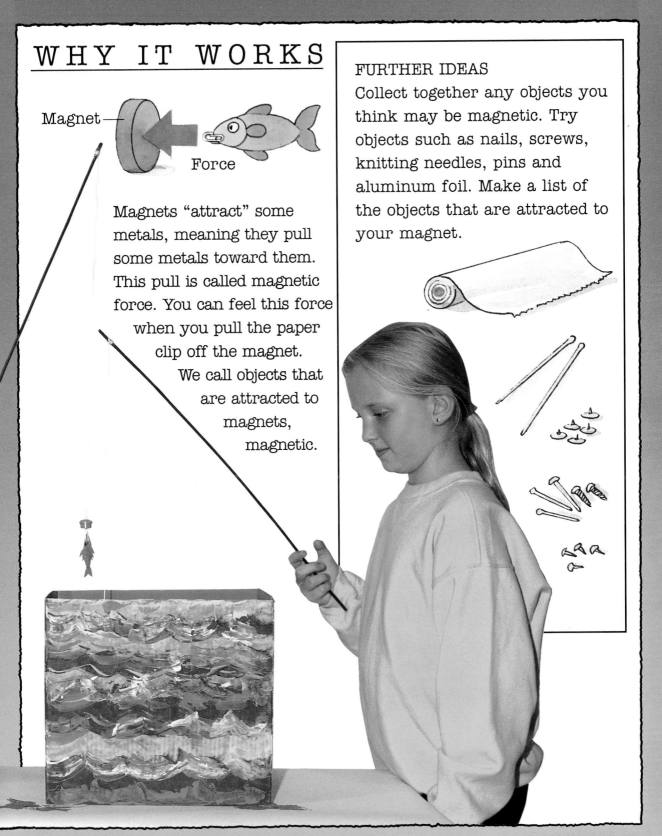

Magnet

Force

Magnets "attract" some metals, meaning they pull some metals toward them. This pull is called magnetic force. You can feel this force when you pull the paper clip off the magnet.

We call objects that are attracted to magnets, magnetic.

## FURTHER IDEAS

Collect together any objects you think may be magnetic. Try objects such as nails, screws, knitting needles, pins and aluminum foil. Make a list of the objects that are attracted to your magnet.

# LONG-RANGE FORCE

How far away can the magnetic force work? Scientists use magnets that will attract objects from many feet away. Your magnet can attract objects a few inches away. When a magnet and object touch, they "stick" together as if fixed with glue.

## MAKE A FLYING BUTTERFLY

**1** Find a clean cardboard box. Ask an adult to cut away two opposite sides leaving a "U" shape (shown right).

GET AN ADULT TO HELP YOU WITH THIS

**2** Tape a strong bar-shaped magnet along one side of the box (see left).

**3** On thin paper, draw and cut out a butterfly shape. Push a thumbtack into one wing (see right). Tie a length of thread to the tack.

**4** Tape the loose end of the thread to the side of the box opposite the magnet. When the thread is pulled taut, the butterfly should almost touch the magnet.

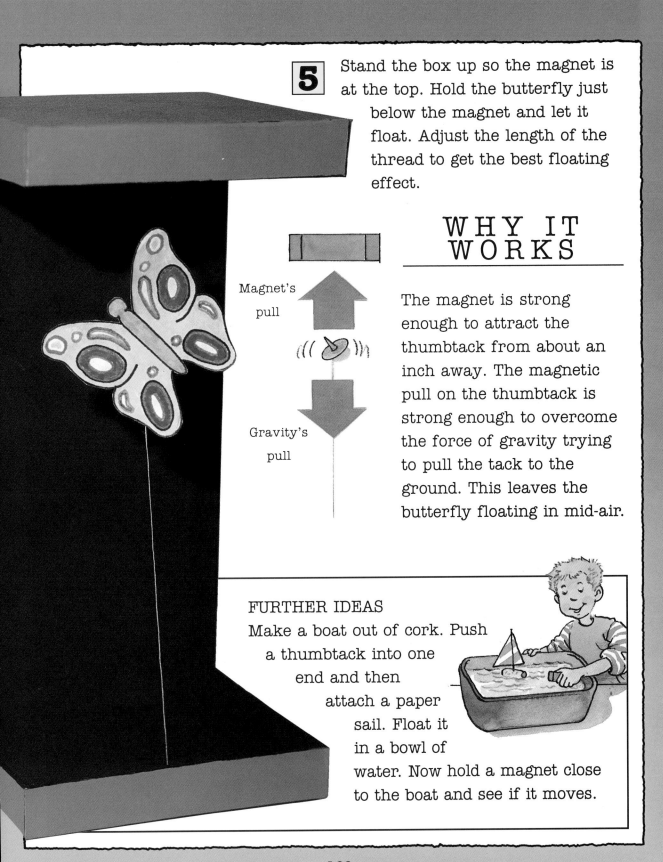

**5** Stand the box up so the magnet is at the top. Hold the butterfly just below the magnet and let it float. Adjust the length of the thread to get the best floating effect.

# WHY IT WORKS

Magnet's pull

Gravity's pull

The magnet is strong enough to attract the thumbtack from about an inch away. The magnetic pull on the thumbtack is strong enough to overcome the force of gravity trying to pull the tack to the ground. This leaves the butterfly floating in mid-air.

## FURTHER IDEAS
Make a boat out of cork. Push a thumbtack into one end and then attach a paper sail. Float it in a bowl of water. Now hold a magnet close to the boat and see if it moves.

# THROUGH AND THROUGH

You can stick paper notes to the metal door of a refrigerator with a magnet. The paper and paint cannot block the magnetic force. If the magnetism is strong enough it can work straight through materials as if they were not there. This can be useful for making things move without touching them.

## MAKE A RACING GAME

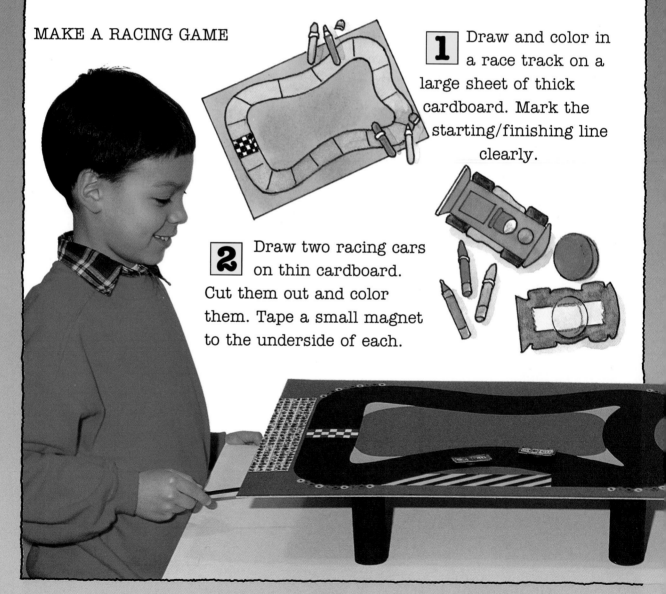

**1** Draw and color in a race track on a large sheet of thick cardboard. Mark the starting/finishing line clearly.

**2** Draw two racing cars on thin cardboard. Cut them out and color them. Tape a small magnet to the underside of each.

**3** Find four cardboard tubes of the same size. Place one under each corner of the race track so it is raised.

**4** Find two long, thin sticks. Tape a small magnet to one end of each.

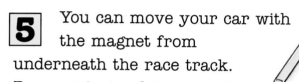

**5** You can move your car with the magnet from underneath the race track. Race against a friend, taking care not to mix up each other's cars!

# WHY IT WORKS

The magnets under the car and on the stick are attracted to each other. The magnetic force goes through the race track, although the race track does slightly weaken the force.

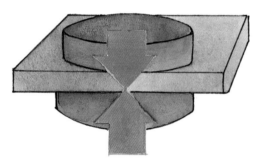

FURTHER IDEAS
Without getting your fingers wet, try to remove a steel paper clip from a glass of water. Move your magnet along the outside of the glass.

# CHAIN REACTION

You may have noticed that when magnetic metals touch a magnet they will attract magnetic metals too. We can use this characteristic to build a "chain" of magnetic objects outward from a permanent magnet. Permanent magnets stay magnetic unless they are dropped or get too hot.

MAKE A MAGNETIC SCULPTURE

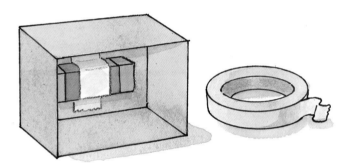

**1** Find a small cardboard box. Tape a small magnet to the inside of the bottom of the box. Turn the box upside down.

**2** Decorate the box with your own pattern and color it with bright colors.

**3** Place a few steel paper clips on top of the box above the magnet. Build up a sculpture by adding pins, tacks and nails.

**4** Change the shape until you are satisfied with your sculpture. You can reshape it endlessly.

# WHY IT WORKS

When a magnetic metal is attracted to a permanent magnet it becomes a magnet too. It can attract other objects but only while it is touching a permanent magnet. This is called "induced" magnetism.

FURTHER IDEAS
Hang a magnet over the edge of a box and tape it into place. Try to form a chain by hanging paper clips from the end of the magnet.

# MAGNETIC METALS

There are many different metals, but only three pure metals can be magnetized. These are iron, nickel and cobalt. None of the other pure metals – gold, silver, aluminum – can be made into magnets. But if you mix pure metals together their magnetic characteristics can be altered.

## MAKE A COIN TESTER

**1** Ask an adult to cut a slot at one end of a shoe box (see right). The slot should be just bigger than your largest coin.

GET AN ADULT TO HELP YOU WITH THIS

**2** Cut out a strip of cardboard. Fold into an "L" shape. Tape into place just to the left of the slot.

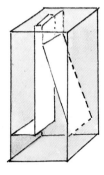

**3** Cut another strip of cardboard, creasing it $^3/_4$ inch from the top. Tape this end to the right of the slot. Tape the other end to the side of the box.

**4** Cut another strip of cardboard. Fold into the shape shown (right). Make sure it fits into the triangular space between the first pieces.

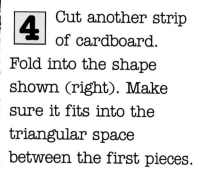

**5** Find a strong magnet. Tape it inside the box just to the right of the slot.

**6** Drop your coins into the slot. Most will fall to the left side of the box. If you drop iron or steel washers into the slot they will fall to the right side of the box.

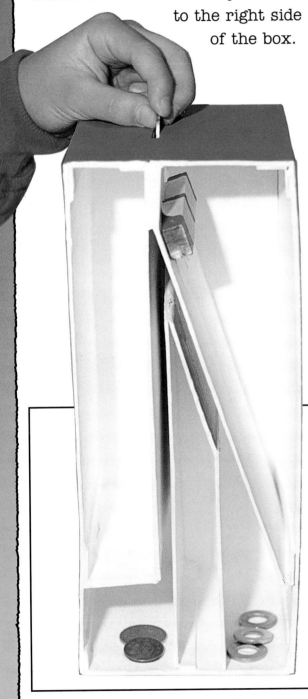

## WHY IT WORKS

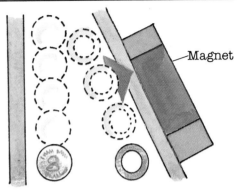

Magnet

Most coins are made from non-magnetic metals such as a copper mix. When you drop them into the box they are not attracted to the magnet and so fall straight down. When you drop iron or steel objects they are attracted by the magnet and are pulled over to the right side of the box.

### FURTHER IDEAS
Tableware is often made of stainless steel. Make a ramp out of cardboard and roll spoons or forks down it. Put a magnet under the ramp. See how it affects the path of the tableware. Why not try toy cars as well?

# PUSH AND PULL

Magnets have two points where their power is strongest. These are called poles. Every magnet has a north and a south pole. When iron or steel touches a permanent magnet it has poles too (pages 172-173). A good way of testing whether an object is a permanent magnet or not is to see if it will "repel", or push away, another magnet.

MAKE A MAGNET FLOAT

**1** Find a cardboard box. Ask an adult to cut away the sides and the middle of the box to leave the shape (shown at right).

GET AN ADULT TO HELP YOU WITH THIS

**2** Tape down a strong bar magnet to the base of the box (left).

**3** Copy the shape (shown at right) onto a piece of cardboard and cut out. Tape an identical magnet to the cardboard. Fold the cardboard around the magnet.

**4** Hold the second magnet on top of the first with both north and south poles facing the same way, tape them together.

# WHY IT WORKS

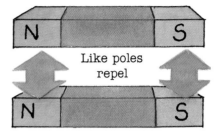

Like poles repel

**5** The top magnet should "float" above the bottom. Try pushing the top magnet.

Magnetic poles of the same type repel each other. Gravity is trying to pull the top magnet down, but the two magnets are repelling each other with such force that the top one is held above the bottom. The top magnet would spring away if it wasn't taped in place.

## FURTHER IDEAS

Find three horseshoe-shaped magnets. Thread them onto two pencils (shown at right). Line up the poles. See if you can make the magnets float. Try doing the same thing with ring-shaped magnets. Which works best?

# USEFUL MAGNETS

Doctors have used magnets to pull tiny bits of iron out of a patient's eye. The advantage of using a magnet is that nothing needs to touch the injured eye. The magnet's ability to attract some materials but not others has been used in many ways. Giant magnets are used to sort out different waste metals.

## MAKE A TREASURE HUNT

**1** Make a desert island by filling a bowl almost to the top with clean, dry sand.

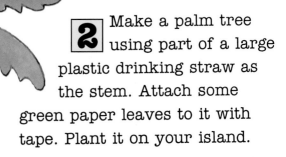

**2** Make a palm tree using part of a large plastic drinking straw as the stem. Attach some green paper leaves to it with tape. Plant it on your island.

**3** Make a treasure chest out of colored cardboard. Now find some treasure to put in it. An iron or steel bolt will do.

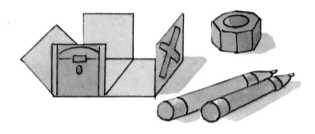

**4** Bury the treasure chest in the sand. Make sure it is fairly near to the surface.

Magnet

Treasure

**5** Search for the treasure using a magnet. You can take turns with a friend to find it.

# WHY IT WORKS

You can hunt for the treasure by moving the magnet over the surface of the sand. When you hold the magnet directly over the steel treasure, the magnet strongly attracts it. The magnetic force goes straight through the sand.

FURTHER IDEAS
Sort out aluminum soda cans that can be recycled by testing each can with a magnet. Aluminum cans are not magnetic.

# VERY ATTRACTIVE

Magnets pull magnetic materials such as iron and steel toward them. This pull is called attraction. The stronger the magnet, the stronger its attractive force. Modern household items have many ingenious uses for magnetic attraction. Did you know that a magnet is often used on a refrigerator door to hold it firmly closed?

MAKE A FUNNY FACE

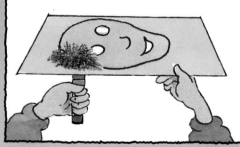

**1** Draw the shape of a face on a sheet of thin cardboard. Make the eyes, nose and mouth especially large. Don't draw in any hair or eyebrows.

**2** Ask an adult to make some iron filings for you by filing down a nail. Pour the iron filings onto the cardboard in a few places.

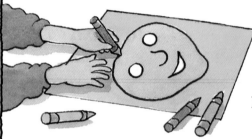

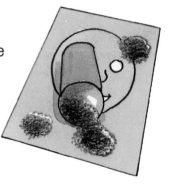

**3** Hold the cardboard with one hand and bring a magnet under it with the other. The magnet will attract the iron filings through the cardboard.

**4** Arrange the iron filings with the magnet to give your face hair, eyebrows and a beard. Move the magnet away from your funny face.

# WHY IT WORKS

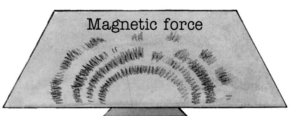

Magnetic force

Magnet

The magnetic force pulls on each tiny piece of iron filing. As you move the magnet under the cardboard the filings are dragged along. When you move the magnet away the iron filings stay in place.

FURTHER IDEAS
Test the strength of your magnet. Use it to move a pin through one page of a book, then through two pages, then three pages and so on until the pages block the magnetic force.

# INVISIBLE PATTERNS

Magnetic objects close to a magnet are attracted to it. There is a "field" (space) around the magnet where the magnetic force works. We cannot see this field but can feel its pull on objects. Scientists have discovered that birds use the Earth's magnetic field to guide them on long journeys.

### SEE A MAGNETIC FIELD

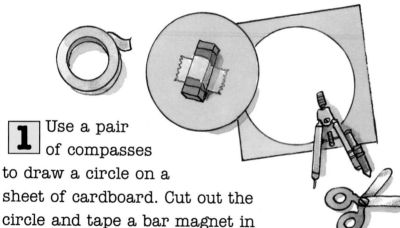

**1** Use a pair of compasses to draw a circle on a sheet of cardboard. Cut out the circle and tape a bar magnet in the center.

**2** Turn the cardboard over so the magnet is underneath. Evenly sprinkle some iron filings (see page 180) over the surface of the cardboard.

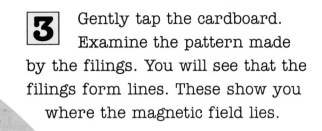

**3** Gently tap the cardboard. Examine the pattern made by the filings. You will see that the filings form lines. These show you where the magnetic field lies.

## WHY IT WORKS

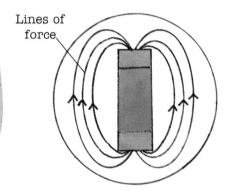

Lines of force

Each filing is attracted to the magnet along invisible lines of force. These make up the magnetic field. The filings are small enough to show the direction in which the field is pulling.

FURTHER IDEAS
Try the experiment again using a horseshoe or ring-shaped magnet. What kind of pattern do the iron filings make?

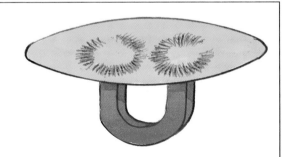

# NORTH AND SOUTH

For centuries travelers have found their way with the help of a compass. Inside a compass is a small magnetic pointer. It spins around but always comes to rest pointing north. From knowing where north is, it is easy to locate south, west and east.

## MAKE A COMPASS

**1** Stroke a nail with one end of a magnet. Make sure you pass the magnet in one direction only. Stroke the nail about 20 times.

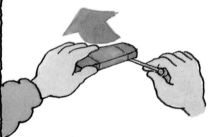

**2** Ask an adult to slice a piece of cork. Now tape the magnetized nail to it.

GET AN ADULT TO HELP YOU WITH THIS

**3** Float the cork in a basin of water. Leave until the nail stops moving. Make sure there are no magnetic objects nearby.

# WHY IT WORKS

**4** The nail will point either north or south. Find out which way it is pointing, then make labels for north, south, west and east.

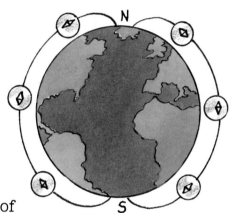

The north pole of a magnet seeks out the north pole of the Earth. It is as if the Earth contained a gigantic magnet. The north pole of the Earth attracts any smaller magnets so that when allowed to, they always point north.

## FURTHER IDEAS

Tie a piece of thread around the middle of a bar magnet. Suspend the magnet from the back of a chair. Watch to see if the poles point north-south. What happens when other magnetic objects are close to the magnet?

# HIDDEN MAGNETS

You may be surprised how important magnets are in modern machines. Computers use magnetic floppy disks to store huge amounts of information. Tape recorders and video recorders use magnetic tape to store film, sound, and music. These are hidden magnets.

THE AMAZING MAGIC FINGER

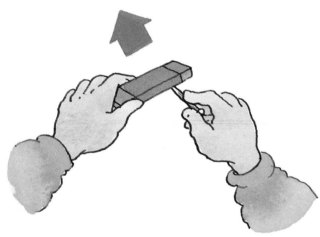

**1** Magnetize a steel nail by stroking it in one direction with a magnet. Stroke at least 20 times (see page 184).

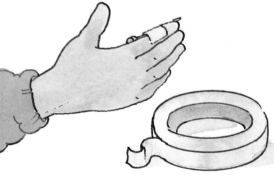

**2** Carefully tape the nail to your index finger. Make sure the point cannot hurt anyone.

**3** Find an old glove that fits your hand snugly. Put it on to hide the magnetized nail.

**4** Bring your magic finger close to a compass needle. Amaze your friends by making the compass needle swing around.

# WHY IT WORKS

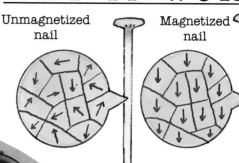

Unmagnetized nail    Magnetized nail

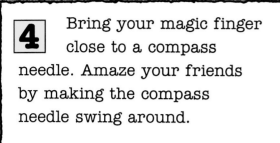

The metal in the nail is made up of millions of tiny crystals. Each can behave like a tiny magnet but they point in different directions.
Stroking the nail with a magnet makes each crystal point the same way. This causes the nail to become magnetized.

FURTHER IDEAS
Use your magic finger for other magic tricks. Impress your friends by balancing a pin or nail right on the end of your finger.

# ELECTROMAGNETISM

An electromagnet is a coil of wire around an iron core. You may have seen a crane that has an electromagnet instead of a hook to carry things. Powerful electromagnets can lift heavy iron loads, even whole cars. The load is dropped by switching off the electromagnet.

## MAKE AN ELECTROMAGNET

**1** Take a cardboard box. Make holes in the center of three sides. Cut two strips of cardboard. Make three holes in each strip (see right).

Holes

**2** Push three pieces of stick through the holes in the strips of cardboard and the box (left). This is your crane arm.

**3** Color some smaller boxes to make them look like cars or an iron bar. Glue a steel washer to the top of each one.

**4** Take 2 to 3 feet of plastic-coated wire and coil around an iron nail. Connect the wire to the terminals of a battery.

**5** Hide the battery in the box. Push the nail and wire through the hole in the front of the crane. Use the electromagnet to pick up paper clips. Switch it off by removing the wire from the battery.

## WHY IT WORKS

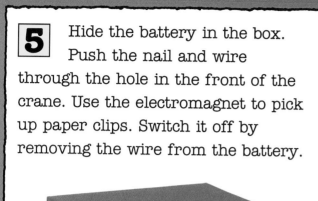

Nail becomes magnetized

Electricity flowing along a wire has a magnetic field around it. The field is made stronger by coiling the wire. The nail inside the coils becomes magnetized by the field. Each part of the iron nail lines up facing the same direction, running from north to south.

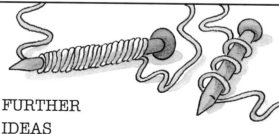

FURTHER IDEAS
Experiment with your electromagnet by changing the number of coils around the nail. What happens when there are fewer coils? What happens when there are more?

# CONTENTS

# CHAPTER *Eight*

HEARING
SOUNDS

# WHAT IS A SOUND?

All sounds are made by something moving. Gently rest your fingertips on your throat as you talk. You can feel your throat vibrating. Vocal cords in your throat move as you speak and make the air in your throat and mouth vibrate. The vibrating air makes sounds.

## MAKE A BANGER

**1** Take a square sheet of paper and decorate it. Fold it in half diagonally to make a triangle (see right).

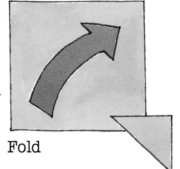

Fold

**2** Fold the top right-hand corner downward.

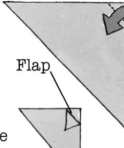

Flap

Fold

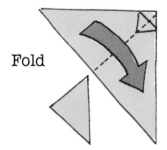

**3** Fold the triangle in half (see left). Make sure the folded corner is on the inside.

**4** Make a crease down the middle but do not fold in half.

Crease

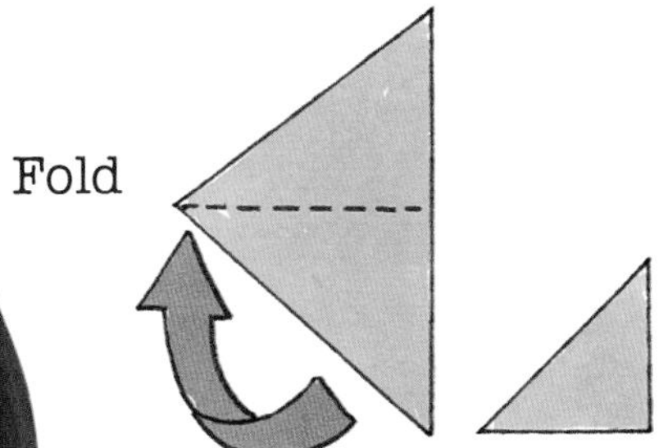

Fold

**5** From the open end of the triangle fold the top layer of paper over along the crease. Flip the triangle over and repeat.

**6** Grasp the three pointed ends of the triangle together. Flick your wrist down to make the banger work.

# WHY IT WORKS

Flicking your wrist makes the folded paper jump out of place. The paper pushes hard against the air. The pushed air reaches your ears as a "bang."

Air

FURTHER IDEAS
Try making different-sized bangers. Follow the same steps with the largest square of paper you can find. Repeat with the smallest square of paper.

# MAKING A SOUND

Sounds travel through the air to reach our ears. On a very windy day, the wind can blow sounds away from you so it is difficult to hear a conversation. If sounds have traveled a long way then they lose some loudness. Sounds made close to us seem louder.

## MAKE A BULL ROARER

**1** You will need a long cardboard tube, scissors, a ruler, about 19 inches of clothing elastic and 3 to 6 feet of string.

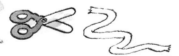

**2** Loop the elastic through the tube. Knot the two ends together firmly.

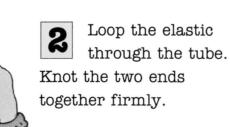

**3** Knot one end of the string around the elastic at the opening of the tube.

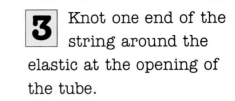

**4** Take the other end of the string in your hand and swing the bull roarer around. Listen to the sound it makes.

# WHY IT WORKS

As the tube spins around, air enters and pushes the elastic rapidly backward and forward. Air leaving the tube carries the sounds made from these movements.

Air carrying sound out

Air in

## FURTHER IDEAS

Experiment with the bull roarer by using a shorter length of string. If you have room, try a longer length. Listen carefully. How does the difference in length affect the sound?

# GOOD VIBRATIONS

Pleasant sounds can come from musical instruments. All musical instruments have parts that move to make vibrations. Vibrations are caused by something moving back and forth very quickly and smoothly. A drum has a head that vibrates when it is hit with a stick. The harder you hit the drum, the bigger the vibrations and the louder the sound.

MAKE A DRUM

**1** You will need a large, empty tin can and a clean plastic bag. Carefully cut a circle out of the plastic bag. Make sure it is larger than the can.

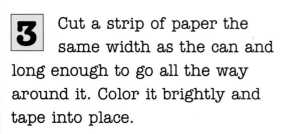

**2** Stretch the circle of plastic as tightly as you can over the rim of the empty can. Hold it in place with tape.

**3** Cut a strip of paper the same width as the can and long enough to go all the way around it. Color it brightly and tape into place.

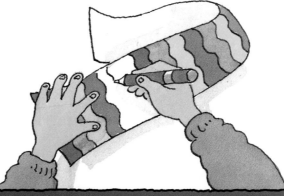

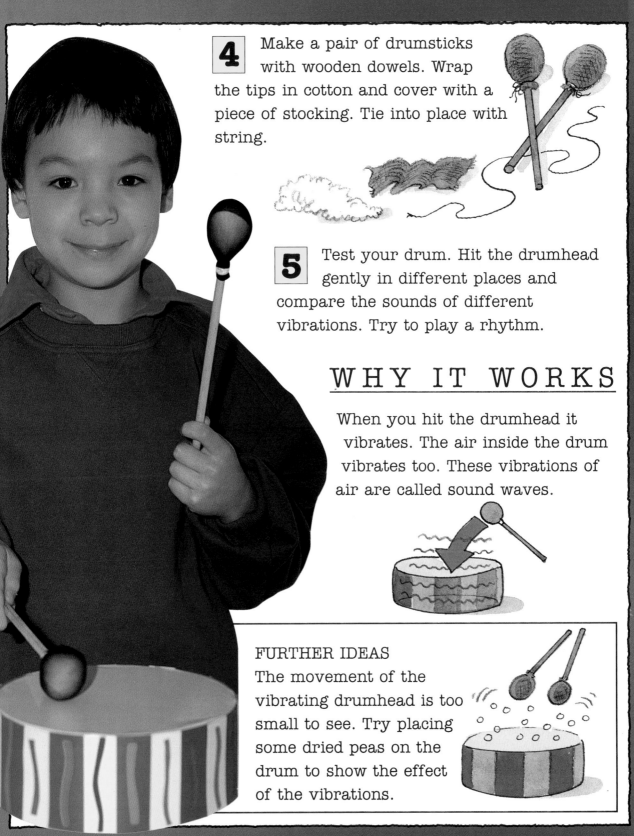

**4** Make a pair of drumsticks with wooden dowels. Wrap the tips in cotton and cover with a piece of stocking. Tie into place with string.

**5** Test your drum. Hit the drumhead gently in different places and compare the sounds of different vibrations. Try to play a rhythm.

# WHY IT WORKS

When you hit the drumhead it vibrates. The air inside the drum vibrates too. These vibrations of air are called sound waves.

FURTHER IDEAS
The movement of the vibrating drumhead is too small to see. Try placing some dried peas on the drum to show the effect of the vibrations.

# THE SOUND DRUM

We cannot see sounds but we can see their effects. Sounds travel through the air just like waves in the sea. If the waves are strong enough they can move things in their path. The human ear has an eardrum that moves when hit by sound waves entering the ear.

MAKE A SOUND DRUM

**1** Roll a strong sheet of cardboard into a tube. Make sure the cardboard overlaps so that it can be taped together.

**2** Cut a circle larger than the end of your tube out of a clean plastic bag. Tape it as tightly as possible over one end of the tube.

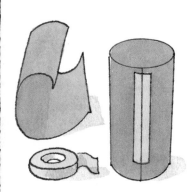

**3** Cut a cardboard circle the same size. Cut a hole in the middle of it. Tape the circle over the other end of the tube.

**4** Make a target out of a long strip of tissue paper. Cut one end into a long fringe.

**5** Point the hole in the bottom of your sound drum toward your target. Tap the plastic drumhead. What happens to your target?

## WHY IT WORKS

Tapping the drumhead pushes sound waves through the hole in the bottom of the drum. It also forces rings of air out through the hole, which moves the paper fringe.

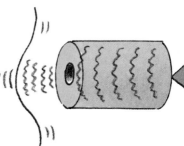

FURTHER IDEAS
You need a partner to help you. Take turns to hit the sound drum and hold the target. What is the farthest distance you can hit the target from?

# LISTEN CLOSELY

If you are ill a doctor may use a stethoscope to listen to your heart or lungs. You may have a problem breathing or your heart may not be making the sounds it is supposed to. These sounds are normally too quiet to hear. A stethoscope magnifies them so they can be heard.

## MAKE A STETHOSCOPE

**1** Cut out two large paper circles. Color them brightly. Make a long cardboard tube. Decorate this too.

**2** Cut a hole in the center of each circle the same size as the tube end. Cut from the hole to the edge of the circle. Tape the edges to form two cones.

**3** Tape one cone shape over each end of the tube. Make the fit as snug as possible.

sound in

**4** Now try out your stethoscope. Put your ear to one cone and place the other on a friend's chest.

# WHY IT WORKS

As sound waves spread out they become smaller and harder to hear. The first cone stops them from spreading by collecting them together. They move along the tube and out through the second cone into your ear.

FURTHER IDEAS
Use your stethoscope to compare the sound of your heartbeat with your friend's heartbeat. Try to think of other quiet sounds to listen to, such as a friend whispering or a ticking watch.

# BOUNCING SOUNDS

Bats have very poor eyesight yet can fly around safely in complete darkness. They can avoid hitting obstacles by bouncing squeaky sounds off them. Bouncing sounds are called echoes. You can hear echoes in places such as large halls or gyms when sounds bounce off the walls.

BOUNCE AN ECHO

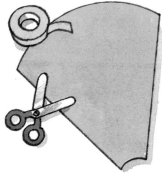

**2** One cone is a hearing aid, the other a megaphone to magnify sounds.

**1** Cut the shape shown here out of cardboard. Overlap the edges and tape to make a cone. Repeat so you have two large cones.

## 3
Cut out two strips of cardboard. Tape them along the sides of your hearing aid and megaphone to make handles.

Hearing aid

Megaphone

# WHY IT WORKS

When a sound wave hits something it can either be absorbed or bounce off. Smooth, flat surfaces bounce sounds best. The sound of your voice bounces off the mirror just as light would.

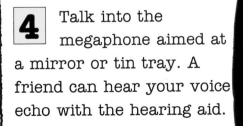

## 4
Talk into the megaphone aimed at a mirror or tin tray. A friend can hear your voice echo with the hearing aid.

## FURTHER IDEAS
Try to bounce sounds off other surfaces. You could compare a cork tile, an egg carton and a wooden block. Which reflects sound waves best?

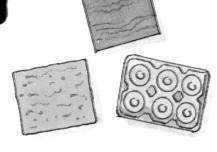

# KEEPING SOUNDS IN

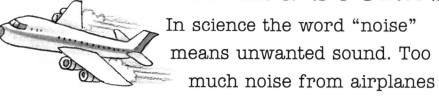

In science the word "noise" means unwanted sound. Too much noise from airplanes or discos is bad for your health. It can keep you from sleeping and even damage your eardrums. A radio studio is soundproofed. Noise is kept out so that it cannot be heard when programs are broadcast.

MAKE A SOUNDPROOF BOX

**1** You need a large cardboard box and a shoe box, both with lids. The shoe box must easily fit inside the cardboard box.

**2** Decorate the outside of the cardboard box. Use brightly colored paints. When dry, place the shoe box inside the larger box.

**3** Pack the space between the boxes with crumpled newspapers. Add a little paper to the inner box.

# WHY IT WORKS

Sound waves from the alarm cannot escape from the soundproof box. Most sound waves are absorbed by the cardboard and the newspaper. You may hear just a few sound waves leaking out.

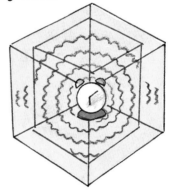

**4** Set off an alarm clock and place it in the inner box. Close the lids of both boxes. What can you hear?

FURTHER IDEAS
Try to improve the soundproofing by replacing the newspaper with egg cartons or sawdust. Make it a fair test by using the same alarm clock each time.

# VIBRATING AIR

An orchestra has percussion, wind, and stringed instruments. Wind instruments include flutes, clarinets, and recorders. They are all made out of a tube. When the instrument is played, air inside the tube vibrates and makes sound. Instruments make different sounds because they vary in shape and size.

## MAKE A CLARINET

**1** Use stiff cardboard to make a cone as shown on page 202. Make sure the small opening at the top is less than half an inch across.

**2** Use sharp scissors to cut a "V" shape from the end of a drinking straw.

**3** Hold the cut end of the straw between your thumb and finger. Pinch the ends together to flatten them.

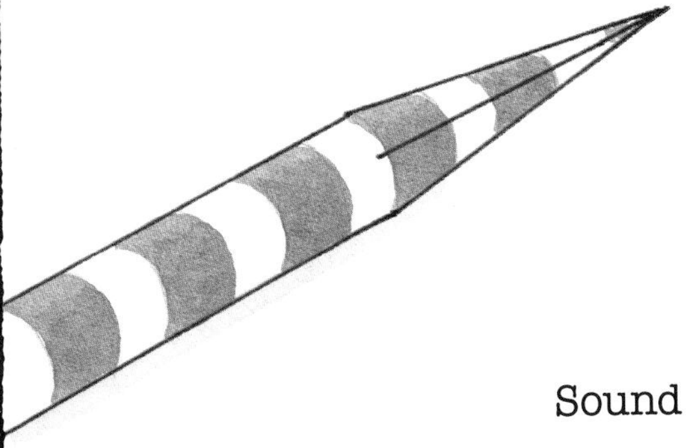

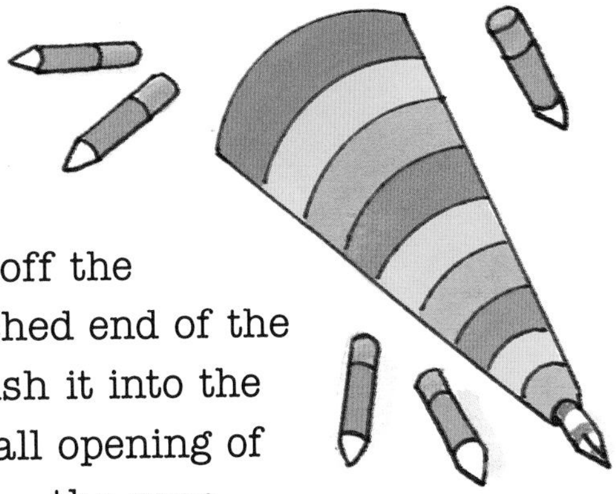

**4** Cut off the pinched end of the straw. Push it into the small opening of the cone.

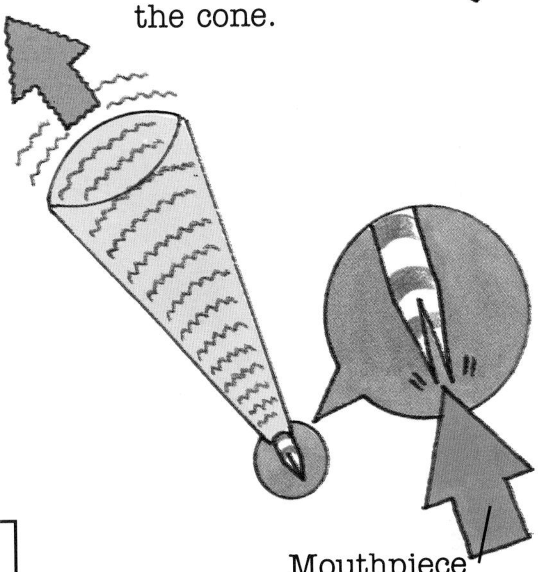

Sound out

**5** Try out your clarinet. Put the mouthpiece inside your mouth and blow into the cone. Feel it vibrate as you play a note.

Mouthpiece

FURTHER IDEAS
Make more clarinets using cones of different sizes. Each needs a straw mouthpiece as before. Compare the kinds of notes you get with long and short clarinets. Using your different-sized clarinets, can you and your friends play a tune?

# WHY IT WORKS

Blowing through the sharp edges of the straw makes them vibrate. The vibrating straw makes all the air in the cone vibrate and causes sound. We hear these sound waves escaping from the cone.

# DIFFERENT PITCHES

Most musical instruments can make a wide range of notes – from low or deep notes that you may be able to feel, to high notes you can only just hear.

Notes differ in pitch. Pitch measures how high or low a note is.

MAKE A XYLOPHONE

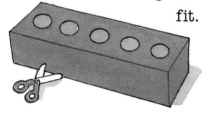

GET AN ADULT TO DO THIS FOR YOU

**1** Cut five circles in the lid of a box, big enough for glass bottles to fit.

**2** Check that the bottles fit snugly into place. Tape a sheet of cardboard to stand up behind them.

**3** Fill each bottle with a different amount of water. Line them up with the fullest at one end and the emptiest at the other.

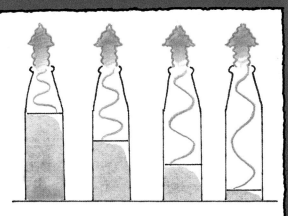

# WHY IT WORKS

Above the water level each bottle contains a tube of air. Hitting the bottles makes the air vibrate. Longer tubes of air (emptier bottles) vibrate more slowly. Slower vibrations make deeper (lower-pitched) sounds.

**4** Tap the neck of each bottle with a stick or wooden spoon. Note the different sounds they make. See if you can play a tune.

FURTHER IDEAS
You can make the air in the bottles vibrate another way. Rest your lip on the bottle top and blow.

# VIBRATING STRINGS

Stringed instruments include violins, harps, and guitars. Musicians hit or pluck the strings to make them vibrate. Each string is of a different thickness and tautness so each makes a different note. Musicians also change the notes by altering the length of the vibrating string.

## MAKE A GUITAR

**1** Wash out a large margarine tub. Cut an oval-shaped hole in the lid with a sharp knife or pair of scissors.

GET AN ADULT TO DO THIS FOR YOU

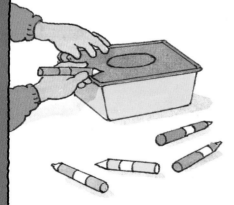

**2** Use brightly colored magic markers to decorate the outside of the tub and lid.

**3** Wrap six rubber bands of differing thickness lengthwise around the tub. Leave a space between each rubber band.

**4** Pluck each rubber band with your finger. Compare the sounds made by plucking the ends or middle of each rubber band.

Slower vibrations - lower notes

Faster vibrations - higher notes

# WHY IT WORKS

A vibrating rubber band makes the air in the tub vibrate. This makes sound waves which escape through the hole in the lid. Thin rubber bands vibrate much faster than thicker ones. Faster vibrations make higher notes.

FURTHER IDEAS
Place a pencil between the rubber bands and the lid of the tub. This alters the length of the rubber bands and changes the notes they make. Experiment with the pencil in different places along the tub.

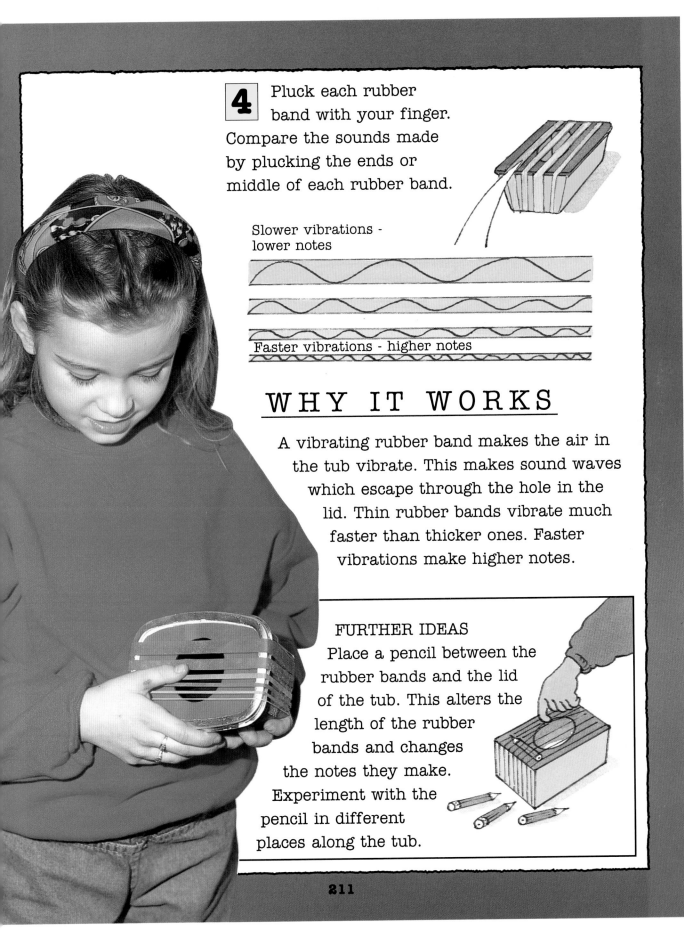

# TUNING UP

Musicians have to "tune" their instruments. For a stringed instrument this means adjusting each string to just the right tautness to play the correct note. If a string is too slack, it cannot vibrate properly. If it is too taut then the string might snap.

## MAKE A SONOMETER

**1** You will need a large sheet of thick cardboard. Divide it roughly into thirds. Decorate one side with colored magic markers.

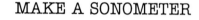
GET AN ADULT TO DO THIS FOR YOU

**2** Very carefully use a sharp knife to cut a notch into the sides of two wooden pencils.

**3** Find a piece of nylon fishing line about three feet long. Firmly push a thumbtack into one end of the cardboard. Tie one end of the thread to the thumbtack.

**4** Tape the notched pencils into place. Lay the fishing line in the two notches. Tie the other end of the line around a plastic cup weighted down with marbles or stones.

**5** Hang the cup over the edge of a table. Pluck the fishing line. Listen to the sound change when you add marbles to the cup.

# WHY IT WORKS

Hanging more weight from the fishing line pulls it tighter. This causes it to vibrate faster. The faster the vibrations are, the higher the note sounds to us.

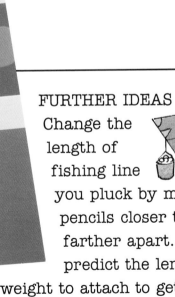

FURTHER IDEAS
Change the length of fishing line you pluck by moving the pencils closer together or farther apart. Try to predict the length of line and weight to attach to get the highest and lowest possible notes.

# FARAWAY SOUNDS

Listening to the ground is an excellent way of listening to faraway sounds. This is because sounds travel faster through the ground than through air. You may have seen a bandit in a cowboy film put his ear to a railway track. Today railway workers use this method to listen for trains. They hear sound trapped in the rails before they see the train.

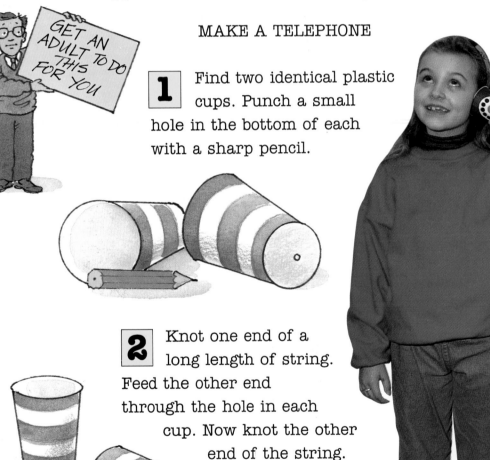

GET AN ADULT TO DO THIS FOR YOU

## MAKE A TELEPHONE

**1** Find two identical plastic cups. Punch a small hole in the bottom of each with a sharp pencil.

**2** Knot one end of a long length of string. Feed the other end through the hole in each cup. Now knot the other end of the string.

**3** Check that the string cannot be easily tugged out of place. Decorate each telephone cup. Use brightly colored magic markers.

# WHY IT WORKS

The sounds you make travel along the string as tiny vibrations (you can just feel them if you touch the string). They travel through the plastic cup and the air to reach your ear.

**4** With a partner, each take a cup and pull the string taut. Put your cup to your ear. Ask your partner to talk into his or hers. Try to have a conversation.

### FURTHER IDEAS
Tie a fork and spoon to a piece of string. Hold the other end of the string to one ear; cover up your other ear. You can "feel" the sound of the jangling utensils. The sounds travel up through the string.

# GLOSSARY

**Acid**
A liquid that turns blue litmus (an indicator) red. Many occur naturally; hydrochloric acid is found in the stomach and helps food digestion.

**Alkali**
A liquid that turns red litmus (an indicator) blue.

**Arch**
A shape, roughly semicircular, that is capable of supporting a great deal of weight.

**Atom**
The smallest complete particle that everything is made up of. Atoms are made up of smaller particles called electrons, protons, and neutrons.

**Attract**
To pull something toward you.

**Ballast**
Extra weight carried by vessels. It can be solid or liquid. Ballast helps keep a boat stable. When pumped out, it helps increase buoyancy.

**Buoyancy**
The ability of a substance to float. Buoyancy depends on the density of the object.

**Charge**
Electric charge can be either positive or negative. Inside atoms, electrons carry a negative charge and protons carry a positive charge.

**Chlorophyll**
Chemical pigment that gives green plants their color. It traps the energy contained in sunlight needed for photosynthesis.

**Circuit**
A complete path around which an electric current can flow.

**Compass**
An instrument with a magnetized pointer. The pointer always points north because it always lines itself with the Earth's magnetic field.

**Compress**
To squeeze together into less space.

**Conductor**
Any material that allows electricity to pass through it.

**Convection currents**
Circular movements in fluids caused by warm substances rising, cooling, and then falling again.

**Crystal**
A solid body in which the atoms are arranged in a rigid structure.

**Current**
A flow of negative charge (electrons) around a circuit.

**Density**
The weight or heaviness of an object when it takes up a given amount of space.

**Drag**
The resistance of air or water. A force that holds back moving objects.

**Eardrum**
A sheet of skin inside your ear. Sounds in the air set it vibrating just like a drumhead. Messages to the brain tell you what the sound is like.

**Echo**
The reflection or bouncing back of a sound from a surface.

**Elastic**
An elastic object will recover its original shape after being molded.

**Electric motor**
A machine that turns electricity into movement by using a magnet.

**Electrolyte**
A liquid in which a chemical reaction takes place when an electric current flows through it.

**Electromagnet**
A coil of wire with an iron bar inside it. It becomes a magnet only when electricity is flowing through the coil.

**Electroscope**
A device used by scientists to measure how much static electricity is contained in an object.

**Energy**
When a force moves an object, energy is passed to the object (where it may be saved). Heat, light and power are familiar forms of energy.

**Filter**
A process to purify substances by removing impurities.

**Force**
A push, pull, or twist that makes an object move or change direction. For example, throwing a ball is exerting force on the ball which makes it move.

**Freeze**
When a substance turns from a liquid into a solid as its temperature drops.

**Frequency**
The number of sound vibrations that happen in one second.

**Friction**
A force that occurs when two surfaces rub against each other. It always slows movement, and brings motion to a stop if no other force is applied to overcome it.

**Gravity**
The pulling force of the Earth that makes things fall, and gives things weight.

**Grip**
The action of a surface on another as a result of friction.

**Gyroscope**
A spinning top that stays upright even if its surroundings are moved.

**Hydraulics**
The use of liquids, particularly water, in engineering. Hydraulic systems are used for transmitting energy.

# GLOSSARY

**Hydrometer**
Instrument used to measure the density of a liquid by how deeply it sinks into the liquid.

**Image**
The "picture" of an object usually formed by a lens or photograph.

**Indicator**
Shows the chemical conditions of a substance by changing color. Litmus turns red for acids, green for alkalis and blue for neutrals.

**Induced magnetism**
Magnetism caused in magnetic material such as iron or steel, when a permanent magnet is brought very close.

**Insulator**
Any material that does not let electricity pass through it.

**Jet**
A fast-moving flow of water or air forced through a small outlet.

**Light ray**
A very narrow beam of light.

**Line of force**
A line that shows the magnetic effect around a magnet.

**Litmus**
An indicator that turns red in acids and blue in alkalis.

**Lodestone**
A type of rock which is a natural magnet.

**Magnetic field**
The area around a magnet where the magnetic force works.

**Magnetic material**
Material that can be made into or attracted to a magnet.

**Magnetic pole**
Place on a magnet where the magnetic force is strongest. Poles can be north and south.

**Magnetize**
To turn a magnetic material into a magnet.

**Melt**
To change from a solid to a liquid when the temperature rises.

**Microbe**
A microscopic living organism.

**Möbius strip**
A surface that has only one side. It is made by joining the two ends of a strip that has been twisted around once.

**Molecule**
Smallest particle of a substance that still has the substance's properties. A molecule may contain several atoms.

**Note**
A steady sound or tone of the same pitch or frequency.

**Oxidize**
To combine a substance with oxygen.

**Particle**
A tiny piece of a substance.

**Percussion**
Musical instruments played by hitting two things together; for example, a drum and drumstick.

**Permanent magnet**
A magnet that keeps its magnetism unless it is dropped, knocked, or gets too hot.

**Photosynthesis**
A chemical process where light energy trapped by chlorophyll combines with water and air to help make a plant grow.

**Pigment**
The substance added to paints and dyes to give them their color.

**Pitch**
The highness or lowness of a sound. Pitch depends on the frequency of the vibration causing the sound.

**Plastic**
When a body can be shaped into a new form, it is said to be plastic. Its properties allow it to be molded and then retain its new shape.

**Port**
The left side of a boat or ship as you look forward.

**Power**
The rate at which energy is changed from one form to another. The power of moving car engines is measured in brake horsepower (bhp).

**Pressure**
The force which presses down on a given area.

**Primary color**
There are three primary colors of paints and dyes, from which all other colors are made: red, yellow, and blue.

**Prism**
A transparent wedge, usually of glass, used to split white light into the colors of the rainbow.

**Propeller**
A rotating object with spiral arms used to drive a boat or other vessel forward.

**Pulley**
A system of wheels and rope that allows heavy loads to be lifted more easily.

**Reflect**
When light or sound is bounced back from a surface.

**Repel**
To push apart. Two south or two north poles repel each other.

**Resistance**
The ability that a material has to stop or resist the flow of electric current through it.

# GLOSSARY

**Rigid**
When an object is stiff and inflexible, it is said to be rigid. Its structure will not allow it to be bent or formed into any other shape.

**Rudder**
A flat steering object found under the stern of and underneath a boat.

**Saturated**
When a substance has been filled to its fullest possible extent.

**Shadow**
Place of darkness created by an object blocking light.

**Sound wave**
A regular pattern of vibrations that move through the air or other materials.

**Starboard**
The right side of a boat or ship as you look forward.

**Stethoscope**
Instrument used by doctors to hear sounds within the body which are normally too quiet to hear.

**Structure**
The arrangement of parts to form an entire object.

**Temperature**
The level of heat that a body has. It is measured in degrees of Celsius, Fahrenheit, and Kelvin.

**Terminal**
The part of a battery to which wires can be attached.

**Tessellation**
The ability of shapes to fit together neatly and cover an area without overlapping or leaving any spaces.

**Thermal**
An ascending current of warm air.

**Tiller**
The handle used to turn a rudder.

**Vibration**
A rapid backward and forward movement.

**Vocal cord**
Flaps of elastic tissue in the human throat which vibrate as air from the lungs is pushed over them, producing the sounds of the human voice.

**Volume**
The amount of space something takes up.

**Weaving**
To form a fabric by interlacing fibers. The weft threads are woven through the warp threads, to create the finished cloth.

**Woodwind**
Wind instruments made from wood or sometimes silver; for example, a clarinet or a flute.

# INDEX

# INDEX

# INDEX

# T H E
# *Knowledge*
# FACTORY

© Aladdin Books Ltd 1996

Designed and produced by
Aladdin Books Ltd
28 Percy Street
London W1P 0LD

First published in the United States by
Copper Beech Books, an imprint of
The Millbrook Press
2 Old New Milford Road
Brookfield, Connecticut

Printed in U.S.A.
All rights reserved

Some of the material in this book was
previously in other Aladdin Books' series.

Library of Congress Cataloging-in-Publication Data

# T H E
# *Knowledge*
# FACTORY

Copper Beech Books
Brookfield, Connecticut

# CONTENTS

## Technology

## History

## Geography and the Environment

# INTRODUCTION

The *Know*ledge *Fact*ory is no ordinary book – it includes absolutely everything you ever wanted to know. All the information, topics, illustrations, and pictures you could possibly want, right at your fingertips. The *Know*ledge *Fact*ory has a clearly defined contents and an easy-to-use index. It allows you to access various information at the turn of a page. You can pick it up anytime of day, and browse through it at your leisure. Your friends will be astounded and impressed with your great knowledge of almost every subject; from animals, to the latest advances in space technology.

## *Animals*

Animal life is a massive and very complex subject. There are thousands of different amazing species within each animal group. All animals have evolved through time and have adapted to their particular environments in many extraordinary ways! For example, what if giraffes had short necks or if an elephant didn't have a trunk? These questions, and many more, are answered in this book. You can learn everything you need to know about your cat, dog, or bird; even how spiders trap their prey with spun silk and how beetles have survived through the ages.

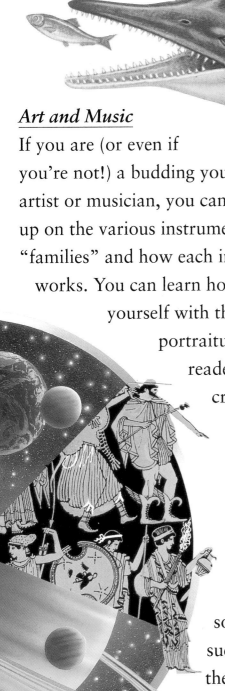

### Art and Music

If you are (or even if you're not!) a budding young artist or musician, you can read up on the various instrument "families" and how each instrument works. You can learn how to paint yourself with the art of self-portraiture; and if you are an avid reader of the comics you can create your own cartoon strips.

### Geography and the Environment

The Earth is an amazing and mysterious place. In this day and age, environmental and geographical topics are very important in our society. This book covers many important areas such as saving energy and recycling. After reading these topics you will be able to tell your friends about these subjects, and each of you can play a part in helping the Earth. You will answer questions like, what if the Earth stood still, and what happens when a volcano erupts?

## Prehistory

Prehistory is an exciting topic for everyone. There are many things we can learn from studying the past, such as; what are our origins, how did the dinosaurs become extinct, and how did the first humans live? We can peer back through time and see how the Earth looked and learn about how it developed. We are able to learn about our lives now, compared to that of the first humans. How they hunted with their primitive, yet very inventive tools – and also used them to fight off the vicious saber-toothed tiger!

## Technology

The enormous technological advances of the 20th Century have radically changed the way we live. What would people do without cars? Would there be no computer age if the microchip had not been invented? In the last half of this century, humans have been able to exceed the boundaries of the Earth. We have landed on the moon, sent probes to explore the farthest planets in our solar system. The technological advances in medicine have saved many lives, and helped rebuild many limbs with artifical implants.

## Science

Science covers a broad range of material – from the study of UFSs and aliens to the multiple parts of the brain. We can learn about the effects of sunlight on the Earth and what we would do if the sun went out and left us in complete darkness!

Scientific discoveries are the stepping stones for the future, *and* the link to the past.

## History

Who was Robin Hood? Was he a real person, or just an infamous character created by some people sitting around a campfire?

In this book you can discover the answer for yourself. You will explore medieval castles and ride out west with the North American cowboys and cowgirls. You may even encounter a pirate or two as you sail through the pages!

In the end... The *Know*ledge *Fact*ory has everything you could ever want to know. It will take you on an exciting journey through the world of knowledge. If you wish to find a specific topic check out the concise contents list and use the helpful index at the back of the book. With brilliant pictures and fun-to-read text, it gives you all of those weird and wonderful *facts* you always needed to *know*.

# ROBIN HOOD

Who has not heard of Robin Hood? He has acquired such fame that today all kind-hearted bandits are known as "Robin Hoods." And yet no one even knows who the real Robin Hood was, or even if he existed at all.

A document of 1239 mentions a Yorkshireman described as "Robert Hood, outlaw." Tales of Robin the outlaw were circulating by the mid-13th century, and the first written reference appears in the poem *Vision of Piers Plowman* (1378).

In the early poems, printed more than a century later, Robin is more like a real medieval bandit. He kills bloodily and enjoys it. Slaying Guy of Gisborne, he sticks his head on the end of his bow! But with time, as characters and adventures were added (*above*) by writers like Sir Walter Scott (as in the novel *Ivanhoe*), Robin was transformed into the romantic figure we recognize today.

THE MERRY MEN. Robin Hood stories became popular because they satisfy people's needs – ordinary men and women can triumph over privileged and corrupt masters.

Robin's adventures have been turned into dozens of films (*above*), most of which have little to do with the rough life of the medieval bandit!

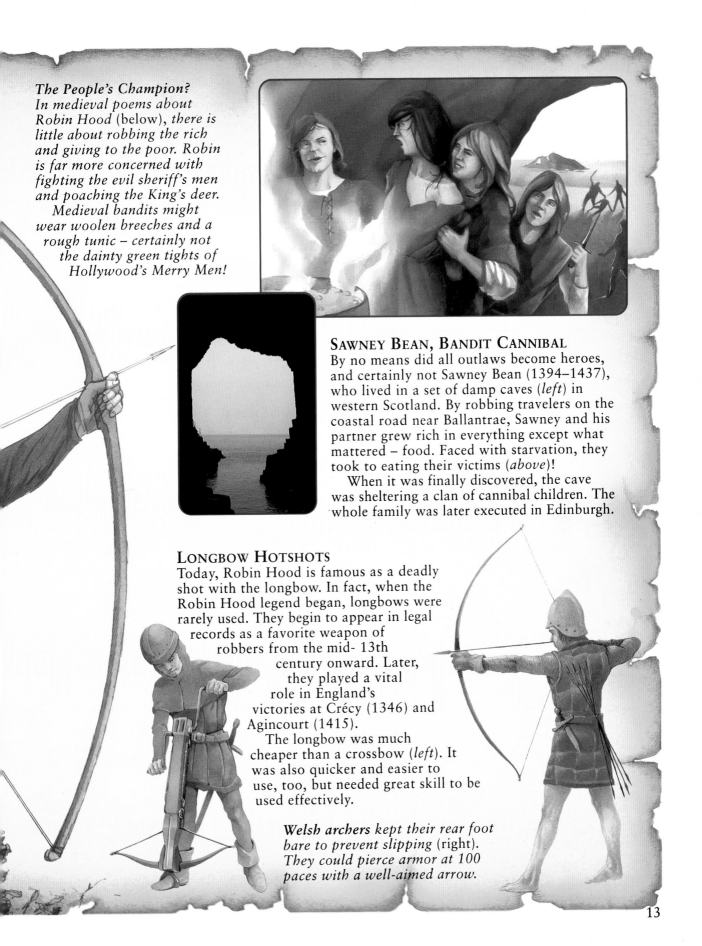

### The People's Champion?
*In medieval poems about Robin Hood* (below), *there is little about robbing the rich and giving to the poor. Robin is far more concerned with fighting the evil sheriff's men and poaching the King's deer.*
*Medieval bandits might wear woolen breeches and a rough tunic – certainly not the dainty green tights of Hollywood's Merry Men!*

## SAWNEY BEAN, BANDIT CANNIBAL
By no means did all outlaws become heroes, and certainly not Sawney Bean (1394–1437), who lived in a set of damp caves (*left*) in western Scotland. By robbing travelers on the coastal road near Ballantrae, Sawney and his partner grew rich in everything except what mattered – food. Faced with starvation, they took to eating their victims (*above*)!

When it was finally discovered, the cave was sheltering a clan of cannibal children. The whole family was later executed in Edinburgh.

## LONGBOW HOTSHOTS
Today, Robin Hood is famous as a deadly shot with the longbow. In fact, when the Robin Hood legend began, longbows were rarely used. They begin to appear in legal records as a favorite weapon of robbers from the mid- 13th century onward. Later, they played a vital role in England's victories at Crécy (1346) and Agincourt (1415).

The longbow was much cheaper than a crossbow (*left*). It was also quicker and easier to use, too, but needed great skill to be used effectively.

*Welsh archers kept their rear foot bare to prevent slipping* (right). *They could pierce armor at 100 paces with a well-aimed arrow.*

# WHAT IF GIRAFFES HAD SHORT NECKS?

Some do! The okapi is a type of giraffe found in the tropical rain forests of central Africa. Unlike its taller relative, the giraffe of the African plains, all of its food is within easy reach among the lush jungle vegetation. As a result, it does not need the long neck of the plains giraffe. The tree branches of the African plains are found well above the ground, so the giraffe needs a long neck to stretch up and eat the leaves that can be over 19 ft (6 m) high. The giraffe's unique feature has evolved over years of evolution, so that it is now perfectly suited to its way of life.

## Designed by committee

The odd shape of the giraffe, with its big head, long neck, long front legs, and short back legs, has often been described as an animal put together by a committee. However, the peculiar body has evolved naturally over time. The result may look odd, but it works.

## Lookout post

Not only does the giraffe's tall neck allow it to reach the highest branches, it lets it see over long distances. High above the grassy plains, the giraffe can spot danger, such as a bush fire or a prowling hunter, or even new trees to eat, from several miles away.

Okapi

# All creatures great and small

Just as the neck of the giraffe has developed over millions of years, so nature has created a whole host of different mammals. There are currently over 4,000 species of mammals, ranging from enormous whales to tiny mice, and from peaceful cows to aggressive tigers. Each of these has developed its own method of survival, involving a bizarre array of physical features. These include the hump of a camel, the stripes of a zebra, or the trunk of an elephant. All of these strange-looking features have evolved to help the animal survive in its environment.

**The long and short of it**

A giraffe, like all other mammals, including the okapi, has only seven vertebrae in its neck. However, these neck bones are greatly elongated (stretched), allowing the giraffe's head to stand way above the ground.

Giraffe

# What if dinosaurs were still alive?

Then we would not be here! Mammals and dinosaurs first appeared at the same time, about 200 million years ago. However, it was the dinosaurs who were first to develop and rule the Earth. Mammals could not compete, and they had to be very small to survive. Then, mysteriously, the dinosaurs died out about 65 million years ago, and mammals were able to develop into their many and various forms (see above). If the dinosaurs were still here, then the largest mammal would probably be about the size of a cat.

# WARPLANES

In less than a century warplanes have developed beyond recognition. The first dogfight between two aircraft took place in October 1914. Since then, air power has been decisive in almost every major war. Today's warplanes carry a wide variety of armaments, including fast-firing cannons, and sophisticated guided missiles and bombs. Some planes, such as the Stealth fighter and the F-15 Eagle, are developed for one purpose only. "Multi-role" warplanes are designed to be able to carry out different functions by modifying a basic aircraft frame.

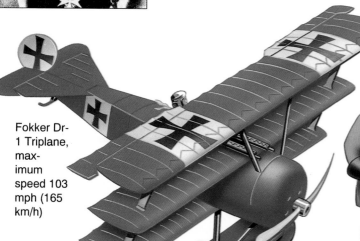

Fokker Dr-1 Triplane, maximum speed 103 mph (165 km/h)

World War I pilot dressed in warm clothes against the cold

## Early warplanes

World War I planes were maneuverable but had few technological aids. The pilot relied on his own flying skills. The top flying ace was German pilot Manfred von Richthofen, known as the "Red Baron," above. His planes – an Albatros, and later a Fokker Triplane – were painted scarlet. Official war records show that he shot down 80 enemy planes, before being killed in 1918.

## World War II

Different planes had different roles during World War II. Fighters were small and fast, but could not carry many armaments or fly long distances. Bombers such as the Boeing B-29 Superfortress shown here were bigger, with enough fuel for long flights. But they were slower, and vulnerable to enemy fighters.

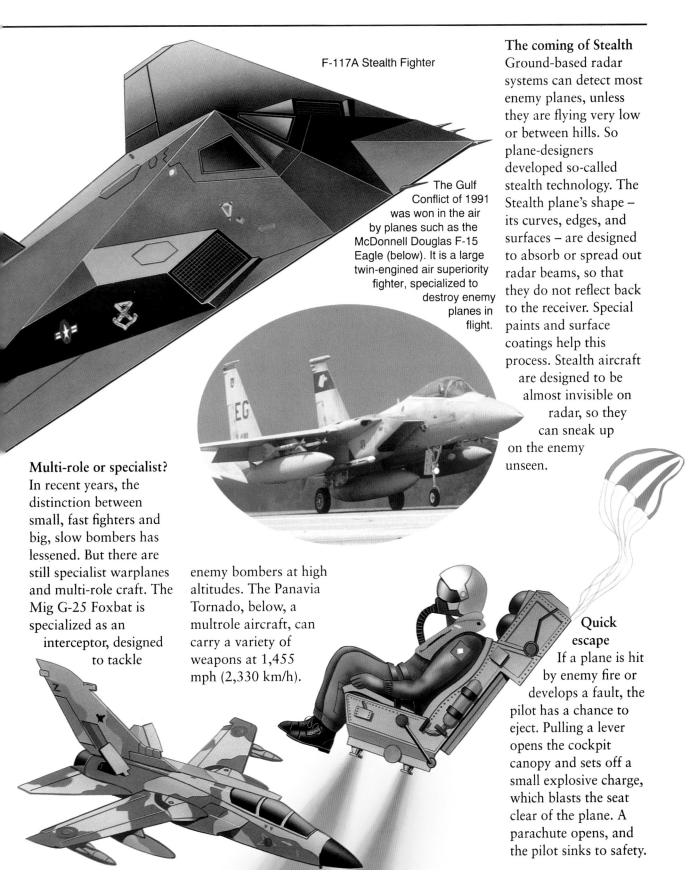

F-117A Stealth Fighter

**The coming of Stealth**
Ground-based radar systems can detect most enemy planes, unless they are flying very low or between hills. So plane-designers developed so-called stealth technology. The Stealth plane's shape – its curves, edges, and surfaces – are designed to absorb or spread out radar beams, so that they do not reflect back to the receiver. Special paints and surface coatings help this process. Stealth aircraft are designed to be almost invisible on radar, so they can sneak up on the enemy unseen.

The Gulf Conflict of 1991 was won in the air by planes such as the McDonnell Douglas F-15 Eagle (below). It is a large twin-engined air superiority fighter, specialized to destroy enemy planes in flight.

**Multi-role or specialist?**
In recent years, the distinction between small, fast fighters and big, slow bombers has lessened. But there are still specialist warplanes and multi-role craft. The Mig G-25 Foxbat is specialized as an interceptor, designed to tackle enemy bombers at high altitudes. The Panavia Tornado, below, a multrole aircraft, can carry a variety of weapons at 1,455 mph (2,330 km/h).

**Quick escape**
If a plane is hit by enemy fire or develops a fault, the pilot has a chance to eject. Pulling a lever opens the cockpit canopy and sets off a small explosive charge, which blasts the seat clear of the plane. A parachute opens, and the pilot sinks to safety.

# BLOOD

No matter how frightened the brain is, it never faints at the sight of blood, because blood brings life. Blood carries vital oxygen, energy in the form of blood sugars, nourishing nutrients for growth and repair, the chemical messengers called hormones, and dozens of other essential substances. So smile and be thankful for this red, endlessly flowing river of life.

*A heavy ball*

## BLOOD GROUPS

All blood is not the same. Each body has its own blood group. Doctors found this when they tried transfusing blood (opposite), and often failed. One set of blood groups is A, B, AB, or O. Another is Rh positive or negative, named because it was discovered in rhesus monkeys.

*Red blood cell*

*Platelet*

*White blood cell*

## SELF-SEALING SYSTEM

If a blood vessel springs a small leak, it soon seals and mends itself, by forming a sticky scab. Some car radiators do the same (with water).

## BLOOD CELLS

Red cells carry oxygen. White cells fight germs. Platelets help blood to clot.

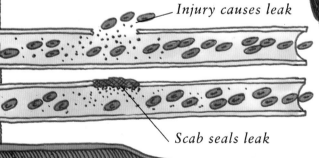

*Injury causes leak*

*Scab seals leak*

## THREE TUBES FOR BLOOD

Big arteries carry blood from the heart. They divide into capillaries, which are tiny. These join into veins, and return blood to the heart.

*Capillary*

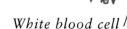

*Main artery*

*Small artery*

*Arteriole*

 *$O_2$ and nutrients out*

 *$CO_2$ and wastes in*

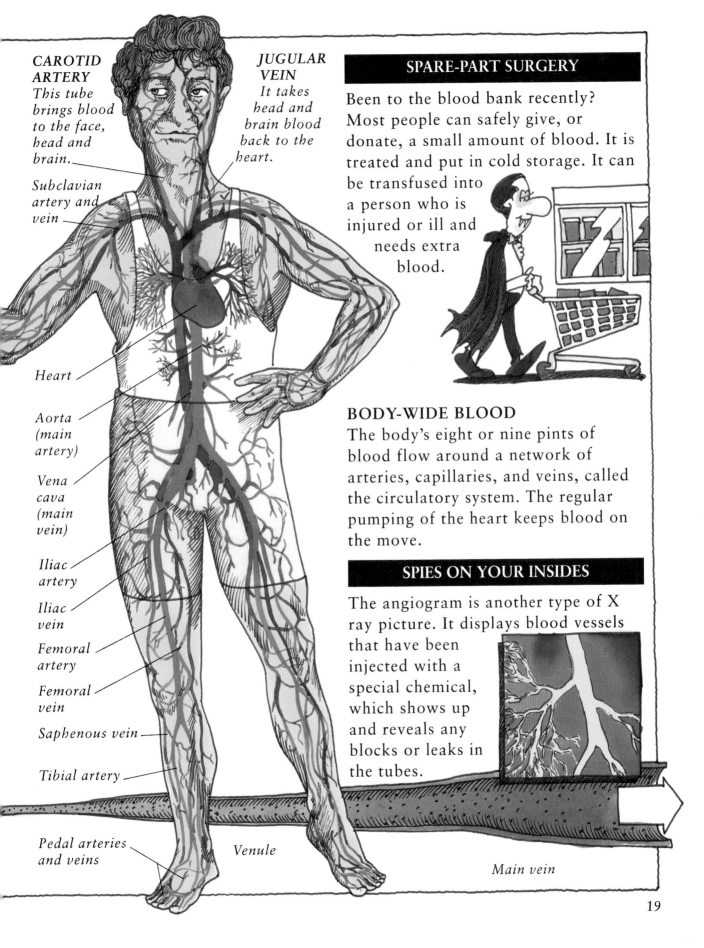

**CAROTID ARTERY**
*This tube brings blood to the face, head and brain.*

**JUGULAR VEIN**
*It takes head and brain blood back to the heart.*

*Subclavian artery and vein*

*Heart*

*Aorta (main artery)*

*Vena cava (main vein)*

*Iliac artery*

*Iliac vein*

*Femoral artery*

*Femoral vein*

*Saphenous vein*

*Tibial artery*

*Pedal arteries and veins*

*Venule*

## SPARE-PART SURGERY

Been to the blood bank recently? Most people can safely give, or donate, a small amount of blood. It is treated and put in cold storage. It can be transfused into a person who is injured or ill and needs extra blood.

## BODY-WIDE BLOOD

The body's eight or nine pints of blood flow around a network of arteries, capillaries, and veins, called the circulatory system. The regular pumping of the heart keeps blood on the move.

## SPIES ON YOUR INSIDES

The angiogram is another type of X ray picture. It displays blood vessels that have been injected with a special chemical, which shows up and reveals any blocks or leaks in the tubes.

*Main vein*

# MEASURING EARTHQUAKES

The scientists who study the seismic waves released from the focus of an earthquake are called seismologists. Special measuring instruments, called seismographs, record the pattern of the seismic waves. Seismologists use these patterns to determine the strength and duration of an earthquake, as well as the amount of movement along a fault line. Taking readings at several different points on the earth's surface also helps them to pinpoint the exact location of the earthquake's focus.

Two different scales are used to measure the strength of an earthquake. The most common one is the Richter scale, devised by American seismologist, Charles Richter, in 1935. It calculates the magnitude of an earthquake from seismograph recordings that measure the amount of energy released. An increase of 1 point on the Richter scale means that an earthquake is 10 times stronger than one with the next value below. An earthquake measuring less than 5 on the Richter scale causes minimal damage, while a major earthquake measures 7 or more. The second scale is the Mercalli scale, which calculates the intensity of an earthquake by assessing the damage it causes.

I: Felt by only a very few people. II: Felt by a few, on upper floors.

VII: Bricks loosen. Difficult to stand. VIII: Damage to weak structures.

V: Buildings tremble and trees shake. VI: Felt by all. Plaster cracks.

III: Similar to a passing vehicle. IV: Felt by many people indoors.

**Jagged tracings (right) are made as the seismograph records the movements of the ground during an earthquake. Scientists can distinguish between the primary, secondary, and surface waves.**

IX: Pipes crack. Buildings collapse. X: Huge ground cracks. Landslides.

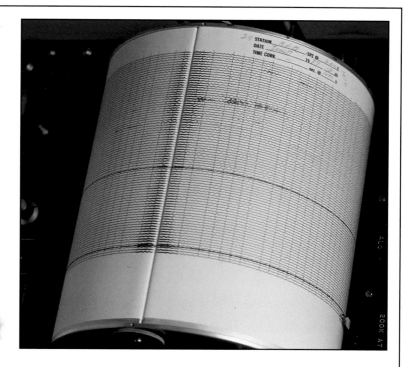

XI: Most buildings destroyed. *Tsunamis*. XII: Total destruction. Surface waves seen.

◄ **The Mercalli scale was invented in 1902 by Italian seismologist, Giuseppe Mercalli, and modified during the 1930s by American scientists. The scale describes effects that range from tiny swaying movements (I) to total devastation (XII).**

### Seismographs

One type of seismograph records the horizontal movements of the earth, and the other type vertical movements. A weight is attached to a frame by a sensitive spring. As the ground trembles, the weight remains stationary but the frame moves and a pen records the movement on paper wrapped around a rotating drum. This recording is called a seismogram.

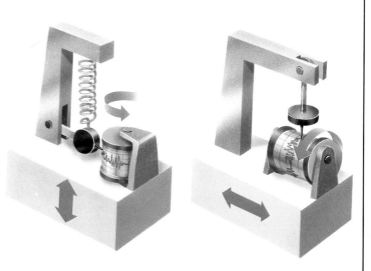

# THE PREHISTORIC OCEANS

During the Mesozoic era (which includes the Triassic, the Jurassic, and the Cretaceous periods), the world's oceans were home to many large marine reptiles. Some of these creatures are familiar to us today, like the crocodiles and turtles. Others, like *Ichthyosaurus* (fish lizard), look similar to dolphins, but were reptiles not mammals. Marine reptiles were a very important part of the Mesozoic oceans, but they were not the only creatures to live in them. Some of the most familiar and plentiful fossils, such as the ammonites and "Devil's Toenail," lived in the seas at that time.

## Snake stones

Ammonites were molluscs (animals with a shell), distantly related to snails and shellfish. They floated in the water, catching food with their tentacles. When people first found these coiled fossils, they thought that they were snakes that had been turned to stone.

A variety of molluscs including this entolium lived on the seabed.

Entolium

Ammonite

## Layers of history

An age can be given to the rocks by looking at the fossils they contain, or by comparing sequences of layers of rock. The layers of rock are called strata. They were originally all more or less level, but movements of the Earth's crust have caused them to move about, sinking and rising.

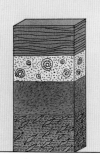

Rock strata

Plesiosaurs had long necks that they used to snatch small fish from the water.

Plesiosaurs

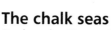

## The chalk seas

During the Upper Cretaceous, the world's oceans contained micro-organisms that are now preserved as chalk rock. They lived in the surface of the sea, and when they died, their bodies sank to the seabed, forming chalk.

Ichthyosaur

Ichthyosaurs were dolphinlike reptiles that grew up to 50 feet in length.

### Child scientist

In 1810, Mary Anning found her first whole ichthyosaur fossil at Lyme Regis in England (below). She was only eleven years old at the time. During her life, Mary Anning found many specimens, some of which she sold to British scientists. You may have heard the rhyme "She sells sea shells on the sea shore." which was possibly written about her.

Lyme Regis

### Sea dragons

Since the discovery of their fossils, many attempts to produce reconstructions of marine reptiles have been made. Most of the earlier drawings (below) show seas full of fish, ammonites, and reptiles all in dramatic poses, or looking like Scotland's Loch Ness Monster, not at all like the modern, graceful images of them.

Pliosaurs had very short necks, and skulls more adapted to kill larger animals, possibly even ichthyosaurs and plesiosaurs.

Pliosaur

# THE TELESCOPE AND MICROSCOPE

Do you believe that the Moon is made of green cheese, and that germs don't exist? If you had a telescope and a microscope, you could see for yourself. Telescopes look at outer space, to reveal the mysteries of the universe. Microscopes look into inner space, to show us what our own bodies are made of.

Many inventors and scientists fooled around with curved pieces of glass, called lenses. From the 1200s, lenses of various strengths were used in eyeglasses. Two lenses, specially shaped and put near to each other, make distant things look bigger and nearer. This was probably discovered by Hans Lippershey in Holland, in 1608.

Early spectacles

Within a year, the famous Galileo heard about the new invention, and made his own versions. They magnified up to 30 times. He scanned the dark skies and discovered mountains on the Moon, spots on the Sun, and moons going around Jupiter. He was the first real telescope-user.

Galileo

## Types of telescopes

Christian Huygens, who worked on pendulum clocks, also invented better telescopes. In about 1757 a British optician, John Dollond, sandwiched two lenses closely together. These compound lenses gave better, clearer images.

In 1668 the great Isaac Newton designed a telescope with a curved mirror in place of one lens. This was called a reflector. Today, the biggest optical telescopes are reflectors. They look deep into space, to tell us about our Moon and Sun, the planets and stars, and the beginning of the universe.

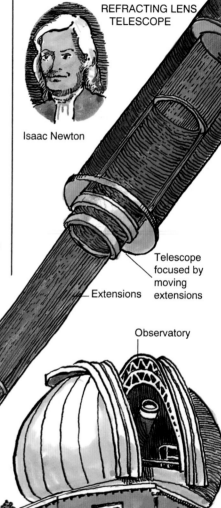

REFRACTING LENS TELESCOPE

Isaac Newton

Telescope focused by moving extensions

Extensions

Observatory

Eyepiece lens

GALILEO'S TELESCOPE

REFRACTING LENS TELESCOPE

Eyepiece lens

Convex lens

Mirror

NEWTONIAN REFLECTOR

Eyepiece

Mirror

# THE TELESCOPE AND MICROSCOPE

## Seeing the invisible

Around 1590, Dutch lens-maker Zacharias Janssen also put two lenses near to each other. He noticed that a tiny thing at one end looked much bigger from the other end – provided the lenses were the right distance apart.

Scientists showed an interest. They realized that a whole tiny world was waiting to be discovered. In 1655, Robert Hooke first used the word "cell" for a microscopic part of a living thing, in his book Micrographia, "Small Drawings." Hooke showed that tiny creatures such as ants had a heart, stomach and other body parts – just like bigger animals, but smaller!

LEEUWENHOEK'S MICROSCOPE

Lens

Object

## Draper turned lens-maker

By the 1680s Anton van Leeuwenhoek, in Holland, made fascinating discoveries through the microscope. His homemade microscopes could magnify over 250 times. Through them he saw new wonders such as red blood cells, tiny one-celled creatures like amoebas, the eggs of fleas, insect eyes, and stacks of cells in the thinnest leaf.

Anton van Leeuwenhoek

After Leeuwenhoek, many people looked through microscopes. The science of microbiology began. Soon people were looking at germs, and working out how they invaded the body and caused diseases.

Microscopes became more powerful, with strong lights and changeable lenses that could magnify over one thousand times. Today, medicine and biology would be lost without microscopes.

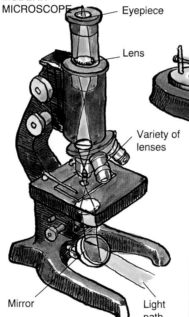

MODERN MICROSCOPE

Eyepiece

Lens

Variety of lenses

Mirror

Light path

## How they work

In a microscope, light waves from the tiny and nearby object are bent inwards by the convex (bulging) lens. They are bent again at the second lens, the eyepiece, so that you see a clear and enlarged view.

In a telescope, much the same happens. But the light waves come from far, far away, so they are parallel when they reach the telescope.

EARLY MICROSCOPE

Eyepiece

Metal body

Focusing screw

Object

## Wow! Big, small, and far-out

• The telescope with the biggest one-piece lens is at the Yerkes Observatory, in the USA. The lens is 40 inches across.

• Electron microscopes use electron beams instead of light rays. They magnify over one million times.

• Radio telescopes detect not light rays, but radio waves from stars, quasars and pulsars. They can "see" billions of miles, to the far side of the Universe.

Radio telescopes

# WHAT IS DROUGHT?

Drought is a long period with no rain or with much less rainfall than is normal for a particular area. Almost one-third of the land on Earth is prone to drought, which affects more than 600 million people.

During a drought, the soil becomes parched and cracked. The hard-baked surface cannot absorb any water, and so very little moisture is retained in the soil. The dry and dusty topsoil is worn away by wind and rain, leaving behind patches of barren land.

Drought is a natural disaster that can affect any country in the world. However, its effects are made much worse in the developing world by a number of factors. They include overpopulation, overgrazing, and cutting down trees to provide firewood.

**Hot, dry winds and very high temperatures, combined with a lack of rainfall and the evaporation of moisture in the ground, produce the conditions of drought. In some areas, periods of drought alternate with periods of flood, continually destroying food crops and farmland.**

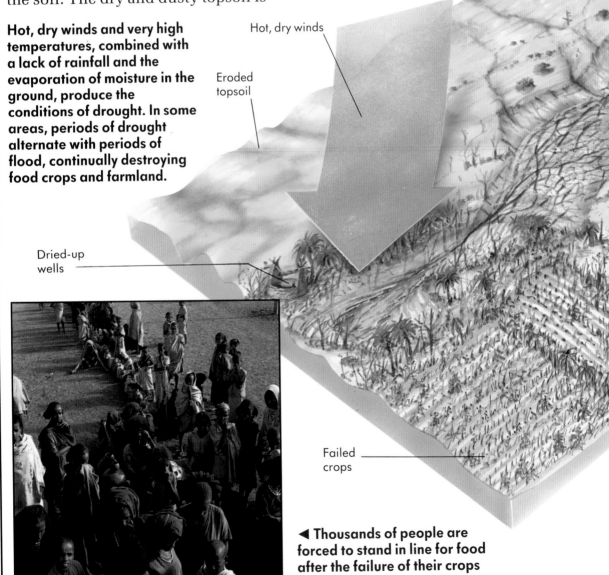

Hot, dry winds

Eroded topsoil

Dried-up wells

Failed crops

**◄ Thousands of people are forced to stand in line for food after the failure of their crops through drought.**

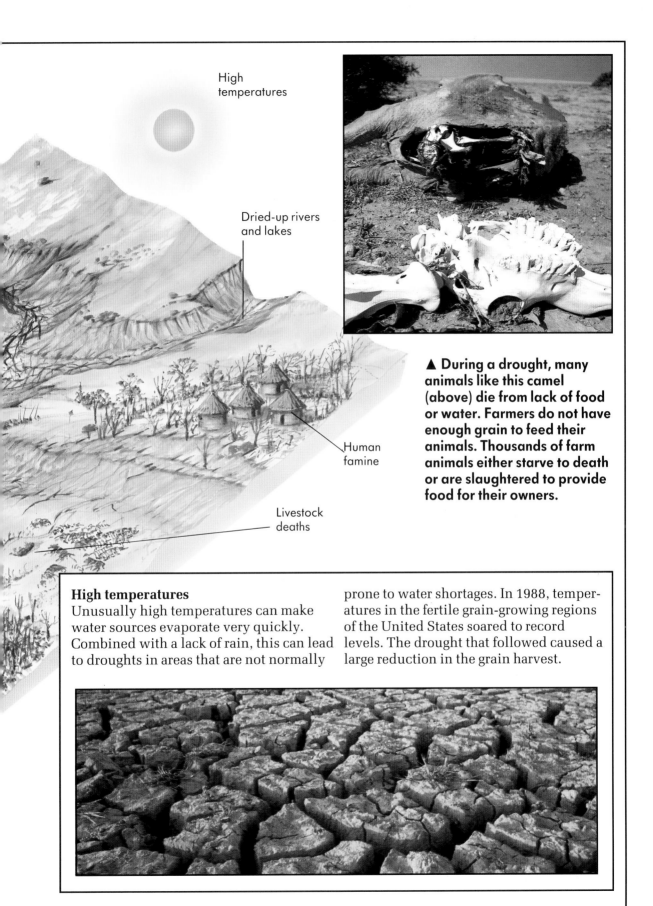

High
temperatures

Dried-up rivers
and lakes

Human
famine

Livestock
deaths

▲ **During a drought, many animals like this camel (above) die from lack of food or water. Farmers do not have enough grain to feed their animals. Thousands of farm animals either starve to death or are slaughtered to provide food for their owners.**

## High temperatures

Unusually high temperatures can make water sources evaporate very quickly. Combined with a lack of rain, this can lead to droughts in areas that are not normally prone to water shortages. In 1988, temperatures in the fertile grain-growing regions of the United States soared to record levels. The drought that followed caused a large reduction in the grain harvest.

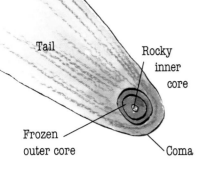

Tail

Rocky inner core

Frozen outer core

Coma

**Inside a comet**

A typical comet has a small center, or core, a few miles across. It's made from pieces of grit, dust, and crystals of frozen gases such as methane, ammonia, carbon dioxide, and water (ice).

# WHAT IF COMETS DIDN'T RETURN?

Ancient civilizations thought a comet was a god breathing into the heavens or sending a fireball to destroy the Earth. At regular intervals they would streak across the night sky, creating fear and panic in all who saw them. Comets are really just lumps of ice and rock that boil and fizz as they near the Sun, sending out a huge tail of dust and vapor. In the 1700s it was noticed that some comets kept returning, orbiting the Sun in a stretched-out circle, called a *parabola*. Some just disappear into deep space.

## Crash, bang, smash

If a comet hit a planet, there would be a massive explosion. This was seen when the comet Shoemaker-Levy 9 collided with Jupiter in 1994. A series of explosions punched huge holes in the atmosphere, stirring up gases from Jupiter's interior.

# How do we know comets will return?

The British astronomer Edmond Halley noticed that the paths of comets observed in 1531 and 1607, and the one he saw in 1682, were all the same – was it the same comet returning each time? He predicted it would return in 1758. It did, and has since been called Halley's comet. From his theories, astronomers were able to plot comets' long orbits around the Sun.

# How do we know what's inside a comet?

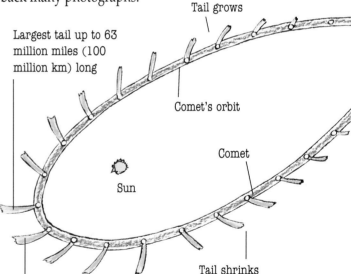

From observing its orbit and how fast it travels, by studying the light and other waves it gives out, and with space probes and telescopes. In 1986, five space probes passed near Halley's comet, on its regular visit. Europe's Giotto got within 375 miles (600 km) of the core, which is only 10 miles (16 km) long and 5 miles (8 km) wide, and sent back many photographs.

# What if a comet didn't have a tail?

For much of its lifetime, it doesn't. As a comet travels close to the Sun and warms, its icy crust boils, throwing out gases that make a glowing outer layer, called the *coma*. The solar wind blows dust and other particles from the coma to form a tail that reflects the Sun's glow, and points away from the Sun. Then the comet heads into space, and the tail disappears.

Largest tail up to 63 million miles (100 million km) long

Tail grows

Comet's orbit

Comet

Sun

Tail shrinks

Tail points away from Sun

# How long do comets last?

Some fall to pieces after a few hundred years, while others may last millions of years. It depends partly on how often the comet travels near the Sun. Halley's comet has been seen every 75-76 years for over 2,000 years!

# HOW INSECTS FEED

Insects have adapted to make use of every possible food source. Some feed on plants and some on animals. Some suck juices, while some munch on solid food. Many insects consume their prey while it is still alive; many more eat it when it is dead. Some insects are specialized to eat wood or pollen, feathers or blood, even dung. Some eat each other. Many insects feed on humans, causing illness by infecting people with tiny disease organisms. Insects that eat our food can cause famine. Those that eat building materials can cause great damage.

Insect species have different kinds of mouthparts, specialized to cope with their particular diet. All have four main structures. The mandibles are hard jaws for biting, the maxillae are secondary jaws. The labrum and the labium form the upper and lower lips. Caterpillars of butterflies and moths have strong jaws to munch leaves.

Ant

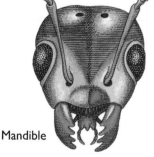

Mandible

Labium

### Biting
Ants' saw-shaped mandibles are closed by strong muscles to chomp on solid food. Behind the mandibles, the maxillae taste the food. The labium and labrum chew it and push it into the mouth.

A monarch butterfly caterpillar consumes a leaf.

### Food chains
Insects form very important links in food chains, eating plants and in turn being eaten by other insects and larger animals. In temperate climates such as Europe, when the weather warms in spring and the buds on trees begin to burst, thousands of insect eggs hatch into grubs which begin to feed and grow. They provide food for the young of nesting birds such as blackbirds and robins. Swallows return from their warm wintering grounds in South Africa just as the grubs are turning into adult insects. This provides an airborne feast for the swallows (right) to feed to their young as they hatch.

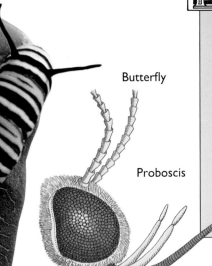

## Locust pests

In Africa, the feeding habits of migratory locusts make them one of the most feared of pests. These insects are usually solitary, and dull in color. But when rains come to the parched savannahs and grass begins to grow, they begin to reproduce rapidly, and become brightly colored. They gather in swarms of billions. Such a swarm can strip a field of crops in minutes, leaving the farmer with no food.

Butterfly

Proboscis

## Sucking

Butterfly and moth mouthparts have evolved into a long strawlike tube, or proboscis, to enable the insect to suck liquid nectar from flowers. The proboscis is kept rolled up between feeds. The housefly (left) squirts digestive juices down its proboscis onto its food. When the food has gone mushy, the fly sucks it up.

Fly

Mosquito

## Piercing

Insects such as shieldbugs and mosquitoes puncture the hard skin of plants or animals to suck out juices. Their mandibles have evolved into needlelike tubes. The insect feels for a suitable place to puncture with the soft labium which surrounds its "needle." Then it stabs its prey, and pumps in digestive fluids before it sucks the victim's juices out.

Mandibles

## Wood-boring beetles

The furniture beetle lays its eggs in cracks in old, dead wood. The wood provides a food source for the larvae, whether it is a dead tree or a valuable piece of antique furniture. Undetected, the larvae, or "woodworm," tunnel through the wood, and eventually pupate. Flight holes suddenly appear in the wood as the adult insects leave to mate and lay eggs on a new food source. Flight holes have sometimes been faked in new furniture, to make it appear older, and therefore more valuable.

## Insects as food

Although few people from Western countries consider eating insects, they are nutritious, and are eaten as delicacies in many parts of the world. Australian Aborigines eat adult bogong moths, and the fat "witchetty" grubs of the giant wood moth. In Africa mosquito pie is eaten, and in Asia stir-fried locust is popular.

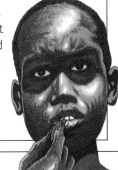

# ESTIMATING TIME

Hours are artificial units of time, first introduced by the Ancient Egyptians when they observed that shadows follow a similar pattern of movement each day. Shadow clocks and sundials were early time-measurement tools. In the 14th century, the sandglass, or hourglass, was popular, but it could only be used to estimate periods of time, varying from minutes to hours. It could not indicate the time of day. Onboard ship, a four-hour glass timed "watch" for the crew, until John Harrison invented the more accurate chronometer in 1735. This also calculated longitude and latitude. Early sandglasses were filled with powdered eggshell or marble dust.

## TIME IS RUNNING OUT

**1**

**1.** Wash and dry two small bottles thoroughly. Make an open-ended cylinder of cardboard and slide it over the top of one bottle. Cut out a disc of cardboard to fit inside and make a hole in its center.

**2**

**2.** Make sure the other bottle is absolutely dry. Now, carefully pour a measured amount of salt into it.

**3**

**3.** Position the empty bottle on top of the salt-filled bottle by sliding the cardboard cylinder over the neck of the lower bottle.

**4**

**4.** Check that the cardboard "seal" around the middle is secure. Carefully turn your timer over and observe what happens.

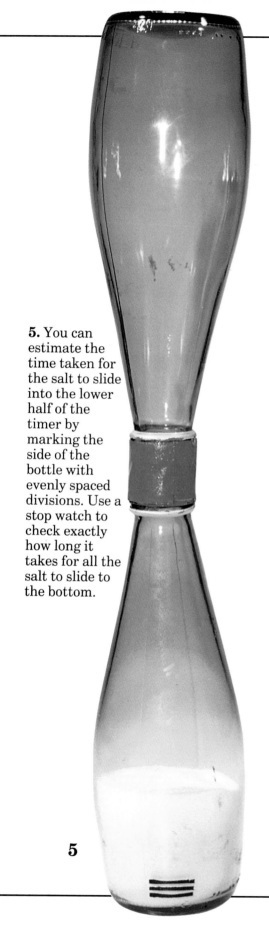

**5.** You can estimate the time taken for the salt to slide into the lower half of the timer by marking the side of the bottle with evenly spaced divisions. Use a stop watch to check exactly how long it takes for all the salt to slide to the bottom.

**5**

## WHY IT WORKS

The upper vessel of the timer holds just enough salt to run through a hole, of a given size, in a given period of time. The force of gravity pulls the salt down through the hole and into the bottom container. The salt grains must be absolutely dry, so they don't stick. The size of the hole between the two vessels will determine the speed at which the grains will flow, but once established, the rate of flow will not vary. The total period of time depends on the quantity of salt.

Salt

## BRIGHT IDEAS

Remove the regulator from between the two bottles and replace it with another, in which a hole of a different diameter has been made. Repeat this exercise a number of times, changing the size of the hole each time. What do you discover?

Design a sandglass that will run for exactly 3 minutes - use it as an eggtimer when you boil an egg.

Can you design another kind of sandglass that runs for a much longer period of time? Shape a funnel from cardboard, and insert it into the neck of a measuring container. Fill the funnel with sand and time how long it takes to pour through into the container below. Standardize your method of reading the scale - the top of the mound of sand will be concave.

Funnel

Sand

Scale

# SEASHORE LIFE

The seashore is one of the harshest surroundings for living things. Twice a day these creatures are covered by water, then dry out as the tide goes out. They are exposed to heat, cold, and buffeting waves. Conditions keep changing. But each tide brings in a new supply of food in the form of microscopic sea creatures. In spite of the difficulties, many sea animals live on shores. Seaweeds grow among rocks where the water is shallow enough for them to get the light they need. There is a huge number of kinds, but by observation and taking notes you will find you soon get to know the main ones. The seashore is one of the places that is most fun for a naturalist. There is always something to see, and you are never sure what will be in the next pool.

**SHORE ZONES**
**If you map seaweed types on a rocky shore you will find they live at different levels on the beach. The same is true for many of the animals.**

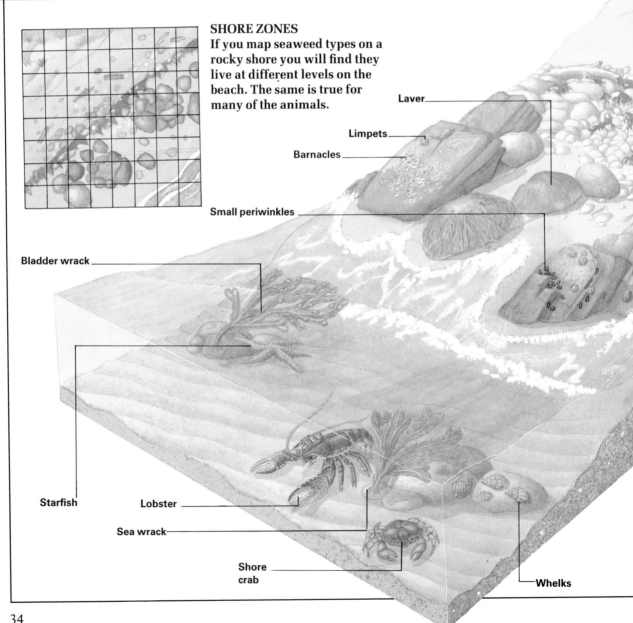

Laver

Limpets

Barnacles

Small periwinkles

Bladder wrack

Starfish

Lobster

Sea wrack

Shore crab

Whelks

## SEARCHING THE BEACH

To discover which animals live along a shore, especially at the lower levels, follow the tide out down the beach. Many animals will have hidden in crevices and beneath rock ledges, others may be lurking in rocky tide pools, so you should be able to get close enough to study them.

Gulls are successful scavengers. You will see them swoop down to catch crabs or to gobble up any small fish that may have become tangled in seaweed and stranded by the tide.

**Black headed gull**

**Sea bindweed**

**Hermit crab**

**Common dog whelk**

### VARYING TIDES
The height of the tides varies throughout a month, but parts of the shore are only wetted by the highest spring tides. Some sea creatures can only survive where they are just splashed by spray.

**Splash zone**

**SPRING TIDE**
**HIGH TIDE**
**LOW TIDE**

# LARGER SPECIES

Seals swim near the shore and may climb out to rest if they don't see you. Dolphins and porpoises sometimes play close by the shore. Search the strandline for the remains of these and other dead animals washed up on the beach after storms.

### MAKING TRACKS
Seals are graceful swimmers, but are clumsy on land. If they cross sand they may leave tracks like these.

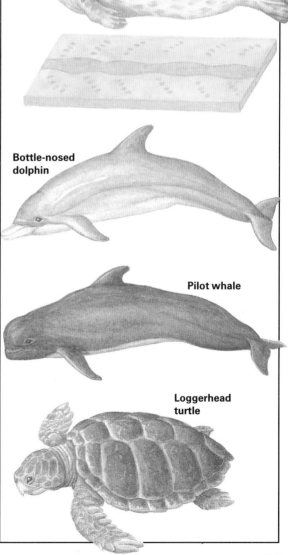

**Gray seal and tracks**

**Bottle-nosed dolphin**

**Pilot whale**

**Loggerhead turtle**

# COWGIRLS

Cowboys lived at a time when most women stayed at home looking after children and working around the house. If they went out riding, they usually sat sidesaddle. Their long dresses made it hard to rush around and do the same work as men.

In the West, however, things were sometimes rather different. The women who traveled with the wagon trains often worked alongside the men. When they settled, some managed ranches when their menfolk were away, or after they had died. A few even put on men's clothing and joined the drovers on horseback. This caused confusion among the men, who did not know what to make of such "cowgirls." The women they were used to were either nymphs or the mothers and daughters of the homestead. Cowboys therefore regarded cowgirls with a mixture of fear and scorn. One or two women, such as "Cattle Annie" and "Little Britches" (*below*), even joined outlaw gangs. Later, pioneering women worked in rodeo and "Wild West" shows.

## CALAMITY JANE

Martha Jane Canary (*above*) was born in Montana in 1852. Her parents died when she was young, forcing her to look after herself. She tried all sorts of jobs, such as cooking and dancing, but found them all rather boring.

In search of excitement, she took to wearing men's clothes and doing men's work. She was a mule driver, railroad laborer and even joined the army, acting as a scout in the Indian Wars.

After that she drifted west, drawing crowds to the saloons with her swashbuckling behavior. Having lived with Wild Bill Hickok for a time, after his death she joined Buffalo Bill's Wild West Show. Sadly, she was now drinking heavily and was soon fired. She spent the rest of her days in drunken poverty. Dying in 1903, she was buried beside Wild Bill.

## BELLE STARR

For sheer excitement, few women could match the career of Belle Starr (*left*), known as the "Bandit Queen." Raised as Myra Belle Shirley in a wealthy middle-class home, Belle soon tired of her respectable life and went to live as a bandit.

She shocked people by having two children by men friends and wearing a revolver on a gun belt over her dress. Yet she still rode her horse, *Venus*, sidesaddle, like a lady (*right*). She was found guilty of many robberies and had several spells in prison. She married the rustler Sam Starr, and after his death continued to run the ranch as a hideout for outlaws. But one evening, while riding alone, she was killed in an ambush by a fellow bandit.

**C**OWGIRLS ON SCREEN. Until the 1960s, women in Westerns were usually portrayed as either flirtatious prairie nymphs or as domestic, pretty, and willing to follow their menfolk.

More recent films, such as *Bad Girls* (*left*), have depicted them as tough fighters, but their true role in settling the West is still to be shown.

### Cattle Annie and Little Britches

*For a time "Oklahoma's Girl Bandits" – Jennie Stevens and Annie McDougal – were the most famous girls in the West. Meeting some of the Doolin gang at a dance, the girls decided to run away from home and join them. Before long, "Cattle Annie" and "Little Britches," as Jennie was known, were robbing with the Doolin gang. But the law was closing in. The girls were finally cornered by Marshal Tilghman and his assistant. Tracking the girls down was one thing – but capturing them was quite another (left). By the time the girls were handcuffed, both men were nursing painful bruises. After two years in prison, Annie married and settled down. Jennie went to New York, where she died of consumption.*

# WHAT IS THE WEATHER?

From sunshine and showers to blizzards and hurricanes, the weather is a combination of wind, rain, clouds, and temperature. Believe it or not, all our weather is caused by the air around our planet warming up and cooling down. The average weather in one particular region is called the climate. In some climates, the weather stays much the same all year round. But in many parts of the world, the weather changes at certain times of year. A climate appears to stay the same, but may change quite a lot over thousands of years.

**Earth moves around the Sun once a year.**

**Earth spins once a day.**

## The Sun and Earth

The Earth moves slowly around the Sun once every year. Because the Earth is tilted, places are closer to the Sun at different times of year. This affects the amount of light and heat these places receive, and produces a pattern of changes in the weather called the seasons. The Earth also spins on its axis once every 24 hours, giving us night and day.

### The atmosphere

The Earth is surrounded by a thick blanket of air called the atmosphere, which is made up of five layers. Weather happens only in the layer nearest to the Earth – the troposphere. This stretches up about 7 miles above the surface of the planet, not much higher than the top of Mount Everest. The troposphere is the warmest layer of the atmosphere and contains the most moisture.

Auroras are produced when radiation from the Sun hits the outer layers of the atmosphere.

50 miles

30 miles

Weather occurs in this layer, the troposphere.

7 miles

### Sun gods

Many ancient peoples worshiped the Sun as a god. They made sacrifices to the gods to keep the Sun shining. In the Aztec religion, the Sun was the warrior, Huitzilopochtli, who died every evening to be born again the next day, driving away the stars and Moon with a shaft of light.

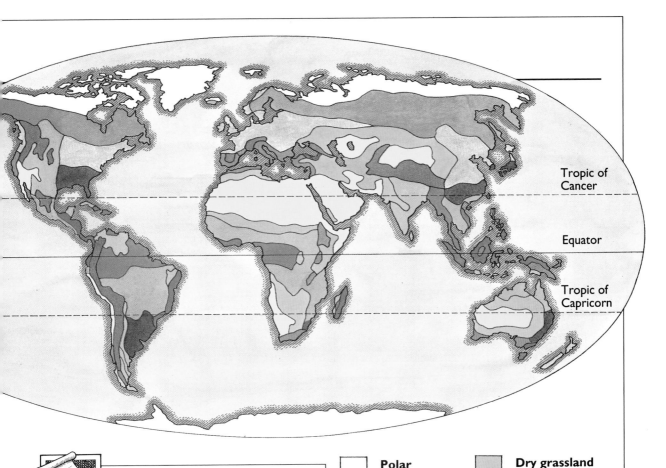

Tropic of Cancer

Equator

Tropic of Capricorn

## Air pressure

Air pressure is caused by the force of gravity in the Earth's atmosphere pulling air down toward the surface. In 1643, Galileo's pupil, Toricelli, invented the first instrument for measuring air pressure – the mercury barometer. Before weather maps were developed in the early 1800's, the barometer was the most important tool in weather forecasting. High pressure usually indicates fine, settled weather, and low pressure means cloudy, rainy weather. The French physicist, Jean de Borda (1733-1799), was the first to show that changes in air pressure are also related to wind speed. An aneroid (non-liquid) barometer measures the effect of air pressure on a chamber that has part of the air removed.

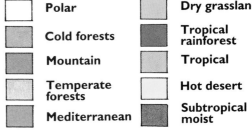

Aneroid barometer

| | Polar | | Dry grassland |
| --- | --- | --- | --- |
| | Cold forests | | Tropical rainforest |
| | Mountain | | Tropical |
| | Temperate forests | | Hot desert |
| | Mediterranean | | Subtropical moist |

## World climates

Climates depend on how near to the equator a place is, how high it is above sea level, and how far it is from the sea. World climates can be divided into the following categories:

**Polar** – Cold and snowy, strong winds
**Cold forest** – Short summers and long, cold winters
**Mountain** – Cold and snowy high up
  **Temperate forests** – Neither too hot nor too cold, rain all year round
    **Mediterranean** – Long, hot, dry summers and cool, wet winters
    **Dry grasslands** – Hot, dry summers and cold, snowy winters
    **Tropical rainforest** – Hot, rainy, humid, wet
   **Tropical** – Hot all year, wet and dry seasons
  **Hot desert** – Hot and dry, hardly any rain
 **Subtropical moist** – Warm to hot summers, cool winters and moderate rain all year round.

# CATS

The cat family, the Felidae, are all very similar in shape though they come in different sizes. They are all agile hunters that stalk and pounce on their prey. They have excellent stereoscopic vision, they can see in color and in the dark. They have a special layer at the back of the eye, called the tapetum, which reflects light back to the retina, so they can see in low light. All cats have sensitive whiskers for nighttime hunting.

## Small Cats

There are 28 species of "small cats." Apart from their size they are very similar to big cats. Small cats can purr, but they cannot roar. Big cats can roar, but cannot purr. The domestic cat (bottom), is descended from the wild cat, which was found in Europe and North Africa. The bobcat, and the lynx (top), are peculiar in having ear tufts and short tails. Many small cats, like the ocelot, have spotted coats for camouflage in the forest.

### Cheshire Cat

The grinning Cheshire cat, in *Alice's Adventures in Wonderland*, by Lewis Carroll, caused some difficulty when the Queen of Hearts ordered "Off with its head." The Cheshire cat was able to make its body invisible. The executioner was puzzled as to how he could cut a head off a body that was not there. While the king debated the matter the queen threatened to have all the court executed. Meanwhile the cat had disappeared!

### Witch's Cats

Cats have lived alongside people for some 5,000 years, ridding homes of mice and rats. But in the Middle Ages they became associated with witchcraft and the devil. They were cruelly persecuted along with their owners. The Christian Church also tried to rid the world of them because they were symbols of paganism.

### Record Breakers

The cheetah is the fastest land animal in the world. It can reach speeds of 60 miles per hour. It can move so fast because it stores energy in its springlike backbone. When it runs its backbone alternately stretches and coils, swinging its long legs forward and backward.

## Big Cats

Tigers, cheetahs, leopards, and jaguars are solitary hunters. They usually stalk medium-sized grazers no bigger than themselves. Lions take larger prey, and hunt in prides. Prides consist of a full-grown male and several breeding females and their cubs. Big cats hunt only when they are hungry, gorging on the kill and then dozing for several days.

Tiger

Jaguar

Lion

### Agility

Cats are supposed to have "nine lives" — they almost always land on their feet. They do this by a reflex action controlled by the organ of balance in the inner ear. It tells the brain which way up the cat is. The brain matches this information with messages from the eyes. The neck muscles turn the head to the upright position and the body follows — all before the cat hits the ground. Cats are agile climbers, clinging on with their claws. They have powerful legs and can spring straight up into the air, landing on their prey on all fours.

# WHAT IF THE SUN WENT OUT?

Who turned off the lights? Why is it suddenly so cold? If the Sun no longer bathed our world in light and warmth, we might last a short time with fires, electric light, and oil or gas heat. But plants could not grow in the dark, and animals would perish from the cold. Soon all life would cease, and our planet would be dark and frozen. In fact this will happen, but not for billions of years. Our Sun is a fairly typical star, and stars do not last forever. They form, grow old, and either fade away or explode in a supernova, a massive explosion.

## From the cradle to the grave

Throughout the universe there are massive clouds of gas, called *nebulae.* In some of these, the dust and particles clump together, and over millions of years, these clumps will form stars. Other nebulae are the wispy remains of a *supernova*, a star that has exploded.

## What is a red giant?

An enormous human with red clothes? No, it is a star that has been growing and shining for billions of years, and is nearing the end of its life. As it ages, the star swells and its light turns red. Our Sun will do this in millions of years. It will expand to the size of a Red Giant, scorching our planet, before it explodes. Then all that will be left is a tiny white dwarf star that will slowly fade over millions of years.

## How can we see a black hole?

When a really big star explodes, its core collapses and leaves behind a remnant whose gravity is so strong that nothing can escape its pull. This remnant is called a black hole. Because light cannot escape, it is impossible to actually see a black hole. However, its presence can be detected by the effect it has on objects around, such as gases, and waves, including light rays and X rays.

## Great balls of fire

A typical star is made mainly of hydrogen gas. Huge forces squeeze together its atoms to form helium. This process is called *nuclear fusion*. As the atoms fuse they release energy, which radiates from the core, through the radiation zone. The energy is then carried to the surface by circular convection currents. Finally at the photosphere, the energy is radiated into space as light and other types of rays and waves.

Radiation zone

Convection zone

Photosphere surface

## Silent explosion

Sound waves can't pass through the vacuum of space, so we can't hear a star explode. But we can see it, as a glow that appears in the night sky, which then fades. It leaves behind a cloud, called a *nebula*.

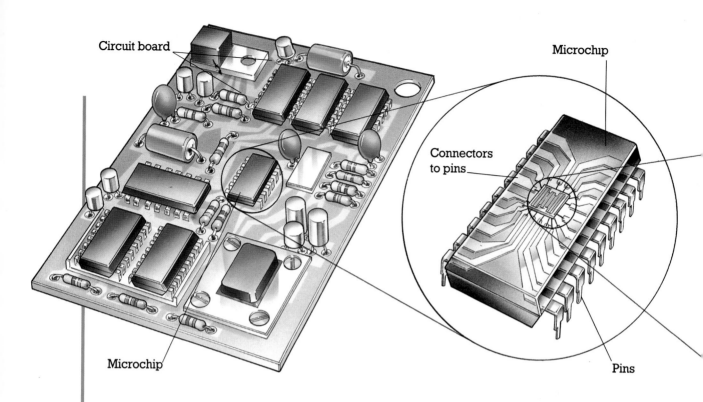

Circuit board

Microchip

Connectors to pins

Pins

Microchip

Inside a computer, electronic circuits are formed from components mounted on circuit boards (see above left), which are linked together by metal tracks on the boards. Many of the components are microchips (see above right). Each of them contains a tiny chip of silicon and this itself contains circuits composed of thousands of microscopically small components (see diagrams opposite).

# THE MICROCHIP

Computers process information by first changing it into pulses of electric current that are then directed through complex electrical pathways or circuits. The majority of the electronic components on the computer's circuit boards are microchips. Most of them look like blocks of black or gray plastic with a row of metal pins along each side (see above right). The plastic block is to protect the chip which is buried inside, its metal pins connected to the metal tracks in the circuit board. The chip itself is often no bigger than a fingernail, although some are smaller. It is made from a slice of pure silicon on which intricately shaped layers of chemicals are added to form thousands of individual components. Silicon is one of a group of materials called semiconductors. Its resistance to an electrical current decreases as its temperature rises. This electrical resistance can also be changed by a process called "doping." This involves adding small amounts of different materials to the silicon. Some provide extra charged particles called electrons, forming n-type silicon. Others create a shortage of electrons forming p-type silicon.

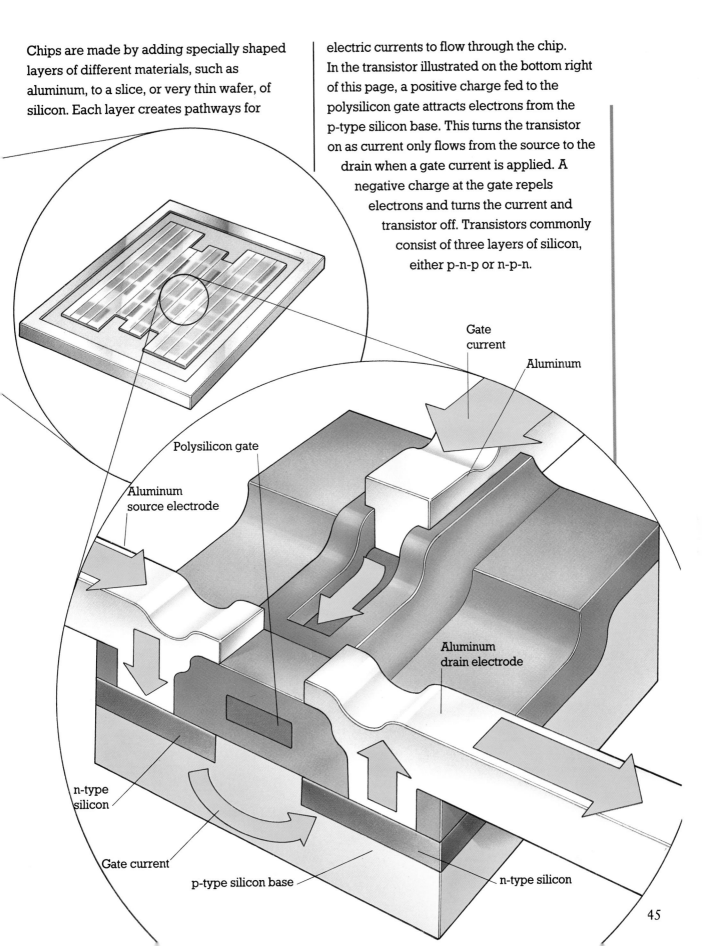

Chips are made by adding specially shaped layers of different materials, such as aluminum, to a slice, or very thin wafer, of silicon. Each layer creates pathways for electric currents to flow through the chip. In the transistor illustrated on the bottom right of this page, a positive charge fed to the polysilicon gate attracts electrons from the p-type silicon base. This turns the transistor on as current only flows from the source to the drain when a gate current is applied. A negative charge at the gate repels electrons and turns the current and transistor off. Transistors commonly consist of three layers of silicon, either p-n-p or n-p-n.

Gate current

Aluminum

Polysilicon gate

Aluminum source electrode

Aluminum drain electrode

n-type silicon

Gate current

p-type silicon base

n-type silicon

# THE THINKING BRAIN

The main part of the brain that we use to think, decide and reason is the cortex – the thin gray layer on the wrinkled domes of the two cerebral hemispheres. The cortex looks the same all over. But brain research has "mapped" it to show its different parts are specialized for different jobs. We have maps on the brain!

**PERSONALITY**
*Are you a good, kind person? Of course! The frontal lobes take part in the complex behaviors we call personality.*

## LEFT BRAIN, RIGHT BRAIN

In most people, the two halves of the cortex seem to have different tendencies. The right side is most involved in creative and artistic abilities such as painting, drawing, writing and playing music.

*Artistic brilliance*

*Scientific excellence*

The left side tends to take over in logical and rational thinking, as when solving mathematical sums, doing scientific experiments, playing chess and working out what to say.

## SENSOR AND MOTOR

These two drawings show how we would look, if each part of our body was in proportion to the area of cortex dealing with it. One is for skin's touch, the sensory cortex. The other is for muscle movement, the motor cortex.

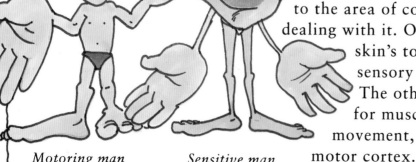

*Motoring man*          *Sensitive man*

## MUSCLE CONTROL
*The motor cortex is in overall control of the muscles, ordering them to work so that we can move.*

## THE INS AND OUTS
Information whizzes around the brain and body along nerves, as tiny electrical blips called nerve signals. Sensory signals come into the brain from the eyes, ears and other senses. Motor signals go out to the muscles.

### TOUCH
*The somato-sensory cortex is the "touch center." It receives information from all over our skin, about things we touch, and whether they feel hot or cold, or press hard, or cause pain.*

### SIGHT
*The visual cortex receives and processes information from the eyes. It works out shapes, colors and movements, and identifies what we see. It is the site of the "mind's eye."*

### SMELL AND TASTE
*The olfactory cortex sorts out smelly signals from the nose. The gustatory cortex is part of the touch area and receives tastes.*

### HEARING
*Information from our ears, in the form of nerve signals, travels to the auditory cortex. Here it is sorted out and analyzed. We can identify most sounds by comparing them with sound patterns in our memory banks. For a strange or unusual sound, we may turn the head to see what has made it.*

*1 Signals come in from the senses.*

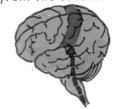

*2 The brain decides what to do.*

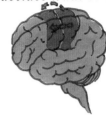

*3 Signals go out to the muscles.*

## SPIES ON YOUR INSIDES

Another scanning method for looking inside the brain is PET (positron emission tomography). The PET scan shows where the brain is busiest and most active.

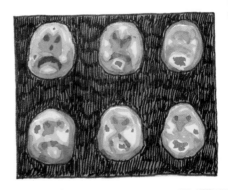

# WHAT ARE OUR ORIGINS?

For thousands of years humankind has been preoccupied by the question of its origins. Many cultures have myths and legends explaining how and why humans were created. In the last 200 years there have also been some scientific explanations. Information from fossils has convinced many scientists that human beings developed over millions of years. However, we still do not know the whole story, and there are many unanswered questions about the exact pattern of human development.

### Digging up the bones

Early human fossils are found buried in the ground. Scientists use picks, trowels and brushes (left) to dig carefully around artefacts on the dig site. The smallest fragments may be very important.

The dig site (right) is carefully mapped so that every find can be located. Dozens of people are often needed for the slow, careful work.

### Charles Darwin

Charles Darwin (1809-1882) was a naturalist who travelled to South America and the Pacific with the British scientific expedition aboard H.M.S. *Beagle*. Wherever he went he studied as many plants and animals as possible and found many similarities between the different species.

### Reconstruction

Sometimes a lucky find will be a complete skeleton. One example of this is "Lucy," the fossilised remains of an ape-like creature called *Australopithecus*, found in Ethiopia in 1973. The form of the pelvic bone showed the remains to be female, and the formation of the teeth suggested she was about 20 years old. Only 40% of Lucy's bones were found, but because skeletons are symmetrical we know what the missing bones look like.

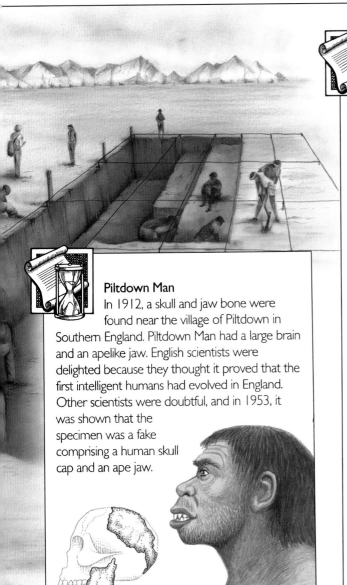

## Famous discoveries

The most important discoveries of early humans have been made in the past 100 years. By 1900, only a few skulls and skeletons had come to light, but many stone tools and pieces of art had been found. During the twentieth century the pace of discovery has quickened, and our understanding of human origins has improved immensely.

Eugène Dubois (1858-1941) found the remains of Java Man, a form of *Homo erectus*, in 1891, the first significant early human fossil. The specimens provoked such fierce debate that Dubois later claimed the bones came from a giant gibbon.

### Piltdown Man

In 1912, a skull and jaw bone were found near the village of Piltdown in Southern England. Piltdown Man had a large brain and an apelike jaw. English scientists were delighted because they thought it proved that the first intelligent humans had evolved in England. Other scientists were doubtful, and in 1953, it was shown that the specimen was a fake comprising a human skull cap and an ape jaw.

Raymond Dart (1893-1990) was the first to suggest that the earliest human ancestors came from Africa. Here he discovered one of the most important human fossils, the skull of an *Australopithecus*. At first many scientists did not believe that the fossil was human.

Richard Leakey (1944- ) has found many human fossils in Africa, notably part of a skull of the oldest known *Homo habilis* fossil dating back 1.9 million years. He also discovered a 1.6 million year old *Homo erectus* skull.

Donald Johanson (1947- ) found a series of human fossils in Ethiopia, including Lucy (see left), and he gave *Australopithecus afarensis* its name. He has argued that the first humans could walk upright, but that they had ape sized brains.

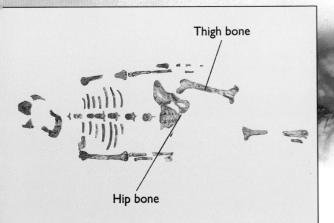

**Thigh bone**

**Hip bone**

# CASTLE PEOPLE

**A medieval castle housed the lord and his family, his soldiers as well as the servants, who looked after them. In fact, the bailey was a very busy and crowded place.**

There was a lot of work involved in running a castle. Blacksmiths or armorers were very important. They had to shoe horses, repair tools and look after the soldiers' armor. The soldiers patrolled the countryside on horses. They had to be looked after in stables. Carpenters made furniture and repaired carts. Other men looked after the buildings and repaired the walls. There was usually a plumber to make new lead roofs and pipes. "Plumber" literally means someone who works with lead.

Life in the Middle Ages was hard. People had to work very hard either growing food or in someone else's service. They did not live as long as they do today – many died of diseases, like the plague, and others died in wars. A 40-year-old was considered old.

# COOKING IN A CASTLE

This is the kitchen at Glastonbury Abbey. Sometimes kitchens were built in the bailey. Several men worked in the kitchens preparing food. Food was obtained from the surrounding countryside but in a siege people had to survive on animals living within the bailey or on salted or dried food. Some castles had their own fishponds and dovecots. They provided fresh food throughout the year. Women rarely worked in the kitchen but they did wash the laundry. They had to make their own soap from animal fat and water mixed with vegetable ash. Candles were also made from animal fat.

# CROCODILES AND ALLIGATORS

The 22 species of crocodilians are all lurking predators, which also scavenge meat from any dead carcass left by another hunter. They live in tropical regions, in or near water, and spend much of the day basking in the sun to keep warm. The powerful tail and rear limbs are used to propel the animal through the water. The caimans of South America have the shortest, broadest snouts and eat the most varied diet, including frogs, snakes, lizards, birds, and mammals. The gavial of the Indian region has a long, narrow snout and eats mainly fish.

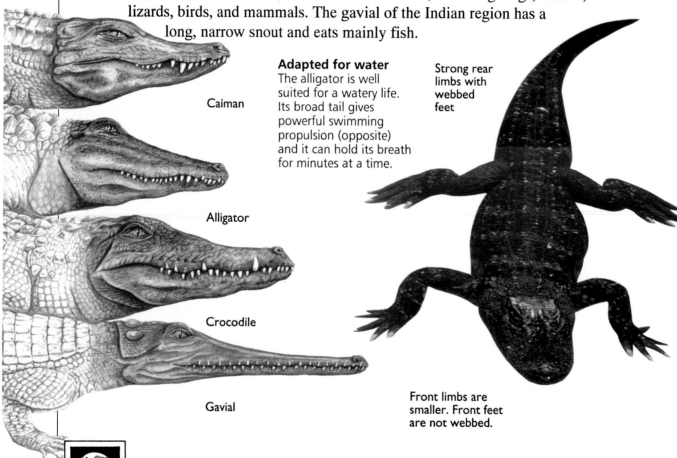

Caiman

Alligator

Crocodile

Gavial

**Adapted for water**
The alligator is well suited for a watery life. Its broad tail gives powerful swimming propulsion (opposite) and it can hold its breath for minutes at a time.

Strong rear limbs with webbed feet

Front limbs are smaller. Front feet are not webbed.

## Crocodilians worldwide
The map shows the distribution of some of the main species of crocodilians. The two main groups are the crocodiles, with 14 species, and alligators, with 7 species, which includes the caimans. The Estuarine crocodile is the only one that lives in salt water.

Key
- Common caiman
- American alligator
- American crocodile
- Nile crocodile
- Estuarine crocodile
- Gavial

## The swishing tail
The tail is arched from side to side by powerful muscles running down the animal's body. The main part of the body is relatively stiff and takes little part in swimming.

## With a crocodile's help
The crocodile features in many stories. In *The Just So Stories* by Rudyard Kipling (1902) a crocodile seizes a young elephant by its nose, which is "no bigger than a boot." The elephant tries to get away, and its nose stretches – which is how, supposedly, the elephant got its trunk!

## From rare to common
American alligators live in the southeastern United States. They were hunted so much for their skins and because they threatened people and livestock, that they became in danger of extinction (dying out completely). Wildlife laws were introduced in 1969 to protect them. In 1987 the species was declared to be out of danger of extinction. Today they are more common and a few are hunted (below).

## Crocodile swimming
The main swimming power for crocodilians comes from the deep tail, which swishes from side to side like a fish's tail. This pushes the animal forward. The front legs are usually held up against the underside of the body, for better streamlining. The rear legs can be used for steering, and for paddling at slow speeds. By thrusting its rear feet forward and up, with its webbed toes spread, a crocodile can suddenly stop moving forward and sink down under the water.

## Crocodile songs
Crocodilians feature in various plays and also in popular songs. These include *See You Later Alligator* (1956), the early rock'n'roll jive-talking hit by Bill Haley and the Comets, and *Crocodile Rock* (1973) by Elton John.

**Bill Haley**

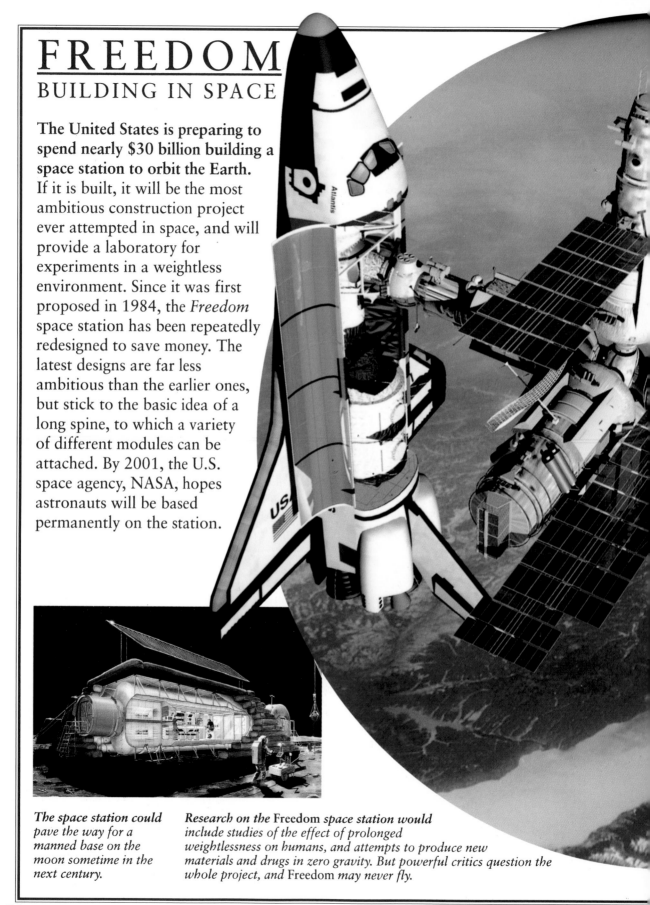

# FREEDOM
## BUILDING IN SPACE

The United States is preparing to spend nearly $30 billion building a space station to orbit the Earth. If it is built, it will be the most ambitious construction project ever attempted in space, and will provide a laboratory for experiments in a weightless environment. Since it was first proposed in 1984, the *Freedom* space station has been repeatedly redesigned to save money. The latest designs are far less ambitious than the earlier ones, but stick to the basic idea of a long spine, to which a variety of different modules can be attached. By 2001, the U.S. space agency, NASA, hopes astronauts will be based permanently on the station.

*The space station could pave the way for a manned base on the moon sometime in the next century.*

*Research on the* Freedom *space station would include studies of the effect of prolonged weightlessness on humans, and attempts to produce new materials and drugs in zero gravity. But powerful critics question the whole project, and* Freedom *may never fly.*

The first stage in building the station would be to create the basic structure and attach the solar panels. The space shuttle would be used to carry the U.S.-built modules to the station and attach them, with the international modules following.

*The **ultimate prize could** be a base on Mars, the only planet in the solar system, apart from earth, which appears remotely habitable. The first manned visit to Mars is planned sometime in the next century.*

*Latest designs for* Freedom, *are a greatly simplified version of the original. One major change is the removal of costly windows.*

# COLORS OF THE RAINBOW

Sunlight appears colorless but really it is made up of different colors. Sometimes you can see these colors — on the surfaces of bubbles or if there is oil on water. You may also see the colors across the sky in the form of a rainbow. In each case "white" light is being separated into different colors called the spectrum.

## HOW A RAINBOW IS MADE

When the Sun comes out during a shower you may see a rainbow. The sunlight shines on the droplets of rain and gets separated into the colors of the spectrum. From a distance the light appears as a colored arc across the sky. People divide the rainbow into seven bands of color — red, orange, yellow, green, blue, indigo and violet. The colors always appear in the same order, with red on the outside and violet on the inside of the arc. The diagram shows how light which enters each raindrop is reflected, bent and separated into all the colors of the spectrum, which together form a rainbow in the sky.

△ It is impossible to reach the end of a rainbow — you can only see it shining in the sky at a distance.

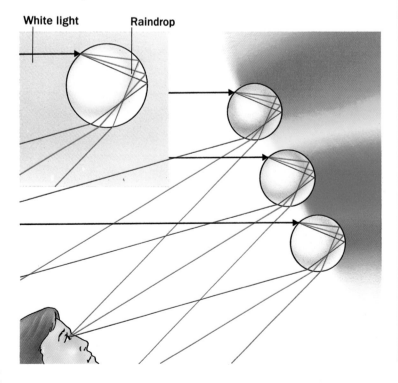

White light    Raindrop

## MAKE A RAINBOW

You can see the colors of the spectrum by making your own rainbow. On a sunny day fill a pan of water and rest a mirror at an angle inside it. Stand the pan in front of a window so that sunlight falls onto the mirror. Then hold a piece of white cardboard in front of the mirror and move it around until you see a rainbow appear on it. You may have to move the mirror to get this right. The mirror and the water act as a "prism" — they separate white light into the colors of the spectrum.

## THE NORTHERN LIGHTS

Sometimes dazzling displays of colored lights appear in the sky at night in parts of the world which are far from the equator. These lights are caused by huge explosions on the surface of the Sun known as "flares." During a flare, millions of tiny particles are sent out from the Sun. They travel very fast and some eventually reach the Earth's atmosphere. The Earth's magnetism bends the paths of the particles so they only reach the Earth's atmosphere near the poles. As they travel through the air they bump into other particles. These collisions produce light. In the North they can be seen best in parts of Canada, but they can also be seen in northern Scotland and Scandinavia. They are called the Northern Lights or "Aurora borealis." Similar lights can be seen in the South where they are called "Aurora australis."

△ The Northern Lights make an impressive display of color which looks like a constantly moving curtain in the sky.

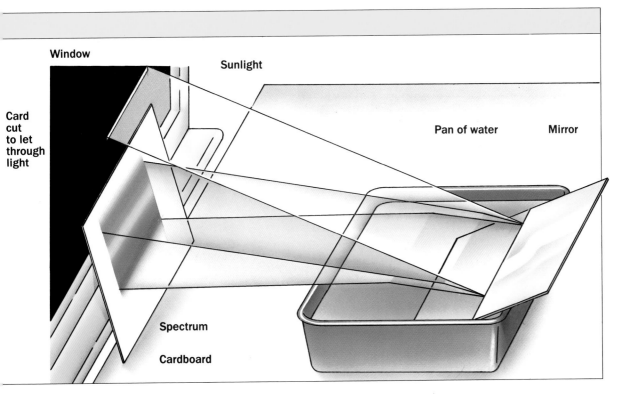

Window

Sunlight

Card cut to let through light

Pan of water

Mirror

Spectrum

Cardboard

57

# MAKING A POND ENVIRONMENT

If you have a yard you can construct a real pond, but failing this, a coldwater aquarium can be stocked with plants and animals to make a "natural" habitat. One secret of success is to make sure that the animals have enough oxygen. Choose an aquarium with a big surface, not one that is tall and narrow. Do not overcrowd it, and above all do not put in fierce hunters such as diving beetles and dragonfly larvae that will eat other insects and small fish.

## FISH

**Goldfish make good pond fish, as they can survive in stagnant water. Sticklebacks are found in all kinds of water. Minnows can live in ponds, but prefer clear, moving water.**

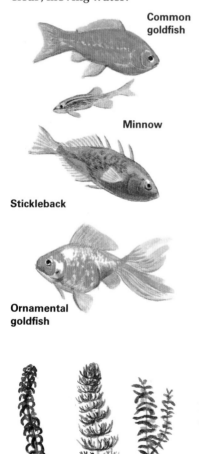

**Common goldfish**

**Minnow**

**Stickleback**

**Ornamental goldfish**

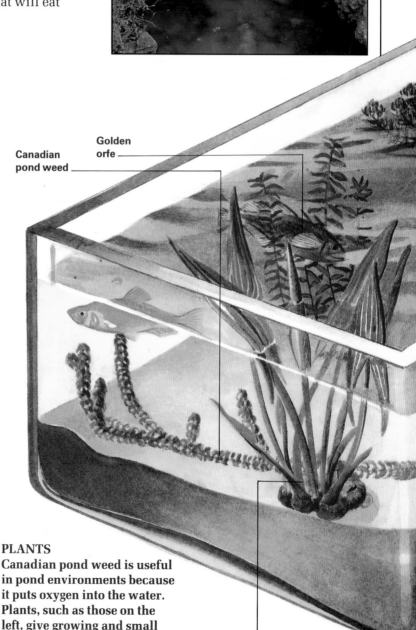

Canadian pond weed

Golden orfe

Arrowhead

## PLANTS

Canadian pond weed is useful in pond environments because it puts oxygen into the water. Plants, such as those on the left, give growing and small animals somewhere to hide.

58

## FROG SPAWN
You can follow a frog's growth from spawn (eggs) to tadpoles and then tiny frogs over about 12 weeks.

**Frog spawn**

## MOLLUSKS
Snails climb on the plants and over the sides of a pond. They eat the green algae that would otherwise cover these surfaces.

**Great diving beetle**

**Common snail**

**Stonefly nymph**

**Hornwort**

## INSECTS
Water insects include plant and meat eaters among the many kinds of beetles and bugs. They often arrive attached to new plants.

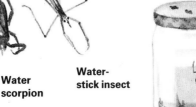

**Great diving beetle**

**Water scorpion**

**Water-stick insect**

A fine mesh net will catch pond animals. Try sweeping the water, plants, and mud with it. A light colored tray into which your catch can be deposited is useful to pick out interesting specimens. A magnifying glass is handy for seeing small creatures, and a covered bucket or jar will help you to take your catch home. Only take common species from a pond.

**Plastic bucket**

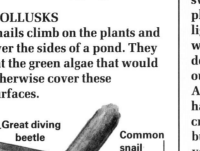

**Fishing net**

**Magnifying glass**

**Notebook and pencil**

# THE THUNDER OF GUNS

When guns were first introduced in the early 14th century, they had more influence on siege warfare than battle tactics. By 1425, there was not a castle that could not be battered into swift submission by cannon fire.

Armored knights hung on longer. The final proof that they were no longer needed came at the Battle of Ravenna (1512), when French cannons destroyed a large Spanish army. By the 17th century, the wide use of handguns meant that armor was all but stripped away (*left*).

Chivalric ideals survived, however. Knightly honors were given for feats of bravery and other services, and chivalric orders, such as the Burgundian Order of the Golden Fleece, were still admired.

## HAIL THE MIGHTY CANNON

The first cannons were cast from bronze, brass, or iron bars. Gunpowder, a mixture of charcoal, potassium nitrate, and sulfur was made on the spot because of the danger of transporting it.

The gun was loaded by pouring powder down the barrel and holding it in place with wadding. A cannon ball was then rolled down the barrel and secured with more wadding.

**To fire the gun** (above) *the gunpowder was lit through a small hole in the rear. The explosion blasted the ball out of the barrel toward its target. Gunners were protected from arrows by a wooden screen.*

*Watch Out for the Big Bang!*
*Gunners cover their ears from the blast (above). In the early days, cannons frequently exploded upon firing. Also, the ignition of the slow-burning powder was so random that accuracy was almost impossible.*

## A TUDOR SUMMIT

Though knights were no longer a powerful force on the battlefield, many of the traditions and customs survived.

In 1520, King Henry VIII led the elite of English chivalry to meet the elite of Francis I's French knights on the Field of the Cloth of Gold *(left)*.

By now the jousting and feasting were supposed to demonstrate Anglo-French friendship, rather than a show of military force.

### Fantasy Land

*Scholars believe the original Camelot was in the English counties of Cornwall, Hampshire, or Somerset.*

*None of this is relevant to the musical* Camelot, *which places the court of King Arthur in a singing and dancing medieval fantasy land* (right)!

**D**ON QUIXOTE. Miguel de Cervantes Saavedra mirrored the decline of Spanish chivalry in his two-part novel *Don Quixote de la Mancha* (1605-1615). It is a story about a Spanish landowner who adores tales of the knights of old. Wishing to live like the knights, he takes the name Don Quixote and sets out to perform great deeds of chivalry, accompanied by his loyal friend Sancho Panza *(left)*.

**Don Quixote** *attacks windmills he thinks are giants and flocks of sheep he mistakes for armies! When all his adventures prove romantic follies, he returns home to die.*

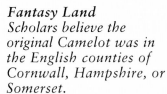

### Arise, Sir Francis!

*No longer was the honor of knight reserved for mounted warriors. When Francis Drake returned from sailing around the world, on April 4, 1581 Queen Elizabeth knighted him on board his ship (right). He hadn't been near a horse for almost three years!*

# WHERE BIRDS LIVE

With their adaptations for flight and feeding, birds are able to live all over the world. They range from the freezing Poles to the baking deserts, and from rushing rivers to steamy jungles. Flight has given them the mobility to exploit a wide variety of food supplies and habitats. Being warm-blooded, they also have the advantage of maintaining a constant body temperature and staying active whatever the weather.

### Antarctica
The 16 species of penguin all live in the Southern Hemisphere. Six species, including these emperor penguins, are even found in Antarctica itself, despite the extremely cold temperatures and wind. Emperors are the largest of all penguin species. They grow to about three feet (1 m) tall.

### The tropics
About two-thirds of all species of birds live in the world's tropical rain forests. They include trogons and parrots. Rain forest birds are often brightly colored. The bright green feathers of this rainbow lorikeet blend in with the foliage. Even its colorful markings could be mistaken for flowers or fruits in the lush forest.

### Bird-watching
The best places to observe birds are parks, gardens, or wooded areas. Sit very quietly and try to keep out of sight. In a forest you will see that different species prefer a particular part of the woods. Some birds will feed on the ground, others might nest among shrubs, and some will sing from tree branches. Watch patiently and note down the colors, shape, and behavior of different types of birds, and where and when you saw them.

## Desert

Roadrunners live in the North and Central American deserts. They rarely fly, but can race at great speeds after their prey – insects, lizards, and snakes. They survive the scorching heat of the desert by staying in the shade until dusk, when the air and ground cool off.

## Mountains

Some birds of prey, like this golden eagle, soar above high mountains. They glide on rising currents of air, keeping a lookout for prey below. They nest on cliff faces where they can rear their eaglets, protected from predators.

Never disturb nests or harm birds or eggs.

Keep a scrapbook to record the birds you see. Later you can compare it with a bird identification book.

## National birds

Birds can be found virtually all over the world. Many nations have adopted as symbols birds that are native to the country or which migrate through the region. Often they are chosen for their beauty, rarity, or some other special feature. Some birds have even been incorporated onto national flags or emblems. Try to think of other ways in which birds have been used as symbols.

## Australia

The black swan of Australia is revered as it is one of only three swan species in the Southern Hemisphere. It is all black with white wing feathers and a red bill.

## Papua New Guinea

The flag of this country carries the silhouette of a bird of paradise, which is native to New Guinea. These birds are famed for their dazzling plumage and courtship displays.

## The United States

The bald eagle was adopted as the national emblem of the United States in 1782. It was chosen because it is such a powerful, noble-looking bird.

## Egypt

Egypt's national flag shows a bird of prey, which symbolizes strength. Kestrels were held sacred in Ancient Egypt, and were often mummified.

## Uganda

The national flag of Uganda in East Africa shows an African balearic crane, also known as a crowned crane. They are residents of this region and are held in special regard because of their striking appearance and amazing dance.

# MAKING AN ASTRONAUT'S HELMET

This mask, a must for all space games, is based on a shell made of papier mâche. It is a vital piece of equipment when visiting alien worlds.

You could cut zigzag shapes from paper and glue them on to decorate the visor.

You could add a stars and stripes flag, painted on or made with pieces of straw.

Measure and pierce two small eyeholes in the mask with scissors. Alternatively, you could make the visor from transparent plastic so that you can see out more easily.

1 To make papier mâche, mix flour and a little water in a bowl, until you have a thick paste. Tear a newspaper into strips. Blow up a balloon and stand it in another bowl. Dip a strip in the paste, run it through your fingers to remove excess paste, and lay it on the balloon. Repeat this until the top half of the balloon is covered with at least three layers of newspaper. Leave it to dry overnight. Burst the balloon. 2 Trim the bottom of the papier mâche shape flat with scissors. 3 Cut two segments from an egg carton to make earpieces, and tape them on the sides of the helmet. 4 Cut out a circular piece of paper bag to make the visor, and tape it into the helmet. 5 The astronaut's eyes are two Ping Pong balls, and the nose is a cork. Cut eyebrows from an egg carton and tape all these features to the visor. Splay one end of a drinking straw, and tape it to the top of the helmet to make a radio receiver. Pierce a hole through the straw, cut another straw in half and puch it though the hole, to form a crosspiece.

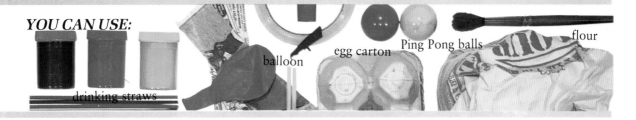

balloon

egg carton

Ping Pong balls

flour

drinking straws

# STEP BY STEP

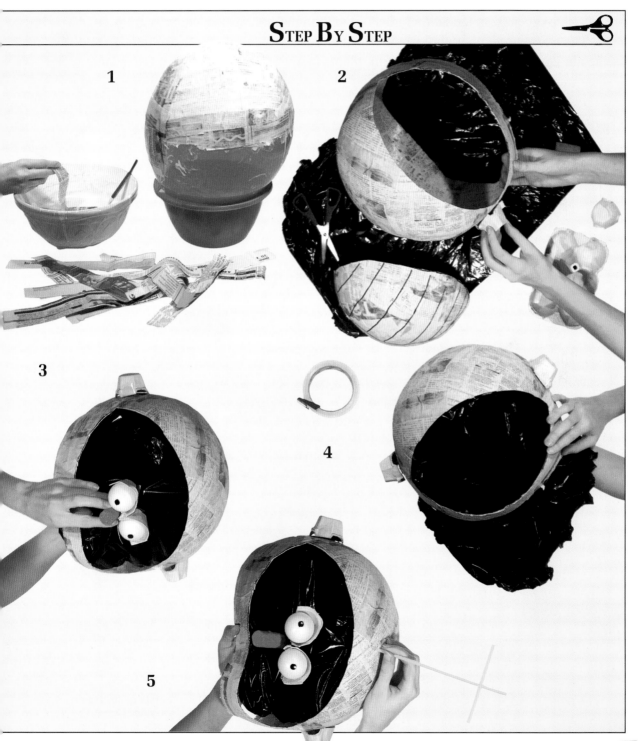

1

2

3

4

5

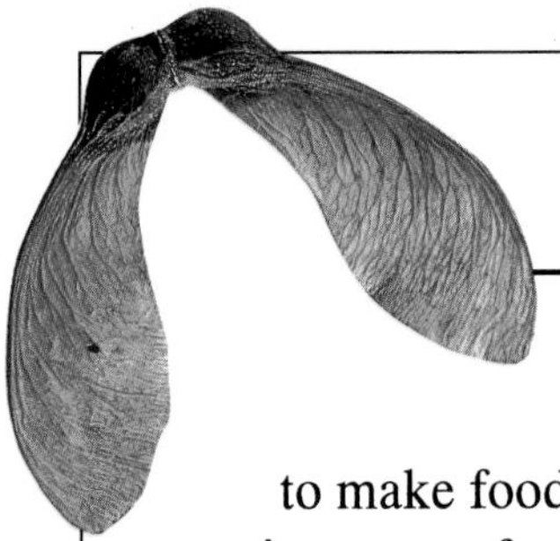

# PLANTS AND AIR

Air is just as vital to the survival of plants as it is to animals. Plants need carbon dioxide from the air to make food during the process of photosynthesis. But they also take in oxygen from the air and give out carbon dioxide, just as animals do. The waste product of photosynthesis is oxygen, which plants release into the air. During the history of the earth, plants gradually built up the oxygen in the atmosphere. Only after there was enough oxygen in the air, could animals develop.

oxygen

### Dispersal record
You could make your own nature diary to keep a record of seeds which are spread by the wind, such as sycamore or dandelion seeds. Stick the seeds into your scrapbook and write down the date and where you found them. In spring and summer, look out for plants that use the wind to spread their pollen, such as tree catkins.

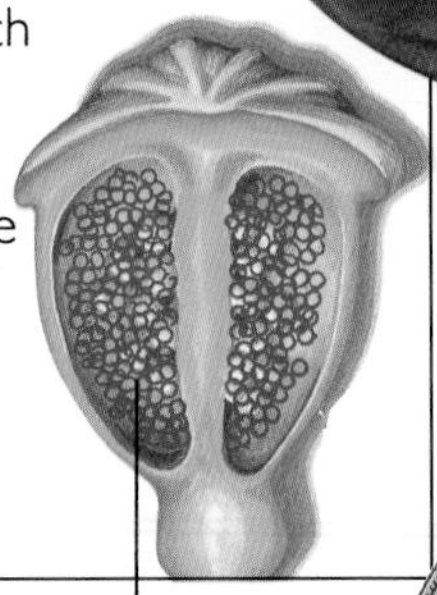

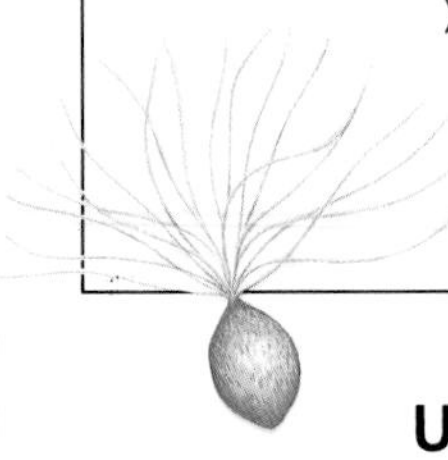

poppy seeds

## Using the wind
Pollen and seeds that float on the wind are usually very light, but some use other floating devices such as little "wings," parachutes or air sacs. Seeds move away from the parent plant to reduce the competition for light, water and food nutrients.

water and minerals

A giant puffball can produce 7,000 billion spores in a lifetime. The spores (simple seeds) puff out in clouds every time the wind blows against them. Even an ordinary field mushroom can release 100 million spores in an hour.

dandelion spores

Land plant roots obtain the oxygen they need from water in the soil

water

The epidermis is covered in a waxy layer called the cuticle. Though this prevents the leaf losing water, it also prevents carbon dioxide from entering. So there are stomata (usually on the shady side) to let carbon dioxide in.

carbon dioxide

hairs

waxy epidermis that acts as "skin"

palisade cells that turn light into food

mesophyll, a spongy middle layer

food- and water-carrying cells

stomata (also below, under microscope)

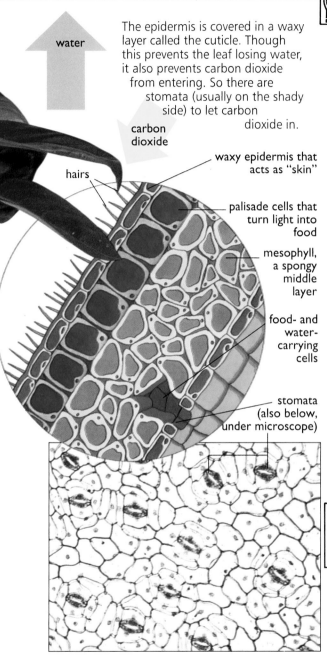

## Hay fever
Many people suffer from an allergic reaction to plant pollen called hay fever. Symptoms include a runny nose, sneezing, and watery eyes, but they are seasonal since plants only release pollen in spring and summer. Pollen counts are often given as part of weather forecasts to warn sufferers when to expect problems.

## Plant "breathing"
Water plants take in gases from the water all over their surface. Land plants breathe through little holes called stomata in the leaves or stem. Woody stems have small raised pores called lenticels instead of stomata. The stomata or lenticels open and close to control the flow of gases and water vapor in and out of the leaf or stem. On a leaf, the stomata are mostly on the underside. There may be from 20 to over 1,000 stomata per square inch, depending on the species. The stomata usually open during daylight hours when the plant is busy taking in and giving out gases during photosynthesis.

## Plants on mountains
At high altitudes, there is less oxygen for plants to breathe and less carbon dioxide for them to make their food. So mountain plants tend to grow slowly and function at a slow rate. The thin mountain air also fails to protect the mountain slopes from strong sunlight during the day and cold at night. Mountain plants tend to be short to hug the ground for warmth and to trap moisture, often growing in closely packed cushions for mutual protection.

## Food from air
Plants make their own food from carbon dioxide and water, using the energy in sunlight. This process is called photosynthesis. The food that plants make is a sort of sugar called a carbohydrate. Some food is broken down during respiration to release energy.

# WHAT IF THE CONTINENTS DIDN'T MOVE?

The land under your feet may seem solid and still. But each main landmass, or continent, is drifting very slowly across the face of the Earth, by less than 2 inches (5 cm) each year. The Earth's outer "skin," or crust, is made up of 12 giant, curved plates, like a vast, ball-shaped puzzle. They are called *lithospheric (curved-rock) plates.* As the plates rub against each other, their edges crack or get pushed deeper. Some plates enlarge, while others shrink. This has been going on since the Earth began, 4.5 billion years ago.

We would see some strange animal meetings!

The plates under the ocean are thinner. Molten rock from deep below becomes solid, adds to the plate, pushing it sideways.

An oceanic plate pushes into a continental plate. The oceanic plate is forced down and an ocean trench forms.

Continent

Ocean

Magma (molten rock)

# Rock steady

Pangaea

Without continental drift, there could be no metamorphic rocks, like marble. These form when other rocks are squeezed incredibly hard in the roots of new mountains. Igneous rocks, like granite, form when melted rock, such as the lava from volcanoes, cools and solidifies. Sedimentary rocks, such as chalk, form when tiny particles settle in a lake or sea, and get pressed and cemented together.

Metamorphic rock

Igneous rock

Sedimentary rock

# Mapping out the world

About 250 million years ago all the continents were joined into one vast land mass, the super-continent of Pangaea. The continuous ocean around it was the Tethys Sea. If continental drift had stopped, the map would still look like this. A journey from North America to Europe, or South America to Africa, could be by car!

The layers of rock in the continental plate are crumpled by movements. This creates huge folds – mountains.

# Highs and lows!

The world would be much flatter and less exciting without continental drift. The deepest part of the oceans, the Marianas Trench in the Pacific, and the highest mountain, Mount Everest in the Himalayas, wouldn't exist.

Fold mountains

69

# DINOSAURS

Dinosaurs, the word means "terrible lizards," were reptiles which became extinct about 65 million years ago. They lived on the earth for over 140 million years, but the last ones suddenly died out. This was possibly due to a rapid cooling of the planet's climate. Before that time most of the earth was warm and damp so that even in the Arctic Circle there were tropical plants and dinosaurs that ate them. Dinosaurs vanished from the earth millions of years before people evolved. We have to reconstruct what they might have looked like from their fossils. Today the animals that are related most closely to them are crocodiles and birds. Up to now scientists have discovered many hundreds of species of dinosaur.

The Protoceratops, when fully grown to six feet in length, had horns. The discovery of complete nests of fossil eggs (below) told scientists how dinosaurs looked after their young. The baby Protoceratops was about one foot long. The size of dinosaurs varied a lot.

The Brachiosaurus, for example, was 75 feet long and weighed 80 tons. The Cynognathus, from which the tooth (below right) came, was only five feet long. This reptile lived 200 million years ago.

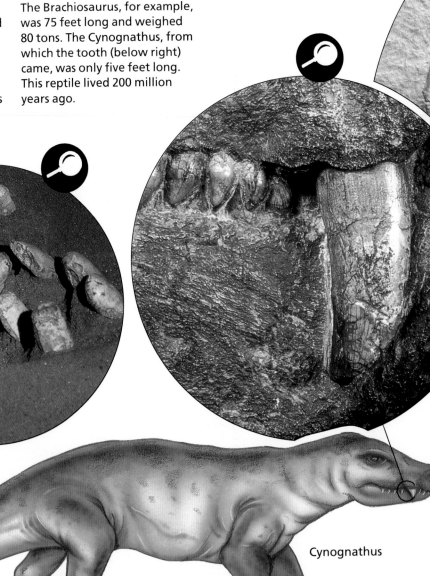

Eggs

Cynognathus

Not all creatures that lived during the "Age of the Dinosaurs" were dinosaurs. Dinosaurs lived on the land. In the air were flying reptiles called pterosaurs, and in the sea were various types of swimming reptiles including plesiosaurs and ichthyosaurs.

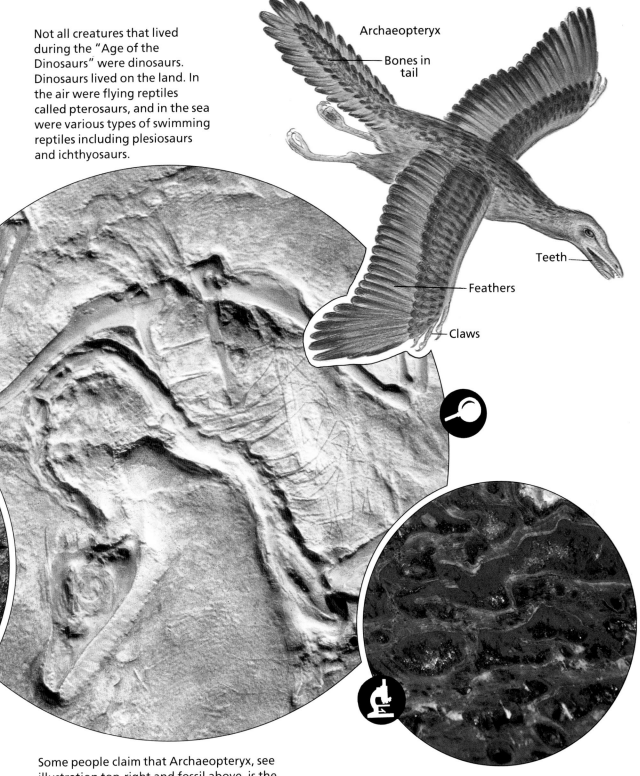

Archaeopteryx

Bones in tail

Teeth

Feathers

Claws

Some people claim that Archaeopteryx, see illustration top right and fossil above, is the missing link between extinct dinosaurs and the birds which we all know today. It was about the same size as a modern crow and ate insects and small reptiles. These strange flying animals had feathers, jaws with sharp teeth, wing claws for climbing trees, and a long bony tail.

Sometimes geologists, investigating rock layers, come across a cluster of fossilized bones. Under a microscope (see above) these can appear to be very beautiful. Paleontologists, scientists who specialize in fossils, will often have to study these finds in detail.

71

Many of the ideas of Ancient Greece were so intelligent or entertaining that they have attracted people from many times. During the Middle Ages, the long centuries in which Christianity dominated Europe, most Greek literature was lost forever. But from the fifteenth century people rediscovered how interesting the Greeks had been.

From that time until the present day, some schools have taught ancient Greek. Greek writings on politics and religion are still read with respect by many people. And modern scientists, when they want new words for new notions, often make them up – like "catalyst" and "electron" – from the language of the Greeks.

**The Olympic Games**
Today's Olympic Games are not very old. They began in 1896. They are modeled on the ancient Greek games, which were held every four years at Olympia. Like the modern Olympics (right), the ancient games were the supreme contest for athletes. Ancient Greek states, like nations today, used athletes for propaganda. They fixed races and bribed umpires!

## The theater

Drama seems to have originally grown from a simple chorus, which sang in honor of the god Dionysus. The illustration shows a famous playwright of Ancient Greece – Aeschylus – with his players. Plays were presented in theaters specially built into a hillside so that as many people as possible could see. Some of these theaters are still used today (above), and their design has been copied in many modern theaters.

Doric  Ionic  Corinthian

## Architecture

Greek architecture is famous for its tall columns. They decorated important buildings, such as the Parthenon (above) in ancient times. Today, many towns have buildings in the Greek style, especially buildings where people go to think, like libraries and museums.

# WHAT ARE MAMMALS?

Mammals are the most successful animals with backbones on Earth today. There are about 4,500 species, and they live in all habitats, from the coldest to the hottest, on land, in the sea, and in the air. Each one looks different, but in certain ways they are all alike. Mammals have large brains and keen senses. They communicate by sounds, smells, and visual means. They are warm-blooded, have an efficient circulation system and they care for their young. Human beings can even change their environment.

### Mother's Milk

One of the reasons for the success of mammals is the care that they give to their young. Mothers provide instant food until the babies are big enough to feed themselves. This food, a liquid secretion called *milk*, contains nutrients and immunity to some diseases. It is made by mammary glands under the mother's skin, and the baby sucks it from nipples during nursing.

### First Mammals

The last 65 million years, since the dinosaurs died out, has been the "Age of Mammals." But the first mammals appeared long before this, about 200 million years ago. They evolved from a group of mammal-like reptiles that were successful even before the reign of the dinosaurs. *Megazostrodon* and *Purgatorius* were among the first true mammals. These tiny animals hid in trees and undergrowth, hunting insects at night.

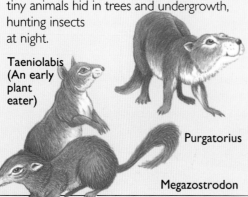

Taeniolabis (An early plant eater)

Purgatorius

Megazostrodon

### Warm Blood

Mammals can live in any climate because they are warm-blooded, or *endothermic*. This means they can keep their bodies at the same temperature no matter how cold or hot the weather is. Endotherms generate heat by chemical reactions that go on inside the body tissues. They keep this heat in with layers of insulating fat and fur. If they get too hot, most mammals can produce sweat. Sweat is a liquid secreted onto the skin surface which evaporates and cools the body.

## Food, Clothes, and Shelter

When people migrated from the warmth of Africa, where they first evolved, to colder northern latitudes, they began to use the skins of other mammals to keep themselves warm. In the far north, where there were no caves and no trees to build huts, they used colossal mammoth bones and tusks for the framework of shelters. This may have led to the first man-made extinctions, about 10,000 years ago, when the mammoths died out.

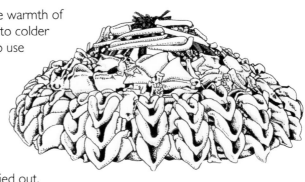

## Vertebrates

Mammals belong to the group of animals known as *vertebrates*. They all have backbones as part of their internal skeletons. Skeletons provide support and protection for internal organs and enable movement. A gorilla's skeleton (left) is similar to that of an orangutan.

## Aesop's Fables

Aesop was a Greek storyteller who lived in the 6th century B.C. He used animal stories to show people how to deal with life's little problems, and to teach right from wrong. One story (below) tells of a race between a slow tortoise (a reptile) and a swift hare (a mammal). The hare is so far ahead, and so confident of victory, he takes a nap. The tortoise plods

along steadily, passing the hare, who wakes up to see his opponent crossing the finishing line. The tale teaches that persistence can be more important than speed.

## Adaptable Mammals

After the demise of the dinosaurs, mammals soon adapted to fill every habitat. Some mammals are perfectly adapted to a particular habitat. Dolphins are so well adjusted to life in the water they can no longer live on land. Others survive by being adaptable. The wolf lives by its wits, eating almost anything it can find, and taking advantage of any situation.

# SPARE-PART SURGERY

**Surgeons estimate that within 50 years one person in ten will have at least one artificial part inside them.**

The materials first used to make artificial parts included wood and gold. Today's bioengineers have a vast range of metals, plastics and other "inert" substances that the body will not reject. Some of the most commonly implanted artificial parts are hip, knee, ankle, and shoulder joints, which banish the pain and stiffness caused by arthritis. Steel plates and pins are used to hold broken bones in place and aid rapid healing. Artificial blood vessels of woven plastic fibers replace arteries damaged by disease, and robotic hands now provide increasing dexterity.

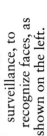

# SILICON CHIP
## RESTORING SIGHT

The retina of the human eye detects light rays shining on it and responds by sending electrical nerve signals to the brain. In certain forms of blindness the retina does not respond in this way. In the future a silicon chip could replace the retina and enable some blind people to see. The thumbnail-sized chip would be connected directly to the optic nerve that leads to the brain. Similar artificial eyes could be used for surveillance, to recognize faces, as shown on the left.

The silicon chip would be inserted in the eye behind the lens, so that light was focused onto it. Signals from the chip would pass along the optic nerve to the brain.

The
*chip*
*contains*
*hundreds*
*of light-*
*sensitive cells.*
*All the cells operate*
*at once, processing*
*data very fast.*

The latest
artificial limbs are
a huge
improvement on
previous versions.
Here a champion
at the
Paralympic
Games shows
how the
revolutionary
"flex foot"
enables him to
run. The foot
has a joint that
bends (flexes)
and then springs
back. The latest
artificial hands
can be connected
to nerves in the
arm. Tiny
electrical signals
from the nerves
control motors
and levers, to
reproduce some of
the movements of
real hands.

㉓

㉑
㉒
㉔

⑲

*Above, a victim of the*
*siege of Sarajevo is fitted*
*with a new artificial*
*hand.*

Real hands can both grip and feel. The
pincer movement between fingers and
thumb is especially important for
picking things up. Advances in the
robot industry have produced
artificial hands with touch-
feedback that can grip
items lightly or
firmly. Some
patients prefer
simpler devices.

**Artificial implants**
1. Skull plate  2. Eye  3. Nose bridge
4. Hearing aid  5. Jaw plate
6. Chin implant  7. Electronic larynx
8. Valve to control water on the brain
9. Shoulder joint  10. Filter to prevent blood
clotting in the lungs  11. Artificial heart
12. Elbow hinge  13. Artificial arm
14. Radial bone-bead  15. Metal forearm plate
16. Stoma appliance  17. Wristbones
18. Tendon  19. Thumblwristbone connection
20. Hip joint  21. Femoral bone
22. Knee hinge  23. Artificial leg
24. Big toe

# The String Family

The violin is the smallest member of the string family, and the highest in pitch. It was also the first to be invented. The violin's immediate relatives – the viola, cello, and double bass – can also be either bowed or plucked. As the body of the instrument gets bigger, so its range of notes becomes lower.

### VIOLA, CELLO, AND DOUBLE BASS

The viola (below) is slightly bigger than the violin, and is held in the same way. The cello (right) is even bigger, and is played sitting down. The instrument is held between the player's knees, and rests on an endpin or spike. Largest and deepest is the double bass (far right), which has the same strings as the violin, but in the reverse order. Bass players play sitting on a high stool, or standing up.

## THE CONCERT HARP

The other member of the string family with a regular place in the symphony orchestra is the concert harp. Each string of the harp produces one note when plucked; each of these notes can be lowered or raised half a tone by means of pedals. The characteristic sound of the harp makes it instantly recognizable, even when the whole orchestra is playing. Also related are the guitar and the zither, which is a folk instrument.

## THE STRINGS IN THE ORCHESTRA

The stringed instuments form the mainstay of the modern Western symphony or chamber orchestra. Together the strings cover a range of over seven octaves. It is even possible to have an orchestra made solely of string players – a string orchestra. The variety of effects possible with stringed instruments, such as *pizzicato* makes them very popular with composers.

## GEOGRAPHY OF THE ORCHESTRA

The diagram below shows how a symphony orchestra is usually laid out. The stringed instruments are spread across the front of the platform in a semicircle, ranging from the violins on the left to the double basses on the far right. The conductor stands at the front, surrounded by string players. If the piece is a concerto, the soloist stands or sits next to the conductor.

POSITIONS OF THE STRINGS

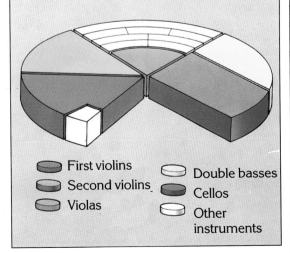

First violins
Second violins
Violas
Double basses
Cellos
Other instruments

## ALTO AND BASS CLEFS

The lower stringed instruments read music written in different clefs, although both the viola and the cello sometimes use the treble clef. The viola usually plays music written in the alto clef (below left) and the cello uses the bass clef (right). So does the double bass, but its notes sound an octave lower than written.

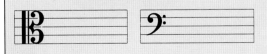

# PLOTTING THE STARS

Astronomy is the study of the stars, planets and other objects in the universe. For centuries, astronomers have striven to learn more about our Universe. Through observation and careful measurement, using scientific tools like the telescope, we now know that the Sun is the center of our solar system. Accurate measurement of star distance is a science developed over the centuries by astronomers like Tycho Brahe (1546-1601). Centuries ago, sailors calculated time at night by observing the movements of star clusters near the fixed Pole Star. Watches aboard ship were timed from the position of these constellations in the sky.

## STAR TIME

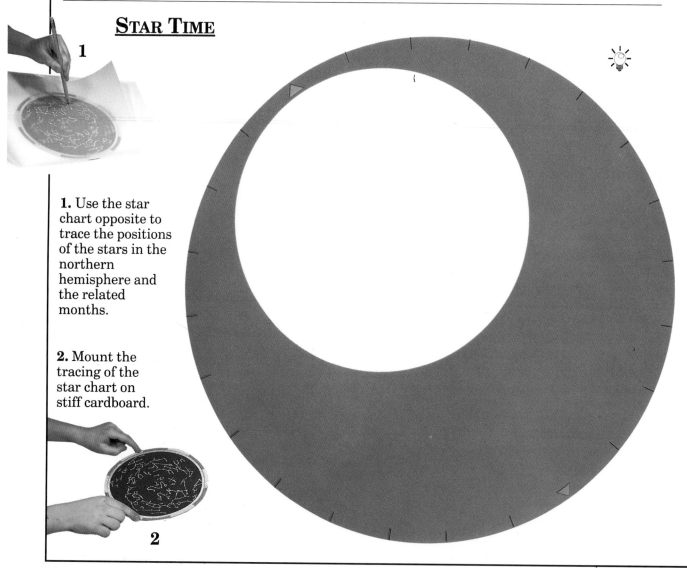

**1**

**1.** Use the star chart opposite to trace the positions of the stars in the northern hemisphere and the related months.

**2.** Mount the tracing of the star chart on stiff cardboard.

**2**

**3.** Trace the shape on the opposite page onto cardboard. Mark the 24 hours of the day, starting with Noon at the bottom.

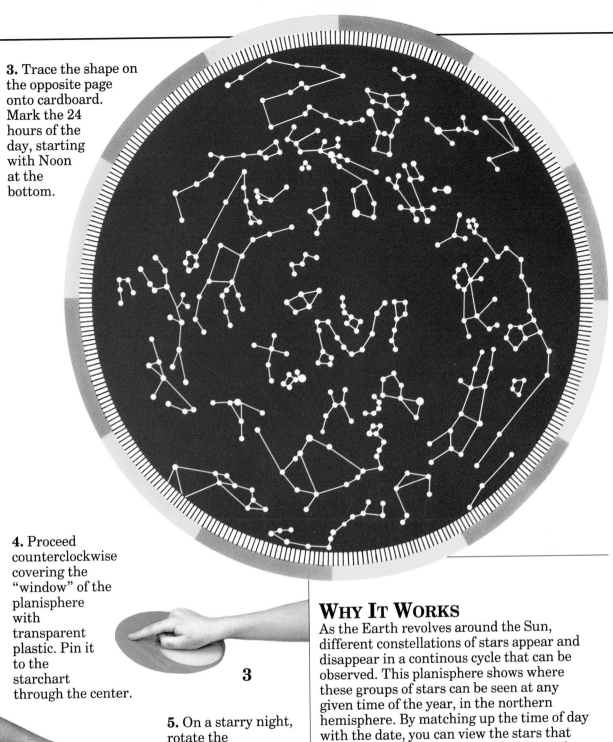

**4.** Proceed counterclockwise covering the "window" of the planisphere with transparent plastic. Pin it to the starchart through the center.

**3**

**4**

**5.** On a starry night, rotate the planisphere until the time of day, marked on the edge, is lined up with the appropriate month at the bottom of the star chart. Compare what you see with the stars in the sky.

## WHY IT WORKS

As the Earth revolves around the Sun, different constellations of stars appear and disappear in a continous cycle that can be observed. This planisphere shows where these groups of stars can be seen at any given time of the year, in the northern hemisphere. By matching up the time of day with the date, you can view the stars that should be visible in the night sky through the cut out "window." The planisphere should be held up and viewed from underneath. The stars visible through the window should match those in the sky. The Sun is a star. It is the only star close enough to look like a ball. The other billions of stars are so far away, they appear to be pinpoints of light.

# AIR POLLUTION

The Earth's atmosphere is polluted naturally by sandstorms and the dust and gases from volcanoes. But the most serious kind of air pollution comes from people. Factories, power stations, and vehicle exhausts pump harmful gases into the air, contributing to global warming, causing acid rain, and destroying the ozone layer. On a much smaller scale, air pollution causes all sorts of breathing problems. There are no simple solutions to air pollution, but people could reduce air pollution by saving energy and reducing harmful emissions from vehicle exhausts and power stations.

### Noise pollution
Loud noises not only annoy people but can damage hearing. Noise is measured in decibels, with 0 decibels being the lowest sound audible to human ears. A level of 160 decibels, such as the noise of a jet airplane taking off at close range, will cause damage to hearing.

Air pollution is at its worst over big cities where millions of people live, work, and travel about in cars, buses, and trucks. Factory chimneys can be fitted with devices to cut down air pollution, but this is expensive. If better public transport and cycle lanes were available in towns and cities, people would be less likely to use their cars, reducing the overall amount of pollution.

### Smoking
Smoking cigarettes adds to the general levels of air pollution as well as damaging our health. Cigarette smoke contains chemicals that can cause cancer, a gas which stops oxygen being taken into the blood and a substance called nicotine which raises blood pressure and makes the heart beat faster. No-smoking areas cut down on this pollution and save non-smokers breathing in other people's cigarette smoke.

## Volcanic pollution

When a volcano erupts, dust is blasted high above the troposphere and may take weeks to be carried around the world. It is above the weather zone, so cannot be washed out of the air by rain. It will eventually fall to Earth after a few years.

## Radioactive pollution

In 1986, part of a nuclear reactor at Chernobyl in the Ukraine exploded, releasing dangerous radioactive pollution into the atmosphere. This was carried around the world by winds and rain, polluting countries many thousands of miles away. The radioactivity was passed on from plants, which took it from the air, to animals eating plants. People were also affected (such as young children) and health and farming problems persist today.

## Detecting pollution

To find out more about the air pollution in your local area, try putting out squares of card covered in grease or vaseline. Put them in different places and leave them for a week or so. Which card collects the most dirt? How does the weather affect the amount of dirt in the air?

Plants called lichens are very sensitive to air pollution. If there are no lichens in your area, the air is very dirty. Leafy or bushy lichens indicate clean air, while the presence of flat, crusty lichens – like the orange circles on rooftops and walls – mean the air is very dirty.

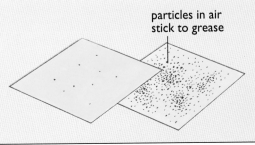

particles in air stick to grease

# GOING WEST

European settlers arrived in North America in the early 17th century. For over a hundred years they remained largely on the Atlantic seaboard, but by the beginning of the 19th century, the United States was on the move, heading west. By 1820 the frontier was across the Mississippi. Texas was annexed twenty-five years later and by 1853, apart from Alaska, the frontiers of the United States were as they stand today.

Two events followed this expansion. One was the migration of thousands of Americans to start new lives on the Great Plains and beyond. The other was the Civil War (1861–65). The era of the cowboy was about to begin.

STEER ROPERS. One of the biggest differences between screen cowboys and real ones is racial. The movie cowboys are generally white and English-speaking. Many real cowboys were non-white, and the working language of nearly all cowboys was Spanish.

One in seven cowboys was an African American, including two of the most skilled and famous, Nat Love (*above left*) and John Ware. There were also many Native Americans and Mexican cowboys. But the movie makers had different ideas. When cowboys passed through the filter of Hollywood, only the white ones were left (*above right*), thus creating one of the most powerful myths of modern culture.

*Wagon trains were the final phase of westward expansion. First came the explorers and trappers, then the cattlemen, and finally farmers and their families in the long trains of wagons. The three great trail routes ran west from St. Louis and Natchez on the Mississippi, and Fort Smith on the Arkansas River.*

## ABRAHAM LINCOLN

Born of pioneer parents in 1809, Lincoln (*left*) trained as a lawyer and became President of the United States in 1860.

He guided the North (also known as the Union) through the Civil War, firmly believing that slavery was a moral evil. He abolished slavery in 1863. He was assassinated in 1865.

## HANDS FOR HIRE

Men – and a few women – became cowboys for all kinds of reasons. The Civil War, fought between the Northern and Southern states over the issue of slavery, had put almost three million men in arms. When the North won in 1865, many returned home to find there was no work.

These included some of the 200,000 ex-slaves who had fought for their freedom with the North. A number of discharged troops, black and white, signed up as cowboys (*below*). They were joined by a few young men leaving prosperous homes in the northeast in search of adventure. But the life of the cowboy was anything but romantic. It was dirty, often dull, and always hard.

**Discharge**
*After the Civil War, many ex-soldiers became cowboys.*

# BEETLES

In terms of numbers, the group of beetles, or Coleoptera, has been more successful than any other kind of animal. There are at least 370,000 known species in the world, and new ones are being discovered all the time. Beetles are armor-plated insects. The head and thorax are covered in tough cuticle, formed into strange, threatening shapes in many species. Despite their heavy appearance, most beetles fly very well. Beetle grubs undergo complete metamorphosis to become adult.

Some species of beetles are herbivores (plant-eaters), others are carnivores (meat-eaters). Some kill prey and eat it. Many perform the important function of consuming the dead bodies of animals, some eating the flesh, others eating fur or feathers. Some feed on animal dung. Some beetle pests consume grains or vegetables. Colorado beetles attack potato crops. Others attack vegetation, such as elm bark beetles that spread Dutch elm disease.

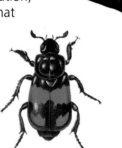

Weevil

Burying beetle

Most beetles have biting jaws to seize their prey. In weevils the jaws are located on the end of a long nose or rostrum.

## Light show

Glowworms, or fireflies, are neither worms nor flies. They are beetles that produce light to attract mates. During dark evenings, males and females flash signals to each other, like morse code signals from a lantern. The code is different for each species. In South-East Asia, whole trees pulse with thousands of these tiny lights. The light is made by a chemical reaction involving an enzyme which releases energy in the form of light.

### Holy beetle

The female scarab beetle rolls a ball of dung to her burrow. She lays her eggs in the dung, and the larvae feed on it. The scarab beetle was sacred to the ancient Egyptians. They compared the insect's behavior with the action of their god Ra, who, they believed, rolled the sun across the sky each day. Egyptian craftsmen made scarab jewelry, using gold, lapis lazuli, and semi-precious stones.

**Rove beetle**          **Chafer beetle**

Many kinds of beetles have fierce-looking jaws and horns. These are often for show, to frighten off predators, or for fighting between males. Stag beetles (left) are so named because the male has fearsome, antlerlike jaws. Sparring stag beetles wrestle, each trying to turn his opponent over. In beetles, the front pair of wings form tough, often colorful wing cases, called elytra. These fold back when the insect is not flying, to protect the delicate wings beneath. In flight, the wing cases are raised.

**Elytron**

### Insect machines

Some engineers have used insects as inspiration in the design and manufacture of machines. In the late 1940's the vehicle manufacturer Volkswagen pioneered a family car with a rounded beetle shape. Its success was phenomenal, and over 19 million Volkswagen Beetles were produced and exported to nearly 150 countries worldwide.

### Heralds of death

Deathwatch beetles are wood borers. The larvae live in the dead wood of trees or in cut timber such as the roof timbers of a house. At mating time the males and females call to each other from the tunnels they have bored, tapping their jaws on the wood, and making an ominous ticking noise. In the days before pest control and when illnesses were difficult to treat, this sound in old houses was thought to foretell a death in the family, ticking away the last minutes of someone's life.

# HOT-AIR FLIGHT

Have you seen a hot-air balloon? More than 200 years ago, two French brothers, Joseph and Jacques Montgolfier, discovered that rising hot air could be captured and used for flight. They made a huge balloon from linen and paper and built a fire underneath it. The balloon trapped the hot air and smoke rising from the fire and lifted the two men into the air. As the air cooled, the balloon floated back down to the ground. Since that first flight, people have used hot-air balloons for pleasure, for racing, and even for warfare. You can make your own hot-air balloon.

## BALLOON LIFT-OFF

**1**

**1** To make a balloon that traps hot air to fly, you need four large sheets of tissue paper. Fold each sheet in half and lightly copy this shape on to one using a pencil. When you are happy with the outline cut out your first "panel."

**3**

**3** Unfold your first panel and spread glue on the edge of one half. Stick the second panel on top and press down. Repeat with the next panel until all four panels are joined into a balloon.

**4** Make a small "passenger basket" from a piece of folded oak tag. Attach the basket to the open end of the balloon with four lengths of thread.

**2**

**2** Use the first panel to help you mark out the next three. Cut them out and trim them carefully to make sure they are all the same size.

**4**

**5** Take the balloon outside for your first flight. Blow up the balloon with hot air from a hair dryer and watch it lift off.

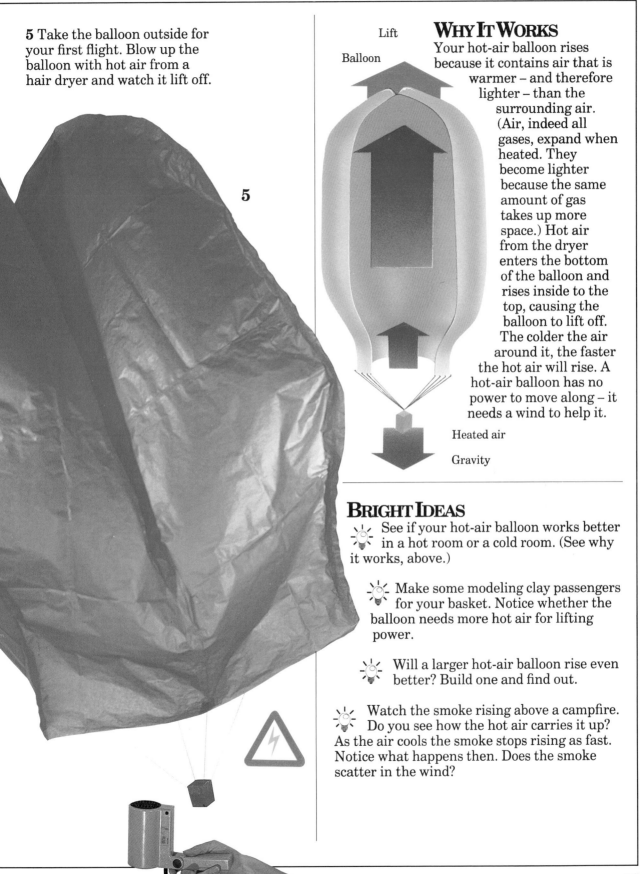

5

Lift

Balloon

Heated air

Gravity

## WHY IT WORKS

Your hot-air balloon rises because it contains air that is warmer – and therefore lighter – than the surrounding air. (Air, indeed all gases, expand when heated. They become lighter because the same amount of gas takes up more space.) Hot air from the dryer enters the bottom of the balloon and rises inside to the top, causing the balloon to lift off. The colder the air around it, the faster the hot air will rise. A hot-air balloon has no power to move along – it needs a wind to help it.

## BRIGHT IDEAS

See if your hot-air balloon works better in a hot room or a cold room. (See why it works, above.)

Make some modeling clay passengers for your basket. Notice whether the balloon needs more hot air for lifting power.

Will a larger hot-air balloon rise even better? Build one and find out.

Watch the smoke rising above a campfire. Do you see how the hot air carries it up? As the air cools the smoke stops rising as fast. Notice what happens then. Does the smoke scatter in the wind?

# CREATING A SUPERHERO

A comic strip is a series of pictures that tell a story, from the adventures of mischievous school friends to the exploits of fantasy superheroes. The next two pages are about creating your own comic strip, and the first step is to invent the characters.

What do Superman, the Incredible Hulk, and the Teenage Mutant Ninja Turtles have in common? Most superheroes are concocted from a recipe of certain ingredients. Looking at these ingredients can help you build your own characters.

## Factor X
Some superheroes come from other planets but most are from Earth; they are ordinary people or (animals) who have acquired a special ability, often as a result of some extraordinary event. This is sometimes linked to radiation, but not always; Popeye gets his great strength from an ordinary can of spinach.

A superhero has his or her own territory, a particular location to patrol. Cities are popular, and, of course, the far reaches of outer space.

## Missions and superskills
All superheroes have a cause - to fight villains like the one shown above left, or to right a particular injustice in the world. Your superhero will need a mission and a special ability - think about the superpower you would most like to have for yourself!

A superpower can be extra strength, vision, or hearing, or it can be something new, from X-ray vision to the ability to change shape. A superhero associated with an animal takes on the creature's powers - so the owl girl above might be able to see in the dark. Other favorite crime fighters are themselves animals.

## Developing a script

Your superhero can be developed by thinking about costume, weaknesses, likes and dislikes, sidekicks and friends. But the best way of learning about your superhero is to set out on an adventure and see how he performs!

What makes a good storyline? Cartoon scripts often contain certain key ingredients. The strip begins with a problem: a crime or mystery which is often the the work of the villain. It may be almost too late before the hero learns of the trouble and decides to step in.

Meanwhile problems may mount up, and friends may be captured or wounded. In the nick of time comes a moment of inspiration, and the tide turns. Triumph! There is often a celebration before the hero heads home. Develop your plot along these lines and your superhero is ready to go!

▷ *"My superhero. Cartoonman, is a cool customer; here you can see him studying his script, unconcerned by the battle raging around him. To find out what problems lie in store for him, see the script in the box above.*

*Cartoonman's first adventure*
*Rocketwoman is guiding her spaceship across the galaxy when the engine develops a fault. Forced to crash land on an unknown planet, she is besieged by alien lifeforms. Using his superhearing, Cartoonman learns of the danger. He speeds to the planet and soon has things sorted out. Returning Rocketwoman to her own planet, he receives a hero's send off and returns to base.*

# SUNLIGHT

The Sun is a star that gives us light and heat energy. The Sun is about 93 million miles from the Earth. All plants grow toward the sun. If you see a field of sunflowers, like the one pictured here, you will notice that they all face the same way, toward the Sun. Plants use the Sun's energy to make their own food. This energy is trapped by the green chlorophyll in a plant's leaves. During a process called photosynthesis, oxygen is released into the air as the sunlight is used to convert nutrients from the soil into food. The Greek word "photo" means light. Bioethanol is a fuel made by fermenting the food produced by plants like wheat. One day it could replace gasoline.

## LEAVES

**1.** Half fill a shallow container with soil and scatter watercress seeds on the top. Keep the soil moist and place the tray in a sunny position. Leave it until the seeds sprout.

**3.** Leave the tray in its sunny position. You may have to wait as long as two weeks. Keep the soil moist while the cress is growing.

**3**

**1**

**2.** Cut out your initials from some cardboard, and place it over the seedlings. Make sure the sunlight cannot reach the plants beneath.

**4**

**2**

**4.** During this growing time do not remove the cardboard. You may want to turn the tray occasionally to allow an equal amount of light to reach every part of the tray.

**5.** When you observe that the watercress is fully grown, remove the cardboard. You should be able to see your initials in the seedlings. They will be a much darker green than the rest of the cress, where the light could not reach.

## WHY IT WORKS

Sunlight is used by plants to convert nutrients from the soil into chemical energy for growth. When the leaves are covered, sunlight cannot be absorbed. No food can be manufactured inside the plant. Plants absorb carbon dioxide and water. These are converted by the green chlorophyll in the leaves into oxygen and simple sugars. The sugars are converted into food for the plant while the remaining oxygen and water is released into the air through small holes called stomata. These are located on the underside of the leaves. This process is called photosynthesis.

Sunlight

Carbon dioxide absorbed

Oxygen and water released

Water absorbed

## BRIGHT IDEAS

☼ Starch is produced when leaves photosynthesize. You can test for starch. Ask an adult to help you. Remove some cress from different parts of the tray and soak them in rubbing alcohol to remove any green chlorophyll. Then place them on a clean surface and put drops of dilute iodine on the surface of each. Where starch is present, the leaves will turn blue, where there is no starch they will turn brown.

☼ Plants always grow toward the sun. This is called phototropism. Plant a seedling in a pot and place it in a shoe box. Place a hole at one end of the box for the light to enter. The shoot will appear through the hole.

**5**

*One of the greatest problems with cars is finding somewhere to put them. Renault's concept car, the Matra Zoom, gets around this problem by making itself smaller, tucking its rear wheels under itself for parking, and stretching them out again for the open road. Other manufacturers have turned to electronics. Volkswagen's concept car, the Futura, is fitted with lasers and ultrasound sensors to measure the space, and to park the car.*

*Matra Zoom*

# SMART CARS
## DRIVING MADE EASIER

**The car of the future will make driving easier and safer.**
Onboard computers will control many parts of the car, including the suspension and anti-lock brakes. Communication links will provide driver information.

*Driving position*

*Parking position*

*Route-planners linked to a central computer will guide the driver. In a strange area, the planners will suggest the best route. At home, where routes are familiar, they will warn of road works, congestion, and accidents. Systems like these are already being tested and could be common within about five years. The dashboard of the future will be designed to provide lots of clear information. Speed, fuel level, and warnings of dangers ahead may be shown as "head-up displays" on the screen, close to the driver's line of sight.*

Once on a highway, cars will be driven automatically a few feet apart, using sensors to prevent crashes. This technique, called "platooning" and already tested in California, is safer and makes much better use of roads. If someone pulls out unexpectedly, all the cars will automatically slow to prevent a crash. Onboard route maps will show the way, or direct the driver by voice control. Each car will be centrally monitored, with systems that can override the driver.

*Driving in the future is unlikely to be free. Some of today's road and fuel taxes will be replaced by "road pricing" systems, which will charge for the use of busy city streets or highways. The ADEPT plan, being developed by 16 European countries, would use beacons on the roadside and meters in the cars to deduct payments from the user's "Smart card." Charges could be based on the distance traveled, limited to a city center, or levied only when the roads are congested. The congestion meter would be activated by microwave beacons located on the outskirts of the charging area.*

THIS SIDE UP

# THE AIR BAG
## HOW LIVES ARE SAVED

Air bags are triggered by the rapid deceleration in a crash. Instantly, a small explosive charge fires, inflating the bag with gas. In a 30-mph crash into a solid barrier, the charge fires in under ten milliseconds – blinking the eye takes fifteen times as long. By 20 milliseconds, the driver is moving forward and the bag is expanding fast. At 80 milliseconds, the car has stopped dead and the driver's head has hit the air bag, which vents gas to absorb the energy. The driver bounces back unhurt. Air bags were developed in the United States where many people are reluctant to wear seat belts. It was important to develop a restraint that was automatic, and did not rely on the drivers remembering to use it. Combining the air bag and seat belt will virtually eliminate serious head and facial injuries, even in faster crashes.

*Seat belts have cut road deaths dramatically, but not everybody wears them. Even when they are worn, they do not offer complete protection. In frontal crashes at 20-30 mph, almost a third of the drivers hit their heads on the steering wheel even if they are belted up. The airbag prevents this, inflating in a fraction of a second to provide a soft cushion absorbing the impact of the crash. Air bags are a masterpiece of engineering, although there have been a few problems. Some materials burn due to the friction caused by the inflating bag.*

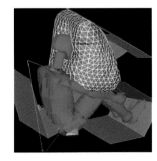

# THE BODY SYSTEMS

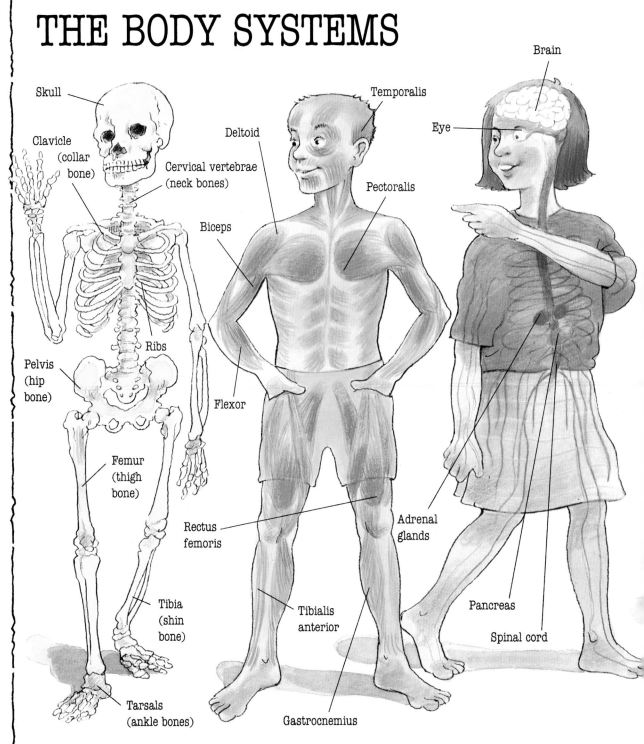

Skull

Clavicle (collar bone)

Cervical vertebrae (neck bones)

Biceps

Ribs

Pelvis (hip bone)

Femur (thigh bone)

Rectus femoris

Tibia (shin bone)

Tarsals (ankle bones)

Temporalis

Deltoid

Pectoralis

Flexor

Adrenal glands

Tibialis anterior

Gastrocnemius

Brain

Eye

Pancreas

Spinal cord

**The Skeleton**
206 bones provide a rigid framework moved by muscles and protect soft parts like the brain.

**Muscles**
Over 640 muscles pull bones, so you can move. Muscles are two-fifths of our total body weight.

**Nerves, Senses, and Glands**
The nerves and glands control the body's systems, using either chemical or electrical messages.

Jugular vein

Aorta (main artery)

Heart

Windpipe (trachea)

Saliva gland

Liver

Gullet

Lungs

Kidneys

Stomach

Ureter

Large intestine

Femoral artery and vein

Bladder

Anus

Small intestine

## Circulation

The body's cardiovascular system circulates blood through the blood vessels pumped by the heart. The blood spreads oxygen and nutrients, and collects any of the body's waste products.

## Respiration and excretion

In respiration, the lungs absorb oxygen from the air, and excrete, or get rid of, carbon dioxide. The kidneys excrete wastes by filtering them from the blood, to form urine.

## Digestion

The mouth, gullet, stomach, and intestines break down food and absorb nutrients into the body. The pancreas makes digestive juices, and the liver processes and stores nutrients.

# WHAT IS A VOLCANO?

Volcanoes are openings in the surface of the earth, from which molten rock, called magma, and gases can escape.

The earth is made up of three layers – the crust, the mantle and the core. The crust is the outermost layer of rock and can be quite thin. The continental crust is between 20 and 30 miles thick, but the oceanic crust is only about 3 miles thick.

The crust feels solid but it consists of giant plates (see illustration, right) which float on the upper mantle. The upper mantle is made of hot, molten rock called magma which is always moving. Pressure in the mantle forces magma to the surface.

Volcanic eruptions occur where the rising magma finds a way through a crack or weakness in the earth's crust, usually at the edges of plates. These are called plate margins.

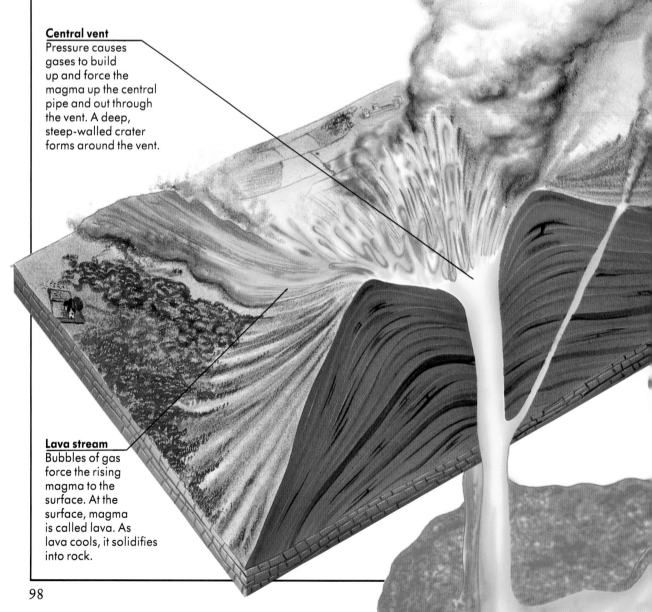

**Central vent**
Pressure causes gases to build up and force the magma up the central pipe and out through the vent. A deep, steep-walled crater forms around the vent.

**Lava stream**
Bubbles of gas force the rising magma to the surface. At the surface, magma is called lava. As lava cools, it solidifies into rock.

## Layers

The steep slopes are built up of alternate layers of ash, and hardened lava. Sometimes lava bursts through in other places and forms other cones on the sides of the central cone.

## Ash

The clouds of ash and gas that pour from the volcano help to form the cone shape around its vent. The ash consists of tiny pieces of lava, which harden into rock called tuff.

## Plate movements

200 million years ago, all the land was joined together in one big continent called Pangaea. Gradually the pieces drifted apart and formed the seven continents we have today. Active volcanoes are usually found in definite zones, near plate margins. They are mostly caused by plate movement.

Active volcanoes marked in red

200 million years ago — 100 — 50 — Present day

## Types of volcanoes

Thick, slow moving andesite lava builds up high, cone-shaped volcanoes. Andesite volcanoes are very violent. Shield volcanoes form when runny lava escapes through a fissure and flows a long way. The volcano has broad sloping sides like a shield.

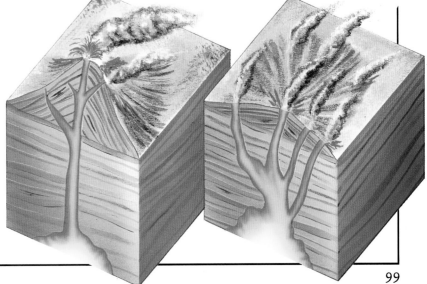

## Magma

Magma collects in a chamber in the upper mantle. It is formed when two plates collide. The edge of one plate is dragged down under the other and melts into magma.

99

# HOOFED ANIMALS

Ungulates walk on the tips of their toes which are protected by hard hooves. Hooves are made from keratin, the same horny material as claws and nails. Solid hooves are an adaptation for running away from predators. Ungulates are divided into three groups: the elephants and their relatives (such as hyraxes); the perissodactyls or odd-toed ungulates, such as horses and zebras; and the artiodactyls or even-toed ungulates, such as cattle.

## Odds and Evens

The skeletons of ungulate feet show how they walk on the tips of their toes. Originally all mammals had five digits or toes. But as ungulates evolved they lost toes to improve their speed. Some ungulates, like elephants, still have five toes. Pig trotters have two large hooves and two small hooves which do not touch the ground. Rhinos (upper left) walk on three toes, deer have four (lower left) but walk upon two, and horses have only one.

## Diseases

Foot-and-mouth disease affects animals with cloven (split) hooves, such as cattle and sheep. It spreads rapidly through the herds and can bankrupt farmers. Some animal diseases spread to humans. Sleeping sickness is transferred from cattle to humans via the blood-sucking tsetse fly (below).

## Mythical Horses

In Ancient Greek mythology, the winged Pegasus flew up to heaven and was tamed by the goddess Athena with a magical golden bridle. The Unicorn is a white horse with a spiral horn growing from its forehead. It is said that whoever drinks from its horn is protected from poisoning.

## Migration

Many animals make seasonal migrations to new habitats, to find better living conditions. Huge herds of wildebeest walk hundreds of miles across the African plains in search of grass and water. The urge to move is so strong they will tackle any obstacle. Many die on the way, drowning in rivers, falling down gorges, or caught by predators.

## Ungulate Relatives

Camels (left) and llamas are even-toed ungulates. But they do not walk on the tips of their toes like other cloven-hoofed animals. The weight is carried by soft pads behind their hooves. Camels are ideally suited for desert life. Their wide feet do not sink in the sand, their humps store food for long-distance travel, and their stomachs can hold 22 gallons of water. Rhinos are primitive relatives of horses. They have stumpy feet with three hoofed toes, and thick, hairless skin folded into armorlike plates.

## Horsemanship

Man's first association with horses was to hunt them for meat. Horses were domesticated in Asia about 6,000 years ago. Until the horse collar was invented, horses were not used to pull heavy loads, but for pulling warriors in chariots. In the Middle Ages horses were bred to be strong enough to carry knights in full armor. These thoroughbreds are among the 150 breeds known today.

Zebras (left) are closely related to horses and donkeys. They live in sociable groups, grazing on the African plains.

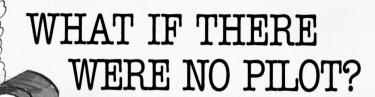

# WHAT IF THERE WERE NO PILOT?

Sometimes there isn't. At least, not a human pilot actually operating the controls. Many modern planes have an automatic pilot. It's not a robot sitting in the pilot's seat, but a set of controls incorporated into the main controls. The real pilot sets the plane's speed, height and direction, then switches to automatic, for a break. Of course, if something happens, alarms activate, and the real pilot takes the controls. In very modern planes, the computer-based auto-pilot can even take off and land the aircraft.

## How do pilots "fly by wire?"

Computer screens are wired up to show speed, direction, engine conditions, and other information. Small levers and switches activate the flaps, rudder, and other control surfaces. This happens by sending electrical signals along wires to motors. This system is all controlled by the avionics system.

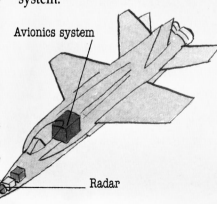

Avionics system

Radar

## What is a "black box?"

It's not usually black or box-shaped. It may be bright orange and cylindrical. But it's the usual name for an aircraft's flight data recorder. This device continually records the plane's speed, height, direction, and other information from the instruments, as well as radio signals and voice communications. It is specially made to be fireproof, shockproof, and waterproof. In the event of emergency or disaster, it can be recovered, and its recordings give valuable information about what happened.

## Tires, skis, skids, and floats

Airplanes can be equipped with a variety of landing gear, depending on their size and the conditions. Jet liners require wheels to withstand the pressure. Seaplanes need floats to keep them above water. Gliders and early rocket planes use skids, while planes that have to land on snow and ice use skis!

## Do you have to be strong to fly a plane?

Not really. Some controls are simple electrical switches and knobs. Others are levers, like the control column and rudder pedals, but they are well-balanced with counterweights and cables, so they aren't too heavy to move. But to fly a plane well, you do have to be alert and physically fit, with good coordination and quick reactions.

## When can you see two sets of controls and instruments?

In the "head-up display." There are not really two sets. Part of the main display is reflected or projected upward onto the front windshield or canopy, or into the pilot's special helmet visor. The pilot can look ahead and see outside, and the controls at the same time.

# FLOWERS

The main function of a tree's flowers is to produce seeds that will grow into new trees. Flowers contain the tree's reproductive parts. They can be male or female or contain both male and female parts. Willows and poplars have male flowers on one tree and female on another. Most conifers have separate clusters of male and female flowers on the same tree. The wind carries pollen from the male flowers to fertilize the female flowers.

A flower's shape, color, and smell are designed to transfer male pollen grains to the female parts efficiently. Pollen is mainly transferred by insects or wind. Plants that rely on insect carriers have evolved brightly-colored, sweetly-scented flowers that have a landing platform for insects. In warm climates, birds and bats transfer pollen when they fly from flower to flower sipping nectar.

APPLE BLOSSOMS

### Looking into flowers
Flowers vary from species to species in their shape, color, and size. Many trees in temperate (moderate, seasonal) climates are wind-pollinated, so they have unspectacular flowers because they do not rely on attracting insects.

Nikau palm flowers

Palms have small flowers which grow in large clusters. The pollinated flowers later develop into dates, coconuts, or other fruits, depending on the species.

Walnut trees grow male hanging catkin flowers 2-4 inches (5-10 cm) long. The female flowers are rounded and stand upright.

### Cones of Norway spruce

Pine flowers are very inconspicuous. The red or yellow clustered flowers develop into cones about a year after being fertilized.

Walnut catkin and flowers

There are many different kinds of magnolia trees, but all are known for their beautiful flowers which lure insects.

Magnolia flowers

HONEYBEE

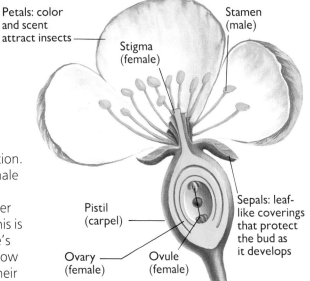

Petals: color
and scent
attract insects

Stigma
(female)

Stamen
(male)

Pistil
(carpel)

Sepals: leaf-
like coverings
that protect
the bud as
it develops

Ovary
(female)

Ovule
(female)

This flower has both male
and female parts. Stamens
produce millions of pollen
grains at a time, each grain
is only .008 inches across.

## Pollination

For a new seed to grow, male pollen grains must reach the female ovules, which are contained in the ovary. This is called pollination. Even if a flower contains both male and female parts, it very rarely pollinates itself. Pollen usually travels from the male parts of a flower to the female parts of a different flower – this is called cross-pollination. The design of a tree's flowers shows how they are pollinated. Willow catkins use the wind to carry their pollen. Their dangling shape allows the wind to scatter the pollen grains. Flowers pollinated by insects, such as bees and butterflies, attract them with their color, smell, and a store of sweet nectar to eat. Pollen sticks to the insects' legs and hairy backs, and is carried to the next flower they visit, where it may join with an ovule.

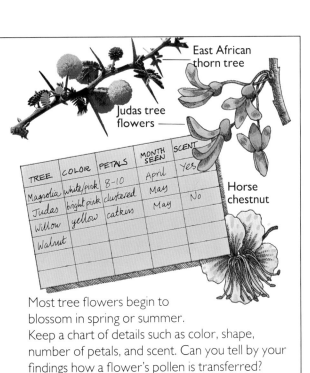

East African
thorn tree

Judas tree
flowers

Horse
chestnut

| TREE | COLOR | PETALS | MONTH SEEN | SCENT |
|------|-------|--------|------------|-------|
| Magnolia | white/pink | 8-10 | April | Yes |
| Judas | bright pink | clustered | May | No |
| Willow | yellow | catkins | May |  |
| Walnut |  |  |  |  |

Most tree flowers begin to blossom in spring or summer.
Keep a chart of details such as color, shape, number of petals, and scent. Can you tell by your findings how a flower's pollen is transferred?

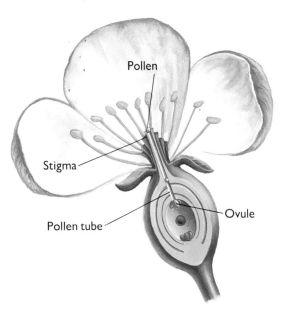

Pollen

Stigma

Pollen tube

Ovule

The sticky top of the pistil, called the stigma, catches the pollen. Then the pollen puts out long tubes which join with the ovule. This is called fertilization.

# RECYCLING
## REUSING MATERIALS

**Many materials can be recycled and used again. Energy can be saved provided recycling uses less energy than the original production process.**
Recycling aluminum drink cans uses only a twentieth as much energy as making new ones from bauxite ore. Steel has always been recycled and scrap iron is often added to the process. About a quarter of the materials in every new car are recycled from an old car. Cars contain many different materials that are expensive to separate when the product is scrapped. Some car manufacturers have come up with better designs to make recycling easier, saving a lot of energy and making expensive raw materials go farther. The average family in a developed country throws away about two tons of waste material each year. Much of this waste could be used again. Fuel pellets made of garbage, comprising mainly paper, will burn well to generate heat. Plants for sorting garbage are expensive to build but they start paying for themselves in a few years.

*Using fewer different materials in cars would make recycling easier. Plastics are difficult to recycle, but BMW has come up with a car that is made from a large proportion of recycled* *or recyclable plastic (below). The parts shown in green are recyclable plastics, those shown in blue are made from recycled plastics.*

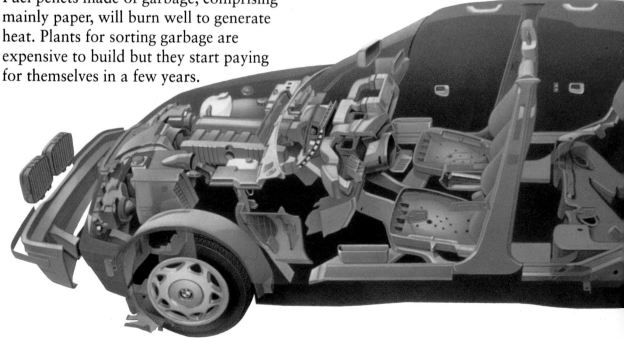

# T I R E   P O W E R
## E N E R G Y   F R O M   R U B B E R

The main reason for burning garbage is to dispose of it efficiently. But waste also has an energy content and the easiest way to recover energy is by burning. Old car tires are among the hardest things to dispose of because they contain rubber, steel, and fabrics that cannot easily be separated. Often, old tires are piled in huge heaps, that can easily catch fire and burn for weeks on end. A use has now been found for old tires. A British power station (left) has been built that generates electricity, by burning tires, leaving only ash behind. This solves the problem of piles of old tires and also generates useful amounts of energy.

*The French car company PSA, is moving toward the fully recyclable car. At present, about 70 percent of the average scrapped car is recycled, either as second-hand parts or as scrap metal. The remaining 30 percent is crushed into blocks as inert compacted waste. Much of this is plastic, which is hard to recycle. In the new cars, plastics used will be ground and made into a fuel with properties similar to coal.*

# STUDYING THE PAST

The past is divided into two main eras: the prehistoric and the historic. History began between 4,500 and 5,000 years ago, when writing was first used to record events. Little information was recorded at first, but in time the historical records became more detailed. Information about prehistoric times is more difficult to obtain – the main evidence is what we can dig up out of the gound. Even in studies of historic times, a lot of useful information can come from such archaeological digs.

**The earliest humans lived a long time ago, and the only remains they left behind were their teeth and bones, which sometimes turned into fossils. The study of fossils – animal or human – is known as paleontology. In time, our ancestors began to make tools out of sticks, and then out of pebbles. Stone tools were very durable and they have survived more often than bones. Other human activities, such as building huts and making fires, also left evidence behind.**

**Over the centuries, human activities became more complicated, and with each stage there is more evidence to find – complex stone tools appear, then stone carvings and cave paintings, then buildings, pottery and metal tools. The study of such man-made objects is called archaeology.**

## Teeth

Teeth are harder than bones and they are often the only part of the body to be preserved, An electron microscope can reveal how fragments of bone leave a particular type of scratch mark, showing that meat was on the menu. Soil particles from tubers and roots leave a deeper type of scratch mark.

## Footprints

Very occasionally footprints are preserved in mud or volcanic ash, if it dries to a hard surface and is then covered by more sediment.

## Bones

Bones eventually rot, but where they are preserved by sediment, they may turn into fossils. In this process, minerals from the rock gradually replace the bone itself, creating a stone 'replica' of the bone.

## Plants

Plants produce pollen grains which have a characteristic shape and pattern for each species of plant. They are also very tough and are often preserved. They can be seen in rocks using a microscope, and can reveal what the climate was like at the time, and what sort of food plants our ancestors ate.

# Dating a site

Finding out the age of a site is very important. One method of dating is based in radioactive materials, which occur naturally and 'decay' at a fixed rate. A radioactive form of carbon, carbon-14, is found in the carbon dioxide gas in the atmosphere, and therefore in all living plants and animals. Once they die, no more carbon is taken into the body, and the carbon-14 already present slowly decays.

By measuring the amount remaining scientists can work out how long ago organisms died. Carbon dating works well, but only for objects less than 70,000 years old.
Older archaeological sites are more difficult, but the ages of some can be worked out using potassium-argon dating, which measures that radiation from a radioactive form of potassium found in volcanic ash.

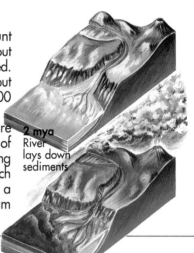

**2 mya**
River lays down sediments

**1.9 mya**
Volcano erupts and lays down ash in the sediments

**1.3 mya**
More sediments accumulate

**Present day**
Erosion exposes sediments

**mya** = million years ago

### Wood and hide
Although wooden tools and animal hides are not preserved on prehistoric sites such as this, they would survive on more recent sites.

### Fire
Fire leaves burned stones and baked clay, although it is not always easy to tell if the fire was a natural one or man-made campfire. In later sites the signs are clearer, because people built hearths and used them often.

### Fire
In prehistoric sites, any wooden tools have long since rotted away, but stone tools are often preserved. The way in which the tool is used leaves a particular 'polish' on its surface. By looking at this tool under a microscope scientists would know that is had been used to scrape animal skins – which shows that skins were used for making bags, tents, or clothing.

Studying our past requires a lot of detective work – especially on prehistoric sites such as this one, dating from half a million years ago. Archaeologists must be able to piece together fragments of evidence to build up a picture of how our ancestors lived. As well as human bones, the remains of animals which were eaten are often found at camp-sites. They show if the people hunted big game or small. Cut marks on the bones from stone tools reveal how the animal was butchered.
Once people began burying their dead, far more human bones were preserved.

# THE SPACE AGE BEGINS

World War II ended in 1945, but the Cold War, an era of confrontation between the United States and the Soviet Union, began soon after. Both countries developed rockets to display their military might and national pride. Under a brilliant leader, Sergei Korolyev, the Soviets had by 1956 built a giant rocket, the SS-6, capable of carrying a two-ton bomb 4,000 miles. To demonstrate the rocket, Korolyev was ordered to launch a satellite, a small object that would stay in space, and circle around the Earth. On October 4 1957, the satellite Sputnik 1 was launched. The Space Age had begun.

## Launchers

Sputnik's SS-6 launcher was big and simple, but very effective. It consisted of a central core, with four strap-on boosters to increase lift off power.

Compared to the Soviet design, the American rockets (below) were lighter and more delicate in construction. They used high-technology fuel tanks instead of the thick-walled steel tanks of the SS-6. Less power meant that American satellites had to be light. This gave a boost to the development of min-iaturized electronic devices such as new transistors, which were soon used in portable radios and other everyday objects.

A-1
Sputnik

Vanguard

Juno 1

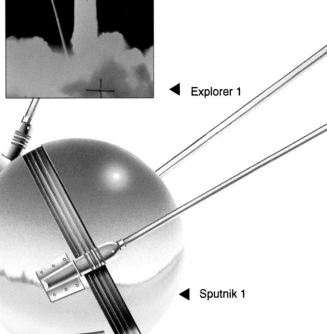
◀ Explorer 1

◀ Sputnik 1

### The response to Sputnik

By late 1957, the United States was ready to match Sputnik with a satellite of its own. But the first launch, of a Vanguard rocket with a tiny 3.4 pound satellite, was a dismal failure. It rose only a few feet before crashing back to the launch pad and exploding in a ball of flame. In desperation, the United States turned to Wernher von Braun, whose satellite project had been in need of money.

### American success

Von Braun put together a Jupiter C rocket and a satellite called Explorer. This was launched successfully on January 31, 1958 (see the photo on the opposite page). Explorer 1 was a much smaller satellite than either of the first two Sputniks which preceded it into space. Other early American launches met with less success: a Mercury rocket suffered premature engine cut-off during its launch in 1960 (above left).

In April 1958, the National Aeronautics and Space Administration (NASA) was created, to survey the Moon and put a man into space. It has been a force in world science and politics ever since.

▲ NASA's first office building in Washington D.C.

### Sputnik

Sputnik 1 (left) was a simple metal sphere that weighed 184 pounds. Its transmitter emitted a series of beeps. In November 1957, the much larger Sputnik 2 carried a passenger: the dog Laika, who became the first space traveler.

### Voices from the sky

A satellite is an object that goes around another. Scientists realized that artificial radio satellites could relay radio, TV, and telephone signals around the Earth. The first was Telstar, (below right) launched by the U.S. in 1962. In 1965, Early Bird became the first geostationary satellite. People could watch the Beatles (below) live on TV beamed from another continent.

### The van Allen belts

One of the instruments on Explorer 1 was designed to count and measure electrically charged particles in space. This instrument led to the first space discovery. James van Allen, the scientist responsible, noticed that at certain heights the counter seemed to stop working, and he realized it had been overloaded. The reason was a region in space dense with charged particles - now known as the van Allen belts. These sometimes disrupt radio communications.

# THE BITS OF THE BRAIN

The top half of your head is filled with a large lump of pinkish-gray, wrinkled looking substance, that feels like a mixture of pudding and jelly. But don't worry. All brains are like this. The human brain is the most amazing bio-computer. It can think, remember, predict, solve, create, invent, control, and coordinate.

## BRAIN POWER

Are you smarter than a rabbit? Almost certainly. Your brain is much bigger than the rabbit's brain. Are you smarter than a sperm whale? Again, almost certainly, even though this huge beast's brain is five times bigger than your own. Intelligence is not just a matter of brain size. It depends on the relative sizes of the brain parts, and how they are connected. The cortex, the wrinkly gray part, is huge in the human brain. This is where intelligence, thinking, and complicated behavior are based.

## SPIES ON YOUR INSIDES

The CAT (computerized axial tomography) scanner pictures a "slice" of the brain, with no discomfort or risk. It beams weak X rays through the head and displays the results on a computer TV screen.

Computer

**CORTEX**
*The outer gray part, where thinking takes place.*

*X rays beamed from all angles as camera goes around head.*

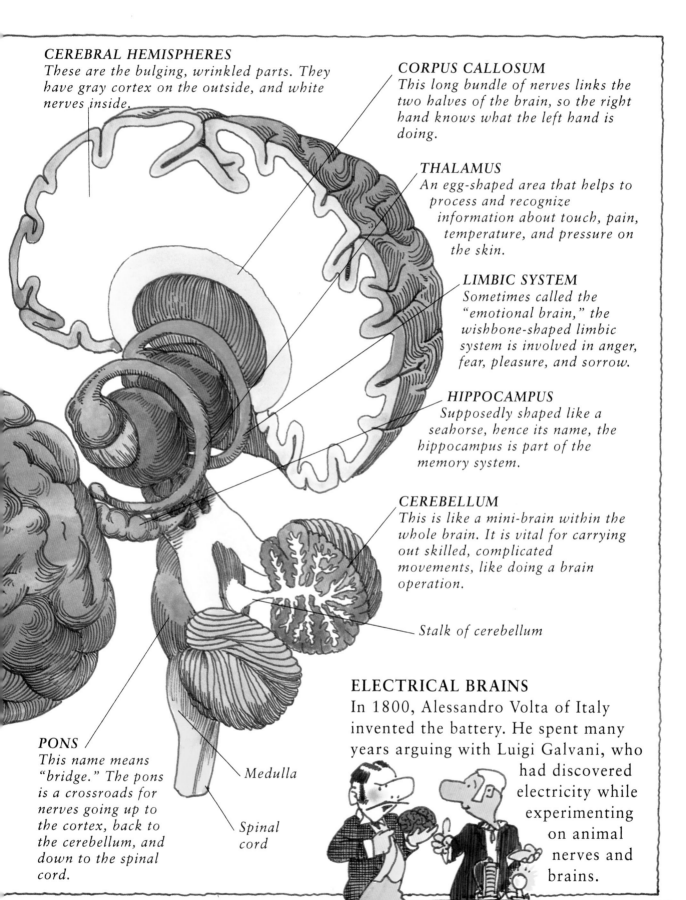

**CEREBRAL HEMISPHERES**
These are the bulging, wrinkled parts. They have gray cortex on the outside, and white nerves inside.

**CORPUS CALLOSUM**
This long bundle of nerves links the two halves of the brain, so the right hand knows what the left hand is doing.

**THALAMUS**
An egg-shaped area that helps to process and recognize information about touch, pain, temperature, and pressure on the skin.

**LIMBIC SYSTEM**
Sometimes called the "emotional brain," the wishbone-shaped limbic system is involved in anger, fear, pleasure, and sorrow.

**HIPPOCAMPUS**
Supposedly shaped like a seahorse, hence its name, the hippocampus is part of the memory system.

**CEREBELLUM**
This is like a mini-brain within the whole brain. It is vital for carrying out skilled, complicated movements, like doing a brain operation.

Stalk of cerebellum

**PONS**
This name means "bridge." The pons is a crossroads for nerves going up to the cortex, back to the cerebellum, and down to the spinal cord.

Medulla

Spinal cord

**ELECTRICAL BRAINS**
In 1800, Alessandro Volta of Italy invented the battery. He spent many years arguing with Luigi Galvani, who had discovered electricity while experimenting on animal nerves and brains.

113

# Marsupials

Marsupials, or pouched mammals, differ from humans in that they carry their underdeveloped newborns in a pouch outside the mother's stomach. They feed on grass and other plant life, and mostly inhabit grasslands and forests. There are several types of marsupials, such as kangaroos, wombats, opossums, wallabies, and Koala bears.

The Red Kangaroo is the largest of the marsupials. It can grow as large as 6½ feet long and 200 pounds in weight. However, at birth they are only ¾ inch long and $\frac{1}{30}$ oz. The baby is born after only five weeks in its mother's womb, and spends the next six months inside her pouch feeding on her milk.

*The babies of most mammals grow and develop inside their mother's body until they are fully formed. They get all their nutrients from a sack inside the womb called a* placenta. *But female marsupials do not have placentas; their babies come out of the womb at a very early stage and suckle milk constantly until they can look after themselves.*

marsupial mouse

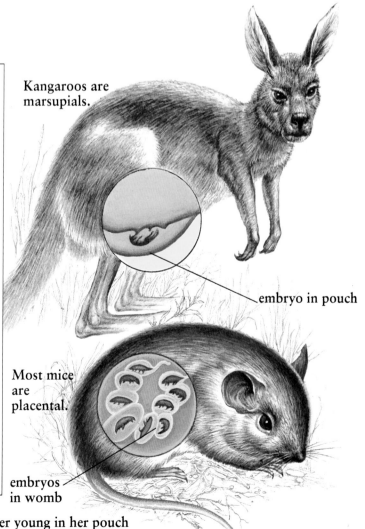

Kangaroos are marsupials.

embryo in pouch

Most mice are placental.

embryos in womb

◁ A mother Gray Kangaroo with her young in her pouch

# SPEED AND ACCELERATION

Speed is how fast something is moving. Velocity describes both speed and direction. When a car turns a corner, speed may stay the same, but velocity changes. Speed describes how far an object travels in a period of time. For example, a snail moves at about 0.03 miles per hour, while Concorde travels about 1,300 miles per hour. A speedometer, like the one pictured here, indicates how fast a car is moving. Acceleration is how much the speed increases in a period of time. A decrease in speed is called deceleration.

## AT FULL SPEED

**1**

**2.** Tape one end of the road to the narrow end of a shoe box. It can be lifted to different heights.

**3**

**1.** Cut the road from stiff cardboard as wide as a shoe box, but twice as long. Secure a small peice of cardboard in the middle of one side with a paper fastener.

**2**

**3.** Cut out one quarter of a circle. Divide it into angles of 10 degrees, and cut slits along the edge. Attach to the side of the box.

**4.** Check that the piece of cardboard on the road is in the correct position to slide into a notch. Pierce a hole in the lid of the plastic bottle. Cut off the bottom section. Tape over the hole, invert and fill with paint. Mount on top of the car.

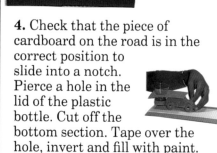

**4**

## WHY IT WORKS

By observing the distance between the drops of paint on the inclined ramps you can estimate the speed of the vehicle. When they are close together, the speed is slowest. If the spaces are uniform, the vehicle must be traveling at a constant speed. If the spaces widen, the vehicle has accelerated, if they narrow it has decelerated. The bigger the mass of an object, the greater the force needed to make it move. When the slope is steeper, the truck accelerates faster. The spaces between the drops are wider apart toward the bottom of the slope. The speed can be calculated by dividing the distance by the time taken.

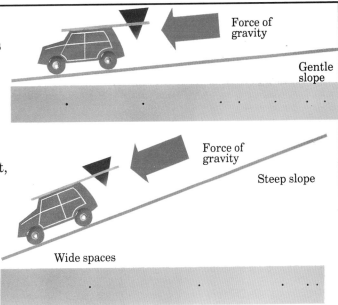

Force of gravity

Gentle slope

Force of gravity

Steep slope

Wide spaces

## BRIGHT IDEAS

Use a variety of toy cars on a sloping ramp and experiment with differing angles. Which car travels furthest? Did you use the same "push" each time to ensure a controlled experiment?

Run the same car down a variety of angles, and allow it to run into a shoe box each time. Measure the distance that the box has moved. The distance that it moves depends on the speed.

Try running on a beach at various speeds. Use a stop-watch to time yourself and measure the spaces between the footprints. Your footprints will be further apart, the faster you run.

**5**

**5.** Set the angle of the road. Place a long piece of paper over the road to record your results each time. Position the car at the top of the slope. Remove the tape just before it is released. Time each run accurately. Be careful not to push the car.

# WATER AT WORK

From industry to agriculture to generating power for factories and homes, we make water work for us. To make the paper for this book, about 4 gallons of water were used, and other industrial processes, such as making cars, use vast amounts of water. Some power stations use water to generate electricity, while others need large quantities of water to cool machinery – you can often see water vapor escaping into the atmosphere through huge cooling towers (shown above).

## Water power

Water generates power when it flows from a higher to a lower place. Waterwheels were originally used to capture the energy of flowing water and use it to turn millstones that ground corn or wheat into flour. Today, turbines use moving water to generate electricity. Modern turbines are huge machines weighing thousands of tons. They are usually placed at the bottom of a dam to make the best use of the energy made by falling water.

Waterwheel

The Itaipú Dam (shown above), on the Paraná River in Brazil, is one of the world's largest hydro-electric dams. Its 18 turbines can produce 13 million kilowatts of electricity.

## Industry

In the United States, industry uses around 320 million gallons of water each day. Water is used for washing, cleaning, cooling, dissolving substances and even for transporting materials, such as logs for the timber industry (above). About 7,100 gallons of water are needed to make a car and eight quarts of water are used to produce just one quart of lemonade. The largest industrial users of water are paper, petroleum, chemicals, and the iron and steel-making industries.

### Dam problems

Dams can cause problems for people and for the environment. Before a dam is built, people and animals have to be cleared from the area. If trees or plants are left to rot under the water, they make the water acidic and the acid may corrode (eat away) the machinery inside the dam. Reservoirs may become clogged by mud and silt which cannot be washed away downstream.

## Irrigation

Crop plants, such as wheat or rice, need large quantities of water to grow properly. In places where there is not enough water, or the supply varies with the seasons, farmers irrigate the land. Most irrigation systems involve a network of canals and ditches to carry water to the crops. The sprinkler irrigation system (below) has an engine and wheels and moves across a field spraying crops with a fine mist of water.

Flood irrigation is used to grow rice. The fields of young rice plants are flooded, covering them in water. These fields are called paddy fields (above). It takes about 9,900 pounds of water to grow just one pound of rice.

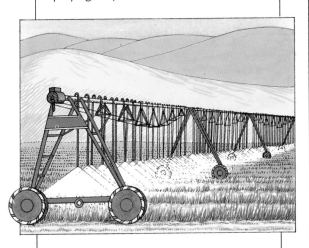

An Archimedes screw lifts water up a spiral screw to a higher level. The device was invented by the Greek scientist Archimedes over 2,000 years ago. It is still used in some parts of the world today.

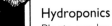

## Hydroponics

Plants can be grown without soil using a watering technique called hydroponics. A carefully controlled mixture of nutrients are dissolved in water and passed over the roots of plants which are suspended in a tank of water. Hydroponics does not produce better or larger crops, but it is important in the study of plants and can be used in areas where soil is not easily available, such as on board a ship or in Arctic areas.

## Solar salt

For centuries, salt has been a vital part in people's diets and has even been used instead of money. In countries such as China, India and France, salt is harvested from seawater and used for food flavoring or to make industrial chemicals. Seawater is left in shallow pools in the hot sun so the water evaporates, or disappears, into the air. Salt crystals are left behind and can be raked by hand or collected by machines. The salt is then taken to a refinery where it is crushed, ground and sorted before being packaged and sold. Evaporating seawater is the oldest method of obtaining salt. This kind of salt is called solar salt.

# DINOSAUR EXTINCTION

The most intriguing question about dinosaurs has always been "why did they die out?" There is no simple answer to this question, even though many hundreds of scientists are studying the problem. They are not studying the extinction of the dinosaurs alone, but the whole question of extinction. Many other plants and animals have died out in the past, and it is important to understand how and why this happened. Having this information could help save many species that are under threat in the modern world. Humans are causing extinctions now, because of pollution and other damage to the environment. Maybe the dinosaurs can tell us how to save the earth today, because of their extinction 65 million years ago!

## Early ideas
Some of the early dinosaur scientists, 100 years ago, thought the dinosaurs died out because the air changed, and they could not breathe. Others thought that the dinosaurs disappeared simply because they became too big. They were too heavy to move without falling over, and could not find enough food to survive.

One theory is that a huge killer meteorite hit the earth. Smaller meteorites have fallen since then, making craters like this one in Arizona.

## Survivors
Whatever happened 65 million years ago, most plants and animals were not wiped out. Among the reptiles, the crocodiles, turtles, tortoises, lizards, and snakes survived. So too did the mammals, birds, amphibians, fish, and most plants and sea creatures.

Tortoise

Crocodile

Perhaps huge amounts of lava poured out of volcanoes in India. This sent up vast clouds of dust that blacked out the sun, and made the earth icy cold.

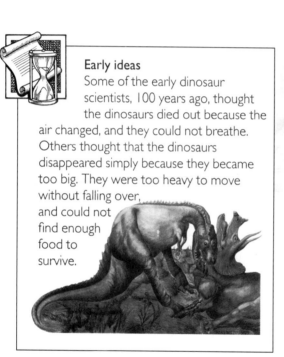

## Dinosaurs and people in films

A lot of dinosaur films in the past have shown people and dinosaurs living at the same time. There are often epic battles between spear-waving cavemen and dinosaurs. No human being, however, could have wrestled with a dinosaur, since the dinosaurs died out 60 million years before the first humans lived!

Evidence from fossil leaves (above) shows that climates became colder. Perhaps that was enough to kill off the dinosaurs?

## Measuring rates of extinction

You've probably heard the expression "dead as a Dodo." The Dodo is just one of millions of species of plants and animals that have died out. Extinction is quite normal. However, sometimes so many species die out all at the same time that something unusual must have been going on. One of these mass extinctions happened when the dinosaurs died out.

**Dodo**

## The final curtain

Dinosaurs were not the only animals to die out 65 million years ago. The flying pterosaurs also disappeared, as did the swimming plesiosaurs and some other reptile groups and shellfish in the sea. Many other plants and animals, however, did survive, and life on earth had returned to "normal" about 10 million years later. "Normality," of course, also meant a world without the dinosaurs. 160 million years of domination by these beasts had ended.

# MOTORCYCLES
## FASTER AND SAFER

The quickest way through the traffic is on a motorcycle. But while cars have been getting safer and more economical, motorcycles have gone the other way. Better and better performances from bigger and bigger engines may be exciting, but fuel economy has suffered. A typical, modern "superbike" has an engine as powerful as most cars, and gets no more than 40 miles per gallon. Meanwhile, little progress has been made toward creating a safer bike, or one that protects the rider from the cold and wet. "A rider simply gets colder, and wetter, and uses more fuel on a bike than in a car," says British motorcycle enthusiast Royce Creasey, who designed his own improved machine, the *Voyager*.

*The BMW C1, a prototype machine, protects the rider from the weather with a full roof and the option of fitting side panels for long journeys. Anti-lock brakes and an air-bag can be fitted, and there is space for luggage. Most car journeys are short (an average of just four miles) and are made alone; perfect for a motorcycle.*

*The safety of the C1 is provided by a strong, aluminum space frame, made of tubes welded together. In a crash, this would distort in a controlled fashion,* *providing a motorcycle for the first time with "crumple zones" just like those of a modern car. Computer simulation shows that the C1, in fact, provides the same protection in a head-on collision as a small car. The frame would also protect the rider from glancing blows and from being thrown over the handlebars, a major cause of serious injury.*

*Rear wheel*

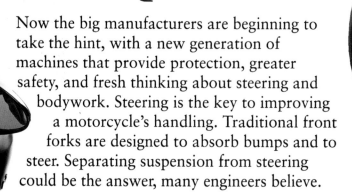

Now the big manufacturers are beginning to take the hint, with a new generation of machines that provide protection, greater safety, and fresh thinking about steering and bodywork. Steering is the key to improving a motorcycle's handling. Traditional front forks are designed to absorb bumps and to steer. Separating suspension from steering could be the answer, many engineers believe.

*The rotor draws the fuel through the inlet port, and into the cavity.*

*As the rotor continues to turn, the fuel is compressed into a smaller space. The spark plug fires.*

*The burning fuel expands into the larger space beyond the plugs, driving the rotor around. As the rotor turns, it exposes the exhaust ports, and the burned fuel escapes.*

# THE WANKEL ENGINE
## HOW ROTARY ENGINES WORK

The ultimate engine for a motorcycle is one that does not vibrate as pistons and connecting rods hurl themselves to and fro thousands of times a minute. Such an engine was designed in 1956 by German engineer Felix Wankel, and fitted in the late 1980s to the *Norton Commander*, claimed to be "the smoothest motorcycle in the world." The Wankel engine has a triangular rotor, geared to the drive shaft, and rotating in the combustion chamber. As it turns, the rotor draws in fuel, compresses it, ignites it, and finally exhausts it like a normal four-stroke. It works: but wear on the rotors, poor fuel consumption, and high emission levels count against it.

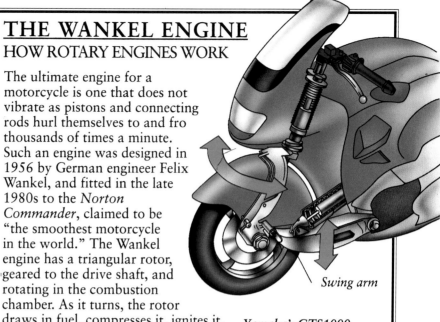

*Swing arm*

*Yamaha's GTS1000 makes a break with traditional front forks. The wheel is mounted on a swing arm with a single shock-absorber. The steering column does not have to absorb shocks at the same time as steering.*

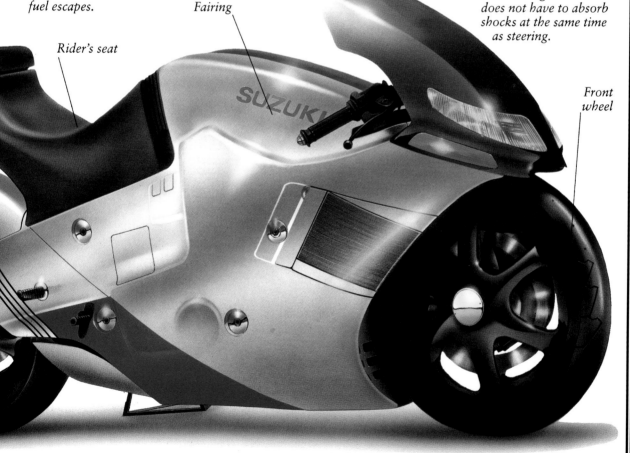

*Fairing*

*Rider's seat*

*Front wheel*

# *Popular* PYRAMIDS

Central and South America saw the rise and fall of many civilizations, such as the Olmecs, Toltecs, Maya, Incas, and Aztecs, before the arrival of European settlers in the sixteenth century. These peoples first built great mounds of earth, then developed flat-topped pyramids by casing the mounds in stone with steep steps. These were places where gods and people could meet. The pyramids had temples on top, but some had burials underneath. The Europeans destroyed hundreds of ancient cities, and many treasures and artifacts were lost.

**SACRIFICE AND CEREMONY**
*To please their gods, the Maya offered their own blood at special rites. Sometimes they also offered human lives. The Aztecs believed that their many gods needed human hearts to stay strong, and sacrificed thousands of people to them. Aztec and Mayan sacrifices were made before shrines on flat-topped pyramids, like that at Tikal in Guatemala (right). Mysterious picture writing has been found on some Mayan pyramids, and is now being translated.*

**INCA PYRAMID MOUNDS**
*The Incas ruled a vast area of South America in the fifteenth century. In the city of Cuzco in Peru they built a great temple called the Coricancha (right) for their sun-god, Inti. There they offered food and beer and sacrificed animals to their god.*

**THE MODERN MONUMENT**
*A glass pyramid (right) is the entrance to the Louvre Museum in Paris.*

*Did other peoples mummify their dead?*
Mummification is a very old practice in South America. Mummies of the Nazca people in Peru date from about 200 B.C. to A.D. 500. Human sacrifices were sometimes buried in the Andean mountains, where they were naturally preserved in the snow and ice.

**REMEMBERING THE DEAD**
*Stone or ceramic funeral masks were used in the traditional funeral rites of several Native American cultures, similar to those of the Egyptians.*

**NORTH AMERICA**
*Some Native North American people also built pyramids. The Mississippians built towns in A.D. 700–1500. The important buildings were set on great mounds of earth (above). Many cultures buried their dead in earth mounds with gifts.*

### A lasting impression
In modern times, architects have used pyramid shapes and Egyptian decorations as part of their designs. For Example, the casino based on the Great Pyramid which was built in Las Vegas. It is the same size as Khufu's tomb, and is guarded by a giant Sphinx! Decorations, such as those on the Empire State Building or these apartments in San Francisco (below), are directly influenced by Egyptian pyramid paintings, while tiles and decorations often show decorative papyrus-leaf designs.

*Biblical buildings*
*The early people of Mesopotamia built mud-brick temples on platforms on the ruins of older temples. The platforms grew taller over the years and became huge, stepped mounds similar to early pyramids.*

*We call them ziggurats. The great ziggurat Etemenanki was built by King Nebuchadnezzar (630-562 B.C.) in Babylon, home of the famous Hanging Gardens. It might have given rise to the story of the Tower of Babel (right).*

# BABY MAMMALS

Young mammals do not have to fend for themselves until they are almost fully grown. Some, like mice, are born with their eyes closed, have no fur and are cared for in a cosy nest. Others, like zebra foals, are able to run with their mothers very soon after birth. All mammal babies, however, are fed on milk. Mothers, and sometimes fathers, keep their babies clean and warm, teach them the skills they will need in adult life, and protect them from predators. Baby mammals spend a lot of time playing, which strengthens their bodies and improves their co-ordination.

## Multi-birth

Wolves grow up in large families. This mother wolf suckles four cubs. She provides shelter in a den and the rest of the adult pack protect them. Babies brought up in dens or nests are happy to be left alone while the mother goes out to search for food. She cannot take them with her until they are much bigger and stronger.

### Number of Babies

Having lots of babies at a time is an insurance policy. Parents divide their energy between all the babies in the hope that at least one of them will survive attacks from predators (below). Having only one baby at a time is too risky; if the baby dies the parents have wasted all their energy.

## Only Child

The mother sloth hangs upside down and carries her single infant on her stomach. This way she does not need to leave it alone in a den and can protect it all the time. The baby suckles for about one month, but stays put for another five months, reaching out to grab leaves as its mother slowly creeps along the branches. Eventually, it slowly wanders off on its own.

## Baby Face

All parents find their babies attractive. This ensures that they will care for their young. The features of all baby mammals are similar — huge eyes set in round faces. These features often appeal to cartoonists and animators. The film *Watership Down*, about a rabbit warren endangered by human destruction, stars young rabbits who have appealing features and individual personalities.

## Growth Rates

The rate at which a baby animal grows depends partly on its size. A harvest mouse is independent at 16 days — a giraffe grows for ten years. A gorilla baby also takes ten years to grow. It is much smaller than a giraffe, but it has a much bigger brain. The fastest growth rate of any baby mammal is that of the baby blue whale. During the last two months of pregnancy it puts on 220 pounds of weight daily.

The simplest family is a mother and her babies. In some cases a father is present. Elephants form stable families where babies are looked after by sisters and aunts. The leader is an old female called the *matriarch*.

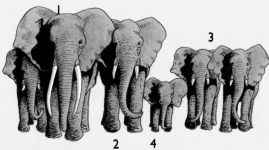

Meet the family...

1. Sire Bull

2. Matriarch

3. Sisters and Aunts

4. Infant

127

# WHAT IF ROCKETS HADN'T BEEN INVENTED?

We would still be wondering about the empty space above us, instead of launching astronauts into space and sending probes on space missions. A rocket can fly fast enough to get into space. To do this, it must reach the speed called *escape velocity*, 17,700 mph ( 28,500 km/h), to escape from the pull of Earth's gravity. A rocket engine can work in airless space, unlike jets and other engines, as explained below. The other way to get into space might be a gigantic gun that fires spacecraft and satellites into space. However, any astronaut would be crushed by the g-forces of acceleration!

## Dawn of the rocket age

The first rockets used a type of gunpowder and flew in warfare in China, in A.D. 1232. The first modern rocket to use the liquid fuel that today's rockets use was launched by American scientist Robert Goddard in 1926.

## Why can't jets fly in space?

Like a jet engine, a rocket burns fuel in a type of continuous explosion. Hot gases blast out of the back, and thrust the engine forward. Space has no air, which is needed for the burning that takes place inside the jet engine. A rocket must carry its own supply of oxygen.

Rocket

Combustion chamber    Oxidizer Fuel

Jet

Fuel

Air

Combustion chamber

Compressor turbine

**Rockets and jets**
Rockets carry their own oxidizer substance. Jets, however, need oxygen from the air to burn their fuel.

# Up, up, and away in my beautiful balloon

Special weather balloons go higher than 31 miles (50 km). They carry radiosondes that measure temperature, air pressure, and humidity, and send back the results by radio. The balloon is quite small and floppy when it takes off, but it gradually expands as it rises, as the air pressure decreases. However, no weather balloon could carry a heavy satellite high enough, or give it the required speed to put it in orbit.

## Would we have fabulous firework displays?

Perhaps, but we would have to power the rockets by other types of engines, maybe a mini jet engine. Firework rockets use solid fuel such as gunpowder or other fuel-oxidizer mixtures to launch into the air. Many space rockets use liquid fuel, and have the propellant and oxidizer in liquid form.

## Multi-staged rockets

A staged rocket may have two, three, or more rockets, placed on top of each other in decreasing size. The biggest one launches the entire rocket, then stops firing and falls away. The rocket's weight is now less and so is the effect of the Earth's gravity, so the second-stage rocket is much smaller, and so on with the remaining stages. Extra rockets, called boosters, may assist the main rocket engine at launch and then fall away, as in the space shuttle.

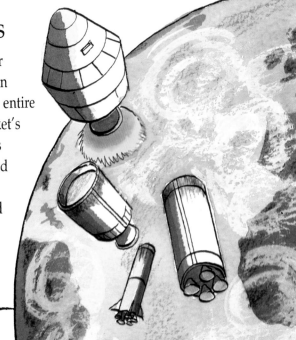

# THE WORLD OF WOODWIND

The woodwind family includes the clarinet, oboe, English horn, bassoon, and saxophone, which use a single or double reed to make the air vibrate inside the instrument. Many different kinds of musicians play woodwind instruments, from the musician on the street corner to the folk or jazz player, and the professional in the concert hall.

Woodwind instruments are important in the orchestra, and are also used in chamber music, played by a small group of musicians. The wind quintet is a popular combination for chamber music, but almost any group of instruments can play. The position of woodwind in the orchestra is shown below right.

Flutes and other woodwind instruments are used as solo concert instruments or are accompanied by the piano, harp, or guitar. Baroque music now performed by the flute and piano was probably written for another keyboard instrument, the harpsichord. A good performer will communicate with both the accompanist and the audience.

If you get the chance, join a chamber group or an orchestra. Look for these orchestral pieces with famous woodwind passages:
Debussy, *L'après-midi d'un faune*
Stravinsky, *Petrouchka* and *Firebird*
Saint-Saëns, *Carnival of the Animals*
Prokofiev, *Peter and the Wolf*
Rossini, *William Tell Overture*

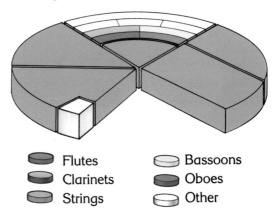

- Flutes
- Clarinets
- Strings
- Bassoons
- Oboes
- Other

## JAMES GALWAY

James Galway is one of the best known flutists performing today. He is famous for his golden flute and the recordings he has made of concertos by Khachaturian and Rodrigo — the second of these was actually written for Galway. These pieces show off his bright, brilliant sound, and his superb tongue and finger technique.

Flute     Oboe     French Horn     Clarinet     Bassoon

The standard woodwind instruments are the flute, clarinet, oboe, and bassoon. Each instrument has larger or smaller relatives which produce a lower or higher sound. The little cousin of the flute is the piccolo, which is pitched an octave higher.

The clarinet, oboe, and bassoon all have vibrating reeds. The oboe has a double reed and a conical shape, opening out at the bottom. It produces a mellow sound. Richard Strauss and Vaughan Williams have written concertos for the oboe.

The clarinet has a single reed which vibrates against the mouthpiece. It has a beautiful, flowing sound and a range of three and a half octaves. Clarinets emerged in the 18th century, and were improved by Boehm. The bass clarinet is pitched an octave lower.

The bassoon has a distinct tone, which can sound comic or sorrowful. It, too, has a double reed. Its relative, the contrabassoon, plays an octave lower. The wind quintet (above) is completed by the horn, a member of the family of brass instruments.

# WHAT IS ELECTRICITY?

Electricity is an invisible form of energy which is stored in electrons and protons. These are the tiny particles in atoms (below) which make up all matter. Electricity is created when there is an imbalance of negatively charged electrons and positively charged protons. Current electricity is made up of moving electrons which travel through wires. In static electricity the electrons remain still. Electricity is a powerful and useful source of energy, but it can also be very dangerous.

### Discovering electricity

Electricity was first discovered by the ancient Greeks, about 2,000 years ago. A Greek scientist called Thales noticed that a piece of amber (the hard fossilized sap from trees) attracted straw or feathers when he rubbed it with a cloth. The word "electricity" comes from the Greek word for amber – "elektron."

In 1600, William Gilbert (left), a doctor to Queen Elizabeth I of England, was the first person to use the word "electric." He carried out experiments and discovered that materials such as diamond, glass and wax behaved in a similar way to amber.

the atom's nucleus – made up of protons (green) and neutrons (black)

### From the stars

The Sun and other stars send out radio waves through space. They are a form of electrical and magnetic energy which travel through space at the speed of light. They are picked up by huge dishes called radio telescopes. The radio waves are changed into electrical signals that give astronomers information about distant galaxies.

## Investigating static electricity

Static electricity, used inside photocopiers and paint-spraying machines, can be generated by rubbing different materials together.

You can test materials for static charges, which are either positive or negative. Opposite charges attract things and like charges repel things. Experiment by rubbing different materials such as paper, plastic, metal, wood, and rubber with a cloth. Do they attract or repel things? Make a chart of your results.

## Electrons everywhere

A particle accelerator (above) is used for research into atoms. By smashing atoms together, scientists have discovered over 200 particles, even smaller than atoms. A beam of electrons in an electron microscope (above left) enlarges objects millions of times.

negatively charged electron

## Switch on the light

In fluorescent lights, an electric current makes gas glow. Neon gas makes red light, sodium gas yellow light, and mercury gas makes blue light.

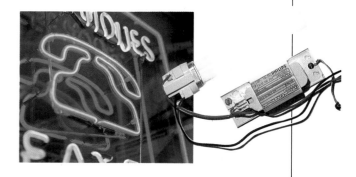

## Electricity for life

Most animals rely on electrical signals which provide them with information about their environment and control the way their body works. A network of nerve cells collects the information and sends out instructions. Invertebrates such as an octopus (right) have simple nerve nets.

Humans have more complex systems. The brain has an intricate network of nervous tissue (below). Our brain buzzes with tiny electrical signals, which trigger our heart-beats, to make our muscles move and sustain our body processes.

# SEASONS

A season is a time of year with a particular kind of weather. Each season has a different effect on plant and animal life. Areas around the poles have only two seasons – six months of summer, when it is light nearly all the time, and six months of winter, when it is dark most of the time. Places near the equator have less defined seasons. Often there are only two, one wet and one dry. It is hot all year round, and the length of the day stays the same all year. Temperate regions between the equator and the poles, have four seasons – spring, summer, fall, and winter. The days are longer in summer and shorter in winter.

## Life in the fall and winter

During these seasons, the weather may turn cooler, wetter, and more windy. There is little food for animals to eat. Some gather stores of food in the fall to help them survive the winter. Plants also rest over the winter when it is too cold for them to grow and water in the soil is frozen. Areas closer to the equator remain warm.

People in the north-east of Brazil (above) can still spend time on the beach, even in the winter.

Winter in Canada (above) often brings snow.

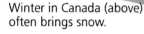

### Seasonal festivals

In the northern hemisphere, the Christian festival of Easter happens in springtime. Easter symbols, such as spring flowers and eggs, represent new life and the resurrection (or rising from the dead) of Jesus Christ. Some Hindu festivals are connected with the annual cycle of the seasons. Pongal, or Sankranti, marks the end of the south-east monsoon and the reaping of the harvest. Beautiful kilars (decorative designs) are traced on floors with moistened rice flour.

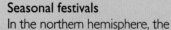

## Life in spring and summer

Spring in temperate climates brings warmer weather and the days get longer. Day and night are almost the same length. The warmth and spring showers encourage plants and trees to grow and buds to burst open. Many animals have their young in spring so that they will have time to grow strong enough to survive the cold autumn and winter seasons. Summer in the Mediterranean climate of Spain is very hot and dry. Olive trees (top left) are suited to this environment, and olive groves flourish.

Summer in Southeast Asia (above) and parts of eastern Africa can be very wet when the monsoon rains arrive between April and July.

### Hibernation and migration

To survive cold, hot, or dry seasons, animals may move away or migrate to warmer, cooler, or wetter places. The arctic tern migrates from one end of the world to the other and back again, covering about 25,000 miles a year. But other migrations, such as that of the wildebeest on the African grasslands, are over much shorter distances. Instead of moving away, other animals, such as dormice, stay put and go into a deep sleep in a safe place. This behavior is called hibernation in a cold climate and aestivation in a hot climate.

**Dormouse**

**Arctic tern**

**Spring bud**

### The four seasons

The Italian composer, violinist, and conductor Antonio Vivaldi (1678-1741) wrote four famous violin concertos called "The Four Seasons" in about 1725. Each one consists of three pieces which convey the characteristics of each season. It is one of Vivaldi's best known compositions. Vivaldi wrote nearly 50 operas, church music, and hundreds of concertos for almost every instrument known at the time.

# Tricks and IMAGINATION

In the 20th century, UFOs and aliens have become a familiar part of our culture. Many science fiction books are bestsellers, films like *E.T.*, *Close Encounters of the Third Kind*, *Alien*, and *Star Trek* attract enormous audiences, and organizations have been set up around the world to record and investigate UFO sightings. This fascination has led to some clever hoaxes. Many fake photographs of UFOs have been made by photographing miniature models in close-up, or by tampering with photographic negatives. Some people have faked UFO sightings and evidence of landings by spacecraft. There have even been suggestions that extraterrestrials are living in secret on Earth...and a few people have claimed to be aliens!

**THE REAL UFOS**
*During World War II, U.S. pilots reported seeing fiery balls in the sky, which they nicknamed "foo fighters." They were thought to be natural phenomena or UFOs. In fact, the Germans had invented disk-shaped anti-radar craft whose fuel caused a fiery "halo." Since then, Russia and the U.S. may have created a disk-shaped supersonic craft, using UFO reports as a cover-up.*

**STRANGE SIGHTS IN OUTER SPACE**
*Many reports of moving lights in the sky are often found later to be sightings of falling meteors or comets. Venus, the brightest planet in the night sky, is clearly visible with the naked eye and has frequently been mistaken for a UFO.*

**SKY LIGHTS**
*Ball lightning has scared people for centuries. It appears as a red, yellow, orange, or green fiery ball and is seen during storms, usually after ordinary lightning. No one knows why it occurs.*

## Fake photographs

A photograph of a UFO, apparently taken by an airline pilot over Venezuela in 1965, was believed to be genuine until 1971. A U.S. photographic expert pointed out that the UFO was too sharply outlined to be a distant object and could not have created the shadow underneath it. The "UFO" was a button, placed over a picture of the sky and re-photographed. The shadow had been chemically burned in during the processing of the film. This is one of the most convincing UFO fakes ever, but there have been many more since then!

### NATURAL UFOs

*Horizontal formations of cloud can look saucer-like, especially when light shines on them. Unusual weather conditions can cause strange signals on radar screens, which may be mistaken for UFOs.*

### THE CROWDED SKIES

*All kinds of flying objects have been mistaken for UFOs over the years, including planes, airships, weather balloons, satellites, kites, and even flocks of birds.*

### NEW THEORIES

*A report has suggested a link between alien stories and the drama of birth. Aliens are often described as having big heads and short limbs, like unborn babies. Do tales of bright tunnels resemble a baby's experience of being born?*

*How are movie UFOs created?*
For many years, special effects teams have used small models to create UFO effects. The models are photographed in a series of pictures which, when played back at speed, give the illusion of movement. Recently, hi-tech computer programs have made it possible to achieve even more spectacular extraterrestrial action, allowing animators to move and manipulate all sorts of images.

# THE FIRST FISHES

Fossil fishes are first recorded in rocks of Cambrian era, but preservation is quite poor. By the Ordovician, however, the fossils show enough detail for scientists to give names to the fishes. Fishes found in these rocks often had armor instead of scales and many did not have jaws. During the Devonian that followed, many new types of fishes evolved, including sharks and rays, and bony fishes. The Late Devonian also saw the evolution of *Eusthenopteron,* a fish that developed lungs and could walk on land using its strong front fins.

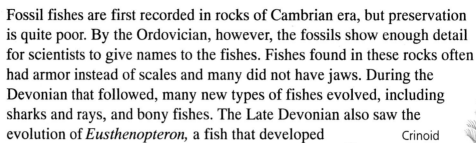

Crinoid

## Rare cones

Nautiloids are molluscs and are related to ammonites. During the Ordovician, most had straight, cone-shaped shells, instead of the familiar coiled shells of ammonites. At the end of the Permian period, all the straight cones became extinct. The coiled cones survived, and evolved to produce a variety of ammonites.

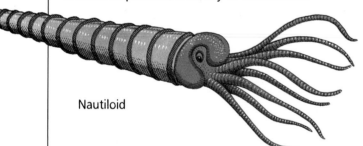

Nautiloid

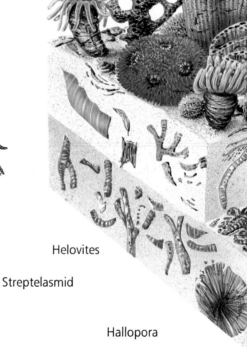

Helovites

Streptelasmid

Hallopora

### Protective armor

Some of the Devonian fishes were completely encased in an armor made up of bony plates, while others also relied on scales for protection. The osteostracans did not have armor that covered all of the body; it was limited to the head. The placoderms were a group of armored fishes that evolved many strange shapes. Their heads and forequarters were covered with heavy armor. These species were not very successful and did not survive the Devonian. Some, like *Coccosteus,* were probably good swimmers. Not all Devonian fish had armor; thelodonts and anaspids were covered with small scales.

## Ancient corals

Many rocks of the earlier part of the Paleozoic contain the remains of coral reefs. Corals are first known from the Cambrian, but it was not until the Silurian that large coral reefs became common. Two types of coral built the reefs. Colonial corals (for example *Favosites*) are made up of many animals all living in the same stony coral. Solitary corals only have one animal living in them. The reefs were home to other creatures including crinoids, nautiloids, trilobites, and fishes. Ancient corals tended to be larger than today's and lived singly, like sea anemones.

**Alive and kicking**
Coelacanths are known from fossils in rocks ranging from the Devonian to the Cretaceous, when it was thought they became extinct. In 1938, a strange fish was caught by fishermen off the southeastern coast of Africa. Scientists noticed the similarity between this fish with its leglike fins (called *Latimeria*), and fossils of prehistoric fish, and decided that the coelacanths are still alive today! *Latimeria* lives in the deep waters of the Indian Ocean.

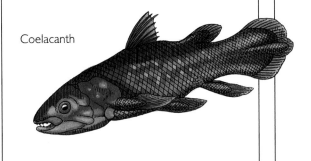

Coelacanth

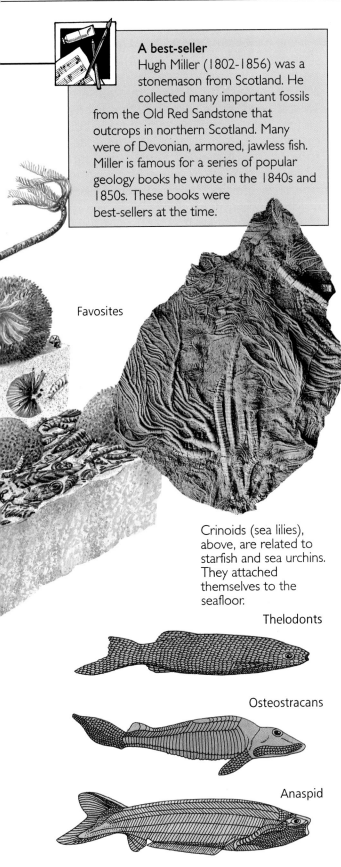

Favosites

Crinoids (sea lilies), above, are related to starfish and sea urchins. They attached themselves to the seafloor.

Thelodonts

Osteostracans

Anaspid

## Jawless fish

Most of the earliest fish did not have jaws. They belong to class Agnatha, which means "no jaws." They had a simple hole for a mouth and many must have grubbed about for organic debris in the sediment under the water. Today, there are two living groups of agnathans, the lampreys and the hagfish. It is thought that the class Gnathostomata (all of the vertebrates with jaws) evolved from jawless fish. The jaws were formed from some of the bones that supported the gills.

Dinithys

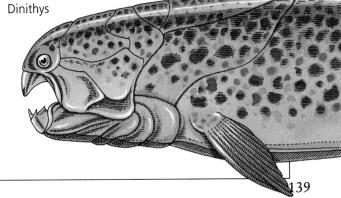

Different objects reflect different colors. This is because of a variety of substances they contain called pigments. Different pigments reflect different combinations of colors. Paints and dyes contain pigments. They can be used to change the color of things by changing the colors they reflect.

## BLUE AND YELLOW MAKE GREEN

Many objects contain more than one pigment. You can mix paints to see how the pigments combine to give different colors. Mixing pigments is quite different from mixing lights. The primary colors of pigments are said to be red, blue and yellow — but more accurately they are magenta, cyan and yellow. All colors can be made by mixing these primary colors. Mixing blue with yellow makes green. This is because blue paint (cyan) reflects violet, blue and green light. Yellow pigment appears yellow because it reflects red, orange, yellow and green light. The only color which both pigments reflect is green. Mixing all three primary colors makes black, since between them the pigments absorb all colors of light.

Printed color photographs are made by combining dots of the primary colors on the page. Use a magnifying glass to look at the dots that make up the photograph on the opposite page. Apart from magenta, cyan, and yellow, black is used to give extra contrast.

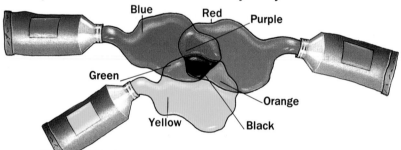

Blue   Red   Purple
Green
Yellow   Orange   Black

▷ These materials have been dyed bright colors to make them more attractive. Dyes can be made from plants or they may be man-made.

## USING CHROMATOGRAPHY

You can separate the pigments used in colored pens and inks. This is called chromatography. Cut a strip of blotting paper and draw a line of ink about 2 inches from one end. Hang the strip so that the end nearest the ink just dips into a dish of water. The pigments will soon spread up the paper. Each pigment travels at a different speed and so they separate. When the color is at the top of the paper take it out and let it dry.

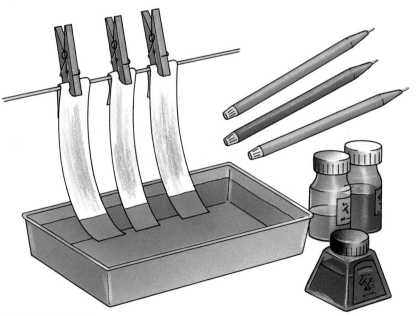

## MAKING DYES

You can make vegetable dyes to color material. You can use cherries (red), onion skins (yellow) and spinach (green), as well as many others. Ask an adult to boil the leaves or fruit in a pan with a little water and simmer the mixture for 15 minutes. When it has cooled, put a coffee filter into a funnel and pour the liquid through it into a pan. Leave the material you want to dye in the pan for a few minutes and then let it dry.

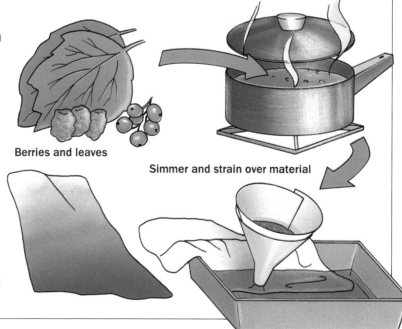

Berries and leaves

Simmer and strain over material

# FIGHTING SHIPS

Fighting ships were conceived as fighting platforms for troops to board and capture the enemy vessels. The early Egyptian galleys were probably the first real fighting ships, and although sails were added through the ages, galleys with banks of oarsmen were still in service until the 17th century. The great ships or galleons like the *Mary Rose* (which sank because she was made top heavy) were followed by the ships-of-the-line, like *Victory*. They used their broad sides of cannon fire to cripple opposing ships before boarding and capturing the enemy. The French *Gloire* (1859) was the first warship to carry iron armor plates, followed in 1860 by the English all-iron, screw-driven *Warrior*.

## Battleships
In *Warrior* (below), iron replaced wood, steam replaced sail, and guns replaced cannon. *Dreadnought* was one of the first new class of

battleships. It was launched in 1906, had ten 12-inch guns and a crew of 800 men. It was the first steam turbine-powered battleship.

HMS *Dreadnought*

## Triremes
The trireme (above) appeared in the Mediterranean around 500 B.C. A typical Greek trireme was about 130ft long and 20ft wide. It had three banks of oars operated by 170 oarsmen, and also carried warriors for combat. It attacked and sank other ships by ramming.

Fire control radar

Bridge

SAM launcher

Automatic gun

## Aircraft carriers
The first aircraft carriers were introduced between the two World Wars and during World War II they were the most important ship type.

Modern navies are based around aircraft carriers. The biggest carriers in the world are the *Nimitz* (below) class of the U.S. Navy. Their flight decks are 1080 feet long and they carry about 90 aircraft and helicopters.

## New Developments

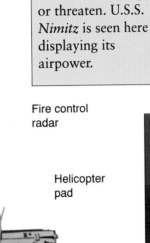

High-tech developments are likely in naval craft. The U.S. Navy's *Sea Shadow*, shown left, can avoid detection by radar.

## Gunboat diplomacy

One of the main jobs of today's fighting ships is to wait near political trouble spots. This military "show of strength" known as "gunboat diplomacy" can be used to support or threaten. U.S.S. *Nimitz* is seen here displaying its airpower.

Long range search

Navigation radar

Target information radar

Fire control radar

Helicopter pad

Battleships in the Gulf conflict used their huge guns and launched cruise missiles.

HMS *Glasgow*, a Sheffield (type 42) class destroyer.

## The modern ship

The use of iron and explosive shells revolutionized battleships. Modern fighting ships, such as the destroyer above, are fast, light, and crammed full of electronics. The gas turbine engines give it a top speed of 29 knots. Armament includes light guns, torpedoes, and surface-to-air (SAM) missiles for attacking aircraft. These are controlled by the computerized fire-control system. A helicopter is carried for antisubmarine operations. In a conflict, the ship's main role is to defend the fleet's aircraft carriers.

## High-speed boats

Some countries operate high-speed patrol boats around their coasts. They often include hydrofoils and hovercraft as well as gas turbine boats. Iranian gunboats sank several oil tankers in the Gulf with torpedoes, during the Iran/Iraq war of 1984/1985.

# AIR AND THE EARTH

The Earth is surrounded by the atmosphere, a big layer of air which formed about 4,500 million years ago. It is held in place by the pull of the Earth's gravity. The atmosphere works like a shield, keeping out harmful rays from the Sun and reducing the impact of rocks from space as they fly toward the Earth's surface. Life is only possible on Earth because the atmosphere prevents it getting too hot or cold.

### Measuring air pressure

Atmospheric pressure is endlessly changing – it pushes on us from all directions because of the gas molecules constantly jostling with each other.

To feel the effect of atmospheric pressure try this simple test. Place a piece of paper flat on a table, by the edge. Then slip a ruler between the paper and the table and lever the paper upward with the ruler. The force you feel working against you is atmospheric pressure.

### Colors of the sky

Sunlight is composed of all the colors of the rainbow. Molecules of gas in the atmosphere scatter the blue light more than the other colors. So extra blue light reaches our eyes and we see the sky as blue on clear days.

At sunrise or sunset, the Sun is low in the sky and has to shine through a thicker layer of atmosphere. More light is scattered aside by dust and gas molecules in the air and only the orange and red light gets through.

On the Moon, the sky looks black because there is no atmosphere with dust and gases to scatter the light.

### Layers in the atmosphere

The atmosphere can be divided into five main layers, although there are no physical barriers and the gases in the air move freely about. More than 75 percent of the atmosphere is in the troposphere, and all life and weather is in this layer. Above this, the stratosphere contains the ozone layer, which absorbs ultraviolet rays from the Sun. In the upper atmosphere, where the air is very thin, are the mesosphere, thermosphere and exosphere. In the thermosphere the air can reach temperatures as high as 4,000 degrees F.

144

## Space suits

Out in space, there is no air at all, so to travel to and from space or work outside their spacecraft, astronauts wear special space suits. These act as a kind of miniature atmosphere, providing air pressure (blood pressure would cause astronauts' bodies to explode otherwise), temperature control and pure oxygen. The early space suits used for walking on the Moon have been developed into sophisticated Manned Maneuvering Units. First used in 1984, these have an autopilot that keeps the astronaut in position using nitrogen gas-jets.

Exosphere – up to 650 miles

## Altitude

As you go higher and higher above the Earth, there is less and less air and the atmosphere becomes thinner. On high mountains, there is not enough oxygen in the air for climbers to breathe properly so they may take oxygen tanks with them. Mountain animals, and people living at high altitudes, develop large hearts and lungs to enable them to take more oxygen from the air.

Altitude sickness happens when people do not get enough oxygen. They may experience symptoms such as headaches, nausea, coughing, and sleeplessness.

Only 47 percent of the total radiation from the Sun ever reaches the Earth's surface. The rest is absorbed by the ozone layer (in the stratosphere) or is reflected back into the stratosphere by clouds.

Thermosphere – up to 300 miles

Mesosphere – up to 55 miles

Stratosphere – up to 33 miles

Tropopause

Troposphere – up to 14 miles

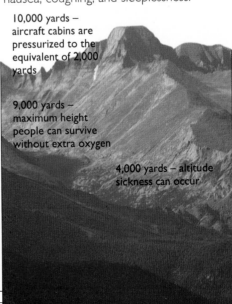

10,000 yards – aircraft cabins are pressurized to the equivalent of 2,000 yards

9,000 yards – maximum height people can survive without extra oxygen

4,000 yards – altitude sickness can occur

145

# INCA RELIGION

Religion cemented the unity of the Inca empire. At its heart was the cult of Inti, the Sun. Other important deities were Mamaquilla (the Moon), Pachamama (Mother Earth), Mamacocha (Mother Water) and Illapa (Thunder). These gods all represented Viracocha, the Creator. The Incas also worshiped holy sites, called *huacas*. The High Priest of the Sun and his assistants belonged to the imperial family. Mamacunas (chosen women) lived in convents. It was their duty to teach the *acllas* (virgins).

## The Inca Calendar
The Incas observed the sun, moon and stars. They established a solar calendar of twelve months, in accordance with the sun's position in the sky, which was marked by special stones (below). The Inca calendar cycle was respected throughout the empire.

## The Sapa Inca
To assert his power, each ruler claimed to be the son of the Sun. As the Sun ruled the skies, so the Supreme Inca ruled on Earth. When the Sapa Inca died, it was said that the Sun had summoned him. The bodies of dead rulers were mummified and were consulted as oracles (right). Their wishes were interpreted by the living Sapa Inca.

## Ceremony and Sacrifice
Religion was the focus for the entire Inca empire. One third of everything was passed on to the cult of Inti and the priests (right), who held an important position in Inca society. Llamas and guinea pigs formed part of this "taxation." If these were free from blemishes they were sacrificed to the air, frost, and water in order to ensure a good harvest. Sacrifices were also made to the Sun as it rose every day over the city of Cuzco.

146

## The cult of the Sun

Inti, the Sun, was worshiped as the "giver of life." Temples for the cult of Inti were built throughout the empire. At Cuzco's main temple the Incas kept gold images of the Sun (main picture). Herds and produce belonging to the Sun were used in rituals and as offerings. The cult's festivals were closely tied to the growing of crops (above). Inti Raimi, the Feast of the Sun, was celebrated on the winter solstice in the month belonging to June.

### Egyptian sun worship

From very early times the sun was also worshiped in the Nile Valley. During the Old and Middle Kingdoms of Egypt (c.2666-1640 B.C.), the supreme deity was Ra, the Sun God (below). His symbols were the pyramid and the obelisk, and he was shown sailing the heavens in a boat. The

cult of Ra showed itself most clearly in the raising of magnificent temples. For Egyptians, Ra was embodied in the Pharaohs, who were worshiped in the same way as Ra himself.

### Mummification

The Incas revered the remains of their ancestors. After the death of each emperor, his internal organs were removed and buried, and his body preserved. Dressed in fine fabrics and surrounded by precious objects, the bodies remained in the palace that each had inhabited in life. Thousands of years before, the Egyptians had also mummified their dead, and in South America, the Paracas people placed mummy bundles in deep caves (right).

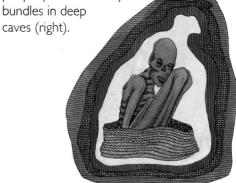

147

# WHAT ARE AMPHIBIANS?

**Major groups:** earthworm-like caecilians (150 species), newts and salamanders (350), eel-like sirens and species with minute limbs (4), frogs and toads (2,700).
**Distribution:** all wetlands except in polar regions.
**Largest:** Japanese and Chinese giant salamanders – 1.8m (6ft) long, 65kg (143lb) in weight.
**Smallest:** Arrow-poison frog – 8.5mm (0.3 in) long.

The name amphibian comes from two Greek words – *amphi* meaning both, and *bios* life. Young amphibians live in water. Like fish, they breathe using gills, use a tail and fins for swimming, and have a lateral line system. Adult amphibians are adapted mainly for life on land. They breathe using lungs or through their skin, have two pairs of limbs for walking or jumping, and have eyes, ears and a nose like those of true land vertebrates. Yet few adult amphibians are entirely independent of water. Most breed in water because their eggs need moisture, and amphibians dry out if their skin cannot be kept moist. Some American tree frogs, for example, spend their entire lives in trees, using rainwater "puddles" that collect at the bases of leaves to keep moist and for laying their eggs.

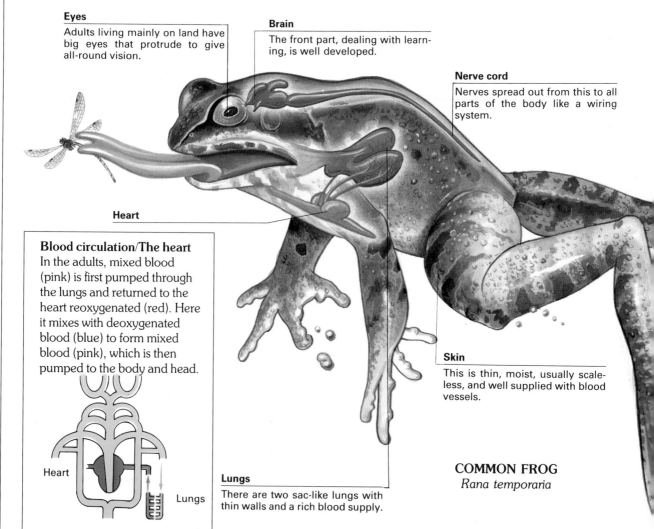

**Eyes**
Adults living mainly on land have big eyes that protrude to give all-round vision.

**Brain**
The front part, dealing with learning, is well developed.

**Nerve cord**
Nerves spread out from this to all parts of the body like a wiring system.

**Heart**

**Blood circulation/The heart**
In the adults, mixed blood (pink) is first pumped through the lungs and returned to the heart reoxygenated (red). Here it mixes with deoxygenated blood (blue) to form mixed blood (pink), which is then pumped to the body and head.

Heart

Lungs

**Lungs**
There are two sac-like lungs with thin walls and a rich blood supply.

**Skin**
This is thin, moist, usually scaleless, and well supplied with blood vessels.

**COMMON FROG**
*Rana temporaria*

# Metamorphosis

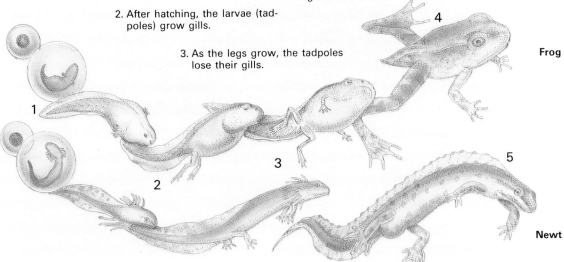

1. Female frogs and newts lay egg masses called spawn.

2. After hatching, the larvae (tadpoles) grow gills.

3. As the legs grow, the tadpoles lose their gills.

4. Frogs lose their tail as they grow into adults.

5. Newts keep their tails and some species grow a frill along the back.

**Frog**

**Newt**

A common feature of most amphibians, and certainly of the familiar frogs and toads, is that they undergo a complete change in appearance and internal body structure during their life history. The gradual change from aquatic larva to land-living adult is known as metamorphosis. In newts and salamanders this change is less dramatic.

The adult amphibians breed in water. The female produces eggs (spawn) that are protected by a layer of jelly. After a few days to several weeks the larvae, or tadpoles, hatch. Those of frogs and toads feed on tiny water plants, whereas newt larvae eat insect larvae and small soft-shelled animals. Then, the tadpoles start to take on adult features. They begin to lose their gills, and as their lungs grow they come to the surface to breathe. They start to eat insects such as flies and worms. Legs begin to grow – first the back ones and then the front ones – and the tail gets shorter and shorter (in frogs and toads) until it disappears. The young adults are then ready to come out on land.

**Skeleton**

Except for lack of ribs, this is like the skeleton of true land vertebrates.

**FROG SKELETON**

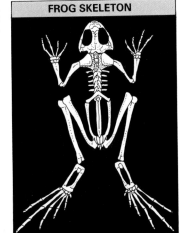

**Webbed feet**

Skin between the toes of the hind feet helps to push against the water.

# CHEMICAL REACTIONS

Have you ever wondered why cakes rise in the oven or what the bubbles in soda are actually made of ? The answer in each case is the same – carbon dioxide. Carbon dioxide is a gas which is formed when two atoms of oxygen join with one atom of carbon. The formula for carbon dioxide is $CO_2$. There are actually small amounts of carbon dioxide in the air and green plants give out $CO_2$ during the hours of darkness. The $CO_2$ in cakes, however, is not drawn from the air. It is produced when acids react with carbonates or bicarbonates which are present in the ingredients.

## VOLCANIC ERUPTION

**1.** Make a volcano which erupts with a foam of vinegar and baking powder. Form a cone shape around an old plastic cup or bowl. Glue the cone firmly to a base.

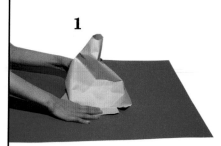

**2.** Cover the cone with 5 or 6 layers of newspaper and glue and leave to dry. Next, cover the base with glue and sprinkle with sawdust or sand. Paint the base and volcano.

**3.** When dry, a coat of sealing mixture (3 parts water to 1 part glue) will help to protect the paintwork when the volcano erupts. Once again, allow the whole thing to dry well before the next step.

**4.** Next, prepare the ingredients which will produce the reaction. You will need a small amount of baking powder or bicarbonate of soda and some vinegar mixed with a little red food-coloring.

**5.** Put a teaspoon of the baking powder into the volcano then pour in a little vinegar. The reaction should be fast and a red liquid containing carbon dioxide will foam up over the sides of your volcano as it "erupts."

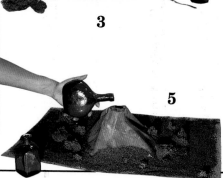

## WHY IT WORKS

The vinegar is an acid and it reacts with the sodium bicarbonate (which is an alkali) in the baking powder. This reaction produces carbon dioxide gas. If you add water to baking powder you would also get a reaction, although it would be a slower one. This is because the baking powder contains acidic salts which become acids when the water is added. These acids react with the sodium bicarbonate to produce $CO_2$. It is partly this reaction which causes cakes to rise in the oven.

Vinegar     Baking powder     Carbon dioxide

## BRIGHT IDEAS

Why not make your own fizzing lemonade? Mix the juice of 4 lemons with 1 quart of water then add sugar until your mixture tastes good. When you want a drink, pour out a glass, add half a teaspoon of bicarbonate of soda, stir, and drink at once!

**6.** Obviously, the more ingredients you use, the bigger the size of the eruption. A fizzing noise, known as effervescence, can be heard – this is the sound of the carbon dioxide gas being produced.

6

# FAMOUS COMPOSERS

The following list of famous composers have written music for piano, flute, trumpet, or violin. Some have written for all of these. The composers below span the Baroque (c.1600-1750), Classical (c.1750-1820), Romantic (c.1820-1900) periods as well as the new developments of the 20th century and present day. The Baroque period featured very elaborate, rich music, with new forms of vocal work. The Classical period emphasized a balance and elegance in the different sections of a piece of music. In the Romantic period composers believed music should be highly imaginative and emotional. The 1900s has seen many developments, such as new ideas in harmony, and popular music such as jazz.

---

**BACH, Johann Sebastian (1685-1750)**
A very famous German composer of the Baroque period. He was also a choirmaster and a brilliant organist. He wrote sonatas, suites, and cantatas and other orchestral works for many different instruments. His fugues (pieces in which the notes of a theme follow themselves up and down the keyboard) are particularly famous. Bach wrote much music for the organ, including "chorales" based on old German hymn tunes. He also wrote many works for the flute, including "The Musical Offering," written for Frederick the Great, and the B minor suite.

**BARTOK, Béla (1881-1945)**
Hungarian composer who developed a national style based on the folk and gypsy music of his country. This is clear in his writing for the violin.

J.S.Bach

**BEETHOVEN, Ludwig van (1770-1827)**
One of the greatest composers in history. A German composer who was revolutionary in that he broke away from the tradition of writing religious music, and wrote music to be listened to for its own sake. He wrote many dramatic concertos and sonatas for the piano. From the age of 30, Beethoven's hearing began to fail, and some of his greatest works were composed when he was deaf. His violin concerto, a powerful piece, opens with four ominous drumbeats. The virtuoso violin concerto went on to become a very popular form in the course of the 19th century.

**BERLIOZ, Hector (1803-69)**
A French composer who wrote his violin concerto in memory of a young girl. It begins with just the four open strings.

**BERNSTEIN, Leonard (1918-91)**
An American composer and conductor whose music is inspired by jazz, Broadway musicals, and traditional Jewish music.

**BIEDERBECKE, Bix (1903-1931)**
Jazz pianist, cornet-player, and composer, who wrote "Singin' the Blues" and "In A Mist."

**BIRTWISTLE, Harrison (b.1934)**
A present-day English composer who has written concertos for trumpet with orchestral accompaniment.

Bix Biederbecke

**BOULEZ, Pierre (b.1925)**
A French composer and conductor whose sonatine contains modern techniques which give the flute a wide range of expression.

**BRAHMS, Johann (1833-97)**
A great German composer, who has been regarded as the leading composer of Romantic symphonies, concertos, and chamber music. When he wrote his famous violin concerto it was first thought to be unplayable. It was called a concerto "not for but against the violin."

**BRITTEN, Benjamin (1913-76)**
A versatile English composer who has written work for particular performers, and for amateurs and children, such as "The War Requiem."

**BRUCH, Max (1838-1920)**
A German composer who wrote two very popular violin concertos.

**BYRD, William (1543-1623)**
An English composer

Claude Debussy

known for his religious music, and for being one of the first composers of keyboard music. The Renaissance period, between 1400 and 1600, saw the beginning of the great age of keyboard music. Byrd composed for the virginal, a stringed keyboard instrument similar to the harpsichord.

**CHAMINADE, Cécile Louise Stephanie (1857-1944)**
French composer and pianist whose flute concerto has a delightful Hollywood-style opening and furious technical sections.

**CHOPIN, Frédéric (1810-49)**
One of the greatest pianist-composers who wrote for solo piano. He discovered a new, poetic character

for the new 19th century piano.

**COPLAND, Aaron (1900-1991)**
American composer who wrote several film, ballet, and theatre scores.

**CORELLI, Arcangelo (1653-1713)**
A celebrated violinist and teacher, who was the first to write specifically for the violin. But even the hardest pieces he wrote seem quite easy by modern technical standards.

**COUPERIN, François (1668-1733)**
Couperin composed music for harpsichord and organ. Today this music is often played on the piano.

**DEBUSSY, Claude (1862-1918)**
A French pianist-composer. By the 19th century grand pianos had a beautiful sound and touch, and Debussy was very inspired by this. He created musical "impressions" of natural phenomena like rain, sunlight, and snow. His "L'apres-midi d'un faune" begins with a haunting flute solo, and his "Syrinx"

is possibly the best-known solo piece for the flute.

**DELIUS, Frederick (1862-1934)**
English composer who is famous for his rich harmonies and romantic music.

**DVORAK, Antonin (1841-1904)**
Czech composer whose symphonies, concertos and chamber music are colorful, and

George Gershwin

dramatic, reflecting the character of Czech music.

**ELGAR, Sir Edward William (1857-1934)**
A British violinist and composer of the Romantic tradition. He wrote many orchestral works, including "The Enigma Variations."

# COMETS

From time to time an object looking like a star with a tail appears in the sky. This is a comet. The solid portion of a comet is a mixture of water, ice, frozen gases, and rock. Comets travel far out in space away from the planets in elongated orbits. When their orbits bring them close to the sun, frozen gases on the rocky body vaporize and form the bright tail which always points away from the sun. Some comets are well known. Halley's comet, for example, returns every 76 years. Amateur astronomers have been very successful in discovering new comets, so keep your eyes and notebooks open.

## COMETS
A few comets are visible to the unaided eye. Others have to be viewed through binoculars or telescopes. Although many comets are well known, new comets are spotted from time to time and are always named after the person who first saw and recorded them.

## ORBITS OF COMETS

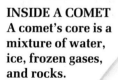

Very long orbit

Long orbit

Short orbit

Saturn's orbit    Jupiter's orbit

## INSIDE A COMET
A comet's core is a mixture of water, ice, frozen gases, and rocks.

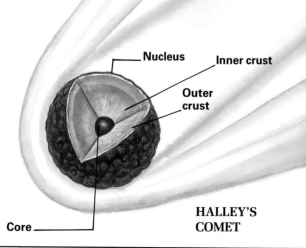

Nucleus    Inner crust

Outer crust

Core

HALLEY'S COMET

# ASTEROIDS

There are thousands of pieces of rock and iron orbiting in our solar system. We call them asteroids. One group of vast boulders orbits the sun in a "belt" between Mars and Jupiter. Another group, the Trojans, occupies the same orbit as Jupiter. This includes the largest asteroid, Ceres, which is over 600 miles across. A third group orbits close to Earth. The Martian moons, Phobos and Deimos, may be asteroids that have been captured by the planet's gravitational field.

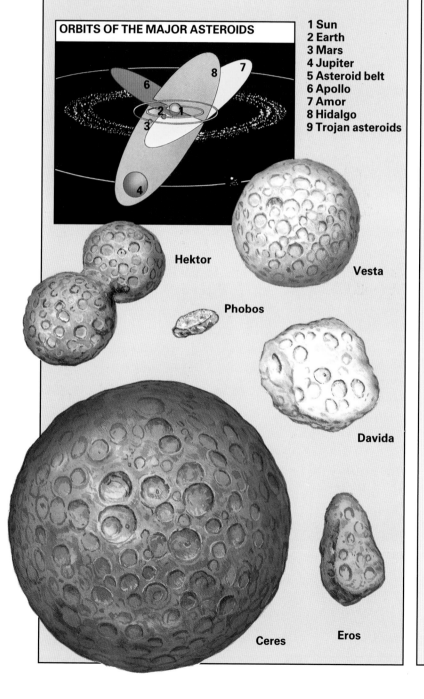

**ORBITS OF THE MAJOR ASTEROIDS**

1 Sun
2 Earth
3 Mars
4 Jupiter
5 Asteroid belt
6 Apollo
7 Amor
8 Hidalgo
9 Trojan asteroids

Hektor

Vesta

Phobos

Davida

Ceres

Eros

# METEORS

Meteors, which are sometimes produced when asteroids collide, appear as streaks of light whenever chunks of debris from space enter Earth's atmosphere and burn up. Meteors can be seen on almost any night. Regular meteor showers also occur when Earth passes through a stream of particles left by a comet. The Orionid shower, for example, (October 16th-26th) is caused by particles from Halley's comet.

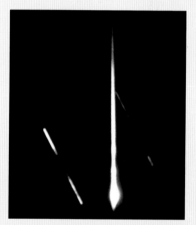

**Because of their brief appearance, meteors are also known as "shooting stars."**

**ROCKS FROM SPACE**
A meteor that reaches Earth without burning up is called a meteorite.

155

# THE ALL-SEEING BRAIN

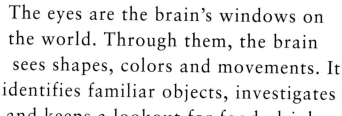

The eyes are the brain's windows on the world. Through them, the brain sees shapes, colors and movements. It identifies familiar objects, investigates strange ones, and keeps a lookout for food, drink, comfort, danger, and computer games.

## BRIGHT OR DIM?

No, not you – the light. The hole in the front of the eye, the pupil, gets smaller in bright light. This prevents too much light from damaging the retina. Eye color is the color of the iris.

*Bright light (blue eye)* *Dim light (brown eye)*

*Eyebrow-raising muscle*

*Eyelid-closing muscle*

**SPIES ON YOUR INSIDES**

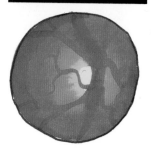

### BLINKING EYES
*Blinking smears tear fluid over the eye surface, to wipe off dust and germs.*

The doctor looks into the eye with a light-and-lens instrument, the ophthalmoscope. It shows the retina, blood vessels, and gives clues to the eye's health.

## SEEING
The cornea and lens bend light rays to focus a clear image onto the retina.

*Cornea*
*Iris*
*Pupil*
*Lens*

*Object*

*Cornea and lens*

*Upside down image*

*Nerve signals to brain*

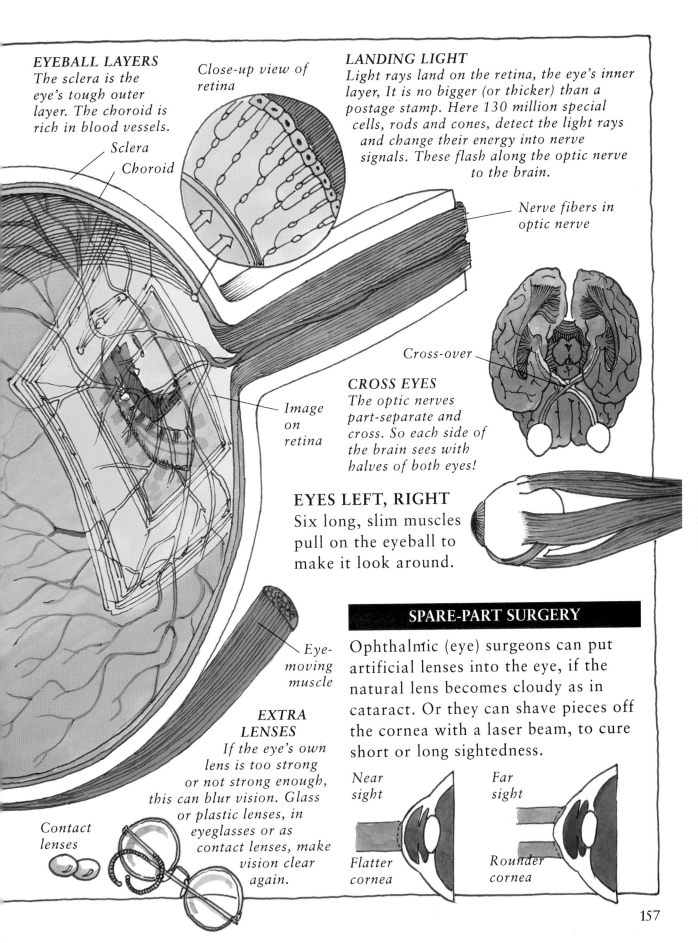

**EYEBALL LAYERS**
The sclera is the eye's tough outer layer. The choroid is rich in blood vessels.

Sclera

Choroid

Close-up view of retina

**LANDING LIGHT**
Light rays land on the retina, the eye's inner layer, It is no bigger (or thicker) than a postage stamp. Here 130 million special cells, rods and cones, detect the light rays and change their energy into nerve signals. These flash along the optic nerve to the brain.

Nerve fibers in optic nerve

Cross-over

Image on retina

**CROSS EYES**
The optic nerves part-separate and cross. So each side of the brain sees with halves of both eyes!

**EYES LEFT, RIGHT**
Six long, slim muscles pull on the eyeball to make it look around.

Eye-moving muscle

**EXTRA LENSES**
If the eye's own lens is too strong or not strong enough, this can blur vision. Glass or plastic lenses, in eyeglasses or as contact lenses, make vision clear again.

Contact lenses

**SPARE-PART SURGERY**

Ophthalmic (eye) surgeons can put artificial lenses into the eye, if the natural lens becomes cloudy as in cataract. Or they can shave pieces off the cornea with a laser beam, to cure short or long sightedness.

Near sight

Far sight

Flatter cornea

Rounder cornea

# Exploring the
# DEPTHS

**PRESSURE SUITS**
*Wearing some diving suits feels like wearing a submarine! The Wasp and Jim (left) are popular designs, in which a diver can reach 1,650 feet (500 m) with*
enough air for three days.
*However, the suits are expensive and clumsy to use.*

The early films of Hans and Lottie Hass and Jacques Cousteau allowed many people to explore the wonders of the underwater world on their own TV sets. Now, with modern diving suits and camera equipment, ordinary people can plunge into the oceans and examine their watery secrets for themselves. Louis Boutan, the inventor of the first underwater camera, would have been amazed to see the disposable waterproof cameras now for sale. Some resorts now offer submarine trips rather than boat tours. Soon you may be able to buy a submersible of your own!

*Do submarines ever get lost?*
On September 1, 1973, a small submersible, the *Pisces III*, was rescued from 1,580 feet (480 m) below sea level. Two men had been trapped inside for three days, after losing control of the craft and straying out of radio contact with their surface ship. It took two crewed submersibles and a robot vehicle to find and recover the submarine.

**OCEAN FLYERS**
Deep Flight One *(above) is a new craft that "flies" underwater. It is very strong, but weighs only as much as a large car.* Deep Flight Two *may soon take people down to the depths more easily than the clumsy* Trieste.

### FISHING THE DEEP

*Scientists can catch animals from the deep-sea floor by using special underwater sleds with nets. The sled is towed by a ship over the muddy seabed, on the end of a cable up to 9 miles (15 km) long. It can carry instruments to examine the water, and video or still cameras.*

### SNAPPING THE OCEANS

*Scientists have started dropping their cameras into the sea! The* Bathysnap *(left) is a special camera that sinks to the seabed and takes pictures of the mysterious animals that live deep down. When the film is finished, the camera is automatically released from the heavy weights which hold it and floats to the surface.*

## Say "Cheese!"

Louis Boutan took the first underwater photograph in 1893 (left), but his camera was heavy and clumsy. Today's cameras are small and light and have brought many of the ocean's mysteries to life. Special lamps emphasize colors and scenery. Remote-controlled still and video cameras can explore the seabed, sending back images to scientists on research ships. These pictures can be transmitted live to laboratories and museums worldwide.

### YELLOW SUBMARINE

*The British scientist Robert Leeds has recently designed a small "yellow submarine" (right), shaped like a flying saucer, for commercial use.*

*It will be tested in 1996 and, if it is declared safe, you may soon be able to hire one and go fish-watching down to a depth of 165 feet (50 m).*

# USING HOLOGRAMS

Holograms are used in three main ways: as an art form, to record information, and as a security measure to prevent something being copied. Some shops now specialize in selling holographic works. Holograms have even been added to the exhibitions of painting and sculpture in major art galleries.

One of the most important uses of holograms in the future will be to store information. The 3-D image in a hologram contains much more detail than a normal photograph. It can be turned to show parts of the image that are normally hidden and to reveal how different objects or parts of objects relate to each other in space. Information can also be recorded in a hologram in the on-off binary code computers use.

Until recently, holograms were only made in laboratories in small numbers and they could only be viewed in laser light. Today, holograms can be made in large numbers and they can be seen in daylight. Because of this, holograms will become common in packaging, store windows and street signs.

Although holograms can be made more easily now by specialist companies, they are still almost impossible to copy. This is why they are printed onto security items, for instance credit and identity cards. In this way, holograms help to prevent fraud.

Holograms like this bird are often printed on credit cards to make it difficult to copy them.

Science has helped to create the new visual art forms of our age – photography, movies, television and now holography (as seen in the gallery above). Holograms are increasingly being used to record 3-D images of complex objects. Designers and architects can now produce holograms which show how their work will look from computer programs, and dentists can keep holographic records of patients' teeth or dental plates (below).

**Information stored as holograms**

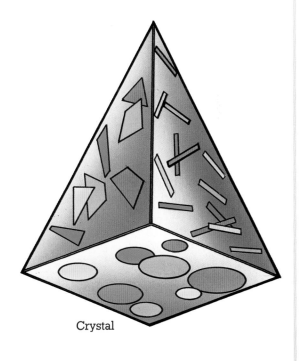

Crystal

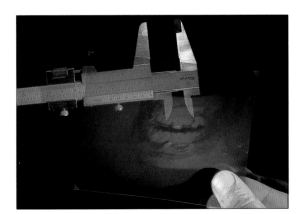

Crystals are materials with a regular geometrical shape formed from sheets (or planes) of particles. Some crystals can store a different hologram on each plane. In 1969, the U.S. Bell Laboratories found that 1,000 holograms could be stored in a crystal of lithium niobate. As the crystal is tilted, the hologram on each plane appears.

# THE AGE OF THE KNIGHT

Between about 900 and 1400 the mounted knight was the most valued European battle weapon. Knights were more than just warriors. They formed a privileged group at the top of society. The division of land was geared to the cost of putting an armored knight into the field and knightly behavior, known as *chivalry*, was held up as an example for everyone to follow.

Nevertheless, the importance of mounted knights in battle is easily exaggerated. They looked magnificent and could make devastating charges. But medieval warfare was primarily about capturing enemy castles, not cavalry attacks.

Commanders usually avoided battle if they could. Besides, in an extended fight a knight with his head inside a steel helmet often had no idea what was going on!

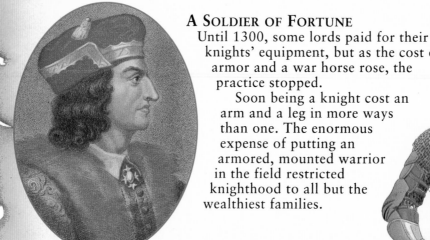

## A SOLDIER OF FORTUNE

Until 1300, some lords paid for their knights' equipment, but as the cost of armor and a war horse rose, the practice stopped.

Soon being a knight cost an arm and a leg in more ways than one. The enormous expense of putting an armored, mounted warrior in the field restricted knighthood to all but the wealthiest families.

*Knight in 1200*

## CASTLES COUNT!

Large-scale battles between mounted knights were rare and usually of little significance.

The capture of mighty Château-Gaillard from French King John (*above*) in 1204, for example, had more impact on the history of France than any cavalry conflict.

*Château-Gaillard* (above) *dominated the countryside for miles around.*

### The Sword in the Stone
*British director John Boorman used the name* Excalibur – *Arthur's magical sword (right) – as the title of his remake of the legend (left).*

*Arthur found the weapon sticking into a stone and returned it to the Lady of the Lake when he died.*

THE LEGEND OF KING ARTHUR is a blend of ancient British and French myth, spiced with Christianity, and a dash of fact.

The real Arthur may have been a Romano-Briton who fought the Anglo-Saxon invaders in the 6th century A.D. Arthur, the romantic hero of Camelot was created by the 12th-century monk Geoffrey of Monmouth.

Geoffrey set the tales in his own time, with his own religious message. This is why they feature knights in armor, Christian chivalry, and glamorous ladies in long pointed hats!

### The Power of the Sword
*The sword, ideal for stabbing and slashing, was the basic weapon of every knight.*

*Knight in 1500*

### CHAOS AT BOUVINES *(above)*
King John lost his French possessions with the fall of Château-Gaillard. When he tried to get them back, he was heavily defeated in 1214 at Bouvines, Flanders (modern Belgium).

The battle was a rare example of a major conflict between mounted knights. After the first assault, the fight deteriorated into total chaos!

# WHAT ARE REPTILES?

There are probably more than 10 million different kinds, or species, of animals in the world. About 6,500 are reptiles – "cold-blooded" creatures with a bony internal skeleton and scaly skin, that breed by laying eggs. Despite their small proportion of total animal species, reptiles are one of the best-known animal groups. They include slithering snakes, speedy lizards, slow tortoises, flippered turtles, and fearsome crocodiles. Those giants of the distant past, the dinosaurs, were also reptiles.

### Reptile eggs
Reptiles are vertebrates – animals with backbones. Like another group of vertebrates, birds, they lay tough-shelled eggs. The shell houses and protects the baby animal as it develops inside, using the food store in the egg known as yolk. The eggs of turtles, snakes, and most kinds of lizards have tough, leathery, slightly flexible shells. Those of tortoises, crocodiles, and lizards such as geckoes have hard, brittle shells, more like a bird's egg. However, some lizards and snakes do not lay eggs. The young develop inside their mother and are born fully formed.

### Hatching
Baby reptiles have a hard, horny scale on the mouth, called the egg tooth. They use it to crack their way out of the egg.

### The lizard group
There are about 3,750 species of lizards, from tiny wall and sand lizards to big, sturdy monitors and iguanas. Lizards are the most widespread reptile group.

### The crocodile group
There are about 22 species of crocodiles, alligators, caimans, and gavials, called crocodilians. They have powerful tails and mostly live in swamps, lakes, and rivers.

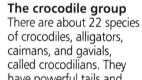

### A reptile puzzle
The worm lizards are a small group of reptiles, with about 140 species. Neither worms nor lizards, they are in a reptile group of their own, called the amphisbaenids. Most have no legs and live in tropical and subtropical places, burrowing in the soil of forests to prey on worms, insects, and other creatures. The biggest amphisbaenids are 30 ins (75 cms) long.

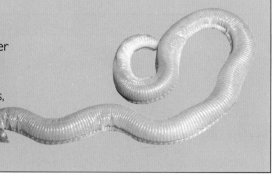

## The skeleton

The skeleton of a reptile is similar to other vertebrates, being composed of a skull, a line of bones called vertebrae making up the spinal column, and four legs. The vertebrae carry on past the hips to form the tail.

Skull

Leg bones

Main vertebrae (backbones) of spinal column

Front foot bones

## Dragons galore

Myths, legends, and stories from all over the world feature dragons, sometimes called "great worms." The typical dragon is a reptile-like creature. It has scaly skin, breathes fire, flies on vast wings, guards stolen treasure, attacks humans, and is evil and cunning. One of the most famous is Smaug, the huge and terrible dragon from J R R Tolkien's exciting folk story *The Hobbit*, written in 1937.

## Inside a reptile

A reptile such as this crocodile has all the main internal parts common to other vertebrate animals, like frogs, birds, or mammals such as yourself. These include a brain, heart, stomach, intestines, kidneys, and the bones of the skeleton.

### The snake group

There are about 2,400 species of snakes, from tiny thread snakes to huge pythons. They have long, slim, flexible bodies, and most lack all traces of legs.

### The turtle group

There are about 240 species of turtles, tortoises, and terrapins, called chelonians. Many have domed shells of bone and horn.

### Snakeless zone

The island of Ireland has no snakes. Christian legend says that they were banished by Saint Patrick (389-461 A.D.), patron saint of Ireland, because they were evil. A more likely biological explanation is that snakes have never managed to spread to Ireland from mainland Britain because of the wide barrier of the Irish Sea.

# FUTURE CITIES
## DESIGNING BETTER CITIES

**Most of the world's population live in cities; and the cities we live in were almost all built before the invention of the car, the telephone, or electricity.**

As a result, most cities are congested and polluted, and use energy inefficiently. Designing better cities is difficult because technology moves so fast: what makes sense on the drawing board may be out of date by the time the city is built. To escape from 19th century squalor, 20th century planners went for clean, "garden cities" in which workplaces and homes were placed far apart. That forced people into cars, replacing factory pollution with exhaust fumes. Housing developments on the edges of cities provided good houses, but a boring environment that bred crime and disillusionment. *Lu Jia Zui*, a new plan for a district of Shanghai by the Richard Rogers Partnership, attempts to design a future city without these problems. Grouped around a park, *Lu Jia Zui* will

be served by steetcars and a light rail system, with frequent stops so that nobody will have to walk more than a quarter of a mile. The plan for *Lu Jia Zui* is flexible, to allow for change. A computer program allows changes in population, parking, energy-use, and the

*One solution to expanding urban populations could be to build out into the sea (below). Land has been reclaimed from the sea in the past, but the concept of a floating city – like a futuristic Venice – looks more and more probable. Reclaimed land could also provide the wide open spaces of parkland that may no longer exist in the older cities.*

movement of people to be analyzed and incorporated into the design. Housing and commercial developments are mixed in all six sections of the city. To maximize the daylight admitted to the buildings, a model was tested for summer and winter conditions.

*Lu Jia Zui (right) will lie close to the famous Shanghai waterfront, the Bund. A light rail system will circulate around the central area, with parking for cars, and connections to the Shanghai subway.*

# S A V I N G   S P A C E
## G O I N G   U N D E R G R O U N D

As the population of the world increases, space has become more and more valuable. Building downward instead of upward is one solution to an over-populated and over-polluted environment. This vision of the future (below) shows what an underground city might look like. Shielded from the outside weather conditions by a huge, glass dome, the underground city can create its own climatic conditions. Air from the outside could be cleaned and filtered before being pumped around the multi-story city, while natural light penetrates the building through a central atrium. Natural insulation from the surrounding earth would help to save the energy usually needed to heat or cool a conventional building above the surface.

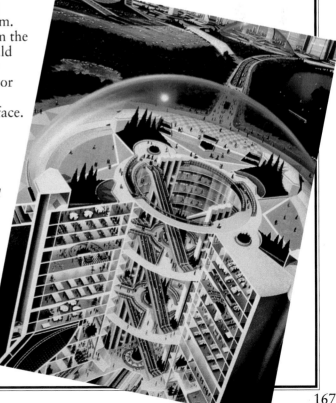

*Energy (right) would be provided both as heat, and as electricity, with all the buildings designed to be energy-efficient. The buildings have been arranged to maximize natural light, which cuts energy costs by 15 percent. All areas of the city are within easy reach of open spaces, with private cars banned from the inner areas.*

# HOW SOUNDS ARE HEARD

When sound waves enter our ears, they strike the eardrum which vibrates back and forth. This in turn causes tiny bones called ossicles to vibrate. These vibrations are turned by our "inner ear" into electrical signals that pass along nerves to the brain. When the signals reach the brain, we hear sounds. People cannot hear some sounds because they are too high or too low – not everyone can hear the high-pitched squeak of a bat. Dogs can hear higher pitched sounds than people, and a scientist called Sir Francis Galton (1822–1911) invented a whistle for calling dogs which was too high for people to hear. This kind of sound is called ultrasonic sound, or ultrasound.

## WHY IT WORKS

The sound waves from your friend's voice make the plastic wrap vibrate. These vibrations are transmitted into your cardboard "ossicles" and can be seen by watching the mirror for movements. This is a simple model of how a real ear works.

Vibrations in the air (sound waves) enter the outer ear and make the eardrum itself vibrate. The three bones, the malleus, the incus, and the stapes, together known as the ossicles, transmit the vibrations through the middle ear

to the oval window, or vestibular fenestra. The force of the vibrations on the oval window is over 20 times greater than that of the original vibrations on the eardrum. The oscillations (or vibrations) of the stapes makes the fluid in the part of the inner ear called the cochlea vibrate. The cochlea also contains fibers that pick up the vibrations and send messages along nerves to the brain. Other parts of the ear control our balance – these are called semicircular canals.

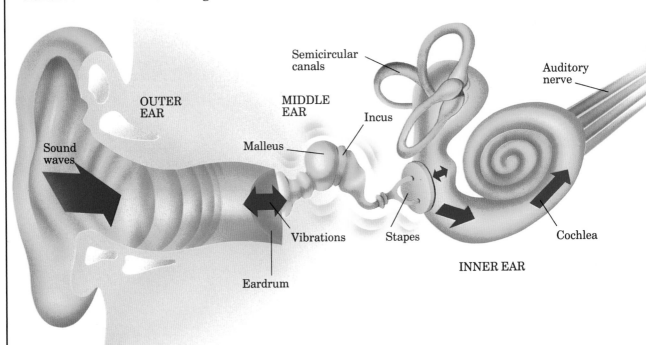

# HEAR THIS?

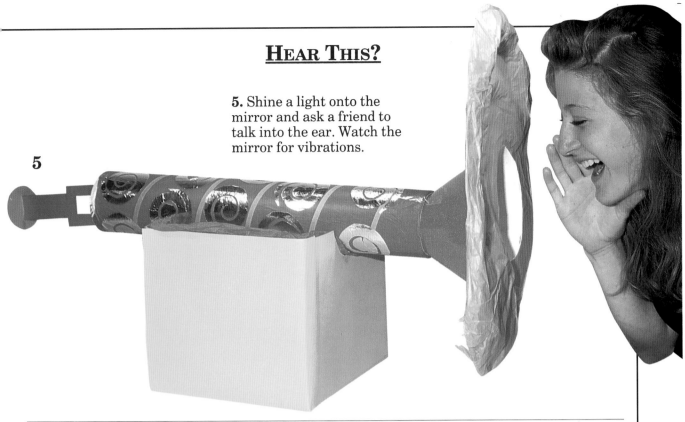

**5.** Shine a light onto the mirror and ask a friend to talk into the ear. Watch the mirror for vibrations.

**5**

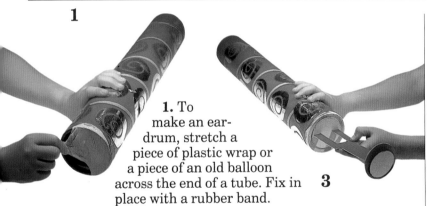

**1**

**1.** To make an eardrum, stretch a piece of plastic wrap or a piece of an old balloon across the end of a tube. Fix in place with a rubber band.

**3**

**2.** Make a set of "ossicles" with two disks and a fork shape of thin cardboard held together with double sided tape.

**2**

**3.** Attach a small mirror or a disk of shiny foil to one end, and attach the other to the plastic wrap "eardrum" on the tube. Your middle ear is complete.

**4.** Make an outer ear from a cone of cardboard with a hole at its end. With careful use of pink tissue paper you can achieve quite a realistic look!

**4**

## BRIGHT IDEAS

Watch the oval window of your ear again. How does it respond to shouting, whispering, whistling etc? The vibrations of your oval window could be a result of blowing on the eardrum, rather than the vibrations of sound waves. Use a radio to create sound without blowing.

A hundred years ago, people who suffered from hearing loss used ear trumpets. Find out about these devices! Can you make your own?

Listen to sounds blindfolded. Put your hand over one ear and try to tell which direction a sound is coming from. Listen to the same sound with both ears. Can you hear a difference? It is easier to hear the direction of sound with both ears.

# BEFORE THE DINOSAURS

The earth had already passed through most of its history before the dinosaurs appeared. Earth is about 4,600 million years old, and the first dinosaurs came on the scene 230 million years ago. The first living things were tiny creatures, like viruses or bacteria, which lived in the warm oceans 3,500 million years ago. Their fossils can only be seen through a microscope. Larger plants and animals arose 1,000 million years ago, and familiar forms, like shellfish, corals, and fish, existed by 500 million years ago. Fish were the first animals with backbones, and they gave rise to land-living amphibians 375 million years ago, and reptiles a little later. The reptiles ruled the earth from 275 million years ago until mammals became dominant over 65 million years ago.

### Early views of dinosaurs

The first dinosaurs were named in England in 1824 (*Megalosaurus* from Oxfordshire) and 1825 (*Iguanodon* from Sussex). The only fossils at that time were odd bones and teeth, and scientists originally thought that these new animals were either large lizards, or rhinoceros-like giants. It was only later, when complete skeletons were found, that the mistakes were realized. Long before the dinosaurs were named in England, fossilized bones and teeth had been found in China. Written records of "dragon bones" and "dragon teeth" exist from the third century.

### Cretaceous Period

The last phase of the age of dinosaurs, a time of great success. Flowering plants came on the scene and, with them, social insects such as ants and bees.

**TODAY**

65 mya

mya= million years ago

An early illustration of Iguanodon shows a ferocious, dragonlike monster.

### Cainozoic Era

The most recent phase of earth history, the last 65 million years of the Age of Mammals. During this time, all modern plants and animals appeared, including humans.

It is hard to understand the huge amounts of time involved in the history of life on earth. When you remember that the first cars ran on the roads only 100 years ago, think how much can happen in spans of millions of years. This chart shows some of the main divisions of geological time over the past 400 million years, and some of the common backboned animals.

## Devonian Period
Fish were abundant, and amphibians appeared.

## Carboniferous Period
Amphibians, like bloated crocodiles, were the common backboned animals. They lived in warm coal swamps.

360 mya

286 mya

## Permian Period
A drier time in many parts of the world, and ruled by various kinds of reptiles.

245 mya

208 mya

## Triassic Period
Dinosaurs arose halfway through this time, about 230 million years ago.

## Jurassic Period
The age of the giant dinosaurs, the great long-necked plant-eaters. Also time of origin of the birds.

144 mya

## Dating rocks
Layers of rock can be placed in order by looking at the fossils in them. But, the exact ages, in millions of years, are worked out by studying the radioactive decay of rock particles. When the elements that made up the earth were formed, all possible particles were present. Now, the older the rock is, the more the radioactive elements have decayed. It is possible, therefore, to give an age to rocks by looking at the rates of radioactive decay.

## Geological periods
The units of geological time were named during the 19th century. The names reflect something of the life at the time, or commonly refer to a part of the world. The main units are the eras: Paleozoic (ancient life), Mesozoic (middle life), and Cei nozoic (recent life). The Mesozoic Era, the Age of Reptiles, includes three periods: the Triassic, Jurassic, and Cretaceous. Triassic (three parts) refers to the three main divisions of rocks of that age in Germany. Jurassic was named after the Jura Mountains in Germany, and Cretaceous is based on "Creta" (chalk), a common rock of that particular age in history.

Rock strata

# WHAT IF A BAT COULDN'T HEAR?

Clicks

Echoes

**Bat sonar**

The bat's sound pulses are so high-pitched that you or I couldn't hear them. However, a bat's hearing is so sensitive, it can hear these clicks and their echoes. The bat can find its way and catch its flying food even in complete darkness. The system is like radar, but with sound waves instead of radio waves. It's known as sonar or echolocation.

It would fly through the dark night – and crash into things! Mammals possess an amazing array of senses to detect the outside world. Hearing is only one of these. They are able to see in very poor light, smell the very faintest odors, taste an enormous variety of different foods, and detect touches and vibrations that are as light as a feather.

**Dolphin sonar**

Predatory members of the whale group, such as dolphins and killer whales, have a sonar system like the bat's (above). The sound pulses are concentrated, or focused, into a beam by a large lump in the forehead, the melon.

melon

## What if whales could sing?

All whales make underwater sounds, varying from shrill clicks and squeaks and squawks, to haunting low moans and groans. Beluga and humpback whales are so noisy that their calls can be heard underwater more than 125 miles (200 km) away. The "songs" of a whale can last between 6 and 35 minutes, and are used by the whales to communicate with each other.

# Nighttime eye-shine

If you've ever shone a flashlight into a cat's eyes, you will have seen that they appeared to glow in the dark. A cat's eye has a mirrorlike layer inside, the tapetum. Light rays come into the eye and some are detected by the light-sensitive layer, the retina. Others pass through the retina, bounce off the tapetum, and get sensed by the retina on the way out. This gives the eye two chances to detect light rays. Other nocturnal (nighttime) animals, such as opossums, have this too.

The pupil opens wider in dark conditions, to let in more light.

The retina detects light and turns it into nerve signals, which go to the brain.

The tapetum is a layer behind the retina. It reflects the light back onto the retina.

# What if a lion had eyes on the side of its head?

It would leap at its prey, and probably miss! Most hunters, such as seals, cats, and foxes, have two forward-facing eyes at the front of the head. This gives them overlapping fields of vision (right), and allows them to judge distances well, for pursuit and pounce. Most hunted mammals, such as deer, zebras, and rabbits, have eyes on the sides of their head. Although this means that they can't judge distances well, it does give them a good overall view for spotting any predators that may be creeping up on them (right).

# Something in the air

Dogs sniff everything, from the food they eat, to other dogs, especially when it is time to mate. The scent in the air enters the nose and attaches to an organ called the *olfactory bulb.* This is very large and very sensitive in a dog's nose. It then sends signals to the brain.

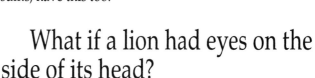

Olfactory bulb

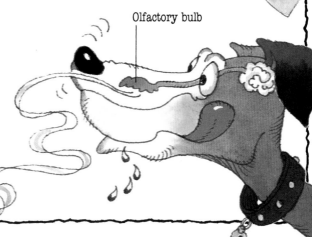

# HIEROGLYPHICS

The Ancient Egyptians spoke a language related to the languages of the Middle East and North Africa. Those who could, wrote using a system of picture writing, called hieroglyphics. The Egyptians began using hieroglyphics in about 3000 B.C., shortly after the first known examples of writing appeared in Sumer (now southeastern Iraq). Each picture, or hieroglyph, could stand for an object and a sound. Some represented one letter; others up to five letters. These were always consonants. Vowels were not written down.

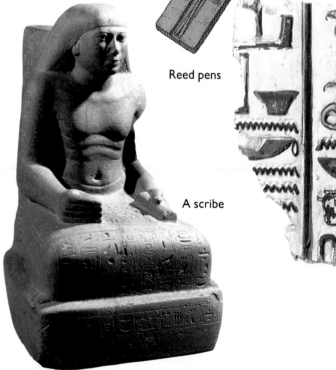

Ink blocks

Reed pens

A scribe

### Breaking the code

Hieroglyphics were last used in about A.D. 394. For more than 1,400 years no one could read or understand them. In 1799, however, a soldier in Napoléon Bonaparte's army in Egypt found a large stone slab — the Rosetta Stone. On the stone was a text carved by Egyptian priests in 196 B.C. to mark the crowning of King Ptolemy V. The same text was written out in Ancient Egyptian hieroglyphs, demotic script (a simpler form of hieroglyphs), and Greek. By comparing the three, a French scholar called Jean-François Champollion, was finally able to crack the code in 1822.

Champollion

The Rosetta Stone

### Writing hieroglyphs

The word "hieroglyph" is Greek for sacred carvings. Egyptian hieroglyphs were usually written or carved by highly trained men called scribes. Egyptian society was based on keeping records, and scribes were therefore very important. Many rose to positions of great authority because they could read and write. Use the symbols below to write your own hieroglyphic message.

| | | | | | | | | | |
|---|---|---|---|---|---|---|---|---|---|
| * | i | y | y | * | w | * | b | p | f |

## Papyrus paper

The Egyptians wrote on a paper-like material, called papyrus, made of reeds. The pith was taken out of the reeds and cut into strips. These were laid flat in layers, covered with cloth, and pounded with heavy stones or a mallet to weld them together. The papyrus was then polished to give a smooth, flat surface. Sheets of papyrus were often put together to form a roll.

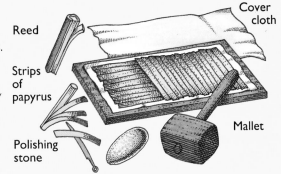

Reed

Strips of papyrus

Cover cloth

Polishing stone

Mallet

For daily use, two simpler, less formal shorthand scripts were created. Hieratic script (left) was used in the Old Kingdom. By about 700 B.C., demotic (from the Greek word *demotikos,* meaning "popular") script was in use.

B

A

There were many different ways of writing hieroglyphs. They could be written from left to right, right to left or top to bottom. If an animal faced right (A), you read from right to left. If it faced left (B), you read from left to right.

B

A

Hieroglyphs (above) were not used in everyday life. They were reserved for important inscriptions, such as those on tombs and temples and for affairs of state.

The name or symbol of a ruler appeared in hieroglyphs within an oval frame called a cartouche (shown left).

K
L  I  O  P  A  D
R
A

P  O  L  Y  S
T  O  M

Champollion solved the puzzle of the Rosetta Stone using names like Ptolemy and Cleopatra (left and above). See if you can spot which letters appear in both names.

*No translation

m   n   r   h   h   ch   h (soft)   s   s   sh   q   k   g (hard)   t   tj   d   dj

# DOGS

The dog family, or Canidae, includes dogs, wolves, jackals, and foxes. Dogs tend to take advantage of any situation, feeding on carrion, insects, and even fruit and leaves, if they cannot hunt. They can all run at speed for long distances, but are less agile than cats. Dogs are intelligent, sociable animals and most live as tightly-knit family groups or packs, at least for part of the year. They communicate by sounds, body postures, and their highly developed sense of smell.

## Domestic Dogs

The earliest remains of a domestic dog are believed to be over 11,000 years old. Abandoned wolf pups may have been taken into the home as pets, guard dogs, or hunters. Dogs treat the families they live with as members of their pack, taking their place in the hierarchy. As with other domestic animals, many different breeds have been produced, each with different characteristics.

## Big Bad Wolf

Wolves have had a bad image for centuries because they kill domestic animals and game if they have to. There are many stories, but few proven cases, of attacks on people. Fairy stories about the Big Bad Wolf and legends of werewolves (right) reflect the fear of wolves. It has lead to centuries of persecution. Today the gray wolf, which once roamed most of the northern hemisphere, is an endangered animal. Efforts to re-introduce it involve improving its image.

## Hot and Cold Foxes

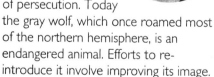

The Arctic fox, as its name suggests, lives in the cold Arctic tundra. It can survive temperatures as low as -58°F. It has a coat of thick fur all over its body, even on the pads of its paws, and on its small, rounded ears. They are so well insulated that they loose very little heat.

176

### Pavlov

Ivan Pavlov was a Russian doctor who spent a lot of time finding out how the human body works. He used dogs for his experiments. He discovered he could train them to salivate with a bell, not just in response to food. When the body learns to perform a function in response to an artificial cue it is called a conditioned reflex.

### Peter and the Wolf

The Russian composer Prokofiev wrote this musical fairy tale for children in 1936. The story is told by a narrator and all the characters – Peter, his grandfather, the wolf, the bird, the cat, and the duck – are played by different musical instruments from the orchestra. The wolf is portrayed by three horns.

### Canine Relatives

The closest relatives of the domestic dog are wolves, coyotes, and jackals. Members of a wolf pack hunt together cooperatively to bring down large prey. The North American coyote is one of the few wild animals that is increasing in numbers today. An adaptable animal, it eats anything it can find. A breeding pair of African jackals stay mated for life.

Wolf

Coyote

Jackal

### Working Dogs

Many domestic dogs work for their living, helping on the farm or with field sports, racing and guarding or guiding their owners. Huskies, bred for their strength and resilience, work together in teams, pulling sleds across the snow.

The tiny Fennec fox, the smallest of all the wild dogs, lives in hot African deserts. It keeps itself cool by sleeping in a burrow during the hottest part of the day. It uses its huge ears as radiators to get rid of excess body heat. They are also useful for listening to the sounds of the tiny animals on which it feeds.

# *Spooky* PLACES

Stonehenge is only one of many mysterious places. Ancient sites often seem to attract supernatural events, such as sightings of ghosts and aliens. One theory is that standing stones and earthworks (banks of earth built by early peoples) were placed at the crossing points of the magnetic energy lines that cross the Earth, to form a bridge to the sky. *Ley lines* are a network of straight lines which seem to link sites such as standing stones and barrows (mounds of earth covering graves) with holy places. Ancient trackways follow these lines; some scientists believe that they match the lines of force around the Earth's surface.

### THE VANISHING CREW
*On a calm afternoon in December 1872, the* Mary Celeste *was seen drifting in the Atlantic Ocean. Her log ended on November 25. The entire crew had vanished. Had they been attacked by a giant octopus, sucked into a whirlpool, abducted by aliens...or simply drowned?*

### MYSTERIOUS MONUMENTS
*On the slopes of Easter Island, in the Pacific Ocean, stand dozens of giant stone statues. They were probably made in A.D. 1000–1500, in the quarries of the extinct volcano Rano Raruku. They are believed to represent spirits of ancestors, who magically protected the islanders.*

Florida

Bermuda

Puerto Rico

*What was Stonehenge used for?*
Scientists believe that this great monument was a tribal gathering place and religious center, although no one can be sure. It is thought that the layout of the stones was used to predict important astronomical events. Tribal ceremonies were probably held there at certain times of the year.

### DEADLY TRIANGLE
*Off the coast of Florida is an area known as the Bermuda Triangle, where over 200 ships and planes have vanished mysteriously. Some disappearances can be explained as the result of unusual weather, but the rest are a puzzle. Many people think that there could be strange energies at work there.*

## PICTURES IN THE SAND
In 1927, a pilot, flying a light aircraft over the Nazca plains of Peru, looked down and saw thousands of vast lines and pictures drawn in the desert. The pictures included a spider, a monkey, and a hummingbird with a wingspan of 200 feet (60 m, above). Archaeologists think they were created 1,000–2,500 years ago by the Nazca people, who moved the dark stones to expose the light sand underneath.

## Visitors from the skies

In 1969, Erich von Däniken wrote a book called *Chariots of the Gods?*, in which he suggested that aliens had visited Earth 10,000 years ago.

He claimed that they came from an advanced civilization and created many ancient wonders, like the Easter Island statues and Stonehenge. He said that some South American carvings (above) and a cave painting in Australia's Kimberley Mountains were images of alien visitors. Von Däniken said that early peoples worshiped the aliens and that many ancient myths were reports of their arrival in fiery chariots or spaceships.

## POWERFUL STONES
The standing stones at Carnac, France are just one ancient site apparently chosen to match the Earth's energy lines. Thousands of huge stones are arranged in parallel rows, but no one knows why.

## THE LOST CONTINENT
The ancient Greek philosopher Plato described a vast continent in the Atlantic known as Atlantis, which suddenly vanished. Huge undersea walls, from about 9500 B.C., have been found in the Bahamas. Could these have been the walls of Atlantis? Or did the legend arise from the flooding of the island of Crete in 1950 B.C.?

Bacteria are so small that they can be seen only with the aid of a microscope. They have cells with a very simple structure. The cells of plants and animals are more complex and measure between 0.001 and 0.002 inches across.

The amount of oxygen in the atmosphere gradually increased with the greater number of cyanobacteria. At first it probably killed off many of the bacteria, but gradually they adapted to use the oxygen for their own purposes. The development of different types of bacteria led to the evolution of other organisms that obtained their energy simply by feeding off more primitive ones. The next important stage occurred when more complex cells acquired the ability to photosynthesize through the development of chloroplasts (see below). These were the first true plant cells.

## Simple to complex cells

The cells of plants and animals are much more complicated than those of bacteria. Plants, for example, have tiny egg-shaped structures called chloroplasts inside their cells. By separating them from the rest of the cell, scientists have shown that they do the work of photosynthesis – using sunlight to make food. What is most striking about chloroplasts is how much they resemble cyanobacteria – the single-celled creatures that originally pumped oxygen into the air. It is now believed that chloroplasts are the descendants of cyanobacteria that made a home inside larger cells many millions of years ago.

Plant and animal cells include other egg-shaped structures known as mitochondria. These are responsible for the reactions in which food is broken down and oxygen is used to produce energy. Like chloroplasts, mitochondria are probably descended from bacteria that had learned to cope with oxygen, and which then began living inside larger cells that had "swallowed" them.

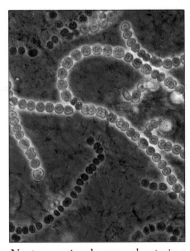

*Nostoc*, a simple cyanobacterium

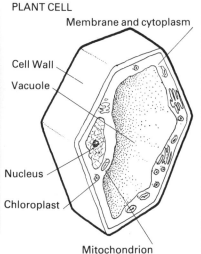

PLANT CELL

Membrane and cytoplasm

Cell Wall

Vacuole

Nucleus

Chloroplast

Mitochondrion

Single-celled desmids have a cellulose cell wall.

# Plant evolution

The first plants were single-celled organisms formed when cyanobacteria took refuge inside larger cells. Those larger cells already contained mitochondria, descended from other bacteria. From their point of view, there was a lot to gain by giving the bacteria a home. The mitochondria helped them to cope with oxygen, and the chloroplasts made food for them.

These ancestral plants probably lived at the surfaces of seas and lakes, as many of their descendants – the unicellular algae – do today. In time, the single-celled plants began to evolve into many-celled forms, by dividing into two without separating. Some formed balls of cells, others hollow cylinders, and some formed strings of cells. Many organisms with these arrangements (shown below) live today as pondweeds and seaweeds.

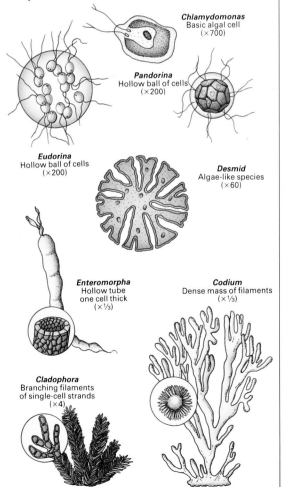

**Chlamydomonas**
Basic algal cell
(×700)

**Pandorina**
Hollow ball of cells
(×200)

**Eudorina**
Hollow ball of cells
(×200)

**Desmid**
Algae-like species
(×60)

**Enteromorpha**
Hollow tube
one cell thick
(×⅓)

**Codium**
Dense mass of filaments
(×⅓)

**Cladophora**
Branching filaments
of single-cell strands
(×4)

# On to land

For millions of years, algae were the only forms of plant life. Like today's algae, they were largely confined to water because they would dry out on land and because they had no supporting structure to hold up their leaf-like fronds. To begin with, therefore, there were no plants on land. Then a small alga began to grow around the edges of ponds, just out of the water. In time, it evolved a semi-waterproof covering, and developed root-like structures to draw up water from the soil. These pioneering algae gave rise to the mosses, simple plants which still need damp places in which to grow. Later on, more advanced groups of plants such as ferns appeared. These had a waterproof covering on their leaves and were the first plants to develop roots and woody stems, allowing them to grow taller.

Mosses need a layer of moisture to reproduce.

The cycad is an ancient primitive plant.

# WHAT ARE FLOODS?

Floods are the waters which cover an area of land that is normally dry. They have affected almost every corner of the earth at some time or another, but those which cause the greatest amount of damage are the result of extreme weather conditions.

Tropical storms, which are called typhoons, hurricanes, or cyclones in different parts of the world, whip up the winds over the oceans and create huge waves. These waves, known as storm surges, race toward the shore and crash onto the coastline. The country of Bangladesh has suffered serious flooding on many occasions, as cyclones in the Bay of Bengal send huge sea waves crashing over the low-lying coastal areas. Other enormous waves which produce severe flooding are the so-called tidal waves, or *tsunamis*, which result from earthquakes or volcanic eruptions.

The millions of tons of rock, soil, and mud unleashed during a landslide can block a river valley or dam, causing water levels to rise dramatically. Flooding can also follow a seiche, the violent movement of lake waters following an earthquake. The most frequent cause, however, is when heavy rains and melting snow and ice make inland rivers and dams burst. This problem is made worse in areas where large numbers of trees have been cleared. Stripped of their vegetation, the hillsides cannot hold the excess water, which runs off and causes flooding in lowland areas.

◄ During powerful storms, strong winds whip up high waves that pound down on the coastline. Sea defenses are often smashed to pieces, causing serious flooding in areas along the coast and extensive damage to property.

► Sudden, violent bursts of water surging down narrow mountain valleys or dry river beds are called flash floods. These raging torrents of water, such as the one shown right at El Oued in Algeria, can flood an area for just a few hours, or even minutes, before subsiding.

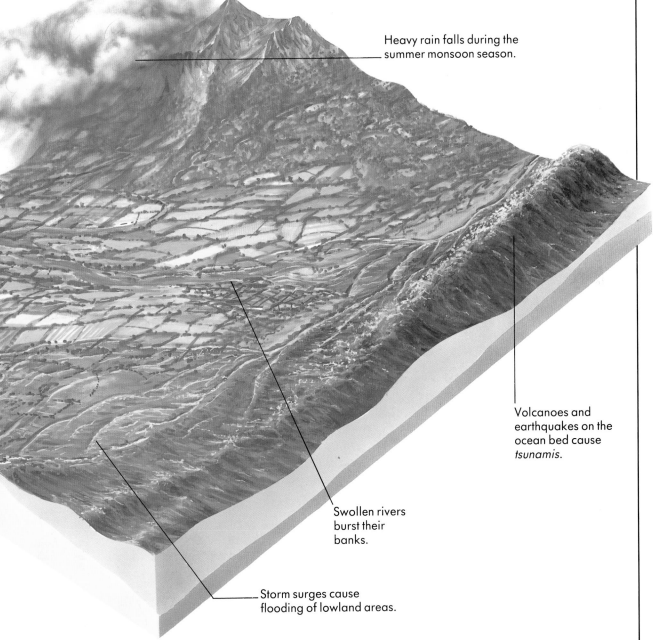

Heavy rain falls during the summer monsoon season.

Volcanoes and earthquakes on the ocean bed cause *tsunamis*.

Swollen rivers burst their banks.

Storm surges cause flooding of lowland areas.

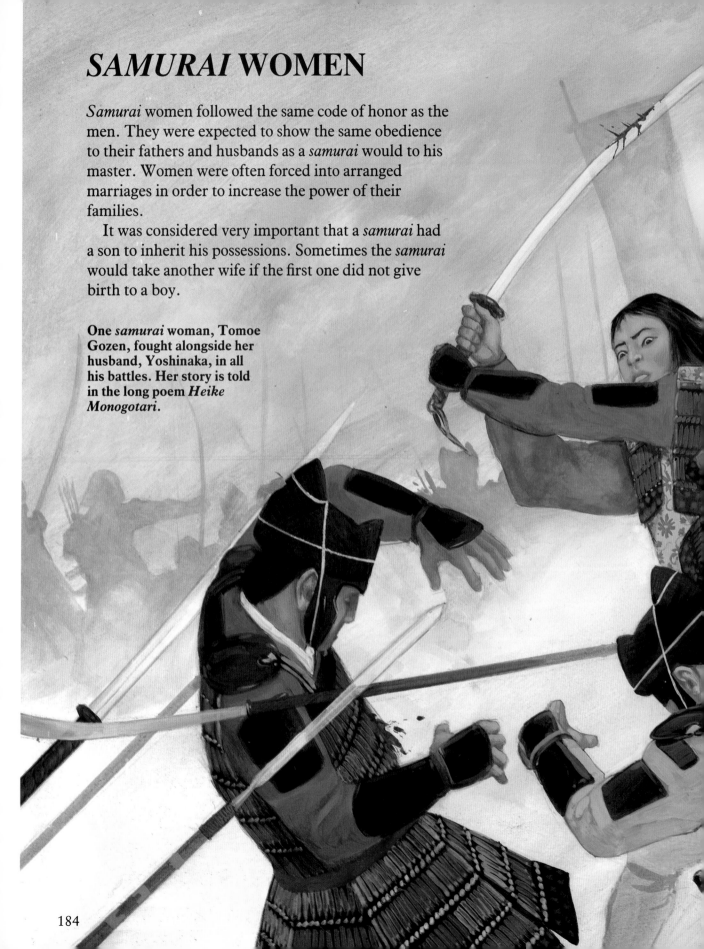

# SAMURAI WOMEN

*Samurai* women followed the same code of honor as the men. They were expected to show the same obedience to their fathers and husbands as a *samurai* would to his master. Women were often forced into arranged marriages in order to increase the power of their families.

It was considered very important that a *samurai* had a son to inherit his possessions. Sometimes the *samurai* would take another wife if the first one did not give birth to a boy.

One *samurai* woman, Tomoe Gozen, fought alongside her husband, Yoshinaka, in all his battles. Her story is told in the long poem *Heike Monogotari*.

184

Some *samurai* women learned to fight and they defended their homes against enemies. One *kabuki* play tells of two sisters, Miyagino and Shinobu, whose father was murdered by a *samurai* called Shiga. They swore to avenge their father's death. In secret they trained themselves to fight, then they went to the local leaders and asked permission to challenge Shiga to a duel. In the fight that followed, Shiga was killed and the family honor was satisfied. The story of Miyagino and Shinobu is still performed on the Japanese stage to this day. It shows the courage of *samurai* women.

## *SAMURAI* CHILDREN

In the Edo period, schools were set up for the sons of *samurai*. Calligraphy and Chinese writings were the main subjects taught, as well as the *samurai* codes. Girls learned *ikebana*, the art of flower arranging, and the tea ceremony from their mothers. At the age of 13, boys had the front part of their heads shaved. This was a sign that they had become men.

Girls wore their hair parted in the middle and falling over their shoulders. By the time they grew up, it touched the ground. Boys liked to catch dragonflies and make them fight each other. Girls caught fireflies and kept them in jars to use as lanterns.

13 year-old boy

Young boy

Young girl

# BIRDS

Birds, the champions of the air, are the most plentiful of the earth's warm-blooded animals. Scientists have estimated that there may be over 100,000 million birds in the world altogether. Their success is largely due to their ability to fly, which gives them versatility in finding food and places to live. Birds come in all different sizes and colors.

Brilliantly colored macaws live in noisy flocks in the world's rain forests. The species shown here are endangered in the wild.

Blue and yellow macaw

Scarlet macaw

### The first birds
All living things change over thousands of years to improve their chances of survival. This process of change is called evolution. Birds evolved from reptiles about 150 million years ago. Their feathers developed from the scales which covered their ancestors. Wings gradually evolved from front legs. One of the first birds was *Archaeopteryx* ("ancient wing"). It was about the size of a gull and had the sharp teeth of a lizard. It was a poor flier and used to climb trees and then glide away.

**Archaeopteryx**

### Legend and symbol
Birds have been so successful that they can be found virtually everywhere. Over the years, different cultures have come into contact with birds and attached various meanings to them. Bird flight has always inspired awe in earthbound humans. Birds have often been viewed as bearers of good fortune. However, crows, vultures, and other carrion-scavenging birds are commonly associated with evil or horror.

### The phoenix
This bird was worshiped in ancient Egypt, but exists only in legend. The phoenix was said to set itself on fire and then rise from its own ashes.

### The dove
The dove as a symbol of peace originated with the biblical story of Noah, who sent a dove from his Ark to find dry land.

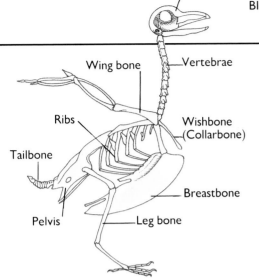

- Skull
- Wing bone
- Vertebrae
- Ribs
- Wishbone (Collarbone)
- Tailbone
- Breastbone
- Pelvis
- Leg bone

## Inside a bird

Birds are vertebrates, with an internal skeleton and backbone. Flying birds have very light skeletons, to reduce the amount of weight they have to carry in flight. Many of their bones are hollow. The inside of the bone looks like a honeycomb. Birds also have lightweight beaks, instead of heavy, bony jaws.

### Bird records

There is an amazing variety of different bird species. Although all birds share similar body structure, they differ enormously in color, size, and shape. Some birds are so plentiful that they become pests. Others, like the California condor, are extremely rare.

### Largest and smallest

The ostrich is the largest bird in the world. It can grow up to 9 feet (2.7m) tall. The smallest bird is the bee hummingbird of Cuba, which is no larger than a bumblebee.

### Most common

The domestic fowl, also known as the chicken, is the world's most common bird. In the wild, the red-billed quelea of Africa is the most numerous bird.

### Heaviest

The heaviest flying bird ever recorded was a mute swan that weighed 50 lb (23 kg). The Kori bustard can also grow to this weight.

Hyacinth macaw

Scarlet macaw

Ostrich

Domestic fowl

Mute swan

### The white stork

In Europe, the stork is a symbol of good luck. In legend, the stork delivers newborn babies to homes.

### The pelican

The pelican got its reputation for being a dutiful parent in the Middle Ages (5-15th centuries). It was fabled to pierce its chest and feed its young with its blood.

# THE REUSABLE SPACECRAFT

Conventional rockets are used just once, then thrown away. The space shuttle is different; it takes off vertically, like a rocket, enters space as a spacecraft, and then returns and lands on a runway like an aircraft. The idea was to make spaceflight simpler and cheaper, but the results have been disappointing. To put a satellite into orbit with NASA's space shuttle costs up to $250 million, no less than a conventional rocket. The popular dream of ordinary people paying for a space ride is still many years away.

**Development**

The design of the shuttle drew on experience from a series of rocket planes developed in the United States. The first of these, the Bell X-1, launched in mid-air from beneath a B29 bomber, was the first aircraft to exceed the speed of sound in 1947. Later models (below) showed the rounded shape and V-shaped delta wings of the shuttle, designed to resist the intense heat of reentry and then to glide swiftly to a landing.

**X-15**

The Bell X-15 rocket plane (above), tested in the 1960s, reached speeds of more than 4,000 mph and attained heights of 67 miles, the very edge of space.

Satellite payload

Fuel tanks

Payload handling controls

X 24A

M2F3

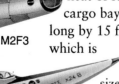

X 24B

**The shuttle**

The shuttle is built of aluminum alloy, covered with ceramic tiles to protect it from the heat of reentry. The cargo bay is 60 feet long by 15 feet wide, which is about the size of a railway freight wagon. The doors are made of carbon-fiber reinforced plastic. The stubby wings allow the shuttle to glide, though very fast, and land at more than 200 mph The flight deck is the upper level at the front, with the galley and sleeping berths below in the mid deck area. Each shuttle costs about $1.1 billion.

Airlock

Oxidizer tank

## First flight

The space shuttle Columbia lifted off for its maiden flight in 1981. In general, the shuttle program has been successful. It launches satellites regularly, carries out experiments in space, and also does secret military work. It has made dramatic rescues.

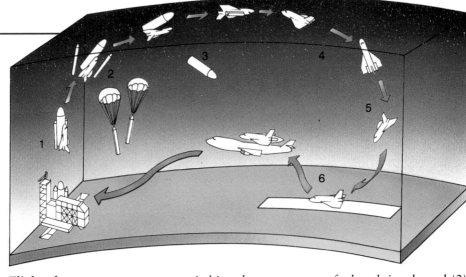

Space radiator

Forward control thrusters

Nose wheels

## Flight plan

The flight sequence of the shuttle appears above. For lift-off (1), the shuttle uses its three main engines, plus two boosters. Extra fuel is carried in a huge internal tank. After two minutes, the boosters burn out and parachute into the sea (2). Six minutes later, the main engines stop, and the fuel tank is released (3). The final step into space is made by smaller orbital engines (4). After landing (5), a Boeing 747 returns the shuttle to the launch pad (6).

## International rescue

In 1992 (below) three shuttle astronauts spent more than eight hours on a space walk, wrestling a four-ton communications satellite, Intelsat-VI, into the cargo bay. There they fitted a new rocket motor and sent the satellite off on its true orbit, 22,300 miles above the Earth.

## Disaster

In America's worst space disaster, hot gases leaked through a joint in the booster casing during the launch of Challenger in 1986. A tongue of flame burned into the main tank and ignited the fuel, blowing the shuttle to pieces and killing its seven crew members, among them Christa McAuliffe, a teacher. The disaster set back the program by nearly three years, as engineers struggled to prevent it from ever happening again.

# USING PENCILS AND PASTELS

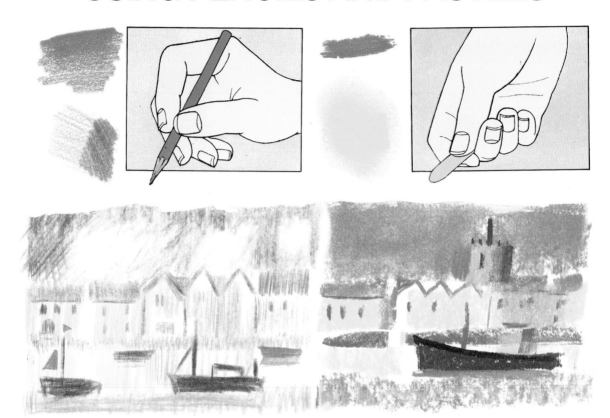

### Colored pencils

Colored pencils are one of the most basic coloring tools. Many bright and wonderful colors are available. Artists like David Hockney frequently choose to use them. Although they are often used as colors in their own right, they mix and can be laid down on top of one another to achieve different effects.

### Chalk pastels

Chalk pastels are pure pigment bound together with gum. They blend well if you rub them with your finger – this is messy, but effective. Pastel can be put on smoothly with the side of the chalk, or quite thickly if you press firmly with the end. As with most drawing materials, price and quality vary.

### Colored pencil and wash

Water-soluble pencils are fun to experiment with. Lines drawn with them will blur to make an area of flat color if you lay a wash of clean water over them with a paint brush.

# COLOR THEORY

The six colors you can see in the color wheel on the left are divided into two groups. Red, yellow and blue are called the *primary* colors. Orange, green and purple are the *secondary* colors, and are a mix of the two primaries on either side. In fact nearly all colors can be mixed from the primaries; some ways of mixing colors are shown below. The more colors are mixed together, the duller they become. The colors that are opposite each other on the color wheel are known as *complementaries*. When placed side by side, they bring out the best in each other. For example, red looks redder next to green, and vice versa.

△ *"Make a color wheel for yourself with the primary and secondary colors. Then try again, blending the secondaries from your primary colors."*

Colors can be mixed in various ways. In *cross-hatching*, shades of colored pencil are laid on top of each other.

Colors appear darker or lighter, depending on how hard you press down with your pencil or crayon.

Strokes of yellow wax crayon laid over blue produce a light green. Blue laid over yellow makes a darker green.

Wax crayons can be blended with a finger. If colors are rubbed too much, they will get dirty.

Felt-tip colors can be blended by overlapping groups of tiny dots. This technique is used in color printing.

191

# WHAT IS ENERGY?

Energy is the ability to do things. Without it we couldn't get up in the morning, or turn on the lights, or drive the car. Plants wouldn't grow, the rain wouldn't fall, the Sun wouldn't shine. Everything we do needs a supply of energy, which is used to make things work: The word energy is Greek, and means "the work within." Energy comes in many forms, which can be stored and used in different ways.

The universe was born 15 billion years ago in an incredibly hot ball of energy (left). It began to expand at an astonishing rate, creating matter, and cooling rapidly as it grew. After 10,000 years, atoms appeared and in two billion years began to group together to form stars and galaxies. Whirling gases around the stars condensed into the planets, like Earth and Mars, about five billion years ago.

### Matter and energy

Energy and matter seem very different, but they're not: in fact, matter can be turned into energy. This is how the Sun produces its enormous energy, and how nuclear power stations and nuclear bombs work. The physicist Albert Einstein showed that the amount of energy produced is given by the equation $E = mc^2$, where E is energy, m is mass, and c is a very large number – the speed of light.

The energy we need comes from food. Some foods, like sugar or fat, contain more energy than others. In the body, food is digested to release its energy, which then flows through the bloodstream to the muscles. An active person needs more food than somebody who sits down all day.

## Aristotle and Galileo

The Greek philosopher Aristotle (384-322 B.C.) was among the first to try to explain energy. He believed that a heavier stone would fall faster than a lighter one – but he never tested it. If he had, he would have found that both fell at the same rate. They did not fall simply because they were heavy, but because they had energy from being lifted. It was the Italian physicist Galileo Galilei (1564-1642) who first began to understand this and to challenge many of Aristotle's incorrect theories.

All machines need a source of energy. Viking longboats were driven by muscle power, which is limited. But the gasoline or diesel engines in a modern mechanical digger are far more powerful. Until the invention in the 19th century of engines that could turn heat from coal or oil into work, the methods by which people altered their environment were very different.

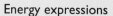

## Energy expressions

There are many sayings which use ideas about heat and energy. To "get into hot water" means to get into some kind of difficult situation. To "go full steam ahead" means to do something with all your energy. To "blow hot and cold" is to change your attitude toward something many times. Do you know these sayings: to "be too hot to handle." to "be firing on all cylinders?"

## Tidal waves

The energy of earthquakes under the sea can travel across the oceans as huge waves called tsunamis. The tsunamis, or tidal waves, are barely visible out at sea, but when they reach land they sweep ashore, causing destruction. Systems around the Pacific Ocean warn people to move if a tsunami approaches.

Sound is a form of energy, created by vibrations, such as the sound of a tuning fork. It is transmitted through the air in waves, which travel at about 700 mph (1,126 kph). The vibrations of the air are picked up by our ear drums, which vibrate in time, sending signals to our brains.

# CLIMATE CHANGE

Weather changes from day to day, season to season, and even over longer periods of time. The climate of a region may change altogether. For example, the Sahara used to be a grassland thousands of years ago. Now it's a desert. Because of the pollution we continually pump into the atmosphere, we could be drastically changing the atmosphere ourselves. Recent winters in the Alps have seen many places without their usual cover of snow. This could be a sign of climatic change.

## THE GREENHOUSE EFFECT

The amount of carbon dioxide in the atmosphere has increased slightly in the last 100 years. It is believed this increase is caused by the burning of fossil fuels and destruction of rainforests. If the buildup continues, more heat will be trapped in the atmosphere and an increase in the average temperature over the earth may occur (global warming).

**Some heat escapes.** ——————

**Cities and factories produce waste gases.**

**Heat is reflected back toward the earth.**

## ICE AGES

There have been several Ice Ages when the climate of the earth was colder than average. Ice that spread from the poles and glaciers covered much of Europe and North America. The last Ice Age ended 10,000 years ago. Some scientists think that the world is returning to an Ice Age climate. But more people fear global warming.

**Heat radiation from the sun**

## CFCs

CFCs are chemicals used in aerosol cans, refrigerators and in making styrofoam. If released into the air, they break down when exposed to ultraviolet light, giving off chlorine. The danger is that this chlorine may attack the ozone that forms a protective layer from ultraviolet radiation in the atmosphere. Already, environmentalists have detected ozone damage.

**Rainforest destruction**

# WEATHER WATCH

You can keep tabs on the weather in your area. You can make a rain gauge and measure how much falls each day. You can record wind direction, either with a weather vane or a wind sock. You may be able to estimate wind speeds, too. How damp is the atmosphere? You can get complicated instruments to measure this, or you could just use an old pinecone, and notice whether it is open (dry) or closed (damp). Measure the temperature, too. Put a thermometer outside, but in the shade. You could make a chart of temperature and rainfall for each month. You would need to keep up your record for a long time, though, before you could even begin to guess whether the climate was changing!

**Homemade rain gauge made from a plastic bottle that has the top cut off and sitting upside down in the base.**

**Make a card for each month and measure temperature, rainfall and record other observations such as animals seen or trees.**

**Take average rainfall and temperature and make graphs for each. Use symbols for such things as falling leaves.**

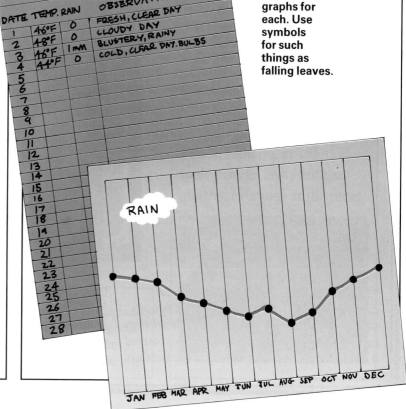

FEBRUARY

| DATE | TEMP. | RAIN | OBSERVATIONS |
|------|-------|------|--------------|
| 1 | 46°F | 0 | FRESH, CLEAR DAY |
| 2 | 48°F | 0 | CLOUDY DAY |
| 3 | 46°F | 1mm | BLUSTERY, RAINY |
| 4 | 44°F | 0 | COLD, CLEAR DAY. BULBS |
| 5 | | | |
| 6 | | | |
| 7 | | | |
| 8 | | | |
| 9 | | | |
| 10 | | | |
| 11 | | | |
| 12 | | | |
| 13 | | | |
| 14 | | | |
| 15 | | | |
| 16 | | | |
| 17 | | | |
| 18 | | | |
| 19 | | | |
| 20 | | | |
| 21 | | | |
| 22 | | | |
| 23 | | | |
| 24 | | | |
| 25 | | | |
| 26 | | | |
| 27 | | | |
| 28 | | | |

RAIN

JAN FEB MAR APR MAY JUN JUL AUG SEP OCT NOV DEC

# Fantastic VOYAGES

With the development of the rocket, people's dreams of space travel finally came true. Rockets burn fuel to produce gases that escape through a nozzle, causing the rocket to thrust forward. Their engines are the only kind that can work in space, and they must carry all their fuel and oxygen to burn it. The secret of reaching space is the multi-stage rocket, in which various parts burn out and fall off, one after another. Since the first rockets went into space, spacecraft have explored the solar system to its very limits, and people have walked on the Moon.

**A VISION OF THE FUTURE**
*The French author Jules Verne was well known for his futuristic visions. In 1865 he wrote a book about a journey to the Moon. His space travelers were fired from a gun – which in real life would have killed them – and had to fly around the Moon, and then come back, because they had no way of landing.*

**THE ROCKET PIONEERS**
*The principles of rocketry were developed by Konstantin Tsiolkovsky, a Russian teacher, at the beginning of the twentieth century. Robert Goddard, an American physicist whose early rocket is shown bottom left, and Werner von Braun (above) from Germany went on to build and launch successful rockets. Von Braun's V-2 rocket (top left) was used by the Nazis as a devastating weapon during the last year of World War II (1939–1945).*

## NASA
The National Aeronautics and Space Administration (NASA) put the first person on the Moon in July 1969. But unstaffed NASA missions to the planets have taught us more. For example, the landings on Mars by Viking spacecraft found no signs of life there, despite many people's claims that it could exist.

Heat radiation
from the
sun

Rainforest
destruction

# WEATHER WATCH

You can keep tabs on the weather in your area. You can make a rain gauge and measure how much falls each day. You can record wind direction, either with a weather vane or a wind sock. You may be able to estimate wind speeds, too. How damp is the atmosphere? You can get complicated instruments to measure this, or you could just use an old pinecone, and notice whether it is open (dry) or closed (damp). Measure the temperature, too. Put a thermometer outside, but in the shade. You could make a chart of temperature and rainfall for each month. You would need to keep up your record for a long time, though, before you could even begin to guess whether the climate was changing!

**Homemade rain gauge** made from a plastic bottle that has the top cut off and sitting upside down in the base.

**Make a card for each month** and measure temperature, rainfall and record other observations such as animals seen or trees.

**Take average rainfall and temperature** and make graphs for each. Use symbols for such things as falling leaves.

FEBRUARY

| DATE | TEMP. | RAIN | OBSERVATIONS |
|------|-------|------|--------------|
| 1 | 46°F | 0 | FRESH, CLEAR DAY |
| 2 | 48°F | 0 | CLOUDY DAY |
| 3 | 46°F | 1 mm | BLUSTERY, RAINY |
| 4 | 44°F | 0 | COLD, CLEAR DAY. BULBS |
| 5 | | | |
| 6 | | | |
| 7 | | | |
| 8 | | | |
| 9 | | | |
| 10 | | | |
| 11 | | | |
| 12 | | | |
| 13 | | | |
| 14 | | | |
| 15 | | | |
| 16 | | | |
| 17 | | | |
| 18 | | | |
| 19 | | | |
| 20 | | | |
| 21 | | | |
| 22 | | | |
| 23 | | | |
| 24 | | | |
| 25 | | | |
| 26 | | | |
| 27 | | | |
| 28 | | | |

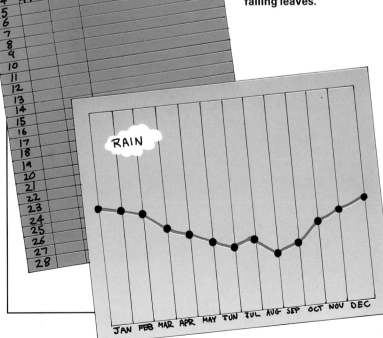

RAIN

JAN FEB MAR APR MAY JUN JUL AUG SEP OCT NOV DEC

# The Early MYSTERIES

Bones of dinosaurs and other large animals were first described by scientists in the 1600s, but even the Romans had dug up such remains. These probably inspired legends. Elephant skulls, which have an opening in the middle of the head, almost certainly inspired the one-eyed Cyclops featured in the ancient Greek poem *The Odyssey*, and for centuries, people believed that large fossils were the remains of animals drowned in the biblical flood.

### DINO-WARS
*In the late 19th century, a "war" broke out between two American paleontologists, Othniel Marsh and Edward Drinker Cope. Each wanted to collect, name, and describe more dinosaurs than the other. This fight led to many major discoveries, which now fill museums throughout the country.*

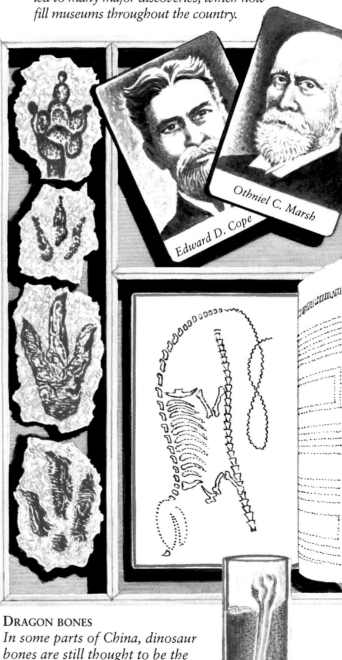

Edward D. Cope

Othniel C. Marsh

### GIANT PRINTS
*In 1835, Edward Hitchcock described some giant footprints found in Massachusetts. Some people believed they had been left by Noah's raven, but Hitchcock said they had come from huge birds. Only after his death were they recognized as dinosaur tracks.*

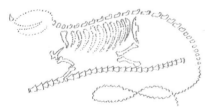

**"MANTELL" PIECE** *Gideon Mantell, an English doctor, was one of the first people to identify dinosaur bones. He realized they belonged to giant reptiles. He reconstructed a dinosaur (above) and named it Iguanodon.*

### DRAGON BONES
*In some parts of China, dinosaur bones are still thought to be the remains of dragons and are ground up for medicinal purposes.*

### NAMING DINOSAURS

*Richard Owen, a great 19th-century paleontologist, invented the name "dinosaur" which means "terrible lizard." He first made his ideas public at a meeting in England in 1841.*

### DINOSAURS AT THE MOVIES

*Dinosaurs have appeared in many films, from* King Kong *to* Jurassic Park *(above). The first dinosaur film was made in 1912 and starred a friendly sauropod called Gertie (above right).*

### NESTING DINOSAURS

*An expedition to Mongolia made one of the first discoveries of dinosaur eggs, in 1923. A dinosaur found with them was thought to have been an egg thief, but new findings show that it was the parent sitting on the nest.*

### Dinosaurs at the Palace

The first model dinosaurs were displayed at Crystal Palace, London, in 1853. They look strange now, but they amazed everyone at the time!

*Who first wrote about dinosaur bones?* The first description of a dinosaur bone was published by Robert Plot in England, in 1676. He thought it was part of a giant human. The bone is now lost.

# THE LEGACY OF ROME

Even today, over 1,500 years after the decline of the empire, Rome still has an enormous influence over our lives. Many of our buildings were copied from the Roman style of architecture. Our legal and political systems can be traced back to Roman times. In addition, there is a huge quantity of historical evidence, from literature and coins, to surviving roads and aqueducts, to keep the memory of Rome well and truly alive.

The Radcliffe Camera is a library in Oxford, England. Its architect, James Gibbs (1683-1754), modeled it on a Roman basilica. The dome, the pillars, and the ornate, classical style are reminiscent of many of the magnificent buildings of the Roman Empire. Several major cities have been built on sites chosen by the Romans. For example, Londinium (modern day London) was founded by the Romans in A.D.43 as a seaport. Can you find out any other examples of towns or cities which were built by the Romans, and which remain today?

### The Roman revival
In the early 15th century, writers, artists, sculptors, and architects began to draw inspiration from ancient Greece and Rome. Ruins were studied and statues were dug up. Ancient myths and legends were used as the basis for paintings, such as the French artist Claude's depiction of Aeneas at Delos (shown right). Latin literature also provided inspiration for Renaissance writers. The English poet Pope was greatly influenced by the Latin writer Juvenal throughout his work.

The European
Community flag

The period of Roman Empire demonstrated the possibility of one government controlling large areas. Roman citizenship gave people a sense of identity. Today the European Community can be seen to reflect Roman ideals of unity, albeit with modern goals of a single monetary and taxation system, and a central government.

## Herbal medicine

For centuries, the healing properties of plants and herbs have been used by different cultures, including the Romans. Try growing your own herbs from seed in a patch of garden or in a small pot. Place them in a sunny, sheltered spot and remember to water them well. Some of the medicinal properties of herbs are listed below.

Basil for the stomach

Lemon balm for headaches

Sage for sore throats

Camomile (antiseptic)

## Pompeii

Much of the evidence that we have today about ancient Rome comes from archaeological excavations such as Pompeii (below). The town has been well preserved under the volcanic ash and lava which engulfed it in A.D. 79. Its forum, basilica, theaters, temples, lavish villas, and tiny sleeping quarters offer a complete picture of Roman life. The ruins also provide us with a valuable insight into many aspects of Roman civilization and culture.

The archaeological remains of Pompeii, which was destroyed by the volcano, Vesuvius, in A.D. 79.

## The French Empire

The Imperial system used by the Romans was later copied by rulers of other European countries. The Frankish king, Charlemagne, revived the idea of the Roman Empire in the West. It was termed the Holy Roman Empire by subsequent Frankish and German leaders. The Holy Roman Empire was destroyed by Napoleon Bonaparte who modeled his own empire on that of Rome and even called himself emperor.

# WHAT IF AN ELEPHANT HAD NO TRUNK?

The long trunk is one of the main features of the animal, and it couldn't survive without it. The trunk is the nose and upper lip, that have joined together and grown very long. The elephant uses its trunk for many vital actions, especially eating and drinking. Without a trunk, this plant-eater would not be able to pick up grass and leaves to eat. It also uses the trunk to smell, breathe, feel, and to suck up water. If the elephant crosses a deep river, it can even use its trunk as a snorkel!

### Trunk call

The hairy tip of the trunk is very sensitive to touch. The two holes are nostrils that lead to the long nose tube. Through this the elephant breathes and trumpets its calls. Muscles bend the trunk in any direction.

### Sniffing and smelling

Elephants lift their trunks high to sniff the air for predators, fire, and other dangers, and to catch the scent of their herd and other creatures. They also smell food before eating it.

## The daily grind

Long, thin, sharp, fang-shaped teeth are good for catching, killing, and ripping up meaty prey – but they are no good for chewing or grinding up leaves, grass, fruits, and other plant parts. Herbivores (plant-eaters) need wide, broad, fairly flat teeth to mash and pulp their food thoroughly. This is because plants are made from tough fibers that need to be broken down, so that a herbivore's intestines can extract the nutrients.

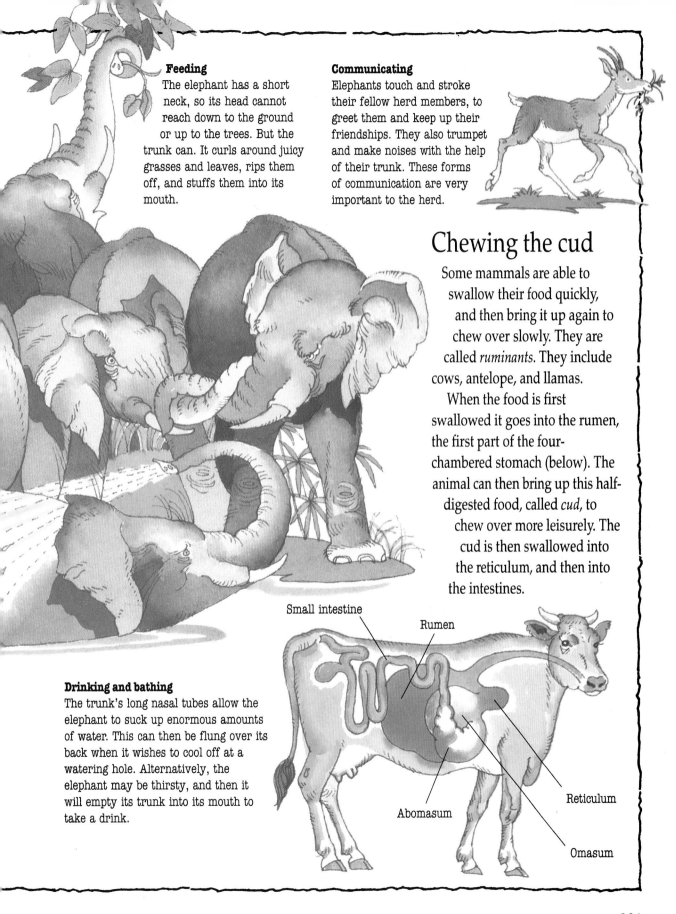

### Feeding

The elephant has a short neck, so its head cannot reach down to the ground or up to the trees. But the trunk can. It curls around juicy grasses and leaves, rips them off, and stuffs them into its mouth.

### Communicating

Elephants touch and stroke their fellow herd members, to greet them and keep up their friendships. They also trumpet and make noises with the help of their trunk. These forms of communication are very important to the herd.

# Chewing the cud

Some mammals are able to swallow their food quickly, and then bring it up again to chew over slowly. They are called *ruminants*. They include cows, antelope, and llamas.

When the food is first swallowed it goes into the rumen, the first part of the four-chambered stomach (below). The animal can then bring up this half-digested food, called *cud*, to chew over more leisurely. The cud is then swallowed into the reticulum, and then into the intestines.

### Drinking and bathing

The trunk's long nasal tubes allow the elephant to suck up enormous amounts of water. This can then be flung over its back when it wishes to cool off at a watering hole. Alternatively, the elephant may be thirsty, and then it will empty its trunk into its mouth to take a drink.

Small intestine

Rumen

Abomasum

Reticulum

Omasum

201

# Fantastic VOYAGES

**A VISION OF THE FUTURE**
*The French author Jules Verne was well known for his futuristic visions. In 1865 he wrote a book about a journey to the Moon. His space travelers were fired from a gun – which in real life would have killed them – and had to fly around the Moon, and then come back, because they had no way of landing.*

With the development of the rocket, people's dreams of space travel finally came true. Rockets burn fuel to produce gases that escape through a nozzle, causing the rocket to thrust forward. Their engines are the only kind that can work in space, and they must carry all their fuel and oxygen to burn it. The secret of reaching space is the multi-stage rocket, in which various parts burn out and fall off, one after another. Since the first rockets went into space, spacecraft have explored the solar system to its very limits, and people have walked on the Moon.

**THE ROCKET PIONEERS**
*The principles of rocketry were developed by Konstantin Tsiolkovsky, a Russian teacher, at the beginning of the twentieth century. Robert Goddard, an American physicist whose early rocket is shown bottom left, and Werner von Braun (above) from Germany went on to build and launch successful rockets. Von Braun's V-2 rocket (top left) was used by the Nazis as a devastating weapon during the last year of World War II (1939–1945).*

## NASA

The National Aeronautics and Space Administration (NASA) put the first person on the Moon in July 1969. But unstaffed NASA missions to the planets have taught us more. For example, the landings on Mars by Viking spacecraft found no signs of life there, despite many people's claims that it could exist.

*Can we make time stand still?*
If we can ever design a spacecraft that is able to travel at the speed of light, time on board will stand still, according to Albert Einstein's theories. An astronaut could travel for 1,000 years and come back no older than the day he or she set off. But it is unlikely that technology will ever develop enough to build such a fast craft.

### ALONE IN SPACE

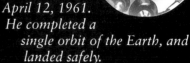

*The first person in space, Major Yuri Gagarin, was launched by the former Soviet Union in Vostok 1 on April 12, 1961. He completed a single orbit of the Earth, and landed safely.*

### PROBING DEEP SPACE

*The first space probes to leave the solar system were Pioneer 10 and 11, then two Voyager spacecraft. The Voyager craft took closeup pictures of Jupiter and Saturn in 1979, then Voyager 2 went on to visit Uranus and Neptune. The latest mission, Galileo, was launched in 1989 but will reach the outer planets slowly, by a complicated route.*

### LITTER-BUGS

*The landscapes of the solar system are dotted with equipment left behind by various expeditions.*

### EARTH'S CALLING CARD

*Pioneer 10, which was launched in 1972, carries a plaque of information, or "calling card," in case it should ever meet other intelligent life. It has a diagram showing what human beings look like, and a sky map to identify where our solar system is.*

# TRUMPET AND BRASS

Your trumpet is a member of a large family of trumpets, all named after the notes they correspond to on the piano. Your instrument is probably a B$^b$ trumpet; there is also a C trumpet, a D trumpet, and so on. The higher the trumpet, the shorter the instrument will be.

Try the following test with a piano. Play the first open note of a scale, your middle C, on your trumpet. Now play a B$^b$ on the piano, or ask someone to play it for you. The notes should sound the same on both instruments. Your C equals the piano's B$^b$, so your trumpet is called a B$^b$ trumpet. An E$^b$ trumpet playing the same open note would sound the same as E$^b$ on a piano.

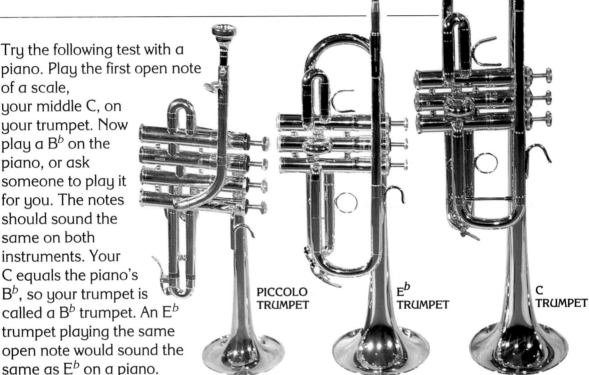

PICCOLO TRUMPET

E$^b$ TRUMPET

C TRUMPET

## ROTARY VALVE TRUMPET

The trumpets that are mostly used in the United States and Britain are known as piston trumpets. This name refers to the type of valve that is used in the instrument to produce a wider range of notes. In countries such as Germany and Austria, rotary valve trumpets are played instead. Rotary valves look similar to the valves used on French horns. Although they look different from piston trumpets, rotary valve trumpets are played in almost the same way.

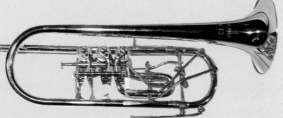

## BRASS FAMILY

The **euphonium** (right) has a warm, deep, lyrical sound. The **trombone** (below) is the only modern brass instrument that uses a slide to produce a full range of notes.

The **sousaphone** was invented by John Philip Sousa for marching bands. The **tuba** (below) is another large member of the brass family. It was invented 150 years ago, for Russian military bands.

The **French horn** is a descendant of a hunting horn. It would measure over 16 feet (5 m) long if stretched out. The musician places one hand in the bell to improve the sound.

The **tenor horn** is used mainly in the brass band, where its warm, soft sound adds color. You can expect to see three or four tenor horns in many brass bands.

## LOUIS ARMSTRONG

Louis Armstrong was one of the strongest influences in the history of jazz. He learned to play while at reform school (he had been arrested for firing blanks from a pistol in the street). He was soon in demand as a cornetist, and eventually formed his own bands. His influence on many musicians is widely acknowledged.

# WHAT IS LIGHT?

Light is a mixture of electrical and magnetic energy that travels faster than anything else in the universe. It takes less than one tenth of a second for light to travel from New York to London. Light is made up of tiny particles of energy called photons. The light moves along in very small waves that travel forward in straight lines, called rays. Light can travel through air and transparent substances, but can also travel through empty space. This is how sunlight reaches the earth. Light is similar to other forms of electromagnetic energy which have different wavelengths.

**Radio waves**
These have the longest wavelength. They are used for satellite communication and to carry TV and radio signals.

**Visible light**
Appears white or colorless, but is made up of colors, each with a different wavelength.

| Radio | Micro | Infrared | Visible |
|-------|-------|----------|---------|

**Electromagnetic spectrum**
This shows different kinds of electromagnetic energy arranged in order of their wavelengths. Wavelength is the distance between two consecutive waves.

**Microwaves**
Very short radio waves used in microwave ovens. They are also used in radar.

**Infrared rays**
Invisible rays, but we can feel the heat from them. They can be used to detect cancer and arthritis, or to take photographs in the dark.

**Different ways of seeing**
Most animals see visible light like we do. However, others have evolved sight which detects different wavelengths along the spectrum. Some insects see in ultraviolet light, which is invisible to most mammals and birds (except pigeons). Insect-pollinated flowers have lines which guide insects to their nectar. These lines only appear in ultraviolet light. The insects follow the guide lines to the nectar, scattering pollen on the way. This process helps the flowers to reproduce.

Bees cannot see the color red. They are strongly attracted by yellow and blue flowers which usually have strong ultraviolet markings. These markings attract bees to the flowers, and even pinpoint the location of the nectaries.

## Ultraviolet rays

These cause us to tan and help the skin to produce vitamin D. Large amounts are dangerous and may cause skin cancer, although most ultraviolet light from the sun is absorbed by the ozone layer.

## Gamma rays

These have the shortest wavelength. They are given off by naturally radioactive materials, such as uranium, and are part of the fallout after a nuclear explosion. They can travel through lead and cement, and damage living tissue.

| UV | X rays | Gamma |
|----|--------|-------|

## X Rays

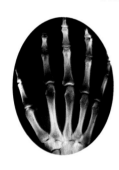

Called "X" by their discoverer because he was unsure of their nature. They pass through flesh, but are absorbed by bones and teeth, causing them to show up on x ray film. Small doses are safe, but large amounts are harmful to living tissue.

### Taking the straight path

Try this experiment to prove that light travels in straight lines. Cut out two pieces of cardboard, about 8 in square. Make a hole in the center of each piece of cardboard, and stick a knitting needle through both holes, ensuring that they are aligned. Fix the cardboards onto a flat surface with modeling clay. Turn off the light and shine a flashlight through the holes. What happens? Try putting certain materials like cellophane, paper, or a book, between the two cards when the flashlight is on. Describe what happens to the ray of light.

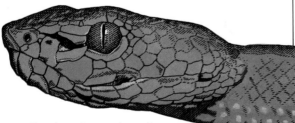

Certain snakes, such as pit vipers and pythons, detect prey by sensing the infrared light or "heat" they give out. They have special heat sensors which form an image from the infrared emissions. This helps them to hunt at night.

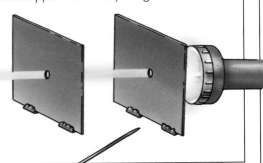

# WATER POLLUTION

Humans use enormous quantities of water. Not only do we drink it, we use it to wash and bathe. We irrigate farm crops and gardens. We use it to flush away waste in the sewage system. Flowing water provided the first source of energy to power machines. Today's factories still use water to make things, or sometimes just to cool machinery. Hydroelectric power is an important source of energy in some countries. Our need for water makes it hard to find enough. We dam valleys to trap water in reservoirs – but this may disturb a river's flow. We sink boreholes – but these may dry out the land and stop springs flowing. Many human activities leave water dirty, and sometimes full of unwanted and dangerous chemicals. How to stop this pollution is one of the biggest problems we now face.

## POLLUTING WATER

Detergents and poisonous chemicals are an obvious danger to water. But even chemicals that make things thrive, such as fertilizers, can create problems. If they run off the land into water they can make tiny water plants grow too well. These may use up all the oxygen in the water.

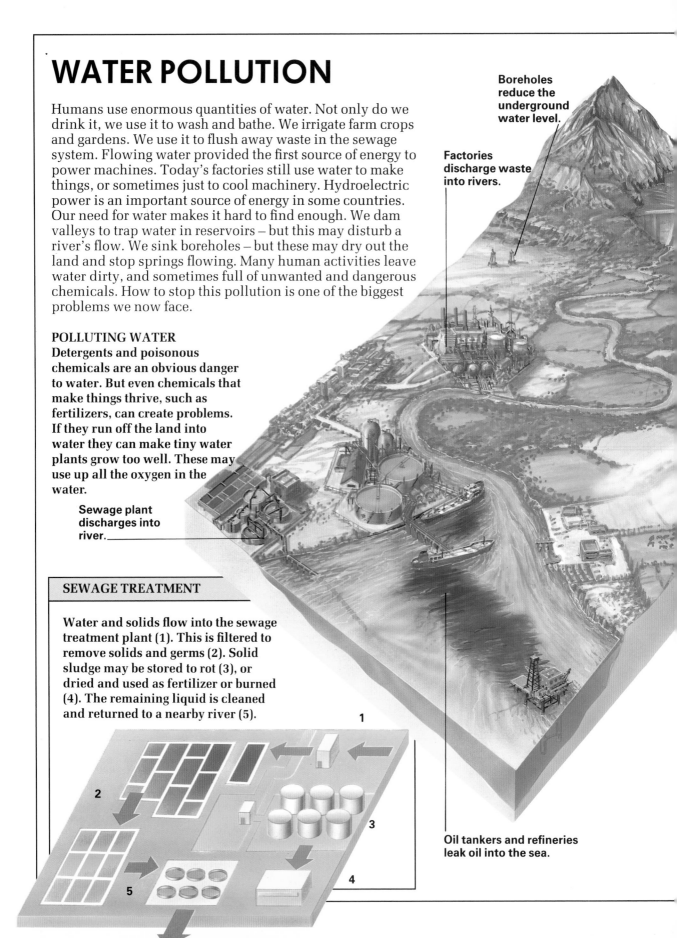

Boreholes reduce the underground water level.

Factories discharge waste into rivers.

Sewage plant discharges into river.

Oil tankers and refineries leak oil into the sea.

## SEWAGE TREATMENT

Water and solids flow into the sewage treatment plant (1). This is filtered to remove solids and germs (2). Solid sludge may be stored to rot (3), or dried and used as fertilizer or burned (4). The remaining liquid is cleaned and returned to a nearby river (5).

1

2

3

4

5

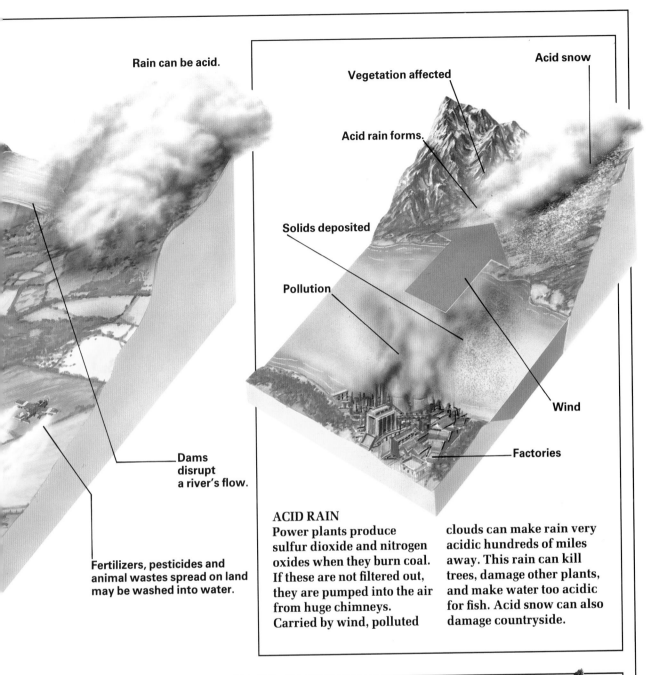

Rain can be acid.

Acid snow

Vegetation affected

Acid rain forms.

Solids deposited

Pollution

Wind

Dams disrupt a river's flow.

Factories

Fertilizers, pesticides and animal wastes spread on land may be washed into water.

## ACID RAIN

Power plants produce sulfur dioxide and nitrogen oxides when they burn coal. If these are not filtered out, they are pumped into the air from huge chimneys. Carried by wind, polluted clouds can make rain very acidic hundreds of miles away. This rain can kill trees, damage other plants, and make water too acidic for fish. Acid snow can also damage countryside.

## DANGER IN THE FOOD CHAIN

Some substances that are used to control pests break down soon after they are used. But some do not, and these may be passed up the food chain to animals which are not the original target of the poison. The poison can build up to harmful levels in animals at the top of the chain.

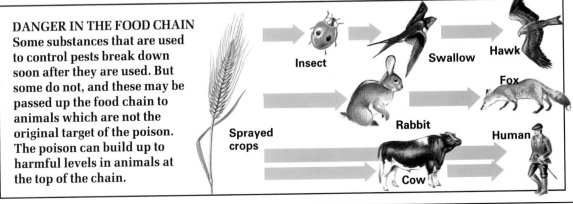

Insect

Swallow

Hawk

Fox

Rabbit

Human

Sprayed crops

Cow

# WHO WERE THE VIKINGS?

The Viking Age lasted from the end of the eighth century A.D. until the end of the eleventh century A.D. The Vikings, or Norsemen, came from Scandinavia, from the present-day countries of Denmark, Sweden, and Norway. The Vikings are most famous as fierce warriors who looted and conquered many parts of Europe in a series of terrifying raids. However, they were also successful and adventurous traders and explorers, talented poets, and skilled shipbuilders and craftsmen.

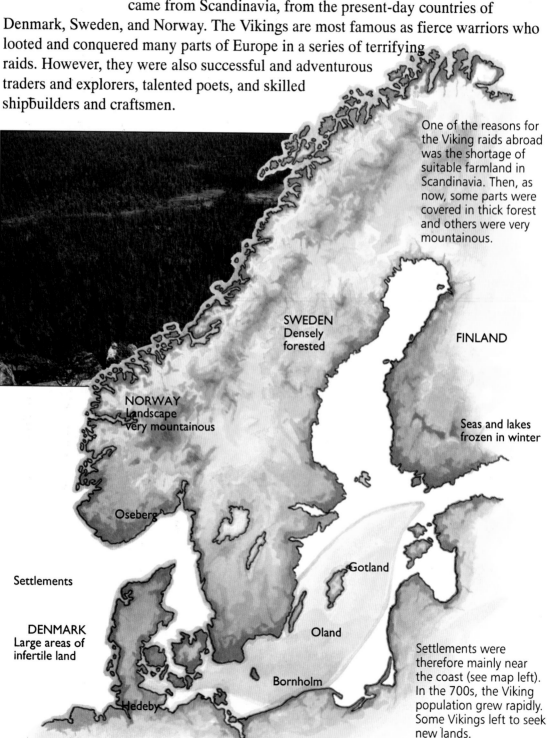

One of the reasons for the Viking raids abroad was the shortage of suitable farmland in Scandinavia. Then, as now, some parts were covered in thick forest and others were very mountainous.

SWEDEN
Densely forested

FINLAND

Seas and lakes frozen in winter

NORWAY
Landscape very mountainous

Oseberg

Gotland

Settlements

Oland

DENMARK
Large areas of infertile land

Bornholm

Settlements were therefore mainly near the coast (see map left). In the 700s, the Viking population grew rapidly. Some Vikings left to seek new lands.

Hedeby

GERMANY                    POLAND

## Classes of society

Viking society was divided into different classes, based on wealth and land ownership. A king, or chief, ruled over each community. Below him came the rich noblemen, or jarls. The English word "earl" comes from the word "jarl." The kings and jarls were the most powerful landowners. Below them came the freemen, or karls. They included farmers, merchants, and craftsmen. At the bottom of the ladder were the slaves, who were known as thralls.

JARLS
Noblemen

KARLS
Freemen

THRALLS
Slaves

## The Viking name

The Scandinavians did not call themselves Vikings. This was a name used by early writers. The word "Viking" may come from the old Icelandic word "vik.," meaning bay or creek. The phrase "a-Viking" also means to go exploring.

## The first raid

*"...never before has such terror appeared in Britain as we have now suffered from this pagan race..."*
This account by the Northumbrian priest Alcuin marks the beginning of the Viking reign of terror after their attack on the Holy Island of Lindisfarne in June, A.D. 793. The Vikings looted the monastery there, killed some of the monks, and carried others off to be slaves. The attack on Lindisfarne was terrifying because it was a holy place, known and respected throughout Europe. Also, like other monasteries around the coast of Britain, Lindisfarne had believed itself to be immune to attacks from the sea.

**The original monastery at Lindisfarne was completely destroyed by the Vikings. It was later rebuilt (below).**

## Vikings at work

The majority of Vikings spent quite short periods away from home on raids. They worked as farmers, growing oats, barley, rye, and vegetables, and tending cattle, pigs, sheep, and goats. Fruits, such as apples, and hazelnuts and walnuts were also grown and stored for use during the winter. Reindeer, rabbit, hare, and wild bears were hunted by the Vikings, and cod, salmon, and trout were plentiful in the Scandinavian fjords and rivers. Other Vikings were merchants, traveling far and wide to trade their goods. Some were specialized craftsmen – silversmiths, blacksmiths, and woodcarvers. Most famous of all were the skills of the Viking shipbuilders and sailors.

The Gila Monster of the North American deserts is a lizard with a venomous bite. Its venom is powerful enough to subdue its bird and mammal prey.

The Australian Stump-tailed Skink is able to store food in its tail, as fat, and can go for months without food.

Gila Monster

Stump-tailed Skink

# Desert Lizards

The Lizard group is by far the largest group of reptiles living today. Lizards can be found in many different environments. Many species of lizards live in the deserts. Lizards are well adapted to living in dry habitats. Their bodies are geared to retain water; they have very dry and scaly skin which loses water at a very slow rate.

Lizards also burn fat very slowly, therefore they are able to go for long periods of time without food. This is useful in dry desert areas where food is quite scarce.

A Frilled Lizard runs on its back legs to keep its body away from the hot sand. ▷

# SUBMARINES

Most of the world's submarines are warships. They are designed to carry and fire torpedoes and missiles, or to lay mines, to destroy enemy vessels. Only the smallest submarines, called submersibles, are used for non-military, or civilian, work. Submersibles are built for repairing oil rigs, laying pipes on the seabed, and to study the underwater world.

There are two main types of submarine. The most common is the diesel-electric. This is powered by a diesel engine when on the surface of the water and by an electric motor when submerged. The second type is the nuclear submarine. This is powered at all times by a nuclear reactor. Diesel-electric submarines are the easiest and cheapest to build.

Military submarines are given code letters that describe their engines or the weapons they carry. For example, diesel-electric attack subs are coded SS, and nuclear powered ones SSN. Attack subs are designed to find and destroy enemy warships. Submarines that carry missiles which can be guided to a ship or target on land are coded SSG or, if nuclear powered, SSGN.

**The nuclear powered hunter-killer submarine is fast and well-armed.**

A submersible – for underwater research.

A nuclear missile-carrying submarine.

Submarines range in size from submersibles less than 6m (20ft) long to the 170m (558ft) Soviet Typhoon class submarine. This is nuclear powered and carries "ballistic" missiles (SSBN class).

A diesel-electric submarine.

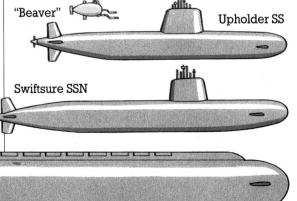

"Beaver"

Upholder SS

Swiftsure SSN

Typhoon SSBN

# WORKING WITH PHOTOS

"From this day on, painting is dead." Many people believed this when photography was first invented. Artists today haven't actually given up painting, but a great many have used photographs in picture making.

### Picture puzzles

Cutting up and reassembling a photograph is a little like making your own jigsaw puzzle. This process will produce a new image which can be intriguing, bizarre or funny.

You will need a collection of images from postcards or magazines. These pictures can be cut up, using scissors or a craft knife. Cutting paper with a craft knife held against a metal ruler will produce a clean edge. There are many ways in which the pieces that you cut can be reassembled. A few are shown here, and others are suggested for you to try.

### Squares, strips and fans

Photographs can be cut into squares, as described below, or they can be cut into straight strips or curves. Curved strips can be spread out evenly, or shaped into a fan. Fanning will elongate your image. On the right, fanning has emphasized the curve of the goose's neck. This technique is very effective with photographs of figures in action.

### Two into one *will* go

Another project with strips is shown at the bottom of the opposite page. This project works best with two images that complement each other, as the shape of the bird's head and the hill do there. Cut both pictures into strips, and intersperse the two images. When the pictures are combined, the shapes will interact with one another.

◁"The image on the left is composed of squares. To cut squares more accurately, mark out the lines on the back of your image first.

The illustration shows only one of the many ways in which the squares can be reassembled. Try rotating each square by 90°, and see what happens. Try again, rotating all the squares by 180° and sticking them upside down."

△ *"Here the photograph from the opposite page has been treated very differently. Try replacing strips like these in reverse order, or removing every other one and putting the rest together again."*

▽ *"The round hill echoes the shape of the bird's head below. Look for similar shapes for your own collage."*

# SOUND WAVES

Sound waves are similar to light waves in some ways. Like a beam of light can be reflected from a mirror, so a sound can be reflected from a surface like a wall. If you shout loudly in your school hall, the sound waves travel to the wall and are bounced back, reaching your ears a split second later – this is an echo. Bats make use of echoes when finding their way, or hunting. They give out a very high pitched sound that bounces back from objects or insects, telling them how far away things are. We can also use this method to find objects that we cannot see. Sonar uses sound to locate objects at the bottom of the sea, such as shipwrecks and shoals of fish.

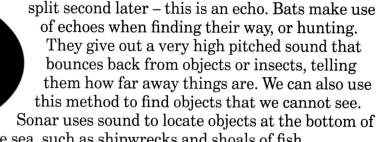

## FIRING WAVES

**1.** This cannon will send a narrow "beam" of sound waves. Begin by making a pair of wheels for your cannon using circles of cardboard, paper plates, thread spools, and a wooden stick.

**1**

**2.** Make a large tube of stiff cardboard for the cannon itself, 18-20 inches in diameter, and four feet long. Make the back of the cannon by covering a circle of cardboard with plastic wrap. Attach **2** with tape.

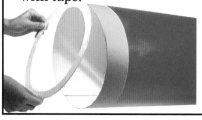

**3**

**3.** The front of the cannon is a disk of stiff cardboard with a 1 in hole in the center. You could decorate this with a disk of colored paper.

**4**

**4.** Tape the ends of the cannon firmly with double sided tape – this will enable you to fix the ends onto the tube and not into it.

**5.** Fix the tube to the wheels with tape, and weight the back end of the cannon so that it does not tip forward. Aim the cannon at a wall and tap the plastic wrap quite firmly – from a distance you should get an echo. Make a curtain from 0.5 in strips of foil. Fire your cannon at the curtain. You should see the sound waves making the foil vibrate.

**5**

218

## WHY IT WORKS

When you strike the piece of plastic wrap (diaphragm) on the cannon, the vibrations lead to sound waves being formed. The waves travel outward from the diaphragm, making the air particles around move back and forth in the same direction. When the waves leaving the front of the cannon meet a solid object, some of them are reflected while some continue traveling through the object, making it move slightly like the air particles. A bat uses sound to find objects in the dark. It produces sounds and then listens for the echoes to be reflected. This is called echolocation.

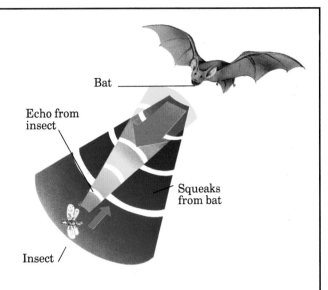

Bat

Echo from insect

Squeaks from bat

Insect

## BRIGHT IDEAS

🔆 Which surfaces are best for echoing? Can you make an echo in a bathroom, a kitchen, a cafeteria, a hall, a subway? Try other places, too. Do you think hard surfaces are better than soft surfaces for giving echoes? Which sounds echo the best?

🔆 Try shouting, knocking two stones together, banging two blocks of wood together, whistling, and talking. Do short, sharp sounds echo better than long soft ones?

🔆 The cannon channels the sound waves in one direction. Make a megaphone to channel your voice. Make a narrow cone, and then a wide cone. Shout to a friend through each cone. Shout again, aiming the megaphone 30 feet to their side. What happens? Which cone makes your voice sound louder, and which can you hear best from the side? Can you figure out why?

219

# SAVING ENERGY

In the 1970s, the oil-producing nations twice increased the price of oil. Though it has since declined, the shock made many nations think carefully about saving energy. More efficiency, less waste, and greater efforts to recycle materials are the results. Homes, offices, and factories now use less energy, while the fuel consumption of cars has improved. More could be done, but the high cost of saving energy is often seen as a disadvantage.

Industry has always recycled valuable materials; a quarter of every new car is made of metal from old cars. Paper can also be used again, once it has been bleached to remove ink. Recycled paper is never as clean and crisp as new paper, so it can't be used for high-value products. Often, it may simply be cheaper to plant more trees and use them as raw material.

### Insulation

A simple experiment shows the value of insulation in saving energy. Use two identical mugs and wrap an old scarf around one. Fill both with hot water at the same temperature. Take the temperature of each at regular intervals and plot them on graph paper. Also try a thermos flask. Why is that so much better?

BMW has produced a totally recyclable car, in which every item can be dismantled and re-used.

Scientific research has shown that the lead in car exhaust fumes is dangerous to the body, even in small quantities. Lead-free gasoline was introduced to reduce pollution but it doesn't save energy because it burns less smoothly than leaded gas.

### Pedal power

Bicycles are the most energy-efficient form of transportation in towns. They don't burn fuel and are quicker in heavy traffic. The police in Seattle use bicycles instead of cars. The biggest drawback is the danger from other vehicles.

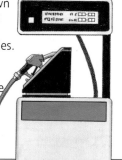

a bottle recycling plant

### Brighter bulbs

Compact fluorescent light bulbs use about a fifth as much energy to produce the same light output as normal light bulbs. They also last longer but cost more. This means they are most effective in lights that stay on for many hours. However, they do not produce heat, so more energy may be used in heating your home.

Recycling of domestic waste makes sense, but not if it involves driving many miles to put a few bottles in a recycling bin. That would use far more energy in gas than could ever be saved by recycling glass. Separating waste into different garbage cans at home sounds more sensible. But often the prices paid for waste materials are too low to cover costs.

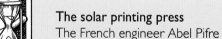

The world has huge coal reserves, but less gas or oil. The oil looks as if it will run out in only 20 years. This is misleading: oil companies do not explore for new oil if they have enough to be going on with.

Nuclear fuel that has already been used once can be reprocessed to extract plutonium and unused uranium. This process takes place in a reprocessing plant (left) where the used fuel is dissolved in nitric acid and waste products are chemically removed.

### The solar printing press

The French engineer Abel Pifre showed this invention in Paris in 1882. Sunlight shone on to a mirror and focused on a steam boiler. The steam produced powered an engine which in turn worked the press.

# THE PIRATE SCHOONER

Pirates operated in every kind of ship, from galleys to junks. Usually they had no choice – they sailed in whatever vessel they captured. The type of schooner shown here was built from the mid-18th century onward. It was an ideal craft: fast, maneuverable, and with a shallow draft that allowed her to hide in rivers and bays. The sail plan, with square sails only at the tops of the masts, allowed the boat to sail close to the wind. "Schooner" comes from the American verb scoon, meaning to skim along the water.

Note that this ship is not heavily armed. Cannons were expensive to operate, their weight slowed the ship down, and they were only used against unarmed vessels. Besides, no pirate wanted a gunfight. They aimed to strike fast and get away as quickly as possible.

*Captain's Cabin*
*Placed at the stern, this was out of the worst of the weather and could be easily defended in case of mutiny. It was also the store-room for charts and money.*

powder  wadding  shot

## UNDER FIRE
Cannons (*above*) were loaded through the muzzle with powder, wadding, and shot. A gun's recoil, capable of breaking a man's leg, was absorbed by ropes. A single cannon ball weighed 20 lb (9 kg). To get greater range and hit a vessel on the waterline, gunners skimmed shots off the sea (*below left*). Double balls and shrapnel (*below right and middle*) were used against the rigging to do the most damage.

*Sail Locker*
*A storm could carry away the entire rigging, so all ships carried spare sails. They had to be kept dry to prevent rotting.*

*Stores and Armory*
*These were kept at the bottom of the boat due to their weight. To prevent damage they were tied down in rough weather.*

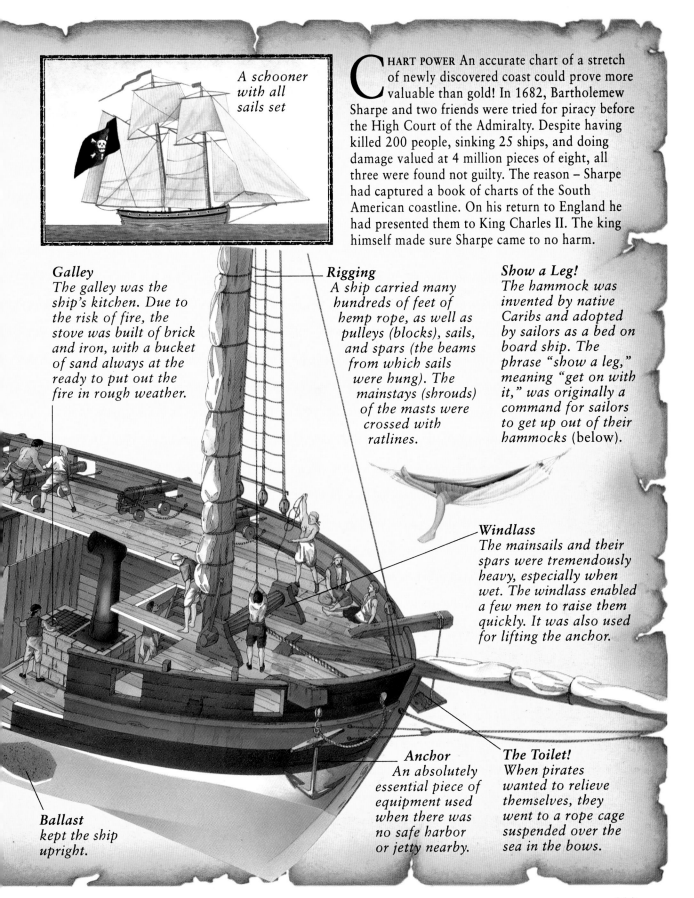

A schooner with all sails set

**C**HART POWER An accurate chart of a stretch of newly discovered coast could prove more valuable than gold! In 1682, Bartholemew Sharpe and two friends were tried for piracy before the High Court of the Admiralty. Despite having killed 200 people, sinking 25 ships, and doing damage valued at 4 million pieces of eight, all three were found not guilty. The reason – Sharpe had captured a book of charts of the South American coastline. On his return to England he had presented them to King Charles II. The king himself made sure Sharpe came to no harm.

**Galley**
The galley was the ship's kitchen. Due to the risk of fire, the stove was built of brick and iron, with a bucket of sand always at the ready to put out the fire in rough weather.

**Rigging**
A ship carried many hundreds of feet of hemp rope, as well as pulleys (blocks), sails, and spars (the beams from which sails were hung). The mainstays (shrouds) of the masts were crossed with ratlines.

**Show a Leg!**
The hammock was invented by native Caribs and adopted by sailors as a bed on board ship. The phrase "show a leg," meaning "get on with it," was originally a command for sailors to get up out of their hammocks (below).

**Windlass**
The mainsails and their spars were tremendously heavy, especially when wet. The windlass enabled a few men to raise them quickly. It was also used for lifting the anchor.

**Ballast**
kept the ship upright.

**Anchor**
An absolutely essential piece of equipment used when there was no safe harbor or jetty nearby.

**The Toilet!**
When pirates wanted to relieve themselves, they went to a rope cage suspended over the sea in the bows.

# WHAT ARE INSECTS?

Insects are the most successful of all animal groups, making up 85 percent of the whole animal kingdom. There are as many as 10,000 insects living on every square yard of the Earth's surface. There are many different kinds of insects, but all share a common body design, adapted to cope with every possible environment, and to eat every possible kind of food. All adult insects have a segmented body which is divided into three parts: head, thorax, and abdomen.

An insect's skin is made of a tough substance called chitin. This forms a hard shell, or exoskeleton, which protects the insect's organs. The leg and wing muscles are securely anchored to the exoskeleton. It is waterproof, and prevents the insect from drying out. But it does not allow air through. Holes in the skin, called spiracles, lead to breathing tubes. The exoskeleton does not grow. As an insect gets bigger, it must shed its old skin, and grow a new one. The outer skin, or cuticle, is patterned and colored for camouflage or warning.

Antennae

Compound eye

Mouthparts

Thorax

Six jointed legs

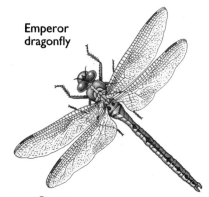

**Emperor dragonfly**

**Common cockroach**

**Bush cricket**

**Firebug**

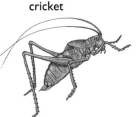

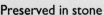

All insects have three pairs of jointed legs, and most have four wings. Insects from some easily recognizable insect groups are shown above.

## Preserved in stone

Insects first appeared on Earth about 370 million years ago. Early species had no wings; they fed on the sap and spores of the newly-evolved land plants. Insects were the first creatures to conquer the air, 150 million years before birds first flew. This is a fossil of an early dragonfly that lived 300 million years ago, in the steamy Carboniferous forests with the ancestors of the dinosaurs.

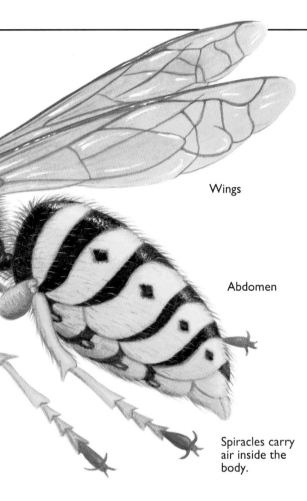

Wings

Abdomen

Spiracles carry air inside the body.

The head contains a simple brain which receives messages from the sense organs and controls the muscles. The thorax is made of three segments fused together. It carries the legs and wings. The abdomen contains the organs for digestion and reproduction.

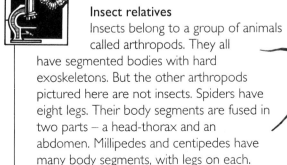

Seven-spotted ladybird (beetle)

Bluebottle (fly)

Privet hawkmoth

Wood ant

Insect relatives

Insects belong to a group of animals called arthropods. They all have segmented bodies with hard exoskeletons. But the other arthropods pictured here are not insects. Spiders have eight legs. Their body segments are fused in two parts – a head-thorax and an abdomen. Millipedes and centipedes have many body segments, with legs on each.

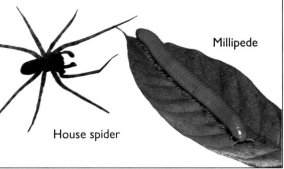

Millipede

House spider

# THE FIRST MOTORISTS

After the experiments of the 1880s, the first car-making factories were set up in Germany and France during the 1890s. Engineers improved Daimler's engines, making them more powerful and reliable. Frenchman Emile Levassor was probably first to think of the car as a machine in its own right, and not just a cart without a horse. In 1891 he moved the engine from the back to the front, away from the mud and stones thrown up by the wheels. He also replaced the belt drive between engine and road wheels, with a clutch and a gearbox. The car as we know it today was quickly taking shape.

Napier 1913

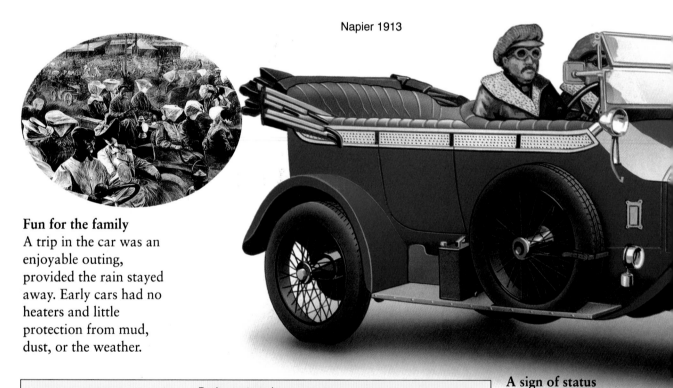

**Fun for the family**
A trip in the car was an enjoyable outing, provided the rain stayed away. Early cars had no heaters and little protection from mud, dust, or the weather.

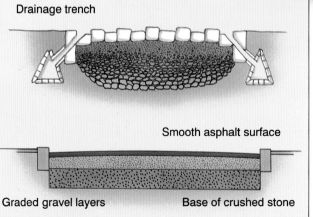

**Roads to run on**
Cars were faster than horse-drawn carts, so they needed better roads. Instead of packed-down layers of earth and stone (top right), engineers devised smooth surfaces of tarmac or asphalt.

Drainage trench

Smooth asphalt surface

Graded gravel layers          Base of crushed stone

**A sign of status**
Big houses, fine furniture and beautiful horses had been signs of wealth for centuries. Around 1900 a new symbol of status appeared: the car. As yet, the car was not a useful means of transportation. Roads were muddy, rutted cart tracks, and refueling places were scarce.

### Flying the red flag

Under a law passed in Britain in 1865, steam traction engines were allowed to lumber along roads, provided they did not exceed 4 mph (6.5 kph) and a man with a red flag walked about 170 feet in front. The red flag was abandoned in 1878, but a footman still had to walk 60 feet in front. This law applied to any similar vehicle, including the first cars. In 1896 the footman was abandoned too, and the speed limit raised to almost 12 mph (20 kph).

Gas pump 1905

### Buying a car

At first, only the rich could afford a car. But many people gathered in car showrooms to gaze at these newfangled pieces of machinery, which seemed to have little practical use.

### Stopping for fuel

In the early days many car owners carried cans of spare fuel with them. There were no detailed maps and finding a gasoline station on a long journey was mostly a matter of luck.

### The maker's name

Car manufacturers were soon competing to produce the best, fastest, or cheapest vehicles. Companies such as Buick and Austin designed easily recognized nameplates.

### Advertising

The growing car business involved designers, engineers, manufacturers, mechanics, and of course advertisers. As roads became busier, they became valuable places for posters, advertising the latest cars to drivers.

# SCALES, SHARPS, AND FLATS

Some scales have natural notes, which are the white keys on a piano. A scale is C major, when it starts on C. Scales that begin on other notes use sharps and flats, which are the black keys on the piano.

The sign for a sharp is shown on the left. A sharp raises the pitch of a note by a half step. A flat sign is shown below left. It lowers the pitch of a note by a half step. Sometimes sharps or flats appear in the "key signature" near the treble clef. They tell us the scale or key that the music is based on.

If no sharp or flat appears in the key signature, the key is C major. In the second line below, the key is G major, with F# in the key signature.

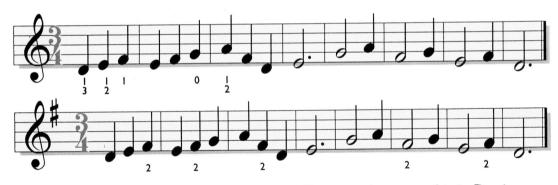

For every major key there is also a minor one. The first exercise below is in F major; the second is in D minor. Both have B♭ in the key signature.

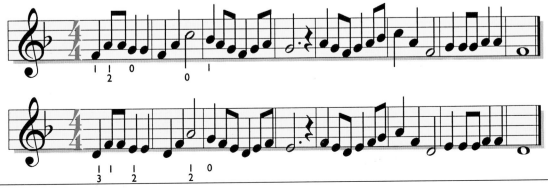

## KEY SIGNATURES

Sharps or flats in the key signature do not appear in the music itself. The scales of D major and B minor have $F^{\#}$ and $C^{\#}$ in the key signature.

The scales of $B^b$ major and G minor both have $B^b$ and $E^b$ in their key signature. Remember to play these notes flat in the music itself.

Practice the exercises below, looking out for the key-signature. See if you can tell if they are written in a major or a minor key.

### MAJOR AND MINOR

In the Middle Ages early forms of scales, or "modes," were used by choirs of monks in Christian churches. The monks would sing just one melody line, with no accompaniment. By the 13th century the music was sung in two or more parts; what we call "harmony" was born. Many modes gradually disappeared, leaving us with mainly the major and minor scales that we recognize today.

# UFOs and ALIENS

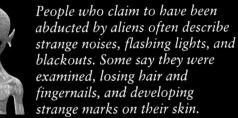

40 million UFO sightings have been recorded since 1947, when the first "flying saucers" were reported. The most common sightings are of glowing balls of light, moving quickly. There have been reports of crash landings by mysterious objects and of alien abductions. In 1948, the U.S. Air Force set up an investigation into UFOs. By 1969, when the project ended, about 12,000 incidents had been recorded. A quarter were caused by natural phenomena or known objects, but the rest remained unidentified. It has yet to be proved that there are intelligent life forms elsewhere in space – or that they are visiting Earth.

### KIDNAPPED!

*People who claim to have been abducted by aliens often describe strange noises, flashing lights, and blackouts. Some say they were examined, losing hair and fingernails, and developing strange marks on their skin.*

### TIME TRAVELERS

*No other planet in our solar system can support life, so UFOs must come from planets orbiting another star like our Sun. It would take thousands of years to reach us from the nearest star. Some people think that aliens can "beam" their ships across space and time.*

### MYSTERY AT ROSWELL

*In 1995, British ufologists unveiled an old film showing U.S. scientists examining the corpse of an alien (below). It has been linked to a reported UFO crash near Roswell, NM, in 1947. The U.S. government claimed the wreckage was a weather balloon, but others said they were hiding a "spy" balloon...or a UFO. The film is now being tested – perhaps the truth will be known at last.*

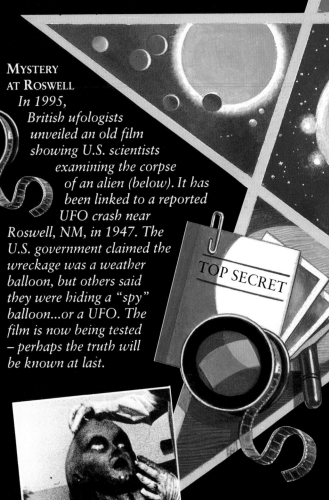

*Where do UFOs come from?*
Most ufologists believe that aliens visit Earth from distant galaxies which human science and technology are not yet advanced enough to find. However, some people have a theory that UFOs come from a hollow area in the center of the Earth and fly into space through a hole at the North Pole!

## CLOSE ENCOUNTERS
*UFO sightings are called Close Encounters. A Close Encounter of the First Kind is seeing a UFO. The Second Kind includes evidence such as landing marks. The Third Kind is when a witness sees or meets alien beings. In 1947, a pilot saw some strange disks in the sky. He told reporters that they looked like "saucers" and the name "flying saucers" caught on.*

## FACING THE ALIENS
*UFOs appear in many shapes and sizes! On April 24, 1964, a police officer claimed that he saw an egg-shaped craft land and two small, human-like creatures climb out. The aliens saw him, rushed back to the ship, and took off. Scorch marks were later found where the ship had been standing.*

## Tracking alien beings
Everyone has seen imaginary UFOs in films such as *Close Encounters of the Third Kind* (below), but ufologists investigate UFO sightings by real-life witnesses. They use hi-tech equipment to measure radio waves and magnetic effects which might be caused by UFOs, and track mysterious craft on radar screens. Amateur ufologists watch the skies using telescopes and cameras. If they spot a UFO, they record its position, movement, color, and shape, and send this data to UFO organizations. Permanent observers now keep watch for UFOs around the world.

## ENCOUNTER OVER IRAN
*On September 9, 1976, a UFO was seen over Iran. Two planes went to investigate, but their controls jammed. The UFO, which was about 160 feet long, seemed to fire at them before speeding away.*

# WHAT IS A HURRICANE?

A hurricane is a large, spinning wind system that develops over warm seas near the equator. These areas are known as the tropics. Technically, hurricanes are called tropical revolving storms, but they also have local names. They are called hurricanes when they occur over the Atlantic Ocean, typhoons in the Far East, and cyclones in the Indian Ocean. By definition, all are characterized by rotating winds that exceed speeds of 75 mph on the Beaufort wind scale.

The tropics are the hottest parts of the world, and experience the most extreme weather conditions. Air heated by the sun rises swiftly, which creates areas of very low pressure. As the warm air rises, it becomes loaded with moisture that condenses into massive thunderclouds. Cool air rushes in to fill the void that is left, but because of the constant turning of the earth on its axis, the air is bent inward and then spirals upward with great force. The swirling winds rotate faster and faster, forming a huge circle that can be up to 1,200 miles across.

▲ The typhoon that hit Manila in the Philippines in 1988 caused severe flooding. People were forced to cling to items like tires to survive.

► The shattered remains of Darwin in Australia after Cyclone Tracy hit the area on Christmas Day in 1974. Tracy's winds reached 150 mph and battered the city for over four hours. 48,000 inhabitants were evacuated and 8,000 homes destroyed.

### Extreme conditions

A spectacular part of tropical storms is the long, low thunderclouds that can be seen rolling across this landscape. The tinges of gray-black at the edges of the clouds are the result of undercurrents of cold air that force the moisture in the warmer air above to condense very quickly. It is these clouds that bring the torrential downpours of rain that accompany most thunderstorms. Thunder and lightning can also occur.

# EARLY MAMMALS

Mammals evolved from a group of reptiles that existed long before the dinosaurs. Throughout the Triassic, certain carnivorous reptiles, the cynodonts, grew to resemble mammals. These mammallike reptiles were fairly small, about the size of a dog. The first true mammals were small, shrewlike beasts, such as *Megazostrodon* (below). It was probably covered with hair and was "warm-blooded." Today, mammals can be divided into three groups: the monotremes, marsupials, and placental mammals.

Barylambda lived in the Early Tertiary.

Megazostrodon

## What is a mammal?

Mammals are "warm-blooded" animals covered in hair. They are able to produce heat inside their bodies. Most give birth to live young, although the monotremes lay eggs. All feed their young milk. Some mammals look after their young in special pouches. Such animals are called marsupials, and include the kangaroos and wallabies. Mammals have adapted to live on land, in the sea (for example, seals, porpoises, and whales), and in the air (for example, bats).

A marsupial protects and feeds its underdeveloped embryo in a pouch.

### Causing a sensation

William Buckland (1784-1856) worked as Professor of Geology at Oxford University and as the Dean of Westminster, England. He was an eccentric character who kept many strange pets, including a bear and a jackal. He is most famous for describing the carnivorous dinosaur *Megalosaurus*. He also described the first Jurassic mammal, *Amphitherium*. His announcement that mammals had lived at the time of great reptiles caused a great sensation at the time!

William Buckland

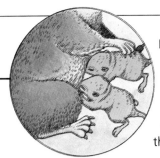

Placental mammals (such as humans and rodents) feed their unborn young through a placenta. They produce milk to feed their young after they are born.

## Mammalian evolution

From the Triassic period until the end of the Cretaceous, 155 million years later, mammals were very small, never growing larger than a cat. At the start of the Tertiary period they evolved very quickly and filled many of the niches left by the dinosaurs. Today, mammals are found on every continent and have even traveled to the Moon!

Meniscotherium

Lions

Monotremes are mammals that lay eggs. Their oldest fossils are known from Early Cretaceous rocks. Today, monotremes like the spiny anteater and duck-billed platypus live in Australia.

## Mammals vs dinosaurs

Mammals and dinosaurs shared the Earth for 155 million years. For many years, it was thought the mammals were responsible for the extinction of the dinosaurs. Scientists described the dinosaurs of the Cretaceous as slow and stupid, claiming they were not able to compete with the active and intelligent mammals. We now know that mammals did not kill off the dinosaurs, even though they would have eaten dinosaur eggs given the chance!

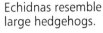

Echidnas resemble large hedgehogs.

Planetetherium

## Earliest mammals

The earliest known true mammals, from the end of the Triassic, 190 million years ago, were found in South Wales, China, North America, and Southern Africa. During the age of dinosaurs, they hunted at night and many of their rodent descendants are still nocturnal.

# AZTEC RELIGION

The Aztecs regarded themselves as "the people of the sun." Huitzilopochtli (hummingbird-on-the-left) was the god of war and the sun, and was the most important god to the Aztecs. They did, however, worship many other gods, including Tezcatlipoca (smoking mirror), and Quetzalcoatl (plumed serpent). The Aztecs believed it was essential to offer the gods a stream of human sacrifices, in order to regenerate the cosmos and help the sun on its daily journey across the sky.

## The gods

Aztec deities were depicted in gold, jade, stone, clay, wood, and other materials. Tezcatlipoca's emblem was an obsidian mirror. His mask was made from a human skull decorated with a mosaic of turquoise, lignite, and shell. Quetzalcoatl was the plumed serpent god. His turquoise mosaic mask (top) has a pair of serpents entwined around the eyes, nose, and mouth. Mictlantecuhtli was Lord of the Region of Death. This sandstone carving (right) shows him with a skull mask.

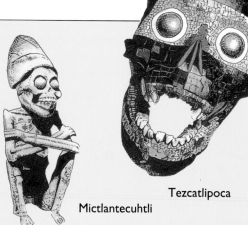

Mictlantecuhtli

Tezcatlipoca

## Human sacrifice

Human sacrifice was practiced by the Aztecs on a huge scale. Victims, regarded as the gods' messengers, were thrown on the sacrificial stone and their hearts cut out (right). Sacrificial knives (left) were highly decorated, inlaid with turquoise, jade, and shell.

## Temples

The Aztec city was dominated by the great double temple of Huitzilopochtli and Tlaloc (right). To mark its inauguration in 1487, 20,000 captive warriors were sacrificed. This huge monument, dedicated to warfare and agriculture, was built in seven stages. Aztec builders increased the size of the massive pyramid by building each new construction onto earlier ones.

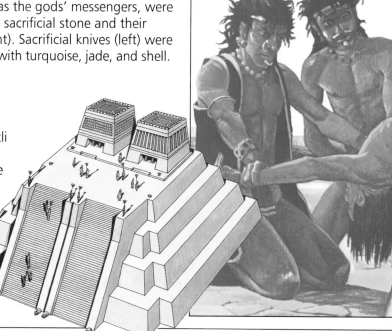

## Time and the cosmos

The Aztec Calendar Stone (right) commemorates the five world-creations. To count time, the Aztecs used a solar calendar of 365 days and a sacred calendar of 260 days. The combination of these led to cycles of 52 years. Each year had many festivals, such as the Flying Dance, which saw five men climb a pole. While one played music, four "flew" to the ground, suspended on ropes (left).

### Pyramids

Egyptian pyramids were monumental tombs. Built of stone with a rubble core, they covered or contained a burial chamber, and were thought to guarantee the well-being of kings in the afterlife. Early pyramids had stepped sides (bottom), but later ones were given straight sides to represent the sun's rays. Although they knew nothing of Egyptian pyramids, the Maya of ancient Mexico and the Aztecs after them built very similar structures. These stepped pyramids had temples at the summit, unlike Egyptian pyramids and were rarely used as tombs (right).

# WHALES AND PORPOISES

**There are 2 major types:**
Toothed whales (66 species), including river dolphins, beaked whales, dolphins and porpoises.
Whalebone (baleen) whales (10 species), including gray whale, rorquals and right whales.
**Biggest species:** Blue whale – more than 100 ft (30 m) long and weighing 140 tons.

The whale family comprises mammals completely adapted to life in water. The majority of the 80 or so species live in the open seas, and of these, many inhabit warm tropical waters, while others spend much of their lives in the cool polar seas. All are mammals that during evolution returned to the sea, where animal life began. They still have a fish-like appearance. Among them are the biggest animals ever to have lived on Earth, with the Blue whale at 140 tons. Whales have no hind limbs or external ears. Their forelimbs take the form of paddles, and they have a tail with flukes. Beneath the skin is a layer of blubber, or fat, which helps to conserve body heat in the water.

## Breathing

Whales can stay under water for an hour or more. Yet they breathe air with their lungs and must surface to replace the oxygen their bodies need. They store oxygen in their muscles and on a dive use this and the oxygen in their lungs to stay alive. As they surface, they open the blowhole on top of their head and blow out the used air. Then they take one or more deep breaths. Underwater, the blowhole is closed by a valve and the windpipe is sealed off from the throat to prevent water entering the lungs when the animal feeds.

A fin whale blows water out of its blowhole.

## Birth

Most whales do not reach maturity for many years. Pregnancy lasts from 8 months, for small dolphins, to 16 months or more for the big whales such as the blue, fin and sperm whales. Mostly only one offspring is produced. The baby is born under water tail-first. Immediately it surfaces, or its mother nudges its head out of the water, to take its first breath. The baby suckles milk from nipples hidden in folds on the mother's underside. Care of the young lasts weeks or months and is often carried out by all the females in a group.

A mother dolphin and her offspring

# Feeding

Whales are divided into two main groups by the different types of jaws and feeding methods.

Toothed whales have narrow lower jaws and, as adults, cone-shaped pointed teeth in the lower or both jaws. The teeth number from 2 to 120 depending on the species. In narwhals, one of the two upper jaw teeth is greatly enlarged to form a spirally twisted tusk 6.5 feet (2 m) in length. Toothed whales feed mainly on fish and squid.

Baleen, or whalebone, whales lack teeth and the upper jaws V-shaped and has up to 300 plates of horny material similar to matted hair and fingernails. These plates of baleen hang down from the jaw and act as strainers to sift out plankton, the tiny aquatic animals and plants. When baleen whales are not feeding, the plates are enclosed within the broad lower jaw.

A southern right whale feeding on plankton

A killer whale hunts in the Arctic Ocean.

# Migration

There tend to be many separate populations of whales. Some inhabit just the Northern Hemisphere, others the Southern, and within each there are Pacific, Atlantic and Indian Ocean groups. Within each area, groups of whales may migrate many thousands of miles each year, following definite circuits. These sometimes take them close to the mainland or among the pack ice of polar regions. Most toothed whales migrate to keep up with the movements of the fish on which they feed. Among baleen whales, the males move north in summer and return to the tropics in winter for the breeding season.

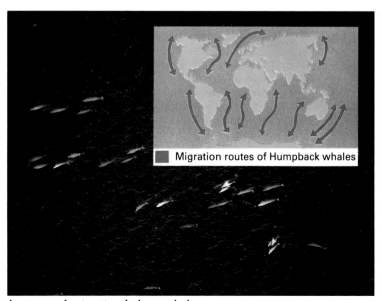

Migration routes of Humpback whales

A group of migrating beluga whales

# NEW BICYCLES
## CHANGING CONCEPTS

**The shape of the bicycle, unaltered for nearly a century, has been transformed in the past ten years.**

New materials, new designs, and wind tunnel testing have made bikes lighter, stronger and faster. Designing bikes is like designing aircraft: both have to minimize wind drag, maximize efficiency, respond quickly to the controls, yet be as light as possible. The key to the bike is the frame. Nowadays, the tubes in a racing-bike are made of aircraft-grade aluminum alloy, the gears of titanium, and flat disks are used instead of spoked wheels to reduce wind resistance. Brakes and gear mechanisms may be combined so that less time is needed to switch from applying the brakes to changing the gears.

*The Lotus bike replaces the normal frame with a solid "wing" made of reinforced carbon-fiber. Designed for racing on a circular track, it has no gears or brakes. The rear wheel is a flat disk to minimize drag, but the front one is spoked. The flat handlebars allow the rider to lie almost horizontal.*

*Rider's seat*

*Rear wheel*

*British inventor, Clive Sinclair's Zike is a recent attempt to produce a light, powered bike. Batteries in the frame produce electricity to drive the Zike, which can also be pedaled. Designed for town use, the Zike has small wheels and a suspension system.*

*Rider's seat*

*Drive chain*

*Suspension forks*

Handlebars are a key factor, because they control the position of the rider. The lower the rider, the less wind resistance; but careful wind tunnel testing is needed to create optimum airflow. Riders in races like the Tour de France use drop handlebars with a curved horseshoe-shaped bar on top, which they can tuck their elbows behind for sprinting. These became popular after American cyclist, Greg Le Mond, won the 1989 tour using them. Clipless pedals, which operate like ski bindings, are safer than the traditional toe clip.

*The most expensive mountain bikes, like the Cannondale Super V, use air-sprung shock-absorbers to soak up the bumps. The movement of the front suspension can be adjusted.*

*Solid "wing"*

*Three-pronged front wheel*

# SAILING ON A BICYCLE
## HOW THE LOTUS BIKE WORKS

Most bikes lose speed in a crosswind. That is because drag increases sharply when the air is flowing past them at an angle. The Lotus bike, by contrast, is designed to go faster in those conditions by using its flat frame as a sail, taking advantage of the wind.

To achieve this result, the bike was put into a wind tunnel with its rider, Chris Boardman, in the saddle, and wind resistance was measured at different angles. By adjusting the shape and curvature of the frame, and ensuring that it and the solid rear wheel acted as a unit, it was predicted that on a circular track, a fraction of a second would be gained every lap.

Boardman went on to win an Olympic Gold at Barcelona. The precise position of the rider, allowing air to flow between him and the bike, was also perfected.

*The world's oddest bike is Behemoth, designed by Steve Roberts. It has 105 gears, carries four computers, a satellite navigation system, a refrigerator and solar cells to power them all. Behemoth – it stands for Big Electronic Human-Energized Machine Only Too Heavy – is a mobile office on which Roberts has pedaled 19,311 miles across the United States.*

# MAKING CARTOON STRIPS AND ANIMATION

## Cartoon strips

Cartoon strips are a sequence of individual cartoons that tell a story. From cave paintings to the Bayeux tapestry, from Mickey Mouse to Superman, the principle is to show developing action through a series of images. Have a look through some of your own cartoon books to see the vast range of styles that can be used.

We often enjoy strip cartoons without noticing the techniques artists use to show closeup or long distance views, to indicate drama, tension, or a change of pace. Filmmakers and animators use similar techniques to produce the same kinds of effects.

## Cartooning in color

Cartoon strips are usually in color. Many color materials are available. Colored pencils are easy to use. You can create pale and dark tones by pressing lightly or heavily, and new colors by laying one color over another (left). Watercolor and gouache (middle picture) are both good for cartooning. Watercolor is washed on thinly and is transparent. Gouache is denser and opaque. For both you will need to use thick paper, as thin paper will wrinkle up.

Felt-tips (right) are also versatile. Chunky, wedge-shaped ones cover the paper quickly and evenly; thin ones are good for outlines.

## Animation

Animation is a way of bringing pictures to life by making them appear to move. When we watch a modern cartoon film, we seem to see a smooth sequence of movement. It's hard to believe we are actually looking at thousands of single pictures, each one slightly different from the last. They change in front of our eyes so quickly we can't see when one image replaces another.

Later in the book we will look at the techniques animators use. You can practice some of these tricks yourself. If you enjoy being precise and working carefully, you can get some very impressive results.

## Painting on acetate

For the purposes of animation, cartoons are painted on sheets of clear plastic called acetate. Both sides of the acetate are used, as shown below. The image is drawn on one side with a special oil-based pen called an o.h.p. (overhead projector pen). The image is colored in on the other side using gouache or acrylic paint. This may be done quite messily, because when the acetate is turned over again, the brush marks will be invisible. Small pads of acetate are available and can be bought in art stores. Try cartooning on acetate yourself; the result will look very effective positioned on a window with light shining through it.

# MEDICINE

**If you had a headache, would you let someone drill a hole in your skull to release the "evil spirits?" Medicine started like that! Most people nowadays expect doctors to cure them of life's aches and pains, and to heal serious diseases. Good medical care is sometimes not appreciated. It is just taken for granted.**

Medicine began in the mists of prehistory. Some people found that they could cure an illness with a potion of plant juices, or a smear of animal fluids. They were the first doctors.

Some skulls over 10,000 years old have holes bored in them. The bone had grown back after being drilled, so these people must have survived after their "operation," trepanning.

A few early treatments worked, but many did not. Some were very harmful. Even so, if a medicine worked, people had respect and wonder for the doctor. As a result, doctors became powerful, and some were made into gods.

Trepanned skull

## The father of medicine

One of the first proficient doctors was Hippocrates of Ancient Greece. He tried to rid medicine of magic and superstitions, and make it more scientific. He taught that a doctor's main aim was to help the patient, by finding the cause of an illness, and treating it. The results should be checked, so medicines could be improved. Hippocrates' main ideas are still followed today.

Hippocrates

## Deadening pain

Surgery has been around for thousands of years. The only way of deadening the pain of the knife and saw was to get the patient very drunk on alcohol or to use opium. In 1842, Dr. Crawford Long operated on a patient using ether as an anaesthetic, to deaden pain and other sensations. Today we could not imagine even a very small operation, without an anaesthetic.

Joseph Lister

## Killing germs on the body

Until the 1860s, patients who had operations often suffered and died, because their wounds became infected with germs. British surgeon Joseph Lister began to use antiseptics (germ-killing substances) to clean his operating instruments and the patient's cuts. Within a few years, surgery became much safer.

Alexander Fleming

## Killing germs in the body

In 1928, British scientist Alexander Fleming discovered a substance which could kill bacteria (types of germs). It was made by a pinhead-sized mold called *Penicillium*, so he named it penicillin. This was the first antibiotic (bacteria-killing) drug. Many other antibiotics have been discovered, and they have saved millions of lives.

## Seeing inside the body

X rays were discovered by German professor Wilhelm Roentgen in 1895. People were amazed that they could pass through the body, except for bones. Soon X rays were showing up broken bones and suspicious lumps and bumps.

Doctors have many modern methods of seeing into the body. CAT scans and NMR scans show the inside parts in amazing detail. Thin tubes called endoscopes can be pushed into the body, to examine and photograph the insides.

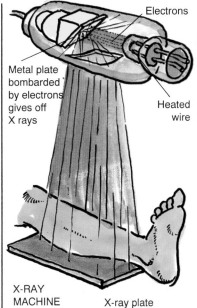

Electrons

Metal plate bombarded by electrons gives off X rays

Heated wire

X-RAY MACHINE

X-ray plate

Broken bone

X-ray film

ENDOSCOPE

Biopsy forceps control

Eyepiece

Tube tip control

Water supply

Laser light source

Cat Scanner

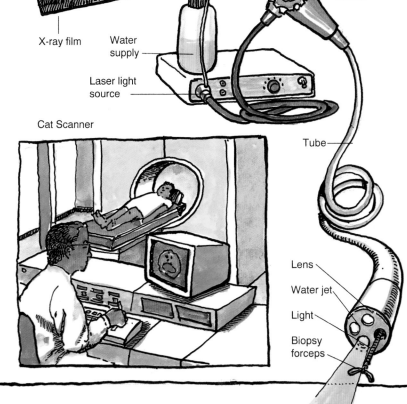

Tube

Lens

Water jet

Light

Biopsy forceps

## Whoops! Not a good idea

• Malaria is a serious illness spread by the bites of certain mosquitoes, which lay their eggs in water. Years ago, people thought malaria was spread by stale air (malaria means "bad air"). So they put sweet-smelling flowers in pots of water by the bedside. The mosquitoes laid their eggs in the water, hatched out and bit the sleeping people, and the illness spread even faster!

• "Ring-a-ring-a-roses, A pocket full of posies, A-tishoo, A-tishoo, All fall down." A nice nursery rhyme? In fact, it is about one of the worst diseases ever, the Great Plague. People kept roses and bunches of flowers, hoping the scent would keep the plague away. One of the first symptoms of the plague was sneezing. In a few days, most of them fell down dead.

# NATURE'S BALANCE

The living world performs a delicate balancing act. Living things can only exist where conditions are right and they depend on each other for survival. Only a few living things can survive without oxygen from the earth's atmosphere. They all need water. They need the right climate and the right temperature, not too wet and not too dry, not too hot and not too cold. Above all, each living thing forms part of a system, depending on others for survival.

**ECOSYSTEMS IN SCALE**
Parrots in a rainforest and fish on a coral reef are part of different ecosystems. Taken together, creatures, plants and their habitat make up an ecosystem. The largest ecosystems into which the earth's land is divided are called biomes. For example, the tropical forest biome, which includes all tropical forests on every continent, takes up about one-fifth of all land. A community consists of the animals and plants in a small area. Within a community are populations, for example, all the rabbits in one wood.

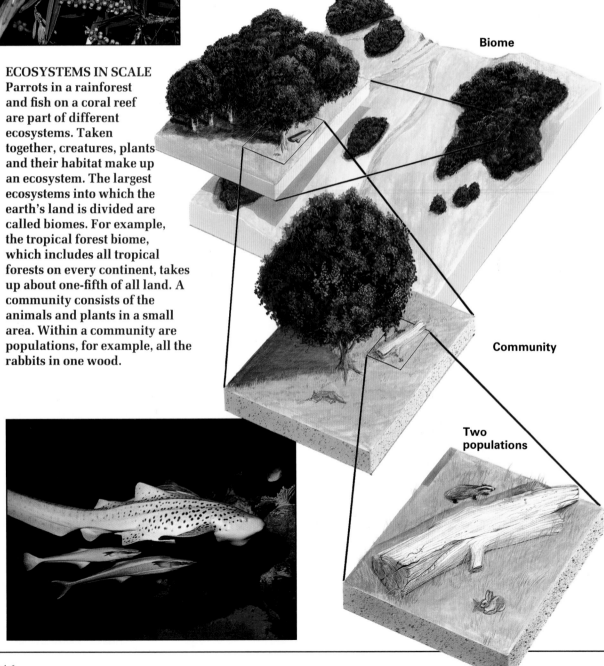

**Biome**

**Community**

**Two populations**

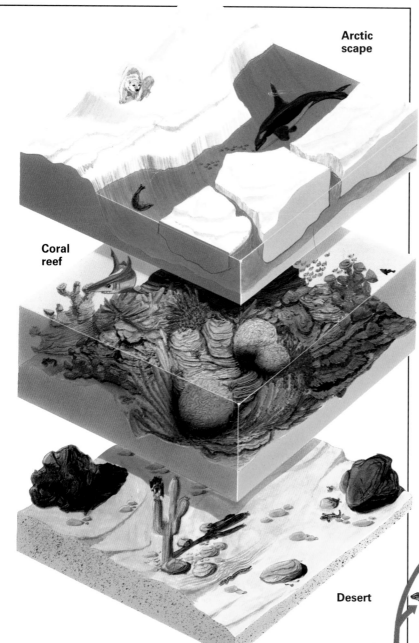

**Arctic scape**

**Coral reef**

**Desert**

## FOOD WEBS

In a simple food chain an underwater plant makes its own food. A shrimp comes along and eats the plant. A fish eats the shrimp, which is eaten in turn by a seal. Later, a whale eats the seal. People catch and eat the whale. In fact, food chains are very rarely as simple as this. Most animals eat several different foods. Several other animals may eat them. Food chains are all interwoven, forming a food web, like the one shown below. These can sometimes be very complicated indeed. But they show how living things in an ecosystem depend on each other for survival.

**FOOD WEBS**

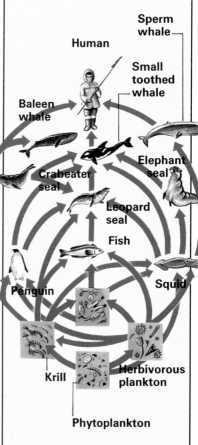

Sperm whale

Human

Small toothed whale

Baleen whale

Elephant seal

Crabeater seal

Leopard seal

Fish

Squid

Penguin

Krill

Herbivorous plankton

Phytoplankton

## MAKING A LIVING

Some ecosystems are more complex than others. A desert has few kinds of animal and plant life. This is partly because conditions are so harsh. But there are also few ways of making a living here. In a tropical forest, on the other hand, there is a bounty of trees, flowers, and other plants. Birds, monkeys, frogs, snakes and vast numbers of insects will all coexist.

The way that an animal makes its living is known as its "niche." Coral reefs, perhaps the oldest ecosystems, are teeming with niches. Taking up just a small space on the planet, they support one-third of all fish species. In the Arctic, where there are few niches, things look simpler. But even the simplest eco-system has a lot going on in it.

# THE COAL SWAMPS

During the Carboniferous period, the surface of the Earth was dominated by large expanses of tropical forest. These forests contained giant lycopod ferns over 130 feet tall, club mosses, and giant horsetails. The tropical swamps were home to many kinds of large amphibians (vertebrates that need to return to water to lay their eggs). Over millions of years, dead plant material was slowly fossilized to produce coal, a carbon-rich rock.

### Mazon Creek fossils

The rocks containing the Mazon Creek creatures are recovered from the spoil heaps produced by coal mining. These fossils are an example of exceptional preservation of invertebrates. Some of the plants and animals lived in the sea, like those illustrated here. Others would have lived in freshwater streams and ponds. The fossils are found in nodules (rounded lumps) of ironstone, a rock that is rich in iron and preserves soft parts of animals. These include worms, jellyfish, insects, scorpions, and spiders.

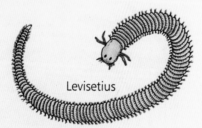

Levisetius

Octomedusa

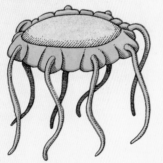

Pterochiton

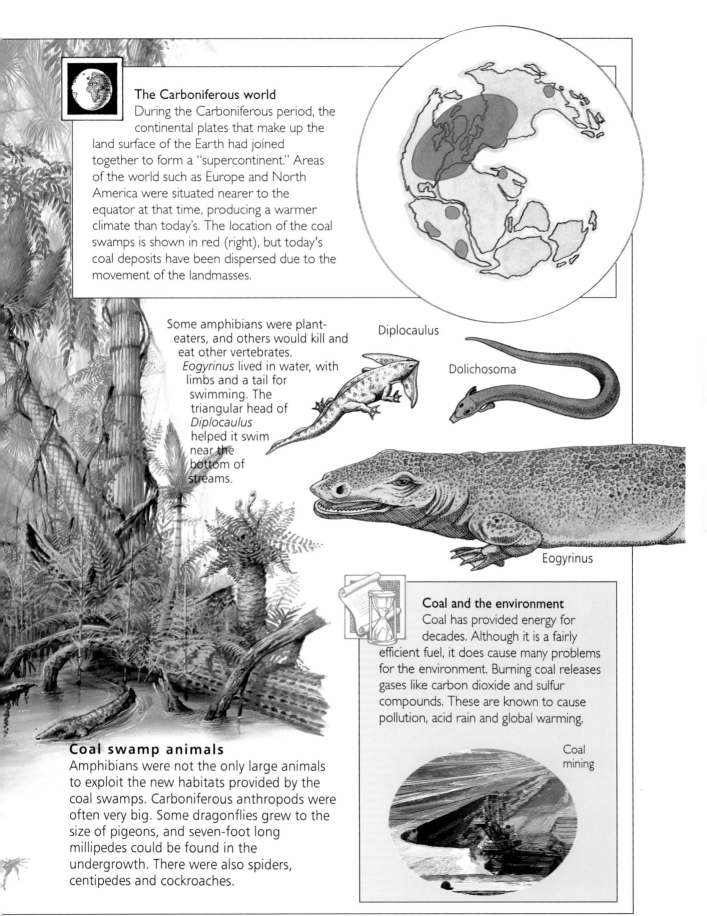

## The Carboniferous world

During the Carboniferous period, the continental plates that make up the land surface of the Earth had joined together to form a "supercontinent." Areas of the world such as Europe and North America were situated nearer to the equator at that time, producing a warmer climate than today's. The location of the coal swamps is shown in red (right), but today's coal deposits have been dispersed due to the movement of the landmasses.

Some amphibians were plant-eaters, and others would kill and eat other vertebrates. *Eogyrinus* lived in water, with limbs and a tail for swimming. The triangular head of *Diplocaulus* helped it swim near the bottom of streams.

Diplocaulus

Dolichosoma

Eogyrinus

## Coal and the environment

Coal has provided energy for decades. Although it is a fairly efficient fuel, it does cause many problems for the environment. Burning coal releases gases like carbon dioxide and sulfur compounds. These are known to cause pollution, acid rain and global warming.

Coal mining

## Coal swamp animals

Amphibians were not the only large animals to exploit the new habitats provided by the coal swamps. Carboniferous anthropods were often very big. Some dragonflies grew to the size of pigeons, and seven-foot long millipedes could be found in the undergrowth. There were also spiders, centipedes and cockroaches.

# Early Explorers
# AND DISCOVERERS

Throughout history, people have tried to understand the pyramids. Early Christians thought they were places where priests watched the stars. In the nineteenth century, some people believed that the measurements of the Great Pyramid were inspired by God, and that from them they could predict the future! But by then, scholars could read ancient Egyptian writing and they had started to dig up historic sites. The pyramids were finally known to be the last resting places of Egypt's ancient Kings.

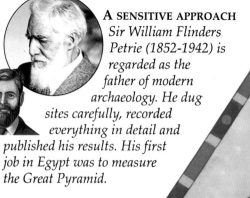

**A SENSITIVE APPROACH**
*Sir William Flinders Petrie (1852-1942) is regarded as the father of modern archaeology. He dug sites carefully, recorded everything in detail and published his results. His first job in Egypt was to measure the Great Pyramid.*

**EARLY ADVENTURER**
*Jean de Thevenot (1633-67, below) was one of the first explorers of ancient Egyptian sites.*

**THE BURIED SPHINX**
*In Egyptian legend, the Sphinx (the statue which guards the pyramids) appeared to a prince in a dream. It promised to make him king if he cleared away the sand covering its body. He did so, and became Tuthmosis IV.*

**NAPOLÉON'S NIGHTMARE**
*Napoléon Bonaparte, the Emperor of France, led an invasion of Egypt in 1798. Legend has it that he ventured into the Great Pyramid alone, only to emerge pale, shaken, and gasping for air. What secrets did he encounter in the darkness? We will never know...*

## TREASURE HUNTERS
*In the early nineteenth century, great damage was done by collectors and their agents. They entered the tombs in all sorts of ways, including blasting their way in. Giovanni Belzoni was a former circus strongman, who was hired by a collector to gather ancient Egyptian artifacts. He had no idea of preservation – one of his writings describes how he clumsily crushed Late-Period mummies as he forced his way into a tomb.*

## Preserving the treasures
Many museums and universities have carried out excavations in Egypt. The objects found are treated by experts, then stored for future research. X rays, medical scanners (below), robot photography and many other modern techniques are used to help scientists understand the secrets of the tombs.

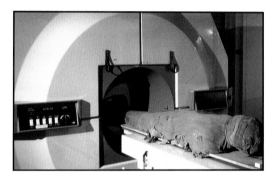

## PYRAMID GRAFFITI
*Belzoni even carved his name on the stones of the pyramids!*

*When did tourists start to arrive?*
In 1869, Thomas Cook, a British travel agent, bought a steamboat in Egypt and offered a new service – a package vacation. He charged one amount to cover everything – travel to Egypt, a Nile cruise and a guide. Until then, visitors to Egypt had to arrange all these details for themselves, which could be both very difficult and extremely expensive.

## UNCHARTED TERRITORY
*After the Arab invasion of Egypt, few people were able to visit the country. Little was known about the pyramids, the Nile Valley and its surroundings, or the culture and history of ancient Egypt.*

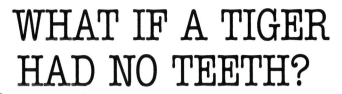

# WHAT IF A TIGER HAD NO TEETH?

Carnassial teeth

It would soon go hungry and starve. The tiger uses its claws to catch and scratch prey. But it needs its teeth to deliver the deadly bites, and to slice the meat off the bones for eating. The tiger has two main kinds of teeth for these jobs. The long, sharp canines or "fangs" are at the front of the mouth. They stab, wound, and skin the victim, making it bleed, suffocate, and die.

The large, ridge-edged carnassial teeth at the back of the mouth come together like the blades of scissors when the tiger closes its jaws. These very strong teeth carve off and slice up the meat, and can even crunch gristle (cartilage) and soft bones.

Canine teeth

## Purr-fect claws

A cat's claws are vital for its survival in the wild. With these incredibly sharp weapons, the hunter can slash, stab, and pin prey that will become its food. However, these deadly claws need to be kept razor sharp for the next kill. To ensure this, most cats can withdraw, or retract, their claws into sheaths in the toes.

This allows the cat to run, walk, and jump without scraping its sharp talons along the ground. It keeps them sharp, unbroken, and clean. It keeps them from getting blunt or getting tangled in twigs, grass, bark, and other things. When the cat needs its claws to climb a tree or to slash and pin its prey, it makes them stick out of the toes.

**Claws indoors**

The cat's claw is equivalent to your fingernail or toenail. But the claw can swing or pivot on its toe bone. A muscle in the lower leg pulls on a long, stringlike tendon that is attached to the bone and claw. This pulls the sharp claw out of its protective sheath.

Bone

Tendon

Claw

## Plant-eating carnivore

When the giant panda of China was first discovered, it posed a problem to scientists. It has the sharp, fanglike teeth of a carnivore (meat-eater), and is indeed a close relative of the meat-eating raccoon. However, its diet consists almost solely of bamboo shoots. Even though it can eat meat, the panda chooses the young shoots of this type of grass. Unfortunately, bamboo is very low in nutritional value. As a result, it must spend nearly all of its time sitting around, lazily eating in order to consume enough to survive.

## Highly-sprung hunter

The fastest hunter on land owes its speed to its flexible backbone. Without this powerful spring running along its spine, the cheetah would not be able to catch and kill the nimble prey that it hunts, such as gazelle and springbok.

As this big cat sprints, the spine flexes, stretching the body out, and allowing the legs to cover even more distance with each stride. This makes the cheetah the world's fastest runner, at over 60 mph (100 km/h).

As the cheetah's legs come together, the spine bends up in the middle.

As the cheetah extends its legs, the spine flattens and arches backward.

As a result the legs can stretch further apart, letting the cheetah run faster.

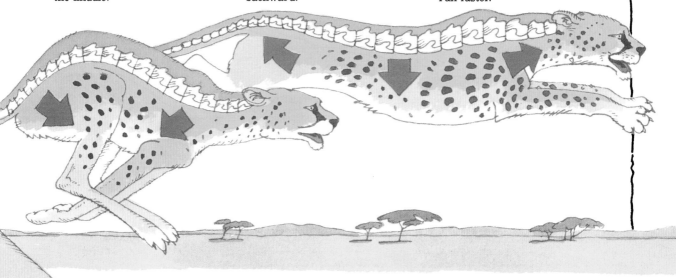

# VIRTUAL REALITY
## COMPUTER ILLUSIONS

**Computers have been used to create three-dimensional images for many years.** "Virtual reality" allows us to take a walk inside those models, to make us feel that we are really there. Virtual reality technology uses computers to work directly on our senses – particularly vision, hearing, and touch – to create the illusion of reality, being in a computer-created spaceship or at Cluny Abbey. The user wears a special headset fitted with goggles. Computer-created images are sent to the headset. As the user moves, sensors feed data back to the computer, so that the view of the image changes, just as it would if you were moving through a real building or landscape.

In some virtual reality systems, it is possible to pick up imaginary objects, using a glove fitted with sensors that give the impression of gripping and lifting.

*Virtual reality environments like the one above have many uses. Engineers have used virtual reality to plan telephone networks.*

*Architects have been using three-dimensional computer-aided design programs for several years. But a virtual reality design program like the one used to create Cluny Abbey would enable them to walk inside their buildings before they are constructed.*

Virtual reality can be used for entertainment or for serious scientific research. Scientists at the University of North Carolina use it to build up molecules of drugs. Virtual reality not only allows them to see how atoms bind together but to feel when they don't.

*The 1000SD is the first virtual reality computer game. Put on the headset and you find yourself in a computer-generated world. The design of the headset allows you complete freedom of movement. All your actions are controlled by a joystick.*

*The nave of Cluny Abbey, France (below), has been rebuilt inside a computer as an exercise in virtual reality. From the archaeological discoveries, and drawings made before it was knocked down, experts created the model with the help of IBM France.*

## CLUNY MONASTERY
### RECONSTRUCTING THE PAST

Virtual reality is a powerful tool for archaeologists. It is now possible to re-create from plans and sketches what it felt like to walk through buildings long since lost. The monastery at Cluny, in southeast France, was a great center of culture and learning during the 11th and 12th centuries. What is known of Cluny comes from excavations during the 1900s. Virtual reality still has some way to go before it is truly convincing. The graphics alone present some big problems. The headset has to respond to your movement and to send images to your eyes at least as fast as a movie.

# THE KEYBOARD FAMILY

The keyboard was one of the most important musical inventions. The system of scales and keys we know today is largely based on it. The keyboard has been used in a wide variety of instruments besides the piano and the older harpsichord, just some of which are shown here.

French musician Jean-Michel Jarre (above right) pioneered the use of synthesizers and electronic sounds.

## ELECTRIC KEYBOARDS

Electric organs and pianos are played very like an ordinary piano, but the sounds, like those of the synthesizer, are electronic. These instruments are very popular with jazz musicians and pop groups.

## ELECTRIC ORGAN

Electric organs began to appear in movies and theaters in the 1920s. They were technically very advanced for their time, and could produce many extraordinary sounds. Visually these organs made a dramatic impact on audiences, as they rose up from the pit in front of the screen or stage during intervals in performances, with their many lights flashing.

## SYNTHESIZER

Synthesizers (above) generate electronic signals which are fed though amplifiers and speakers. These signals can produce many different sounds.

## CELESTA
The keyboard of a celesta plays a set of tuned metal bars inside the instrument. Tchaikovsky's "Dance of the Sugar Plum Fairy" is written for it.

## ACCORDION
The accordion (right) is a kind of portable organ, with a keyboard down one side. Learning to play the keyboard at this angle takes a great deal of practice.

## CHURCH ORGAN
A large church or concert organ (right) often has three or four keyboards (known as "manuals"), plus a pedal keyboard, which is played with the feet. There are also a variety of "stops" — knobs or handles that the organist pulls out or pushes in to select whole groups or sets of pipes. All these devices are needed because many organs have a large number of pipes, with a range of different sound qualities, as well as notes of different pitch. Electric organs which were used in movies or theaters are now sometimes used in churches. The organ shown on the opposite page is reused in this way.

# MUSCLES AND MOVEMENT

All the body's movements are powered by muscles. Muscle tissue is specialized to contract, or get shorter. The body has three main kinds of muscles. One is the skeletal muscles, attached to the bones of the skeleton, which you use to move about. There are more than 600 skeletal muscles, from the huge gluteus in the buttock to tiny finger and toe muscles. The other kinds of muscles are cardiac muscle in the heart (top left above) and smooth muscles in the stomach, intestines and other internal organs (left above).

## Inside a muscle

A skeletal muscle has a bulging central part known as the body. This tapers at each end into a rope-like tendon, which anchors the muscle to a bone. As the muscle contracts, the tendons pull on their bones and move the body. The muscle body is divided into bundles of hair-fine fibers called myofibers. These long cells contain proteins that slide past one another to make the cell shorter in length.

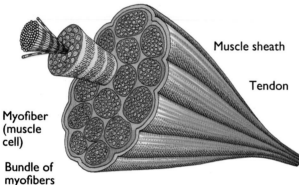

Muscle sheath

Tendon

Myofiber (muscle cell)

Bundle of myofibers

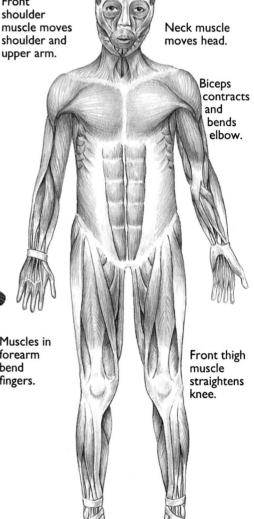

Front shoulder muscle moves shoulder and upper arm.

Neck muscle moves head.

Biceps contracts and bends elbow.

Muscles in forearm bend fingers.

Front thigh muscle straightens knee.

Shin muscle bends ankle by pulling up foot.

## Changing fashions

Bulging muscles have been in and out of fashion through the centuries. A few hundred years ago, plump bodies were seen as desirable. Today some men and women like to look slim. Other people work hard at body-building, training and lifting weights in the gym. They strive to increase the thickness of their muscle fibers through special exercises and diet.

## Stories of the strong

Legends from many different cultures tell of well-muscled, strong men and women. Some are heroes, others are villains. Hercules of Ancient Greece had to undertake 12 "herculean" (very difficult) tasks or labors. In the Bible, the boy David fought and killed the giant Goliath with his slingshot. Samson was a hero who fought the Philistines, but he lost his strength when Delilah tricked him into having his hair shorn. Blinded and chained, he pushed the columns of the Gaza Temple and brought it crashing down on himself and his captors, as pictured right.

Triceps contracts, straightening elbow. Biceps relaxes and stretches.

## Master of art and science

During the Renaissance period, from about the 14th century, there was a rebirth of fascination in the beauty of the human form, and a scientific interest in the structure and workings of the body. Foremost in this field was the genius of art and science, Leonardo da Vinci (1452-1519). He performed amazing dissections of the body, especially the muscle system, and drew them with unparalled skill and mastery, as shown here.

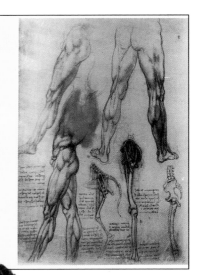

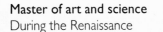

Biceps contracts, bending elbow. Triceps relaxes.

Quadriceps contracts, straightening knee. Hamstring muscles relax and stretch.

Quadriceps and hamstrings tensed to maintain crouched position.

## Muscle pairs

A muscle contracts to pull on its bone. But it cannot do the reverse – actively get longer and push the bone the other way. So many of the body's muscles are arranged in opposing pairs, attached across the same joint. One partner of the pair pulls the bones one way, bending the joint. The other pulls the other way and straightens the joint, while its partner relaxes. Even a simple movement also involves many other muscles that keep the body balanced.

# MT. ST. HELENS

Mount St. Helens is a volcanic peak in the Cascade Mountains of Washington State. On May 18, 1980, a huge explosion ripped the mountain apart, releasing clouds of ash and dust (below).

Geologists knew that the volcano could erupt at any time. It had been dormant since 1857, but a series of small earthquakes during the 1970s suggested that magma was rising into the mountain. There were other warning signs too. The side of the mountain was bulging, and steam was escaping.

At 8:32 am, an earthquake broke the bulging side loose, causing the worst landslide ever recorded. Rock and lava cascaded down the mountainside and clouds of hot gases and ash plunged the valley into darkness. The eruption killed 63 people, flattened forests, and destroyed wildlife over 400 sq miles.

The volcano continued to erupt violently for days and there were smaller eruptions for several months.

**Effect On Environment**
After the eruption the countryside resembled a desert of ash and charred remains (below). Yet five years later, wildlife could be found once again in the area. Other, more long-term effects have resulted from the 30 million tons of ash flung into the atmosphere (right). The effect of the ash on the amount of sunlight reaching the ground may have caused changes in the weather worldwide.

# PROBLEMS OF SIZE

The most obvious thing about dinosaurs is their size: they were all big. Even though some, like *Compsognathus*, were no bigger than chickens, there is no doubt that dinosaurs lived at a different scale from the mammals. The mammals, the hairy backboned animals like mice, cats, horses and humans, are said to rule the earth today. However, the largest living mammal today, the elephant, is a mere midget at 5 tons, compared to the sauropod dinosaurs, many of which weighed from 50 to 100 tons. Most mammals are actually very small – think of mice, rats, shrews, voles, bats, and hedgehogs – and no dinosaur was ever as small as that!

What is the biggest size that a dinosaur could have reached? Could they have reached 200 tons, 500 tons, 1,000 tons? There is a limit for land-living animals caused by the fact that they must be able to lift their great weight on their legs and move. Beyond about 140 tons, a dinosaur would have needed such thick legs to hold up its body weight that it could not have moved at all.

The depth of dinosaur footprints shows how heavy these animals were.

Iguanodon

Tyrannosaurus rex

### Weighing dinosaurs
Use a scale model of a dinosaur to calculate how much it would have weighed. Lower the model into a container of water and measure how much is displaced. This is the volume. If the model is to a scale of one-twentieth, the volume is multiplied by 20 x 20 x 20, giving the dinosaur's volume. Living reptiles are 0.9 times as heavy as their volume of water, so multiply by 0.9, to give the weight in grams.

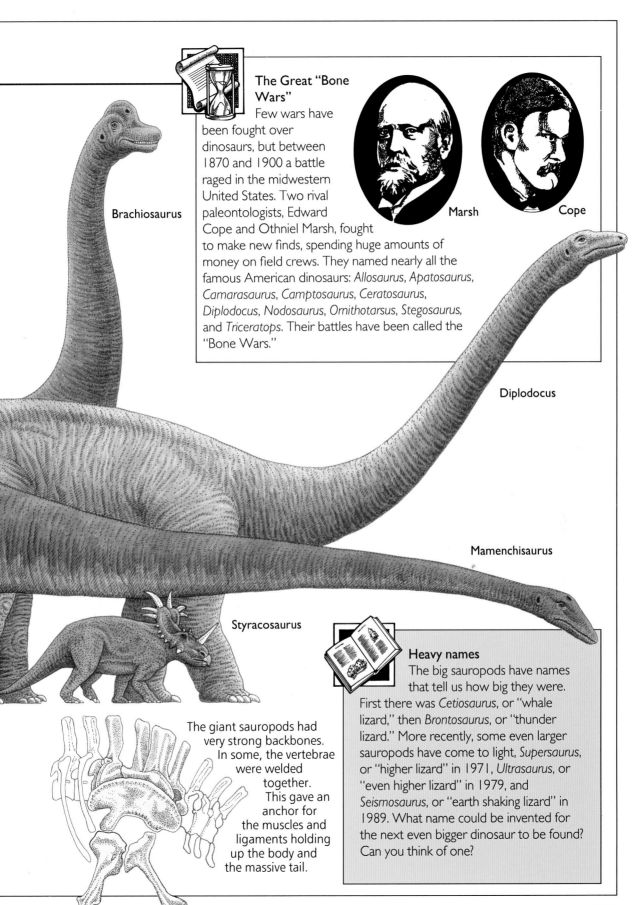

**The Great "Bone Wars"**
Few wars have been fought over dinosaurs, but between 1870 and 1900 a battle raged in the midwestern United States. Two rival paleontologists, Edward Cope and Othniel Marsh, fought to make new finds, spending huge amounts of money on field crews. They named nearly all the famous American dinosaurs: *Allosaurus, Apatosaurus, Camarasaurus, Camptosaurus, Ceratosaurus, Diplodocus, Nodosaurus, Ornithotarsus, Stegosaurus,* and *Triceratops.* Their battles have been called the "Bone Wars."

Marsh

Cope

Brachiosaurus

Diplodocus

Mamenchisaurus

Styracosaurus

The giant sauropods had very strong backbones. In some, the vertebrae were welded together. This gave an anchor for the muscles and ligaments holding up the body and the massive tail.

**Heavy names**
The big sauropods have names that tell us how big they were. First there was *Cetiosaurus,* or "whale lizard," then *Brontosaurus,* or "thunder lizard." More recently, some even larger sauropods have come to light, *Supersaurus,* or "higher lizard" in 1971, *Ultrasaurus,* or "even higher lizard" in 1979, and *Seismosaurus,* or "earth shaking lizard" in 1989. What name could be invented for the next even bigger dinosaur to be found? Can you think of one?

# ROMAN GODS

The Romans worshiped a great many gods and spirits – about 30,000 in all. These included the major gods and goddesses, such as Jupiter, the chief god, Neptune, god of the sea, Venus, goddess of love and beauty, and Minerva, goddess of wisdom and war. Each household also worshiped its own protective spirits – the Lares, Penates, and Manes. After Augustus's death, the emperors were considered gods, too. People all over the empire were allowed to worship their own local gods, as long as they also paid homage to the Roman gods. Large and impressive temples, often modeled on Greek examples, were built as places of worship for the state deities.

One of the household Lares; the guardian of houses.

## Household gods

Every Roman house had its own shrine to the household gods (Lares), called a Lararium, where worship was carried out daily. The family offered gifts such as wine, bread, and fruit, and also gave sacrifices to the gods. Outside the home, people worshiped the Roman gods in shrines and temples (right).

### Festivals

Roman festivals were regarded as holy days (holidays), during which people did not have to work.

Under Augustus there were about 130 public holidays, and this number increased under later emperors. The festivals were usually celebrated with games and races.

The Rites of Bona Dea was held in early December. The festival was for women only, and men were forbidden to attend.

*Compitalia* occurred in early January. Farmers built a shrine and made sacrifices to ensure the prosperity of their farms. During *Parilia*, in April, people danced around a bonfire onto which offerings were thrown.

## Religious persecution

During the empire, many Romans felt the empty rituals of the state religion could no longer meet their spiritual needs. Foreign cults such as those of Mithras, Isis, and Cybele encouraged their followers to take part in ceremonies, and spread across the empire. Christianity was not tolerated by the Romans, however. Its followers refused to worship the state gods and were often cruelly persecuted.

## Vestals

Vesta was the goddess of the hearth. The six Vestal virgins had to perform symbolic household duties for the state. This included tending the fire dedicated to Vesta which burned in her temple in the forum. The virgins had to remain unmarried for 30 years. Those who did not were buried alive.

## Offerings and sacrifices

People tried to discover the will of the gods with sacrifices. Sheep, chickens, bulls, and pigs were the main sacrificial animals. The priests removed their innards and read them to discover the gods' intentions.

## Looking heavenward

The positions of the stars and the planets at the time of a person's birth were considered very significant by the Romans.

**Mercury**

## Ceremonies

Special ceremonies marked important events in the lives of all Romans. A newborn baby was placed at its father's feet. The father raised the child in his arms as a sign of acceptance into the family. Funerals were very grand affairs, with professional mourners hired to wail over the body. In Republican times, death masks and mourning robes were worn. This practice was stopped during the empire.

Many of the stars and planets were named after Roman and Greek gods and goddesses. For example, Mercury was named after the messenger of the gods, who was also the god of trade and thieves. Venus was the goddess of love and beauty and Mars was the god of war. Jupiter was the king of the gods – the god of thunder and of lightning. Can you find out who the other planets were named after?

**Jupiter**

Roman marriages were usually arranged. The couple clasped hands (shown right) as a symbol of their marriage.

**Venus**

# WHAT ARE BIRDS?

There are 27 groups of birds.
**Biggest group:** Passerines, the perching birds. This includes familiar types such as crows and sparrows (5,150 species).
**Smallest group:** Struthioniformes, with just one species, the ostrich.
**Most common species:** African quelea finch – more than 100 billion.
**Rarest species:** California condor – fewer than 10 in the wild.

There are about 8,500 different species or kinds of birds, making them the most numerous backboned animals living on land. They range in size from tiny hummingbirds only 2.2 inches long to the ostrich, which may be more than 7 feet tall. They are found on every continent and in all habitats from tropical forests and desert to arctic tundra and ice. But they all have in common the fact that they are warm-blooded – that is, they can keep their bodies at a constant temperature, usually about 104°F. The front limbs – legs in most reptiles and mammals – have become modified as wings, usually used for flight, and feathers provide the main body covering, with scales on the legs and toes. Feathers trap heat under them and provide large surfaces needed for flight. Birds have no teeth, but have lightweight beaks (made of horn) covering the jaws.

## Flight

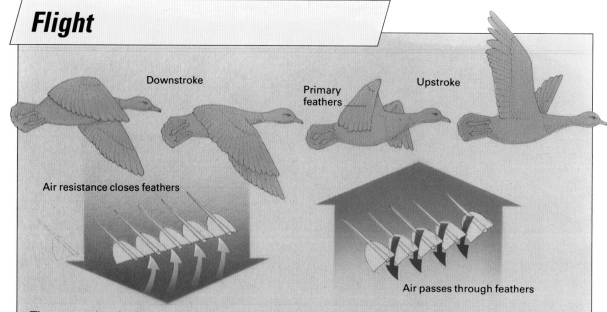

Downstroke

Primary feathers

Upstroke

Air resistance closes feathers

Air passes through feathers

The streamlined shape of a bird helps it slip easily through the air as it flies, driven through the air by its wings acting as propellers. The power to work the wings comes from large muscles on the bird's chest on each side of the breastbone. Tendons run from these to the wing bones. There is little muscle in the wings themselves, which are light and easy to swing. The inner part of the wings helps give the bird lift as it moves forward. It acts rather like the wing of an airplane. The outer part of the wings, with its long primary feathers, gives the forward push, with the primaries bending so that they help the animal forward on the upstroke as well as the downstroke. As the bird makes a downstroke the feathers are flattened against the air, making an airtight surface. On the upstroke they are turned so that air can spill between them. Flying actions and the wing shapes are adapted to the animals' needs and the type of country they inhabit.

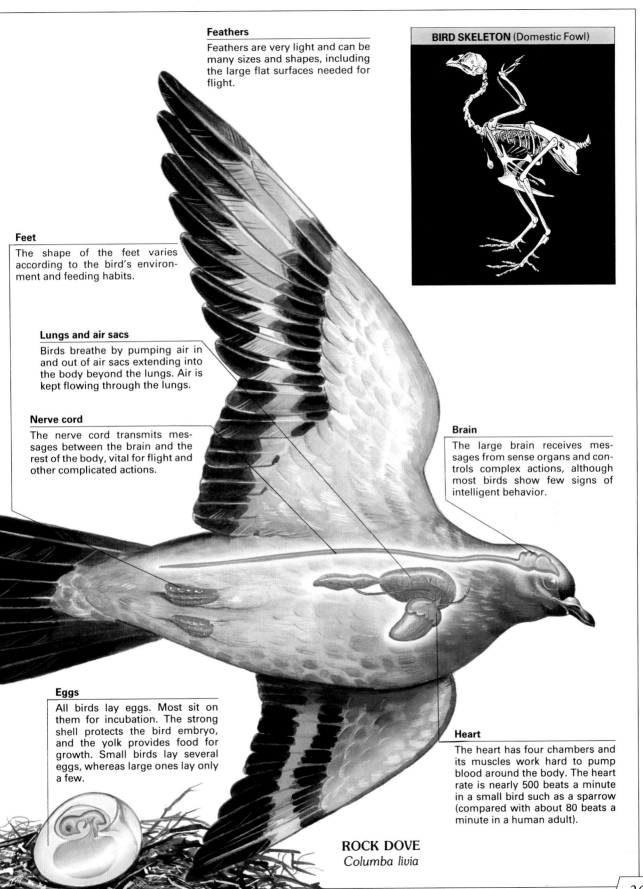

**Feathers**

Feathers are very light and can be many sizes and shapes, including the large flat surfaces needed for flight.

**BIRD SKELETON** (Domestic Fowl)

**Feet**

The shape of the feet varies according to the bird's environment and feeding habits.

**Lungs and air sacs**

Birds breathe by pumping air in and out of air sacs extending into the body beyond the lungs. Air is kept flowing through the lungs.

**Nerve cord**

The nerve cord transmits messages between the brain and the rest of the body, vital for flight and other complicated actions.

**Brain**

The large brain receives messages from sense organs and controls complex actions, although most birds show few signs of intelligent behavior.

**Eggs**

All birds lay eggs. Most sit on them for incubation. The strong shell protects the bird embryo, and the yolk provides food for growth. Small birds lay several eggs, whereas large ones lay only a few.

**Heart**

The heart has four chambers and its muscles work hard to pump blood around the body. The heart rate is nearly 500 beats a minute in a small bird such as a sparrow (compared with about 80 beats a minute in a human adult).

**ROCK DOVE**
*Columba livia*

# THE ATOMIC BOMB

In a split second in 1945, the world changed forever. In the Pacific, World War II was dragging on. At 7:30 a.m. on August 6, the Allies dropped the first atomic bomb, over the Japanese city of Hiroshima. Killing and destruction were immense. In a few days, the war ended. The shadow of atomic and nuclear weapons has been with us ever since.

"Little Boy" was a metal-cased bomb about 6 feet long. Exploding over Hiroshima, it killed some 75,000 people and flattened three-fifths of the city. Thousands more died later from injuries, burns and radiation sickness.

Little Boy

## How the bomb worked

"Little Boy" had gigantic destructive power because it turned matter into energy. The matter was in the form of the radioactive substance uranium-235.

At the critical moment, two pieces of uranium-235 crashed together in the bomb. Some of the uranium atoms split, in a process called nuclear fission. The resulting atomic fragments weighed less than the original atoms, because parts of them were converted to energy – in the form of light, heat, and radioactivity. The fission

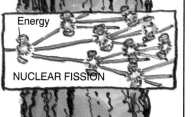
Energy
NUCLEAR FISSION

also made more fast-moving atomic fragments, which collided with other uranium atoms, splitting them too, and so on, in a split-second chain reaction.

## Nuclear weapons today

After the war, enough atomic bombs were made to blast the whole world to pieces many times.

Then came hydrogen bombs, which were even more powerful. Their energy was released when atomic bits of hydrogen joined together, in atomic fusion. Different types of hydrogen bombs form the bulk of today's nuclear weapons.

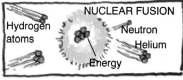
NUCLEAR FUSION
Hydrogen atoms
Neutron
Helium
Energy

## Power to destroy

• One of the most powerful chemical high-explosives is TNT.

• An atomic bomb or A-bomb is a million times more powerful than a TNT bomb of the same size.

• A hydrogen bomb or H-bomb is a thousand times more powerful than an A-bomb of the same size.

# FUSION POWER – *HALF AN INVENTION?*

**A safe, cheap, reliable source of energy, that won't pollute the world or run out. Sounds like a dream? It has been. But in the 1990s, scientists are trying to make the dream real. Fusion power could not only change the world, but save it, too.**

The hydrogen bombs described opposite work by nuclear fusion. But their energy is released all at once, in a massive BANG. Could the process be controlled in a fusion reactor? Experiments in the past few years show – hopefully, yes.

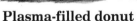

**A TYPICAL NUCLEAR FISSION POWER STATION**

Control rods

Heat exchanger

Steam

Turbine

Electricity

Generator

Condenser

Reactor core

### Plasma-filled donut
A fusion reactor will be shaped like a donut, and called a torus. Inside, two forms of hydrogen called deuterium and tritium must be heated to an incredible 1,800,000,000°F, as they whirl around. At this temperature they are not solid, liquid or gas. They are another form of matter, plasma.

Some of the atomic bits in the plasma of deuterium and tritium join together, or fuse. They produce atomic bits of another substance, helium, and also give out vast amounts of heat and other energy. The heat could power electricity generators, as in a normal power station.

### Copying the Sun
Today's nuclear power stations use fission reactors which split atoms, like the atomic bomb (opposite). In theory, fusion power could be cleaner, less dangerous and less polluting. But it will take many years and experiments before fusion power changes the world.

Even so, we already rely on it! Bits of hydrogen atoms fuse to form helium, creating light and heat and other energy – in the Sun.

### Cold fusion fails
• In the early 1990s there was a great argument about "cold fusion," where fusion power might be made at ordinary temperatures. A few scientists claimed they'd got it to work. Others repeated the experiments, but they didn't work. No one has proved "cold fusion" since.

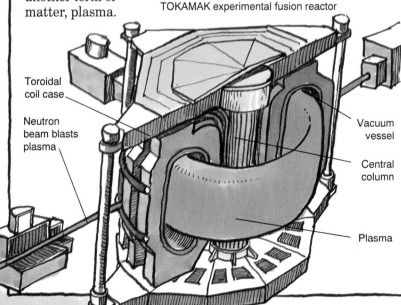

TOKAMAK experimental fusion reactor

Toroidal coil case

Neutron beam blasts plasma

Vacuum vessel

Central column

Plasma

# DRAWING THE HUMAN FIGURE

When the American space program launched the rocket *Pioneer 10* into outer space, they attached a plaque to inform extraterrestrials about the planet earth. The plaque featured a drawing of two figures – a man and a woman. It's strange to think that other beings might look very different to us. Imagine that you've been given the task of showing aliens what humans look like. For an accurate picture you will need to show the body in proportion.

### Getting things in proportion

Proportion is about comparing the size of one thing to another. For the artist, it is about showing different sizes correctly on paper. The drawings on the right show the proportions of the human figure. The length of the body is often measured in relation to the head. The average adult, whether male or female, is seven heads tall. The torso is three heads long from the chin to the top of the legs, and divides into thirds at the nipple line and navel. The distance from the top of the legs to the soles of the feet also measures three heads. Children's heads are larger in proportion to the rest of their bodies. Adult or child, with your arms stretched out sideways, the distance between your fingertips measures the same as your height – try it!

### Foreshortening

Here the story gets more complicated; these proportions appear to change as we move about. Parts of the body appear larger or smaller, depending on whether they are near or far from the person looking at them. We found out about this in the project on perspective.

If someone's leg or arm is pointing directly at you, part of its length will be hidden. This is known as *foreshortening*. You can see it on the right in the drawings of the figures sitting and crouching, and also in the sketches at the bottom of the opposite page.

### Practicing foreshortening

Foreshortening takes a more dramatic turn when you look at the figure from an unusual angle. As shown in the drawings left and middle opposite, a person with his arm outstretched toward you, or lying down, will seem to have an enormous hand or enormous feet. Have a go at drawing someone in these positions. It takes a lot of practice to get these things to look right, but you can have fun on the way as long as you don't mind making mistakes. The third picture is a sketch of the artist looking down at his own body and drawing himself at work. Try it. If you shut one eye, you can even see your nose, and include it in the picture, as he did.

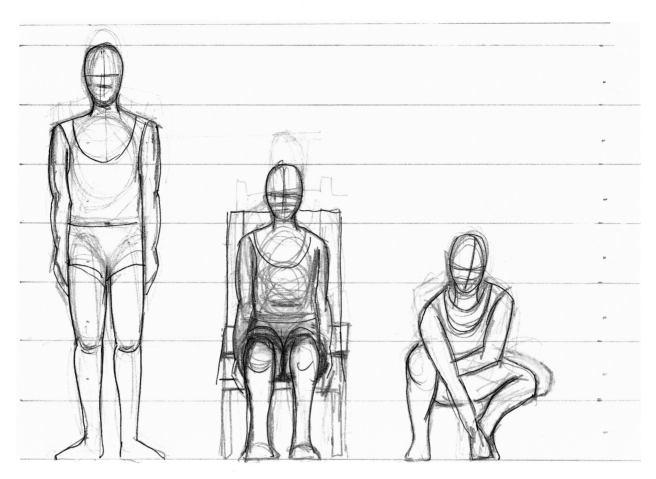

△ *"Above I have drawn the proportions of the standing figure. You might want to copy this first. Try it again from memory, and then check the measurements against a real person."*

△ *"The seated figure shows how two heads have been 'lost' from the height; the space from hips to knees has become foreshortened. Again, check this against the real thing."*

△ *"The crouching figure is more complicated, as the top half is also foreshortened as it leans toward you. The legs are foreshortened differently. Can you see how?"*

# THE MILKY WAY

It is important for an astronomer to know what lies both in and outside our galaxy. Although the stars in the sky seem to be so far away that they are separate from us, the sun and almost all of the stars that we can see actually belong to a single star system called the Milky Way galaxy. The Milky Way contains about 300 trillion stars mingled with clouds of gas and dust. Its shape is similar to a pair of plates placed rim to rim, forming a flattened disk. If we could see it from above, it would look like a vast spiral of light slowly spinning through space. It is so big that even if we could travel at the speed of light, it would take 100,000 years to cross from one side to the other.

**WHAT YOU CAN SEE**
In some directions, the sky is dense with stars. This is because we are looking through the disk of stars that make up the Milky Way. In other directions, there are few stars against the black backdrop of space. This is the view out of the galaxy, either above it or below the disk of the Milky Way, where there are fewer visible stars.

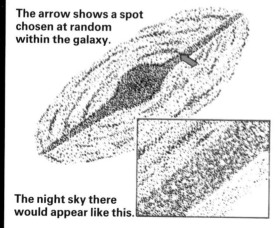

**The arrow shows a spot chosen at random within the galaxy.**

**The night sky there would appear like this.**

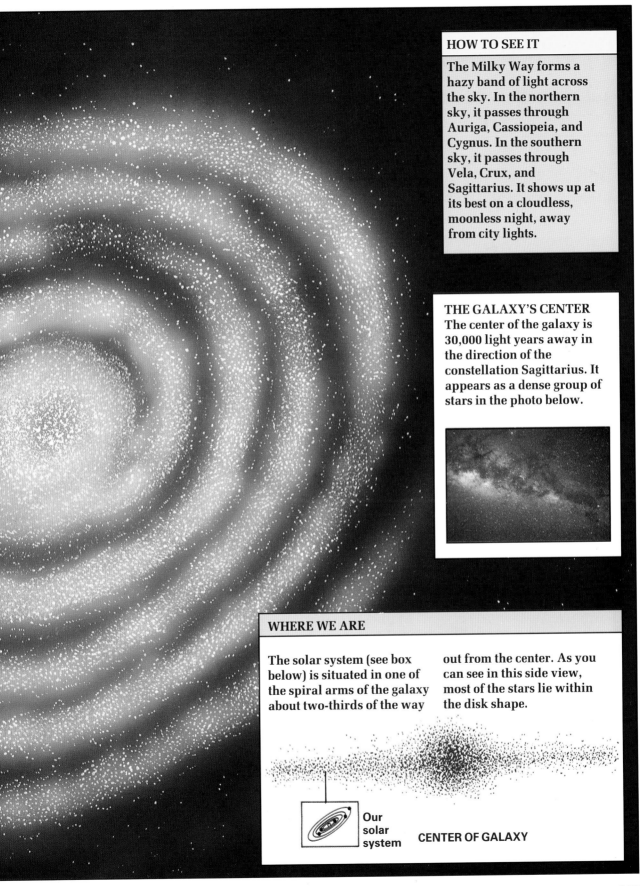

HOW TO SEE IT

The Milky Way forms a hazy band of light across the sky. In the northern sky, it passes through Auriga, Cassiopeia, and Cygnus. In the southern sky, it passes through Vela, Crux, and Sagittarius. It shows up at its best on a cloudless, moonless night, away from city lights.

THE GALAXY'S CENTER
The center of the galaxy is 30,000 light years away in the direction of the constellation Sagittarius. It appears as a dense group of stars in the photo below.

WHERE WE ARE

The solar system (see box below) is situated in one of the spiral arms of the galaxy about two-thirds of the way out from the center. As you can see in this side view, most of the stars lie within the disk shape.

Our solar system

CENTER OF GALAXY

# *Underwater* HUNTS

*The flagship of King Henry VIII of England, the* Mary Rose, *was raised from the English seabed in 1982. It sank in 1545, and has told historians a lot about life in Tudor times. It was pulled up by the* Tor Mog, *the biggest lifting barge in existence.*

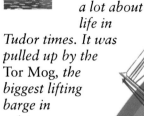

Many people dream of finding sunken treasure...but few have succeeded. Time, money, and equipment are needed to do so. However, finding treasure has been made much easier with modern technology. Once treasure is found, it is possible to go back to an exact spot in the sea using a Global Positioning System. This takes readings from satellites in space and is accurate to within a few yards.

Not all treasure is made of gold – 24,000 valuable plates were raised from a wreck called the *Diana* in 1994. The ship sank near Singapore in 1817 in only 106 feet (32 m) of water, but was quickly buried in sand.

### Liquid riches
Oil is known as the sea's "black gold." Countries like Saudi Arabia and Brunei have become rich by collecting oil from beneath their seas. Most oil rigs can work only in less than 660 feet (200 m) of water. Now special drilling ships are finding oil in much deeper places. Computers keep the ship in the right spot while it drills through the seabed.

### SEARCHING FOR WRECKS
Many wrecks are found by sonar equipment (left). Waves of sound are sent to the seabed. When they bounce back, the pattern they make shows up lumps and bumps.

*What is the oldest shipwreck?*
The oldest known wreck dates from the 14th century B.C., and still lies off the coast of Turkey.
*Do the oceans contain any other natural treasures?*
Sea water contains tiny amounts of gold, but not enough to be extracted (unfortunately!). Other valuable elements, such as magnesium and bromine, can be taken from the water.

### A TERRIBLE DISASTER
In 1912, the biggest ocean liner ever, the Titanic, collided with an iceberg. Over 1,500 people died as the ship sank to the seabed, 2.4 miles (4 km) below. It was found in 1985 (below), using hi-tech equipment. Submersibles have since taken scientists to see the sad remains.

0 5 5 4
2 9 1 6
0 5 4

### TREASURE!
In 1994, salvage expert Bob Hudson raised a haul of silver coins using a remote-controlled grab. They came from the John Barry, *a ship sunk by a torpedo in the Arabian Sea in 1944. Other recent finds have included gold bars and valuable pottery.*

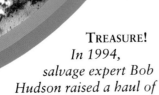

### NATURE'S GIFTS
Manganese nodules are found on the seabed below about 2.5 miles (4 km). They contain valuable metals such as copper and nickel and take millions of years to form. Specialized mining systems are being developed to collect them.

# COWBOYS AND INDIANS

Cowboy hostility toward Native Americans – popularly known in the movies as Indians – is another myth of the Wild West. The myth arose because many of the best stories set good against evil, and cowboy films were no exception. The heroes were the cowboys. Searching for villains, film directors and organizers of Wild West shows often selected Indians because their appearance and tactics were good entertainment. The truth was quite different. America's westward expansion was marked by frequent fighting between immigrant and Native Americans, but cowboys were rarely involved.

The Indian Wars that began in 1864 were generally fought between Native groups and the U.S. Army. Real cowboys had little reason to dislike the Indians. In fact, many cowboys *were* Native Americans. Excellent horsemanship, good local knowledge and the ability to survive in tough conditions made them ideal cattlemen. No drover taking cattle through Indian territory wanted to make his difficult job still harder by stirring up trouble with the local people.

## CUSTER'S LAST STAND

No Native group resented the arrival of the White Man into its territory more than the Sioux. Things came to a head in 1874, when gold was discovered on Sioux territory in Dakota. Miners came in the thousands, ignoring the rights of the locals. The Sioux attacked, destroying the settlers' camps. One of the U.S. army officers given the task of settling the disturbance was Colonel George Armstrong Custer. On June 25, 1876, Custer led his troop of 215 men right into a Sioux ambush. They were wiped out in under an hour (*above*).

**W**HITEWASH. Another cowboy myth is that all cattlemen were descended from white Europeans. Mexicans and Native and African Americans all joined the cowboy ranks, and the cowboy language was not English but Spanish.

Almost one in seven cowboys was black. Nat Love, for example, won many rodeo competitions for his skill with the rope and revolver. John Ware, another African American cowboy, had the reputation of being the best bronco tamer in the West.

*Indian Territory*
*Anyone taking cattle across an Indian reservation had to pay them a dollar per head of cattle. The trail boss often employed Native Americans (left) to negotiate the fee.*

*Friendly Trade*
*Real-life cowboys much preferred talking with Native Americans to fighting them. While on the trail, they often depended on Indian traders for fresh food and other essential supplies (above).*

**T**HE LONE RANGER was one of the most popular TV cowboys of the 1950s. The masked figure on a white horse helped folk in their fight against lawlessness. He was accompanied by an Indian, Tonto. The white hero and his loyal Native American servant was typical of the way Hollywood depicted the Native Americans. It helped perpetuate the lie of white supremacy so resented by non-white Americans.

# Spiders

Spiders are arachnids, a large group of arthropods, or animals with segmented bodies and jointed appendages, that live on land. Arachnids, like all arthropods, have an external skeleton. Spiders have eight legs, several eyes (which see very little), and they can produce silk from glands in their abdomen. Spiders use this silk in many ways, but mainly to trap their prey – insects and other small invertebrates.

Spiders also use camouflage to catch their prey. The dull colors of many garden spiders, and their stillness, allow them to trap unwary victims. The *Myrmecium* spider even looks so much like the ants on which it feeds, that it can live in the nest.

Crab spiders are adapted to the flowers they live on.

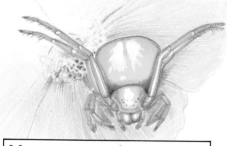

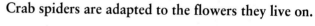

*Myrmecium spiders wave their front pair of legs about to look like an insect's antennae. They fool their prey and so can get close enough to attack them.*

**Ant-mimic spider**

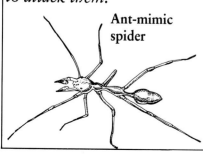

278

# GEARS

Today's cyclists have a much easier time than the men and women who rode the very first bicycles over 100 years ago. The draisienne was a popular bicycle in 1820 – but it was a heavy thing without pedals; you had to free-wheel along, like you would on a scooter! About 1885, J.K. Starley produced the first commercially successful safety bicycle with pedals that used a chain to drive the rear wheel, leaving the front wheel free for steering. The bicycle continued to improve, and today modern machines make climbing steep hills and traveling at high speeds possible by the clever use of special, toothed wheels, called gears.

## BRIGHT IDEAS

 Turn your bicycle upside down and turn the pedals slowly to make the wheels turn. Be careful not to trap your fingers. By pushing a piece of paper into the spokes when the wheel is still, you will be able to count how many times the wheel turns for each full turn of the pedals. In which gear is it easiest to go fast?

**6.** When both feet are attached to the bike, one leg should be up when the other is down. The left foot should be fixed to the keyhole shaped cam, not directly to the pedal wheel. The front wheel can also be fixed with a fastener.

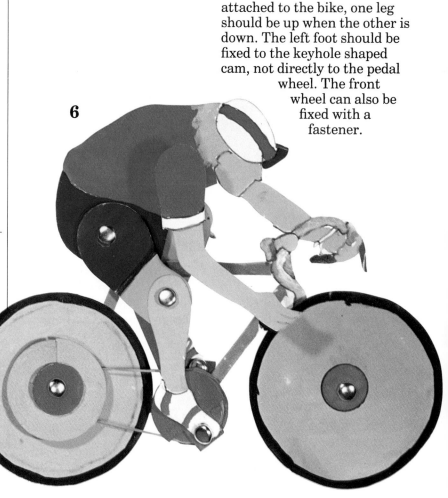

**6**

# Pedal Power

**1.** Draw a pattern of your cyclist. The body of the cyclist and the frame are one piece. The wheels and the cyclist's legs are separate.

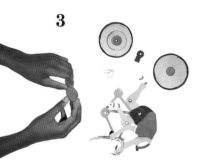

**1**

**2.** Paint your pieces realistically. The back wheel is made up of 3 separate disks of thick cardboard, held with a paper fastener. The smallest 2 are your gear wheels.

**2**

# Why It Works

As we turn the pedals on a bike, the large pedal gear turns the smaller gear wheel on the back wheel by means of the chain. In the bottom picture, if the pedal gear has 50 teeth and the rear gear has 10 teeth then the wheel will turn five times for every turn of the pedals. This is called a high gear and would be best for going fast on flat ground. In the top picture, if the rear gear also has 50 teeth, it will only turn once for every turn of the pedals. This is a low gear and would be good for climbing hills.

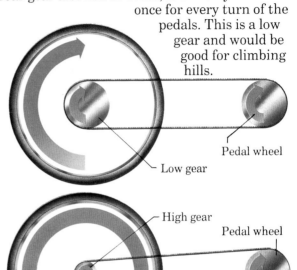

Pedal wheel

Low gear

High gear

Pedal wheel

**3**

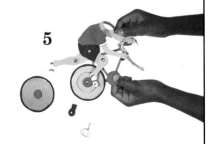

**3.** Join the legs of the cyclist at the knee and the hip. Cut out a thick piece of cardboard, 1in across. It should be thick enough to support a rubber band. The cyclist's foot will pedal this around.

**5**

**4**

**4.** Attach the disk to the bike with a piece of stick, so it turns. A small cam (the blue keyhole shape) is attached to the straw on the other side, and then to the other foot with a fastener.

**5.** Attach a rubber band from the back wheel to the pedal wheel. As the back wheel turns, the cyclist's legs will begin to pedal. If the rubber band is moved to the smaller gear, the cyclist will pedal faster.

# PERCUSSION INSTRUMENTS

The percussion section is a very important part of any band or orchestra. It is helpful in creating the complete musical sound desired, by providing the beat and aiding with the rhythm of a musical piece. Some common percussion instruments are the bass and snare drums, cymbals, the triangle, and the tambourine. A percussion instrument can be an exciting accompaniment to any woodwind, string, keyboard, and/or brass instrument.

Japanese bamboo flute

Wind instruments make a sound when air is blown into them. Woodwind instruments have holes which can be covered to change notes.

Percussion instruments produce sound when they are hit, scraped or shaken with the correct amount of force.

Chinese mandoline

Chinese wind gong

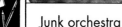

### Junk orchestra
Even if you do not have access to many instruments, it is still possible to make your own band with things you find around the home. Invite some friends over and look around for materials you can use to make music. Be creative!

Stick tacks into a wood block at lengths as shown. Stretch rubber bands between pairs of tacks and pluck away.

Turn some empty cans bottom up and hit them with something that serves as a drumstick.

Bind two lids from jars together with tape to make your own castanets.

## Counting time

Music is a sequence of melodic sounds built around a rhythm, or pattern of beats. In a piece of music, the rhythms are organized into groups of beats, called bars. Musical notes have different values which stand for varying lengths of time.

These values are given below. The notes in each bar of 4/4 time (below) add up to the value of four quarter notes. Try writing some more bars of four beats using the notes provided.

o — Whole note

♩ — Quarter note

♩ — Half note

♪ — Eighth note

In a brass instrument, musicians vibrate their lips to make the air in the pipes move. The notes are changed by altering the length of the pipe.

Trumpet

Stringed instruments contain stretched strings which are plucked or scraped to produce musical notes. Shorter strings, tighter strings, or lighter strings have a higher pitch.

## The story so far...

We can roughly date the beginnings of the musical styles we listen to today. Some folk music dates back hundreds of years. Classical music began during the 18th century and jazz sprung out of the American South in the early 1900's with blues developing from spirituals around the same time. Rock music dates from the 1950's, with its offspring soul arising in the 1960's. Reggae developed in the West Indies during the 1970's, and in the 1980's rap became popular worldwide. Popular music often influences dance styles.

Jazz

Keyboard instruments have a series of keys which activate small hammers to strike or pluck the strings. Pipe organ keys activate columns of air.

Piano

283

# HOW A TREE GROWS

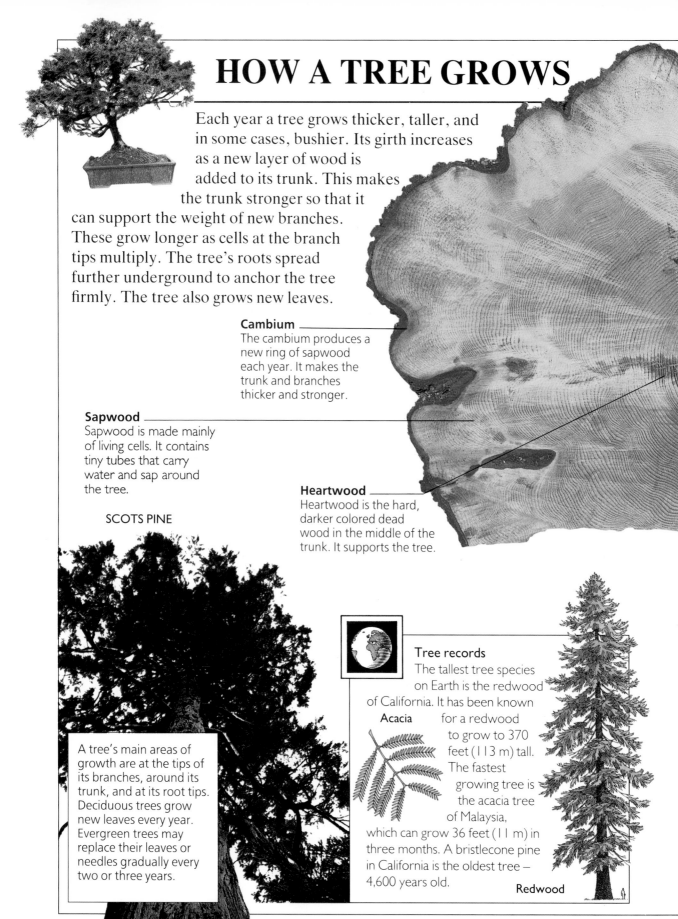

Each year a tree grows thicker, taller, and in some cases, bushier. Its girth increases as a new layer of wood is added to its trunk. This makes the trunk stronger so that it can support the weight of new branches. These grow longer as cells at the branch tips multiply. The tree's roots spread further underground to anchor the tree firmly. The tree also grows new leaves.

**Cambium**
The cambium produces a new ring of sapwood each year. It makes the trunk and branches thicker and stronger.

**Sapwood**
Sapwood is made mainly of living cells. It contains tiny tubes that carry water and sap around the tree.

SCOTS PINE

**Heartwood**
Heartwood is the hard, darker colored dead wood in the middle of the trunk. It supports the tree.

A tree's main areas of growth are at the tips of its branches, around its trunk, and at its root tips. Deciduous trees grow new leaves every year. Evergreen trees may replace their leaves or needles gradually every two or three years.

**Tree records**
The tallest tree species on Earth is the redwood of California. It has been known for a redwood to grow to 370 feet (113 m) tall. The fastest growing tree is the acacia tree of Malaysia, which can grow 36 feet (11 m) in three months. A bristlecone pine in California is the oldest tree — 4,600 years old.

Acacia

Redwood

# 160-YEAR-OLD OAK TRUNK

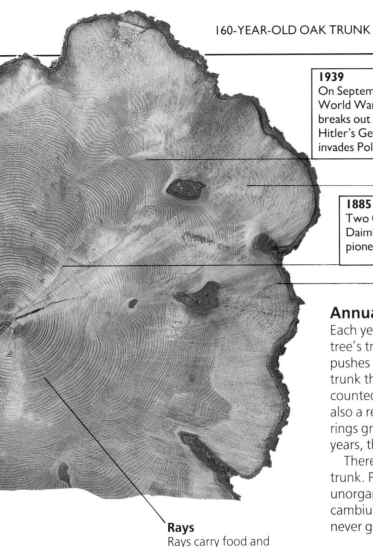

**1939**
On September 3, World War II breaks out after Hitler's Germany invades Poland.

**1969**
American astronaut Neil Armstrong becomes the first man to step on the moon.

**1885**
Two German inventors, Daimler and Benz, pioneer the automobile.

**1990**
What important events happened during this year?

**Rays**
Rays carry food and water sideways through the sapwood.

## Annual growth rings

Each year, the layer of cambium inside the tree's trunk produces a ring of new wood. This pushes the cambium outward and makes the trunk thicker. These annual rings can be counted to find out how old a tree is. They are also a record of past weather conditions. Wide rings grow in years with plenty of rain. In dry years, the rings are narrow and close together.

There are no annual rings inside a palm tree trunk. Palm trunks contain a mass of unorganized fibers. They do not contain cambium to make new wood, so the trunk never gets wider, only taller.

### Making a bonsai tree

Bonsais are dwarf trees that are planted in Japanese and Chinese ornamental gardens. Although real bonsais are skillfully sculpted, you can use this shortcut to make your own. You will need to get a dwarf conifer, a shallow tray, compost, scissors, wire, and clippers. Trim the roots of the tree. Then wind wire around the roots to restrict root growth. Plant the tree in the tray and trim the branches to the shape you want. Ensure the tree gets water and light.

3 Snip out branches

2 Bind the root ball with wire

1 Trim the roots

# CLOUDS

Clouds are made up of millions of droplets of water or ice, which are so small and light they can float in the air. Clouds form when warm air rises. This happens when air is heated by the Sun or if it has to rise up over mountains or when cold air pushes it up from underneath. High in the sky, invisible water vapor in the air cools and turns into droplets of liquid water which gather together to make clouds. The shape, color, and height of clouds helps people to predict changes in the weather. Fog or mist are clouds that form down at ground level.

Cold front

Warm front

Cold air pushes warm air up.

Warm air slides up over cold air.

**cumulonimbus** – storm clouds. May rise to great heights while the bases are near the ground.

## Warm and cold fronts

Clouds often form where warm air meets cold air – this is called a weather front. The cold air may push up under the warm air, forcing it to rise rapidly. This is a cold front. The passing of the front brings colder weather behind. Or the warm air may slide slowly up over the cold air, forming a warm front. Warmer weather would follow this front. In both warm and cold fronts, warm air rises, cools and may form clouds. A weather front is a sign of change in the weather, with rain and sometimes storms as a result.

**cumulus** – heaped-up piles of fair-weather clouds.

**cirrus** – high ice clouds, often first to form along a weather front.

## Heavens above

If someone asked you where heaven is, you'd probably point upward toward the sky. Throughout history, heaven has been portrayed as a spiritual place above the clouds. This illustration by Gustave Dore (1832-1883) depicts a typical heavenly scene with winged angels supported by cotton- wool clouds. Films too, such as *Matter of Life and Death* (1946) show heaven as a timeless place with expansive floors of cloud.

**altocumulus** – sometimes referred to as a mackerel sky – sign of unsettled weather to come.

**stratocumulus** - not as even in thickness as a stratus.

## Clouds in my coffee

When you look at the clouds, do they make you feel dreamy or sad or happy or hopeful? Clouds are quite often used to convey emotions in poetry and songs. Listen to the lyrics (words) of songs. How many can you think of that mention clouds, storms, or rain?

**stratus** – rain or drizzle blanket clouds

## Recycling the clouds

One of the ways clouds form is when the Sun heats water on the surface of the Earth. Some of the liquid water turns to water vapor and is absorbed into the air. This change from liquid water to water vapor is called evaporation. As the warm air, which is now full of moisture, rises up into the sky, it cools down. This makes the moisture turn back, or condense, into liquid water again, forming clouds. This is called the water cycle.

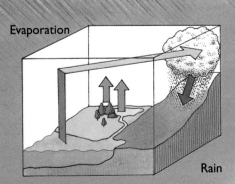

Evaporation

Rain

# DINOSAUR HABITATS

A great deal is known about the lands in which the dinosaurs lived. Dinosaur fossils are found in rocks, and these rocks can give us some idea of what their world was like: how hot it was, whether it rained or not, how far the land was from the sea, what the plants were like, and what other kinds of animals lived at the same time. These clues come from the study of the *geology* of dinosaur sites; that is, everything that can be learned from the rocks. A geologist who finds fossil mud cracks near a dinosaur skeleton will know that there must once have been pools of water drying out. If a geologist finds some fossil leaves or small shells or fish mixed up with the dinosaur bones, these plants and animals must have been living at the same time, perhaps in a pond where the dinosaur died while drinking.

## How fossils formed

Fossils are the remains of plants or animals that once lived on the earth. Dinosaur fossils are usually odd bones or whole skeletons. After a dinosaur dies (1), the flesh rots or is eaten away. Only the hard bones are left, and mud and sand may be washed around the skeleton, covering it over. Then, after millions of years, the mud and sand may turn into rock, and the spaces in the bone become filled with heavy minerals (2). Later, the fossil bones may be found buried deep in the rock or exposed at the surface.

### Continental drift

The continents have not always been where they are now. In fact, all of the continents were joined together during the Age of Dinosaurs. This meant that plants and animals could move all over their world without having to cross great oceans. It was about 100 million years ago that the Atlantic Ocean began to open up.

**Present-day**

**100 million years ago**

**200 million years ago**

**50 million years ago**

The Jurassic period was a time of high rainfall and lush, tropical conditions. Plant groups of all kinds spread, and huge forests of conifers were established. This climate and vegetation were favorable to dinosaurs, and it was during this time that the gigantic sauropods first appeared.

### Collecting fossils

Everyone can collect fossils. Find out from your local museum or library where your nearest fossil sites are. These may be coastlines where there are rocks on the beach, or old quarries. Fossils are found in sandstone, mudstone, or limestone. Be sure to check whether you may go on to the land. Also, take grown-ups with you, since many old quarries and cliffs are very dangerous.

# BUFFALO BILL

William Frederick Cody (1846–1917) did more than any other individual to create the fiction of the exciting "Wild West." Born in Iowa, he had first-hand knowledge of the West, having been a pony express rider, buffalo hunter, and scout in the Indian Wars. He had, though, never been a cowboy.

He didn't let this worry him, and when he noticed a growing public interest in the American West in the early 1880s, "Buffalo Bill" decided to cash in. In 1883 he organized Buffalo Bill's Wild West Show (*below*).

The three-hour entertainment was largely myth, but it was what the audiences wanted, and all over America and Europe they flocked to see it. Cowboys and Indians, dressed in spotless costume, enacted battles and hold-ups. Artists gave daring demonstrations of riding, roping, and marksmanship.

Real life stars were taken on, such as Sitting Bull, Calamity Jane, and the sureshot Annie Oakley. The show eventually lost popularity to the movies, and Bill died heavily in debt. But by then the myth of the Wild West was established.

## BUFFALO BILL'S INDIANS
Buffalo Bill had fought against the Indians and had great admiration for their courage and skills. But his show demanded colorful villains to set off against his mythical cowboys. Indians fitted the bill perfectly.

However, the image of them that was burned into the audience's mind did the Native American peoples a great injustice.

## BUCK TAYLOR

William Levi "Buck" Taylor (*right*) was the star of the Wild West Show. A real Texas cowboy who worked at Cody's ranch, he was a fine horseman who knew a trick or two with the rope.

Buck set the trend for "authentic" cowboy dress – the Stetson, spurs, checkered shirt, bright neckerchief, jeans, and elaborately tooled boots.

### Dime Novels
*In the early 20th century, thousands of simple adventure stories featured the reinvented cowboy, no longer a cattleman but a noble fighter.*

### Nice Shooting!
*Annie Oakley could slice a card in two with a single bullet. Even more amazing was her ability to shoot through the pips of cards thrown into the air (left). Her life was turned into the musical* Annie Get Your Gun.

### MISSIE MAKES A HIT

Phoebe Ann Oakley Mozee was born in Ohio in 1860. At fifteen she won her first major shooting contest, and in 1886 she entered Buffalo Bill's Wild West Show as "Little Missie" or "The Peerless Wing and Rifle Shot." Annie was the darling of audiences the world over. She shot cigarettes from her husband's mouth and coins from between his fingers. One trick involved releasing two clay pigeons, leaping on a table, picking up a gun, and shooting them before they hit the ground!

291

# WHAT IF SHARKS STOPPED SWIMMING?

They would sink to the bottom and stay there. Most fish have an inner body part like an adjustable gas bag, called a swim bladder. The fish adjusts the amount of gas in the bladder to float up or down. Sharks and other cartilaginous fish lack swim bladders and can only stay up by swimming, using their rigid fins like a plane's wings.

Sharks cannot pump water over their gills, like other fish. They need to swim to get oxygen from the water into their blood. If they were to stop they would need a current of water to stay alive.

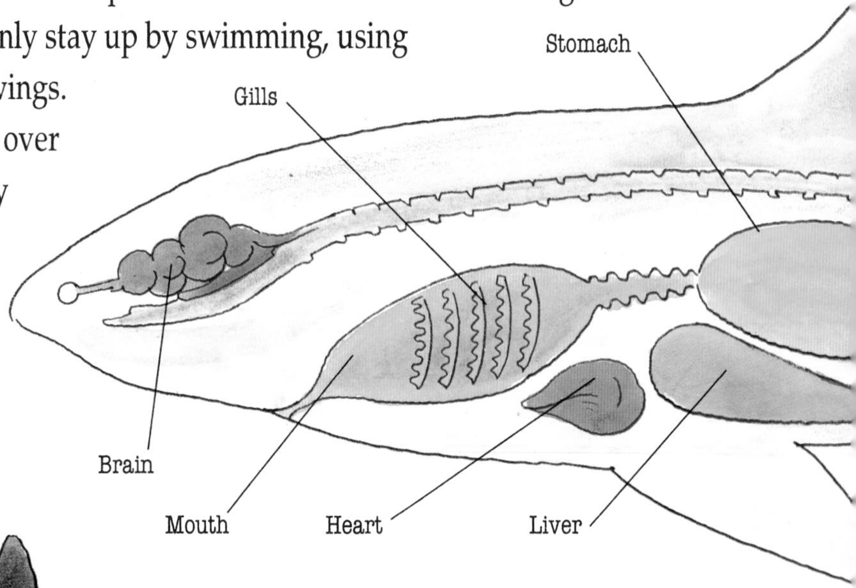

Stomach

Gills

Brain

Mouth    Heart    Liver

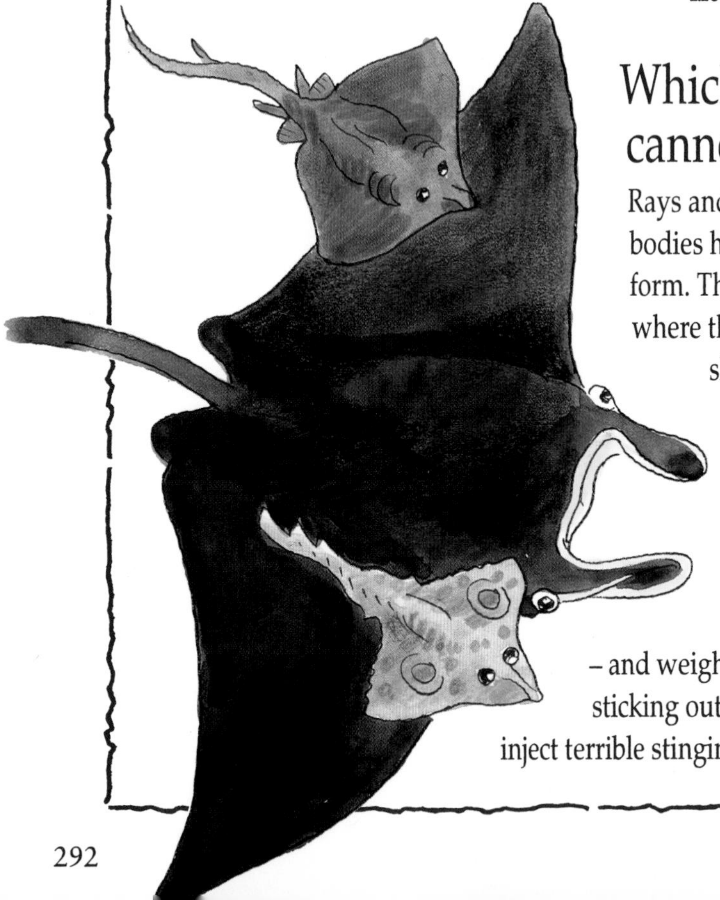

## Which fish have wings but cannot fly?

Rays and skates are flattened cartilaginous fish. Their bodies have developed into a squashed, wing-shaped form. This is perfect for their bottom-dwelling lifestyle, where they scavenge or eat seabed creatures. While skates have a tail they can use to swim like other fish, a ray cannot swish its body from side to side, so it flaps its wings up and down to "fly" through the water.

The largest ray is the Pacific manta or devilfish. It has a "wingspan" of more than 20 feet (6 m) – about the same as a hang-glider – and weighs almost two tons. Stingrays have a sharp spine sticking out of the tail, which they can jab into enemies to inject terrible stinging poison.

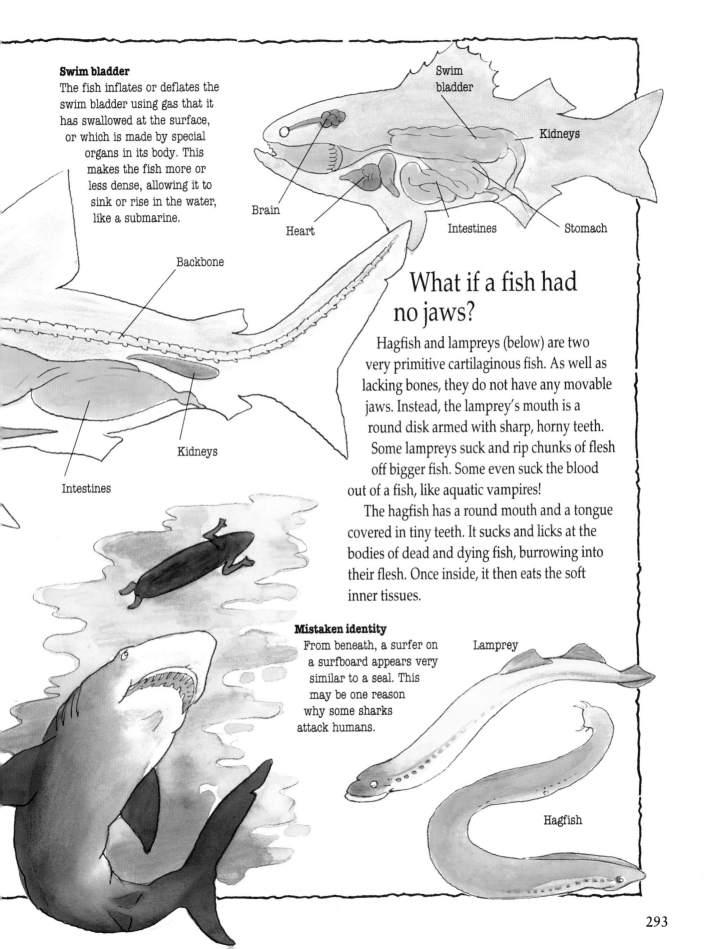

**Swim bladder**

The fish inflates or deflates the swim bladder using gas that it has swallowed at the surface, or which is made by special organs in its body. This makes the fish more or less dense, allowing it to sink or rise in the water, like a submarine.

Swim bladder

Kidneys

Brain

Heart

Intestines

Stomach

Backbone

Kidneys

Intestines

# What if a fish had no jaws?

Hagfish and lampreys (below) are two very primitive cartilaginous fish. As well as lacking bones, they do not have any movable jaws. Instead, the lamprey's mouth is a round disk armed with sharp, horny teeth. Some lampreys suck and rip chunks of flesh off bigger fish. Some even suck the blood out of a fish, like aquatic vampires!

The hagfish has a round mouth and a tongue covered in tiny teeth. It sucks and licks at the bodies of dead and dying fish, burrowing into their flesh. Once inside, it then eats the soft inner tissues.

**Mistaken identity**

From beneath, a surfer on a surfboard appears very similar to a seal. This may be one reason why some sharks attack humans.

Lamprey

Hagfish

293

# ROCKET ENGINE

A rocket is not propelled forwards by the explosive gases rushing from its engine pushing against the surrounding air. For a start, there is no air in space. Three centuries ago the great English scientist Isaac Newton explained it this way: "For every action, there is an equal and opposite reaction." If a shot-putter wearing ice skates throws the shot forward, he moves backward because of the momentum he has created, not because of the shot pushing against the air. Action-and-reaction is the principle of the rocket engine.

A working rocket engine is a "controlled explosion." It burns fuel in an oxidizer (usually oxygen), in a combustion chamber. This creates hot gases under enormous pressure. The gases accelerate out of the back of the chamber. Engineers found that by making a small exit, or throat, from the chamber, the gases accelerate even more, giving extra thrust. They then added a conical nozzle to the throat. This restricts the gases and accelerates them still more, and also helps with guiding the rocket.

**Liquid hydrogen tank**

The propellant (fuel and oxidizer) tanks are made of specially developed aluminum alloys. They are shaped like giant aerosol cans since they are designed to do the same job – withstand high pressure from within. As the propellants are consumed and the tanks gradually empty, sloshing about of their contents has to be overcome.

## THE ENGINE SYSTEMS

The principle of a rocket engine is simple, but there are many practical problems. Engineers have designed various systems to overcome these. In the Space Shuttle main engine, oxygen oxidizer and hydrogen fuel are first pressurized, mixed and preburned, to form hot gases. These gases are then introduced together in an exact mixture in the combustion chamber. The ultracold fuel circulates in a heat-exchanger, to warm itself before preburning and to cool the chamber and nozzle.

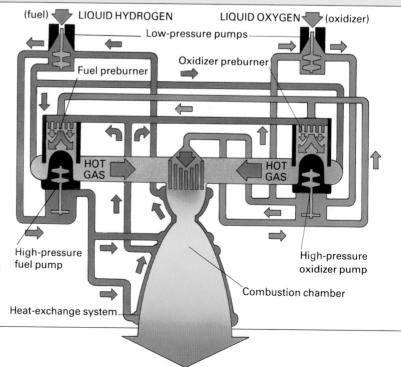

(fuel) LIQUID HYDROGEN — Low-pressure pumps — LIQUID OXYGEN (oxidizer)

Fuel preburner

Oxidizer preburner

HOT GAS

HOT GAS

High-pressure fuel pump

High-pressure oxidizer pump

Combustion chamber

Heat-exchange system

Apollo, the United States' moon program, was launched by the Saturn V rocket. This had a third stage fueled by liquid hydrogen and oxygen. These liquids were fed at high pressure and carefully-controlled rates into the combustion chamber.

### Liquid oxygen tank

In this rocket stage, the liquid oxygen tank is contained within the liquid hydrogen tank. The design saves space and weight. Although the liquid oxygen tank is smaller, the weight of its contents is greater than that of liquid hydrogen. A specially adapted Saturn V third stage formed the orbiting space laboratory Skylab in 1973.

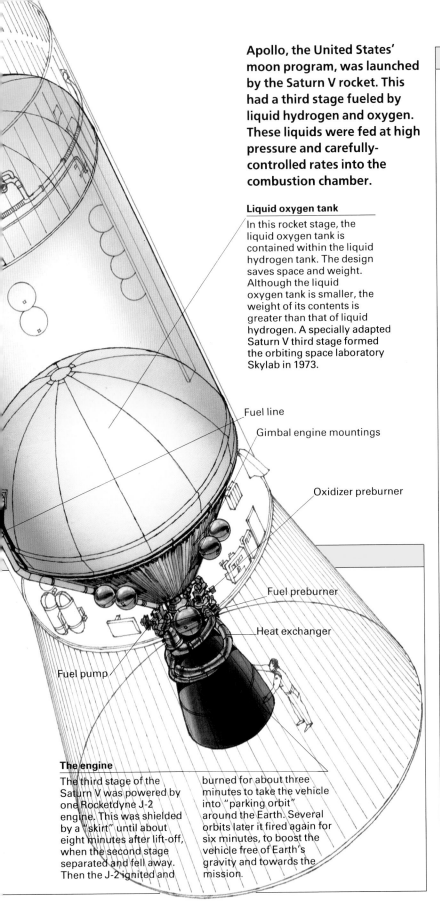

Fuel line

Gimbal engine mountings

Oxidizer preburner

Fuel preburner

Heat exchanger

Fuel pump

### The engine

The third stage of the Saturn V was powered by one Rocketdyne J-2 engine. This was shielded by a "skirt" until about eight minutes after lift-off, when the second stage separated and fell away. Then the J-2 ignited and burned for about three minutes to take the vehicle into "parking orbit" around the Earth. Several orbits later it fired again for six minutes, to boost the vehicle free of Earth's gravity and towards the mission.

## SOLID-FUEL ROCKET

The solid-fuel rocket engine does not burn gunpowder, like a toy firework, but a specially mixed propellant. But once ignited it cannot be turned off. It is used mainly as a booster, strapped to the main engine.

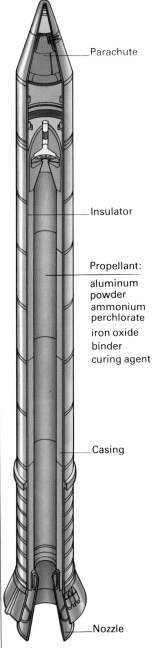

Parachute

Insulator

Propellant:
aluminum powder
ammonium perchlorate
iron oxide
binder
curing agent

Casing

Nozzle

# UNDERSTANDING COLOR

Learning about colors is a bit like learning to speak a different language. If the first few pages of this book seem like hard work, think of them as needing to learn a new vocabulary so that you can express yourself with confidence in future.

**All colors have three qualities**
These qualities are brightness, tone and hue. The brightness or dullness of a color compares with a loud or soft note in music. Tone means how light or dark a color is when compared to another color. A note in music has an equivalent high or low sound. Lastly, each color also has a hue, which is equivalent to the actual note in music. The hue is the actual color you are left with when

**Playing scales in color**
Brightness, tone and hue are illustrated in the color charts on the right. The top one demonstrates a progression of brightness to dullness, the middle shows light to dark tones, and the bottom one is a progression of the color pink to green in the same tone and brightness, to demonstrate hue. If colors of the same tone and brightness are placed side by side, as shown below, they seem to shimmer and dance together in front of your eyes. It is difficult to get this right, but if you learn to recognize when it *is* right you are beginning to get some real control with color-mixing.

differences in tone and brightness have been removed.

## Seeing hue

The idea of this project is to make a picture in which all the colors are the same tone and as much as possible the same brightness. What you will then see is their hue. Choose some colors; experiment with mixing them and painting them in simple patches. The patches below have been made into buildings. First mix your colors. Look at them on the palette and change them around until they are all the same tone before you start painting. Use black to darken or quiet colors if they look too light or too bright. Try to keep the colors clean and flat.

◁ *"To keep colors on separate brushes clean, I stand the brushes bristles up in a can with holes punched in the lid. Alternatively, you could use a container filled with scrunched-up chicken wire."*

**Black** is introduced here as a way of making colors darker in tone and less bright. It can also be used as a color in its own right. Like white, it may appear to be affected by colors that surround it. Sometimes painters use lines of black to separate the colors in their pictures, as panes of colored glass are separated. This can have the effect of bringing order to a chaotic image.

# Changing Views of
# THE UNIVERSE

*How big is the universe?*
The universe is so big that light, which travels at 186,000 miles (300,000 km) per second, would take billions of years to reach us from its furthest edges.

The first challenge to Ptolemy's Earth-centered universe came from Nicolaus Copernicus, in 1543. He realized that the movement of the planets was explained more easily if the Sun, not the Earth, lay at the center. But he did not dare publish his theories until the year of his death. Like Ptolemy, he believed that the planets moved in circles, but Johannes Kepler (1571-1630) showed that their orbits were elliptical (oval-shaped). To explain this, Isaac Newton (1643-1727) discovered the laws of gravity (the force which attracts objects toward each other). In the twentieth century, Albert Einstein's theories linked gravity, space, and time to explain the shape of the universe.

**REDRAWING THE UNIVERSE**
*Copernicus did not support Ptolemy's idea that all the stars circled the Earth once a day. He also realized that it could not explain all the movements of the Sun, Moon, and planets. His own theory declared the Earth an ordinary planet instead of the center of the universe.*

**THE PULL OF THE EARTH**
*Isaac Newton's theory of gravity applies equally to an apple falling from a tree and to the movement of the planets. He said that all objects are pulled together by a force based on their mass (the matter they contain) and their distance apart. This is why planets' orbits are elliptical.*

### EARLY OBSERVATIONS

*Galileo used his telescope to confirm that Copernicus had been right to put the Sun at the center of the universe. The telescope was invented in 1608 by a Dutch*

*eyeglass-maker, Hans Lippershey, who called it a "looker." He found that two lenses in a tube could magnify distant objects. When Galileo heard of this, he quickly built his own telescope, which he used to make many amazing discoveries.*

### SEEING INTO SPACE

*Tycho Brahe (1546–1601) was a Danish astronomer who built an observatory and kept precise records of the stars and planets. His assistant, Johannes Kepler (1571–1630), later used these records to show that the planets moved in elliptical (oval-shaped) orbits, rather than in circles.*

### A MODERN GENIUS

*Albert Einstein (1879–1955) was one of the greatest physicists of the twentieth century. His theory combines space and time so that objects are given a position in time as well as in space. Gravity works by bending this space-time, making objects follow a curved path.*

**Fact or fiction?**
Some of the most fantastic predictions of science fiction have come true. But so far we have not met aliens, or discovered a "warp drive" to travel at the speed of light. If Einstein was right, such speeds are impossible, so most of the universe will always be out of our reach.

# OUR ENVIRONMENT

A picture of the earth taken from space (photo left) shows land and sea, and swirling clouds. It gives clues about the climate on different parts of the earth, which in turn determines the different habitats below. The temperature and the amount of rain affect what kind of plants will grow. If the right balance of sunlight, warmth, and moisture exists, plants will grow. Where rainfall is high and temperatures constant, as around the equator, great rainforests grow. Where it is too dry for trees, grasslands may still thrive. If it is very dry, as in the desert, little grows.

**About 11 percent of the earth's land can be cultivated. By the year 2000 about half of this land will be farmed.**

The natural habitats of the world are very varied. Some, like the rainforests, have been destroyed by humans. In other cases, humans have altered landscapes and created artificial habitats which have much in common with natural habitats.

**About two fifths of the land should be forest, but much has been cut down.**

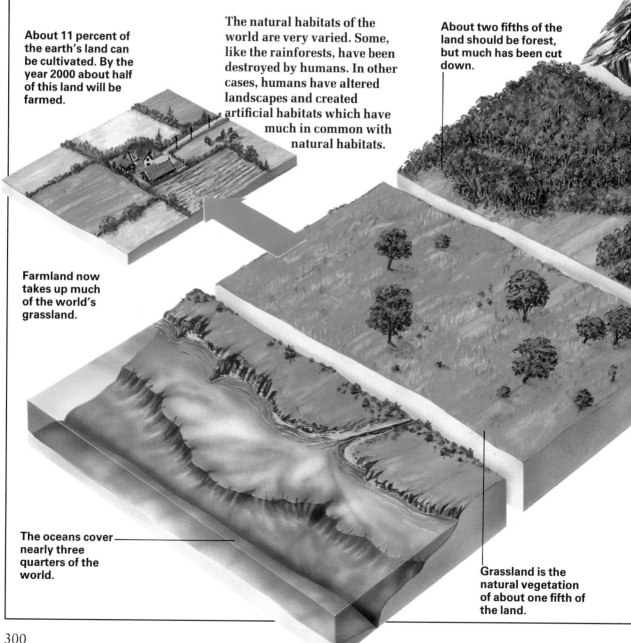

**Farmland now takes up much of the world's grassland.**

**The oceans cover nearly three quarters of the world.**

**Grassland is the natural vegetation of about one fifth of the land.**

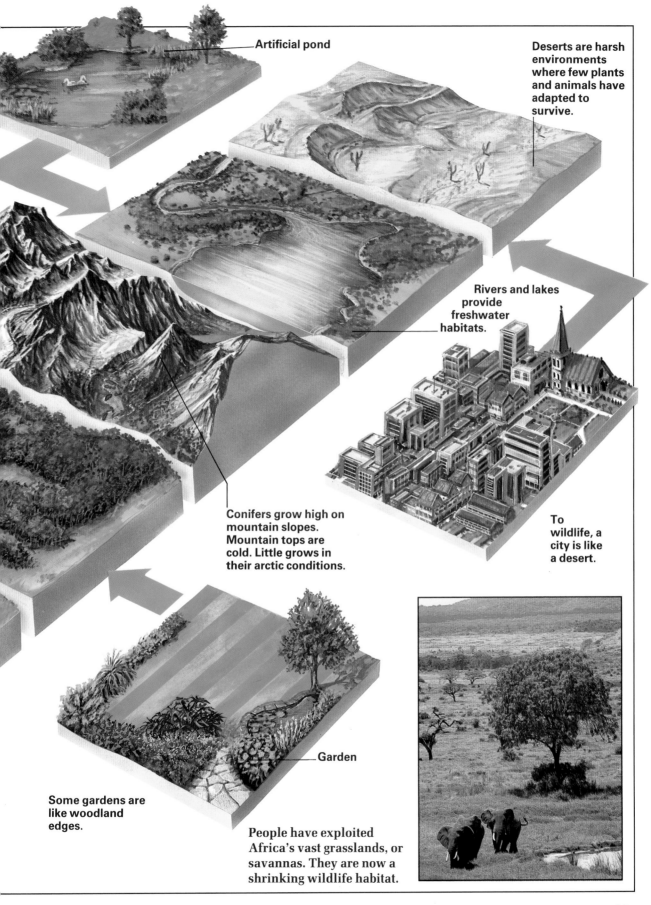

Artificial pond

Deserts are harsh environments where few plants and animals have adapted to survive.

Rivers and lakes provide freshwater habitats.

Conifers grow high on mountain slopes. Mountain tops are cold. Little grows in their arctic conditions.

To wildlife, a city is like a desert.

Some gardens are like woodland edges.

Garden

People have exploited Africa's vast grasslands, or savannas. They are now a shrinking wildlife habitat.

# ANCIENT GREEK LAW

By 700 B.C., Greece was divided into small, independent city states. Greek society was made up of citizens (men who were born in the city state) and non-citizens (women, foreigners, and slaves). Most city states were governed by an oligarchy – a small group of rich noblemen, called aristocrats. Resentment of their power led to revolts. Tyrants, or absolute rulers, were then appointed to restore order. In 508 B.C., however, a different system called democracy (*demos* = people; *kratos* = rule) was introduced in Athens. It gave all male citizens a say in the government. Other city states soon followed Athens' lead.

## A woman's place

In Ancient Greece, women were thought of as non-citizens. Their lives were controlled by men – first their fathers, then their husbands. They could not inherit or own property, or take part in the running of the city. Greek women usually got married when they were about 15. The marriage was arranged and the husband was often much older than his bride. A woman's role in life was to look after the household, spin and weave cloth and raise the children. Spartan women had more freedom and were encouraged to take exercise so that they would have healthy, strong babies. This was frowned on by other Greek societies.

## Slaves

Slaves were used as servants or laborers. Some were prisoners of war; others were bought and sold in slave markets. They had no legal rights.

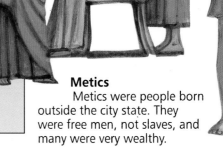

## Metics

Metics were people born outside the city state. They were free men, not slaves, and many were very wealthy.

## Greek *gymnasia*

A *gymnasium* was a center for sport and learning. Apart from training facilities, there might also be a llecture hall. In the 4th century B.C., the philosopher Plato and his brilliant pupil, Aristotle, taught in the *gymnasia* throughout Athens. Each eventually founded his own school, which both became very famous.

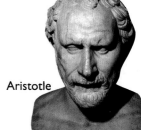

Aristotle

## Jury service

There were no lawyers or judges in Ancient Greece. Citizens conducted their own legal cases and trial was by a jury of about 200 citizens. A *kleroteria* used colored balls to pick the jury for the day. Each juror was given two bronze tokens — one for a "guilty" verdict, one for an "innocent" verdict.

**Bronze tokens**

*Kleroteria*

## Citizens

Citizens were the most privileged social class in Ancient Greece. Only citizens could take part in the government of their city state, own land, or speak in a law court. Citizens were also expected to serve in the army.

## Changing fashions

Greek fashion changed over the years, although the basic dress for men and women remained a *chiton* (tunic), *himation* (cloak), and leather sandals. There were two basic styles of women's dress. The Doric chiton was wrapped around the body, while the Ionic chiton fastened at intervals across the shoulders. Hair styles also changed. Curly hair (below right) was the fashion during the Hellenistic Period.

An Ionic chiton

## Education

In Athens, there were three types of schooling. A teacher called a *grammatistes* taught reading, writing, and arithmetic; a *kitharistes* taught music and poetry; a *paidotribes* taught athletics. A slave called a *paidagogos* was sometimes hired to supervise a boy's education. However, it was only the sons of wealthier citizens who could afford a higher education. Girls were taught domestic duties at home by their mothers.

303

# POISONOUS SNAKES

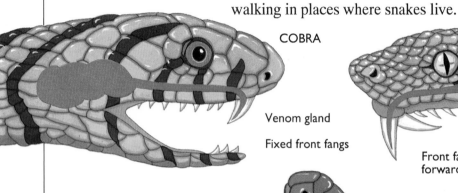

There are nearly 2,400 species of snakes around the world. But only about one-sixth of these have venom (poison) strong enough to harm other creatures. Only a few dozen have venom powerful enough to seriously harm or kill a person. Poisonous snakes use their venom to paralyze or kill their prey. Occasionally they will bite in self-defense, for example, if a careless person treads on them. Just in case, it is best to treat all snakes with respect, and to take great care when walking in places where snakes live.

COBRA

Venom gland

Fixed front fangs

Front fangs hinge forward to strike

VIPER

Venom

BOOMSLANG

Venom gland

Grooved fangs

## Venom and fangs

Snake venom is made in venom glands on either side of the head. The snake injects its venom into the victim when it bites, using its long teeth, called fangs. Back-fanged snakes such as the deadly boomslang and the twig snake have grooved fangs at the rear of the mouth. Cobras, including coral snakes, have fangs at the front. Vipers, including adders, sidewinders and rattlesnakes, have long, hinged fangs that fold back when not in use.

### Snake charming

In some parts of the world people "charm" snakes by playing flute music, as the snake sways to and fro, as though dancing or hypnotized. Often poisonous snakes such as cobras are used, though they sometimes have their venom glands or fangs removed. In fact, the snake can hardly hear the flute. It may react to the rocking body of the charmer and to the vibrations from his or her tapping foot.

Above: Coral snake

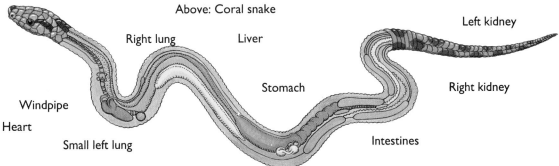

Right lung     Liver     Left kidney

Windpipe

Heart     Stomach     Right kidney

Small left lung     Intestines

### Mimicry
Some poisonous snakes advertise their identity with bright warning colors so that other animals do not attack. Certain nonpoisonous snakes have similar colors. They are mimics, pretending to be dangerous, so that they fool enemies and gain the same protection.

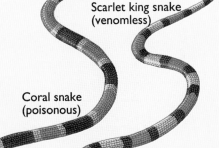

Scarlet king snake (venomless)

Coral snake (poisonous)

## Inside a snake
Snakes are long and thin. Their internal organs have an unusual design, to fit within the body shape. Instead of two lungs side by side, there is only one working lung, the right one. The left lung is either very small or absent altogether. The right kidney is in front of the left one.

### "Poor venomous fool"
Cleopatra was the queen of Egypt from 51 BC. Julius Caesar defeated her, and her lover Mark Antony committed suicide. So she placed an asp (cobra) at her breast, and allowed its bite to kill her. The story is told in Shakespeare's *Antony and Cleopatra*.

# SPORTING TRUCKS

Custom trucks originated in the United States among drivers who owned their trucks. They tried to make their trucks look different from all the others on the road by painting them with startling designs and pictures. Customization may also include replacing some of the standard parts of a truck, such as the exhaust "stack" (a vertical exhaust pipe), and the fuel tank, with highly polished chromium plated parts. The demand for customized trucks is so great in the United States that many manufacturers now supply their trucks in a range of different color schemes. These serve as a starting point for the owner's unique "paint job."

Articulated truck tractors are mostly used to pull especially heavy loads along public highways at normal speeds, but the powerful tractors without their trailers are capable of traveling at very high speeds. Truck racing is one of the fastest growing motor sports in Europe.

Trucks have also taken part in ordinary car rallies including the annual Paris-Dakar race.

A truck "Superprix" race at the Brands Hatch circuit in England.

Truck racing using truck tractor units started in the United States, and then rapidly spread to Europe. There is now a European Truck Racing Championship. Every year, professional racing teams supported by many of the truck manufacturers compete for the title. The races test the trucks' top speeds and road-holding to the limit. The majority of the drivers still earn their living by driving ordinary trucks on the roads when they are not racing. Truck racing drivers do not yet receive the enormous amounts of money that Formula 1 racing drivers enjoy.

As with motor car racing, many of the improvements in ordinary truck design, engine efficiency and safety are made as a result of experimentation on the race-track.

A "funny car" with outsize wheels.

A Leyland Land train doing a "wheelie" at an exhibition event.

# WORKING WITH FABRIC

You don't have to be able to sew or knit to enjoy the rich world of cloth. Fabrics open up an entirely new range of possibilities, enabling you to achieve effects you can't get any other way.

## Many textures

Most households have a bag of cloth scraps tucked away. Collect as many different kinds of fabric as you can. Silk, corduroy, velvet, burlap, muslin – each material has its own unique character, a particular color, weave, texture and pattern.

Buttons, sequins, lace, yarn, and felt can all be brought in. You will also need a pair of sharp scissors, strong glue, pins or staples, and thick cardboard or cork to use as a base.

## What do your scraps suggest?

Study your fragments and see what they remind you of. You could try a head like the one opposite, or an animal, landscape, or abstract pattern. Work as you have with paper, experimenting with your fragments in different positions before sticking or stapling them down.

▽ *"The odds and ends I collected suggested the crazy face and clothes of a clown. I chose pink nylon for the face and a background of cotton twill, and began by laying down these basic ingredients."*

▽ *"I chose shiny red cotton for the clown's nose, and small cotton patchwork squares for his jacket. I tried strands of yarn for the hair, but finally opted for a coarse tweed material."*

309

# REFLECTION

When light rays hit a surface, they bounce off again, like a ball bouncing off a wall. This is called reflection. The way light behaves when it hits a reflective surface is used by people and animals to see more clearly. Cats have eyes designed to reflect as much light as possible, because they need to see in the dark. Inside high-quality periscopes on board submarines, prisms (blocks of glass) are used to bend beams of light around corners, making objects at the surface visible. Light can be made to reflect off a surface. Mirrors can also be used inside a periscope.
Make your own periscope and let nothing spoil your view!

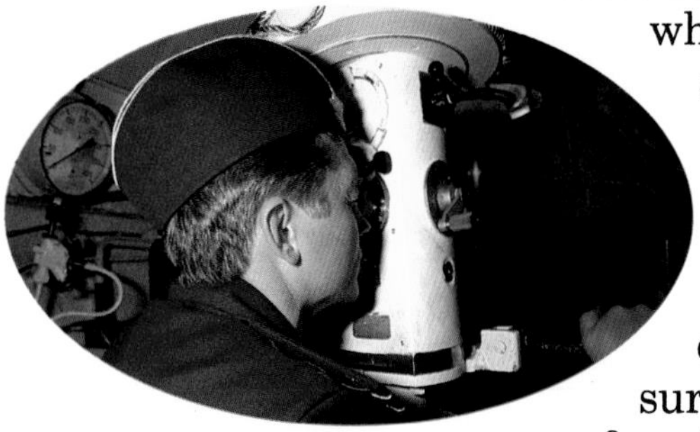

## UP PERISCOPE!

**1**

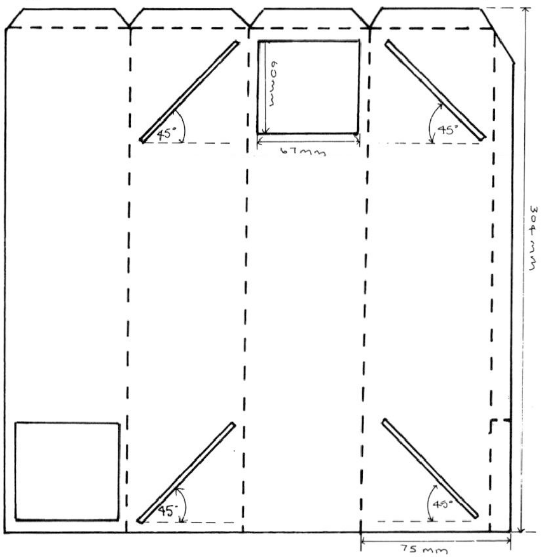

**2**

**1.** Use a ruler and pencil to measure and draw a plan of your periscope like the one shown here. Cut out the two windows and the four slits. Fold along the dotted lines.

**2.** Take two flat mirrors of the same size and put masking tape around the edges. These should be slightly wider than the periscope.

**4.** Slide the mirrors into the slits so that the reflecting faces are opposite each other. The edges of the mirrors will protrude from the periscope case. Make sure that they are secure. If they are not, they may slide out and break.

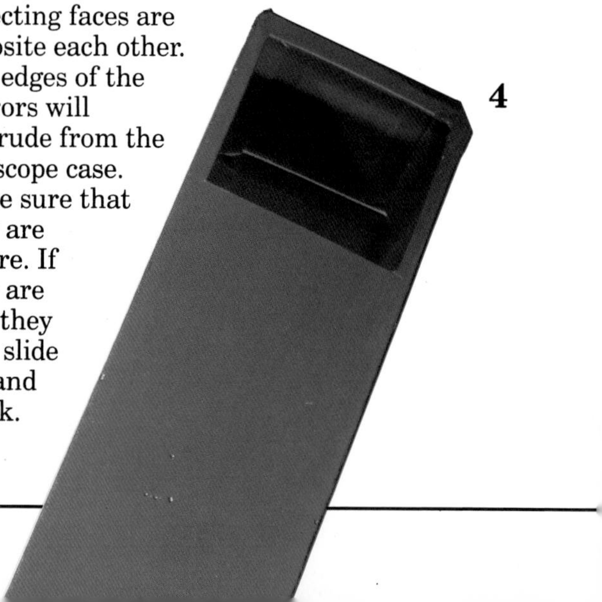

**3.** Use glue or colored masking tape to stick down the folded sides and flaps. Paint the outside of your periscope.

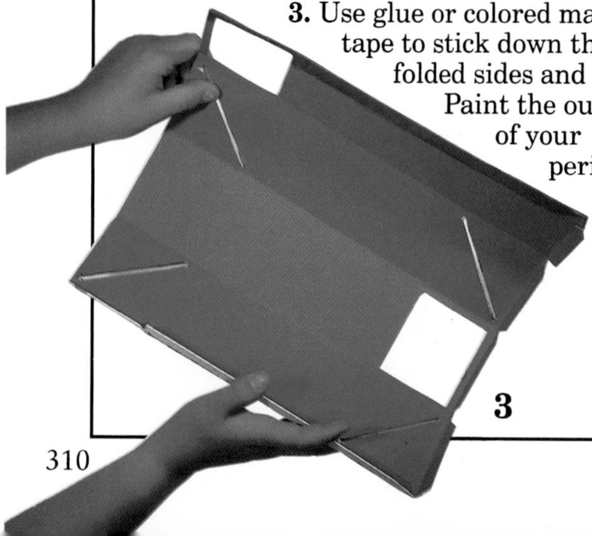

**3**

**4**

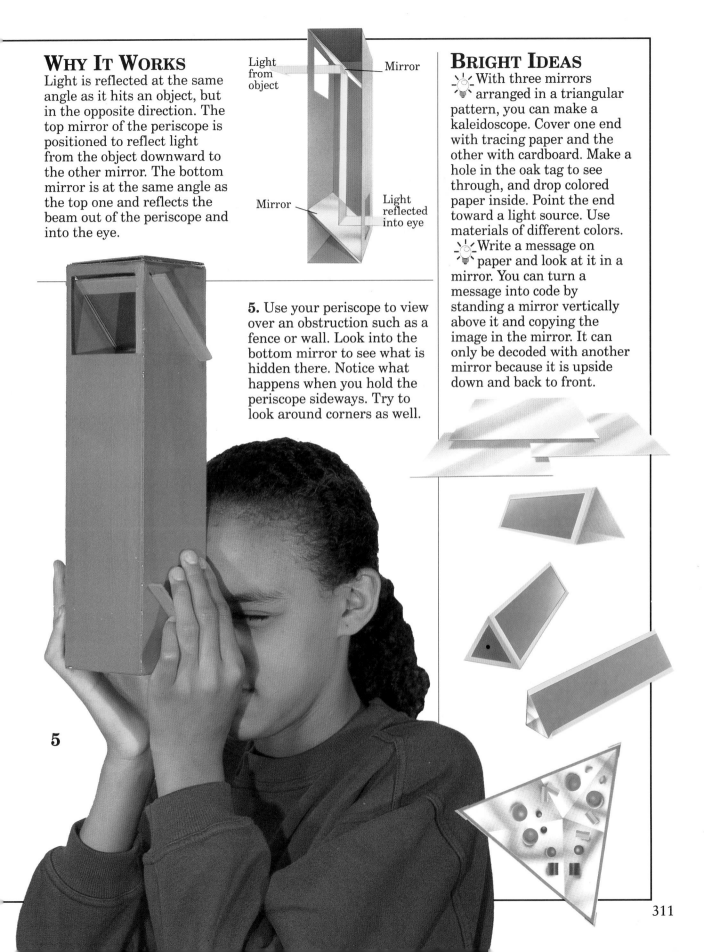

## WHY IT WORKS

Light is reflected at the same angle as it hits an object, but in the opposite direction. The top mirror of the periscope is positioned to reflect light from the object downward to the other mirror. The bottom mirror is at the same angle as the top one and reflects the beam out of the periscope and into the eye.

Light from object

Mirror

Mirror

Light reflected into eye

**5.** Use your periscope to view over an obstruction such as a fence or wall. Look into the bottom mirror to see what is hidden there. Notice what happens when you hold the periscope sideways. Try to look around corners as well.

## BRIGHT IDEAS

With three mirrors arranged in a triangular pattern, you can make a kaleidoscope. Cover one end with tracing paper and the other with cardboard. Make a hole in the oak tag to see through, and drop colored paper inside. Point the end toward a light source. Use materials of different colors.

Write a message on paper and look at it in a mirror. You can turn a message into code by standing a mirror vertically above it and copying the image in the mirror. It can only be decoded with another mirror because it is upside down and back to front.

5

# Life in the Oceans

## The ocean ecosystem

The ocean is a giant ecosystem – plants and animals depend upon each other, and nothing is ever wasted. Like the land, the ocean gets its energy for life from the sun. The energy is passed from plant to animal and from animal to animal in the form of food.

### Rock pool world

Every rock pool is a miniature ecosystem. Winkles and limpets graze on the seaweed. Crabs and small fish chew on the shellfish and are in turn picked off by seabirds. Every time the tide comes in, it brings bits of food and refreshes the water.

### The great white shark

The great white shark (below) is a high-speed killing machine with super senses. It is one of the ocean's top predators (hunters). Its favorite prey are seals and sea lions, but it will take a bite from anything it can catch. It can grow to more than 19 feet (6 meters) long, and has razor-sharp teeth.

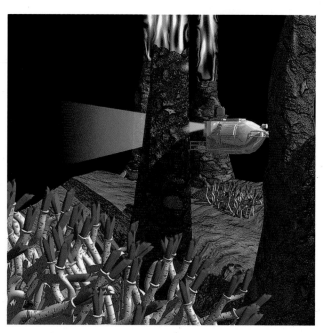

### Creatures from the deep

Deep on the ocean floor, communities of giant worms, crabs, and tiny fish live around hydrothermal vents — holes where superhot water full of minerals gushes up from deep in the earth's crust (above). Tiny bacteria feed on the minerals and provide food for other creatures.

# Food chains and webs

Minute, floating plants, called plant plankton, form the basis of the ocean food chain. They are eaten by tiny surface animals that are, in turn, eaten by larger creatures. When they eventually die, they are eaten by detritus (waste) feeders on the seabed, such as sea cucumbers.

sun

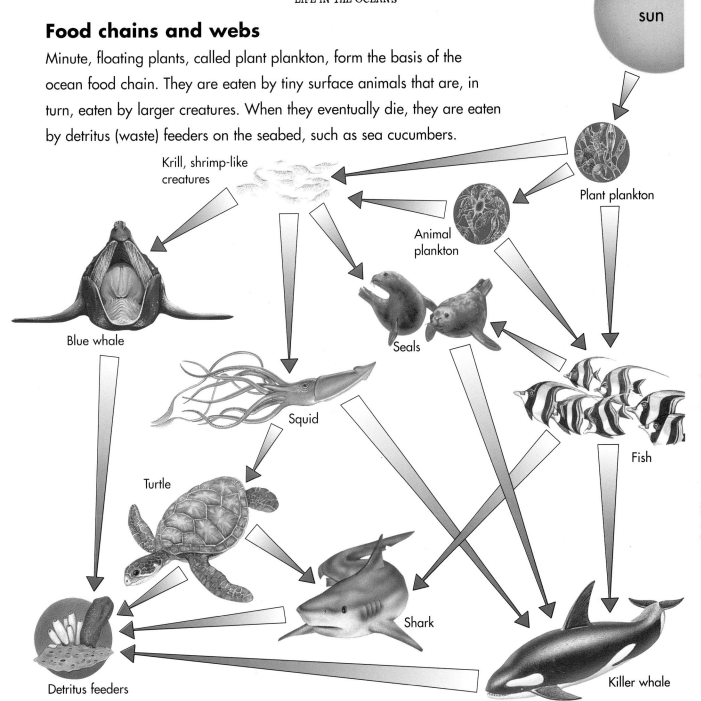

Plant plankton

Krill, shrimp-like creatures

Animal plankton

Blue whale

Seals

Squid

Fish

Turtle

Shark

Detritus feeders

Killer whale

**TALKING POINT**

**Q:** Sharks are among the ocean's top predators (hunters). Do they have any enemies?

**A:** Yes, they do. Big sharks, like great white sharks, have few enemies, but people kill 4.5 million sharks every year for food, sport, or just because they are in the way. All predators are important because they kill weak, sick, and old animals. This helps to keep other species strong.

313

# THE SALEM WITCH TRIALS

Salem, Massachusetts, 1692. A group of girls aged between 4 and 20 sit around the fire listening to stories of a female slave, Tituba. Two of the girls become hysterical. Shortly afterward, adults complain that the girls have been bewitched.

Arrests are made (*right*) and a trial is held. Of the 150 people accused, 19 people are hanged, one is crushed to death with stones, and two die in prison. Even dogs are executed for witchcraft!

The trials went on until 1693, when local ministers helped to stop the craze. The executions were the last for witchcraft in North America, and also signaled the end of witch trials in Europe as well.

*Tumbling Like Hogs* (below) *Young girls from Salem on trial for witchcraft. One of the accused was said to have "tumbled about like a hog." No one is quite sure what went on. Some historians think that a local minister, Samuel Paris, used the beliefs of ignorant farmers to accuse villagers who opposed him.*

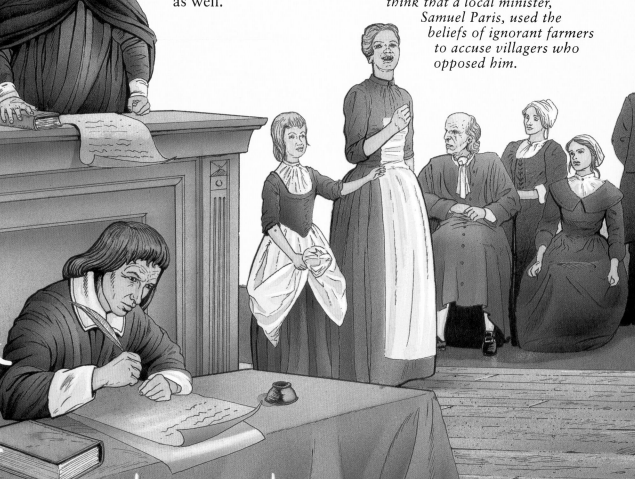

## PILGRIM FATHERS

The colony of Massachusetts was founded by religious refugees who left England in 1620. Known as the "Pilgrim Fathers" (*below*), many of them possessed a strong puritanical faith. They genuinely believed that the devil might appear at any moment. As an English colony, Massachusetts followed English law, so witchcraft was punishable by death.

Sixteen other witches had already been hanged in the region by 1692.

### The Last Witch?

*The Swiss woman Anna Goddi, hanged in 1782, was the last person in Europe to be executed for witchcraft.*

## HOLY MOTION POTION

Evil spirits can be driven from a person or place by exorcism. This is a special religious ceremony that a priest may perform only with a bishop's permission.

In earlier times, people believed evil spirits entered and left people by the body's natural openings. This led to some very odd rituals and experiences! Those possessed by a demon might be given a "holy potion" to drink, made up of oil, herbs, and sherry!

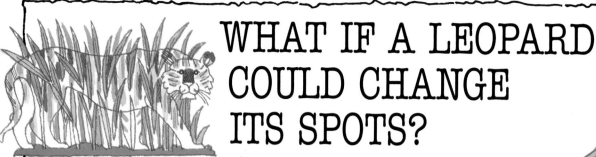

# WHAT IF A LEOPARD COULD CHANGE ITS SPOTS?

A leopard's spots are designed to break up its outline and keep it hidden, especially when it's crawling through the long grass, or lying on a tree branch. Many mammals have this type of camouflage – both the hunted and the hunters, including tigers. If these animals were brightly colored, or if they had strange patterns on their fur, they would stand out, and enemies could spot them at once!

### Dappled deer

Adult red deer tend to graze in open areas. But baby red deer, called fawns, hide by lying still among ferns or heather, under a bush, or in a thicket. The sunlight shining through the leaves creates light and shadow below. So the fawn's coat has similar light and dark patches to conceal it in the dappled sunlight.

## What if a polar bear had no fur coat?

Its naked, pinkish body would show up clearly against the white background of snow and ice. So the polar bear would have trouble trying to sneak up on seals to eat, and it would get very hungry. It would also be extremely cold. This is another job of a mammal's hairy coat – to protect against the cold (or heat, as in the case of a camel). The polar bear's fur coat is extremely thick and warm, as well as extra white. Without it, the bear would quickly freeze to death.

# Stop blubbering!

All mammals have a layer of a soft, fatty substance just under the skin, covering the muscles and other inner parts. When this is very thick, it's called *blubber*. It makes the seal's body smooth and sleek, and acts as a store of energy should food ever get scarce.

However, its major role is as a wraparound blanket of fat to help the fur keep out the cold, especially when the animal is swimming in the icy seawater. Some seals can have a layer blubber that is more than 4 in (10 cm) thick.

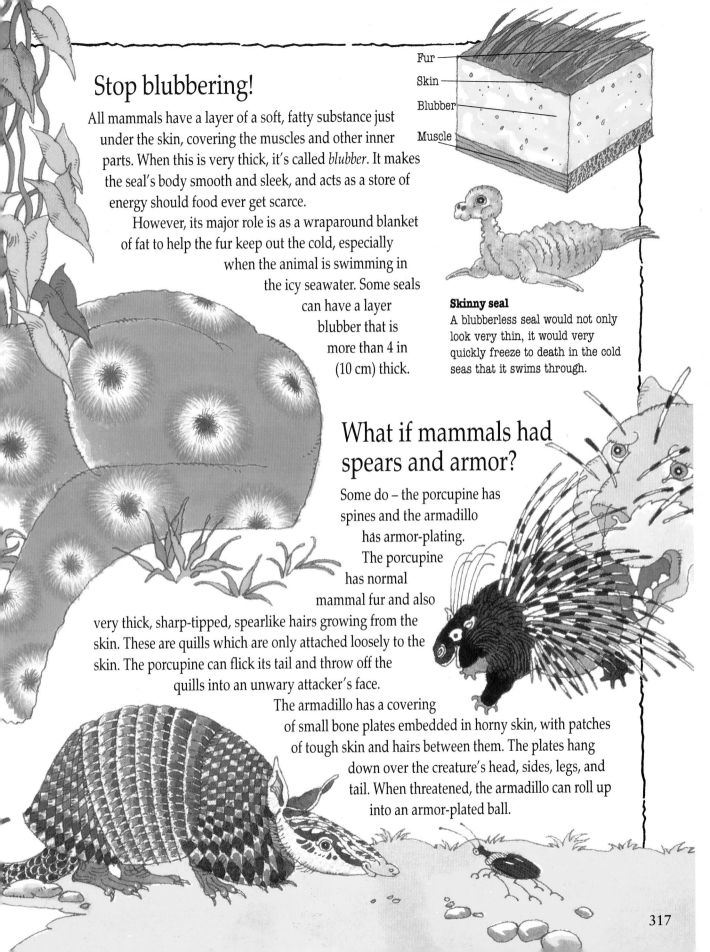

Fur
Skin
Blubber
Muscle

**Skinny seal**
A blubberless seal would not only look very thin, it would very quickly freeze to death in the cold seas that it swims through.

# What if mammals had spears and armor?

Some do – the porcupine has spines and the armadillo has armor-plating. The porcupine has normal mammal fur and also very thick, sharp-tipped, spearlike hairs growing from the skin. These are quills which are only attached loosely to the skin. The porcupine can flick its tail and throw off the quills into an unwary attacker's face.

The armadillo has a covering of small bone plates embedded in horny skin, with patches of tough skin and hairs between them. The plates hang down over the creature's head, sides, legs, and tail. When threatened, the armadillo can roll up into an armor-plated ball.

317

# CARS FOR EVERYONE

During the early 1900s, most cars became larger, more comfortable – and more costly. In America, however, entrepreneur Henry Ford was working in the other direction. Ford understood that there were only a limited number of rich people. His aim was to build small cars in huge numbers, so that they were cheap enough for the average person to buy. This would allow families to travel by car where they wanted. It was part of the freedom offered by the "American Dream," in which Ford believed so strongly. And the dream came true, with the Model T Ford.

◀ Model T, 1914

Ford production line, 1913

## The Model T

Production of the "Tin Lizzie" (so-called because the body was made of thin vanadium steel) began in 1908. The car had a four cylinder, three-liter, 20-horsepower engine, and a top speed of about 40 mph (65 kph). The Model T was designed to be inexpensive and long-lasting.

## Production line

Ford claimed that "the way to make automobiles is to make one automobile like another automobile, to make them all alike." At first the Model Ts were made on Ford's new invention, the production line, in his Detroit factory. In 1913 he introduced the moving assembly line, which has since been copied around the world.

## Mass motoring

When the Model T ceased production in 1927, more than 15 million had been made. Cheap motoring meant more crowded roads. Without clear road markings and signs, driving was a hazardous business.

## "How many tunes does it play, mister?"

Cars in country areas were a source of bafflement. This postcard shows how the handcrank could be mistaken for the wind-up mechanism of a barrel organ!

HOW MANY TUNES DOES IT PLAY, MISTER?

## Increasing choice

In the years before World War I, car manufacturers set up in most industrial countries. The home of mass production was America. European makers concentrated on the more expensive models built with hand tools, a development of the skilled tradition in building luxury horse-drawn carriages. Many famous names date from this period.

Peugeot 1905

Fiat 1914

Benz 1907

Mercedes 1914

| Car versus Horse (1904) | |
|---|---|
| Total cost over five years A pair of horses, including food, stabling, vet's bills : | $4,780 |
| Standard car, cost new: | $1,583 |
| gas and oil: | $760 |
| new set of tires: | $122 |
| wages for boy to clean and maintain: | $633 |
| repairs and spares: | $682 |
| minus resale price: | $487 |
| Total: | $3,293 |

## The cost of cars

Ford set the cost trend with the Model T, and the more that were made, the cheaper they became. A basic version cost $825 when it was introduced, and $260 some years later.

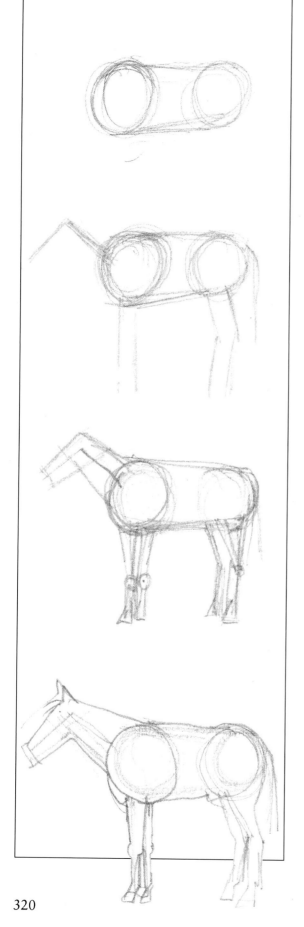

# DRAWING ANIMALS

The variety in the world of nature provides a constant source of wonder and excitement to the artist. From camels to crocodiles, from bats to bulls, animals provide a wonderful opportunity to experiment with lines and mark-making.

The texture of an animal's coat is particularly important. Let your eyes enjoy the softness of cats, the roughness of dogs, the sleekness of horses, and the prickliness of porcupines.

### Back to basics
"Treat nature by means of the cylinder, sphere and cone," said the artist Paul Cézanne.

◁ *"In this example you can see how a drawing can 'evolve,' or be built up gradually. The basic shapes develop step by step into a particular horse. At each stage, more detail is added until, finally, the animal has its own special presence. Make your own version of this sequence of drawings all in one go. You might want to put the figure of a rider on the horse's back to make your drawing more interesting."*

▽ *"In the final stages, I added tone to make my horse look more solid and to complete my picture."*

The simple shapes we studied earlier are the basis for animal forms, and can be used to make your drawings look convincing. The drawings on the left show how the figure of a horse evolves from a few basic shapes. Try this out with your own drawing and then try a similar method with other animals. What basic shapes might develop into a cow, a dog or a cat?

### Animals don't stay still
What all living creatures have in common is that they move and won't pose for you. As with a moving human figure, however, the combination of photographs, your imagination and, most important, your eyes, can work very well.

### Field studies
Don't be afraid to draw from real life whenever possible. Even if your drawing doesn't have a textbook likeness, it may well have a special quality about it. There is nothing so exciting for the artist as confronting the real thing armed only with a pencil and pad. Use a rough sketch book; the less expensive the better, so you will not feel that what you do has to be perfect. Learn to draw quickly and directly, and your pictures will take on a life of their own.

### Caught on the hop
Below you can see an example of how an animal moves. When drawing animals in motion, it is important to let your subject draw itself for you. Look at the animal and allow your pencil to follow the forms in front of you without looking at the paper.

Make a sequence of drawings as the animal moves. When it changes position, don't be frustrated. Keep the same drawing going if it is only a slight change. If your subject changes into a different pose entirely, begin another drawing. Return to the previous one when the original pose is taken up again.

# BREATHING

Like any living thing, the brain needs oxygen. After a few minutes without oxygen, it would start to fade and die – and we wouldn't want that.

Oxygen is an invisible gas that makes up one-fifth of the air around the body. But it cannot seep through the skull bones, straight into the brain. It must first go down the windpipe into the lungs, then into the blood, and finally to the brain.

Rib breathing muscles

## HIC, PUFF, PANT

Sometimes the smooth in-out movements of breathing are interrupted. Hiccups are uncontrolled in-breaths, usually when the main breathing muscle, the diaphragm, gets stretched by a too-full stomach just below it. When the body is very active, its muscles need more oxygen, so the breathing gets faster and we pant.

### TUBE-CLEANING
*Tiny hairs, cilia, and slimy mucus line the breathing tubes. The mucus traps dust and germs; the cilia wave to sweep it upward, to be swallowed.*

## SPIES ON YOUR INSIDES

Modern X-ray machines can do wondrous things, especially when helped by computers. In the bronchoscopy, the breathing tubes are lined with a special fluid that shows up on the X-ray picture. A computer can color the picture to make it easier to see the details.

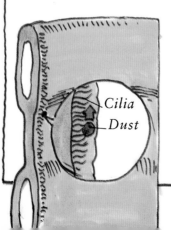

*Cilia*
*Dust*

*RIBS*
*These long, springy bones form a protective cage for the delicate heart and lungs. They are hinged so that they move up and down when breathing.*

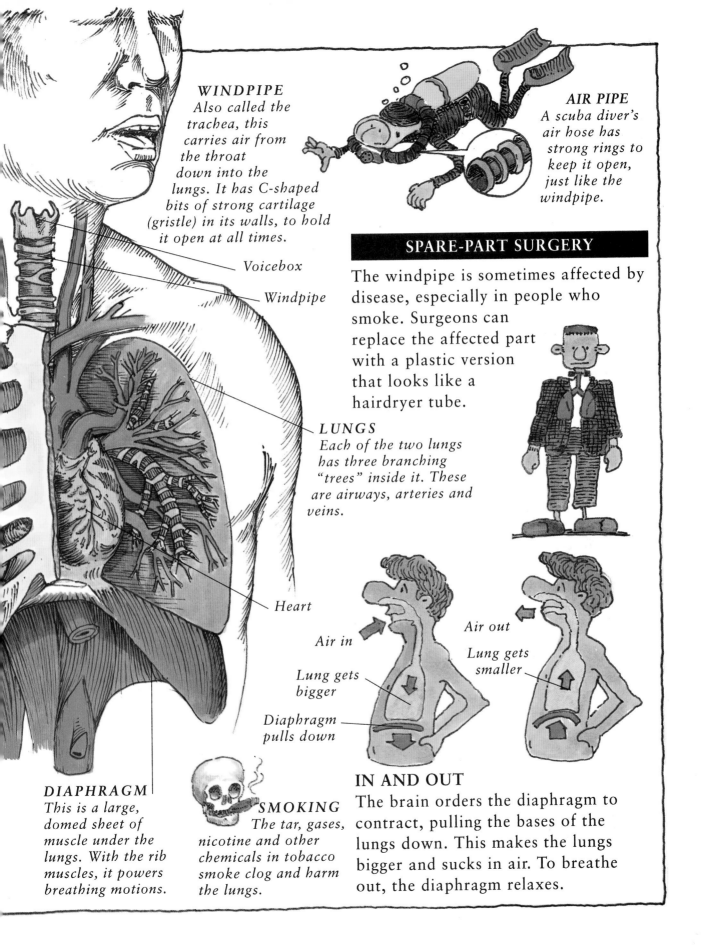

## WINDPIPE
Also called the trachea, this carries air from the throat down into the lungs. It has C-shaped bits of strong cartilage (gristle) in its walls, to hold it open at all times.

## AIR PIPE
A scuba diver's air hose has strong rings to keep it open, just like the windpipe.

Voicebox

Windpipe

## SPARE-PART SURGERY
The windpipe is sometimes affected by disease, especially in people who smoke. Surgeons can replace the affected part with a plastic version that looks like a hairdryer tube.

## LUNGS
Each of the two lungs has three branching "trees" inside it. These are airways, arteries and veins.

Heart

Air in

Lung gets bigger

Diaphragm pulls down

Air out

Lung gets smaller

## DIAPHRAGM
This is a large, domed sheet of muscle under the lungs. With the rib muscles, it powers breathing motions.

## SMOKING
The tar, gases, nicotine and other chemicals in tobacco smoke clog and harm the lungs.

## IN AND OUT
The brain orders the diaphragm to contract, pulling the bases of the lungs down. This makes the lungs bigger and sucks in air. To breathe out, the diaphragm relaxes.

# WHEN A VOLCANO ERUPTS

Volcanoes are in a sense the safety valves in the earth's crust, releasing the buildup of pressure caused by gases beneath the earth's surface.

The strength of a volcanic eruption depends on the type of magma and the amount of gases trapped in it. The magma formed when plates pull apart is very fluid. The gases in it have time to escape and there is no violent eruption. When plates collide, however, the magma formed is much thicker and stickier. Gases become trapped in it and escape explosively in a huge cloud of steam and dust thousands of feet high.

A volcano may be quiet for many years before it erupts again. Often its slopes are covered with grass and trees, like an ordinary mountain. A thin wisp of vapor rising from the crater may be the only sign that it is a still-active volcano.

Surges of red-hot lava flood out of the volcano's crater at speeds of up to 600 ft per second. Lava will flow from the volcano as long as there is enough pressure to force it to the surface. After such violent eruptions, the entire volcano often collapses into its empty magma chamber, forming a steep-sided depression. This is called a caldera.

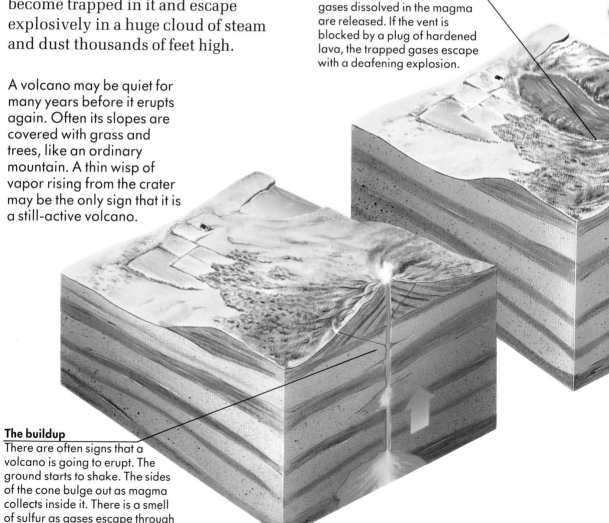

**The explosion**
When a volcano erupts, the gases dissolved in the magma are released. If the vent is blocked by a plug of hardened lava, the trapped gases escape with a deafening explosion.

**The buildup**
There are often signs that a volcano is going to erupt. The ground starts to shake. The sides of the cone bulge out as magma collects inside it. There is a smell of sulfur as gases escape through cracks in the rocks.

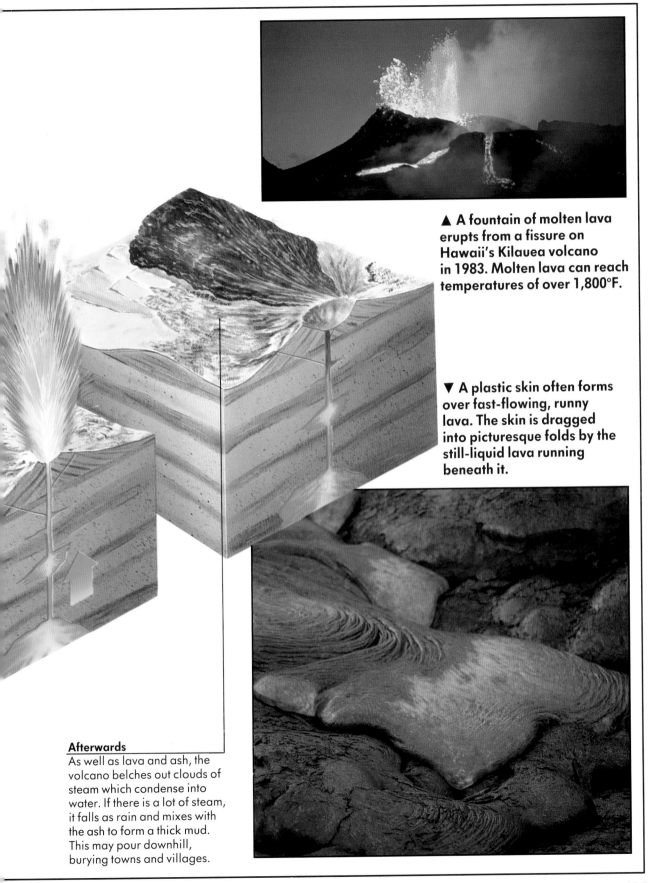

▲ A fountain of molten lava erupts from a fissure on Hawaii's Kilauea volcano in 1983. Molten lava can reach temperatures of over 1,800°F.

▼ A plastic skin often forms over fast-flowing, runny lava. The skin is dragged into picturesque folds by the still-liquid lava running beneath it.

**Afterwards**

As well as lava and ash, the volcano belches out clouds of steam which condense into water. If there is a lot of steam, it falls as rain and mixes with the ash to form a thick mud. This may pour downhill, burying towns and villages.

# ANCIENT EGYPTAIN BURIAL CUSTOMS

The Ancient Egyptians were firm believers in life after death. They went to great lengths to prepare themselves for death, burial, and the life to come. They believed that a dead person's soul traveled into an underworld called Duat. Here it had to pass through many trials and ordeals before it could reach the next world, the Kingdom of the West. There, it could lead a life very like the one it had known in Egypt, but free from trouble. The Ancient Egyptians believed that a person had three souls — the *ka*, the *ba*, and the *akh*. They could only survive in the next world if the body was preserved and not left to rot. This led to bodies being mummified.

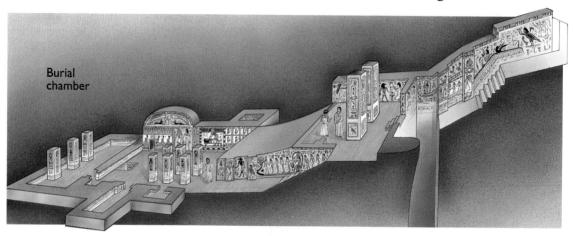

Burial chamber

The tombs of the New Kingdom kings were cut deep into the rocks of a valley at Thebes. They consist of a central tunnel with rooms leading off to the burial chamber (see above). Many Middle Kingdom tombs contain tomb models. Nonroyal tombs from all periods show activities from everyday life, such as grinding corn or plowing the fields. Hundreds of magical statues of servants, called *shabti*, have been found in the tombs of wealthy Egyptians. If Osiris ordered you to work in the fields or do some other menial task in the underworld, you could get the *shabti* to do it for you.

Model of woman grinding corn

The Egyptians filled their tombs with objects which they might need in the afterlife. These included clothes, food and furniture. Tomb walls were painted with scenes from daily life. Osiris, the Ruler of the Dead, was supposed to bring these to life.

*Shabti* figure of Amenhotep II

### Poor burials
Very few Egyptians could afford splendid tombs or grand coffins. Poor people were often buried in simple holes in the hot sand or in a small tomb cut into the ground. However, all Egyptians, whether rich or poor, believed that if they had led a good, virtuous life, Osiris would reward them with a happy eternal life.

Wooden model of a funerary boat

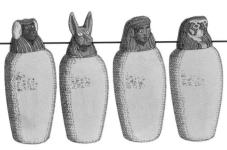

Canopic jars

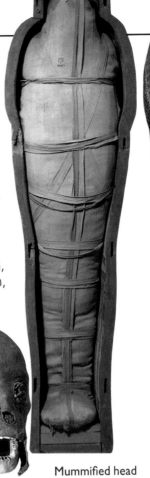

## Mummification

Bodies were mummified to keep them from rotting. The process was so successful that many have survived, remarkably intact, to the present day. There were different degrees of mummification, depending on how rich a person was. In general, though, the first step was to remove the brain, liver, lungs, and intestines. These were stored in special jars, called canopic jars (shown above).

The heart was left in place (see below). Then the body was packed in crystals of natron salt to dry it out. The body was padded with cloth to make it look fleshier, then oiled and wrapped in strips of linen before being placed in its coffin. The process took about 70 days.

Mummified head

### Funerary texts

Passages of prayers, spells, and hymns were carved on tomb walls. These were intended to guide the dead person through the afterlife, to protect them from evil and provide for their future needs. The texts were later written down on papyrus scrolls and became known as The Book of the Dead. The texts and spells were often accompanied by colorful illustrations, such as the one shown below.

In the Judgement Hall, the dead person would stand trial before the god, Osiris. The engraving, right, shows Anubis (the figure on the left with the head of a jackal) preparing to weigh the dead person's heart against a feather, the symbol of truth. If he had led a sinful life, his heart would tip the scales and he would be punished. If he had led a good life, his heart and the feather would balance and he could go on to join his ancestors. The verdict is recorded by Thoth, god of wisdom.

# RODENTS AND RABBITS

**Within the order Rodentia there are 3 main groups:** Squirrel group, with kangaroo rats, marmots and beavers (377 species). Porcupine group, with African mole-rats and, from South America, guinea pigs, chinchillas (188). Mouse group, with rats, hamsters and jerboas (over 1,137). The order Lagomorpha includes rabbits, hares and pikas (58 species).

Rodents, a group that includes mice, rats and rabbits, are extremely successful mammals, found in nearly all habitats except the sea. Most live on the ground, although there are many – such as squirrels – that are good at climbing or living in trees. Others, like beavers and some voles, live in and around fresh water. Many use burrows for shelters and homes, but mole-rats and other species are adapted to a life burrowing underground and almost never come to the surface. The secrets of their success include their feeding methods and their ability to reproduce fast. Hares, rabbits and the similar pikas share some of the same adaptations but are not so varied.

## Teeth and jaws

Rodents have a pair of large incisor teeth at the top and bottom of the front of the mouth. These grow continuously, and are used for gnawing into tough plant food, a process that wears the teeth down as fast as they grow. The enamel on the front of the incisors is hardest, so the teeth wear into a chisel shape. Along the side of the jaws are flattened chewing teeth. Rabbits have two pairs of chisel-shaped incisor teeth. They make good use of food by passing it through the gut twice, eating the feces produced the first time.

A porcupine shows its long front incisors.

## Breeding

Many rodents produce great numbers of offspring. This is not so much because their litters are large – while some species produce as many as 17 young at a time, a more typical number is 4 – but because the young themselves become able to breed at an early age. In species such as mice, pregnancy lasts just a few weeks and those less than a year old may start to produce litters. In favorable conditions populations build up fast. Rabbits, too, breed fast. With no deaths, the offspring of a single pair could reach 33 million in 3 years.

House mice produce litters several times a year.

# Homes

Rodents make their homes in a variety of places. Many climbing species rest in tree holes. Others make a ball nest from sticks, as do some squirrels, or from grasses or bark, as do harvest mice and dormice. Most rodent homes are not elaborate, but wood rats and stick-nest rats build large mounds of twigs to serve as weatherproof houses. These may have several compartments, including a place to store food and a latrine. The most elaborate aboveground structures are made by beavers, which make dams of sticks and mud to control water levels around the 'lodge' containing the family. Many rodents seek refuge down burrows. Some construct complex systems of tunnels with escape holes, nest chambers, storage places and latrines. Prairie dogs build a raised lip of soil around the entrance to keep out floodwater. The longest tunnels are those of mole-rats – more than 400m (440yd) long. The homes of rabbits are similar but less varied.

A beaver's dam and lodge in Alaska

Squirrels sometimes nest in holes in trees.

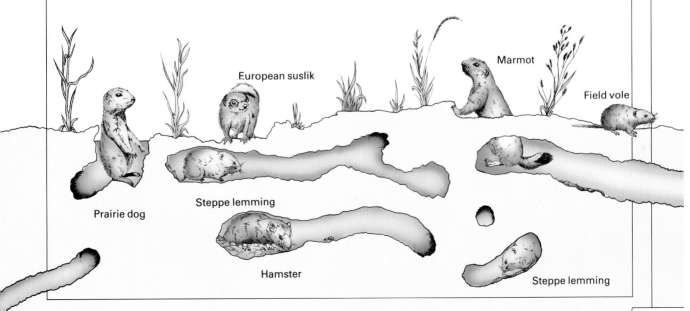

European suslik

Marmot

Field vole

Prairie dog

Steppe lemming

Hamster

Steppe lemming

# SATELLITES
## SPACE COMMUNICATION

**Communications satellites (comsats) are capable of relaying computer data, radio, telephone, and TV signals across the world in seconds.**

Today, there are hundreds of comsats in orbit around the Earth. Now there are plans to build a satellite network far bigger than any of the present systems. Made up of 840 satellites, the network would provide communications services even to the remotest parts of the world. The network would provide a global information network, linking computers in homes and offices.

*Consisting of 18 satellites 11,000 miles above the Earth, GPS works out the position of the ship or plane by calculating the time the satellite's signal takes to reach the receiver on earth.*

## S A T E L L I T E S
### HOW THEY ARE LAUNCHED

Comsats are launched into orbit by rockets (above) or carried into space by space shuttles. Satellites are equipped with booster engines that guide them into orbit and help to keep them there. Earth stations receive telephone, TV, or radio signals and send them to the satellite. The satellite amplifies the signals and retransmits them to earth using a device called a transponder.

Equipped with portable satellite transmitters, journalists can now use comsats to send live broadcasts home without having to rely on the facilities of local TV stations. Aircraft and shipping use a satellite navigation system called the American Global Positioning System (GPS). Portable receivers, such as the Sony Pyxis, make GPS more widely available.

*Equipped with portable satellite transmitters (right), newspaper and TV correspondents no longer have to relay live broadcasts via a local TV station with access to a satellite, neither do they have to rely on telephone links.*

*The Gulf War of 1991 provided an excellent opportunity to test the portable satellite transmitters in action (below). Reporting a war is difficult as well as dangerous, because normal communications are often disrupted. Portable transmitters could transform the coverage of wars and events in remote places.*

**SONY**

**PYXIS**

GLOBAL POSITIONING SYSTEM

*The Global Positioning System was originally designed for military purposes, but it can also be used by sailors, climbers, explorers, and scientists. The small Sony receiver, called Pyxis (left) after the Pyxis or Compass constellation has opened up GPS to many more people. GPS allows users to know their position anywhere on earth within 30 ft, their speed to within inches per second, and the time to within fractions of a second. With the aid of GPS, scientists in Cumbria, England, have tracked the movements of individual sheep to see why some are still picking up radioactivity from the 1986 Chernobyl disaster.*

**SONY**

POS    NAV    TRACK    EDIT    SET    MARK

EXTENSION

CLEAR    RECALL    ⇦    ⇨    ENTER

GLOBAL POSITIONING SYSTEM    IPS-360

*Astronauts maneuver a satellite into orbit from the space shuttle (above). Other spacecraft can launch satellites but only the space shuttle can be reused. Space shuttles have made it possible to retrieve satellites so they can be serviced in space. Those that need repairs can be brought back to Earth.*

# FUN WITH SOUND

Some of the most difficult instruments to play in the orchestra are the reed instruments, for example an oboe or a bassoon. The reed is held to the musician's mouth and blown to make the reed vibrate. An inexperienced player, though, can blow and blow without getting a sound from the reed! Organs, too, create their sounds by blowing through reeds, though in this case, the air is pumped through by bellows. Originally, reeds were made from the reeds that commonly grow by the edge of water.

## WHY IT WORKS

When you blow, the tips of the reed vibrate. This sets the air inside the straw vibrating too, which transmits sound waves to our ears. Inside the tube there is a column of air that also vibrates in response to the vibrating of the reed. You can vary the length of the column of air depending on where you place your fingers. The larger the column of air, the slower the vibrations and the lower the pitch of the note becomes.

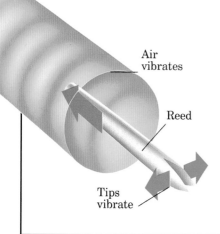

Air vibrates

Reed

Tips vibrate

# REED SOUNDS

**1.** Begin by finding (or making) a tube of cardboard or oak tag. It needs to be about 20 in long and 1 inch in diameter. Paint your tube and leave it to dry.

**2.** When dry, carefully mark out the position of the finger holes of your reed instrument. Start with the first hole about 6 inches from one end and continue along the length of the tube. Make the hole with a sharp pencil.

**3.** Next, make the reed – you will need a 4 inch length of plastic drinking straw or art straw for this. Squash the straw flat at one end and cut a 0.5 inch piece from the center outward toward the edge. Repeat on the other side.

**4.** Place a cork or stopper in the end of the tube that has the finger holes. Next, practice blowing the reed. Place the squashed end into your mouth so that the cut parts are just inside your lips. Hold it lightly and blow gently.

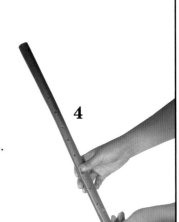

**5.** If at first your reed makes no sound, carefully open out the cut flaps so that they are just a millimeter or two apart. Try again. By making very fine adjustments to this gap, your reed will eventually work. When it does, put the end of the reed into the tube and change notes by covering different holes.

## BRIGHT IDEAS

Make more reeds. Change the length of the reeds and find out whether longer reeds played on their own make notes with a lower pitch. Make a cone of oak tag and place it on the end of your reed. It will act as an amplifier, making the sound louder.

Put the end of a hollow tube into a bowl of water and blow across the top. Move the tube up and down, so changing the amount of air inside it; what do you notice about the pitch of the sound?

You can turn your reed pipe into a flute! Make another, larger hole 4 in from the end. Make the first finger hole, 2 in from this, larger too. Now hold the pipe sideways underneath your mouth and blow across the first hole to create a flutelike sound.

# H i - T e c h
# S P O O K S

Modern science is developing at a breathtaking speed. New technology enables us to explore and understand more about our world and our universe. Scientific techniques, like radiocarbon dating, help historians and archaeologists to unravel the mysteries of the past. Space laboratories, radiotelescopes, and space probes are constantly investigating the mysteries of the skies at close quarters. Satellites give scientists information about the atmosphere and the weather. As technology advances, we may discover new explanations for phenomena that we now consider supernatural.

*Are the mind and the brain the same? Although many people believe that our thoughts and feelings can be explained scientifically, there do seem to be differences between the mind and the brain. When we dream, for example, our minds are not linked to our bodies and brains as closely as when we are awake.*

**PROBING THE MIND**
*Some scientists believe that our thoughts are due to electrical and chemical charges in the brain, which they can monitor with an electroencephalograph (EEG) machine. This shows changes in brain activity at various times.*

**ALIEN CROP RAIDERS?**
*In the 1980s, strange circles began to appear in cornfields all over England. They were almost perfectly circular and the crops had been flattened without harm to the stalks. People said they were made by aliens or caused by the weather. High-tech gadgets have been used in attempts to recreate such circles, but without success.*

**PHOTOGRAPHING THE BEAST**
*Infrared film has been used in the tracking of several ferocious creatures which have terrorized sheep on British moors since the 1980s. Some witnesses describe huge black dogs. Others say there must be a new breed of wild cat or that big cats have escaped from wildlife parks. There are still many different theories about the strange beasts' identities.*

### LIVING COLORS

In 1939, the Soviet scientists Semyon and Valentina Kirlian invented a method of photography which showed an aura, or halo, around living objects. They said that live cells give off colored electrical energy which alters according to mood, but many scientists dismiss their theory.

### SCANNING THE SKIES

Scientists use radiotelescopes to search for alien messages. The Parkes radiotelescope (right), in Australia, monitors radio waves from space to check for signals which could be messages. In 1995, U.S. scientists set up Project BETA, to scan the nearest 1,000 stars for possible life.

### The modern miracles

Hi-tech equipment has revealed the truth of the Turin Shroud (below). Believed for centuries to be the death wrappings of Christ, the shroud is in fact a medieval fake. But its mystery continues to puzzle scientists – no one is sure how the startling image of Christ was produced.

In 1995, thousands of people reported seeing Hindu statues drinking milk. Some said this was a miracle, but others said that the statues were made of porous stone or full of absorbent material.

### INTO SPACE

Space probes are constantly exploring the mysteries of the skies. In 1986, Giotto (below) flew through Halley's Comet, seen for centuries as a bad omen. Pioneer 10 and 11 carry greetings to any life-forms they may encounter in space.

# AVALANCHES

When an avalanche strikes, more than 130 million cubic yards of snow and ice blast down a mountainside. As the ice mass falls, it collects large amounts of debris such as rocks and tree stumps on its way. In a populated mountain area, whole villages are crushed, hundreds of people and animals are buried alive, power and water supplies are cut off, and roads and railroad lines disappear – all in a matter of minutes.

The world's greatest single avalanche disaster occurred in 1962 in Peru. More than 3,500 people died and eight villages and towns were destroyed in just 7 minutes. When the avalanche finally came to rest, after a journey of almost 10 miles, the pile of snow and ice was over 60 feet deep.

Trapped under the hard, packed snow, an avalanche victim can barely move and is unlikely to survive for more than a couple of hours. Victims die from the cold, from a lack of oxygen, or from the injuries that occurred when they were first struck. Only about 5 percent of all avalanche victims are rescued alive.

6:18 p.m.
The deadly torrent of ice and rocks misses Yungay, but crushes the village of Ranrahirca, killing 2,700 people.

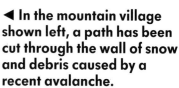

◀ **In the mountain village shown left, a path has been cut through the wall of snow and debris caused by a recent avalanche.**

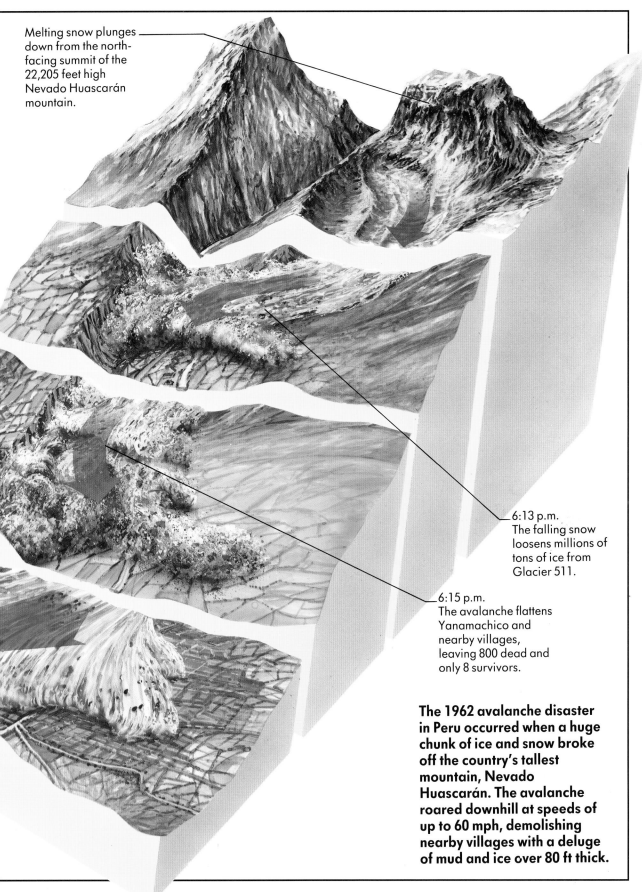

Melting snow plunges down from the north-facing summit of the 22,205 feet high Nevado Huascarán mountain.

6:13 p.m.
The falling snow loosens millions of tons of ice from Glacier 511.

6:15 p.m.
The avalanche flattens Yanamachico and nearby villages, leaving 800 dead and only 8 survivors.

**The 1962 avalanche disaster in Peru occurred when a huge chunk of ice and snow broke off the country's tallest mountain, Nevado Huascarán. The avalanche roared downhill at speeds of up to 60 mph, demolishing nearby villages with a deluge of mud and ice over 80 ft thick.**

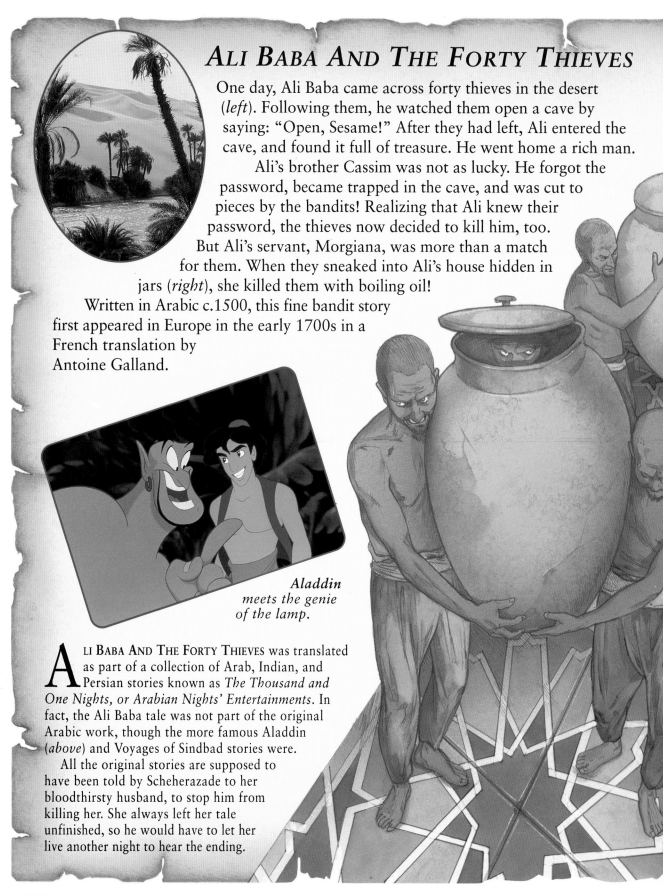

# ALI BABA AND THE FORTY THIEVES

One day, Ali Baba came across forty thieves in the desert (*left*). Following them, he watched them open a cave by saying: "Open, Sesame!" After they had left, Ali entered the cave, and found it full of treasure. He went home a rich man.

Ali's brother Cassim was not as lucky. He forgot the password, became trapped in the cave, and was cut to pieces by the bandits! Realizing that Ali knew their password, the thieves now decided to kill him, too.

But Ali's servant, Morgiana, was more than a match for them. When they sneaked into Ali's house hidden in jars (*right*), she killed them with boiling oil!

Written in Arabic c.1500, this fine bandit story first appeared in Europe in the early 1700s in a French translation by Antoine Galland.

**Aladdin**
*meets the genie
of the lamp.*

ALI BABA AND THE FORTY THIEVES was translated as part of a collection of Arab, Indian, and Persian stories known as *The Thousand and One Nights, or Arabian Nights' Entertainments*. In fact, the Ali Baba tale was not part of the original Arabic work, though the more famous Aladdin (*above*) and Voyages of Sindbad stories were.

All the original stories are supposed to have been told by Scheherazade to her bloodthirsty husband, to stop him from killing her. She always left her tale unfinished, so he would have to let her live another night to hear the ending.

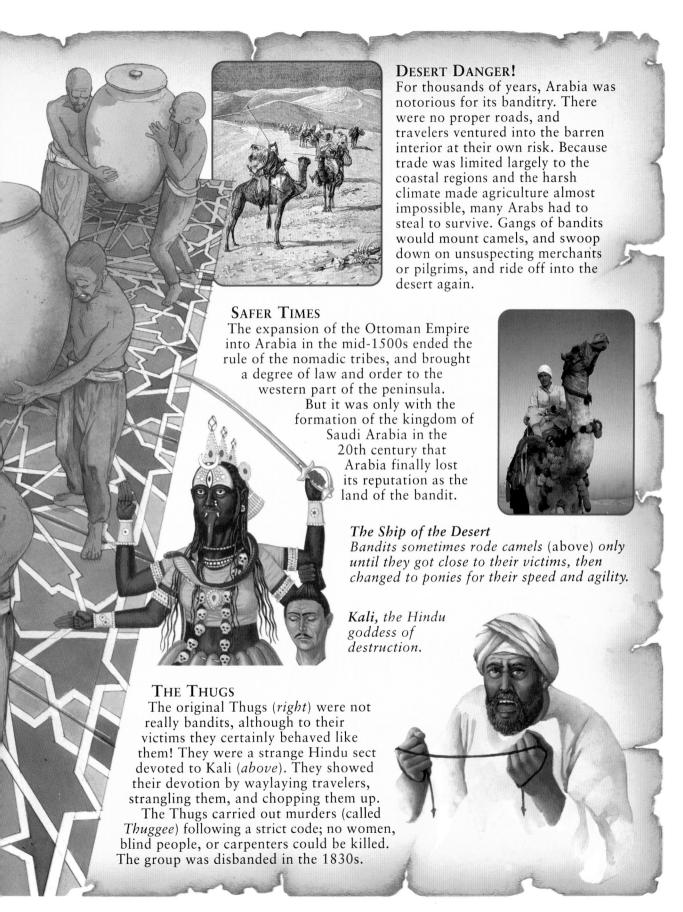

## DESERT DANGER!

For thousands of years, Arabia was notorious for its banditry. There were no proper roads, and travelers ventured into the barren interior at their own risk. Because trade was limited largely to the coastal regions and the harsh climate made agriculture almost impossible, many Arabs had to steal to survive. Gangs of bandits would mount camels, and swoop down on unsuspecting merchants or pilgrims, and ride off into the desert again.

### SAFER TIMES

The expansion of the Ottoman Empire into Arabia in the mid-1500s ended the rule of the nomadic tribes, and brought a degree of law and order to the western part of the peninsula. But it was only with the formation of the kingdom of Saudi Arabia in the 20th century that Arabia finally lost its reputation as the land of the bandit.

*The Ship of the Desert*
*Bandits sometimes rode camels* (above) *only until they got close to their victims, then changed to ponies for their speed and agility.*

*Kali, the Hindu goddess of destruction.*

### THE THUGS

The original Thugs (*right*) were not really bandits, although to their victims they certainly behaved like them! They were a strange Hindu sect devoted to Kali (*above*). They showed their devotion by waylaying travelers, strangling them, and chopping them up.

The Thugs carried out murders (called *Thuggee*) following a strict code; no women, blind people, or carpenters could be killed. The group was disbanded in the 1830s.

# FISH OF SHORES & REEFS

The shallow waters along the seashore provide a wide range of fish habitats, from tidal mudflats to sandbanks and rocky coasts. In tropical areas, coral reefs can support a great variety of life. Nutrients are plentiful, and the bright sun provides lots of light, so many seaweeds and other plants can grow. These plants are the basic food for all the forms of animal life, including myriad worms, crabs, starfish and shellfish, which thrive in the warm, shallow waters. They, in turn, provide food for a dazzling array of fish. In contrast, the shoreline of a wide beach is much emptier of fish.

## Nooks and crannies
The blenny and rock goby use rocks and boulders to shelter from predators and ambush prey. The clingfish can stick to overhanging rocks with its suckerlike fins.

Clingfish

Lumpsucker

Rock goby

Grunion

Butterfish

Blenny

## Tropical paradise
Many people dream of "getting away from it all" on a deserted tropical island. In 1719 the English writer Daniel Defoe based his adventure story *Robinson Crusoe* on the experiences of a real sailor named Alexander Selkirk. The book tells of a lonely castaway struggling to survive on a small island, beset by lack of food, water and shelter, and plagued by insect pests, pirates and islanders. Not such a paradise?

## Traditional fishing
Around the world's coastlines, people use various traditional fishing methods to catch what they need from the sea. The Inuit people of northern North America fish from the shore or along coastal rivers, using nets, and spears, harpoons and hooks carved from natural materials such as walrus tusks or whalebone. However, these traditional ways of life are becoming ever more difficult to preserve.

## The perils of the tide

Shores and reefs can be treacherous places for fish, because of the tides. As the tide falls, it can leave fish marooned in pools. The butterfish is named from its tough, slippery, slimy skin. This enables it to wriggle from under rolling pebbles, and prevents it from drying out as it flaps over the rocks from one pool to another. Shore fish such as gobies and blennies can withstand great variations in temperature and salinity (salt concentration), as well as buffeting by waves and rolling boulders.

### Partners in life

Certain fish team up with quite different animals, in relationships beneficial to both. Clownfish swim among the stinging tentacles of anemones. Their bodies are covered in mucus that provides a barrier to the stings. The clownfish are safe from attack while the anemone consumes the food they drop. This partnership is called symbiosis.

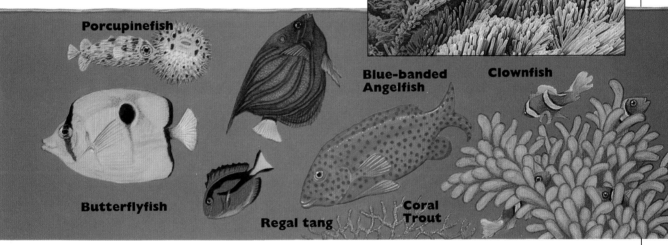

**Porcupinefish**

**Blue-banded Angelfish**

**Clownfish**

**Butterflyfish**

**Regal tang**

**Coral Trout**

### Warm and shallow

Coral reefs are rich environments for fish and other sea life, but they form only in certain places around the world. The water must be very clean, and warm – preferably around 75°F all year – with a salt concentration of between 25 and 40 parts per thousand. The basis of the reef is the coral polyp, a tiny animal like a miniature jellyfish. Polyps grow in their millions and build hard, chalky cup-shaped skeletons around their bodies, for protection. As they die, more polyps grow on top. Over hundreds of years, billions of coral skeletons accumulate, and the rocky reef grows. The corals are food for hundreds of fish.

# THE TANK

The battle tank is the main weapon of modern land combat. Its job is to disable or destroy enemy tanks. Every tank is also therefore itself the target of another tank. It may also be attacked by a range of lethal weapons carried by soldiers and aircraft. To survive so that it can do the job it was designed for, it must be able to protect itself from these attacks.

The design of every tank is a combination of three important factors – mobility, protection and firepower. A powerful engine driving a pair of metal tracks gives it mobility. It is protected by

hull. The hull must be large enough to hold the engine, fuel, weapon systems, ammunition and the tank's electronic systems, with enough space left over for the tank's crew of three or four.

A tank's electronic systems include fire control and radio communications. Fire control is a computerized system that helps the gunner to aim the main gun accurately. The tank may also be equipped with specialized instruments

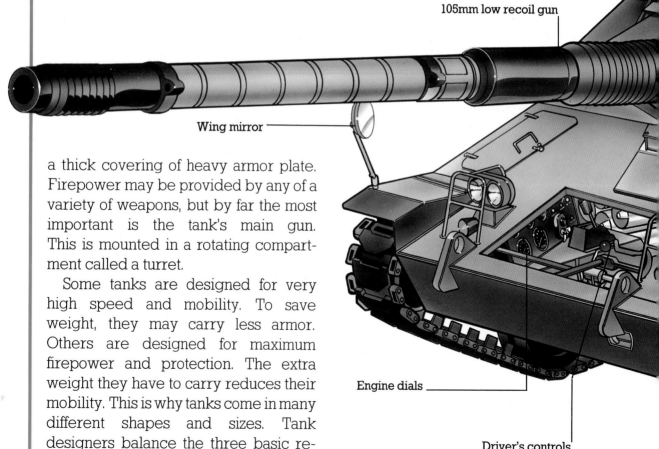

105mm low recoil gun

Wing mirror

Engine dials

Driver's controls

a thick covering of heavy armor plate. Firepower may be provided by any of a variety of weapons, but by far the most important is the tank's main gun. This is mounted in a rotating compartment called a turret.

Some tanks are designed for very high speed and mobility. To save weight, they may carry less armor. Others are designed for maximum firepower and protection. The extra weight they have to carry reduces their mobility. This is why tanks come in many different shapes and sizes. Tank designers balance the three basic requirements in different ways.

The structure of the tank has two main components, the turret and the body, or

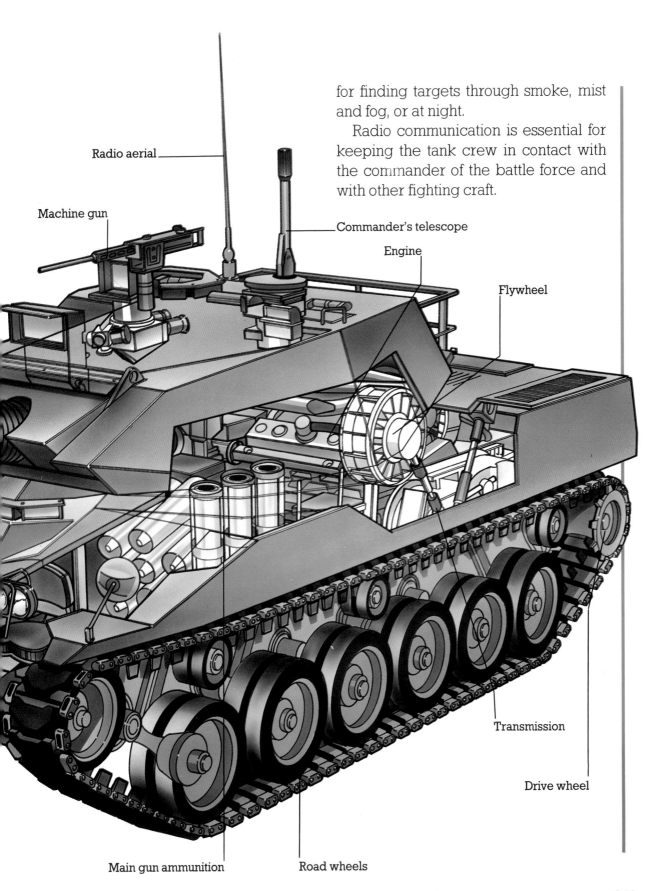

for finding targets through smoke, mist and fog, or at night.

Radio communication is essential for keeping the tank crew in contact with the commander of the battle force and with other fighting craft.

Radio aerial

Machine gun

Commander's telescope

Engine

Flywheel

Transmission

Drive wheel

Main gun ammunition

Road wheels

343

# PAINTING SELF-PORTRAITS

Painters paint self-portraits for all kinds of reasons, but the most obvious has to be that your own face is always there when you want it. Have a good look in the mirror and see what shape yours is. Ask yourself what kind of person you are and how you can show this in a painting. Are you cheerful or sad? Do you shout a lot or do you keep things bottled up? Do you like to do things quickly, or do you take your time? Using some of the ideas from the previous projects, try to combine careful observation and the expression of feeling in a portrait of yourself.

## Getting set up

Begin by getting comfortable. Place your paper or board on an easel or rest it against a wall or the back of a chair. Arrange yourself in such a way that you can look straight from the mirror to your painting without turning your head too much.

Make a pencil sketch as you did earlier, taking care to establish the particular proportions of your face. Mix your colors, and change them around until you are satisfied that they represent you.

## Showing how you feel

Do several pictures of yourself in different moods and change the colors and the way you put on the paint accordingly. After the first painting, you may want to dispense with the mirror and paint your "inner self" from imagination.

△ *"These three portraits use color to convey mood. This boy in shades of pink looks gentle and thoughtful."*

## Features and expressions

Here are examples of the same face with three very different expressions, looking in turn angry, frightened and perplexed. These emotions are conveyed chiefly through the shape of the mouth and eyes. Notice, however, that the eyebrows, hair, even the nose and ears can also express emotion. Lines and shapes turning upward look cheerful and full of life; turning down they look sad or fierce. To convey perplexity the lines are undecided and may turn in both directions.

△ *"I have tried to convey the scattiness and good humor of this boy through the use of bright colors and jagged strokes."*

△ *"My third sitter seemed anxious and sad. I chose gloomy colors and applied them with nervous, scratchy strokes."*

# WHAT ARE ELEMENTS?

Everything in the world is made up of elements. An element is a simple chemical substance which itself is made of tiny particles called atoms. Diamonds (right) are made from the element, carbon. There are 105 elements known to man. Some, like iron or copper, were used in ancient times, while others have been made by modern scientists. Many elements can be combined to make new substances – copper and tin can be melted together to make an alloy (mixture) called bronze. The periodic table arranges all the known elements in a special way.

## PERIODIC TABLE

**1.** Each square contains the symbol for a different element. The symbol comes from the common name or Latin name of the element; C stands for carbon and Al for aluminum. The Latin for iron is ferrum, so the symbol is Fe.

| H | | | | | | | |
|---|---|---|---|---|---|---|---|
| Li | Be | | | | | | |
| Na | Mg | | | | | | |
| K | Ca | SC | Ti | V | Cr | Mn | Fe | Co |
| Rb | Sr | Y | Zr | Nb | Mo | Tc | Ru | Rh |
| Cs | Ba | La | Hf | Ta | W | Re | Os | Ir |
| Fr | Ra | Ac | | | | | | |

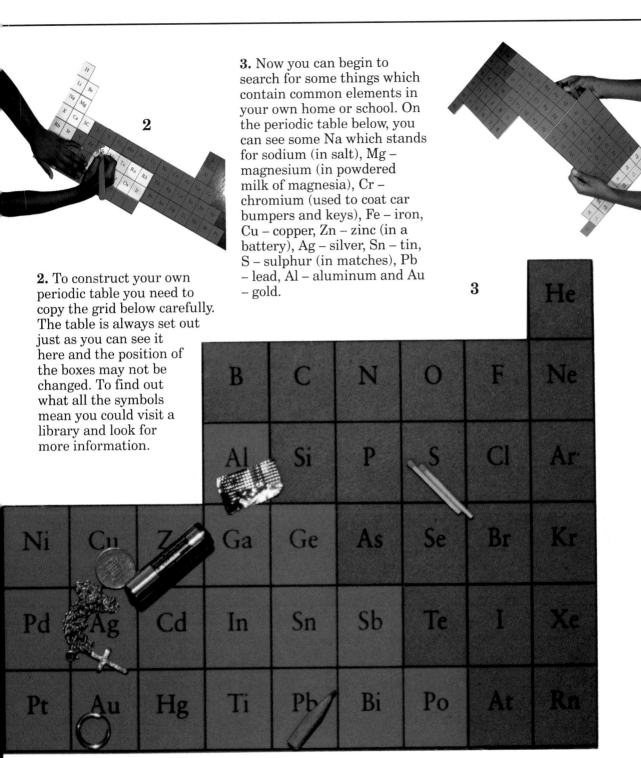

**2**

**2.** To construct your own periodic table you need to copy the grid below carefully. The table is always set out just as you can see it here and the position of the boxes may not be changed. To find out what all the symbols mean you could visit a library and look for more information.

**3.** Now you can begin to search for some things which contain common elements in your own home or school. On the periodic table below, you can see some Na which stands for sodium (in salt), Mg – magnesium (in powdered milk of magnesia), Cr – chromium (used to coat car bumpers and keys), Fe – iron, Cu – copper, Zn – zinc (in a battery), Ag – silver, Sn – tin, S – sulphur (in matches), Pb – lead, Al – aluminum and Au – gold.

**3**

| | | | | | He |
|---|---|---|---|---|---|
| B | C | N | O | F | Ne |
| Al | Si | P | S | Cl | Ar |
| Ni | Cu | Z | Ga | Ge | As | Se | Br | Kr |
| Pd | Ag | Cd | In | Sn | Sb | Te | I | Xe |
| Pt | Au | Hg | Ti | Pb | Bi | Po | At | Rn |

Now try to find some... C – carbon (soot, pencil lead, diamonds and charcoal are all forms of carbon), Hg – mercury (the silver stuff in thermometers), Pt – platinum (a metal used in jewelry making) and Cl – chlorine (added to drinking water to kill bacteria).

# WHAT IF THE EARTH STOOD STILL?

Direction of Earth's spin

Axis of spin

If it were daytime, the first thing you might notice was that the Sun stopped moving across the sky. You'd wait for evening – but it would never come. It'd be daylight forever! The Earth spins around like a gigantic top on an imaginary line called its axis, that goes through the North and South Poles. It makes one complete turn every 24 hours, giving us the cycle of day and night. As your area of the surface turns, the Sun appears to move across the sky in daytime, and the stars and Moon move across at nighttime.

A still Earth would heat up unbearably on the daytime side.

Daytime on the side facing the Sun

## A hard day's night!

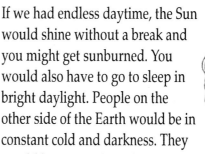

If we had endless daytime, the Sun would shine without a break and you might get sunburned. You would also have to go to sleep in bright daylight. People on the other side of the Earth would be in constant cold and darkness. They would become pale and sick.

On the shady side, it would be dark, cold, and soon freeze over.

# No more seasons in the Sun?

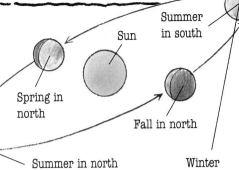

Besides spinning like a top, the Earth also goes around the Sun in a long, curved path called its *orbit*. One orbit takes one year. The Earth's spinning axis is tilted, so some parts of its surface are closer to the Sun during certain times in the orbit. On these closer parts it is warmer – and summer. If the Earth stopped orbiting and stood still, the seasons would cease, too. It would be endless summer in some areas, and everlasting winter in others!

Summer in south

Sun

Spring in north

Fall in north

Summer in north and winter in south

Winter in north

Nighttime on the side away from the Sun

# What would happen to clocks and calendars?

Clocks would keep ticking, and we might continue to use them to tell time. But this would be less useful. We could no longer say things like "It gets dark at 8 o'clock." The calendar would be less useful, too. Without seasons, every month would have the same weather and you would soon get very bored!

# How might animals react?

They'd get very confused! Their internal "body clocks" need the pattern of night and day to stay accurate. With no day or night, they wouldn't know when to eat or sleep. With no seasons, they wouldn't know if they should begin a winter's sleep (hibernation) or set off for a long fall or spring journey (migration).

# The best place to live

A still Earth would have a very narrow strip on each side, one in constant dawn, and the other in continuous dusk. These areas would not get too bright and hot or too dark and cold. They'd be the best places to live.

# TYPES OF DINOSAURS

Dinosaurs are probably the best-known form of prehistoric life. They ruled the Earth from the Late Triassic until the end of the Cretaceous, a total of 165 million years. Although we usually think of dinosaurs as one group (or order) of animal, two distinct types existed. The first were the saurischian, or lizard-hipped dinosaurs. Saurischian dinosaurs included the theropods (meat-eaters) and the giant sauropods (plant-eaters). The second group were the ornithischians, or bird-hipped dinosaurs. Most plant-eating dinosaurs were ornithischians.

### The first dinosaurs

In 1842, Sir Richard Owen recognized that some large bones found years before were different from living reptiles and he grouped them together as the "Dinosauria." The first creature to be described was *Megalosaurus*, a large carnivorous dinosaur found in the Jurassic rocks of the Cotswolds in England. Two others were herbivores, and of Cretaceous age. *Hylaeosaurus* was an armored dinosaur.

## The Jurassic world

By the Jurassic, dinosaurs ruled the Earth. During the early Jurassic, the most common dinosaurs were the prosauropods, ancestors of the sauropods (reptile feet); small ornithischians, for example, the fabrosaurs; and the carnivorous *Megalosaurus*. By the Middle Jurassic, the giant sauropods like *Cetiosaurus* and *Brachiosaurus* came into their own. Other herbivores included stegosaurs (plated reptiles), and a selection of ornithopods (bird feet) such as the hypsilophodonts. These animals were hunted by *Megalosaurus* and *Ornithomimius*.

Jurassic

## The Triassic world

The Triassic world was dominated by many groups of large vertebrates including rhynchosaurs and thecodontians. Dinosaurs evolved from the thecodontians, and first appeared in great numbers during the Late Triassic.

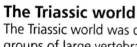

Masrocnemus

Rhynchosaur

Triassic

### Dinostars

One of the most successful dinosaur films is Steven Spielberg's *Jurassic Park* (right), based on the book of the same name by Michael Crichton. Jurassic Park is a dinosaur theme park created by a businessman. But things go horribly wrong! The dinosaurs were brought to life for the movie by computer graphics and model animation. It's probably the most realistic dinosaur film ever made.

Cretaceous

We know from fossils that many dinosaurs laid eggs. Some fossil eggs (below) have been found containing babies.

### Cretaceous world

At the end of the Cretaceous, the reign of the dinosaurs ended. This may have been caused by a meteorite hitting the Earth. Evidence for this comes from the iridium layer (marked by the white circle below) which is a rare element found at the Cretaceous-Tertiary boundary. Other theories suggest dinosaurs died out due to a change in climate.

Iridium layer

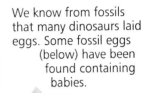

### Hot-blooded or not?

Dinosaurs used to be thought of as large, slow, stupid reptiles. But today, even though scientists think they led more active lives, the question of their metabolism (how their bodies produced heat) has still not been decided. Some people think that dinosaurs were warm-blooded, like mammals, generating their own body heat without having to use the sun's rays to warm them up. However, most scientists agree that the large size of their bodies probably meant that a dinosaur stayed warm, even though it could not produce heat internally. This meant they could act in an almost "warm-blooded" manner.

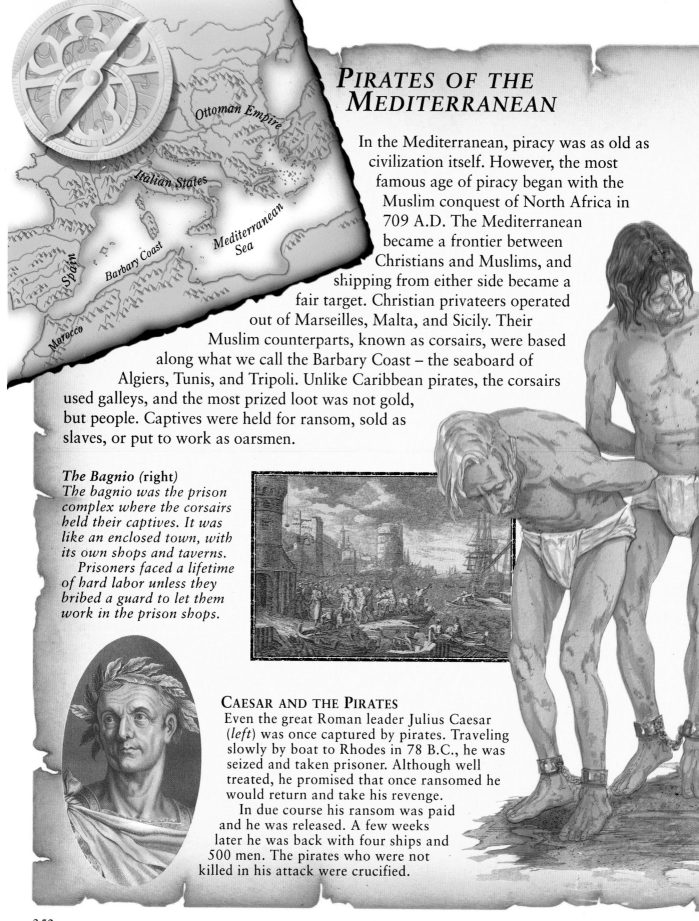

# PIRATES OF THE MEDITERRANEAN

In the Mediterranean, piracy was as old as civilization itself. However, the most famous age of piracy began with the Muslim conquest of North Africa in 709 A.D. The Mediterranean became a frontier between Christians and Muslims, and shipping from either side became a fair target. Christian privateers operated out of Marseilles, Malta, and Sicily. Their Muslim counterparts, known as corsairs, were based along what we call the Barbary Coast – the seaboard of Algiers, Tunis, and Tripoli. Unlike Caribbean pirates, the corsairs used galleys, and the most prized loot was not gold, but people. Captives were held for ransom, sold as slaves, or put to work as oarsmen.

**The Bagnio** (right)
*The bagnio was the prison complex where the corsairs held their captives. It was like an enclosed town, with its own shops and taverns.*
*Prisoners faced a lifetime of hard labor unless they bribed a guard to let them work in the prison shops.*

## CAESAR AND THE PIRATES
Even the great Roman leader Julius Caesar (*left*) was once captured by pirates. Traveling slowly by boat to Rhodes in 78 B.C., he was seized and taken prisoner. Although well treated, he promised that once ransomed he would return and take his revenge.
In due course his ransom was paid and he was released. A few weeks later he was back with four ships and 500 men. The pirates who were not killed in his attack were crucified.

**Bombardment of Algiers**
*When the Napoleonic Wars ended in 1815, the British and Dutch bombarded Algiers to end the threat from the Barbary Coast forever. As a result, 3,000 prisoners were freed.*

**Prisoners of the Corsairs**
*Once taken prisoner by the corsairs, European captives were chained and taken to the bagnio. If they were lucky, perhaps because their native country had a treaty with the corsairs, they would be ransomed. If not, they would either work for the master of the bagnio or be sold as slaves. An alternative was to adopt the Muslim religion, or "turn Turk." This might bring some freedom, but it led to problems if ever they met Christians.*

# THE CAMERA

A camera is a device designed specially to record images on light-sensitive film. There are many different types of camera, but they all work in much the same way. The Single-Lens Reflex, or SLR, camera shown here is an example of one of the most popular types.

A camera is basically a lightproof box. A lens is fixed to one side and film is positioned inside the box opposite the lens. Light is prevented from entering the box by a shutter, a type of blind, behind the lens. When closed, the shutter stops light passing through a hole, the aperture, in the camera body. Light entering the lens of an SLR is reflected upward by a mirror. At the top of this camera, a specially shaped block of glass called a penta-prism reflects the light out through the viewfinder. Other types of cameras have separate viewfinder and shutter-lens systems.

When a camera user wishes to take a photograph, or "shot," almost the exact image that will be recorded on the film can be seen in the viewfinder. At the right moment, the shutter is opened by pressing a button known as the shutter release. If the camera is an SLR, the mirror flips up out of the way, allowing the light to pass through the lens and reach the film. The lens bends the rays of light so that they produce a sharp image on the film. The amount the light rays have to be bent, or refracted, depends on how far away the objects are from the camera. Refraction is adjusted by rotating the focusing ring on the lens. Some cameras use a fixed-focus lens that is suitable for photo-

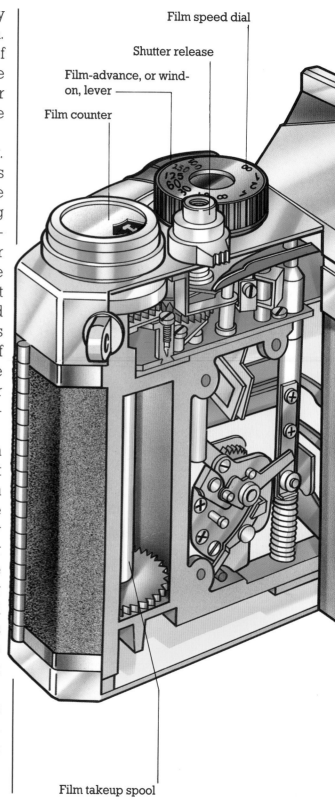

Film speed dial

Shutter release

Film-advance, or wind-on, lever

Film counter

Film takeup spool

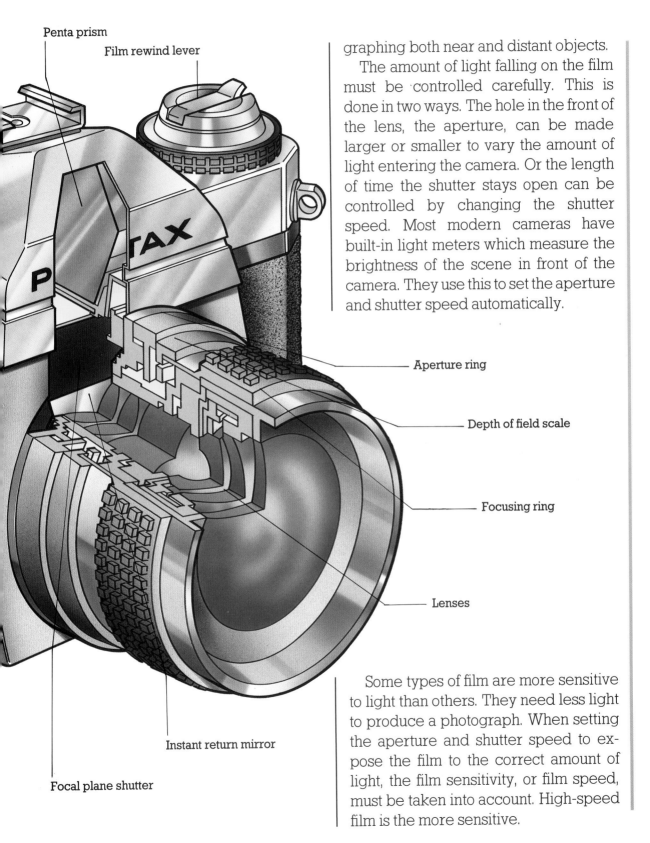

**Penta prism**

**Film rewind lever**

PENTAX

**Aperture ring**

**Depth of field scale**

**Focusing ring**

**Lenses**

**Instant return mirror**

**Focal plane shutter**

graphing both near and distant objects.

The amount of light falling on the film must be controlled carefully. This is done in two ways. The hole in the front of the lens, the aperture, can be made larger or smaller to vary the amount of light entering the camera. Or the length of time the shutter stays open can be controlled by changing the shutter speed. Most modern cameras have built-in light meters which measure the brightness of the scene in front of the camera. They use this to set the aperture and shutter speed automatically.

Some types of film are more sensitive to light than others. They need less light to produce a photograph. When setting the aperture and shutter speed to expose the film to the correct amount of light, the film sensitivity, or film speed, must be taken into account. High-speed film is the more sensitive.

# WHAT ARE PLAGUES?

A plague is an invasion by large numbers of animals or insects. The animals often carry disease, and they eat enormous quantities of growing crops and stored grain. This can bring about a severe famine.

Some of the most destructive plagues consist of swarms of locusts. A single swarm may contain up to 50 billion insects.

Plagues of locusts have threatened several African countries in recent years. Rains in 1988 helped to relieve the drought. However, when combined with warmer weather, they provided ideal conditions for the locusts to breed. As a result, swarms of migratory locusts swept across North and Central Africa, destroying the much-needed harvest there.

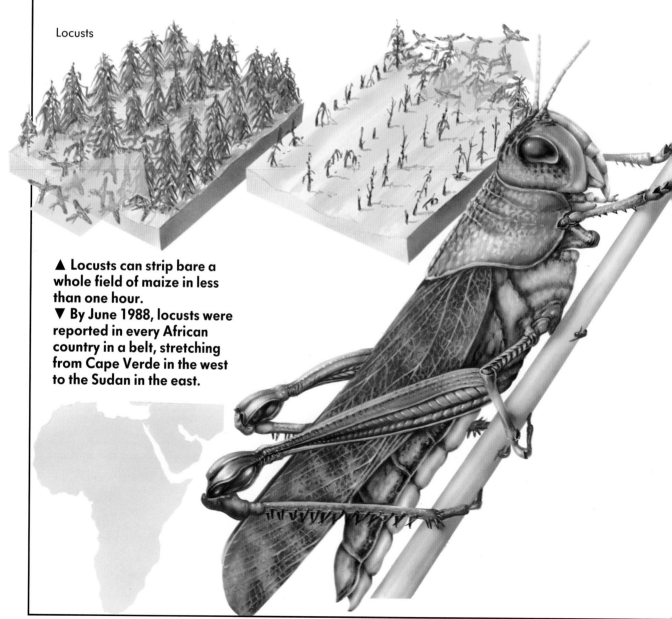

Locusts

▲ Locusts can strip bare a whole field of maize in less than one hour.
▼ By June 1988, locusts were reported in every African country in a belt, stretching from Cape Verde in the west to the Sudan in the east.

► Locusts fly thousands of miles in search of food. Locust invasions, such as the one in Dakar, Senegal, shown right, have plagued farmers throughout the world since ancient times. Locusts will eat any kind of vegetation, and can consume more than their own body weight of food in just one day.

▼ ◄ A locust is a type of adult grasshopper with wings. Its body is about 3 inches long. The female locust can produce hundreds of eggs in a single breeding season. As locusts become crowded and restless, they begin to migrate in swarms to other areas. The swarms can be so large, they block out the sunlight.

### Kangaroos

Animal plagues can also involve large mammals such as kangaroos and goats. More than 3 million kangaroos are killed in Australia each year. Australian farmers consider that some of the 50 different kinds of kangaroo are pests. They feed and drink in the same areas as the farmers' sheep and cattle.

Controlling the kangaroo population has proved difficult as they cannot easily be contained by fencing.

# UNDERSTANDING PERSPECTIVE

Perspective, which means "looking through," is a way of creating the illusion of three-dimensional space on the flat surface of a picture. The kind of perspective that is usually most familiar is based on the idea that the painting on the wall is like a window through which we can see the real world.

**Getting angles right**

Everyone knows how difficult it can sometimes be to get a particular angle of a building or table exactly right, so that it looks as if it were moving toward or away from us. People who find this skill difficult to master often give up the idea of being good at art before they have discovered all the

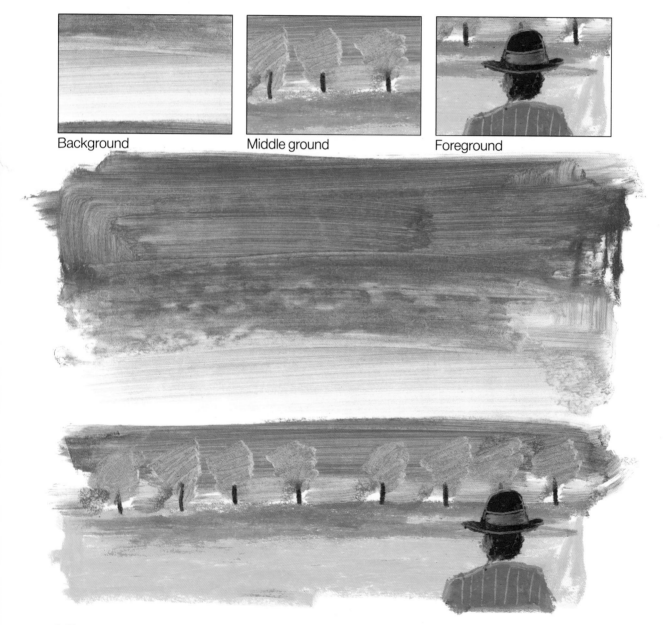

Background

Middle ground

Foreground

other aspects of painting that are exciting and enjoyable.

## Creating distance

There are at least four different ways of showing that one thing is behind or in front of another. Many pictures combine several or all four, though some use none at all.

◁ *"The sky in my picture opposite shows that a strong blue can appear to be in front of a paler, thinner blue as it fades toward the horizon. I used the brightest colors in the foreground and middle distance. I applied the paint thickly and more vigorously in those areas too."*

For the painter perhaps the most appropriate way of portraying distance is through color. As a rule, dark and dull colors tend to go back, or recede, in space. Light and bright ones tend to come forward. Think of how the rays of a yellow sun reach out from a background of blue sky.

The strongest contrasts in tone should be in the foreground. Colors in a landscape seem to get bluer and mistier the further away they are, and the same effect can be achieved in painting. Recession can also be emphasized by using thinner paint in the middle and background. Paint a landscape and test out these theories.

## A sense of space

The diagrams below illustrate some of the other ways of showing perspective. The first is an example of "linear" or line perspective. Lines that would in fact run parallel in the real world, like the roadsides in the diagram, appear to meet at a point on the horizon called the "vanishing point."

The second diagram shows an example of overlapping. The hill that blocks out part of another hill must be in front of it; the human figure blocks them all out and so must be the nearest thing to you. In the third diagram the darker, stronger and "speedier" lines and tones in the foreground appear to be in front of the softer, "slower" lines.

1. Linear

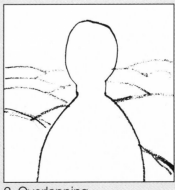

2. Overlapping

3. Tonal

# WHAT IF AIRCRAFT DIDN'T HAVE WINGS?

Most of them would speed along the runway... and crash at the end, without taking off. Wings make a plane rise into the air, by providing lift. The wing shape also tells you how fast a plane goes. Slower planes, especially gliders, have very long, thin wings that stick out sideways. These wings have a very narrow chord (the distance from the front of the wing – leading edge – to the rear of the wing – trailing edge). This is the same design as the wings of gliding birds, like the albatross. Faster planes have swept-back wings, usually with a bigger chord, like fast hunting birds such as hawks.

## An uplifting experience

Some aircraft don't get their lift from wings. It comes from a jet engine or propeller facing straight down, which pushes the aircraft into the air. A strange test craft from the 1950s, called the "Flying Bedstead," did this. So does the Harrier Jump Jet, which can take off straight up, and hover in mid-air. Hovercraft use lifting fans, like propellers facing downward, to create a cushion of air.

# What if a plane flew upside down?

First, how does a wing work? Seen end-on, a wing has a special shape, known as the airfoil section. It is more curved on top than below. As the plane flies, air going over the wing has farther to travel than air beneath. This means the air over the top moves faster, which produces low pressure, so the wing is pushed upward – a force known as *lift* – which raises the plane. If a plane flew upside down, the wing would not give any lift. To overcome this, the plane tilts its nose up at a steep angle. Air hitting the wing then pushes it up, keeping the plane in the air.

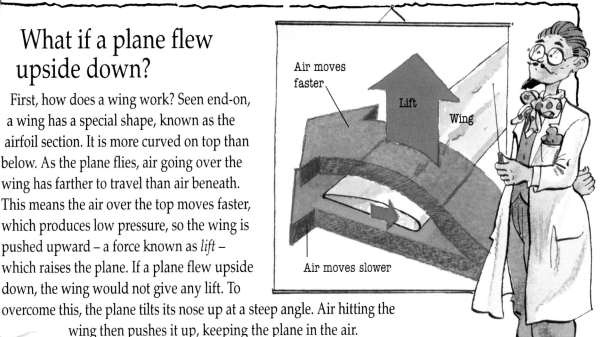

Air moves faster

Lift

Wing

Air moves slower

# Can planes fly in space?

A few can, like the X-15 rocket planes of the 1960s and the space shuttles of today. First, they need engine power to blast up there. The X-15 was carried up on a converted B-52 bomber, while today the shuttle uses massive rocket boosters. Once in space, there's no air (or anything else), so wings can't work by providing lift. The power for all maneuvers in space comes from small rocket thrusters.

# How do spy planes fly so high?

Spy planes, such as the U-2 and the Blackbird, need to fly high, at 100,000 ft (30,000 m) or higher, so they are beyond detection by enemy planes or radar. However, as air is very thin at such heights, they need very special wing designs, with an extra-curved top surface, to give the greatest possible lift. With the arrival of spy satellites, the use of spy planes declined, until recently. A new generation of pilotless, remote-control spy planes, such as DarkStar, has arrived.

# THE TELEPHONE

"Can I order tickets for Friday by phone, please."
"Did you hear about the great party last week!"
"Emergency, which service do you require?"
"Hello, is that you, Mom?"
A world without telephones would be a difficult place. We could only talk to people and pass on urgent messages when they were in front of us. Even modern fax machines and computer modems rely on telephone lines.

For thousands of years, communication was face-to-face. Only a few simple methods, like smoke signals from a fire, or the beating of drums, could be used to send messages quickly across long distances.

By the 1830s, battery power had arrived. People realized that if they had very long wires, they could send electric signals over great distances, using an on-off switch. The telegraph system was invented, and Samuel Morse came up with his dot-dash code.

The Morse key

### Sound to electricity

Soon after the telegraph, inventors dreamed of making the electric signals copy the pattern of someone's voice.

Alexander Graham Bell was a doctor and speech teacher for deaf people. He knew about voices and sounds. In about 1876, he made a simple machine that changed sounds to electrical signals. The signals flashed along a wire, almost a million times faster than sounds went through the air. A similar machine at the other end of the wire changed the signals back into sounds.

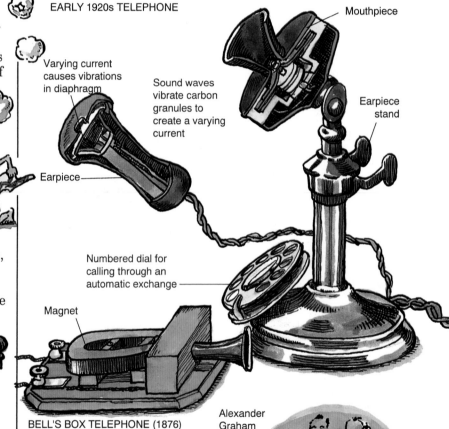

EARLY 1920s TELEPHONE

Mouthpiece

Varying current causes vibrations in diaphragm

Sound waves vibrate carbon granules to create a varying current

Earpiece stand

Earpiece

Numbered dial for calling through an automatic exchange

Magnet

BELL'S BOX TELEPHONE (1876)

Alexander Graham Bell

# THE TELEPHONE

## Coast-to-coast phones

In 1877, Bell showed that his machine could send signals almost 20 miles, from Boston to Salem, Massachusets. Within a few years, telephones were being installed in important buildings and in the homes of rich people.

At first, when you called someone, all the connections were made by hand. Operators worked switches and plugs in the local exchange. The first automatic switches arrived in 1892. By 1915, Americans could phone coast-to-coast. Today, many phone systems use satellite links.

## All the same signals

There are probably almost one billion phones in the world. We use them for shopping, passing on messages, doing business, finding out information (such as the sports scores), and simply chatting.

When you talk into a telephone, it converts your voice to electrical signals. The phone lines can carry any similar type of small signals. So they can pass on signals from computers, teletypes, radios, televisions, fax machines and many other gadgets.

## How the telephone works

A telephone has two main parts. These are called the mouthpiece and the earpiece.

In the mouthpiece, sounds make a flat piece of metal vibrate. This squashes and stretches tiny pieces of carbon in a container. Electricity goes through carbon pieces more easily when they are squashed, and less when they are stretched. So sounds are converted to very fast-changing electrical pulses or signals.

The signals go along the wire to the earpiece of the other telephone. They pass through a coil of wire, called an electromagnet. The magnetism produced pulls on a nearby sheet of metal. The strength of the magnetism varies with the fast-changing signals, so the metal moves back and forth very quickly. This makes the sound waves that you hear.

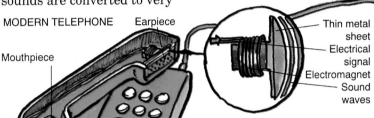

MODERN TELEPHONE — Earpiece

Mouthpiece

Thin metal sheet
Electrical signal
Electromagnet
Sound waves

Electrical signal

Carbon granules

Soundwaves

## Whoops, a bit of trouble

• Alexander Graham Bell first spoke on the phone by accident. A test system was set up in his workroom, when he spilled some acid. He called to his assistant, Thomas Watson, "Mr Watson, come here, I want you!" In the next room, Watson heard the words over the test system. The first phone call was a plea for help!

• Many phones now have push buttons instead of a circular dial. But people still say, "Dial this number."

• Most phones have a bleeper or buzzer instead of a bell. Yet people still say, "Give me a ring.".

# INDEX

# INDEX

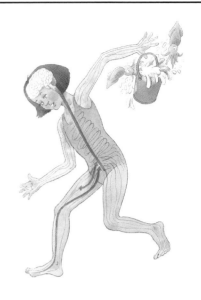

# INDEX